Mobil
Travel Guide

On the
Road
with Your
Pet

Acknowledgements

We gratefully acknowledge the help of our representatives for their efficient and perceptive inspections of the lodging and dining establishments listed; the establishments' proprietors for their cooperation in showing their facilities and providing information about them; and the many users of previous editions who have taken the time to share their experiences.

Mobil Travel Guide is also grateful to all the highly talented writers who contributed entries to this book.

Mobil, Mobil 1, Exxon, Speedpass, and Mobil Travel Guide are trademarks of Exxon Mobil Corporation or one of its subsidiaries. All rights reserved. Reproduction by any means, including, but not limited to, photography, electrostatic copying devices, or electronic data processing is prohibited. Use of information contained herein for solicitation of advertising or listing in any other publication is expressly prohibited without written permission from Exxon Mobil Corporation. Violations of reserved rights are subject to prosecution.

Copyright © 2004 EMTG, LLC. All rights reserved. Except for copies made by individuals for personal use, this publication may not be reproduced in whole or in part by any means whatsoever without written permission from Mobil Travel Guide, 1460 Renaissance Drive, Suite 401, Park Ridge, IL 60068; 847/795-6700; info@mobil travelguide.com

Printing Acknowledgement: North American Corporation of Illinois

www.mobiltravelguide.com

The information contained herein is derived from a variety of third-party sources. Although every effort has been made to verify the information obtained from such sources, the publisher assumes no responsibility for inconsistencies or inaccuracies in the data or liability for any damages of any type arising from errors or omissions.

Neither the editors nor the publisher assumes responsibility for the services provided by any business listed in this guide or for any loss, damage, or disruption in your travel for any reason.

ISBN: 0-7627-3099-4

Manufactured in the United States of America.

10 9 8 7 6 5 4 3

Contents

Welcome

Dear Traveler,

Since its inception in 1958, Mobil Travel Guide has served as a trusted advisor to auto travelers in search of value in lodging, dining, and destinations. Now in its 46th year, the Mobil Travel Guide is the hallmark of our ExxonMobil family of travel publications, and we're proud to offer an array of products and services from our Mobil, Exxon, and Esso brands in North America to facilitate life on the road.

Whether you're looking for business or pleasure venues, our nationwide network of independent, professional evaluators offers their expertise on thousands of travel options, allowing you to plan a quick family getaway, a full-service business meeting, or an unforgettable Five-Star celebration.

Your feedback is important to us as we strive to improve our product offerings and better meet today's travel needs. Whether you travel once a week or once a year, please take the time to contact us at www.mobiltravelguide.com. We hope to hear from you soon.

Best wishes for safe and enjoyable travels.

Lee R Raymond

Lee R. Raymond
Chairman and CEO
Exxon Mobil Corporation

A Word to Our Readers

T ravelers are on the roads in great numbers these days. They're exploring the country on day trips, weekend getaways, business trips, and extended family vacations, visiting major cities and small towns along the way. Because time is precious and the travel industry is ever-changing, having accurate, reliable travel information at your fingertips is critical. Mobil Travel Guide has been providing invaluable insight to travelers for more than 45 years, and we are committed to continuing this service well into the future.

The Mobil Corporation (known as Exxon Mobil Corporation since a 1999 merger) began producing the Mobil Travel Guide books in 1958, following the introduction of the US highway system in 1956. The first edition covered only five southwestern states. Since then, our books have become the premier travel guides in North America, covering the 48 contiguous states and Canada. Now, ExxonMobil presents the latest editions of our annual travel guides, with a fresh new look. We also recently introduced road atlases and specialty publications, a robust new Web site, as well as the first fully integrated, auto-centric travel support program called MobilCompanion, the driving force in travel. (See the inside back cover for more information).

Since its founding, Mobil Travel Guide has served as an advocate for travelers seeking knowledge about hotels, restaurants, and places to visit. Based on an objective process, we make recommendations to our customers that we believe will enhance the quality and value of their travel experiences. Our trusted One- to Five-Star rating system is the oldest and most respected lodging and restaurant inspection and rating program in North America. Most hoteliers, restaurateurs, and industry observers favorably regard the rigor of our inspection program and understand the prestige and benefits that come with receiving a Mobil Travel Guide star rating.

The Mobil Travel Guide process of rating each establishment includes:

- Unannounced facility inspections
- Incognito service evaluations for Mobil Four- and Five-Star properties
- A review of unsolicited comments from the general public
- Senior management oversight

For each property, more than 450 attributes, including cleanliness, physical facilities, employee attitude, and courtesy, are measured and evaluated to produce a mathematically derived score, which is then blended with the other elements to form an overall score. These quantifiable scores allow comparative analysis among properties and form the basis that Mobil Travel Guide uses to assign its Mobil One- to Five-Star ratings.

This process focuses largely on guest expectations, guest experience, and consistency of service, not just physical facilities and amenities. It is fundamentally a relative rating system that rewards those properties that continually strive for and achieve excellence each year. Indeed, the very best properties are consistently raising the bar for those that wish to compete with them. These properties proactively respond to consumers' needs even in today's uncertain times.

Only facilities that meet Mobil Travel Guide's standards earn the privilege of being listed in the guide. Deteriorating, poorly managed establishments are deleted. A Mobil Travel Guide listing constitutes a positive quality recommendation; every listing is an accolade, a recognition of achievement. Our One- to Five-Star rating system highlights its level of service. Extensive in-house research is constantly underway to determine new additions to our lists.

- The Mobil Five-Star Award indicates that a property is one of the very best in the country and consistently provides gracious and courteous service, superlative quality in its facility, and a unique ambience. The lodgings and restaurants at the Five-Star level consistently and proactively respond to consumers' needs and continue their commitment to excellence, doing so with grace and perseverance.
- Also highly regarded is the Mobil Four-Star Award, which honors properties for outstanding achievement in overall facility and for providing very strong service levels in all areas. These award-winners provide a distinctive experience for the ever-demanding and sophisticated consumer.
- The Mobil Three-Star Award recognizes an excellent property that provides full services and amenities. This category ranges from exceptional hotels with limited services to elegant restaurants with a less-formal atmosphere.

- A Mobil Two-Star property is a clean and comfortable establishment that has expanded amenities or a distinctive environment. A Two-Star property is an excellent place to stay or dine.
- A Mobil One-Star property is limited in its amenities and services but focuses on providing a value experience while meeting travelers' expectations. The property can be expected to be clean, comfortable, and convenient.

Allow us to emphasize that we do not charge establishments for inclusion in our guides. We have no relationship with any of the businesses and attractions we list and act only as a consumer advocate. In essence, we do the investigative legwork so that you won't have to.

Keep in mind, too, that the hospitality business is ever-changing. Restaurants and lodgings—particularly small chains and standalone establishments—change management or even go out of business with surprising quickness. Although we make every effort to double-check information during our annual updates, we nevertheless recommend that you call ahead to make sure the place you've selected is still open and offers all the amenities you're looking for. We've provided phone numbers; when available, we also list fax numbers and Web site addresses.

We hope that your travels are enjoyable and relaxing and that our books help you get the most out of every trip you take. If any aspect of your accommodation, dining, or sightseeing experience motivates you to comment, please drop us a line. We depend a great deal on our readers' remarks, so you can be assured that we will read your comments and assimilate them into our research. General comments about our books are also welcome. You can write to us at Mobil Travel Guide, 1460 Renaissance Drive, Suite 401, Park Ridge, IL 60068, or send an e-mail to info@mobiltravelguide.com.

Take your Mobil Travel Guide books along on every trip you take. We're confident that you'll be pleased with their convenience, ease of use, and breadth of dependable coverage.

Happy travels!

How to Use This Book

Lodging Listings

Lodgings are usually listed under the city or town in which they are located. In large cities, lodgings located within 5 miles of major commercial airports are listed under a separate "Airport Area" heading that follows the city section.

Travelers have different wants and needs when it comes to accommodations. To help you pinpoint properties that meet your particular needs, each lodging property is classified by type according to the following characteristics:

- **Motels/Motor Lodges.** These accommodations are in low-rise structures with rooms that are easily accessible to parking, which is usually free. Properties have small, functional lobbies, and guests enter their rooms from the outdoors. Service is often limited, and dining may not be offered in lower-rated motels. Shops and businesses are generally found only in higher-rated properties, as are bell staff, room service, and restaurants serving three meals daily.

- **Hotels.** A hotel is an establishment that provides lodging in a clean, comfortable environment. Guests can expect private bathrooms as well as some measure of guest services, such as luggage assistance, room service, and daily maid service.

- **Resorts.** A resort is an establishment that provides lodging in a facility that is typically located on a larger piece of land. Recreational activities are emphasized and often include golf, spa, and tennis. Guests can expect more than one food and beverage establishment on the property, which aims to provide a variety of food choices at a variety of price points.

- **All Suites.** In an all-suites property, guest accommodations consist of two rooms: a bedroom and a living room. Higher-rated properties offer facilities and services comparable to regular hotels.

- **B&Bs/Small Inns.** The hotel alternative for those who prefer the comforts of home and a personal touch. It may be a structure of historic significance and often is located in an interesting setting. Breakfast is usually included and often is treated as a special occasion. Cocktails and refreshments may be served in the late afternoon or evening. Rooms are often individually decorated, but telephones, televisions, and private bathrooms may not be available in every room.

- **Guest Ranches.** Like resorts, guest ranches specialize in stays of three days or more. These lodgings also offer meal plans and extensive outdoor activities. Horseback riding is usually a feature; stables and trails are found on the ranch property, and trail rides and daily instruction are part of the program. Many guest ranches are working ranches, ranging from casual to rustic, and guests are encouraged to participate in ranch life. Eating is often family style and may include cookouts. Western saddles are assumed; phone ahead to inquire about English saddle availability.

- **Extended Stay.** These hotels specialize in stays of three days or more and usually offer weekly room rates. Service is often limited, and dining may not be offered at lower-rated properties.

Because most lodgings offer the following features and services, information about them does not appear in the listings unless exceptions exist:

- Year-round operation with a single rate structure
- Major credit cards accepted (note that Exxon or Mobil Corporation credit cards cannot be used to pay for room or other charges)
- Air-conditioning and heat, often with individual room controls
- Bathroom with tub and/or shower in each room
- Cable television
- Cots and cribs available
- Daily maid service
- Elevators
- In-room telephones

Each lodging listing gives the name, address/location (when no street address is available), neighborhood and/or directions from downtown (in major cities), phone number(s), fax number, total number of guest rooms, and seasons open (if not year-round). Also included are details on business, luxury, recreational, and dining facilities on the property or nearby. A key to the symbols at the end of each listing can be found on the inside front cover of this book.

For every property, we also provide pricing information. Because lodging rates change frequently, we often opt to list a pricing category rather than specific prices; however, we provide specific room rates wherever possible. The pricing categories break down as follows:

- **$** = Up to $150
- **$$** = $151-$250
- **$$$** = $251-$350
- **$$$$** = $351 and up

All prices quoted by the Mobil Travel Guide are in effect at the time of publication; however, prices cannot be guaranteed. In some locations, short-term price variations may exist because of special events or holidays. Whenever possible, these price variations are noted. Certain resorts have complicated rate structures that vary with the time of year; always confirm rates when making your plans.

QUALITY RATINGS
The Mobil Travel Guide has been rating lodgings and restaurants in the United States since the first edition was published in 1958. For years, the guide was the only source of such ratings, and it remains among the few guidebooks to rate restaurants across the country and in Canada.

All listed establishments have been inspected by experienced field representatives and/or evaluated by a senior staff member. Our ratings are based on detailed inspection reports of the individual properties, on written evaluations of staff members who stay and dine anonymously, and on an extensive review of reader comments. Rating categories reflect both the features a property offers and its quality in relation to similar establishments.

Here are the definitions for the star ratings for lodgings:
- ★ : A Mobil One-Star lodging is a limited-service hotel, motel, or inn that is considered a clean, comfortable, and reliable establishment.
- ★★ : A Mobil Two-Star lodging is considered a clean, comfortable, and reliable establishment that has expanded amenities, such as a full-service restaurant on the premises.
- ★★★ : A Mobil Three-Star lodging is well appointed, with a full-service restaurant and expanded amenities, such as a fitness center, golf course, tennis courts, 24-hour room service, and optional turndown service.
- ★★★★ : A Mobil Four-Star lodging provides a luxury experience with expanded amenities in a distinctive environment. Services may include, but are not limited to, automatic turndown service, 24-hour room service, and valet parking.
- ★★★★★ : A Mobil Five-Star lodging provides consistently superlative service in an exceptionally distinctive luxury environment, with expanded services. Attention to detail is evident throughout the hotel, resort, or inn, from bed linens to staff uniforms.

TERMS AND ABBREVIATIONS IN LISTINGS
The following terms and abbreviations are used throughout the Mobil Travel Guide lodging listings to indicate which amenities and services are available at each establishment. We've done our best to provide accurate and up-to-date information, but things do change, so if a particular feature is essential to you, please contact the establishment directly to make sure that it is available.

Continental breakfast Usually coffee and a roll or doughnut.

D Followed by a price, indicates the room rate for a double room—two people in one room in one or two beds (the charge may be higher for two double beds).

Each additional The extra charge for each additional person beyond the stated number of persons.

In-room modem link Every guest room has a connection for a modem that's separate from the main phone line.

Kitchen(s) A kitchen or kitchenette that contains a stove or microwave, sink, and refrigerator and is either part of the room or a separate, adjoining room. If the kitchen is not fully equipped, the listing will indicate "no equipment" or "some equipment."

Laundry service Either coin-operated laundry facilities or overnight valet service is available.

Luxury level A special section of a lodging, spanning at least an entire floor, that offers increased luxury accommodations. Management must provide no less than three of these four services: separate check-in and check-out, concierge, private lounge, and private elevator service (with key access). Complimentary breakfast and snacks are commonly offered.

Movies Prerecorded videos are available for rental or check-out.

Valet parking An attendant is available to park and retrieve your car.

VCR VCRs are present in all guest rooms.

VCR available VCRs are available for hookup in guest rooms.

SPECIAL INFORMATION FOR TRAVELERS WITH DISABILITIES

The Mobil Travel Guide D symbol indicates establishments that are at least partially accessible to people with mobility problems. Our criteria for accessibility are unique to our publications. Please do not confuse them with the universal symbol for wheelchair accessibility.

When the D symbol follows a listing, the establishment is equipped with facilities to accommodate people using wheelchairs or crutches or otherwise needing easy access to doorways and rest rooms. Travelers with severe mobility problems or with hearing or visual impairments may or may not find the facilities they need. Always phone ahead to make sure that an establishment can meet your needs.

All lodgings bearing our D symbol have the following facilities:

- ISA-designated parking near access ramps
- Level or ramped entryways to buildings
- Swinging building entryway doors a minimum of 39 inches wide
- Public rest rooms on the main level with space to operate a wheelchair and handrails at commode areas
- Elevator(s) equipped with grab bars and lowered control buttons
- Restaurant(s) with accessible doorway(s), rest rooms with space to operate a wheelchair, and handrails at commode areas
- Guest room entryways that are at least 39 inches wide
- Low-pile carpet in rooms
- Telephones at bedside and in the bathroom
- Beds placed at wheelchair height
- Bathrooms with a minimum doorway width of 3 feet
- Bath with an open sink (no cabinet) and room to operate a wheelchair
- Handrails at commode areas and in the tub
- Wheelchair-accessible peepholes in room entry door
- Wheelchair-accessible closet rods and shelves

Making the Most of Your Trip

A few hardy souls might look back with fondness on a trip during which the car broke down, leaving them stranded for three days, or a vacation that cost twice what it was supposed to. For most travelers, though, the best trips are those that are safe, smooth, and within budget. To help you make your trip the best it can be, we've assembled a few tips and resources.

Saving Money

ON LODGING

Many hotels and motels offer discounts—for senior citizens, business travelers, families, you name it. It never hurts to ask—politely, that is. Sometimes, especially in the late afternoon, desk clerks are instructed to fill beds, and you might be offered a lower rate or a nicer room to entice you to stay. Simply ask the reservation agent for the best rate available. Also, make sure to try both the toll-free number and the local number. You may be able to get a lower rate from one than the other.

Becoming a member of MobilCompanion will entitle you to discounted rates at many well-known hotels around the country. For more information, call 877/785-6788 or visit www.mobilcompanion.com.

Timing your trip right can cut your lodging costs as well. Look for bargains on stays over multiple nights, in the off-season, and on weekdays or weekends, depending on the location. Many hotels in major metropolitan areas, for example, have special weekend packages that offer considerable savings on rooms: they may include breakfast, cocktails, and dinner discounts.

Another way to save money is to choose accommodations that give you more than just a standard room. Rooms with kitchen facilities enable you to cook some meals yourself, reducing your restaurant costs. A suite might save money for two couples traveling together. Even hotel luxury levels can provide good value, as many include breakfast or cocktails in the price of a room.

State and city taxes, as well as special room taxes, can increase your room rate by as much as 25 percent per day. We are unable to include information about taxes in our listings, but we strongly urge you to ask about taxes when making reservations so that you understand the total cost of your lodgings before you book.

Watch out for telephone-usage charges that hotels frequently impose on long-distance, credit-card, and other calls. Before phoning from your room, read the information given to you at check-in, and then be sure to review your bill carefully when checking out. You won't be expected to pay for charges that the hotel didn't spell out. Consider using your cell phone if you have one; or, if public telephones are available in the hotel lobby, your cost savings may outweigh the inconvenience of using them.

Here are some additional ways to save on lodgings:

- Stay in B&B accommodations; they're generally less expensive than standard hotel rooms, and the complimentary breakfasts cut down on food costs.
- If you're traveling with children, find lodgings at which kids stay free.
- When visiting major cities, stay just outside the city limits; these rooms are usually less expensive than those in downtown locations.
- Consider visiting national parks during the low season, when prices of lodgings near the parks drop 25 percent or more.
- When calling a hotel, ask whether it is running any special promotions or if any discounts are available; many times reservationists are told not to volunteer deals unless specifically asked about them.
- Check for hotel packages; some offer nightly rates that include a rental car or discounts on major attractions.

ON DINING

There are several ways to get a less expensive meal at a more expensive restaurant. Early-bird dinners are popular in many parts of the country and offer considerable savings. If you're interested in sampling a Mobil Four- or Five-Star establishment, consider going at lunchtime. Although the prices are probably still relatively high at midday, they may be half of those at dinner, and you'll experience the same ambience, service, and cuisine.

As a member of MobilCompanion, you can enroll in iDine. This program earns you up to 20 percent cash back at more than 1,900 restaurants on meals purchased with the credit card you register; the rebate appears on your credit card bill. For more information about MobilCompanion and iDine, call 877/785-6788 or go to www.mobilcompanion.com.

ON ENTERTAINMENT

Although many national parks, monuments, seashores, historic sites, and recreation areas may be used free of charge, others charge an entrance fee (ranging from $1 to $6 per person or $5 to $20 per carload) and/or a usage fee for special services and facilities. If you plan to make several visits to national recreation areas, consider one of the following money-saving programs offered by the National Park Service:

- **National Parks Pass.** This annual pass is good for entrance to any national park that charges an entrance fee. If the park charges a per-vehicle fee, the pass holder and any accompanying passengers in a private noncommercial vehicle may enter. If the park charges a per-person fee, the pass applies to the holder's spouse, children, and parents as well as the holder. It is valid for entrance fees only; it does not cover parking, camping, or other fees. You can purchase a National Parks Pass in person at any national park where an entrance fee is charged; by mail from the National Park Foundation, PO Box 34108, Washington, DC 20043-4108; by calling 888/GO-PARKS; or at www.nationalparks.org. The cost is $50.

- **Golden Eagle.** When affixed to a National Parks Pass, this sticker, available to people who are between 17 and 61 years of age, extends coverage to sites managed by the US Fish and Wildlife Service, the US Forest Service, and the Bureau of Land Management. It is good until the National Parks Pass to which it is affixed expires and does not cover usage fees. You can purchase one at National Park Service, Fish and Wildlife Service, and Bureau of Land Management fee stations. The cost is $15.

- **Golden Age Passport.** Available to citizens and permanent US residents 62 and older, this passport is a lifetime entrance permit to fee-charging national recreation areas. The fee exemption extends to those accompanying the permit holder in a private noncommercial vehicle or, in the case of walk-in facilities, to the holder's spouse and children. The passport also entitles the holder to a 50 percent discount on federal usage fees charged in park areas, but not on concessions. Golden Age Passports must be obtained in person and are available at most

National Park Service units that charge an entrance fee. The applicant must show proof of age, such as a driver's license or birth certificate (Medicare cards are not acceptable proof). The cost is $10.

- **Golden Access Passport.** Issued to citizens and permanent US residents who are physically disabled or visually impaired, this passport is a free lifetime entrance permit to fee-charging national recreation areas. The fee exemption extends to those accompanying the permit holder in a private noncommercial vehicle or, in the case of walk-in facilities, to the holder's spouse and children. The passport also entitles the holder to a 50 percent discount on usage fees charged in park areas, but not on concessions. Golden Access Passports must be obtained in person and are available at most National Park Service units that charge an entrance fee. Proof of eligibility to receive federal benefits (under programs such as Disability Retirement, Compensation for Military Service-Connected Disability, and the Coal Mine Safety and Health Act) is required, or an affidavit must be signed attesting to eligibility.

A money-saving move in several large cities is to purchase a CityPass. If you plan to visit several museums and other major attractions, CityPass is a terrific option because it gets you into several sites for one substantially reduced price. Currently, CityPass is available in Boston, Chicago, Hollywood, New York, Philadelphia, San Francisco, Seattle, and southern California (which includes Disneyland, Sea World, and the San Diego Zoo). For more information or to buy one, call 888/330-5008 or visit www.citypass.net. You can also buy a CityPass from any participating CityPass attraction.

Here are some additional ways to save on entertainment and shopping:

- Check with your hotel's concierge for various coupons and special offers; they often have two-for-one tickets for area attractions and coupons for discounts at area stores and restaurants.

- Purchase same-day concert or theater tickets for half-price through the local cheap-tickets outlet, such as TKTS in New York City or Hot Tix in Chicago.

- Visit museums on their free or "by donation" days, when you can pay what you wish rather than a specific admission fee.

- Save receipts from purchases in Canada; visitors to Canada can get a rebate on federal taxes and some provincial sales taxes.

ON TRANSPORTATION

Transportation is a big part of any vacation budget. Here are some ways to reduce your costs:

- If you're renting a car, shop early over the Internet; you can book a car during the low season for less, even if you'll be using it in the high season.
- Rental car discounts are often available if you rent for one week or longer and reserve in advance.
- Get the best gas mileage out of your vehicle by making sure that it's properly tuned up and keeping your tires properly inflated. If your tires need to be replaced, you can save money on a new set of Michelins by becoming a member of MobilCompanion.
- Travel at moderate speeds on the open road; higher speeds require more gasoline.
- Fill the tank before you return your rental car; rental companies charge to refill the tank and do so at prices of up to 50 percent more than at local gas stations.
- Make a checklist of travel essentials and purchase them before you leave; don't get stuck buying expensive sunscreen at your hotel or overpriced film at the aiport.

FOR SENIOR CITIZENS

Look for the senior-citizen discount symbol SC in this book's listings. Always call ahead to confirm that a discount is being offered, and be sure to carry proof of age. At places not listed in this book, it never hurts to ask if a senior-citizen discount is offered. Additional information for mature travelers is available from the American Association of Retired Persons (AARP), 601 E St NW, Washington, DC 20049; phone 202/434-2277; www.aarp.org.

Tipping

Tips are expressions of appreciation for good service. However, you are never obligated to tip if you receive poor service.

IN HOTELS

- Door attendants usually get $1 for hailing a cab.
- Bell staff expect $2 per bag.
- Concierges are tipped according to the service they perform. Tipping is not mandatory when you've asked for suggestions on sightseeing or restaurants or for help in making dining reservations. However, a tip of $5 is appropriate when a concierge books you a table at a restaurant known to be difficult to get into. For obtaining theater or sporting event tickets, $5 to $10 is expected.
- Maids should be tipped $1 to $2 per day. Hand your tip directly to the maid, or leave it with a note saying that the money has been left expressly for the maid.

IN RESTAURANTS

Before tipping, carefully review your check for any gratuity or service charge that is already included in your bill. If you're in doubt, ask your server.

- Coffee shop and counter service waitstaff usually receive 15 percent of the bill, before sales tax.
- In full-service restaurants, tip 18 percent of the bill, before sales tax.
- In fine restaurants, where gratuities are shared among a larger staff, 18 to 20 percent is appropriate.
- In most cases, the maitre d' is tipped only if the service has been extraordinary, and only on the way out. At upscale properties in major metropolitan areas, $20 is the minimum.
- If there is a wine steward, tip $20 for exemplary service and beyond, or more if the wine was decanted or the bottle was very expensive.
- Tip $1 to $2 per coat at the coat check.

AT AIRPORTS

Curbside luggage handlers expect $1 per bag. Car-rental shuttle drivers who help with your luggage appreciate a $1 or $2 tip.

Staying Safe

The best way to deal with emergencies is to avoid them in the first place. However, unforeseen situations do happen, so you should be prepared for them.

IN YOUR CAR

Before you head out on a road trip, make sure that your car has been serviced and is in good working order. Change the oil, check the battery and belts, make sure that your windshield washer fluid is full and your tires are properly inflated (which can also improve your gas mileage). Other inspections recommended by the vehicle's manufacturer should also be made.

Next, be sure you have the tools and equipment needed to deal with a routine breakdown:

- Jack
- Spare tire
- Lug wrench
- Repair kit
- Emergency tools
- Jumper cables
- Spare fan belt
- Fuses
- Flares and/or reflectors
- Flashlight
- First-aid kit
- In winter, a windshield scraper and snow shovel

Many emergency supplies are sold in special packages that include the essentials you need to stay safe in the event of a breakdown.

Also bring all appropriate and up-to-date documentation—licenses, registration, and insurance cards—and know what your insurance covers. Bring an extra set of keys, too, just in case.

En route, always buckle up! In most states, wearing a seatbelt is required by law.

If your car does break down, do the following:

- Get out of traffic as soon as possible—pull well off the road.
- Raise the hood and turn on your emergency flashers or tie a white cloth to the roadside door handle or antenna.
- Stay in your car.
- Use flares or reflectors to keep your vehicle from being hit.

If you are a member of MobilCompanion, remember that En Route Support is always ready to help when you need it. Just give us a call and we'll locate and dispatch an emergency roadside service to assist you, as well as provide you with significant savings on the service.

IN YOUR HOTEL OR MOTEL

Chances are slim that you will encounter a hotel or motel fire, but you can protect yourself by doing the following:

- Once you've checked in, make sure that the smoke detector in your room is working properly.
- Find the property's fire safety instructions, usually posted on the inside of the room door.
- Locate the fire extinguishers and at least two fire exits.
- Never use an elevator in a fire.

For personal security, use the peephole in your room door and make sure that anyone claiming to be a hotel employee can show proper identification. Call the front desk if you feel threatened at any time.

PROTECTING AGAINST THEFT

To guard against theft wherever you go:

- Don't bring anything of more value than you need.
- If you do bring valuables, leave them at your hotel rather than in your car.
- If you bring something very expensive, lock it in a safe. Many hotels put one in each room; others will store your valuables in the hotel's safe.

- Don't carry more money than you need. Use traveler's checks and credit cards or visit cash machines to withdraw more cash when you run out.

For Travelers with Disabilities

To get the kind of service you need and have a right to expect, don't hesitate when making a reservation to question the management about the availability of accessible rooms, parking, entrances, restaurants, lounges, or any other facilities that are important to you, and confirm what is meant by "accessible."

The Mobil Travel Guide D symbol indicates establishments that are at least partially accessible to people with special mobility needs (people using wheelchairs or crutches or otherwise needing easy access to buildings and rooms). Keep in mind that our criteria for accessibility are unique to our publication and should not be confused with the universal symbol for wheelchair accessibility. Further information about these criteria can be found in the earlier section "How to Use This Book."

A thorough listing of published material for travelers with disabilities is available from the Disability Bookshop, Twin Peaks Press, Box 129, Vancouver, WA 98666; phone 360/694-2462; disabilitybookshop. virtualave.net. Another reliable organization is the Society for Accessible Travel & Hospitality (SATH), 347 Fifth Ave, Suite 610, New York, NY 10016; phone 212/447-7284; www.sath.org.

Border Crossing Regulations

MEXICO

Proof of citizenship—a passport or a certified birth certificate—is required for travel into Mexico. A driver's license is not acceptable. Aliens must carry their alien registration cards, and naturalized citizens should carry their naturalization certificates. If you are planning to stay for more than 24 hours or if you are a naturalized citizen or a resident alien, get a copy of current border regulations from the nearest Mexican consulate or tourism office before crossing, and make sure that you understand them. A helpful booklet, *Know Before You Go,* may be obtained free of charge from the nearest office of the US Customs Service.

If you take your car for the day, you may find it more convenient to unload all baggage before crossing than to go through a thorough customs inspection upon your return. You will not be permitted to bring any plants, fruits, or vegetables into the United States.

Federal regulations permit each US citizen 21 years of age or older to bring back 1 quart of alcoholic beverage duty free. However, state regulations vary; check locally before entering Mexico. New regulations may be issued at any time.

Your automobile insurance is not valid in Mexico; for short visits, get a one-day policy before crossing. US currency is accepted in all border cities. Mexico does not observe Daylight Savings Time.

For more information about traveling to Mexico, including safety information, look for the US State Department's Consular Information Sheet at travel.state.gov/mexico.html, or request it by fax by calling 202/647-3000.

CANADA

Citizens of the United States should be aware of these conditions when entering Canada:

- Visas are not required.
- Visitors may tour the provinces for up to three months without paying a fee.
- Proof of citizenship, such as a passport, birth certificate, or voter registration card, is required. A driver's license is not acceptable proof of citizenship.
- Naturalized citizens will need their naturalization certificates or their US passports to reenter the United States.
- Children under 18 traveling on their own should carry a letter from a parent or guardian giving them permission to travel in Canada.
- Drivers are advised to carry their motor vehicle registration cards.
- If the car is not registered in the driver's name, a letter from the registered owner authorizing use of the vehicle should be available.
- If the car is a rental, carry a copy of the rental contract stipulating permission for use in Canada.
- Ask your car insurer for a Canadian Non-Resident Inter-Province Motor Vehicle Liability Insurance Card. This card ensures that your insurance company will meet the minimum insurance requirements in Canada.
- The use of seatbelts by drivers and passengers is compulsory in all provinces.
- Rabies vaccination certificates are required for dogs or cats.
- A permit is required for the use of citizens band (CB) radios.

The Canadian dollar's rate of exchange with the US dollar varies; contact your local bank for the latest figures.

For the most current and detailed listing of Customs regulations and sources, ask for the annually revised brochure *Canada: Travel Information,* available upon request from the Canadian consulate or embassy in your area.

Important Toll-Free Numbers and Online Information

Hotels and Motels

Adams Mark 800/444-2326
www.adamsmark.com
AmericInn 800/634-3444
www.americinn.com
AmeriHost Inn Hotels 800/434-5800
www.amerihostinn.com
Amerisuites 800/833-1516
www.amerisuites.com
Baymont Inns 877/BAYMONT
www.baymontinns.com
Best Inns & Suites 800/237-8466
www.bestinn.com
Best Value Inns 888/315-BEST
www.bestvalueinn.com
Best Western International 800/WESTERN
www.bestwestern.com
Budget Host Inn 800/BUDHOST
www.budgethost.com
Candlewood Suites 888/CANDLEWOOD
www.candlewoodsuites.com
Clarion Hotels 800/252-7466
www.choicehotels.com
Comfort Inns and Suites 800/252-7466
www.choicehotels.com
Country Hearth Inns 800/848-5767
www.countryhearth.com
Country Inns & Suites 800/456-4000
www.countryinns.com
Courtyard by Marriott 888/236-2427
www.courtyard.com
Cross Country Inn 800/621-1429
www.crosscountryinns.com
Crowne Plaza Hotels and Resorts 800/227-6963
www.crowneplaza.com
Days Inn 800/544-8313
www.daysinn.com
Delta Hotels 800/268-1133
www.deltahotels.com
Destination Hotels & Resorts 800/434-7347
www.destinationhotels.com
Doubletree Hotels 800/222-8733
www.doubletree.com
Drury Inns 800/378-7946
www.druryinn.com
Econolodge 800/553-2666
www.econolodge.com
Economy Inns of America 800/826-0778
www.innsofamerica.com

Embassy Suites 800/362-2779
www.embassysuites.com
ExelInns of America 800/FOREXEL
www.exelinns.com
Extended StayAmerica 800/EXTSTAY
www.extstay.com
Fairfield Inn by Marriott 888/236-2427
www.fairfieldinn.com
Fairmont Hotels 877/441-1414
www.fairmont.com
Four Points by Sheraton 888/625-5144
www.starwood.com
Four Seasons 800/545-4000
www.fourseasons.com
Hampton Inn/Hampton Inn and Suites 800/426-7866
www.hamptoninn.com
Hard Rock Hotels, Resorts and Casinos 800/HRDROCK
www.hardrock.com
Harrah's Entertainment 800/HARRAHS
www.harrahs.com
Harvey Hotels 800/922-9222
www.bristolhotels.com
Hawthorn Suites 800/527-1133
www.hawthorn.com
Hilton Hotels and Resorts (US) 800/774-1500
www.hilton.com
Holiday Inn Express 800/HOLIDAY
www.sixcontinentshotel.com
Holiday Inn Hotels and Resorts 800/465-4329
www.holiday-inn.com
Homestead Studio Suites 888/782-9473
www.stayhsd.com
Homewood Suites 800/225-5466
www.homewoodsuites.com
Howard Johnson 800/406-1411
www.hojo.com
Hyatt 800/633-7313
www.hyatt.com
Ian Schrager . . . . Contact individual hotel
www.ianschragerhotels.com
Inter-Continental 888/567-8725
www.intercontinental.com
Joie de Vivre 800/738-7477
www.jdvhospitality.com
Kimpton Hotels 888/546-7866
www.kimptongroup.com
Knights Inn 800/843-5644
www.knightsinn.com

La Quinta 800/531-5900
www.laquinta.com

Le Meridien 800/543-4300
www.lemeridien.com

Leading Hotels of the World 800/223-6800
www.lhw.com

Loews Hotels 800/235-6397
www.loewshotels.com

MainStay Suites 800/660-6246
www.choicehotels.com

Mandarin Oriental 800/526-6566
www.mandarin-oriental.com

Marriott Conference Centers 888/236-2427
www.conferencecenters.com

Marriott Hotels, Resorts, and Suites 888/236-2427
www.marriott.com

Marriott Vacation Club International 800/845-5279
www.marriott.com/vacationclub

Microtel Inns & Suites 800/771-7171
www.microtelinn.com

Millennium & Copthorne Hotels 866/866-8086
www.mill-cop.com

Motel 6 . . . . 800/4MOTEL6
www.motel6.com

Omni Hotels 800/843-6664
www.omnihotels.com

Pan Pacific Hotels and Resorts 800/327-8585
www.panpac.com

Park Inn & Park Plaza 888/201-1801
www.parkhtls.com

The Peninsula Group . . . . Contact individual hotel
www.peninsula.com

Preferred Hotels & Resorts Worldwide 800/323-7500
www.preferredhotels.com

Quality Inn 800/228-5151
www.qualityinn.com

Radisson Hotels 800/333-3333
www.radisson.com

Raffles International Hotels and Resorts 800/637-9477
www.raffles.com

Ramada International 888/298-2054
www.ramada.com

Ramada Plazas, Limiteds, and Inns 800/2RAMADA
www.ramadahotels.com

Red Lion Inns 800/733-5466
www.redlion.com

Red Roof Inns 800/733-7663
www.redroof.com

Regal Hotels 800/222-8888
www.regal-hotels.com

Regent International 800/545-4000
www.regenthotels.com

Relais & Chateaux 800/735-2478
www.relaischateaux.com

Renaissance Hotels 888/236-2427
www.renaissancehotels.com

Residence Inns 888/236-2427
www.residenceinn.com

Ritz-Carlton 800/241-3333
www.ritzcarlton.com

Rockresorts 888/FORROCKS
www.rockresorts.com

Rodeway Inns 800/228-2000
www.rodeway.com

Rosewood Hotels & Resorts 888/767-3966
www.rosewood-hotels.com

Scottish Inn 800/251-1962
www.bookroomsnow.com

Select Inn 800/641-1000
www.selectinn.com

Sheraton 888/625-5144
www.sheraton.com

Shilo Inns 800/222-2244
www.shiloinns.com

Shoney's Inns 800/552-4667
www.shoneysinn.com

Signature/Jameson Inns 800/822-5252
www.jamesoninns.com

Sleep Inns 800/453-3746
www.sleepinn.com

Small Luxury Hotels of the World 800/525-4800
www.slh.com

Sofitel 800/763-4835
www.sofitel.com

SpringHill Suites 888/236-2427
www.springhillsuites.com

SRS Worldhotels 800/223-5652
www.srs-worldhotels.com

St. Regis Luxury Collection 888/625-5144
www.stregis.com

Staybridge Suites by Holiday Inn 800/238-8000
www.staybridge.com

Summerfield Suites by Wyndham 800/833-4353
www.summerfieldsuites.com

Summit International 800/457-4000
www.summithotels.com

Super 8 Motels 800/800-8000
www.super8.com

The Sutton Place Hotels 866/378-8866
www.suttonplace.com

Swissotel 800/637-9477
www.swissotel.com

TownePlace Suites 888/236-2427
www.towneplace.com

Travelodge 800/578-7878
www.travelodge.com

Universal 800/23LOEWS
www.loewshotel.com

Vagabond Inns 800/522-1555
www.vagabondinns.com
W Hotels 888/625-5144
www.whotels.com
Wellesley Inn and Suites 800/444-8888
www.wellesleyinnandsuites.com
WestCoast Hotels 800/325-4000
www.westcoasthotels.com
Westin Hotels & Resorts 800/937-8461
www.westin.com
Wingate Inns 800/228-1000
www.wingateinns.com
Woodfin Suite Hotels 800/966-3346
www.woodfinsuitehotels.com
Wyndham Hotels & Resorts 800/996-3426
www.wyndham.com

Airlines

Air Canada 888/247-2262
www.aircanada.ca
Alaska 800/252-7522
www.alaskaair.com
American 800/433-7300
www.aa.com
America West 800/235-9292
www.americawest.com
ATA 800/435-9282
www.ata.com
British Airways 800/247-9297
www.british-airways.com
Continental 800/523-3273
www.flycontinental.com
Delta 800/221-1212
www.delta-air.com
Island Air 800/323-3345
www.islandair.com
Mesa 800/637-2247
www.mesa-air.com
Northwest 800/225-2525
www.nwa.com
Southwest 800/435-9792
www.southwest.com
United 800/241-6522
www.ual.com
US Airways 800/428-4322
www.usairways.com

Car Rentals

Advantage 800/777-5500
www.arac.com
Alamo 800/327-9633
www.goalamo.com
Allstate 800/634-6186
www.bnm.com/as.htm

Avis 800/831-2847
www.avis.com
Budget 800/527-0700
www.budgetrentacar.com
Dollar 800/800-4000
www.dollarcar.com
Enterprise 800/325-8007
www.pickenterprise.com
Hertz 800/654-3131
www.hertz.com
National 800/227-7368
www.nationalcar.com
Payless 800/729-5377
www.800-payless.com
Rent-A-Wreck.com 800/535-1391
www.rent-a-wreck.com
Sears 800/527-0770
www.budget.com
Thrifty 800/847-4389
www.thrifty.com

Introduction

When you go on vacation or visit family for the holidays, what do you do with your pet? For more and more Americans, the answer is that our pets come along. For many people, the idea of leaving a dog or cat behind is unbearable—it just wouldn't be a vacation!

Pets can enhance your travel adventures in many ways. Traveling with your pet is a great way to meet new people. Animals are great conversation starters, and animal lovers are everywhere! While you probably can't spend hours dancing at the local hotspot or checking out the art museums, you can enjoy a picnic in a meadow or a barbecue in a park—and you'll never be left eating alone. While your pet will not encourage you to browse the outlet malls, he will probably insist on a walk around town and may even convince you to explore a few hiking trails.

In return for his companionship and fun, your pet will require much of your time, just as he does at home. In fact, if you decide to include him, your pet will probably be a major focus during your trip. Even the most adaptable pet will require a lot of your attention. You must always keep your pet's needs in mind, and that means planning your days around where he can and cannot go. Often, this means you aren't as free to spend leisurely hours sightseeing, shopping, or dining out. If these activities are really important to you, and if you think you would not enjoy a vacation where you can't stop wherever you want for as long as you like, consider hiring a pet sitter or finding a good boarding kennel for your pet.

When you take your pet with you, your travel plans become a lot more complicated. The number and variety of hotels, motels, and resorts that accept pets is certainly growing, as you'll see in this book, but some within the travel industry are still cautious to put out the welcome mat. Along the way, most pets are not allowed in most shops and public attractions. And most restaurants are not allowed, by law, to admit animals. (Outdoor cafés are an exception.)

Most important, if you don't think your pet will enjoy traveling, it is unfair to both him and you to make him come along anyway. While most pets have a remarkable ability to adapt to new situations, those who don't can get stressed out very quickly and even become ill. You want your pet to enjoy the trip as much as you do!

Take Your Pet or Leave Him?

Deciding to travel with your pet can be a difficult decision. We can't imagine spending time without them. And we may think our pets will pine away if we're not around. While there's no doubt they miss us when we're gone, for some pets being on the road is even worse than being without you. Try not to let your emotions take precedence over practical concerns, such as your pet's age, temperament, and health. Consider what you want out of the trip and how you will handle the responsibility of taking care of your pet on the road.

The most important consideration is, of course, your pet. Always try to see things from her point of view. Most cats, for example, really would prefer to stay home. The best candidates for travel are pets who are even tempered, well behaved, sociable, and in good health. If your pet is anxious, aggressive, or likely to be highly stressed by new situations or time spent confined, it is probably better for her if you make alternative plans, such as boarding or pet sitting in your home.

While it is legal to transport an eight-week-old kitten or puppy by airplane, it is advisable to wait until an animal is at least 12 weeks old. At eight weeks, animals are susceptible to many diseases because their immune systems are not fully developed. It's also important to control the environment of very young puppies and kittens so they don't have experiences that may frighten them. This is difficult to do while traveling.

Some trips are inappropriate for pets because of the environment, time of year, and nature of the journey. A friend of mine decided to take her six-year-old Labrador Retriever on a cross-country drive from New York to Arizona. She left at the end of June. By the time she reached the Grand Canyon, it was mid-July. The heat was tough on her but almost unbearable for her dog. As a result, she spent a lot of her time worrying about her dog and not much time sightseeing. If she had made the trip at a different time of year, the adventure might have been more pet-friendly.

Who Should Stay and Who Should Go?

Bring	Don't Bring
Calm pets	Anxious pets
Well-behaved pets	Pets who are noisy, boisterous, or not housetrained
Friendly pets	Unfriendly pets
Well-socialized pets	Unsocialized pets
Pets who enjoy new experiences	Fearful pets
Pets over 12 weeks old	Pets under 12 weeks old
If your travel plans are pet-friendly	If your travel plans are not pet-friendly
If the weather permits	If the weather will be uncomfortable for your pet

Be honest with yourself about whether your pet is well trained and socialized enough to go on the road. Think of the things you two are going to be doing together during your trip, and make sure that your pet can do them all without any fuss. While you're on the road is not the time to teach your dog to come when you call or your cat not to scratch the arm of a chair. Traveling with a poorly trained pet is stressful for you and for the animal. Plus, it's not fair to other pet owners: If your pet misbehaves in a hotel, park, or attraction that allows him, next year pets may not be allowed at all.

If you think your pet is not well trained enough to go on this year's trip, work on his training and you'll both be ready for next year.

What does a well-trained pet need to know? A dog should be *reliably* trained in the following:
- The basic four obedience commands: sit, down, stay, and come
- Walking nicely on a loose leash
- Greeting strangers politely
- Greeting other dogs politely
- Getting into and out of a car calmly
- Going through doors without charging ahead
- Getting off (and staying off) the furniture
- Stopping barking on command (and not barking when you're gone)
- Chewing only on appropriate chew toys
- Resting quietly in a crate
- Eliminating only when and where you say it is okay

A cat should be *reliably* trained in the following:
- Being polite (or at least aloof) with strangers
- Not charging through doors when they are opened
- Respecting any boundaries you set (such as staying off the curtains)
- Scratching only where you say it's appropriate
- Chewing only on appropriate items
- Resting quietly in a carrier
- Eliminating only in his litter box

It's a nice bonus for both of you if your cat will walk on a harness and leash, but it's not a necessity for safe and fun travel.

Great Places to Go with Pets

Visiting friends and family. When you stay at someone's home, a lot of the worry is taken out of your trip. Your pet is familiar with the idea of spending time at home alone and can probably be left in your friend's home while you go out during the day. There will be other people there who can help you care for your pet, and probably will provide some extra play time and cuddle time as well. They may enjoy your pet as much as you do, and she may even get a little spoiled.

There are a few things to keep in mind, though. Don't assume the people you are visiting really want a pet in their home. Ask first, and respect their decision. If they have pets, make sure that their pets (and yours) are sociable with other animals. Even if your pet is mild-mannered most of the time, don't tempt Mother Nature by mixing predator and prey. For instance, it is not a good idea to bring your cat to visit a friend who has a canary, or your terrier to visit your cousin who keeps hamsters.

If the person you're visiting has no pets, remember that his house will not be pet-proofed the way yours is. There may be precious objects on a low coffee table that can easily be knocked on the floor, houseplants to dig in, or exposed electrical cords to chew on. Help your friend pet-proof at least one room; when you can't supervise your pet in the house, that room can be her safe haven. Finally, make sure that your pet is not overlooked in all the excitement. Be sure to include her in as many activities as possible so that she has as much fun as you do.

Pet-friendly hotels and resorts. You'll find a lot of them listed in this book. Some simply allow animals. Others offer extras for your pet, ranging from gourmet snacks to grooming and other "spa" services to arranging pet sitters or dog walkers. Some even have pet daycare centers.

Whatever services they offer, just remember that you can't leave your pet in the room all day while you sightsee, come back for a quick walk and/or play session, and then go out again for a long dinner, followed by a movie. Your pet must be included in many of your activities.

Nature parks and camping sites. Trips to these sorts of destinations are fun for both you and your pet, especially if you have a dog. What could be more fun than a walk in the woods? You can even train most dogs to carry a special canine knapsack.

It's tempting to think that pets are welcome at all outdoor areas, but that's not the case. Many national and state parks do not allow pets. Be sure to find out beforehand if your pet can accompany you, and observe all posted regulations, including leash laws.

Some extra cautions if you have a dog: Just like us, dogs who are not usually physically active will not enjoy a physically demanding vacation. If you plan to take your dog hiking or swimming, spend some weeks before your trip getting her into condition. Talk to your veterinarian about setting up a fitness program for your dog.

Some extra cautions if you have a cat: Indoor cats will not enjoy suddenly being outdoors, and may well become very frightened. Even if your cat spends time outdoors when you are home, it is not safe for her to roam when you're on the road. You have no idea what dangers are lurking about, including wild animals, poisons, unsafe conditions, and unkind people. Also, cats lose their homing instincts when they're in unfamiliar territory, and if your cat walks away, she will not be able to find you again. Cats, as well as dogs, should be on leash at any outdoor site.

Doggie destinations. You can take vacations with your dog that will be as much of an adventure for her as they are for you. Dog camps, seminars, and workshops are a terrific way to have fun with your pet, enhance your bond, improve your dog's training, and learn more about your canine companion. You'll find a list of these destinations in Appendix B.

At the moment, there are no camps for pets of the feline persuasion. Cats are not big fans of a structured environment.

The Territory Thing

Dogs and cats are territorial animals. That means they always feel most comfortable on their home turf.

(Territorial instincts are stronger in cats than they are in dogs.) What constitutes "home turf" varies according to your pet and his lifestyle. It could be just your home, or your home and yard, or it might include certain parts of your neighborhood.

A long trip far from home is not the place to introduce your pet to the concept of leaving his territory. You need to spend some time beforehand getting him used to the idea. You can also teach him to regard his crate or carrier as a piece of "portable territory"—a little home away from home that will help him feel secure when he's on unfamiliar turf.

If you put your pet in a crate only when he has misbehaved and put him in the car only to go to the veterinarian, he's not going to like either of those places. That's why practice sessions are so important—and why they should always have a happy ending.

Crate or carrier training. Let's start with the crate or carrier. A crate or carrier is invaluable when your pet is traveling by car, and is required when your pet is traveling by air. Your pet's carrier should be strong and sturdy, with smooth edges. If you're flying, opaque sides are also important to minimize stress. The carrier should have a door with grille bars, several ventilation openings on each side, and a secure door and door latch. If you are traveling by air, your carrier should hold food and water dishes. Choose one that is big enough for your pet to stand up, turn around, and lie down in. Don't make the mistake of choosing a carrier that gives your pet too much extra room. Animals are more likely to be injured in a carrier that is too big. There are many different brands of carriers on the market. Airline-approved carriers are a wise choice because they can be used for both air and car travel and are generally very durable.

The first step is to teach your pet to accept and even enjoy time spent in his crate or carrier. To do so, leave the crate or carrier open and accessible all the time. Put an old towel or blanket in the bottom and a toy inside. When your pet shows an interest in it, toss a few treats inside. Let him investigate it on his own. Most pets will eventually choose to spend some time in the crate, because animals generally like little dens, even when they're in the middle of the living room. When your pet is resting in his crate, give him another treat, and then, briefly and without any fuss, close the door. Open it again in a few seconds, pop in another treat, and tell him what a fantastic pet he is. Slowly increase the time your pet spends in the crate from a few seconds to a few minutes. Make sure that every encounter is pleasant, and never use the crate to punish your pet. To make sure that he regards his crate as a safe place, don't let anyone bother him while he's in it.

Exploring new territory. Once you've established that the carrier or crate is safe territory, start walking your pet around town. Take your dog on a longer walk, outside his home turf, at least once a week. Put your cat in his carrier and take him for a walk, too. Go visit a nearby friend, go to a local pet-friendly shop, or just walk around in the sunshine. Get your pet used to the idea of going a bit farther afield.

Now it's time for a little road trip. Put your pet in his crate or carrier and put him in the car. Go for a drive around the block, come home, set the crate down on the floor, open the door, and offer your pet a treat or some play time. Tell him how wonderful he is. Gradually increase the length of these little trips until your pet can comfortably spend a few hours in the car, get out and visit someone, and then get back in the car for the trip home. Make your destinations fun places such as parks or the homes of people he really likes. Make sure that he meets plenty of new people, and sometimes give them a treat to feed him or let them fuss over him for a moment or two. Now he has learned that trips aren't always to scary places to meet people who hold him down. Sometimes travel can be a lot of fun.

Before You Go

Preparation is the key to traveling successfully with your pet. As we've seen, that includes training your pet and getting the crate or carrier you will use for your trip. It also includes planning your route and making your reservations.

Due to the fast-changing nature of the lodging industry, it is important to call ahead and confirm the pet-friendly status of lodgings before you depart. It's not uncommon for policies to change on short notice. After all, it can take just one irresponsible visitor with a pet to convince a hotel manager that pets just aren't worth the trouble.

Try to select a hotel with more than one floor, or one with rooms that open into an interior corridor. This way, if your pet does bolt through an open door, she'll be less likely to end up on the street. Ask when you make your reservations, and try to get a room with this safety feature in mind.

When confirming your reservations, ask a lot of questions to find out as much as you can. Be sure to double-check the fees and restrictions at each lodging. Accommodations often have restrictions on the number, size, type, or age of animals (puppies are often discouraged). Pets may be restricted to smoking rooms or certain areas of the property. Ask if you are allowed to leave your pet unattended in the room and, if so, whether the pet must be in her travel carrier or crate. Ask about any extra fees, too, and whether they are refundable.

Try to have a confirmation mailed, faxed, or e-mailed to you before your departure. At the very least, take down the name and title of a contact person for each of your lodgings.

If you're traveling by air, you will need to start out very early with your reservations, because most airlines restrict the number of pets they will accept on a single flight. In fact, the airline rules have become so complex that we devote a whole section to them, starting on page A-23.

Check the insurance policies—yours and your pet's. If you have health insurance for your pet, make sure that you understand what is covered and what is not and how you report a claim. Most pet health insurance policies do cover accidents and emergency care anywhere in the United States, but check anyway. If you're traveling outside the United States, find out what, if any, coverage your pet has.

Also check your own homeowner's insurance to find out whether you have any coverage if your pet damages or destroys something in a hotel room or someone's home. (Of course, your well-trained pet would never do such a thing. But her evil twin might, and you could still be blamed.)

Visit the veterinarian. Take your pet for a complete physical before you leave on your trip. The stress of travel can cause even the most minor health concern— one that may have been invisible to you—to turn into a more serious condition. A complete physical for your animal will also give you an opportunity to discuss your travel plans and concerns with your vet. Make sure to tell him where you are going, because your pet may need vaccinations or preventive medicines that are not necessary in your area but are important in the area you are visiting. For example, heartworm and Lyme disease are more of a concern in the Northeast,

while Rocky Mountain spotted fever is a problem in
the West. Your vet will know what precautions you and
your pet should take. If your pet becomes ill after you
have returned from your vacation, he'll know what to
look for as well.

Ask your veterinarian about flea and tick preventives,
too, even if you are not planning a trip to the great
outdoors. The grass at roadside rest stops is filled with
all kinds of creepy crawlies, and you need to keep your
pet safe.

If your pet is on medication, make sure to get an extra
prescription from your veterinarian, just in case. This
is also a good time to ask your vet if he can recommend a veterinarian or clinic at your destination. It
never hurts to be prepared!

If all this is not enough to convince you that your pet
needs a pre-trip check-up, consider that each state
has its own regulations regarding health certificates
for pets who cross state lines. In some states, all that's
required is that the pet be free from contagious diseases. In other states, a certificate of veterinary inspection is required. And some states require formal proof
that the pet has been vaccinated against rabies. It is
unlikely that you will ever be asked to show this paperwork, but if you are asked and you don't have it, your
pet may be quarantined and you can be fined.

Generally speaking, a health certificate from your
veterinarian and certification that your pet has been
vaccinated against rabies will get you anywhere in the
United States (except Hawaii). Still, it's not a bad idea
to check. The United States Department of Agriculture
maintains a database of rules for each state. You'll find
contact information in Appendix B.

There's a lot more to think about concerning your
pet's health, especially when you're on the road. In
fact, there's so much that we've given that information
its own section—Appendix A.

The day before. The day before you go, give your pet
a serious grooming routine. If your pet is normally
bathed, do it now. Comb and brush her and trim her
nails. Make sure she is the neatest, sweetest, freshest pet
in the world when she goes out to meet her public.

What to Pack
While you may love shopping for new things to take
with you on vacation, your pet prefers the old and
familiar. Take along as many familiar items as possible.

These reminders of home will help make unfamiliar
areas seem more like your pet's territory.

The following list may seem a bit daunting, but my
friends with young children insist that their lists are
much longer when they pack for their kids! It's usually
best to keep all of your pet's items in one easy-to-reach
bag. You want to avoid fumbling around for something
for your pet in an overheard bin or the back seat of
your car.

IDENTIFICATION
- A leash and collar or harness with ID tags and your
pet's license tag (if required). Your pet should wear
two ID tags when traveling: one with your permanent address and telephone number and another
that says where you can be reached while you're on
the road. If you will be changing your location often,
one trick is to staple a matchbook from your lodging
(minus the matches!) to a ring on your pet's collar.
You can also buy tags that can be changed by slip-
ping in a new piece of paper.
- Consider having your pet tattooed or microchipped
in addition to wearing traditional ID tags. Both
processes are humane and effective for tracking
pets. For more information about microchipping
and tattooing, talk to your veterinarian and refer to
Appendix B.
- A recent color photo. Taking every imaginable precau-
tion doesn't guarantee that your pet won't get loose
or lost. Consider running off some flyers with a color
photo of your pet and a description, just in case.

FOOD AND WATER
- Food and water bowls. Paper plates and a collapsible
water bowl are light to carry and easy to dispose of,
which is great at roadside rest stops. For dinner in
your hotel, though, your pet may appreciate eating
and drinking from his usual dinner dishes.
- Your pet's food. If it isn't a national brand and you
are not 100 percent certain you can find it everywhere you are going, be sure to bring enough for the
whole trip. A sudden change in your pet's diet could
cause an upset stomach. If you usually add a bit of
moist food to the dry food but prefer not to take
heavy cans with you, bring a few packets of bland
dry soup mix. Sprinkle a bit over the kibble and mix
with warm water to make a tasty gravy.
- If you bring canned food, don't forget a can opener
and a spoon.
- Your pet's usual brands of treats and biscuits.

○ A container of water from your home. This is especially advisable if your pet has a sensitive stomach and may be affected by drinking unfamiliar water. You can also buy bottled water on the road or bring along one of those filtered water pitchers so that you can filter the tap water wherever you go.

○ A spray bottle to squirt water in your pet's mouth, if there is no other way to get him a quick drink.

CLEANUP SUPPLIES

○ Plastic bags (for poop and soiled towels).

○ A lint and hair remover for yourself and to tidy up your lodgings.

○ A room deodorizer.

○ Baby wipes or moist towelettes for quick and easy clean-ups of paws and hands.

○ Old cloths and/or paper towels for lining the carrier and cleanup.

○ A spray bottle of cleaner.

○ Grooming tools to keep your pet clean (and therefore more likely to be welcomed).

○ A flea comb and brush.

SLEEPING

○ A familiar bed, towel, or piece of carpet for your pet to sleep on.

○ An old bath towel or sheet to put on the hotel bed or sofa if you let your pet on the furniture.

TOYS

○ Hollow toys that you can stuff with food are especially good choices for when you want to leave your pet alone in a crate or carrier for a few hours.

○ Toys your pet uses to exercise aerobically, such as balls or flying discs (for dogs) or fishing pole toys (for cats).

MEDICAL SUPPLIES

○ Any medication prescribed by your veterinarian, along with an extra prescription.

○ A first-aid kit (see Appendix A).

○ A slip-on muzzle in case your pet has a medical emergency.

○ Tweezers for removing burrs, ticks, and other nasty things.

○ Health and rabies certificates.

○ Bug or flea spray.

EXTRAS

○ A clip-on miniature fan for the hotel room or the car.

○ A cooling pack or pad for the carrier.

JUST FOR DOGS

○ Chew toys.

○ Short and long leashes.

○ A flashlight for nighttime walks.

JUST FOR CATS

○ A scratching post or pad.

○ A litter box, scoop, a plastic bag to slip over the box, and a couple of large rubber bands or luggage straps to hold the bag in place.

○ The same litter your cat uses at home. If it isn't a national brand and you are not 100 percent certain you can find it everywhere you are going, be sure to bring enough for the whole trip. Cats are extremely particular about their litter and will not use a litter they don't like. A road trip is not the time to switch brands.

Stress and Traveling

Traveling is stressful for people, and it's even more so for pets. The best ways to alleviate stress for your pet are to teach her what you want and to control her environment. A lot of stress comes from not knowing how to act. Be considerate of your pet's stress levels. Don't expect her to meet and greet too many people in one day. Even the most social animals can be overwhelmed if too many people say hello at once or if they are overtired. Control who comes into contact with your pet and how often. Watch your pet for signs of stress (yawning, panting, excessive grooming, or avoiding eye contact) and give her a quiet place to relax if she needs to. A crate or blanket is great for this purpose.

Many animals suffer from a lack of appetite when they are traveling or are under stress in general. If you plan ahead, you can train your pet to eat in the car and/or in her carrier. Feed her in her carrier for at least a few weeks before to your trip. By doing so, you will train your pet to think of her crate as her safe haven *and* a portable dining room.

In the Air

Air travel can be a very stressful and sometimes even a dangerous experience for pets. This is especially true if they are in the baggage or cargo hold instead of in the cabin with you. The International Air Transport Association, which along with the United States Department of Agriculture governs air travel for pets, estimates that half a million dogs and cats travel on commercial airlines in the United States each year. Of those, a reported 99 percent arrive at their destination without incident. However, that leaves approximately 5,000 airline mishaps a year—enough to make any pet owner very cautious of this mode of transportation.

The safest way to fly with a pet is to have him in the cabin with you. However, this is not possible if your pet's carrier will not fit under the seat in front of you or if you are flying with more than one pet. In that case, pet and carrier must be sent in the baggage compartment. When the baggage compartment contains animals, it usually is pressurized. But still, this part of the plane is not designed for comfort. It will be heated in the winter, but not cooled in the summer. The ventilation may be poor. And carriers with pets inside have been subject to rough handling.

The best way to ensure your pet's safety is to ask lots of questions and get answers that sound right to you before you proceed. Just remember that each person you speak with is in some way responsible for the care of your pet, so be considerate!

Each airline has its own guidelines for travel. Find out what an airline's policies are *before* you book your trip, and let the airline know that you will be flying with a pet when you book your ticket. Reconfirm your plans 24 to 48 hours before your flight leaves, especially during peak flying times. If possible, get written confirmation of your arrangements from the airline.

QUESTIONS TO ASK

To travel by plane, all pets need a health certificate that has been issued no more than ten days before the flight and an airline-approved carrier. After that, the rules can get complicated. Because airlines change their rules regarding travel with pets fairly often, we do not list individual airline policies here. Most airlines have information regarding pet travel on their Web sites (see Important Toll-Free Numbers and Online Information). However, we can give you a list of things to ask about when you make your plans:

- **Are there restrictions on what breeds and types of animals may fly?** Many airlines have restrictions on what times of year breeds with short muzzles, such as Bulldogs, Pugs, and Boston Terriers and Himalayan and Persian cats, may fly, because they have more difficulty adjusting to hot weather. They may also have difficulty breathing at high altitudes because of their short nasal passages, and some airlines do not accept them at all.

- **Are there restrictions on what times of the year animals may fly?** Most airlines will not accept animals in the baggage hold if the outside temperature at *every airport where the flight stops* is no less than 32 degrees F and no more than 85 degrees F. Many simply will not accept animals in the baggage compartment during the summer months. Generally, these rules do not apply to pets flying with you in the cabin, but be sure to ask.

- **Are there restrictions on how many animals may fly in the cabin? As baggage?** Most airlines limit the number of animals they will allow on a plane. Some will let you reserve a spot for your pet when you make your reservation. Some accommodate pets in the cabin on a first-come, first-served basis, and your pet may end up being checked as baggage.

- **How much will it cost?** The cost of flying your pet is determined by the individual airline and may be based on the size and weight of your animal, as well as where and how he flies (cabin, baggage, or cargo). If you take your pet in the cabin, the carrier counts as a piece of hand luggage, but you will still have to pay a fee—usually $75 to $100.

- **What are the carrier requirements?** In the cabin, a carrier must be small enough to fit under the seat in front of you. Both soft-sided and molded plastic carriers are usually acceptable. If your pet is traveling in the baggage hold, the crate must be rigid and big enough for your pet to stand up, turn around, and lie down in comfortably. It must be sturdy and well ventilated and contain two plastic food and water dishes (these usually come with the crate). Airlines generally have specifications for size, strength, and ventilation. If you do not have your own carrier, some airlines sell them, but they're usually quite a bit more expensive than carriers you buy from a store or catalog.

- **If a pet can't fly in the cabin, does he fly as checked baggage or as cargo?** Generally, to travel on your flight as checked baggage, the total weight of your pet and his carrier must not exceed 100 pounds. You can check in your pet when you check your own luggage, and he travels on the same flight with you. If the combined weight of the animal and the carrier is greater than 100 pounds, most airlines will allow the pet only to be shipped as cargo. And some airlines require that all animals be shipped as cargo. When flying as cargo, airlines do not guarantee that your pet will be on the same flight as you. You may have to drop your pet off at a cargo terminal, and you may also have to arrange the flight through a cargo agent. Pricing also changes: It will be based on the weight and/or the measurements of the crate. Flying as cargo is one of the most hazardous ways to transport your pet. Make sure that you understand everything you must do. If cargo is your only option, you need to be even more careful to question the airline on every aspect of your pet's journey.

WHEN TO TRAVEL

✪ **Best days to fly.** Weekday flights are usually less hectic than weekend flights. Therefore, both you and your pet are more likely to receive attentive service during the week.

✪ **Best months to fly.** If you must travel in the summer months, book flights only in the early morning or late evening when the temperatures are lowest. In the winter, midday flights are best because temperatures are usually higher than in the morning or evening.

✪ **Best routes to fly.** Direct and nonstop flights are best. Avoid bringing your pet on a flight with a stopover, especially flights that require passengers to change planes. These are the situations in which a mishap is most likely to occur because of scheduling changes or simple human error. If you are making a flight connection to a different airline, you will have to retrieve and recheck your animal and pay another fee.

GUIDELINES FOR PETS
Pets who can travel by plane. Healthy animals over eight weeks old who have been issued a health certificate no more than ten days before flying are legally allowed to fly. However, it is advisable to wait until your pet is at least 12 weeks old. If your pet is under the care of a veterinarian for an existing medical condition, consult your vet regarding the pros and cons of air travel.

Pets who shouldn't travel by plane. If your pet is pregnant, ill, or less than 12 weeks old, he should not fly, because the stress can cause serious complications. You should also consider an alternative method of travel or consult your vet if your pet does not handle new and stressful situations well.

Feeding. In most cases, it is advisable to avoid feeding your pet a large meal within two hours of your departure time. Instead, provide a light meal for your pet four to six hours before departure. Allow small amounts of water periodically in the hours before the trip.

Tranquilizers. The American Veterinary Medical Association advises pet owners not to give a pet a tranquilizer before flying, because some animals have an adverse reaction to the combination of sedatives and high altitude. Tranquilizers may make the animal less able to right himself if his carrier is mishandled and can

also affect your pet's ability to regulate his body temperature. Instead, try to exercise your pet before departure so he will be more likely to relax or even fall sleep.

AIRLINE TRAVEL TIPS
If your pet is flying in the cabin with you. You will be required to leave him in his carrier for the entire flight, so make sure that your pet is used to sleeping there. When you arrive at the security checkpoint, you will be required to remove your pet from his carrier and send the carrier through the X-ray machine. Be sure to have a collar or harness and leash on your pet. To avoid delays, have your pet's health certificate and boarding pass ready when you approach the security gate.

If you're checking your pet as baggage or cargo. The checking-in process can take a bit of time, so get to the airport at least 2 1/2 hours before the flight. Make sure that you have all your paperwork ready and be friendly to everyone at the airline—remember, they will be taking care of your pet. Be sure to bring a health certificate that was issued no more than ten days before the flight.

Have a crate that is airline-approved and the right size for your pet. The crate should be big enough for your pet to stand up, turn around, and lie down in with ease. If it is too large, your pet could be hurt because too much movement means that he is more likely to be banged around. Don't put any toys in the crate, because they increase the possibility of choking. Ready the crate for the trip by securing its fasteners super-tight. Secure a water bowl or bucket that won't spill and that your dog's head can't get caught in. Fill the water bowl with ice that will melt en route. Put in some bedding that can be thrown away at your destination if it is soiled; try to use something that has your scent on it to help your pet feel more secure. Make sure that the crate is clearly identified and boldly marked so you can spot it from a distance. It should have your name and address firmly affixed to it. You can also tape a friendly note to the top of the crate with information regarding your pet. A sample might be, "Hi, my name is Flash. I am a two-year-old Border Collie. I am going to Houston on flight 123 on American Airlines. Thank you for taking good care of me."

After you check your pet in, go to your gate and watch to make sure that your pet is safely loaded. (A brightly marked carrier will make it easy to spot your animal.) Ask one of the airline employees to reconfirm with baggage personnel that your pet is aboard. Also ask them to inform the captain that there are animals in the baggage compartment. Be polite, but insist.

If you must change planes at a stopover, check with the airline personnel again to make sure that your pet has made the connection. If there will be a long delay in the second flight departure, claim your pet, take him for a quick walk, and then reboard him.

Upon arrival, your pet will be delivered to the baggage claim area. Pick him up there as quickly as you can.

On the Road

Travel by car is a far better option for your pet than travel by airplane. It is safer and less stressful. However, there are two major safety concerns for pets: restraint and overheating.

RESTRAINT

A loose animal in a car is a danger to herself and everyone else. If you make a short stop or are involved in an accident, the animal could be badly injured or killed. Your pet has a higher center of gravity than you do, and far less ability to grab onto something. It doesn't take much to send a dog flying into the dash, windshield, or you, or out of the car altogether. In a 30-miles-per-hour collision, an animal becomes a lethal weapon to all the passengers inside. When loose, an animal is also likely to distract you and may get caught under the accelerator or brake pedal. In addition, if you have even a minor accident, a pet who is loose in the car can easily get out and may run across the road and get hit by a car or run away and get lost.

Make sure that your pet is restrained to avoid accidents and injury. Options for restraint include a carrier or crate, a harness attached to a seatbelt, a regular leash tied to a stationary part of the car, or a gate that restricts the animal to a certain part of the car (often the rear deck in a station wagon or sport utility vehicle). If you decide to use a carrier or crate, make sure that it is secured in the car so it won't tip over if you make a sharp turn or stop. Put a sticker or tag on the crate that says, "In case of an accident, take this animal to a veterinarian, and then contact the following people [list names and phone numbers], who have guaranteed to pay all expenses." Remember that you may not be able to speak for your pet if you have been in a serious accident.

Animals who enjoy car rides can be secured with a pet seatbelt or leash, giving them the freedom to move around just a little bit, but still keeping them—and you—safe.

While dogs, especially, like nothing more than to stick their head out the window of a moving car, feeling the wind in their hair and catching bugs in their teeth, allowing this is not a good idea. It's common for animals to need veterinary care when debris becomes embedded in their eyes. All that cold air forced into the lungs can also give a pet respiratory problems. You can open the windows a bit to allow fresh air to circulate, but not enough to enable your pet to stick his head out. If you want to open your windows fully, consider installing window guards or restrain your pet so that she can't put her head out.

OVERHEATING

Leaving your pet in the car unsupervised is a dangerous proposition. Even in mild temperatures, a car can heat up in minutes to a level that can cause heatstroke and even death. On warm days, the temperature in your car can rise to 120 degrees F in a matter of minutes, even with the windows cracked open and even if you park in the shade. Heatstroke can quickly be fatal for dogs and cats. (For information about emergency treatment for heatstroke, see Appendix A.) Dogs and cats do not have efficient internal cooling systems because they don't sweat very much through their skin—rather, they rely on panting. In warm weather, a damp towel draped over the carrier will help to cool the air circulating through the crate while you are in the car with your pet, but it will not do much good in a car that isn't moving.

If you are traveling alone and have a small pet in a portable carrier, take her with you. If you must leave your pet in the car when you go to the rest room, one option is to leave the car running with the air-conditioning on (in warm weather). You'll need to have two sets of car keys with you so you can leave one in the ignition and still lock the car. Be sure to keep your pet secured in the car and away from the car's control panels, and remember that leaving your pet alone even for a moment leaves her susceptible to thieves. Also remember that you can't do this for very long; eventually, fumes in the car will make your pet sick. So this option is only for *short* bathroom breaks.

What if you don't have air-conditioning? You can park in the shade, place your pet in a crate, padlock the crate door, and use a sturdy bicycle lock to lock the crate to the outside of your car. (*Never* leave your pet tied in or to your car.) If it's very hot even in the shade, clip a battery-powered miniature fan to the crate for circulation. Remember that your pet is still susceptible to thieves this way.

What about longer stops? Many attractions have boarding arrangements for pets. Check ahead to find out what facilities are available, or consider daycare at a boarding kennel near the attraction you are interested in visiting. As for those spur-of-the-moment shopping stops, if you are traveling alone, your pet will save you a lot of money!

REST STOPS

When you're on the road, try to keep as close to your pet's normal routine as possible. When you stop for yourself, always be considerate of your pet and allow her time to stretch and relieve herself as well. How often you should stop depends on your pet's age and temperament. For very young or old animals, stops should be more frequent. Traveling can be stressful for even the calmest animal, and stress will make your pet more likely to need to eliminate. So allow your pet a few more opportunities to get out and eliminate than you would at home.

Allowing her to exercise for a bit before you head off will make her more likely to sleep. Many rest stops have grassy areas appropriate for pets, but no matter how well trained your pet is, be sure to keep her on a leash at all times.

At each rest stop, offer your pet some water from home. If you can, take along ice cubes, which are easier on your pet than large amounts of water. Keep feeding to a minimum during travel. Provide a light meal for your pet two to three hours before you leave, and save the big meal for after you stop for the day.

CAR SICKNESS

Consult your vet if your pet has a history of serious car-sickness (you'll also find information in Appendix A). The veterinarian may recommend medication. A holistic approach might also work well for your pet. Many people have had success with Rescue Remedy, which is a mix of flower essences. Discuss this option with your vet as well. Never give your pet any drugs, especially tranquilizers, without your veterinarian's approval.

Other Ways to Travel

With the exception of service dogs, only a few cruise ships accept pets. Some cruise lines permit pets in private cabins, but they are mostly confined to kennels. Contact cruise lines in advance to find out their policies and which of their ships have kennel facilities. If you must use the ship's kennel, make sure that it is clean, well kept, and protected from the elements.

Amtrak and most major bus companies do not allow pets unless they are service dogs. There may be smaller train and bus companies that do permit animals, so call ahead and find out.

In Europe, many countries allow pets on trains, buses, and even public transportation within cities. Generally, it is the passengers' responsibility to feed and exercise their pets at station stops. The basic rules of good manners apply in all cases.

Travel Abroad

Make plans well in advance. Regulations vary from country to country. Ask your travel agent for information, as well as your airline and the embassy or consulate of the country you are traveling to. Great Britain, Japan, and some other countries have quarantine periods for visiting pets, as does Hawaii. The rules keep changing, so be sure to find out *before* you plan your trip.

For travel to Canada, you must carry a certificate issued by a veterinarian that clearly identifies the animal and certifies that the dog or cat has been vaccinated against rabies during the preceding 36 months. The various Canadian provinces may have different requirements, so be sure to contact the government of the province you plan to visit.

For travel to Mexico, you must carry a health certificate prepared by your veterinarian within two weeks of the day you cross the border. The certificate must include a description of your pet, the lot number of the rabies vaccine used, indication of distemper vaccination, and a veterinarian's statement that the animal is free from infectious and contagious diseases. This certificate must be stamped by an office of the US Department of Agriculture (USDA).

Travel Petiquette

Allowing pets to stay is a courtesy offered by lodging owners. Many places roll out the red carpet for travelers with pets, but they are also quick to roll the carpet up and put it away after just one or two bad encounters! You and your pet act as ambassadors for every person who travels with a pet, so please be on your best behavior. Make sure to follow basic rules, such as cleaning up after your pet, as well as any specific rules posted by the management. If no rules are posted, ask about them. Be understanding of people's concerns about pets as well. It's hard to believe, but not everyone likes animals as much as you do!

Use the following guidelines while in lodgings:

- Even if your pet sleeps on the furniture at home, a good pet guest stays off the furniture when visiting. If you simply can't bear the idea of sleeping without Fido or Fluffy, be sure to bring along your own towel or sheet to cover the bed.

- Always clean up after your pet. Also, please clean up any other pet messes you see lying around. It's the right thing to do. (Anyway, someone might think your pet did it!)

- Ask the manager where he or she would prefer you to walk your dog. Walk your dog in areas away from flowerbeds and other public areas. (Be aware that many public areas and lodgings use poisons to get rid of insects and rodents. These are also poisonous to pets. When you register, ask if any poisons are used. See Appendix B for information about the ASPCA Animal Poison Control Center.)

- Be sure to wipe your pet's feet before you enter the room after a walk.

- Always keep your pet on a leash or in her carrier.

- Never leave your pet alone in your room unless she is in her carrier and you are sure she will not disturb other guests. This is for the safety of your pet and the lodging employees. An employee might enter the room to clean and accidentally let your pet slip out of the room. For the safety of employees, if you must leave your pet alone in a room, it is best to hang the Do Not Disturb sign.

- Put your suitcases in front of the door when you're in the room. This way, if you open the door and your pet makes a dash for it, there are obstacles to slow her down.

- Do not bathe your pet in the bathtub in your room.

- If your pet damages any hotel property, discuss the situation with the manager immediately and agree to cover all costs.

- If you have a cat, put some newspaper under the litter box and put the box in the bathroom or in the bathtub so the cat is less likely to track litter on the carpet. If your cat scatters litter out of the box, be sure to clean it up.

- Control who comes into contact with your pet. Allowing too many people to say hello to her may add to her stress (and yours!). The stress of traveling can make even the friendliest animal behave in unexpected ways.

Alabama

Alexander City

Motel/Motor Lodge

★ **JAMESON INN.** *4335 Hwy 280 (35010). Phone 256/234-7099; toll-free 800/526-3766; fax 256/234-9807. www.jamesoninns.com.* 60 rooms, 2 story. S, D $48; each additional $5; suites $53-$58; under 13 free. Pets accepted. Complimentary continental breakfast. Check-out 11 am. TV; cable (premium). In-house fitness room. Pool.

D 🐾 ➰ 🏃 ⬚ SC

Anniston

Motel/Motor Lodge

★ ★ **BEST WESTERN RIVERSIDE INN.** *11900 US Hwy 78 (35135). Phone 205/338-3381; fax 205/338-3183. www.bestwestern.com.* 70 rooms, 2 story. S $35-$40; D $45-$55; each additional $6; under 12 free; race weekends 4-day minimum. Pets accepted, some restrictions. Check-out 11 am. TV. Laundry services. Restaurant. Pool; children's pool. Boats, waterskiing. Pier.

D 🐾 ⚓ ➰ ⬚

Athens

Motel/Motor Lodge

★ **BEST WESTERN ATHENS INN.** *1329 Hwy 72 (35612). Phone 256/233-4030; fax 256/233-4554. www.bestwestern.com.* 88 rooms, 2 story. S $36; D $44; each additional $4; under 12 free. Pets accepted, some restrictions; fee. Complimentary continental breakfast. Check-out noon. TV; cable (premium). Pool.

D 🐾 ⚓ ⚡ ➰ ⬚

Auburn

Motel/Motor Lodge

★ **BEST WESTERN UNIVERSITY CONVENTION CENTER.** *1577 S College St (36830). Phone 334/821-7001. www.qualityinn.com.* 122 rooms, 3 story. S, D $42-$69; each additional $5; suites $64-$84; under 18 free;

higher rates Auburn University football games (2-day minimum). Pets accepted. Complimentary continental breakfast. Check-out 11 am. TV; cable (premium). In-room modem link. Restaurant, bar. In-house fitness room. Pool.

D 🐾 ➰ 🏃 ⬚ SC

Hotel

★ ★ ★ **AUBURN UNIVERSITY HOTEL.** *241 S College St (36830). Phone 334/821-8200; toll-free 800/228-2876; fax 334/826-8755. www.auhcc.com.* This hotel and conference center, with elegantly furnished rooms, is located in scenic Auburn, near Auburn University. 248 rooms, 6 story. S, D $59-$125; each additional $10; suites $165-$250; under 18 free; higher rates football games. Pets accepted. Check-out noon. TV. In-room modem link. Restaurant, bar. Health club privileges. In-house fitness room. Pool. Located on eastern edge of campus opposite Samford Hall.

D 🐾 ➰ 🏃 ⬚ SC

Birmingham

Motels/Motor Lodges

★ **BAYMONT INN.** *513 Cahaba Park Cir (35242). Phone 205/995-9990; fax 205/995-0563. www.baymontinns.com.* 102 rooms, 3 story. S $41.95; D $47.95; each additional $7; suites $55.95-$62.95; under 18 free. Pets accepted, some restrictions; fee. Complimentary continental breakfast. Check-out noon. TV; cable (premium). In-room modem link.

D 🐾 ⬚ SC

★ **LA QUINTA INN.** *905 11th Ct W (35212). Phone 205/324-4510; fax 205/252-7972. www.laquinta.com.* 106 rooms, 3 story. S, D $57-$77; each additional $10; under 18 free. Pets accepted, some restrictions. Complimentary continental breakfast. Check-out noon. TV. Pool.

D 🐾 ➰ ⬚ SC

Hotel

★ ★ **PICKWICK HOTEL AND SUITES.** *1023 20th St S (35205). Phone 205/933-9555; toll-free 800/255-7304; fax 205/933-6918. www.pickwickhotel.com.* 63 rooms, 8 story. S, D $86-$89; each additional $10; suites $109; under 12 free; weekend rates. Pets accepted; fee. Complimentary continental breakfast. Check-out noon. TV. In-room modem link. Health club privileges. Free covered parking. In historical area. Art Deco décor.

D 🐾 🏃

Clanton

Motels/Motor Lodges

★ **DAYS INN.** *2000 Holiday Inn Dr (35046). Phone 205/755-0510; fax 205/755-0510. www.daysinn.com.* 100 rooms, 2 story. S, D $45-$56; each additional $5; under 19 free. Pets accepted; fee. Check-out noon. TV. In-room modem link. Restaurant, bar. Room service. Pool; children's pool. Free airport transportation.

⌨ 🏊 🖥 SC

★ **KEY WEST INN.** *2045 7th Ave S (35045). Phone 205/755-8500; fax 205/280-0044.* 43 rooms, 2 story. S $42; D $46; each additional $5; under 18 free; higher rates fishing tournaments. Pets accepted; fee. Check-out noon. TV. In-room modem link. Laundry services. Totally nonsmoking.

D ⌨ 🖥 SC

Cullman

Motel/Motor Lodge

★ **DAYS INN.** *1841 4th St SW (35055). Phone 256/739-3800; toll-free 800/329-7466. www.daysinn.com.* 117 rooms, 2 story. S, D $41-$52; each additional $5; family, weekly rates. Pets accepted, some restrictions; fee. Complimentary full breakfast. Check-out noon. TV; cable (premium). In-room modem link. Restaurant. Pool.

⌨ 🏊 🖥 SC

Demopolis

Motels/Motor Lodges

★ **BEST WESTERN.** *1100 Hwy 80 E (36732). Phone 334/289-5772; fax 334/289-5775. www.bestwestern.com.* 70 rooms. S $45.95; D $49.95; each additional $2; under 12 free; weekly rates. Pets accepted; fee. Complimentary continental breakfast. Check-out 11 am. TV; VCR available (movies $6). In-room modem link. Health club privileges. In-house fitness room. Pool. Business center.

D ⌨ 🏊 🏋 🖥 🚶

★ **WINDWOOD INN.** *628 Hwy 80 E (36732). Phone 334/289-1760; toll-free 800/233-0841; fax 334/289-1768.* 90 rooms. S $29-$32; D $31-$35; each additional $5; kitchen units $34-$43; under 12 free. Pets accepted, some restrictions. Check-out 11 am. TV; cable (premium). Pool.

⌨ 🏊 🖥 SC

Dothan

Motels/Motor Lodges

★ ★ **COMFORT INN.** *3593 Ross Clark Cir NW (36303). Phone 334/793-9090; toll-free 800/474-7298; fax 334/793-4367. www.comfortinn.com.* This hotel is conveniently located just 5 miles from Dothan Airport. Within a short distance are area amusement parks, trails, and gardens. 122 rooms, 5 story. Pets accepted, some restrictions; fee. Complimentary continental breakfast. Check-out 1 pm, check-in 2 pm. TV; cable (premium), VCR available (movies). In-room modem link. Restaurant. In-house fitness room. Health club privileges. Outdoor pool. **$**

D ⌨ 🏊 🏋 🖥 ✈ SC

★ **DAYS INN.** *2841 Ross Clark Cir (36301). Phone 334/793-2550; fax 334/793-7962. www.daysinn.com.* 2 story. S $31-$38; D $36-$48; each additional $5; family rates; some weekend rates. Pets accepted; fee. Check-out noon. TV; cable (premium). In-room modem link. Restaurant adjacent open 24 hours. Pool.

⌨ 🏊 🖥

★ ★ **HOLIDAY INN.** *2195 Ross Clark Cir SE (36301). Phone 334/794-8711; toll-free 800/777-6611; fax 334/671-3781. www.holiday-inn.com.* 144 rooms, 2 story. S $50-$56; D $56-$62; each additional $6; under 18 free; suites $64-$74. Pets accepted; fee. Complimentary full breakfast. Check-out noon. TV. In-room modem link. Restaurant, bar. Room service. Pool.

D ⌨ 🏊 🖥 SC

★ ★ **HOLIDAY INN.** *3053 Ross Clark Cir (36301). Phone 334/794-6601; fax 334/794-9032. www.holiday-inn.com.* 102 rooms, 2 story. S, D $57-$62; suites $66-$71; under 18 free; weekend rates. Pets accepted; fee. Check-out noon. TV; cable (premium). In-room modem link. Restaurant, bar. Room service. Pool; children's pool. Business center.

D ⌨ 🏊 🖥 SC 🏋

★ **MOTEL 6.** *2907 Ross Clark Cir SW (36301). Phone 334/793-6013; fax 334/793-2377. www.motel6.com.* 102 rooms, 2 story. S, D $28.99-$34.99; each additional $5-$6; under 17 free. Pets accepted, some restrictions. Check-out noon. TV. In-room modem link. Pool.

D ⌨ 🏊 🖥

★ ★ **RAMADA INN.** *3011 Ross Clark Cir (36301). Phone 334/792-0031; fax 334/794-3134. www.ramada.com.* 159 rooms, 2 story. S $57; D $67; each additional $6; suites $75-$105; under 18 free; weekly rates; some weekend rates. Pets accepted, some restrictions; fee. Complimentary breakfast. Check-out noon. TV; cable (premium), VCR available (movies). Restaurant 6 am-9 pm. Bar; entertainment. Room service. Pool; children's pool. Free airport transportation. Business center.

Eufaula

Motel/Motor Lodge

★ **RAMADA INN.** *US 82 and Riverside Dr (36027). Phone 334/687-2021; fax 334/687-2021. www.ramada.com.* 96 rooms, 2 story. S $44.50-$55; D $49.50-$66.50; each additional $5; suites $61.50-$65.50; under 18 free; golf plans. Pets accepted, some restrictions. Check-out noon. TV; cable (premium). In-room modem link. Restaurant, bar. Room service. Pool.

Evergreen

Motels/Motor Lodges

★ **COMFORT INN.** *83 Bates Rd (36401). Phone 251/578-4701; fax 251/578-3180. www.comfortinn.com.* 58 rooms, 2 story. S $38; D $50; each additional $5. Pets accepted; fee. Check-out 11 am. TV; cable (premium). In-room modem link. Pool.

★ **DAYS INN.** *Rte 2 Box 389 (36401). Phone 251/578-2100. www.daysinn.com.* 40 rooms, 4 suites, 2 story. Mid-June-Labor Day: S, D $48; each additional $5; suites $55-$60; under 12 free; lower rates rest of year. Pets accepted; fee. Complimentary continental breakfast. Check-out 11 am. TV; cable (premium).

Florence

Motel/Motor Lodge

★ **HOMESTEAD EXECUTIVE INN.** *505 S Court St (35630). Phone 256/766-2331; toll-free 800/248-5336; fax 256/766-3567.* 120 rooms, 2 story. S, D $51-$56; each additional $5; under 12 free. Bar 4 pm-1 am; closed Sun. Pets accepted; fee. Check-out noon. TV; cable (premium), VCR available (movies). Restaurant, bar. Room service. Pool; poolside service.

Fort Payne

Motel/Motor Lodge

★ **ECONO LODGE.** *1412 Glenn Blvd SW (35967). Phone 256/845-4013; fax 256/845-2344.* 79 rooms, 2 story. S $38-$42; D $42-$45; each additional $5; under 16 free; higher rates holidays. Pets accepted; fee. Check-out 11 am. TV; cable (premium), VCR available. Pool; children's pool.

Gadsden

Motel/Motor Lodge

★ **KEY WEST INN.** *10535 AL Hwy 168, Boaz (35957). Phone 256/593-0800; fax 256/593-9100. www.keywestinn.net.* 41 rooms, 2 story. Oct-Dec: S, D $46.50-$51.50; each additional $5; under 18 free; lower rates rest of year. Pets accepted, some restrictions; fee. Complimentary continental breakfast. Check-out 11 am. TV; cable (premium).

Greenville

Motel/Motor Lodge

★ **RAMADA INN.** *941 Fort Dale Rd (36037). Phone 334/382-2651. www.ramada.com.* 96 rooms, 2 story. S, D $57; each additional $6; under 18 free. Pets accepted; fee. Check-out noon. TV. In-room modem link. Restaurant, bar. Room service. Pool.

Guntersville

Motels/Motor Lodges

★ **BEST WESTERN.** *751 US Hwy 431 (35957). Phone 256/593-8410. www.bestwestern.com.* 116 rooms, 2 story. S $39-$46; D $48-$60; each additional $5; under 12 free. Pets accepted, some restrictions; fee. Check-out 11 am. TV. Pool; children's pool.

★ **COVENANT COVE LODGE AND MARINA.** *7001 Val Monte Dr (35976). Phone 256/582-1000; fax*

256/582-1385. www.covenantcove.com. 53 rooms, 2 story. Apr-Oct: S, D $47-$56; each additional $5; suites, kitchen units $78-$93; under 19 free; lower rates rest of year. Pets accepted, some restrictions; fee. Complimentary continental breakfast. Check-out 11 am. TV; cable (premium). Laundry services. Bar. Pool.

Huntsville

Motels/Motor Lodges

★ **BAYMONT INN.** 4890 University Dr NW (35816). Phone 256/830-8999; toll-free 800/428-3438; fax 256/837-5720. www.baymontinns.com. 102 rooms, 3 story. S $41.95; D $49.95-$54.95; each additional $5; under 18 free. Pets accepted, some restrictions; fee. Complimentary continental breakfast. Check-out noon. TV. In-room modem link. Pool.

★ **GUESTHOUSE INTERNATIONAL.** 4020 Independence Dr Nw (35816). Phone 256/837-8907; toll-free 800/331-3131; fax 256/837-5435. 112 kitchen suites, 1-2 story. Suites $75-$105; some weekend rates. Pets accepted; fee. Complimentary continental breakfast. Check-out noon. TV; cable (premium), VCR available. Fireplaces. Health club privileges. Pool; whirlpool. Airport transportation. Sports court.

★ ★ **HOLIDAY INN.** 3810 University Dr (35816). Phone 256/837-7171; toll-free 800/345-7720; fax 256/837-9257. www.holidayinn.com. 112 rooms, 2 story. S, D $69; under 12 free; some weekend rates. Pets accepted, some restrictions; fee. Check-out noon. TV; cable (premium). In-room modem link. Laundry services. Restaurant, bar. Room service. Health club privileges. Pool. Free airport transportation.

★ **LA QUINTA INN.** 3141 University Dr NW (35816). Phone 256/533-0756; toll-free 800/687-6667; fax 256/539-5414. www.laquinta.com. 130 rooms, 2 story. S $52; D $58; each additional $6; under 18 free. Pets accepted. Complimentary continental breakfast. Check-out noon. TV. In-room modem link. Health club privileges. Pool.

Hotel

★ ★ ★ **HILTON.** 401 Williams Ave (35801). Phone 256/533-1400; fax 256/534-4581. www.hilton.com. This hotel is adjacent to the Big Springs International Park and a short walk to the Von Braun Civic Center, the Museum of Art, and the Historic District. 279 rooms, 4 story. S $95-$103; D $105-$113; each additional $10; suites $130-$295. Pets accepted, some restrictions. Check-out noon. TV. In-room modem link. Restaurant 6 am-10 pm. Bar 11 am-midnight; entertainment except Sun. Health club privileges. In-house fitness room. Pool; whirlpool; poolside service. Free airport transportation. Business center. Luxury level. Civic Center, city park opposite.

Jasper

Motel/Motor Lodge

★ **TRAVEL RITE INN.** 200 Mall Way (36602). Phone 205/221-1161. 60 rooms, 2 story. S $31-$34; D $40; each additional $3; under 12 free. Pets accepted, some restrictions. Check-out 11 am. TV.

Mobile

Motels/Motor Lodges

★ **DRURY INN.** 824 S Beltline Hwy (36609). Phone 251/344-7700. 110 rooms, 4 story. S $69; D $80; each additional $8; under 18 free. Pets accepted. Complimentary continental breakfast. Check-out noon. TV. In-room modem link. Pool.

★ **GUESTHOUSE INTERNATIONAL.** 5472-A Inn Rd (36619). Phone 251/660-1520; fax 251/666-4240. www.shoneysinn.com. 118 rooms, 3 story. S $50; D $54; each additional $6; suites $62; under 18 free; golf plan. Pets accepted; fee. Check-out noon. TV. Pool.

★ **LA QUINTA INN.** 816 S Beltline Hwy (36609). Phone 251/343-4051; toll-free 800/531-5900; fax 251/343-2897. www.laquinta.com. 2 story. S, D $59-$79; each additional $8; under 18 free. Pets accepted, some restrictions. Complimentary continental breakfast. Check-out noon. TV; cable (premium). In-room modem link. Pool.

★ **RED ROOF INN.** 5450 Coca Cola Rd (36619). Phone 251/666-1044; toll-free 800/733-7633; fax 251/666-1032. www.redroof.com. 108 rooms, 2 story. S $36-$60; D $48.49-$56.99; each additional $8; under 18 free. Pets accepted. Check-out noon. TV.

Montgomery

Motels/Motor Lodges

★ **DAYS INN.** *2625 Zelda Rd (36107). Phone 334/269-9611; toll-free 800/329-7466; fax 334/262-7393. www.daysinn.com.* 104 rooms, 2 story. S, D $45-$60; under 17 free. Pets accepted; fee. Complimentary continental breakfast. Check-out 11 am. TV. In-room modem link. Pool.

D ⌖ ⌖ ⌖ SC

★★ **HOLIDAY INN.** *1185 Eastern Bypass (36117). Phone 334/272-0370; fax 334/270-1046. www.holiday-inn.com.* 211 rooms, 2 story. S, D $80.95-$89.95; suites $160; under 16 free. Pets accepted, some restrictions; fee. Check-out noon. TV. In-room modem link. Restaurant, bar. Room service. In-house fitness room; sauna. Game room. Indoor pool; whirlpool.

D ⌖ ⌖ ⌖ ⌖ ⌖ SC

★ **LA QUINTA INN.** *1280 Eastern Blvd (36117). Phone 334/271-1620; toll-free 800/531-5980; fax 334/244-7919. www.laquinta.com.* 130 rooms, 2 story. S $56; D $63; each additional $6; under 18 free. Pets accepted. Complimentary continental breakfast. Check-out noon. TV; cable (premium), VCR available. In-room modem link. Pool.

D ⌖ ⌖ ⌖ SC

★★ **RAMADA INN.** *1100 W South Blvd (36105). Phone 334/281-1660; fax 334/281-1667. www.ramada.com.* 150 rooms, 4 story. S, D $46-$56; suites $59-$69; under 10 free. Pets accepted, some restrictions; fee. Check-out noon. TV; cable (premium). In-room modem link. Laundry services. Restaurant, bar. Room service. Pool. Free airport transportation.

D ⌖ ⌖ ⌖ ⌖ SC

Opelika

Motels/Motor Lodges

★ **DAYS INN.** *1014 Anand Ave (36801). Phone 334/749-5080; toll-free 800/329-7466. www.daysinn.com.* 43 rooms, 2 story. S $38-$45; D $42-$50; each additional $5; suites $65-$80; under 12 free; higher rates special events. Pets accepted; fee. Complimentary continental breakfast. Check-out 11 am. TV; cable (premium). Indoor pool; children's pool; whirlpool.

D ⌖ ⌖ ⌖ SC

★ **TRAVELODGE.** *1002 Columbus Pkwy (36801). Phone 334/749-1461; toll-free 800/528-1234; fax 334/749-1468. www.bestwestern.com.* 95 rooms, 2 story. S $29-$34; D $36-$46; each additional $7; under 12 free; weekly rates. Pets accepted; fee. TV; cable. In-room modem link. Bar. Indoor pool; whirlpool. Business center.

D ⌖ ⌖ ⌖ SC

Selma

Motel/Motor Lodge

★★ **HOLIDAY INN.** *US Hwy 80 W (36701). Phone 334/872-0461; fax 334/872-0461. www.holiday-inn.com.* 165 rooms, 2 story. Pets accepted, some restrictions. Check-out noon. TV. In-room modem link. Restaurant, bar. Room service. Pool; children's pool. **$**

D ⌖ ⌖ ⌖ SC

Sheffield

Motel/Motor Lodge

★ **KEY WEST INN.** *1800 Hwy 72, Tuscumbia (35674). Phone 256/383-0700; toll-free 800/833-0555; fax 256/383-3191.* 41 rooms, 2 story. Pets accepted; fee. Complimentary continental breakfast. Check-out noon. TV; cable (premium). Laundry services. **$**

D ⌖ ⌖ SC

Troy

Motel/Motor Lodge

★ **SUPER 8.** *1013 Hwy 231 (36081). Phone 334/566-4960; fax 334/566-5858. www.super8.com.* 69 rooms, 2 story. Pets accepted, some restrictions. Complimentary continental breakfast. Check-out 11 am. TV; cable (premium). Pool. **$**

D ⌖ ⌖ ⌖ SC

Arizona

Bisbee

B&B/Small Inn

★ **HOTEL LA MORE/THE BISBEE INN.** *45 OK St (85603). Phone 520/432-5131; fax 520/432-5343. www.bisbeeinn.com.* 20 rooms, 2 story. Pets accepted, some restrictions. Complimentary breakfast. Check-out 11 am, check-in 3 pm. TV in sitting room. Restored 1917 hotel. Totally nonsmoking. **$**

Bullhead City

Motels/Motor Lodges

★ **BEST WESTERN BULLHEAD CITY INN.** *1126 Hwy 95 (86429). Phone 928/754-3000; toll-free 800/780-7234; fax 928/754-5234. www.bestwestern.com.* 88 rooms, 2 story. Pets accepted; fee. Complimentary continental breakfast. Check-out noon. TV; cable (premium). Pool; whirlpool. **$**

★ **LAKE MOHAVE RESORT.** *Katherine Landing (86430). Phone 928/754-3245; fax 928/754-1125.* 49 rooms, 1-2 story. Pets accepted, some restrictions; fee. Check-out 11 am. Restaurant, bar. Boat rental. Spacious grounds. **$**

Canyon de Chelly National Monument

Motel/Motor Lodge

★★ **BEST WESTERN CANYON DE CHELLY INN.** *100 Main St (Rte 7) (86503). Phone 928/674-5874; toll-free 800/327-0354; fax 928/674-3715. www.bestwestern.com.* 99 rooms. Pets accepted; fee. Check-out 11 am. TV. Restaurant. Indoor pool. Navajo décor. **$**

Carefree

Resort

★★★★ **THE BOULDERS RESORT AND GOLDEN DOOR® SPA.** *34631 N Tom Darlington Dr (85377). Phone 480/488-9009; toll-free 800/553-1717; fax 480/488-4118. www.wyndham.com/boulders.* Nestled in the foothills of the Sonoran Desert near Scottsdale, The Boulders Resort and Golden Door® Spa is a most unusual place, with a flair for the dramatic. Mimicking the natural landscape in its architecture, it teases the eye as it blends perfectly with its surroundings of rock outcroppings, ancient boulders, and saguaro cactus plants. The adobe casitas make wonderful homes and are distinguished by overstuffed leather chairs, exposed beams, and Mexican tiles, while one-, two-, and three-bedroom Pueblo Villas are ideal for families traveling together or for those on longer visits. The resort boasts a first-rate tennis facility and two 18-hole championship golf courses. The Golden Door® Spa, an outpost of the famous California spa, is simply divine and is particularly notable for its hot rock massage. A cavalcade of flavors is discovered at the six restaurants, from Mexican and Spanish to Southwestern and continental. 205 rooms, 1-2 story. Service charge $27/day. Pets accepted, some restrictions; fee. Check-out noon, check-in 4 pm. TV; cable (premium), VCR. In-room modem link. Fireplaces. Dining rooms (public by reservation). Bar; entertainment. Room service. In-house fitness room; spa; massage, sauna, steam room. Four heated pools; whirlpool; poolside service. Golf on premise, greens fee $230. Outdoor tennis. Business center. **$$$$**

Chandler

Resort

★★★ **SHERATON SAN MARCOS GOLF RESORT AND CONFERENCE CENTER.** *One San Marcos Pl (85225). Phone 480/812-0900; toll-free 800/528-8071; fax 480/963-6777. www.sanmarcosresort.com.* Located just minutes from Phoenix, this historic resort marries both business and pleasure into a desert oasis. Golf, tennis, and horseback riding are available on site, with great shopping and excursions close by, insuring that there's something for everyone. 307 rooms, 4 story. Pets accepted, some restrictions; fee. Check-out noon, check-in 3 pm. TV; cable (premium). Restaurant, bar. In-house fitness room. Pool; children's pool; whirlpool; poolside service. Golf on premise, greens fee $109 with cart. Outdoor tennis, lighted courts, pro. Business center. Concierge. **$**

Flagstaff

Motels/Motor Lodges

★ **DAYS INN.** *1000 W Rte 66 (86001). Phone 928/774-5221; toll-free 800/329-7466; fax 928/521-0228. www.daysinnflagstaff.com.* 158 rooms, 2 story. Pets accepted, some restrictions; fee. Complimentary continental breakfast. Check-out 11 am, check-in 3 pm. TV; cable (premium). Pool. **$**

D 🐾 ⌕ ⛺ SC

★ ★ **HOLIDAY INN.** *2320 E Lucky Ln (86004). Phone 928/714-1000; toll-free 800/533-2754; fax 928/779-2610. www.holiday-inn.com/flagstaffaz.* 157 rooms, 5 story. Pets accepted; fee. Check-out noon, check-in 3 pm. TV. In-room modem link. Restaurant, bar. Room service. In-house fitness room. Indoor pool; whirlpool. Downhill ski 11 miles. Free airport transporation. **$**

D 🐾 ⌕ ⛺ 🏃 ⛺

★ **QUALITY INN.** *2000 S Milton Rd (86001). Phone 928/774-8771; toll-free 800/228-5151; fax 928/773-9382. www.qualityinnflagstaffaz.com.* 96 rooms, 2 story. Pets accepted; fee. Complimentary continental breakfast. Check-out 11 am, check-in 2 pm. TV. Heated pool. Downhill ski 15 miles. Airport transportation. **$**

D 🐾 ⌕ ⛺ ⛺ SC

★ **RAMADA INN.** *2755 Woodlands Village Blvd (86001). Phone 928/773-1111; toll-free 877/703-0291; fax 928/774-1449. www.ramada.com.* 89 rooms, 2 story. Pets accepted, some restrictions; fee. Complimentary continental breakfast. Check-out 11 am, check-in 3 pm. TV; cable (premium). In-house fitness room; sauna. Heated pool; whirlpool. **$**

D 🐾 ⌕ 🏃 ⛺ SC

All Suites

★ **AMERISUITES.** *2455 S Beulah Blvd (86001). Phone 928/774-8042; fax 928/774-5524. www.amerisuites.com.* 117 rooms, 5 story. Pets accepted. Complimentary continental breakfast. Check-out noon. TV; VCR available. In-room modem link. Laundry services. In-house fitness room. Indoor pool; whirlpool. Free airport, train station, bus depot transportation. Business center. **$**

D 🐾 ⌕ ⛺ 🏃 ✈ ⛺ SC 🏃

★ ★ **EMBASSY SUITES.** *706 S Milton Rd (86001). Phone 928/774-4333; toll-free 800/774-4333; fax 928/774-0216. www.embassysuitesflagstaff.com.* Within walking distance of historic Flagstaff, this hotel offers a complimentary made-to-order breakfast each morning. 119 rooms, 3 story. Pets accepted, some restrictions; fee.

Complimentary full breakfast. Check-out noon. TV; cable (premium). In-room modem link. In-house fitness room. Heated pool; whirlpool. Downhill ski 12 miles. **$**

D 🐾 ⌕ ⛺ 🏃 ⛺

Florence

B&B/Small Inn

★ ★ **RANCHO SONORA INN & RV PARK.** *9198 N Hwy 79 (85232). Phone 520/868-8000; toll-free 800/205-6817. www.ranchosonora.com.* 11 rooms. Pets accepted. Complimentary continental breakfast. Check-out 11 am, check-in 2 pm. TV; cable (premium), VCR available (free movies). Laundry services. Pool; whirlpool. Built in 1930. Original adobe, western, and traditional décor. Courtyard. Some room phones. **$**

D 🐾 ⌕ 🏃 ⛺

Gila Bend

Motel/Motor Lodge

★ ★ **BEST WESTERN SPACE AGE LODGE.** *401 E Pima St (85337). Phone 928/683-2273; toll-free 800/780-7234; fax 928/683-2273. www.bestwestern.com.* 41 rooms, 1 story. Pets accepted. Check-out noon. TV; cable (premium). Restaurant 24 hours. Pool; whirlpool. **$**

D 🐾 ⛺ ⛺ SC

Glendale

Motels/Motor Lodges

★ **HOLIDAY INN EXPRESS.** *7885 W Arrowhead Towne Center Dr (85308). Phone 623/412-2000; fax 623/412-5522. www.holiday-inn.com.* 60 rooms, 2 story. Pets accepted, some restrictions; fee. Complimentary continental breakfast. Check-out 11 am, check-in 3 pm. TV; cable (premium). In-house fitness room. Heated pool; whirlpool. **$**

D 🐾 ⌕ 🏃 ⛺ SC

★ **LA QUINTA INN.** *16321 N 83rd Ave (85382). Phone 623/487-1900; toll-free 800/687-6667; fax 623/487-1919. www.laquinta.com.* 113 rooms, 5 story. Pets accepted, some restrictions. Complimentary continental breakfast. Check-out noon, check-in 3 pm. TV; cable (premium). In-room modem link. Laundry services. In-house fitness room. Pool; whirlpool. **$**

D 🐾 ⌕ 🏃 ⛺ SC

All Suite

★ **WINDMILL SUITES SUN CITY WEST.** *12545 W Bell Rd (85374).* Phone *623/583-0133; fax 623/583-8366. www.windmillinns.com.* 127 rooms, 3 story. Pets accepted. Complimentary continental breakfast. Check-out 11 am, check-in 4 pm. TV; cable (premium). Laundry services. Pool; whirlpool. **$**

D ⌨ ➰ ⊠

Globe

Motel/Motor Lodge

★ **TRAVELODGE.** *2119 Old West Hwy 60 (85502). Phone 928/425-7008; fax 928/425-6410.* 45 rooms, 2 story. Pets accepted; fee. Complimentary continental breakfast. Check-out noon. TV; cable (premium). Laundry services. **$**

D ⌨ ⊠

Grand Canyon National Park (South Rim)

Motel/Motor Lodge

★ **RODEWAY INN RED FEATHER LODGE.** *Hwy 64 (86023). Phone 928/638-2414; toll-free 800/538-2345; fax 928/638-2707. www.redfeatherlodge.com.* 234 rooms, 2-3 story. Pets accepted; fee. Check-out 11 am. In-house fitness room. **$**

D ⌨ ⚡ ⊼ ✈ ⊠

Holbrook

Motels/Motor Lodges

★★ **BEST WESTERN ARIZONIAN INN.** *2508 Navajo Blvd (86025). Phone 928/524-2611; toll-free 877/280-7300; fax 928/524-2253. www.bestwestern.com.* 70 rooms, 2 story. Pets accepted, some restrictions; fee. Check-out 11 am. TV; cable (premium). Restaurant 24 hours. Heated pool. **$**

⌨ ➰ ⊠

★ **COMFORT INN.** *2602 E Navajo Blvd (86025). Phone 928/524-6131; toll-free 800/228-5150; fax 928/524-2281. www.comfortinn.com.* 60 rooms, 2 story. Pets accepted,

some restrictions; fee. Check-out 11 am. TV; cable (premium). Pool. **$**

D ⌨ ➰ ⊠ SC

★ **ECONO LODGE.** *2596 Navajo Blvd (86001). Phone 928/524-1448; toll-free 800/446-6900; fax 928/524-1493. www.econolodge.com.* 63 rooms, 2 story. Pets accepted; fee. Complimentary breakfast. Check-out 11 am. TV; cable (premium). Laundry services. Heated pool. **$**

⌨ ➰ ⊠

★ **HOLIDAY INN EXPRESS.** *1308 Navajo Blvd (86025). Phone 928/524-1466; fax 928/524-1788. www.holiday-inn.com.* 59 rooms, 2 story. Pets accepted; fee. Complimentary continental breakfast. Check-out 11 am. TV. Laundry services. Indoor pool; whirlpool. **$**

D ⌨ ⚡ ➰ ⊠

Kayenta

Resort

★★ **GOULDING'S LODGE.** *1000 Main (84536). Phone 435/727-3231; fax 435/727-3344. www.gouldings.com.* 19 rooms, 2 story. Pets accepted. Check-out 11 am. TV; VCR available. Laundry services. Restaurant. Indoor pool. One building is an old trading post; now it is a museum. Guided jeep tours. John Wayne movies were filmed here. **$**

D ⌨ ⚡ ➰ ⊠

Kingman

Motels/Motor Lodges

★ **BEST WESTERN A WAYFARER'S INN.** *2815 E Andy Devine Ave (86041). Phone 928/753-6271; toll-free 800/548-5695; fax 928/753-9608. www.bestwestern.com.* 101 rooms, 2 story. Pets accepted, some restrictions; fee. Check-out noon. TV; cable (premium). Heated pool. **$**

➰ ⊠

★ **DAYS INN.** *3023 E Andy Devine Ave (86401). Phone 928/753-7500; toll-free 800/329-7466; fax 928/753-4686. www.daysinn.com.* 60 rooms, 2 story. Pets accepted; fee. TV; cable (premium). In-room modem link. Heated pool; whirlpool. **$**

D ⌨ ➰ ⊠ SC

★ **QUALITY INN.** *1400 E Andy Devine Ave (86401). Phone 928/753-4747; toll-free 800/869-3252; fax 928/753-5175. www.qualityinn.com.* 98 rooms, 1-2 story. Pets accepted; fee. Complimentary continental breakfast.

Check-out noon. TV; cable (premium). In-house fitness room; sauna. Pool; whirlpool. **$**

D ⬛🐾🏊🏃✈ SC

Lake Havasu City

Motel/Motor Lodge

★ ★ **HOLIDAY INN.** *245 London Bridge Rd (85204). Phone 928/855-4071; toll-free 888/428-2465; fax 928/855-2379. www.holiday-inn.com.* 162 rooms, 4 story. Pets accepted; fee. Check-out noon. TV; cable (premium). In-room modem link. Restaurant, bar. Room service. Game room. Heated pool. **$**

D 🐾🛎🏊🚭

Litchfield Park

Motel/Motor Lodge

★ **HOLIDAY INN EXPRESS.** *1313 N Litchfield Rd (85338). Phone 623/535-1313; fax 623/535-0950. www.holiday-inn.com.* 90 rooms, 3 story. Pets accepted, some restrictions; fee. Complimentary continental breakfast. Check-out noon. TV; cable (premium). In-room modem link. Laundry services. In-house fitness room. Game room. Pool; whirlpool. **$**

D 🐾🏊🏃🚭

Resort

★ ★ ★ **THE WIGWAM RESORT AND GOLF CLUB.** *300 Wigwam E Blvd (85340). Phone 623/935-3811; toll-free 800/935-3737; fax 623/856-1081. www.wigwamresort.com.* Once a private club for executives of the Goodyear Tire Company, The Wigwam Resort is one of Arizona's finest. Located in the village of Litchfield Park, it is only 20 minutes from downtown Phoenix. The rooms and suites highlight authentic regional design. Whitewashed wood furniture, slate floors, Mexican ceramic tiles, and traditional Southwestern colors distinguish the accommodations. Comfortable and spacious, the rooms could convince some guests to remain within, yet the tempting array of outdoor pursuits lures visitors from their hideaways. Three award-winning golf courses, nine tennis courts, two pools with a waterslide, and a fitness center with spa keep adults satisfied, while Camp Pow Wow puts a smile on the faces of the youngest guests. Five restaurants and bars have something for everyone, from continental cuisine and live entertainment to regional dishes in a traditional Southwestern kitchen. 331 rooms, 1-2 story. Pets accepted, some restrictions; fee. Check-out noon, check-in 4 pm. TV; cable (premium). Room service 24 hours. Dining room, bar. Supervised children's activities (June-Sept and holidays); ages 5-12. In-house fitness room; sauna, steam room. Indoor, outdoor pool; whirlpool; poolside service. Golf, greens fee $120 (including cart). Outdoor tennis, lighted courts. Skeet, trapshooting. Entertainment. Bicycles. Airport transportation. Business center. Concierge. **$$$$**

D 🐾🏌🏃⛷🏊🚶🚭

Marble Canyon

Motel/Motor Lodge

★ **MARBLE CANYON LODGE.** *Hwy 89A (86036). Phone 928/355-2225; toll-free 800/726-1789; fax 928/355-2227.* 58 rooms. Pets accepted. Check-out 11 am. Laundry services. Restaurant, bar. Hiking. 3,500-foot paved landing strip. Shuttle service for river rafting. **$**

D 🐾🛎🚭 SC

Mesa

Motels/Motor Lodges

★ **BEST WESTERN SUPERSTITION SPRINGS INN.** *1342 S Power Rd (85206). Phone 480/641-1164; toll-free 800/780-7234; fax 480/641-7253. www.bestwestern.com.* 59 rooms, 2 story. Pets accepted; fee. Complimentary continental breakfast. Check-out 11 am, check-in 2 pm. TV; cable (premium). In-room modem link. In-house fitness room. Pool; whirlpool. **$**

D 🐾🏊🏃🚭

★ **LA QUINTA INN.** *6530 E Superstition Springs Blvd (85206). Phone 480/654-1970; fax 480/654-1973. www.laquinta.com.* 113 rooms, 6 story. Pets accepted, some restrictions. Complimentary continental breakfast. Check-out noon, check-in 2 pm. TV; cable (premium). In-room modem link. In-house fitness room. Pool; whirlpool. **$**

D 🐾🏊🏃🚭

Hotel

★ ★ ★ **SHERATON MESA HOTEL AND CONVENTION CENTER.** *200 N Centennial Way (85201). Phone 480/898-8300; toll-free 800/456-6372; fax 480/964-9279. www.sheratonmesa.com.* 282 rooms, 12 story. Pets accepted, some restrictions; fee. Check-out noon, check-in 3 pm. TV; cable (premium), VCR available. Restaurant, bar. In-house fitness room. Heated pool; whirlpool. Luxury level. Elaborate landscaping with palm trees, fountain. **$**

D 🐾🏊🏃🚭

Resorts

★ ★ ★ **ARIZONA GOLF RESORT & CONFERENCE CENTER.** *425 S Power Rd (85206). Phone 480/832-3202; toll-free 800/528-8282; fax 480/981-0151. www.azgolfresort.com.* Tropical palms and beautiful lakes set the scene at this 150-acre golf resort. Guest suites, designed in clusters, have BBQs and heated spas. 187 rooms, 1-2 story. Pets accepted. Check-out noon, check-in 3 pm. TV; cable (premium), VCR available. Dining room, bar. In-house fitness room. Pool. Golf on premise. Lighted tennis. **$**

★ ★ ★ **GOLD CANYON GOLF RESORT.** *6100 S Kings Ranch Rd (85218). Phone 480/982-9090; toll-free 800/624-6445; fax 480/983-9554. www.gcgr.com.* Whether taking in beautiful sunsets or hitting the driving range, guests at this golf resort experience attentive service. 101 rooms, 1 story. Pets accepted; fee. Check-out 11 am, check-in 4 pm. TV; VCR available. In-room modem link. Fireplaces. Dining room, bar. Room service. Heated pool; whirlpool; poolside service. 36-hole golf, greens fee $80-$135 (including cart). Lighted tennis. Bicycle rentals. Concierge. In the foothills of the Superstition Mountains on 3,300 acres. **$**

Nogales

Motel/Motor Lodge

★ **SUPER 8.** *547 W Mariposa Rd (85621). Phone 520/281-2242; fax 520/281-0125. www.super8.com.* 117 rooms, 3 story. No elevator. Pets accepted; fee. Check-out noon. TV. Restaurant, bar. Pool; whirlpool. **$**

Resort

★ ★ ★ **RIO RICO RESORT AND COUNTRY CLUB.** *1069 Camino Caralampi (85648). Phone 520/281-1901; toll-free 800/288-4746; fax 520/281-7132. www.rioricoresort.com.* Go back in time with the Old West feel of this picturesque resort with its very own ghost town. 180 rooms, 2-3 story. No elevator. Pets accepted, some restrictions; fee. Check-out noon, check-in 4 pm. TV; cable (premium). Dining room, bar; entertainment weekends. Room service. In-house fitness room; sauna. Heated pool; whirlpool; poolside service. 18-hole golf, pro, putting green, driving range, greens fee $85 (including cart). Outdoor tennis, lighted courts. Lawn games. Horseback riding. Airport transportation. Business center. Stables. Western cook-outs. On mesa top with scenic view. **$$**

Page

Motels/Motor Lodges

★ ★ **BEST WESTERN ARIZONA INN.** *716 Rim View Dr (86040). Phone 928/645-2466; toll-free 800/826-2718; fax 928/645-2053. www.bestwestern.com.* 103 rooms, 3 story. Pets accepted; fee. Check-out noon. TV; VCR (movies). Restaurant, bar. Pool; whirlpool. Airport transportation. **$**

★ **BEST WESTERN PAGE INN.** *207 N Lake Powell Blvd (86040). Phone 928/645-2451; toll-free 800/637-9183; fax 928/645-9552. www.bestwestern.com.* 90 rooms, 3 story. Pets accepted; fee. Complimentary continental breakfast. Check-out 11 am. TV; cable (premium), VCR available (movies). In-room modem link. Heated pool; whirlpool. Free airport transportation. **$**

★ ★ **QUALITY INN.** *287 N Lake Powell Blvd (86040). Phone 928/645-8851; fax 928/645-2523.* 130 rooms, 3 story. Pets accepted, some restrictions. Check-out 11 am. TV. Laundry services. Restaurant, bar. Room service. Pool. **$**

★ ★ ★ **WAHWEAP LODGE.** *100 Lakeshore Dr (86040). Phone 928/645-2433; toll-free 800/528-6154; fax 928/645-1031. www.visitlakepowell.com.* Located on beautiful Lake Powell, this homey lodge offers a spectacular atmosphere. Guest rooms include lake or resort views. 350 rooms, 2 story. Pets accepted. Check-out 11 am. TV. Laundry services. Restaurant, bar. In-house fitness room. Two pools; whirlpool; poolside service. Boats, motorboats, scenic boat trips. Host for national bass fishing tournaments. Free airport transportation. Concierge. **$**

Payson

Hotel

★ ★ **BEST WESTERN PAYSON INN.** *801 N Beeline Hwy (85541). Phone 928/474-3241; toll-free 800/247-9477; fax 928/472-6564. www.innofpayson.com.* 99 rooms, 2 story. Pets accepted; fee. Complimentary continental breakfast. Check-out 11 am. TV; cable (premium). Restaurant, bar. Heated pool; whirlpool. **$**

Phoenix

Motels/Motor Lodges

★ **BEST WESTERN INNSUITES HOTEL PHOENIX.** *1615 E Northern Ave (85020). Phone 602/997-6285; toll-free 800/752-2204; fax 602/943-1407. www.bestwestern.com.* 105 rooms, 2 story. Pets accepted, some restrictions; fee. Complimentary continental breakfast. Check-out noon, check-in 2 pm. TV; cable (premium). In-room modem link. Laundry services. In-house fitness room. Health club privileges. Heated pool; whirlpool. **$**

D 🐾 ≈ 🏃 🚫 SC

★ **HAMPTON INN.** *8101 N Black Canyon Hwy (85021). Phone 602/864-6233; fax 602/995-7503. www.hamptoninn.com.* 147 rooms, 3 story. Pets accepted; fee. Complimentary continental breakfast. Check-out noon. TV; cable (premium). In-room modem link. Heated pool; whirlpool. **$**

D 🐾 ≈ 🚫 SC

★ ★ **HOLIDAY INN.** *1500 N 51st Ave (85043). Phone 602/484-9009; toll-free 800/465-4329; fax 602/484-0108. www.holiday-inn.com.* 147 rooms, 4 story. Pets accepted; fee. Check-out noon, check-in 2 pm. TV; cable (premium), VCR available. Restaurant, bar. In-house fitness room; sauna. Pool; whirlpool; poolside service. **$**

D 🐾 ≈ 🏃 🚫 SC

★ ★ **HOLIDAY INN.** *4300 E Washington St (85034). Phone 602/273-7778; toll-free 800/465-4329; fax 602/275-5616. www.holiday-inn.com/phx-airport.* 299 rooms, 10 story. Pets accepted; fee. Check-out noon, check-in 3 pm. TV; cable (premium). In-room modem link. Restaurant, bar; entertainment Fri, Sat. In-house fitness room. Game room. Heated pool; whirlpool; poolside service. Free airport transportation. **$**

D 🐾 ≈ ✈ 🏃 🚫 SC

★ **HOMEWOOD SUITES.** *2001 E Highland Ave (85016). Phone 602/508-0937; fax 602/508-0854. www.homewood-suites.com.* 124 rooms, 4 story. Pets accepted, some restrictions; fee. Complimentary continental breakfast. Check-out noon, check-in 3 pm. TV; cable (premium), VCR available. In-room modem link. Laundry services. In-house fitness room. Health club privileges. Pool. Business center. **$**

D 🐾 ≈ 🏃 🚫 SC 🏃

★ **LA QUINTA INN.** *2725 N Black Canyon Hwy (85009). Phone 602/258-6271; toll-free 800/531-5900; fax 602/340-9255. www.laquinta.com.* 141 rooms, 2 story. Pets accepted, some restrictions. Complimentary continental breakfast. Check-out noon, check-in 1 pm. TV; cable (premium). Laundry services. Heated pool. **$**

D 🐾 ≈ 🚫 SC

★ ★ **QUALITY INN.** *5121 E Lapuente Ave (85044). Phone 480/893-3900; toll-free 800/562-3332; fax 480/496-0815. www.qualityinn.com.* 182 rooms, 4 story. Pets accepted; fee. Complimentary continental breakfast. Check-out noon, check-in 3 pm. TV. In-room modem link. Laundry services. Restaurant. Heated pool; whirlpool. **$**

🐾 ≈

Hotel

★ ★ ★ **SHERATON CRESCENT HOTEL.** *2620 W Dunlap Ave (85021). Phone 602/943-8200; toll-free 800/423-4126; fax 602/371-2856. www.sheratoncrescent.com.* Imagine luxury and fun as the setting at this hotel in the heart of downtown Phoenix. Guests can enjoy suites that include Italian marble bathrooms and splash it up at the 166-foot Monsoon Mountain water slide. 354 rooms, 8 story. Pets accepted, some restrictions. Check-out noon, check-in 3 pm. TV; cable (premium), VCR available. Restaurant, bar. In-house fitness room; sauna, steam room. Pool; whirlpool; poolside service. Lighted tennis. Lawn games. Business center. Luxury level. **$**

🐾 ✈ ≈ 🏃 🏃

All Suites

★ ★ **EMBASSY SUITES.** *1515 N 44th St (85008). Phone 602/244-8800; fax 602/244-8114. www.embassysuites.com.* 229 rooms, 4 story. Pets accepted; fee. Complimentary full breakfast. Check-out noon, check-in 3 pm. TV; cable (premium). Laundry services. Restaurant, bar. Pool; whirlpool; poolside service. Airport transportation. **$**

D 🐾 ≈ ✈ 🚫

★ ★ **HILTON SUITES.** *10 E Thomas Rd (85012). Phone 602/222-1111; toll-free 800/932-3322; fax 602/212-9537. www.phoenixsuites.hilton.com.* This high-rise suite hotel is conveniently located near museums, shopping, and many PGA golf courses. Ideal for families and small groups. 226 rooms, 11 story. Pets accepted; fee. Complimentary full breakfast. Check-out noon, check-in 3 pm. TV; cable (premium), VCR available. In-room modem link. Restaurant, bar. In-house fitness room; sauna. Health club privileges. Indoor pool; whirlpool. Business center. Concierge. **$**

D 🐾 ≈ 🏃 🚫 🏃

Extended Stay

★ ★ **RESIDENCE INN BY MARRIOTT.** *801 N 44th St (85008). Phone 602/273-9220. www.residenceinn.com.* Guests can take advantage of the on-site sport court or unwind in the Southwestern-style guest rooms featuring separate living and sleeping areas. 200 rooms, 4 story. Pets accepted; fee. Complimentary continental breakfast. Check-out noon, check-in 3 pm. TV; cable (premium). In-room modem link. Laundry services. In-house fitness room. Outdoor pool. Outdoor tennis. **$**

Prescott

Motels/Motor Lodges

★ ★ **BEST WESTERN PRESCOTTONIAN.** *1317 E Gurley St (86301). Phone 928/445-3096; fax 928/778-2976. www.bestwestern.com.* 121 rooms, 2-3 story. No elevator. Pets accepted. Check-out noon, check-in 2 pm. TV. In-room modem link. Laundry services. Restaurant, bar. Pool; whirlpool. **$**

★ **DAYS INN.** *7875 E Hwy 69 (86314). Phone 928/772-8600; fax 928/772-0942. www.daysinn.com.* 59 rooms, 2 story. Pets accepted; fee. Complimentary continental breakfast. Check-out 11 am. TV; cable (premium). Pool; whirlpool. **$**

Safford

Motels/Motor Lodges

★ **BEST WESTERN DESERT INN.** *1391 Thatcher Blvd (85546). Phone 928/428-0521; toll-free 800/707-2336; fax 928/428-7653. www.bestwestern.com.* 70 rooms, 2 story. Pets accepted, some restrictions; fee. Check-out 11 am. TV. Laundry services. Bar. Heated pool. **$**

★ **COMFORT INN.** *1578 W Thatcher Blvd (85546). Phone 928/428-5851; fax 928/428-4968. www.comfortinn.com.* 45 rooms, 2 story. Pets accepted, some restrictions; fee. Complimentary continental breakfast. Check-out 11 am. TV; cable (premium). In-room modem link. Heated pool. **$**

Scottsdale

Motels/Motor Lodges

★ ★ **BEST WESTERN SCOTTSDALE AIRPARK SUITES.** *7515 E Butherus Dr (85260). Phone 480/951-4000; toll-free 800/334-1977; fax 480/483-9046. www.scottsdalebestwestern.com.* 120 rooms, 4 story. Pets accepted; fee. Complimentary full breakfast. Check-out noon, check-in 3 pm. TV. In-room modem link. Laundry services. Restaurant, bar. Room service. In-house fitness room. Heated pool; whirlpool; poolside service. **$**

★ **COUNTRY INN & SUITES BY CARLSON.** *10801 N 89th Pl (85260). Phone 480/314-1200; toll-free 800/456-4000; fax 480/314-7367. www.countryinns.com/scottsdaleaz_central.* 163 rooms, 3 story. Pets accepted, some restrictions; fee. Complimentary continental breakfast. Check-out noon. TV; cable (premium). In-room modem link. Laundry services. In-house fitness room. Heated pool; children's pool; whirlpool. **$**

★ **HAMPTON INN.** *4415 N Civic Center Plz (85251). Phone 480/941-9400; fax 480/675-5240. www.hampton innoldtown.com.* 135 rooms, 5 story. Pets accepted; fee. Complimentary continental breakfast. Check-out noon, check-in 3 pm. TV; cable (premium). Laundry services. Pool. **$**

★ ★ **HOSPITALITY SUITE RESORT.** *409 N Scottsdale Rd (85257). Phone 480/949-5115; fax 480/941-8014. www.hospitalitysuites.com.* 210 rooms, 3 story. Pets accepted, some restrictions; fee. Complimentary full breakfast. Check-out 11 am, check-in 2 pm. TV; cable (premium). Laundry services. Restaurant, bar. Room service. Health club privileges. Three heated pools; whirlpool; poolside service. Lighted tennis. Lawn games. Free airport transportation. **$**

★ **LA QUINTA INN.** *8888 E Shea Blvd (85260). Phone 480/614-5300; fax 480/614-5333. www.laquinta.com.* 140 rooms, 3 story. Pets accepted. Complimentary continental breakfast. Check-out noon. TV; cable (premium). Laundry services. In-house fitness room. Pool; whirlpool. **$**

Resorts

★ ★ **DOUBLETREE HOTEL.** *4949 E Lincoln Dr (85253). Phone 602/952-0420; toll-free 800/222-8733; fax 602/840-8576. www.doubletree.com.* Camelback Mountain is a beautifully striking backdrop at this Hilton chain. On-site recreations include a one-million-gallon lagoon pool; shopping, golf, and the famed Biltmore Country Club Resort are also nearby. 262 rooms, 1 story. Pets accepted, some restrictions; fee. Check-out noon, check-in 4 pm. TV; cable (premium). Restaurant, bar. Room service. In-house fitness room; sauna. Two heated pools; whirlpool; poolside service. Lighted tennis. Lawn games. Bicycle rentals. Racquetball. **$**

★ ★ ★ ★ **FOUR SEASONS RESORT SCOTTSDALE AT TROON NORTH.** *10600 E Crescent Moon Dr (85255). Phone 480/515-5700; fax 480/515-5599. www.fourseasons.com.* The Four Seasons Resort Scottsdale at Troon North basks in the abundant golden sunshine synonymous with the Southwest. Blending with the natural surroundings, this two-story resort rests within a 40-acre nature preserve. The rooms and suites are housed in 25 casitas clustered around the grounds. Native American pottery and textiles add local flavor and set a sense of place in the rooms, where fireplaces warm the interiors and windows frame expansive views of the stunning desert. Extra luxuries like plunge pools, alfresco garden showers, and outdoor kiva fireplaces characterize the gracious suites. Influenced by the location, the spa offers desert nectar facials and moonlight massages, and the landscaped pool deck provides a pleasurable place for relaxation. Three restaurants reflect the resort's casually elegant attitude in their ambience and menu. A veritable mecca for golfers, the resort grants priority tee times at Troon North's two courses, considered among the best in the world. 210 rooms, 2 story. Pets accepted, some restrictions. Check-out noon, check-in 4 pm. TV; cable (premium), VCR available. In-room modem link. Room service 24 hours. Restaurant, bar. In-house fitness room; spa; massage, sauna, steam room. Pool; whirlpool; poolside service. Golf, greens fee $248. Outdoor tennis, lighted courts. Business center. Concierge. **$$$$**

★ ★ ★ **MARRIOTT CAMELBACK INN RESORT, GOLF CLUB & SPA.** *5402 E Lincoln Dr (85253). Phone 480/948-1700; toll-free 800/242-2635; fax 480/951-8469. www.marriott.com.* Since the 1930s, the Camelback Inn has appealed to travelers seeking the very best in the American Southwest. This special hideaway, reminiscent of a hacienda, is situated on 125 acres in Arizona's beautiful Sonoran Desert. Supremely comfortable, the rooms and suites share the distinctive charms of the region while providing modern luxuries. To further indulge guests, the suites even offer private pools. Outdoor enthusiasts explore the region on horseback, enjoy the thrill of whitewater rafting, or marvel at the view from above in a hot-air balloon, while tennis courts, three heated pools, and a comprehensive fitness center keep guests occupied closer to home. Set at the base of Mummy Mountain, the spa is a peaceful retreat. All cravings are satisfied here, with a total of seven dining venues ranging from quick and casual to more formal settings ideal for lingering over sensational meals. 453 rooms, 1-2 story. Pets accepted, some restrictions; fee. Check-out noon, check-in 4 pm. TV; cable (premium), VCR available. In-room modem link. Dining room, bar. Room service. Supervised children's activities (holidays only); ages 5-12. In-house fitness room; spa; sauna, steam room. Three pools; whirlpool; poolside service. Golf, greens fee $90-$155 (including cart). Outdoor tennis, lighted courts. Lawn games. Entertainment. Bicycle rental. Business center. Concierge. **$$$$**

★ ★ ★ **RENAISSANCE SCOTTSDALE RESORT.** *6160 N Scottsdale Rd (85253). Phone 480/991-1414; fax 480/951-3350. www.renaissancehotels.com.* Nestled in the famous Camelback Mountain, this 25-acre oasis is a beautifully intimate experience. Whether shopping at the Borgata, shaping up with Splash Aerobics, or chowing down at a private Western-style dinner, guests will enjoy a variety of Southwestern flair. 171 rooms, 3 story. Pets accepted, some restrictions. Check-out noon, check-in 4 pm. TV; cable (premium), VCR available (movies). Fireplaces. Restaurant, bar. Room service. Health club privileges. Pool; poolside service. Lighted tennis. Lawn games, bicycle rentals. Concierge. **$**

All Suites

★ **AMERISUITES.** *7300 E 3rd Ave (85251). Phone 480/423-9944; toll-free 800/833-1516; fax 480/423-2991. www.amerisuites.com.* 128 rooms, 6 story. Pets accepted, some restrictions. Complimentary continental breakfast. Check-out noon, check-in 3 pm. TV; cable (premium), VCR available. Laundry services. In-house fitness room. Pool. Parking lot. Business center. **$**

★★ **CHAPARRAL SUITES RESORT.** *5001 N Scottsdale Rd (85250). Phone 480/949-1414; toll-free 800/ 528-1456; fax 480/947-2675. www.chaparralsuites.com.* 311 rooms, 4 story. Pets accepted, some restrictions; fee. Complimentary full breakfast. Check-out noon, check-in 3 pm. TV; cable (premium), VCR available (movies). Laundry services. Restaurant, bar. In-house fitness room. Game room. Two heated pools; poolside service. Lighted tennis. Free airport transportation. Concierge. **$**

D🐾🏋🏊🚏🍴🏕

★ **SUMMERFIELD SUITES SCOTTSDALE.** *4245 N Drinkwater Blvd (85251). Phone 480/946-7700; toll-free 800/833-4353; fax 480/946-7711. www.wyndham.com.* 163 rooms, 3 story. Pet accepted; fee. Complimentary full breakfast. Check-out noon, check-in 4 pm. TV; cable (premium), VCR available. Laundry services. In-house fitness room. Pool; whirlpool. Bike rentals. Concierge. **$**

D🐾🏊🏕✈🚏

Extended Stay

★★ **RESIDENCE INN BY MARRIOTT.** *6040 N Scottsdale Rd (85253). Phone 480/948-8666; toll-free 800/ 331-3131; fax 480/443-4869. www.residenceinn.com.* 122 rooms, 2 story. Pets accepted; fee. Complimentary continental breakfast. Check-out noon, check-in 3 pm. TV; cable (premium), VCR available. Laundry services. In-house fitness room. Heated pool; whirlpool; poolside service. **$**

D🐾🏊🏕🚏

Sedona

Motels/Motor Lodges

★ **BEST WESTERN INN OF SEDONA.** *1200 W Hwy 89A (86336). Phone 928/282-3072; toll-free 800/ 292-6344; fax 928/282-7218. www.innofsedona.com.* 110 rooms, 3 story. Pets accepted; fee. Complimentary continental breakfast. Check-out 11 am. TV; cable (premium). In-room modem link. In-house fitness room. Pool; whirlpool. Airport transportation. Concierge. **$**

D🐾🏊🏕🚏 SC

★ **DESERT QUAIL INN.** *6626 State Rte 179 (86351). Phone 928/284-1433; toll-free 800/385-0927; fax 928/284-0487. www.desertquailinn.com.* 41 rooms, 2 story. Pets accepted, some restrictions; fee. Check-out 11 am. TV. In-room modem link. Laundry services. Pool. **$**

D🐾🏊🚏

★ **SKY RANCH LODGE.** *1105 Airport Rd (86339). Phone 928/282-6400; toll-free 888/708-6400; fax 928/282-7682. www.skyranchlodge.com.* 94 rooms, 1-2 story. Pets

accepted; fee. Check-out 11 am. TV. Laundry services. Pool; whirlpool. **$**

D🐾🏊🚏

All Suites

★★★ **HILTON SEDONA RESORT AND SPA.** *90 Ridge Trail Dr (86351). Phone 928/284-4040; fax 928/ 284-6940. www.hiltonsedona.com.* 219 rooms, 3 story. Pets accepted; fee. Check-out noon. TV; cable (premium). In-room modem link. Fireplaces. Laundry services. Restaurant, bar. Room service. Supervised children's activities. In-house fitness room; spa, massage. Pool; children's pool; whirlpool; poolside service. 18-hole golf; pro, pro shop, cart available, greens fee $59-$109. Outdoor tennis, lighted courts. Concierge. **$**

D🐾🏋⛳🍴🏊🍴🚏

Show Low

Motels/Motor Lodges

★★ **BEST WESTERN PAINT PONY LODGE.** *581 W Deuce of Clubs Ave (85901). Phone 928/537-5773; fax 928/537-5766. www.bestwestern.com.* 50 rooms, 2 story. Pets accepted; fee. Complimentary continental breakfast. Check-out 11 am. TV; cable (premium). In-room modem link. Restaurant, bar. Room service. Cross-country ski 17 miles. Free airport transportation. **$**

🐾🚏

★ **DAYS INN.** *480 W Deuce of Clubs Ave Hwy 60 (85901). Phone 928/537-4356; fax 928/537-8692. www.daysinn.com.* 122 rooms, 2 story. Pets accepted; fee. Complimentary full breakfast. Check-out noon. TV; cable (premium). Laundry services. Restaurant. Pool. Free airport transportation. **$**

D🐾🏊🚏

Sierra Vista

Motel/Motor Lodge

★ **SUPER 8.** *100 Fab Ave (85635). Phone 520/459-5380; fax 520/459-6052. www.innworks.com.* 52 rooms, 2 story. Pets accepted; fee. Complimentary continental breakfast. Check-out 11 am. TV. Laundry services. Pool. **$**

D🐾🏊🚏 SC

Hotel

★ **WINDEMERE HOTEL AND CONFERENCE CENTER.** *2047 S Hwy 92 (85635). Phone 520/459-5900; toll-free 800/825-4656; fax 520/458-1347. www.windemere-hotel.com.* 149 rooms, 3 story. Pets accepted; fee.

Complimentary breakfast. Check-out 11 am. TV. Laundry services. Restaurant, bar; entertainment. Room service. Health club privileges. Pool; whirlpool. **$**

D ⬛ ⬛ ⬛ ⬛ SC

Tempe

Motels/Motor Lodges

★ **COUNTRY INN & SUITES BY CARLSON.** *1660 W Elliot (85284). Phone 480/345-8585; fax 480/345-7461. www.countryinns.com.* 139 rooms, 3 story. Pets accepted; fee. Complimentary continental breakfast. Check-out noon, check-in 3 pm. TV; cable (premium). Laundry services. Health club privileges. Pool; children's pool; whirlpool. Free airport transportation. **$**

D ⬛ ⬛ ⬛ ⬛ SC

★ ★ **HOLIDAY INN.** *915 E Apache Blvd (85281). Phone 480/968-3451; toll-free 800/553-1826; fax 480/968-6262. www.holiday-inn.com/phx-tempeasu.* 194 rooms, 4 story. Pets accepted, some restrictions; fee. Check-out 1 pm, check-in 1 pm. TV; cable (premium). Laundry services. Restaurant, bar. Room service. In-house fitness room. Health club privileges. Pool; whirlpool; poolside service. **$**

D ⬛ ⬛ ⬛ ⬛ ⬛

★ **HOLIDAY INN EXPRESS.** *5300 S Priest Dr (85283). Phone 480/820-7500; toll-free 800/465-4329; fax 480/730-6626. www.holiday-inn.com.* 160 rooms, 4 story. Pets accepted, some restrictions; fee. Complimentary continental breakfast. Check-out noon, check-in 2 pm. TV; cable (premium). In-house fitness room. Pool; whirlpool. **$**

D ⬛ ⬛ ⬛ ⬛ SC

★ **RODEWAY INN.** *1550 S 52nd St (85281). Phone 480/967-3000; fax 480/966-9568. www.rodewayinn.com.* 100 rooms, 2 story. Pets accepted; fee. Complimentary continental breakfast. Check-out noon, check-in 3 pm. TV; cable (premium). Laundry services. Pool; whirlpool. Free airport transportation. **$**

D ⬛ ⬛ ⬛ ⬛

All Suite

★ ★ **INNSUITES HOTELS TEMPE.** *1651 W Baseline Rd (85283). Phone 480/897-7900; fax 480/491-1008. www.innsuites.com.* 103 rooms, 2 story. Pets accepted, some restrictions; fee. Complimentary continental breakfast. Check-out noon, check-in 2 pm. TV; cable (premium). In-room modem link. Laundry services. Restaurant. In-house fitness room. Pool; whirlpool. Lighted tennis. Business center. Free airport transportation. **$**

D ⬛ ⬛ ⬛ ⬛ ⬛ ⬛ SC ⬛

Tombstone

Motel/Motor Lodge

★ ★ **BEST WESTERN LOOKOUT LODGE.** *US Hwy 80 (85638). Phone 520/457-2223; toll-free 877/652-6772; fax 520/457-3870. www.bestwestern.com.* 40 rooms, 2 story. Pets accepted; fee. Complimentary continental breakfast. Check-out 11 am. TV. Pool. **$**

D ⬛ ⬛ ⬛ ⬛ ⬛ ⬛

Tucson

Motels/Motor Lodges

★ **BEST WESTERN INN HOTEL AND SUITES.** *6201 N Oracle Rd (85704). Phone 520/297-8111; toll-free 888/554-4535; fax 520/297-2935. www.bestwestern.com.* 159 rooms, 2 story. Pets accepted, some restrictions; fee. Complimentary breakfast buffet. Check-out noon, check-in 2 pm. TV; cable (premium). Laundry services. Room service. In-house fitness room. Pool; whirlpool. Lighted tennis. **$**

D ⬛ ⬛ ⬛ ⬛ ⬛ SC

★ **CLARION HOTEL.** *102 N Alvernon Way (85711). Phone 520/795-0330; toll-free 800/227-6086; fax 520/326-2111. www.clarionhotel.com.* 174 rooms, 3 story. Pets accepted. Complimentary breakfast. Check-out noon, check-in 3 pm. TV; cable (premium). In-room modem link. In-house fitness room. Pool; children's pool. Business center. **$**

D ⬛ ⬛ ⬛ ⬛ SC ⬛

★ **RAMADA.** *6944 E Tanque Verde Rd (85715). Phone 520/886-9595; fax 520/721-8466. www.ramadafoothillstucson.com.* 176 rooms, 2 story. Pets accepted, some restrictions; fee. Complimentary continental breakfast. Check-out noon, check-in 3 pm. TV; cable (premium). In-room modem link. Laundry services. Outdoor pool; whirlpool. Free parking. **$**

D ⬛ ⬛ ⬛ SC

★ ★ **SMUGGLER'S INN.** *6350 E Speedway Blvd (85710). Phone 520/296-3292; toll-free 866/517-6870; fax 520/722-3713. www.smugglersinn.com.* 150 rooms, 2 story. Pets accepted, some restrictions; fee. Complimentary continental breakfast. Check-out noon, check-in 4 pm. TV; cable (premium), VCR available. Laundry services. Restaurant, bar. Room service. Outdoor pool; whirlpool. Free parking. **$**

D ⬛ ⬛ ⬛

Hotels

★★ **CLARION HOTEL.** *88 E Broadway (85701). Phone 520/622-4000; fax 520/620-0376. www.clarionhotel.com.* 184 rooms, 8 story. Pets accepted, some restrictions; fee. Complimentary breakfast. Check-out noon, check-in 2 pm. TV; cable (premium). In-room modem link. Laundry services. Restaurant. In-house fitness room. Pool; whirlpool. Business center. **$**

★★ **DOUBLETREE HOTEL.** *445 S Alvernon Way (85711). Phone 520/881-4200; fax 520/323-5225. www. doubletree.com.* Ten minutes from downtown and the airport, this Hilton chain is a nice resting place for business and leisure travelers alike. Directly across the street is the expansive Reid Park. 302 rooms, 2-9 story. Pets accepted; fee. Check-out noon, check-in 3 pm. TV; cable (premium), VCR available. Restaurant, bar. Room service. In-house fitness room. Pool; whirlpool; poolside service. Lighted tennis. Business center. **$**

★★ **RADISSON HOTEL CITY CENTER.** *181 W Broadway Blvd (85701). Phone 520/624-8711; toll-free 800/333-3333; fax 520/624-9963. www.radisson.com.* 309 rooms, 12 story. Pets accepted, some restrictions; fee. Check-out noon, check-in 3 pm. TV; cable (premium). Restaurant, bar. In-house fitness room. Outdoor pool; poolside service. Free garage parking. Airport transportation. Concierge. **$**

★★ **SHERATON TUCSON HOTEL AND SUITES.** *5151 E Grant Rd (85712). Phone 520/323-6262; fax 520/325-2989. www.sheraton.com.* 216 rooms, 4 story. Pets accepted; fee. Complimentary continental breakfast. Check-out noon, check-in 3 pm. TV; cable (premium). Laundry services. Restaurant, bar. In-house fitness room; steam room. Outdoor pool; poolside service. Free parking. **$**

Resorts

★★★ **THE GOLF VILLAS.** *10950 N La Canada (85737). Phone 520/498-0098; toll-free 888/388-0098; fax 520/498-5150. www.thegolfvillas.com.* Luxury one-, two-, and three-bedroom villas afford golf course views. Guests have use of an extensive array of recreational facilities at El Conquistador Country Club across the street. 79 rooms, 2 story. Pets accepted; fee. Check-out noon, check-in 3 pm. TV; cable (premium), VCR available. In-house fitness room; sauna. Pool. Hiking trail. Valet parking available. Business center. Concierge service. **$$**

★★★ **HILTON EL CONQUISTADOR.** *10000 N Oracle Rd (85737). Phone 520/544-5000; fax 520/544-1222. www.hilton.com.* This resort and country club lures visitors with its extensive golf and tennis facilities, including 45 holes and 31 lighted courts, but just gazing at the sunsets and spectacular Santa Catalina Mountain views is therapeutic. The grounds, 2,000 feet below the Pusch Ridge cliffs, feature 428 rooms, five restaurants, and 45,000 square feet of meeting space. 428 rooms. Pets accepted. Check-out noon, check-in 4 pm. TV; cable (premium), VCR available. Fireplaces. Dining rooms, bar; entertainment. Room service. Supervised children's activities; ages 5-12. In-house fitness room; massage, sauna. Pools; whirlpool; poolside service. 45-hole golf, pro, putting green, driving range, greens fee (including cart) $95-$135 ($48-$60 in summer). Outdoor tennis, lighted courts, pro. Lawn games. Bicycles. Hiking and nature trails. Breakfast and evening horseback rides; hayrides. Business center. Concierge. Pro shop. **$$**

★★★ **OMNI TUCSON NATIONAL GOLF RESORT/SPA.** *2727 W Club Dr (85742). Phone 520/297-2271; toll-free 800/528-4856; fax 520/297-7544. www.omnihotels.com.* Breathtaking views, championship golf, and first-class service make the Omni Tucson National Golf Resort & Spa a favorite of leisure travelers. Just outside Tucson, the resort enjoys a peaceful location in the Sonoran Desert. Golf is the centerpiece here, where the 27-hole course is the home of the annual PGA Tucson Open; however, all guests are well taken care of with two pools, a comprehensive fitness center, and tennis, basketball, and sand volleyball courts, as well as a 13,000-square-foot spa featuring the finest therapies and treatments. The rich colors of the Southwest dictate a soothing ambience in the guest rooms. These comfortable retreats are enhanced by expansive views of the verdant golf course or majestic mountains. Some accommodations feature full kitchens, but with four grills, lounges, and restaurants turning out delicious meals, most guests leave the cooking to the resort's talented professionals. 167 rooms, 2 story. Pets accepted; fee. Check-out noon, check-in 4 pm. TV; cable (premium), VCR available. Restaurant, bar; entertainment. In-house fitness room; massage, sauna, steam room. Pool; whirlpool; poolside service. Golf; greens fee $85-$179. Outdoor tennis, lighted courts. Lawn games. Concierge. **$$**

★★★ **WESTWARD LOOK RESORT.** *245 E Ina Rd (85704). Phone 520/297-1151; toll-free 800/722-2500; fax 520/297-9023. www.westwardlook.com.* This oasis in the Sonoran Desert features suite-sized accommodations in a breath-taking setting, combining historic ambience with contemporary luxury. 246 rooms, 2 story. Pets accepted;

fee. Check-out noon, check-in 4 pm. TV; cable (premium). Restaurant, bar; entertainment Thurs-Sat. Room service. In-house fitness room; spa, massage. Three pools; whirlpool. Lighted tennis. Lawn games. Bicycles. Free parking. Business center. Concierge. **$**

All Suites

★ ★ **EMBASSY SUITES.** *7051 S Tucson Blvd (85706). Phone 520/573-0700; toll-free 800/362-2779; fax 520/741-9645. www.embassysuites.com.* 204 rooms, 3 story. Pets accepted, some restrictions. Complimentary full breakfast. Check-out 1 pm, check-in 3 pm. TV; cable (premium). Laundry services. Restaurant, bar. In-house fitness room. Pool; whirlpool; poolside service. Airport transportation. **$$**

★ **WINDMILL SUITES AT ST. PHILLIPS PLAZA.** *4250 N Campbell Ave (85718). Phone 520/577-0007; toll-free 800/547-4747; fax 520/577-0045. www.windmillinns.com.* 122 rooms, 3 story. Pets accepted. Complimentary continental breakfast. Check-out 11 am. TV; cable (premium). Laundry services. Pool; whirlpool. Bicycles. **$$**

Wickenburg

Motel/Motor Lodge

★ ★ **BEST WESTERN RANCHO GRANDE.** *293 E Wickenburg Way (85390). Phone 928/684-5445; toll-free 800/528-1234; fax 928/684-7380. www.bwranchogrande.com.* 80 rooms, 1-2 story. Pets accepted. Check-out noon. TV; VCR available. Pool; whirlpool. Outdoor tennis. Free airport transportation. **$**

Willcox

Motels/Motor Lodges

★ ★ **BEST WESTERN PLAZA INN.** *1100 W Rex Allen Dr (85643). Phone 520/384-3556; toll-free 800/528-1234; fax 520/384-2679. www.bestwestern.com.* 91 rooms, 2 story. Pets accepted; fee. Complimentary full breakfast. Check-out noon. TV. Laundry services. Restaurant, bar. Room service. Pool. **$**

★ **DAYS INN.** *724 N Bisbee Ave (85643). Phone 520/384-4222; toll-free 800/329-7466; fax 520/384-3785. www.daysinn.com.* 73 rooms, 2 story. Pets accepted; fee. Complimentary continental breakfast. Check-out 11 am. TV; cable (premium). Laundry services. Pool. **$**

Williams

Motels/Motor Lodges

★ ★ **HOLIDAY INN.** *950 N Grand Canyon Blvd (86046). Phone 928/635-4114; toll-free 800/465-4329; fax 928/635-2700. www.holiday-inn.com.* 120 rooms, 2 story. Pets accepted. Check-out 11 am. TV. Laundry services. Restaurant, bar. Room service. Indoor pool; whirlpool. Downhill ski 5 miles. **$**

★ **MOTEL 6.** *831 W Bill Williams Ave (86046). Phone 928/635-9000; fax 928/635-2300. www.motel6.com.* 52 rooms, 2 story. Pets accepted, some restrictions. Check-out 11 am. TV. In-room modem link. Laundry services. Indoor pool; whirlpool. **$**

★ **MOUNTAINSIDE INN.** *642 E Rte 66 (86046). Phone 928/635-4431; fax 928/635-2292. www.mtnsideinn.com.* 96 rooms, 2 story. Pets accepted; fee. Check-out noon. TV. Restaurant, bar. Room service. Pool; whirlpool. Downhill ski 4 miles. **$**

Winslow

Motels/Motor Lodges

★ ★ **BEST WESTERN ADOBE INN.** *1701 N Park Dr (86047). Phone 928/289-4638; fax 928/289-5514. www.bestwestern.com.* 72 rooms, 2 story. Pets accepted; fee. Check-out 11 am. TV; cable (premium), VCR available. Laundry services. Restaurant, bar. Room service. Indoor pool; whirlpool. **$**

★ **ECONO LODGE.** *1706 N Park Dr (86047). Phone 928/289-4687; toll-free 800/228-5050; fax 928/289-9377. www.econolodge.com.* 73 rooms, 2 story. Pets accepted; fee. Check-out 11 am. TV; cable (premium), VCR available. Laundry services. Pool. **$**

Yuma

Motels/Motor Lodges

★ **INTERSTATE 8 INN.** *2730 S 4th Ave (85364). Phone 928/726-6110; toll-free 800/821-7465; fax 928/726-7711.* 120 rooms, 2 story. Pets accepted, some restrictions. Check-out 11 am. TV; cable (premium), VCR available. Laundry services. Pool; whirlpool. **$**

★★ **SHILO INN.** *1550 S Castle Dome Ave (85365). Phone 928/782-9511; toll-free 800/222-2244; fax 928/ 783-1538. www.shiloinns.com.* 134 rooms, 4 story. Pets accepted. Complimentary full breakfast. Check-out noon. TV; cable (premium), VCR available. In-room modem link. Laundry services. Restaurant, bar. In-house fitness room; sauna, steam room. Pool; whirlpool; poolside service. Airport transportation. **$**

★ **TRAVELODGE.** *711 E 32nd St (85365). Phone 928/726-4721; toll-free 800/835-1132; fax 928/344-0452. www.travelodge.com.* 80 rooms, 2 story. Pets accepted, some restrictions; fee. Complimentary continental breakfast. Check-out noon. TV; cable (premium), VCR available (movies). Laundry services. Restaurant, bar. Health club privileges. Pool; whirlpool. **$**

All Suites

★★ **BEST WESTERN INNSUITES HOTEL.** *1450 S Castle Dome Ave (85365). Phone 928/783-8341; toll-free 800/922-2034; fax 928/783-1349. www.bestwestern.com.* 166 rooms. Pets accepted, some restrictions; fee. Complimentary continental breakfast. Check-out noon. TV; cable (premium), VCR available. In-room modem link. Laundry services. In-house fitness room. Pool; whirlpool. Outdoor tennis, lighted courts. Business center. **$**

★ **RADISSON SUITES.** *2600 S 4th Ave (85364). Phone 928/726-4830; fax 928/341-1152. www.radisson.com.* 164 rooms, 13 story. Pets accepted. Complimentary continental breakfast. Check-out noon. TV; cable (premium). Health club privileges. Pool; whirlpool. Free airport transportation. **$**

Arkansas

Arkadelphia

Motels/Motor Lodges

★ ★ **BEST WESTERN CONTINENTAL INN.** *136 Valley Rd (71923). Phone 870/246-5592; fax 870/246-3583. www.bestwestern.com.* 59 rooms, 2 story. S, D $52; each additional $5; family rates; higher rates holidays. Pets accepted. Check-out 11 am. TV; cable (premium), VCR available. Laundry services. Restaurant. Room service. Pool.

D ◆ ≈ ⊠ SC

★ ★ **QUALITY INN.** *I-30 and AR 7 (71923). Phone 870/246-5855; toll-free 800/342-4876; fax 870/246-8552. www.qualityinn.com.* 63 rooms, 2 story. Pets accepted. Check-out noon. TV; cable (premium). Pool. $

D ◆ ≈ ⊠ SC

Batesville

Motel/Motor Lodge

★ **RAMADA INN.** *1325 N St. Louis St (71701). Phone 870/698-1800. www.ramada.com.* 124 rooms, 2 story. Pets accepted, some restrictions. Check-out noon. TV; cable (premium). Laundry services. Restaurant. Room service. Pool; whirlpool. $

D ◆ ≈ ⊠

Blytheville

Motels/Motor Lodges

★ **HAMPTON INN.** *301 N Access Rd (72315). Phone 870/763-5220; fax 870/762-1397. www.hamptoninn.com.* 87 rooms, 2 story. S $41.50; D $45.50; each additional $4; under 12 free. Pets accepted, some restrictions; fee. Complimentary continental breakfast. Check-out noon. TV; cable (premium). Restaurant. Pool.

D ◆ ⬤ ≈ ⊠

★ ★ **HOLIDAY INN.** *1121 E Main (72315). Phone 870/ 763-5800; fax 870/763-1326. www.holiday-inn.com.* 153 rooms, 2 story. Mar-mid-Sept: S, D $65; under 19 free; weekend rates; lower rates rest of year. Bar 4 pm-1 am,

closed Sun; entertainment. Pets accepted; fee. Check-out noon. TV; cable (premium). Restaurant, bar; entertainment. Room service. Steam room. Indoor, outdoor pool; whirlpool; poolside service.

D ◆ ≈ ⊠

Conway

Motels/Motor Lodges

★ ★ **BEST WESTERN.** *I-40 and Hwy 64 (72033). Phone 501/329-9855; fax 501/327-6110. www.bestwestern.com.* 70 rooms, 2 story. Pets accepted, some restrictions. Check-out noon. TV; cable (premium). In-room modem link. Restaurant. Health club privileges. Pool. $

D ◆ ≈ ✈

★ **COMFORT INN.** *150 Hwy 65 N (72032). Phone 501/329-0300; fax 501/329-8367. www.comfortinn.com.* 60 rooms, 2 story. Pets accepted; fee. Complimentary continental breakfast. Check-out 11 am. TV; cable (premium). Health club privileges. Pool; whirlpool. $

D ◆ ≈ ⊠ SC

Dumas

Motel/Motor Lodge

★ **REGENCY INN.** *722 Hwy 65 S (72033). Phone 870/382-2707; fax 870/382-2836.* 52 rooms, 2 story. Pets accepted, some restrictions; fee. Complimentary continental breakfast. Check-out noon. TV. Laundry services. Pool. $

D ◆ ≈ ⊠ SC

El Dorado

Motel/Motor Lodge

★ ★ **BEST WESTERN KING'S INN CONFERENCE CENTER.** *1920 Junction City Rd (71730). Phone 870/862-5191; fax 870/863-7511. www.bestwestern.com.* 131 rooms, 2 story. S $59-$65; D $65-$71; each additional $7; weekend rates. Pets accepted, some restrictions; fee. Check-out noon. TV; cable (premium). Restaurant. Room service. Sauna. Two pools, one indoor; children's pool; whirlpool. Lighted tennis. Airport transportation. On 8 acres.

D ◆ ⬤ ⌖ ≈ ⊠

Eureka Springs

Motels/Motor Lodges

★ ★ **1876 INN.** *2023 E Van Buren (72632). Phone 479/ 253-7183; toll-free 800/643-3030.* 72 rooms, 3 story. Pets accepted, some restrictions; fee. Check-out 11 am. TV. In-room modem link. Restaurant. Pool; whirlpool. **$**

★ **THE ALPEN DORF.** *6554 US 62 (72632). Phone 479/253-9475; toll-free 800/771-9872; fax 479/253-2928.* 30 rooms, 2 story. Pets accepted; fee. Check-out 11 am. TV. Pool. **$**

★ ★ **BEST WESTERN INN OF THE OZARKS.** *Hwy 62 W (72632). Phone 479/253-9768. www.bestwestern.com.* 122 rooms, 2 story. Pets accepted, some restrictions. Check-out 11 am. TV; cable (premium), VCR available. In-room modem link. Restaurant 6:30 am-9 pm. Bar. Lighted tennis. **$**

★ **COLONIAL MANSION INN.** *154 Huntsville Rd (72632). Phone 479/253-7300; toll-free 800/638-2622; fax 479/253-7309.* 30 rooms, 2 story. Pets accepted, some restrictions. Complimentary continental breakfast. Check-out 11 am. TV. Pool. **$**

★ **DAYS INN.** *120 W Van Buren St (72632). Phone 479/253-8863; toll-free 800/329-7466; fax 479/253-7885. www.daysinn.com.* 24 rooms, 2 story. Pets accepted, some restrictions; fee. Complimentary continental breakfast. Check-out 11 am. TV; cable (premium), VCR available (movies). Pool. **$**

★ **ROAD RUNNER INN.** *3034 Mundell Rd (72632). Phone 479/253-8166; toll-free 888/253-8166; fax 479/ 253-0231.* 12 kitchen units, shower only, 2 story. Closed mid-Nov-mid Mar. Pets accepted, some restrictions. Check-out 11 am. TV. **$**

Hotel

★ **BASIN PARK HOTEL.** *12 Spring St (72632). Phone 479/253-7837; toll-free 877/643-4972; fax 479/253-6985. www.basinpark.com.* 61 rooms, 6 story. Pets accepted, some restrictions. Complimentary continental breakfast. Check-out 11 am. TV; VCR available (movies). Restaurant, bar. Historic hotel built in 1905. Overlooks Basin Park and Spring. **$**

Fayetteville

Motels/Motor Lodges

★ **BEST WESTERN WINDSOR SUITES.** *1122 S Futrall (72701). Phone 479/587-1400; fax 479/756-5522. www.bestwestern.com.* 68 rooms, 2 story. S $55-$70; D $60-$75; each additional $5; suites $65-$105; under 18 free; higher rates special events. Pets accepted, some restrictions; fee. Complimentary continental breakfast. Check-out 11 am. TV; cable (premium), VCR available. In-room modem link. Laundry services. In-house fitness room. Indoor pool; whirlpool. Business center.

★ **DAYS INN.** *2402 N College Ave (72703). Phone 479/ 443-4323. www.daysinn.com.* 150 rooms, 2 story. Pets accepted, some restrictions; fee. Complimentary continental breakfast. Check-out noon. TV; cable (premium), VCR available. Pool. **$**

★ **RAMADA INN.** *3901 N College Ave (72703). Phone 479/443-3431; fax 479/443-1927.* 120 rooms, 2 story. S $49-$59; D $55-$65; each additional $6; under 18 free. Pets accepted, some restrictions; fee. Check-out noon. TV; cable (premium). Restaurant. Room service. Health club privileges. Pool. Outdoor tennis.

★ **RED ROOF INN.** *1000 S Futrall Dr (72701). Phone 479/442-3041; toll-free 800/REDROOF; fax 479/442-0744. www.redroof.com.* 80 rooms, 2 story. Pets accepted, some restrictions. Check-out noon. TV; cable (premium). Laundry services. Pool. **$**

Hotel

★ ★ ★ **RADISSON HOTEL.** *70 N East Ave (72701). Phone 479/442-5555; fax 479/442-2105. www.radisson.com.* This hotel is located in the full historic beauty of the Ozarks. Explore the nearby Civil War Battlefields and Eureka Springs. 235 rooms, 15 story. Pets accepted, some restrictions. TV; cable (premium), VCR available. Restaurant, bar. Indoor, outdoor pools. Free parking. Free airport transportation. **$**

Forrest City

Motel/Motor Lodge

★ ★ **BEST WESTERN.** *1306 N Hwy 17, Brinkley (72021). Phone 870/734-1650; fax 870/734-1657. www.bestwestern.com.* 100 rooms, 2 story. Pets accepted. Complimentary full breakfast. Check-out noon. TV. Restaurant. In-house fitness room. Pool. **$**

[D] [🐾] [⛷] [≋] [🏃] [⊠]

Fort Smith

Hotel

★ ★ **HOLIDAY INN.** *700 Rogers Ave (72901). Phone 479/783-1000; fax 479/783-0312. www.holiday-inn.com.* 9 story. S, D $109; each additional $10; suites $97.50-$130; weekend rates. Pets accepted; fee. Check-out noon. TV; cable (premium). In-room modem link. Restaurant; entertainment. In-house fitness room. Indoor pool; whirlpool. Valet parking. Free airport transportation.

[D] [🐾] [≋] [🏃] [✈] [⊠]

Greers Ferry Lake Area

Motel/Motor Lodge

★ **BUDGET INN.** *616 W Main St (72543). Phone 501/362-8111; toll-free 888/297-0955.* 25 rooms. S $36; D $42; each additional $5; suites, studio rooms $47. Pets accepted. Check-out 11 am. TV. Pool.

[🐾] [≋] [⊠] [SC]

Helena

Motel/Motor Lodge

★ **DELTA INN.** *1207 Hwy 49 W (72390). Phone 870/572-7915; fax 870/572-3757.* 94 rooms. S $37; D $42; each additional $5; under 16 free. Pets accepted, some restrictions. Complimentary continental breakfast. Check-out 11 am. TV; cable (premium). Pool.

[D] [🐾] [≋] [✈] [⊠]

Hope

Motels/Motor Lodges

★ **BEST WESTERN OF HOPE.** *I-30 and Hwy 278 (71801). Phone 870/777-9222; toll-free 800/429-4494; fax 870/777-9077. www.bestwestern.com.* 75 rooms, 2 story. S $49-$54; D $59-$64; under 12 free. Pets accepted. Check-out noon. TV; cable (premium). Laundry services. Pool.

[D] [🐾] [⛷] [≋] [⊠]

★ **SUPER 8.** *2000 Holiday Dr (71801). Phone 870/777-8601; fax 870/777-3142. www.super8.com.* 100 rooms, 2 story. S $26.88; D $35.88; each additional $7; under 12 free. Pets accepted. Complimentary continental breakfast. Check-out noon. TV; cable (premium). Pool. Outdoor tennis. Lawn games. Landscaped grounds; bridges.

[D] [🐾] [⛷] [✈] [≋] [⊠]

Hot Springs & Hot Springs National Park

Motels/Motor Lodges

★ ★ **QUALITY INN.** *1125 E Grand Ave (71901). Phone 501/624-3321; fax 501/624-5814. www.qualityinn.com.* 138 rooms, 2 story. S, D $54-$64; each additional $5; under 18 free. Pets accepted; fee. Check-out 11 am. TV; cable (premium). In-room modem link. Game room. Pool; whirlpool.

[D] [🐾] [⛷] [🏃] [≋] [⊠]

★ **TRAVELODGE.** *1204 Central Ave (71901). Phone 501/321-1332; toll-free 800/225-1360. www.travelodge.com.* 88 rooms, 16 kitchen units, 2 story. S $44-$50; D $49-$56; each additional $5; suites from $62; kitchen units $54-$58; under 17 free. Pets accepted, some restrictions. Check-out 11 am. TV; cable (premium). Restaurant 7 am-1 pm; 5-10 pm. Pool. Room service.

[D] [🐾] [≋] [⊠]

★ **VELDA ROSE.** *218 Park Ave (71901). Phone 501/623-3311; toll-free 888/624-3311; fax 501/623-8871. www.veldarose.com.* 191 rooms, 9 story. S $62-$72; D $72-$82; each additional $10; suites $89-$250; under 18 free. Pets accepted. Check-out noon. TV; cable (premium). In-room modem link. Restaurant, bar; entertainment. Pool; children's pool.

[🐾] [🍴] [≋] [⊠]

Resorts

★ ★ **CLARION RESORT.** *4813 Central Ave (71913). Phone 501/525-1391; toll-free 800/432-5145; fax 501/525-0813. www.clariononthelake.com.* 149 rooms, 7 story. May-Sept: S $89.95-$155.95; D $99.95-$165.95; each additional $10; under 12 free; lower rates rest of year. Pets accepted, some restrictions; fee. Check-out 11 am. TV; cable (premium). Laundry services. Restaurant. Health club privileges. Pool. Outdoor tennis. Boat rentals, waterskiing.

⊠⚓⛵🏌🏊⛷SC

★ ★ **LAKE HAMILTON RESORT.** *2803 Albert Pike Rd (71913). Phone 501/767-8606; toll-free 800/426-3184; fax 501/767-8576. www.lakehamiltonresort.com.* 104. suites, 3 story. Jan-Oct: suites $79-$94; under 18 free; lower rates rest of year. Closed Dec. Pets accepted; fee. Check-out noon, check-in 2 pm. TV. In-room modem link. Laundry services. Restaurant, bar; entertainment. Room service. In-house fitness room; sauna. Game room. Two pools, one indoor; whirlpool. Outdoor tennis, lighted courts. Boat dock, launching ramp, rentals; motorboats; waterskiing. Fishing guides. Airport transportation. Scenic view from all rooms.

D⊠⚓⛵🏌🏊🎣🏌✈⛷SC

Jonesboro

Motels/Motor Lodges

★ **DAYS INN.** *2406 Phillips Dr (72401). Phone 870/932-9339; fax 870/931-5289. www.daysinn.com.* 46 rooms. S, D $31.95; each additional $5; suites $37.95-$40.95; under 12 free. Pets accepted; fee. Complimentary continental breakfast. Check-out 11 am. TV; cable (premium).

D⊠⚓⛵⛷

★ ★ **HOLIDAY INN.** *3006 S Caraway Rd (72401). Phone 870/935-2030; fax 870/935-3440. www.holiday-inn.com.* 179 rooms, 2 story. S, D $65; each additional $7; suites $65-$100. Pets accepted, some restrictions. Check-out noon. TV; cable (premium). Laundry services. Restaurant, bar; entertainment. Room service. In-house fitness room. Game room. Indoor pool; whirlpool. Airport transportation.

D⊠⚓⛵🏌🏊🎣⛷

★ **HOLIDAY INN EXPRESS.** *2407 Phillips Dr (72401). Phone 870/932-5554; toll-free 800/465-4329; fax 870/932-2586. www.sixcontinentshotel.com.* 103 rooms, 4 story. S, D $59; each additional $7; suites $70; under 18 free. Pets accepted. Complimentary continental breakfast. Check-out noon. TV; cable (premium). In-room modem link. Health club privileges.

D⊠⚓⛷SC

Little Rock

Motels/Motor Lodges

★ **DAYS INN.** *3200 Bankhead Dr (72206). Phone 501/490-2010; fax 501/490-2229. www.daysinn.com.* 115 rooms, 2 story. S, D $48-$53; each additional $5; kitchens, $58-$63; under 18 free. Pets accepted, some restrictions; fee. Complimentary continental breakfast. Check-out noon. TV; cable (premium). In-room modem link. Laundry services. Pool. Free airport transportation.

D⊠⚓🏊✈⛷

★ **LA QUINTA INN.** *2401 W 65th St (72209). Phone 501/568-1030; fax 501/568-5713. www.laquinta.com.* 113 rooms, 2 story. S $59-$64; D $66-$75; each additional $7; suites $89; under 18 free. Pets accepted; fee. Complimentary continental breakfast. Check-out noon. TV; cable (premium). In-room modem link. Pool.

D⊠⚓🏊⛷

★ **LA QUINTA INN.** *11701 I-30 (72209). Phone 501/455-2300; fax 501/455-5876. www.laquinta.com.* 145 rooms, 3 story. S, D $64-$79; each additional $7; suites $139-$147; under 18 free. Pets accepted, some restrictions. Complimentary continental breakfast. Check-out noon. TV; cable (premium), VCR available. In-room modem link. Restaurant, bar. Health club privileges. Pool; whirlpool.

D⊠⚓🏊⛷

★ **MOTEL 6.** *7501 I-30 (72209). Phone 501/568-8888; toll-free 800/466-8356; fax 501/568-8355. www.motel6.com.* 130 rooms, 3 story. S $31.99, D $37.99; each additional $3; suites $48.44; under 17 free. Pets accepted. Check-out noon. TV; cable (premium). In-room modem link. Pool.

D⊠⚓🏊⛷SC

★ **RED ROOF INN.** *7900 Scott Hamilton Dr (72209). Phone 501/562-2694; fax 501/562-1723. www.redroof.com.* 108 rooms, 2 story. S $30-$35; D $36-$46; under 18 free. Pets accepted, some restrictions. Check-out noon. TV; cable (premium). In-room modem link.

D⊠⚓⛷

Hotel

★ ★ **HOLIDAY INN.** *201 S Shackleford Rd (72211). Phone 501/223-3000; toll-free 800/465-4329; fax 501/223-2833. www.holiday-inn.com.* 261 rooms, 5 story. S, D $88-$99; each additional $8; suites $135-$299; under 18 free; weekly, weekend rates. Pets accepted, some restrictions; fee. Check-out noon. TV; cable (premium). In-room modem link. Laundry services. Restaurant, bar; entertainment. Room service. In-house fitness room; sauna. Game room. Indoor pool; whirlpool; poolside service. Free airport, train station transportation. Concierge.

D 🐾 ⊠ 🏃 ⊠ SC

Magnolia

Motel/Motor Lodge

★ ★ **BEST WESTERN COACHMAN'S INN.** *420 E Main St (71753). Phone 870/234-6122; fax 870/234-1254. www.bestwestern.com.* 84 rooms, 2 story. S $49-$59; D $59-$69. Pets accepted, some restrictions; fee. Complimentary continental breakfast. Check-out noon. TV; cable (premium). In-room modem link. Restaurant. Pool.

D 🐾 🕹 ⊠ ⊠

Morrilton

Motel/Motor Lodge

★ ★ **BEST WESTERN INN.** *356 Hwy 95 (22902). Phone 501/354-0181; toll-free 800/251-1962; fax 501/354-1458.* 55 rooms, 2 story. S, D $38-$52; each additional $4; under 12 free; higher rates special events. Pets accepted, some restrictions; fee. Check-out noon. TV; cable (premium). Pool.

🐾 ⊠ ⊠ SC

Mountain Home

Motels/Motor Lodges

★ ★ **BAXTER INN.** *1350 Hwy 62 SW (72653). Phone 870/425-5101.* 100 rooms, 2 story. S $49; D $52; each additional $7; under 18 free. Pets accepted, some restrictions. Check-out noon. TV; cable (premium), VCR available. In-room modem link. Restaurant; entertainment. Room service. Health club privileges. Pool. Airport transportation.

D 🐾 🕹 🕹 ⊠ ✈ ⊠

★ ★ **BEST WESTERN CARRIAGE INN.** *963 Hwy 62 E (72653). Phone 870/425-6001. www.bestwestern.com.* 82 rooms, 2 story. S $43-$57; D $50-$62; each additional $6; under 12 free. Pets accepted, some restrictions. Check-out noon. TV; cable (premium). Restaurant. Room service. Pool. Continental breakfast.

🐾 🕹 🕹 ⊠ ⊠

Resort

★ **TEAL POINT RESORT.** *715 Teal Point Rd (72653). Phone 870/492-5145; toll-free 888/789-1023; fax 870/492-5215.* No room phones. June-Sept: cottages $62-$139;

each additional $5; family rates; lower rates rest of year. Pets accepted, some restrictions; fee. Check-out 9 am, check-in 3 pm. TV. Restaurant 1 mile. Game room. Pool. Lawn games. Boats, rentals. Fishing guides.

🐾 🕹 ⊠

Newport

Motel/Motor Lodge

★ ★ **PARK INN.** *901 Hwy 367 N (72112). Phone 870/523-5851; toll-free 800/633-2275; fax 870/523-9890.* 58 rooms. S $52; D $62; each additional $3; under 18 free. Pets accepted. Check-out noon. TV; cable (premium), VCR available (movies). Restaurant, bar. Health club privileges. Pool. Some rooms with cathedral ceiling.

D 🐾 ⊠ ⊠

Pine Bluff

Motel/Motor Lodge

★ ★ **RAMADA.** *Two Convention Center Dr (71601). Phone 870/535-3111; fax 870/534-5083. www.ramada.com.* 84 suites, 5 story. S, D $69; each additional $5; suites $79-$89; under 18 free. Pets accepted; fee. Check-out 11 am. TV. In-room modem link. Restaurant, bar. In-house fitness room; sauna. Game room. Indoor pool; whirlpool.

D 🐾 🕹 ⊠ 🏃 ⊠

Russellville

Motel/Motor Lodge

★ ★ **HOLIDAY INN.** *2407 N Arkansas (72476). Phone 479/968-4300; toll-free 800/465-4329. www.holiday-inn.com.* 149 rooms, 2 story. S $58; D $68; each additional $10; under 18 free. Pets accepted. Complimentary continental breakfast. Check-out noon. TV; cable (premium). In-room modem link. Restaurant. Room service. Pool. Airport transportation.

D 🐾 ⊠ ⊠ SC

Springdale

Motel/Motor Lodge

★ ★ **HOLIDAY INN.** *1500 S 48th St (72762). Phone 479/751-8300; toll-free 800/465-4329; fax 479/751-8300. www.holiday-inn.com.* 206 rooms, 8 story. S, D $119; suites $135-$160; under 18 free. Pets accepted, some restrictions; fee. Check-out noon. TV; cable (premium), VCR available. In-room modem link. Laundry services. Restaurant, bar. In-house fitness room. Indoor pool; whirlpool. Free airport transportation. Business center.

D 🐾 🛏 🏃 🚭 SC 🚶

Stuttgart

Motel/Motor Lodge

★ **BEST WESTERN DUCK INN.** *704 W Michigan St (72160). Phone 870/673-2575. www.bestwestern.com.* 72 rooms, 2 story. Mid-Nov-mid-Jan: S $55-$75; D $60-$85; each additional $5; suites $85; family rates; lower rates rest of year. Pets accepted. Check-out noon. TV; cable (premium), VCR. Indoor pool.

D 🐾 🛏 🚭 SC

California

Alturas

Motels/Motor Lodges

★ **BEST WESTERN TRAILSIDE INN.** *343 N Main St (96161). Phone 530/233-4111; toll-free 800/528-1234; fax 530/233-3180. www.bestwestern.com.* 38 rooms, 4 kitchen units, 2 story. May-Oct: S, D $60-$70; each additional $5; kitchen units $10 additional; lower rates rest of year. Pets accepted, some restrictions; fee. Complimentary continental breakfast. Check-out 11 am. TV; cable (premium). In-room modem link. Pool. Downhill, cross-country ski 10 miles. Totally nonsmoking.

★ **HACIENDA MOTEL.** *201 E 12th St (96101). Phone 530/233-3459.* 20 rooms, 2 kitchen units. S $35; D $39; each additional $3; kitchen units $5 additional; under 8 free. Pets accepted. Check-out 11 am. TV; cable (premium). Restaurant nearby. Downhill, cross-country ski 10 miles.

Anaheim

Hotels

★ ★ ★ **HILTON.** *777 W Convention Way (92802). Phone 714/750-4321; fax 714/740-4460. www.anaheim.hilton.com.* 1,574 rooms, 14 story. S $89-$300; D $119-$330; each additional $30; suites $800-$1,600; under 18 free; family rates. Pets accepted, some restrictions. Check-out noon. TV; cable (premium). Restaurant, bar; entertainment. In-house fitness room; sauna. Game room. Two heated pools, one indoor; whirlpool; poolside service. Covered parking. Business center. Concierge. Luxury level.

★ ★ ★ **MARRIOTT.** *700 W Convention Way (92802). Phone 714/750-8000; toll-free 800/228-9290; fax 714/750-9100. www.marriotthotels.com/laxah.* Appropriate for business or leisure, this hotel is located two blocks south of Disneyland and adjacent to the convention center. 1,033 rooms, 19 story. Pets accepted. Check-out noon, check-in 4 pm. TV; cable (premium). Continental

breakfast in lobby. Restaurant, bar. In-house fitness room; sauna. Game room. Two pools; one indoor; whirlpools, poolside service. Valet parking. Airport, Disneyland transportation. Business center. Concierge. Luxury level. **$$$**

Arcadia

Extended Stay

★ ★ **RESIDENCE INN BY MARRIOTT.** *321 E Huntington Dr (91006). Phone 626/446-6500; fax 626/446-5824. www.residenceinn.com.* 120 kitchen units, 2 story. Suites $149-$189; higher rates Rose Bowl (4-day minimum). Pets accepted; fee. Complimentary continental breakfast. Check-out noon. TV; cable (premium), VCR available. Laundry services. Health club privileges. Pool; whirlpool. Airport transportation available.

Bakersfield

Motels/Motor Lodges

★ **BEST WESTERN HILL HOUSE.** *700 Truxton Ave (93301). Phone 661/327-4064; toll-free 800/300-4230; fax 661/327-1247.* 97 rooms, 2 story. Pets accepted; fee. Complimentary continental breakfast. Check-out 11 am. TV; cable (premium). Restaurant, bar. Pool. **$**

★ **LA QUINTA INN.** *3232 Riverside Dr (93308). Phone 661/325-7400; toll-free 800/687-6667; fax 661/324-6032. www.laquinta.com.* 129 rooms, 3 story. Pets accepted; fee. Complimentary continental breakfast. Check-out noon. Check-in 2 pm. TV; cable (premium). **$**

★ **QUALITY INN.** *1011 Oak St (93304). Phone 661/325-0772; toll-free 800/228-5050; fax 661/325-4646.* 89 rooms, 2 story. Pets accepted, some restrictions; fee. Complimentary full breakfast. Check-out noon, check-in 10 am. TV; cable (premium). Sauna. Indoor pool; whirlpool. **$**

★ **SUPER 8.** *901 Real Rd (93309). Phone 661/322-1012; fax 661/322-7636. www.super8.com.* 90 rooms, 3 story. Pets accepted; fee. Check-out 11 am. Check-in 1 pm. TV; cable (premium). Outdoor pool; whirlpool. **$**

Barstow

Motel/Motor Lodge

★ **DAYS INN.** *1590 Coolwater Ln (92311). Phone 760/256-1737; toll-free 800/329-7466; fax 760/256-7771. www.daysinn.com.* 113 rooms, 2 story. S $44-$49; D $53-$59; under 12 free; weekly rates. Pets accepted; fee. Complimentary continental breakfast. Check-out 11 am. TV; cable (premium). Laundry services. Pool.

D ⬛ ⬛ ⬛ SC

Beaumont

Motel/Motor Lodge

★ ★ **BEST WESTERN EL RANCHO MOTOR INN.** *480 E 5th St (92223). Phone 909/845-2176; fax 909/845-7559.* 52 rooms, 2 story. S $59; D $69; each additional $3; suites $70-$85. Pets accepted, some restrictions; fee. Complimentary continental breakfast. Check-out 11 am. TV; cable (premium). Restaurant 7 am-9 pm. Bar 11 am-11 pm. Pool.

D ⬛ ⬛ ⬛ ⬛

Berkeley

Hotel

★ ★ ★ **DOUBLETREE BERKELEY MARINA.** *200 Marina Blvd (94710). Phone 510/548-7920; toll-free 800/243-0625; fax 510/548-7944. www.radisson.com/berkeleyca.* Directly on the bay and only 15 minutes from the city. 369 rooms, 4 story. Pets accepted, some restrictions. Check-out noon. TV; cable (premium). In-room modem link. Room service 24 hours. Restaurant, bar. Babysitting services available. In-house fitness room; massage, sauna. Pool; children's pool; whirlpool; poolside service. Dockage. Valet parking. Business center. Luxury level. $

D ⬛ ⬛ ⬛ ⬛ ⬛

Beverly Hills

Hotels

★ ★ ★ **AVALON HOTEL.** *9400 W Olympic Blvd (90212). Phone 310/277-5221; toll-free 800/535-4715; fax 310/277-4928. www.avalon-hotel.com.* Marilyn Monroe once bunked here. Ergo the Avalon channels the mid-century modernist spirit of Monroe's age, en route becoming one of the coolest scenes in Beverly Hills thanks to noted designer Kelly Wearstler. The sleek lobby serves as a Beverly Hills meeting spot overlooking the hourglass-shaped swimming pool and funneling patrons into Blue On Blue restaurant and bar. Each of its rooms is different and options range from see-and-be-seen poolside quarters, to cityscape tower rooms and junior suites with kitchenettes. Aura Spa provides in-room massages. 88 rooms, suites, 5 story. Mar-May; S, D$179-$299; suites $239-$339; each additional $35; under 18 free; lower rates rest of year. Pets accepted; fee. Check-out noon, check-in 3 pm. TV; cable (premium); VCR, CD available. Room service 24 hours. Restaurant, bar. In-house fitness room. Pool. Tennis, 10 courts. Valet parking. Concierge.

D ⬛ ⬛ ⬛ ⬛ ⬛ ⬛ SC

★ ★ ★ ★ ★ **THE BEVERLY HILLS HOTEL.** *9641 Sunset Blvd (90210). Phone 310/276-2251; toll-free 800/283-8885; fax 310/281-2905. www.beverlyhillshotel.com.* Hovering above Sunset Boulevard in a magnificent setting of lush gardens, The Beverly Hills Hotel epitomizes the glamour of Hollywood. Affectionately known as the "pink palace," this legendary hotel has long been the favorite hideaway of the silver screen's biggest stars. Taking a cue from its most famous guests, the hotel evokes the allure of 1940s Hollywood in its public and private rooms. The guest rooms and suites are an ideal refuge with soothing pastel color schemes and luxurious furnishings. Fireplaces add a romantic touch, and terraces and balconies focus attention on the beautiful gardens. Guests seeking a true getaway opt for the bungalows privately tucked away along paths of fragrant tropical plants. A variety of dining venues attract producers and stars, but visitors in the know head for the pool, where the scene is best viewed from a fantastic private cabana. 203 rooms, 1-4 story. Pets accepted, some restrictions; fee. Check-out noon, check-in 3 pm. TV; cable (premium); VCR available. In-room modem link. Fireplaces. Restaurant, bar. Room service. Babysitting services available. In-house fitness room; massage. Outdoor pool; whirlpool; poolside service. Outdoor tennis. Valet parking. Airport transportation. Business center. Concierge. $$$$

D ⬛ ⬛ ⬛ ⬛ ⬛ ⬛

★ ★ ★ **THE BEVERLY HILTON.** *9876 Wilshire Blvd (90210). Phone 310/274-7777; toll-free 800/445-8667; fax 310/285-1313. www.beverlyhills.hilton.com.* Traditional Hollywood glamour can be yours at this elegant haven adjacent to Century City and Westwood. 581 rooms, 8 story. Pets accepted; fee. Check-out noon. Check-in 3 pm. TV; cable (premium), VCR available. In-room modem link. Room service 24 hours. Dining room, bar. In-house fitness room. Pool; children's pool; poolside service. Garage, valet parking. Business center. Concierge. Lanai rooms around pool. $$$

D ⬛ ⬛ ⬛ ⬛ SC ⬛

★ ★ ★ ★ ★ **THE PENINSULA BEVERLY HILLS.** *9882 S Santa Monica Blvd (90212). Phone 310/551-2888; toll-free 800/462-7899; fax 310/788-2319. www.peninsula.com.* The Peninsula embodies the grace and elegance synonymous with Beverly Hills. This French Renaissance-style hotel remains close to the enticing boutiques of Rodeo Drive and Century City, yet feels very private and secluded. Meticulously maintained, the luscious gardens are a kaleidoscope of colors and fragrances, from rare and exotic plantings to familiar favorites. The sun-filled lobby mimics the bounty of the gardens in its sophisticated, tropical-inspired décor. The guest rooms and suites, fitted with the Peninsula's renowned amenities, are the last word in luxury. Swimmers drink in a view of the city from the rooftop lap pool, while spa-goers retreat to the Zen-like spa, complete with fitness center. Dining is exceptional, from the delicious West Coast cuisine of The Belvedere and the wonderful afternoon tea of the Living Room to the health-conscious spa menu at the Rooftop Garden. *Secret Inspector's Notes:* Not only is this is the place to see and be seen in Beverly Hills, but the personalized service will keep you coming back. The staff takes pains to make sure that you are enjoying every moment; they are warm, engaging, and gracious and make you feel like you're a star no matter who you are. Make sure to reserve a spa treatment in a private bungalow adjacent to the rooftop pool! 196 rooms, 5 story. Pets accepted; fee. TV; cable (premium), VCR available. In-room modem link. Room service 24 hours. Restaurant, bar. Babysitting services available. In-house fitness room; spa, massage, sauna. Outdoor pool; whirlpool. Valet parking. Airport transportation. Business center. Concierge. **$$$$**

⬛ 🐾 🏊 🧍 ✈ 🚫 🚶

★ ★ ★ ★ ★ **RAFFLES L'ERMITAGE BEVERLY HILLS.** *9291 Burton Way (90210). Phone 310/278-3344; toll-free 800/800-2113; fax 310/278-8247. www.lermitagehotel.com.* Satisfying the cool quotient in Beverly Hills with its stylish and serene décor, Raffles L'Ermitage is the haven of choice for the jet set. Conveniently located, this hotel maintains a sanctuary-like ambience in the heart of Beverly Hills. The guest rooms and suites are a harmony of European and Asian influences with light woods, simple furnishings, and shoji-style screens. All accommodations are outfitted with high-tech accoutrements, including 40-inch televisions, Bose speakers, and ten jacks for audiovisual needs and DSL lines. Hipsters flock to JAAN's sensuous setting and delicious French dishes infused with Indochine flavors. The Living Room and Writer's Bar encourage visitors to sink into their inviting surroundings and enjoy cocktails or light meals. The rooftop pool provides guests with a bird's-eye view of the prestigious neighborhood, while the Amrita spa takes guests to a higher level of relaxation with its Ayurvedic techniques. *Secret Inspector's Notes:* It's true that the cool quotient is high, but guests feel comfortable and relaxed in this Beverly Hills haven. The staff is generally warm and friendly and also ultra-hip! 123 rooms, 8 story. Pets accepted, some restrictions; fee. TV; cable (premium), DVD available. In-room modem link. Restaurant, bar. Room service. Babysitting services available. In-house fitness room; sauna, steam room, spa, massage. Outdoor pool; whirlpool. In/out garage parking. Airport transportation. Concierge. Luxury level. **$$$$**

⬛ 🐾 🏊 🧍 ✈ 🚫

★ ★ ★ ★ **THE REGENT BEVERLY WILSHIRE.** *9500 Wilshire Blvd (90212). Phone 310/275-5200; toll-free 800/545-4000; fax 310/274-2851. www.regenthotels.com.* For a taste of the good life, savvy travelers check in at the Regent Beverly Wilshire, a Four Seasons Hotel. Located at the intersection of Rodeo Drive and Wilshire Boulevard, it doesn't get any better than this prestigious address in the heart of world-famous Beverly Hills. Bridging old and new, this Italian Renaissance-style hotel is a happy marriage of two distinctive sensibilities. The guest rooms of the Beverly Wing are a triumph of contemporary décor, while the Wilshire Wing's rooms appeal to classic-minded guests. The service is exemplary, as guests have come to expect from the Four Seasons, from the attentive room service to the helpful staff in the business and fitness centers. The Dining Room is a vision, with its Murano glass chandeliers, mahogany-paneled walls, and sumptuous seating. A very British afternoon tea is served at the Lobby Lounge, and the convivial bar is a perfect place to sit back and watch the glamorous parade of this star-studded city. 395 rooms, 10 and 12 story. Pets accepted, some restrictions. Covered parking, valet. Check-out noon, check-in 3 pm. TV; cable (premium), VCR available (movies). In-room modem link. Room service 24 hours. Restaurant, bar; entertainment. In-house fitness room; sauna, steam room, spa, massage. Outdoor pool; whirlpool; poolside service. Business center. Concierge. **$$$$**

⬛ 🐾 🏊 🧍 🚫 🚶

Big Bear Lake

B&B/Small Inn

★ ★ ★ **EAGLES NEST BED AND BREAKFAST.** *41675 Big Bear Blvd (92315). Phone 909/866-6465; toll-free 888/866-6465; fax 909/866-6025. www.eaglesnestlodge bigbear.com.* High in the Bernardino Mountains and in the heart of Bear Valley, this bed-and-breakfast is conveniently located to Snow Summit and Big Bear Mountain ski resorts. 5 rooms, 2 story. S, D $110-$150; weekly rates. Pets accepted, some restrictions. Check-out 11 am, check-in 2 pm. TV. Full breakfast. Fireplaces. Downhill, cross-country ski 1/4 mile. Lodge décor. Totally non-smoking.

🐾 🐟 ⚡ 🚫 🚶

Bishop

Motels/Motor Lodges

★ **BEST WESTERN BISHOP HOLIDAY SPA LODGE.** *1025 N Main St (93514). Phone 760/873-3543; toll-free 800/576-3543; fax 760/872-4777.* 89 rooms, 1-2 story. S $59-$89; D $69-$99; each additional $10; higher rates holidays. Pets accepted; fee. Check-out 11 am. TV; cable (premium). Laundry services. Pool; whirlpool. Cross-country ski 20 miles.

D ➰ ⛷ ⛵ ➰ ➷ SC

★ **BISHOP THUNDERBIRD MOTEL.** *190 W Pine St (93514). Phone 760/873-4215; fax 760/873-6870.* 23 rooms, 2 story. Pets accepted; fee. Check-out 11 am. TV; cable (premium). Cross-country ski 20 miles. **$**

➰ ➷ ➷ SC

★ **COMFORT INN.** *805 N Main St (93514). Phone 760/873-4284; toll-free 800/576-4080; fax 760/873-8563.* 54 rooms, 2 story. S $69-$79; D $79-$89; each additional $5; suites $139-$200; higher rates holidays. Pets accepted; fee. Complimentary continental breakfast. Check-out 11 am. TV; cable (premium). Laundry services. Pool; whirlpool. Fish cleaning, freezer facilities.

D ➰ ⛷ ➰ ➷ SC

Blythe

Motels/Motor Lodges

★ **BEST VALUE INN.** *850 W Hobson Way (92225). Phone 760/922-5145; fax 760/922-8422. www.bestvalueinn.com.* 50 rooms, 34 with shower only, 1-2 story. S, D $45-$65; each additional $5; under 14 free; weekly rates. Pets accepted, some restrictions. Complimentary continental breakfast. Check-out 11 am. TV; cable (premium). Restaurant adjacent. Pool.

D ➰ ➰ ➷ SC

★ **BEST WESTERN SAHARA MOTEL.** *825 W Hobson Way (92225). Phone 760/922-7105; fax 760/922-5836. www.bestwestern.com.* 47 rooms. S $55-$95; D $66-$115; each additional $5; under 12 free; higher rates special events. Pets accepted, some restrictions. Complimentary continental breakfast. Check-out noon. TV; cable (premium), VCR. Pool; whirlpool.

➰ ➰ ➷

★ **LEGACY INN.** *903 W Hobson Way (92225). Phone 760/922-4146; toll-free 877/737-5342; fax 760/922-8481.*

48 rooms, 2 story. S $50; D $58; each additional $5; under 18 free; higher rates special events. Pets accepted. Complimentary continental breakfast. Check-out noon. TV; cable (premium). Restaurant opposite. Pool.

➰ ➰

Bodega Bay

B&B/Small Inn

★ ★ ★ **THE INN AT OCCIDENTAL.** *3657 Church St (95465). Phone 707/874-1047; toll-free 800/522-6324; fax 707/874-1078. www.innatoccidental.com.* Tucked among the towering redwoods and only minutes from the Wine Country and the Pacific's coastline is this lovely Victorian bed-and-breakfast. 18 rooms. Pets accepted, some restrictions. Children over 12 years only. Complimentary full breakfast. Check-out noon, check-in 3 pm. Fireplaces. Totally nonsmoking. **$$$**

D ➰ ➷

Borrego Springs

Motel/Motor Lodge

★ ★ **BORREGO SPRING RESORT.** *1112 Tilting T Dr (92004). Phone 760/767-5700; toll-free 888/826-7734; fax 760/767-5710. www.borregospringsresort.com.* 100 rooms, 2 story. Pets accepted; fee. Complimentary continental breakfast. Check-out noon, check-in 4 pm. TV. In-room modem link. Laundry services. Restaurant. Babysitting services available. In-house fitness room. Outdoor pool; whirlpool. 27-hole golf, greens fee $54-$64, putting green, driving range. Lighted tennis. Free airport transportation. **$$**

➰ ⛹ ⛷ ➰ 🏃

B&B/Small Inn

★ ★ **BORREGO VALLEY INN.** *405 Palm Canyon Dr (92004). Phone 760/767-0311; toll-free 800/333-5810; fax 760/767-0900. www.borregovalleyinn.com.* 15 rooms. Closed July-Aug; Jun-Sept (weekdays). Pets accepted; fee. Complimentary continental breakfast. Check-out 11 am, check-in 4 pm. TV; cable (premium), VCR available. In-room modem link. Some fireplaces. Outdoor pool; whirlpool. Free airport transportation. Totally nonsmoking. **$$**

D ➰ ➰ ✈ ➷

Bridgeport

Motels/Motor Lodges

★ **SILVER MAPLE INN.** *310 Main St (93517). Phone 760/932-7383; fax 760/932-7811. www.silvermapleinn.com.* 20 rooms. No A/C. S, D $70-$115; each additional $5. Pets accepted. Check-out 11 am. TV; cable (premium). Lawn games.

D 🐾 🛶 ⚓ 🎿 🔀

★ **WALKER RIVER LODGE.** *100 Main St (93517). Phone 760/932-7021; toll-free 800/388-6651; fax 760/932-7914. www.walkerriverlodge.com.* 36 rooms, 1-2 story. Mid-Apr-Oct: S $75-$140; D $80-$155; each additional $10; kitchen units $95-$200; lower rates rest of year. Pets accepted. Check-out 11 am. TV; cable (premium). Restaurant adjacent. Pool; whirlpool. Cross-country ski 12 miles. Fish freezer.

D 🐾 🛶 ⚓ 🏊 🔀 SC

Buena Park

Motel/Motor Lodge

★ **COLONY INN.** *7800 Crescent Ave (90620). Phone 714/527-2201; toll-free 800/982-6566; fax 714/826-3826. colonyinnbuenapark.com.* 2 story, 8 suites. S $49; D $55; suites, family units $75; under 12 free. Pets accepted; fee. Complimentary continental breakfast. Check-out 11 am. TV; cable (premium). Pool; children's pool.

D 🐾 🏊 🔀 SC

Hotel

★ ★ **BEST WESTERN INNSUITES HOTEL & SUITES.** *7555 Beach Blvd (90620). Phone 714/522-7360; toll-free 888/522-5885; fax 714/523-2883. www.bestwestern.com.* 176 rooms, 2 story. S, D $79-$88; suites $88-$200; under 18 free. Pets accepted, some restrictions; fee. Check-out noon. TV; cable (premium). In-house fitness room; sauna. Game room. Pool; whirlpool. Free Disneyland transportation.

🐾 🏊 🏋 🔀 SC

Burbank

Hotel

★ ★ ★ **HILTON BURBANK AIRPORT AND CONVENTION CENTER.** *2500 N Hollywood Way (91505). Phone 818/843-6000; toll-free 800/445-8667; fax 818/842-9720. www.burbankairport.hilton.com.* The location of this hotel is key for travelers looking to visit attractions in the greater LA area. Minutes from Disneyland, Universal Studios, and NBC, this hotel is also located across the street from the Burbank-Glendale-Pasadena Airport. 488 rooms, 8-9 story. S $200; D $229; each additional $20; suites $248-$540; under 18 free; family, weekend rates. Pets accepted; fee. Check-out noon. TV; cable (premium). Laundry services. Room service 24 hours. Restaurant, bar. In-house fitness room. Two pools; whirlpool; poolside service. Free airport transportation. Business center. Concierge.

D 🐾 🏊 🏋 ✈ 🔀 🚶

Calistoga

B&B/Small Inns

★ ★ **THE ELMS BED & BREAKFAST INN.** *1300 Cedar St (94515). Phone 707/942-9476; toll-free 888/399-ELMS; fax 707/942-9479. www.theelms.com.* 7 rooms, 3 story. No elevator. No room phones. Pets accepted, some restrictions; fee. Complimentary full breakfast. Check-out 11 am, check-in 4 pm. TV. Whirlpool. Concierge service. Built in 1871; antiques. Totally nonsmoking. **$$**

🐾 🔀 🔀

★ ★ ★ **MEADOWLARK COUNTRY HOUSE AND INN.** *601 Petrified Forest Rd (94515). Phone 707/942-5651; fax 707/942-5023. www.meadowlarkinn.com.* 8 rooms, 2 story. Pets accepted. Complimentary full breakfast. Check-out 11:30 am, check-in 3:30 pm. TV in sitting room; cable; VCR. Sauna. Outdoor pool; whirlpool. Totally nonsmoking. **$$**

🐾 🏊 🔀

Cambria

B&B/Small Inn

★ **CAMBRIA SHORES INN.** *6276 Moonstone Beach Dr (93428). Phone 805/927-8644; toll-free 800/433-9179; fax 805/927-4070. www.cambriashores.com.* 24 rooms. No A/C. Memorial Day-Labor Day, weekends, holidays: S $85-$150; D $95-$160; lower rates rest of year. Pets accepted, some restrictions; fee. Complimentary continental breakfast. Check-out 11 am. TV.

🐾 🔀 🔀

Carlsbad

Motel/Motor Lodge

★ **INNS OF AMERICA.** *751 Raintree Dr (92009). Phone 760/931-1185; fax 760/931-0970. www.innsofamerica.com.* 125 rooms, 3 story. D $129. Pets accepted; fee. Complimentary continental breakfast. Check-out 11 am, check-in 3 pm. TV; cable (premium). Laundry services. Heated pool.

Resort

★ ★ ★ ★ **FOUR SEASONS RESORT AVIARA.** *7100 Four Seasons Point (92009). Phone 760/603-6800; fax 760/603-6801. www.fourseasons.com/aviara.* The Four Seasons Resort Aviara is a world away from everyday distractions, yet it is only 30 minutes from San Diego. This splendid resort is nestled on 200 lush acres overlooking the Batiquitos Lagoon, the Pacific Ocean, and a nature preserve that's home to a wide variety of wildlife. The architecture pays homage to the region's history in its Spanish colonial design. An unpretentious elegance is felt throughout the property, especially in the guest rooms. Recognized for its 18-hole course designed by Arnold Palmer, the resort is a favorite of golfers. Carefully preserving the natural landscape, the course is a visual and athletic delight. Relaxation is guaranteed at this resort, whether poolside or at the spa. From the Pool Bar & Grill, California Bistro, and Argyle, with views over the verdant links, to Vivace, with floor-to-ceiling windows framing the Pacific Ocean, dining is always with a view. *Secret Inspector's Notes:* Do not overlook the spa! It is an oasis of calm and light, with a staff that attends to your every need. 329 rooms, 44 suites, 5 story. S, D $395-$505; suites $615-$4,200; under 17 free; golf plans. Pets accepted, some restrictions; fee. Valet parking. Check-out noon, check-in 3 pm. TV; cable (premium), VCR available. In-room modem link. Restaurant 6-10:30 pm. Bar to midnight; entertainment. Room service 24 hours. Supervised children's activities; ages 5-11. In-house fitness room; sauna, steam room. Spa. Massage. Two heated pools; children's pool; whirlpool; poolside service. 18-hole golf, greens fee $185; weekends $195. 6 lighted tennis courts. Business center. Concierge.

Carmel

Motels/Motor Lodges

★ ★ **BEST WESTERN CARMEL MISSION INN.** *3665 Rio Rd (93923). Phone 831/624-1841; toll-free 800/*348-9090; fax 831/624-8684. www.carmelmissioninn.com.* 165 rooms, 4 story. Pets accepted, some restrictions; fee. Check-out noon, check-in 4 pm. TV; cable (premium). In-room modem link. Fireplaces. Restaurant, bar. Room service. Babysitting services available. In-house fitness room. Outdoor pool. Business center. **$**

★ **WAYSIDE INN.** *Mission St and 7th Ave (93921). Phone 831/624-5336; toll-free 800/433-4732; fax 831/626-6974. www.innsbythesea.com.* 22 rooms, 4 kitchen units, 2 story. No A/C. S, D $109-$289; each additional $15; suites $200-$350; under 14 free; weekends (2-day minimum). Pets accepted, some restrictions. Complimentary continental breakfast. Check-out noon. TV; cable (premium), VCR available. In-room modem link. Many fireplaces. Restaurant nearby.

B&B/Small Inns

★ ★ **CARMEL GARDEN COURT INN.** *4th and Torres St (93921). Phone 831/624-6926; toll-free 800/313-7770; fax 831/624-4935. www.carmelgardencourtinn.com.* 10 rooms, 2 story. No A/C. Pets accepted, some restrictions; fee. Complimentary continental breakfast. Check-out 11 am, check-in 4 pm. TV; VCR available. Fireplaces. Totally nonsmoking. **$$**

★ ★ **CYPRESS INN.** *Lincoln and 7th St (93921). Phone 831/624-3871; toll-free 800/443-7443; fax 831/624-8216. www.cypress-inn.com.* 33 rooms, 2 story. Pets accepted, some restrictions; fee. Complimentary continental breakfast. Check-out noon, check-in 4 pm. TV; cable (premium) in library. Fireplaces. Bar. Massage. Whirlpool. Concierge. **$**

★ **VAGABOND HOUSE INN.** *Dolores St and 4th Ave (93921). Phone 831/624-7738; toll-free 800/262-1262; fax 831/626-1243. www.vagabondshouseinn.com.* 13 rooms, 1-2 story. story. No A/C. Pets accepted, some restrictions; fee. Children over 10 years only. Complimentary continental breakfast. Check-out noon, check-in 3 pm. TV; cable (premium). Many fireplaces, kitchenettes. **$**

Carmel Valley

B&B/Small Inns

★ ★ **CARMEL VALLEY LODGE.** *8 Ford Rd (93924). Phone 831/659-2261; toll-free 800/641-4646; fax 831/659-4558. www.valleylodge.com.* 27 kitchen units, 1-2 story. No A/C. Apr-Oct: S, D $159-$199; each additional $15;

kitchen units, cottages $249-$329; higher rates: holidays, special events; weekends, holidays (2-3-day minimum); lower rates rest of year. Pets accepted, some restrictions; fee. Complimentary continental breakfast. Check-out noon, check-in 3 pm. TV; VCR available. In-house fitness room; sauna. Pool; whirlpool.

D 🐾 ⛱ ⊠ SC

★★ **LOS LAURELES LODGE.** *313 Carmel Valley Rd (93924). Phone 831/659-2233; fax 831/659-0481. www.loslaureles.com.* 6 suites. No A/C. Apr-Oct: S, D $90-$155; suites $175-$595; under 17 free; weekends, holidays (2-day minimum); lower rates rest of year. Pets accepted, some restrictions; fee. Check-out noon, check-in 3 pm. TV; cable (premium). Fireplaces. Restaurant. The main building was built in the 1890s; once the home of Muriel Vanderbilt.

🐾 ⛱ ⊠ SC

Chico

Motels/Motor Lodges

★★ **HOLIDAY INN.** *685 Manzanita Ct (93923). Phone 530/345-2491; toll-free 800/310-2491; fax 530/893-3040. www.holiday-inn.com.* 172 rooms, 5 story. S $92; D $101; each additional $10; suites $100-$160; under 19 free. Pets accepted; fee. Check-out 11 am. TV; cable (premium). In-room modem link. Bar; entertainment. Restaurant. Room service. Health club privileges. Pool; whirlpool. Free airport transportation.

D 🐾 ⛱ ✈ ⊠

★ **VAGABOND INN.** *630 Main St (95928). Phone 530/895-1323; toll-free 800/522-1555; fax 530/343-2719. www.vagabond.com.* 43 rooms, 2 story. S $42-$69; D $52-$79; higher rates special events; each additional $5; kitchen units $8 additional; under 16 free. Pets accepted; fee. Complimentary continental breakfast. Check-out 11 am. TV; cable (premium). Pool.

🐾 ⛱ ⊠ SC

Claremont

Motel/Motor Lodge

★★ **RAMADA INN.** *840 S Indian Hill Blvd (91711). Phone 909/621-4831; toll-free 800/322-6559; fax 909/621-0411. www.ramada.com.* 122 rooms, 2 story. S $74; D $79; each additional $8; under 12 free. Pets accepted, some restrictions; fee. Complimentary continental breakfast. Check-out noon. TV; cable (premium). Health club privileges. Pool; children's pool; whirlpool. Lighted tennis.

🐾 🎾 ⛱ ⊠

Coleville

Motel/Motor Lodge

★ **ANDRUSS MOTEL.** *106964 US 395 (96107). Phone 530/495-2216.* 13 kitchen units. S $46-$54; D, kitchen units $54; each additional $4. Pets accepted, some restrictions; fee. Check-out 11 am. TV; cable (premium). Pool. Lawn games. Fish cleaning, freezing facilities.

D 🐾 🎣 ⛱ 🎿 ⊠

Corona

Motel/Motor Lodge

★ **DYNASTY SUITES.** *1805 W 6th St (92882). Phone 909/371-7185; toll-free 800/842-7899; fax 909/371-0401. www.dynastysuites.com.* 56 rooms, 2 story. S, D $59.95; each additional $5. Pets accepted, some restrictions; fee. Complimentary continental breakfast. Check-out noon. TV; cable (premium), VCR available (movies). Pool; whirlpool.

D 🐾 ⛱ ⊠ SC

Coronado

Motel/Motor Lodge

★★ **CROWN CITY INN.** *520 Orange Ave (92118). Phone 619/435-3116; toll-free 800/422-1173; fax 619/435-6752. www.crowncityinn.com.* 33 rooms, 2 story. D $109-$129; higher rates holidays. Pets accepted, some restrictions; fee. Check-out 11 am, check-in 3 pm. TV; cable (premium). Laundry services. Restaurant. Room service. Heated pool.

🐾 ⛱ ⊠

Resorts

★★★ **LOEWS CORONADO BAY RESORT.** *4000 Coronado Bay Rd (92118). Phone 619/424-4000; toll-free 800/23-LOEWS; fax 619/424-4400. www.loewshotels.com.* Tucked onto a private 15-acre peninsula off Coronado, this resort features a private marina. 450 rooms. Pets accepted. Check-out noon, check-in 3 pm. TV; cable (premium), VCR available. In-room modem link. Restaurant; entertainment. Room service 24 hours. Children's activity center, babysitting services available. In-house fitness room; spa, massage, sauna. Health club privileges. Game room. Beach. Outdoor pool; children's pool. Outdoor tennis, lighted courts. Lawn games, bicycles, boats. Business center. Concierge. **$**

D 🐾 🎾 ⛱ ⊠ 🚶

★ ★ ★ **MARRIOTT CORONADO ISLAND RESORT.** *2000 2nd St (92118). Phone 619/435-3000; fax 619/435-4183. www.marriott.com.* Get hypnotized by the sparkling San Diego city lights at this bayfront resort 5 miles from the Gaslamp Quarter. The crisp white entrance is a minimalist beginning to the 16 tropical acres that are home to waterfalls, exotic wildlife, and award-winning restaurants. For something special, reserve one of 28 villas with a private entrance and pool. 300 rooms, 3 story. Pets accepted, some restrictions. Check-out noon. Check-in 4 pm. TV; cable (premium), VCR available. Room service 24 hours. Restaurant. Spa, sauna. Indoor pool; whirlpool; poolside service. Lighted tennis. Bicycle rental. Valet parking. Business center. Concierge. **$$**

Costa Mesa

Motels/Motor Lodges

★ **RAMADA LIMITED.** *1680 Superior Ave (92627). Phone 949/645-2221; toll-free 800/272-6232; fax 949/650-9125. www.ramadalimitednewport.com.* 140 rooms, 35 suites, 3 story. Mid-May-mid-Sept: S, D $69-$79; each additional $5; suites $109-$169; under 17 free; lower rates rest of year. Pets accepted, some restrictions. Complimentary continental breakfast. Check-out noon. TV; cable (premium). In-house fitness room. Pool; whirlpool. Free airport transportation.

★ **VAGABOND INN.** *3205 Harbor Blvd (92626). Phone 714/557-8360; toll-free 800/522-1555; fax 714/662-7596. www.vagabondinncostamesa.com.* 128 rooms, 5 suites, 2 story. Pets accepted, some restrictions; fee. Complimentary continental breakfast. Check-out noon, check-in 1 pm. TV; cable (premium). In-house fitness room. Health club privileges. Outdoor pool. Mission-style building. Free airport transportation. **$**

Hotels

★ ★ **HILTON.** *3050 Bristol St (92626). Phone 714/540-7000; fax 714/540-9176. www.doubletreehotels.com.* 484 rooms, 7 story. D $125-$395; each additional $15; under 18 free. Pets accepted, some restrictions; fee. Check-out noon, check-in 3 pm. TV; cable (premium). In-room modem link. Restaurant, bar; entertainment Fri-Sun. Room service. In-house fitness room; massage, sauna. Game room. Pool; whirlpool; poolside service. Valet parking. Free airport transportation. Business center. Concierge. Luxury level.

★ ★ ★ **THE WESTIN SOUTH COAST PLAZA.** *686 Anton Blvd (92626). Phone 714/540-2500; fax 714/662-6696. www.westin.com.* Connected to the South Plaza Mall and close to the Anaheim Convention Center, Disneyland, and John Wayne Airport, this hotel is great for the business traveler or the proper shopper. Visit the close-by performing arts center and restaurants. 400 rooms, 16 story. D $195-$300; each additional $20; under 18 free; weekend package plans. Pets accepted, some restrictions. Check-out 1 pm, check-in 3 pm. TV; cable (premium). In-room modem link. Restaurant 6:30 am-10 pm. Bar noon-midnight; entertainment weekends. Room service 24 hours. Health club privileges. In-house fitness room. Heated pool; poolside service. Lighted tennis. Parking, valet parking. Free airport transportation. Business center. South Coast Plaza retail center and village adjacent.

★ **WYNDHAM ORANGE COUNTY HOTEL.** *3350 Ave of the Arts (92626). Phone 714/751-5100; fax 714/751-2704. www.wyndham.com.* 238 rooms, 35 suites, 6 story. Pets accepted; fee. Check-out noon, check-in 3 pm. TV. Restaurant, bar. Room service. Babysitting services available. In-house fitness room. Outdoor pool; whirlpool. Free airport transportation. Fireplaces. **$**

Crescent City

Motel/Motor Lodge

★ **SUPER 8.** *685 US 101 S (95616). Phone 707/464-4111; fax 707/465-8916. www.super8.com.* 49 rooms, 2 story. No A/C. Mid-June-Labor Day: S $65; D $69-$74; each additional $5; under 13 free; lower rates rest of year. Pets accepted, some restrictions; fee. Check-out 11 am. TV; cable (premium). Laundry services.

Davis

Motel/Motor Lodge

★ **BEST WESTERN UNIVERSITY LODGE.** *123 B St (95616). Phone 530/756-7890; fax 530/756-0245. www.bestwestern.com.* 53 rooms, 2 story. S $85; D $89. Pets accepted; fee. Check-out noon. TV; cable (premium). Restaurant opposite. In-house fitness room. University of California 1 block.

Death Valley National Park

Motel/Motor Lodge

★ **STOVEPIPE WELLS VILLAGE.** *Hwy 190 (92328). Phone 760/786-2387; fax 760/786-2389. www.stovepipewells.com.* 83 rooms. No room phones. S, D $70-$92; each additional $10; under 13 free. Pets accepted; fee. Check-out 11 am. Restaurant, bar. Pool. Landing strip. Panoramic view of mountains, desert, dunes.

⬛🐾🏊🏖

Dunsmuir

Motel/Motor Lodge

★ **CEDAR LODGE MOTEL.** *4201 Dunsmuir Ave (96025). Phone 530/235-4331; fax 530/235-4000. www.cedarlodgedunsmuir.com.* 16 rooms. May-Oct: S $45; D $50; each additional $4; kitchen units $10 additional; family units from $65; lower rates rest of year. Pets accepted, some restrictions; fee. Check-out 10 am. TV. Downhill, cross-country ski 16 miles. Large exotic bird aviary. Near Sacramento River.

🐾⛷✈🏖

Resort

★★ **RAILROAD PARK RESORT.** *100 Railroad Park Rd (96025). Phone 530/235-4440; toll-free 800/974-7245; fax 530/235-4470. www.rrpark.com.* 28 rooms, 4 cabins. June-Sept: S, D $80-$100; each additional $8; cabins $80-$10. Pets accepted; fee. Check-out 11 am. Restaurant, bar. Game room. Pool; whirlpool. Lawn games. RV hookups. Rooms in authentic railroad cars; 1/4 mile from Sacramento River.

⬛🐾⛷🏊🏖

El Cajon

Motel/Motor Lodge

★ **TRAVELODGE.** *1220 W Main St (92020). Phone 619/442-2576; toll-free 800/525-9055; fax 619/579-7562. www.travelodge.com.* 39 rooms, 2 story. Pets accepted, some restrictions; fee. Check-out 11 am, check-in 1 pm. TV. Pool. **$**

⬛🐾🏖 SC

El Centro

Motels/Motor Lodges

★ **CALIPATRIA INN AND SUITES.** *700 N Sorensen Ave (92233). Phone 760/348-7348; toll-free 800/830-1113; fax 760/348-2667.* 40 rooms, 7 suites. S, D $50-$80; each additional $10; suites $90-$135; under 12 free; higher rates special events. Pets accepted. Complimentary continental breakfast. Check-out noon. TV; cable (premium), VCR available. In-room modem link. Restaurant nearby. Pool; whirlpool.

⬛🐾🏊✈🏖

★★ **RAMADA INN.** *1455 Ocotillo Dr (92243). Phone 760/352-5152; toll-free 800/805-4000; fax 760/337-1567. www.ramada.com.* 147 rooms, 2 story. Pets accepted, some restrictions; fee. Check-out noon, check-in 3 pm. TV; cable (premium), VCR available. Restaurant open 24 hours, bar. Room service 24 hours. In-house fitness room. Outdoor pool; children's pool; whirlpool. Free airport transportation. **$**

⬛🐾🏊🚶✈🏖

★★ **VACATION INN.** *2015 Cottonwood Cir (92243). Phone 760/352-9523; toll-free 866/708-6000; fax 760/353-7620.* 170 rooms, 2 story. Pets accepted; fee. Complimentary continental breakfast. Check-out noon, check-in 3 pm. TV; cable (premium). In-room modem link. Restaurant. Bar. In-house fitness room. Outdoor pool; whirlpool; poolside service. **$**

⬛🐾🏊🚶🏖

Resort

★★★ **BARBARA WORTH GOLF RESORT AND CONVENTION CENTER.** *2050 Country Club Dr (92250). Phone 760/356-2806; toll-free 800/356-3802; fax 760/356-4653. www.bwresort.com.* 104 rooms, 2 story. S, D $80-$84; each additional $5; kitchen suites $135-$141; under 13 free; weekly, monthly rates; golf plans. Pets accepted. Check-out noon. TV; cable (premium). In-room modem link. Restaurant, bar. Room service. In-house fitness room. Pool; children's pool; whirlpool. Greens fee $33. Business center.

⬛🐾⛳🏊🚶✈🏌

Escondido

Hotels

★★ **CASTLE CREEK INN & SPA.** *29850 Circle R Way (92026). Phone 760/751-8800; toll-free 800/253-5341;*

fax 760/751-8787. www.castlecreekinn.com. 30 rooms, 2 story. D $139-$179; under 12 free. Pets accepted; fee. Check-out 11 am, check-in 3 pm. TV; cable. Restaurant 7 am-7 pm. In-house fitness room; sauna. Pool. Tennis.

★ **COMFORT INN.** 1290 W Valley Pkwy (92029). Phone 760/489-1010; toll-free 800/541-6012; fax 760/489-7847. www.comfortinn.com. 93 rooms, 3 story. Pets accepted, some restrictions; fee. Complimentary continental breakfast. Check-out noon, check-in 3 pm. TV. In-room modem link. In-house fitness room. Outdoor pool; whirlpool. $

Resort

★★★ **QUAILS INN HOTEL.** 1025 La Bonita Dr (92069). Phone 760/744-0120; toll-free 800/447-6556; fax 760/744-0748. www.quailsinn.com. The price is right for this clean, quiet getaway with lake- or pool-view rooms. 140 rooms, 2 story. S, D $99; each additional $10; suites, kitchen cottages $199-$300; under 12 free; package plans. Pets accepted, some restrictions; fee. Check-out noon. TV; cable (premium), VCR available. Room service. In-house fitness room. Pool; whirlpool. Boat rental. Extensive grounds. On Lake San Marcos.

Eureka

Motel/Motor Lodge

★★ **RED LION.** 1929 Fourth St (95501). Phone 707/445-0844; fax 707/445-2752. www.redlion.com. This hotel is just 15 minutes from the Eureka/Arcata Municipal Airport. Golf, whitewater rafting, and charter fishing are nearby. 176 rooms, 3-4 story. S $69-$99; D $75-$109; suites $129-$169; under 18 free; weekend rates. Pets accepted; fee. Check-out noon. TV; cable (premium), VCR available. In-room modem link. Restaurant, bar; entertainment weekends. Room service. Pool; whirlpool. Free airport transportation.

Hotel

★★ **EUREKA INN.** 518 7th St (95501). Phone 707/442-6441; fax 707/442-0637. www.eurekainn.com. Since opening in 1922, this inn has hosted such guests as Robert Kennedy, Sir Winston Churchill, and Mickey Mantle. 104 rooms, 4 story. No A/C. S, D $99-$114; suites $129-$159, each additional $10; under 16 free. Pets accepted, some restrictions. Check-out noon. TV. Restaurant 6:30 am-2 pm, 5:30-10 pm. Bar; entertainment Thurs-Sat. Saunas.

Pool; whirlpool. Free airport transportation. Fireplace in lobby. Historic Tudor-style building.

B&B/Small Inn

★★ **OLD TOWN BED AND BREAKFAST INN.** 1521 3rd St (95501). Phone 707/443-5235; toll-free 888/508-5235; fax 707/442-4390. www.oldtownbandb.com. 4 rooms, 2 story. No A/C. Pets accepted, some restrictions; fee. Complimentary full breakfast. Check-out 11 am, check-in 4-6 pm. Some fireplaces. Built in 1871, the oldest lodging in town; Greek Revival Victorian home with antique furnishings. Bay 1 1/2 blocks. Totally non-smoking. $$

Fort Bragg

B&B/Small Inn

★★ **CLEONE GARDENS INN.** 24600 N Hwy 1 (95437). Phone 707/964-2788; toll-free 800/400-2189; fax 707/964-2523. www.cleonegardensinn.com. 10 rooms, 1-2 story. No A/C. Pets accepted; fee. Check-out 11 am, check-in 1:30 pm. TV; cable. Some refrigerators, fireplaces. Some room phones. Walking trails. $

Fort Ross State Historic Park

B&B/Small Inn

★★★ **TIMBER COVE INN.** 21780 North Coast Hwy 1, Jenner (95450). Phone 707/847-3231; fax 707/847-3704. www.timbercoveinn.com. 50 rooms, 2 story. Pets accepted, some restrictions; fee. Check-out 11 am, check-in 3 pm. Many fireplaces. Restaurant, bar. Room service. $$

Fremont

Motel/Motor Lodge

★★ **BEST WESTERN GARDEN COURT INN.** 5400 Mowry Ave (94538). Phone 510/792-4300; toll-free 800/541-4909; fax 510/792-2643. www.bestwestern.com. 122 rooms, 2-3 story. S, D $109-$179; under 14 free; weekend rates. Pets accepted; fee. Complimentary continental breakfast. Check-out noon. TV; cable (premium). Health club privileges; sauna. Pool; whirlpool.

D 🐾 🏊 🎿 SC

Hotel

★ ★ ★ **MARRIOTT.** *46100 Landing Pkwy (94538). Phone 510/413-3700. www.marriott.com.* 357 rooms, 10 story. S, D $169-$330; under 17 free. Pets accepted, some restrictions; fee. Check-out 11 am. TV; cable (premium). Restaurant, bar. In-house fitness room. Indoor pool. Valet parking. Business center.

🐾 🏊 🎿 🚶

All Suite

★ ★ ★ **W SILICON VALLEY, NEWARK.** *8200 Gateway Blvd (94560). Phone 510/494-8800. www.whotels.com.* 174 suites, 10 story. S, D $200-$575; each additional $25. Pets accepted; fee. Check-out noon. TV; cable (premium), VCR available. Restaurant 6:30 am-11 pm. Bar. In-house fitness room; spa. Pool. Valet parking.

🐾 🏊 🚶

Extended Stay

★ ★ **RESIDENCE INN BY MARRIOTT.** *5400 Farwell Pl (94536). Phone 510/794-5900; toll-free 800/331-3131; fax 510/793-6587. www.marriott.com.* 80 kitchen units, 2 story. Suites $99-$199; weekly, monthly rates. Pets accepted; fee. Complimentary continental breakfast. Check-out noon. TV; cable (premium). Laundry services. Health club privileges. Pool; whirlpool.

D 🐾 🏊 🎿 SC

Fresno

Hotel

★ ★ ★ **RADISSON HOTEL & CONFERENCE CENTER FRESNO.** *2233 Ventura St (93721). Phone 559/268-1000; fax 559/441-2954.* This hotel is situated adjacent to the Fresno Convention Center. Yosemite National Park and Sequoia-Kings Canyon Park are both within driving distance. 357 rooms, 8 story. D $119-$149; each additional $10; under 18 free. Pets accepted, some restrictions; fee. Check-out noon, check-in 3:30 pm. TV. Restaurant, bar. In-house fitness room; sauna. Indoor, outdoor pool; whirlpool; poolside service. Free airport transportation.

D 🐾 🏊 🚶 🎿

Fullerton

Hotel

★ ★ ★ **MARRIOTT FULLERTON ANAHEIM.** *2701 Nutwood Ave (92831). Phone 714/738-7800; fax 714/738-0288. www.marriott.com.* 224 rooms, 6 story. S, D $114-$179; suites $350. Pets accepted, some restrictions; fee. Check-out noon. TV; cable (premium). Restaurant, bar. Room service. In-house fitness room; sauna. Pool; whirlpool; poolside service. Business center.

D 🐾 🏊 🚶 🎿 🚶

Garberville

Motel/Motor Lodge

★ **SHERWOOD FOREST MOTEL.** *814 Redwood Dr (95542). Phone 707/923-2721; fax 707/923-3677. www.sherwoodforestmotel.com.* 32 rooms. May-Oct: S $55-$60; D $64-$78; each additional $5; suites, kitchen units $84-$102; lower rates rest of year. Pets accepted, some restrictions. Check-out 11 am. TV; cable (premium). Laundry services. Restaurant adjacent. Pool; whirlpool. Free airport transportation.

D 🐾 🏊 🎿

Grass Valley

Motel/Motor Lodge

★ **HOLIDAY LODGE.** *1221 E Main St (95945). Phone 530/273-4406; toll-free 800/742-7125; fax 530/477-2878. www.holidaylodge.biz.* 36 rooms, 1-2 story. Mid-Apr-mid-Oct: S, D $60-$85; each additional $10; gold panning, holiday rates; lower rates rest of year. Pets accepted; fee. Check-out 11 am. TV. Pool. Continental breakfast.

🐾 🏊 🎿 SC

Guerneville

B&B/Small Inn

★ ★ **RIDENHOUR RANCH HOUSE INN.** *12850 River Rd (95446). Phone 707/887-1033; toll-free 888/877-4466; fax 707/869-2967. www.ridenhourinn.com.* 8 rooms, 3 story, 1 cabins. Pets accepted, some restrictions; fee. Complimentary breakfast. Check-out 11 am, check-in 3 pm. Whirlpool. Totally nonsmoking. **$**

🐾 🎿

Half Moon Bay

Motel/Motor Lodge

★ **HOLIDAY INN EXPRESS.** *230 S Cabrillo Hwy (94019). Phone 650/726-3400; fax 650/726-1256. www.hiexpress.com/halfmoonbay.* 52 rooms, 2 story. July-Aug: S, D $119-$139; each additional $10; under 18 free; higher rates holidays, special events; lower rates rest of year. Pets accepted, some restrictions; fee. Complimentary continental breakfast. Check-out noon. TV. In-room modem link.

B&B/Small Inn

★★ **ZABALLA HOUSE.** *324 Main St (94019). Phone 650/726-9123; fax 650/726-3921. www.zaballahouse.com.* 17 rooms, 2 story. S, D $115-$205; each additional $10. Pets accepted, some restrictions; fee. Complimentary breakfast buffet; afternoon refreshments. Check-out 11 am, check-in 3-7 pm. Some TV; cable in some rooms. Oldest building in town still standing (1859); some antiques. Totally nonsmoking.

Hanford

B&B/Small Inns

★★★ **INN AT HARRIS RANCH.** *24505 W Dorris (93210). Phone 559/935-0717; toll-free 800/942-2333; fax 559/935-5061. www.harrisranch.com.* Stay in rooms with private patios amidst fresh flowers and archways of columns on this hacienda. Fly in on the hotel's private airstrip. 153 rooms, 3 story. Pets accepted, some restrictions; fee. Check-out noon, check-in 3 pm. TV; cable (premium). Laundry services. Restaurant, bar. In-house fitness room. Outdoor pool; whirlpool. Private 2,800-foot paved and lighted airstrip on site. $

★★ **IRWIN STREET INN.** *522 N Irwin St (93230). Phone 559/583-8000; toll-free 866/583-7378; fax 559/583-8793. www.irwinstreetinn.com.* 2 story, 3 suites. S, D $69-$89; suites $125-$150; under 12 free. Pets accepted; fee. Check-out noon, check-in 3 pm. Continental breakfast. TV; cable (premium), VCR available. Restaurant 6:30 am-9 pm; Sun to 2 pm. Wading pool. Historic buildings (late 1800s), restored; many antiques. Totally nonsmoking.

Healdsburg

Motel/Motor Lodge

★ **BEST WESTERN DRY CREEK INN.** *198 Dry Creek Rd (95448). Phone 707/433-0300; toll-free 800/222-5784; fax 707/433-1129. drycreekinn.com.* 103 rooms, 3 story. Pets accepted; fee. Complimentary continental breakfast. Check-out noon, check-in 3 pm. TV; cable (premium). In-room modem link. Laundry services. In-house fitness room. Outdoor pool; whirlpool. **$$**

Hotel

★★★ **HOTEL HEALDSBURG.** *25 Matheson St (95448). Phone 707/431-2800; toll-free 800/889-7188; fax 707/431-0414. www.hotelhealdsburg.com.* 55 rooms, 3 story. Pets accepted, some restrictions; fee. Complimentary continental breakfast. Check-out 1 pm, check-in 3 pm. TV; cable (premium). In-room modem link. Laundry services. Restaurant, bar. Room service. Babysitting services available. In-house fitness room; spa. Outdoor pool; whirlpool; poolside service. Valet parking. Concierge. **$$$$**

Hemet

Motel/Motor Lodge

★ **BEST WESTERN INN OF HEMET.** *2625 W Florida Ave (92545). Phone 909/925-6605; toll-free 800/605-0001; fax 909/925-7095. www.bestwestern.com.* 70 rooms, 29 kitchen units, 2 story. S $64; D $70-$88; each additional $6; kitchen units $70-$104; weekly, monthly rates; higher rates: Ramona Pageant, special events. Pets accepted, some restrictions; fee. Complimentary breakfast. Check-out 11 am. TV; cable (premium). Restaurant adjacent open 24 hours. Health club privileges. Pool; whirlpool. Lawn games.

Hollywood

Motel/Motor Lodge

★★ **BEST WESTERN HOLLYWOOD HILLS HOTEL.** *6141 Franklin Ave (90028). Phone 323/464-5181; toll-free 800/287-1700; fax 323/962-0536. www.bestwestern.com.* 86 rooms, 3-4 story. S $79-$109; D $89-$119; each additional $10; under 12 free; weekly rates;

higher rates Rose Bowl. Pets accepted, some restrictions; fee. Check-out noon. TV; cable (premium). Laundry services. Restaurant. Pool.

D ◨ 🐾 🏊 🏃 ⊠

Hotels

★★★ **ARGYLE HOTEL.** *8358 Sunset Blvd (90069). Phone 323/654-7100; toll-free 800/225-2637; fax 323/654-9287. www.argylehotel.com.* Stay where the stars have stayed! With 15 stories of elegance, this hotel has it all. The Art Deco architecture is stunning. 64 rooms, 44 suites, 15 story. Pets accepted; fee. Check-out noon, check-in 3 pm. TV; cable (premium), VCR available. In-room modem link. Restaurant, bar. Room service. In-house fitness room; massage, sauna. Outdoor pool; whirlpool; poolside service. Valet parking. Concierge. **$$**

D ◨ 🐾 🏊 🏃 ⊠

★★★ **CHATEAU MARMONT.** *8221 Sunset Blvd (90046). Phone 323/656-1010; toll-free 800/242-8328; fax 323/655-5311. www.designhotels.com.* Sleep in a slice of Hollywood history at the classic Chateau Marmont, a hipster from the Greta Garbo era. Just above Sunset Boulevard, Chateau Marmont cossets the glitterati, particularly those who take one of its elite bungalows, within the heart of happening West Hollywood. It's favored by fashion photo shoots, starlet-toting publicists and deal-making producers, so the poolside people watching may be worth the room price alone. The main castle-like building dates to 1929, but renovation efforts have kept amenities and décor contemporary. 63 rooms, 7 story, 54 kitchen units. Pets accepted; fee. Check-out noon, check-in 2 pm. TV; cable (premium), VCR. In-room modem link. Room service 24 hours. Restaurant, bar. In-house fitness room. Outdoor pool; poolside service. Valet parking. Neo-Gothic chateau-style building; old Hollywood landmark. **$$$$**

🐾 🏊 🏃 ⊠

★★★ **LE MONTROSE SUITE HOTEL.** *900 Hammond St (90069). Phone 310/855-1115; toll-free 800/776-0666; fax 310/657-9192. www.lemontrose.com.* In West Hollywood, the Art Nouveau-styled Le Montrose furnishes its spacious suites with sunken living rooms, fireplaces and refrigerators, many with kitchenettes, and private balconies suitable to families or long-term stays. Venture up to the roof for a dip in the pool and Jacuzzi, or a set on the tennis court. The noteworthy restaurant, The Library, is reserved exclusively for guests and their friends. A well-equipped health club helps encourage residential stays. 132 suites, 5 story. Suites $185-$575; under 18 free. Pets accepted; fee. Check-out noon. TV; cable (premium), VCR available. In-room modem link. Fireplaces. Restaurant. Room service

24 hours. In-house fitness room; massage, sauna. Pool; whirlpool; poolside service. Lighted tennis. Concierge.

D ◨ 🐾 🏊 🏃 ⊠

Idyllwild

B&B/Small Inn

★★ **FIRESIDE INN.** *54540 N Circle Dr (92549). Phone 909/659-2966; toll-free 877/797-3473; fax 909/659-4286. thefireside-inn.com.* 7 cabins, 2 A/C rooms. No room phones. Pets accepted, some restrictions. Check-out 11 am, check-in 2 pm. TV; cable (premium), VCR available. In wooded area near village center. **$**

🐾 🛏 🏊 🏃 ⊠

Indio

Motels/Motor Lodges

★ **BEST WESTERN DATE TREE HOTEL.** *81909 Indio Blvd (92201). Phone 760/347-3421; toll-free 800/292-5599; fax 760/347-3421. www.bestwesterncalifornia.com.* 119 rooms, 2 story. Jan-Apr: S, D $59.99-$149.99; each additional $6; suites, kitchen units $79-$179.99; under 18 free; weekly rates; higher rates special events; lower rates rest of year. Pets accepted; fee. Complimentary continental breakfast. Check-out noon. TV; cable (premium). In-room modem link. In-house fitness room. Game room. Pool; whirlpool. Lawn games.

D 🐾 🛏 🏊 ⊠

★ **QUALITY INN.** *43505 Monroe St (92201). Phone 760/347-4044; fax 760/347-1287. www.qualityinnindio.com.* 62 rooms, 2 story. Dec-May: S $69-$99; D $69-$129; under 18 free; higher rates: late Dec, Bob Hope Classic, Date Festival, Fri, Sat Dec-May; lower rates rest of year. Pets accepted. Complimentary breakfast. Check-out 11 am. TV; cable (premium). Restaurant nearby. Pool; whirlpool.

D 🐾 🏊 🏃 ⊠

Inverness

B&B/Small Inns

★★★ **MANKA'S INVERNESS LODGE.** *30 Callendar Way (94937). Phone 415/669-1034; toll-free 800/585-6343; fax 415/669-1598. www.mankas.com.* In a small coastal village surrounded by national park land, is this old-time lodge and restaurant. 14 rooms, 4 with shower only, 2 story, 4 cabins. No A/C. D $185-$515. Pets accepted; fee. Check-out noon, check-in 4-6 pm. Some

refrigerators, balconies, fireplaces. 1917 hunting lodge and cabins. Restaurant. Hiking. Totally nonsmoking.

★ ★ **OLEMA INN.** *10000 Sir Francis Drake Blvd (94950). Phone 415/663-9559; fax 415/663-8783. www.theolemainn.com.* 6 rooms, 2 with shower only. 2 story. No A/C, room phones. Pets accepted. Complimentary continental breakfast. Check-out 11 am, check-in 3 pm. Restaurant, bar; entertainment Sun, Fri. Country inn built in 1876. Totally nonsmoking. **$**

Jackson

Motel/Motor Lodge

★ **JACKSON GOLD LODGE.** *850 N Hwy 49 and 88 (95642). Phone 209/223-0486; toll-free 888/777-0380; fax 209/223-2905.* 36 rooms, 2 story. S, D $48-$85; each additional $6; kitchen units $85. Pets accepted, some restrictions; fee. Complimentary continental breakfast. Check-out 11 am. TV. Pool.

Joshua Tree National Park

Motels/Motor Lodges

★ **BEST WESTERN GARDEN INN & SUITES.** *71487 Twentynine Palms Hwy (92277). Phone 760/367-9141; fax 760/367-2584. www.bestwestern.com.* 84 rooms, 2 story. S, D $79-$85; each additional $10; kitchen suites $98-$119; under 12 free. Pets accepted; fee. Complimentary continental breakfast. Check-out 11 am. TV. In-room modem link. In-house fitness room. Pool; whirlpool.

★ **CIRCLE C LODGE.** *6340 El Rey Ave (92277). Phone 760/367-7615; fax 760/361-0247. www.circleclodge.com.* 12 kitchen units. S $74; D $90; each additional $10; under 15 free. Pets accepted; fee. Check-out 11 am. TV; cable (premium), VCR. Pool; whirlpool.

Hotels

★ ★ **OASIS OF EDEN INN & SUITES.** *56377 29 Palms Hwy (92284). Phone 760/365-6321; toll-free 800/606-6686; fax 760/365-9592. www.oasisofeden.com.* 39 rooms, 14 theme rooms, 6 kitchen units. 1-2 story.

Jan-May: S, D $59-$89; each additional $5; kitchen units $69-$99; theme rooms $99-$299; family, weekly, monthly rates; lower rates rest of year. Pets accepted, some restrictions; fee. Complimentary continental breakfast. Check-out 11 am. TV; cable (premium), VCR available (movies). Pool; whirlpool.

Laguna Beach

Motel/Motor Lodge

★ **LAGUNA BRISAS SPA HOTEL.** *1600 S Coast Hwy (92651). Phone 949/497-7272; toll-free 800/532-7204; fax 949/497-8306. www.lagunabrisas.com.* 66 rooms, 4 story. D $169-$189; each additional $10; under 16 free; 2-day minimum: weekends, July, Aug, holidays. Pets accepted, some restrictions; fee. Complimentary continental breakfast. Check-out noon, check-in 4 pm. TV; cable (premium), VCR available. Massage. Ocean view sun deck. Heated pool; whirlpool.

Resorts

★ ★ ★ **MARRIOTT LAGUNA CLIFFS RESORT.** *25135 Park Lantern (92629). Phone 949/661-5000; toll-free 800/533-9748; fax 949/487-3277. www.marriott.com.* This hotel has great views of the Pacific Ocean. 346 rooms, 3 and 4 story. June-Sept: S, D $318-$375; suites $475-$1,500; under 16 free; seasonal rates available. Pets accepted, some restrictions; fee. Check-out 11 am, check-in 4 pm. TV; cable (premium), VCR available. In-room modem link. Restaurant, bar. Room service. Supervised children's activities (summer); ages 2-12 years. Health club privileges. In-house fitness room; massage, sauna. Pool; whirlpool; poolside service. Lighted tennis. Bicycle rentals. Valet parking. Business center. Concierge. Opposite beach. Park. Located on the cliffs above the bay with 42 acres of lawn and parkland.

★ ★ ★ ★ **ST. REGIS MONARCH BEACH RESORT AND SPA.** *One Monarch Beach Resort (92629). Phone 949/234-3200. www.stregis.com.* Tucked away on 200 acres facing the Pacific Ocean, The St. Regis Monarch Beach Resort and Spa is a place for exceptional holidays. Well-heeled travelers swoon over the luscious, secluded setting and the playful yet sophisticated design. The guest rooms are ravishing, from the swirled rugs and sensual furnishings to the glimmering silk fabrics and decorative accents. Private balconies flaunt ocean or golf course views, and all rooms are fitted with the finest amenities. This full-service resort entices guests to partake in a round of golf, a game of tennis, or a treatment at the

Gaucin spa, while three heated pools complete the beautifully landscaped pool deck. Nature trails encourage others to take the less-traveled path to private beaches. The joie de vivre of this resort extends to the restaurants, where chic settings focus attention on the gorgeous views. 400 rooms, 74 suites, 7 story. S, D $355-$845; suites $950-$5,500; each additional $25; under 17 free. Pets accepted, some restrictions; fee. Check-out noon. TV; cable (premium), VCR available. Restaurant. Bar. In-house fitness room. Spa. Golf. Valet parking. Business center. Tuscan-style architecture.

B&B/Small Inn

★ ★ **CASA LAGUNA INN.** *2510 S Pacific Coast Hwy (92651). Phone 949/494-2996; toll-free 800/233-0449; fax 949/494-5009. www.casalaguna.com.* 20 rooms. July-Aug: S, D $150-$250; suites $200-$395; lower rates rest of year; weekly rates. Pets accepted, some restrictions; fee. Complimentary continental breakfast. Check-out 11 am, check-in 2 pm. TV; DVD. Spanish architecture, individually decorated rooms. Totally nonsmoking.

La Jolla

Motel/Motor Lodge

★ **ANDREA VILLA INN.** *2402 Torrey Pines Rd (92037). Phone 858/459-3311; toll-free 800/411-2141; fax 858/459-1320. www.andreavilla.com.* 55 rooms, 20 kitchen units, 2 story. June-mid-Sept: S, D $119-$135, kitchen units $139-$179; monthly rates; lower rates rest of year. Pets accepted, some restrictions; fee. Complimentary continental breakfast. Check-out noon. TV; cable (premium). Health club privileges. Whirlpool.

Hotels

★ ★ ★ **LA VALENCIA.** *1132 Prospect St (92037). Phone 858/454-0771; toll-free 800/451-0772; fax 858/456-3921. www.lavalencia.com.* Enjoy the wonderful, scenic ocean view from a well-furnished, cozy room. Marvel at the Spanish mosaics and Mediterranean colonnades found on the property or take the short trip to one of the many boutiques and galleries nearby. 131 rooms, 7 kitchen units, 11 story. S, D $275-$775; suites $750-$3,500; weekends (2-day minimum), summer, holidays (3-day minimum). Pets accepted, some restrictions; fee. Check-out noon. TV; cable (premium), VCR. In-room modem link. Some fireplaces. Restaurant 6:30 am-11 pm. Bar; entertainment. Room service 24 hours. In-house

fitness room; sauna. Whirlpool; poolside service. Valet parking. Concierge. Beach opposite.

★ ★ ★ **MARRIOTT SAN DIEGO LA JOLLA.** *4240 La Jolla Village Dr (92037). Phone 858/587-1414; fax 858/546-8518. www.marriott.com.* 360 rooms, suites, 15 story. S, D $238-$358; suites $299-$650; under 18 free; weekend rates. Pets accepted; fee. Check-out noon. TV; cable (premium). In-room modem link. Restaurant, bar. Room service. In-house fitness room; massage, sauna. Game room. Indoor pool; whirlpool; poolside service. Golf privileges. Valet parking. Concierge. Luxury level.

Extended Stay

★ ★ **RESIDENCE INN BY MARRIOTT.** *8901 Gilman Dr (92037). Phone 858/587-1770; toll-free 800/876-1778; fax 858/552-0387. www.residenceinnlajolla.com.* 288 suites, 2 story. Suites $149-$289; weekly rates. Pets accepted; fee. Complimentary continental breakfast. Check-out noon, check-in 4 pm. TV; cable (premium). In-room modem link. Laundry services. Two heated pools; five whirlpools. Airport transportation.

Lake Arrowhead

Motel/Motor Lodge

★ **LAKE ARROWHEAD TREE TOP LODGE.** *27992 Rainbow Dr (92352). Phone 909/337-2311; toll-free 800/358-8733; fax 909/337-1403. www.arrowheadtreetop.com.* 20 rooms, 1-2 story. S, D $65-$241. Pets accepted, some restrictions; fee. Check-out 11 am. TV; VCR available. Pool. Private nature trail.

Lodi

B&B/Small Inn

★ ★ ★ **WINE AND ROSES HOTEL.** *2505 W Turner Rd (95242). Phone 209/334-6988; fax 209/371-6049. www.winerose.com.* 36 rooms, 2 story. Pets accepted; fee. Check-out 11 am, check-in 3 pm. TV; VCR available. Restaurant, bar. Room service. In-house fitness room; spa. Lawn games. Historic inn built in 1902; individually decorated rooms; fireplace in sitting room. Totally nonsmoking. **$$**

Lompoc

Motel/Motor Lodge

★ ★ **QUALITY INN.** *1621 N H St (90802). Phone 805/735-8555; toll-free 800/638-7949; fax 805/735-8566. www.qualityinn.com.* 218 rooms, 92 kitchen units, 4 story. S, D $74-$84; kitchen units $85-$129; each additional $10; under 18 free. Pets accepted, some restrictions; fee. Check-out noon. TV; cable (premium). Full breakfast buffet. Health club privileges. Massage. Pool; whirlpool.

D ⟨icons⟩ SC

Lone Pine

Motel/Motor Lodge

★ ★ ★ **DOW VILLA MOTEL.** *310 S Main St (93545). Phone 760/876-5521; toll-free 800/824-9317; fax 760/876-5643. www.dowvillamotel.com.* 42 rooms, 2 story. S, D $60-$82; suites $115-$125; golf packages. Pets accepted; fee. Check-out noon. TV; cable (premium), VCR available. Restaurant open 24 hours. Pool; whirlpool. Motel for motion picture casts since the early 1920s.

D ⟨icons⟩ SC

Long Beach

Motel/Motor Lodge

★ ★ **GUESTHOUSE INTL.** *5325 E Pacific Coast Hwy (90804). Phone 562/597-1341; toll-free 800/990-9991; fax 562/597-5171. www.guesthouselb.net.* 143 rooms, 2 story. S, D $109; suites $109-$149; each additional $10; under 18 free; weekly rates; higher rates Grand Prix. Pets accepted; fee. Check-out noon. TV; cable (premium), VCR available. In-room modem link. Restaurant, bar. Pool. Health club privileges. Airport transportation.

D ⟨icons⟩

Hotel

★ ★ **HILTON LONG BEACH.** *701 W Ocean Blvd (90831). Phone 562/983-3400; toll-free 800/345-6565; fax 562/983-1200. www.longbeach.hilton.com.* Located in downtown Long Beach, this hotel is within four blocks of the beach, convention center, and Catalina Island landing. 393 rooms, 15 story. Pets accepted, some restrictions; fee. Check-out noon, check-in 3 pm. TV; cable (premium). In-room modem link. Restaurant, bar. In-house fitness room; steam room. Outdoor pool; whirlpool. Valet parking. Business center. Concierge. **$$**

D ⟨icons⟩

Los Angeles

Hotels

★ ★ ★ **THE CENTURY PLAZA HOTEL AND SPA.** *2025 Ave of the Stars (90067). Phone 310/277-2000; toll-free 800/228-3000; fax 310/551-3355. www.centuryplazala.com.* Given that The Century Plaza Hotel and Spa is adjacent to Beverly Hills, it's no wonder that it resonates star power. This glitzy contemporary hotel is situated on 7 acres dotted with reflecting pools and lush tropical plants. All guest rooms have balconies with views of the Los Angeles cityscape and the tree-lined boulevards of Beverly Hills. The accommodations are styled handsomely with Asian decorative objects and warm tones, while leather headboards and striking light fixtures enhance the contemporary feel. Asian influences abound at Spa Mystique, from the feng shui design principles used in the 27 treatment rooms and four outdoor cabanas to the popular treatments on the menu. Surrounded by manicured grounds, the heated outdoor pool provides yet another urban oasis. All tastes are suited at The Century Plaza, whether at the signature Breeze Restaurant or at the casual and light alternatives of the Lobby Bar and Café Mystique. 728 rooms, 19 story. Pets accepted; fee. Check-out noon, check-in 4 pm. TV; cable (premium), VCR available. In-room modem link. Laundry services. Restaurant, bar; entertainment. Room service 24 hours. In-house fitness room; spa, massage. Outdoor pool; whirlpool; poolside service (summer). Valet parking. Business center. Concierge. **$$$**

D ⟨icons⟩ SC

★ ★ ★ **FOUR SEASONS HOTEL LOS ANGELES.** *300 S Doheny Dr (90048). Phone 310/273-2222; toll-free 800/332-3442; fax 310/859-3824. www.fourseasons.com.* The Four Seasons Hotel Los Angeles at Beverly Hills makes every guest feel like a star. A bastion of chic, the hotel is only 1 mile from the exclusive boutiques of Rodeo Drive. Refreshing and elegant, the guest rooms are luxuriously appointed with European élan and Californian comfort. The hotel is honed to perfection, down to the smallest details. Enlivened by rich colors and abundant floral displays, the Florentine-style Gardens Restaurant is a showpiece for California-Pacific cuisine, and the Café is a sun-filled Mediterranean-style bistro. Bathed by the glorious southern California sun, the heated outdoor pool is a popular gathering spot, and the Poolside Café satisfies hungry sun worshippers with spa cuisine and traditional favorites. The spa is a standout, from tequila massages to European body kurs. The marvelous California sunset massage, conducted in a private candlelit cabana, is a sensational massage that's not to be missed. 285 rooms, 16 story. Pets accepted, some restrictions. Check-out noon, check-in 3 pm. TV; cable (premium), VCR available. In-room modem link. Restaurant, bar. Babysitting services available. In-house fitness room; spa, massage. Outdoor pool; whirlpool. Underground parking. Business center. Concierge. **$$$$**

⊡ 🐾 🏊 🖼 🏃

★★★★★ **HOTEL BEL-AIR.** *701 Stone Canyon Rd (90077). Phone 310/472-1211; toll-free 800/648-4097; fax 310/476-5890. www.hotelbelair.com.* Special memories are made at the Hotel Bel-Air. Close to the action of Los Angeles, this magical hotel transports visitors to a romantic, unhurried world. It enjoys a parklike setting on 12 acres of gardens dotted with intimate courtyards, trickling fountains, winding creeks, and intoxicating aromas. The centerpiece of the garden is the signature Swan Lake, where visitors marvel at the graceful movements of these elegant creatures. A favorite of guests seeking anonymity, the guest rooms are spread throughout the grounds, lending a special privacy to each accommodation. Reflecting a timeless décor, the rooms are luxurious. Amenities are plentiful, including Kiehl's products in the guest rooms and a well-equipped fitness center. The pool offers a wonderful way to spend the afternoon. Guests are romanced and charmed in the restaurants as well, whether dining in the distinguished Restaurant and the beautiful garden setting of the Terrace or enjoying the unique in-kitchen Table One. 92 rooms. Pets accepted, some restrictions; fee. Check-out noon, check-in 3 pm. TV; cable (premium), VCR (movies). In-room modem link. Some wood-burning fireplaces. Restaurant, bar; entertainment. Room service 24 hours. Babysitting services available. In-house fitness room; massage. Outdoor pool; poolside service. Valet parking. Airport transportation. Business center. Concierge. **$$$$**

⊡ 🐾 🏊 🧍 🖼 🏃

★★★ **LE MERIDIEN BEVERLY HILLS.** *465 S La Cienega Blvd (90048). Phone 310/247-0400; toll-free 800/645-5687; fax 310/247-0315. www.lemeridien beverlyhills.com.* Le Meridien expertly blends European panache with the lively spirit of its famous neighborhood. Centrally located on Restaurant Row in Beverly Hills, the hotel provides a convenient base for visitors soaking up the glamour of Rodeo Drive or conducting business in nearby Wilshire. The guest rooms show off the flair of French architect Pierre Yves Rochon. Spacious and stylish, the accommodations offer the latest and most luxurious amenities. Many rooms include terraces overlooking peaceful courtyard gardens. Business and fitness centers round out the experience at this cool contemporary hotel, and the heated outdoor pool provides a respite

from working, touring, or shopping. The hip design of the Café Noir Bar & Lounge makes it a happening spot, and the star-studded Cannes Film Festival is celebrated at Le Festival, where vintage photographs line the walls and Mediterranean dishes top the tables. 297 rooms, 6 story. S, D $310-$415; each additional $25; suites $600-$1,800; under 12 free. Pets accepted, some restrictions; fee. Check-out 1 pm. TV; cable (premium), VCR available. In-room modem link. Restaurant, bar; entertainment. Room service 24 hours. In-house fitness room. Massage. Pool. Valet parking. Business center. Concierge.

⊡ 🐾 🏊 🧍 🖼 🏃

★★★★ **ST. REGIS HOTEL & SPA LOS ANGELES.** *2055 Avenue of the Stars (90067). Phone 310/277-6111; fax 310/277-3711. www.stregis.com.* Los Angeles' west side is home to the sublime St. Regis Hotel and Spa. This sleek modern tower commands impressive views of the downtown skyline, Santa Monica coastline, and Hollywood Hills from its Century City location. Abundant floral displays and impressive marble columns set a stunning tone in the lobby, and French doors open out to private balconies in all guest accommodations. Regal and dignified, the guest rooms are the last word in luxury, from 300-thread-count bed linens to oversized marble baths. The rooftop pool affords fantastic viewing from the privacy of a private cabana. Dealmakers unwind at the spa, where a full range of treatments beautify and soothe. Reflecting the hotel's distinguished personality, Encore shows off the talents of its chef in a refined yet airy setting enhanced by parquet floors and floor-to-ceiling windows. 297 rooms, 30 story. Pets accepted; fee. Check-out noon, check-in 3 pm. TV; cable (premium). In-room modem link. Restaurant, bar; entertainment. Room service 24 hours. In-house fitness room; spa, sauna, steam room. Indoor pool; whirlpool. Business center. Concierge. **$$$**

🐾 🏊 🧍 🖼 🏃

Los Angeles International Airport Area

Motel/Motor Lodge

★★ **TRAVELODGE.** *5547 W Century Blvd (90045). Phone 310/649-4000; toll-free 800/421-3939; fax 310/649-0311. travelodgelax.com.* 147 rooms, 2 story. S, D $64-$79; each additional $8; under 18 free. Pets accepted, some restrictions; fee. Check-out noon. TV; cable (premium),

VCR. Restaurant, bar. Room service. In-house fitness room. Pool. Free airport transportation.

[D] [icons] [SC]

Hotels

★ ★ ★ **HILTON LOS ANGELES AIRPORT.** *5711 W Century Blvd. (90045). Phone 310/410-4000; fax 310/410-6250. www.hilton.com.* 1,244 rooms, 17 story. S $88-$200; each additional $20; suites $299-$399; family, weekend rates. Pets accepted; fee. Check-out noon. TV; cable (premium), VCR available. In-room modem link. Restaurant, bar. In-house fitness room; sauna. Pool; pool-side service. Valet parking. Free airport transportation. Business center. Luxury level.

[D] [icons]

★ ★ ★ **MARRIOTT LOS ANGELES AIRPORT.** *5855 W Century Blvd (90045). Phone 310/641-5700; toll-free 800/229-9290; fax 310/337-5358. www.marriotthotels.com.* 1,023 rooms, 18 story. D $149-$218; suites from $325; family, weekend rates. Pets accepted. Check-out noon, check-in 3 pm. TV; cable (premium), VCR available. In-room modem link. Laundry services. Restaurant, bar; entertainment. In-house fitness room. Heated pool; whirlpool; poolside service. Parking, valet parking. Free airport transportation. Business center. Concierge. Luxury level.

[D] [icons]

★ **QUALITY INN.** *5249 W Century Blvd (90045). Phone 310/645-2200.* 283 rooms, 10 story. D $79-$96; each additional $10; under 18 free; weekend rates. Pets accepted, some restrictions; fee. Check-out noon, check-in 3 pm. TV; cable (premium), VCR available. Restaurant, bar. In-house fitness room. Pool; poolside service. Free airport transportation. Business center.

[D] [icons] [SC] [icon]

★ ★ ★ **THE WESTIN LOS ANGELES AIRPORT.** *5400 W Century Blvd (90045). Phone 310/216-5858; fax 310/417-4545. www.westin.com.* 772 rooms, 12 story. D $129-$159; each additional $20; under 18 free; weekend rates. Pets accepted; fee. Check-out noon, check-in 3 pm. TV; cable (premium). In-room modem link. Laundry services. Restaurant, bar; entertainment. Room service 24 hours. In-house fitness room; sauna. Heated pool; whirlpool. Covered parking. Free airport transportation. Business center. Luxury level.

[D] [icons]

All Suites

★ ★ ★ **EMBASSY SUITES.** *1440 E Imperial Ave (90245). Phone 310/640-3600; fax 310/322-0954.*

www.embassysuites.com. Fauna and fish-filled pools in the courtyard add a nice touch. 349 suites, 5 story. D $109-$224; each additional $15; under 18 free; weekend rates. Pets accepted, some restrictions; fee. Complimentary full breakfast. Check-out noon, check-in 3 pm. TV; cable (premium). In-room modem link. Restaurant, bar. In-house fitness room. Near beach. Indoor pool; whirlpool. Parking. Free airport transportation. Business center. Spanish mission architecture.

[D] [icons]

★ ★ ★ **SUMMERFIELD SUITES EL SEGUNDO.** *810 S Douglas Ave (90245). Phone 310/725-0100; fax 310/725-0900. www.summerfieldsuites.com.* 122 kitchen suites, 3 story. Jan-Aug: $149-$229; family rates; package plans; lower rates rest of year. Pets accepted, some restrictions; fee. Complimentary continental breakfast. Check-out noon. TV; cable (premium), VCR (movies). In-room modem link. Bar. Health club privileges. In-house fitness room. Pool; whirlpool. Airport transportation. Concierge.

[D] [icons]

Los Gatos

Motel/Motor Lodge

★ ★ **LOS GATOS LODGE.** *50 Los Gatos-Saratoga Rd (95032). Phone 408/354-3300; toll-free 800/231-8676; fax 408/354-5451. www.losgatoslodge.com.* 129 rooms, 2 story. S, D $135; under 16 free. Pets accepted, some restrictions. Check-out noon. TV. Restaurant, bar; entertainment Fri, Sat. Pool; whirlpool. Lawn games.

[D] [icons]

Madera

Motel/Motor Lodge

★ ★ **BEST WESTERN MADERA VALLEY INN.** *317 N G St (93637). Phone 559/664-0100; toll-free 877/673-5164; fax 559/664-0200. www.bestwestern.com.* 93 rooms, 5 story. S, D $80; each additional $4; suites $85; under 12 free. Pets accepted; fee. Check-out noon. TV; cable (premium). Restaurant, bar. Room service. Health club privileges. In-house fitness room. Pool. Free airport transportation.

[icons]

Mammoth Lakes

Motels/Motor Lodges

★ **ECONO LODGE.** *3626 Main St (93546). Phone 760/934-6855; toll-free 800/228-5050; fax 760/934-8208. www.econolodge.com.* 32 rooms, 2 story. No A/C. S, D $69-$169; ski plans. Pets accepted; fee. Complimentary continental breakfast. Check-out 10 am. TV; cable (premium). Pool; whirlpool. Downhill/cross-country ski 3 miles. Mountain view from some rooms.

🐾 🏊 🎿 🗻 SC

★ **SHILO INN.** *2963 Main St (93546). Phone 760/934-4500; toll-free 800/222-2244; fax 760/934-7594. www.shiloinns.com.* 70 rooms, 4 story. S, D $70-$225; under 12 free. Pets accepted; fee. Complimentary continental breakfast, coffee in rooms. Check-out noon. TV; cable (premium). In-room modem link. Laundry services. Restaurant adjacent. In-house fitness room. Indoor pool; whirlpool. Downhill, cross-country ski 5 miles. Garage parking. Free airport transportation.

D 🐾 🎿 🏊 🏃 🎿 🗻 SC

Manhattan Beach

Hotel

★ ★ ★ **MARRIOTT MANHATTAN BEACH.** *1400 Parkview Ave (90266). Phone 310/546-7511; toll-free 800/228-9290; fax 310/796-0322. www.marriott.com.* Located ten minutes from LA's international airport on 26 beautifully landscaped acres. 385 rooms, 7 story. Pets accepted; fee. Check-out noon, check-in 3 pm. TV; cable (premium), VCR available. In-room modem link. Restaurant, bar. Room service. In-house fitness room. Outdoor pool; whirlpool. Golf on premise, greens fee. Valet, garage parking. Airport transportation. Business center. Concierge. Luxury level. **$$**

D 🐾 🏌 🏊 🏃 🎿 🗻 🏃

All Suite

★ **TOWNEPLACE SUITES BY MARRIOTT.** *14400 Aviation Blvd (90250). Phone 310/725-9696; fax 310/725-0086. www.towneplacesuites.com.* Guests planning on a longer stay will find comfort in the spacious rooms featuring fully equipped kitchens and large work spaces. 144 rooms, 4 story. D $85-$139. Pets accepted; fee. Check-out noon, check-in 3 pm. TV; cable (premium). In-room modem link. In-house fitness room. Outdoor pool. Business center.

🐾 🏊 🏃 🗻 🏃

Marina del Rey

Hotel

★ ★ ★ **THE RITZ-CARLTON, MARINA DEL REY.** *4375 Admiralty Way (90292). Phone 310/823-1700; toll-free 800/241-3333; fax 310/823-2403. www.ritzcarlton.com.* Moments from central Los Angeles, The Ritz-Carlton, Marina del Rey introduces guests to a different side of this West Coast capital. Situated on 5 acres on the world's largest manmade marina, this hotel is a waterside resort within a city. An instant calm washes over visitors who daydream while watching yachts bob on gentle waves. Joggers rejoice in the hotel's location along the 21-mile coastal Promenade, running from Malibu to Manhattan Beach. The guest rooms are gracefully appointed, with picture-perfect views of the marina adding to the soothing ambience. Sprinkled with art and antiques, the accommodations are refreshingly elegant. A heated outdoor pool is only steps from the ocean, and seasonal dining service is available at the poolside grill, Wave. Capturing the sophistication of nautical design with light woods and white walls, Jer-ne takes diners on a satisfying culinary journey. 304 rooms, 12 story. Pets accepted, some restrictions; fee. Valet parking. Check-out noon, check-in 3 pm. TV; cable (premium), VCR in suites. In-room modem link. Room service 24 hours. Restaurant, bar. In-house fitness room; sauna, steam room, spa, massage. Outdoor pool; whirlpool; poolside service. Supervised children's activities; ages 5-13. Outdoor tennis. Bicycle rental. Business center. Concierge. Luxury level. **$$$**

D 🐾 🎾 🏊 🏃 🗻 SC 🏃

Mendocino

B&B/Small Inns

★ ★ ★ **BLACKBERRY INN.** *44951 Larkin Rd (95460). Phone 707/937-5281; toll-free 800/950-7806. www.blackberryinn.biz.* Guests can stay in one of the theme rooms, each offering a unique stay modeled after a Western movie set. 16 rooms. No A/C. Pets accepted, some restrictions; fee. Complimentary continental breakfast. Check-out 11 am, check-in 3 pm. TV; cable. Many fireplaces; some refrigerators, in-room whirlpools. Some room phones. **$$**

D 🐾 🐕 🗻 🏃

★ ★ **INN AT SCHOOLHOUSE CREEK.** *7051 N Hwy 1 (95460). Phone 707/937-5525; toll-free 800/731-5525; fax 707/937-2012. www.schoolhousecreek.com.* 13 rooms, 4 suites, 3 kitchen units. No A/C. Some room phones. Pets accepted, some restrictions; fee. Complimentary continental breakfast. Check-out 11 am, check-in 2 pm. TV; cable (premium), VCR (movies). Fireplaces. Lawn games. Concierge service. Built in 1862; on 8 1/2 acres; gardens, meadows, forests. Totally nonsmoking. **$$**

★ ★ ★ **THE STANFORD INN BY THE SEA.** *Hwy 1 at Comptche Ukiah Rd (95460). Phone 707/ 937-5615; toll-free 800/331-8884; fax 707/937-0305. www.stanfordinn.com.* Feel at home at this inn situated on organic gardens and a farm located on the rugged Mendocino coast. Take in the panoramic view of the gardens and ocean while enjoying fine artwork and wood-burning stoves in the rooms. 41 rooms, 3 story. No A/C. Pets accepted, some restrictions; fee. Complimentary full breakfast. Check-out noon, check-in 4 pm. TV; cable (premium), VCR (movies $4). In-room modem link. Fireplaces. Restaurant. In-house fitness room; sauna. Indoor pool; whirlpool. Bike, canoe rentals. Free airport transportation. Business center. Concierge. Big River llamas on grounds. Tropical greenhouse. Totally nonsmoking. Free airport transportation. **$$$$**

Merced

Motel/Motor Lodge

★ ★ **BEST WESTERN SEQUOIA INN.** *1213 V St (95340). Phone 209/723-3711; toll-free 800/735-3711; fax 209/722-8551. www.bestwestern.com.* 98 rooms, 2 story. S $109-$129; D $64-$69; each additional $5; under 18 free. Pets accepted; fee. Complimentary continental breakfast. Check-out noon. TV; cable (premium). Restaurant, bar. Room service. Pool.

Modesto

Motel/Motor Lodge

★ **VAGABOND INN.** *1525 McHenry Ave (95350). Phone 209/521-6340; fax 209/575-2015. www.vagabondinn.com.* 99 rooms, 2 story. S, D $64-$84; each additional $5; under 18 free. Pets accepted, some restrictions; fee. Complimentary continental breakfast. Check-out noon. TV; cable (premium). Heated pool.

Hotel

★ ★ ★ **DOUBLETREE HOTEL.** *1150 9th St (95354). Phone 209/526-6000; fax 209/526-6096. www.doubletree.com.* This hotel has two restaurants, an outdoor heated pool, Jacuzzi, and sauna, as well as fax and data ports for business travelers. A visit to the theater located across the street provides evening entertainment. 258 rooms, 10 story. Jan-Nov: S $114; D $134; each additional $15; suites $250-$500; under 18 free; family rates; package plans; lower rates rest of year. Pets accepted; fee. Check-out noon. TV. In-room modem link. Restaurant, bar; entertainment Fri, Sat. In-house fitness room; sauna. Pool; whirlpool. Valet parking. Free airport transportation. Business center.

Monterey

Motel/Motor Lodge

★ ★ **BEST WESTERN THE BEACH RESORT.** *2600 Sand Dunes Dr (93940). Phone 831/394-3321; toll-free 800/242-8627; fax 831/393-1912. www.monterey beachhotel.com.* 196 rooms, 4 story. Pets accepted; fee. Check-out noon, check-in 4 pm. TV; cable (premium). In-room modem link. Restaurant, bar. Room service. In-house fitness room. Beach. Outdoor pool. Business center. Concierge. Totally nonsmoking. **$$**

Hotel

★ ★ ★ **HYATT REGENCY MONTEREY.** *One Old Golf Course Rd (93940). Phone 831/372-1234; toll-free 800/ 233-1234; fax 831/375-3960. www.montereyhyatt.com.* Located steps from Pebble Beach Company's Del Monte Golf Course. 575 rooms, 46 suites, 4 story. No A/C. Pets accepted, some restrictions; fee. Check-out noon, check-in 3 pm. TV; cable (premium), VCR available. In-room modem link. Fireplaces. Laundry services. Restaurant, bar. Room service. Babysitting services available. In-house fitness room; massage. Game room. Outdoor pool; whirlpool. Outdoor tennis, lighted courts. Bicycles. Airport transportation. Business center. Concierge. Luxury level. Situated on 23 landscaped acres. **$$**

B&B/Small Inn

★ ★ **BEST WESTERN VICTORIAN INN.** *487 Foam St (93940). Phone 831/373-8000; toll-free 800/ 232-4141; fax 831/373-4815. www.victorianinn.com.* 68 rooms, 3 story. Pets accepted; fee. Complimentary continental breakfast. Check-out noon, check-in 4 pm. TV; cable (premium), VCR available. In-room modem link. Fireplaces. Babysitting services available. Whirlpool. Parking. Victorian furnishings. Two blocks from bay. **$$**

Morro Bay

Motels/Motor Lodges

★ ★ **BEST WESTERN EL RANCHO.** *2460 N Main St (93442). Phone 805/772-2212; toll-free 800/528-1234. www.bestwestern.com.* 27 rooms. S, D $49-$89; each additional $7; under 12 free. Pets accepted; fee. Check-out 11 am. TV; VCR available. Laundry services. Restaurant. Pool. Redwood lobby, etched glass door.

★ **DAYS INN.** *1095 Main St (93442). Phone 805/772-2711; fax 805/772-2711. www.daysinn.com.* 46 rooms, 2 story. No A/C. Memorial Day-Sept: S, D $60-$125; each additional $6; lower rates rest of year. Pets accepted; fee. Complimentary continental breakfast. Check-out 11 am. TV; cable (premium).

Mountain View

Extended Stay

★ ★ **RESIDENCE INN BY MARRIOTT.** *1854 W El Camino Real (94040). Phone 650/940-1300; toll-free 800/331-3131; fax 650/969-4997. www.marriott.com.* 112 kitchen units, 2 story. S, D $229-$259; weekly, weekend, monthly rates. Pets accepted; fee. Complimentary continental breakfast. Check-out noon. TV; cable (premium). Laundry services. Health club privileges. Pool; whirlpool.

Mount Shasta

Motels/Motor Lodges

★ ★ **BEST WESTERN TREE HOUSE MOTOR INN.** *111 Morgan Way (96067). Phone 530/926-3101; toll-free 800/545-7164; fax 530/926-3542. www.bestwestern.com.* 95 rooms, 2-3 story. S $69-$79; D $79-$94; each additional $5; suites $89-$154. Pets accepted; fee. Complimentary full breakfast. Check-out noon. TV. In-room modem link. Restaurant, bar. Indoor pool; whirlpool. Downhill, cross-country ski 10 miles. Business center. View of Mount Shasta.

★ **FINLANDIA MOTEL.** *1612 S Mt. Shasta Blvd (96067). Phone 530/926-5596. www.finlandiamotel.com.* 25 rooms, 1-2 story. S, D $41-$64$56; suites $48-$75. Pets

accepted, some restrictions; fee. Check-out 11 am. TV. Downhill ski 9 miles, cross-country ski 8 miles.

★ **SWISS HOLIDAY LODGE.** *2400 S Mt. Shasta Blvd (96067). Phone 530/926-3446; fax 530/926-3091.* 21 rooms, 2 story. S $36-$52; D $42-$72; each additional $5; suite $105. Pets accepted; fee. Complimentary continental breakfast. Check-out 11 am. TV; cable (premium). Pool; whirlpool. Downhill, cross-country ski 10 miles. View of Mount Shasta. Totally nonsmoking.

Napa

Motel/Motor Lodge

★ **CHABLIS INN.** *3360 Solano Ave (94558). Phone 707/257-1944; toll-free 800/443-3490; fax 707/226-6862. www.chablisinn.com.* 34 rooms, 2 story. Pets accepted; fee. Check-out noon, check-in 3 pm. TV; cable (premium). In-room modem link. Outdoor pool; whirlpool. **$$**

B&B/Small Inn

★ ★ ★ **BEAZLEY HOUSE.** *1910 1st St (94559). Phone 707/257-1649; toll-free 800/559-1649; fax 707/257-1518. www.beazleyhouse.com.* This lovely bed-and-breakfast is a great stop for travelers touring the wine country. Visitors will enjoy the great landscape and wonderful gardens along with the friendly service. 11 rooms, 2 story. Pets accepted. Complimentary full breakfast. Check-out noon, check-in 3 pm. Health club privileges. Built in 1902. Totally nonsmoking. **$$**

Newport Beach

Hotels

★ ★ ★ ★ **FOUR SEASONS HOTEL NEWPORT BEACH.** *690 Newport Center Dr (92660). Phone 949/759-0808; toll-free 800/332-3442; fax 949/720-1718. www.fourseasons.com.* The Four Seasons Hotel Newport Beach embodies the best of a resort within a city. In the heart of southern California, this 20-story tower is angled toward the Pacific Ocean and only minutes from the glorious beaches. This full-service resort allows its guests to reap the rewards of a refreshing sleep, a delicious meal, or a perfectly lazy day spent by the pool. All the guest rooms have private balconies overlooking the beautiful grounds.

The accommodations are West Coast casual blended with European élan; shades of lemon, lime, and peach enhance the restful appearance. The pool sparkles, and its 17-foot fireplace warms visitors on chilly evenings. Guests can stay in touch poolside, where dataports and telephone jacks are available. The nearby Pelican Hill Golf Club and Grill provide leisure and culinary diversions, while the hotel's signature Pavilion restaurant is a lovely spot for dining at any time of day. 189 rooms, 96 suites, 20 story. S, D $330-$410; each additional $30; suites $475-$4,350; under 18 free; weekend rates; package plans. Pets accepted, some restrictions. Check-out noon, check-in 3 pm. TV; cable (premium), VCR available (movies). In-room modem link. Restaurant, bar; entertainment. Room service 24 hours. Supervised children's activities; ages 5-12 (summer). In-house fitness room; sauna, spa, massage. Pool; whirlpool; poolside service. Golf privileges. Two lighted tennis courts. Bicycles. Valet parking. Complimentary airport transportation. Business center. Concierge. Oceanfront views available.

★ ★ ★ THE SUTTON PLACE HOTEL. *4500 MacArthur Blvd (92660). Phone 949/476-2001; toll-free 800/243-4141; fax 949/476-0153. www.suttonplace.com.* 435 rooms, 10 story. S, D $190-$250; each additional $25; suites $310-$875; under 16 free; weekend rates. Pets accepted, some restrictions; fee. Check-out noon, check-in 3 pm. TV; cable (premium), VCR available (movies). In-room modem link. Restaurant, bar; entertainment. Room service 24 hours. Health club privileges. In-house fitness room; massage, sauna. Pool; whirlpool; poolside service. Lighted courts. Free airport transportation. Business center. Concierge. Luxury level. European décor.

Resort

★ ★ ★ MARRIOTT NEWPORT BEACH HOTEL AND TENNIS CLUB. *900 Newport Center Dr (92660). Phone 949/640-4000; toll-free 800/228-9290; fax 949/640-5055. www.marriott.com.* 586 rooms, 16 story. Pets accepted, some restrictions. Check-out noon, check-in 4 pm. TV; cable (premium). In-room modem link. Laundry services. Room service 24 hours. Restaurant, bar. Babysitting services available. In-house fitness room; massage. Health club privileges. Outdoor pool; whirlpool; poolside service. Outdoor tennis, lighted courts. Valet parking. Free airport transportation. Business center. Concierge. Luxury level. Beautiful landscaping. **$$**

Oakhurst

Motel/Motor Lodge

★ COMFORT INN. *40489 Hwy 41 (93644). Phone 559/683-8282; fax 559/658-7030. www.comfortinn.com.* 113 rooms, 2 story. Apr-Nov: S, D $69-$99; each additional $6; suites $125; kitchen unit $225; under 18 free; lower rates rest of year. Pets accepted; fee. Complimentary continental breakfast. Check-out 11 am. TV; cable (premium), VCR available. Pool; whirlpool.

Oakland

Hotels

★ ★ BEST WESTERN INN AT THE SQUARE. *233 Broadway (94607). Phone 510/452-4565; toll-free 800/528-1234; fax 510/452-4634. www.innatthesquare.com.* 100 rooms, 2-3 story. Pets accepted; fee. Complimentary continental breakfast. Check-out 11 am, check-in 2 pm. TV; cable (premium). In-room modem link. Restaurant. In-house fitness room. Outdoor pool. **$**

★ ★ CLARION HOTEL. *1800 Madison St (94612). Phone 510/832-2300; toll-free 800/933-4683; fax 510/832-7150. www.lakemerritthotel.com.* 41 suites, 6 story. S, D $179; each additional $10; suites $219-$299; under 17 free. Pets accepted; fee. Check-out 11 am. TV; VCR available. In-room modem link. Restaurant, bar. Health club privileges. Valet parking. Concierge. Restored Mediterranean/Art Deco landmark (1927) offers views of Lake Merritt.

★ ★ ★ HILTON OAKLAND AIRPORT. *1 Hegenberger Rd (94621). Phone 510/635-5000; fax 510/383-4062. www.oaklandairport.hilton.com.* This hotel offers its guests a resortlike atmosphere to relax. 363 rooms, 3 story. Pets accepted, some restrictions; fee. Check-out noon, check-in 2 pm. TV; cable (premium), VCR available. In-room modem link. Restaurant, bar; entertainment. Room service. In-house fitness room. Outdoor pool; poolside service. Free airport transportation. Business center. **$**

Ojai

Motel/Motor Lodge

★ **BEST WESTERN CASA OJAI.** *1302 E Ojai Ave (93023). Phone 805/646-8175; toll-free 800/255-8175; fax 805/646-8247. www.bestwestern.com.* 44 rooms, 2 story. Mid-May-mid-Sept: S $75-$120; D $80-$120; each additional $10; under 12 free; lower rates rest of year. Pets accepted, some restrictions; fee. Complimentary continental breakfast. Check-out noon. TV; VCR available. In-room modem link. Pool; whirlpool.

⬜ 🐾 🏊 🏊

Resort

★ ★ ★ **OJAI VALLEY INN & SPA.** *905 Country Club Blvd (93023). Phone 805/646-5511; toll-free 800/422-6524; fax 805/646-7969. www.ojairesort.com.* 3 story. S, D $279-$340; suites, cottages $390-$2,500; family rates. Pets accepted; fee. Check-out noon, check-in 4 pm. TV; cable (premium). In-room modem link. Room service 24 hours. Restaurant, bar; entertainment. Supervised children's activities; ages 3-12. In-house fitness room; sauna, steam room. Three pools; whirlpool; poolside service. 18-hole golf; pro, putting green, driving range; greens fee from $80. Outdoor tennis, lighted courts, pro. Lawn games. Bicycles. Hiking, horseback riding, mountain biking. Business center. Concierge. On 220 acres. Aviary. Mountain views.

⬜ 🐾 ⛳ ⛳ 🏋 🚴 🏊 🎾 🏊 🚶

Ontario

Motels/Motor Lodges

★ **BEST WESTERN ONTARIO AIRPORT.** *209 N Vineyard Ave (91764). Phone 909/937-6800; toll-free 800/528-1234; fax 909/937-6815. www.bestwestern.com.* 150 rooms, 2 story. S, D $69-$79; each additional $5; under 12 free. Pets accepted; fee. Complimentary continental breakfast. Check-out noon. TV; cable (premium). Restaurant adjacent. In-house fitness room. Pool; whirlpool. Free airport transportation.

🐾 🏊 🏋 ✈ 🏊

★ ★ **HOLIDAY INN.** *3400 Shelby St (91764). Phone 909/466-9600; toll-free 800/642-2617; fax 909/941-1445. www.holiday-inn.com.* 150 kitchen units, 3 story. S, D $109. Suites $119-$129; 1-bedroom suites $139-$149;

each additional $10; under 18 free; weekly rates. Pets accepted; fee. Complimentary full breakfast. Check-out noon. TV; cable (premium), VCR available. Laundry services. Restaurant, bar. Room service. In-house fitness room; sauna. Game room. Pool; whirlpool. Free airport transportation. Business center.

 ⬜ 🐾 🏊 🏋 ✈ 🏊 🚶

Hotels

★ ★ ★ **DOUBLETREE HOTEL.** *222 N Vineyard Ave (91764). Phone 909/937-0900; fax 909/937-1999. www.doubletree.com.* 484 rooms, 3-4 story. S, D $161-$179; each additional $15; suites $375-$650; under 18 free; weekend rates. Pets accepted, some restrictions; fee. Check-out 1 pm. TV; cable (premium), VCR available. Restaurant, dining room, bar; entertainment. Room service. In-house fitness room. Pool; whirlpool; poolside service. Free airport transportation. Luxury level.

⬜ 🐾 🏊 🏋 🏊 **SC**

★ ★ ★ **MARRIOTT ONTARIO AIRPORT.** *2200 E Holt Blvd (91761). Phone 909/975-5000; toll-free 800/284-8811; fax 909/975-5050. www.marriotthotels.com/ontca.* Perfect for business and leisure travelers, this hotel offers many amenities, including a full-service health club that features racquetball, basketball, a sauna, and lap pool. Visitors will enjoy the choice between the four restaurants. 299 rooms, 3 story. S, D $89-$169; suites $250; weekend rates. Pets accepted; fee. Check-out noon. TV; cable (premium). In-room modem link. Restaurant, bar. In-house fitness room; sauna, steam room. Pool; whirlpool; poolside service. Outdoor tennis, lighted courts. Racquetball. Free airport transportation. Concierge.

⬜ 🐾 ⛳ 🏃 🏊 🏋 🏊 **SC**

Orange

Extended Stay

★ ★ **RESIDENCE INN BY MARRIOTT.** *3101 West Chapman Ave (92868). Phone 714/978-7700; toll-free 800/423-9315; fax 714/978-6257. www.marriott.com.* 104 kitchen units, 2 story. S, D $104-$124; family, weekly rates. Pets accepted; fee. Complimentary continental breakfast. Check-out noon. TV; cable (premium), VCR available. Laundry services. Health club privileges. Pool; whirlpool. Airport, train station, bus depot transportation.

⬜ 🐾 🏊 🏋 🏊

Oroville

B&B/Small Inn

★ ★ ★ **LAKE OROVILLE BED AND BREAKFAST.**
240 Sunday Dr (95916). Phone 530/589-0700; fax 530/589-3800. www.now2000.com/lakeoroville. Eat a hearty breakfast and stroll 40 acres of rolling hills at this relaxing escape. The guest rooms are quaintly decorated. The quiet sunroom is great for watching sunsets. 6 rooms. Pets accepted; fee. Complimentary full breakfast. Check-out 11:30 am, check-in 3-6 pm. TV available; VCR available (movies). Game room. Bicycles available. Hiking trails. Totally nonsmoking. **$**
D 🐾 ⤒ SC

Oxnard

Motel/Motor Lodge

★ ★ **CASA SIRENA MARINA RESORT.** *3605 Peninsula Rd (93035).* Phone 805/985-6311; toll-free 800/447-3529; fax 805/985-4329. www.casasirenahotel.com. 273 rooms. Some A/C, 2-3 story. S, D $120-$149; each additional $10; suites $179-$275; kitchen units $179; package plans. Pets accepted, some restrictions; fee. Check-out noon. TV. In-room modem link. Restaurant, bar. Room service. In-house fitness room; sauna. Game room. Pool; whirlpool. Outdoor tennis; lighted courts. Marina. Free airport, train station, bus depot transportation. View of harbor. Park adjacent.
D 🐾 ⤒ ⤒ ⤒ ⤒ ⤒ SC

Hotel

★ ★ ★ **RADISSON HOTEL OXNARD.** *600 E Esplanade Dr (93030).* Phone 805/485-9666; fax 805/485-2061. www.radisson.com. 163 rooms, 6 story. S, D $149; each additional $10; suites $129-$169; under 18 free. Pets accepted, some restrictions; fee. Check-out noon. TV; cable (premium). In-room modem link. Restaurant, bar; entertainment. Health club privileges. Pool; whirlpool. Free airport transportation.
D 🐾 ⤒ ⤒

Extended Stay

★ ★ **RESIDENCE INN BY MARRIOTT.** *2101 W Vineyard Ave (93030).* Phone 805/278-2200; fax 805/983-4470. www.marriott.com. 252 kitchen units, 1-2 story. S, D $135-$175; under 17 free; golf, tennis packages. Pets accepted; fee. Complimentary breakfast buffet. Check-out noon. TV; cable (premium). In-room modem link. Pool;

whirlpool; poolside service. Greens fee. Lighted courts. Free airport transportation.
D 🐾 ⤒ ⤒ ⤒ ⤒

Palm Desert

Extended Stay

★ ★ **RESIDENCE INN BY MARRIOTT.** *38305 Cook St (92211).* Phone 760/776-0050; fax 760/776-1806. www.residenceinn.com. Nestled around the Santa Rosa Mountains, this hotel offers spacious guest suites—some featuring balconies with views. 130 rooms, 2 story. D $199-$249. Pets accepted, some restrictions. Complimentary buffet breakfast. Check-out noon, check-in 4 pm. TV; cable (premium), VCR. In-room modem link. Laundry services. In-house fitness room. Outdoor pool. Outdoor tennis. Business center. Concierge.
🐾 ⤒ ⤒ ⤒ ⤒ ⤒ ⤒

Palm Springs

Motels/Motor Lodges

★ **THE CHASE HOTEL AT PALM SPRINGS.**
200 W Arenas Rd (92262). Phone 760/320-8866; toll-free 877/532-4273; fax 760/323-1501. www.chasehotelpalmsprings.com. 26 kitchen units, 1-2 story. Pets accepted; fee. Complimentary continental breakfast. Check-out noon, check-in 3 pm. TV. Outdoor pool. Lawn games. Concierge. **$**
D 🐾 ⤒ ⤒ ⤒

★ **COMFORT SUITES CATHEDRAL CITY.** *69-151 E Palm Canyon Dr (92234).* Phone 760/324-5939; toll-free 800/892-5085; fax 760/324-3034. www.comfortinn.com. 97 kitchen units, 3 story. Jan-May: kitchen suites $99-$179; under 16 free; higher rates weekends; lower rates rest of year. Pets accepted, some restrictions; fee. Complimentary continental breakfast. Check-out noon. TV; cable (premium). Restaurant opposite. Pool; whirlpool. Golf privileges.
D 🐾 ⤒ ⤒ SC

★ **MOTEL 6.** *660 S Palm Canyon Dr (92262).* Phone 760/327-4200; toll-free 800/466-8356; fax 760/320-9827. www.motel6.com. 148 rooms, 3 story. Shower only. Sept-mid-Apr: S $56.99; D $60.99; each additional $3; under 17 free. Pets accepted, some restrictions. Check-out noon. TV; cable (premium). Laundry services. Pool.
D 🐾 ⤒ ⤒ SC

★ **PLACE IN THE SUN.** *754 E San Lorenzo Rd (92264). Phone 760/325-0254; toll-free 800/779-2254; fax 760/322-3479. www.aplaceinthesunhotel.com.* 16 rooms. Pets accepted; fee. Complimentary continental breakfast. Check-out noon, check-in 2 pm. TV. Laundry services. Outdoor pool; whirlpool. Lawn games. Free airport transportation. **$**

⬛⬛⬛

★ ★ **RAMADA INN.** *1800 E Palm Canyon Dr (92264). Phone 760/323-1711; toll-free 800/245-6907; fax 760/327-6941. www.ramada.com.* 255 rooms, 3 story. Pets accepted, some restrictions; fee. Check-out noon, check-in 3 pm. TV. In-room modem link. Laundry services. Restaurant, bar; entertainment. In-house fitness room; sauna. Outdoor pool; whirlpool; poolside service. Outdoor tennis. Free airport transportation. **$**

⬛⬛⬛⬛⬛⬛⬛⬛SC

★ **SUPER 8.** *1900 N Palm Canyon Dr (92262). Phone 760/322-3757; fax 760/323-5290. www.innworks.com.* 61 rooms, 2 story. Late Dec-May: S $68; D $73; each additional $5; suites $90-$110; under 12 free; lower rates rest of year. Pets accepted, some restrictions; fee. Complimentary continental breakfast. Check-out 11 am. TV. Laundry services. Pool; whirlpool.

⬛⬛

Resorts

★ ★ ★ **HILTON PALM SPRINGS RESORT.** *400 E Tahquitz Canyon Way (92262). Phone 760/320-6868; toll-free 800/522-6900; fax 760/320-2126. www.hilton.com.* Located steps from shopping, fine and fast food restaurants, theater, and art galleries. 260 rooms, 60 suites, 3 story. Pets accepted; fee. Check-out noon, check-in 3 pm. TV; cable (premium), VCR available. In-room modem link. Restaurant, bar. Room service. Babysitting services available. In-house fitness room; spa, sauna. Outdoor pool; whirlpool. Valet parking. Business center. Concierge. Free airport transportation. **$$$**

⬛⬛⬛⬛⬛⬛⬛SC⬛

★ ★ ★ **LA MANCHA RESORT AND SPA.** *444 N Avenida Caballeros (92262). Phone 760/323-1773; toll-free 800/673-7901; fax 760/323-5928. www.la-mancha.com.* Located in the Coachella Valley, this hideaway for movie stars is a wonderful place to relax and is very romantic. 49 kitchen units, 1-2 story. Pets accepted, some restrictions; fee. Check-out noon, check-in 3 pm. TV; VCR available (movies). In-room modem link. Fireplaces. Dining room, bar. Room service. Babysitting services available. Spa, sauna. Pool; whirlpool; poolside service. Lighted tennis courts. Lawn games. Bicycles. Free airport transportation. Concierge. **$$**

⬛⬛⬛⬛⬛⬛⬛

★ ★ ★ **MIRAMONTE RESORT.** *45000 Indian Wells Ln (92210). Phone 760/341-2200; toll-free 800/327-2926; fax 760/837-1637. www.miramonte-resort.com.* 222 rooms, 3 story. Pets accepted, some restrictions; fee. Check-out noon, check-in 4 pm. TV; cable (premium), VCR available. Restaurant. Babysitting services available. In-house fitness room; spa. Outdoor pool; whirlpool. Business center. **$$**

⬛⬛⬛⬛⬛⬛SC⬛

★ ★ ★ **PALM SPRINGS RIVIERA RESORT.** *1600 N Indian Canyon Dr (92262). Phone 760/327-8311; toll-free 800/444-8311; fax 760/327-4323. www.psriviera.com.* Situated on 24 acres, this resort is 1 mile from downtown Palm Springs and provides spectacular moutain views. 476 rooms, 2-3 story. Pets accepted, some restrictions; fee. Check-out noon, check-in 3 pm. TV. In-room modem link. Restaurant, bar; entertainment. Room service. Babysitting services available. In-house fitness room; massage. Outdoor pool; children's pool; whirlpool. Outdoor tennis, lighted courts. Lawn games. Concierge. **$$**

⬛⬛⬛⬛⬛⬛⬛⬛⬛

B&B/Small Inns

★ ★ **BALLANTINES HOTEL.** *1420 N Indian Canyon Dr (92262). Phone 760/320-1178; toll-free 800/780-3464; fax 760/320-5308. www.ballantineshotels.com.* 14 rooms. Pets accepted, some restrictions; fee. Complimentary continental breakfast. Check-out noon, check-in 2 pm. TV; VCR available. Outdoor pool; whirlpool. **$$**

⬛⬛⬛⬛⬛⬛

★ ★ ★ **CASA CODY BED AND BREAKFAST INN.** *175 S Cahuilla Rd (92262). Phone 760/320-9346; toll free 800/231-2639; fax 760/325-8610. www.casacody.com.* 23 rooms. Pets accepted; fee. Complimentary continental breakfast. Check-out 11 am, check-in 2 pm. TV; cable, VCR available. Fireplaces. Babysitting services available. Indoor pool; whirlpool. **$$**

⬛⬛⬛⬛

★ ★ ★ **ESTRELLA RESORT.** *415 S Belardo Rd (92262). Phone 760/320-4117; toll-free 800/237-3687; fax 760/323-3303. www.estrella.com.* Located in scenic Palm Springs within walking distance of the famous Follies, restaurants, art galleries, and shops. Three acres of courtyards, gardens, and lawns are here to enjoy. 73 rooms, 2 story. Pets accepted, some restrictions; fee. Complimentary continental breakfast. Check-out noon, check-in, check-in 3 pm. TV; VCR available. In-house fitness room; spa. Health club privileges. Outdoor pool; children's pool; whirlpool. Free airport transportation. Concierge service. Built in 1929. **$$**

⬛⬛⬛⬛SC

Palo Alto

Hotels

★ ★ ★ **GARDEN COURT HOTEL.** *520 Cowper St (94301). Phone 650/322-9000; toll-free 800/824-9028; fax 650/324-3609. www.gardencourt.com.* Located downtown, this hotel is in the heart of Silicon Valley near Stanford University, shopping, and restaurants. The Mediterranean-style architecture with rooms overlooking the courtyard of flowers provides an intimate feeling. Four-poster beds, down comforters, and plush terry robes enhance this feeling. 62 rooms, 4 story. S, D $299-$350; each additional $20; suites $365-$575. Pets accepted, some restrictions; fee. Check-out noon. TV; cable (premium), VCR available. In-room modem link. Fireplaces. Room service 24 hours. Restaurant, bar. In-house fitness room. Bicycles. Valet parking. Concierge. Open-air, flower-laden courtyard reminiscent of a European village square.

D ◗ 🏊 🏃 🖾

★ ★ ★ **SHERATON PALO ALTO HOTEL.** *625 El Camino Real (94301). Phone 650/328-2800; fax 650/327-7362. www.sheraton.com.* This resort hotel is surrounded by flower gardens, ponds, and fountains. The property is located at the entrance to Stanford University and near the Stanford Shopping Center. Guest rooms offer generous work stations for business travelers. 4 story. S, D $149-$309; each additional $10; under 18 free; weekend rates. Pets accepted, some restrictions; fee. Check-out noon. TV; cable (premium), VCR available. In-room modem link. Restaurant, bar. Room service. In-house fitness room. Poolside service. Valet parking. Business center. Concierge.

D ◗ 🏊 🖾 🏃 🖾 🏃

Pasadena

Resort

★ ★ ★ ★ **THE RITZ-CARLTON HUNTINGTON HOTEL AND SPA.** *1401 S Oak Knoll Ave (91106). Phone 626/568-3900; fax 626/568-3700. www.ritzcarlton.com.* The Ritz-Carlton Huntington Hotel & Spa has been painting a rosy picture for lucky guests since 1907. This historic hotel, acquired by Ritz-Carlton in 1991, is nestled at the foothills of the San Gabriel Mountains on 23 beautiful acres. Its relaxed, rural setting belies its convenient location in Pasadena, near Los Angeles. Oriental carpets, crystal chandeliers, and antique furniture comprise the resolutely classic interiors. The guest rooms reflect the great tradition of this hotel while incorporating modern necessities. Dining at the Terrace Restaurant is a treat, from its alfresco setting with a view of the Picture Bridge to its appetizing dishes. The Grill specializes in seafood and meats in a casual environment, while the lounge and pool bar entertain day and night. From refreshing spa treatments and bike rentals to tee times and tennis lessons, this resort has it covered. 392 rooms, 3-8 story. S, D $350-$2,500; suites, cottages $415-$2,500; under 18 free; package plans. Pets accepted, some restrictions; fee. Check-out noon, check-in 3 pm. TV; cable (premium), VCR available. Room service 24 hours. Restaurant, bar; entertainment. Spa. Pool; whirlpool; poolside service. Lighted tennis. Lawn games. Bicycle rental. Valet parking. Business center. Concierge. Luxury level.

D ◗ 🏃 🖾 🏃 🖾 🏃

Pebble Beach

Resort

★ ★ ★ ★ **THE LODGE AT PEBBLE BEACH.** *Seventeen Mile Dr (93953). Phone 831/624-3811; toll-free 800/654-9300; fax 831/625-8590. www.pebblebeach.com.* Distinguished by its impressive architecture and spectacular oceanside setting, The Lodge at Pebble Beach is the jewel in the crown of the world-class Pebble Beach resort. Exclusive and refined, the fashionably appointed rooms and suites are supremely comfortable. All feature balconies, and the spa rooms even feature private gardens with outdoor whirlpools. In addition to its famous golf, the Lodge encourages its guests to unwind by the pool, enjoy a vigorous workout in the fitness center, or play a tennis match in its state-of-the-art facility. Its four restaurants offer a variety of casually elegant settings and run the gamut from casual American fare and succulent seafood to updated, lightened versions of French classics. The Lodge's spa celebrates the diversity of natural resources indigenous to the Monterey Peninsula in its treatments and therapies, and the shops tantalize visitors with an array of apparel, jewelry, and art. 161 rooms, 2-3 story. Service charge $15/day. Pets accepted, some restrictions; fee. Check-out noon, check-in 4 pm. TV; cable (premium), VCR available. In-room modem link. Fireplaces. Room service 24 hours. Restaurant, bar. Babysitting services available. In-house fitness room; spa, massage, sauna, steam room. Beach. Outdoor pool; children's pool; whirlpool. Golf; greens fee $350. Outdoor tennis. Horses/riding. Valet parking. Business center. Concierge. Bicycling. Free airport transportation. **$$$$**

D ◗ 🏃 🏌 🏃 🖾 🏃 🖾 🏃

Pismo Beach

Motel/Motor Lodge

★ ★ **BEST WESTERN CASA GRANDE INN.** *850 Oak Park Rd (93420). Phone 805/481-7398; fax 805/481-*

4859. www.bestwestern.com. 114 rooms, 21 suites, 2-3 story. June-mid-Sept: S $75-$90; D $85-$120; each additional $10; suites $100-$140; family rates; holidays (2-day minimum); lower rates rest of year. Pets accepted; fee. Complimentary continental breakfast. Check-out 11 am. TV; cable (premium), VCR available. Restaurant, bar. In-house fitness room; sauna. Game room. Pool; whirlpool.

All Suite

★ ★ **OXFORD SUITES RESORT.** 651 Five Cities Dr (93449). Phone 805/773-3773; toll-free 800/982-7848; fax 805/773-5177. oxfordsuites.com. The friendly staff welcome guests with a reception featuring beer, wine, juice, and sodas along with light hors d'ouevres. 133 suites, 2 story. S, D $79-$129; each additional $10; under 10 free. Pets accepted, some restrictions; fee. Complimentary full breakfast. Check-out noon. TV; VCR available. Laundry services. Pool; children's pool; whirlpool.

Placerville

Motels/Motor Lodges

★ **BEST WESTERN CAMERON PARK INN.** 3361 Coach Ln (95682). Phone 530/677-2203; toll-free 800/601-1234; fax 530/676-1422. www.bestwestern.com. 62 rooms, 1-2 story. S $51-$65; D $56-$70; each additional $5; suites $75-$104; under 16 free; family rates. Pets accepted; fee. Complimentary continental breakfast. Check-out noon. TV; cable (premium), VCR available. Restaurant adjacent. Health club privileges. Outdoor pool. Golf privileges. Business center.

★ **BEST WESTERN PLACERVILLE INN.** 6850 Greenleaf Dr (95667). Phone 530/622-9100; toll-free 800/854-9100; fax 530/622-9376. 105 rooms, 3 story. No elevator. S, D $70-$80; each additional $10; under 12 free. Pets accepted; fee. Check-out 11 am. TV. Pool; whirlpool.

Pleasanton

All Suite

★ **CANDLEWOOD SUITES.** 5535 Johnson Dr (94588). Phone 925/463-1212; fax 925/463-6080. www.candlewoodsuites.com. 126 suites, 4 story. S, D $123-$179; under 18 free; package plans. Pets accepted, some restrictions; fee. Check-out noon. TV; cable (premium), VCR (movies). In-room modem link. Restaurant adjacent. Room

service 5-9 pm. In-house fitness room. Pool privileges; whirlpool.

Extended Stay

★ ★ **RESIDENCE INN BY MARRIOTT.** 11920 Dublin Canyon Rd (94588). Phone 925/227-0500. www.residenceinn.com. 135 rooms, 3 story. S, D $69-$179; suites $279; each additional $25; under 17 free. Pets accepted, some restrictions; fee. Check-out noon. TV; cable (premium), VCR available. In-room modem link. Laundry services. In-house fitness room. Pool; whirlpool.

Rancho Cordova

Motel/Motor Lodge

★ **INNS OF AMERICA.** 12249 Folsom Blvd (95742). Phone 916/351-1213; fax 916/351-1817. www.innsofamerica.com. 124 rooms, 3 story. S, D $89; each additional (up to 4) $5. Pets accepted, some restrictions. Complimentary continental breakfast. Check-out 11 am. TV; cable (premium). Laundry services. Pool.

Rancho Santa Fe

B&B/Small Inn

★ ★ ★ **INN AT RANCHO SANTA FE.** 5951 Linea Cielo (92067). Phone 858/756-1131; toll-free 800/843-4661; fax 858/759-1604. www.theinnatranchosantafe.com. Originally designed in 1924, this pristine inn is 20 miles north of San Diego and 7 miles inland. 89 rooms. Pets accepted. Check-out noon, check-in 3 pm. TV; VCR available. Fireplaces. Restaurant. Room service. In-house fitness room; massage. Outdoor pool; whirlpool; poolside service. Outdoor tennis. Lawn games. **$$**

Redding

Motels/Motor Lodges

★ ★ **BEST WESTERN HOSPITALITY HOUSE MOTEL.** 532 N Market St (96003). Phone 530/241-6464; toll-free 800/700-3019; fax 530/244-1998. www.bestwestern.com. 61 rooms, 2 story. S $44-$64; D $50-$70; each additional $6; suite $99; under 18 free.

Pets accepted, some restrictions; fee. Complimentary full breakfast. Check-out 11 am. TV. Restaurant. Pool.

★ ★ **BRIDGE BAY RESORT.** *10300 Bridge Bay Rd (96003). Phone 530/275-3021; toll-free 800/752-9669; fax 530/275-8365.* 40 rooms, 2-day minimum suites, 8 kitchen units, 1-2 story. May-Sept: S $89; each additional $6; suites $120-$160; under 12 free; lower rates rest of year. Pets accepted; fee. Check-out 11 am. TV. Restaurant, bar. Pool.

★ **LA QUINTA INN.** *2180 Hilltop Dr (96002). Phone 530/221-8200; toll-free 800/687-6667; fax 530/223-4727. www.laquinta.com.* 133 rooms, 3 story. S, D (up to 4) $60; suites $99; under 18 free. Pets accepted. Complimentary continental breakfast. Check-out noon. TV. In-room modem link. Laundry services. Restaurant. In-house fitness room. Pool; whirlpool.

★ ★ **RED LION.** *1830 Hilltop Dr (96002). Phone 530/221-8700; toll-free 800/733-5466; fax 530/221-0324. www.redlion.com.* 193 rooms, 2 story. May-Sept: S, D $79-$105; each additional $15; suites $250; under 18 free; package plans; lower rates rest of year. Pets accepted, some restrictions; fee. Check-out 1 pm. TV; VCR available (movies). In-room modem link. Restaurant. Dining room. Bar; entertainment Thurs-Sat. Room service. Health club privileges. In-house fitness room. Pool; children's pool; whirlpool; poolside service. Free airport transportation.

★ ★ **RIVER INN MOTOR HOTEL.** *1835 Park Marina Dr (96001). Phone 530/241-9500; toll-free 800/995-4341; fax 530/241-5345.* 79 rooms, 2-3 story. No elevator. S, D $60-$75; each additional $5; under 12 free. Pets accepted, some restrictions; fee. Check-out 11 am. TV; cable (premium). Restaurant, bar. Sauna. Pool; whirlpool.

Redlands

Motel/Motor Lodge

★ **BEST WESTERN SANDMAN MOTEL.** *1120 W Colton Ave (92374). Phone 909/793-2001; fax 909/792-7612. www.bestwestern.com.* 65 rooms, 2 story. S $59; D $45; each additional $4; kitchen units $5 additional; under 12 free. Pets accepted. Complimentary continental breakfast. Check-out 11 am. TV; cable (premium). Pool; whirlpool.

Redwood City

Hotel

★ ★ ★ **HOTEL SOFITEL.** *223 Twin Dolphin Dr (94065). Phone 650/598-9000; toll-free 800/763-4835; fax 650/598-9383. www.sofitel.com.* This hotel is within 5 minutes of the airport. 42 suites, 9 story. S, D $99-$189; each additional $20; suites $329-$479; under 12 free. Pets accepted; fee. Check-out noon. TV; cable (premium), VCR available. In-room modem link. Restaurant, bar; entertainment Mon-Sat. Room service 24 hours. In-house fitness room. Valet parking. Free airport transportation. Business center. Concierge. Elegant atmosphere; Baccarat chandeliers.

Sacramento

Motels/Motor Lodges

★ **BEST WESTERN HARBOR INN AND SUITES.** *1250 Halyard Dr (95691). Phone 916/371-2100; toll-free 800/528-1234; fax 916/373-1507. www.bestwestern.com.* 138 rooms, 2-4 story. Pets accepted; fee. Complimentary continental breakfast. Check-out 11 am, check-in 3 pm. TV; cable (premium). Outdoor pool; whirlpool. **$**

★ ★ **CLARION HOTEL.** *700 16th St (95814). Phone 916/444-8000; toll-free 800/443-0880; fax 916/442-8129. www.clarionhotel.com.* 238 rooms, 2-4 story. S, D $86-$94; each additional $20; suites $135-$265; under 18 free; weekend rates. Pets accepted; fee. Check-out noon. TV; cable (premium), VCR available. In-room modem link. Restaurant, bar. Room service. Health club privileges. Pool; poolside service. Airport transportation.

★ **LA QUINTA INN.** *4604 Madison Ave (95841). Phone 916/348-0900; fax 916/331-7160. www.laquinta.com.* 122 rooms, 3 story. Pets accepted, some restrictions. Check-out noon, check-in 3 pm. TV; cable (premium). In-room modem link. Restaurant. Health club privileges. Outdoor pool; whirlpool. Continental breakfast. **$**

★ ★ **RED LION.** *1401 Arden Way (95815). Phone 916/922-8041; fax 916/922-0386. www.redlion.com.* 376 rooms, 2-3 story. S, D $125-$148; each additional $15; suites $150-$395; under 18 free. Pets accepted, some restrictions; fee. Check-out noon. TV; cable (premium).

Restaurant, bar; entertainment Tues-Sat. Room service. In-house fitness room. Three pools; whirlpool; poolside service. Valet parking.

★ **VAGABOND INN.** *1319 30th St (95816). Phone 916/454-4400; fax 916/736-2812. www.vagabondinns.com.* 81 rooms, 3 story. S, D $45-$65; each additional $5; under 18 free. Pets accepted, some restrictions; fee. Check-out noon. TV. In-house fitness room. Pool.

★ **VAGABOND INN.** *909 3rd St (95814). Phone 916/446-1481; fax 916/448-0364. www.vagabondinns.com.* 108 rooms, 3 story. S $73-$83; D $83-$93; each additional $5; under 17 free. Pets accepted, some restrictions. Complimentary continental breakfast. Check-out noon. TV; cable (premium). Free airport transportation.

Hotels

★ ★ ★ **DOUBLETREE HOTEL.** *2001 Point West Way (95815). Phone 916/929-8855; fax 916/924-4913. www.doubletree.com.* The comfortable guest rooms and suites are conveniently located just 6 miles from the California State Capitol. Across the street, the Arden Fair Mall features 160 stores. 448 rooms, 4 story. S, D $119-$199; each additional $15; suites $200-$500; under 18 free. Pets accepted, some restrictions; fee. Check-out noon. TV; cable (premium), VCR available. In-room modem link. Restaurant, bar. Room service. Health club privileges. In-house fitness room. Pool; whirlpool; poolside service. Free airport, train station, bus depot transportation. Business center.

★ **LA QUINTA INN.** *200 Jibboom St (95814). Phone 916/448-8100; toll-free 800/531-5900; fax 916/447-3621. www.laquintainn.com.* 165 rooms, 3 story. Pets accepted. Complimentary continental breakfast. Check-out noon, check-in 3 pm. TV; cable (premium). In-room modem link. Guest laundry. In-house fitness room. Pool. Free airport transportation. On Sacramento River. **$**

★ ★ ★ **RADISSON HOTEL SACRAMENTO.** *500 Leisure Ln (95814). Phone 916/922-2020; toll-free 800/333-3333; fax 916/649-9463. www.radissonsac.com.* This hotel's unique resort surroundings offers guests a varied choice of diversions: a lakeside pool and spa, rental paddle boats for the lake, a 35-mile trail for jogging or bicycling along the American River, and a scenic "par" course, complete with a complimentary health drink. A courtesy shuttle service is available to surrounding areas. The 21,000-square-foot trade show area includes a 16,000-square-foot ballroom, the largest hotel ballroom in Sacramento. 307 rooms, 2 story. S, D $69-$129; each additional $10; suites $159-$448; under 18 free; weekend rates. Pets accepted; fee. Check-out noon. TV; VCR available. Restaurant, bar; entertainment. Room service 24 hours. In-house fitness room. Pool; whirlpool; poolside service. Business center. Concierge.

All Suite

★ ★ **HAWTHORN SUITES.** *321 Bercut Dr (95814). Phone 916/441-1200; toll-free 800/767-1777; fax 916/444-2347. www.hawthorn.com.* 272 suites, 3 story. Pets accepted, some restrictions; fee. Complimentary full breakfast. Check-out noon, check-in 3 pm. TV; cable (premium), VCR available. Restaurant, bar. Room service. In-house fitness room. Health club privileges. Outdoor pool; whirlpool. Free transportation. **$$**

St. Helena

Motel/Motor Lodge

★ **EL BONITA.** *195 Main St (94574). Phone 707/963-3216; toll-free 800/541-3284; fax 707/963-8838. www.elbonita.com.* 41 rooms, 3 suites. June-Oct: S, D $159-$185; suites $199-$279; each additional $8; lower rates rest of year. Pets accepted; fee. Complimentary continental breakfast. Check-out 11:30 am. TV; cable (premium). Restaurant nearby. Sauna. Pool; whirlpool.

B&B/Small Inn

★ ★ ★ **HARVEST INN.** *1 Main St (94574). Phone 707/963-9463; toll-free 800/950-8466; fax 707/963-4402. www.harvestinn.com.* This renaissance of courtly English Tudor architecture is nestled among 8 acres of landscape and is reminiscent of the country gentry style. Even the meeting space at Harvest Inn has country inn charm. Hot air ballooning, gliding, Calistoga mud baths, and winery tours are nearby. 57 rooms, 1-2 story. Apr-Oct: S, D $240-$470; suites $550-$675; weekends (2-day minimum); lower rates rest of year. Pets accepted, some restrictions; fee. Complimentary continental breakfast. Check-out 11 am, check-in after 4 pm. TV; VCR available (movies). In-room modem link. Fireplaces. Room service. Pool; whirlpool. Concierge. Overlooks vineyards.

San Bernardino

Motel/Motor Lodge

★ **LA QUINTA INN.** *205 E Hospitality Ln (92408). Phone 909/888-7571; toll-free 800/687-6667; fax 909/884-3864. www.laquinta.com.* 153 rooms, 3 story. S $65-$70; D $95-$120; suites $120-$150; each additional $8; under 18 free. Pets accepted, some restrictions. Complimentary continental breakfast. Check-out noon. TV; cable (premium). Health club privileges. Pool.

San Clemente

Hotel

★ ★ **HOLIDAY INN.** *111 S Ave De La Estrella (92672). Phone 949/361-3000; toll-free 800/469-1161; fax 949/361-2472. www.holidayinnsanclementeresort.com.* 72 rooms, 3 story. Pets accepted; fee. Check-out noon, check-in 3 pm. TV; cable (premium), VCR available. In-room modem link. Restaurant. Room service. Outdoor pool; whirlpool. $$

San Diego

Motels/Motor Lodges

★ **LA QUINTA INN.** *10185 Paseo Montril (92129). Phone 858/484-8800; toll-free 800/684-6667; fax 858/538-0476. www.lq.com.* 120 rooms, 4 story. Pets accepted. Complimentary continental breakfast. Check-out noon, check-in 2 pm. TV; cable (premium). In-room modem link. Outdoor pool. $

★ **OLD TOWN INN.** *4444 Pacific Hwy (92110). Phone 619/260-8024; toll-free 800/643-3025; fax 619/296-0524. www.oldtown-inn.com.* 74 rooms, 1-3 story. Pets accepted, some restrictions; fee. Complimentary continental breakfast. Check-out 11 am. Check-in 3 pm. TV; cable (premium). Outdoor pool. $

Hotels

★ ★ **DOUBLETREE HOTEL.** *7450 Hazard Center Dr (92108). Phone 619/297-5466; fax 619/688-4088. www.doubletreesandiego.com.* Located in the heart of San Diego, this comfortable hotel offers guests a place to relax and enjoy nearby attractions like the San Diego Zoo, SeaWorld, and Mission Valley's premier shopping district. 300 rooms, 8 suites, 11 story. Pets accepted, some restrictions; fee. Check-out noon, check-in 3 pm. TV; cable (premium). In-room modem link. Laundry services. Restaurant, bar; entertainment. Room service. Babysitting services available. In-house fitness room; sauna. Indoor pool; outdoor pool; whirlpool. Outdoor tennis, lighted courts. Garage, valet parking. Luxury level. $

★ ★ **HOLIDAY INN.** *1355 N Harbor Dr (92101). Phone 619/232-3861; toll-free 800/877-8920; fax 619/235-4924. www.holidayinn.com.* 602 rooms, 14 story. Pets accepted, some restrictions; fee. Check-out noon, check-in 3 pm. TV; cable (premium). In-room modem link. Restaurant. In-house fitness room. Outdoor pool; whirlpool. Parking. Business center. Many bay view rooms. Cruise ship terminal opposite. Outside glass-enclosed elevator. Free transportation. $

★ ★ **HORTON GRAND HOTEL.** *311 Island Ave (92101). Phone 619/544-1886; toll-free 800/542-1886; fax 619/239-3823. www.hortongrand.com.* 132 rooms, 4 story. Pets accepted, some restrictions; fee. Check-out noon, check-in 3 pm. TV. Fireplaces. Restaurant, bar. Valet parking. Airport transportation. Victorian building; built 1886. Oldest building in San Diego. Skylight in lobby; bird cages. $$

★ ★ ★ **MARRIOTT SAN DIEGO HOTEL AND MARINA.** *333 W Harbor Dr (92101). Phone 619/234-1500; toll-free 800/228-9290; fax 619/234-8678. www.sdmarriott.com.* Situated on the bay in downtown San Diego, adjoining the Convention Center and Seaport Village, this hotel is perfect for both business and leisure travelers. It is seven minutes from the San Diego Lindbergh International Airport and within walking distance of major shops. 1,358 rooms, 25 story. Pets accepted. Check-out noon, check-in 3 pm. TV; cable (premium). In-room modem link. Restaurant, bar; entertainment. Room service 24 hours. Babysitting services available. In-house fitness room; sauna, steam room. Game room. Outdoor pool; whirlpool. Outdoor tennis, lighted courts. Bayside; marina. Valet parking. Business center. Concierge. Luxury level. Large chandeliers in lobby. $$$

★ ★ ★ **MARRIOTT SAN DIEGO MISSION VALLEY.** *8757 Rio San Diego Dr (92108). Phone 619/692-3800; toll-free 800/842-5329; fax 619/692-0769. www.marriott.com/marriott.sanmv.* 352 rooms, 5 suites, 17 story. Pets accepted, some restrictions; fee. Check-out 11 am, check-in 4 pm. TV; cable (premium), VCR available. In-room modem link. Laundry services. Restaurant, bar. Room service. Sauna, steam room. Outdoor pool. Garage, valet parking. Business center. Luxury level. **$**

D ⊕ ⊷ ⊷ ⊀ ⊷ ✕ ⊀

★ ★ **RADISSON HOTEL.** *1433 Camino Del Rio S (92108). Phone 619/260-0111; toll-free 800/333-3333; fax 619/497-0813. www.radisson.com/sandiegoca.* Located in the heart of beautiful San Diego and accessible to main attractions like the Mission Valley Mall and the San Diego Zoo, this hotel offers a relaxing and comfortable stay with luxurious guest rooms and superb service. 261 rooms, 15 suites, 12 story. Pets accepted, some restrictions; fee. Check-out noon, check-in 4 pm. TV; cable (premium), VCR available. In-room modem link. Laundry services. Restaurant, bar. Room service. Babysitting services available. In-house fitness room; health club privileges. Outdoor pool; whirlpool. Concierge. Luxury level. Free transportation. **$**

D ⊕ ⊷ ⊷ ⊀ ⊷ ✕ ⊷ SC

★ ★ **RED LION.** *2270 Hotel Circle N (92108). Phone 619/297-1101; toll-free 800/733-5466; fax 619/297-6049. www.redlion.com.* A family-oriented resort, this property is in the center of San Diego's Mission Valley, close to the Fashion Valley shopping center, SeaWorld, Old Town, and the San Diego Zoo. The gardens—with tropical flowers, palm trees, and ponds filled with koi—create an island setting. 416 rooms, 8 story. Pets accepted, some restrictions; fee. Check-out noon, check-in 3 pm. TV; cable (premium). In-room modem link. Restaurant, bar. Room service. Babysitting services available. In-house fitness room; massage, steam room. Outdoor pool; whirlpool. Parking. Business center. **$**

D ⊕ ⊷ ⊷ ⊷ ✕ ⊀

★ ★ **SHELTER POINTE HOTEL & MARINA.** *1551 Shelter Island Dr (92106). Phone 619/221-8000; toll-free 800/566-2524; fax 619/221-5953. www.shelterpointe.com.* 206 rooms, 32 suites, 5 kitchen units, 3 story. Pets accepted, some restrictions; fee. Check-out noon. Check-in 4 pm. TV; cable (premium). In-room modem link. In-house fitness room; massage, sauna. Outdoor pool; whirlpool. Outdoor tennis, lighted courts. Free airport transportation. Concierge. On bay. **$$**

D ⊕ ⊷ ⊷ ⊷ ⊷ ✕ ⊷

★ ★ ★ **SHERATON SUITES SAN DIEGO.** *701 A St (92101). Phone 619/696-9800; toll-free 800/962-1367; fax 619/696-1555. www.sheraton.com.* This hotel is located in downtown San Diego, minutes from the historic Gaslamp Quarter, the San Diego Convention Center, and San Diego's international airport. 264 suites, 27 story. Pets accepted; fee. Check-out noon, check-in 3 pm. TV; cable (premium). In-room modem link. Restaurant, bar. Room service 24 hours. Babysitting services available. In-house fitness room. Health club privileges. Indoor pool; whirlpool. Valet parking. Business center. Concierge. **$$**

D ⊕ ⊷ ⊷ ⊀ ⊷ ✕

Extended Stay

★ ★ **RESIDENCE INN BY MARRIOTT.** *5995 Pacific Mesa Ct (92121). Phone 858/552-9100; fax 858/552-9199. www.residenceinn.com.* 150 rooms, 3 story. D $139-$189. Pets accepted, some restrictions; fee. Complimentary buffet breakfast. Check-out noon, check-in 4 pm. TV; cable (premium). In-room modem link. Laundry services. In-house fitness room. Outdoor pool.

⊷ ⊷ ✕ ⊷

San Francisco

Motel/Motor Lodge

★ **PACIFIC HEIGHTS INN.** *1555 Union St (94123). Phone 415/776-3310; toll-free 800/523-1801; fax 415/776-8176. www.pacificheightsinn.com.* 40 rooms, 2 story. No A/C. Pets accepted; fee. Complimentary continental breakfast. Check-out noon, check-in 2 pm. TV. In-room modem link. **$**

⊷ ⊷

Hotels

★ **BERESFORD ARMS.** *701 Post St (94102). Phone 415/673-2600; toll-free 800/533-5349; fax 415/474-0449. www.beresford.com.* 95 rooms, 8 story. No A/C. Pets accepted. Complimentary continental breakfast. Check-out noon, check-in 3 pm. TV; VCR (movies). In-room modem link. Valet parking. **$**

D ⊷ ⊷ SC

★ ★ **BEST WESTERN TUSCAN INN AT FISHERMAN'S WHARF.** *425 Northpoint St (94133). Phone 415/561-1100; toll-free 800/648-4626; fax 415/561-1199. www.tuscaninn.com.* 221 rooms, 12 suites, 4 story. Pets accepted, some restrictions; fee. Check-out noon, check-in 3 pm. TV; cable (premium), VCR available. Fireplaces. Restaurant, bar. Room service. Babysitting services available. Valet parking. Concierge. European-style boutique hotel following the tradition of a classic inn. Three blocks from Pier 39. **$$**

D ⊷ ⊷ SC

★ ★ ★ **CAMPTON PLACE HOTEL.** *340 Stockton St (94108). Phone 415/781-5555; toll-free 800/235-4300; fax 415/955-5536. www.camptonplace.com.* Just steps from the upscale shopping of bustling Union Square, Campton Place maintains an intimacy and a blissful quietude unlike other hotels. With just 110 guest rooms, this intimate hotel makes guests feel at home with attentive service and thoughtful touches. Luxury is in the details here. The accommodations are casually elegant, employing shades of terracotta and cream alongside polished wood furnishings. Attractive artwork adorns the walls of each room, enhancing the residential ambience of the hotel. Campton Place's dedication to excellence is evident at the restaurant, considered one of San Francisco's top tables. A native of the Gascony and Basque regions of France, the chef dazzles diners with his sinfully delicious French country meals. 110 rooms, 17 story. Pets accepted; fee. Check-out noon, check-in 3 pm. TV; VCR available (movies). In-room modem link. Room service 24 hours. Restaurant, bar. Babysitting services available. In-house fitness room. Valet parking. Concierge. **$$$$**

⊡ 🐾 🏄 ⊠

★ ★ **CLARION HOTEL.** *761 Post St (94109). Phone 415/673-6040; toll-free 800/794-6011; fax 415/563-6739. www.hotel-cosmo.com.* Most rooms have expansive city views. 144 rooms, 17 story. No A/C. Pets accepted, some restrictions. Check-out noon, check-in 3 pm. TV; cable. Restaurant, bar. In-room modem link. Babysitting services available. Valet parking. Complimentary transportation is available. **$**

🐾 SC

★ ★ ★ **CROWNE PLAZA.** *480 Sutter St (94108). Phone 415/398-8900; toll-free 800/2CROWNE; fax 415/989-8823. www.crowneplaza.com.* Centrally located in the heart of San Francisco. 403 rooms, 30 story. Pets accepted; fee. Check-out noon, check-in 3 pm. TV; cable (premium), VCR available. Restaurant, bar. Babysitting services available. In-house fitness room. Business center. **$$**

⊡ 🐾 🏄 ⊠ SC 🏃

★ ★ **DIVA HOTEL.** *440 Geary St (94102). Phone 415/885-0200; toll-free 800/553-1900; fax 415/346-6613. www.hoteldiva.com.* 114 rooms, 7 story. Pets accepted, some restrictions; fee. Complimentary continental breakfast. Check-out noon, check-in 2 pm. TV; cable (premium), VCR available. Restaurant. Room service. In-house fitness room. Valet parking. Business center. Concierge. **$$**

⊡ 🐾 🏄 ⊠ 🏃

★ ★ ★ ★ ★ **FOUR SEASONS HOTEL SAN FRANCISCO.** *757 Market St (94103). Phone 415/633-3000; fax 415/633-3001. www.fourseasons.com.* Occupying 12 levels of a residential tower, it's no wonder that the Four Seasons Hotel San Francisco feels so much like home. The hotel sparkles, from its floor-to-ceiling windows to its impressive art and sculpture collection. This showpiece of contemporary design is in a perfect location, with the shopping of Union Square only two blocks away and the Museum of Modern Art just around the bend. The guest rooms and suites are a wonderful blend of sophisticated city living and extra-luxurious amenities. Every detail has been considered in this stunning environment, even the strategically placed lights highlighting elegantly appointed floral arrangements throughout the lobby. In the guest rooms, large windows frame unparal-

leled views of San Francisco's lively streets or its glittering bay. A refined elegance pervades the Four Seasons, whether in the stunning lobby or the restaurant. The Sports Club/LA, adjacent to the hotel, takes a comprehensive approach to fitness with state-of the-art equipment and cutting-edge classes. The center's Splash is the city's premier day spa, attracting hotel guests and city dwellers alike. *Secret Inspector's Notes:* You'll feel like you have gone to heaven upon checking in to this hotel. All of the fabrics and amenities are the richest and most luxurious you'll find, but just wait: there's more. They take technology seriously here, as is evidenced in both the guest rooms and the business center. Also take note of the exquisite artifacts found throughout the hotel. 277 rooms, 10 story. Pets accepted, some restrictions. Check-out noon, check-in 3 pm. TV; cable (premium), VCR available. Restaurant, bar. Babysitting services available. In-house fitness room; spa. Indoor pool. Valet parking. Business center. **$$$**

⊡ 🐾 ⊿ 🏄 ⊠ 🏃

★ ★ **HARBOR COURT HOTEL.** *165 Stuart St (94105). Phone 415/882-1300; toll-free 800/346-0555; fax 415/882-1313. www.harborcourthotel.com.* 131 rooms, 8 story. Pets accepted. Check-out noon, check-in 3 pm. TV; cable (premium). In-room modem link. Restaurant. In-house fitness room; sauna. Indoor pool; whirlpool. Concierge. On waterfront. **$$**

⊡ 🐾 ⊿ 🏄 ⊠ SC

★ ★ **HOLIDAY INN.** *50 Eighth St (94103). Phone 415/626-6103; toll-free 800/243-1135; fax 415/552-0184. www.holiday-inn.com.* 394 rooms, 14 story. Pets accepted, some restrictions; fee. Check-out noon, check-in 3 pm. TV; cable (premium). In-room modem link. Restaurant, bar. Room service. Babysitting services available. In-house fitness room. Outdoor pool. Business center. **$**

⊡ 🐾 ⊿ 🏄 ⊠ 🏃

★ ★ **THE HOTEL JULIANA.** *590 Bush St (94108). Phone 866/325-9457; toll-free 888/242-7835; fax 415/986-2880. www.julianahotel.com.* 107 rooms, 9 story. Pets accepted, some restrictions. Check-out noon, check-in 3 pm. TV; cable (premium). In-room modem link. Babysitting services available. In-house fitness room. **$$**

⊡ 🐾 🏄

★ ★ ★ **HOTEL MONACO.** *501 Geary St (94102). Phone 415/292-0100; toll-free 800/214-4220; fax 415/292-0111. www.monaco-sf.com.* Bright colors, cheerful ambience, and a whimsical style greet visitors of this luxury hotel, housed in a remodeled Beaux Arts building that showcases a fanciful mural in the lobby. Guest rooms continue the theme of patterns and colors, from the walls to the canopied beds, with multi-hued headboards and bedding (courtesy of Frette). Complimentary amenities include morning coffee, afternoon tea, an evening wine reception, and a shoe shine. The Grand Café next door is worth a visit, as is the on-site, full-service spa. 235 rooms, 7 story. Pets accepted. Check-out noon, check-in 3 pm. TV; cable (premium), VCR available. In-room modem link. Restaurant, bar. Babysitting services available. In-house fitness room; spa, massage. Valet parking. Business center. Concierge. **$$**

D ⬛ ⬛ 🛏 ⬛ 🚶

★★★ **HOTEL NIKKO SAN FRANCISCO.** *222 Mason St (94102). Phone 415/394-1111; toll-free 800/ NIKKOUS; fax 415/394-1159. www.nikkohotels.com.* Situated between Union Square, the Theater District, and SoMa, this high-end hotel caters to international and business travelers. Despite its imposing size, the hotel achieves an understated harmony and serenity, in keeping with its Japanese influence. Notable features include the striking two-story lobby, which visitors enter via stairs, escalator, or elevator, and the 8-foot, hand-blown glass orange lamps. Extensive amenities include a fully staffed fitness center and spa, an indoor, atrium-style swimming pool, and a tanning cabana. The hotel's Anzu restaurant serves fabulous sushi and sake martinis. 532 rooms, 25 story. Pets accepted, some restrictions. Check-out noon, check-in 4 pm. TV; cable; VCR available. Room service 24 hours. Restaurant, bar. Babysitting services available. In-house fitness room; spa, sauna, steam room. Indoor pool; whirlpool; poolside service. Valet parking. Business center. Concierge. Luxury level. **$$$**

D ⬛ ⬛ 🛏 ⬛ 🚶

★★★ **HOTEL PALOMAR.** *12 Fourth St (94103). Phone 415/348-1111; toll-free 877/294-9711; fax 415/348-0302. www.hotelpalomar.com.* Hotel Palomar personifies sophisticated exuberance. Occupying the fifth through ninth floors of a historic building just off Union Square, this hotel captures the imagination of its guests with its eclectic style. Full of character, the hotel's playful décor is most evident in the guest rooms, where leopard-print carpets reside alongside cool furnishings and contemporary artwork. Residents of the one-of-a-kind Renee Magritte Suite sleep under a ceiling of blue sky and white clouds while enjoying prints of this modern master's work. Guests are properly cosseted in this joyous hotel, from business services and complimentary car service to pet-friendly policies and in-room spa services. Fifth Floor, with its modern French cuisine and dazzling décor and convivial scene, is one of downtown San Francisco's hippest dining establishments. 198 rooms, 5 story. Pets accepted, some restrictions. Check-out noon, check-in 3 pm. TV; cable (premium), VCR available, CD available. Restaurant, bar. Supervised children's activities. In-house fitness room. Valet parking. Concierge. **$$$**

D ⬛ 🛏 ⬛

★★ **HOTEL VINTAGE COURT.** *650 Bush St (94108). Phone 415/392-4666; toll-free 800/654-1100; fax 415/433-*

4065. www.vintagecourt.com. 107 rooms, 8 story. Pets accepted. Complimentary continental breakfast. Check-out noon, check-in 3 pm. TV; cable (premium), VCR available. In-room modem link. Restaurant. Babysitting services available. Valet parking. **$**

D ⬛ ⬛

★★★★ **MANDARIN ORIENTAL, SAN FRANCISCO.** *222 Sansome St (94104). Phone 415/276-9888; toll-free 800/622-0404; fax 415/433-0289. www.mandarinoriental.com.* Savvy travelers in search of the ultimate in skyscraper style head for the Mandarin Oriental, San Francisco. Occupying the top levels of the city's third tallest building, the Mandarin Oriental offers unsurpassed views of the lovely city by the bay. Situated in the heart of the downtown business district, the hotel is also a convenient base for exploring major attractions and sites. The guest rooms and suites are spacious and incorporate Asian decorative objects and furnishings, although it is the jaw-dropping views that attract most of the attention. All accommodations feature dazzling city or bay views, and binoculars are provided for better viewing opportunities. Guests are invited to dine on Pacific Rim cuisine at Silks or enjoy continental dishes at the Mandarin Lounge. 158 rooms, 13 story. Pets accepted, some restrictions; fee. Check-out noon, check-in 3 pm. TV; cable (premium), VCR available, CD available. In-room modem link. Room service 24 hours. Restaurant, bar; entertainment Mon-Sat. Babysitting services available. In-house fitness room; massage. Valet parking. Business center. Concierge. **$$$$**

D ⬛ 🛏 ⬛ ⬛ 🚶

★★★ **MARRIOTT FISHERMAN'S WHARF.** *1250 Columbus Ave (94133). Phone 415/775-7555; fax 415/771-9076. www.sfwmarriott.com.* Centrally located on Fisherman's Wharf and by Ghirardelli Square, Pier 39, and Underwater World, this hotel offers something for everyone. Guest rooms are well-appointed and spacious. 285 rooms, 5 story. Pets accepted, some restrictions; fee. Check-out noon, check-in 4 pm. TV; cable (premium), VCR available. In-room modem link. Restaurant, bar. Babysitting services available. In-house fitness room; sauna. Valet parking. Business center. Concierge. Marble floor in lobby. **$$**

D ⬛ 🛏 ⬛ SC 🚶

★★ **MONTICELLO INN.** *127 Ellis St (94102). Phone 415/392-8800; toll-free 800/669-7777; fax 415/598-2650. www.monticelloinn.com.* Built in 1906, this inn maintains its charming historic elegance while providing modern amenities and superb service. With all of the personal touches of home, guests can enjoy the extensive library and serene atmosphere. 91 rooms, 28 suites, 5 story. Pets accepted, some restrictions. Check-out noon, check-in 3 pm. TV; cable (premium). In-room modem link. Restaurant, bar. Valet parking. Concierge. 18th-century décor. **$$**

D 🐾 ≈ SC

★ ★ ★ **OMNI SAN FRANCISCO HOTEL.** *500 California St (94104). Phone 415/677-9494; toll-free 800/788-6664; fax 415/677-4108. www.omnisanfrancisco.com.* 362 rooms, 17 story. Pets accepted, some restrictions; fee. Check-out noon, check-in 3 pm. TV; cable (premium), VCR (movies). In-room modem link. Room service 24 hours. Restaurant, bar. Babysitting services available. In-house fitness room. Valet parking. Business center. Concierge. **$$**

D 🐾 🏃 ≈ 🚶

★ ★ ★ **PAN PACIFIC SAN FRANCISCO HOTEL.** *500 Post St (94102). Phone 415/771-8600; toll-free 800/533-6465; fax 415/398-0267. www.panpacific.com.* Located on fashionable Post Street in Union Square, this hotel is one of only two US outposts of its luxury Pacific Rim chain. The architecture and design of the public spaces and 329 rooms and suites is Asian-inspired. The penthouse-level terrace is the highlight of the 14,000 square feet of meeting space with its panoramic views of the Bay. 329 rooms, 21 story. Pets accepted, some restrictions; fee. Check-out noon, check-in 3 pm. TV; cable (premium), VCR available. In-room modem link. Room service 24 hours. Restaurant. Bar. Babysitting services available. In-house fitness room. Valet parking. Business center. Concierge. **$$**

D 🐾 🏃 ≈ 🚶

★ ★ ★ **PRESCOTT HOTEL.** *545 Post St (94102). Phone 415/563-0303; toll-free 800/624-4657; fax 415/563-6831. www.prescotthotel.com.* Smack in the middle of Union Square shopping, the Prescott Hotel has undergone a thorough renovation in recent years. Guest rooms are not large, but they are comfortable, with hardwood floors and Ralph Lauren décor of coordinating fabrics; baths come stocked with Aveda shampoos and other amenities. The private, inviting club-level lounge comes equipped with a personal concierge, an evening bar service, and other extras. The adjoining Postrio restaurant is part of the famed, though no longer quite as trendy, Wolfgang Puck empire. 164 rooms, 7 story. Pets accepted. Complimentary breakfast. Check-out noon, check-in 3 pm. TV; VCR available. In-room modem link. Room service. Restaurant. Dining room. Bar. Babysitting services available. In-house fitness room. Pool privileges. Concierge. Luxury level. **$$$**

D 🐾 ≈ 🏃 ≈ SC

★ ★ ★ **RENAISSANCE STANFORD COURT HOTEL.** *905 California St (94108). Phone 415/989-3500; toll-free 800/227-4736; fax 415/391-0513. www.renaissancehotels.com.* Located on San Francisco's most prestigious Nob Hill, this grand hotel pampers their guests with elegance and superb service. From the amazing lobby dome

of Tiffany-style stained glass to the Beaux Arts fountain, there is elegance and a quality of service that makes it truly extraordinary. 393 rooms, 8 story. Pets accepted, some restrictions. Check-out noon, check-in 3 pm. TV; cable (premium). In-room modem link. Restaurant, bar. Room service. In-house fitness room; massage. Health club privileges. Valet parking. Business center. Concierge. **$$**

D 🐾 🏃 ≈ 🚶

★ ★ ★ **SERRANO HOTEL.** *405 Taylor St (94102). Phone 415/885-2500; fax 415/351-7654. www.serranohotel.com.* Spanish-revival architecture fused with eclectic furnishings sets this elegant hotel apart. This hotel provides personalized service amidst a sophisticated setting. 236 rooms. Pets accepted. Check-out noon, check-in 3 pm. TV; cable (premium). Restaurant, bar. Babysitting services available. In-house fitness room; spa. Business center. **$$**

D 🐾 🏃 ≈ 🚶

★ ★ ★ **THE WESTIN ST. FRANCIS.** *335 Powell St (94102). Phone 415/397-7000; fax 415/774-0124. www.westin.com.* A luxurious landmark overlooking Union Square, The Westin St. Francis proudly displays its rich heritage while injecting modernity into its historic building. Reminiscent of a palace, the two-level lobby makes a grand statement with its stately columns, sweeping staircase, and gilded details. The accommodations redefine elegance with dark woods, jewel tones, and regal furnishings. Handsome and classic, the guest rooms have been updated with state-of-the-art technology, and terrific city views delight visitors. Great care is taken to ensure the comfort and convenience of all guests, with business and fitness facilities, airline ticket windows, and rental car counters located within the hotel. Noted for its frozen vodka martini and caviar cart, Compass Rose has an inviting setting complemented by nightly live entertainment. The Oak Room is a more casual alternative, while Caruso's Coffee Bar is perfect for those on the go. 1,195 rooms, 32 story. Pets accepted, some restrictions; fee. Valet parking. Check-out noon, check-in 3 pm. TV; cable (premium), VCR available. Room service 24 hours. Restaurant, bar. Babysitting services available. In-house fitness room; spa, steam room. Business center. Concierge. **$$**

D 🐾 🏃 ≈ 🚶

★ ★ ★ **W SAN FRANCISCO.** *181 Third St (94103). Phone 415/777-5300; fax 415/817-7823. www.whotels.com.* Another chic spot in this national chain's list of hotels geared to meet the ever-increasing demands of tech-savvy business clientele. In the South of Market district and adjacent to the Museum of Modern Art, the stylishly modern rooms all contain a signature "heavenly bed." The eclectic and aptly named restaurant, XYZ, finishes off the dramatic three-story lobby. 423 rooms, 31 story.

Pets accepted; fee. Check-out noon, check-in 3 pm. TV; cable (premium), VCR available. In-room modem link. Restaurant, bar. Room service. Babysitting services available. In-house fitness room; massage. Indoor pool; whirlpool. Valet parking. Business center. Concierge. **$$$$**

⬚⬚⬚⬚⬚

B&B/Small Inns

★ ★ ★ **INN SAN FRANCISCO.** *943 S Van Ness Ave (94110). Phone 415/641-0188; toll-free 800/359-0913; fax 415/641-1701. www.innsf.com.* Built in 1872 and known as one of San Francisco's most exquisite bed-and-breakfast inns, this mansion offers an unsurpassed ambience and serene elegance. The guest rooms are all lovingly appointed with fresh flowers and antique furnishings. Step outside and enjoy the gazebo while surrounded by an enchanting English garden. 21 rooms, 2 story. Pets accepted, some restrictions. Complimentary breakfast. Check-out noon, check-in 2 pm. TV; cable (premium), VCR available. Fireplaces. Whirlpool. Limited parking available. **$$**

⬚⬚

★ ★ ★ **THE SHERMAN HOUSE.** *2160 Green St (94123). Phone 415/563-3600; toll-free 800/424-5777; fax 415/563-1882. www.theshermanhouse.com.* Numerous magazines, from *Architectural Digest* to *Condé Nast Traveler,* have featured this historic 1876 Pacific Heights mansion, and it's no wonder. A luxury hotel since the 1970s, the 14 rooms here have individual décor, but all boast upholstered walls, fireplaces, canopy beds with down comforters, and black granite bathtubs. French-California cuisine is served in the guests-only dining room. Located a block away from shopping on popular Union Street, the "intimate grand" hotel also boasts views of the bay from the back garden. 14 rooms, 3 story. No elevator. Pets accepted, some restrictions. Check-out noon, check-in 4 pm. TV; cable (premium), VCR available, CD available. In-room modem link. Many fireplaces. Dining room (by reservation) 5:30-9 pm. Room service 24 hours. Free valet parking. Concierge service. Butler service. Totally nonsmoking. **$$$**

⬚⬚⬚

★ ★ ★ **WASHINGTON SQUARE INN.** *1660 Stockton St (94133). Phone 415/981-4220; toll-free 800/388-0220; fax 415/397-7242. www.washingtonsquareinnsf.com.* 15 rooms, 2 story. No A/C. Pets accepted, some restrictions. Complimentary continental breakfast. Check-out noon, check-in 3 pm. TV; VCR available. In-room modem link. Valet parking. Concierge. Opposite historic Washington Square. Totally nonsmoking. **$$**

⬚⬚

San Francisco Airport Area

Hotels

★ ★ ★ **MARRIOTT SAN FRANCISCO AIRPORT.** *1800 Old Bayshore Hwy (94010). Phone 650/692-9100; toll-free 800/228-9290; fax 650/692-8016. www.marriott.com/sfobg.* Perched along the waterfront, this hotel is just 1 mile south of the airport and convenient to the city and Silicon Valley. There is a lounge with a great view of the bay and several dining options. 685 rooms, 22 suites, 11 story. S, D $79-$239; suites $269-$399; under 18 free; weekend, weekly rates. Restaurant. Pets accepted. Check-out noon. TV; cable (premium), VCR available. In-room modem link. Bar; piano bar. Room service to midnight (weekends to 1 am). Health club privileges. In-house fitness room; sauna. Heated indoor pool; whirlpool; poolside service. Valet parking. Free airport transportation. Concierge. Luxury level.

⬚⬚⬚⬚⬚⬚

★ ★ ★ **THE WESTIN SAN FRANCISCO AIRPORT.** *1 Old Bayshore Hwy (94030). Phone 650/692-3500; toll-free 800/228-3000; fax 650/872-8111. www.westin.com.* Travelers will find this hotel's location very convenient; only 25 minutes from downtown San Francisco and five minutes from the airport. 393 rooms, 7 story. S, D $119-$349; each additional $20; suites $550-$600; under 18 free; weekend rates. Pets accepted; fee. Check-out 1 pm. TV; cable (premium), VCR available. In-room modem link. Room service 24 hours. Restaurant, bar; entertainment. In-house fitness room. Indoor pool; whirlpool; poolside service. Valet parking. Free airport transportation. Business center. Concierge.

⬚⬚⬚⬚⬚⬚⬚⬚

San Jose

Hotels

★ ★ ★ **DOUBLETREE HOTEL.** *2050 Gateway Pl (95110). Phone 408/453-4000; fax 408/437-2899. www.doubletree.com.* Set in a contemporary architectural design featuring two high-rise towers, this pleasant hotel is located in the heart of the Silicon Valley and features spacious guest rooms. 505 rooms, 10 story. S, D $89-$259; each additional $20; suites $695-$895; under 17 free; weekend rates. Pets accepted, some restrictions; fee. Check-out noon. TV; cable (premium), VCR available. In-room modem link. Laundry services. Room service 24 hours. Restaurant, bar; entertainment. In-house fitness room; sauna. Pool. Parking, valet parking. Free airport transportation. Business center. Concierge. Luxury level.

⊡ ⬛ ⬛ ⬛ ⬛ ⬛ ⬛

★ ★ ★ **THE FAIRMONT SAN JOSE.** *170 S Market St (95113). Phone 408/998-1900; toll-free 800/866-5577; fax 408/995-5037. www.fairmont.com.* The 20-story twin-tower complex of The Fairmont San Jose is a perfect match for its location in the heart of Silicon Valley, the nerve center of the computer industry. The hotel provides its guests with the best. Cream and pastel tones create a light, breezy décor synonymous with California's relaxed style. Spacious and comfortable, the accommodations are a welcome respite from the hustle and bustle of the city. Business travelers seek the services of the well-equipped business center, while others head for the fitness center and spa to work off the pressures of the day. From The Grill on the Alley's steaks and seafood and the Fountain Restaurant's traditional American menu to the sophisti-cated Chinese dishes of Pagoda, the hotel's three restau-rants offer something for everyone. 805 rooms, 20 story. S, D $140-$359; each additional $25; suites $329-$1,800; holiday plans. Pets accepted, some restrictions; fee. Covered parking. Check-out 1 pm. TV; cable (premium). In-room modem link. Restaurant 6:30 am-10:30 pm; Fri, Sat to 11 pm. Bar 11-1:30 am; entertainment. Room service 24 hours. In-house fitness room; massage, sauna, steam room. Heated pool; poolside service. Business cen-ter. Concierge service.

⊡ ⬛ ⬛ ⬛ ⬛ ⬛ ⬛

★ ★ ★ **HILTON SAN JOSE AND TOWERS.** *300 Almaden Blvd (95110). Phone 408/287-2100; fax 408/947-4489.* Perfect for business or pleasure, this hotel offers an extensive array of services in the beautiful downtown area of San Jose. It is connected directly with the McEnery Convention Center and only 3 miles from the San Jose International Airport. 355 rooms, 16 story. S $119-$259; D $134-$274; each additional $15; suites $395; under 18 free; weekend rates. Pets accepted, some restrictions. Check-out noon. TV; cable (premium). In-room modem link. Laundry services. Restaurant, bar. In-house fitness room; massage. Heated pool; whirlpool; poolside service. Valet, garage parking. Business center. Concierge. Luxury level.

⊡ ⬛ ⬛ ⬛ ⬛ ⬛ ⬛ ⬛

All Suite

★ ★ ★ **SUMMERFIELD SUITES.** *1602 Crane Ct (95112). Phone 408/436-1600; fax 408/436-1075. www.wyndham.com.* Located 1 mile from the San Jose International Airport and just minutes from Valley Fair Mall and Great America, this hotel provides for a com-fortable stay. 98 kitchen units, 2-3 story. S, D $209-$259.

Pets accepted, some restrictions; fee. Complimentary con-tinental breakfast. Check-out noon. TV; cable (premium), VCR (movies). Laundry services. Health club privileges. In-house fitness room. Pool; whirlpool. Free airport transportation.

⬛ ⬛ ⬛ ⬛

Extended Stay

★ ★ **RESIDENCE INN BY MARRIOTT.** *2761 S Bascom Ave (95008). Phone 408/559-1551; toll-free 800/331-3131; fax 408/371-9808. www.residenceinn.com/sjcba.* 80 kitchen units, 2 story. Suites $169-$189. Pets accepted; fee. Complimentary continental breakfast. Check-out noon. TV; cable (premium). Laundry services. Health club privileges. Pool; whirlpool. Free airport transportation.

⊡ ⬛ ⬛ ⬛ ⬛ SC

San Juan Capistrano

Motel/Motor Lodge

★ **BEST WESTERN CAPISTRANO INN.** *27174 Ortega Hwy (92675). Phone 949/493-5661; toll-free 800/441-9438; fax 949/661-8293. www.bestwestern.com.* 108 rooms, 2 story. Mar-Sept: S, D $109-$89; each additional $6; kitchen units $89-$109; under 12 free; lower rates rest of year. Pets accepted; fee. Check-out noon. TV; cable (premium), VCR available. In-room modem link. Health club privileges. Pool; whirlpool.

⊡ ⬛ ⬛ ⬛ ⬛

San Luis Obispo

Motels/Motor Lodges

★ ★ **BEST WESTERN ROYAL OAK HOTEL.** *214 Madonna Rd (93405). Phone 805/544-4410; toll-free 800/545-4410; fax 805/544-3026. www.bestwestern.com.* 99 rooms, 2 story. May-mid-Nov: S, D $69-$99; each addi-tional $7; under 12 free; higher rates: special events, some holidays; lower rates rest of year. Pets accepted, some restric-tions; fee. Complimentary continental breakfast. Check-out noon. TV; cable (premium). In-room modem link. Laundry services. Restaurant. Room service. Pool; whirlpool.

⊡ ⬛ ⬛ ⬛ SC

★ ★ ★ **SANDS SUITES & MOTEL.** *1930 Monterey St (93401). Phone 805/544-0500; toll-free 800/441-4657; fax 805/544-3529. www.sandsuites.com.* 70 rooms, 1-2 story. May-Sept: S $59-$79; D $69-$89; each additional $7; suites $69-$139; under 12 free; higher rates: special events, holidays; lower rates rest of year. Pets accepted; fee. Complimentary continental breakfast. Check-out 11 am. TV; VCR (free movies). In-room modem link. Laundry services. Pool; whirlpool. Free airport, train station, bus depot transportation.

San Pedro

Hotel

★ ★ ★ **HILTON PORT OF LOS ANGELES.** *2800 Via Cabrillo Marina (90731). Phone 310/514-3344; toll-free 800/HILTONS; fax 310/514-8945. www.portoflosangeles sanpedro.hilton.com.* Just 19 miles from LAX and 6 miles from downtown Long Beach, this newly remodeled hotel overlooks Cabrillo Marina and is convenient to the World Cruise Center and Catalina Island. 226 rooms, 3 story. Pets accepted; fee. Check-out noon, check-in 3 pm. TV; cable (premium). Restaurant, bar. In-house fitness room; sauna. Outdoor pool; whirlpool. Lighted tennis. On marina. Free parking. Business center. **$$**

San Rafael

Hotel

★ ★ **FOUR POINTS BY SHERATON.** *1010 Northgate Dr (94903). Phone 415/479-8800; fax 415/755-6160. www.fourpoints.com/sanrafael.* 235 rooms, 4 story. Pets accepted. Check-out noon, check-in 3 pm. TV; cable (premium). In-room modem link. Restaurant, bar. Room service. Babysitting services available. In-house fitness room. Outdoor pool; whirlpool. **$**

B&B/Small Inn

★ ★ ★ **GERSTLE PARK INN.** *34 Grove St (94901). Phone 415/721-7611; toll-free 800/726-7611; fax 415/721-7600. www.gerstleparkinn.com.* This century-old estate, nestled in the foothills of San Rafael, re-opened in December 1995 as an elegant inn. 12 rooms. No A/C. Pets accepted, some restrictions. Complimentary full breakfast. Check-out noon, check-in 3 pm. TV. In-room modem link. Concierge service. Built in 1895. Some in-room Jacuzzis. Totally nonsmoking. **$$**

San Simeon

Motel/Motor Lodge

★ ★ **BEST WESTERN CAVALIER OCEANFRONT RESORT.** *9415 Hearst Dr (93452). Phone 805/927-4688; toll-free 800/826-8168; fax 805/927-6472. www.cavalierresort.com.* 90 rooms, 2 story. No A/C. May-Oct: S, D $109-$259; each additional $6; lower rates rest of year. Pets accepted. Check-out noon. TV; cable (premium), VCR available. In-room modem link. Fireplaces. Restaurant, bar. Room service. In-house fitness room. Pool; whirlpool.

Santa Barbara

Resorts

★ ★ ★ ★ **BACARA RESORT & SPA.** *8301 Hollister Ave (93117). Phone 805/968-0100; fax 805/968-1800. www.bacararesort.com.* Bacara Resort & Spa, with its spectacular setting and a dash of old-time Hollywood glamour, is a jetsetter's fantasy. This resort sparkles from its majestic location atop a bluff overlooking the Pacific Ocean. It is truly a delight for the senses, with its magnificent stretch of beach, three infinity-edge pools, and romantic Spanish colonial architecture. Rustic tiles set a relaxed elegance in the accommodations, where luxurious amenities are de rigueur. Fresh sea breezes attest to the notion that serenity is paramount here, and the spectacular spa is no exception. From citrus avocado body polishes to earth crystal therapies, this spa is sublime. Guests adopt a healthy lifestyle while staying here; golf, tennis, yoga, and meditation are just some of their passions. Mediterranean flavors and feeling mingle at The Bistro; Miro amazes with its Californian cuisine; and the Spa Café breathes new life into healthy eating. 360 rooms, 4 story. Pets accepted, some restrictions; fee. Check-out noon, check-in 4 pm. TV; cable (premium), VCR available. In-room modem link. Fireplaces. Room service 24 hours. Restaurant, bar. Children's activity center, babysitting services available. In-house fitness room; spa; massage. Outdoor pool; whirlpool. Golf. Lighted tennis. Business center. Concierge. **$$$$**

★ ★ ★ **DOUBLETREE HOTEL.** *633 E Cabrillo Blvd (93103). Phone 805/564-4333; toll-free 800/879-2929; fax 805/564-4964. www.doubletree.com.* This resort's 360 guest rooms and suites are dispersed among the property's expansive gardens and courtyards, which are the setting of many a fairy tale wedding. Service is attentive, and dog lovers appreciate the resort's pet-friendly policy. 360 rooms, 3 story. Pets accepted, some restrictions. Check-out 11 am, check-in 4 pm. TV; cable (premium), VCR available (free movies). In-room modem link. Room service 24 hours. Restaurant, bar; entertainment. Seasonal children's activity center. In-house fitness room; spa; massage. Game room. Outdoor pool; whirlpool; poolside service. Lighted courts. Lawn games. Valet parking. Free airport transportation. Concierge. **$$**

★ ★ ★ ★ **FOUR SEASONS RESORT SANTA BARBARA.** *1260 Channel Dr (93108). Phone 805/ 969-2261; toll-free 800/332-3442; fax 805/565-8323. www.fourseasons.com.* Perfectly situated on 20 lush acres facing the Pacific Ocean, the Four Seasons Resort Santa Barbara is a veritable Eden. Nicknamed "America's Riviera" because of its temperate climate and golden beaches, Santa Barbara offers a wonderful getaway. The resort pays tribute to the region's Spanish colonial history with its red-tiled roof and arches in the hacienda-style main building. The guest rooms, located in the main building and also in separate cottages, are warm and inviting retreats imbued with international design influences and local flavor. Crisp white cabanas line the sparkling pool of this full-service resort, where the beach is only steps away and the spa is a sybarite's fantasy. The lovely garden setting of the Patio is matched by its delicious Mediterranean and Pacific Rim cuisine, while La Marina is a visual and culinary wonder with dramatic ocean views and artful regional dishes. 213 rooms, 2 story. Pets accepted, some restrictions. Valet parking. Check-out 1 pm, check-in 4 pm. TV; cable (premium), VCR available. In-room modem link. Laundry services. Room service 24 hours. Restaurant, bar; entertainment. Children's activity center, babysitting services available. In-house fitness room; spa, massage, sauna. Pool; whirlpool; poolside service. Lighted tennis. Lawn games. Bicycles. Business center. Concierge. **$$$$**

★ ★ ★ **SAN YSIDRO RANCH.** *900 San Ysidro Ln (93108). Phone 805/969-5046; toll-free 800/368-6788; fax 805/565-1995. www.sanysidroranch.com.* Cottages and guest rooms nestle into the Montecito hillside overlooking picturesque Santa Barbara. Originally a way station for Franciscan monks in the 1760s, the resort is homey and quiet. 38 rooms. Pets accepted; fee. Check-out noon, check-in 3 pm. TV; cable (premium), VCR (movies). In-room modem link. Fireplaces. Room service 24 hours. Dining room, bar; entertainment. In-house fitness room; massage. Outdoor pool; children's pool; poolside service.

Outdoor tennis. Lawn games. 550 acres in the mountains. Summer activities. **$$$$**

All Suite

★ ★ **PACIFICA SUITES.** *5490 Hollister Ave (93111). Phone 805/683-6722; toll-free 800/338-6722; fax 805/683-4121. www.pacificasuites.com.* Winding pathways connect guest rooms with the lobby and the adjacent Sexton House, an exquisitely restored 1880s landmark that houses four elegant conference rooms. 87 suites, 2 story. Pets accepted, some restrictions; fee. Complimentary continental breakfast. Check-out noon, check-in 3 pm. TV; VCR available. In-room modem link. Health club privileges. Outdoor pool; whirlpool. Free airport transportation. **$**

B&B/Small Inns

★ ★ **CASA DEL MAR.** *18 Bath St (93101). Phone 805/963-4418; toll-free 800/433-3097; fax 805/966-4240. www.casadelmar.com.* 21 rooms, some kitchen units, 2 story. Pets accepted, some restrictions; fee. Complimentary continental breakfast. Check-out noon, check-in 3 pm. TV. In-room modem link. Whirlpool. **$**

★ ★ **OLD YACHT CLUB INN.** *431 Corona Del Mar Dr (93103). Phone 805/962-1277; toll-free 800/676-1676; fax 805/962-3989. www.oldyachtclubinn.com.* 14 rooms, 2 story. No A/C. Pets accepted, some restrictions; fee. Check-out 11 am, check-in 3-7 pm. Bicycles. Totally nonsmoking. **$$**

Santa Clara

Motels/Motor Lodges

★ **GUESTHOUSE INTERNATIONAL.** *2930 El Camino Real (95051). Phone 408/241-3010; toll-free 800/334-3928; fax 408/247-0623. www.guesthouse.net.* 16 kitchen units, 2 story. S $89-$200; D $99-$200; each additional $10; kitchen units $149-$250; under 17 free. Pets accepted; fee. Complimentary continental breakfast. Check-out 11:30 am. TV; VCR available. In-room modem link. Pool.

★ **VAGABOND INN.** *3580 El Camino Real (95051). Phone 408/241-0771; toll-free 800/522-1555; fax 408/247-3386. www.staynight.com/vagabondsc.* 70 rooms, 2 story.

S, D $109-$139; each additional $5; under 18 free. Pets accepted, some restrictions; fee. Complimentary continental breakfast. Check-out noon. TV; cable (premium). In-room modem link. Laundry services. Pool.

⬛⬛⬛⬛

Hotels

★ ★ ★ **MARRIOTT SANTA CLARA-SILICON VALLEY.** *2700 Mission College Blvd (95054). Phone 408/988-1500; toll-free 800/228-9290; fax 408/727-4353. www.marriott.com.* This hotel is located close to many of Silicon Valley's major technology corporations. In addition to the nearby Santa Clara Convention Center and San Jose McEnery Convention Center, the hotel has 23,000 square feet of its own meeting space. 755 rooms, 15 story. S, D $89-$239; suites $500-$1,200; under 18 free; weekend plans. Pets accepted; fee. Check-out noon. TV; cable (premium), VCR available. In-room modem link. Laundry services. Restaurant, bar. Room service. In-house fitness room; massage. Pool; whirlpool; poolside service. Outdoor tennis, lighted courts. Valet parking. Airport transportation. Business center. Concierge. Luxury level.

⬛⬛⬛⬛⬛⬛⬛⬛

★ ★ ★ **THE WESTIN SANTA CLARA.** *5101 Great America Pkwy (95054). Phone 408/986-0700; toll-free 800/937-8461; fax 408/980-3990. www.westin.com.* This hotel is adjacent to the Santa Clara Convention Center. 505 rooms, 14 story. S, D $79-$395; each additional $20; suites $499-$900; under 18 free; weekend, holiday rates. Pets accepted; fee. Check-out noon. TV; cable (premium), VCR available. In-room modem link. Room service 24 hours. Restaurant, bar. Health club privileges. In-house fitness room. Pool; whirlpool; poolside service. Free self-parking, valet parking, fee. Business center. Concierge. Near airport.

⬛⬛⬛⬛⬛⬛⬛

Santa Maria

Motel/Motor Lodge

★ ★ **BEST WESTERN BIG AMERICA.** *1725 N Broadway (93454). Phone 805/922-5200; toll-free 888/326-3380; fax 805/922-9865. www.bigamerica.com.* 2 story, 16 suites. S, D $77-$89; suites $75-$130; under 18 free; weekly rates. Pets accepted, some restrictions. Complimentary continental breakfast. Check-out noon. TV; cable (premium), VCR available (movies). Restaurant, bar. Room service. Pool; whirlpool. Free airport transportation.

⬛⬛⬛⬛⬛⬛

Santa Monica

Hotels

★ ★ ★ **THE FAIRMONT MIRAMAR HOTEL SANTA MONICA.** *101 Wilshire Blvd (90401). Phone 310/576-7777; fax 310/458-7912. www.fairmont.com.* This hotel is conveniently located one block from the beach and two blocks from shopping and movies. 362 rooms, 10 story. D $249-$429; each additional $20; under 17 free; weekend rates. Pets accepted, some restrictions; fee. Check-out noon, check-in 3 pm. TV; cable (premium), VCR available (movies). In-room modem link. Room service 24 hours. Restaurant, bar. In-house fitness room; massage; sauna. Beach opposite. Pool; whirlpool; poolside service. Valet parking. Concierge.

⬛⬛⬛⬛⬛⬛

★ ★ ★ **GEORGIAN HOTEL.** *1415 Ocean Ave (90401). Phone 310/395-9945; fax 310/451-3374. www.georgianhotel.com.* 112 rooms, 8 story. D $235-$285; each additional $25; package plans. Pets accepted, some restrictions; fee. Check-out noon, check-in 3 pm. TV; cable (premium), VCR available. In-room modem link. Restaurant. Health club privileges. In-house fitness room. Valet parking.

⬛⬛⬛⬛⬛⬛

★ ★ ★ **LE MERIGOT–A JW MARRIOTT BEACH HOTEL AND SPA SANTA MONICA.** *1740 Ocean Ave (90401). Phone 310/395-9700; toll-free 800/926-9524; fax 310/395-9200. www.lemerigothotel.com.* Recalling the grand hotels of the French Riviera, Le Merigot brings a bit of Europe to the Santa Monica coastline. Not far from the world-famous pier, the resort conveys quiet luxury. The guest rooms are at once classic and contemporary. Infused with a breath of fresh air, they reflect the elegance synonymous with European resorts. Frette linens dress the plush, oversized beds, while multi-line telephones, dataports, and high-speed Internet access make staying in touch with those back home easy and convenient. Creature comforts are plentiful here, especially at the spa, where guests unwind in the eucalyptus steam room or redwood sauna before surrendering to the fantastic treatments. Injected with bits of whimsy, Cézanne has a bold and stunning décor. The artistic culinary creations, largely inspired by the bounty of local farmers markets, delight hotel guests and locals alike. 175 rooms, 6 story. Pets accepted; fee. Check-out noon, check-in 3 pm. TV; cable (premium). In-room modem link. Room service 24 hours. Restaurant, bar. In-house fitness room; spa. Beach. Indoor pool; whirlpool. Valet parking. Business center. Concierge. **$$$**

⬛⬛⬛⬛⬛⬛

★ ★ ★ **VICEROY HOTEL.** *1819 Ocean Ave (90401). Phone 310/451-8711; fax 310/394-6657. www.viceroysanta monica.com.* 161 rooms. Pets accepted; fee. Check-out noon, check-in 3 pm. TV; cable (premium). In-room modem link. Room service 24 hours. Restaurant, bar. In-house fitness room; massage. Two lap pools; poolside service. Concierge. **$$**

Santa Nella

Motels/Motor Lodges

★ **BEST WESTERN ANDERSEN'S INN.** *12367 S Hwy 33 (95322). Phone 209/826-5534; fax 209/826-4353. www.bestwestern.com.* 94 rooms, 2 story. S $65; D $75; each additional $7; under 18 free. Pets accepted, some restrictions; fee. Complimentary continental breakfast. Check-out 11 am. TV; cable (premium). Restaurant adjacent. Heated pool.

★ ★ **RAMADA.** *13070 S Hwy 33, at I-5 (95322). Phone 209/826-4444; toll-free 800/546-5697; fax 209/826-8071. www.ramada.com.* 161 rooms, 2 story. S, D $74.95; each additional $10; under 13 free. Pets accepted; fee. Check-out noon. TV; cable (premium). Restaurant, bar. Pool; whirlpool. Spanish-style mission structure.

Santa Rosa

Hotel

★ ★ ★ **VINEYARD CREEK HOTEL.** *170 Railroad St (95401). Phone 707/636-7100; toll-free 888/920-0008; fax 707/636-7136. www.vineyardcreek.com.* 155 rooms, 1-2 story. Pets accepted, some restrictions; fee. Check-out noon, check-in 3 pm. Fireplaces. Restaurant, bar. Babysitting services available. In-house fitness room; spa, massage. Outdoor pool; whirlpool. **$$**

Solvang

Motel/Motor Lodge

★ **ROYAL COPENHAGEN INN.** *1579 Mission Dr (93463). Phone 805/688-5561; toll-free 800/624-6604; fax 805/688-7029. www.royalcopenhageninn.com.* 48 rooms, 1-2 story. S, D $80-$90; each additional $10; suites $125.

Pets accepted. Complimentary continental breakfast. Check-out 11 am. TV. Pool.

Sonoma

Motel/Motor Lodge

★ **BEST WESTERN SONOMA VALLEY INN.** *550 2nd St W (95476). Phone 707/938-9200; toll-free 800/334-5784; fax 707/938-0935. www.sonomavalleyinn.com.* 75 rooms, 2 story. Apr-Dec: S, D $119-$249; each additional $10; under 12 free; lower rates rest of year. Pets accepted; fee. Complimentary continental breakfast in rooms. Check-out noon. TV; cable (premium). Many fireplaces. Free guest laundry facilities. Restaurant nearby. In-house fitness room. Pool; whirlpool. Totally nonsmoking.

Resort

★ ★ ★ **RENAISSANCE LODGE AT SONOMA RESORT AND SPA.** *1325 Broadway (95476). Phone 707/935-6600; toll-free 800/HOTELS-1; fax 707/935-6829. www.thelodgeatsonoma.com.* 182 rooms, 2 story. Pets accepted, some restrictions; fee. Check-out noon, check-in 4 pm. TV; cable (premium), VCR available. Restaurant, bar. In-house fitness room; spa. Pool; whirlpool; poolside service. Business center. Concierge. **$$$**

Sonora

Motel/Motor Lodge

★ ★ **DAYS INN.** *160 S Washington St (95370). Phone 209/532-2400; toll-free 800/580-4667; fax 209/532-4542. www.daysinn.com.* 64 rooms, 3 story. S, D $63-$83; each additional $5; suites $99-$169; under 18 free; ski plans. Pets accepted, some restrictions; fee. Complimentary continental breakfast. Check-out 11 am. TV; cable (premium). Restaurant, bar. Pool.

B&B/Small Inn

★ ★ **1859 HISTORIC NATIONAL HOTEL, A COUNTRY INN.** *18183 Main St (95327). Phone 209/984-3446; toll-free 800/894-3446; fax 209/984-5620. www.national-hotel.com.* 9 rooms, 2 story. No room phones. S, D $90-$130; each additional $10. Pets accepted, some restrictions; fee. Children over 10 years only. Complimentary breakfast. Check-out noon, check-in 2 pm. TV available. Dining room 11 am-10 pm; Sun to 9 pm. Bar 9 am-10 pm. Room service. Continuously operated since 1859. Totally nonsmoking.

⬛⬛⬛

Stockton

Motels/Motor Lodges

★ **HOWARD JOHNSON.** *1672 Herndon Rd (95350). Phone 209/537-4821; toll-free 800/446-4656; fax 209/537-1040. www.hojo.com.* 50 rooms, 25 with shower only, 1-2 story. Apr-Sept: S $70; D $80; each additional $10; under 18 free. Pets accepted. Complimentary continental breakfast. Check-out 11 am. TV; cable (premium), VCR available. In-room modem link. Restaurant nearby. Pool.

⬛⬛⬛⬛

★ **RED ROOF INN.** *2654 W March Ln (95207). Phone 209/478-4300; fax 209/478-1872. www.redroof.com.* 123 rooms, 3 story. S $52; D $59; each additional $4; suites $80-$100; under 18 free. Pets accepted, some restrictions. Complimentary continental breakfast. Check-out 11 am, check-in 2 pm. TV; cable (premium). In-room modem link. Pool; whirlpool.

⬛⬛⬛⬛⬛

Sunnyvale

Hotel

★★ **MAPLE TREE INN.** *711 E El Camino Real (94087). Phone 408/720-9700; toll-free 800/423-0243; fax 408/738566S. www.mapletreeinn.com.* 18 rooms, 2-3 story. S, D $69-$180; each additional $10; suites, kitchen unit $150-$175; under 12 free; weekend, holiday rates; higher rates Stanford graduation. Pets accepted. Complimentary continental breakfast. Check-out noon. TV; cable (premium). In-room modem link. Room service. Pool. Health club privileges.

⬛⬛⬛⬛

All Suite

★★ **SUMMERFIELD SUITES SUNNYVALE.** *900 Hamlin Ct (94089). Phone 408/745-1515; fax 408/745-0540. www.wyndham.com.* An all-suite hotel offering amenities to please any family of travelers. On the property is a six-hole mini golf course. 138 kitchen units, 2-3 story. S, D $89-$200; weekend rates. Pets accepted, some restrictions; fee. Complimentary breakfast buffet. Check-out noon. TV; cable (premium), VCR available. In-room modem link. Health club privileges. In-house fitness room. Pool; whirlpool. Free airport transportation.

⬛⬛⬛⬛⬛

Extended Stay

★★ **RESIDENCE INN BY MARRIOTT.** *750 Lakeway (94086). Phone 408/720-1000; fax 408/737-9722. www.residenceinn.com.* 231 kitchen units, 2 story. S $179; D $199; suites $219. Pets accepted, some restrictions; fee. Complimentary continental breakfast. Check-out noon, check-in 3 pm. TV; cable (premium). In-house fitness room. Pool; two whirlpools. Outdoor tennis. Lawn games. Free airport transportation. Concierge.

⬛⬛⬛⬛⬛⬛

Tehachapi

Motels/Motor Lodges

★★ **BEST WESTERN MOUNTAIN INN.** *416 W Tehachapi Blvd (93561). Phone 661/822-5591; toll-free 800/780-7234; fax 661/822-6197. www.bestwestern.com.* 74 rooms, 2 story. S $55-$65; D $65-$75; each additional $3; under 18 free. Pets accepted; fee. Check-out noon. TV; cable (premium). Laundry services. Restaurant. Pool.

⬛⬛⬛⬛⬛ SC

★★ **TRAVELODGE.** *500 Steuber Rd (93561). Phone 661/823-8000; fax 661/823-8006. www.travelodge.com.* 81 rooms, 2 story. S $49-$52; D $56-$59; each additional $7; suites $61-$64; kitchen unit $90; under 18 free. Pets accepted; fee. Check-out 11 am. TV; cable (premium). In-room modem link. Restaurant, bar. Whirlpool.

⬛⬛⬛ SC

Three Rivers

Motels/Motor Lodges

★ **BEST WESTERN HOLIDAY LODGE.** *40105 Sierra Dr (93271). Phone 559/561-4119; toll-free 888/523-9909; fax 559/561-3427. www.bestwestern.com.* 54 rooms, 1-2 story. May-Oct: S $61-$105; D $71-$105; each additional $4; suites $77-$91; lower rates rest of year. Pets accepted; fee. Check-out 11 am. TV. Fireplaces. Pool; whirlpool. Continental breakfast.

⬛⬛⬛⬛⬛⬛

★ **LAZY J RANCH MOTEL.** *39625 Sierra Dr (93271). Phone 559/561-4449; toll-free 888/315-BEST; fax 559/561-4889.* 20 rooms. S $45-$60; D $46-$70; each additional $5; suites $150-$170; kitchen units $88-$98; weekly rates; some holidays (3-day minimum). Pets accepted, some restrictions; fee. Check-out 11 am. TV; VCR available. Laundry services. Pool. Cross-country ski 20 miles. On river.

⬛⬛⬛⬛⬛⬛

★ **SIERRA LODGE.** *43175 Sierra Dr (93271). Phone 559/561-3681; toll-free 800/367-8879; fax 559/561-3264. www.sierra-lodge.com.* 22 kitchen units, 1-3 story. No elevator. May-Sept: S, D $49-$72; each additional $3; suites $85-$165; lower rates rest of year. Pets accepted; fee. Complimentary continental breakfast. Check-out 11 am. TV; cable (premium). Pool.

⊡ 🐾 ⇌ ⇳ SC

Vacaville

Motel/Motor Lodge

★ **BEST WESTERN HERITAGE INN.** *1420 E Monte Vista Ave (95688). Phone 707/448-8453; fax 707/447-8649. www.bestwestern.com.* 41 rooms, 2 story. Pets accepted, some restrictions. Complimentary continental breakfast. Check-out 11 am, check-in 2 pm. TV; cable (premium). In-room modem link. Outdoor pool. **$**

D 🐾 ⇌ ⇳

Vallejo

Motels/Motor Lodges

★ **BEST WESTERN HERITAGE INN.** *1955 E 2nd St (94510). Phone 707/746-0401; toll-free 800/528-1234; fax 707/745-0842. www.bestwestern.com.* 100 rooms, 3 story. S, D $65-$120; each additional $5; suites $130; under 17 free; weekly, monthly rates. Pets accepted; fee. Complimentary continental breakfast. Check-out 11 am. TV; cable (premium). Restaurant nearby. Pool; whirlpool.

D 🐾 ⇌ ⇳ SC

★ **RAMADA INN.** *1000 Admiral Callaghan Ln (94591). Phone 707/643-2700; toll-free 800/677-1148; fax 707/642-1168. www.ramada.com.* 130 rooms, 36 suites, 3 story. May-Sept: S $95-$100; D $110; each additional $10; suites $116; under 18 free. Pets accepted, some restrictions; fee. Complimentary continental breakfast. Check-out noon. TV; cable (premium). In-room modem link. Health club privileges. Pool; whirlpool.

D 🐾 🐕 ⇌ ⇳ SC

Ventura

Motel/Motor Lodge

★ **VAGABOND INN.** *756 E Thompson Blvd (93001). Phone 805/648-5371; toll-free 800/522-1555; fax 805/648-5613.* 82 rooms, 2 story. S $56-$61; D $66-$75; each additional $5; higher rates special events. Pets accepted;

fee. Complimentary continental breakfast. Check-out noon. TV; cable (premium). In-room modem link. Restaurant. Pool; whirlpool.

🐾 ⇌ ⇳ SC

Walnut Creek

All Suite

★ ★ ★ **EMBASSY SUITES.** *1345 Treat Blvd (94596). Phone 925/934-2500; toll-free 800/362-2779; fax 925/256-7233. www.embassysuites.com.* This attractive all-suite hotel offers guests all the comforts of home. Located adjacent to the Bay Area Rapid Transit station, this hotel offers easy access to San Francisco, Sacramento, and the Napa Valley. 249 suites, 8 story. S, D $129-$209; each additional $15; under 18 free. Pets accepted; fee. Complimentary full breakfast. Check-out noon. TV; cable (premium), VCR available. In-room modem link. Laundry services. Restaurant, bar. Room service. In-house fitness room. Indoor pool; whirlpool. Parking.

D 🐾 ⇌ 🏃 ⇳ SC

Hotel

★ ★ ★ **MARRIOTT SAN RAMON.** *2600 Bishop Drive (94583). Phone 925/867-9200; fax 925/275-9443. www.marriotthotels.com.* Conveniently located between San Francisco and the Silicon Valley, this hotel is tailored for the business traveler. 368 rooms, 6 story. S, D $209; suites $350-$800; under 18 free; weekend rates. Pets accepted; fee. Check-out noon. TV; cable (premium), VCR available. In-room modem link. Restaurant, bar. Health club privileges. In-house fitness room; sauna. Pool; whirlpool. Business center. Concierge. View of Mount Diablo.

D 🐾 ⇌ ⇳ 🏃

Westwood Village

Hotel

★ ★ ★ **W LOS ANGELES WESTWOOD.** *930 Hilgard Ave (90024). Phone 310/208-8765; fax 310/824-0355. www.whotel.com.* 257 suites, (1-3 bedroom), 16 story. S, D $235-$650; weekend rates. Pets accepted; fee. Check-out noon. TV; cable (premium), VCR available (movies). In-room modem link. Restaurant, bar; entertainment Fri-Sun. Room service 24 hours. Health club privileges. In-house fitness room; massage. Valet parking. Concierge.

D 🐾 ⇌ 🏃 ⇳ 🚶

Whittier

Motel/Motor Lodge

★ **VAGABOND INN.** *14125 E Whittier Blvd (90605). Phone 562/698-9701; toll-free 800/522-1555; fax 562/698-8716. www.vagabondinn.com.* 49 rooms, 3 story. S, D $65-$90; each additional $5; under 18 free. Pets accepted; fee. Complimentary continental breakfast. Check-out noon. TV. Pool.

⊡ 🐾 ☒ ☒ SC

Willits

Motel/Motor Lodge

★ **BAECHTEL CREEK INN & SPA.** *101 Gregory Ln (95490). Phone 707/459-9063; toll-free 800/459-9911; fax 707/459-0226. www.baechtelcreekinn.com.* 46 rooms, 2 story. June-Oct: S $59-$69, D $79-$109; each additional $3; under 12 free; lower rates rest of year. Pets accepted, some restrictions; fee. Complimentary continental breakfast. Check-out 11 am. TV. In-room modem link. Pool; whirlpool.

⊡ 🐾 ☒ ☒ SC

Willows

Motels/Motor Lodges

★ **BEST VALUE INN.** *452 N Humboldt Ave (95988). Phone 530/934-7026; toll-free 800/814-6301; fax 530/934-7028.* 41 rooms, 2 story. S, D $39-$69; each additional $6; under 6 free. Pets accepted; fee. Check-out 11 am. TV; cable (premium). Pool.

🐾 ☒ ☒ SC

★ ★ **BEST WESTERN GOLDEN PHEASANT INN.** *249 N Humboldt Ave (95988). Phone 530/934-4603; toll-free 800/338-1387; fax 530/934-4275.* 104 rooms. S $55-$69; D $69-$89; each additional $10; suites $90; under 12 free. Pets accepted; fee. Complimentary continental breakfast. Check-out 11 am. TV; VCR available (movies $3.50). Fireplaces. Restaurant 6-10 am, 11:30 am-9 pm. Bar from 10 am. Room service. Free airport transportation.

⊡ 🐾 ☒ ☒

★ **COMFORT INN.** *400 C St (95987). Phone 530/473-2381; fax 530/473-2418.* 60 rooms, 2 story. S $50; D $55; each additional $5. Pets accepted; fee. Complimentary continental breakfast. Check-out noon. TV. Pool; whirlpool.

⊡ 🐾 ☒ ☒ SC

Yosemite National Park

Motels/Motor Lodges

★ ★ **MINERS INN MOTEL.** *5181 Hwy 49 N (95338). Phone 209/742-7777; toll-free 888/646-2244; fax 209/966-2343. yosemite-rooms.com.* 78 rooms, 2 story. Apr-Oct: S $49-$59; D $59-$75; each additional $6; suites $149; kitchen units $125; under 6 free; lower rates rest of year. Pets accepted; fee. Check-out 11 am. TV; cable (premium). In-room modem link. Fireplaces. Restaurant 6:30 am-10 pm, bar; entertainment Fri, Sat. Pool; whirlpool.

⊡ 🐾 🏊 ☒ ☒

★ ★ **YOSEMITE VIEW LODGE.** *11156 Hwy 140 (95318). Phone 209/379-2681; fax 209/379-2704. www.yosemite-motels.com.* 280 kitchen units, 2-3 story. Apr-Oct: S $99-$129; D $99-$139; each additional $10; ski plans; holidays (2-day minimum); lower rates rest of year. Pets accepted, some restrictions; fee. Check-out 11 pm. TV; cable (premium). Laundry services. Restaurant, bar. Two pools, one indoor; whirlpool. Downhill, cross-country ski 20 miles. On river.

⊡ 🐾 🏊 ☒ ☒ ☒

Hotels

★ **BEST VALUE MARIPOSA LODGE.** *5052 Hwy 140 (95338). Phone 209/966-3607; fax 209/742-7038. www.mariposalodge.com.* 44 rooms. Apr-Oct: S, D $65-$76; each additional $6; lower rates rest of year. Pets accepted, some restrictions; fee. Check-out 11 am. TV; cable (premium), VCR available. In-room modem link. Pool; whirlpool. Free airport transportation.

⊡ 🐾 ☒ ☒

★ ★ **GROVELAND HOTEL AT YOSEMITE NATIONAL PARK.** *18767 Main St (95321). Phone 209/962-4000; toll-free 800/273-3314; fax 209/962-6674. www.groveland.com.* 17 rooms, 3 suites, 2 separate two-story buildings (one is Ca. Monterey Colonial Adobe). S, D $135-$155; each additional $15 for under 12 years and $25 for over 12 years; suites $210. Pets accepted. Complimentary innkeeper breakfast. Check-out noon, check-in 2 pm. TV in common room/bar/some rooms; VCR available (movies). In-room modem link. Restaurant. Bar. Room service. Downhill, cross-country ski 20 miles. Concierge. Built in 1849; European antiques. Totally nonsmoking.

⊡ 🐾 🛴 🛷 🏊 ✕ ☒

Yountville

Hotel

★ ★ ★ **VINTAGE INN.** *6541 Washington St (94599). Phone 707/944-1112; toll-free 800/351-1133; fax 707/944-1617. www.vintageinn.com.* 80 rooms, 2 story. Pets accepted; fee. Complimentary buffet breakfast. Check-out noon, check-in 4 pm. TV; cable (premium), VCR available. Fireplaces. In-house fitness room; massage, steam room. Outdoor pool; whirlpool. Outdoor tennis. Business center. Mountain and vineyard views. Coincierge. **$$$**

Colorado

Alamosa

Motels/Motor Lodges

★ ★ **BEST WESTERN ALAMOSA INN.** *1919 Main St (81101). Phone 719/589-2567; toll-free 800/459-5123; fax 719/589-0767. www.bestwestern.com/alamosainn.* 53 rooms, 2 story. Pets accepted, some restrictions; fee. Complimentary continental breakfast. Check-out 11 am, check-in 2 pm. TV; cable (premium). Restaurant, bar. Indoor pool; whirlpool. Airport transportation. **$**

★ ★ **HOLIDAY INN.** *333 Santa Fe Ave (81101). Phone 719/589-5833; toll-free 800/669-1658; fax 719/589-4412. www.holiday-inn.com.* 126 rooms, 2 story. Pets accepted; fee. Check-out noon, check-in 3 pm. TV; VCR available. In-room modem link. Restaurant, bar. Room service. Sauna. Game room. Indoor pool; whirlpool. Airport transportation. Business center. **$**

B&B/Small Inn

★ ★ ★ **COTTONWOOD INN.** *123 San Juan Ave (81101). Phone 719/589-3882; toll-free 800/955-2623; fax 719/589-6437. www.cottonwoodinn.com.* With easy access to Sedona and the Grand Canyon, this inn features a lovely courtyard setting. 10 rooms, 2 story. Pets accepted, some restrictions; fee. Complimentary continental breakfast. Check-out 11 am, check-in 4 pm. TV. Whirlpool. Totally nonsmoking. **$**

Aspen

Motel/Motor Lodge

★ ★ **INNSBRUCK INN.** *233 W Main St (81611). Phone 970/925-2980; fax 970/925-6960. www.preferredlodging.com.* 30 rooms, 2 story. Pets accepted; fee. Complimentary continental breakfast. Check-out 11 am, check-in 3 pm. TV; cable (premium), VCR available. In-room modem link. Pool; whirlpool. Downhill, cross-country ski 1/2 mile. **$**

Hotels

★ **ASPEN MOUNTAIN LODGE.** *311 W Main St (81611). Phone 970/925-7650; fax 970/925-5744. www.aspenmountainlodge.com.* 38 rooms, 4 story. No elevator. Closed late Apr-mid-May. Pets accepted, some restrictions; fee. Complimentary buffet breakfast. Check-out 11 am, check-in 4 pm. TV. In-room modem link. Outdoor pool; whirlpool. Downhill, cross-country ski 6 blocks. Four-story river rock fireplace. **$$**

★ ★ **HOTEL ASPEN.** *110 W Main St (81611). Phone 970/925-3441; toll-free 800/527-7369; fax 970/920-1379. www.aspen.com/ha.* 45 rooms, 2-3 story. No elevator. Pets accepted; fee. Complimentary continental breakfast. Check-out 11 am, check-in 4 pm. TV; cable (premium), VCR available. In-room modem link. Fireplaces. Health club privileges. Pool; whirlpool. Downhill ski 8 blocks. Free ski shuttle. Parking $1/day. Totally nonsmoking. **$$**

★ ★ ★ **HOTEL JEROME.** *330 E Main St (81611). Phone 970/920-1000; toll-free 800/331-7213; fax 970/925-2784. www.hoteljerome.com.* Built to rival the Ritz in Paris, the Hotel Jerome has been an Aspen landmark since 1889. Located in the heart of downtown, this historic hotel is within walking distance of the town's boutiques and restaurants, yet only minutes from the slopes (with complimentary transportation a nice bonus). Guests feel cosseted here; the general concierge meets every demand, and the ski concierge assists with rentals, tickets, and insight on the trails. The boutique-style rooms are magnificent, reflecting the hotel's Victorian heritage with carved armoires and beautiful beds. Every amenity is supplied here, and after a long day of skiing or hiking, guests appreciate the extra touches. The dashing J Bar, a popular watering hole since the 1890s, is still one of the hottest places in town. 91 rooms, 3-4 story. Pets accepted, some restrictions; fee. Parking. Check-out 11 am, check-in 4 pm. TV; cable (premium), VCR (movies, fee). In-room modem link. Room service 24 hours. Restaurant, bar. Babysitting services available. In-house fitness room; massage. Pool; whirlpool; poolside service. Downhill ski 4 blocks, cross-country ski 1 mile. Free airport transportation. Concierge. **$$$$**

★ ★ ★ ★ **THE ST. REGIS, ASPEN.** *315 E Dean St (81611). Phone 970/920-3300; toll-free 888/454-9005; fax 970/925-8998. www.stregisaspen.com.* The St. Regis radiates luxury in its superb location at the base of Aspen Mountain. From its elegant interpretation of Western style to its white-glove service, this hotel is the very definition of refinement. Memorable skiing is guaranteed here, with a terrific location between the gondola and lift, gracious shuttles from door to door, and easy transportation to nearby Aspen Highlands, Buttermilk Mountain, and Snowmass. Aspen's picture-perfect vistas attract hikers, while its clear streams appeal to anglers. The sparkling outdoor pool and accompanying lounge are ideal for whiling away warm afternoons. Well-heeled guests succumb to the sumptuous accommodations, where overstuffed leather chairs and stunning appointments create cocoonlike shelters. Guests beat a path to Olives, where renowned chef Todd English creates his inspired dishes from the Mediterranean. Live entertainment is enjoyed in the Lobby Lounge, and Whiskey Rocks is a hip gathering place, perfect after a long day spent in the great outdoors. *Secret Inspector's Notes:* The St. Regis Aspen is *the* place to stay for guests who want to be treated well. The staff is incredibly warm, welcoming, and accommodating. Everything at this hotel oozes with luxury; whether you're skiing or not, you feel like a VIP amidst Aspen's mountain beauty. 257 rooms, 6 story. Closed late Oct-mid-Nov. Pets accepted; fee. Valet parking. Check-out noon, check-in 3 pm. TV; cable (premium), VCR available (movies). In-room modem link. Room service 24 hours. Restaurant, bar; entertainment. Babysitting services available. In-house fitness room; massage; sauna, steam room. Outdoor pool; children's pool; whirlpool; poolside service. Downhill skiing 1 block, cross-country skiing 1 1/2 miles. Bicycles, hiking. Business center. Concierge. Luxury level. **$$$**

D 🔒 🛋 💺 🏊 ➳ ✈ 🔅 SC 🚶

Resorts

★ **LIMELITE LODGE.** *228 E Cooper St (81611). Phone 970/925-3025; toll-free 800/433-0832; fax 970/925-5120. www.aspen.com/limelite.* 63 rooms, 1-3 story. No elevator. Pets accepted. Complimentary continental breakfast. Check-out 11 am. TV; cable (premium), VCR available. In-room modem link. Sauna. Two pools; whirlpool. Downhill ski 3 blocks. **$**

D 🔒 🏊 ➳ 🔅 SC

★ ★ ★ ★ ★ **THE LITTLE NELL.** *675 E Durant Ave (81611). Phone 970/920-4600; toll-free 800/525-6200; fax 970/920-6345. www.thelittlenell.com.* Tucked away at the base of a mountain, The Little Nell provides its guests with a perfect location either to hit the slopes for a day of skiing or to pound the streets in search of Aspen's latest fashions. Offering unparalleled luxury, it captures the essence of an elegant private hideaway while maintaining the services usually associated with larger resorts. Romantic in winter, The Little Nell delights visitors throughout the year with its European *savoir faire* and breathtaking views. The rooms and suites are heavenly cocoons with fireplaces, overstuffed furniture, and luxurious bathrooms. Some suites feature vaulted ceilings showcasing glorious mountainside views, while others overlook the charming former mining town. A well-equipped fitness center challenges guests to vigorous workouts, while the outdoor pool and Jacuzzi soothe tired muscles. The Little Nell's Montagna is one of the hottest tables in town with its inventive reinterpretation of American cuisine. *Secret Inspector's Notes:* Lively crowds and frequent celebrity sightings (even Antonio Banderas) make the aprés-ski scene at The Little Nell's Garden Bar and Hotel Lounge Bar a worthy destination regardless of whether you are a guest at the hotel. 92 rooms, 4 story. Closed late Apr-mid-May. Pets accepted. Check-out noon, check-in 4 pm. TV; cable (premium), VCR available. In-room modem link. Fireplaces. Restaurant, bar; entertainment. In-house fitness room; massage; steam room. Outdoor pool; children's pool; whirlpool; poolside service. Downhill ski on site. Parking. Free airport transportation. Business center. Concierge. **$$$$**

D 🔒 🛋 🏊 ➳ ✈ 🚶

B&B/Small Inn

★ ★ ★ **HOTEL LENADO.** *200 S Aspen St (81611). Phone 970/925-6246; toll-free 800/321-3457; fax 970/925-3840. www.hotellenado.com.* In the heart of Aspen, this hotel offers personalized touches and a comfortable retreat for travelers year-round. A four-poster bed adorns each room. 19 rooms, 3 story. Pets accepted, some restrictions. Complimentary full breakfast (in season), continental breakfast (off season). Check-out noon, check-in 4 pm. TV; cable (premium), VCR available. In-room modem link. Bar. Whirlpool. Downhill, cross-country ski 6 blocks. **$$$$**

D 🔒 🏊 ➳

Boulder

Hotel

★ ★ **BOULDER BROKER INN.** *555 30th St (80303). Phone 303/444-3330; toll-free 800/338-5407; fax 303/444-6444. www.boulderbrokerinn.com.* The Victorian-style guest rooms of this small inn are spacious and bright. Close to the University of Colorado. 118 rooms, 4 story. Pets accepted, some restrictions. Complimentary breakfast. Check-out noon. TV; cable (premium). In-room modem link. Restaurant, bar; entertainment. Room service. Health club privileges. Pool; whirlpool; poolside service. Airport transportation. Business center. Concierge. **$**

D 🔒 ➳ 🔅 SC 🚶

Extended Stay

★ **RESIDENCE INN BY MARRIOTT.** *3030 Center Green Dr (80301). Phone 303/449-5545; toll-free 800/331-3131; fax 303/449-2452. www.residenceinn.com.* 224

rooms, 2 story. Pets accepted; fee. Complimentary continental breakfast. Check-out noon, check-in 3 pm. TV; cable (premium). In-room modem link. Health club privileges. Pool; whirlpool. Outdoor tennis, lighted courts. **$**

Breckenridge

Resort

★ ★ ★ **LODGE & SPA AT BRECKENRIDGE.** *112 Overlook Dr (80424). Phone 970/453-9300; toll-free 800/736-1607; fax 970/453-0625. www.thelodgeatbreck.com.* With exposed wood beams and richly colored fabrics, the décor of this small, full-service spa is sophisticatedly rustic. 47 rooms, 4 story. Pets accepted; fee. Check-out 11 am. TV; cable (premium), VCR available. In-room modem link. Fireplaces. Restaurant, bar. Room service. In-house fitness room; massage; sauna, steam room. Indoor pool; whirlpool; poolside service. Downhill, cross-country ski 2 miles. Free valet parking. Business center. Concierge. **$**

Broomfield

Resort

★ ★ ★ **OMNI INTERLOCKEN RESORT.** *500 Interlocken Blvd (80021). Phone 303/438-6600; toll-free 800/843-6664; fax 303/438-7224. www.omnihotels.com.* Metropolitan Denver is home to the wonderful Omni Interlocken Resort. Situated midway between Denver and Boulder in the area's technology corridor, the resort is part of the Interlocken Advanced Technology Park. Sharing space with leading businesses and the FlatIron Crossings shopping center, this all-season resort is a premier recreational destination. Set against the backdrop of the Rocky Mountains, the 300-acre property has something for everyone. Golfers needing to brush up on their game head for the L. A. W. s Academy of Golf for its celebrated instruction before hitting the three 9-hole courses. The well-equipped fitness center and pool keep guests active, while the full-service spa attends to every need. Indigenous Colorado materials are used throughout the resort, enhancing the local flavor of the design. The guest rooms are comfortably elegant and include 21st-century amenities like WebTV and high-speed Internet connections. Three restaurants run the gamut from traditional to pub style. 390 rooms, 11 story. Pets accepted; fee. Check-out noon. TV; cable (premium), VCR available. In-room modem link. Room service 24 hours. Restaurant, bar. Supervised children's activities (summer). In-house fitness room; massage; sauna, steam room. Game room.

Pool; whirlpool; poolside service. Golf, greens fee $65-$105 (including cart). Bike rentals. Hiking trail. Free valet parking. Business center. Concierge. **$**

Buena Vista

Motels/Motor Lodges

★ **BEST WESTERN VISTA INN.** *733 US Hwy 24 N (81211). Phone 719/395-8009; toll-free 800/809-3495; fax 719/395-6025. www.bestwestern.com.* 41 rooms, 2 story. Pets accepted, some restrictions; fee. Check-out 11 am. Check-in 2 pm. TV; cable (premium). In-room modem link. Three hot springs whirlpools. Cross-country ski 1 mile. Bicycles, fishing, hiking. **$**

★ **GREAT WESTERN SUMAC LODGE.** *428 Hwy 24 S (81212). Phone 719/395-8111; toll-free 888/786-2290; fax 719/395-2560.* 30 rooms, 2 story. Pets accepted; fee. Check-out 11 am. TV; cable (premium). In-room modem link. Mountain view. **$**

Burlington

Motel/Motor Lodge

★ **CHAPARRAL MOTOR INN.** *405 S Lincoln (80807). Phone 719/346-5361; toll-free 800/456-6206; fax 719/346-8502.* 39 rooms. Pets accepted, some restrictions; fee. Check-out 11 am. TV; cable (premium). Pool; whirlpool. **$**

Cañon City

Motels/Motor Lodges

★ ★ **BEST WESTERN ROYAL GORGE.** *1925 Fremont Dr (81212). Phone 719/275-3377; toll-free 800/231-7317; fax 719/275-3931. www.bestwestern.com.* 67 rooms, 2 story. Pets accepted, some restrictions; fee. Check-out 11 am. TV; cable (premium). In-room modem link. Laundry services. Restaurant, bar. Pool; whirlpool; poolside service. **$**

★ ★ ★ **CANON INN.** *3075 E US 50 (81212). Phone 719/275-8676; toll-free 800/525-7727; fax 719/275-8675. www.canoninn.com.* Located at the mouth of Royal Gorge, this simple hotel offers spectacular vistas. 152 rooms, 2 story. Pets accepted, some restrictions; fee. Check-out 11 am. TV; cable (premium). Laundry services. Restaurant, bar. Room service. Pool; whirlpool. Free airport transportation. $

D 🐾 ≈ 🏊

Colorado Springs

Motels/Motor Lodges

★ **DRURY INN.** *8155 N Academy Blvd (80920). Phone 719/598-2500; toll-free 800/325-8300. www.drury-inn.com.* 118 rooms, 4 story. Pets accepted, some restrictions. Complimentary continental breakfast. Check-out noon. TV. In-room modem link. In-house fitness room. Indoor, outdoor pool; whirlpool. $

D 🐾 ≈ 🏋 🏊 SC

★ **VILLAGER PREMIER COLORADO SPRINGS.** *725 W Cimarron St (80905). Phone 719/473-5530; fax 719/473-8763.* 208 rooms, 2 story. Pets accepted; fee. Complimentary continental breakfast. Check-out noon. TV; cable (premium). In-room modem link. Pool. $

D 🐾 🏋 ≈ 🏊

Hotels

★ ★ ★ **DOUBLETREE HOTEL.** *1775 E Cheyenne Mountain Blvd (80906). Phone 719/576-8900; toll-free 800/222-8733; fax 719/576-4450. www.doubletree.com.* This contemporary hotel is situated at the base of the mountains in Colorado Springs. 299 rooms, 5 story. Pets accepted; fee. Check-out noon. TV; cable (premium). In-room modem link. Restaurant, bar; entertainment. Room service. In-house fitness room; sauna. Indoor pool; whirlpool. Airport transportation. $

D 🐾 ≈ 🏋 🏊

★ ★ **RADISSON INN & SUITES COLORADO SPRINGS AIRPORT.** *1645 Newport Rd (80916). Phone 719/597-7000; fax 719/597-4308. www.radisson.com.* Adjacent to the municipal airport and 10 minutes from downtown, this full-service hotel affords a comfortable stay. 200 rooms, 2 story. Pets accepted, some restrictions; fee. Complimentary full breakfast. Check-out noon. TV; cable (premium). In-room modem link. Room service 24 hours. Restaurant, bar. In-house fitness room. Game room. Indoor pool; whirlpool; poolside service. Free airport transportation. Business center. Concierge. $

D 🐾 ≈ 🏋 ✈ 🏊 SC 🏃

★ ★ **RADISSON INN COLORADO SPRINGS NORTH.** *8110 N Academy Blvd (80920). Phone 719/598-5770; fax 719/598-3434. www.radisson.com.* This hotel is the closest option to the US Air Force Academy. 200

rooms, 2-4 story. Pets accepted, some restrictions; fee. Check-out noon. TV; cable (premium). In-room modem link. Restaurant, bar. Room service. In-house fitness room; sauna. Indoor pool; whirlpool. Free airport transportation. $

D 🐾 ≈ 🏋 ✈ 🏊 SC

Cortez

Motels/Motor Lodges

★ **BEST WESTERN TURQUOISE INN & SUITES.** *535 E Main St (81321). Phone 970/565-3778; toll-free 800/547-3376; fax 970/565-3439. www.cortezbestwestern.com.* 77 rooms, 2 story. Pets accepted; fee. Complimentary continental breakfast. Check-out 11 am, check-in 3 pm. TV; cable (premium). In-room modem link. Fireplaces. Outdoor pool; whirlpool. Free airport transportation. $

🐾 ≈ ✈ 🏊

★ **HOLIDAY INN EXPRESS.** *2121 E Main St (81321). Phone 970/565-6000; toll-free 800/626-5652; fax 970/565-3438. www.coloradoholiday.com.* 100 rooms, 3 story. Pets accepted, some restrictions. Complimentary continental breakfast. Check-out 11 am, check-in 3 pm. TV; cable (premium), VCR available. In-room modem link. Laundry services. In-house fitness room; sauna. Indoor pool; whirlpool. Free airport transportation. $

D 🐾 ≈ 🏋 ✈ 🏊 SC

Craig

Motel/Motor Lodge

★ ★ **HOLIDAY INN.** *300 S Hwy 13 (81625). Phone 970/824-4000; toll-free 800/465-4329; fax 970/824-3950. www.holiday-inn.com.* 152 rooms, 2 story. Pets accepted, some restrictions; fee. Check-out 11 am. TV; cable (premium), VCR available. Laundry services. Restaurant, bar. Room service. In-house fitness room. Game room. Indoor pool; whirlpool; poolside service. $

D 🐾 ≈ 🏊

Delta

Motels/Motor Lodges

★ ★ **BEST WESTERN SUNDANCE.** *903 Main St (81416). Phone 970/874-9781; toll-free 800/626-1994; fax 970/874-5440. www.bestwesternsundance.com.* 41 rooms, 2 story. Pets accepted, some restrictions; fee. Complimentary full breakfast. Check-out 11 am. TV;

cable (premium). In-room modem link. Restaurant, bar. Room service. In-house fitness room. Pool; whirlpool. **$**

D 🐾 ≈ 🏃 ⊠ SC

★ **COMFORT INN.** *180 Gunnison River Dr (81416). Phone 970/874-1000; toll-free 800/228-5150; fax 970/874-4154. www.comfortinn.com.* 47 rooms, 2 story. Pets accepted; fee. Complimentary continental breakfast. Check-out 11 am, check-in 2 pm. TV; cable (premium), VCR available (movies). Health club privileges. Sauna. Game room. Pool privileges; whirlpool. **$**

D 🐾 ≈ ⊠ SC

Denver

Motels/Motor Lodges

★ ★ **HOLIDAY INN.** *10 E 120th Ave (80233). Phone 303/452-4100; fax 303/457-1741. www.holiday-inn.com.* 235 rooms, 6 story. Pets accepted; fee. Check-out noon. TV. In-room modem link. Restaurant, bar. In-house fitness room. Health club privileges. Indoor pool; whirlpool. **$**

D 🐾 ≈ 🏃 ⊠

★ **LA QUINTA INN.** *3500 Park Ave W (80216). Phone 303/458-1222; fax 303/433-2246. www.laquinta.com.* 106 rooms, 3 story. Pets accepted, some restrictions. Complimentary continental breakfast. Check-out noon. TV; cable (premium). In-room modem link. Pool. **$**

D 🐾 ≈ ⊠

★ **LA QUINTA INN DENVER AIRPORT SOUTH.** *3975 Peoria Way (80239). Phone 303/371-5640; toll-free 800/687-6667; fax 303/371-7015. www.laquinta.com.* 112 rooms, 2 story. Pets accepted. Complimentary continental breakfast. Check-out noon. TV; cable (premium). In-room modem link. Pool. Free airport transportation. **$**

D 🐾 ≈ ⊠ SC

★ ★ **QUALITY INN.** *12100 W 44th Ave (80033). Phone 303/467-2400; toll-free 800/449-0003; fax 303/467-0198. www.qualityinn.com.* 108 rooms, 5 story. Pets accepted; fee. Check-out 11 am. TV; cable (premium). Restaurant, bar. Room service. In-house fitness room. Whirlpool. **$**

D 🐾 🏃 ⊠ SC

Hotels

★ ★ **ADAM'S MARK.** *1550 Court Pl (80202). Phone 303/893-3333; fax 303/626-2542. www.adamsmark.com.* 1,225 rooms, 8 and 22 story. Pets accepted, some restrictions; fee. Check-out noon. TV; cable (premium). In-room modem link. Room service 24 hours. Restaurant, bar; entertainment. In-house fitness room; sauna, steam room. Health club privileges. Pool; poolside service.

Airport transportation. Business center. Concierge. Luxury level. **$$$**

D 🐾 ≈ 🏃 ⊠ 🏃

★ ★ ★ **HOTEL MONACO DENVER.** *1717 Champa St (80202). Phone 303/296-1717; toll-free 800/397-5380; fax 303/296-1818. www.monaco-denver.com.* This boutique hotel has a cool feel and a fun, comfortable design. The guest rooms resemble Mackenzie-Childs pottery, with swirls of patterns and other colorful touches. Amenities are somewhat limited, but arrangements can be made for most needs. 189 rooms, 7 story. Pets accepted. Check-out noon. TV; cable (premium), VCR available. Room service 24 hours. Restaurant, bar. In-house fitness room. Bike rental. Valet parking. Business center. Concierge. **$$**

D 🐾 🏃 ⊠ SC 🏃

★ ★ ★ **HOTEL TEATRO.** *1100 14th St (80202). Phone 303/228-1100; toll-free 888/727-1200; fax 303/228-1101. www.hotelteatro.com.* This downtown boutique hotel is located in a historic landmark building adjacent to the theater district. Handsome guest rooms are designed for the business traveler with printers, copiers, and fax machines as well as three telephones in each room. Large, luxurious bathrooms and a sophisticated décor make this an ideal hotel for both business and leisure guests. 111 rooms, 9 story. Pets accepted, some restrictions. Check-out noon, check-in 3 pm. TV; cable (premium). In-room modem link. Room service 24 hours. Restaurant, bar. Supervised children's activities. In-house fitness room. Health club privileges. Valet parking. Concierge. **$$$**

🐾 🏃 ⊠

★ ★ ★ **LOEWS DENVER HOTEL.** *4150 E Mississippi Ave (80246). Phone 303/782-9300; fax 303/758-6542. www.loewshotels.com.* Pretty flower arrangements and furniture adorn the entrance of this hotel in the Cherry Creek section of Denver. 183 rooms, 11 story. Pets accepted. Check-out 11 am. TV; cable (premium), VCR available (movies). Room service 24 hours. Restaurant, bar. In-house fitness room. Health club privileges. Valet parking. Business center. Concierge. **$$**

D 🐾 🐕 🏃 ⊠ 🏃

★ ★ ★ **THE MAGNOLIA HOTEL.** *818 17th St (80202). Phone 303/607-9000; toll-free 888/915-1110; fax 303/607-0101. www.themagnoliahotel.com.* 244 rooms, 10 story. Pets accepted. Complimentary continental breakfast. Check-out 11 am. TV; cable (premium). In-room modem link. In-house fitness room. Valet parking. Airport transportation. Business center. Concierge. **$$**

🐾 🏃 🏃

★ ★ ★ **MARRIOTT DENVER CITY CENTER.** *1701 California St (80202). Phone 303/297-1300; toll-free 800/228-9290; fax 303/298-7474. www.marriott.com.*

Located in downtown Denver, this property is within walking distance of Coors Field, and several restaurants and shops. 614 rooms, 19 story. Pets accepted. Check-out noon. TV; cable (premium), VCR available. In-room modem link. Restaurant, bar. Room service. In-house fitness room; sauna. Indoor pool; whirlpool. Valet parking. Business center. Concierge. Luxury level. **$$**

⬛🐾🏊🏋️🎿🚶

★ ★ ★ **MARRIOTT DENVER SOUTHEAST.** *6363 E Hampden Ave (80222). Phone 303/758-7000; toll-free 800/228-9290; fax 303/691-3418. www.marriott.com.* 607 rooms, 11 story. Pets accepted, some restrictions; fee. Check-out noon, check-in 4 pm. TV; cable (premium), VCR available. In-room modem link. Laundry services. Restaurant, bar. In-house fitness room. Game room. Indoor, outdoor pool; whirlpool; poolside service. Covered parking. Airport transportation. Business center. Concierge. Luxury level. **$**

D🐾🏊🏋️🎿SC🚶

★ ★ ★ **MARRIOTT DENVER TECH CENTER.** *4900 S Syracuse St (80237). Phone 303/779-1100; toll-free 800/228-9290; fax 303/740-2523. www.marriott.com.* A block of rooms is designated for business travelers, and the hotel will even provide secretarial services. 626 rooms, 2-10 story. Pets accepted, some restrictions; fee. Check-out noon. TV; cable (premium), VCR available. In-room modem link. Restaurant, bar. In-house fitness room; sauna. Health club privileges. Indoor, outdoor pool; whirlpool. Valet parking. Business center. **$$**

D🐾🏊🏋️🎿SC🚶

★ ★ ★ **WARWICK HOTEL DENVER.** *1776 Grant St (80203). Phone 303/861-2000; toll-free 800/525-2888; fax 303/832-0320. www.warwickdenver.com.* The combination of European-style hospitality and service and traditional American décor make this hotel warm and inviting. Convenient to many of Denver's major attractions, this hotel is ideally located for both business and leisure travelers and has spectacular views of the Rocky Mountains. 263 rooms, 16 story. Pets accepted; fee. Check-out noon, check-in 3 pm. TV; cable (premium). In-room modem link. Restaurant, bar. Room service. Health club privileges. Pool; poolside service. Concierge. **$$**

D🐾🏊🎿SC

★ ★ ★ **THE WESTIN TABOR CENTER.** *1672 Lawrence St (80202). Phone 303/572-9100; toll-free 800/937-8461; fax 303/572-7288. www.westin.com/taborcenter.* Centrally located to downtown Denver and adjacent to the 16th Street Mall, this hotel boasts some of the largest guest rooms in the city. Many of the rooms have views of the nearby Rocky Mountains. 430 rooms, 19 story. Pets accepted; fee. Check-out 1 pm. TV; cable (premium), VCR available. In-room modem link. Room service 24 hours.

Restaurant, bar; pianist Tues-Sat. In-house fitness room. Health club privileges; sauna, steam room. Indoor, outdoor pool; whirlpool; poolside service. Business center. Luxury level. **$$**

D🐾🏊🏋️🎿🚶

★ ★ ★ **THE WESTIN WESTMINSTER.** *10600 Westminster Blvd (80020). Phone 303/410-5000; toll-free 800/937-8461; fax 303/410-5005. www.westin.com.* 369 rooms, 14 story. Pets accepted; fee. Check-out noon. TV; cable (premium). In-room modem link. Fireplace. Room service 24 hours. Restaurant, bar. Supervised children's activities. In-house fitness room; sauna. Indoor pool; whirlpool; poolside service. Hiking trail. Valet parking. Business center. Concierge. **$**

D🐾🏊🏊🏋️🎿🚶

All Suite

★ ★ ★ **EMBASSY SUITES.** *4444 Havana St (80239). Phone 303/375-0400; toll-free 800/345-0087; fax 303/371-4634. www.placetostay.com.* 210 rooms, 7 story. Pets accepted, some restrictions; fee. Complimentary full breakfast. Check-out 1 pm. TV; cable (premium), VCR available. In-room modem link. Restaurant, bar. In-house fitness room; sauna, steam room. Indoor pool; whirlpool. Free airport transportation. **$**

D🐾🏊🏋️🎿

B&B/Small Inn

★ **HOLIDAY CHALET.** *1820 E Colfax Ave (80218). Phone 303/321-9975; toll-free 800/626-4497; fax 303/377-6556.* 10 rooms, 3 story. Pets accepted, some restrictions. Complimentary breakfast. Check-out noon. TV; VCR. Concierge. Restored brownstone built in 1896. Totally nonsmoking. **$**

🐾🎿SC

Denver International Airport Area

Hotel

★ ★ ★ **DOUBLETREE HOTEL.** *3203 Quebec St (80207). Phone 303/321-3333; fax 303/329-5233. www.doubletree.com.* 571 rooms, 9 story. Pets accepted; fee. Check-out noon, check-in 3 pm. TV; VCR available. In-room modem link. Room service 24 hours. Restaurant, bar. In-house fitness room; sauna. Indoor pool; whirlpool. Free airport transportation. Business center. **$**

D🐾🍴🏊🏋️🎿🚶

Dillon

Motels/Motor Lodges

★ ★ **BEST WESTERN PTARMIGAN LODGE.** *652 Lake Dillon Dr (80435). Phone 970/468-2341; toll-free 800/842-5939; fax 970/468-6465. www.bestwestern.com.* 69 rooms, 1-2 story. No A/C. Pets accepted; fee. Complimentary continental breakfast. Check-out 11 am. TV; cable (premium). Bar. Sauna. Whirlpool. Downhill, cross-country ski 5 1/2 miles. Boating. Free ski area transportation. **$**

★ **DAYS INN.** *580 Silverthorne Ln (80498). Phone 970/468-8661; toll-free 800/520-4267; fax 970/468-1421. www.daysinn.com.* 73 rooms, 4 story. Pets accepted. Complimentary continental breakfast. Check-out 11 am. TV; cable (premium). Laundry services. Sauna. Wading pool; whirlpool. Downhill, cross-country skiing 6 miles. **$**

B&B/Small Inn

★ **NEW SUMMIT INN.** *1205 N Summit Blvd (80443). Phone 970/668-3220; toll-free 800/745-1211; fax 970/668-0188. www.newsummitinn.com.* 31 rooms, 2 story. Pets accepted, some restrictions; fee. Complimentary continental breakfast. Check-out 10 am. TV. Laundry services. Sauna. Whirlpool. **$**

Durango

Motels/Motor Lodges

★ ★ **BEST WESTERN LODGE AT DURANGO MOUNTAIN.** *49617 Hwy 550 N (81301). Phone 970/247-9669; toll-free 800/637-7727; fax 970/247-9681. www.bestwestern.com.* 32 rooms, 2 story. Pets accepted; fee. Complimentary continental breakfast. Check-out 11 am. Check-in 3 pm. TV; cable (premium), VCR available (movies fee). In-room modem link. Restaurant. In-house fitness room. Game room. Indoor pool; whirlpool. Downhill, cross-country ski adjacent. **$**

★ **DAYS INN.** *1700 County Rd 203 (81301). Phone 970/259-1430; toll-free 866/338-1116; fax 970/259-5741. www.daysinndurango.com.* 94 rooms, 3 story. Pets accepted, some restrictions. Complimentary continental breakfast. Check-out 11 am, check-in 2 pm. TV; cable (premium). In-room modem link. Laundry services.

In-house fitness room; spa, massage, sauna. Indoor pool; whirlpool. **$**

★ **RODEWAY INN.** *2701 N Main Ave (81301). Phone 970/259-2540; toll-free 800/752-6072; fax 970/247-9642. www.rodewayinndurango.com.* 30 rooms, 2 story. Pets accepted, some restrictions; fee. Complimentary continental breakfast. Check-out 11 am, check-in 2 pm. TV; cable (premium). In-room modem link. Laundry services. Indoor pool; whirlpool. **$**

Hotel

★ ★ ★ **DOUBLETREE HOTEL.** *501 Camino Del Rio (81301). Phone 970/259-6580; fax 970/259-4398. www.doubletree.com.* Overlooking the magnificent Animas River, this hotel is just two blocks from the historic Durango and Silverton Train and the downtown entertainment center. 159 rooms, 3 story. Pets accepted, some restrictions; fee. Check-out noon, check-in 3 pm. TV; cable (premium). In-room modem link. Restaurant, bar. Room service. In-house fitness room; sauna. Indoor pool; whirlpool. Airport transportation. Concierge. **$**

Resorts

★ **IRON HORSE INN & CONFERENCE CENTER.** *5800 N Main Ave (81301). Phone 970/259-1010; toll-free 800/748-2990; fax 970/385-4791. www.ironhorseinndurango.com.* 143 rooms. Pets accepted, some restrictions. Complimentary continental breakfast. Check-out 11 am; check-in 3 pm. TV; cable (premium). In-room modem link. Fireplaces. Restaurant. In-house fitness room; sauna. Game room. Indoor pool; whirlpool. Lawn games. Free airport transportation. **$**

★ ★ ★ **TAMARRON RESORT.** *40292 US 550 N (81301). Phone 970/259-2000; toll-free 800/678-1000; fax 970/382-7822. www.lodgeattamarron.com.* Pine trees surround this scenic resort, located on a 750-acre site in the San Juan Mountains. 210 rooms, 4 story. Pets accepted; fee. Check-out 11 am, check-in 4 pm. TV; cable (premium), VCR available. In-room modem link. Room service 24 hours. Restaurant, bar. Supervised children's activities (Memorial Day-Labor Day); ages 4-15. In-house fitness room; spa, massage, sauna, steam room. Game room. Indoor, outdoor pool; whirlpool; poolside service. Golf, greens fee $75. Downhill ski 15 miles, cross-country ski on site; rental equipment available. Bicycle rentals. Fishing/hunting guides. Hiking, sleighing, tobogganing, snowmobiles. Valet parking. Airport transportation. Concierge. **$**

76 COLORADO/DURANGO

B&B/Small Inns

★★ **LELAND HOUSE BED & BREAKFAST SUITES.** *721 E 2nd Ave (81301). Phone 970/385-1920; toll-free 800/664-1920; fax 970/385-1967. www.lelandhouse.com.* 10 air-cooled rooms, 2 story. Pets accepted, some restrictions; fee. Complimentary full breakfast. Check-out 11 am, check-in 3 pm. TV; cable (premium), VCR available. In-room modem link. Fireplaces. Restored apartment building (1927); many antiques. Totally nonsmoking. **$**

★★★ **NEW ROCHESTER HOTEL.** *726 E 2nd Ave (81301). Phone 970/385-1920; toll-free 800/664-1920; fax 970/385-1967. www.rochesterhotel.com.* Built in 1892, this hotel offers guest rooms named after historic figures from the Old West. 15 rooms, 2 story. Pets accepted, some restrictions; fee. Complimentary continental breakfast. Check-out 11 am, check-in 3 pm. TV; cable (premium), VCR available. Totally nonsmoking. **$**

Englewood

Motel/Motor Lodge

★ **HAMPTON INN.** *9231 E Arapahoe Rd (80112). Phone 303/792-9999; fax 303/790-4360. www.hamptoninn.com.* 150 rooms, 5 story. Pets accepted; fee. Complimentary continental breakfast. Check-out noon, check-in 3 pm. TV; cable (premium), VCR available. In-room modem link. In-house fitness room. Health club privileges. Pool. **$**

Estes Park

Motel/Motor Lodge

★★ **OLYMPUS MOTOR LODGE.** *2365 Big Thompson Hwy 34 (80517). Phone 970/586-8141; toll-free 800/248-8141; fax 970/586-8143. www.estes-park.com/olympus.* 17 rooms. Pets accepted, some restrictions; fee. Check-out 10 am. TV. Restaurant. Lawn games. Airport transportation. **$**

Fort Collins

Motels/Motor Lodges

★ **BEST WESTERN UNIVERSITY INN.** *914 S College Ave (80524). Phone 970/484-1984; fax 970/484-1987. www.bestwestern.com.* 75 rooms, 2 story. Pets

accepted, some restrictions; fee. Complimentary continental breakfast. Check-out 11 am, check-in 3 pm. TV; cable (premium). In-room modem link. In-house fitness room. Pool. **$**

★★ **HOLIDAY INN.** *3836 E Mulberry St (80524). Phone 970/484-4660; fax 970/484-2326. www.holiday-inn.com.* 198 rooms, 4 story. Pets accepted, some restrictions; fee. Check-out noon, check-in 4 pm. TV; cable (premium), VCR available. In-room modem link. Laundry services. Restaurant, bar. Room service. In-house fitness room; sauna. Game room. Indoor pool; children's pool; whirlpool. **$**

Hotel

★★★ **MARRIOTT FORT COLLINS.** *350 E Horsetooth Rd (80525). Phone 970/226-5200; fax 970/282-0561. www.marriott.com.* Located just 3 miles from Colorado State University, the Marriott is a great place to stay during parents' weekend. 256 rooms, 6 story. Pets accepted, some restrictions; fee. Check-out noon, check-in 4 pm. TV; cable (premium), VCR available. In-room modem link. Restaurant, bar. Room service. In-house fitness room. Indoor, outdoor pool; whirlpool. Cross-country ski 15 miles. Business center. Concierge. Luxury level. **$**

Fort Morgan

Motels/Motor Lodges

★ **BEST WESTERN PARK TERRACE INN.** *725 Main (80701). Phone 970/867-8256; toll-free 888/593-5793; fax 970/867-8257. www.bestwestern.com.* 24 rooms, 2 story. Pets accepted; fee. Check-out 11 am. TV; cable (premium). In-room modem link. Pool; whirlpool; poolside service. **$**

★ **CENTRAL MOTEL.** *201 W Platte Ave (80701). Phone 970/867-2401.* 19 rooms. Pets accepted. Check-out 11 am, check-in 2 pm. TV; cable (premium). **$**

Glenwood Springs

Motel/Motor Lodge

★ **RUSTY CANNON MOTEL.** *701 Taughenbaugh Blvd (81650). Phone 970/625-4004; fax 970/625-3604. www.rustycannonmotel.com.* 89 rooms, 2 story. Pets accepted, some restrictions. Check-out 11 am, check-in 3 pm. TV; cable (premium). In-room modem link. Sauna. Outdoor pool. Ski privileges. Horseback riding. **$**

Golden

Motel/Motor Lodge

★ **LA QUINTA INN.** *3301 Youngfield Service Rd (80401). Phone 303/279-5565; toll-free 800/687-6667; fax 303/279-5841. www.laquinta.com.* 129 rooms, 3 story. Pets accepted. Complimentary continental breakfast. Check-out noon. TV; cable (premium). In-room modem link. Laundry services. Health club privileges. Pool. **$**

Granby

Resort

★★ **INN AT SILVERCREEK.** *62927 US 40 (80451). Phone 970/887-2131; toll-free 800/927-4386; fax 970/887-4083. www.silvercreeklodging.com.* 342 rooms, 3 story. No A/C. Pets accepted, some restrictions; fee. Check-out 11 am, check-in 4 pm. TV; cable (premium). Fireplaces. Bar. In-house fitness room; sauna. Pool; whirlpool. Outdoor tennis, lighted courts. Downhill ski 1 mile. Fishing. Racquetball. Sleigh rides. Whitewater rafting. **$**

Grand Junction

Motels/Motor Lodges

★ **BUDGET HOST INN.** *721 Horizon Dr (81506). Phone 970/243-6050; toll-free 800/888-5736; fax 970/243-0310. www.budgethost.com.* 54 rooms, 2 story. Pets accepted; fee. Complimentary continental breakfast. Check-out 11 am, check-in 3 pm. TV; cable (premium). Laundry services. Pool. **$**

★★ **HOLIDAY INN.** *755 Horizon Dr (81506). Phone 970/243-6790; toll-free 888/489-9796. www.holiday-inn.com.* 292 rooms. Pets accepted. Check-out 11 am, check-in 4 pm. TV; cable (premium), VCR available. In-room modem link. Restaurant, bar; entertainment. Room service. In-house fitness room; sauna. Game room. Indoor, outdoor pool; children's pool; whirlpool. Airport transportation. **$**

★★ **RAMADA INN.** *752 Horizon Dr (81506). Phone 970/243-5150; fax 970/242-3692. www.ramadagj.com.* 100 rooms, 2 story. Pets accepted, some restrictions; fee. Check-out noon, check-in 3 pm. TV; cable (premium), VCR available. In-room modem link. Laundry services. Restaurant. Outdoor pool; whirlpool. Free airport transportation. **$**

Hotel

★★ **GRAND VISTA HOTEL.** *2790 Crossroads Blvd (81506). Phone 970/241-8411; toll-free 800/800-7796; fax 970/241-1077. www.grandvistahotel.com.* 158 rooms, 6 story. Pets accepted, some restrictions; fee. Check-out noon, check-in 3 pm. TV; cable (premium). In-room modem link. Restaurant, bar. Room service. Health club privileges. Indoor pool; whirlpool. Free airport transportation. **$**

Greeley

Motel/Motor Lodge

★★ **BEST WESTERN REGENCY HOTEL.** *701 8th St (80631). Phone 970/353-8444; toll-free 800/780-7234; fax 970/353-4269. www.bestwestern.com.* 148 rooms, 3 story. Pets accepted, some restrictions; fee. Complimentary continental breakfast. Check-out 11 am. TV; cable (premium). In-room modem link. Restaurant, bar. Room service. Health club privileges. Indoor pool. **$**

Gunnison

Motel/Motor Lodge

★ **RAMADA INN.** *1011 W Rio Grande Ave (81230). Phone 970/641-2804; fax 970/641-1420. www.ramada.com.* 36 rooms, 2 story. Pets accepted, some restrictions; fee. Complimentary continental breakfast. Check-out 11 am, check-in 3 pm. TV. Indoor pool; whirlpool. **$**

Idaho Springs

B&B/Small Inn

★★★ **ST. MARY'S GLACIER BED AND BREAKFAST.** *336 Crest Dr (80452). Phone 303/567-4084.* Looking to ski in July? Visit North America's highest bed-and-breakfast where the snow stays year-round!

Only an hour from Denver, this log retreat borders the Arapaho National Forest. Romantic guest rooms feature hand-sewn quilts, and many have private decks with spectacular views. 7 rooms, 3 story. No A/C. No elevator. Pets accepted, some restrictions; fee. Complimentary full breakfast. Check-out 11 am, check-in 4-7 pm. TV in common room; VCR available (movies). In-room modem link. Game room. Totally nonsmoking. **$**

La Junta

Motels/Motor Lodges

★ ★ **BEST WESTERN BENT FORT'S INN.** *10950 US 50 (81054). Phone 719/456-0011; fax 719/456-2550. www.bestwestern.com.* 38 rooms, 2 story. Pets accepted. Complimentary breakfast. Check-out 11 am. TV. In-room modem link. Restaurant, bar. Room service. Pool. Free airport transportation. **$**

★ ★ **QUALITY INN.** *1325 E Third St (81050). Phone 719/384-2571; toll-free 800/525-8682; fax 719/384-5655.* 76 rooms, 2 story. Pets accepted, some restrictions; fee. Complimentary breakfast. TV; cable (premium), VCR available (movies). Restaurant, bar. Room service. In-house fitness room. Indoor, outdoor pool; whirlpool; poolside service. Free airport transportation. **$**

Lake City

Motel/Motor Lodge

★ ★ **MELODY C. CRYSTAL LODGE.** *2175 US 149S (81235). Phone 970/944-2201; toll-free 800/984-1234; fax 970/944-2503. www.crystallodge.net.* 28 rooms, 1-2 story. No A/C. No room phones. Pets accepted, some restrictions; fee. Check-out 10 am, check-in noon. TV; cable (premium), VCR available. Restaurant. Whirlpool. Cross-country ski 1 mile. Surrounded by San Juan Mountains. Totally nonsmoking. **$**

Lakewood

Motel/Motor Lodge

★ ★ **HOLIDAY INN.** *7390 W Hampden Ave (80227). Phone 303/980-9200; toll-free 800/465-4329; fax 303/980-*

6423. www.holiday-inn.com. 190 rooms, 6 story. Pets accepted, some restrictions; fee. Check-out noon. TV; cable (premium). In-room modem link. Restaurant, bar. Room service. In-house fitness room; sauna. Health club privileges. Pool; whirlpool. **$**

Lamar

Motels/Motor Lodges

★ ★ **BEST WESTERN COW PALACE INN.** *1301 N Main St (81052). Phone 719/336-7753; toll-free 800/678-0344; fax 719/336-9598. www.bestwestern.com.* 95 rooms, 2 story. Pets accepted. Complimentary breakfast buffet. Check-out 11 am. TV; cable (premium), VCR available. Restaurant, bar. Room service. Health club privileges. Indoor pool; whirlpool; poolside service. Free airport transportation. **$**

★ **BLUE SPRUCE.** *1801 S Main St (81052). Phone 719/336-7454; fax 719/336-4729.* 30 rooms. Pets accepted; fee. Complimentary continental breakfast. Check-out 11 am. TV; cable (premium). Pool. Free airport transportation. **$**

Limon

Motels/Motor Lodges

★ **BEST WESTERN LIMON INN.** *925 T Ave (80828). Phone 719/775-0277; fax 719/775-2921. www.bestwestern.com.* 47 rooms, 2 story. Pets accepted; fee. Complimentary continental breakfast. Check-out 11 am. TV; cable (premium). In-room modem link. Indoor pool. **$**

★ **PREFERRED MOTOR INN.** *158 E Main (80828). Phone 719/775-2385; fax 719/775-2901.* 57 rooms. Pets accepted; fee. Check-out 10 am. TV; cable (premium). Indoor pool; whirlpool. Free airport transportation. **$**

★ **SAFARI MOTEL.** *637 Main St (80828). Phone 719/775-2363; toll-free 800/330-7021; fax 719/775-2316.* 28 rooms, 1-2 story. Pets accepted; fee. Check-out 10 am. TV; cable (premium). In-room modem link. Pool. **$**

Longmont

Hotel

★★ **RAINTREE PLAZA HOTEL.** *1900 Ken Pratt Blvd (80501). Phone 303/776-2000; toll-free 800/843-8240; fax 303/678-7361. www.raintreeplaza.com.* 211 rooms, 2 story. Pets accepted; fee. Complimentary continental breakfast. Check-out noon. TV; cable (premium). In-room modem link. Laundry services. Restaurant, bar. Room service. In-house fitness room; sauna, steam room. Pool. Valet parking. Airport transportation. **$**

Manitou Springs

Motel/Motor Lodge

★ **REDWING MOTEL.** *56 El Paso Blvd (80829). Phone 719/685-5656; toll-free 800/733-9547; fax 719/685-9547. www.pikes-peak.com/redwing.* 27 rooms, 2 story. Pets accepted; fee. Check-out 10 am. TV. Pool. **$**

Mesa Verde National Park

Motel/Motor Lodge

★★ **FAR VIEW LODGE IN MESA VERDE.** *1 Navajo Hill, Mile 15 (81328). Phone 970/529-4421; fax 970/533-7831.* 150 rooms, 1-2 story. No A/C. No room phones. Closed late Oct-mid-Apr. Pets accepted, some restrictions; fee. Check-out 11 am. Room service 24 hours. Restaurant, dining room, bar. Hiking trails. Mesa Verde tours available. Camping sites, trailer facilities. Educational programs. View of canyon. Totally non-smoking. **$**

Monte Vista

Motels/Motor Lodges

★★ **BEST WESTERN MOVIE MANOR.** *2830 W US 160 (81144). Phone 719/852-5921; toll-free 800/771-9468; fax 719/852-0122. www.bestwestern.com.* 60 rooms, 2 story. Pets accepted, some restrictions; fee. Check-out 11 am, check-in noon. TV; cable (premium). Restaurant, bar. Drive-in movies visible from rooms; speakers in most rooms. **$**

★ **COMFORT INN.** *1519 Grand Ave (81144). Phone 719/852-0612; fax 719/852-3585. www.comfortinn.com.* 44 rooms, 2 story. Pets accepted. Complimentary continental breakfast. Check-out 11 am, check-in noon. TV; cable (premium). In-room modem link. Indoor pool; whirlpool. **$**

Montrose

Motels/Motor Lodges

★ **BEST WESTERN RED ARROW.** *1702 E Main St (81402). Phone 970/249-9641; toll-free 800/468-9323; fax 970/249-8380. www.bestwestern.com/redarrow.* 62 rooms, 2 story. Pets accepted; fee. Check-out 11 am. TV; cable (premium), VCR available. In-room modem link. Restaurant. In-house fitness room. Pool; whirlpool. Lawn games. Free airport transportation. Business center. Concierge. **$**

★ **BLACK CANYON.** *1605 E Main St (81401). Phone 970/249-3495; toll-free 800/348-3495; fax 970/249-0990. www.toski.com/black-canyon.com.* 49 rooms, 1-2 story. Pets accepted; fee. Check-out 11 am, check-in. TV; cable (premium). Outdoor pool. **$**

★ **SAN JUAN INN.** *1480 S Townsend (81401). Phone 970/249-6644; toll-free 888/681-4159; fax 970/249-9314. www.sanjuaninn.com.* 51 rooms, 2 story. Pets accepted, some restrictions; fee. Complimentary continental breakfast. Check-out 11 am, check-in 2 pm. TV; cable (premium). Indoor pool; whirlpool. Free airport transportation. **$**

Ouray

Motels/Motor Lodges

★★ **OURAY VICTORIAN INN & TOWNHOMES.** *50 3rd Ave (81427). Phone 970/325-7222; toll-free 800/846-8729; fax 970/325-7225. www.ouraylodging.com.* 38 rooms, 2 story. No A/C. Pets accepted, some restrictions. Complimentary continental breakfast (Oct-May). Check-out 11 am. TV; cable (premium). In-room modem link. Two whirlpools. On river. **$**

★ **SUPER 8.** *373 Palomino Trail (81432). Phone 970/626-5444; toll-free 800/368-5444; fax 970/626-5888. www.super8.com.* 52 rooms, 2 story. Pets accepted, some restrictions; fee. Check-out 11 am. TV; cable (premium). In-room modem link. Sauna. Pool; whirlpool. Mountain views. **$**

Pagosa Springs

Motels/Motor Lodges

★★ **BEST VALUE HIGH COUNTRY LODGE.** *3821 E Hwy 160 (81147). Phone 970/264-4181; toll-free 800/862-3707; fax 970/264-4185. www.highcountrylodge.com.* 35 rooms, 2 story. Pets accepted; fee. Complimentary continental breakfast. Check-out 11 am, check-in 2:30 pm. TV. In-room modem link. Restaurant. Whirlpool. Downhill ski 20 miles, cross-country ski 3 miles. **$**

★ **RED LION INN & SUITES.** *3565 Hwy 60 W (81147). Phone 970/731-3400; toll-free 888/221-8088; fax 970/731-3402. www.pagosaspringsinn.com.* 97 rooms, 3 story. Pets accepted, some restrictions; fee. Check-out noon, check-in 3 pm. TV; cable (premium). In-house fitness room. Game room. Indoor pool; whirlpool. Cross-country ski 3 miles. **$**

Pueblo

Motel/Motor Lodge

★★ **BEST WESTERN INN AT PUEBLO WEST.** *201 S McCulloch Blvd (81007). Phone 719/547-2111; toll-free 800/448-1972; fax 719/547-0385. www.bestwestern.com/innatpueblow.* 79 rooms, 2 story. Pets accepted; fee. Check-out 11 am. TV; cable (premium). Restaurant. In-house fitness room. Pool. **$**

Salida

Motel/Motor Lodge

★ **TRAVELODGE.** *7310 W US Hwy 50 (81201). Phone 719/539-2528; toll-free 800/234-1077; fax 719/539-7235. www.salidatravelodge.com.* 27 rooms, 2 story. Pets accepted, some restrictions; fee. Check-out 11 am, check-in 2 pm. TV; cable (premium), VCR available. Outdoor pool; whirlpool. Downhill, cross-country ski 18 miles. Fishing, rafting. **$**

Silverton

B&B/Small Inns

★★ **ALMA HOUSE BED AND BREAKFAST.** *220 E 10th St (81433). Phone 970/387-5336; toll-free 800/267-5336; fax 970/387-5974.* 10 rooms, 2 1/2 story. No room phones. Pets accepted, some restrictions; fee. Complimentary full breakfast. Check-out 11 am, check-in 2 pm. TV; cable (premium). Built 1898. Victorian furnishings. Totally nonsmoking. **$**

★★★ **WYMAN HOTEL.** *1371 Greene St (81433). Phone 970/387-5372; toll-free 800/609-7845; fax 970/387-5745. www.silverton.org/wymanhotel.* 18 rooms, 2 story. Closed Nov, Dec, Mar, Apr. Pets accepted, some restrictions; fee. Complimentary full breakfast. Check-out 10:30 am, check-in after 3 pm. TV; cable (premium), VCR available. In-room modem link. Built 1902. Victorian furnishings. Totally nonsmoking. **$**

Snowmass Village

Motel/Motor Lodge

★★★ **SILVERTREE HOTEL.** *100 Elbert Ln (81615). Phone 970/923-3520; toll-free 800/837-4255; fax 970/923-5192. www.silvertreehotel.com.* This year-round mountain resort provides skiing right from the hotel with over 5,000 acres of ski area. Summer brings balloon rides, hiking, and jazz concerts. 260 rooms, 2-7 story. No A/C. Pets accepted, some restrictions. Check-out 11 am. TV; cable (premium). In-room modem link. Laundry services. Restaurant; entertainment. Room service. Children's activity center, babysitting services available. In-house fitness room; massage, steam room. Outdoor pool; children's pool; whirlpool; poolside service. Downhill, cross-country ski on site. Lawn games, bicycles. Free local airport transportation. Business center. Concierge. **$$$**

Resort

★★ **WILDWOOD LODGE.** *40 Elbert Ln (81615). Phone 970/923-3550; toll-free 800/445-1642; fax 970/923-5494. www.wildwood-lodge.com.* 140 rooms, 3 story. Closed early Apr-May. Pets accepted, some restrictions.

Complimentary continental breakfast. Check-out 11 am, check-in 4 pm. TV; cable (premium), VCR available. In-room modem link. Laundry services. Restaurant. Room service. Children's activity center, babysitting services available. Health club privileges. Outdoor pool; children's pool; whirlpool; poolside service. Downhill, cross-country ski 1 block. Free airport transportation. Concierge. **$$**

Steamboat Springs

Motels/Motor Lodges

★ **ALPINER LODGE.** *424 Lincoln Ave (80488). Phone 970/879-1430; toll-free 800/538-7519; fax 970/879-6044. www.steamboat-lodging.com.* 33 rooms, 2 story. Pets accepted; fee. Check-out 10 am. TV; cable (premium). In-room modem link. Downhill ski 1 mile, cross-country ski 1/2 mile. **$**

★ ★ **BEST WESTERN PTARMIGAN INN.** *2304 Apres Ski Way (80477). Phone 970/897-1730; toll-free 800/538-7519; fax 970/879-6044. www.steamboat-lodging.com.* 77 rooms, 3-4 story. Late Nov-mid-Apr: S, D $72-$234; each additional $10; under 18 free; higher rates late Dec; package plans; varied lower rates rest of year. Closed early Apr-late May. Pets accepted, some restrictions; fee. Check-out 10 am. TV; VCR. In-room modem link. Laundry services. Restaurant, bar. Room service. Sauna. Pool; whirlpool. Downhill, cross-country ski on site. View of Mount Werner and the valley.

★ ★ **HOLIDAY INN.** *3190 S Lincoln Ave (80477). Phone 970/879-2250; toll-free 800/654-3944; fax 970/879-0251. www.holidayinnsteamboat.com.* 82 rooms, 2 story. Pets accepted, some restrictions; fee. Check-out 11 am. TV; cable (premium), VCR available. In-room modem link. Restaurant, bar. Room service. In-house fitness room. Game room. Pool; children's pool; whirlpool. Downhill, cross-country ski 1 mile. Lawn games. **$**

Sterling

Motels/Motor Lodges

★ **BEST WESTERN SUNDOWNER.** *Overland Trail St (80751). Phone 970/522-6265; toll-free 800/780-7234. www.bestwestern.com.* 30 rooms. Pets accepted, some restrictions; fee. Complimentary continental breakfast. Check-out 11 am. TV; cable (premium), VCR available. In-room modem link. In-house fitness room. Pool; whirlpool. **$**

★ **COLONIAL MOTEL.** *915 S Division Ave (80751). Phone 970/522-3382; toll-free 888/522-2901.* 14 rooms. Pets accepted, some restrictions; fee. Check-out 10 am. TV; cable (premium). In-room modem link. **$**

★ ★ **RAMADA.** *22246 E Hwy 6 (80751). Phone 970/522-2625; toll-free 800/835-7275; fax 970/522-1321. www.ramada.com.* 100 rooms, 2 story. Pets accepted, some restrictions; fee. Check-out noon. TV; cable (premium). In-room modem link. Restaurant, bar. In-house fitness room; sauna. Game room. Indoor pool; whirlpool. **$**

Telluride

Hotel

★ ★ ★ **COLUMBIA HOTEL.** *300 W San Juan Ave (81435). Phone 970/728-0660; toll-free 800/201-9505; fax 970/728-9249. www.columbiatelluride.com.* 21 rooms, 4 story. No A/C. Pets accepted, some restrictions; fee. Check-out 11 am. TV; cable (premium), VCR available. In-room modem link. Fireplaces. Laundry services. Restaurant, bar. Room service. In-house fitness room. Downhill, cross-country ski/snowboard on site. **$$**

Resort

★ ★ ★ **WYNDHAM - THE PEAKS RESORT.** *136 Country Club Dr (81435). Phone 970/728-6800; toll-free 800/789-2220; fax 970/728-6175. www.peaksresort.com.* 174 rooms, 6 story. Closed mid-Apr-mid-May, mid-Oct-mid-Nov. Pets accepted; fee. Check-out noon, check-in 4 pm. TV; cable (premium), VCR. In-room modem link. Dining room, bar. Room service. Supervised children's activities. Babysitting services available. In-house fitness room; spa, massage, sauna. Indoor, outdoor pool; children's pool; whirlpool; poolside service. Golf; greens fee $160 (including cart). Outdoor tennis, lighted courts. Downhill, cross-country ski on site; rentals. Hiking, sleighing, snowmobiles. Valet parking. Free airport transportation. Business center. Concierge. **$$$**

Trinidad

Motels/Motor Lodges

★ **BUDGET HOST INN.** *10301 Santa Fe Trail (81082). Phone 719/846-3307; toll-free 800/BUDHOST; fax 719/846-3309. www.trinidadco.com/budgethost.* 26 rooms. Pets accepted, some restrictions; fee. Complimentary continental breakfast. Check-out 11 am. TV. Whirlpool. Lawn games. Free airport transportation. Features 107-foot oil derrick. Located along the Mountain Branch of the Santa Fe Trail. **$**

D 🐾 🛉 🛟 SC

★ **BUDGET SUMMIT INN.** *9800 Santa Fe Trail Dr (81082). Phone 719/846-2251.* 44 rooms, 2 story. Pets accepted; fee. Complimentary continental breakfast. Check-out 11 am. TV. In-room modem link. Laundry services. Whirlpool. Lawn games. **$**

D 🐾 🛟

★ ★ **HOLIDAY INN.** *3125 Toupal Dr (81082). Phone 719/846-4491; fax 719/846-2440. www.holiday-inn.com.* 113 rooms, 2 story. Pets accepted. Check-out noon. TV; cable (premium). In-room modem link. Restaurant, bar. Room service. In-house fitness room. Game room. Indoor pool; whirlpool; poolside service. Lawn games. **$**

D 🐾 🖘 🛏 🛉 🛟

Walsenburg

Motel/Motor Lodge

★ ★ **BEST WESTERN RAMBLER.** *I-25, exit 52 (81089). Phone 719/738-1121; fax 719/738-1093. www.bestwestern.com.* 35 rooms. Pets accepted, some restrictions. Check-out 11 am. TV. In-room modem link. Restaurant. Pool. **$**

D 🐾 🛏 🛟

Winter Park

Motel/Motor Lodge

★ **HIGH MOUNTAIN LODGE INC.** *425 County Rd 5001 (66211). Phone 970/726-5958; fax 970/726-9796. www.himtnlodge.com.* 12 air-cooled rooms, 2 story. Mid-Dec-early Apr: $80/person; weekly rates; higher rates special events; lower rates rest of year. Closed May. Pets accepted, some restrictions; fee. Complimentary full breakfast. Check-out 10 am. TV in recreation room; VCR available. Fireplaces. Laundry services. Bar. In-house fitness room; massage, sauna. Game room. Indoor pool; whirlpool. Downhill, cross-country ski 9 miles. Lawn games. Concierge. Opposite stream.

D 🐾 🖘 🛏 🛉

Hotels

★ ★ **THE VINTAGE RESORT.** *100 Winter Park Dr (80482). Phone 970/726-8801; toll-free 800/472-7017; fax 970/726-9230. www.vintagehotel.com.* 170 rooms, 5 story. Pets accepted; fee. Check-out 11 am. TV; cable (premium). In-room modem link. Restaurant, bar. In-house fitness room; sauna. Game room. Pool; whirlpool. Downhill, cross-country ski. **$**

D 🐾 🖘 🛏 🛉 🛟

★ **WINTER PARK MOUNTAIN LODGE.** *81699 US 40 (80482). Phone 970/726-6328; fax 970/726-1094.* 162 rooms, 5 story. Pets accepted, some restrictions. Complimentary continental breakfast. Check-out 10 am, check-in 4 pm. TV. Restaurant. Indoor pool; whirlpool. **$**

D 🐾 🛏

Connecticut

Branford

Motel/Motor Lodge

★ **DAYS INN.** *375 E Main St (06405). Phone 203/488-8314; toll-free 800/329-7466; fax 203/483-6885. www.daysinn.com.* 74 rooms, 2 story. S $75-$80; D $90-$99; each additional $10; suites $245; under 16 free. Pets accepted, some restrictions; fee. Complimentary continental breakfast. Check-out 11 am. TV; cable (premium), VCR available. Restaurant. Pool. Business center.

D 🐾 ➰ ⬛ SC 🚶

Bridgeport

Motel/Motor Lodge

★ ★ **HOLIDAY INN.** *1070 Main St (06604). Phone 203/334-1234; fax 203/367-1985. www.holiday-inn.com.* 234 rooms, 9 story. S $79-$119; D $89-$129; each additional $10; suites $179-$450; under 16 free; family, weekend rates. Pets accepted, some restrictions; fee. Check-out noon. TV. In-room modem link. Restaurant, bar. In-house fitness room. Indoor, outdoor pool. Free covered parking. Free airport, train station, bus depot transportation. Business center.

D 🐾 🛗 ➰ 🚶 🎿 ⬛ 🚶

Cornwall Bridge

B&B/Small Inn

★ **CORNWALL INN AND RESTAURANT.** *270 Kent Rd; Rte 7 (06754). Phone 860/672-6884; toll-free 800/786-6884; fax 860/672-0352. www.cornwallinn.com.* 14 rooms, 2 story. No room phones. Pets accepted, some restrictions; fee. Complimentary continental breakfast. Check-out 11 am, check-in 2 pm. TV. Dining room, bar. Pool. Restored 19th-century country inn; antiques. **$**

D 🐾 ➰

Danbury

Motel/Motor Lodge

★ ★ **HOLIDAY INN.** *80 Newtown Rd (06810). Phone 203/792-4000; toll-free 800/465-4329; fax 203/797-0810. www.danburyholidayinn.com.* 114 rooms, 4 story. Apr-Dec: S, D $124; suites $109-$114; under 18 free; lower rates rest of year. Pets accepted; fee. Check-out noon. TV; cable (premium), VCR available. In-room modem link. Room service 24 hours. Restaurant, bar. Health club privileges. Pool; poolside service. Free airport transportation.

D 🐾 🏊 ⬛ SC

East Haddam

B&B/Small Inn

★ ★ **BISHOPSGATE INN.** *7 Norwich Rd (06423). Phone 860/873-1677; fax 860/873-3898. www.bishopsgate.com.* 6 rooms, 2 story. D $100-$150; each additional $15; suite $150. Pets accepted, some restrictions. Children over 5 years only. Complimentary breakfast. Check-out 11 am, check-in 2 pm. Near Connecticut River. Colonial house (1818) furnished with period pieces. **$**

D 🐾 🛗 🎿 ➰

Farmington

Hotel

★ ★ **THE FARMINGTON INN.** *827 Farmington Ave (06032). Phone 860/677-2821; toll-free 800/648-9804; fax 860/677-8332. www.farmingtoninn.com.* 72 rooms, 2 story. S, D $119-$149; each additional $10; suites $109-$149; under 16 free. Pets accepted, some restrictions. Complimentary continental breakfast. Check-out 11 am. TV; cable (premium), VCR available. In-room modem link. Health club privileges. Golf on premise. Cross-country ski 1 1/2 miles.

D 🐾 🛗 ⚡ 🎿 🚶 ➰ SC

All Suite

★ ★ **CENTENNIAL INN SUITES.** *5 Spring Ln (06032). Phone 860/677-4647; toll-free 800/852-2052; fax 860/676-0685. www.centennialinn.com.* 112 kitchen units, 2 story. S, D $119-$209; family, weekend rates. Pets accepted; fee. Complimentary continental breakfast.

Check-out noon. TV; cable (premium), VCR available. In-room modem link. Fireplaces. Laundry services. In-house fitness room. Pool; whirlpool. Downhill ski 15 miles. Business center. On 12 wooded acres.

Hartford

Motel/Motor Lodge

★ ★ **HOLIDAY INN.** 363 Roberts St (06108). Phone 860/528-9611; toll-free 800/465-4329; fax 860/289-0270. www.holiday-inn.com. 130 rooms, 5 story. S, D $65-$85; under 18 free; weekend rates. Pets accepted; fee. Check-out noon. TV; cable (premium). In-room modem link. Laundry services. Restaurant, bar. Room service. In-house fitness room. Indoor pool.

Hotels

★ ★ **CROWNE PLAZA.** 50 Morgan St (06120). Phone 860/549-2400; toll-free 800/227-6963; fax 860/549-7844. www.crowneplaza.com. Located in the heart of downtown Hartford, this popular hotel is within walking distance of Hartford's popular theater district. 350 rooms, 18 story. Pets accepted, some restrictions; fee. Check-out noon, check-in 3 pm. TV; cable (premium), VCR available. In-room modem link. Restaurant, bar. In-house fitness room. Outdoor pool; poolside service. Free airport transportation. Business center. $

★ ★ ★ **SHERATON HARTFORD HOTEL.** 100 E River Dr (06108). Phone 860/528-9703; toll-free 888/530-9703; fax 860/289-4728. www.sheraton.com. 199 rooms, 8 story. S $219; each additional $10; suites $150-$200; under 18 free; weekend rates. Pets accepted, some restrictions; fee. Check-out 11 am. TV; cable (premium). In-room modem link. Laundry services. Restaurant, bar. Room service. Health club privileges. Indoor pool.

Lakeville

Motel/Motor Lodge

★ ★ **INN AT IRON MASTERS.** 229 N Main St (06039). Phone 860/435-9844; fax 860/435-2254. www.inn atironmasters.com. 28 rooms. Apr-Nov: S $95-$135; D $105-$145; each additional $15; under 15 free; lower rates rest of year. Pets accepted, some restrictions. Check-out 11 am. TV. Restaurant, bar. Continental breakfast.

Resort

★ ★ ★ **INTERLAKEN INN.** 74 Interlaken Rd (06039). Phone 860/435-9878; toll-free 800/222-2909; fax 860/435-2980. www.interlakeninn.com. Whether visitors are looking for a family or romantic setting, this cozy lakeside inn has accommodations to suit every need. With recreational activities and tranquil surroundings, guests will find a perfect getaway at this 30-acre spread. 80 rooms, 2 story. May-Oct: S, D $129-$199; each additional $15; suites $265; higher rates special events; lower rates rest of year. Pets accepted, some restrictions; fee. Check-out noon, check-in 3 pm. TV; cable (premium), VCR available. In-room modem link. Restaurant. Room service. In-house fitness room; sauna. Pool. 9-hole golf, pro. Outdoor tennis. Lawn games. Rowboats, canoes, sailboats, paddleboats.

B&B/Small Inn

★ ★ **WAKE ROBIN INN.** Rte 41 (06039). Phone 860/435-2515; fax 860/435-2000. www.wakerobininn.com. 39 rooms, 2 story. Pets accepted, some restrictions; fee. Check-out noon, check-in 3 pm. TV; cable (premium). On hill. $$

Madison

B&B/Small Inn

★ ★ **MADISON BEACH HOTEL.** 94 W Wharf Rd (06443). Phone 203/245-1404; fax 203/245-0410. www. madisonbeachhotel.com. 35 rooms, 4 story. No elevator. Closed Jan-Feb. Pets accepted, some restrictions; fee. Complimentary continental breakfast. Check-out 11 am, check-in after 2pm. TV; cable (premium). Restaurant, bar. Lawn games. $

Manchester

All Suite

★ ★ **CLARION HOTEL.** 191 Spencer St (06040). Phone 860/643-5811; toll-free 800/992-4004. www.clarion suites.com. 104 kitchen units, 2 story. S, D $99-$139; under 16 free; weekend rates. Pets accepted; fee. Complimentary full breakfast. Check-out noon. TV; VCR available. Laundry services. In-house fitness room. Pool; whirlpool. Downhill, cross-country ski 20 miles. Lawn games. Free airport, railroad station transportation.

Extended Stay

★★ **RESIDENCE INN BY MARRIOTT.** *201 Hale Rd (06040). Phone 860/432-4242; fax 860/432-4243. www.residenceinn.com.* Guests can take advantage of the on-site sport court, or unwind in guest suites featuring fully equipped kitchens and separate living and sleeping areas. 96 rooms, 3 story. D $99-$199. Pets accepted; fee. Complimentary buffet breakfast. Check-out noon, check-in 3 pm. TV; cable (premium). In-room modem link. Laundry services. In-house fitness room. Outdoor pool.

⌨️🐾🎿❄️

Middletown

Motel/Motor Lodge

★ **COMFORT INN.** *111 Berlin Rd (Hwy 372) (06416). Phone 860/635-4100; toll-free 800/228-5150; fax 860/632-9546. www.comfortinn.com.* 77 rooms, 4 story. S $54; D $61; each additional $6; under 18 free. Pets accepted, some restrictions; fee. Complimentary continental breakfast. Check-out 11 am. TV; VCR available. Health club privileges.

D 🐾 ❄️ SC

Mystic

B&B/Small Inns

★ **APPLEWOOD FARMS INN.** *528 Colonel Ledyard Hwy (06339). Phone 860/536-2022; toll-free 800/717-4262; fax 860/536-6015. www.visitmystic.com/applewoodfarmsinn.* 5 rooms, 1 suite, 2 story. No room phones. S $109; D $125, each additional $25; suite $250; weekly rates; weekends (2-day minimum), holidays (3-day minimum). Pets accepted, some restrictions. Children over 8 years only. Complimentary breakfast. Check-out 11 am, check-in 3 pm. House built in 1826, once used as town hall; many fireplaces, colonial atmosphere.

🐾 ❄️

★★ **INN AT MYSTIC.** *Rtes 1 and 27 (06355). Phone 860/536-9604; toll-free 800/237-2415; fax 860/572-1635. www.innatmystic.com.* Built on a hillside overlooking the harbor and sound, this remarkable inn offers simple elegance during any season. With complimentary tours of the gardens, afternoon tea and pastries, and luxurious guest rooms, this inn is a special treat. 67 rooms, 2 story. Pets accepted, some restrictions; fee. Check-out 11 am, check-in 3 pm. TV; cable (premium), VCR available. Fireplaces. Restaurant, bar. Room service. Outdoor pool. Outdoor tennis. Long Island Sound 1/4 mile. **$**

🐾🎿🏊❄️

New London

Motel/Motor Lodge

★ **RED ROOF INN.** *707 Colman St (06320). Phone 860/444-0001; fax 860/443-7154. www.redroof.com.* 108 rooms, 2 story. May-Oct: S $39.99-$57; D $34.99-$77; each additional $5; under 18 free; higher rates special events; lower rates rest of year. Pets accepted, some restrictions. Check-out noon. TV; cable (premium), VCR available. In-room modem link.

D 🐾 🐾 🎿 ❄️

Old Lyme

B&B/Small Inn

★★★ **OLD LYME INN.** *85 Lyme St (06371). Phone 860/434-2600; toll-free 800/434-5352; fax 860/434-5352. www.oldlymeinn.com.* Located in the historic district of Old Lyme, this bed-and-breakfast is close to Essex, Mystic Seaport, Mystic Aquarium, and art galleries. Guests can also enjoy outlet shopping and visiting the local museums. 13 rooms, 2 story. Pets accepted, some restrictions. Complimentary continental breakfast. Check-out noon, check-in 3-11 pm. TV; VCR available. Restaurant, bar. Business center. Built in 1850, former farm; antiques, murals. **$$**

D 🐾 ❄️ 🎿

Plainfield

Motel/Motor Lodge

★ **PLAINFIELD MOTEL.** *66 E Main St (06354). Phone 860/564-2791.* 35 rooms. S, D $56-$89; each additional $10. Pets accepted; fee. Check-out noon. TV; cable (premium). Laundry services. Pool.

D 🐾 🏊 ❄️

Putnam

Motel/Motor Lodge

★★ **KINGS INN.** *5 Heritage Rd (06260). Phone 860/928-7961; toll-free 800/541-7304; fax 860/963-2463.* 4 rooms, 1-2 story. S $62-$72; D $68-$78; each additional $8; under 12 free; weekly rates. Pets accepted. Complimentary continental breakfast. Check-out 11 am. TV; cable (premium), VCR available. Bar. Pool.

🐾 🐾 🏊 🎿 ❄️ SC

Simsbury

Motel/Motor Lodge

★ **IRON HORSE INN.** *969 Hopmeadow St (06070). Phone 860/658-2216; toll-free 800/245-9938; fax 860/651-0822. www.ironhorseofsimsbury.com.* 27 kitchen units, 2 story. S $79; D $89; under 12 free; weekly rates. Pets accepted, some restrictions; fee. Complimentary continental breakfast. Check-out 11 am. TV. In-room modem link. Sauna. Pool.

🐾🏊🎿🛏️ SC

Southbury

Hotel

★ ★ ★ **HILTON SOUTHBURY.** *1284 Strongtown Rd (06488). Phone 203/598-7600; fax 203/598-0261. www.hilton.com.* Located in the Litchfield Hills area between Boston and New York, this hotel is sprawled in a country setting near numerous local antique centers and shops. The Quassy Amusement Park and several ski areas are also nearby. 198 rooms, 3 story. S $95-$140; suites $125-$315; under 12 free; ski plans; weekend, holiday rates. Pets accepted, some restrictions. Check-out noon. TV; cable (premium), VCR available. In-room modem link. Restaurant, bar. Room service. In-house fitness room; sauna. Indoor pool; whirlpool; poolside service.

D 🐾 🏋️ 🌀 🏊 🎿 🛏️

Wethersfield

Motel/Motor Lodge

★ **BEST WESTERN CAMELOT INN.** *1330 Silas Deane Hwy (06109). Phone 860/563-2311; toll-free 800/228-2828; fax 860/529-2974. www.ramada.com.* 112 rooms, 4 story. S, D $42-$59; under 18 free. Pets accepted, some restrictions; fee. Complimentary continental breakfast. Check-out noon. TV; cable (premium), VCR available. In-room modem link. Laundry services. Bar; entertainment Fri, Sat. Health club privileges. Downhill ski 20 miles.

D 🐾 🏊 🛏️ SC

Windsor Locks

Hotel

★ ★ ★ **SHERATON BRADLEY AIRPORT HOTEL.** *1 Bradley International Airport (06096). Phone 860/627-5311; toll-free 877/422-5311; fax 860/627-9348. www.sheraton.com/bradleyairport.* 237 rooms, 8 story. Sept-June: S, D $139-$205; each additional $15; suites $225-$300; under 5 free; lower rates rest of year. Pets accepted. Check-out noon. TV; VCR available. Restaurant, bar; entertainment Tues-Thurs. In-house fitness room; sauna. Indoor pool. Concierge. Free train station transportation.

D 🐾 🏊 🏋️ 🎿 ✈️ 🛏️ SC

All Suite

★ ★ **HOMEWOOD SUITES.** *65 Ella Grasso Tpke (06096). Phone 860/627-8463; fax 860/627-9313. www.homewoodsuites.com.* 132 kitchen units, 2-3 story. S, D $99-$140. Pets accepted, some restrictions; fee. Complimentary continental breakfast. Check-out noon. TV; VCR available. In-room modem link. Laundry services. In-house fitness room. Pool. Lawn games. Free airport, train station transportation. Business center.

🐾 🏊 🏋️ ✈️

Delaware

Lewes

B&B/Small Inn

★ ★ ★ **INN AT CANAL SQUARE.** *122 Market St (19958). Phone 302/644-3377; toll-free 888/644-1911; fax 302/644-3565. www.theinnatcanalsquare.com.* Adjacent to the beautiful historic district, this charming bed-and-breakfast is the only waterfront inn in Lewes. 26 rooms, 4 story. Pets accepted, some restrictions. Complimentary continental breakfast. Check-out 11 am, check-in 3 pm. TV; cable (premium). In-room modem link. Restaurant. Concierge. On canal. **$**

D ⊷ ⇌ SC

Newark

Motels/Motor Lodges

★ **HOWARD JOHNSON.** *1119 S College Ave (19713). Phone 302/368-8521; toll-free 800/654-2000; fax 302/368-9868. www.hojo.com.* 142 rooms, 2 story. S, D $55; each additional $10; under 18 free. Pets accepted; fee. Complimentary continental breakfast. Check-out noon. TV. In-room modem link. Health club privileges. Pool.

D ⊷ ⇌ ✗ ⇌ SC

★ ★ **QUALITY INN.** *1120 S College Ave (19713). Phone 302/368-8715; toll-free 800/228-5150; fax 302/368-6454. www.qualityinn.com.* 102 rooms, 2 story. S $50-$54; D $56-$60; each additional $6; under 18 free. Pets accepted; fee. Complimentary continental breakfast. Check-out 11 am. TV; VCR available (movies). In-room modem link. Pool.

D ⊷ ⇌ ⇌ SC

New Castle

Motel/Motor Lodge

★ **RODEWAY INN.** *111 S DuPont Hwy (19720). Phone 302/328-6246; toll-free 800/321-6246; fax 302/328-9493. www.rodewayinn.com.* 40 rooms. S $49-$59; D $55-$69; each additional $5; under 18 free. Pets accepted; fee. Complimentary continental breakfast. Check-out noon. TV.

⊷ ↻ ✗ ⇌

Rehoboth Beach

Motel/Motor Lodge

★ **SEA ESTA MOTEL III.** *1409 DE 1 (19971). Phone 302/227-4343; toll-free 800/436-6591; fax 302/227-3049. www.seaesta.com.* 33 kitchen units, 3 story. July-Aug: S, D $100-$150; each additional $10; under 12 free; lower rates rest of year. Pets accepted; fee. Check-out 11 am. TV; cable (premium). Covered parking.

D ⊷ ⇌

Wilmington

Motel/Motor Lodge

★ **BEST WESTERN BRANDYWINE VALLEY INN.** *1807 Concord Pike (19803). Phone 302/656-9436; toll-free 800/537-7772; fax 302/656-8564. www.bestwestern.com.* 95 rooms, 2 story. Pets accepted. Check-out noon. TV; cable (premium), VCR available. In-room modem link. In-house fitness room. Pool; children's pool; whirlpool. **$**

D ⊷ ⇌ ✗ ⇌

Hotel

★ ★ ★ **HOLIDAY INN.** *630 Naamans Rd (19703). Phone 302/792-2700; fax 302/798-6182. www.holiday-inn.com.* 193 rooms, 7 story. S, D $99-$136; each additional $15; suites $150-$275; under 12 free; weekend rates. Pets accepted; fee. Check-out noon. TV; cable (premium). In-room modem link. Restaurant, bar. In-house fitness room. Pool. Free airport transportation.

D ⊷ ⇌ ✗ ⇌ SC

District of Columbia

Washington

Hotels

★★★★ **FOUR SEASONS HOTEL WASHINGTON DC.** *2800 Pennsylvania Ave NW (20007). Phone 202/342-0444; fax 202/944-2076. www.fourseasons.com.* This Four Seasons Hotel is nestled within Washington's lovely and historic Georgetown neighborhood. Just outside the hotel's doors are enticing shops, energetic nightlife, and delectable dining. The warm and inviting atmosphere of the Four Seasons is instantly recognizable in the gracious lobby, where bountiful floral displays and Oriental rugs set a refined, residential tone. The guest accommodations are some of the most spacious in the city and are magnificently appointed with polished formal furnishings, beautiful fabrics, and exquisite attention to detail. The views of Rock Creek Park and the C & O Canal further enhance the relaxing mood. Popular fitness classes are offered in the extremely well-equipped fitness center, complete with a lap pool, while the seven spa treatment rooms provide a restful alternative for personal well-being. Consistently delicious meals are available at Seasons, or you can retreat to the cozy Garden Lounge for afternoon tea or cocktails. Not only is the food memorable, but the politically-charged crowd is unparalleled! *Secret Inspector's Notes:* No time to finish your e-mails before lunch? No problem! When dining at Seasons for lunch, guests are greeted not only with gracious charm but also with the offer of wireless connectivity from an available laptop. 260 rooms, 6 story. Pets accepted, some restrictions. Check-out noon. TV; cable (premium), VCR available (movies). In-room modem link. Room service 24 hours. Valet parking, fee. Business center. Concierge. **$$$$**

★★ **HARRINGTON HOTEL.** *436 11th St NW (20004). Phone 202/628-8140; toll-free 800/424-8532; fax 202/347-3924. www.hotel-harrington.com.* 260 rooms, 11 story. Pets accepted, some restrictions. Check-out noon. TV; cable (premium). Laundry services. Restaurant, bar. **$**

★★★★ **HAY-ADAMS HOTEL.** *16th and H sts NW (20006). Phone 202/638-6600; toll-free 800/424-5054; fax* *202/638-2716. www.hayadams.com.* The Hay-Adams seems to radiate the power of the nation's capital. Set on Lafayette Square across from the White House, the hotel has been welcoming notables since the 1920s. Reading like a Who's Who of American history, the Hay-Adams' guest list is truly fascinating. If only these walls could talk! Originally designed as the private residences of two influential men, the hotel retains the majestic style of its former incarnation. The guest rooms are a happy marriage of historic preservation and 21st-century conveniences; intricately carved plaster ceilings and ornamental fireplaces unite with high-speed Internet access and multiline telephones. Windows frame views of the White House, St. John's Church, and Lafayette Square, further convincing visitors that they are in the center of Washington's universe. All-day dining is available at Lafayette, while the Off the Record bar is a popular watering hole for politicians and hotel guests. 145 rooms, 8 story. Pets accepted, some restrictions. Check-out noon, check-in 3 pm. TV; cable (premium). Room service 24 hours. Restaurant, bar. Babysitting services available. Parking. Concierge. **$$$$**

★★ **HOTEL WASHINGTON.** *515 15th and Pennsylvania Ave NW (20004). Phone 202/638-5900; toll-free 800/424-9540; fax 202/638-1595. www.hotelwashington.com.* 344 rooms, 11 story. Pets accepted. Check-out 1 pm, check-in 3 pm. TV; cable (premium). In-room modem link. Restaurant, bar. In-house fitness room; sauna. Business center. One of the oldest continuously operated hotels in the city. Original Jardin d'Armide tapestry (1854). **$$**

★★★ **THE JEFFERSON.** *1200 16th St NW (20036). Phone 202/347-2200; toll-free 800/235-6397; fax 202/331-7982. www.loweshotels.com.* Just four blocks from the White House, this Beaux Arts hotel, dating to 1923, is a masterpiece of quiet luxury. The antique-filled public rooms recall the elegance of the past, and the museum-quality collection of artwork and original documents signed by Thomas Jefferson is astounding. The guest rooms are a stylish blend of old and new. The seamless, attentive service is outstanding and satisfies every need. A fitness center is available, as are privileges at the University Club, with its Olympic-size pool. The restaurant feels like old Washington with its faux tortoiseshell walls and leather chairs, yet its New American cuisine is all the rage. 100 rooms, 8 story. Pets accepted, some restrictions. Check-out 1 pm. TV; cable (premium), VCR (movies). In-room modem link. Bar, restaurant. Room service 24 hours. Health club privileges. Garage, valet parking, fee. Concierge. Opened in 1923; individually decorated rooms have four-poster beds. **$$$**

★ ★ ★ **LOEWS L'ENFANT PLAZA HOTEL.** *480 L'Enfant Plaza SW (20024). Phone 202/484-1000; fax 202/646-4456. www.loewshotels.com.* Sitting just blocks from the DC Mall, this hotel cannot be beat for its central location. 370 rooms. Pets accepted. Check-out 1 pm. TV; cable (premium), VCR available. In-room modem link. Restaurant, bar. In-house fitness room. Pool; poolside service. Valet parking. Business center. Concierge. **$$**

D ♦ ⇌ ⫞ ⊠ ⫞

★ ★ ★ **MARRIOTT WARDMAN PARK HOTEL.** *2660 Woodley Rd NW (20008). Phone 202/328-2000; fax 202/234-0015. www.marriott.com.* Located in a prestigious area of the capital, this hotel is just minutes from the National Zoo. 1,350 rooms, 10 story. Pets accepted, some restrictions. Check-out noon. TV; cable (premium), VCR available. Restaurant, bar. In-house fitness room; sauna. Pool. Valet parking, fee. Business center. Concierge. **$$**

D ♦ ⇌ ⫞ ⊠ ⫞

★ ★ ★ **MONARCH HOTEL.** *2401 M St NW (20037). Phone 202/429-2400; toll-free 877/222-2266; fax 202/457-5010. www.monarchdc.com.* This recently renovated property is within walking distance of Georgetown and minutes from many national attractions. 415 rooms, 10 story. Pets accepted, some restrictions; fee. Check-out 1 pm. TV; cable (premium), CD player available. In-room modem link. Room service 24 hours. Restaurant, bar; entertainment. In-house fitness room; sauna, steam room. Indoor pool; whirlpool. Squash, racquetball courts. Valet parking, fee. Business center. Concierge. **$$**

D ♦ ⇌ ⫞ ⊠ SC ⫞

★ ★ ★ **OMNI SHOREHAM HOTEL.** *2500 Calvert St NW (20008). Phone 202/234-0700; toll-free 800/843-6664; fax 202/265-7972. www.omnihotels.com.* A retreat in the middle of the city, this hotel is located on 11 acres in Rock Creek Park, offering picturesque views. 836 rooms, 8 story. Pets accepted, some restrictions; fee. Check-out noon. TV; cable (premium), VCR available. Restaurant, bar; entertainment. In-house fitness room; sauna. Pool; children's pool; poolside service. Valet parking. Business center. **$**

D ♦ ⇌ ⫞ ⊠ SC ⫞

★ ★ ★ **PARK HYATT WASHINGTON.** *1201 24th St NW (20037). Phone 202/789-1234; fax 202/457-8823. www.hyatt.com.* The awe-inspiring monuments and world-class museums of Washington, DC are within easy reach of the Park Hyatt. Located in the city's West End, the hotel is several blocks from Georgetown and downtown. The Park Hyatt maintains a handsome style throughout the hotel, from the gleaming lobby with its palette of gold and cream to the guest rooms and suites, which include the latest technology while maintaining a cozy ambience. Rivaling a small museum, the hotel boasts an impressive art collection: Picasso, Léger, Matisse, and Miró adorn the walls of the public and private spaces. Melrose is

recognized for its distinguished cuisine, served in the formal dining room or outside on the terrace during warmer months. The health club is comprehensive, including the latest exercise equipment, indoor pool; whirlpool; and sauna. 223 rooms, 10 story. Pets accepted. Check-out noon, check-in 3 pm. TV; cable (premium), VCR available. Room service 24 hours. Restaurant, bar. In-house fitness room; spa, steam room, sauna, massage. Indoor pool; whirlpool; poolside service. Valet parking. **$$$**

D ♦ ⇌ ⫞ ⊠

★ ★ ★ **RENAISSANCE MAYFLOWER HOTEL.** *1127 Connecticut Ave NW (20036). Phone 202/347-3000; toll-free 800/HOTELS-1; fax 202/466-9082. www.renaissancehotels.com.* If you like to get comfortable in stately old hotels, you'll want to book a room at this high-rise property in the heart of the city's business district. Built in 1925 for Calvin Coolidge's inauguration, this hotel played host to the likes of Franklin Delano Roosevelt and J. Edgar Hoover. You'll find popular shops and restaurants just outside its front doors; the White House is only four blocks away. Be ready for the eye-pleasing view when you check in: all the gilded trim, crystal chandeliers, and Oriental rugs in the block-long lobby will awe you. The guest rooms themselves are quite homey, so you'll likely feel right at home in yours. For business travelers, each room has a desk with work lamp, a two-line phone with a dataport, and a speakerphone. For groups, the Mayflower offers state-of-the-art meeting facilities. 660 rooms, 10 story. Pets accepted, some restrictions; fee. Check-out noon, check-in 3 pm. TV; cable (premium). In-room modem link. Room service 24 hours. Restaurant, bar; entertainment. Babysitting services available. In-house fitness room; health club privileges. Valet parking, fee. Business center. Concierge. Foreign currency exchange. **$**

D ♦ ⫞ ⊠ ⫞

★ ★ ★ ★ **THE RITZ-CARLTON, WASHINGTON DC.** *1150 22nd St NW (20037). Phone 202/835-0500; fax 202/974-5519. www.ritzcarlton.com.* A convenient West End location, stylish accommodations, and superior service make The Ritz-Carlton, Washington, DC a favorite of sophisticated travelers. The supremely knowledgeable staff truly pampers its guests. The Ritz-Carlton's attention to detail is marvelous, and it continues to exceed expectations with innovative amenities. On-call technology butlers assist with computer woes, while the Luggage-less Travel program is offered to frequent guests, inviting them to leave behind items for their next visit. Traditional European décor defines the 300 rooms and suites, and Club Level accommodations are treated to five food and beverage presentations daily. Perhaps most impressive is the Sports Club/LA access granted to all guests of The Ritz-Carlton. Adjacent to the hotel, this massive 100,000-square-foot complex is a veritable nirvana for fitness buffs with cutting-edge fitness programming, multiple athletic courts, and a pool. The complex also includes Splash, one of Washington's leading day spas. 300 rooms, 15 story. Pets accepted, some restrictions. Check-out noon, check-in 3 pm. TV; cable (premium). In-room modem link. Restaurant, bar. Babysitting services available. In-house fitness room; spa. Indoor pool; whirlpool. Business center. Concierge. **$$$**

★ ★ ★ THE RITZ-CARLTON GEORGETOWN.

3100 South St NW (20007). Phone 202/835-0500; toll-free 800/241-3333; fax 202/974-5519. www.ritzcarlton.com. Embassy delegations often stay at this elegant, intimate hotel that blends contemporary décor with a historical setting. It's located on the banks of the Potomac River in Washington Harbour, an entertainment/residential/office complex located on land that was once the site of the original village of George Towne. Many of its executive suites and deluxe rooms offer gorgeous river views, and each comes with all the extra creature comforts you'd expect from a Ritz-Carlton, including feather duvets, goosedown pillows, and oversized marble baths. But don't spend all your time in your cushy room. Sip one of the fire-red martinis served in the Degrees Bar and Lounge, and then dine in Fahrenheit, which dishes out American/ Italian cuisine. Soothe yourself with a facial or a full-body massage at the Boutique Spa, or tone those muscles at the fully equipped fitness center. 86 rooms. Pets accepted, some restrictions. Check-out noon, check-in 3 pm. TV; cable (premium). Restaurant, bar. Babysitting services available. In-house fitness room; spa. **$$$$**

★ ★ ★ ★ THE ST. REGIS, WASHINGTON, DC.

923 16th and K sts NW (20006). Phone 202/638-2626; toll-free 800/562-5661; fax 202/638-4231. www.sheraton.com. The St. Regis is a treasure in the nation's capital. Since 1926, the St. Regis has been a preferred residence of discerning travelers visiting Washington. Just a stone's throw from the White House, the hotel enjoys a prime city location with nearly all of Washington's attractions nearby. Stepping into this esteemed hotel offers an enchanting glimpse of a grander time. Its gilded lobby of coffered ceilings and sparkling chandeliers is a work of art. Reflecting its Italian Renaissance roots, the 193 rooms and suites recall the splendor of European palaces with silk-covered walls and antique furnishings. English-style butlers attend to the individual needs of each guest. Formal afternoon tea is served to the gentle strains of a harp, and dining at the Library Restaurant completes this sublimely elegant experience. 193 rooms, 8 story. Pets accepted, some restrictions; fee. Check-out 1 pm, check-in 3 pm. TV; cable (premium), VCR available. In-room modem link. Room service 24 hours. Restaurant, bar. Babysitting services available. In-house fitness room. Health club privileges. Valet parking. Concierge. **$$$**

★ ★ ★ SWISSOTEL WASHINGTON - THE WATERGATE.

2650 Virginia Ave NW (20037). Phone 202/965-2300; toll-free 800/424-2736; fax 202/337-7915. www.swissotel.com. Neighboring the Kennedy Center along the Potomac River, this luxury hotel is walking distance to the Mall and historic Georgetown. Views from the expansive guest rooms make any stay a pleasure. 232 rooms, 13 story. Pets accepted, some restrictions; fee. Check-out noon. TV; cable (premium), VCR available. In-room modem link. Room service 24 hours. Restaurant, bar. In-house fitness room; massage. Sauna, steam room. Indoor pool; whirlpool. Valet parking. Business center. Concierge. **$$**

★ ★ ★ WILLARD INTER-CONTINENTAL WASHINGTON.

1401 Pennsylvania Ave NW (20004). Phone 202/ 628-9100; toll-free 800/327-0200; fax 202/637-7326. www.w ashington.interconti.com. The Willard Inter-Continental is steeped in history. Only two blocks from the White House, this legendary Beaux Arts hotel has been at the center of Washington's political scene since 1850. The Willard's lobby has always served as a drawing room to the world; it is here that Lincoln held fireside staff meetings, Grant escaped the rigors of the White House to enjoy brandy and cigars, and the term "lobbyist" was coined. Henry Clay shared the secret of the mint julep in the Round Robin Bar, while the Willard Room's continental cuisine makes history today. This landmark's guest rooms and suites are a traditional blend of Edwardian and Victorian styles furnished in deep jewel tones. The Jenny Lind suite is perfect for honeymooners with its mansard roof and canopy bed, while the Oval suite, inspired by the office of the same name, makes guests feel like masters of the universe. 341 rooms, 12 story. Pets accepted. Check-out noon, check-in 3 pm. TV; cable (premium), VCR available. In-room modem link. Room service 24 hours. Restaurant, bar. Babysitting services available. In-house fitness room. Valet parking, covered parking. Business center. Concierge. **$$$$**

All Suites

★ ★ RIVER INN.

924 25th St Nw (20037). Phone 202/337-7600; toll-free 800/424-2741; fax 202/337-6520. www.theriverinn.com. 126 rooms. Pets accepted; fee. Check-out noon. TV; cable (premium). In-room modem link. Restaurant, bar. Health club privileges. Parking. **$**

★ WASHINGTON SUITES GEORGETOWN.

2500 Pennsylvania Ave NW (20037). Phone 202/333-8060; toll-free 877/736-2500; fax 202/338-3818. www.washington suiteshotel.com. 123 rooms, 10 story. Pets accepted, some restrictions; fee. Check-out noon. TV; cable (premium). In-room modem link. Health club privileges. **$**

Florida

Altamonte Springs

Motels/Motor Lodges

★ **CROSBY'S MOTOR INN.** *1440 W Hwy 441 (32712). Phone 407/886-3220; fax 407/886-7458.* 61 rooms, 2 story. Pets accepted; fee. Check-out 11 am. TV; cable (premium). Laundry services. Pool. **$**

★ **HAMPTON INN.** *151 N Douglas Ave (32714). Phone 407/869-9000; toll-free 800/426-7866; fax 407/788-6746. www.orlandohamptoninn.com.* 210 rooms, 2 story. Pets accepted; fee. Complimentary continental breakfast. Check-out noon. TV; cable (premium). Laundry services. In-house fitness room. Pool; whirlpool. Business center. **$**

★ **LA QUINTA INN.** *150 S Westmonte Dr (32714). Phone 407/788-1411; toll-free 800/531-5900; fax 407/788-6472. www.laquinta.com.* 118 rooms, 2 story. Pets accepted, some restrictions. Complimentary continental breakfast. Check-out noon. TV; cable (premium). Health club privileges. **$**

Extended Stay

★ ★ **RESIDENCE INN BY MARRIOTT.** *270 Douglas Ave (32714). Phone 407/788-7991; fax 407/869-5468. www.residenceinn.com.* 128 rooms, 2 story. Pets accepted, some restrictions; fee. Complimentary continental breakfast. Check-out noon. TV; cable (premium). Fireplaces. Laundry services. Health club privileges. Pool; whirlpool. **$**

Amelia Island

B&B/Small Inns

★ ★ ★ **1857 FLORIDA HOUSE INN.** *20 S 3rd St (32034). Phone 904/261-3300; toll-free 800/258-3301; fax 904/277-3831. www.floridahouseinn.com.* This gem on the National Register of Historic Places is in the heart of the Fernandina Beach Historic District and is Florida's oldest surviving hotel. Operating since 1857, this inn is only 2 miles from the Atlantic. 15 rooms, 2 story. Pets accepted, some restrictions; fee. Complimentary full breakfast.

Check-out 11 am, check-in 2 pm. TV; VCR available. Dining room, bar. Wraparound veranda with rocking chairs. Totally nonsmoking. **$$**

★ ★ **GOODBREAD HOUSE B&B.** *209 Osborne St (31558). Phone 912/882-7490. www.stmaryswelcome.com.* 5 rooms, 2 story. Pets accepted. Complimentary full breakfast. Check-out noon, check-in 2 pm. TV; cable. Built in 1870. Totally nonsmoking. **$**

★ ★ ★ **HOYT HOUSE BED & BREAKFAST.** *804 Atlantic Ave (32034). Phone 904/277-4300; toll-free 800/432-2085; fax 904/277-9626. www.hoythouse.com.* Located in the downtown historic district, this charming yellow and blue Victorian was built in the Queen Anne style. 10 rooms, 2 story. Pets accepted, some restrictions; fee. Complimentary full breakfast. Check-out 11 am, check-in 3 pm. TV; VCR available (free movies). Built in 1905 by a local merchant. Totally nonsmoking. **$$**

Arcadia

Motel/Motor Lodge

★ ★ **BEST WESTERN ARCADIA INN.** *504 S Brevoad Ave (34266). Phone 863/494-4884; toll-free 877/886-0797; fax 863/494-2006. www.bestwestern.com.* 38 rooms. Pets accepted; fee. Complimentary continental breakfast. Check-out 10 am. TV. **$**

Aventura

Hotel

★ ★ **RESIDENCE INN BY MARRIOTT.** *19900 W Country Club Dr (33180). Phone 786/528-1001; fax 786/528-1002. www.marriott.com.* 191 rooms. Pets accepted, some restrictions; fee. Complimentary continental breakfast. Check-out 11 am, check-in 3 pm. In-house fitness room. Outdoor pool; whirlpool. **$$**

Bartow

Motel/Motor Lodge

★ **DAVIS BROTHERS MOTEL AND LOUNGE.** *1035 N Broadway Ave (33830). Phone 863/533-0711; fax 863/533-0924.* 102 rooms, 2 story. Pets accepted, some restrictions; fee. Check-out noon. TV. Laundry services. Pool; children's pool. **$**

D 🐾 ➿ ⛱

Boca Raton

Hotel

★ ★ ★ **RENAISSANCE BOCA RATON HOTEL.** *2000 NW 19th St (33431). Phone 561/368-5252; toll-free 800/394-7829; fax 561/750-5437. www.renaissancehotels .com.* A resortlike setting with Mediterranean style. The rich, red-tile roof and waterfall-pool deck are the perfect backdrop for business or pleasure. 189 rooms, 5 story. Pets accepted, some restrictions; fee. Check-out noon, check-in 3 pm. TV; cable (premium). In-room modem link. Room service 24 hours. Restaurant, bar. Health club privileges. Pool; whirlpool; poolside service. Business center. Concierge. Luxury level. **$$**

D 🐾 ➿ ⛱ SC 🏃

All Suite

★ ★ **RADISSON SUITE HOTEL.** *7920 Glades Rd (33434). Phone 561/483-3600; fax 561/479-2280. www.radisson.com/bocaratonfl_suites.* 200 rooms, 7 story. Pets accepted; fee. Complimentary continental breakfast. Check-out noon, check-in 3 pm. TV; cable (premium), VCR available (movies fee). In-room modem link. Laundry services. Restaurant, bar. In-house fitness room. Outdoor pool; whirlpool. **$$**

D 🐾 ➿ 🏃 🏃

Extended Stay

★ ★ **RESIDENCE INN BY MARRIOTT.** *525 NW 77th St (33487). Phone 561/994-3222; fax 561/994-3339. www.residenceinn.com.* 120 rooms, 2 story. Pets accepted, some restrictions; fee. Complimentary continental breakfast. Check-out noon, check-in 3 pm. TV; VCR available. In-room modem link. Laundry services. Pool; whirlpool. **$**

D 🐾 ➿ ⛱ SC

Boynton Beach

Motel/Motor Lodge

★ **ANN MARIE MOTEL.** *911 S Federal Hwy 1 (33435). Phone 561/732-9283; toll-free 800/258-8548; fax 561/732-9283. www.annmariemotel.com.* 16 rooms. Pets accepted, some restrictions; fee. Complimentary continental breakfast. Check-out 11 am. TV; VCR (movies fee). Pool. **$**

D 🐾 ➿

Bradenton

Motels/Motor Lodges

★ **COMFORT INN.** *4450 W 47th St (34210). Phone 941/795-4633; toll-free 800/437-7275; fax 941/795-0808. www.comfortinn.com.* 130 rooms, 3 story. Pets accepted, some restrictions; fee. Complimentary continental breakfast. Check-out noon. TV. Health club privileges. Pool; whirlpool. **$**

D 🐾 ➿ ⛱ SC

★ **HOWARD JOHNSON.** *6511 W 14th St (34207). Phone 941/756-8399; toll-free 800/446-4656; fax 941/755-1387. www.hojo.com.* 50 rooms, 2 story. Pets accepted, some restrictions; fee. Complimentary continental breakfast. Check-out 11 am. TV; cable (premium). In-house fitness room. Pool. **$**

🐾 ➿ 🏃

★ **RAMADA INN.** *5218 17th St E (34222). Phone 941/729-8505; toll-free 888/298-2054; fax 941/729-1110. www.ramada.com.* 73 rooms, 2 story. Pets accepted; fee. Complimentary continental breakfast. Check-out 11 am. TV; cable (premium). Laundry services. Heated pool; whirlpool. **$**

D 🐾 ➿ ⛱

★ **SHONEY'S INN LAKESIDE.** *4915 E 17th St (34222). Phone 941/729-0600; toll-free 800/222-2222; fax 941/722-5908. www.shoneysinn.com.* 63 rooms, 2 story. Pets accepted, some restrictions; fee. Complimentary continental breakfast. Check-out 11 am. TV; cable (premium). In-room modem link. Pool; whirlpool. **$**

D 🐾 🐾 ➿ ⛱ SC

Brooksville

Resort

★ ★ **BEST WESTERN WEEKI WACHEE RESORT.** *6172 Commercial Way (34606). Phone 352/596-2007; toll-free 800/490-8268; fax 352/596-0667. www.bestwestern.com.* 122 rooms, 2 story. Late Dec-May: S, D $59-$79; each additional $6; under 18 free; lower rates rest of year. Pets accepted. Complimentary continental breakfast. Check-out 11 am. TV; cable (premium). Restaurant, bar. Pool; children's pool. Lawn games.

D 🐾 ➿ ⛱ SC

Cape Coral

Motel/Motor Lodge

★ **QUALITY INN.** *1538 Cape Coral Pkwy E (33904). Phone 239/542-2121; toll-free 800/638-7949; fax 239/542-6319. www.qualityinn.com.* 143 rooms, 5 story. Pets accepted, some restrictions; fee. Check-out 11 am. TV. Laundry services. In-house fitness room. Pool; poolside service. **$**

⊡ ✎ ⌷ ⌷ ⌷ SC

Clearwater

Motels/Motor Lodges

★ **KNIGHTS INN.** *34106 US 19 (34684). Phone 727/789-2002; fax 727/784-6206. www.knightsinn.com.* 114 rooms. Jan-Apr: S, D $83; under 18 free; weekly rates; lower rates rest of year. Pets accepted; fee. Check-out 11 am. TV; cable (premium). Laundry services. Pool.

✎ ⌷ ⌷

★ **LA QUINTA INN.** *3301 Ulmerton Rd (34622). Phone 727/572-7222; toll-free 800/687-6667; fax 727/572-0076. www.laquinta.com.* 117 rooms. Pets accepted, some restrictions. Complimentary continental breakfast. Check-out noon. TV; cable (premium). In-room modem link. Laundry services. In-house fitness room; sauna. Pool; whirlpool. Free airport transportation. **$**

⊡ ✎ ⌷ ⌷ ⌷ ⌷ SC

Resort

★ ★ ★ **SAFETY HARBOR RESORT AND SPA.** *105 N Bayshore Dr (34695). Phone 727/726-1161; toll-free 800/237-0155; fax 727/726-4268. www.safetyharborspa.com.* This retreat on Tampa Bay offers extensive spa treatments and salon services, including five natural mineral springs. Lounge along the 28 miles of white sand on the Gulf. 189 rooms, 3-6 story. Feb-mid-Apr: S, D $179-$199; each additional $20; AP available; under 13 free; special rates holidays; lower rates rest of year. Pets accepted; fee. Complimentary continental breakfast. TV; cable (premium). Laundry services. Dining room, bar. Room service. In-house fitness room. Three pools; whirlpool. Lawn games, bicycles. Business center. Concierge. 300-seat theater.

⊡ ✎ ⌷ ⌷ ⌷ ⌷ ⌷ ⌷ ⌷ ⌷

Extended Stay

★ ★ **RESIDENCE INN BY MARRIOTT.** *5050 Ulmerton Rd (33760). Phone 727/573-4444; fax 727/572-*4446. *www.residenceinn.com.* 88 rooms, 2 story. Pets accepted; fee. Complimentary continental breakfast. Check-out noon. TV; cable (premium). In-room modem link. Fireplaces. Health club privileges. Pool; whirlpool. Lawn games. **$**

⊡ ✎ ⌷ ⌷ SC

Cocoa

Motels/Motor Lodges

★ **BEST WESTERN COCOA INN.** *4225 W King St (32926). Phone 321/632-1065; fax 321/631-3302. www.bestwestern.com.* 120 rooms, 2 story. Pets accepted; fee. Complimentary continental breakfast. Check-out 11:30 am. TV. Bar. Game room. Pool. **$**

✎ ⌷ ⌷

★ **DAYS INN.** *5600 State Rd 524 (32926). Phone 321/636-6500; toll-free 800/329-7466; fax 321/631-0513. www.daysinn.com.* 121 rooms, 2 story. Pets accepted, some restrictions; fee. Check-out 11 am. TV; cable (premium). Pool. **$**

✎ ⌷ ⌷ SC

★ ★ **RAMADA.** *900 Friday Rd (32926). Phone 321/631-1210; toll-free 800/228-2828; fax 321/636-8661. www.ramada.com.* 99 rooms, 2 story. Pets accepted, some restrictions; fee. Check-out 11 am. TV; cable (premium). Laundry services. Restaurant, bar. Room service. Pool. Lawn games. Private lake. **$**

⊡ ✎ ⌷ ⌷ ⌷ SC

Cocoa Beach

Motel/Motor Lodge

★ **DAYS INN.** *5500 N Atlantic Ave (32931). Phone 321/784-2550; toll-free 877/233-9330; fax 321/868-7124. www.cocoabeachlodging.com.* 103 rooms, 2 story. Pets accepted, some restrictions. Check-out 11 am. TV. In-room modem link. In-house fitness room. Pool. **$**

⊡ ✎ ⌷ ⌷ ⌷ ⌷ SC

Coconut Grove

Hotels

★ ★ ★ **GROVE ISLE CLUB AND RESORT.** *4 Grove Isle Dr (33133). Phone 305/858-8300; toll-free 180/884-7683; fax 305/858-5908. www.groveisle.com.* Situated on a secluded private island on Biscayne Bay, this resort's tropical rooms and suites have glossy, terra-cotta-tiled floors and floor-to-ceiling windows that open onto private terraces. 49 rooms, 5 story. Pets accepted. Complimentary continental breakfast. Check-out noon, check-in 3 pm. TV; cable (premium), VCR available. In-room modem link. Restaurant, bar. Room service. Babysitting services available. In-house fitness room. Outdoor pool; whirlpool. Outdoor tennis, lighted courts. Valet parking. Marina. **$$$**

★ ★ ★ **THE RITZ-CARLTON, COCONUT GROVE.** *2700 Tigertail Ave (33133). Phone 305/644-4680; fax 305/644-4681. www.ritzcarlton.com.* Elegance and grace are the calling card of The Ritz-Carlton, Coconut Grove. From the magnificent lobby to the sophisticated interiors, this hotel calls to mind the grandeur of the Renaissance from its serene spot overlooking Biscayne Bay in Miami's chic Coconut Grove neighborhood. Dazzling water, skyline, or tropical garden views from expansive private balconies are just the beginning at this palatial hotel recognized for its impeccable service, where technology, travel, bath, and even bow-wow butlers cater to you and your four-legged friend's every whim. The spacious spa calms body and mind, and a shimmering pool with fabulous views over Coconut Grove is paradise for sunbathers and people watchers. The lobby lounge serves cocktails and afternoon tea to the soothing sounds of a cascading waterfall, while local denizens and in-the-know guests book a table at Bizcaya Grill for its cosmopolitan take on the traditional steak house. 115 rooms, 4 story. Pets accepted, some restrictions; fee. Check-out noon, check-in 3 pm. TV; cable (premium), VCR available. In-room modem link. Room service 24 hours. Restaurant, bar; entertainment. Babysitting services available. In-house fitness room; spa, sauna, steam room. Outdoor pool; whirlpool. Valet parking. Airport transportation. Business center. Concierge. Luxury level. **$$$**

★ ★ ★ **WYNDHAM GRAND BAY COCONUT GROVE.** *2669 S Bayshore Dr (33133). Phone 305/858-9600; toll-free 800/327-2788; fax 305/858-0339. www.wyndham.com.* Offering splendid views of Biscayne Bay, this hotel is a favorite for those who want to enjoy all that downtown Miami has to offer and still stay close to the action in Coconut Grove. The service, food offerings, and other amenities are top notch. 177 rooms, 12 story. Pets accepted; fee. Check-out noon, check-in 3 pm. TV; cable (premium), VCR available. In-room modem link. Room service 24 hours. Restaurant, bar; entertainment. Babysitting services available. In-house fitness room; massage, sauna. Outdoor pool; whirlpool. Valet parking. Business center. Concierge. **$$**

Coral Gables

Hotel

★ ★ ★ **OMNI COLONNADE HOTEL.** *180 Aragon Ave (33134). Phone 305/441-2600; toll-free 800/843-6664; fax 305/445-3929. www.omnicolonnade.com.* European design and mahogany furnishings give this hotel, with its 1926 colonnade lobby, a charming feel. Although kid-friendly, it particularly serves the modern business traveler. 157 rooms, 14 story. Pets accepted, some restrictions; fee. Check-out noon, check-in 3 pm. TV; cable (premium), VCR available. In-room modem link. Restaurant, bar; entertainment. Room service. In-house fitness room; health club privileges, sauna. Outdoor pool; whirlpool. Valet parking, fee. Concierge. Rotunda off the lobby is part of original Colonnade building. **$$$**

Crystal River

Motel/Motor Lodge

★ **COMFORT INN.** *4486 N Suncoast Blvd (34428). Phone 352/563-1500; fax 352/563-5426. www.comfortinn.com.* 66 rooms, 2 story. Pets accepted; fee. Complimentary continental breakfast. Check-out 11 am. TV; cable (premium). In-room modem link. Lighted tennis. Pool. **$**

Resort

★ ★ **BEST WESTERN CRYSTAL RIVER RESORT.** *614 NW US 19 (34428). Phone 352/795-3171; toll-free 800/780-7234; fax 352/795-3179. www.bestwestern.com.* 114 rooms, 2 story. Pets accepted; fee. Check-out noon. TV; cable (premium), VCR available (movies). Restaurant, bar. Heated pool; whirlpool. On the Crystal River; dock, launching ramp, boat rentals, guides; scuba diving. **$**

Dania

Hotel

★ ★ ★ **SHERATON FT. LAUDERDALE AIRPORT HOTEL.** *1825 Griffin Rd (33004). Phone 954/920-3500; toll-free 800/947-8527; fax 954/920-3571. www.sheraton.com.* 250 rooms, 12 story. Pets accepted; fee. Check-out 1 pm, check-in 3 pm. TV; cable (premium). In-room modem link. Restaurant, bar. Room service. In-house fitness room.

Pool; whirlpool; poolside service. Outdoor tennis, lighted courts. Free airport transportation. **$$**

D ⊠ ⊠ ⊠ ⊠ ⊠

Daytona Beach

Motel/Motor Lodge

★ **QUALITY INN.** 2323 S Atlantic Ave (32118). Phone 386/255-0476; toll-free 800/874-7517; fax 386/255-3376. www.qualityinn.com. 110 rooms, 6 story. Pets accepted; fee. Complimentary continental breakfast. Check-out 11 am. TV. In-room modem link. Laundry services. Health club privileges. Game room. On beach. Pool; children's pool. Outdoor tennis. **$**

D ⊠ ⊠ ⊠ ⊠ SC

Resort

★★★ **RADISSON RESORT.** 640 N Atlantic Ave (32118). Phone 386/239-9800; toll-free 800/333-3333; fax 386/253-0735. www.radisson.com. 206 rooms, 11 story. Pets accepted; fee. Check-out 11 am, check-in 4 pm. TV; cable (premium). Laundry services. Restaurant, bar. In-house fitness room. Game room. Outdoor pool; children's pool; poolside service. **$**

D ⊠ ⊠ ⊠ ⊠ SC

Deerfield Beach

Hotel

★ **COMFORT INN.** 1040 E Newport Center Dr (33442). Phone 954/570-8887; toll-free 800/538-2777; fax 954/428-7638. www.choicehotels.com. 101 rooms, 4 story. Pets accepted, some restrictions; fee. Complimentary continental breakfast. Check-out noon, check-in 3 pm. TV; cable (premium), VCR available. In-room modem link. Outdoor pool; whirlpool. **$**

D ⊠ ⊠ ⊠ SC

De Funiak Springs

Motel/Motor Lodge

★★ **BEST WESTERN CROSSROADS INN.** 2343 Freeport Rd (32435). Phone 850/892-5111; fax 850/892-2439. www.bestwestern.com. 100 rooms, 2 story. Pets accepted, some restrictions. Complimentary breakfast. Check-out noon. TV; cable (premium). In-room modem link. Restaurant, bar. Pool. **$**

D ⊠ ⊠ ⊠ SC

DeLand

Motel/Motor Lodge

★★★ **HOLIDAY INN.** 350 E International Speedway Blvd (32724). Phone 386/738-5200; toll-free 800/465-4329; fax 386/734-7552. www.holiday-inn.com. This centrally located hotel is convenient to the Daytona beaches and Blue Springs State Park and about an hour from Disney, Universal Orlando, and SeaWorld. 148 rooms, 6 story. Pets accepted; fee. Check-out noon. TV; cable (premium), VCR available. In-room modem link. Restaurant, bar. Room service. In-house fitness room. Health club privileges. Pool; whirlpool. **$**

D ⊠ ⊠ ⊠ ⊠ SC

Englewood

Resort

★ **DAYS INN.** 2540 S McCall Rd (34224). Phone 941/474-5544; toll-free 800/887-5412; fax 941/475-2124. www.daysinn.com. 84 rooms, 2 story. Pets accepted, some restrictions; fee. Check-out noon. TV. Restaurant. Pool. **$**

D ⊠ ⊠ ⊠ SC

Fort Lauderdale

Motels/Motor Lodges

★ **WELLESLEY INN.** 13600 NW 2nd St (33325). Phone 954/845-9929; fax 954/845-9996. www.wellesleyinnandsuites.com. Located near the largest outlet mall in Florida, the Wellesley Inn is also convenient to the area's business center. 74 rooms, 30 suites, 4 story. Dec-Mar: S, D $59-$79; suites $69-$109; lower rates rest of year. Pets accepted, some restrictions. Complimentary continental breakfast. Check-out noon. TV; cable (premium). Heated pool.

D ⊠ ⊠ ⊠

★★★ **WELLESLEY INN.** 7901 SW 6th St (33324). Phone 954/473-8257; fax 954/473-9804. www.wellesleyinnandsuites.com. The Wellesley brand is a top performer in mid-priced chains and is geared to business travelers. This property is adjacent to the Broward Mall and the Fountains Shoppes. 105 rooms, 4 story. D $99-$119. Pets accepted, some restrictions; fee. Complimentary continental breakfast. Check-out 11 am. TV; cable (premium). In-room modem link. Health club privileges. Heated pool.

D ⊠ ⊠ ⊠

Hotels

★ ★ ★ **MARRIOTT FORT LAUDERDALE NORTH.** *6650 N Andrews Ave (33309). Phone 954/771-0440; fax 954/772-9834. www.marriott.com.* 315 rooms, 17 story. Pets accepted, some restrictions; fee. Check-out noon, check-in 3 pm. TV; cable (premium). In-room modem link. Room service 24 hours. Restaurant, bar. In-house fitness room; sauna. Outdoor pool; whirlpool. Business center. Concierge. Luxury level. **$$**

◨ ◨ ◨ ◨ ◨ ◨ ◨ ◨ ◨

★ ★ ★ **SHERATON SUITES PLANTATION, FT. LAUDERDALE WEST.** *311 N University Dr (33324). Phone 954/424-3300; fax 954/452-8887. www.sheraton.com.* Geared to please the meeting planner, this hotel has a 16,000-square-foot outdoor rotunda. Take a break to shop at the adjacent Fashion Mall at Plantation or swim in the rooftop pool. 263 suites, 9 story. Mid-Dec-mid-Apr: S $209-$254; D $229-$289; each additional $20; under 18 free; weekend rates; lower rates rest of year. Pets accepted, some restrictions; fee. Check-out noon. TV; cable (premium), VCR. In-room modem link. Room service 24 hours. Restaurant, bar. In-house fitness room; sauna. Pool; whirlpool; poolside service. Valet parking. Airport transportation. Concierge.

◨ ◨ ◨ ◨ ◨ ◨

★ ★ ★ **THE WESTIN FORT LAUDERDALE.** *400 Corporate Dr (33334). Phone 954/772-1331; fax 954/772-0330. www.westin.com.* Overlooking a peaceful lagoon, this hotel is convenient to downtown yet minutes from beaches. 293 rooms, 15 story. Pets accepted, some restrictions; fee. Check-out 1 pm. TV; cable (premium). In-room modem link. Room service 24 hours. Restaurant, bar. Supervised children's activities. In-house fitness room; sauna. Pool; whirlpool; poolside service. Paddleboats. Business center. Blue-mirrored tile building surrounded by palm trees; 20-foot poolside waterfall, 5-acre lake. **$$**

◨ ◨ ◨ ◨ ◨ ◨ ◨

All Suites

★ **AMERISUITES.** *1851 SE 10th Ave (33316). Phone 954/763-7670; fax 954/763-6269. www.amerisuites.com.* 128 rooms, 6 story. Pets accepted, some restrictions. Complimentary continental breakfast. Check-out 11 am, check-in 3 pm. TV; cable (premium), VCR available. In-room modem link. In-house fitness room. Outdoor pool. Free airport transportation. Business center. **$**

◨ ◨ ◨ ◨ ◨

★ ★ **DOUBLETREE HOTEL.** *2670 E Sunrise Blvd (33304). Phone 954/565-3800; toll-free 800/222-8733; fax 954/561-0387. www.doubletree.com.* 229 rooms, 14 story. Pets accepted; fee. Check-out noon, check-in 3 pm. TV; cable (premium). In-room modem link. Restaurant,

bar. Room service. In-house fitness room; steam room. Outdoor pool; whirlpool; poolside service. Valet parking. Business center. Concierge. Overlooks Intracoastal Waterway; dockage. **$$**

◨ ◨ ◨ ◨ ◨ ◨

B&B/Small Inn

★ **LA CASA DEL MAR.** *3003 Granada St (33304). Phone 954/467-2037; fax 954/467-7439. www.lacasadelmar.com.* 11 rooms, 3 story. Pets accepted, some restrictions. Complimentary full breakfast. Check-out 11 am, check-in 2 pm. TV; cable (premium), VCR available. Outdoor pool. Totally nonsmoking. **$**

◨ ◨ SC

Extended Stay

★ ★ **RESIDENCE INN BY MARRIOTT.** *130 N University Dr (33324). Phone 954/723-0300; fax 954/474-7385. www.residenceinn.com.* Separate living and sleeping areas make this branch of the Marriott chain a comfortable place to work. The property is located near the Broward and Plantation Fashion Malls as well as various local corporations. 138 suites, 4 story. Mid-Dec-mid-Apr: suites $119-$219; family, weekly rates; lower rates rest of year. Pets accepted; fee. Complimentary breakfast buffet. Check-out noon. TV; cable (premium). In-room modem link. Health club privileges; in-house fitness room. Pool; whirlpool. Lawn games. Concierge. Sports court.

◨ ◨ ◨ ◨ ◨ SC

Fort Myers

Motels/Motor Lodges

★ **LA QUINTA INN.** *4850 S Cleveland Ave (33907). Phone 239/275-3300; fax 239/275-6661. www.laquinta.com.* 130 rooms, 2 story. Pets accepted. Complimentary continental breakfast. Check-out 11 am. TV; cable (premium). In-room modem link. Health club privileges. Heated pool. **$**

◨ ◨ ◨ ◨

★ **TA KI-KI MOTEL.** *2631 First St (38916). Phone 239/334-2135; fax 239/332-1879. www.takikimotel.com.* 23 rooms. Pets accepted. Check-out 11 am. TV. Heated pool. On river; boat dock. **$**

◨ ◨ ◨

Hotel

★ ★ ★ **RADISSON INN SANIBEL GATEWAY.** *20091 Summerlin Rd (33908). Phone 239/466-1200; fax 239/466-3797. www.radisson.com.* The Southwestern architecture and tropical grounds are enticing. Take a swim in the heated pool that has an underwater music system. 158 rooms, 3 story. Pets accepted; fee. Check-out noon. TV; cable (premium). In-room modem link. Restaurant, bar. Room service. Pool; whirlpool. **$**

D 🐾 ⇔ 🖼 SC

Fort Myers Beach

Resort

★ ★ **BEST WESTERN BEACH RESORT.** 684 *Estero Blvd (33931). Phone 239/463-6000; toll-free 800/ 336-4045; fax 239/463-3013. www.bestwestern.com.* 75 rooms, 5 story. Pets accepted, some restrictions; fee. Complimentary continental breakfast. Check-out 11 am. TV; cable (premium). Heated pool. In-room modem link. Game room. Lawn games. On the Gulf. **$**

D 🐾 🛪 ⇔ 🖼 SC

Fort Pierce

Motels/Motor Lodges

★ **DAYS INN.** 6651 *Darter Ct (34945). Phone 772/466-4066; fax 772/468-3260. www.daysinn.com.* 125 rooms, 2 story. Pets accepted; fee. Check-out 11 am. TV; cable (premium). Heated pool. Restaurant. **$**

D 🐾 ⇔ 🖼 SC

★ **HOLIDAY INN EXPRESS.** 7151 *Okeechobee Rd (34945). Phone 772/464-5000; toll-free 800/465-4329; fax 772/461-9573. www.holiday-inn.com.* 100 rooms, 2 story. Pets accepted, some restrictions; fee. Complimentary continental breakfast. Check-out noon. TV; cable (premium). Laundry services. Pool; children's pool. **$**

D 🐾 ⇔ 🖼 SC

Gainesville

Motels/Motor Lodges

★ **ECONO LODGE UNIVERSITY.** 2649 *SW 13th St (32608). Phone 352/373-7816; toll-free 800/446-6900; fax 352/372-9099. www.econolodge.com.* 53 rooms, 2 story. Pets accepted, some restrictions; fee. Complimentary continental breakfast. Check-out 11 am. TV; cable (premium). Pool. **$**

D 🐾 🛪 ⇔ 🖼

★ **LA QUINTA INN.** 920 *NW 69th Terrace (32605). Phone 352/332-6466; fax 352/332-7074. www.laquinta.com.* 135 rooms, 4 story. Pets accepted. Complimentary continental breakfast. Check-out noon. TV; VCR available (movies). In-room modem link. Health club privileges. Heated pool. **$**

D 🐾 ⇔ 🖼

B&B/Small Inn

★ ★ **MAGNOLIA PLANTATION BED & BREAKFAST INN.** 309 *SE 7th St (32601). Phone 352/375-6653; toll-free 800/201-2379; fax 352/338-0303. www.magnoliabnb.com.* 5 rooms, 3 story. Some room phones. Pets accepted, some restrictions. Complimentary full breakfast. Check-out 11 am, check-in 2 pm. TV in parlor; VCR. Restored Second Empire house (1885). Totally nonsmoking. **$**

🐾 🖼

Hollywood

Motel/Motor Lodge

★ **DAYS INN.** 2601 *N 29th Ave (33020). Phone 954/923-7300; fax 954/921-6706. www.daysinn.com.* 114 rooms, 7 story. Pets accepted; fee. Complimentary continental breakfast. Check-out noon, check-in 3 pm. TV. In-room modem link. Bar. In-house fitness room. Pool; whirlpool. Free airport transportation. **$**

D 🐾 ⇔ 🏃 ✈ 🖼

Homestead

Motels/Motor Lodges

★ ★ **DAYS INN.** 51 *S Homestead Blvd (33030). Phone 305/245-1260; toll-free 800/329-7466; fax 305/247-0939. www.daysinn.com.* 100 rooms, 2 story. Pets accepted; fee. Complimentary continental breakfast. Check-out 11 am. TV; cable (premium). Restaurant, bar; entertainment. Room service. Pool. **$**

D 🐾 ⇔ 🖼 SC

★ **HAMPTON INN.** 124 *E Palm Dr (33034). Phone 305/247-8833; toll-free 800/426-7866; fax 305/247-6456. www.hamptoninn.com.* 122 rooms, 2 story. Pets accepted, some restrictions. Complimentary continental breakfast. Check-out noon. TV; cable (premium). In-room modem link. Pool. **$**

D 🐾 ⇔ 🖼 SC

Homosassa Springs

Hotel

★★ **THE CROWN HOTEL.** *109 N Seminole Ave (34450). Phone 352/344-5555; toll-free 888/856-4455; fax 352/726-4040. www.thecrownhotel.com.* 34 rooms, 3 story. Pets accepted, some restrictions; fee. Complimentary continental breakfast. Check-out 11 am. TV. In-room modem link. Restaurant, bar. Health club privileges. Pool. Hotel built in the late 19th century; Victorian décor; leaded, cut glass windows in lobby; gold-plated bathroom fixtures. **$**

⬛🐾≋⛱SC

Jacksonville

Motels/Motor Lodges

★ **BEST INN.** *8220 Dix Ellis Trail (32256). Phone 904/739-3323; toll-free 800/237-8466; fax 904/739-3323.* 109 rooms, 2 story. Pets accepted, some restrictions; fee. Complimentary continental breakfast. Check-out noon. TV; cable (premium). Pool. **$**

⬛🐾≋⛱SC

★★ **BEST WESTERN.** *300 N Park Ave (32073). Phone 904/264-1211; toll-free 800/533-1211; fax 904/269-6756. www.bestwestern.com.* 201 rooms, 2 story. Pets accepted; fee. TV; cable (premium). Restaurant, bar. Room service. Health club privileges. Pool; children's pool. **$**

⬛🐾≋⛱

★★★ **HOLIDAY INN.** *9150 Baymeadows Rd (32256). Phone 904/737-1700; toll-free 800/828-1191; fax 904/737-0207. www.holiday-inn.com.* 240 rooms, 4 story. Pets accepted. Check-out noon. TV; cable (premium). In-room modem link. Laundry services. Restaurant, bar. Room service. In-house fitness room. Game room. Pool. **$**

⬛🐾≋🏋⛱

★★★ **HOLIDAY INN.** *14670 Duval Rd (32256). Phone 904/741-4404; toll-free 800/465-4329; fax 904/741-4907. www.holiday-inn.com.* 489 rooms, 6 story. Pets accepted. Check-out noon. TV; cable (premium), VCR available. In-room modem link. Restaurant, bar. Room service. In-house fitness room. Game room. Indoor pool; outdoor pool; poolside service. Lighted tennis. Business center. Luxury level. Free airport transportation. **$**

⬛🐾🏌≋🏋✈🚶

★ **LA QUINTA INN.** *8555 Blanding Blvd (32244). Phone 904/778-9539; toll-free 800/687-6667; fax 904/779-5214. www.laquinta.com.* 128 rooms, 7 story. Pets accepted, some restrictions. Complimentary continental breakfast. Check-out noon. TV. In-room modem link. Laundry services. Health club privileges. Pool. **$**

⬛🐾≋⛱

★ **LA QUINTA INN.** *8255 Dix Ellis Trail (32256). Phone 904/731-9940; fax 904/731-3854. www.laquinta.com.* 106 rooms, 2 story. Pets accepted, some restrictions. Complimentary continental breakfast. Check-out noon. TV; cable (premium). Pool. In-room modem link. Laundry services. Health club privileges. **$**

⬛🐾≋⛱

★★ **RAMADA INN.** *3130 Hartley Rd (32257). Phone 904/268-8080; toll-free 800/393-1117; fax 904/262-8718. www.ramada-inn.com.* 152 rooms, 2 story. Pets accepted; fee. Complimentary full breakfast. Check-out noon. TV. Large stone fireplace in lobby. Restaurant, bar. Room service. Game room. Pool; children's pool. **$**

⬛🐾≋⛱

★ **RED ROOF INN.** *6099 Youngerman Cir (32244). Phone 904/777-1000; fax 904/777-1005. www.redroof.com.* 108 rooms, 2 story. Pets accepted, some restrictions. Check-out 11 am. TV. In-room modem link. Pool. **$**

⬛🐾≋⛱

All Suites

★ **AMERISUITES.** *8277 Western Way Cir (32256). Phone 904/737-4477; toll-free 800/833-1516; fax 904/739-1649. www.amerisuites.com.* 112 rooms, 6 story. Pets accepted; fee. Complimentary continental breakfast. Check-out 11 am. TV; cable (premium), VCR available. In-room modem link. In-house fitness room. Pool. Business center. **$**

⬛🐾≋🏋⛱SC🚶

★★ **HOMEWOOD SUITES.** *8737 Baymeadows Rd (32256). Phone 904/733-9299; fax 904/448-5889. www.homewood-suites.com.* 116 rooms, 2-3 story. Pets accepted; fee. Complimentary continental breakfast. Check-out noon. TV; cable (premium), VCR available. In-room modem link. In-house fitness room. Pool; whirlpool. Business center. **$**

⬛🐾≋🏋⛱SC🚶

Extended Stay

★★ **RESIDENCE INN BY MARRIOTT.** *8365 Dix Ellis Trail (32256). Phone 904/733-8088; toll-free 800/331-3131; fax 904/731-8354. www.residenceinn.com.* 112 rooms, 2 story. Pets accepted, some restrictions; fee. Complimentary continental breakfast. Check-out noon. TV; cable (premium). In-room modem link. Health club privileges. Heated pool; whirlpools. **$**

⬛🐾≋⛱

Jacksonville Beach

Resort

★ ★ ★ **MARRIOTT AT SAWGRASS RESORT.**
1000 PGA Tour Blvd (32082). Phone 904/285-7777; toll-free 800/457-GOLF; fax 904/285-0906. www.marriott.com. A getaway for the entire family, this resort boasts 99 holes of golf and is the official course of the Players Championship. The location is convenient to historic St. Augustine and Jacksonville. 508 rooms, 7 story. Pets accepted, some restrictions; fee. Check-out noon, check-in 4 pm. TV; cable (premium), VCR available. In-room modem link. Some fireplaces. Dining room, bar. Room service. Supervised children's activities, ages 3-12. In-house fitness room; sauna, steam room. Pool; children's pool; whirlpool; poolside service. Greens fee. Lighted tennis. Bicycles. Private beach access, boating. Business center. Four stocked ponds. **$**

Jupiter

Motel/Motor Lodge

★ **HOLIDAY INN EXPRESS.** *13950 US 1 (33408). Phone 561/622-4366; toll-free 800/465-4329; fax 561/625-5245. www.holiday-inn.com.* 108 rooms, 2 and 3 story. Pets accepted; fee. Complimentary continental breakfast. Check-out 11 am. TV. In-room modem link. Laundry services. Health club privileges. Pool. **$**

Hotel

★ ★ **JUPITER BEACH RESORT.** *5 N A1A (33477). Phone 561/746-2511; toll-free 800/228-8810; fax 561/747-3304. www.jupiterbeachresort.com.* Jupiter has a smaller, more natural appeal than its Palm Beach neighbor, and this casual Caribbean-style resort fits in perfectly. Relax at the private beach or dine and be seen at Sinclair's Ocean Grill. 153 rooms, 9 story. Pets accepted, some restrictions; fee. Check-out noon. TV; cable (premium), VCR available. In-room modem link. Restaurant, bar; entertainment. In-house fitness room. Pool; poolside service. Outdoor tennis, lighted courts. Bicycle rentals. Sailing, snorkeling available. Valet parking. Concierge. **$**

Key Biscayne

Resort

★ ★ ★ ★ **THE RITZ-CARLTON, KEY BISCAYNE.** *455 Grand Bay Dr (33149). Phone 305/365-4500; fax 305/365-4513. www.ritzcarlton.com.* The Ritz-Carlton, Key Biscayne serves up family fun in an elegant setting. Only 6 miles from the Miami coast on the southernmost barrier island in the United States, this resort exudes the intimacy of a private island escape. From its 12 acres of oceanfront property and its beachfront Ritz Kids Pavilion to its 20,000-square-foot spa and 11-court tennis center, this resort has something for everyone. Concierges anticipate every need at the two ocean-view pools, one with a waterfall. The guest rooms capture the spirit of the West Indies with British colonial furnishings and pastel colors. A bevy of restaurants and lounges entice guests to kick back and relax while enjoying delicious cuisine. Aria, the resort's signature restaurant, calls to mind the grace of the Mediterranean with its ocean views. Seemingly scripted from the restaurant menu, the spa offers scrumptious treatments like the Key lime coconut body scrub, and soaking in the giant whirlpools is enough to soothe away any negative memories of life at home. *Secret Inspector's Notes:* This Ritz-Carlton resort is in a brilliantly selected location, a tropical spot only a short drive from the Miami airport. From the time you cross the bridge into Key Biscayne, you feel as though you have left the modern world behind, and this brand-new oasis and its staff will do what they can to make sure that it remains forgotten until you leave. Some of the staffing newness is still being worked out in the spa and restaurants, but this hotel should be on your list of winter vacation spots to frequent in the future. By the time you get there, it should be as close to perfection as you can get without a passport. 402 rooms, 10 story. Pets accepted, some restrictions; fee. Check-out noon, check-in 3 pm. TV; cable (premium), VCR available. In-room modem link. Room service 24 hours. Restaurant, bar; entertainment. Children's activity center, babysitting services available. In-house fitness room; sauna, spa, massage, steam room. Beach. Outdoor pool; children's pool; whirlpool. Outdoor tennis, lighted courts. Airport transportation. Business center. Concierge. Luxury level. **$$$**

Key West

Motels/Motor Lodges

★ **KEY LODGE INN AND SUITES.** *1004 Duval St (33040). Phone 305/296-9915; toll-free 800/845-8384. www.keylodge.com.* 23 rooms. Pets accepted; fee. Complimentary continental breakfast. Check-out 11 am. TV. Pool. **$**

D 🐾 ⛱

★ **SUGAR LOAF LODGE.** *US Hwy 1, Mile Marker 17 (33044). Phone 305/745-3211; toll-free 800/553-6097; fax 305/745-3389. www.sugarloaflodge.com.* 55 rooms, 1-2 story. Pets accepted; fee. Check-out 11 am, check-in 3 pm. TV. Restaurant, bar; entertainment. Room service. Pool. Lawn games, marina, charter boats, kayaks, canoes. **$**

D 🐾 🎣 🎿 ⛱

B&B/Small Inns

★★ **CENTER COURT HISTORIC INN & COTTAGES.** *915 Center St (33040). Phone 305/296-9292; toll-free 800/797-8787; fax 305/294-4104. www.centercourtkw.com.* Located in Old Town and just blocks from Duval Street, these units are recognized for their historical preservation. Some date back to the late 1880s and are filled with local art and Caribbean décor. 41 rooms, 1-2 story. Pets accepted; fee. Complimentary continental breakfast. Check-out 11 am, check-in 3 pm. TV; VCR available (movies). In-room modem link. Pool; whirlpool. Concierge. Built in 1880; tropical foliage. Totally nonsmoking. **$**

D 🐾 ⛱ 🎿 ⊠

★ **FRANCES STREET BOTTLE INN.** *535 Frances St (33040). Phone 305/294-8530; toll-free 800/294-8530; fax 305/294-1628. www.bottleinn.com.* 7 rooms, 2 story. Pets accepted; fee. Complimentary continental breakfast. Check-out 11 am, check-in 2 pm. TV; cable (premium). Collection of antique bottles and undersea articles. Victorian coach house built in 1890. Totally nonsmoking. **$**

D 🐾 ⊠

Kissimmee

Motels/Motor Lodges

★★ **HOWARD JOHNSON.** *2323 E Hwy 192 (34744). Phone 407/846-4900; toll-free 800/521-4656; fax 407/994-0188. www.hojo.com.* 190 rooms, 2 story. Pets accepted; fee. Check-out noon. Laundry services. Restaurant. Game room. Pool. **$**

D 🐾 ⛱ ⊠

★ **MASTERS INN - ORLANDO/MAIN GATE.** *2945 Entry Point Blvd (34747). Phone 407/396-7743; toll-free 800/633-3434; fax 407/396-6307. www.mastersinn.com.* 117 rooms, 3 story. Pets accepted, some restrictions; fee. Complimentary continental breakfast. Check-out 11 am. TV; cable (premium). Laundry services. Pool. **$**

D 🐾 ⛱ ⊠ SC

Hotel

★★ **TRAVELODGE.** *5711 Irlo Bronson Memorial Hwy (34746). Phone 407/396-4222; toll-free 800/327-1128; fax 407/396-1834. www.orlandotravellodgehotel.com.* 446 rooms, 8 story. Pets accepted, some restrictions; fee. Check-out 11 am, check-in 4 pm. TV; cable (premium). Laundry services. Restaurant, bar; entertainment. Sauna. Game room. Pool; children's pool; whirlpool. Free Walt Disney World transportation. **$**

D 🐾 ⛱ ⊠

Resort

★★ **HOLIDAY INN.** *5678 US 192 E (34746). Phone 407/396-4488; toll-free 800/366-5437; fax 407/396-8915. www.familyfunhotel.com.* 614 rooms, 2 story. Pets accepted, some restrictions; fee. Check-out 11 am, check-in 4 pm. TV; VCR (movies). Laundry services. Restaurant. Room service. Supervised children's activities, ages 3-12. Game room. Pool; children's pool; whirlpool; poolside service. Outdoor tennis, lighted courts. Free Walt Disney World transportation. **$**

D 🐾 🎿 ⛱

Lakeland

Motel/Motor Lodge

★ **COMFORT INN.** *1817 E Memorial Blvd (33801). Phone 863/688-9221; toll-free 800/228-5150; fax 863/687-4797. www.comfortinn.com.* 64 rooms, 2 story. Pets accepted; fee. Complimentary continental breakfast. Check-out 11 am. TV; VCR available. Pool. **$**

D 🐾 ⛱ ⊠

Hotel

★ **WELLESLEY INN.** *3520 US 98 N (33809). Phone 863/859-0100; toll-free 800/444-8888; fax 863/859-0106. www.wellesleyinnandsuites.com.* Spend an afternoon shopping and then put your feet up and relax at this hotel located just 1 mile from the Lakeland Square Mall. 106 rooms, 6 story. Pets accepted, some restrictions; fee. Complimentary continental breakfast. Check-out 11 am. TV; cable (premium). Health club privileges. **$**

D 🐾 ⛱ ⊠ SC

Marathon

Motel/Motor Lodge

★ ★ **RAINBOW BEND.** *57784 Overseas Hwy (33050). Phone 305/289-1505; fax 305/743-0257.* 24 rooms, 1-2 story. Pets accepted, some restrictions; fee. Complimentary full breakfast. Check-out noon. TV; cable (premium), VCR available (movies). Laundry services. Restaurant. Pool; whirlpool. Sailboats, canoes, fishing pier. **$**

D 🐾 🛲 ⇔ ⇗

Marco Island

Hotel

★ ★ **BOATHOUSE.** *1180 Edington Pl (34145). Phone 239/642-2400; toll-free 800/5286345; fax 239/642-2435. www.theboathousemotel.com.* 20 rooms, 2 story. Nov-May: S, D $58-$92; each additional $10-$20; weekly rates in season; lower rates rest of year. Pets accepted; fee. Check-out 11 am. TV. Pool. On entrance to Collier Bay; dockage.

D 🐾 🛲 ⇔

Marianna

Motel/Motor Lodge

★ **COMFORT INN.** *2175 State Rd 71 (32448). Phone 850/526-5600; toll-free 800/638-7949; fax 850/482-7899. www.comfortinn.com.* 80 rooms, 2 story. Pets accepted; fee. Complimentary continental breakfast. Check-out 11 am. TV; cable (premium). Laundry services. Pool. **$**

🐾 ⇔

Melbourne

Hotel

★ ★ ★ **HILTON OCEANFRONT MELBOURNE BEACH.** *3003 N FL A1A (32903). Phone 321/777-5000; toll-free 877/843-8786; fax 321/777-3713. www.hilton.com.* Situated on one of the Space Coast's most beautiful beaches, this hotel is just 10 minutes from Melbourne's International Airport. An oceanfront heated pool and Jacuzzi and the white sandy beaches of the Atlantic are a lure for sunbathers. 118 rooms, 11 story. Pets accepted; fee. Check-out noon. TV; cable (premium). Restaurant, bar; entertainment. In-house fitness room. Poolside service. **$**

D 🐾 ⇔ 🏃 ⇗

All Suite

★ ★ **QUALITY INN.** *1665 N FL A1A (32903). Phone 321/723-4222; toll-free 800/876-4222; fax 321/768-2438. www.qualitysuites.com.* 208 rooms, 9 story. Pets accepted; fee. Check-out noon. TV; cable (premium), VCR available. Restaurant, bar. Health club privileges. Game room. Pool; whirlpool; poolside service. Buffet breakfast. **$**

D 🐾 🛲 ⇔ ⇗ SC

Miami

All Suite

★ **AMERISUITES.** *11520 SW 88th St (33176). Phone 305/279-8688; toll-free 800/833-1516; fax 305/279-7907. www.amerisuites.com.* 67 suites, 5 story. Pets accepted, some restrictions. Complimentary continental breakfast. Check-out 11 am. TV; cable (premium), VCR available. Pool. In-room modem link. Room service. Business center. Concierge. **$**

D 🐾 🛲 ⇔ ⇗ SC 🏃

Hotels

★ ★ ★ ★ **MANDARIN ORIENTAL MIAMI.** *500 Brickell Key Dr (33131). Phone 305/913-8288; fax 305/913-8337. www.mandarinoriental.com.* With its secluded waterfront location, award-winning spa, and soothing interior design, it is clear that serenity is paramount at the Mandarin Oriental Miami. While close to downtown, Coconut Grove, and South Beach, the Mandarin Oriental enjoys a peaceful spot on Brickell Key, a 44-acre island overlooking Biscayne Bay. Two-story floor-to-ceiling windows showcase waterfront views in the vibrant lobby, while the rooms and suites are blissfully tranquil. Bathed in the glorious Miami sunlight, the rooms highlight contemporary Asian-influenced design with bamboo hardwood floors, simple furnishings, and white fabrics. Achieve balance at the three-level spa, where the ancient traditions of Chinese, Balinese, and Thai cultures blend harmoniously in the treatments and therapies. The Mandarin Oriental's Asian influences extend to dining, especially at Café Sambal, where a sushi and sake bar delight visitors. Latin, French, and Caribbean flavors tempt the palate at trend-setting Azul, while M-Bar is notable for its creative martini menu. 329 rooms, 20 story. Pets accepted, some restrictions; fee. Check-out noon, check-in 3 pm. TV; cable (premium). In-room modem link. Room service 24 hours. Restaurant, bar; entertainment. In-house fitness room; spa, sauna, steam room. Pool; children's pool; whirlpool; poolside service. Valet parking. Business center. Concierge. **$$$$**

D 🐾 ⇔ 🏃 🍽 ⇗

★ ★ ★ **MAYFAIR HOUSE HOTEL.** *3000 Florida Ave (33133). Phone 305/441-0000; toll-free 800/433-4555; fax 305/448-4819. www.mayfairhousehotel.com.* Nestled in the heart of Miami's famous Coconut Grove, Mayfair House features an exotically designed avant-garde building around a lush, central courtyard. Each suite features its own unique name, character, and design, as well as hand-carved mahogany furniture and a Japanese-style hot tub or luxurious Roman tub. Stained glass windows and antique artwork provide beauty throughout this 12,000-square-foot space. Just steps from the hotel, you'll find fine restaurants, upscale shopping, and hot nightclubs. Just down the street, don't miss The Martini Bar for elegant nightlife and great live music, and Tu Tu Tango for Spanish tapas. 179 rooms, 5 story. Pets accepted, some restrictions; fee. Check-out 1 pm, check-in 4 pm. TV; cable (premium), DVD available. Room service 24 hours. Restaurant, bar. In-house fitness room; spa, massage. Health club privileges. Outdoor pool; whirlpool. Valet parking, fee. Business center. Concierge. **$$**

★ ★ ★ **SOFITEL.** *5800 Blue Lagoon Dr (33126). Phone 305/264-4888; fax 305/261-7871. www.sofitel.com.* A French-inspired hotel with American hospitality on Blue Lagoon Lake. From French cuisine to fresh-cut flowers, you'll notice the European difference. 281 rooms, 15 story. Pets accepted, some restrictions; fee. Check-out noon. TV; cable (premium). In-room modem link. Room service 24 hours. Restaurant, bar; entertainment. In-house fitness room. Pool; poolside service. Outdoor tennis, lighted courts. Complimentary valet parking. Airport transportation. Business center. Concierge. On lagoon. **$$**

★ **WELLESLEY INN.** *8436 NW 36th St (33166). Phone 305/592-4799; fax 305/471-8461. www.wellesleyonline.com.* Located within walking distance to the Doral Country Club and close to the airport and shopping areas. 104 rooms, 4 story. Pets accepted, some restrictions; fee. Complimentary continental breakfast. Check-out 11 am, check-in 3 pm. TV; cable (premium). In-room modem link. Laundry services. Pool. Free airport transportation. **$**

★ **WELLESLEY INN.** *7925 NW 154th St (33016). Phone 305/821-8274; fax 305/828-2257. www.wellesleyinn andsuites.com.* 100 rooms, 4 story. Pets accepted, some restrictions; fee. Complimentary continental breakfast. Check-out 11 am, check-in 2 pm. TV; cable (premium). In-room modem link. Laundry services. Outdoor pool. **$**

B&B/Small Inn

★ **MIAMI RIVER INN.** *118 SW South River Dr (33130). Phone 305/325-0045; toll-free 800/468-3589; fax 305/325-9227. www.miamiriverinn.com.* 40 rooms, 2-3 story. Pets accepted, some restrictions; fee. Complimentary continental breakfast. Check-out noon, check-in 1 pm. TV. In-room modem link. Laundry services. Pool. Lawn games. Valet parking. Restored 1908 houses once owned by Miami's founders. Opposite river. **$**

Miami Beach

Hotels

★ ★ ★ **ABBEY HOTEL.** *300 21st St (33139). Phone 305/531-0031; toll-free 888/612-2239; fax 305/672-1663. www.abbeyhotel.com.* A boutique hotel, newly updated by designer Harry Schnaper, in the Deco District's north end. Get pampered with complimentary in-room breakfast or visit the chic indoor-outdoor lobby lounge. You can spy the beach from the roofdeck and lounge. 50 rooms, 3 story. Valet parking. Pets accepted, some restrictions; fee. Check-out 11 am, check-in 3 pm. TV; cable (premium), VCR available, CD available. In-room modem link. Restaurant, bar. Room service. In-house fitness room. Concierge. **$**

★ ★ ★ **FONTAINEBLEAU HILTON RESORT.** *4441 Collins Ave (33140). Phone 305/538-2000; toll-free 800/445-8667; fax 305/531-2845. www.fontainbleauhilton resort.com.* A Miami Beach landmark, this three-building resort sits on 20 tropical acres. With 190,000 square feet of meeting space, it is a major business destination, but not without significant draws for leisure travelers, like the half-acre multi-pool with waterfalls. 876 rooms, 17 story. Pets accepted, some restrictions; fee. Check-out 11 am, check-in 3 pm. TV; cable (premium). In-room modem link. Restaurant, bar; entertainment. Children's activity center; babysitting services available. In-house fitness room; sauna, steam room. Beach. Outdoor pool; children's pool; whirlpool; poolside service. Lawn games. On ocean; dockage, catamarans, jet skis, paddle boats, parasailing. Business center. Concierge. Luxury level. **$$$**

★ ★ ★ **HOTEL OCEAN.** *1230 Ocean Dr (33139). Phone 305/672-2579; fax 305/672-7665. www.hotelocean.com.* Guests of the Hotel Ocean, located in the heart of Miami's famous South Beach, can easily stroll along Ocean Boulevard, where shops, restaurants, and the warm Atlantic Ocean await. Lincoln Bouevard is also within easy walking distance, providing more shops, restaurants, and a wide array of art galleries and boutiques. Nightlife on the beach never stops, and the hotel's concierge can help with club suggestions and theater reservations, as well as fishing tours and other outdoor activities. Rooms range from singles to deluxe suites, and all feature access to the hotel's extensive health club, fitness center, heated pool; and spa services. 27 rooms, 5 story. Pets accepted; fee. Complimentary continental breakfast. Check-out noon, check-in 3 pm. TV; cable (premium), VCR available. In-room modem link. Restaurant, bar. Babysitting services available. Valet parking. Concierge. Luxury level. **$$$**

★ ★ ★ ★ **LOEWS MIAMI BEACH HOTEL.** *1601 Collins Ave (33139). Phone 305/604-1601; toll-free 800/ 356397; fax 305/531-8677. www.loewshotels.com.* Sun-splashed and sexy, South Beach is back with its seductive Latin rhythms and distinctive pastel-colored buildings. From its beachfront location and central spot in the historic Art Deco district to the hottest restaurants and clubs only a short walk away, staying at the Loews Miami Beach Hotel ensures that you never miss a beat. Overlooking the wide, golden beaches synonymous with southern Florida, the Loews is a premier resort destination. Its architecture puts a modern spin on Art Deco while incorporating one of South Beach's landmarks, the St. Moritz. Palm trees gently sway in the breeze while the shimmering pool encourages guests to take a dip. Groovy furnishings and bright splashes of color give the guest rooms a distinctly South Beach sizzle. Creative South American dishes are to be enjoyed at the Gaucho Room, where animal prints and black-and-white photographs set an energetic and lively tone for the evening. 720 rooms, 18 story. Pets accepted. Check-out noon, check-in 4 pm. TV; cable (premium), VCR available. Room service 24 hours. Restaurant, bar. Supervised children's activities. In-house fitness room; sauna, steam room. Pool; whirlpool. Valet parking. Business center. Concierge. **$$**

★ ★ **NEWPORT BEACHSIDE RESORT.** *16701 Collins Ave (33160). Phone 305/949-1300; toll-free 800/ 327-5476; fax 305/947-5873. www.newportbeachresort .com.* A mock lighthouse greets visitors at this oceanfront resort with 500 feet of beach and a focus on water sports. You can lounge at the fishing pier, dive in the artificial reef, or visit the onsite scuba center. 220 rooms, 12 story. Pets accepted. Check-out 11 am, check-in 3 pm. TV; cable (premium). In-room modem link. Restaurant, dining room, bar. Supervised children's activities, from age 3. Babysitting services available. In-house fitness room. Game room. Beach. Outdoor pool; children's pool; whirlpool; poolside service. Lawn games. On ocean; fishing pier; water sport rentals. Valet parking, fee. **$$**

★ ★ **RALEIGH MIAMI BEACH.** *1775 Collins Ave (33139). Phone 305/534-6300; toll-free 800/848-1775; fax 305/538-8140. www.raleighhotel.com.* 93 rooms, 9 story. Pets accepted. Check-out noon, check-in 3 pm. TV; cable (premium), VCR available, CD available. Room service 24 hours. Restaurant, bar. In-house fitness room. Valet parking available. Concierge. **$$**

★ ★ ★ **RENAISSANCE EDEN ROC MIAMI BEACH RESORT AND SPA.** *4525 Collins Ave (33140). Phone 305/531-0000; toll-free 800/327-8337; fax 305/672-9796. www.edenrocresort.com.* Built in 1956 by Morris Lapidus, this star-attracting beachfront icon recently underwent a $24 million renovation. The futuristic Spa of Eden boasts a rock-climbing arena, and the ocean and bay view rooms are brightly colored with Italian marble baths. 349 rooms, 15 story. Pets accepted, some restrictions; fee. Check-out 11 am, check-in 3 pm. TV; cable (premium). In-room modem link. Restaurant, bar. Children's activity center, babysitting services available. In-house fitness room; spa. Game room. Beach. Outdoor pool; whirlpool; poolside service. Valet parking. Business center. Concierge. Restored landmark hotel. **$$**

★ **RITZ PLAZA.** *1701 Collins Ave (33139). Phone 305/534-3500; toll-free 800/522-6400; fax 305/604-8605. www.ritzplaza.com.* 132 rooms, 12 story. Pets accepted, some restrictions. Check-out noon, check-in 3 pm. TV; cable (premium). In-room modem link. Restaurant, bar. Beach. Outdoor pool; poolside service. Airport transportation. **$$**

★ ★ ★ **THE TIDES.** *1220 Ocean Dr (33139). Phone 305/604-5070; fax 305/604-5180. www.islandoutpost.com.* Modern elegance abounds in this cream-and-white-themed contemporary hotel where the best suite will cost you $3,000 per night and bring you all the luxury and pampering you'd expect at a high-class hotel. Renovated by John Pringle, every one of the elegant rooms overlooks the beach and the Atlantic Ocean. Step out the back door, and you can feel the sand between your toes as you make your way to the warm ocean waters of the Atlantic. Step out the front door and you're just minutes away from the fine dining, shopping, art galleries, theater, and nightclubs and that make South Beach famous. 45 rooms, 10 story. Pets accepted, some restrictions; fee. Check-out noon, check-in 4 pm. TV; cable (premium), VCR available. In-room modem link. Room service 24 hours. Restaurant, bar. Babysitting services available. Outdoor pool; poolside service. Valet parking. Business center. Concierge. **$$$$**

Resort

★ ★ **CROWNE PLAZA.** *1545 Collins Ave (33139). Phone 305/604-5700; fax 305/604-2059. www.royalpalmcp.crowne plaza.com.* 370 rooms, 17 story. Pets accepted, some restrictions; fee. Complimentary continental breakfast. Check-out noon. Check-in 4 pm. TV; cable (premium), VCR (movies). In-room modem link. Room service 24 hours. Restaurant, bar. In-house fitness room; massage, sauna, steam room. Pool; whirlpool; poolside service. Valet parking. Business center. Concierge. **$$**

D ⌖ ⇌ ⅄ ⋈ ⚲

All Suites

★ ★ ★ **ALEXANDER ALL SUITE OCEANFRONT RESORT.** *5225 Collins Ave (33140). Phone 305/865-6500; fax 305/341-6555. www.alexanderhotel.com.* The West Indies Caribbean décor will relax you at this exclusive all-suite resort on Millionaire's Row. Climb the spiral staircase to Shula's Steak House, take a dip in the lagoon pools, or enjoy the view from your terrace. 150 suites, 17 story. Pets accepted, some restrictions; fee. Check-out noon, check-in 3 pm. TV; cable (premium), VCR available. In-room modem link. Laundry services. Restaurant, bar; entertainment. Room service. In-house fitness room; massage, sauna, steam room. Outdoor pool; poolside service. On ocean; marina, water sport equipment. Valet parking. Concierge. **$$$**

D ⌖ ⇌ ⅄ ⋈ SC

★ ★ ★ **CASA GRANDE HOTEL.** *834 Ocean Dr (33139). Phone 305/672-7003; toll-free 800/688-7678; fax 305/673-3669. www.casagrandehotel.com.* Located in the midst of Miami's famous Art Deco district, the elegant Casa Grande Hotel is both convenient for corporate travelers (it's walking distance from the Convention Center) and family friendly. The Casa Grande claims the only private beach club on the strip. The central location provides easy access to Miami Beach's great restaurants and cafés, as well as clubs and other nightlife attractions. It's also just across the street from Lummus Park, one of the most famous Atlantic Ocean beaches on Miami Beach's long coastline, where you'll find paved walking trails and a great playground for children. 34 rooms, 5 story. Pets accepted; fee. Check-out noon, check-in 3 pm. TV; cable (premium), VCR available. Babysitting services available. Health club privileges. Beach. Valet parking. **$$$**

D ⌖ ⚓ ⋈ SC

B&B/Small Inn

★ ★ **BAY HARBOR INN & SUITES, MIAMI BEACH.** *9660 E Bay Harbor Dr (33154). Phone 305/868-4141; fax 305/867-9094. www.bayharborinn.com.* 45 rooms, 2 story. Pets accepted, some restrictions; fee. Complimentary continental breakfast. Check-out 11 am, check-in 3 pm. TV. In-room modem link. Restaurant. In-house fitness room. Pool. Valet parking available. Business center. Inn (1948) located on scenic Indian Creek. **$**

D ⌖ ⇌ ⅄ ⋈ SC ⚲

Miami International Airport Area

Motels/Motor Lodges

★ ★ **COMFORT INN.** *5301 NW 36th St (33166). Phone 305/871-6000; toll-free 800/941-9996; fax 305/871-4971. www.comfortinn.com.* 274 rooms, 11 story. Pets accepted, some restrictions; fee. Complimentary continental breakfast. Check-out noon, check-in 3 pm. TV; cable (premium), VCR available. In-room modem link. Laundry services. Restaurant, bar. In-house fitness room. Outdoor pool. Outdoor tennis, lighted courts. Free airport transportation. Business center. Concierge. **$**

D ⌖ ⚓ ⇌ ⅄ ✈ ⋈ ⚲

★ **HAMPTON INN.** *3620 NW 79th Ave (33166). Phone 305/513-0777; fax 305/513-9019. www.hamptoninn.com.* 127 rooms, 6 story. Pets accepted; fee. Complimentary continental breakfast. Check-out 11 am, check-in 3 pm. TV; cable (premium). In-room modem link. Babysitting services available. In-house fitness room. Pool. Free airport transportation. Business center. **$**

D ⌖ ⚓ ⇌ ⅄ ✈ ⋈ SC ⚲

Hotels

★ ★ **CROWNE PLAZA.** *950 NW Le Jeune Rd (33126). Phone 305/446-9000; toll-free 800/2-CROWNE; fax 305/441-0725. www.crowneplaza.com.* 304 rooms, 5 story. Pets accepted, some restrictions; fee. Check-out noon, check-in 3 pm. TV; cable (premium). Restaurant, bar. In-house fitness room; sauna. Indoor pool; whirlpool. Free airport transportation. Business center. **$**

D ⌖ ⚓ ⇌ ⅄ ✈ ⋈ ⚲

★ **HOLIDAY INN EXPRESS.** *5125 NW 36th St (33166). Phone 305/887-2153; fax 305/887-3559. www.hiexpress.com.* 110 rooms, 6 story. Pets accepted, some restrictions; fee. Complimentary continental breakfast. Check-out noon, check-in 3 pm. TV; cable (premium). In-room modem link. Pool. Greens fee $28-$59. Free airport transportation. **$**

D ⌖ ⚲ ⅄ ⇌ ✈ ⋈ SC

★ **SLEEP INN.** *105 Fairway Dr (33166). Phone 305/ 871-7553; toll-free 800/753-3746; fax 305/871-5441. www.sleepinn.com.* 119 rooms, 2 story. Pets accepted; fee. Complimentary continental breakfast. Check-out noon. TV; cable (premium). In-room modem link. Laundry services. In-house fitness room. Pool. Free airport transportation. **$**

D ⬛ 🏌 ➰ ⬛

Naples

Motel/Motor Lodge

★ **RED ROOF INN.** *1925 Davis Blvd (34104). Phone 239/774-3117; toll-free 800/843-7663; fax 239/775-5333. www.redroof.com.* 157 rooms, 3 story. Pets accepted. Check-out 11 am. TV; cable (premium). Laundry services. Pool; whirlpool. Lawn games. Marina adjacent. **$**

D ⬛ ➰ ⬛

Hotel

★ ★ ★ **WELLESLEY INN.** *1555 Fifth Ave S (34102). Phone 239/793-4646; fax 239/793-5248. www.wellesleyinn andsuites.com.* 104 rooms, 3 story. Pets accepted, some restrictions. Complimentary continental breakfast. Check-out 11 am. TV; cable (premium). Health club privileges. Pool. **$**

D ⬛ ➰ ⬛ SC

Resort

★ ★ **WORLD TENNIS CENTER RESORT.** *4800 N Airport Pulling Rd (34105). Phone 239/263-1900; toll-free 800/292-6663; fax 239/649-7855. www.worldtenniscenter .com.* 86 rooms, 2 story. Pets accepted, some restrictions. Check-out 11 am, check-in 3 pm. TV. Pool; whirlpool; poolside service. Outdoor tennis, lighted courts. Mediterranean village atmosphere on 82 1/2 acres. **$$**

D ⬛ 🎾 🏌 ➰ SC

New Port Richey

Motel/Motor Lodge

★ **TRAVELODGE.** *11736 US 19 N (34668). Phone 727/863-1502; fax 727/378-0003. www.travelodge.com.* 151 rooms, 2 story. Pets accepted; fee. Check-out 11 am. TV; cable (premium). In-room modem link. Laundry services. Restaurant. Health club privileges. Pool. **$**

D ⬛ ➰ ⬛

Ocala

Motel/Motor Lodge

★ ★ **HOLIDAY INN.** *3621 W Silver Springs Blvd (34475). Phone 352/629-0381; toll-free 800/465-4329; fax 352/629-8813. www.holiday-inn.com.* 269 rooms, 2 story. Pets accepted; fee. Check-out noon. TV; cable (premium). In-room modem link. Restaurant, bar; entertainment. Room service. Pool. Free train station, bus depot transportation. **$**

D ⬛ ➰ ⬛ SC

Okeechobee

Motels/Motor Lodges

★ **BUDGET INN.** *201 S Parrott Ave (34974). Phone 863/ 763-3185; fax 863/763-3185.* 24 rooms. Pets accepted; fee. Check-out 11 am. TV. In-room modem link. Pool. **$**

⬛ ➰ ⬛ SC

★ **ECONOMY INN.** *507 N Parrott Ave (34972). Phone 863/763-1148; toll-free 800/285-0946; fax 863/763-1149.* 24 rooms. Pets accepted; fee. Check-out 11 am. TV. **$**

⬛ ⬛ SC

Orlando

Motels/Motor Lodges

★ **HOWARD JOHNSON.** *7050 Kirkman Rd (32819). Phone 407/351-2000; toll-free 800/327-3808; fax 407/363-1835. www.howardjohnsonhotelorlando.com.* 356 rooms, 2 story. Pets accepted, some restrictions; fee. Check-out noon, check-in 3 pm. TV. Laundry services. Restaurant, bar; entertainment. Game room. Two pools, children's pool; poolside service. Lawn games. Miniature golf. Free transportation to area attractions. **$**

D ⬛ ➰

★ ★ **QUALITY INN.** *9000 International Dr (32819). Phone 407/996-8585; toll-free 800/228-5151; fax 407/996-6839. www.qualityinn.orlando.com.* 1,088 rooms, 10 story. Pets accepted, some restrictions; fee. Check-out 11 am, check-in 3 pm. TV. Restaurant, bar. Health club privileges. Game room. Pool. **$**

D ⬛ ➰ ⬛

Hotels

★ ★ ★ **HARD ROCK HOTEL.** *5800 Universal Blvd (32819). www.loewshotels.com.* The Hard Rock Hotel at Universal Orlando sits on 14 lushly landscaped acres and boasts a classic California Mission design. You'll find classic rock 'n' roll memorabilia throughout the public areas, and you'll hear classic rock 'n' roll music virtually everywhere—including underwater at the massive zero-entry pool with a 260-foot waterslide. Little ones will enjoy the "Little Rock" pool. Guests don't miss a beat when they return to their rooms, where CD sound systems keep the tunes going. Kids' suites cater to little ones with whimsical décor and are great for families, with a king-size bed for mom and dad. Thirsty guests can choose from several cocktail venues, including the Lobby Lounge, the oh-so-trendy Velvet Bar, and the poolside Hard Rock Beach Club. The full-service Sunset Grill (featuring an open kitchen) and an Orlando version of the world-famous Palm restaurant, among other dining spots, satisfy hungry appetites. 621 rooms, 7 story. Pets accepted, some restrictions; fee. Check-out 11 am. TV; cable (premium), VCR available. In-room modem link. Room service 24 hours. Restaurant, bar; entertainment. In-house fitness room; sauna, steam room. Pool; whirlpool; poolside service. Airport transportation. Free transportation to SeaWorld and Wet 'n Wild. Business center. Concierge. Luxury level. **$$**

★ ★ ★ **PORTOFINO BAY HOTEL.** *5601 Universal Studios Plaza (32819). Phone 407/503-1000; toll-free 800/ BEASTAR; fax 407/503-1003. www.loewshotels.com.* The Portofino Bay Hotel at Universal Orlando re-creates the famed Italian fishing village of the same name. Nestled around a harbor, the buildings feature trompe l'oeil paintings that add to the authenticity of this luxurious resort. As you sit by the faithfully replicated harbor's edge listening to strolling musicians, it's hard to imagine that thrill rides are just beyond the landscaping. Tranquil guest rooms feature fluffy white duvets and warm wood furnishings. The hotel boasts eight different eateries, including the romantic Delfino Riviera, the full-service Trattoria del Porto, and Mama Della's, a family-style Italian restaurant. For drinks, try the Bar American or, for a more casual cocktail, head to the Thirsty Fish at the water's edge. Three pools, a fitness center, a day spa, and Campo Portofino for little ones round out the resort experience. 723 rooms, 6 story. Pets accepted, some restrictions. Check-out 11 am. TV; cable (premium), VCR available. In-room modem link. Room service 24 hours. Restaurant, bar; entertainment. In-house fitness room; spa, sauna, steam room. Three pools, whirlpool; poolside service. Airport transportation. Free transportation to SeaWorld and Wet 'n Wild. Business center. Concierge. **$$$**

Resort

★ ★ ★ **ROYAL PACIFIC RESORT.** *6300 Hollywood Way (32819). Phone 407/503-3000. www.loewshotels.com.* The Royal Pacific Resort, Universal Orlando's newest resort property, offers a South Seas theme. The 53-acre resort has 1,000 luxury rooms and suites and features a towering bamboo forest and an authentic Kul-Kul tower—a Balinese structure used to celebrate special occasions. Don't miss the open-air Orchid Court, filled with hundreds of brilliantly colored orchids, exotic palm trees, hand-carved stone statues, and hand-painted panels. Bamboo accents, dark woods, and richly colored fabrics lend an air of the tropics to the accommodations. Guests have six restaurants and lounges to choose from, including Emeril Lagasse's second Universal Orlando restaurant, Tchoup Chop, which offers a fine-dining South Pacific culinary experience, and the full-service Islands Dining Room. Relax for cocktails at the Bula Bar & Grille, the Orchid Court Lounge, or the massive 12,000-square-foot Lagoon pool—Orlando's largest pool. 946 rooms. Pets accepted, some restrictions; fee. Check-out 11 am. TV. In-room modem link. Room service 24 hours. Restaurant, bar. In-house fitness room; spa, sauna, steam room. Interactive play area. Pool; children's pool; whirlpool. Airport transportation. Free transportation to SeaWorld and Wet 'n Wild. Business center. Concierge. Luxury level. **$$**

Extended Stay

★ ★ **RESIDENCE INN BY MARRIOTT.** *7975 Canada Ave (32819). Phone 407/345-0117; toll-free 800/ 227-3978; fax 407/352-2689. www.residenceinn.com.* 176 rooms, 2 story. Pets accepted, some restrictions; fee. Complimentary continental breakfast. Check-out 11 am. Health club privileges. Pool. Lighted sports court. **$**

★ ★ **RESIDENCE INN BY MARRIOTT.** *11000 Westwood Blvd (32821). Phone 407/313-3600; fax 407/ 313-3611. www.residenceinn.com.* 350 rooms, 6 story. Pets accepted, some restrictions; fee. Complimentary buffet breakfast. Check-out 11 am, check-in 4 pm. TV; cable (premium). In-room modem link. Laundry services. Restaurant. In-house fitness room. Outdoor pool. Concierge. **$**

Ormond Beach

Motel/Motor Lodge

★ **COMFORT INN.** *507 S Atlantic Ave (32176). Phone 386/677-8550; toll-free 800/456-8550; fax 386/673-6260. www.comfortinn.com/hotel/fl448.* 47 rooms, 4 story. Pets accepted, some restrictions; fee. Complimentary continental breakfast. Check-out 11 am, check-in 3 pm. TV. Beach. Outdoor pool; children's pool. **$$**

D ⊠ ⊠ ⊠ ⊠

Palm Beach

Hotels

★ ★ ★ **BRAZILIAN COURT HOTEL.** *301 Australian Ave (33480). Phone 561/655-7740; toll-free 800/552-0335; fax 561/655-0801. www.braziliancourt.com.* This Mediterranean-style hideaway originally opened on New Year's Day 1926. It sits between Lake Worth and the Atlantic, with Worth Avenue shopping just steps away. The Chancellor Grille Room and Terrace restaurants both overlook the Fountain Courtyard. 80 rooms, 2-3 story. Pets accepted, some restrictions; fee. Check-out noon, check-in 3 pm. TV; cable (premium), VCR (movies, CD players available in suites). In-room modem link. Laundry services. Restaurant, bar; entertainment. Babysitting services available. In-house fitness room; spa, massage. Outdoor pool; poolside service. Valet parking. Concierge. **$$$$**

D ⊠ ⊠ ⊠ ⊠ ⊠

★ ★ ★ **CHESTERFIELD PALM HOTEL.** *363 Cocoanut Row (33480). Phone 561/659-5800; toll-free 800/243-7871; fax 561/659-6707. www.chesterfieldpb.com.* Striped awnings welcome guests to this member of Small Luxury Hotels of the World. The rooms, Churchill-esque restaurant, pool, and spa are the perfect combination of an English country house and Palm Beach luxury. The marble bathrooms are a treat. 53 rooms, 3 story. Pets accepted; fee. Check-out noon, check-in 3 pm. TV; cable (premium), VCR available. In-room modem link. Room service 24 hours. Restaurant, bar. Health club privileges. Pool; whirlpool; poolside service. Free valet parking. Business center. Concierge. Cigar room. **$$$**

⊠ ⊠ ⊠ ⊠

★ ★ ★ **HILTON PALM BEACH OCEANFRONT RESORT.** *2842 S Ocean Blvd (33480). Phone 561/586-6542; toll-free 800/433-1718; fax 561/585-0188. www.hilton.com.* Enter through the striped awning of this oceanfront resort and experience casual, relaxed ambience. Jog along the Intracoastal Waterway path, snorkel at the nearby manmade reef, or take a dip in the pool. Private balconies offer tempting views. 134 rooms, 5 story. Pets accepted, some restrictions; fee. Check-out noon, check-in 4 pm. TV; cable (premium), VCR (free movies). In-room modem link. Restaurant, bar. Room service. Health club privileges, sauna. Pool; whirlpool; poolside service. Valet parking. Business center. Concierge. **$$**

D ⊠ ⊠ ⊠ ⊠ ⊠

★ **PLAZA INN.** *215 Brazilian Ave (33480). Phone 561/832-8666; toll-free 800/233-2632; fax 561/835-8776. www.plazainnpalmbeach.com.* Elegant and affordable, this historic inn is just one block from the beach and four from Worth Avenue shopping. Sink into one of the uniquely decorated, antique-filled rooms or relax in the Stray Fox Pub and Piano Bar. 47 rooms, 3 story. Pets accepted. Complimentary continental breakfast. Check-out noon, check-in 2 pm. TV. Dining room, bar. Babysitting services available. Health club privileges. Outdoor pool; whirlpool; poolside service. **$**

⊠ ⊠ ⊠ SC

★ ★ ★ ★ ★ **THE RITZ-CARLTON, PALM BEACH.** *100 S Ocean Blvd (33462). Phone 561/533-6000; toll-free 800/241-3333; fax 561/585-3532. www.ritzcarlton.com.* Tucked away on 7 oceanfront acres on the southern tip of Palm Beach Island, The Ritz-Carlton, Palm Beach remains close to the area's attractions and activities. This Mediterranean-style resort is a classically refined seaside getaway. The rooms and suites artfully blend Florida's characteristic décor with European elegance. Views of the Atlantic Ocean or the manicured grounds are particularly alluring. Guests partake in a host of recreational activities here, from water sports and tennis to spa treatments and Ritz Kids programs, and some of South Florida's best golf courses are just a short drive away. Four restaurants showcase the talents of the chefs. The Restaurant's creative take on local dishes makes it a favorite, while the Grill is perfect for meat and seafood lovers. Others adopt the fun-loving spirit of the tropics at the Ocean Café and Bar or enjoy afternoon tea at the Lobby Lounge. *Secret Inspector's Notes:* The service and personal attention at this luxurious getaway will keep you coming back for years to come. The staff's commitment to guest satisfaction is evident throughout the hotel, and you will leave with a smile on your face and a place in your heart for this special resort. Not a single detail at this hotel will disappoint you; you will recommend it above all others as *the* place to stay in Palm Beach. 270 rooms, 6 story. Pets accepted, some restrictions; fee. Valet parking. Airport transportation. Check-out noon, check-in 4 pm. TV; cable (premium), VCR available (movies). In-room modem link. Room service 24 hours. Restaurant, bar; entertainment. Children's activity center, babysitting services available. In-house fitness room; sauna, steam room, massage. Outdoor pool; whirlpool; poolside service. Outdoor tennis. Private cabanas. Beach. Business center. Concierge. Luxury level. **$$$$**

D ⊠ ⊠ ⊠ ⊠ ⊠ ⊠

Resort

★ ★ ★ ★ ★ **FOUR SEASONS RESORT PALM BEACH.** *2800 S Ocean Blvd (33480). Phone 561/582-2800; toll-free 800/432-2335; fax 561/547-1557. www.fourseasons.com.* The Four Seasons Resort unites the best of Palm Beach in one spot. Just minutes from the alluring boutiques of Worth Avenue and the challenges of three championship golf courses, the resort enjoys a secluded setting on a lovely stretch of golden beach. The guest rooms have a sophisticated tropical décor, with floral prints, pastel colors, and casually elegant furnishings. All rooms have terraces or balconies overlooking the Atlantic Ocean or the beautiful garden and pool area. Southeastern regional dishes are the specialty at the refined Restaurant, while the patio setting of the Atlantic Bar & Grill and the canopied terrace of the Ocean Bistro are preferable for casual meals and tropical drinks. Steps from the ocean, the freshwater pool has an idyllic landscaped terrace shaded by leafy palms. A small yet wonderful spa and fitness center with state-of-the-art equipment and yoga and Pilates classes round out the total resort experience. *Secret Inspector's Notes:* While the hotel itself is nice, the restaurant at the Four Seasons Palm Beach is where the true luxury lies. The staff is amazingly warm and eager to please, and the food is filled with surprises and contrasts, contributing to the happy feelings passing through the dining room. The staff at the hotel could learn a few lessons from the exceptional degree of care bestowed on guests at the restaurant, as service at the hotel is lackluster in contrast. The modern fitness center and well-attended pool remind you why you selected this seaside resort in the first place. 210 rooms, 4 story. Pets accepted, some restrictions. Valet parking. Check-out noon, check-in 3 pm. TV; cable (premium), VCR available (movies). In-room modem link. Room service 24 hours. Restaurant, bar. Babysitting services available. In-house fitness room; spa, sauna, steam room, massage. Beach. Outdoor pool; whirlpool; poolside service. Children's activity center. Outdoor tennis, lighted courts. Airport transportation. Business center. Concierge. **$$$$**

D 🐾 🏋 🏌 🏊 🎾 ✈ 🏃

Pensacola

Motels/Motor Lodges

★ ★ **BAY BEACH INN.** *51 Gulf Breeze Pkwy (32561). Phone 850/932-2214; fax 850/932-0932. www.baybeach inn.com.* 168 rooms, 2 story. Pets accepted; fee. Check-out noon. TV; cable (premium). In-room modem link. Laundry services. Restaurant. Health club privileges. Pool; children's pool. On Pensacola Bay; opposite fishing pier. **$**

D 🐾 🏋 🏊 ⛱

★ ★ **RAMADA INN.** *7601 Scenic Hwy (32504). Phone 850/477-7155; fax 850/477-7155. www.ramada.com.* 150 rooms, 2 story. May-Aug: S, D $79; each additional $6; under 18 free; holidays (3-day minimum); lower rates rest of year. Pets accepted, some restrictions; fee. Check-out

noon. TV. In-room modem link. Restaurant, bar; entertainment. Room service. In-house fitness room; sauna. Pool.

D 🐾 🏃 ⛱ SC

★ **RED ROOF INN.** *7340 Plantation Rd (32504). Phone 850/476-7960; fax 850/479-4706. www.redroof.com.* 108 rooms, 2 story. S, D $39.99-$69.99; each additional $10; under 18 free. Pets accepted, some restrictions. Check-out noon. TV.

D 🐾

★ **SUPER 8.** *7220 Plantation Rd (32504). Phone 850/476-8038; fax 850/474-6284. www.super8.com.* 62 rooms, 3 story. Memorial Day-Labor Day: S $37.80-$47; D $39.60-$49; suites $65-$75; under 18 free; family rates; weekly rates; lower rates rest of year. Pets accepted, some restrictions; fee. Check-out 11 am. TV. Pool.

D 🐾 🏋 ⛱ ⛱

Hotel

★ ★ ★ **CROWNE PLAZA.** *200 E Gregory St (32501). Phone 850/433-3336; toll-free 800/348-3336; fax 850/432-7572. www.crowneplaza.com.* 210 rooms, 15 story. S, D $95-$105; each additional $10; suites $175-$408; family rates; package plans. Pets accepted, some restrictions; fee. Check-out 1 pm. TV; cable (premium). Heated pool. In-room modem link. Restaurant, bar. In-house fitness room. Free airport transportation. Lobby is restored 1912 Louisville and Nashville Railroad Depot.

D 🐾 ⛱ 🏌 ✈ ⛱

Port Charlotte

Motel/Motor Lodge

★ **DAYS INN.** *1941 Tamiami Trail (33948). Phone 941/627-8900; toll-free 800/329-7466; fax 941/743-8503. www.daysinn.com.* 126 rooms, 3 story. Jan-Mar: S $59-$109; D $79-$114; each additional $5; under 17 free; lower rates rest of year. Pets accepted, some restrictions. Check-out 11 am. TV; cable (premium). Laundry services. Room service. Health club privileges. In-house fitness room. Pool.

D 🐾 🏌 ⛱ SC

Punta Gorda

Motel/Motor Lodge

★ ★ **BEST WESTERN WATERFRONT.** *300 Retta Esplanade (33950). Phone 941/639-1165; toll-free 800/525-1022; fax 941/639-8116. www.bestwestern.com.* 182 rooms, 2-5 story. Pets accepted; fee. Check-out 11 am. TV; cable (premium). Heated pool. Restaurant, bar; entertainment. Room service. On harbor; boat dock. Wilderness tours. **$**

🅳 🐾 ⚓ ⛱ 🚫

Saint Augustine

Motel/Motor Lodge

★ **DAYS INN.** *2800 N Ponce de Leon Blvd (32084). Phone 904/829-6581; toll-free 800/331-9995; fax 904/824-0135. www.daysinn.com.* 124 rooms, 2 story. S $39-$105; D $44-$105; each additional $5; under 18, $2; under 12 free; higher rates: holidays, special events. Pets accepted; fee. Check-out noon. TV. Restaurant. Pool.

🐾 ⛱

Saint Augustine Beach

Motel/Motor Lodge

★★ **HOLIDAY INN.** *860 A1A Beach Blvd (32080). Phone 904/471-2555; toll-free 800/626-7263; fax 904/461-8450. www.holidayinnstaugustine.com.* 152 rooms, 5 story. Feb-mid-Sept: S, D $77-$130; under 18 free; lower rates rest of year. Pets accepted, some restrictions; fee. Check-out 11 am. TV. Laundry services. Restaurant, bar. Room service. Pool; poolside service. On beach; ocean views.

🅳 🐾 ⚓ ⛱ 🚫 🆂🅲

St. Petersburg

Motels/Motor Lodges

★★ **LA MARK CHARLES BEST VALUE INN.** *6200 34th St N (33781). Phone 727/527-7334; toll-free 800/448-6781; fax 727/526-9294. www.lmcmotel.com.* 93 rooms, 1-2 story. Feb-Apr: S, D $60-$75; each additional $5; suites $79-$95; kitchen units $65-$75; under 12 free; lower rates rest of year. Pets accepted; fee. Check-out 11 am. TV; cable (premium). Restaurant. Heated pool; whirlpool.

🐾 ⛱ 🚫

★ **LA QUINTA INN.** *4999 34th St N (33714). Phone 727/527-8421; toll-free 800/687-6667; fax 727/527-8851. www.laquinta.com.* 120 rooms, 2 story. Pets accepted, some restrictions. Complimentary continental breakfast. Check-out noon. TV; cable (premium). In-room modem link. Laundry services. In-house fitness room. Pool. **$**

🅳 🐾 ⛱ 🏃 🚫

★ **VALLEY FORGE.** *6825 Central Ave (33710). Phone 727/345-0135; fax 727/384-1671.* 27 rooms. Pets accepted, some restrictions; fee. Check-out 11 am. TV; cable (premium), VCR available. Pool. Lawn games. Courtyard. **$**

🐾 ⚓ ⛱ 🚫

Sanibel and Captiva Islands

Resort

★★ **TWEEN WATERS INN.** *15951 Captiva Dr (33924). Phone 239/472-5161; toll-free 866/893-3646; fax 239/472-0249. www.tween-waters.com.* 137 rooms, 2 story. Pets accepted, some restrictions; fee. Check-out noon. TV; cable (premium). Restaurant, bar. In-house fitness room; massage. Game room. Pool; children's pool; poolside service. Outdoor tennis, lighted courts. Lawn games. Concierge. **$$**

🅳 🐾 ⚓ ⛱ 🏃 🚫

Sarasota

Motels/Motor Lodges

★ **COMFORT INN.** *4800 N Tamiami Trail (34234). Phone 941/355-7091; toll-free 800/228-5150; fax 941/359-1639. www.comfortinn.com.* 73 rooms, 2 story. Pets accepted; fee. Complimentary continental breakfast. Check-out 11 am. TV; cable (premium). Pool; whirlpool. **$**

🅳 🐾 ⛱ 🚫 🆂🅲

★★ **RAMADA INN.** *1660 S Tamiami Trail (34229). Phone 941/966-2121; fax 941/966-1124. www.ramada.com.* 148 rooms, 2 story. Feb-Mid-Apr: S, D $89-$119; kitchen units $137-$162; lower rates rest of year. Pets accepted; fee. Check-out noon. TV. Restaurant, bar. Pool; poolside service.

🅳 🐾 ⛱ 🚫 🆂🅲

★ **WELLESLEY INN.** *1803 N Tamiami Trail (34234). Phone 941/366-5128; fax 941/953-4322. www.wellesley innandsuites.com.* 103 rooms, 4 story. Pets accepted, some restrictions. Complimentary continental breakfast. Check-out 11 am. TV; cable (premium). Health club privileges. Pool. Free airport transportation. **$**

🅳 🐾 ⛱ 🚫

Sebring

Motels/Motor Lodges

★ ★ **INN ON THE LAKES.** *3100 Golfview Rd (33872). Phone 863/471-9400; toll-free 800/531-5253.* 161 rooms, 14 suites, 3 story. Jan-mid-Apr: S, D $55-$80; suites $85-$140; weekly, monthly rates; package plans; higher rates special events; lower rates rest of year. Pets accepted, some restrictions; fee. Check-out noon. TV; cable (premium), VCR available. In-room modem link. Restaurant, bar. Room service. Health club privileges. In-house fitness room. Pool; poolside service.

⊡ 🐾 🏊 🏌 🖼

★ ★ **QUALITY INN.** *6525 US 27 N (33825). Phone 863/385-4500; toll-free 800/228-5151; fax 863/382-4793. www.qualityinn.com.* This is the best lodging choice for visitors to Sebring. Guest can enjoy the use of the outdoor pool during the warm seasons. 148 rooms, 2 story. S, D $99-$129; under 18 free; weekend rates; higher rates special events (4-day minimum). Pets accepted, some restrictions; fee. Check-out noon. TV; VCR available. Laundry services. Restaurant, bar; entertainment Wed-Sat. Room service. In-house fitness room; sauna. Pool; children's pool; poolside service. Lawn games.

⊡ 🐾 🏊 🖼 SC

Siesta Key

Resort

★ ★ **TROPICAL SHORES BEACH RESORT.** *6717 Sara Sea Circle Siesta Key (34242). Phone 941/349-3330; toll-free 800/235-3493; fax 941/346-0025. www.tropicalshores.com.* 30 kitchen units, 1-2 story. Pets accepted; fee. Check-out 10 am. TV; cable (premium). Pool. Lawn games. **$$**

⊡ 🐾 🛏 🏊 🖼 SC

B&B/Small Inn

★ ★ **TURTLE BEACH RESORT.** *9049 Midnight Pass Rd (34242). Phone 941/349-4554; fax 941/312-9034. www.turtlebeachresort.com.* 10 kitchen units. 5 with shower only. Pets accepted; fee. Check-out 11 am, check-in 1 pm. TV; VCR available. Pool. Totally nonsmoking. **$$**

🐾 🛏 🏊 🖼

Silver Springs

Motels/Motor Lodges

★ **DAYS INN.** *5001 E Silver Springs Blvd (32688). Phone 352/236-2891; fax 352/236-3546. www.daysinn.com.* 56 rooms, 2 story. Mid-Jan-mid-Apr, mid-June-early Sept: S $45-$65; D $55-$75; each additional $5; under 18 free; lower rates rest of year. Pets accepted; fee. Check-out 11 am. TV; VCR available (movies). Pool. Ocala National Forest nearby.

🐾 🏊 🖼

★ **KNIGHTS INN.** *5565 E Silver Springs Blvd (34488). Phone 352/236-2616; fax 352/236-1941.* 40 rooms, 2 story. Feb-Mar and June-Aug: S $40-$45; D $45-$50; each additional $5; under 18 free; higher rates: races, holidays, football weekends, special events; lower rates rest of year. Pets accepted; fee. Check-out noon. TV; cable (premium). Pool. Lawn games.

⊡ 🐾 🏊 🖼

★ **SUN PLAZA MOTEL.** *5461 E Silver Springs Blvd (34489). Phone 352/236-2343; fax 352/236-1214. www.sunplazamotel.com.* 47 rooms. Late Dec-Apr, June-Labor Day: S $35-$65; D $39-$75; each additional $5; kitchen units $55-$70; lower rates rest of year. Pets accepted, some restrictions; fee. Check-out 11 am. TV. Pool. Lawn games.

🐾 🏊 🖼

Starke

Motel/Motor Lodge

★ **BEST WESTERN MOTOR INN.** *1290 N Temple Ave (32091). Phone 904/964-6744; fax 904/964-3355. www.bestwestern.com.* 51 rooms, 2 story. S, D $58; under 12 free; higher rates special events. Pets accepted, some restrictions; fee. Complimentary continental breakfast. Check-out 11 am. TV. In-room modem link. Pool.

🐾 🏊 🖼

Stuart

Resort

★ ★ ★ **MARRIOTT HUTCHINSON ISLAND RESORT.** *555 NE Ocean Blvd (34996). Phone 772/225-3700; toll-free 800/775-5936; fax 772/225-0003. www.marriott.com.* Set on a 200-acre island on Florida's famed Treasure Coast, this nautical resort is a great location to do business, with 22,000 square feet of meeting space. Recreations also abound with an onsite golf course, tennis courts, and a marina. 290 rooms, 4 story. Pets accepted, some restrictions; fee. Check-out 11 am, check-in 3 pm. TV. In-room modem link. Laundry services. Dining room, bar. Room service. Supervised children's activities, from age 3. Four pools, whirlpool; poolside service. Golf. Outdoor tennis, lighted courts. Bicycles. Full-service marina; store. Deep-sea fishing charters; tour boat; boat rentals. Waterskiing. Business center. Concierge. Onsite tram service. Snorkeling equipment. In-house fitness room. **$$**

Sun City Center

Motel/Motor Lodge

★ ★ **SUN CITY CENTER INN.** *2020 Clubhouse Dr (33573). Phone 813/634-3331; toll-free 800/237-8200; fax 813/634-2053.* 100 rooms, 1-2 story. Dec-early May: S $49-$79; D $79-$92; each additional $5; under 17 free; golf plans; lower rates rest of year. Pets accepted, some restrictions; fee. Check-out 11 am. TV. Restaurant, bar; entertainment. Health club privileges. Pool.

Tallahassee

Motels/Motor Lodges

★ **BEST WESTERN PRIDE INN & SUITES.** *2016 Apalachee Pkwy (32301). Phone 850/656-6312; toll-free 800/827-7390; fax 850/942-4312. www.bestwestern.com.* 78 rooms, 2 story. S, D $46-$58; each additional $5. Pets accepted, some restrictions; fee. Complimentary continental breakfast. Check-out 11 am. TV. Pool.

★ **LA QUINTA INN.** *2905 N Monroe St (32303). Phone 850/385-7172; fax 850/422-2463. www.laquinta.com.* 154 rooms, 3 story. S $74-$85; D $80-$90; each additional $7; under 18 free. Pets accepted. Complimentary continental breakfast. Check-out noon. TV; cable (premium). In-room modem link. Pool.

★ **RED ROOF INN.** *2930 Hospitality St (32303). Phone 850/385-7884; fax 850/386-8896. www.redroof.com.* 107 rooms, 2 story. S, D $41.99-$48.99; each additional $7; under 18 free. Pets accepted, some restrictions. Check-out noon. TV. In-room modem link.

★ **SHONEY'S INN.** *2801 N Monroe St (32303). Phone 850/386-8286; fax 850/422-1074. www.shoneysinn.com.* 113 rooms, 2 story. S, D $49-$73; each additional $5; suites $80-$150. Pets accepted, some restrictions; fee. Complimentary continental breakfast. Check-out noon. TV. Laundry services. Health club privileges. Pool.

Tampa

Motels/Motor Lodges

★ ★ **COMFORT INN.** *820 E Busch Blvd (33612). Phone 813/933-4011; toll-free 800/288-4011; fax 813/932-1784. www.travelodge.com.* 263 rooms, 2-4 story. Pets accepted, some restrictions; fee. Complimentary continental breakfast. Check-out 11 am, check-in 3 pm. TV; cable (premium). Restaurant, bar. Room service. Game room. Indoor pool; outdoor pool; whirlpool. Outdoor tennis, lighted courts. Business center. Free Busch Gardens transportation. **$**

★ ★ **DAYS INN.** *701 E Fletcher Ave (33612). Phone 813/977-1550; toll-free 800/329-7466; fax 813/977-6556. www.daysinn.com.* 240 rooms, 3 story. Pets accepted; fee. Complimentary full breakfast. Check-out noon. TV; cable (premium). Restaurant. Health club privileges. Pool. **$**

★ **HOLIDAY INN EXPRESS.** *4732 N Dale Mabry Hwy (33614). Phone 813/877-6061; toll-free 800/898-4484; fax 813/876-1531. www.holiday-inn.com.* 235 rooms, 1-2 story. Pets accepted; fee. Complimentary continental breakfast. Check-out noon. TV; cable (premium). In-room modem link. Restaurant. In-house fitness room. Game room. Pool. Free airport transportation. Business center. **$**

★ **LA QUINTA INN.** *2904 Melburne Blvd (33605). Phone 813/623-3591; toll-free 800/687-6667; fax 813/620-1375. www.laquinta.com.* 129 rooms, 3 story. Pets accepted, some restrictions. Complimentary continental breakfast. Check-out noon. TV; cable (premium). In-room modem link. Laundry services. Pool. **$**

★ **MASTERS INN–TAMPA FAIRGROUNDS.** *6606 E Martin Luther King Blvd (33619). Phone 813/623-6667; fax 813/263-1495.* 128 rooms, 2 story. Pets accepted, some restrictions; fee. Check-out 11 am. TV; cable (premium). Pool. **$**

★ **RED ROOF INN.** *5001 N US 301 (33610). Phone 813/623-5245; toll-free 800/843-7663; fax 813/623-5240. www.redroof.com.* 108 rooms, 2 story. Pets accepted, some restrictions. Check-out noon. TV; cable (premium). **$**

All Suites

★ **AMERISUITES.** *11408 N 30th St (33612). Phone 813/979-1922; fax 813/979-1926. www.amerisuites.com.* 128 rooms, 6 story. Pets accepted, some restrictions; fee. Complimentary continental breakfast. Check-out 11 am. TV; cable (premium). In-room modem link. In-house fitness room. Heated pool. Business center. **$**

★ **AMERISUITES.** *4811 W Main St (33607). Phone 813/282-1037; fax 813/282-1148. www.amerisuites.com.* 126 rooms, 6 story. Pets accepted, some restrictions. Complimentary continental breakfast. Check-out 11 am. TV; cable (premium). In-room modem link. Laundry services. Restaurant, bar. In-house fitness room. Pool. Free airport transportation. Business center. **$**

★ ★ **BEST WESTERN ALL SUITES HOTEL.** *3001 University Center Dr (33612). Phone 813/971-8930; toll-free 800/786-7446; fax 813/971-8935. www.bestwestern.com.* 150 rooms, 3 story. Pets accepted, some restrictions; fee. Complimentary full breakfast. Check-out noon. TV; cable (premium), VCR available. In-room modem link. Restaurant. Health club privileges. Pool; whirlpool. **$**

★ ★ **WOODFIN SUITES.** *3075 N Rocky Point Dr (33607). Phone 813/281-5677; toll-free 877/433-9644; fax 813/289-0266. www.woodfinsuitehotels.com.* 176 rooms, 1-2 story. Pets accepted, some restrictions; fee. Complimentary continental breakfast. Check-out noon. TV; cable (premium). In-room modem link. Health club privileges. Pool; whirlpool. Dock; watersports, parasailing, fishing. On Tampa Bay. Free airport transportation. **$$**

Tarpon Springs

Motel/Motor Lodge

★ ★ **BEST WESTERN TAHITIAN RESORT.** *2337 US 19 N (34691). Phone 727/937-4121; toll-free 800/528-1234; fax 727/937-3806. www.bestwestern.com.* 140 rooms, 2 story. Pets accepted; fee. Complimentary full breakfast. Check-out 11 am. TV. Laundry services. Restaurant, bar;

entertainment Fri, Sat. Room service. Health club privileges. Pool. **$**

Tavares

Motel/Motor Lodge

★ **INN ON THE GREEN.** *700 E Burleigh Blvd (32778). Phone 352/343-6373; toll-free 800/935-2935; fax 352/343-7216. www.innonthegreen.net/.* 76 rooms, 14 kitchen units, 2 story. Mid-Dec-mid-Apr: S, D $79-$89; each additional $5; kitchen units $15 additional; suites $135-$250; under 12 free; weekly rates; higher rates special events; lower rates rest of year. Pets accepted, some restrictions; fee. Check-out 11 am. TV; cable (premium), VCR available (movies). Pool. Lawn games.

Titusville

Motels/Motor Lodges

★ **DAYS INN.** *3755 Cheney Hwy (32780). Phone 321/269-4480; toll-free 877/767-3297; fax 321/383-0646. www.daysinn.com.* 149 rooms, 2 story. Pets accepted, some restrictions; fee. Check-out 11 am. TV; cable (premium). Laundry services. In-house fitness room. Pool. Lawn games. **$**

★ **RIVERSIDE INN.** *1829 Riverside Dr (32780). Phone 321/267-7900; fax 321/267-7080.* 104 rooms, 2 story. Pets accepted, some restrictions; fee. Check-out 11 am. TV; cable (premium). Bar. In-house fitness room. Pool. On Indian River; overlooks Kennedy Space Center. **$**

Venice

Motel/Motor Lodge

★ ★ **DAYS INN.** *1710 S Tamiami Trail (34293). Phone 941/493-4558; fax 941/493-1593. www.daysinnvenice.com.* 72 rooms, 8 kitchen units, 3 story. Late Jan-mid-Apr: S, D $70-$80; each additional $10; kitchen units $100-$170; under 17 free; higher rates holidays; lower rates rest of year. Pets accepted; fee. Check-out 11 am. TV; cable. Restaurant, bar. Pool.

Vero Beach

Motel/Motor Lodge

★★ **DAYS INN.** 8800 20th St (32966). Phone 772/562-9991; fax 772/562-0716. www.daysinn.com. 115 rooms, 2 story. Pets accepted; fee. Check-out 11 am. TV. In-room modem link. Restaurant. Pool. **$**

⬛🔲🐾⬛⬛⬛⬛

Walt Disney World

Motels/Motor Lodges

★ **COMFORT INN.** 8442 Palm Pkwy (32836). Phone 407/996-7300; toll-free 800/999-7300; fax 407/996-7301. www.comfortinnorlando.com. 710 rooms, 5 story. Pets accepted, some restrictions; fee. Complimentary continental breakfast. Check-out 11 am, check-in 3 pm. TV; cable (premium). Laundry services. Restaurant, bar. Game room. Pool. Free Walt Disney World transportation. **$**

⬛🐾⬛⬛

★★ **DAYS INN.** 12799 Apopka Vineland Rd (32836). Phone 407/239-4441; toll-free 800/224-5058; fax 407/239-0325. www.daysinn.com. 203 rooms, 8 story. Pets accepted, some restrictions; fee. Check-out noon, check-in 4 pm. TV; cable (premium), VCR available. Laundry services. Restaurant. Game room. Pool. Free Walt Disney World transportation. **$**

⬛🐾⬛⬛SC

West Palm Beach

Motels/Motor Lodges

★ **COMFORT INN.** 1901 Palm Beach Lakes Blvd (33409). Phone 561/689-6100; fax 561/686-6177. www.comfortinn.com. 162 rooms, 6 story. Pets accepted, some restrictions; fee. Complimentary continental breakfast. Check-out noon. TV; cable (premium). Laundry services. Restaurant. Pool. **$**

⬛🐾🔲⬛⬛⬛

★★ **DAYS INN.** 2700 N Ocean Dr (33404). Phone 561/848-8661; toll-free 800/329-7466; fax 561/844-0999. www.daysinn.com. 165 rooms, 2 story. Jan-Apr: S, D, kitchen units $159-$179; under 17 free; lower rates rest of year. Pets accepted; fee. Check-out noon. TV; cable (premium). Restaurant, bar. Pool; whirlpool. Lawn games. **$**

⬛🐾🔲⬛⬛

★★ **DAYS INN.** 2300 45th St (33407). Phone 561/689-0450; toll-free 800/543-1613; fax 561/686-7439. www.daysinn.com. 214 rooms, 2 story. Pets accepted; fee. Check-out 11 am. TV; cable (premium). Laundry services. Restaurant. Pool; whirlpool. **$**

🐾⬛⬛SC

B&B/Small Inn

★★★ **HIBISCUS HOUSE.** 501 30th St (33407). Phone 561/863-5633; toll-free 800/203-4927. www.hibiscushouse.com. Mayor David Dunkle built this bed-and-breakfast in 1922 during the Florida land boom. The rooms and suites are all uniquely decorated. 8 rooms, 2 story. Pets accepted. Complimentary full breakfast. Check-out noon, check-in 2 pm. TV. In-room modem link. Pool. Street parking. **$**

⬛🐾⬛⬛

Winter Haven

Motels/Motor Lodges

★ **BUDGET HOST INN.** 970 Cypress Gardens Blvd (32789). Phone 863/294-4229; fax 863/293-2089. 22 rooms, 2 kitchen units. Dec-Apr: S, D $42-$62; each additional $6; kitchen units $8 additional; lower rates rest of year. Pets accepted, some restrictions; fee. Complimentary continental breakfast. Check-out 11 am. TV. Pool. Lawn games.

🐾⬛⬛

★★ **HOWARD JOHNSON.** 1300 3rd St SW (33880). Phone 863/294-7321; toll-free 800/654-2000; fax 863/299-1673. www.hojo.com. 100 rooms, 2 story. Dec-Apr: S, D $74-$95; each additional $7; under 18 free; lower rates rest of year. Pets accepted; fee. Complimentary continental breakfast. Check-out noon. TV; cable (premium). Laundry services. Restaurant, bar. Game room. Heated pool; children's pool. Miniature golf. Lawn games.

⬛🐾⬛⬛SC

★ **SCOTTISH INN.** 1901 Cypress Gardens Blvd (33884). Phone 863/324-3954; fax 863/324-0391. 23 rooms. Dec-Apr: S, D $58-$74; each additional $6; kitchen units $8 additional; weekly rates; lower rates rest of year. Pets accepted; fee. Check-out 11 am. TV. Laundry services.

🐾⬛

Georgia

Adel

Motels/Motor Lodges

★ **DAYS INN.** *1200 W 4th St (30121). Phone 229/896-4574; toll-free 800/329-7466; fax 229/896-4575. www.daysinn.com.* 78 rooms, 2 story. Pets accepted, some restrictions; fee. Check-out 11 am. TV; cable (premium), VCR available. Restaurant. Pool. **$**

⊡ 🐾 🏊 🏖 SC

★ **SUPER 8.** *1103 W 4th St; I-75 exit 10 (31620). Phone 229/896-2244; toll-free 800/800-8000. www.super8.com.* 69 rooms, 2 story. Pets accepted, some restrictions; fee. Check-out noon. TV. Pool. **$**

⊡ 🐾 🏊 🏖 SC

★ **SUPER 8.** *1102 W 4th St (31620). Phone 229/896-4523; toll-free 800/800-8000. www.super8.com.* 50 rooms, 2 story. Pets accepted; fee. Check-out 11 am. TV. Pool. **$**

⊡ 🐾 🏊 🏖 SC

Albany

Motel/Motor Lodge

★ **RAMADA INN.** *2505 N Slappey Blvd (31701). Phone 229/883-3211; fax 229/439-2806. www.ramada-albany.com.* 158 rooms, 2 story. Pets accepted; fee. Check-out noon. TV; cable (premium), VCR available. In-room modem link. Restaurant, bar. Room service. Pool; children's pool. Free airport transportation. **$**

⊡ 🐾 🏊 🏖

Americus

B&B/Small Inn

★ ★ ★ **1906 PATHWAY INN BED & BREAKFAST.** *501 S Lee St (31709). Phone 229/928-2078; toll-free 800/889-1466. www.1906pathwayinn.com.* For a small-town getaway, this English-colonial bed-and-breakfast offers guests relaxation, Southern style. The Old South charm here is warm and inviting. 5 rooms, 2 story. Pets accepted, some restrictions; fee. Complimentary full breakfast. Check-out 11 am, check-in 4 pm. TV; cable (premium), VCR available (movies). Concierge. Southern mansion built in 1906. Totally nonsmoking. **$**

🐾 ⚓ 🏖

Athens

Motels/Motor Lodges

★ **BEST WESTERN COLONIAL INN.** *170 N Milledge Ave (30601). Phone 706/546-7311; toll-free 800/592-9401; fax 706/546-7959. www.bestwestern.com.* 70 rooms, 2 story. Pets accepted; fee. Complimentary continental breakfast. Check-out 11 am, check-in 2 pm. TV; cable (premium). In-room modem link. Outdoor pool. **$**

⊡ 🐾 🏊 🏖 SC

★ **HOLIDAY INN EXPRESS.** *513 W Broad St (30601). Phone 706/546-8122; toll-free 800/465-4329; fax 706/546-1722. www.holiday-inn.com.* 160 rooms, 5 story. Pets accepted, some restrictions; fee. Check-out 11 am, check-in 3 pm. TV; cable (premium), VCR available. In-room modem link. In-house fitness room. Outdoor pool. **$**

⊡ 🐾 🏊 🏋 🏖

Atlanta

Motel/Motor Lodge

★ **BEST WESTERN INN AT THE PEACHTREES.** *330 W Peachtree St (30308). Phone 404/242-4642; toll-free 800/528-1234; fax 404/659-3244. www.bestwestern.com.* 112 rooms, 4 story. Pets accepted; fee. Complimentary full breakfast. Check-out noon, check-in 3 pm. TV; cable (premium). In-house fitness room; health club privileges. Airport transportation. Business center. Near Merchandise Mart and Apparel Mart. **$**

⊡ 🐾 🏋 🏖 SC 🚶

Hotels

★ ★ ★ **CROWNE PLAZA.** *3377 Peachtree Rd (30326). Phone 404/264-1111; fax 404/233-7061. www.crowneplaza.com.* 291 rooms, 11 story. Pets accepted; fee. Check-out 11 am. Check-in 4 pm. TV; cable (premium), VCR available. In-room modem link. Restaurant, bar. Babysitting services available. In-house fitness room; health club privileges. Outdoor pool. Concierge. **$**

⊡ 🐾 🏊 🏋 🏖 SC

★ ★ ★ ★ **FOUR SEASONS HOTEL ATLANTA.** *75 14th St (30309). Phone 404/881-9898; fax 404/873-4692. www.fourseasons.com.* The Four Seasons Hotel is Atlanta's premier address. This Neoclassical granite tower reigns over Midtown, where world-class culture, flourishing businesses, and enticing stores line the streets. Well suited for both business and leisure travelers, this hotel offers its guests the finest accommodations and flawless, intuitive service. Neutral tones and polished woods set a relaxed elegance in the rooms and suites, while striking views of downtown or midtown Atlanta inspire occupants. Visitors swoon over the luxurious amenities, from plush furnishings to sensational beds, and in-room massage and spa therapies ensure pure relaxation. The state-of-the-art fitness center is complete with an indoor pool and sun terrace, perfect for exercise or repose. Park 75's fresh approach to new American cuisine earns praise from locals and hotel guests alike, and its ficus-lined terrace is a pleasing alternative. 244 rooms, 19 story. Pets accepted, some restrictions. Check-out noon, check-in 3 pm. TV; cable (premium), VCR available. In-room modem link. Room service 24 hours. Restaurant, bar; entertainment. Babysitting services available. In-house fitness room; sauna, steam room. Indoor pool; whirlpool. Valet parking. Business center. Concierge. **$$$**

★ ★ ★ **THE GEORGIAN TERRACE HOTEL.**
659 Peachtree St NE (30308). Phone 404/897-1991; toll-free 800/651-2316; fax 404/724-9116. www.thegeorgianterrace. com. This historic property, built in 1911, blends modern conveniences with old-world elegance. Its atrium lobby features arched doorways, plush chairs, and plenty of light, while the richly decorated guest suites offer full kitchens, speakerphones, hair dryers, and full-size washers and dryers. 318 rooms, 19 story. Pets accepted, some restrictions. Check-out noon. Check-in 3 pm. TV; cable (premium), VCR available. In-room modem link. Room service 24 hours. Restaurant, bar. Babysitting services available. In-house fitness room. Outdoor pool. Valet parking, fee. Business center. Concierge. Luxury level. **$$**

★ ★ **HOLIDAY INN.** *4386 Chamblee Dunwoody Rd (30341). Phone 770/457-6363; toll-free 800/465-4329; fax 770/458-5282. www.hiselect.com/altperimeter.* 250 rooms, 5 story. Pets accepted, some restrictions; fee. Check-out noon, check-in 3 pm. TV; cable (premium). In-room modem link. Restaurant, bar. Babysitting services available. In-house fitness room. Outdoor pool. **$**

★ ★ ★ **OMNI HOTEL AT CNN CENTER.** *100 CNN Center (30335). Phone 404/659-0000; toll-free 800/843-6664; fax 404/525-5050. www.omnihotels.com.* Located in downtown Atlanta and conveniently connected to the CNN Center and the Georgia World Congress Center, this well-appointed hotel offers spacious rooms, flawless service, and attention to detail to ensure guests' standards are met and surpassed. Enjoy a stroll at the Centennial Olympic Park located across the street or the use of the Turner Athletic Club with its 50,000-square-foot, state-of-the-art health club for an invigorating workout. 467 rooms, 15 story. Pets accepted, some restrictions; fee. Check-out noon. Check-in 3 pm. TV; cable (premium); VCR available. In-room modem link. Restaurant, bar. Room service. Babysitting services available. Valet parking. Airport transportation. Business center. Concierge. **$$**

★ ★ ★ ★ **THE RITZ-CARLTON, BUCKHEAD.** *3434 Peachtree Rd NE (30326). Phone 404/237-2700; toll-free 800/244-3333; fax 404/240-7195. www.ritzcarlton.com.* The Ritz-Carton, Buckhead is unquestionably the grande dame of Atlanta. This gracious hotel, nestled in the fashionable uptown neighborhood, has long been the favorite of the social set. Southern grace and Ritz-Carlton standards blend here, resulting in a warm and luxurious experience. The guest rooms enchant with European furnishings, antiques, and sublime amenities. Bay windows showcase lovely views of the wooded locale or the downtown skyline. Attentive and exceptional service ensures that all guests are cosseted. The fitness center appeals to athletic-minded visitors, and the indoor pool with sundeck adds a relaxing touch. Afternoon tea in the Lobby Lounge is a Georgia tradition, especially after a day of perusing the area's world-famous stores, and The Café is a popular gathering place to enjoy casual fare. The piéce-de-résistance, however, is the Dining Room, where award-winning French cuisine infused with Asian flavors delights the senses. 553 rooms, 22 story. Pets accepted, some restrictions; fee. Check-out noon, check-in 3 pm. TV; cable (premium), VCR available. In-room modem link. Restaurant, bar; entertainment. Room service. Babysitting services available. In-house fitness room; spa, massage, sauna, steam room. Indoor pool; whirlpool; poolside service. Valet parking, fee. Airport transportation. Business center. Concierge. Luxury level. **$$$**

★ ★ ★ **W ATLANTA AT PERIMETER CENTER.** *111 W Perimeter Ctr (30346). Phone 770/396-6800; toll-free 800/683-6100; fax 770/399-5514. www.whotels.com.* Located in the Perimeter Center Office Complex and within walking distance to numerous restaurants, cinemas, and all the delights downtown Atlanta has to boast. This refreshing hotel offers guests unsurpassed sophisticated elegance combined with all the comforts of home. From the signature pillowtop beds and divine linens to the exquisitely appointed guest rooms, this hotel makes for a truly memorable stay. 275 rooms, 12 story. Pets accepted; fee. Check-out noon, check-in 4 pm. TV; cable (premium). Laundry services. Restaurant, bar. Room service. In-house fitness room; sauna. Outdoor pool; whirlpool; poolside service. Situated in park-like setting. **$$**

★ ★ ★ **THE WESTIN ATLANTA NORTH AT PERIMETER CENTER.** *7 Concourse Pkwy (30328). Phone 770/395-3900; toll-free 888/627-8407; fax 770/395-3935. www.westin.com.* Leave the distraction of the city behind and relax in serene tranquility combined with superb accommodations and amenities. Situated amidst 64 gloriously lush acres of woodlands and with scenic views of the private lake, this elegantly appointed hotel offers guests a respite from life's daily tribulations. Become revitalized in the soothing waters of the outdoor pool, rekindle that dormant energy with a game of squash, run along the scenic trail, or treat yourself to some well-deserved pampering with a massage. 369 rooms, 20 story. Pets accepted; fee. Check-out noon, check-in 3 pm. TV; cable (premium). In-room modem link. Room service 24 hours. Restaurant, bar; entertainment. Babysitting services available. Health club privileges, sauna. Outdoor pool; whirlpool; poolside service. Free parking. Luxury level. **$$**

D 🐾 🏊 ⛷ SC

B&B/Small Inn

★ **BEVERLY HILLS INN.** *65 Sheridan Dr (30305). Phone 404/233-8520; toll-free 800/331-8520; fax 404/233-8659. www.beverlyhillsinn.com.* 18 kitchen units, 3 story. Pets accepted; fee. Complimentary continental breakfast. Check-out noon, check-in 2 pm. TV. In-room modem link. European-style hotel restored to 1929 ambience. **$**

🐾

Extended Stays

★ ★ **RESIDENCE INN BY MARRIOTT.** *2960 Piedmont Rd NE (30305). Phone 404/239-0677; fax 404/262-9638. www.residenceinn.com.* Located only seven minutes from downtown Atlanta, this hotel features spacious guest rooms with full kitchens. 140 rooms, 2 story. Pets accepted, some restrictions; fee. Complimentary buffet breakfast. Check-out noon, check-in 3 pm. TV; cable (premium). In-room modem link. Laundry services. Outdoor pool. Outdoor tennis. **$**

🐾 ⛷ 🏊 ⛷

★ **RESIDENCE INN BY MARRIOTT.** *1901 Savoy Dr (30341). Phone 770/455-4446; toll-free 800/331-3131; fax 770/451-5183. www.residenceinn.com/atlrn.* 144 rooms, 2 story. Pets accepted, some restrictions; fee. Complimentary continental breakfast. Check-out noon, check-in 3 pm. TV; cable (premium), VCR available. In-room modem link. Fireplaces. Laundry services. Health club privileges. Outdoor pool; whirlpool. Tennis. **$**

D 🐾 🏊 ⛷ ⛷ SC

★ **SUMMERFIELD SUITES PERIMETER.** *760 Mt Vernon Hwy (30328). Phone 404/250-0110; toll-free 800/996-3426; fax 404/250-9335. www.wyndham.com.*

Conveniently located just minutes from downtown Atlanta and Buckhead, this hotel offers large, modern suites with all the comforts of home (such as an outdoor barbecue) and friendly service. 122 rooms, 2-3 story. Pets accepted, some restrictions; fee. Complimentary continental breakfast. Check-out noon, check-in 3 pm. TV; cable (premium), VCR (movies fee). In-room modem link. Laundry services. In-house fitness room. Outdoor pool; whirlpool. **$**

D 🐾 🏊 ⛷ ⛷

Atlanta Hartsfield Airport Area

Hotel

★ ★ ★ **HILTON ATLANTA AIRPORT AND TOWERS.** *1031 Virginia Ave (30354). Phone 404/767-9000; toll-free 800/774-1500; fax 404/559-6889. www.atlantaairporthilton.com.* 504 rooms, 17 story. Pets accepted, some restrictions; fee. Check-out 11 am, check-in 3 pm. TV; cable (premium), VCR available. In-room modem link. Room service 24 hours. Restaurant, bar. Babysitting services available. In-house fitness room; massage, sauna. Indoor pool; outdoor pool; whirlpool. Outdoor tennis, lighted courts. Valet parking. Business center. Concierge. Luxury level. Free transportation. **$$**

D 🐾 ⛷ 🏊 🏊 ✈ ⛷ ⛷

Augusta

All Suites

★ **AMERISUITES.** *1062 Claussen Rd (30907). Phone 706/733-4656; fax 706/736-1133. www.amerisuites.com.* 111 rooms, 6 story. Pets accepted; fee. Complimentary breakfast. Check-out noon. TV; cable (premium), VCR available. In-house fitness room; health club privileges. Pool; whirlpool. Business center. **$**

D 🐾 🏊 ⛷ ⛷ ⛷

★ ★ **RADISSON SUITES INN.** *3038 Washinton Rd (30907). Phone 706/868-1800; fax 706/868-7300. www.radisson.com.* Oversized suites with in-room whirlpool, kitchen, and much more make this hotel a popular stop for convenience and comfort. It's located just 10 minutes from the airport and offers a full complimentary breakfast each morning. 176 rooms, 4 story. Pets accepted; fee. Complimentary breakfast. Check-out noon. TV; cable (premium). In-room modem link. Restaurant, bar. Room service. Health club privileges. Pool. Business center. **$**

D 🐾 🏊 ⛷ ⛷

Hotels

★★ RADISSON RIVERFRONT HOTEL. *2 10th St (33870). Phone 706/722-8900; toll-free 800/333-3333; fax 706/823-6513. www.radisson.com.* Offering Southern charm along with warm hospitality and outstanding accommodations, this hotel promises a very comfortable and relaxing stay. Elegantly appointed guest rooms are spacious and well-equipped with everything from work-stations to makeup mirrors and offer views of the beautiful Savannah River, downtown Augusta, and the scenic Riverwalk. The hotel's superb location allows guests to be just minutes from restaurants, antique shops, art galleries, and museums. 237 rooms, 11 story. Pets accepted, some restrictions. Check-out noon. TV; cable (premium). In-room modem link. Restaurant, bar. In-house fitness room; health club privileges, sauna. Pool. On Savannah River. **$**

D 🐾 ⛱ 🏋 ⬕ SC

★★★ SHERATON AUGUSTA HOTEL. *2651 Perimeter Pkwy (30909). Phone 706/855-8100; toll-free 800/325-3535; fax 706/860-1720. www.sheraton.com.* Upon entering the serene and airy atrium lobby, guests are made welcome with towering palm trees, lush plants, and an uncompromising dedication to quality and service. Relax in the elegantly appointed guest rooms. 179 rooms. Pets accepted, some restrictions. Check-out noon. TV; cable (premium), VCR available. In-room modem link. Laundry services. Restaurant, bar. In-house fitness room; sauna. Indoor, outdoor pool. Free airport transportation. Business center. Concierge. **$**

D 🐾 ⛱ 🏋 ⬕ SC 🚶

Brunswick

Motels/Motor Lodges

★★ BEST WESTERN BRUNSWICK INN. *5323 New Jesup Hwy, exit 36B (31523). Phone 912/264-0144; fax 912/262-0992. www.bestwestern.com.* 145 rooms, 2 story. Pets accepted. Complimentary continental breakfast. Check-out 11 am, check-in noon. TV. Laundry services. Restaurant. Outdoor pool. **$**

D 🐾 ⛱ ⬕

★ JAMESON INN BRUNSWICK. *661 Scranton Rd (31520). Phone 912/267-0800; toll-free 800/526-3766; fax 912/265-1922. www.jamesoninns.com.* 62 rooms, 2 story. Pets accepted. Complimentary continental breakfast. Check-out 11 am, check-in 3 pm. TV; cable (premium), VCR available (movies). In-room modem link. In-house fitness room. Outdoor pool. **$**

D 🐾 ⛱ 🏋 ⬕ SC

All Suite

★ EMBASSY SUITES. *500 Mall Blvd (31525). Phone 912/264-6100; toll-free 800/432-3229; fax 912/267-1615. www.embassysuites.com.* This hotel is attached to the Glynn Place Mall and features complimentary breakfast, an outdoor pool, and meeting facilities. Guest suites feature kitchenettes, in-room coffee, and hair dryers. 130 suites, 5 story. Pets accepted, some restrictions; fee. Complimentary continental breakfast. Check-out noon, check-in 3 pm. TV; cable (premium). In-room modem link. In-house fitness room. Outdoor pool. Free airport transportation. **$$**

🐾 ⛱ 🏋 ✈

Calhoun

Motels/Motor Lodges

★ COMFORT INN. *742 Hwy 53 SE (30120). Phone 706/629-8271. www.comfortinn.com.* 120 rooms, 2 story. Pets accepted; fee. Check-out noon. TV. Pool. **$**

D 🐾 ⛱ ⬕

★ HOWARD JOHNSON. *1220 Red Bud Rd (30701). Phone 706/629-9191; toll-free 800/846-3271; fax 706/629-0873. www.hojo.com.* 99 rooms, 2 story. Pets accepted; fee. Check-out noon. TV; cable (premium). In-room modem link. Restaurant. Room service. Pool. **$**

D 🐾 ⛱ ⬕

★★ QUALITY INN. *915 Hwy 53 E SE (30701). Phone 706/629-9501; toll-free 800/225-4686. www.qualityinn.com.* 100 rooms, 2 story. Pets accepted, some restrictions; fee. Complimentary continental breakfast. Check-out 11 am. TV; cable (premium). In-room modem link. Restaurant, bar. Room service. In-house fitness room. Pool. **$**

D 🐾 ⛱ 🏋 ⬕

Hotel

★★★ BARNSLEY GARDENS. *597 Barnsley Gardens Rd (30103). Phone 770/773-7480; fax 770/773-1779. www.slh.com/barnsley.* 70 rooms, 1 story. Pets accepted; fee. Check-out noon. TV; cable (premium). In-room modem link. Restaurant, bar. In-house fitness room; sauna. Game room. Indoor pool; outdoor pool; whirlpool; poolside service. Airport transportation. Business center. Concierge. **$$**

🐾 ⛱ 🏋 🚶

Cartersville

Motels/Motor Lodges

★ **BUDGET HOST INN.** *851 Cass White Rd NW (30121). Phone 770/386-0350; toll-free 800/283-4678; fax 770/387-0591. www.budgethost.com.* 92 rooms, 3 story. Pets accepted; fee. Check-out 11 am. TV. Laundry services. Restaurant. Pool. **$**

[icons] SC

★ ★ **HOLIDAY INN.** *2336 Hwy 411 NE (30184). Phone 770/386-0830; fax 770/386-0867. www.holiday-inn.com.* 144 rooms, 2 story. Pets accepted. Check-out noon. TV; cable (premium). In-room modem link. Restaurant, bar. Room service. In-house fitness room; health club privileges. Pool; whirlpool. Lawn games. **$**

[icons]

Columbus

Motels/Motor Lodges

★ **BAYMONT INN.** *2919 Warm Springs Rd (31909). Phone 706/323-4344; toll-free 800/301-0200; fax 706/596-9622. www.baymontinn.com.* 102 rooms, 3 story. Pets accepted, some restrictions; fee. Complimentary continental breakfast. Check-out noon. TV. In-room modem link. Pool. **$**

[icons] SC

★ **LA QUINTA INN.** *3201 Macon Rd (31906). Phone 706/568-1740; toll-free 800/687-6667; fax 706/569-7434. www.laquinta.com.* 122 rooms, 2 story. Pets accepted. Complimentary continental breakfast. Check-out noon. TV; cable (premium). In-room modem link. Laundry services. Pool. **$**

[icons] SC

Commerce

Motels/Motor Lodges

★ **HOLIDAY INN EXPRESS.** *30747 Hwy 441 S (30529). Phone 706/335-5183; toll-free 800/465-4329; fax 706/335-6588. www.holiday-inn.com.* 96 rooms, 2 story. Pets accepted; fee. Complimentary continental breakfast. Check-out noon. TV; cable (premium). In-room modem link. Laundry services. In-house fitness room. Pool. **$**

[icons] SC

★ **HOWARD JOHNSON.** *148 Eisenhower Dr (30529). Phone 706/335-5581; fax 706/335-7889. www.hojo.com.* 120 rooms, 2 story. Pets accepted; fee. Complimentary continental breakfast. Check-out noon. TV; cable (premium), VCR available (movies). Restaurant. Pool; children's pool. **$**

[icons]

Dalton

Motels/Motor Lodges

★ ★ **BEST WESTERN INN OF DALTON.** *2106 Chattanooga Rd (30720). Phone 706/226-5022; fax 706/226-5002. www.bestwestern.com.* 99 rooms, 2 story. Pets accepted; fee. Check-out noon. TV. In-room modem link. Laundry services. Restaurant, bar; entertainment. Room service. Pool.

[icons]

★ ★ **HOLIDAY INN.** *515 Holiday Dr (30720). Phone 706/278-0500; toll-free 800/753-6510; fax 706/226-0279. www.holiday-inn.com.* 199 rooms, 2 story. Pets accepted; fee. Check-out noon. TV; cable (premium). In-room modem link. Laundry services. Restaurant, bar. Room service. In-house fitness room. Pool; children's pool. **$**

[icons] SC

Douglas

Motel/Motor Lodge

★ ★ **HOLIDAY INN.** *1750 S Peterson Ave; US 441 S (31533). Phone 912/384-9100; toll-free 800/465-4329. www.holiday-inn.com.* 100 rooms, 2 story. Pets accepted; fee. Check-out noon. TV; cable (premium). In-room modem link. Restaurant, bar. Room service. Pool. Free airport transportation.

[icons] SC

Dublin

Motel/Motor Lodge

★ ★ **HOLIDAY INN EXPRESS.** *2192 Hwy 441 S (31040). Phone 478/272-7862; fax 478/272-1077. www.holiday-inn.com.* 124 rooms, 2 story. Pets accepted, some restrictions. Complimentary breakfast. Check-out noon. TV; cable (premium). In-room modem link. Restaurant, bar; entertainment. Room service. In-house fitness room; health club privileges. Pool. Airport transportation.

[icons]

Duluth

Extended Stay

★ ★ **RESIDENCE INN BY MARRIOTT.** *1760 Pineland Rd (30096). Phone 770/921-2202; fax 770/921-8950. www.residenceinn.com.* Enjoy the comforts of home in the spacious guest rooms featuring separate living and sleeping areas and fully-equipped kitchens. 132 rooms, 3 story. Pets accepted, some restrictions; fee. Complimentary buffet breakfast. Check-out noon, check-in 3 pm. TV; cable (premium). In-room modem link. Laundry services. In-house fitness room. Outdoor pool. Business center. **$**

Forsyth

Motels/Motor Lodges

★ **HAMPTON INN.** *520 Holiday Cir (31029). Phone 478/994-9697; toll-free 800/426-7866; fax 478/994-3594. www.hamptoninn.com.* 124 rooms, 4 story. Pets accepted. Complimentary continental breakfast. Check-out noon. TV; cable (premium). In-room modem link. Health club privileges. **$**

★ ★ **HOLIDAY INN.** *480 Holiday Cir (31029). Phone 478/994-5691; fax 478/994-3254. www.holiday-inn.com.* 120 rooms, 2 story. Pets accepted, some restrictions; fee. Check-out noon. TV; cable (premium). In-room modem link. Restaurant, bar. Room service. In-house fitness room. Game room. Pool; children's pool. Business center. Chapel on premises. **$**

Gainesville

Motel/Motor Lodge

★ ★ **HOLIDAY INN.** *726 Jesse Jewell Pkwy (30504). Phone 770/536-4451; fax 770/538-2880. www.holiday-inn .com.* 132 rooms, 2-3 story. Pets accepted, some restrictions. Check-out noon. TV; cable (premium), VCR available. In-room modem link. Restaurant, bar. Room service. Pool. Free transportation. **$**

Hiawassee

Motel/Motor Lodge

★ **SALALE LODGE.** *1340 Hwy 76 E (30546). Phone 706/896-3943; fax 706/896-4773.* 4 rooms, 2 story. Pets accepted, some restrictions; fee. Check-out 11 am. TV; cable (premium). **$**

Jekyll Island

Motels/Motor Lodges

★ ★ **CLARION HOTEL.** *85 S Beachview Dr (31527). Phone 912/635-2261; toll-free 800/253-5955; fax 912/635-4732. www.clarionhotel.com.* 207 rooms, 2-4 story. Pets accepted, some restrictions; fee. Check-out 11 am, check-in 4 pm. TV. In-room modem link. Restaurant. Supervised children's activities (June-Aug), ages 4-12. In-house fitness room. Game room. Outdoor pool; children's pool; whirlpool; poolside service. Outdoor tennis. Lawn games. Airport transportation. Beachfront. **$$**

★ **COMFORT INN.** *711 Beachview Dr (31527). Phone 912/635-2211; toll-free 800/204-0202; fax 912/635-2381. www.comfortinn.com.* 180 rooms, 2 story. Pets accepted; fee. Complimentary continental breakfast. Check-out 11 am, check-in 4 pm. TV. In-house fitness room. Beach. Outdoor pool; children's pool; whirlpool. Airport transportation. **$$**

Hotel

★ ★ **HOLIDAY INN.** *200 S Beachview Dr (31527). Phone 912/635-3311; toll-free 800/753-5955; fax 912/635-3919. www.holiday-inn.com.* 198 rooms, 2-4 story. Pets accepted; fee. Check-out 11 am, check-in 4 pm. TV; cable (premium). In-room modem link. Laundry services. Restaurant, bar; entertainment. Room service. In-house fitness room. Beach. Outdoor pool; children's pool; poolside service. Tennis, lighted courts. Bicycles. **$**

Resort

★ ★ ★ **VILLAS BY THE SEA.** *1175 N Beachview Dr (31527). Phone 912/635-2521; toll-free 800/841-6262; fax 912/635-2569.* A delightful 17-acre oceanside resort, these large privately owned villas are a great getaway for family vacations and romantic getaways alike. With nature trails, white sandy beaches, a children's playground, and the Video Saloon, visitors here will find a relaxing oasis. 182 rooms, 1-2 story. Pets accepted; fee. Check-out 11 am, check-in 4 pm. TV; VCR available. Dining room, bar. Babysitting services available. In-house fitness room. Outdoor pool; children's pool; whirlpool. Bicycle rentals. On 17 acres. Private beach. **$$**

Macon

Motels/Motor Lodges

★ **HAMPTON INN.** *3680 Riverside Dr (31210). Phone 478/471-0660; toll-free 800/426-7866; fax 478/471-2528. www.hamptoninn.com.* 151 rooms, 2 story. Pets accepted, some restrictions; fee. Complimentary continental breakfast. Check-out noon. TV. In-room modem link. Health club privileges. Pool. **$**

★ **HOLIDAY INN EXPRESS.** *2720 Riverside Dr (31204). Phone 478/743-1482; fax 478/745-3967. www.holiday-inn.com.* 93 rooms, 6 story. Pets accepted; fee. Complimentary continental breakfast. Check-out noon. TV; cable (premium). In-room modem link. Health club privileges. Pool. **$**

★ **RODEWAY INN.** *4999 Eisenhower Pkwy (31206). Phone 478/781-4343; fax 478/784-8140. www.rodeway.com.* 55 rooms, 2 story. Pets accepted, some restrictions; fee. Complimentary continental breakfast. Check-out 11 am. TV; cable (premium), VCR available. Laundry services. Pool. **$**

Madison

Motels/Motor Lodges

★ **DAYS INN.** *2001 Eatonton Hwy (30650). Phone 706/342-1839; toll-free 800/329-7466. www.daysinn.com.* 77 rooms, 2 story. Pets accepted; fee. Check-out noon. TV; cable (premium). Restaurant. Pool; children's pool. **$**

★ **HOLIDAY INN EXPRESS.** *10111 Alcovy Rd, Covington (30014). Phone 770/787-4900; toll-free 800/788-1390; fax 770/385-9805. www.holiday-inn.com.* 50 rooms, 2 story. Pets accepted; fee. Complimentary continental

breakfast. Check-out noon. TV; cable (premium). In-room modem link. In-house fitness room. Pool. **$**

Marietta

Motel/Motor Lodge

★ **LA QUINTA INN.** *2170 Delk Rd SE (30067). Phone 770/951-0026; toll-free 800/531-5900; fax 770/952-5372. www.laquinta.com.* 130 rooms, 3 story. Pets accepted, some restrictions. Complimentary continental breakfast. Check-out noon. TV; cable (premium). In-room modem link. Pool. **$**

Extended Stay

★ **HAWTHORN SUITES.** *1500 Parkwood Cir NW, Atlanta (30339). Phone 770/952-9595; fax 770/984-2335. www.hawthornsuiteatlanta.com.* 280 rooms, 2-3 story. Pets accepted, some restrictions; fee. Complimentary full breakfast. Check-out noon, check-in 4 pm. TV; cable (premium). In-room modem link. In-house fitness room; health club privileges. Outdoor pool; whirlpool. Outdoor tennis, lighted courts. Elaborate landscaping, flowers. **$**

Norcross

Motel/Motor Lodge

★ **RED ROOF INN.** *5171 Brook Hollow Pkwy (30071). Phone 770/448-8944; fax 770/448-8955. www.redroof.com.* 115 rooms, 3 story. Pets accepted, some restrictions. Check-out noon. TV; cable (premium). **$**

All Suites

★ **AMERISUITES.** *3530 Venture Pkwy NW, Duluth (30096). Phone 770/623-9699; toll-free 800/833-1516; fax 770/623-4643. www.amerisuites.com.* 114 suites, 6 story. Pets accepted, some restrictions. Complimentary continental breakfast. Check-out noon. TV; cable (premium), VCR available. In-room modem link. In-house fitness room; health club privileges. Pool. Business center. **$**

★ **HOMEWOOD SUITES.** *10775 Davis Dr, Alpharetta (30004). Phone 770/998-1622; toll-free 800/225-5466; fax 770/998-7834. www.homewoodsuites.com.* 6 story. Pets accepted; fee. Complimentary continental breakfast. Check-out noon. TV; cable (premium), VCR available.

In-room modem link. Laundry services. In-house fitness room. Pool. Business center. **$**

D ⬤ ≈ ⌐ ⊠ SC ⬤

★ **HOMEWOOD SUITES.** *450 Technology Pkwy (30092). Phone 770/448-4663; fax 770/242-6979. www.homewoodsuites.com.* 92 rooms, 2-3 story. Pets accepted, some restrictions; fee. Complimentary continental breakfast. Check-out noon. TV. In-room modem link. Laundry services. In-house fitness room; health club privileges. Pool; whirlpool. Business center. **$**

D ⬤ ≈ ⌐ ⊠ SC ⬤

Perry

Motels/Motor Lodges

★★ **NEW PERRY HOTEL.** *800 Main St (31069). Phone 478/987-1000; toll-free 800/877-3779; fax 478/987-5779.* 43 rooms, 3 story. Pets accepted; fee. Check-out noon. TV. Restaurant. Pool. Built in 1925; landscaped grounds. **$**

⬤ ≈

★ **RAMADA INN.** *100 Market Pl Dr (31069). Phone 478/987-8400; toll-free 888/298-2054; fax 478/987-3133. www.ramada.com.* 60 rooms, 2 story. Pets accepted, some restrictions; fee. Complimentary continental breakfast. Check-out 11 am. TV; cable (premium). In-room modem link. Indoor pool; whirlpool. **$**

D ⬤ ≈ ⊠

Rome

Motel/Motor Lodge

★★ **HOLIDAY INN.** *20 Hwy 411 E (30161). Phone 706/295-1100; toll-free 800/465-4329; fax 706/291-7128. www.holiday-inn.com.* 200 rooms, 2 story. Pets accepted; fee. Check-out noon. TV; cable (premium). Restaurant, bar; entertainment. Room service. In-house fitness room; sauna. Indoor/outdoor pool; whirlpool; poolside service. Business center. **$**

D ⬤ ⟲ ⚡ ≈ ⌐ ⊠ ⬤

Savannah

All Suite

★ **HOMEWOOD SUITES.** *5820 White Bluff Rd (31405). Phone 912/353-8500; fax 912/354-3821. www.homewoodsuites.com.* 106 rooms, 2-3 story. Pets

accepted, some restrictions; fee. Complimentary continental breakfast. Check-out 11 am, check-in 3 pm. TV; VCR available. In-room modem link. In-house fitness room. Outdoor pool; whirlpool. Business center. Sports court. **$$**

D ⬤ ≈ ⌐ ⊠ ⬤

Hotels

★ **BAYMONT INN.** *8484 Abercorn St (31406). Phone 912/927-7660; fax 912/927-6392. www.baymontinn.com.* 103 rooms, 3 story. Pets accepted. Complimentary continental breakfast. Check-out noon, check-in 2 pm. TV; cable (premium). In-room modem link. Laundry services. Outdoor pool. **$**

D ⬤ ≈ ⊠ SC

★ **CLUBHOUSE INN.** *6800 Abercorn St (31405). Phone 912/356-1234; toll-free 800/258-2466; fax 912/352-2828. www.clubhouseinn.com.* 138 rooms, 2 story. Pets accepted; fee. Complimentary full breakfast. Check-out 11 am, check-in 3 pm. TV; cable (premium). In-room modem link. Laundry services. Health club privileges. Outdoor pool; whirlpool. **$**

D ⬤ ≈ ⊠ SC

B&B/Small Inns

★★★ **EAST BAY INN.** *225 E Bay St (31401). Phone 912/238-1225; toll-free 800/500-1225; fax 912/232-2709. www.eastbayinn.com.* Just steps away from the waterfront, this romantic inn has many beautiful rooms filled with period furnishings and antiques. Enjoy a cheese and wine reception each evening. 28 rooms, 3 story. Pets accepted; fee. Complimentary continental breakfast. Check-out 11 am, check-in 3 pm. TV. In-room modem link. Restaurant, dining room. Built in 1853; formerly a cotton warehouse. Opposite historic waterfront of Savannah River. **$$**

D ⬤ ⊠

★★ **OLDE HARBOUR INN.** *508 E Factors Walk (31401). Phone 912/234-4100; toll-free 800/553-6533; fax 912/233-5979. www.oldeharbourinn.com.* 24 rooms, 3 story. Pets accepted; fee. Complimentary continental breakfast. Check-out 11 am, check-in 3 pm. TV; cable (premium). Built in 1892, originally housed offices and warehouse of an oil company. **$$**

⬤ SC

Statesboro

Motels/Motor Lodges

★ **DAYS INN.** *461 S Main St (30458). Phone 912/764-5666; toll-free 800/329-7466; fax 912/489-8193. www.daysinn.com.* 44 rooms, 1-2 story. Pets accepted; fee.

Complimentary continental breakfast. Check-out 11 am. TV; cable (premium), VCR available. Pool. **$**

★ **RAMADA INN.** *230 S Main St (30458). Phone 912/764-6121; toll-free 800/272-6232. www.ramada.com.* 129 rooms, 2 story. Pets accepted; fee. Complimentary breakfast buffet. Check-out noon. TV; cable (premium). In-room modem link. Laundry services. Restaurant, bar. Room service. Pool; children's pool. **$**

Tifton

Motel/Motor Lodge

★ **COMFORT INN.** *1104 King Rd (31794). Phone 229/382-4410; toll-free 800/223-5234; fax 229/382-3967. www.comfortinn.com.* 91 rooms, 2 story. Pets accepted, some restrictions; fee. Complimentary continental breakfast. Check-out 11 am. TV. Bar. Indoor/outdoor pool; whirlpool. **$**

Toccoa

Motel/Motor Lodge

★ **SHONEY'S INN.** *14227 Jones St, Lavonia (30553). Phone 706/356-8848; toll-free 800/222-2222; fax 706/356-2951. www.shoneysinn.com.* 60 rooms, 2 story. Pets accepted, some restrictions; fee. Check-out noon. TV; cable (premium). In-room modem link. Pool. **$**

Valdosta

Motels/Motor Lodges

★★ **BEST WESTERN KING OF THE ROAD.** *1403 N St. Augustine Rd (31602). Phone 229/244-7600; fax 229/245-1734. www.bestwestern.com.* 137 rooms, 3 story. Pets accepted, some restrictions. Complimentary continental breakfast. Check-out 11 am. TV. Restaurant, bar; entertainment. Room service. Pool. Airport transportation. **$**

★★ **QUALITY INN.** *1902 W Hill Ave (31601). Phone 229/244-4520; fax 229/247-2404. www.qualityinn.com.* 48 rooms, 2 story. Pets accepted. Complimentary continental breakfast. Check-out noon. TV. Restaurant, bar. Pool. **$**

★ **RAMADA INN.** *2008 W Hill Ave (31601). Phone 229/242-1225; fax 229/247-2755. www.ramada.com.* 102 rooms, 2 story. Pets accepted; fee. Complimentary continental breakfast. Check-out noon. TV. Room service. Health club privileges. Pool. **$**

★ **SHONEY'S INN.** *1828 W Hill Ave (31601). Phone 229/244-7711; fax 229/244-0361. www.shoneysinn.com.* 96 rooms, 2 story. Pets accepted, some restrictions. Check-out noon. TV. Pool. **$**

Waycross

Motel/Motor Lodge

★★ **HOLIDAY INN.** *1725 Memorial Dr (31501). Phone 912/283-4490; toll-free 800/465-4329. www.holiday-inn.com.* 148 rooms, 2 story. Pets accepted; fee. Complimentary full breakfast. Check-out noon. TV; cable (premium). In-room modem link. Laundry services. Restaurant, bar. Room service. In-house fitness room; health club privileges. Game room. Pool. Airport, bus depot transportation. **$**

Idaho

Boise

Motels/Motor Lodges

★ **BOISE CENTER GUESTLODGE.** *1314 Grove St (83702). Phone 208/342-9351; fax 208/336-5828.* 50 rooms, 2 story. Pets accepted, some restrictions. Complimentary continental breakfast. Check-out noon, check-in 1 pm. TV; cable (premium). Pool. Airport transportation. **$**

⊟ ⇌ ⊠ SC

★ **BUDGET HOST INN.** *8002 Overland Rd (83709). Phone 208/322-4404; toll-free 800/733-1481; fax 208/322-7487.* 87 rooms, 2 story. Pets accepted; fee. Check-out noon. TV; cable (premium), VCR available. Pool; whirlpool. **$**

D ⇌ ⊠ ⊠

★ ★ **HOLIDAY INN.** *3300 Vista Ave (83705). Phone 208/344-8365; toll-free 800/465-4329; fax 208/343-9635. www.holiday-inn.com.* 265 rooms, 2 story. Pets accepted; fee. Check-out noon. TV; cable (premium). Laundry services. Restaurant, bar. Room service. In-house fitness room. Pool. Downhill ski 20 miles. Free airport transportation. **$**

D ⇌ ⊠ ⊠ ⊠ SC

★ ★ ★ **OWYHEE PLAZA HOTEL.** *1109 Main St (83702). Phone 208/343-4611; toll-free 800/233-4611; fax 208/336-3860. www.owyheeplaza.com.* This historic property in the Owyhee Mountains offers an outdoor pool, two restaurants, and a complimentary airport shuttle. 100 rooms, 3 story. Pets accepted, some restrictions; fee. Check-out noon, check-in 3 pm. TV; cable (premium), VCR available. In-room modem link. Laundry services. Restaurant, bar; entertainment. Room service. Pool; poolside service. Downhill, cross-country ski 20 miles. Free airport transportation. Built in 1910. **$**

D ⇌ ⊠ ⊠ ⊠ ⊠

★ **RODEWAY INN.** *1115 N Curtis Rd (83706). Phone 208/376-2700; fax 208/377-0324. www.rodeway.com.* 98 rooms, 2 story. Pets accepted; fee. Complimentary full breakfast. Check-out noon, check-in 2 pm. TV; cable (premium). In-room modem link. Laundry services. Restaurant, bar; entertainment. Room service. Sauna. Indoor, outdoor pool; whirlpool. Free parking. Free airport transportation. **$**

D ⇌ ⊠ ⊠ ⊠ SC

★ **SHILO INN.** *4111 Broadway Ave (83705). Phone 208/343-7662; fax 208/344-0318. www.shiloinns.com.* 125 rooms, 4 story. Pets accepted; fee. Complimentary continental breakfast. Check-out noon, check-in 2 pm. TV; cable (premium), VCR available. In-room modem link. Laundry services. Room service. In-house fitness room; sauna, steam room. Pool; whirlpool. Free parking. Free airport transportation. **$**

D ⇌ ⊠ ⊠ ⊠ ⊠

★ **SHILO INN.** *3031 Main St (83702). Phone 208/344-3521; toll-free 800/222-2244; fax 208/384-1217. www.shiloinns.com.* 112 rooms, 3 story. Pets accepted, some restrictions; fee. Complimentary continental breakfast. Check-out noon, check-in 3 pm. TV; cable (premium), VCR available. In-room modem link. Laundry services. In-house fitness room; sauna, steam room. Indoor pool; whirlpool. Downhill, cross-country ski 15 miles. Free parking. Free airport transportation. **$**

D ⇌ ⊠ ⊠ ⊠ ⊠ ⊠ SC

★ **SUPER 8.** *2773 Elder St (83705). Phone 208/344-8871. www.super8.com.* 108 rooms, 3 story. Pets accepted; fee. Complimentary continental breakfast. Check-out 11 am, check-in 3 pm. TV; cable (premium), VCR available. Laundry services. Indoor pool. Free parking. **$**

D ⇌ ⊠ ⊠

Hotel

★ ★ **DOUBLETREE HOTEL.** *2900 Chinden Blvd (83714). Phone 208/343-1871; toll-free 800/222-TREE; fax 208/344-4994. www.doubletree.com.* Right on the banks of the Boise River, this hotel is only 1 mile from the city center, near golf, whitewater rafting, and the Bogus Basin Ski Area. 304 rooms, 2 story. Pets accepted, some restrictions; fee. Check-out noon, check-in 3 pm. TV. In-room modem link. Restaurant, bar. Room service. In-house fitness room. Outdoor pool; children's pool; whirlpool; poolside service. Downhill ski 16 miles. Airport transportation. **$**

D ⇌ ⊠ ⊠ ⊠ ⊠ ⊠

Extended Stay

★ ★ **RESIDENCE INN BY MARRIOTT.** *1401 Lusk Ave (83706). Phone 208/344-1200; toll-free 800/331-3131; fax 208/384-5354. www.residenceinn.com.* 104 rooms, 2 story. Pets accepted; fee. Complimentary full breakfast. Check-out noon, check-in 3 pm. TV; cable (premium). In-room modem link. Laundry services. In-house fitness room. Outdoor pool; whirlpool. Downhill, cross-country ski 20 miles. Lawn games. Free parking. Free airport transportation. **$**

D ⇌ ⊠ ⊠ ⊠ ⊠

Bonners Ferry

Motels/Motor Lodges

★ **KOOTENAI VALLEY MOTEL.** *Hwy 95 (83805). Phone 208/267-7567; fax 208/267-2600. www.visit idaho.org.* 22 rooms, 1 story. Pets accepted, some restrictions; fee. Check-out 11 am, check-in 1 pm. TV; cable (premium). In-room modem link. Whirlpool. Free parking. **$**

⬜🐾🔲

★ **TOWN & COUNTRY MOTEL.** *US 95 S (83805). Phone 208/267-7915.* 12 rooms. Pets accepted; fee. Complimentary continental breakfast. Check-out 11 am, check-in noon. TV; cable. Whirlpool. Free parking. **$**

D🐾🔲

Burley

Motel/Motor Lodge

★★ **BEST WESTERN BURLEY INN & CONVENTION CENTER.** *800 N Overland Ave (83318). Phone 208/678-3501; toll-free 800/599-1849; fax 208/678-9532. www.bestwestern.com.* 126 rooms, 2 story. Pets accepted, some restrictions. Check-out noon. TV; cable (premium). Laundry services. Restaurant, bar. Room service. Pool. Lawn games. Trailer facilities. **$**

D🐾⛷️💤✈️🔲

Caldwell

Motels/Motor Lodges

★ **LA QUINTA INN.** *901 Specht Ave (83605). Phone 208/454-2222; fax 208/454-9334.* 65 rooms, 3 story. Pets accepted, some restrictions. Complimentary continental breakfast. Check-out noon, check-in 2 pm. TV; cable (premium). In-room modem link. Laundry services. In-house fitness room; sauna. Health club privileges. Indoor pool; whirlpool. Lawn games. Free parking. **$**

D🐾🏃🔲SC

★ **SUNDOWNER MOTEL.** *1002 Arthur (83605). Phone 208/459-1585; toll-free 800/588-5268; fax 208/467-5268.* 66 rooms, 2 story. Pets accepted; fee. Complimentary continental breakfast. Check-out 11 am, check-in 2 pm. TV; cable (premium). Free parking. **$**

🐾🔲

Challis

Motels/Motor Lodges

★ **NORTHGATE INN.** *Hwy 93 (83226). Phone 208/879-2490; fax 208/879-5767.* 60 rooms, 3 story. Pets accepted, some restrictions; fee. Check-out 11 am, check-in 3 pm. TV. Free parking. **$**

D🐾🔲SC

★ **VILLAGE INN.** *US 93 (83226). Phone 208/879-2239; fax 208/879-2813.* 54 rooms, 1-2 story. Pets accepted, some restrictions; fee. Check-out 11 am, check-in 2 pm. TV. Restaurant. Whirlpool. Downhill ski 7 miles, cross-country ski 10 miles. Free parking. **$**

D🐾🔲

Coeur d'Alene

Motels/Motor Lodges

★★ **BEST WESTERN COEUR D'ALENE INN.** *414 W Appleway Ave (83814). Phone 208/765-3200; toll-free 800/251-7829; fax 208/664-1962. www.cdainn.com.* 122 rooms, 2 story. Pets accepted; fee. Check-out noon. TV; cable (premium). In-room modem link. Restaurant, bar; entertainment. Room service. In-house fitness room; spa. Pool. Airport, train station, bus depot transportation. **$**

D🐾⛷️🏊🏃✈️🔲SC

★ **DAYS INN.** *2200 Northwest Blvd (83814). Phone 208/667-8668; fax 208/765-0933. www.daysinn.com.* 62 rooms, 2 story. Pets accepted; fee. Complimentary continental breakfast. Check-out noon, check-in 3 pm. TV; VCR available. In-room modem link. In-house fitness room; sauna. Whirlpool. Free parking. **$**

D🐾🏃🔲

★ **HOWARD JOHNSON.** *3705 W 5th Ave (83854). Phone 208/773-4541; toll-free 800/829-3124; fax 208/773-0235. www.hojo.com.* 99 rooms, 2-4 story. Pets accepted; fee. Complimentary continental breakfast. Check-out noon, check-in 2 pm. TV; cable (premium), VCR available. Laundry services. Indoor pool; whirlpool. Free parking. **$**

D🐾🏊🔲

★ **MOTEL 6.** *416 W Appleway Ave (83814). Phone 208/664-6600; fax 208/667-9446. www.motel6.com.* 109 rooms, 2 story. Pets accepted, some restrictions. Check-out noon. TV; cable (premium). Pool. **$**

D🐾🏊🔲

★ **SHILO INN.** *702 W Appleway Ave (83814). Phone 208/664-2300; toll-free 800/222-2244; fax 208/667-2863. www.shiloinns.com.* 139 rooms, 4 story. Pets accepted; fee. Complimentary continental breakfast. Check-out noon, check-in 4 pm. TV; cable (premium), VCR available. In-room modem link. Laundry services. In-house fitness room; sauna, steam room. Indoor pool; whirlpool. Free parking. **$**

D ☎ ⚓ 🛄 ➳ 🏊 🏃 ➘ ≋ SC

★ **SUPER 8.** *505 W Appleway Ave (83814). Phone 208/765-8880; toll-free 800/800-8000. www.super8.com.* 95 rooms, 3 story. Pets accepted, some restrictions; fee. Check-out 11 am. TV; cable (premium), VCR available. **$**

D ☎ ≋ SC

★ ★ **WESTCOAST.** *414 E 1st Ave (83854). Phone 208/773-1611; toll-free 800/325-4000; fax 208/773-4192. www.westcoasthotels.com.* 167 rooms, 2-3 story. Pets accepted, some restrictions; fee. Check-out noon, check-in 2 pm. TV. In-room modem link. Laundry services. Restaurant, bar; entertainment. Room service. In-house fitness room; sauna. Game room. Indoor pool; whirlpool. Outdoor tennis. Lawn games, On river; marina, guest docking, boat rentals. Free parking. Airport transportation. **$**

D ☎ 🛄 ➳ 🏃 ✈ ≋

Resort

★ ★ ★ **COEUR D'ALENE RESORT.** *115 S 2nd St (83814). Phone 208/765-4000; fax 208/664-7276. www.cdaresort.com.* Ski the Rockies in style at this golf and ski resort on the banks of Lake Coeur d' Alene. Besides skiing, there are a variety of water-related activities available, as well as shopping and dining. 336 rooms, 18 story. Pets accepted; fee. Check-out noon, check-in 4 pm. TV; cable (premium). In-room modem link. Laundry services. Restaurant, bar; entertainment. Room service. Supervised children's activities. In-house fitness room; spa, massage, sauna, steam room. Beach. Indoor pool; outdoor pool; children's pool; whirlpool; poolside service. Golf on premises. Outdoor tennis. Cross country ski on site. Marina. Boat rentals. Tour boats. Valet parking. Airport transportation. Business center. Concierge. **$**

D ☎ ⚓ 🛄 ➳ 🛅 🧖 🏊 ➳ 🏃 ✈ ≋ 🏃

B&B/Small Inn

★ ★ **THE ROOSEVELT.** *105 E Wallace Ave (83814). Phone 208/765-5200; toll-free 800/290-3358; fax 208/664-4142. www.therooseveltinn.com.* 15 rooms, 4 story. Pets accepted, some restrictions; fee. Children over 6 years only. Complimentary full breakfast. Check-out noon, check-in 3 pm. TV in common room; VCR available. In-house fitness room; massage, sauna. Whirlpool. Downhill ski 20 miles, cross-country ski 1 mile. Airport transportation. Built in 1905; formerly an elementary school named after Theodore Roosevelt. Totally nonsmoking. **$**

☎ 🏊 🏃 ✈ ≋ 🖼

Driggs

Motels/Motor Lodges

★ **BEST WESTERN TETON WEST.** *476 N Main St (83422). Phone 208/354-2363; fax 208/354-2962. www.bestwestern.com.* 40 rooms, 2 story. Pets accepted; fee. Complimentary continental breakfast. Check-out noon, check-in 3 pm. TV; cable (premium). In-room modem link. Laundry services. Indoor pool; whirlpool. Downhill ski 10 miles, cross-country ski 5 miles. Free parking. **$**

D ☎ ➳ 🏊 ≋ 🖼

★ **TETON MOUNTAIN VIEW LODGE.** *510 Egbert Ave (83452). Phone 208/456-2741; toll-free 800/625-2232; fax 208/456-2232. www.tetonmountainlodge.com.* 24 rooms, 2 story. Pets accepted, some restrictions; fee. Complimentary continental breakfast. Check-out 11 am, check-in 2 pm. TV; cable (premium). In-room modem link. Whirlpool. Free parking. **$**

D ☎ 🛄 ≋

Guest Ranch

★ ★ ★ **TETON RIDGE RANCH.** *200 Valley View Rd (83452). Phone 208/456-2650; fax 208/456-2218. www.tetonridge.com.* More of a lodge or guest house than a dude ranch, this casually elegant property offers well-appointed guest rooms, incredible views of the Grand Tetons and gourmet dining on 4,000 private acres. Horseback riding and fishing are available. 5 rooms. Closed Nov-mid-Dec, Apr-May. Pets accepted. Children over 12 years only. Check-out 11 am, check-in 1 pm. TV in public rooms; cable (premium). In-room modem link. Fireplaces. Massage. Downhill ski 20 miles, cross-country ski on site. Fishing/hunting guides, clean and store. Hiking. Horse stables. Sleighing. Free parking. Airport transportation. Concierge. **$$$$**

☎ ⚓ 🛄 🏃 ✈ ≋

Idaho Falls

Motels/Motor Lodges

★ **COMFORT INN.** *195 S Colorado Ave (83402). Phone 208/528-2804; fax 208/522-3083. www.comfortinn.com.* 52 rooms, 2 story. Pets accepted, some restrictions; fee. Complimentary continental breakfast. Check-out 11 am, check-in 3 pm. TV; cable. In-room modem link. Laundry services. Indoor pool; whirlpool. Valet parking. **$**

★ **SHILO INN.** *780 Lindsay Blvd (83402). Phone 208/523-0088; toll-free 800/222-2244; fax 208/522-7420. www.shiloinns.com.* 162 rooms, 4 story. Pets accepted, some restrictions. Complimentary full breakfast. Check-out noon, check-in 2 pm. TV. In-room modem link. Laundry services. Restaurant, bar. Room service. In-house fitness room; sauna, steam room. Indoor pool; whirlpool. Free parking. Free airport transportation. **$**

Jerome

Motels/Motor Lodges

★ **BEST WESTERN SAWTOOTH INN & SUITES.** *2653 S Lincoln Ave (83338). Phone 208/324-9200; toll-free 800/780-7234; fax 208/324-9292. www.bestwestern.com.* 57 rooms, 2 story. Pets accepted; fee. Complimentary continental breakfast. Check-out noon. TV; cable (premium). Laundry services. In-house fitness room. Indoor pool; whirlpool. **$**

★ **DAYS INN.** *1200 S Centennial Spur (83338). Phone 208/324-6400; fax 208/324-9207. www.daysinn.com.* 73 rooms, 3 story. Pets accepted, some restrictions; fee. Check-out noon. TV; cable (premium), VCR available. In-room modem link. Laundry services. **$**

Kellogg

Motels/Motor Lodges

★ **SILVERHORN MOTOR INN & RESTAURANT.** *699 W Cameron Ave (83837). Phone 208/783-1151; toll-free 800/437-6437; fax 208/784-5081.* 40 rooms, 3 story. Pets accepted. Check-out noon, check-in noon. TV. Laundry services. Restaurant. Room service. Whirlpool. Downhill, cross-country ski 3 miles. Free parking. **$**

★ **SUPER 8.** *601 Bunker Ave (83837). Phone 208/783-1234; toll-free 800/800-8000; fax 208/784-0461. www.super8.com.* 61 rooms, 2 story. Pets accepted, some restrictions; fee. Complimentary continental breakfast. Check-out 11 am, check-in 3 pm. TV; cable (premium), VCR available. In-room modem link. Indoor pool; whirlpool. Downhill ski on site. Free parking. **$**

Lewiston

Motels/Motor Lodges

★ **HOWARD JOHNSON.** *1716 Main St (83501). Phone 208/743-9526; fax 208/746-6212. www.hojo.com.* 66 rooms, 2 story. Pets accepted; fee. Complimentary continental breakfast. Check-out noon, check-in 3 pm. TV; cable (premium). In-room modem link. Laundry services. Pool. **$**

★ ★ **RED LION.** *621 21st St (83501). Phone 208/799-1000; toll-free 800/232-6730. www.redlionlewiston.com.* 183 rooms, 4 story. Pets accepted, some restrictions. Check-out noon, check-in 3 pm. TV; cable (premium). Laundry services. Restaurant, bar. Room service. Pool; whirlpool; poolside service. Airport transportation. Concierge. **$**

★ **RIVERVIEW INN.** *1325 Main St (83501). Phone 208/746-3311; toll-free 800/806-7666; fax 208/746-7955.* 75 rooms, 4 story. Pets accepted. Check-out noon, check-in 3 pm. TV; cable (premium). In-room modem link. In-house fitness room. Pool. **$**

★ **SACAJAWEA SELECT INN.** *1824 Main St (83501). Phone 208/746-1393; toll-free 800/333-1393; fax 208/743-3620. www.selectinn.com.* 90 rooms, 2 story. Pets accepted, some restrictions; fee. Complimentary continental breakfast. Check-out noon, check-in 1 pm. TV; cable (premium). In-room modem link. Laundry services. Restaurant, bar. In-house fitness room. Outdoor pool; whirlpool. Airport transportation. **$**

McCall

Motel/Motor Lodge

★ **BEST WESTERN.** *415 N 3rd St (83638). Phone 208/634-6300; toll-free 800/780-7234; fax 208/634-2967. www.bestwestern.com.* 79 rooms, 2 story. Pets accepted, some restrictions. Check-out 11 am, check-in 2 pm. TV; cable (premium), VCR available. In-room modem link. Laundry services. In-house fitness room. Indoor pool; whirlpool. Downhill, cross-country ski 10 miles. **$**

Montpelier

Motel/Motor Lodge

★ **BEST WESTERN CLOVER CREEK INN.** *243 N 4th St (83254). Phone 208/847-1782; toll-free 800/528-1234; fax 208/847-3519. www.bestwestern.com.* 65 rooms, 2 story. Pets accepted, some restrictions; fee. Complimentary continental breakfast. Check-out 11 am, check-in 2 pm. TV; cable (premium), VCR available. Restaurant. In-house fitness room. Whirlpool. **$**

⬜ 🐾 🏃 🛅

Moscow

Motels/Motor Lodges

★★ **BEST WESTERN UNIVERSITY INN.** *1516 Pullman Rd (83843). Phone 208/882-0550; toll-free 800/325-8765; fax 208/882-7800. www.bestwestern.com.* 173 rooms, 2 story. Pets accepted; fee. Check-out noon, check-in 4 pm. TV. In-room modem link. Restaurant open 24 hours. Bar. Room service. In-house fitness room; sauna. Indoor pool; children's pool; whirlpool. Airport transportation. **$**

⬜ 🐾 🏊 🏃 ✈ 🛅

★ **HILLCREST MOTEL.** *706 N Main St (83843). Phone 208/882-7579; toll-free 800/368-6564; fax 208/882-0310.* 35 rooms. Pets accepted, some restrictions; fee. Check-out 11 am, check-in 1 pm. TV. Laundry services. **$**

🐾 🛅

★★ **MARK IV MOTOR INN.** *414 N Main St (83843). Phone 208/882-7557; toll-free 800/833-4240; fax 208/883-0684. www.ark4motorinn.com.* 86 rooms, 2 story. Pets accepted; fee. Check-out noon, check-in 3 pm. TV; cable (premium). In-room modem link. Restaurant, bar. Room service. Indoor pool; whirlpool. Airport transportation. **$**

⬜ 🐾 🏊 ✈ 🛅 SC

Mountain Home

Motels/Motor Lodges

★ **BEST WESTERN FOOTHILLS MOTOR INN.** *1080 Hwy 20 (83647). Phone 208/587-8477; toll-free 800/604-8477; fax 208/587-5774. www.bestwestern.com/foothillsmotorinn.* 76 rooms, 2 story. Pets accepted; fee. Complimentary continental breakfast. Check-out noon, check-in 3 pm. TV. In-room modem link. Pool; whirlpool. **$**

⬜ 🐾 🏊 🛅

★ **SLEEP INN.** *1180 Hwy 20 (83647). Phone 208/587-9743; toll-free 800/753-3746; fax 208/587-7382. www.sleepinn.com.* 60 rooms, 2 story. Pets accepted; fee. Complimentary continental breakfast. Check-out noon, check-in 3 pm. TV; VCR. In-room modem link. Laundry services. Restaurant. In-house fitness room. **$**

⬜ 🐾 🏃 🛅

Nampa

Motels/Motor Lodges

★ **DESERT INN.** *115 9th Ave S (83651). Phone 208/467-1161; toll-free 800/588-5268; fax 208/467-5268.* 40 rooms, 2 story. Pets accepted, some restrictions; fee. Complimentary continental breakfast. Check-out 11 am, check-in 3 pm. TV; cable (premium). Pool. **$**

⬜ 🐾 🏊 🛅

★ **SHILO INN.** *1401 Shilo Dr (83687). Phone 208/466-8993; fax 208/465-5929. www.shiloinns.com.* 84 rooms, 3 story. No elevator. Pets accepted; fee. Complimentary continental breakfast. Check-out noon, check-in 3 pm. TV; cable (premium). Laundry services. Sauna, steam room. Pool; whirlpool. **$**

⬜ 🐾 🏊 🛅

★★ **SHILO INN.** *617 Nampa Blvd (83687). Phone 208/466-8993; toll-free 800/222-2244; fax 208/465-3239. www.shiloinns.com.* 61 rooms, 3 story. Pets accepted; fee. Complimentary continental breakfast. Check-out noon, check-in 3 pm. TV; cable (premium). Laundry services. Room service. In-house fitness room; sauna. Indoor pool; whirlpool. Free airport transportation. **$**

⬜ 🐾 🏊 🏃 ✈ 🛅

Pocatello

Motels/Motor Lodges

★★ **BEST WESTERN COTTONTREE INN.** *1415 Bench Blvd (83201). Phone 208/237-7650; toll-free 800/662-6886; fax 208/238-1355. www.cottontree.net.* 149 rooms, 1-2 story. Pets accepted, some restrictions. Check-out noon, check-in 2 pm. TV; cable (premium). Laundry services. Restaurant, bar. Room service. Health club privileges. Indoor pool; whirlpool. Free airport transportation. **$**

⬜ 🐾 🏊 ✈ 🛅

★ **COMFORT INN.** *1333 Bench Blvd (83201). Phone 208/237-8155; fax 208/237-8155. www.comfortinn.com.* 52 rooms, 2 story. Pets accepted; fee. Complimentary continental breakfast. Check-out 11 am, check-in 3 pm. TV; cable (premium). Indoor pool; whirlpool. **$**

★★ **HOLIDAY INN.** *1399 Bench Rd (83201). Phone 208/237-1400; toll-free 800/200-8944; fax 208/238-0225. www.holiday-inn.com.* 205 rooms, 2 story. Pets accepted, some restrictions. Complimentary continental breakfast. Check-out noon, check-in 3 pm. TV; cable (premium), VCR available. Laundry services. Restaurant, bar. Room service. In-house fitness room; sauna. Game room. Indoor pool; whirlpool. Free airport transportation. **$**

★★ **RED LION.** *1555 Pocatello Creek Rd (83201). Phone 208/233-2200; toll-free 800/325-4000; fax 208/234-4524. www.redlion.com.* 150 rooms, 2 story. Pets accepted, some restrictions. Check-out noon. TV. Laundry services. Restaurant, bar. Room service. In-house fitness room; sauna. Indoor pool; children's pool; whirlpool. Free airport transportation. Business center. **$**

★ **SUPER 8.** *1330 Bench Blvd (83201). Phone 208/234-0888; fax 208/232-0347. www.super8.com.* 80 rooms, 3 story. Pets accepted; fee. Complimentary continental breakfast. Check-out 11 am, check-in 2 pm. TV. **$**

Priest Lake Area

Resorts

★★ **ELKINS ON PRIEST LAKE.** *404 Elkins Rd (83848). Phone 208/443-2432; fax 208/443-2527. www.elkinsresort.com.* 31 cabins. Closed Mar, Apr. Pets accepted, some restrictions; fee. Check-out 11 am, check-in 4 pm. Restaurant, bar. Game room. Cross-country ski on site. Boats. **$**

★★ **HILLS RESORT.** *4777 W Lakeshore Rd (83856). Phone 208/443-2551; fax 208/443-2363. www.hillsresort.com.* 77 cabins, 1-2 story. No A/C. Pets accepted; fee. Check-out 10:30 am, check-in 4:30 pm. Fireplaces. Laundry services. Dining room, bar. Game room. Outdoor tennis. Cross-country ski on site. Lawn games. Bicycles (rentals). Beach, boats, rowboats, canoes, waterskiing. Sleighing, tobogganing, snowmobiles. **$**

Rexburg

Motels/Motor Lodges

★ **BEST WESTERN COTTONTREE INN.** *450 W 4th St S (83440). Phone 208/356-4646; toll-free 800/662-6886; fax 208/356-7461. www.bestwestern.com.* 98 rooms, 2 story. Pets accepted, some restrictions. Check-out noon, check-in 2 pm. TV. Laundry services. Restaurant. Health club privileges. Indoor pool; whirlpool. **$**

★ **COMFORT INN.** *1565 W Main St (83440). Phone 208/359-1311; toll-free 800/228-5150; fax 208/359-1387. www.comfortinn.com.* 52 rooms, 2 story. Pets accepted. Complimentary continental breakfast. Check-out 11 am, check-in 3 pm. TV. In-house fitness room. Indoor pool; whirlpool. **$**

Sandpoint

Motels/Motor Lodges

★★ **BEST WESTERN EDGEWATER RESORT.** *56 Bridge St (83864). Phone 208/263-3194; toll-free 800/635-2534. www.sandpointhotels.com/edgewater.* 55 rooms, 3 story. No elevator. Pets accepted; fee. Complimentary breakfast. Check-out noon. Check-in 3 pm. TV; VCR available. Restaurant, bar. Room service. Sauna. Indoor pool; whirlpool. **$**

★ **LAKESIDE INN.** *106 Bridge St (83864). Phone 208/263-3717; toll-free 800/543-8126; fax 208/265-4781. www.keokee.com/lakeside.* 50 rooms, 3 story. No elevator. Pets accepted, some restrictions; fee. Complimentary continental breakfast. Check-out 11 am, check-in 2 pm. TV. Laundry services. Sauna. Whirlpool. Lawn games. Free airport transportation. **$**

★★ **QUALITY INN.** *807 N 5th Ave (83864). Phone 208/263-2111; fax 208/263-3289. www.qualityinn.com.* 53 rooms, 2 story. Pets accepted; fee. Check-out noon, check-in 3 pm. TV; VCR available. Laundry services. Restaurant, bar. Indoor pool; whirlpool. Downhill, cross-country ski 11 miles. **$**

Stanley

Motel/Motor Lodge

★★ **MOUNTAIN VILLAGE LODGE.** *Hwy 75 and 21 (83278). Phone 208/774-3661; fax 208/774-3761. www.mountainvillage.com.* 54 rooms, 2 story. Pets accepted; fee. Check-out 11 am, check-in 3 pm. TV; cable (premium), VCR available. Laundry services. Restaurant, bar; entertainment. Lawn games. Airport transportation. **$**

Twin Falls

Motels/Motor Lodges

★ **COMFORT INN.** *1893 Canyon Springs Rd (83301). Phone 208/734-7494; fax 208/735-9428. www.comfortinn.com.* 52 rooms, 2 story. Pets accepted; fee. Complimentary continental breakfast. Check-out 11 am. TV; cable (premium). Indoor pool; whirlpool. **$**

★ **SHILO INN.** *1586 Blue Lakes Blvd N (83301). Phone 208/733-7545; toll-free 800/222-2244; fax 208/736-2019. www.shiloinns.com.* 128 rooms, 4 story. Pets accepted; fee. Complimentary continental breakfast. Check-out noon. TV; cable (premium), VCR available. In-room modem link. Laundry services. In-house fitness room; sauna. Indoor pool; whirlpool. **$**

Wallace

Motel/Motor Lodge

★★ **BEST WESTERN WALLACE INN.** *100 Front St (83873). Phone 208/752-1252; toll-free 800/643-2386; fax 208/753-0981. www.bestwestern.com.* 63 rooms, 2 story. Pets accepted; fee. Check-out noon. TV; cable (premium), VCR available. Restaurant, bar. Room service. In-house fitness room; sauna. Indoor pool; whirlpool; poolside service. Bus depot transportation. **$**

Illinois

Altamont

Motel/Motor Lodge

★ **SUPER 8.** *I-70 and SR 26 S (62411). Phone 618/483-6300; toll-free 800/800-8000; fax 618/483-3323. www.super8.com.* 25 rooms, 2 story. Pets accepted; fee. Check-out 11 am. TV; cable (premium). **$**

D ⬚ ⬚ SC

Alton

Motel/Motor Lodge

★ **SUPER 8.** *1800 Homer Adams Pkwy (62002). Phone 618/465-8885; toll-free 800/800-8000; fax 618/465-8964. www.super8.com.* 61 rooms, 3 story. Pets accepted; fee. Complimentary continental breakfast. Check-out 11 am. TV; cable (premium). In-room modem link. **$**

D ⬚ ⬚

Antioch

Motel/Motor Lodge

★ **BEST WESTERN REGENCY INN.** *350 Hwy 173 (60002). Phone 847/395-3606; fax 847/395-3606. www.bestwestern.com.* 68 rooms, 3 story. Pets accepted, some restrictions; fee. Complimentary continental breakfast. Check-out 11 am. TV; cable (premium), VCR available. In-room modem link. Bar. Indoor pool; whirlpool. **$**

D ⬚ ⬚ SC

Arlington Heights

Motel/Motor Lodge

★ **LA QUINTA INN.** *1415 W Dundee Rd (60004). Phone 847/253-8777; toll-free 800/531-5900; fax 847/818-9167. www.laquinta.com.* 121 rooms, 4 story. Pets accepted. Complimentary continental breakfast. Check-out noon. TV; cable (premium). In-room modem link. In-house fitness room. Heated pool. **$**

D ⬚ ⬚ ⬚ ⬚ SC

Belleville

Motel/Motor Lodge

★ ★ **RAMADA INN.** *6900 N Illinois (62208). Phone 618/632-4747; toll-free 888/298-2054; fax 618/632-9428. www.ramada.com.* 159 rooms, 5 story. Pets accepted; fee. Complimentary continental breakfast buffet. Check-out noon. TV; cable (premium). In-room modem link. Restaurant. Room service. In-house fitness room. Game room. Indoor pool; outdoor pool; whirlpools. **$**

D ⬚ ⬚ ⬚ ⬚ SC

Benton

Motel/Motor Lodge

★ **DAYS INN.** *711 W Main St (62812). Phone 618/439-3183; toll-free 800/329-7466; fax 618/439-3183. www.daysinn.com.* 57 rooms, 2 story. Pets accepted, some restrictions; fee. Check-out noon. TV; VCR available (movies). Restaurant, bar; entertainment. Room service. **$**

D ⬚ ⬚ SC

Bloomington

Motels/Motor Lodges

★ **BEST INN.** *1905 W Market St (61701). Phone 309/827-5333; toll-free 800/237-8466; fax 309/827-5333. www.bestinn.com.* 106 rooms, 2 story. Pets accepted; fee. Complimentary breakfast buffet. Check-out 1 pm. TV. In-room modem link. Pool. **$**

D ⬚ ⬚ ⬚ SC

★ **BEST WESTERN UNIVERSITY INN.** *6 Traders Cir (61761). Phone 309/454-4070; toll-free 800/780-7234; fax 309/888-4505. www.bestwestern.com.* 102 rooms, 2 story. Pets accepted. Complimentary continental breakfast. Check-out 11 am. TV; cable (premium). In-house fitness room; sauna. Game room. Indoor pool. Free airport transportation. **$**

D ⬚ ⬚ ⬚ ⬚ ⬚

★ ★ **HOLIDAY INN.** *8 Traders Cir (61761). Phone 309/452-8300; toll-free 800/465-4329; fax 309/454-6722. www.holiday-inn.com.* 160 rooms, 5 story. Pets accepted; fee. Check-out noon. TV; cable (premium), VCR available (movies). Restaurant, bar. Room service. In-house fitness room; sauna. Game room. Indoor pool; whirlpool. Free airport transportation. Business center. **$**

D ⬚ ⬚ ⬚ ⬚ ⬚ SC ⬚

Hotel

★ ★ ★ **JUMERS CHATEAU.** *1601 Jumer Dr (61704). Phone 309/662-2020; fax 309/662-2020. www.jumers.com.* 180 rooms, 5 story. Pets accepted; fee. Check-out noon. TV; cable (premium). Restaurant, bar; entertainment. Room service. In-house fitness room; sauna. Game room. Indoor pool; whirlpool. Free airport transportation. French décor. **$**

Carbondale

Motel/Motor Lodge

★ **SUPER 8.** *1180 E Main St (62901). Phone 618/457-8822; fax 618/457-4186. www.super8.com.* 63 rooms, 3 story. No elevator. Pets accepted. Check-out 11 am. TV; cable (premium). **$**

Champaign/Urbana

Motels/Motor Lodges

★ **BEST WESTERN PARADISE INN.** *1001 N Dunlap St (61874). Phone 217/356-1824; fax 217/356-1824. www.bestwestern.com.* 62 rooms, 1-2 story. Pets accepted, some restrictions; fee. Complimentary continental breakfast. Check-out 11 am. TV; cable (premium). In-room modem link. In-house fitness room. Pool; children's pool. Free airport transportation. **$**

★ **EASTLAND SUITES.** *1907 N Cunningham (61802). Phone 217/367-8331; toll-free 800/253-8331; fax 217/384-3370. www.eastlandsuitesurbana.com.* 127 rooms, 2 story. Pets accepted; fee. Complimentary full breakfast. Check-out 11 am. TV; cable (premium). Bar. In-house fitness room; sauna. Indoor pool. Free airport transportation. **$**

★ **LA QUINTA INN.** *1900 Center Dr (61820). Phone 217/356-4000; toll-free 800/531-5900; fax 217/352-7783. www.laquinta.com.* 122 rooms, 2 story. Pets accepted; fee. Complimentary breakfast. Check-out noon. TV; cable (premium). In-room modem link. Pool. **$**

★ **RED ROOF INN.** *212 W Anthony Dr (61820). Phone 217/352-0101; toll-free 800/RED-ROOF; fax 217/352-1891. www.redroof.com.* 112 rooms, 2 story. Pets accepted. Check-out noon. TV; cable (premium). **$**

★ **SUPER 8.** *202 Marketview Dr (61820). Phone 217/359-2388; toll-free 800/800-8000; fax 217/359-2388. www.super8.com.* 61 rooms, 2 story. Pets accepted; fee. Complimentary continental breakfast. Check-out 11 am. TV; cable (premium). **$**

Hotels

★ ★ **CHANCELLOR INN.** *1501 S Neil St (61820). Phone 217/352-7891; fax 217/352-8108.* 224 rooms, 4-7 story. Pets accepted, some restrictions; fee. Complimentary continental breakfast. Check-out 1 pm. TV. In-room modem link. Indoor pool; outdoor pool; children's pool. Free airport transportation. Dinner theater. **$**

★ ★ ★ **JUMERS CASTLE LODGE.** *209 S Broadway (61801). Phone 217/384-8800; fax 217/384-9001.* Upon entering this hotel's grand lobby, guests will feel the elegance and style of a time gone by. Guest rooms are beautifully decorated with artwork, fireplaces, and woodwork. The lodge features a German American restaurant and a lounge for your entertainment. 130 rooms, 4 story. Pets accepted, some restrictions; fee. Check-out noon. TV; cable (premium). In-room modem link. Restaurant, bar. Indoor pool; whirlpool. Free airport transportation. **$**

Charleston

Motel/Motor Lodge

★ ★ **BEST WESTERN WORTHINGTON INN.** *920 W Lincoln Ave (61920). Phone 217/348-8161; fax 217/348-8165. www.bestwestern.com.* 67 rooms, 1-2 story. Pets accepted, some restrictions. Complimentary continental breakfast. Check-out 11 am. TV. Restaurant. Outdoor pool. Free airport transportation. **$**

Chicago

Hotels

★ ★ ★ **BURNHAM HOTEL.** *1 W Washington (60602). Phone 312/782-1111; toll-free 877/294-9712; fax 312/782-0899. www.burnhamhotel.com.* Reviving the historic Reliance building (predecessor of the modern skyscraper and early 1900s home of department store Carson Pirie Scott), the Burnham retains the integrity of the landmark architecture, integrating it with a whimsically elegant, clubby ambience. In the Loop near the downtown theater district, major museums, and parks, the hotel is appropriate for business or leisure travel. Rooms and suites offer dramatic views of the Chicago cityscape. The in-house Atwood Café serves upscale American comfort food (including breakfast, lunch, dinner, Sunday brunch, and pre-theater options). The hotel offers complimentary morning coffee, an evening wine reception, and 24-hour room service, as well as pampering pet treatments. 122 rooms, 15 story. Pets accepted. Check-out noon, check-in 3 pm. TV; cable (premium), VCR available. Room service 24 hours. Restaurant, bar. Babysitting services available. In-house fitness room. **$$$**

⊡ 🖛 🛉 🖂

★ ★ ★ **THE FAIRMONT CHICAGO.** *200 N Columbus Dr (60601). Phone 312/565-8000; toll-free 800/866-5577; fax 312/856-1032. www.fairmont.com.* The Fairmont Hotel is at once traditional and contemporary. Just a short distance from the lake and near the renowned shopping of the Magnificent Mile, its sleek tower rests on the edge of leafy Grant Park. The interiors are refined, with rich colors and antique reproductions, and spectacular lakefront views define many of the elegant accommodations. Diners and critics alike are singing the praises of the American dishes at Aria restaurant, and afternoon tea is a special event at the Lobby Lounge. The comprehensive business center keeps travelers in touch with the office, while fitness-minded visitors appreciate the guest privileges at the adjoining Lakeshore Athletic Club and Waves day spa. Noteworthy for its indoor rock-climbing wall, this establishment is often considered the city's top exercise facility. 692 rooms, 41 story. Pets accepted, some restrictions; fee. Check-out noon, check-in 3 pm. TV; cable (premium), VCR available. In-room modem link. Restaurant, bar; entertainment Tues-Sat. Room service 24 hours. Babysitting services available. In-house fitness room; spa. Health club privileges. Indoor, outdoor pool; whirlpool. Valet parking. Business center. Concierge. **$$**

⊡ 🖛 🛋 🛉 🖂 🏃

★ ★ ★ ★ ★ **FOUR SEASONS HOTEL CHICAGO.** *120 E Delaware Pl (60611). Phone 312/280-8800; toll-free 800/332-3442; fax 312/280-9184. www.fourseasons.com/chicagofs.* Located in a 66-story building atop the world-renowned shops of 900 Michigan Avenue, the Four Seasons Hotel Chicago is a well-heeled shopper's paradise. More than 100 world-class stores, including Gucci and Bloomingdale's, await only steps from your door. This palatial skytop hotel exudes glamour, from its gleaming marble lobby with grand staircase to its regal accommodations. Even exercise is refined here, with a marvelous Roman-columned indoor pool. Occupying the 30th through 46th floors of the tower, the guest rooms afford jaw-dropping views of the magnificent skyline and Lake Michigan. From this vantage point, guests truly feel on top of the world. The accommodations have an opulent character enhanced by

jewel tones, rich fabrics, and timeless furnishings. Body and mind are calmed at the spa, where a whimsical element inspires the decadent Champagne cocktail and caviar facials. Edible indulgences include French dishes at Seasons restaurant and continental favorites at The Café. 343 rooms, 66 story. Pets accepted, some restrictions; fee. Check-out noon, check-in 3 pm. TV; cable (premium), VCR available. In-room modem link. Room service 24 hours. Restaurant, bar; entertainment. Babysitting services available. In-house fitness room; spa, sauna, steam room. Indoor pool; whirlpool. Valet parking. Business center. Concierge. **$$$$**

⊡ 🖛 🛋 🛉 🖂 🏃

★ ★ ★ **HOTEL ALLEGRO CHICAGO.** *171 W Randolph St (60601). Phone 312/236-0123; toll-free 800/643-1500; fax 312/236-0917. www.allegrochicago.com.* The stylishly eclectic Hotel Allegro is the result of a 1998 renovation of the Loop's historic Bismarck Hotel. This erstwhile grande dame's classic-contemporary new incarnation is exuberantly colorful, with musical and theatrical icons integrated throughout the décor. The dramatic lobby, with fireplace and baby grand piano, harkens back to the days of the grand hotel (guests can enjoy a complimentary evening wine hour). The Allegro offers multiple dining and cocktail environments, including the adjacent restaurant 312 Chicago; the Encore lounge for lunch, cocktails, or late-night dining; and room service. Special amenities are offered for canine and feline guests. 483 rooms, 19 story. Pets accepted, some restrictions. Check-out noon, check-in 3 pm. TV; cable (premium), VCR available. In-room modem link. Restaurant, bar. Babysitting services available. In-house fitness room. Valet parking. Business center. Concierge. **$$$**

⊡ 🖛 🛉 🖂 🏃

★ ★ ★ **HOUSE OF BLUES, A LOEWS HOTEL.** *333 N Dearborn (60610). Phone 312/245-0333; toll-free 800/22-LOEWS; fax 312/923-2466. www.loewshotels.com.* With its exotic Gothic-Moroccan-East Indian décor, eye-popping art collection, and adjacent live concert venue, the hip House of Blues Hotel appeals to a new generation of travelers. Guest rooms are spacious and well appointed; vast meeting space and related services cater to business travelers. The namesake restaurant serves Southern American fare and hosts a popular Sunday gospel brunch. In the same complex are the chic, wine-themed bistro Bin 36 and Smith & Wollensky Steak House. The location puts guests in the heart of the River North gallery, dining, and entertainment district and close to the Loop and Michigan Avenue. 367 rooms, 15 story. Pets accepted. Check-out noon, check-in 3 pm. TV; cable (premium), VCR available. Restaurant, bar. Babysitting services available. In-house fitness room; spa. Business center. **$$**

🖛 🛉 🖂 🏃

★ ★ ★ **LE MERIDIEN CHICAGO.** *521 N Rush St (60611). Phone 312/645-1500; toll-free 800/543-4300; fax 312/327-0598. www.lemeridien.com.* 311 rooms, 12 story. Pets accepted, some restrictions. Check-out noon, check-in 3 pm. TV; cable (premium), VCR available. Room service 24 hours. Restaurant, bar. Babysitting services available. In-house fitness room. Business center. **$$$$**

★ ★ ★ **OMNI CHICAGO HOTEL.** *676 N Michigan Ave (60611). Phone 312/944-6664; toll-free 800/788-6664; fax 312/266-3015. www.omnihotels.com.* In the center of Michigan Avenue within a mixed-use building sits this property, host to many famous guests of the Oprah Winfrey Show. All accommodations offer spacious sitting rooms with bedrooms hidden behind French doors, great for corporate clientele needing their room to double as an office. The fourth-floor Cielo restaurant provides fantastic views of the street excitement below. 347 rooms, 25 story. Pets accepted, some restrictions; fee. Check-out noon, check-in 3 pm. TV; cable (premium), VCR available. In-room modem link. Room service 24 hours. Restaurant, bar. Children's activity center, babysitting services available. In-house fitness room; health club privileges, sauna. Indoor pool; whirlpool. Valet parking. Business center. Concierge. **$$**

★ ★ ★ **THE PALMER HOUSE HILTON.** *17 E Monroe St (60603). Phone 312/726-7500; toll-free 800/445-8667; fax 312/263-2556. www.hilton.com.* Grand and gilded, the Palmer House Hilton has harbored visitors to the Windy City for 130 years, making it America's longest-operating hotel. This Loop landmark has undergone a full renovation to restore designer-builder Potter Palmer's original French Empire opulence, including the breathtaking Beaux Arts ceiling in the palatial lobby. Amenities include an 11-room penthouse suite, executive levels with private elevator, an entire floor of "deluxe-tech" conference and meeting facilities, a fitness club, and a shopping arcade. Four restaurants and bars include the 1940s-themed Big Downtown restaurant and bar and the retro Polynesian favorite, Trader Vic's. 1,639 rooms, 25 story. Pets accepted. Check-out 11 am, check-in 3 pm. TV; cable (premium), VCR available. In-room modem link. Restaurant, bar; entertainment. In-house fitness room; massage, sauna, steam room. Indoor pool; whirlpool. Airport transportation. Business center. Concierge. **$$**

★ ★ ★ ★ **PARK HYATT CHICAGO.** *800 N Michigan Ave (60611). Phone 312/335-1234; toll-free 800/778-7477; fax 312/239-4000. www.parkhyattchicago.com.* From its stylish interiors to its historic Water Tower Square location, the Park Hyatt is intrinsically tied to the history of Chicago. Occupying a landmark building in the heart of the Magnificent Mile shopping area, the hotel has a sleek, modern attitude. The public and private spaces celebrate the city's long-lasting love affair with architecture and its artists. Mies van der Rohe, Eames, and Noguchi furnishings are showcased throughout the guest rooms, while photography commissioned by the Art Institute of Chicago graces the walls. A health club, spa, and salon are the perfect antidotes to stress, and the flawless service always ensures a carefree visit. The nouvelle cuisine at NoMI is a standout, although the dramatic seventh-floor views from the floor-to-ceiling windows are not for the faint of heart. To escape the urban pace, visitors head to the NoMI Garden for American barbecue favorites. 202 rooms, 18 story. Pets accepted, some restrictions; fee. Check-out noon, check-in 3 pm. TV; cable (premium), VCR available. Room service 24 hours. Restaurant, bar. Babysitting services available. In-house fitness room; spa. Indoor pool; whirlpool. Business center. **$$$$**

★ ★ ★ ★ ★ **PENINSULA CHICAGO.** *108 E Superior St (60611). Phone 312/337-2888; fax 312/751-2888. www.peninsula.com.* Reigning over Chicago's famed Magnificent Mile, the Peninsula Chicago hotel basks in a golden aura. From the sun-filled lobby to the gleaming, gilded details, this hotel simply sparkles. With Tiffany and Ralph Lauren downstairs and Saks and Neiman Marcus across the street, the gracious bellmen outfitted in crisp white uniforms are a shopper's savior. Asian sensibilities are expertly blended with details highlighting the city's Art Deco heritage in the public spaces. Soft lighting, polished woods, and golden hues create glorious shelters in the guest rooms. Proving the point that modern amenities are a hallmark of this property, all rooms are fitted with bedside electronic control panels and flat-screen televisions. Guests escape the pressures of the everyday at the state-of-the-art exercise facility and spa, complete with an outdoor sundeck. Whether taking tea, nibbling flamme-kuchen, sampling Asian specialties, or savoring seafood, guests traverse the world at five distinctive dining venues. *Secret Inspector's Notes:* The Peninsula Chicago is one of the most perfect hotel experiences a traveler can expect in this country. The staff attends to every detail with such attention and care that it is impossible to conceive of the luxury offered at this high-tech hotel until you have experienced it. Nothing can compare to luxuriating in your deep bathtub, watching television while enjoying room service at a culinary level of some of the best restaurants in the city. The bar is a fantastic spot to enjoy a drink and perhaps an appetizer, and the adjacent Pierrot Gourmet serves delightful European fare in a bright setting. Eating breakfast in the palatial lobby restaurant is an impressive an experience as you could find while watching the sun rise over the skyline. Find a way to stay here, whether for a night or a week. Your expectations of hotels will be changed forever. 339 rooms, 20 story. Pets accepted, some restrictions. Check-out noon, check-in 3 pm. TV; cable (premium), VCR available. Room service 24 hours. Restaurant, bar. Babysitting services available. In-house fitness room; spa. Indoor pool; children's pool; whirlpool. Valet parking. Business center. **$$$$**

★ ★ ★ **RENAISSANCE CHICAGO HOTEL.** *1 W Wacker Dr (60601). Phone 312/372-7200; fax 312/372-0093. www.renaissancehotels.com.* This Marriott-owned Loop high-rise features stone and glass exterior towers that rise above the intersection of State and Wacker. The Renaissance is a welcome haven to its audience of business travelers and vacationers looking for a central location accessible to theaters and museums. The handsome lobby sets a posh, executive tone; comfortable rooms boast spectacular views (especially on the higher floors). The Great Street Restaurant in the hotel's atrium serves American breakfast, lunch, and dinner (and a bargain theater menu) with a view of the river. Additional amenities include 24-hour room service, expanded club level rooms, a fitness club and pool, a lobby bar, and a 24-hour Kinko's business center. 553 rooms, 27 story. Pets accepted, some restrictions; fee. Check-out 1 pm, check-in 3 pm. TV; cable (premium), VCR available. In-room modem link. Room service 24 hours. Restaurant, bar. In-house fitness room; sauna, massage. Indoor pool; whirlpool; poolside service. Valet parking. Business center. Concierge. Luxury level. **$$$**

★ ★ ★ ★ ★ **THE RITZ-CARLTON, A FOUR SEASONS HOTEL.** *160 E Pearson St (60611). Phone 312/266-1000; toll-free 800/621-6906; fax 312/266-1194. www.fourseasons.com.* Guests of the esteemed Ritz-Carlton Chicago often wonder if heaven could get any better than this. The unparalleled levels of service, commitment to excellence, and meticulous attention to detail make this one of the country's finest hotels. Gracing the upper levels of prestigious Water Tower Place on the Magnificent Mile, the hotel's guest rooms afford picture-perfect views through large windows. Rich tones and dignified furnishings define the accommodations. Managed by the Four Seasons, The Ritz-Carlton offers guests a taste of the luxe life, from the resplendent décor and seamless service to the superlative cuisine at the four restaurants and lounges. The sublime contemporary French menu and sensational ambience at the Dining Room makes it one of the most coveted tables in town. Human guests, however, are not the only ones to be spoiled—furry visitors feast in-room on filet mignon and salmon! *Secret Inspector's Notes:* The Ritz-Carlton Chicago is elegance taken to the highest possible level and then translated into giddy grandeur and opulence. The staff exudes such cheerfulness and genialness that you wish they would sell it in a bottle. The concierges at this home to the fortunate could not be better; they are capable of handling any request with such a personal

touch that it remains in your mind for many months to follow. Breakfast at the Ritz-Carlton is an exercise in being taken care of, where the sweet waitstaff makes sure that you leave feeling both satiated and nourished. 435 rooms, 31 story. Pets accepted, some restrictions. Check-out noon, check-in 3 pm. TV; cable (premium), VCR available. In-room modem link. Room service 24 hours. Restaurant, bar. Babysitting services available. In-house fitness room; spa, sauna, steam room. Indoor pool; whirlpool. Parking. Business center. Concierge. **$$$**

★ ★ ★ **SHERATON CHICAGO HOTEL AND TOWERS.** *301 E North Water St (60611). Phone 312/464-1000; toll-free 800/233-4100; fax 312/464-9140. www.sheratonchicago.com.* Contemporary yet comfortable, every room of the handsomely appointed Sheraton Chicago Hotel & Towers promises a sweeping view of the cityscape, the Chicago River, or Lake Michigan. The central location is just minutes from the Magnificent Mile, the Loop, Navy Pier, and McCormick Place. The spacious lobby is appointed in imported marble and rich woods, and luxurious fitness facilities feature a pool and sauna. Close to numerous fine restaurants, the Sheraton's five in-house dining options include Shula's Steak House and an indoor-outdoor café overlooking the river. Extensive and elegant meeting facilities, a full-service business center, and club-level rooms cater to business travelers. 1,200 rooms, 34 story. Pets accepted, some restrictions; fee. Check-out noon, check-in 3 pm. TV; cable (premium), VCR available. In-room modem link. Room service 24 hours. Restaurant, bar. In-house fitness room; massage, sauna. Indoor pool. Business center. Concierge. Luxury level. **$$**

★ ★ ★ **THE SUTTON PLACE HOTEL.** *21 E Bellevue Pl (60611). Phone 312/266-2100; toll-free 800/810-6888; fax 312/266-2141. www.suttonplace.com.* Stylish understatement is the mantra of this luxurious hotel, an Art Deco-inspired building housing a handsome, modern interior. The prime Gold Coast location offers immediate access to such attractions as Magnificent Mile shopping, Rush Street nightlife, and some of the city's finest restaurants. Recently renovated, soundproof rooms feature deep-soaking tubs, separate glass-enclosed showers, plush robes, and lavish bath accessories. Room service is 24/7, and destination dining and people-watching are available at the Whiskey Bar & Grill. Popular with corporate travelers, Sutton Place is equally suited to private getaways. 246 rooms, 23 story. Pets accepted, some restrictions; fee. Check-out noon, check-in 3 pm. TV; cable (premium), VCR available. In-room modem link. Room service 24 hours. Restaurant, bar. In-house fitness room; health club privileges. Valet parking. Airport transportation. Business center. Concierge. **$$**

★ ★ ★ **W CHICAGO CITY CENTER.** *172 W Adams St (60603). Phone 312/332-1200; fax 312/332-5909. www.whotels.com.* 390 rooms, 20 story. Pets accepted, some restrictions; fee. Check-out noon, check-in 3 pm. TV; cable (premium), VCR. Restaurant, bar; entertainment Tues-Sat. Babysitting services available. In-house fitness room. **$$**

D ⊁ ⬤ 🛉 ⬜

★ ★ ★ **W CHICAGO LAKESHORE.** *644 N Lakeshore Dr (60611). Phone 312/943-9200; fax 312/255-4411. www.whotels.com.* 578 rooms, 33 story. Pets accepted, some restrictions; fee. Check-out noon, check-in 3 pm. TV; cable (premium), VCR available. Restaurant. In-house fitness room; spa. Indoor pool; whirlpool. Business center. **$$**

⬤ 🛏 🛉 ⬜ 🛉

★ ★ ★ ★ **THE WESTIN CHICAGO RIVER NORTH.** *320 Dearborn (60610). Phone 312/744-1900; toll-free 800/WESTIN-1; fax 312/527-2664. www.westinrivernorth.com.* The Westin Chicago River North enjoys a wonderful location overlooking the Chicago River in the heart of the city's financial and theater districts. This luxury hotel is an impressive sight and offers a welcoming home for business or leisure travelers visiting the Windy City. Attractive and comfortable, the rooms use a blend of brass, black, and caramel tones to create a soothing atmosphere, the furnishings a contemporary interpretation of classic design. Westin's signature Heavenly beds make for luxurious slumber, and the Heavenly baths ensure aquatic therapy. Athletic-minded guests reap the rewards of the full-service fitness center. The Kamehachi Sushi Bar delights fish lovers; the Celebrity Café features all-day dining with a focus on American dishes; and the Hana Lounge entertains nightly with hors d'oeuvres and live music. 424 rooms, 20 story. Pets accepted, some restrictions. Check-out noon, check-in 3 pm. TV; cable (premium), VCR available. In-room modem link. Room service 24 hours. Restaurant, bar. Babysitting services available. In-house fitness room; sauna, spa, massage. Valet parking. Business center. Concierge. **$$**

D ⊁ 🛉 ⬜ 🛉

★ ★ ★ **THE WESTIN MICHIGAN AVENUE CHICAGO.** *909 N Michigan Ave (60611). Phone 312/943-7200; toll-free 800/WESTIN-1; fax 312/397-5580. www.westinmichiganave.com.* For the leisure traveler, this hotel is close to Grant Park, Navy Pier, and many art galleries. 751 rooms, 27 story. Pets accepted, some restrictions; fee. Check-out noon, check-in 3 pm. TV; cable (premium). In-room modem link. Room service 24 hours. Restaurant, bar. Babysitting services available. In-house fitness room; sauna, massage. Valet parking. Business center. Concierge. Luxury level. **$$**

D ⊁ 🛉 ⬜ SC 🛉

★ ★ ★ **THE WHITEHALL HOTEL.** *105 E Delaware Pl (60611). Phone 312/944-6300; toll-free 800/948-4255; fax 312/944-8552. www.thewhitehallhotel.com.* A historic Gold Coast landmark, this venerable hotel is just off the Magnificent Mile and steps from Water Tower Place. Built in 1927 and extensively renovated in recent years, the independent Whitehall retains its stature as a small sanctuary with personal service and sedate, old-world charm. Rooms combine traditional décor (including some four-poster beds) and modern technology. The California-Mediterranean restaurant, Molive, offers an excellent wine program, a bar, and outdoor dining. Additional highlights include club floors, an evening cocktail hour, and complimentary sedan service (within 2 miles). 221 rooms, 21 story. Pets accepted, some restrictions. Check-out noon, check-in 3 pm. In-room modem link. Room service 24 hours. Restaurant, bar. Babysitting services available. In-house fitness room; health club privileges. Valet parking. Concierge. Luxury level. **$$**

D ⊁ ⬤ 🛉 ⬜

Chicago O'Hare Airport Area

Hotels

★ ★ **HOLIDAY INN.** *10233 W Higgins Rd (60018). Phone 847/954-8600; toll-free 800/465-4329; fax 847/954-8800. www.hiselect.com/rosemontil.* 300 rooms, 11 story. Pets accepted, some restrictions; fee. Check-out noon, check-in 3 pm. TV; cable (premium), VCR available. Restaurant, bar. In-house fitness room. Whirlpool. Business center. **$**

⊁ 🛉 🛉 ⬜ 🛉

★ ★ ★ **SOFITEL.** *5550 N River Rd (60018). Phone 847/678-4488; toll-free 800/233-5959; fax 847/678-4244. www.sofitel.com.* 300 rooms, 10 story. Pets accepted; fee. Check-out noon. TV; cable (premium). In-room modem link. Room service 24 hours. Restaurant, bar. In-house fitness room; sauna. Indoor pool. Valet parking. Free airport transportation. Business center. Concierge. Traditional European-style hotel. **$$**

D ⊁ 🛏 🛉 🛉 ⬜ 🛉

All Suite

★ ★ **EMBASSY SUITES.** *5500 N River Rd (60018). Phone 847/678-4000; toll-free 800/EMBASSY; fax 847/928-7659. www.embassyohare.com.* 296 suites, 8 story. Pets accepted, some restrictions; fee. Complimentary breakfast. Check-out noon, check-in 3 pm. TV; cable (premium). In-room modem link. Restaurant, bar. Room service. In-house fitness room. Health club privileges. Indoor pool; whirlpool. Business center. Free airport transportation. **$**

D ◨ ⊠ ⊼ ✈ ⊠ ⊼

Collinsville

Motel/Motor Lodge

★ ★ **HOLIDAY INN.** *1000 Eastport Plaza Dr (62234). Phone 618/345-2800; toll-free 800/551-5133; fax 618/345-9804. www.holiday-inn.com.* 229 rooms, 5 story. Pets accepted; fee. Complimentary full breakfast. Check-out noon. TV; cable (premium). In-room modem link. Room service 24 hours. Restaurant, bar. In-house fitness room; sauna. Health club privileges. Game room. Indoor pool; whirlpool. Free airport transportation. **$**

D ◨ ⊠ ⊼ ⊠ SC

B&B/Small Inn

★ **MAGGIE'S BED & BREAKFAST.** *2102 N Keebler Rd (62234). Phone 618/344-8283.* 5 rooms, 3 story. No room phones. Pets accepted, some restrictions; fee. Complimentary full breakfast. Check-out noon, check-in 4-6 pm. TV; VCR (movies). Game room. Whirlpool. Built in 1900; former boarding house. Totally nonsmoking. No Credit cards accepted. **$**

D ◨ ⊠

Danville

Motels/Motor Lodges

★ **COMFORT INN.** *383 Lynch Dr (61834). Phone 217/443-8004; toll-free 800/228-5150; fax 217/443-8004. www.comfortinn.com.* 56 rooms, 2 story. Pets accepted. Complimentary continental breakfast. Check-out 11 am. TV; cable (premium), VCR (movies). In-room modem link. Game room. Whirlpool. **$**

D ◨ ⊠ SC

★ ★ **RAMADA INN.** *388 Eastgate Dr (61834). Phone 217/446-2400; fax 217/446-3878. www.ramada.com.* 131 rooms, 2 story. Pets accepted; fee. Complimentary continental breakfast. Check-out noon. TV; cable (premium). Restaurant, bar. Room service. In-house fitness room. Pool. Free airport transportation. **$**

D ◨ ⊠ ⊼ ⊠

Decatur

Motel/Motor Lodge

★ **BAYMONT INN.** *5100 Hickory Point Frontage Rd (62526). Phone 217/875-5800; fax 217/875-7537. www.baymontinns.com.* 102 rooms, 2 story. Pets accepted, some restrictions; fee. Complimentary continental breakfast. Check-out noon. TV; cable (premium). In-room modem link. Room service. **$**

D ◨ ⊠

Dixon

Motel/Motor Lodge

★ ★ **BEST WESTERN REAGAN HOTEL.** *443 IL Rte 2 (61021). Phone 815/284-1890; toll-free 800/780-7234; fax 815/284-1174. www.bestwestern.com.* 91 rooms, 2 story. Pets accepted; fee. Complimentary continental breakfast (Mon-Fri). Check-out noon. TV; VCR available (movies). Restaurant, bar. Room service. In-house fitness room. Outdoor pool; whirlpool. **$**

D ◨ ⊠ ⊼ ⊠ SC

Effingham

Motels/Motor Lodges

★ **BEST INN.** *1209 N Keller Dr (62401). Phone 217/347-5141; toll-free 888/237-8466; fax 217/347-5141. www.bestinn.com.* 83 rooms, 2 story. Pets accepted, some restrictions; fee. Complimentary breakfast. Check-out 1 pm. TV. Pool. **$**

D ◨ ⊠ ⊠ SC

★ ★ **BEST WESTERN RAINTREE INN.** *1809 W Fayette Ave (62401). Phone 217/342-4121; fax 217/342-4121. www.bestwestern.com.* 65 rooms, 2 story. Pets accepted, some restrictions. Complimentary continental breakfast. Check-out 11 am. TV; cable (premium). Restaurant, bar. Pool. **$**

◨ ⊠ ⊠ SC

★ **COMFORT INN.** *1310 W Fayette Rd (62401). Phone 217/342-3151; toll-free 800/228-5150; fax 217/342-3555. www.comfortsuites.com.* 65 rooms, 3 story. Pets accepted, some restrictions. Complimentary continental breakfast. Check-out 11 am. TV; cable (premium). In-room modem link. Restaurant. Sauna. Indoor pool. **$**

D ◨ ⊠ ⊠

★ **DAYS INN.** *1412 W Fayette Ave (62401). Phone 217/342-9271; toll-free 800/687-4941; fax 217/342-5850. www.daysinn.com.* 109 rooms, 2 story. Pets accepted; fee. Complimentary continental breakfast. Check-out 11 am. TV; cable (premium). Pool. **$**

D 🐾 ➿ ⛆ SC

★ **ECONO LODGE.** *1600 W Fayette Ave (62401). Phone 217/342-4161; fax 217/342-4164.* 135 rooms, 2 story. Pets accepted; fee. Complimentary continental breakfast. Check-out noon. TV; cable. Restaurant, bar. Room service. Pool. Airport, train station, bus depot transportation. **$**

D 🐾 ➿ ⛆ SC

★ **HAMPTON INN.** *1509 Hampton Dr (62401). Phone 217/342-4499; toll-free 800/426-7866; fax 217/347-2828. www.hamptoninn.com.* 62 rooms, 2 story. Pets accepted, some restrictions. Complimentary continental breakfast. Check-out noon. TV; cable (premium). In-room modem link. Indoor pool. **$**

D 🐾 ➿ ⛆ SC

★ **SUPER 8.** *1400 Thelma Keller Ave (62401). Phone 217/342-6888; toll-free 800/800-8000; fax 217/347-2863. www.super8.com.* 49 rooms, 2 story. Pets accepted, some restrictions. Complimentary breakfast. Check-out 11 am. TV; cable (premium). **$**

D 🐾 ⛆

Evanston

Hotel

★★ **OMNI ORRINGTON HOTEL.** *1710 Orrington Ave (60201). Phone 847/866-8700; fax 847/866-8724. www.omnihotels.com.* Located across from Northwestern University, this elegant hotel features such amenities as an onsite fitness center and access to the Evanston Athletic Club and the Henry Crown Sports Pavilion/Norris Aquatics Center. 277 rooms, 9 story. Pets accepted, some restriction; fee. Check-out noon. TV; cable; VCR available. In-room modem link. Restaurant, bar. Health club privileges. Valet, covered parking. Concierge. Refrigerators. **$**

D 🐾 🏃 ⛆

Freeport

Motel/Motor Lodge

★ **RAMADA INN.** *1300 E South St (61032). Phone 815/235-3121; toll-free 800/272-6232; fax 815/297-9701. www.ramada.com.* 90 rooms, 2 story. Pets accepted; fee.

Check-out noon. TV; cable (premium). Restaurant, bar. In-house fitness room. Game room. Heated pool. **$**

D 🐾 ➿ 🏃 ⛆ SC

Galena

Motel/Motor Lodge

★ **BEST WESTERN QUIET HOUSE & SUITES.** *9923 IL 20E (61036). Phone 815/777-2577; toll-free 800/780-7234; fax 815/777-0584. www.bestwestern.com.* 42 rooms, 3 story. Pets accepted, some restrictions; fee. Check-out 11 am. TV; cable (premium). In-house fitness room. Pool; whirlpools. Downhill, cross-country ski 12 miles. **$**

D 🐾 ➿ ➿ 🏃 ⛆

Galesburg

Motels/Motor Lodges

★ **COMFORT INN.** *907 W Carl Sandburg Dr (61401). Phone 309/344-5445; fax 309/344-5445. www.comfortinn.com.* 46 rooms, 2 story. Pets accepted, some restrictions; fee. Complimentary continental breakfast. Check-out 11 am. TV; cable (premium), VCR available. **$**

D 🐾 ⛆ SC

★★★ **JUMERS CONTINENTAL INN.** *260 S Soangetaha Rd (61401). Phone 309/343-7151; fax 309/343-7151. www.jumers.com.* 147 rooms, 2 story. Pets accepted, some restrictions; fee. Check-out noon. TV; cable (premium), VCR available. Restaurant, bar; entertainment. Room service. Saunas. Indoor pool; whirlpool. Free airport transportation. **$**

D 🐾 ➿ ⛆

★★ **RAMADA INN.** *29 Public Sq (61401). Phone 309/343-9161; toll-free 888/298-2054; fax 309/343-0157. www.ramada.com.* 96 rooms, 7 story. Pets accepted; fee. Check-out noon. TV; cable (premium), VCR available. In-room modem link. Restaurant open 24 hours. Bar. Indoor pool; whirlpool. Near Knox College campus. **$**

D 🐾 ➿ ⛆ SC

Greenville

Motel/Motor Lodge

★ **BEST WESTERN COUNTRY VIEW INN.** *I-70 and IL 127 (62246). Phone 618/664-3030; fax 618/664-3030.* 83 rooms, 2 story. Pets accepted, some restrictions; fee. Complimentary continental breakfast. Check-out 11 am. TV. In-house fitness room. Pool. **$**

🐾 🏊 🏃 🏌 SC

Gurnee

Motel/Motor Lodge

★ **BAYMONT INN.** *5688 N Ridge Rd (60031). Phone 847/662-7600; fax 847/662-5300. www.baymontinns.com.* 106 rooms, 4 story. Pets accepted, some restrictions. Complimentary continental breakfast. Check-out noon. TV; cable (premium). In-room modem link. Laundry services. Indoor pool; whirlpool. **$**

D 🐾 🏊 🏌 SC

Kewanee

Motel/Motor Lodge

★ **KEWANEE MOTOR LODGE.** *400 S Main St (61443). Phone 309/853-4000; fax 309/853-4000.* 29 rooms, 2 story. Pets accepted; fee. Check-out 11 am. TV; cable (premium). **$**

D 🐾 🏌 SC

Lincoln

Motels/Motor Lodges

★ **BUDGET INN.** *2011 N Kickapoo St (62656). Phone 217/735-1202; fax 217/735-1202.* 60 rooms. Pets accepted; fee. Check-out noon. TV; cable (premium). Indoor pool. **$**

D 🐾 🏊 SC

★ **COMFORT INN.** *2811 Woodlawn Rd (62656). Phone 217/735-3960; toll-free 800/221-2222; fax 217/735-3960. www.comfortinn.com.* 52 rooms, 2 story. Pets accepted; fee. Complimentary continental breakfast. Check-out 11 am. TV; cable (premium), VCR available. Game room. Indoor pool; whirlpool. **$**

D 🐾 🏊 🏌 SC

Marion

Motel/Motor Lodge

★ **BEST WESTERN AIRPORT INN.** *150 Express Dr (62959). Phone 618/993-3222; fax 618/993-8868. www.bestwestern.com.* 34 rooms, 2 story. Pets accepted;

fee. Complimentary continental breakfast. Check-out 11 am. TV. Pool. Free airport transportation. **$**

🐾 🏊 ✈ 🏌

Mattoon

Motel/Motor Lodge

★ ★ **RAMADA INN.** *300 Broadway Ave E (61938). Phone 217/235-0313; fax 217/235-6005. www.ramada.com.* 124 rooms, 2 story. Pets accepted, some restrictions. Check-out noon. TV; cable (premium). Restaurant, bar. Sauna. Game room. Indoor pool; outdoor pool; whirlpool. **$**

🐾 🏊 🏌

Moline

Motels/Motor Lodges

★ **HAMPTON INN.** *6920 27th St (61265). Phone 309/762-1711; fax 309/762-1788. www.hamptoninn.com.* 138 rooms, 2 story. Pets accepted; fee. Complimentary continental breakfast. Check-out noon. TV; cable (premium). Free airport transportation. **$**

D 🐾 🏌 SC

★ **LA QUINTA INN.** *5450 27th St (61265). Phone 309/762-9008; fax 309/762-2455. www.laquinta.com.* 125 rooms, 2 story. Pets accepted, some restrictions. Complimentary continental breakfast. Check-out noon. TV; cable (premium). In-room modem link. Restaurant. Downhill ski 15 miles. Airport transportation. **$**

🐾 🏊 🏌

Monmouth

Motel/Motor Lodge

★ ★ **MELINGS.** *1129 N Main St (61462). Phone 309/734-2196; fax 309/734-2127.* 34 rooms, 1-2 story. Pets accepted; fee. Check-out 11 am. TV. Laundry services. Restaurant, dining room, bar. **$**

🐾 🏌

Morris

Motel/Motor Lodge

★ ★ **HOLIDAY INN.** *200 Gore Rd (60450). Phone 815/942-6600; toll-free 800/465-4329; fax 815/942-8255. www.holiday-inn.com.* 120 rooms, 2 story. Pets accepted, some restrictions. Check-out noon. TV; cable (premium). In-room modem link. Restaurant, bar. Room service. Indoor pool; whirlpool. **$**

⊡ 🐾 🏊 🎿

Mount Vernon

Motels/Motor Lodges

★ **BEST INN.** *222 S 44th St (62864). Phone 618/244-4343; toll-free 800/237-8466; fax 618/244-4343. www.bestinns.com.* 153 rooms, 2 story. Pets accepted; fee. Complimentary continental breakfast. Check-out 1 pm. TV; cable (premium). Pool. **$**

⊡ 🐾 🏊 🎿 SC

★ **DRURY INN.** *145 N 44th St (62864). Phone 618/244-4550; toll-free 800/325-8300; fax 618/244-4550. www.druryinn.com.* 82 rooms, 3 story. Pets accepted. Complimentary continental breakfast. Check-out noon. TV. Pool. **$**

⊡ 🐾 🏊 🎿 SC

★ ★ **HOLIDAY INN.** *222 Potomac Blvd (62864). Phone 618/244-7100; toll-free 800/243-7171; fax 618/242-8876. www.holiday-inn.com.* 223 rooms, 5 story. Pets accepted, some restrictions; fee. Check-out 1 pm. TV. Restaurant, bar. Room service. Saunas. Indoor pool; whirlpool. Free airport transportation. **$**

⊡ 🐾 🏊 SC

★ ★ **RAMADA INN.** *405 S 44th St (62864). Phone 618/244-3670; toll-free 800/328-7829; fax 618/244-6904. www.ramada.com.* 188 rooms, 4 story. Pets accepted; fee. Complimentary continental breakfast. Check-out noon. TV; cable (premium). In-room modem link. Restaurant, bar; entertainment. Room service. In-house fitness room; sauna. Health club privileges. Game room. Indoor pool; whirlpool. Free airport, bus depot transportation. Business center. **$**

⊡ 🐾 🏊 🎾 🎿 SC 🏃

Naperville

Motel/Motor Lodge

★ **RED ROOF INN.** *1698 W Diehl Rd (60563). Phone 630/369-2500; toll-free 800/733-7663; fax 630/369-9987. www.redroof.com.* 119 rooms, 3 story. Pets accepted, some restrictions. Check-out noon, check-in 2 pm. TV; cable (premium). In-room modem link. **$**

⊡ 🐾 🎿

Oak Lawn

Motel/Motor Lodge

★ **HAMPTON INN.** *13330 S Cicero Ave, Crestwood (60445). Phone 708/597-3330; toll-free 800/426-7866; fax 708/597-3691. www.hamptoninn.com.* 123 rooms, 4 story. Pets accepted. Complimentary continental breakfast. Check-out noon. TV; cable (premium), VCR available. In-room modem link. In-house fitness room. Indoor pool. Free airport transportation. **$**

⊡ 🐾 🏊 🎾 🎿 SC

Ottawa

Motel/Motor Lodge

★ **TRAVELODGE.** *3000 Columbus St (61350). Phone 815/434-3400; fax 815/434-3904.* 120 rooms, 2 story. Pets accepted, some restrictions. Check-out 11 am. TV. Restaurant, bar. In-house fitness room. Game room. Indoor pool; whirlpool. **$**

🐾 🏊 🎾 🎿 SC

Peoria

Motels/Motor Lodges

★ **COMFORT INN.** *4021 N War Memorial Dr (61614). Phone 309/688-3800; toll-free 800/228-5150; fax 309/688-3800. www.comfortsuites.com.* 66 rooms, 2 story. Pets accepted, some restrictions; fee. Complimentary continental breakfast. Check-out 11 am. TV; cable (premium). In-room modem link. Indoor pool; whirlpool. **$**

⊡ 🐾 🏊 🎿 SC

★ **RED ROOF INN.** *4031 N War Memorial Dr (61614). Phone 309/685-3911; fax 309/685-3941. www.redroof.com.* 108 rooms, 2 story. Pets accepted. Check-out noon. TV; cable (premium), VCR available. **$**

⊡ 🐾 🎿

Hotels

★ ★ **HOLIDAY INN.** *500 Hamilton Blvd (61602). Phone 309/674-2500; toll-free 800/474-2501; fax 309/674-8705. www.holiday-inn.com.* 327 rooms, 9 story. Pets accepted. Check-out noon. TV. In-room modem link. Restaurant, bar. In-house fitness room. Pool. Free airport, bus depot transportation. Business center. Luxury level. **$**

⊡ 🐾 🏊 🎾 🎿 SC 🏃

★ ★ **HOTEL PERE MARQUETTE.** *501 Main St (61602). Phone 309/637-6500; toll-free 800/447-1676; fax 309/671-9445. www.hotelperemarquette.com.* 288 rooms, 12 story. Pets accepted; fee. Check-out noon. TV; cable (premium). In-room modem link. Restaurant, bar. In-house fitness room. Health club privileges. Free airport transportation. Restored 1920s hotel. **$**

D 🐾 🏋 ✈ ⛵ SC

★ ★ ★ **PEORIA CASTLE LODGE.** *117 N Western Ave (61604). Phone 309/673-8040; toll-free 800/285-8637; fax 309/673-9782. www.jumers.com.* 175 rooms, 4 story. Pets accepted; fee. Check-out noon. TV; cable (premium), VCR available. In-room modem link. Restaurant, bar; entertainment. In-house fitness room. Indoor pool; whirlpool. Valet parking. Free airport transportation. Bavarian décor. **$**

D 🐾 ⛵ 🏋 ⛵ SC

Peru

Motels/Motor Lodges

★ **ECONO LODGE.** *1840 May Rd (61354). Phone 815/224-2500; fax 815/224-3693. www.econolodge.com.* 104 rooms, 2 story. Pets accepted; fee. Complimentary continental breakfast. Check-out noon. TV. Restaurant. Pool. **$**

D 🐾 ⛵ ⛵ SC

★ **SUPER 8.** *1851 May Rd (61354). Phone 815/223-1848; toll-free 800/800-8000; fax 815/223-1848. www.super8.com.* 60 rooms, 3 story. Pets accepted, some restrictions; fee. Check-out 11 am. TV; cable (premium). Laundry services. **$**

D 🐾 ⛵ SC

Quincy

Motel/Motor Lodge

★ **TRAVELODGE.** *200 S 3rd St (62301). Phone 217/222-5620; toll-free 800/578-7878; fax 217/224-2582. www.travelodge.com.* 68 rooms, 2 story. Pets accepted; fee. Complimentary continental breakfast. Check-out noon. TV; cable (premium). Laundry services. Restaurant, bar. Room service. Pool. **$**

D 🐾 ⛵ SC

Rockford

Motels/Motor Lodges

★ **EXEL INN.** *220 S Lyford Rd (61108). Phone 815/332-4915; fax 815/332-4843. www.exelinns.com.* 100 rooms, 2

story. Pets accepted, some restrictions. Complimentary continental breakfast. Check-out noon. TV; cable (premium). In-room modem link. Laundry services. In-house fitness room. Health club privileges. **$**

D 🐾 🏋 ⛵

★ **SWEDEN HOUSE LODGE.** *4605 E State St (61108). Phone 815/398-4130; toll-free 800/886-4138; fax 815/398-9203. www.swedenhouselodge.com.* 107 rooms, 2-3 story. Pets accepted, some restrictions. Complimentary continental breakfast. Check-out noon. TV; cable (premium). In-house fitness room. Game room. Indoor pool; whirlpool. **$**

🐾 ⛵ 🏋 ⛵ SC

★ **TRAVELODGE.** *4850 E State St (61108). Phone 815/398-5050; toll-free 800/613-1234; fax 815/398-8180. www.travelodge.com.* 84 rooms, 2-3 story. Pets accepted; fee. Complimentary continental breakfast. Check-out 11 am. TV; VCR available (movies). Bar. In-house fitness room. Indoor pool; whirlpool. Rockford College adjacent. **$**

D 🐾 ⛵ 🏋 ⛵ SC

Extended Stay

★ ★ **RESIDENCE INN BY MARRIOTT.** *7542 Colosseum Dr (61107). Phone 815/227-0013; toll-free 800/331-3131; fax 815/227-0013. www.residenceinn.com.* 94 rooms, 3 story. Pets accepted; fee. Complimentary continental breakfast. Check-out noon. TV; cable (premium). In-room modem link. Laundry services. In-house fitness room. Indoor pool; whirlpool. **$**

D 🐾 ⛵ 🏋 ⛵ SC

Schaumburg

Motel/Motor Lodge

★ **LA QUINTA INN.** *1730 E Higgins Rd (60173). Phone 847/517-8484; fax 847/517-4477. www.laquinta.com.* 127 rooms, 3 story. Pets accepted. Complimentary continental breakfast. Check-out noon, check-in 3 pm. TV; cable (premium). In-room modem link. In-house fitness room. Health club privileges. Outdoor pool. **$**

D 🐾 ⛵ 🏋 ⛵

Hotel

★ ★ ★ **SCHAUMBURG MARRIOTT.** *50 N Martingale Rd (60173). Phone 847/240-0100; toll-free 800/228-9290; fax 847/240-2388. www.marriotthotels.com.* 398 rooms, 14 story. Pets accepted, some restrictions; fee. Check-out 1 pm, check-in 3 pm. TV; cable (premium). In-room modem link. Restaurant, bar. In-house fitness room; sauna. Indoor pool; outdoor pool; whirlpool; poolside service. Business center. Luxury level. **$**

Springfield

Motels/Motor Lodges

★ **BEST INN.** *500 N 1st St (62702). Phone 217/522-1100; toll-free 800/237-8466; fax 217/753-8589. www.bestinn.com.* 90 rooms, 2 story. Pets accepted; fee. Complimentary continental breakfast. Check-out 11 am. TV; cable (premium). In-room modem link. Pool. **$**

★ **COMFORT INN.** *3442 Freedom Dr (62704). Phone 217/787-2250; toll-free 800/228-5150; fax 217/787-2250. www.comfortinn.com.* 67 rooms, 2 story. Pets accepted, some restrictions; fee. Complimentary continental breakfast. Check-out 11 am. TV; cable (premium). In-room modem link. Indoor pool; whirlpool. **$**

★ **DAYS INN.** *3000 Stevenson Dr (62703). Phone 217/529-0171; toll-free 800/329-7466; fax 217/529-9431. www.daysinn.com.* 155 rooms, 2 story. Pets accepted, some restrictions; fee. Complimentary continental breakfast. Check-out noon. TV; cable (premium). Pool. Free airport transportation. **$**

★ **RED ROOF INN.** *3200 Singer Ave (62703). Phone 217/753-4302; toll-free 800/843-7663; fax 217/753-4391. www.redroof.com.* 108 rooms, 2 story. Pets accepted. Check-out noon. TV; cable (premium). In-room modem link. **$**

★ **SUPER 8.** *3675 S 6th St (62703). Phone 217/529-8898; toll-free 800/800-8000; fax 217/529-4354. www.super8.com.* 122 rooms, 3 story. Pets accepted, some restrictions; fee. Complimentary continental breakfast. Check-out 11 am. TV. **$**

Hotel

★ ★ ★ **HILTON SPRINGFIELD.** *700 E Adams (62701). Phone 217/789-1530; toll-free 800/445-8667; fax 217/789-0709. www.hilton.com.* While visiting the only skyscraper in Springfield, guests can enjoy amazing views of the city. The hotel has spacious rooms with options for both short- and long-term needs. 367 rooms, 30 story. Pets accepted, some restrictions; fee. Check-out noon. TV; cable (premium). Restaurant, bar; entertainment. In-

house fitness room. Indoor pool. Free airport transportation. Business center. Luxury level. **$**

Vandalia

Motels/Motor Lodges

★ **DAYS INN.** *1920 N Kennedy Blvd (62471). Phone 618/283-4400; toll-free 800/329-7466; fax 618/283-4240. www.daysinn.com.* 95 rooms, 2 story. Pets accepted; fee. Complimentary continental breakfast. Check-out noon, check-in 2 pm. TV; cable (premium). Game room. **$**

★ **JAY'S INN.** *720 W Gochenour St (62471). Phone 618/283-1200; fax 618/283-4588.* 21 rooms, 2 story. Pets accepted; fee. Check-out noon. TV; cable (premium). Restaurant, bar. **$**

★ **RAMADA INN.** *2707 Veterans Ave (62471). Phone 618/283-1400; fax 618/283-3465. www.ramada.com.* 61 rooms, 2 story. Pets accepted, some restrictions; fee. Complimentary breakfast. Check-out noon. TV; cable (premium), VCR available. In-house fitness room. Pool. **$**

★ **TRAVELODGE.** *1500 N 6th St (62471). Phone 618/283-2363; fax 618/283-2363. www.travelodge.com.* 44 rooms, 2 story. Pets accepted; fee. Check-out noon. TV; cable (premium). Pool. **$**

Wheeling

Resort

★ ★ ★ **MARRIOTT LINCOLNSHIRE RESORT.** *10 Marriott Dr (60069). Phone 847/634-0100; toll-free 800/228-9290; fax 847/634-1278. www.marriott.com.* 390 rooms, 3 story. Pets accepted, some restrictions; fee. Check-out noon, check-in 3 pm. TV; cable (premium). Restaurant, bar; entertainment Thurs-Sat. Room service. In-house fitness room; massage. Game room. Indoor pool; outdoor pool; children's pool; whirlpool; poolside service. Golf on premise, greens fee $68. Indoor tennis. Business center. Concierge. Luxury level. 900-seat theater-in-the-round featuring musical comedies. **$$**

Indiana

Anderson

Motels/Motor Lodges

★ **BEST INN.** *5706 S Scatterfield Rd (46013). Phone 765/644-2000; toll-free 800/237-8466; fax 765/644-2000. www.bestinn.com.* 93 rooms, 2 story. Pets accepted; fee. Complimentary continental breakfast. Check-out 1 pm. TV. **$**

⊡ 🐾 ⇙ SC

★ **ECONO LODGE.** *2205 E 59th St (46013). Phone 765/644-4422; toll-free 800/228-5150; fax 765/644-4422. www.econolodge.com.* 56 rooms, 2 story. Pets accepted; fee. Complimentary continental breakfast. Check-out 11 am. TV. Game room. Indoor pool; whirlpool. **$**

⊡ 🐾 ⇙ ⇘ SC

Auburn

Motel/Motor Lodge

★ **HOLIDAY INN EXPRESS.** *404 Touring Dr (46706). Phone 260/925-1900; fax 260/927-1138. www.holiday-inn.com.* 70 rooms, 3 story. Pets accepted, some restrictions. Complimentary continental breakfast. Check-out noon. TV; cable (premium). In-room modem link. Laundry services. Indoor pool; whirlpool. **$**

⊡ 🐾 ⇙ ⇘

Bedford

Motel/Motor Lodge

★ **MARK III.** *1709 M St (47421). Phone 812/275-5935; toll-free 888/884-5814.* 21 rooms, 2 story. Pets accepted, some restrictions. Check-out 11 am. TV; cable (premium). **$**

🐾 ⇘

Bloomington

Motel/Motor Lodge

★ **HAMPTON INN.** *2100 N Walnut (47404). Phone 812/334-2100; fax 812/334-8433. www.hamptoninn.com.* 131 rooms, 4 story. Pets accepted. Check-out noon. TV; cable (premium), VCR available. In-room modem link. Pool. Downhill, cross-country ski 12 miles. **$**

🐾 ⇙ ⇘

Columbus

Motel/Motor Lodge

★★ **HOLIDAY INN.** *2480 W Jonathan Moore Pike (47201). Phone 812/372-1541; toll-free 800/465-4329; fax 812/378-9049. www.holiday-inn.com.* 253 rooms, 2-7 story. Pets accepted, some restrictions; fee. Check-out 11 am. TV; cable (premium). In-room modem link. Restaurant, bar; entertainment. In-house fitness room; sauna. Health club privileges. Indoor pool; whirlpool. Turn-of-the-century atmosphere. Game rooms. **$**

⊡ 🐾 ⇙ 🏃

Crawfordsville

Motel/Motor Lodge

★★ **HOLIDAY INN.** *2500 N Lafayette Rd (47933). Phone 765/362-8700; toll-free 800/465-4329; fax 765/362-8700. www.holiday-inn.com.* 150 rooms, 2 story. Pets accepted, some restrictions; fee. Check-out noon. TV; cable (premium), VCR available. In-room modem link. Laundry services. Restaurant, bar. In-house fitness room. Game room. Pool. **$**

⊡ 🐾 ⇙ 🏃 ⇘

Elkhart

Motels/Motor Lodges

★ **ECONO LODGE.** *3440 Cassopolis St (46514). Phone 574/262-0540; toll-free 800/424-4777; fax 574/262-0540. www.econolodge.com.* 35 rooms, 2 story. Pets accepted; fee. Complimentary continental breakfast. Check-out 11 am. TV; cable (premium), VCR available. Coin laundry. **$**

⊡ 🐾 ⇘ SC

★ **KNIGHTS INN.** *3252 Cassopolis St (46514). Phone 574/264-4262; toll-free 800/843-5644; fax 574/264-4262. www.knightsinn.com.* 118 rooms. Pets accepted, some restrictions; fee. Check-out 11 am. TV; cable (premium). In-room modem link. Pool. **$**

D ◆ ≋ ⊠

★ **QUALITY INN.** *3321 Plaza Ct (46514). Phone 574/264-0404; fax 574/264-0404. www.qualityinn.com.* 54 rooms, 2 story. Pets accepted. Complimentary continental breakfast. Check-out 11 am. TV; cable (premium). Pool. **$**

D ◆ ≋ ⊠

★ ★ **RAMADA INN.** *3011 Belvedere Rd (46514). Phone 574/262-1581; toll-free 888/298-2054; fax 574/262-1590. www.ramada.com.* 145 rooms, 2 story. Pets accepted, some restrictions. Complimentary continental breakfast. Check-out noon. TV; cable (premium), VCR available. In-room modem link. Restaurant, bar. Room service. Sauna. Game room. Indoor pool; outdoor pool; whirlpool; poolside service. Downhill ski 10 miles, cross-country 5 miles. Business center. **$**

D ◆ ≈ ≋ SC ⚘

★ **RED ROOF INN.** *2902 Cassopolis St (46514). Phone 574/262-3691; toll-free 800/733-7663; fax 574/262-3695. www.redroof.com.* 80 rooms, 2 story. Pets accepted, some restrictions. Check-out noon. TV; cable (premium). Downhill ski 20 miles. **$**

D ◆ ≋ ⊠

Evansville

Motels/Motor Lodges

★ **DRURY INN.** *3901 US 41 N (47711). Phone 812/423-5818; toll-free 800/378-7946; fax 812/423-5818. www.drury-inn.com.* 151 rooms, 4 story. Pets accepted, some restrictions. Complimentary continental breakfast. Check-out noon. TV; cable. In-room modem link. Laundry services. In-house fitness room. Indoor pool; whirlpool. **$**

D ◆ ≋ ⚘ ⊠

★ **ECONO LODGE.** *5006 E Morgan Ave (47715). Phone 812/477-2211. www.econolodge.com.* 52 rooms, 3 story. Pets accepted, some restrictions. Complimentary continental breakfast. Check-out 11 am. TV. Game room. Indoor pool; whirlpool. **$**

D ◆ ≋ ⊠

Fort Wayne

Hotel

★ ★ ★ **MARRIOTT FORT WAYNE.** *305 E Washington Center Rd (46825). Phone 260/484-0411; toll-free 800/228-9290; fax 260/483-2892. www.marriott.com.* 222 rooms, 2-6 story. Pets accepted, some restrictions; fee. Check-out noon. TV; cable (premium). In-room modem link. Laundry services. Restaurant, bar. Room service. In-house fitness room. Game room. Indoor pool; outdoor pool; whirlpool; poolside service. Lawn games. Free airport transportation. **$$**

◆ ≋ ⚘ ✈ ⊠

Extended Stay

★ ★ **RESIDENCE INN BY MARRIOTT.** *4919 Lima Rd (46808). Phone 260/484-4700; toll-free 800/331-3131; fax 260/484-9772. www.residenceinn.com.* 80 kitchen units, 2 story. Pets accepted; fee. Complimentary continental breakfast. Check-out noon. TV; cable (premium), VCR available. Pool. **$**

◆ ≋

French Lick

Motel/Motor Lodge

★ **LANE MOTEL.** *8483 W Hwy 56 (47432). Phone 812/936-9919; fax 812/936-7857.* 43 rooms. Pets accepted; fee. Check-out 11 am. TV; cable (premium). Pool. **$**

D ◆ ≋

Goshen

Motel/Motor Lodge

★ ★ **BEST WESTERN INN.** *900 Lincolnway E (46526). Phone 574/533-0408; toll-free 800/780-7234; fax 574/533-0408. www.bestwestern.com.* 77 rooms, 2 story. Pets accepted, some restrictions. Complimentary continental breakfast. Check-out 11 am. TV; cable (premium), VCR available. In-room modem link. In-house fitness room. **$**

D ◆ ⚘ ⊠

Greenfield

Motel/Motor Lodge

★ **LEES INN.** *2270 N State St (46140). Phone 317/462-7112; toll-free 800/733-5337; fax 317/462-9801. www.leesinn.com.* 100 rooms, 2 story. Pets accepted, some restrictions. Complimentary continental breakfast. Check-out noon. TV. **$**

Hammond

Motel/Motor Lodge

★★ **BEST WESTERN NORTHWEST INDIANA INN.** *3830 179th St (46323). Phone 219/844-2140; fax 219/845-7760. www.bestwestern.com.* 154 rooms, 4 story. Pets accepted; fee. Check-out noon. TV; cable (premium). In-room modem link. Laundry services. Restaurant, bar. Room service. In-house fitness room. Pool; poolside service. Luxury level. **$**

Indianapolis

Motels/Motor Lodges

★ **DRURY INN.** *9320 N Michigan Rd (46268). Phone 317/876-9777; toll-free 800/378-7946; fax 317/876-9777. www.druryinn.com.* 110 rooms, 4 story. Pets accepted, some restrictions. Complimentary breakfast. Check-out noon. TV; cable (premium). In-room modem link. Pool. **$**

★★ **HOLIDAY INN.** *6990 E 21st St (46219). Phone 317/359-5341; toll-free 800/465-4329; fax 317/351-1666. www.holiday-inn.com.* 184 rooms, 6 story. Pets accepted, some restrictions. Complimentary full breakfast. Check-out noon. TV; cable (premium). In-room modem link. Coin laundry. Restaurant, bar. Room service. In-house fitness room. Game room. Indoor pool; whirlpool. **$**

★ **HOMEWOOD SUITES.** *2501 E 86th St (46240). Phone 317/253-1919; toll-free 800/225-5466; fax 317/255-8223. www.homewoodsuites.com.* 116 rooms, 3 story. Pets accepted; fee. Complimentary continental breakfast. Check-out noon, check-in 3 pm. TV; cable (premium), VCR available. In-room modem link. Laundry services.

In-house fitness room; sauna. Pool; whirlpool. Business center. **$**

★ **LA QUINTA INN.** *7304 E 21st St (46219). Phone 317/359-1021; fax 317/359-0578. www.laquinta.com.* 122 rooms, 2 story. Pets accepted. Check-out noon. TV; cable (premium). Laundry services. Heated pool. **$**

Hotel

★★★ **MARRIOTT INDIANAPOLIS EAST.** *7202 E 21st St (46219). Phone 317/352-1231; fax 317/352-9775. www.marriott.com.* 252 rooms, 3-5 story. Pets accepted, some restrictions; fee. Check-out noon. TV; VCR available. In-room modem link. Laundry services. Restaurant, bar. Room service. In-house fitness room. Indoor pool; outdoor pool; children's pool; whirlpool; poolside service. Business center. Luxury level. **$**

Jasper

Motel/Motor Lodge

★ **DAYS INN.** *IN 162 and IN 164 (47546). Phone 812/482-6000; fax 812/482-7207. www.daysinn.com.* 84 rooms, 2 story. Pets accepted; fee. Complimentary continental breakfast. Check-out noon. TV; cable (premium), VCR available. Pool. **$**

Jeffersonville

Motels/Motor Lodges

★ **BEST WESTERN GREEN TREE INN.** *1425 Broadway (47129). Phone 812/288-9281; toll-free 800/950-9281; fax 812/288-9281. www.bestwestern.com.* 107 rooms. Pets accepted, some restrictions. Check-out noon. TV; cable (premium). In-room modem link. Pool. **$**

★★ **RAMADA INN.** *700 W Riverside Dr (47130). Phone 812/284-6711; toll-free 888/298-2054; fax 812/283-3686. www.ramada.com.* 187 rooms, 10 story. Pets accepted; fee. Check-out noon. TV; cable (premium). Restaurant, bar. Game room. Pool. Free airport transportation. On the Ohio River. **$**

Kokomo

Motels/Motor Lodges

★ **HAMPTON INN.** *2920 S Reed Rd (46902). Phone 765/455-2900; toll-free 800/426-7866; fax 765/455-2800. www.hampton-inn.com.* 105 rooms, 5 story. Pets accepted, some restrictions. Complimentary continental breakfast. TV; cable (premium), VCR available (movies). In-room modem link. Laundry services. Health club privileges. In-house fitness room. Indoor pool. **$**

D 🐾 ➰ 🏃 ⊠ SC

★ **MOTEL 6.** *2808 S Reed Rd (46902). Phone 765/457-8211; toll-free 800/466-8356; fax 765/454-9774. www.motel6.com.* 93 rooms, 2 story. Pets accepted. Check-out noon. TV; cable. **$**

D 🐾 ⊠

Lafayette

All Suite

★ **HOMEWOOD SUITES.** *3939 IN 26 E (47905). Phone 765/448-9700; toll-free 800/225-5466; fax 765/449-1297. www.homewood-suites.com.* 84 rooms, 3 story. Pets accepted, some restrictions; fee. Complimentary continental breakfast. Check-out noon. TV; VCR (movies). In-room modem link. Laundry services. In-house fitness room; sauna. Health club privileges. Pool; whirlpool. Lawn games. Free airport transportation. Business center. **$**

D 🐾 ➰ 🏃 ⊠ 🚶

Motel/Motor Lodge

★★ **RAMADA INN.** *4221 IN 26 E (47905). Phone 765/447-9460; toll-free 800/272-6232; fax 765/447-4905. www.ramada.com.* 143 rooms, 4 story. Pets accepted, some restrictions; fee. Complimentary continental breakfast. Check-out noon. TV; VCR available (movies). In-room modem link. Laundry services. Restaurant, bar. Room service. In-house fitness room. Pool. Lawn games. **$**

D 🐾 ➰ 🏃 ⊠ SC

Hotel

★★★ **RADISSON INN.** *4343 IN 26 E (47905). Phone 765/447-0575; toll-free 800/333-3333; fax 765/447-0901. www.radisson.com.* 124 rooms, 6 story. Pets accepted, some restrictions; fee. Check-out noon. TV; cable (premium). In-room modem link. Laundry services. Restaurant, bar. Room service. Sauna. Indoor pool; whirlpool. **$**

D 🐾 ➰ ⊠ SC

B&B/Small Inn

★★ **LOEB HOUSE B&B.** *708 Cincinnati St (47901). Phone 765/420-7737; fax 765/420-7805. www.loebhouseinn.com.* 5 rooms, 3 story. No elevator. Pets accepted, some restrictions. Complimentary full breakfast. Check-out 11 am, check-in 4 pm. TV. In-room modem link. Built in 1882; antiques. Totally nonsmoking. **$**

🐾 ⊠

Logansport

Motel/Motor Lodge

★★ **HOLIDAY INN.** *3550 E Market St (46947). Phone 574/753-6351; fax 574/722-1568. www.holiday-inn.com.* 95 rooms, 2 story. Pets accepted. Check-out noon. TV. Restaurant, bar. Pool. Free airport transportation. **$**

D 🐾 ➰ ⊠ SC

Marion

Motel/Motor Lodge

★ **COMFORT INN.** *1345 N Baldwin Ave (46952). Phone 765/651-1006; toll-free 800/445-1210; fax 765/651-0145. www.choicehotels.com.* 62 rooms. Pets accepted, some restrictions; fee. Complimentary continental breakfast. Check-out noon, check-in 3 pm. TV; cable (premium). In-room modem link. In-house fitness room; sauna. Indoor pool; outdoor pool; whirlpool. **$**

🐾 ➰ 🏃 ⊠

Merrillville

Motel/Motor Lodge

★ **RED ROOF INN.** *8290 Georgia St (46410). Phone 219/738-2430; toll-free 800/733-7663; fax 219/738-2436. www.redroof.com.* 108 rooms, 2 story. Pets accepted. Check-out noon. TV; cable (premium). In-room modem link. **$**

D 🐾 ⊠

Michigan City

Motels/Motor Lodges

★ **KNIGHTS INN.** *201 W Kieffer Rd (46360). Phone 219/874-9500; toll-free 800/843-5644; fax 219/874-5122. www.knightsinn.com.* 103 rooms. Pets accepted; fee. Check-out 11 am. TV; cable (premium). Pool. **$**

D ◧ ≋ ◩

★ **RED ROOF INN.** *110 W Kieffer Rd (46360). Phone 219/874-5251; toll-free 800/733-7663; fax 219/874-5287. www.redroof.com.* 79 rooms, 2 story. Pets accepted. Check-out noon, check-in 1 pm. TV; cable (premium). In-room modem link. **$**

D ◧ ◩

Muncie

Motels/Motor Lodges

★ **DAYS INN.** *3509 N Everbrook Ln (47304). Phone 765/288-2311; fax 765/288-0485. www.daysinn.com.* 62 rooms, 2 story. Pets accepted; fee. Complimentary continental breakfast. Check-out 11 am. TV. **$**

D ◧ ◩

★ **LEES INN AND SUITES.** *3302 N Everbrook Ln (47304). Phone 765/282-7557; toll-free 800/733-5337; fax 765/282-0345.* 92 rooms, 2 story. Pets accepted, some restrictions. Complimentary continental breakfast. Check-out noon. In-house fitness room. Pool; whirlpool. **$**

D ◧ ≋ ⑂ ◩

★★ **RAMADA INN.** *3400 S Madison St (47302). Phone 765/288-1911; toll-free 800/272-6232; fax 765/282-9458. www.ramada.com.* 148 rooms, 2 story. Pets accepted, some restrictions; fee. Complimentary continental breakfast. Check-out noon. TV; cable (premium), VCR available. Laundry services. Restaurant, bar; entertainment. Room service. Pool. **$**

D ◧ ≋ ◩ SC

Hotel

★★★ **RADISSON HOTEL ROBERTS.** *420 S High St (47305). Phone 765/741-7777; toll-free 800/333-3333; fax 765/747-0067. www.radisson.com.* Built in 1921, this hotel offers lots of history and culture along with modern amenities and facilities. It is located in downtown Muncie, near many attractions, restaurants, and shops. 130 rooms, 7 story. Pets accepted, some restrictions; fee. Check-out noon. TV; cable (premium). Room service 24 hours. Restaurant, bar; entertainment. Indoor pool; whirlpool. **$**

D ◧ ≋ ◩

Nashville

Motel/Motor Lodge

★ **SALT CREEK INN.** *551 E IN 46 (47448). Phone 812/988-1149; fax 812/988-1149.* 66 rooms, 2 story. Pets accepted; fee. Check-out 11 am. TV. Downhill ski 5 miles. **$**

D ◧ ◧ ◩ SC

Plymouth

Motel/Motor Lodge

★★ **RAMADA INN.** *2550 N Michigan St (46563). Phone 574/936-4013; toll-free 800/272-6232; fax 574/936-4553. www.ramada.com.* 108 rooms, 2 story. Pets accepted; fee. Check-out noon. TV; cable (premium). In-room modem link. Laundry services. Restaurant, bar. Room service. Pool. **$**

D ◧ ≋ ◩

Richmond

Motel/Motor Lodge

★ **LEES INN AND SUITES.** *6030 National Rd E (47374). Phone 765/966-6559; toll-free 800/733-5337; fax 765/966-7732.* 91 rooms, 2 story. Pets accepted. Complimentary continental breakfast. Check-out noon. TV; cable (premium), VCR available. **$**

D ◧ ◩ SC

South Bend

Motel/Motor Lodge

★★ **HOLIDAY INN.** *515 Dixie Hwy N (46637). Phone 574/272-6600; toll-free 800/465-4329; fax 574/272-5553. www.holiday-inn.com.* 220 rooms, 2 story. Pets accepted; fee. Complimentary continental breakfast. Check-out 11 am. TV; cable (premium). Laundry services. Restaurant, bar. Room service. In-house fitness room; sauna. Game room. Indoor pool; outdoor pool; children's pool; whirlpool. Free airport transportation. **$**

D ◧ ≋ ⑂ ✈ ◩

B&B/Small Inn

★ ★ **OLIVER INN BED & BREAKFAST.** *630 W Washington St (46601). Phone 574/232-4545; toll-free 888/697-4466; fax 574/288-9788. www.oliverinn.com.* 9 rooms, 3 story. Pets accepted, some restrictions; fee. Complimentary continental breakfast. Check-out 11 am, check-in 4-6 pm. TV; cable (premium). Downhill, cross-country ski 20 miles. Lawn games. Airport transportation. Built in 1886; Victorian décor. Totally nonsmoking. **$$**

D ☎ ⌇ ⊠

Extended Stay

★ ★ **RESIDENCE INN BY MARRIOTT.** *716 N Niles Ave (46617). Phone 574/289-5555; fax 574/288-4531. www.marriott.com.* 80 rooms, 2 story. Pets accepted; fee. Complimentary continental breakfast. Check-out noon. TV; cable (premium), VCR available (movies). Laundry services. In-house fitness room. Pool; whirlpool. **$**

D ☎ ⌇ 🏃 ⊠

Terre Haute

Motels/Motor Lodges

★ **DRURY INN.** *3050 S US 41 (47802). Phone 812/234-4268; toll-free 800/282-8733; fax 812/234-4268.* 64 rooms, 4 story. Pets accepted, some restrictions. Check-out noon. TV; cable (premium). **$**

D ☎ ⊠ SC

★ ★ **HOLIDAY INN.** *3300 US 41 S (47802). Phone 812/232-6081; toll-free 800/465-4329; fax 812/238-9934. www.holiday-inn.com.* 230 rooms, 2-5 story. Pets accepted, some restrictions. Check-out noon. TV; cable (premium). In-room modem link. Laundry services. Restaurant, bar. Room service. In-house fitness room. Indoor pool; whirlpool. **$**

D ☎ ⌇ 🏃 ⊠ SC

Warsaw

Motel/Motor Lodge

★ ★ **RAMADA INN.** *2519 E Center St (46580). Phone 574/269-2323; toll-free 800/272-6232; fax 574/269-2432. www.ramada.com.* 156 rooms, 4 story. Pets accepted. Check-out noon. TV; VCR available. In-room modem link. Laundry services. Restaurant, bar. Room service. In-house fitness room; sauna. Game room. Indoor pool; outdoor pool; whirlpool; poolside service. **$**

D ☎ ⌇ 🏃 ✈ ⊠

Iowa

Algona

Motel/Motor Lodge

★ **BURR OAK.** *IA 169 S (50511). Phone 515/295-7213; toll-free 877/745-6315; fax 515/295-2979. www.burroakmotel.com.* 40 rooms. Pets accepted; fee. Complimentary continental breakfast. Check-out 10 am. TV; cable (premium). **$**

D 🐾 🏊

Amana Colonies

Motels/Motor Lodges

★ ★ **BEST WESTERN QUIET HOUSE & SUITES.** *1708 N Highland St (52361). Phone 319/668-9777; fax 319/668-9770. www.bestwestern.com.* 33 rooms, 2 story. Pets accepted; fee. Complimentary continental breakfast. TV; cable (premium). In-house fitness room. Indoor pool; outdoor pool; whirlpool. **$**

D 🐾 🏊 🏋 🏊

★ ★ **HOLIDAY INN.** *2211 U Ave (52361). Phone 319/668-1175; toll-free 800/633-9244; fax 319/668-2853. www.amanaholidayinn.com.* 155 rooms, 2 story. Pets accepted. Check-out 11 am. TV; cable (premium). Restaurant, bar. Room service. In-house fitness room; sauna. Game room. Indoor pool; children's pool; whirlpool; poolside service. Little Amana complex adjacent; old-time general store and winery. **$**

🐾 🏊 🏋

★ **SUPER 8.** *2228 U Ave (52361). Phone 319/668-2800; toll-free 800/800-8000. www.super8.com.* 63 rooms, 2 story. Pets accepted, some restrictions; fee. Complimentary continental breakfast. Check-out 11 am. TV; cable (premium). **$**

D 🐾 🏊 SC

Ames

Motels/Motor Lodges

★ **BAYMONT INN.** *2500 Elwood Dr (50010). Phone 515/296-2500; fax 515/296-2874. www.baymontinns.com.*

89 rooms, 2 story. Pets accepted. Complimentary continental breakfast. Check-out noon. TV; cable (premium). Indoor pool; whirlpool. **$**

🐾 🏊

★ ★ **BEST WESTERN STARLITE VILLAGE.** *2601 E 13th St (50010). Phone 515/232-9260; toll-free 800/903-0009; fax 515/232-9260. www.bestwestern.com.* 131 rooms, 3 story. Pets accepted, some restrictions. Check-out noon. TV; cable (premium), VCR available. Restaurant, bar. Room service. Sauna. Game room. Indoor pool; whirlpool. **$**

D 🐾 🏊 🏊 SC

★ **COMFORT INN.** *1605 S Dayton Ave (50010). Phone 515/232-0689. www.comfortinn.com.* 52 rooms, 2 story. Pets accepted, some restrictions; fee. Complimentary continental breakfast. Check-out 11 am. TV. Indoor pool; whirlpool. **$**

🐾 🏊

★ ★ **THE HOTEL AT GATEWAY CENTER.** *US Hwy 30 and Elwood Dr (50010). Phone 515/292-8600; fax 515/268-2224. www.thegatewayames.com.* 188 rooms, 8 story. Pets accepted. Check-out noon. TV; cable (premium), VCR available. In-room modem link. Restaurant, bar. Room service. In-house fitness room; sauna. Indoor pool; whirlpool. Free airport transportation. Business center. **$**

D 🐾 🏊 🏋 ✈ 🏊 🚶

Atlantic

Motel/Motor Lodge

★ **ECONO LODGE.** *Jct US 71 and I-80, exit 60 (50022). Phone 712/243-4067; fax 712/243-1713. www.econolodge.com.* 51 rooms, 1-2 story. Pets accepted, some restrictions. Check-out 11 am. TV. Pool. **$**

D 🐾 🏊 🏊

Bettendorf

Hotel

★ ★ **JUMERS CASTLE LODGE.** *900 Spruce Hills Dr (52722). Phone 563/359-7141; toll-free 800/285-8637. www.jumers.com.* At this upscale hotel, guests will find surroundings adorned with rich tapestries, fine antiques, and grand elegance. Guest rooms have four-poster beds and will please guests with luxurious comfort. The award-winning restaurant serves both American and German cuisine. 210 rooms. Pets accepted, some restrictions; fee. Check-out noon. TV; cable (premium). Bar;

entertainment. In-house fitness room; sauna. Health club privileges. Indoor pool; outdoor pool; whirlpool. Lawn games. Free airport transportation. **$**

D 🛏 🏊 🏃 ✈ 🖺

Burlington

Motels/Motor Lodges

★ ★ **BEST WESTERN PZAZZ MOTOR INN.** *3001 Winegard Dr (52601). Phone 319/753-2223; toll-free 800/373-1223; fax 319/753-2224. www.bestwestern.com.* 151 rooms, 3 story. Pets accepted. Check-out noon. TV; cable (premium), VCR available. In-room modem link. Restaurant, bar; entertainment. Room service. In-house fitness room; sauna. Game room. Indoor pool; whirlpool. Airport transportation. **$**

D 🛏 🏊 🏃 ✈ 🖺

★ **COMFORT INN.** *3051 Kirkwood (52601). Phone 319/753-0000; toll-free 800/228-5150. www.comfortinn.com.* 52 rooms, 2 story. Pets accepted, some restrictions; fee. Complimentary continental breakfast. Check-out 11 am. TV; cable (premium). In-room modem link. Pool. **$**

D 🛏 🏊 🖺 SC

Cedar Rapids

Motels/Motor Lodges

★ ★ **BEST WESTERN COOPER'S MILL HOTEL.** *100 F Ave NW (52405). Phone 319/366-5323; toll-free 800/858-5511. www.bestwestern.com.* 86 rooms, 4 story. Pets accepted; fee. Check-out noon. TV; cable (premium). In-room modem link. Restaurant, bar. Room service. **$**

🛏 SC

★ ★ **CLARION HOTEL.** *525 33rd Ave SW (52404). Phone 319/366-8671; fax 319/362-1420. www.sheratoncr.com.* 157 rooms, 6 story. Pets accepted; fee. Check-out noon. TV; cable (premium). In-room modem link. Restaurant, bar; entertainment. Room service. In-house fitness room; sauna. Game room. Indoor pool; whirlpool; poolside service. Free airport transportation. **$**

D 🛏 🏊 🏃 ✈ 🖺 SC

★ **COMFORT INN.** *5055 Rockwell Dr (52402). Phone 319/393-8247. www.comfortinn.com.* 59 rooms, 2 story. Pets accepted, some restrictions. Complimentary continental breakfast. Check-out 11 am. TV; cable (premium), VCR available. In-room modem link. **$**

D 🛏 🖺

★ **COMFORT INN.** *390 33rd Ave SW (52404). Phone 319/363-7934; toll-free 800/228-5150. www.comfortinn.com.* 60 rooms, 3 story. Pets accepted, some restrictions. Complimentary continental breakfast. Check-out 11 am. TV; cable (premium). **$**

D 🛏 🖺 SC

★ **DAYS INN.** *3245 Southgate Place SW (52404). Phone 319/365-4339. www.daysinn.com.* 42 rooms, 2 story. Pets accepted, some restrictions; fee. Complimentary continental breakfast. Check-out 11 am. TV. In-room modem link. Indoor pool; whirlpool. **$**

D 🛏 🏊 🖺 SC

Clear Lake

Motel/Motor Lodge

★ ★ **BEST WESTERN HOLIDAY LODGE.** *I-35 S (50428). Phone 641/357-5253; toll-free 800/606-3552; fax 641/357-8153. www.bestwestern.com.* 138 rooms, 5 story. Pets accepted, some restrictions; fee. Complimentary breakfast. Check-out 11 am. TV. Restaurant. Room service. Sauna. Indoor pool; whirlpool. Free airport transportation. **$**

🛏 🏊 ✈ 🖺 SC

Clinton

Motels/Motor Lodges

★ ★ **BEST WESTERN FRONTIER MOTOR INN.** *2300 Lincoln Way St (52732). Phone 563/242-7112; toll-free 800/728-7112; fax 563/242-7117. www.bestwestern.com.* 113 rooms, 1-2 story. Pets accepted; fee. Check-out noon. TV; cable (premium). Restaurant, bar. Room service. In-house fitness room. Indoor pool; whirlpool. Cross-country ski 5 miles. **$**

D 🛏 🏊 🏃

★ **RAMADA INN.** *1522 Lincoln Way (52734). Phone 563/243-8841; fax 563/242-6202. www.ramada.com.* 115 rooms, 2 story. Pets accepted, some restrictions; fee. Check-out noon. TV; cable (premium), VCR available. Bar. Room service. Game room. Indoor pool. **$**

D 🛏 🏊 🖺

Council Bluffs

Motel/Motor Lodge

★ ★ **QUALITY INN.** *3537 W Broadway (51501). Phone 712/328-3171; fax 712/328-2205. www.qualityinn.com.* 89 rooms, 2 story. Pets accepted, some restrictions.

Complimentary continental breakfast. Check-out noon. TV; cable (premium). In-room modem link. Restaurant. Indoor pool. Free airport transportation. **$**

D 🐾 ≈ ✈ ⋈

Davenport

Motels/Motor Lodges

★ ★ **BEST WESTERN STEEPLEGATE INN.** *100 W 76th St (52806). Phone 563/386-6900; toll-free 800/373-6900; fax 563/388-9955. www.bestwestern.com.* 121 rooms, 2 story. Pets accepted; fee. Check-out noon. TV; cable (premium). Restaurant, bar; entertainment. Room service. In-house fitness room. Game room. Indoor pool; whirlpool. Free airport transportation. **$**

D 🐾 ≈ 🏋 ✈ ⋈ SC

★ **COMFORT INN.** *7222 Northwest Blvd (52806). Phone 563/391-8222; fax 563/391-1595. www.comfortinn.com.* 89 rooms, 2 story. Pets accepted; fee. Complimentary continental breakfast. Check-out 11 am. TV; cable (premium), VCR available. In-house fitness room. **$**

D 🐾 🏋 ⋈

★ **HAMPTON INN.** *3330 E Kimberly Rd (52807). Phone 563/359-3921; toll-free 800/426-7866; fax 563/359-1912. www.hamptoninn.com.* 132 rooms, 2 story. Pets accepted, some restrictions; fee. Complimentary continental breakfast. Check-out noon. TV; cable (premium). In-room modem link. In-house fitness room. Indoor pool. Free airport transportation. **$**

D 🐾 ≈ 🏋 ⋈ SC

★ **SUPER 8.** *410 E 65th St (52807). Phone 563/388-9810. www.super8.com.* 61 rooms, 2 story. Pets accepted, some restrictions; fee. Complimentary continental breakfast. Check-out 11 am. TV; cable (premium). **$**

D 🐾 SC

Decorah

Motel/Motor Lodge

★ **SUPER 8.** *810 Hwy 9 E (52101). Phone 563/382-8771; toll-free 800/800-8000. www.super8.com.* 60 rooms, 2 story. Pets accepted, some restrictions. Complimentary continental breakfast. Check-out 11 am. TV; cable (premium), VCR available. In-room modem link. **$**

D 🐾 ⋈ SC

Des Moines

Motels/Motor Lodges

★ ★ **BEST INN.** *5050 Merle Hay Rd (50131). Phone 515/270-1111; fax 515/331-2142. www.bestinn.com.* 91 rooms, 2 story. Pets accepted; fee. Complimentary continental breakfast. Check-out 1 pm. TV; cable (premium), VCR available. Indoor pool; whirlpool. **$**

D 🐾 ≈ ⋈ SC

★ ★ **BEST WESTERN STARLITE VILLAGE OF ANKENY.** *133 SE Delaware Ave (50021). Phone 515/964-1717; toll-free 800/903-0009; fax 515/964-8781. www.bestwestern.com.* 116 rooms, 2 story. Pets accepted, some restrictions; fee. TV. Restaurant, bar. Room service. Indoor pool; whirlpool. **$**

D 🐾 ≈ ⋈ SC

★ **COMFORT INN.** *5231 Fleur Dr (50321). Phone 515/287-3434. www.comfortinn.com.* 55 rooms, 3 story. No elevator. Pets accepted, some restrictions; fee. Complimentary continental breakfast. Check-out 11 am. TV; cable (premium). In-room modem link. Indoor pool; whirlpool. Free airport transportation. **$**

D 🐾 ≈ ✈ ⋈ SC

★ **HEARTLAND INN DES MOINES WEST.** *11414 Forest Ave (50325). Phone 515/226-0414; toll-free 800/334-3277; fax 515/226-9769. www.heartlandinns.com.* 87 rooms, 2 story. Pets accepted, some restrictions; fee. Complimentary continental breakfast. Check-out 11 am. TV; cable (premium). Sauna. **$**

D 🐾 ⋈

★ **MOTEL 6.** *3225 Adventureland Dr (50009). Phone 515/967-5252; fax 515/957-8637. www.motel6.com.* 110 rooms, 2 story. Pets accepted, some restrictions. Check-out 11 am. TV; cable (premium). Indoor pool; whirlpool. **$**

D 🐾 ≈ ⋈ SC

★ ★ **RAMADA INN.** *5055 Merle Hay Rd (50131). Phone 515/276-5411; toll-free 888/298-2054; fax 515/276-0696. www.ramada.com.* 146 rooms. Pets accepted; fee. Check-out noon. TV; cable (premium). Restaurant, bar. Indoor pool; whirlpool. Free airport transportation. **$**

D 🐾 ≈ ⋈ SC

Hotels

★ ★ **HOTEL FORT DES MOINES.** *1000 Walnut St (50309). Phone 515/243-1161; toll-free 800/532-1466; fax 515/243-4317. www.hotelfortdesmoines.com.* This historic hotel, restored to its original beauty, has always been popular in Des Moines. With beautiful facilities for both meetings and social events, the grand style here captures its rich history and architectural wonder. 242 rooms, 11 story. Pets accepted. Check-out noon. TV; cable. In-room modem link. Restaurant, bar. In-house fitness room. Pool; whirlpool. Free airport transportation. **$**

★★★ **MARRIOTT DES MOINES.** *700 Grand Ave (50309). Phone 515/245-5500; fax 515/245-5567. www.marriott.com.* Busy travelers have come to rely on this modern hotel suited to meet every need. Conveniently located in the financial district. 415 rooms, 33 story. Pets accepted, some restrictions. Check-out noon. TV; cable (premium), VCR available. Restaurant, bar. In-house fitness room; sauna. Indoor pool; whirlpool; poolside service. Valet parking; fee. Free airport transportation. Luxury level. **$**

★★★ **MARRIOTT WEST DES MOINES.** *1250 74th Ave (50266). Phone 515/267-1500; fax 515/223-1687. www.marriott.com.* 219 rooms, 9 story. Pets accepted; fee. Check-out noon. TV; cable (premium), VCR available. Restaurant. In-house fitness room. Indoor pool. Business center. **$**

Dubuque

Motels/Motor Lodges

★★ **BEST WESTERN MIDWAY HOTEL.** *3100 Dodge St (52003). Phone 563/556-7760; toll-free 800/336-4392; fax 563/557-7692. www.midwayhotels.com.* 149 rooms, 4 story. Pets accepted, some restrictions; fee. Complimentary breakfast buffet. Check-out 1 pm. TV; VCR (movies). In-room modem link. Restaurant, bar. Room service. In-house fitness room; sauna. Game room. Indoor pool; whirlpool. Free airport transportation. **$**

★ **COMFORT INN.** *4055 McDonald Dr (52003). Phone 563/556-3006. www.comfortinn.com.* 52 rooms, 3 story. Pets accepted, some restrictions. Complimentary continental breakfast. Check-out 11 am. TV; cable (premium). In-room modem link. Indoor pool; whirlpool. Downhill ski 6 miles, cross-country ski 5 miles. **$**

★ **DAYS INN.** *1111 Dodge St (52003). Phone 563/583-3297; toll-free 800/772-3297; fax 563/583-5900. www.daysinn.com.* 154 rooms, 2 story. Pets accepted, some restrictions; fee. Complimentary continental breakfast. Check-out 11 am. TV; cable (premium), VCR available.

Restaurant, bar. In-house fitness room. Pool. Free airport transportation. **$**

★★ **HOLIDAY INN.** *450 Main St (52001). Phone 563/556-2000; toll-free 800/465-4329; fax 563/556-2303.* 193 rooms, 5 story. Pets accepted, some restrictions; fee. Check-out noon. TV; cable (premium), VCR available. Restaurant, bar. Room service. In-house fitness room. Indoor pool. Free airport transportation. Business center. **$**

★ **SUPER 8.** *2730 Dodge St; Hwy 20 (52003). Phone 563/582-8898; toll-free 800/800-8000. www.super8.com.* 61 rooms, 3 story. No elevator. Pets accepted, some restrictions; fee. Complimentary continental breakfast. Check-out 11 am. TV; cable (premium). Downhill ski 7 miles. **$**

★★ **TIMMERMAN'S HOTEL & RESORT.** *7777 Timmerman Dr (61025). Phone 815/747-3181; toll-free 800/336-3181; fax 815/747-6556. www.timmermanhotel.com.* 74 rooms, 3 story. Pets accepted, some restrictions; fee. Complimentary continental breakfast. Check-out noon. TV; VCR (movies). In-room modem link. Restaurant, bar. Room service. Sauna. Game room. Indoor pool; whirlpool. Downhill ski 10 miles, cross-country ski 1/4 mile. **$**

Fairfield

Motel/Motor Lodge

★★ **BEST WESTERN FAIRFIELD INN.** *2200 W Burlington Ave (52556). Phone 641/472-2200; toll-free 800/528-1234; fax 641/472-7642. www.bestwestern.com.* 52 rooms, 2 story. Pets accepted. Complimentary continental breakfast. Check-out noon. TV. Restaurant. Indoor pool; whirlpool. **$**

Fort Madison

Motel/Motor Lodge

★ **MADISON INN.** *3440 Ave L (52627). Phone 319/372-7740; toll-free 800/728-7316; fax 319/372-1315. www.madisoninnmotel.com.* 20 rooms. Pets accepted, some restrictions; fee. Check-out 11 am. TV; cable (premium). In-room modem link. **$**

Grinnell

Motels/Motor Lodges

★ **DAYS INN.** *1902 West St S (50112). Phone 641/236-6710; toll-free 800/325-2525; fax 641/236-5783. www.daysinn.com.* 41 rooms, 2 story. Pets accepted, some restrictions; fee. Complimentary continental breakfast. Check-out 11 am. TV. Indoor pool. **$**

D 🐾 ≋ 🚫 SC

★ **SUPER 8.** *2111 West St S (50112). Phone 641/236-7888; toll-free 800/800-8000. www.super8.com.* 53 rooms, 2 story. Pets accepted, some restrictions; fee. Complimentary continental breakfast. Check-out 11 am. TV; cable (premium). **$**

D 🐾 ≋ SC

Hampton

Motel/Motor Lodge

★ **GOLD KEY.** *1570 B US 65N (50441). Phone 641/456-2566; fax 641/456-3622.* 20 rooms. Pets accepted, some restrictions. Check-out 11 am. TV. **$**

D 🐾 ⚡ 🏋 🚫

Marshalltown

Motel/Motor Lodge

★ **COMFORT INN.** *2613 S Center St (50158). Phone 641/752-6000; fax 641/752-8762. www.comfortinn.com.* 62 rooms, 2 story. Pets accepted, some restrictions; fee. Complimentary full breakfast. Check-out noon. TV; cable (premium). Indoor pool; whirlpool. **$**

D 🐾 ≋ 🚫

Mason City

Motel/Motor Lodge

★ **DAYS INN.** *2301 4th St SW (50401). Phone 641/424-0210; toll-free 800/329-7466; fax 641/424-5284. www.daysinn.com.* 58 rooms, 2 story. Pets accepted. Complimentary continental breakfast. Check-out noon. TV. **$**

D 🐾 ≋ SC

Mount Pleasant

Motel/Motor Lodge

★ **HEARTLAND INN.** *810 N Grand Ave (52641). Phone 319/385-2102; toll-free 800/334-3277; fax 319/385-3223. www.heartlandinns.com.* 59 rooms, 2 story. Pets accepted; fee. Complimentary continental breakfast. Check-out 11 am. TV; cable (premium). Sauna. Indoor pool. **$**

D 🐾 ≋ 🚫 SC

Muscatine

Motel/Motor Lodge

★★ **HOLIDAY INN.** *2915 N Hwy 61 (52761). Phone 563/264-5550; fax 563/264-0451. www.holiday-inn.com.* 112 rooms, 3 story. Pets accepted; fee. Check-out noon. TV; cable (premium). In-room modem link. Laundry services. Restaurant, bar. Room service. In-house fitness room. Health club privileges. Sauna. Indoor pool; children's pool; whirlpool. Business center. **$**

D 🐾 ≋ 🏋 🚫 SC 🚶

Newton

Motels/Motor Lodges

★★ **BEST WESTERN NEWTON INN.** *I-80 at Hwy 14 (50208). Phone 641/792-4200; toll-free 800/373-6350; fax 641/792-0108. www.bestwestern.com.* 118 rooms, 2 story. Pets accepted, some restrictions. Complimentary full breakfast. Check-out noon. TV; cable (premium), VCR available. Restaurant, bar. In-house fitness room; sauna. Game room. Indoor pool; whirlpool. **$**

🐾 ≋ 🏋 🚫 SC

★ **DAYS INN.** *1605 W 19th St S (50208). Phone 641/792-2330; fax 641/792-1045. www.daysinn.com.* 59 rooms, 2 story. Pets accepted; fee. Complimentary continental breakfast. Check-out 11 am. TV; cable (premium), VCR available. **$**

D 🐾 ⚡ 🚫

Okoboji

Motels/Motor Lodges

★★★ **CLUBHOUSE INN.** *1405 US 71 N (51355). Phone 712/332-2161; fax 712/332-7727. www.villageeast.com.* 99 rooms, 2 story. Pets accepted, some restrictions. Check-out 11 am. TV. Restaurant, bar. Room service. In-house fitness room; sauna. Two pools; whirlpool. Golf on premises, greens fee $49. Outdoor tennis, indoor tennis. Cross-country ski on site. **$**

⬛ 🐾 ⛷ ⛷ 🏊 🏋 🏊 🎾 🏊

★★ **FILLENWARTH BEACH.** *87 Lakeshore Dr (51331). Phone 712/332-5646. www.fillenwarthbeach.com.* 93 rooms, 1-3 story. No elevator. Closed Oct-Mar. Pets accepted. Check-out noon. TV; cable, VCR. Supervised children's activities (late May-early Sept). Indoor, outdoor pool. Outdoor tennis. Free sail and cruiser boat rides. Boat dock, canoes, boats. Waterskiing, instruction. Free airport, bus depot transportation. **$$$$** (per week)

⬛ 🐾 ⛷ 🎾 🏊 🏊

Onawa

Motel/Motor Lodge

★ **SUPER 8.** *22868 Filbert Ave (51040). Phone 712/423-2101; fax 712/423-3480. www.super8.com.* 80 rooms. Pets accepted, some restrictions; fee. Check-out 11 am. TV. **$**

⬛ 🐾 ⛷ 🏊 🏊

Osceola

Motel/Motor Lodge

★ **BLUE HAVEN MOTEL.** *325 S Main St (50213). Phone 641/342-2115; toll-free 800/333-3180.* 24 rooms, 1-2 story. Pets accepted, some restrictions; fee. Check-out 11 am. TV; cable (premium). **$**

🐾 🏊 **SC**

Oskaloosa

Motel/Motor Lodge

★ **RED CARPET INN.** *2278 US 63 N (52577). Phone 641/673-8641; toll-free 800/255-2110; fax 641/673-4111.* 41 rooms, 2 story. Pets accepted, some restrictions; fee. Complimentary continental breakfast. TV; cable (premium). **$**

🐾 🏊

Ottumwa

Motel/Motor Lodge

★ **HEARTLAND INN.** *125 W Joseph Ave (52501). Phone 641/682-8526; toll-free 800/334-3277; fax 641/682-7124. www.heartlandinns.com.* 89 rooms. Pets accepted, some restrictions; fee. Complimentary continental breakfast. Check-out noon. TV; cable (premium). Laundry services. Sauna. Pool; whirlpool. **$**

⬛ 🐾 🏊

Shenandoah

Motel/Motor Lodge

★★ **COUNTRY INN.** *US 59 and 48; 1503 Sheridan Ave (51601). Phone 712/246-1550; fax 712/246-4773.* 65 rooms, 1-2 story. Pets accepted, some restrictions. Check-out 11 am. TV; cable (premium). Restaurant, bar. Room service. Airport transportation. **$**

🐾 🏊

Sioux City

Motels/Motor Lodges

★★ **BEST WESTERN CITY CENTRE.** *130 Nebraska St (51101). Phone 712/277-1550; toll-free 800/528-1234; fax 712/277-1120. www.bestwestern.com.* 114 rooms, 2 story. Pets accepted, some restrictions; fee. Check-out noon. TV. Laundry services. Bar. Pool. Free airport transportation. **$**

⬛ 🐾 🏊 🏊 **SC**

★ **SUPER 8.** *4307 Stone Ave (51106). Phone 712/274-1520; toll-free 800/800-8000. www.super8.com.* 60 rooms, 2 story. Pets accepted, some restrictions; fee. Check-out 11 am. TV. Restaurant. Continental breakfast. **$**

⬛ 🐾 🏊 **SC**

Hotel

★★ **SIOUX CITY PLAZA HOTEL.** *707 Fourth St (51101). Phone 712/277-4101; toll-free 800/593-0555; fax 712/277-3168.* Conveniently located on the river downtown, this hotel will happily accommodate both corporate and leisure travelers. 193 rooms, 12 story. Pets accepted, some restrictions; fee. Check-out noon. TV; cable (premium). In-room modem link. Restaurant, bar. In-house fitness room; sauna. Indoor pool. Free airport transportation. **$**

⬛ 🐾 🏊 🎾 🏊

Waterloo

Motels/Motor Lodges

★ ★ **BEST WESTERN STARLITE VILLAGE.** *214 Washington St (50701). Phone 319/235-0321; toll-free 800/903-0009; fax 319/235-6343. www.bestwestern.com.* 219 rooms, 11 story. Pets accepted; fee. Check-out noon. TV. In-room modem link. Restaurant, bar. Indoor pool. Airport, train station, bus depot transportation. **$**

D 🔾 ⛴ ⊠ SC

★ **HEARTLAND INN WATERLOO CROSS-ROADS.** *1809 LaPorte Rd (50702). Phone 319/235-4461; toll-free 800/334-3277; fax 319/235-0907. www.heartlandinns.com.* 118 rooms, 2 story. Pets accepted, some restrictions; fee. Complimentary breakfast. Check-out noon. TV. In-room modem link. In-house fitness room; sauna. **$**

D 🔾 🏋 ⊠

★ **HEARTLAND INN WATERLOO GREYHOUND PARK.** *3052 Marnie Ave (50701). Phone 319/232-7467; toll-free 800/334-3277; fax 319/232-0403. www.heartlandinns.com.* 56 rooms, 2 story. Pets accepted, some restrictions; fee. Complimentary breakfast. Check-out noon. TV. **$**

D 🔾 ⊠ SC

★ ★ **RAMADA INN.** *205 W 4th St (50701). Phone 319/233-7560; fax 319/236-9590. www.ramada.com.* 229 rooms, 10 story. Pets accepted. Check-out noon. TV. In-room modem link. Restaurant, dining room, bar; entertainment. Indoor pool; whirlpool; poolside service. Airport transportation. **$**

D 🔾 ⛴ ⊠

Webster City

Motel/Motor Lodge

★ ★ **BEST WESTERN NORSEMAN INN.** *3086 220th St (50271). Phone 515/854-2281; fax 515/855-2621. www.bestwestern.com.* 33 rooms. Pets accepted, some restrictions. Complimentary continental breakfast. Check-out noon. TV. Bar. **$**

 D 🔾 ⊠

Winterset

Motel/Motor Lodge

★ **VILLAGE VIEW MOTEL.** *711 E US 92 (50273). Phone 515/462-1218; toll-free 800/862-1218; fax 515/462-1231.* 16 rooms, 1 story. Pets accepted, some restrictions; fee. Check-out 11 am. TV; cable (premium), VCR available. **$**

🔾 ⊠ SC

Kansas

Abilene

Motel/Motor Lodge

★ **SUPER 8.** *2207 N Buckeye Ave (67410). Phone 785/263-4545; fax 785/263-7448. www.super8.com.* 62 rooms, 3 story. No elevator. Pets accepted; fee. Check-out 11 am. TV; cable (premium). Complimentary breakfast. **$**

[D] [🐾] [🏊]

Arkansas City

Motel/Motor Lodge

★ **HALLMARK INN.** *1617 N Summit St (67005). Phone 620/442-1400; fax 620/442-4729.* 47 rooms. Pets accepted, some restrictions; fee. Complimentary continental breakfast. Check-out 11 am. TV; cable (premium). Pool. **$**

[🐾] [🏊] [☒]

Belleville

Motel/Motor Lodge

★ ★ **BEST WESTERN BEL VILLA MOTEL.** *215 W US Hwy 36 (66935). Phone 785/527-2231; toll-free 800/780-7234; fax 785/527-2572. www.bestwestern.com.* 40 rooms. Pets accepted, some restrictions. Check-out 11 am. TV; cable (premium). In-room modem link. Pool. **$**

[D] [🐾] [🏊] [☒]

Coffeyville

Motel/Motor Lodge

★ **APPLE TREE INN.** *820 E 11th St (67337). Phone 620/251-0002; fax 620/251-1615.* 64 rooms, 2 story. Pets accepted, some restrictions; fee. Complimentary continental breakfast. Check-out noon. TV; cable (premium). In-room modem link. Indoor pool; whirlpool. **$**

[D] [🐾] [🏊] [☒]

Colby

Motel/Motor Lodge

★ ★ **BEST WESTERN CROWN MOTEL.** *2320 S Range Ave (67701). Phone 785/462-3943; fax 785/462-9845. www.bestwestern.com.* 29 rooms. Pets accepted. Check-out 11 am. TV; cable (premium). In-room modem link. Pool. Airport transportation. **$**

[🐾] [🏊] [✈] [☒] [SC]

Concordia

Motel/Motor Lodge

★ **ECONO LODGE.** *89 Lincoln St (66901). Phone 785/243-4545; fax 785/243-4545. www.econolodge.com.* 48 rooms. Pets accepted, some restrictions; fee. Check-out 11 am. TV; cable (premium). Pool. **$**

[🐾] [🏊] [☒] [SC]

Council Grove

Motel/Motor Lodge

★ ★ **THE COTTAGE HOUSE HOTEL & MOTEL.** *25 N Neosho (66846). Phone 620/767-6828; toll-free 800/717-7903; fax 620/767-6414.* 36 rooms, 1-2 story. Pets accepted; fee. Check-out 11 am. TV; VCR available. In-room modem link. Sauna. Whirlpool. Built in 1867 as a cottage and blacksmith shop; some antiques; gazebo. Continental breakfast. **$**

[🐾] [☒] [SC]

Dodge City

Motels/Motor Lodges

★ ★ **BEST WESTERN SILVER SPUR LODGE AND CONVENTION CENTER.** *1510 W Wyatt Earp Blvd (67801). Phone 620/227-2125; toll-free 800/817-2125; fax 620/227-2030. www.bestwestern.com.* 120 rooms, 2 story. Pets accepted, some restrictions; fee. Check-out noon. TV; cable (premium), VCR available. Bar; dancing. Room service. Outdoor pool. Free airport transportation. **$**

[D] [🐾] [🏊] [☒] [SC]

★ ★ **DODGE HOUSE HOTEL & CONVENTION CENTER.** *2408 W Wyatt Earp Blvd (67801). Phone 620/225-9900; fax 620/227-5012. www.dodgehousehotel.com.* 108 rooms, 2 story. Pets accepted, some restrictions. Check-out 11 am. TV; cable (premium), VCR available. Laundry services. Restaurant, bar. In-house fitness room; sauna. Game room. Indoor pool; whirlpool. Free airport transportation. **$**

🄳 ⬛ ⬛ 🔆 ✈ ⬛

★ **SUPER 8.** *1708 W Wyatt Earp Blvd (67801). Phone 620/225-3924; fax 620/225-5793. www.super8.com.* 64 rooms, 3 story. Pets accepted. Complimentary continental breakfast. Check-out noon. TV; cable (premium), VCR available (movies). Pool. **$**

🄳 ⬛ ⬛ ⬛ SC

El Dorado

Motel/Motor Lodge

★ ★ **BEST WESTERN RED COACH INN.** *2525 W Central St (67042). Phone 316/321-6900; fax 316/321-6900. www.bestwestern.com.* 73 rooms, 2 story. Pets accepted. Check-out 11 am. TV; cable (premium). Restaurant. Room service. In-house fitness room; sauna. Game room. Indoor pool; whirlpool. Airport transportation. **$**

⬛ ⬛ 🔆 ⬛

Emporia

Motels/Motor Lodges

★ ★ **BEST WESTERN HOSPITALITY HOUSE.** *3021 W Hwy 50 (66801). Phone 620/342-7587; toll-free 800/362-2036; fax 620/342-9271. www.bestwestern.com.* 143 rooms. Pets accepted, some restrictions. Complimentary continental breakfast. Check-out noon. TV; cable (premium). In-room modem link. Restaurant, bar. Room service. In-house fitness room; sauna. Game room. Indoor pool; whirlpool. Business center. **$**

🄳 ⬛ ⬛ 🔆 ⬛ SC ⬛

★ **DAYS INN.** *3032 W Hwy 50 (66801). Phone 620/342-1787; fax 620/342-2292. www.daysinn.com.* 39 rooms, 1-2 story. Pets accepted, some restrictions. Complimentary continental breakfast. Check-out 11 am. TV; cable (premium). In-room modem link. Game room. Indoor pool; whirlpool. **$**

🄳 ⬛ ⬛ ⬛

★ ★ **RAMADA INN.** *2700 W 18th Ave (66801). Phone 620/343-2200; toll-free 888/298-2054; fax 620/343-1609. www.ramada.com.* 127 rooms, 2 story. Pets accepted;

fee. Check-out noon. TV; cable (premium). Restaurant. Room service. Sauna. Game room. Indoor pool; outdoor pool; whirlpool. **$**

🄳 ⬛ ⬛ ⬛

Fort Scott

Motel/Motor Lodge

★ **BEST WESTERN FORT SCOTT INN.** *1st and State St (66701). Phone 620/223-0100; toll-free 888/800-3175; fax 620/223-1746. www.bestwestern.com.* 76 rooms, 1-2 story. Pets accepted, some restrictions; fee. Complimentary continental breakfast. Check-out 11 am. TV; cable (premium), VCR available. In-room modem link. Laundry services. In-house fitness room; sauna. Outdoor pool; whirlpool. **$**

⬛ ⬛ 🔆 ⬛ SC

Garden City

Motels/Motor Lodges

★ ★ **BEST WESTERN WHEAT LANDS HOTEL & CONFERENCE CENTER.** *1311 E Fulton St (67846). Phone 620/276-2387; toll-free 800/333-2387; fax 620/276-4252. www.bestwestern.com.* 107 rooms, 1-2 story. Pets accepted. Check-out 1 pm. TV; cable (premium), VCR available. In-room modem link. Bar; entertainment. In-house fitness room. Outdoor pool. Airport transportation. **$**

🄳 ⬛ ⬛ 🔆 ✈ ⬛

★ ★ **GARDEN CITY PLAZA INN.** *1911 E Kansas (67846). Phone 620/275-7471; toll-free 800/875-5201; fax 620/275-4028.* 109 rooms, 2 story. Pets accepted; fee. Check-out noon. TV; cable (premium), VCR available (movies). Restaurant, bar; entertainment. Room service. Sauna. Game room. Indoor pool; whirlpool. Free airport transportation. **$**

🄳 ⬛ ⬛ ⬛

Goodland

Motel/Motor Lodge

★ ★ **BEST WESTERN BUFFALO INN.** *830 W US Hwy 24 (67735). Phone 785/899-3621; toll-free 800/433-3621; fax 785/899-5072. www.bestwestern.com.* 93 rooms, 2 story. Pets accepted. Complimentary breakfast. Check-out 11 am. TV; cable (premium), VCR available. In-room modem link. Laundry services. Bar. Indoor pool; children's pool; whirlpool. Airport transportation. Business center. **$**

D 🐾 ⇌ ⇋ SC 🚶

Great Bend

Motels/Motor Lodges

★ ★ **BEST WESTERN ANGUS INN.** *2920 10th St (67530). Phone 620/792-3541; toll-free 800/862-6487; fax 620/792-8621. www.bestwestern.com.* 90 rooms, 2 story. Pets accepted, some restrictions. Check-out 11 am. TV; cable (premium), VCR available. Restaurant. Room service. In-house fitness room; sauna. Game room. Indoor pool; whirlpool. Airport transportation. Business center. **$**

D 🐾 ⇌ 🏋 🏹 ✈ ⇋

★ ★ **HOLIDAY INN.** *3017 W 10th St (67530). Phone 620/792-2431; fax 620/792-5561. www.holiday-inn.com.* 172 rooms, 2 story. Pets accepted. Check-out noon. TV; cable (premium). In-room modem link. Restaurant, bar. Room service. In-house fitness room; sauna. Health club privileges. Indoor pool; whirlpool. Airport transportation. **$**

D 🐾 ⇌ 🏋 ⇋ SC

Greensburg

Motel/Motor Lodge

★ **BEST WESTERN J-HAWK MOTEL.** *515 W Kansas Ave (67054). Phone 620/723-2121; fax 620/723-2650. www.bestwestern.com.* 30 rooms. Pets accepted, some restrictions. Complimentary continental breakfast. Check-out 11 am. TV; cable (premium). In-room modem link. In-house fitness room. Game room. Indoor pool; whirlpool. Free airport transportation. **$**

D 🐾 🛄 ⇌ 🏋 ✈ ⇋

Hays

Motels/Motor Lodges

★ ★ **BEST WESTERN VAGABOND MOTEL.** *2524 Vine St (67601). Phone 785/625-2511; fax 785/625-8879. www.bestwestern.com.* 92 rooms, 1-2 story. Pets accepted, some restrictions. Check-out noon. TV; cable (premium). In-room modem link. Restaurant, bar. Laundry services. In-house fitness room. Whirlpool. **$**

🐾 🏋 ⇋ SC

★ **BUDGET HOST INN.** *810 E 8th St (67601). Phone 785/625-2563; toll-free 800/283-4678; fax 785/625-3967. www.budgethost.com.* 49 rooms, 1-2 story. Pets accepted, some restrictions. Check-out noon. TV; cable (premium). Laundry services. Outdoor pool. Free airport transportation. **$**

D 🐾 ⇌ ⇋ SC

★ **HAMPTON INN.** *3801 Vine St (67601). Phone 785/625-8103; fax 785/625-3006. www.hamptoninn.com.* 117 rooms, 2 story. Pets accepted, some restrictions. Complimentary continental breakfast. Check-out noon. TV; cable (premium). In-room modem link. Free airport transportation. **$**

D 🐾 ⇌

Hutchinson

Motels/Motor Lodges

★ **COMFORT INN.** *1621 Super Plz (67501). Phone 620/663-7822; fax 620/663-1055. www.comfortinn.com.* 63 rooms, 3 story. Pets accepted, some restrictions. Complimentary continental breakfast. Check-out noon. TV; cable (premium). In-room modem link. Two pools, whirlpool. **$**

D 🐾 ⇌ 🏋 ⇋ SC

★ **ECONO LODGE.** *15 W 4th Ave (67501). Phone 620/663-1211; toll-free 800/228-5151; fax 620/669-3710. www.econolodge.com.* 98 rooms, 2 story. Pets accepted, some restrictions. Complimentary breakfast. Check-out noon. TV; cable (premium), VCR available. In-room modem link. Restaurant, bar. Room service. Outdoor pool. **$**

D 🐾 ⇌ ⇋ SC

Independence

Motels/Motor Lodges

★ ★ **APPLETREE INN.** *201 N 8th St (67301). Phone 620/331-5500; fax 620/331-0641.* 64 rooms, 2 story. Pets accepted, some restrictions. Complimentary continental breakfast. Check-out noon. TV; cable (premium). In-room modem link. Indoor pool; whirlpool. **$**

D 🐾 ⇌ ⇋

★ ★ **BEST WESTERN PRAIRIE INN.** *3222 W Main St (67301). Phone 620/331-7300; fax 620/331-8740. www.bestwestern.com.* 41 rooms. Pets accepted; fee. Complimentary continental breakfast. Check-out 11 am. TV; cable (premium). Pool. **$**

D 🐾 ⇌ ⇋ SC

Iola

Motel/Motor Lodge

★ ★ **BEST WESTERN INN.** *1315 N State St (66749). Phone 620/365-5161; toll-free 800/769-0007; fax 620/365-6808. www.bestwestern.com.* 59 rooms. Pets accepted, some restrictions. Check-out noon. TV; cable (premium). Restaurant. Pool. **$**

D ⌖ ⤢ ⊠ SC

Junction City

Motels/Motor Lodges

★ **DAYS INN.** *1024 S Washington St (66441). Phone 785/762-2727; toll-free 800/329-7466; fax 785/762-2751. www.daysinn.com.* 108 rooms, 2 story. Pets accepted. Complimentary continental breakfast. Check-out noon. TV; cable (premium). In-room modem link. Bar. Sauna. Game room. Indoor pool; outdoor pool; whirlpool. **$**

D ⌖ ⤢ ⊠

★ **RED CARPET INN.** *110 E Flinthills Blvd (66441). Phone 785/238-5188; fax 785/238-7585.* 48 rooms, 1-2 story. Pets accepted; fee. Check-out noon. TV; cable (premium), VCR available. Pool. **$**

D ⌖ ⤢ ⊠

★ **SUPER 8.** *1001 E 6th St (66441). Phone 785/238-8101; toll-free 800/800-8000; fax 785/238-7470. www.super8.com.* 97 rooms, 2 story. Pets accepted, some restrictions; fee. Check-out 11 am. TV; cable (premium). In-room modem link. Laundry services. Restaurant, bar. Room service. In-house fitness room; sauna. Pool; whirlpool. **$**

D ⌖ ⤢ ⫟ ⊠ SC

Larned

Motel/Motor Lodge

★ ★ **BEST WESTERN TOWNSMAN MOTEL.** *123 E 14th St (67550). Phone 620/285-3114; toll-free 800/780-7234; fax 620/285-7139. www.bestwestern.com.* 44 rooms. Pets accepted. Check-out noon. TV; cable (premium). In-room modem link. Outdoor pool. **$**

D ⌖ ⤢ ⊠ SC

Lawrence

Motels/Motor Lodges

★ **DAYS INN.** *2309 Iowa St (66047). Phone 785/843-9100; fax 785/843-1572. www.daysinn.com.* 101 rooms, 3 story. Pets accepted, some restrictions. Complimentary continental breakfast. Check-out noon. TV; cable (premium). In-room modem link. Bar. In-house fitness room. Indoor pool; whirlpool. **$**

D ⌖ ⤢ ⫟ ⊠

★ **WESTMINSTER INN.** *2525 W 6th St (66049). Phone 785/841-8410; toll-free 888/937-8646; fax 785/841-1901.* 60 rooms, 2 story. Pets accepted; fee. Check-out noon. TV; cable (premium). Pool. **$**

D ⌖ ⤢ ⊠

Leavenworth

Motel/Motor Lodge

★ ★ **RAMADA INN.** *101 S 3rd St (66048). Phone 913/651-5500; fax 913/651-6981. www.ramada.com.* 97 rooms, 2 story. Pets accepted; fee. Check-out noon. TV; cable (premium). Restaurant, bar. Room service. Outdoor pool. **$**

D ⌖ ⤢ ⊠

Liberal

Motels/Motor Lodges

★ ★ **GATEWAY INN.** *720 E Pancake Blvd (67901). Phone 620/624-0242; toll-free 800/833-3391; fax 620/624-1952.* 101 rooms, 2 story. Pets accepted; fee. Check-out 11 am. TV; cable (premium). In-room modem link. Restaurant, bar. Pool. Free airport transportation. **$**

D ⌖ ⤢ ⊠ SC

★ ★ **LIBERAL INN.** *603 E Pancake Blvd (67901). Phone 620/624-7254; toll-free 800/458-4667; fax 620/624-7254.* 123 rooms, 2 story. Pets accepted. Check-out noon. TV; cable (premium). In-room modem link. Restaurant. Room service. Indoor pool; whirlpool. Free airport transportation. **$**

D ⌖ ⤢ ✈ ⊠

Manhattan

Motels/Motor Lodges

★ **DAYS INN.** *1501 Tuttle Creek Blvd (66502). Phone 785/539-5391; fax 785/539-0847. www.daysinn.com.* 119 rooms, 2 story. Pets accepted, some restrictions; fee. Complimentary continental breakfast. Check-out noon. TV; cable (premium), VCR available. In-room modem link. Pool. Lawn games. **$**

[D] [⬚] [⬚] [⬚]

★★ **HOLIDAY INN.** *530 Richards Dr (66502). Phone 785/539-5311; fax 785/539-8368. www.holiday-inn.com.* 197 rooms, 3 story. Pets accepted, some restrictions. Check-out noon. TV; cable (premium). In-room modem link. Restaurant, bar. Room service. Sauna. Game room. Indoor pool; children's pool; whirlpool. **$**

[D] [⬚] [⬚] [⬚]

★★ **RAMADA INN.** *1641 Anderson Ave (66502). Phone 785/539-7531; toll-free 800/298-2054; fax 785/539-3909. www.ramada.com.* 116 rooms, 6 story. Pets accepted; fee. Check-out noon. TV; cable (premium), VCR available. In-room modem link. Restaurant, bar. Room service. In-house fitness room. Health club privileges. Pool. Free airport transportation. **$**

[D] [⬚] [⬚] [⬚] [⬚] [SC]

Mankato

Motel/Motor Lodge

★ **CREST-VUE MOTEL.** *E Hwy 36 (66956). Phone 785/378-3515.* 12 rooms. Pets accepted, some restrictions; fee. Check-out 11 am. TV. **$**

[⬚] [⬚]

Marysville

Motels/Motor Lodges

★★ **BEST WESTERN SURF.** *2105 Center St (66508). Phone 785/562-2354; fax 785/562-2354. www.bestwestern.com.* 52 rooms, 2 story. Pets accepted, some restrictions; fee. Complimentary continental breakfast. Check-out 11 am. TV; cable (premium), VCR available. In-house fitness room; sauna. Game room. **$**

[D] [⬚] [⬚] [⬚] [⬚]

★ **THUNDERBIRD INN.** *819 Pony Express Hwy (66508). Phone 785/562-2373; toll-free 800/662-2373; fax 785/562-2531.* 21 rooms. Pets accepted. Check-out 11 am. TV; cable (premium). In-room modem link. **$**

[D] [⬚] [⬚]

McPherson

Motels/Motor Lodges

★★ **BEST WESTERN HOLIDAY MANOR.** *2211 E Kansas Ave (67460). Phone 620/241-5343; toll-free 888/841-0038; fax 620/241-8086. www.bestwestern.com.* 110 rooms, 2 story. Pets accepted, some restrictions; fee. Check-out noon. TV; cable (premium). Restaurant. Room service. Indoor pool; outdoor pool; whirlpool. **$**

[D] [⬚] [⬚] [⬚] [SC]

★★ **RED COACH INN.** *2111 E Kansas Ave (67460). Phone 620/241-6960; fax 620/241-4340.* 88 rooms, 1-2 story. Pets accepted, some restrictions; fee. Check-out noon. TV; cable (premium). In-room modem link. Restaurant. Sauna. Indoor pool; whirlpool. **$**

[D] [⬚] [⬚] [⬚]

Medicine Lodge

Motel/Motor Lodge

★ **COPA MOTEL.** *401 W Fowler Ave (67104). Phone 620/886-5673; toll-free 800/316-2673; fax 620/886-5241.* 54 rooms, 2 story. Pets accepted; fee. Check-out 11 am. TV; cable (premium). **$**

[⬚] [⬚]

Newton

Motel/Motor Lodge

★★ **BEST WESTERN RED COACH INN.** *1301 E 1st St (67114). Phone 316/283-9120; fax 316/283-4105. www.bestwestern.com.* 81 rooms, 1-2 story. Pets accepted, some restrictions. Check-out 11 am. TV; cable (premium), VCR available. Room service. In-house fitness room; sauna. Game room. Indoor pool; whirlpool. Free airport transportation. **$**

[D] [⬚] [⬚] [⬚] [⬚] [SC]

Oakley

Motels/Motor Lodges

★ **1ST INTERSTATE INN.** *I-70 and Hwy 40 (67748). Phone 785/672-3203; fax 785/672-3330. www.1stinns.com.* 29 rooms, 1-2 story. Pets accepted, some restrictions; fee. Check-out 11 am. TV; cable (premium). **$**

⬛ ⬛ SC

★★ **BEST WESTERN GOLDEN PLAINS MOTEL.** *3506 US 40 (67748). Phone 785/672-3254; fax 785/672-3200. www.bestwestern.com.* 26 rooms, 2 story. Pets accepted, some restrictions. Complimentary continental breakfast. Check-out 11 am. TV; cable (premium). Outdoor pool. **$**

⬛ ⬛ ⬛ SC

Ottawa

Motel/Motor Lodge

★ **TRAVELODGE.** *2209 S Princeton St (66067). Phone 785/242-7000; toll-free 888/540-4024; fax 785/242-8572. www.travelodge.com.* 60 rooms, 2 story. Pets accepted; fee. Complimentary continental breakfast. Check-out 11 am. TV; cable (premium). Outdoor pool. **$**

⬛ ⬛ ⬛ ⬛

Overland Park

Motels/Motor Lodges

★ **DRURY INN.** *10951 Metcalf Ave (66210). Phone 913/451-0200; fax 913/451-0200. www.druryinn.com.* 151 rooms, 4 story. Pets accepted, some restrictions. Complimentary continental breakfast. Check-out noon. TV; cable (premium). In-room modem link. Pool. Free covered parking. **$**

⬛ ⬛ ⬛ ⬛

★ **LA QUINTA INN.** *9461 Lenexa Dr (66215). Phone 913/492-5500; fax 913/492-2935. www.laquinta.com.* 106 rooms, 3 story. Pets accepted. Complimentary continental breakfast. Check-out noon. TV; cable (premium). In-room modem link. Pool. **$**

⬛ ⬛ ⬛ ⬛

★ **WHITE HAVEN MOTOR LODGE.** *8039 Metcalf Ave (66204). Phone 913/649-8200; toll-free 800/752-2892; fax 913/901-8199. www.white-haven.com.* 100 rooms, 1-2 story. Pets accepted, some restrictions; fee. Check-out noon. TV; cable (premium). Pool. **$**

⬛ ⬛ ⬛ ⬛

All Suites

★ **AMERISUITES.** *6801 W 112th St (66211). Phone 913/451-2553; toll-free 800/833-1516; fax 913/451-3098. www.amerisuites.com.* 126 rooms, 6 story. Pets accepted, some restrictions. Complimentary breakfast. Check-out 11 am. TV; cable (premium), VCR available. In-room modem link. In-house fitness room. Health club privileges. Outdoor pool. Business center. **$**

⬛ ⬛ ⬛ ⬛ ⬛ SC ⬛

★★ **CHASE SUITE HOTEL OVERLAND PARK.** *6300 W 110th S (66211). Phone 913/491-3333; toll-free 800/433-9765; fax 913/491-1377. www.woodfinsuitehotels .com.* 112 suites, 2 story. Pets accepted; fee. Complimentary breakfast. Check-out noon. TV; cable (premium), VCR available. In-room modem link. In-house fitness room. Pool; whirlpool. Business center. Sports court. **$**

⬛ ⬛ ⬛ ⬛ ⬛ ⬛

Pratt

Motel/Motor Lodge

★★ **BEST WESTERN HILLCREST.** *1336 E 1st (67124). Phone 620/672-6407; toll-free 800/336-2279; fax 620/672-6707. www.bestwestern.com.* 40 rooms. Pets accepted, some restrictions; fee. Complimentary continental breakfast. Check-out 11 am. TV; cable (premium). Pool. **$**

⬛ ⬛ ⬛ ⬛

Salina

Motels/Motor Lodges

★★ **BEST WESTERN MID-AMERICA INN.** *1846 N 9th St (67401). Phone 785/827-0356; fax 785/827-7688. www.bestwestern.com.* 108 rooms, 2 story. Pets accepted; fee. Complimentary continental breakfast. Check-out noon. TV; cable (premium). In-room modem link. Restaurant, bar. Room service. Sauna. Indoor pool; outdoor pool; whirlpool; poolside service. **$**

⬛ ⬛ ⬛ ⬛ SC

★ **COMFORT INN.** *1820 W Crawford St (67401). Phone 785/826-1711; fax 785/827-6530. www.comfortinn.com.* 60 rooms. Pets accepted, some restrictions; fee. Complimentary continental breakfast. Check-out 11 am.

TV; cable (premium). In-room modem link. Indoor pool; whirlpool. **$**

[icons]

★ ★ **RED COACH INN.** *2110 W Crawford (67401). Phone 785/825-2111; toll-free 800/332-0047; fax 785/825-6973.* 112 rooms, 2 story. Pets accepted, some restrictions; fee. Check-out noon. TV; cable (premium). Restaurant. Room service. Sauna. Game room. Indoor pool; whirlpool. Lighted tennis. **$**

[icons]

Topeka

Motels/Motor Lodges

★ **BEST WESTERN MEADOW ACRES MOTEL.** *2950 S Topeka Blvd (66611). Phone 785/267-1681; toll-free 800/780-7234; fax 785/267-1681. www.bestwestern.com.* 82 rooms. Pets accepted, some restrictions; fee. Complimentary continental breakfast. Check-out noon. TV; cable (premium). Indoor pool; whirlpool. **$**

[icons] SC

★ **DAYS INN.** *1510 SW Wanamaker Rd (66604). Phone 785/272-8538; toll-free 800/329-7466; fax 785/272-8538.* 62 rooms, 2 story. Pets accepted; fee. Complimentary continental breakfast. Check-out 11 am. TV; cable (premium). Game room. Indoor pool; whirlpool. **$**

[icons] SC

★ ★ **RAMADA INN.** *420 E 6th St (66607). Phone 785/234-5400; fax 785/233-0460. www.ramada.com.* 360 rooms, 3-11 story. Pets accepted. Check-out noon. TV; cable (premium), VCR available. Restaurant, bar; entertainment. Room service. Pool. Free airport transportation. **$**

[icons]

WaKeeney

Motel/Motor Lodge

★ **BUDGET HOST INN.** *668 S 13th St (67672). Phone 785/743-2121; toll-free 800/283-4678; fax 785/743-2458. www.budgethost.com.* 27 rooms. Pets accepted, some restrictions. Check-out 11 am. TV; cable (premium). Laundry services. Pool. **$**

[icons] SC

Wichita

Motels/Motor Lodges

★ **CANDLEWOOD SUITES.** *711 S Main (67213). Phone 316/263-1061; toll-free 800/946-6200; fax 316/263-3817. www.candlewoodsuites.com.* 64 rooms, 2 story. Pets accepted, some restrictions; fee. Complimentary continental breakfast. Check-out noon. TV; cable (premium), VCR available. In-room modem link. Pool. **$**

[icons]

★ **COMFORT INN.** *658 Westdale Dr (67209). Phone 316/945-2600; toll-free 800/318-2607; fax 316/945-5033. www.comfortsuites.com.* 50 rooms, 3 story. Pets accepted, some restrictions; fee. Complimentary breakfast. Check-out noon. TV; cable (premium), VCR available. Bar. In-house fitness room. Pool. Airport transportation. **$**

[icons]

★ ★ **HOLIDAY INN.** *549 S Rock Rd (67207). Phone 316/686-7131; fax 316/686-0018. www.holiday-inn.com.* 238 rooms, 9 story. Pets accepted; fee. Check-out noon. TV; cable (premium), VCR available (movies). In-room modem link. Restaurant, bar. Pool. Business center. Free airport transportation. **$**

[icons]

★ ★ **HOLIDAY INN.** *5500 W Kellogg (67209). Phone 316/943-2181; toll-free 800/255-6484; fax 316/943-6587. www.holiday-inn.com.* 152 rooms, 5 story. Pets accepted; fee. Check-out noon. TV; VCR available. In-room modem link. Restaurant, bar. Room service. In-house fitness room; sauna. Health club privileges. Indoor pool; whirlpool; poolside service. Free airport transportation. **$**

[icons] SC

★ ★ **RAMADA INN.** *7335 E Kellogg (67207). Phone 316/685-1281; fax 316/685-8621. www.ramada.com.* 192 rooms, 6 story. Pets accepted; fee. Complimentary continental breakfast. Check-out noon. TV; cable (premium), VCR available. In-room modem link. Restaurant, bar. Room service. In-house fitness room. Game room. Indoor pool; whirlpool. Free airport transportation. **$**

[icons] SC

Kentucky

Ashland

Motels/Motor Lodges

★ **DAYS INN.** *12700 KY 180 (41102). Phone 606/928-3600; fax 606/928-6515. www.daysinn.com.* 63 rooms, 2 story. S $46-$59; D $52-$64; each additional $5; under 18 free. Pets accepted; fee. Complimentary continental breakfast. Check-out noon. TV; cable (premium), VCR available. In-room modem link. Laundry services. In-house fitness room. Pool. Business center.

[icons]

★ **KNIGHTS INN.** *7216 KY 60 (41102). Phone 606/928-9501; toll-free 800/497-7560; fax 606/928-4436. www.knightsinn.com.* 124 rooms. S $38; D $43; kitchen units $42-$47; each additional $5; under 18 free. Pets accepted, some restrictions; fee. Complimentary continental breakfast. Check-out noon. TV; cable (premium). Pool.

[icons]

Bardstown

Motels/Motor Lodges

★★ **BARDSTOWN PARKVIEW MOTEL.** *418 E Stephen Foster Ave (40004). Phone 502/348-5983; toll-free 800/732-2384; fax 502/349-6973.* 38 rooms, 1-2 story. June-Labor Day: S $50; D $55; each additional $5; suites, kitchen units $65-$85; lower rates rest of year. Pets accepted, some restrictions. Complimentary continental breakfast. Check-out 11 am. TV. Laundry services. Restaurant, bar. Pool. My Old Kentucky Home State Park opposite.

[icons]

★★ **DAYS INN.** *1875 New Haven Rd (40004). Phone 502/348-9253; fax 502/348-5478. www.holiday-inn.com.* 102 rooms, 2 story. May-Sept: S, D $59-$89; each additional $5; under 19 free; lower rates rest of year. Pets accepted; fee. Check-out 11 am. TV; cable (premium), VCR available (movies). In-room modem link. Restaurant, bar. In-house fitness room. Pool. 9-hole par-3 golf, driving range.

[icons]

★ **HAMPTON INN.** *985 Chambers Blvd (40004). Phone 502/349-0100; fax 502/349-1191. www.hamptoninn.com.* 106 rooms, 2 story. June-Oct: S $59-$70; D $64-$75; higher rates special events; lower rates rest of year. Pets accepted. Complimentary continental breakfast. Check-out noon. TV; cable (premium), VCR available. In-room modem link. In-house fitness room. Indoor pool.

[icons]

Berea

Motel/Motor Lodge

★ **DAYS INN.** *KY 595 and I-75 (40403). Phone 859/986-7373; fax 859/986-3144. www.daysinn.com.* 60 rooms, 2 story. S $43-$45; D $49-$51; each additional $5; family rates. Pets accepted; fee. Check-out 11 am. TV. Pool. Miniature golf.

[icons]

Bowling Green

Motel/Motor Lodge

★★ **HOLIDAY INN.** *3240 Scottsville Rd (42104). Phone 270/781-1500; toll-free 800/465-4329; fax 270/842-0030. www.holiday-inn.com.* 107 rooms, 2 story. S $49-$80; D $90; each additional $10; under 19 free. Pets accepted. Check-out noon. TV; cable (premium). In-room modem link. Restaurant, bar. Room service. In-house fitness room. Pool; children's pool.

[icons]

Cadiz

Motel/Motor Lodge

★ **HOLIDAY INN EXPRESS.** *153 Broadbent Blvd (42211). Phone 270/522-7007; toll-free 800/456-4000; fax 270/522-3893. www.hiexpress.com.* 48 rooms, 2 story. S $52; D $57; each additional $5; under 18 free. Pets accepted; fee. Complimentary continental breakfast. Check-out noon. TV; cable (premium). Pool.

[icons]

Cave City

Motels/Motor Lodges

★ **DAYS INN.** *822 Mammoth Cave St (42127). Phone 270/773-2151. www.daysinn.com.* 110 rooms, 2 story.

Late May-early Sept: S $56; D $66; each additional $5; under 12 free; lower rates rest of year. Pets accepted, some restrictions; fee. Check-out noon. TV; cable (premium), VCR available (movies). Laundry services. Restaurant. Game room. Pool; children's pool.

★ ★ **QUALITY INN.** *Mammoth Cave Rd (42127). Phone 270/773-2181; toll-free 800/321-4245; fax 270/773-3200. www.qualityinn.com.* 100 rooms, 2 story. Memorial Day-Labor Day: S $42-$62; D $48-$68; each additional $6; under 12 free; higher rates special events; lower rates rest of year. Pets accepted; fee. Check-out 11 am. TV; cable (premium). Restaurant. Game room. Pool.

★ **SUPER 8.** *88 Stockpen Rd (42765). Phone 270/524-4888; toll-free 800/800-8000; fax 270/524-5888. www.super8.com.* 50 rooms, 2 story. May-mid-Sept: S $47; D $51; each additional $4; under 12 free; higher rates special events; lower rates rest of year. Pets accepted; fee. Complimentary continental breakfast. Check-out 11 am. TV; cable (premium).

Covington

Motel/Motor Lodge

★ **KNIGHTS INN.** *8049 Dream St (41042). Phone 859/371-9711; toll-free 800/843-5644; fax 859/371-4325. www.knightsinn.com.* 116 rooms. S, D $37-$62; each additional $6; kitchen units $48-$58; under 18 free. Pets accepted, some restrictions; fee. Check-out noon. TV; cable (premium). Pool.

Extended Stay

★ **ASHLEY QUARTERS.** *4880 Houston Rd (41042). Phone 859/525-9997; fax 859/525-9980. www.ashleyquarters.com.* 70 rooms, 2 story. Pets accepted; fee. Check-out noon. TV; cable (premium). In-room modem link. Outdoor pool. Business center. Concierge. **$**

★ ★ **RESIDENCE INN BY MARRIOTT.** *2811 Circleport Dr (41018). Phone 859/282-7400; toll-free 800/331-3131; fax 859/282-1790. www.residenceinn.com.* 96 suites, 3 story. No elevator. Suites $79-$179; higher rates special events. Pets accepted; fee. Complimentary continental breakfast. Check-out noon. TV; cable (premium), VCR available. In-room modem link. Laundry services. In-house fitness room. Pool; whirlpool. Free airport transportation.

Danville

Motels/Motor Lodges

★ **COUNTRY HEARTH INN.** *US 127 (40422). Phone 859/236-8601; fax 859/236-0314.* 81 rooms, 2 story. S, D $55-$65; each additional $6; under 19 free. Pets accepted. Check-out noon. TV; cable (premium). In-room modem link. Restaurant open 24 hours. Pool.

★ **SUPER 8.** *3663 KY 150-127 Bypass (40422). Phone 859/236-8881; toll-free 800/800-8000. www.super8.com.* 49 rooms, 2 story. S $41.88; D $51.88-$56.88; each additional $5; under 12 free. Pets accepted, some restrictions; fee. Check-out 11 am. TV; cable (premium). Laundry services.

Elizabethtown

Motels/Motor Lodges

★ **BEST WESTERN CARDINAL INN.** *642 E Dixie Ave (42701). Phone 270/765-6139; toll-free 800/528-1234; fax 270/737-9944. www.bestwestern.com.* 54 rooms, 2 story. S, D $44-$49; each additional $4; under 18 free; higher rates Kentucky Derby. Pets accepted, some restrictions; fee. Complimentary continental breakfast. Check-out 11:30 am. TV; cable (premium). Laundry services. Pool.

★ **COMFORT INN.** *1043 Executive Dr (42701). Phone 270/769-3030; fax 502/769-2516.* 133 rooms, 2 story. S, D $63.95-$79.95; each additional $6; under 18 free; higher rates Kentucky Derby. Pets accepted. Complimentary continental breakfast. Check-out 11:30 am. TV; cable (premium). Game room. Indoor pool.

★ **DAYS INN.** *2010 N Mulberry St (42701). Phone 270/769-5522; fax 270/769-3211. www.daysinn.com.* 121 rooms, 2 story. S $38-$43; D $43-$50; each additional $5; higher rates Derby weekend. Pets accepted; fee. Check-out 11 am. TV; cable (premium). Restaurant open 24 hours. Game room. Pool.

Frankfort

Motel/Motor Lodge

★ **BLUEGRASS INN.** *635 Versailles Rd (40601). Phone 502/695-1800; toll-free 800/322-1802.* 62 rooms, 2 story. S

$36-$42; D $42-$48; each additional $6; under 14 free; higher rates Kentucky Derby. Pets accepted; fee. Check-out noon. TV. Pool.

Henderson

Motel/Motor Lodge

★ **DAYS INN.** *2044 US 41 N (42420). Phone 270/826-6600; toll-free 800/329-7466; fax 270/826-3055. www.daysinn.com.* 117 rooms, 2 story. S, D $50-$80; each additional $6; suites $70-$100; under 12 free. Pets accepted, some restrictions; fee. Check-out 11 am. TV; cable (premium). Restaurant, bar; entertainment. Room service. Pool.

Hopkinsville

Motels/Motor Lodges

★ **BEST WESTERN HOPKINSVILLE.** *4101 Ft Campbell Blvd (42240). Phone 270/886-9000. www.bestwestern.com.* 111 rooms, 3 story. S, D $50; each additional $5; under 12 free. Pets accepted, some restrictions; fee. Continental breakfast. Check-out noon. TV; cable (premium). Bar. Health club privileges. Pool.

★★ **HOLIDAY INN.** *2910 Fort Campbell Blvd (42240). Phone 270/886-4413. www.holiday-inn.com.* 101 rooms, 5 story. S, D $49-$79; each additional $6; under 19 free. Pets accepted. Check-out noon. TV; cable (premium). In-room modem link. Restaurant, bar. Room service. In-house fitness room; sauna. Indoor pool.

Lexington

Motels/Motor Lodges

★ **DAYS INN.** *5575 Athens Boonesboro Rd (40509). Phone 859/263-3100; toll-free 800/329-7466; fax 859/263-3120. www.daysinn.com.* 56 rooms, 2 story. S $40-$60; D $45-$65; each additional $5; family rates; higher rates special events. Pets accepted; fee. Complimentary continental breakfast. Check-out 11 am. TV. In-room modem link.

★ **HAMPTON INN.** *2251 Elkhorn Rd (40505). Phone 859/299-2613; fax 859/299-9664. www.hamptoninn.com.* 125 rooms, 5 story. S $69-$79; D $79-$89; under 18 free.

Pets accepted, some restrictions. Complimentary continental breakfast. Check-out noon. TV; cable (premium), VCR available. In-room modem link. In-house fitness room. Indoor pool.

★★ **HOLIDAY INN.** *1950 Newton Pike (40511). Phone 859/233-0512; fax 859/231-9285. www.holiday-inn.com.* 303 rooms, 2 story. S $109.95; D $114.95; suites $250; under 18 free. Pets accepted, some restrictions; fee. Check-out noon. TV; cable (premium). In-room modem link. Laundry services. Restaurant, bar. Room service. Supervised children's activities (Memorial Day-Labor Day). In-house fitness room; sauna. Game room. Indoor pool; whirlpool. Business center.

★★ **HOLIDAY INN.** *5532 Athens Boonesboro Rd (40509). Phone 859/263-5241; toll-free 800/394-8407; fax 859/563-4333. www.holiday-inn.com.* 149 rooms, 2 story. S, D $65-$80; each additional $6; under 18 free; higher rates: horse racing, special events. Pets accepted, some restrictions; fee. TV; cable (premium). In-room modem link. Restaurant, bar; entertainment. Room service. In-house fitness room; sauna. Pool; whirlpool.

★ **LA QUINTA INN.** *1919 Stanton Way (40511). Phone 859/231-7551; fax 859/281-6002. www.laquinta.com.* 129 rooms, 3 story. S $64; D $68; each additional $8; under 18 free; higher rates some weekends. Pets accepted, some restrictions. Complimentary continental breakfast. Check-out noon. TV. In-room modem link. Laundry services. Pool.

★★ **QUALITY INN.** *750 Newtown Pike (40511). Phone 859/233-0561; toll-free 800/638-7949; fax 859/231-6125. www.qualityinnnorthwest.com.* 109 rooms, 2 story. S, D $65.95-$89; each additional $5; under 19 free. Pets accepted; fee. Complimentary continental breakfast. Check-out noon. TV. Pool.

★ **RED ROOF INN.** *1980 Haggard Ct (40505). Phone 859/293-2626; toll-free 800/843-7663; fax 859/299-8353. www.redroof.com.* 108 rooms, 2 story. S $35.99-$45.99; D $41.99-$61.99; each additional $7; under 18 free. Pets accepted. Check-out noon. TV; cable (premium).

★ **SHONEY'S INN.** *2753 Richmond Rd (40509). Phone 859/269-4999; toll-free 800/552-4667; fax 859/268-2346. www.shoneysinn.com.* 102 rooms, 2 story. S $57-$67; D $62-$72; each additional $5; under 18 free. Pets accepted, some restrictions; fee. Check-out noon. TV. Pool.

★ **SUPER 8.** *2351 Buena Vista Rd (40505). Phone 859/299-6241; toll-free 800/800-8000. www.super8.com.* 62 rooms, 2 story. Apr-Oct: S $41.99; D $50.99-$60.99; suite $50-$75; each additional $5; under 12 free; weekly rates; higher rates horse racing; lower rates rest of year. Pets accepted; fee. Check-out 11 am. TV; cable (premium).

D ➾ ⛖ SC

Hotel

★★ **RADISSON PLAZA HOTEL.** *369 W Vine St (40507). Phone 859/231-9000; toll-free 800/333-3333; fax 859/281-3737. www.radisson.com.* This hotel is located in the Blue Grass region, on Triangle park. It is connected by skyway to the Rupp Arena, the Lexington Civic Center, and the Victorian Square Shopping Center. 367 rooms, 22 story. S $155; D $165; each additional $10; suites $190-$390; under 18 free; weekend rates. Pets accepted, some restrictions; fee. Check-out noon. TV; cable (premium), VCR available (movies). Restaurant, bar; entertainment. Room service. Health club privileges. In-house fitness room; sauna. Indoor pool; whirlpool; poolside service. Valet parking. Free airport transportation. Business center. Concierge. Luxury level.

D ➾ ⛖ ⚓ ⛖ SC ⚑

Resort

★★★ **MARRIOTT GRIFFIN GATE RESORT.** *1800 Newtown Pike (40511). Phone 859/231-5100; fax 859/255-9944. www.marriott.com.* This resort sits in the heart of Kentucky Bluegrass Country. Although outdoor recreations, including a championship golf course, tennis courts, and an indoor and outdoor pool, would please any leisure guest, dataport and voice mail-equipped rooms, a business center, and corporate-team-challenge programs attract business clientele. Four restaurants include The Mansion, serving fine American cuisine in a beautiful, antebellum mansion. 314 rooms, 7 story. S $110-$154; D $129-$169; suite $295-$850; under 18 free; golf plans. Pets accepted; fee. Check-out noon. TV; cable (premium). In-room modem link. Laundry services. Dining room, bar. Supervised children's activities (summer). In-house fitness room; sauna. Game room. Indoor pool; outdoor pool; whirlpool; poolside service. 18-hole golf, pro, putting green. Greens fee $28-$62. Outdoor tennis, lighted courts, pro. Airport transportation. Business center. Luxury level.

D ➾ ⚑ ⚑ ⚑ ⛖ ⚓ ⚑ ⛖

B&B/Small Inn

★★ **1823 HISTORIC ROSE HILL INN.** *233 Rose Hill Ave (40383). Phone 859/873-5957; toll-free 800/307-0460; fax 859/873-1813. www.rosehillinn.com.* 4 rooms, 2 story. Pets accepted, some restrictions; fee. Complimentary full breakfast. Check-out noon, check-in 3 pm. TV; cable (premium), VCR available. Game room. Lawn games. Built in 1823; 3 acres. Totally nonsmoking. **$**

➾ ⛖

London

Motels/Motor Lodges

★★ **BEST WESTERN HARVEST INN.** *207 W KY 80 (40741). Phone 606/864-2222; toll-free 800/528-1234; fax 606/878-2825. www.bestwestern.com.* 95 rooms, 2 story. June-Oct: S $51; D $60; under 17 free; each additional $5; lower rates rest of year. Pets accepted; fee. Complimentary continental breakfast. Check-out noon. TV; cable (premium). Restaurant. Indoor pool; whirlpool.

D ➾ ⛖ ⛖ SC

★ **BUDGET HOST INN.** *254 W Daniel Boone Pkwy (40741). Phone 606/878-7330; toll-free 800/283-4678. www.budgethost.com.* 46 rooms, 2 story. Memorial Day-Oct: S, D $39-$61; each additional $4; under 12 free; weekly rates; lower rates rest of year. Pets accepted, some restrictions. Complimentary continental breakfast. Check-out noon. TV; cable (premium). Pool.

D ➾ ⛖ ⚓ ⛖ SC

Louisville

Motels/Motor Lodges

★★ **BRECKINRIDGE INN.** *2800 Breckinridge Ln (40220). Phone 502/456-5050; fax 502/451-1577. www.breckinridgeinn.com.* 123 rooms, 2 story. S, D $65-$95; each additional $7; under 12 free. Pets accepted, some restrictions; fee. Check-out noon. TV. Laundry services. Restaurant, bar. Room service. In-house fitness room; sauna. Indoor, outdoor pool. Outdoor tennis, lighted courts. Free airport transportation.

D ➾ ⚑ ⛖ ⚓ ⛖

★★★ **EXECUTIVE INN.** *978 Phillips Ln (40209). Phone 502/367-6161; toll-free 800/626-2706; fax 502/363-1880. www.executiveinnhotel.com.* This hotel has an interesting Tudor-style design with all the charm and warmth of a European hotel. It has richly crafted woodwork and spacious, comfortable rooms overlooking a beautiful courtyard and heated pool, surrounded by magnolia trees and water wheels. 465 rooms, 2-6 story. S $85; D $95; each additional $10; suites $109-$282; under 18 free. Pets accepted; fee. Check-out 1 pm. TV; VCR available. Restaurant, bar. Room service. In-house fitness room; sauna. Indoor pool; outdoor pool; children's pool;

poolside service. Lawn games. Free airport transportation. Tudor-inspired architecture.

D ◨ ➳ ☇ ✕ ✈ ⊠ SC

★ ★ **HOLIDAY INN.** *120 W Broadway (40202). Phone 502/582-2241; toll-free 800/626-1558; fax 502/584-8591. www.holiday-inn.com.* 289 rooms, 12 story. S $95-$115; D $103-$125; each additional $10; suites $350; under 18 free. Pets accepted, some restrictions. Check-out noon. TV; VCR available. In-room modem link. Restaurant, bar. Health club privileges. In-house fitness room. Indoor pool. Free airport transportation. Luxury level.

D ➳ ☇ ☇ ✕ ⊠

★ ★ **HOLIDAY INN.** *4004 Gardiner Point Dr (40213). Phone 502/452-6361; toll-free 800/465-4329; fax 502/451-1541. www.holiday-inn.com.* 200 rooms, 3 story. S, D $98; each additional $7; under 18 free; weekend rates. Pets accepted; fee. Complimentary continental breakfast. Check-out noon. TV; cable (premium). In-room modem link. Restaurant, bar. Room service. In-house fitness room. Game room. Pool; poolside service. Outdoor tennis. Free airport transportation.

D ➳ ☇ ☇ ☇ ✕ ⊠ SC

★ ★ **HOLIDAY INN.** *1325 S Hurstbourne Pkwy (40222). Phone 502/426-2600; toll-free 800/465-4329; fax 502/423-1605. www.holidayinnhurstbourne.com.* 267 rooms, 7 story. S, D $99-$125; suites $125-$275; under 18 free. Pets accepted; fee. Check-out noon. TV; cable (premium). In-room modem link. Restaurant, bar. Room service. In-house fitness room; sauna. Indoor pool. Free airport transportation.

D ➳ ☇ ☇ ⊠ SC

★ **RED ROOF INN.** *9330 Blairwood Rd (40222). Phone 502/426-7621; fax 502/426-7933. www.redroof.com.* 108 rooms, 2 story. S $35.99-$69.99; D $43.99-$79.99; each additional $7-$9; under 18 free. Pets accepted. Check-out noon. TV. In-room modem link.

D ➳ ⊠

★ **SUPER 8.** *4800 Preston Hwy (40213). Phone 502/968-0088; fax 502/968-0088, ext. 347. www.super8.com.* 100 rooms, 3 story. S $43.88; D $53.88; each additional $5; under 12 free. Pets accepted; fee. Complimentary continental breakfast. Check-out 11 am. TV; cable (premium). In-room modem link. Free airport transportation.

D ➳ ☇ ☇ ✈ ⊠

Hotels

★ ★ ★ **EXECUTIVE WEST HOTEL.** *830 Phillips Ln (40209). Phone 502/367-2251; toll-free 800/626-2708; fax 502/363-2087. www.executivewest.com.* Just 6 miles from downtown, this hotel is adjacent to Louisville International Airport. 611 rooms, 8 story. S, D $125; suites $105-$240; under 17 free. Pets accepted; fee. Check-out noon. TV. In-room modem link. Restaurant, bar; entertainment. Room service. Health club privileges. Indoor/outdoor pool; poolside service. Free airport transportation. Kentucky Kingdom Amusement Park opposite.

D ➳ ☇ ✕ ⊠

★ ★ ★ **THE SEELBACH HILTON LOUISVILLE.** *500 4th Ave (40202). Phone 502/585-3200; toll-free 800/333-3399; fax 502/585-9240. www.hilton.com.* Built in 1905 by brothers Otto and Louis Seelbach, this hotel is on the National Register of Historic Places. From presidents to movie stars to authors (F. Scott Fitzgerald wrote about the hotel in *The Great Gatsby*), everyone seems drawn here. The entrance is dramatic with its muraled ceilings, marble columns, and regal staircase leading to the impeccable Oakroom restaurant. 321 rooms, 11 story. S $159-$199; D $174-$214; each additional $10; suites $210-$510; under 18 free; package plans. Pets accepted; fee. Check-out 1 pm. TV; cable (premium), VCR available. In-room modem link. Restaurant, bar; entertainment. Health club privileges. Valet parking. Free airport transportation. Business center. Concierge. Luxury level.

D ➳ ✕ ⊠ SC ☇

B&B/Small Inn

★ ★ **WOODHAVEN BED AND BREAKFAST.** *401 S Hubbards Ln (40207). Phone 502/895-1011. www.innatwoodhaven.com.* 8 rooms, 2 story. Pets accepted, some restrictions. Complimentary full breakfast. Check-out 11:30 am, check-in 3 pm. TV; cable (premium). Gothic Revival house built in 1853. Totally nonsmoking. **$$**

➳ ⊠

Extended Stay

★ ★ **RESIDENCE INN BY MARRIOTT.** *120 N Hurstbourne Pkwy (40222). Phone 502/425-1821; fax 502/425-1672. www.residenceinn.com.* 96 suites, 2 story. 1-bedroom $106-$120; 2-bedroom $119-$149; family rates; weekend rates. Pets accepted; fee. Complimentary continental breakfast. Check-out noon. TV; cable (premium). In-room modem link. Fireplaces. Health club privileges. Heated pool; whirlpool. Sport court.

D ➳ ☇ ⊠

Madisonville

Motels/Motor Lodges

★ ★ **BEST WESTERN PENNYRILE INN.** *Pennyrile Pkwy (42440). Phone 270/258-5201; fax 270/258-9072. www.bestwestern.com.* 60 rooms, 2 story. S $35; D $40-

$49; each additional $3; under 12 free. Pets accepted; fee. Complimentary breakfast buffet. Check-out noon. TV; cable (premium), VCR available (movies). Restaurant open 24 hours. Pool.

D 🐾 ≈ ⊠

★ **DAYS INN.** *1900 Lantaff Blvd (42431). Phone 270/821-8620; fax 270/825-9282. www.daysinn.com.* 143 rooms, 2 story. S $52-$57; D $57-$62; each additional $5; suites $90-$120. Pets accepted; fee. Complimentary continental breakfast. Check-out noon. TV; cable (premium). Restaurant. Room service. Health club privileges. Sauna. Indoor pool.

D 🐾 ≈ ⚡ ⚡ ≈

Mount Vernon

Motels/Motor Lodges

★ **ECONO LODGE.** *1375 Richmond Rd (40456). Phone 606/256-4621; toll-free 800/638-7949; fax 606/256-4622. www.econolodge.com.* 35 rooms, 2-3 story. S 29.50-$32; D $36-$40.50; family rates; higher rates: holiday weekends, special events. Pets accepted. Check-out 11 am. TV. Pool.

D 🐾 ≈ ⊠ SC

★ ★ **KASTLE INN MOTEL.** *I-75 and US 25 exit 59 (40456). Phone 606/256-5156; toll-free 800/965-4366.* 50 rooms, 2 story. S $36-$48; D $42-$56; each additional $8; under 12 free. Pets accepted. Check-out 11 am. TV; cable (premium), VCR available. Restaurant. Pool.

D 🐾 ≈ ⊠

Murray

Motels/Motor Lodges

★ **DAYS INN.** *517 S 12th St (42071). Phone 270/753-6706; fax 502/753-6708. www.daysinn.com.* 41 rooms. S $47.50-$60; D $52.50-$65; each additional $5; under 13 free; higher rates special events. Pets accepted; fee. Complimentary continental breakfast. Check-out 11 am. TV; cable (premium). Health club privileges. Pool.

D 🐾 ⚡ ≈ ⊠

★ **MURRAY PLAZA COURT.** *502 S 12th St (42071). Phone 270/753-2682.* 40 rooms, 2 story. S $33; D $36.30; each additional $5; weekly plans; higher rates special events. Pets accepted. Check-out noon. TV; cable (premium).

🐾

★ **SHONEY'S INN.** *1503 N 12th St (42071). Phone 270/753-5353. www.shoneysinn.com.* 67 rooms, 2 story. S $44-$48; D $49-$53; each additional $5; higher rates special events; crib free. Pets accepted; fee. Check-out noon. TV; cable (premium). In-room modem link. Pool.

D 🐾 ⚡ ⚡ ≈ ⊠

Owensboro

Motel/Motor Lodge

★ ★ **RAMADA INN.** *3136 W 2nd St (42304). Phone 270/685-3941; toll-free 800/465-4329; fax 270/926-2917. www.holiday-inn.com.* 145 rooms, 2 story. S, D $59-$69; suites $95; under 19 free. Pets accepted. Check-out noon. TV; cable (premium). In-room modem link. Restaurant, bar. Room service. In-house fitness room; sauna. Indoor pool; whirlpool. Business center.

D 🐾 ≈ 🏃 ⊠ SC 🚶

Paducah

Motels/Motor Lodges

★ **DRURY INN.** *3975 Hinkleville Rd (42001). Phone 270/443-3313. www.druryinn.com.* 118 rooms, 5 story. S $59-$70; D $65-$80 each additional $8; suites $70-$80; under 18 free. Pets accepted, some restrictions. Complimentary full breakfast. Check-out noon. TV. Health club privileges. Indoor pool; whirlpool.

D 🐾 ⚡ ⚡ ≈ ⊠

★ **HOLIDAY INN EXPRESS.** *3994 Hinkleville Rd (42001). Phone 270/442-8874; fax 270/443-3367. www.hiexpress.com.* 76 rooms, 3 story. S $80.50; D $90.50; each additional $10; under 18 free; higher rates special events. Pets accepted, some restrictions. Complimentary continental breakfast. Check-out 11 am. TV; cable (premium), VCR available. Laundry services. Health club privileges. Game room. Indoor pool; whirlpool.

D 🐾 ≈ ⊠ SC

★ ★ **QUALITY INN.** *1380 Irvin Cobb Dr (42003). Phone 270/443-8751; fax 270/442-0133. www.qualityinn.com.* 101 rooms, 2 story. Mar-Nov: S $39.99-$48.99; D $48.99-$58.99; each additional $7; family, weekly rates; higher rates special events; lower rates rest of year. Pets accepted; fee. Complimentary continental breakfast. Check-out 11 am. TV; cable (premium). Pool.

D 🐾 ≈ ⊠

Prestonsburg

Motel/Motor Lodge

★ **DAYS INN.** *512 S Mayo Trail (41240). Phone 606/ 789-3551; toll-free 800/329-7466; fax 606/789-9299. www.daysinn.com.* 72 rooms, 2 story. S $45-$70; D $55-$70; each additional $5; under 12 free; higher rates Apple Festival. Pets accepted; fee. Complimentary continental breakfast. Check-out 11 am. TV; cable (premium). In-house fitness room. Pool.

⊡ 🐾 ⇌ 🏋 ⇌ SC

Richmond

Motels/Motor Lodges

★ **DAYS INN.** *2109 Belmont Dr (40475). Phone 859/ 624-5769; toll-free 800/329-7466; fax 859/624-1406. www.daysinn.com.* 70 rooms, 2 story. S $42; D $47; each additional $5; under 18 free. Pets accepted, some restrictions; fee. Check-out 11 am. TV; cable (premium). Pool.

⊡ 🐾 ⇌ ⇌ SC

★ **LA QUINTA INN.** *1751 Lexington Rd (40475). Phone 859/623-9121; toll-free 800/575-5339; fax 859/623-3160. www.laquinta.com.* 95 rooms, 2 story. S, D $59; under 17 free. Pets accepted, some restrictions; fee. Continental breakfast. Check-out noon. TV; cable (premium). In-room modem link. Heated pool.

🐾 ⫟ ⇌ ⇌

★ **SUPER 8.** *107 N Keeneland Dr (40475). Phone 859/624-1550; toll-free 800/800-8000; fax 859/624-1553. www.super8.com.* 63 rooms, 2 story. S $39.88; D $49.88; each additional $5; under 18 free; weekly rates; higher rates college events, races. Pets accepted; fee. Complimentary continental breakfast. Check-out 11 am. TV; cable (premium).

⊡ 🐾 🐾 ⇌

Somerset

Motel/Motor Lodge

★ **KNIGHTS INN.** *1532 S KY 27 (42501). Phone 606/ 678-4195; toll-free 800/256-3446; fax 606/679-3299.* 100 rooms, 1-2 story. S $42; D $50; each additional $5; under 12 free. Pets accepted; fee. Check-out noon. TV; cable (premium). Restaurant. Room service. Pool; children's pool. Lawn games.

⊡ 🐾 ⇌ ⇌ SC

Walton

Motel/Motor Lodge

★ **DAYS INN.** *11177 Frontage Rd (41094). Phone 859/485-4151; fax 859/485-1239. www.daysinn.com.* 137 rooms, 2 story. S, D $39-$55; each additional $7. Pets accepted, some restrictions; fee. Check-out 11 am. TV. Pool.

⊡ 🐾 ⇌ ⇌

Williamsburg

Motel/Motor Lodge

★ **SUPER 8.** *30 W KY 92 (40769). Phone 606/549-3450; fax 606/549-8161. www.super8.com.* 100 rooms, 2-3 story. No elevator. S, D $65; under 18 free. Pets accepted; fee. Complimentary continental breakfast. Check-out noon. TV; cable (premium). In-room modem link. Room service. Pool.

⊡ 🐾 ⇌ ⇌

Williamstown

Motel/Motor Lodge

★ **DAYS INN.** *211 KY 36 W (41097). Phone 859/ 824-5025; toll-free 800/329-7466; fax 859/824-5028. www.daysinn.com.* 50 rooms, 1-2 story. S $36-$40; D $45-$51; each additional $5; under 12 free. Pets accepted, some restrictions; fee. Check-out 11 am. TV. Pool.

🐾 ⇌ ⇌ SC

Winchester

Motel/Motor Lodge

★ ★ **DAYS INN.** *1100 Interstate Dr (40391). Phone 859/744-9111; fax 859/745-1369. www.daysinn.com.* 64 rooms, 2 story. S, D $59; under 19 free; higher rates special events. Pets accepted, some restrictions; fee. Check-out 11 am. TV; cable (premium). Laundry services. Restaurant. Room service. Pool.

🐾 ⇌ ⇌ SC

Louisiana

Alexandria

Motels/Motor Lodges

★ **BEST WESTERN OF ALEXANDRIA INN & SUITES.** *2720 W MacArthur Dr (71303). Phone 318/445-5530; toll-free 888/338-2008; fax 318/445-8496. www.bestwestern.com.* 198 rooms, 2 story. S $52; D $58; each additional $6; suites $81-$125; under 18 free. Pets accepted, some restrictions. Complimentary continental breakfast. Check-out noon. TV; cable (premium). Bar. Health club privileges. Indoor pool; children's pool; whirlpool. Airport transportation.

★ **DAYS INN.** *1146 MacArthur Dr (71303). Phone 318/443-1841; fax 318/448-4845. www.daysinn.com.* 70 rooms, 2 story. S, D $42; each additional $3; under 17 free. Pets accepted, some restrictions; fee. Complimentary continental breakfast. Check-out 11 am. TV. Pool.

★ **RAMADA INN.** *742 MacArthur Dr (71301). Phone 318/448-1611; fax 318/473-2984. www.ramada.com.* 121 rooms, 2 story. S $36-$40; D $40-$50; each additional $10; suites $57-$62; studio rooms $38-$50; under 17 free. Pets accepted; fee. Check-out noon. TV; cable (premium), VCR available. Pool; children's pool. Airport transportation.

Bastrop

Motels/Motor Lodges

★ **COUNTRY INN.** *1815 E Madison (71220). Phone 318/281-8100; fax 318/281-5895. www.countryinn-motel.com.* 30 rooms, 2 story. S $33-$38; D $38-$43; each additional $5; under 12 free. Pets accepted; fee. Check-out noon. TV; cable (premium).

★ **PREFERRED INN.** *1053 E Madison (71220). Phone 318/281-3621; toll-free 800/227-8767; fax 318/283-1501. www.preferredinns.com.* 109 rooms, 1-2 story. S $30-$48; D $32-$52; suites $44-$65; studio rooms $46-$63; under 12 free. Pets accepted; fee. Complimentary continental

breakfast. Check-out noon. TV; cable (premium). Restaurant. Room service. Pool. Free airport transportation. Business center.

Baton Rouge

Motels/Motor Lodges

★ **LA QUINTA INN.** *2333 S Acadian Thrwy (70808). Phone 225/924-9600; fax 225/924-2609. www.laquinta.com.* 142 rooms, 2 story. S, D $71-$81; suites $125; under 18 free; higher rates special events. Pets accepted, some restrictions. Complimentary continental breakfast. Check-out noon. TV; cable (premium). In-room modem link. Health club privileges. Pool. Airport transportation.

★ **SHONEY'S INN.** *9919 Gwen Adele Dr (70816). Phone 225/925-8399; toll-free 800/552-4667; fax 225/927-1731. www.shoneysinn.com.* 195 rooms, 2 story. S, D $55; suites $70; under 18 free; weekend rates. Pets accepted, some restrictions; fee. Complimentary continental breakfast. Check-out noon. TV; cable (premium). In-room modem link. Restaurant. Pool.

All Suite

★★ **WOODFIN SUITES.** *5522 Corporate Blvd (70808). Phone 225/927-5630; toll-free 800/433-9669; fax 225/926-2317. www.woodfinsuitehotels.com.* 80 kitchen suites, 2 story. Suites $129-$169; weekend rates. Pets accepted; fee. Complimentary breakfast buffet. Check-out noon. TV; cable (premium), VCR available. In-room modem link. Room service. Health club privileges. Pool; whirlpool. Outdoor tennis.

Bossier City

Extended Stay

★★ **RESIDENCE INN BY MARRIOTT.** *1001 Gould Dr (71111). Phone 318/747-6220; toll-free 800/331-3131; fax 318/747-3424. www.residenceinn.com.* 72 kitchen units, 2 story. S $105-$135; D $125-$165. Pets accepted; fee. Complimentary continental breakfast. Check-out noon. TV; cable (premium). In-room modem link. Health club privileges. Pool; whirlpool.

Kenner

Motel/Motor Lodge

★ **LA QUINTA INN.** *2610 Williams Blvd (70062). Phone 504/466-1401; toll-free 800/687-6667; fax 504/466-0319. www.laquinta.com.* 130 rooms, 5 story. S, D $85-$135; under 18 free. Pets accepted. Complimentary continental breakfast. Check-out noon. TV. In-room modem link. Laundry services. Pool. Free airport transportation.

D 🐾 🛏 🖎 SC

Hotel

★ ★ ★ **HILTON NEW ORLEANS AIRPORT.** *901 Airline Dr (70062). Phone 504/469-5000; toll-free 800/872-5914; fax 504/466-5473. www.hilton.com.* This first-class hotel in the airport area caters to business travelers, but with a 21-station fitness center, outdoor pool and hot tub, tennis courts, and putting green, this hotel is great for leisure travelers as well. 317 rooms, 6 story. S $115-$177; D $127-$189; each additional $12; suites $325-$450; family rates; weekend rates. Pets accepted, some restrictions; fee. Check-out 1 pm. TV; cable (premium), VCR available. In-room modem link. Restaurant, bar. In-house fitness room. Pool; whirlpool; poolside service. Outdoor tennis, lighted courts. Free airport transportation. Business center.

D 🐾 ✈ 🛏 🏃 ✈ 🖎 🚶

Lafayette

Motels/Motor Lodges

★ **COMFORT INN.** *1421 SE Evangeline Thrwy (70501). Phone 337/232-9000; toll-free 800/800-8752; fax 337/233-8629. www.comfortinn.com.* 200 rooms, 2 story. S $69-$79; D $74-$84; each additional $5; suites $115-$125; under 18 free; family rates; higher rates Crawfish Festival. Pets accepted. Complimentary continental breakfast. Check-out noon. TV; cable (premium). Restaurant, bar. Room service. In-house fitness room. Pool. Free airport transportation.

D 🐾 🛏 🏃 🖎 SC

★ **LA QUINTA INN.** *2100 NE Evangeline Thrwy (70507). Phone 37/233-5610; toll-free 800/531-5900; fax 337/235-2104. www.laquinta.com.* 140 rooms, 2 story. S, D $65-$72; each additional $7; under 18 free. Pets accepted. Complimentary continental breakfast. Check-out noon. TV; cable (premium). In-room modem link. Health club privileges. Pool.

D 🐾 🛏 🖎 SC

★ **RED ROOF INN.** *1718 N University Ave (70507). Phone 337/233-3339; toll-free 800/843-7663; fax 337/233-7206. www.redroof.com.* 108 rooms, 2 story. S $35-$45; D $41-$49; each additional $8; under 18 free; higher rates special events. Pets accepted. Check-out noon. TV.

D 🐾 🛏 SC

Metairie

Motels/Motor Lodges

★ **LA QUINTA INN.** *5900 Veterans Memorial Blvd (70003). Phone 504/456-0003; fax 504/885-0863. www.laquinta.com.* 153 rooms, 3 story. S, D $82; suites $150; under 18 free. Pets accepted. Complimentary continental breakfast. Check-out noon. TV; cable (premium). In-room modem link. Health club privileges. Pool. Free airport transportation.

D 🐾 🛏 ✈ 🖎

★ ★ **QUALITY INN.** *2261 N Causeway Blvd (70001). Phone 504/833-8211; toll-free 800/638-7949; fax 504/833-8213. www.qualityinn.com.* 204 rooms, 10 story. S, D $89-$119; under 18 free; weekend rates; higher rates special events. Pets accepted; fee. Check-out noon. TV; cable (premium), VCR available. In-room modem link. Restaurant. Room service. In-house fitness room; sauna. Free airport transportation.

D 🐾 🏃 ✈ 🖎 SC

Monroe and West Monroe

Motels/Motor Lodges

★ **LA QUINTA INN.** *1035 US 165 Bypass (71203). Phone 318/322-3900; fax 318/323-5537. www.laquinta.com.* 130 rooms, 2 story. S $55; D $61; each additional $5; suites $75; under 18 free. Pets accepted, some restrictions; fee. Complimentary continental breakfast. TV. In-room modem link. Pool. Free airport transportation.

D 🐾 🛏 ✈ 🖎

★ **RED ROOF INN.** *102 Constitution (71292). Phone 318/388-2420; fax 318/388-2499. www.redroof.com.* 97 rooms, 3 story. S $36.99-$47.99; D $41.99-$52.99; each additional $6; under 18 free. Pets accepted; fee. Check-out noon. TV; cable (premium).

🐾 🐾

Morgan City

Motel/Motor Lodge

★ ★ **HOLIDAY INN.** *520 Roderick St (70381). Phone 985/385-2200; fax 985/384-3810. www.holiday-inn.com.* 219 rooms, 2 story. S, D $69-$79; each additional $10; suites $89-$99; under 18 free. Pets accepted; fee. Check-out noon. TV; cable (premium). In-room modem link. Restaurant, bar. Room service. Health club privileges. Pool.

D 🐾 🐞 🛏 🏊

New Iberia

Motel/Motor Lodge

★ ★ **HOLIDAY INN.** *2915 Hwy 14 (70560). Phone 337/367-1201; fax 337/367-7877. www.holiday-inn.com.* 177 rooms, 2 story. S, D $62; each additional $6; under 18 free. Pets accepted, some restrictions; fee. Check-out 11 am. TV; cable (premium), VCR available. In-room modem link. Restaurant, bar. Room service. Pool.

D 🐾 🛏 🏊 SC

New Orleans

Motel/Motor Lodge

★ **FRENCH QUARTER COURTYARD HOTEL.** *1101 N Rampart St (70116). Phone 504/522-7333; toll-free 800/290-4233; fax 504/522-3908. www.neworleans.com/sqch.* 51 rooms, 2-3 story. S, D $69-$259; under 17 free; higher rates special events. Pets accepted; fee. Complimentary continental breakfast. Check-out noon. TV. Bar open 24 hours. Pool; poolside service. Valet parking.

D 🐾 🛏 🏊

Hotels

★ ★ **AMBASSADOR HOTEL.** *535 Tchoupitoulas St (70130). Phone 504/527-5271; toll-free 888/527-5271; fax 504/527-5270. www.ahno.com.* 165 rooms, 4 story. Pets accepted, some restrictions; fee. Check-out 11 am, check-in 3 pm. TV. In-room modem link. Restaurant, bar. Room service. Valet parking. Airport transportation. Concierge. **$$**

D 🐾 🏊

★ ★ ★ **CHATEAU SONESTA NEW ORLEANS.** *800 Iberville St (70112). Phone 504/586-0800; toll-free 800/SONESTA; fax 504/586-1987. www.chateausonesta.com.*

Be right in the center of the action at this hotel with balconies overlooking Bourbon Street or, if more tranquil scenery is preferred, overlooking the pool. The hotel is also convenient to the St. Charles Streetcar and the waterfront. 251 rooms, 4 story. Pets accepted, some restrictions; fee. Check-out noon, check-in 3 pm. TV; cable. In-room modem link. Restaurant, bar; entertainment. Room service. In-house fitness room. Pool; poolside service. Parking, valet parking. Concierge. **$$$**

D 🐾 🏊 🏃 🛏

★ ★ ★ **OMNI ROYAL ORLEANS.** *621 St. Louis St (70140). Phone 504/529-5333; toll-free 800/788-OMNI; fax 504/529-7089. www.omniroyalorleans.com.* Located in the French Quarter, this hotel offers views of the area and the Mississippi River from Spanish wrought-iron balconies or from the observation deck on the roof. Also on the rooftop is a heated pool for guest use. 346 rooms, 7 story. Pets accepted, some restrictions; fee. Check-out noon, check-in 4 pm. TV; cable (premium), VCR available. In-room modem link. Restaurant, bar; entertainment. Room service 24 hours. In-house fitness room. Outdoor pool. Valet parking. Business center. Concierge. **$$$**

D 🐾 🏊 🏃 🛏 SC 🏃

★ ★ ★ **ROYAL SONESTA HOTEL.** *300 Bourbon St (70130). Phone 504/586-0300; toll-free 800/477-4556; fax 504/586-0335. www.royalsonestano.com.* Offering amazing style and elegance, this hotel is located in the heart of the French Quarter on Bourbon Street near many world-class restaurants, art and antique shops, nightclubs, and other attractions. 484 rooms, 7 story. Pets accepted, some restrictions; fee. Check-out noon, check-in 3 pm. TV; VCR available. In-room modem link. Restaurant, bar; entertainment. In-house fitness room. Outdoor pool. Business center. Luxury level. **$$$**

D 🐾 🏊 🏃 🛏 🏃

★ ★ ★ ★ **WINDSOR COURT HOTEL.** *300 Gravier St (70130). Phone 504/523-6000; toll-free 800/262-2662; fax 504/596-4513. www.windsorcourthotel.com.* Not far from the French Quarter in the city's business district, the Windsor Court Hotel welcomes guests with open arms. This elegant hotel brings a bit of the English countryside to New Orleans. Set around a courtyard, the hotel has 324 guest accommodations, more than half of which are suites. Traditional English furnishings and unique artwork define the rooms, while bay windows focus attention on lovely views of the city or the Mississippi River. This full-service hotel also includes a pool, sundeck, and comprehensive business and fitness centers under its roof. In a city hailed for its works of culinary genius, the Windsor Court is no exception. The Grill Room is one of the hottest tables in town; the Polo Club Lounge is ideal for enjoying brandy and cigars; and Le Salon is the "in" spot for afternoon tea. *Secret Inspector's Notes:* The staff makes the difference here. Personalized service and a sense of enthusiasm pervade the hotel. You'll feel as if you've come home—and you won't want to leave! 324 rooms, 23 story. Pets accepted, some restrictions; fee. Check-out noon, check-in 3 pm. TV; cable (premium), VCR. In-room modem link. Room service 24 hours. Restaurant, bar; entertainment. Health club privileges. Massage, sauna, steam room. Outdoor pool; whirlpool; poolside service. Valet parking. Airport transportation. Concierge. **$$$**

★ ★ ★ **W NEW ORLEANS.** *333 Poydras St (70130). Phone 504/525-9444; toll-free 800/522-6963; fax 504/ 581-7179. www.whotels.com.* This style-soaked chain is designed for savvy business travelers, but leisure guests won't mind the down comforters, Aveda products, and great fitness center. Zoe Bistro offers creative French food, and the lobby's Whiskey Blue bar delivers a dose of nightlife. 423 rooms, 23 story. Pets accepted, some restrictions; fee. Check-out noon, check-in 3 pm. TV; cable (premium). In-room modem link. Restaurant, bar. In-house fitness room. Outdoor pool. Concierge. Luxury level. **$$$**

All Suite

★ ★ **IBERVILLE SUITES.** *910 Iberville St (70112). Phone 504/523-2400; fax 504/524-1321. www.ibervillesuites.com.* 230 rooms, 7 story. Pets accepted; fee. Complimentary continental breakfast. Check-out noon, check-in 3 pm. TV; cable (premium). In-room modem link. Restaurant, bar. Babysitting services available. In-house fitness room; spa, sauna. Game room. Indoor pool; whirlpool. Airport transportation. Business center. Concierge. **$$**

B&B/Small Inn

★ ★ **CHIMES BED & BREAKFAST.** *1146 Constantinople St (70115). Phone 504/488-4640; toll-free 800/729-4640; fax 504/488-4639. www.historiclodging.com/ chimes.* 5 rooms. Oct-May: S, D $115-$155; weekends (3-day minimum); higher rates Jazz Fest; lower rates rest of year. Pets accepted; fee. Complimentary full breakfast. Check-out, check-in hours vary. TV; cable (premium). Totally nonsmoking.

Ruston

Motel/Motor Lodge

★ ★ **DAYS INN.** *1801 N Service Rd (71270). Phone 318/251-2360. www.daysinn.com.* 60 rooms, 2 story. S, D $55-$60; each additional $5; under 18 free. Pets accepted, some restrictions; fee. Complimentary continental breakfast. Check-out noon. TV. In-room modem link. Pool.

Hotel

★ ★ **RAMADA INN.** *401 N Service Rd (71270). Phone 318/255-5901; fax 318/255-3729. www.ramada.com.* 228 rooms, 1-2 story. S, D $49-$79; each additional $10; suites $129; under 19 free. Pets accepted; fee. Check-out noon. TV. In-room modem link. Restaurant. Room service. Two pools; children's pool.

Shreveport

Hotel

★ ★ ★ **SHERATON SHREVEPORT HOTEL.** *1419 E 70th St (71105). Phone 318/797-9900; fax 318/798-2923. www.sheraton.com.* 267 rooms, 6 story. S, D $109; each additional $10; suites $250-$450; under 18 free. Pets accepted; fee. Check-out noon. TV; cable (premium). In-room modem link. Restaurant, bar. In-house fitness room. Pool. Free airport transportation. Business center. Concierge. Luxury level. Free airport transportation.

Slidell

Motels/Motor Lodges

★ **LA QUINTA INN.** *794 E I-10 Service Rd (70461). Phone 985/643-9770; fax 985/641-4476. www.laquinta.com.* 177 rooms, 2 story. S, D $69.99-$86.99; each additional $6; under 18 free; higher rates special events. Pets accepted, some restrictions. Complimentary continental breakfast. Check-out noon. TV; cable (premium), VCR available. In-room modem link. Bar. Health club privileges. Game room. Pool.

★ **RAMADA INN.** *798 E I-10 Service Rd (70461). Phone 985/643-9960; toll-free 800/272-6232; fax 985/643-3508. www.ramada.com.* 149 rooms, 2 story. May-Aug: S $69-$79; D $64-$74; each additional $8; under 18 free; higher rates: Mardi Gras, Sugar Bowl, other special events; lower rates rest of year. Pets accepted, some restrictions; fee. Check-out noon. TV. In-room modem link. Restaurant, bar; entertainment. Health club privileges. Pool; children's pool; poolside service.

[D] [🐾] [≈] [⛳] [SC]

Thibodaux

Motel/Motor Lodge

★ **HOWARD JOHNSON.** *201 N Canal Blvd (70301). Phone 985/447-9071; toll-free 800/952-2968; fax 985/447-5752. www.hojo.com.* 118 rooms, 2 story. S $50-$150; D $55-$150; each additional $5; suites $80-$150; under 18 free; higher rates special events. Pets accepted, some restrictions; fee. Complimentary full breakfast. Check-out noon. TV; cable (premium), VCR available. In-room modem link. Restaurant, bar. Room service. In-house fitness room; sauna. Game room. Pool; poolside service. Lighted tennis courts.

[D] [🐾] [🎾] [≈] [🚶] [⛳]

Maine

Augusta

Motels/Motor Lodges

★★ **BEST WESTERN SENATOR INN & SPA.** *284 Western Ave; I-95 (04330). Phone 207/622-5804; toll-free 877/772-2224; fax 207/622-8803. www.bestwestern.com.* 125 rooms, 1-2 story. July-Aug: S $79-$99; D $89-$109; each additional $9; suites $149-$189; under 18 free; lower rates rest of year. Pets accepted, some restrictions; fee. Complimentary full breakfast. Check-out noon. TV; cable (premium), VCR available (movies). In-room modem link. Laundry services. Restaurant, bar. Room service. In-house fitness room; massage, sauna. Game room. Indoor, outdoor pool.

★★ **COMFORT INN.** *281 Civic Center Dr (04330). Phone 207/623-1000; toll-free 800/808-1188; fax 207/623-3505. www.comfortinn.com.* 99 rooms, 3 story. Pet accepted. Complimentary continental breakfast. Check-out 11 am, check-in 3 pm. TV; cable (premium). Restaurant, bar. In-house fitness room; sauna. Indoor pool. Cross-country ski 10 miles. **$**

★ **MOTEL 6.** *18 Edison Dr (04330). Phone 207/622-0000; toll-free 800/440-6000; fax 207/622-1048. www.motel6.com.* 68 rooms, 2 story. Late June-Sept: S $32.99; D $38.99; each additional $3; under 18 free. Pets accepted. Check-out noon. TV; cable (premium). Laundry services.

★ **TRAVELODGE.** *390 Western Ave (04330). Phone 207/622-6371; toll-free 888/515-6375; fax 207/621-0349. www.travelodge.com.* 98 rooms, 2 story. Mid-June-late Oct: S, D $60-$70; each additional $10; under 18 free; lower rates rest of year. Pets accepted; fee. Complimentary continental breakfast. Check-out 11 am. TV; cable (premium). Laundry services. Restaurant, bar. Pool; children's pool.

Bailey Island

Motel/Motor Lodge

★ **COOK'S ISLAND VIEW MOTEL.** *Rte 24 (04003). Phone 207/833-7780.* 18 rooms. No A/C. Closed Nov-May. Pets accepted. Check-out 11 am. TV. Pool. **$**

Bangor

Motels/Motor Lodges

★★ **BEST INN.** *570 Main St (04401). Phone 207/942-1234. www.bestinn.com.* 50 rooms, 1 suite, 2 story. June-Oct: S $50-$75; D $60-$80; each additional $5; under 18 free; lower rates rest of year. Pets accepted, some restrictions. Complimentary continental breakfast. Check-out 11 am. TV. Restaurant, bar. Free parking.

★★ **BEST WESTERN WHITE HOUSE INN.** *155 Littlefield Ave (04401). Phone 207/862-3737; fax 207/862-3737. www.bestwestern.com.* 66 rooms, 3 story. May-Oct: S, D $60-$100; each additional $5; family room $79-$99; under 12 free; lower rates rest of year. Pets accepted, some restrictions; fee. Complimentary continental breakfast. Check-out 11 am. TV; VCR available (movies). In-room modem link. Bar. Sauna. Pool. Downhill, cross-country ski 4 miles. Lawn games.

★ **COMFORT INN.** *750 Hogan Rd (04401). Phone 207/942-7899; fax 207/942-6463. www.comfortinn.com.* 96 rooms, 2 story. Mid-June-Oct: S $49-$89; D $59-$99; each additional $5; under 19 free; lower rates rest of year. Pets accepted, some restrictions; fee. Complimentary continental breakfast. Check-out noon. TV; cable (premium). In-house fitness room. Game room. Pool. Cross-country ski 10 miles. Free airport transportation.

★ **DAYS INN.** *250 Odlin Rd (04401). Phone 207/942-8272; toll-free 800/329-7466; fax 207/942-1382. www.daysinn.com.* 101 rooms, 2 story. July-Oct: S $50-$65; D $55-$85; each additional $6; under 12 free; lower rates rest of year. Pets accepted; fee. Complimentary continental breakfast. Check-out 11 am. TV; cable (premium), VCR available. In-room modem link. Room service. Game room. Indoor pool; whirlpool. Downhill, cross-country ski 12 miles. Free airport transportation.

[D] [🐾] [⤢] [⛱] [✈] [⊠]

★ **ECONO LODGE.** *327 Odlin Rd (04401). Phone 207/945-0111; toll-free 800/393-0111; fax 207/942-8856. www.econolodge.com.* 128 rooms, 4 story. S $29.95-$65.95; D $39.95-$85.95; under 19 free. Pets accepted; fee. Check-out 11 am. TV; cable (premium). In-room modem link. Laundry services. Downhill, cross-country ski 7 miles.

[D] [🐾] [⤢] [⊠] [SC]

★ ★ **FOUR POINTS BY SHERATON.** *308 Godfrey Blvd (04401). Phone 207/947-6721; toll-free 800/228-4609; fax 207/941-9761. www.fourpoints.com.* 101 rooms, 9 story. S, D $98-$155; each additional $15; under 18 free. Pets accepted, some restrictions; fee. Check-out noon. TV; cable (premium). In-room modem link. Restaurant, bar. In-house fitness room. Pool. Downhill ski 7 miles, cross-country ski 7 miles. Validated parking. Airport transportation. Business center. Enclosed walkway to airport.

[D] [🐾] [⤢] [⛱] [✈] [⊠] [SC] [🏃]

Hotels

★ ★ **HOLIDAY INN.** *500 Main St (04401). Phone 207/947-8651; toll-free 800/799-8651; fax 207/942-2848. www.holiday-inn.com/bangor-civic.* 121 rooms, 4 story. May-Oct: S, D $59-$99; suites $115-$200; under 19 free; lower rates rest of year. Pets accepted, some restrictions. Check-out noon. TV; cable (premium). In-room modem link. Restaurant, bar; entertainment. Room service. Health club privileges. Pool. Downhill ski 10 miles. Free airport transportation. Opposite Civic Center.

[D] [🐾] [⤢] [⛱] [✈] [⊠] [SC]

★ ★ **HOLIDAY INN.** *404 Odlin Rd (04401). Phone 207/947-0101; toll-free 800/914-0101; fax 207/947-7619. www.holiday-inn.com/bangor-odlin.* 207 rooms, 3 story. July-Oct: S $89-$99; D $99-$109; each additional $10; under 19 free; lower rates rest of year. Pets accepted, some restrictions. Check-out noon. TV; cable (premium), VCR available. In-room modem link. Restaurant, bar; entertainment. Room service. Health club privileges. Indoor pool; outdoor pool; whirlpool. Downhill ski 15 miles, cross-country ski 10 miles. Free airport transportation.

[D] [🐾] [⤢] [⛱] [✈] [SC]

Bath

Motel/Motor Lodge

★ ★ **HOLIDAY INN.** *139 Richardson St (04530). Phone 207/443-9741; fax 207/442-8281. www.holiday-inn.com.* 141 rooms, 4 story. Late June-early Oct: S, D $85-$119; each additional $10; under 19 free; lower rates rest of year. Pets accepted, some restrictions. Check-out noon. TV; cable (premium). In-room modem link. Restaurant, bar; entertainment. In-house fitness room; sauna. Pool; whirlpool.

[D] [🐾] [⤢] [⛱] [⊠] [SC]

Belfast

Motels/Motor Lodges

★ ★ **BELFAST HARBOR INN.** *RR 5 Box 5230, Rte 1 (04915). Phone 207/338-2740; toll-free 800/545-8576; fax 207/338-5205. belfastharborinn.com.* 61 rooms, 2 story. July-Aug: S, D $79-$139; each additional $10; under 12 free; weekly rates; lower rates rest of year. Pets accepted, some restrictions; fee. Complimentary continental breakfast. Check-out 11 am. TV; cable (premium). Restaurant. Pool. Downhill, cross-country ski 15 miles. Overlooks Penobscot Bay.

[D] [🐾] [⤢] [⛱]

★ **GULL MOTEL.** *US Rte 1, Searsport Ave (04915). Phone 207/338-4030.* 14 rooms, 2 story. July-Labor Day: S, D $39-$79; each additional $5, under 12 $3; lower rates rest of year. Pets accepted, some restrictions; fee. Check-out 11 am. TV. Overlooks bay.

[🐾]

B&B/Small Inn

★ ★ **BELFAST BAY MEADOWS INN.** *192 Northport Ave (04915). Phone 207/338-5715; toll-free 800/335-2370. www.baymeadowsinn.com.* 19 rooms, 1-3 story. Pets accepted; fee. Complimentary full breakfast. Check-out 11 am, check-in 3:30-6:30 pm. TV in some rooms; VCR available (free movies). Turn-of-the-century country inn. Overlooks bay. Totally nonsmoking. **$**

[🐾] [⊠]

Bethel

Resort

★ ★ **BETHEL INN AND COUNTRY CLUB.** *On the Common (04217). Phone 207/824-2175; toll-free 800/654-0125; fax 207/824-2233. www.bethelinn.com.* No A/C. May-Oct, Dec-Mar: S $99-$149; D $200-$300; each additional $55; MAP: suites $90-$175; EP: townhouses $79-$129/person; lower rates rest of year. Pets accepted, some restrictions; fee. Check-out 11 am, check-in 2 pm. TV; VCR available. Dining room, bar; entertainment. Supervised children's activities (July 7-Labor Day); ages 5-12. In-house fitness room; sauna, massage. Heated pool; whirlpool; poolside service. 18-hole golf, putting green, driving range, greens fee $35-$40. Tennis. Downhill ski 7 miles, cross-country ski on site. Lawn games. Canoes, sailboats.

B&B/Small Inn

★ ★ **BRIAR LEA INN & RESTAURANT.** *150 Mayville Rd (04217). Phone 207/824-4717; toll-free 877/311-1299; fax 207/824-7121. briarleainnrestaurant.com.* 6 rooms, 3 with shower only. No A/C. No room phones, Pets accepted, some restrictions; fee. Complimentary breakfast. Check-out 11 am, check-in 4 pm. TV; VCR available. Restaurant. Downhill, cross-country skiing. Built in 1850s; farmhouse atmosphere. **$**

Bingham

Motel/Motor Lodge

★ **BINGHAM MOTOR INN & SPORTS COMPLEX.** *Rte 201 (04920). Phone 207/672-4135; fax 207/672-4138. www.binghammotorinn.com.* 20 rooms, 4 kitchen units. July-Labor Day, hunting season: S $44.86-$48; D $52.34-$58; each additional $5; kitchen units $5 additional; weekly; lower rates rest of year. Pets accepted, some restrictions. Check-out 10 am. TV. Pool. Downhill ski 3 miles. Lawn games.

Boothbay Harbor

Motels/Motor Lodges

★ ★ **LAWNMEER INN.** *65 Hendrix Hill Rd (04575). Phone 207/633-2544; toll-free 800/633-7645; fax 207/633-0762. www.lawnmeerinn.com.* 32 rooms, 1-2 story. Some

A/C. July-Labor Day: D $88-$140; each additional $25; lower rates: mid-May-June, weekdays after Labor Day-mid-Oct. Closed rest of year. Pets accepted, some restrictions; fee. Check-out 11 am. TV. Restaurant, bar. Lawn games. Built in 1898. On inlet; dock.

★ **PINES MOTEL.** *Sunset Rd (04538). Phone 207/633-4555. www.gwi.net/~pinesmo.* 29 rooms. July-Aug: S $70; D $85; each additional $8; lower rates May-June, after Sept-mid-Oct. Closed rest of year. Pets accepted. Check-out 11 am. TV. Pool. Tennis. Lawn games. In wooded area; view of harbor.

★ ★ **SMUGGLER'S COVE MOTOR INN.** *Rte 96 (04544). Phone 207/633-2800; toll-free 800/633-3008; fax 207/633-5926. www.smugglerscovremotel.com.* 60 rooms, 6 kitchen units, 2 story. Late June-Labor Day: S, D $69-$169; each additional $10; kitchen units $85-$140; under 12 free; weekly rates; lower rates after Labor Day-mid-Oct. Closed rest of year. Pets accepted, some restrictions; fee. Check-out 11 am. TV. Restaurant, bar. Pool.

★ **THE WATER'S EDGE MOTEL.** *549 Ocean Point Rd (04544). Phone 207/633-2505. www.watersedge-linekinbay.com.* 20 kitchen units, 1-2 story. No A/C. No room phones. Late June-late Aug: S, D $85-$120; lower rates mid-May-late June, late Aug-mid-Oct. Closed rest of year. Pets accepted; fee. Check-out 10 am. TV. Lawn games.

Brunswick

Motels/Motor Lodges

★ ★ **TRAVELODGE.** *21 Gurnet Rd, Cooks Corner (04011). Phone 207/729-5555; toll-free 800/578-7878; fax 207/729-5149. www.travelodge.com.* 184 rooms, 3 story. July-Aug: S, D $74-$86; each additional $10; suites $125; under 19 free; lower rates rest of year. Pets accepted. Check-out noon. TV; VCR available. Restaurant, bar. Room service. In-house fitness room; sauna. Game room. Indoor pool; children's pool; whirlpool. Lawn games.

★ **VIKING MOTOR INN.** *287 Bath Rd (04011). Phone 207/729-6661; toll-free 800/429-6661. www.vikingmotorinn.com.* 28 rooms, 10 kitchen units. July-Oct: S $39-$69; D $49-$79; each additional $5; under 12 free; weekly rates off season; lower rates rest of year. Pets accepted, some restrictions; fee. Check-out 10 am. TV. Pool. Lawn games.

Bucksport

Motels/Motor Lodges

★ **BEST WESTERN JED PROUTY MOTOR INN.** *52 Main St (04416). Phone 207/469-3113; toll-free 800/528-1234. www.bestwestern.com.* 40 rooms, 2-4 story. July-Oct: S $89; D $99; each additional $10; suites $125; under 12 free; lower rates rest of year. Pets accepted, some restrictions. Check-out 11 am. TV. In-room modem link. On the Penobscot River.

⌧⌧⌧⌧

★ **BUCKSPORT MOTOR INN.** *70 US Rte 1 (04416). Phone 207/469-3111; toll-free 800/626-9734; fax 207/469-1045.* 24 rooms. Aug: S $40-$72; D $45-$72; each additional $5; lower rates rest of year. Pets accepted, some restrictions; fee. Check-out 11 am. TV.

⌧⌧⌧

Eastport

B&B/Small Inn

★★ **TODD HOUSE.** *1 Capen Ave (04631). Phone 207/853-2328.* This authentic New England Cape once housed soldiers during the War of 1812. 6 rooms, 2 story. No A/C. No room phones. Pets accepted, some restrictions. Complimentary continental breakfast. Check-out 11 am, check-in 2 pm. TV in most rooms; cable. Near the ocean; view of bay. $

⌧⌧⌧

Ellsworth

Motels/Motor Lodges

★★ **COLONIAL TRAVELODGE.** *321 High St (04605). Phone 207/667-5548; fax 207/667-5549. www.acadia.net/colonial.* 68 rooms, 18 kitchen units, 2 story. July-Aug: S $78-$110; D $88-$120; each additional $6; suites $125; kitchen units $78-$94; under 17 free; weekly rates; lower rates rest of year. Pets accepted, some restrictions. Complimentary continental breakfast (June-Sept). Check-out 11 am. TV. Restaurant. Health club privileges. Indoor pool; whirlpool. Cross-country ski 15 miles.

⌧⌧⌧⌧⌧

★★ **HOLIDAY INN.** *215 High St (04605). Phone 207/667-9341; toll-free 800/465-4329; fax 207/667-7294. www.holidayinnellsworth.com.* 103 rooms, 2 story. July-Aug: S $109-$119; D $119-$129; each additional $10; under 19 free; lower rates rest of year. Pets accepted, some restrictions; fee. Check-out noon. TV; cable (premium). In-room modem link. Laundry services. Restaurant, bar. Room service. In-house fitness room; sauna. Indoor pool; whirlpool; poolside service. Outdoor, indoor tennis. Cross-country ski 15 miles. Near river.

⌧⌧⌧⌧⌧⌧⌧

★ **TWILITE MOTEL.** *147 Bucksport Rd (04605). Phone 207/667-8165; toll-free 800/395-5097; fax 207/667-0289. www.twilitemotel.com.* 22 rooms. July-Labor Day: S, D $50-$86; each additional $5; lower rates rest of year. Pets accepted, some restrictions; fee. Complimentary continental breakfast. Check-out 10 am. TV; VCR available.

⌧⌧⌧

Freeport

Motel/Motor Lodge

★ **COASTLINE INN.** *209 US 1 (04032). Phone 207/865-3777; toll-free 800/470-9494; fax 207/865-4678. coastlineinnmaine.com.* 108 rooms, 2 story. July-Oct: S $49-$89; D $59-$99; under 12 free; weekly rates (off season); lower rates rest of year. Pets accepted. Complimentary continental breakfast. Check-out 11 am. TV; cable (premium), VCR available.

⌧⌧⌧

Hotel

★★ **FREEPORT INN.** *31 US Rte 1 (04032). Phone 207/865-3106; toll-free 800/998-2583; fax 207/865-6364. www.freeportinn.com.* 80 rooms, 3 story. No elevator. May-Oct: S, D $60-$100; each additional $10; lower rates rest of year. Pets accepted, some restrictions. Check-out 11 am. TV. In-room modem link. Restaurant. Pool. Lawn games. On 25 acres; river; canoe.

⌧⌧⌧⌧

Greenville Junction

Motels/Motor Lodges

★ **CHALET MOOSEHEAD LAKEFRONT MOTEL.** *Birch St (04441). Phone 207/695-2950; toll-free 800/290-3645. www.mooseheadlodging.com.* 27 rooms, 2 story. Pets accepted, some restrictions; fee. Check-out 10 am. TV; cable (premium). Lawn games. Boat rentals. On Moosehead Lake; dockage, paddleboats. Canoes. Seaplane rides nearby. $

⌧⌧⌧⌧⌧

★ **KINEO VIEW MOTOR LODGE.** *Rte 15 (04441). Phone 207/695-4470; toll-free 800/659-8439; fax 207/695-4656. www.kineoview.com.* 12 rooms, 2 story. No A/C. Memorial Day-mid-Oct: D $65-$75; each additional $5; under 13 free; weekly rates; lower rates rest of year. Pets accepted; fee. Complimentary continental breakfast in season. Check-out 10:30 am. TV. Game room. Downhill ski 9 miles, cross-country ski on site. Lawn games.

Hotel

★ **GREENWOOD.** *Rte 15; Rockwood Rd (04442). Phone 207/695-3321; toll-free 800/477-4386; fax 207/695-2122. www.greenwoodmotel.com.* 16 rooms, 2 story. Mid-May-mid-Sept: S $39.95-$59; D $44.95-$64; each additional $5; hunting plans; lower rates rest of year. Pets accepted, some restrictions; fee. Complimentary continental breakfast. Check-out 10:30 am. TV; cable (premium). Pool. Downhill, cross-country ski 3 miles. Lawn games. Hiking trails.

Houlton

Motel/Motor Lodge

★ **SCOTTISH INN.** *239 Bangor St (04730). Phone 207/532-2236; fax 207/532-9893.* 43 rooms. May-mid-Nov: S, D $44-$48; each additional $6; lower rates rest of year. Pets accepted, some restrictions; fee. Check-out 11 am. TV; cable (premium).

Kennebunk

B&B/Small Inn

★ ★ **THE KENNEBUNK INN.** *45 Main St (04043). Phone 207/985-3351; fax 207/985-8865. www.thekennebunkinn.com.* 24 rooms, 3 story. Some room phones. Mid-June-late Oct: S, D $55-$95; each additional $10; suites $160; under 5 free; lower rates rest of year. Pets accepted, some restrictions. Complimentary continental breakfast. Check-out 11 am, check-in 3 pm. TV in some rooms. Dining room. Built in 1799; turn-of-the-century décor.

Kennebunkport

Hotel

★ ★ **SEASIDE HOUSE & COTTAGES.** *Goochs Beach (04046). Phone 207/967-4461; fax 207/967-1135. www.kennebunkbeach.com.* 22 rooms, 10 cottages kitchen units, (1-week minimum), 1-2 story. No A/C. July-late Aug: S $79-$189; D $89-$199; lower rates rest of year. Cottages closed Nov-Apr. Pets accepted, some restrictions; fee. Check-out 11 am. TV. Lawn games. Boat ramps. Private beach.

Resort

★ ★ ★ **THE COLONY HOTEL.** *140 Ocean Ave, PO Box 511 (04046). Phone 207/967-3331; toll-free 800/552-2363; fax 207/967-8738. www.thecolonyhotel.com/maine.* Located on a rock promontory overlooking the Atlantic Ocean and the mouth of the Kennebunk river, this hotel provides guests with many activities. There is a heated saltwater pool, beach, and gardens on the premises and nearby are golf, tennis, kayaking, bicycling, boating, shopping, and touring of art galleries. Maine lobster and local seafoods are the featured cuisine and afteroon tea is served daily. 125 rooms, in hotel, annex and motel, 2-4 story. No A/C. July-early Sept (weekends 2-day minimum in hotel), MAP: D $175-$375; each additional $30; EP available off season; lower rates mid-May-June, Sept-late Oct. Closed rest of year. Pets accepted; fee. Check-out 11 am, check-in 3 pm. TV in some rooms. In-room modem link. Dining room 7:30-9:30 am, 6:30-8:30 pm; Sun brunch 11 am-2 pm; poolside lunches in season. Bar; entertainment. Room service. Lawn games. Bicycles. On trolley route. Family operated since 1948. Private beach. Totally nonsmoking.

B&B/Small Inn

★ ★ ★ **THE CAPTAIN JEFFERDS INN.** *5 Pearl St (04046). Phone 207/967-2311; toll-free 800/839-6844; fax 207/964-0721. www.captainjefferdsinn.com.* This historic inn built in 1804 has been restored and is furnished with antiques and period reproductions. Each room has private bath, fresh flowers, down-filled comforter, fireplace, porch, CD player, and whirlpool. A three-course breakfast is included, as well as afternoon refreshments. 16 rooms, 3 story. No room phones. Closed last 2 weeks in Dec. Pets accepted, some restrictions; fee. Children over 8 years only. Complimentary breakfast. Check-out 11 am, check-in 3 pm. TV in sitting room; VCR available. Federal-style house built by a merchant sea captain. Near harbor. Totally nonsmoking. **$$$**

Kingfield

Hotel

★ ★ **THE HERBERT HOTEL.** *Main St (04947). Phone 207/265-2000; toll-free 800/THEHERB; fax 207/265-4597.* 33 rooms, 4 suites, 3 story. No A/C. No room phones. Dec 25-Mar: S $45-$59; D $69-$79; each additional $10; suites $90-$150; under 12 free; MAP available; weekly rates; package plans; lower rates rest of year. Pets accepted; fee. Complimentary continental breakfast. Check-out 11 am, check-in noon. TV in sitting room. Dining room. Room service. Massage. Downhill, cross-country ski 14 miles. Built in 1917; elaborate fumed oak woodwork. On river.

🅳 🐾 ⚓ 🎿 🛫 ☒ ▨

Lincoln

Motel/Motor Lodge

★ **BRIARWOOD MOTOR INN.** *Outer West Broadway (04457). Phone 207/794-6731. www.angelfire.com/me4/ briarwood.* 24 rooms, 2 story. July-Aug: S $45; D $50; each additional $5; lower rates rest of year. Pets accepted; fee. Check-out 11 am. TV; cable (premium). Downhill ski 11 miles, cross-country ski 2 miles.

🅳 🐾 ⚓ 🎿 🛫 ▨

Lubec

Motel/Motor Lodge

★ **EASTLAND.** *Rte 189 (04652). Phone 207/733-5501; fax 207/733-2932.* 20 rooms. Some A/C. Mid-June-Oct: S $38-$45; D $52-$62; each additional $4; under 17, $2; lower rates rest of year. Pets accepted, some restrictions; fee. Check-out 10 am. TV; cable (premium). Airport for small planes adjacent.

🅳 🐾 ⚓ ▨

Machias

Motel/Motor Lodge

★ **BLUEBIRD MOTEL.** *RR 1 Box 45 (04654). Phone 207/255-3332.* 40 rooms. Mid-June-mid-Sept: S $48-$54; D $52-$60; each additional $4; lower rates rest of year. Pets accepted, some restrictions. Check-out 11 am. TV.

🐾 ▨

Millinocket

Motels/Motor Lodges

★ **BEST WESTERN HERITAGE MOTOR INN.** *935 Central St (04462). Phone 207/723-9777; toll-free 800/528-1234; fax 207/723-9777. www.bestwestern.com.* 49 rooms, 2 story. June-Aug: S $69; D$79; each additional $10; under 12 free; lower rates rest of year. Pets accepted. Complimentary continental breakfast. Check-out 11 am. TV. Restaurant, bar. In-house fitness room.

🅳 🐾 🏋 ▨ SC

★ **KATAHDIN INN.** *740 Central St (04462). Phone 207/723-4555; toll-free 877/902-4555; fax 207/723-6480. www.katahdininn.com.* 82 rooms, 10 suites, 3 story. June-Oct: S $65-$75; D $70-$80; each additional $5; suites $90; under 18 free; ski plans; lower rates rest of year. Pets accepted, some restrictions. Complimentary breakfast buffet. Check-out noon. TV; VCR available. Laundry services. Bar. In-house fitness room. Indoor pool; children's pool; whirlpool. Cross-country ski 10 miles.

🅳 🐾 ⚓ 🎿 ≋ 🏋 🛫 ▨

Newport

Motel/Motor Lodge

★ **LOVLEY'S MOTEL.** *Rte 100 Pittsfield Rd (04953). Phone 207/368-4311; toll-free 800/666-6760.* 63 rooms, 3 kitchen units, 1-2 story. June-Nov: S $29.70-$49.90; D $39.90-$89.90; each additional $5; kitchen units $8 additional; lower rates rest of year. Pets accepted. Check-out 11 am. TV; cable (premium). Laundry services. Heated pool, whirlpool. Lawn games, gliders.

🅳 🐾 ≋ ▨

Norway

Motel/Motor Lodge

★ **GOODWIN'S MOTOR INN.** *191 Main St (04281). Phone 207/743-5121; toll-free 800/424-8803.* 24 rooms. S $40; D $48; under 12 free; higher rates special events. Pets accepted; fee. Check-out 11 am. TV. Downhill, cross-country ski 6 miles. Two family units.

🐾 ☒ ▨

B&B/Small Inn

★ ★ ★ **WATERFORD INN.** *258 Chadbourne Rd (04088). Phone 207/583-4037. www.waterfordinn.com.* This 19th-century, eight-room farmhouse is surrounded by fields and woods and is furnished with both the old and the new. A pond, an old red barn, and hundreds of birds are outside; inside are antiques, art, barnwood, and brass as well as pewter and a library. 8 rooms, 2 story. No room phones. Pets accepted; fee. Complimentary breakfast. Check-out 11 am, check-in 2 pm. Dining room. Downhill ski 20 miles, cross-country ski on site. Lawn games. Built in 1825. **$**

⬛🦮⛴🛗🏊🚭

Old Orchard Beach

Motel/Motor Lodge

★ **FLAGSHIP MOTEL.** *54 W Grand Ave (04064). Phone 207/934-4866; toll-free 800/486-1681. www.flagshipmotel.com.* 27 rooms, 2 story. July-Labor Day: D $79-$105, suites $89-$110; each additional $8; under 12 free; lower rates mid-May-June, after Labor Day-mid-Oct. Closed rest of year. Pets accepted, some restrictions; fee. Check-out 11 am. TV. Pool.

🦮🏊🚭

Orono

Motels/Motor Lodges

★ **BEST WESTERN BLACK BEAR INN & CONFERENCE CENTER.** *4 Godfrey Dr (04473). Phone 207/866-7120; fax 207/866-7433. www.bestwestern.com.* 68 rooms, 3 story. July-Oct: S $75; D $80; each additional $5; suites $109-$119; under 12 free; lower rates rest of year. Restaurant 5-8 pm; closed Sun. Pets accepted; fee. Complimentary continental breakfast. Check-out 11 am. TV; cable (premium), VCR available. Restaurant. In-house fitness room; sauna. Business center.

⬛🦮🏋🚭SC🏃

★ **MILFORD MOTEL ON THE RIVER.** *154 Main St (04461). Phone 207/827-3200; toll-free 800/282-3330. www.mint.net/milford.motel.* 22 rooms, 2 story. Mid-June-Aug: S, D $64-89; suites $84; under 18 free; weekly rates; lower rates rest of year. Pets accepted, some restrictions. Check-out 10 am. TV; cable (premium). On river.

🦮⛴🚭

★ **UNIVERSITY MOTOR INN.** *5 College Ave (04473). Phone 207/866-4921; toll-free 800/321-4921; fax 207/866-4550. www.universitymotorinn.com.* 48 rooms, 2 story.

June-Sept: S $59; D $69; each additional $4-$6; under 13 free; higher rates: University of Maine graduation, homecoming; lower rates rest of year. Pets accepted, some restrictions. Complimentary continental breakfast. Check-out 11 am. TV. Pool.

⬛🦮⛴🏊🚭

Portland

Motels/Motor Lodges

★ ★ **BEST WESTERN MERRY MANOR INN.** *700 Main St (04106). Phone 207/774-6151; fax 207/871-0537. www.bestwestern.com.* 151 rooms, 1-3 story. No elevator. June-late Oct: S $109.95; D $119.95; each additional $10; under 12 free; lower rates rest of year. Pets accepted, some restrictions. Check-out 11 am. TV; cable (premium), VCR available (movies). In-room modem link. Restaurant. Health club privileges. Heated pool.

⬛🦮⛴🛗🏊🚭

★ ★ **HOWARD JOHNSON.** *155 Riverside St (04103). Phone 207/774-5861; fax 207/774-5861. www.hojoportland.com.* 119 rooms, 3 story. July-mid-Oct: S $75-$110; D $80-$120; each additional $10; under 18 free; lower rates rest of year. Pets accepted; fee. Check-out noon. TV; cable (premium). Restaurant, bar; entertainment Fri, Sat. Room service. In-house fitness room. Indoor pool; whirlpool. Free airport transportation.

⬛🦮🏊🏋✈🚭SC

Hotel

★ ★ ★ **MARRIOTT PORTLAND AT SABLE OAKS.** *200 Sable Oaks Dr (04106). Phone 207/871-8000; fax 207/871-7971. www.marriot.com.* This hotel is located on a hill close to historic downtown Portland. 227 rooms, 6 story. Late May-early Nov: S, D $129-$159; suites $125-$300; lower rates rest of year. Pets accepted, some restrictions; fee. Check-out noon. TV; cable (premium), VCR available. In-room modem link. Restaurant, bar. Room service. In-house fitness room; sauna. Indoor pool; whirlpool; poolside service.

⬛🦮🏊🏋🏋🚭

Resort

★ ★ ★ **INN BY THE SEA.** *40 Bowery Beach Rd (04107). Phone 207/799-3134; toll-free 800/888-4287; fax 207/799-4779. www.innbythesea.com.* This resort is located close to the historic city of Portland on the coast. Every guest room has a porch or deck with a view of the ocean. Recreational activities include an outdoor pool, tennis, shuffleboard, walking or jogging, and volleyball. Amenities for guests include terry robes and turndown with 24-hour business and concierge service. 43 kitchen units, 3 story. No A/C. July-Aug: S, D $180-$549; package plans off-season; lower rates rest of year. Pets accepted. Check-out noon. TV; cable (premium), VCR (movies). In-room modem link. Restaurant. Room service. Health club privileges. Poolside service. Lighted tennis. Lawn games. Bicycles. Concierge. Totally nonsmoking.

B&B/Small Inn

★★ **INN AT ST. JOHN.** *939 Congress St (04102). Phone 207/773-6481; toll-free 800/636-9127; fax 207/756-7629. www.innatstjohn.com.* 32 rooms, 4 story. Some A/C. No elevator. July-Oct: S, D $49-$134; each additional $6; under 13 free; lower rates rest of year. Pets accepted, some restrictions. Complimentary continental breakfast. Check-out 11 am, check-in varies. TV; cable (premium). Laundry services. Free airport, bus depot transportation. Built in 1896; European motif, antiques.

Presque Isle

Motel/Motor Lodge

★ **NORTHERN LIGHTS.** *72 Houlton Rd (04769). Phone 207/764-4441; fax 207/769-6931. www.northern lightsmotel.com.* 13 rooms. S $38.95; D $64.95; each additional $5; under 12 free. Pets accepted. Check-out 11 am. TV.

Rockland

Motel/Motor Lodge

★★ **NAVIGATOR MOTOR INN.** *520 Main St (04841). Phone 207/594-2131; toll-free 888/246-4595; fax 207/594-7763. www.navigatorinn.com.* 81 rooms, 6 kitchen units, 4-5 story. Mid-June-Aug: D $80-$149; each additional $10; under 16 free; lower rates rest of year. Pets accepted. Check-out 11 am. TV. Restaurant, bar. Room service. Downhill ski 10 miles, cross-country ski 2 miles.

B&B/Small Inn

★★ **CRAIGNAIR INN.** *5 Third St (04859). Phone 207/594-7644; toll-free 800/320-9997; fax 207/596-7124. www.craignair.com.* 20 rooms, 16 share bath, 2-3 story. No A/C. Pets accepted; fee. Complimentary full breakfast. Check-out 11 am, check-in 3 pm. TV in common room; VCR available (movies). Restaurant. Room service. Built

in 1930; boarding house converted to an inn in 1947. Totally nonsmoking. **$**

Rumford

Motels/Motor Lodges

★ **LINNELL MOTEL & RESTINN CONFERENCE CENTER.** *986 Prospect Ave (04276). Phone 207/364-4511; toll-free 800/446-9038; fax 207/369-0800. www.linnellmotel.com.* 50 rooms, 1-2 story. S $50; D $60; each additional $5; kitchen units $55-$60; under 12 free. Pets accepted; fee. Complimentary continental breakfast. Check-out 11 am. TV. Downhill, cross-country ski 3 miles.

★★ **MADISON RESORT INN.** *US Rte 2 (04276). Phone 207/364-7973; toll-free 800/258-6234; fax 207/369-0341. www.madisoninn.com.* 60 rooms, 38 A/C, 2 story. S, D $89-135; each additional $15; kitchen units $95-$125; under 12 free. Pets accepted, some restrictions. Check-out 11 am. TV; VCR available (movies). Restaurant, bar. In-house fitness room; sauna. Pool; whirlpool. Downhill, cross-country ski 10 miles. Lawn games. On river; boats, canoes.

Waterville

Motels/Motor Lodges

★★ **BEST WESTERN WATERVILLE INN.** *356 Main St (04901). Phone 207/873-3335. www.bestwestern.com.* 86 rooms, 2 story. July-Oct: S $69-$94; D $79-$104; each additional $10; under 18 free; higher rates Colby graduation weekend; lower rates rest of year. Pets accepted, some restrictions; fee. Check-out noon. TV; VCR available (movies). Restaurant, bar. Health club privileges. Pool.

★★ **HOLIDAY INN.** *375 Main St (04901). Phone 207/873-0111; toll-free 800/785-0111; fax 207/872-2310. www.acadia.net/hiwat-cm.* 138 rooms, 3 story. May-Oct: S $85; D $95; each additional $10; suite $150; under 19 free; lower rates rest of year. Pets accepted, some restrictions. Check-out noon. TV; cable (premium), VCR available. In-room modem link. Laundry services. Restaurant, bar. Room service. In-house fitness room; sauna. Indoor pool; whirlpool.

Wells

Motel/Motor Lodge

★ **N'ER BEACH MOTEL.** *395 Post Rd Rte (04090). Phone 207/646-2636; fax 207/641-0968.* 47 rooms, 1-2 story, 21 kitchen units. Late-June-Aug: S, D $69-$109; kitchen units $89-$139; weekly rates for kitchen units; lower rates Apr-late June, after Labor Day-mid-Nov. Closed rest of year. Pets accepted, some restrictions; fee. Check-out 11 am. TV. Heated pool. Beach nearby. Lawn games.

York

Motel/Motor Lodge

★ **YORK COMMONS INN.** *362 US 1 (03909). Phone 207/363-8903; toll-free 800/537-5515; fax 207/363-1130. www.yorkcommonsinn.com.* 90 rooms. Mid-June-mid-Oct: S, D $89-$99; each additional $5; under 18 free; lower rates rest of year. Pets accepted, some restrictions; fee. Complimentary breakfast. TV. Indoor pool.

Maryland

Aberdeen

Motels/Motor Lodges

★ **DAYS INN.** *783 W Bel Air Ave (21001). Phone 410/ 272-8500; fax 410/272-5782. www.daysinn.com.* 49 rooms, 2 story. S $43; D $47; each additional $4; under 16 free. Pets accepted, some restrictions; fee. Complimentary continental breakfast. Check-out 11 am. TV; cable (premium). Pool.

D 🐾 ≈ ⩳

★★ **HOLIDAY INN.** *1007 Beards Hill Rd (21001). Phone 410/272-8100; toll-free 800/465-4329; fax 410/272-1714. www.holiday-inn.com.* 122 rooms, 5 story. S, D $95-$115; each additional $10; suites $150; kitchen units $105-$120; under 18 free; weekend rates. Pets accepted. Check-out noon. TV; cable (premium), VCR available. Restaurant, bar. Health club privileges. In-house fitness room. Indoor pool.

D 🐾 ≈ 🏋 ⩳ SC

Annapolis

Hotels

★★★ **LOEWS ANNAPOLIS HOTEL.** *126 West St (21401). Phone 410/263-7777; toll-free 800/526-2593; fax 410/263-0084. www.loewsannapolis.com.* Located in the heart of downtown Annapolis, this hotel is within walking distance of many of the city's historical sites. 217 rooms, 6 story. Pets accepted, some restrictions. Check-out noon. TV; cable (premium). In-room modem link. Restaurant, bar. In-house fitness room. Health club privileges. Valet parking. Business center. Concierge. Luxury level. $

D 🐾 🏋 ⩳ SC 🚶

★★ **RADISSON HOTEL ANNAPOLIS.** *210 Holiday Ct (21401). Phone 410/224-3150; toll-free 800/333-3333; fax 410/224-3413. www.radisson.com.* 220 rooms, 6 story. Pets accepted, some restrictions; fee. Check-out noon. TV;

cable (premium). In-room modem link. Restaurant, bar. Room service. Pool. $

D 🐾 ≈ ⩳ SC

Baltimore

Hotel

★★★ **BROOKSHIRE INNER HARBOR SUITE HOTEL.** *120 E Lombard St (21202). Phone 410/625-1300; toll-free 800/647-0013; fax 410/649-2635. www.harbormagic.com.* 97 rooms, 11 story. Pets accepted, some restrictions. Complimentary full breakfast. Check-out noon, check-in noon. TV; cable (premium), VCR available. In-room modem link. Laundry services. Restaurant, bar. Room service. In-house fitness room. Health club privileges. Valet parking. $$

D 🐾 🏋 ⩳ SC

B&B/Small Inns

★★★ **ADMIRAL FELL INN.** *888 S Broadway, Historic Fell's Point (21231). Phone 410/522-7377; toll-free 800/292-4667; fax 410/522-0707. www.admiralfell.com.* Conveniently located downtown on the scenic historic waterfront is this renovated urban inn. From the custom-designed, Federal-style furnishings and meeting rooms, which offer guests an empowering view of the skyline and harbor, to the warm and attentive service, this hotel is a delight to both the business and leisure traveler. Enjoy a stroll along the quaint brick sidewalks to the numerous antique shops, gourmet restaurants, galleries, and friendly pubs. 83 rooms, 5 story. Pets accepted. Complimentary continental breakfast. Check-out noon, check-in 4 pm. TV; cable (premium). Dining room, bar. Health club privileges. $$

D 🐾 ⩳ SC

★★ **INN AT HENDERSON'S WHARF.** *1000 Fell St (21231). Phone 410/522-7777; toll-free 800/522-2088; fax 410/522-7087. www.hendersonswharf.com.* 38 rooms. Pets accepted; fee. Complimentary continental breakfast. Check-out noon, check-in 3 pm. TV; cable (premium). In-room modem link. Laundry services. In-house fitness room. 19th-century tobacco warehouse. On waterfront; dockage available. $$

D 🐾 🏋 ⩳ SC

Baltimore/ Washington International Airport Area

Motel/Motor Lodge

★ **HAMPTON INN.** *829 Elkridge Landing Rd (21090). Phone 410/850-0600; toll-free 800/426-7866; fax 410/691-2119. www.hamptoninn.com.* 139 rooms, 5 story. Pets accepted. Complimentary continental breakfast. Check-out noon. TV; cable (premium). In-room modem link. Laundry services. Free airport, train transportation. **$**

⬚ 🐾 ✈ ⬚ SC

Bethesda

Motel/Motor Lodge

★ ★ **HOLIDAY INN.** *5520 Wisconsin Ave (20815). Phone 301/656-1500; fax 301/656-5045. www.holiday-inn.com.* 215 rooms, 12 story. Pets accepted, some restrictions; fee. Check-out noon. TV; cable (premium), VCR available. In-room modem link. Laundry services. Restaurant, bar. Health club privileges. Pool. Business center. **$**

⬚ 🐾 ⬚ ⬚ 🚶

Bowie

Motel/Motor Lodge

★ **FOREST HILLS MOTEL.** *2901 Crain Hwy (20774). Phone 301/627-3969; fax 301/627-4058.* 13 rooms. Shower only. Apr-Oct: S $42-$44; D $46-$49; under 13 free; lower rates rest of year. Pets accepted; fee. Check-out 11 am. TV.

⬚ 🐾

Chesapeake Bay Bridge Area

B&B/Small Inn

★ ★ **HUNTINGFIELD MANOR.** *4928 Eastern Neck Rd (21661). Phone 410/639-7779; toll-free 800/720-8788;* *fax 410/639-2924. www.huntingfield.com.* 6 rooms, 2 story. No room phones. S, D $85-$125; each additional $25; under 3 free. Pets accepted, some restrictions. Complimentary continental breakfast. Check-out noon, check-in 2 pm. Telescope-type house on a working farm that dates back to the middle 1600s.

⬚ 🐾 ⬚

Cumberland

Motels/Motor Lodges

★ **DAYS INN.** *11100 New Georges Creek Rd SW (21532). Phone 301/689-2050; fax 301/689-2050. www.daysinn.com.* 100 rooms, 2 story. May-Oct: S $66-$78; D $71-$83; each additional $5; suites $86; under 18 free; weekly rates; lower rates rest of year. Pets accepted; fee. Complimentary continental breakfast. Check-out 11 am. TV. In-room modem link. In-house fitness room. Pool privileges. Cross-country ski 15 miles.

⬚ 🐾 ✈ 🚶 ⬚ SC

★ ★ **HOLIDAY INN.** *100 S George St (21502). Phone 301/724-8800; toll-free 877/426-4672; fax 301/724-4001. www.holiday-inn.com.* 134 rooms, 5 story. D $89-$109; under 18 free. Pets accepted; fee. Check-out noon. TV; cable (premium), VCR available. In-room modem link. Restaurant, bar; entertainment. Room service. Outdoor pool. Airport transportation. Business center.

⬚ 🐾 ⬚ ⬚ 🚶

Hotel

★ ★ **OAK TREE INN.** *12310 Winchester Rd (21502). Phone 301/729-6700.* 82 rooms, 3 story. Pets accepted, some restrictions; fee. Check-out noon, check-in 2 pm. TV; cable (premium). Laundry services. Restaurant. In-house fitness room. **$**

⬚ 🐾 🚶 ⬚

Easton

Motel/Motor Lodge

★ **DAYS INN.** *7018 Ocean Gateway (21601). Phone 410/822-4600; toll-free 800/329-7466; fax 410/820-9723. www.daysinn.com.* 80 rooms, 2 story. Apr-Nov: S $69-$89; D, suites $79-$102; under 18 free; higher rates Waterfowl Festival; lower rates rest of year. Pets accepted; fee. Complimentary continental breakfast. Check-out 11 am. TV; cable (premium). Pool; children's pool.

⬚ 🐾 ⬚ ⬚ SC

Frederick

Motel/Motor Lodge

★ **HAMPTON INN.** *5311 Buckeystown Pike (21704). Phone 301/698-2500; toll-free 800/426-7866; fax 301/695-8735. www.hamptoninn.com.* 160 rooms, 6 story. S, D $69-$100; suites $150; under 18 free. Pets accepted, some restrictions; fee. Complimentary continental breakfast. Check-out noon. TV; cable (premium). In-room modem link. Laundry services. Restaurant, bar; entertainment. Health club privileges. In-house fitness room. Pool.

D 🐾 ➽ 🏃 🛰 SC

Gaithersburg

Motels/Motor Lodges

★ **COMFORT INN.** *16216 Frederick Rd (20877). Phone 301/330-0023; toll-free 800/228-5150; fax 301/258-1950. www.comfortinn.com.* 127 rooms, 7 story. Apr-Oct: S, D $49-$109; each additional $10; under 18 free; monthly rates; lower rates rest of year. Pets accepted. Complimentary full breakfast. Check-out 11 am. TV; cable (premium). In-room modem link. Laundry services. Health club privileges. In-house fitness room. Pool. Business center.

D 🐾 ➽ 🏃 🛰 SC 🚶

★ ★ **HOLIDAY INN.** *2 Montgomery Village Ave (20879). Phone 301/948-8900; toll-free 800/465-4329; fax 301/258-1940. www.holiday-inn.com.* 301 rooms, 2-8 story. S $114-$124; D $124-$149; suites $300-$350; kitchen units $119-$139; under 18 free. Pets accepted. Check-out noon. TV; cable (premium). In-room modem link. Laundry services. Restaurant, bar. Room service. In-house fitness room. Game room. Indoor pool; whirlpool; poolside service. Business center.

D 🐾 ➽ 🏃 🛰 SC 🚶

Hagerstown

Motels/Motor Lodges

★ ★ **FOUR POINTS BY SHERATON.** *1910 Dual Hwy (21740). Phone 301/790-3010; toll-free 800/325-3535; fax 301/733-4559. www.fourpoints.com.* 108 rooms, 2 story. S $60-$75; D $64-$79; each additional $6; suites $150; under 18 free. Pets accepted, some restrictions. Complimentary continental breakfast. Check-out noon. TV; cable (premium). Restaurant, bar. Room service.

In-house fitness room; sauna. Pool; whirlpool. Free airport transportation.

D 🐾 ➽ 🏃 🛰 SC

★ ★ **VENICE INN.** *431 Dual Hwy (21740). Phone 301/733-0830; fax 301/733-4978.* 220 rooms, 2-5 story. Apr-Oct: S $58-$68; D $63-$73; each additional $6; suites $125-$250; under 18 free; lower rates rest of year. Pets accepted, some restrictions. Check-out noon. TV; cable (premium), VCR (movies). Restaurant, bar; entertainment. Room service. In-house fitness room. Game room. Pool. Airport transportation.

D 🐾 ➽ 🏃 🛰

Laurel

Motel/Motor Lodge

★ **COMFORT INN.** *14402 Laurel Pl (20707). Phone 301/206-2600; toll-free 800/628-7760; fax 301/725-0056. www.comfortinn.com.* 119 rooms, 5 story. S, D $80-$100; each additional $10; suites $95-$125; under 18 free; weekly, weekend rates; higher rates: cherry blossom, Memorial Day weekend. Pets accepted; fee. Complimentary continental breakfast. Check-out noon. TV; cable (premium). In-house fitness room. Indoor pool; whirlpool. Airport transportation.

D 🐾 ➽ 🏃 🛰

Ocean City

Motel/Motor Lodge

★ **SAFARI MOTEL.** *1-13th St (21842). Phone 410/289-6411; toll-free 800/787-2183.* 46 rooms, 3 and 4 story. July-Aug: S, D $119; under 14 free; lower rates mid-Apr-June, Sept-Oct. Closed rest of year. Pets accepted, some restrictions; fee. Check-out 11 am. TV; cable (premium).

🐾

Hotel

★ ★ **CLARION HOTEL.** *10100 Coastal Hwy (21842). Phone 410/524-3535; fax 410/524-3834. www.clarioninn.com.* This hotel offers a wide range of shops, restaurants, lounges, and services, including many recreational facilities. 250 rooms, 16 story. June-Aug: S, D $230-$300; each additional $15; suites, kitchen units $350; studio rooms $320; condos $1,600-$2,700/weekly; under 17 free; higher rates holiday weekends (3-day minimum); lower rates rest of year. Pets accepted, some restrictions; fee. Check-out 11 am. TV; cable (premium), VCR available. In-room modem link. Restaurant, bar; entertainment. In-house fitness room; sauna, steam room. Game room. Pool; whirlpool; poolside service in season. Airport transportation. Business center.

D ⊠ ↟ ⌧ ⌕ ⊠ ⅃

Pocomoke City

Motel/Motor Lodge

★ ★ **QUALITY INN.** *825 Ocean Hwy (21851). Phone 410/957-1300; fax 410/957-9329. www.qualityinn.com.* 64 rooms. Memorial Day-Labor Day: S $60-$75; D $65-$82; each additional $5; under 18 free; higher rates Pony Penning. Pets accepted. Complimentary continental breakfast. Check-out 11 am. TV; cable (premium). In-room modem link. Pool; children's pool.

D ⊠ ↟ ⌧ ⊠

B&B/Small Inn

★ ★ **RIVER HOUSE INN.** *201 E Market St (21863). Phone 410/632-2722; fax 410/632-2866. www.riverhouseinn.com.* 8 rooms, 3 story. No elevator. No room phones. Apr-Oct: S, D $100-$175; each additional $20; suite $100; guest house $160; under 16 free; golf rates; package plans; weekends (2-day minimum); lower rates rest of year. Pets accepted; fee. Fireplaces. Greens fee. Lawn games. Built in 1860. On river. Totally nonsmoking.

⊠ ↟ ⊠ SC

Rockville

All Suite

★ ★ ★ **WOODFIN SUITES.** *1380 Piccard Dr (20850). Phone 301/590-9880; toll-free 800/237-8811; fax 301/590-9614. www.woodfinsuiteshotel.com.* 203 suites, 3 story. S, D $165-$230; each additional $15; 2-bedroom suites $275; under 12 free. Pets accepted; fee. Complimentary full breakfast. Check-out noon. TV; cable (premium). In-room modem link. Restaurant, bar. In-house fitness room. Pool; whirlpool. Business center.

D ⊠ ↟ ⌧ ⊠ SC ⅃

Salisbury

Motels/Motor Lodges

★ **COMFORT INN.** *2701 N Salisbury Blvd (21801). Phone 410/543-4666; toll-free 800/638-7949; fax 410/749-2639. www.comfortinn.com.* 96 suites, 2 story. Mid-May-mid-Sept: S $74.95-$97.95; D $85.95-$108.95; each additional $8; suites $97.95-$120.95; under 18 free; higher rates weekends; lower rates rest of year. Pets accepted, some restrictions. Complimentary continental breakfast. Check-out 11 am. TV; cable (premium). Pool privileges. Lawn games.

D ⊠ ⌧ ⊠ SC

★ **HOWARD JOHNSON.** *2625 N Salisbury Blvd (21801). Phone 410/742-7194; toll-free 800/465-4329; fax 410/742-5194. www.hojo.com.* 123 rooms, 2 story. Mid-June-mid-Sept: S $49-$99; D $49-$107; each additional $8; under 18 free; lower rates rest of year. Pets accepted; fee. Complimentary breakfast buffet. Check-out 11 am. TV; cable (premium). Laundry services. Restaurant, bar. Health club privileges. Pool.

D ⊠ ⌧ ⊠ SC

★ ★ **RAMADA INN.** *300 S Salisbury Blvd (21801). Phone 410/546-4400; fax 410/546-2528. www.ramada.com.* 156 rooms, 5 story. July-Aug: S, D $87-$135; each additional $10; under 18 free; lower rates rest of year. Pets accepted, some restrictions; fee. Check-out noon. TV; cable (premium). Restaurant, bar. Room service. Health club privileges. Indoor pool. Free airport transportation. On river.

D ⊠ ⌧ ⊠ SC

Waldorf

Motel/Motor Lodge

★ **DAYS INN.** *US 301 (20603). Phone 301/932-9200; fax 301/843-9816. www.daysinn.com.* 100 rooms, 3 story. S, D $65-$75; suite $119-$135. Each additional $5; under 18 free. Pets accepted; fee. Complimentary continental breakfast. Check-out 11 am. TV; cable (premium). Laundry services.

 D ⊠ ⊠

Massachusetts

Amherst

Motel/Motor Lodge

★ **HOWARD JOHNSON.** *401 Russell St, Rte 9 (01035). Phone 413/586-0114; fax 413/584-7163. www.hojo.com.* 100 rooms, 3 story. S $59-$109; D $69-$109; each additional $10; suites $79-$152; under 18 free; higher rates special events. Pets accepted, some restrictions; fee. Complimentary breakfast. Check-out noon. TV; cable (premium). In-room modem link. Health club privileges. In-house fitness room. Pool. Downhill ski 16 miles, cross-country ski 12 miles.

Andover and North Andover

Hotel

★ ★ **ANDOVER WYNDHAM HOTEL.** *123 Old River Rd (01810). Phone 978/975-3600; fax 978/975-2664. www.wyndham.com.* 293 rooms, 6 suites, 5 story. D $155-$350 under 18 free; family rates; package plans. Pets accepted; fee. Check-out noon, check-in 3 pm. TV; cable (premium), VCR available. In-room modem link. Restaurant, bar; entertainment weekends. Room service. In-house fitness room; sauna. Indoor pool; whirlpool. Lawn games. Airport transportation.

Boston

Hotels

★ ★ ★ ★ **BOSTON HARBOR HOTEL.** *Rowes Wharf (02110). Phone 617/439-7000; toll-free 800/752-7077; fax 617/345-6799. www.bhh.com.* Privileged guests rest their weary heads at the Boston Harbor Hotel. Boston's rich heritage comes alive here at Rowes Wharf, once a home to revolutionaries and traders. Occupying an idyllic waterfront location, the hotel is across the street from the financial district and three blocks from the Freedom Trail and Faneuil Hall Market. The Boston Harbor Hotel shares an especially civilized lifestyle with its guests. Here, guests need not worry about the snarls

of traffic, thanks to the hotel's fantastic airport ferry service. This full-service hotel takes care of every possible amenity, ensuring satisfaction and comfort. Rooms and suites are beautifully appointed in rich colors; to pay a few dollars more for one with a view is well worth it. The views of the harbor are sensational, whether enjoyed in the privacy of a guest room or in one of the public spaces. Meritage presents diners with an inventive menu and an extensive wine list in striking contemporary surroundings. 230 rooms, 26 suites, 8 story. S, D $275-$425; each additional $50; suites $475-$1,800; under 18 free; weekend rates. Pets accepted, some restrictions. Check-out 1 pm. TV; cable (premium), VCR available. In-room modem link. Room service 24 hours. Restaurant, bar. In-house fitness room; spa, sauna, steam room. Indoor pool; whirlpool; poolside service. Valet, self-parking. Business center. Concierge. Some rooms recently renovated. Cancel 24 hours in advance.

★ ★ ★ **THE COLONNADE HOTEL.** *120 Huntington Ave (02116). Phone 617/424-7000; toll-free 800/962-3030; fax 617/424-1717. www.colonnadehotel.com.* Located in the historic area of Boston's Back Bay, this luxury hotel offers guests attentive service and spacious rooms, as well as a health club and rooftop pool. The Hynes Convention Center is conveniently located next door and Back Bay's elite shopping street is just blocks away. 292 rooms, 1 story. Sept-mid-Nov: S, D $169-$299; suites $279-$995; under 12 free; weekly, weekend and holiday rates; higher rates: marathon, graduation; lower rates rest of year. Pets accepted. Check-out noon. Check-in. TV; cable (premium), VCR available. In-room modem link. Room service 24 hours. Restaurant, bar. Supervised children's activities (May-Sept); ages 8-13. In-house fitness room. Pool; poolside service. Business center. Concierge.

★ ★ ★ **THE FAIRMONT COPLEY PLAZA BOSTON.** *138 St. James Ave (02116). Phone 617/267-5300; toll-free 800/527-4727; fax 617/247-6681. www.fairmont.com.* Ideally situated in the heart of the theater district, this landmark hotel was built in 1925 and considered by many as the Grande Dame of Boston. Named after the great American painter John Singleton Copley, this traditional hotel still provides guests with elegant surroundings and superb service. The lobby flaunts an exquisite high-domed ceiling with ornate furnishings, as well as dramatic marble pillars and some remarkable imported rugs. 379 rooms, 7 story. S, D $259-$479; each additional $30; suites $379-$1,500; under 18 free; package plans. Pets accepted; fee. Check-out noon, check-in 3 pm. TV; cable (premium), VCR available. In-room modem link. Room service 24 hours. Restaurant, bar. In-house fitness room. Valet parking. Business center. Concierge.

★ ★ ★ ★ ★ FOUR SEASONS HOTEL BOSTON.
200 Boylston St (02116). Phone 617/338-4400; fax 617/423-0154. www.fourseasons.com. The Four Seasons Hotel would make any Boston Brahmin proud. Discriminating travelers are drawn to this refined hotel where the finer things in life may be enjoyed. The Four Seasons offers its guests a prime location overlooking Beacon Hill's Public Garden and the State Capitol. All of Boston is easily explored from here, and the hotel makes it carefree with courtesy town car service. Antiques, fine art, sumptuous fabrics, and period furniture create a magnificent setting in the rooms and suites, while impeccable and attentive service heightens the luxurious experience. Aquatic workouts with a view are available at the indoor pool with floor-to-ceiling windows overlooking the city, and the fitness center keeps guests in tiptop shape. Aujourd'Hui is an epicurean's delight with its sensational New American cuisine and distinguished dining room. The Bristol presents diners with a casually elegant alternative. 274 rooms, 15 story. Pets accepted, some restrictions. Check-out 1 pm, check-in 3 pm. TV; cable (premium), VCR available (movies). In-room modem link. Laundry services. Room service 24 hours. Restaurant, bar; entertainment. Babysitting services available. In-house fitness room; spa, massage, sauna. Indoor pool; whirlpool; poolside service. Valet, garage parking. Business center. Concierge. **$$$$**

D 🐾 ⇌ 🕇 📐 🏃

★ ★ ★ HILTON BOSTON BACK BAY.
40 Dalton St (02115). Phone 617/236-1100; toll-free 800/874-0663; fax 617/867-6104. www.hilton.com. Just steps away from all, this hotel is ideally situated in the heart of Boston's historic Back Bay and adjacent to the Hynes Convention Center. From the meeting facilities with the state-of-the-art audio and visual equipment to the fitness room and indoor sky-lit swimming pool, this hotel charms both the business and leisure traveler. 385 rooms, 26 story. S, D $109-$429; each additional $20; suites $550-$1,200; family rates; package plans. Pets accepted, some restrictions; fee. Check-out noon. Check-in 3 pm. TV; cable (premium). In-room modem link. Restaurant, bar. In-house fitness room. Indoor pool. Business center. Concierge.

D 🐾 ⇌ 🕇 📐 SC 🏃

★ ★ ★ HILTON BOSTON LOGAN AIRPORT.
85 Terminal Rd (02128). Phone 617/569-9300; fax 617/568-6800. www.hilton.com. Experience quiet elegance and superb service at this state-of-the-art luxury hotel centrally located inside the Boston Logan Airport. 603 rooms, 10 story. D $99-$399; each additional $20; family, weekend rates. Pets accepted, some restrictions. Check-out 11 am, check-in 3 pm. TV; cable (premium). In-room modem link. Restaurant, bar. In-house fitness room. Pool; poolside service. Free airport transportation. Business center. Concierge.

D 🐾 ⇌ 🕇 ✈ 📐 🏃

★ ★ ★ LE MERIDIEN BOSTON.
250 Franklin St (02110). Phone 617/451-1900; toll-free 800/543-4300; fax 617/423-2844. www.lemeridienboston.com. Le Meridien is an elegant choice while visiting Boston. Just a stone's throw from Faneuil Hall, the Freedom Trail, and other historic sites, this hotel is a perfect base for retracing the steps of famous patriots. A sense of old-world Europe is felt throughout Le Meridien, from the discreet façade with its signature red awnings to the magnificent lobby done in jewel tones. The guest rooms are equally delightful, and many offer wonderful views of the gardens of Post Office Square. Extra touches are provided to ensure exceedingly comfortable visits. The remarkable French cuisine at Julien is only the beginning, where sparkling chandeliers and glittering gold leaf details will make any guest feel like royalty. Once the Governor's Reception Room of Boston's Federal Reserve Bank, the Julien Bar is a sensational place, while the Mediterranean dishes of Café Fleuri have universal appeal. 343 rooms, 9 story. S, D $310-$395; each additional $25; suites $400-$790; under 12 free; weekend rates. Pets accepted, some restrictions; fee. Check-out 1 pm. TV; cable (premium), VCR available. In-room modem link. Room service 24 hours. Restaurant, bar. In-house fitness room; massage, sauna. Pool. Valet parking. Business center. Concierge. Renaissance Revival building.

D 🐾 ⇌ 🕇 📐 🏃

★ ★ ★ NINE ZERO.
90 Tremont St (02108). Phone 617/772-5800; toll-free 800/434-7347; fax 617/772-5810. 190 rooms, 19 story. Pets accepted, some restrictions. Check-out noon, check-in 3 pm. TV; cable (premium). Internet access. Restaurant, bar. Room service. In-house fitness room; massage. Valet parking. **$$$**

D 🐾 🕇 📐

★ ★ ★ ★ THE RITZ-CARLTON, BOSTON.
15 Arlington St (02117). Phone 617/536-5700; fax 617/536-9340. www.ritzcarlton.com. Distinguished and refined, The Ritz-Carlton is unquestionably the grande dame of Boston. This lovely hotel, faithfully restored to its 1920s splendor, has been a cherished city landmark for many years. Located across from Boston Common, this aristocratic hotel opens its doors to a rarefied world of genteel manners and distinguished surroundings. The guest rooms are a celebration of traditional style; luxurious marble bathrooms encourage soothing soaks. The suites include wood-burning fireplaces, and the hotel even offers a considerate fireplace butler service. The sun-filled Café is an ideal place for shoppers to take a break from the boutiques of Newbury Street, while a proper afternoon tea can be enjoyed in the Lounge. The Bar has a fascinating history, having survived Prohibition, and its wood-paneled walls and roaring fireplace exude a clubby feel. Long considered a local institution, The Dining Room continues to delight guests with its polished service and sophisticated

cuisine. 275 rooms, 42 suites, 17 story. S, D, suites $435-$725; presidential suite $2,500; each additional $20; under 12 free. Pets accepted, some restrictions. TV, cable. Room service 24 hours. Restaurant. In-house fitness room; sauna. Airport transportation available. Concierge.

D 🏃🏼 🏋 ✈ 🔲

★ ★ ★ ★ **THE RITZ-CARLTON, BOSTON COMMON.** *10 Avery St (02111). Phone 617/574-7100; toll-free 800/241-3333; fax 617/574-7200. www.ritzcarlton.com.* While only a short skip across the park from its sister property, The Ritz-Carlton, Boston Common is a world apart from its traditional counterpart with its modern sensibility of clean lines, neutral tones, and hip atmosphere. This contemporary construction attracts the fashionable set seeking the high levels of service synonymous with Ritz-Carlton properties. Flanked by the financial and theater districts, The Ritz-Carlton, Boston Common is convenient for business and leisure travelers alike. The rooms and suites have a distinctly serene feel with muted tones of taupe, cream, and celadon and polished woods. JER-NE Restaurant is a feast for the tongue and the eyes with its inventive creations and sensational décor. An open kitchen enables guests to watch the talented chefs in action, while the bar has a vibrant scene. After a night of indulgence, Ritz-Carlton guests often head to the massive Sports Club/LA, a veritable temple of fitness. *Secret Inspector's Notes:* Be sure to obtain a fitness menu from the Sports Club/LA prior to arriving, as the classes offered and the level of personal training available are far superior to those in many gyms around the country. 193 rooms, 4 story. Pets accepted, some restrictions; fee. Complimentary continental breakfast. Check-out noon, check-in 3 pm. TV; cable (premium). In-room modem link. Room service 24 hours. Restaurant, bar. Babysitting services available. In-house fitness room; health club privileges, spa, massage. Indoor pool. Valet parking. Business center. Concierge. Luxury level. **$$$$**

D 🏃🏼 🏊 🏋 🔲 🏃

★ ★ ★ **SEAPORT HOTEL.** *1 Seaport Ln (02210). Phone 617/385-4500; toll-free 877/732-7678; fax 617/385-4001.* Located on Boston's scenic waterfront and within minutes of Logan International Airport, this hotel features spacious guest rooms, each with a picturesque view of the Boston Harbor or skyline. 426 rooms, 18 story. D $139-$299; each additional $25; suites $500-$1,500; under 12 free; package plans. Pets accepted, some restrictions. Check-out 1 pm. TV; cable (premium), VCR available. In-room modem link. Restaurant, bar. In-house fitness room; massage, sauna. Indoor pool. Garage parking. Business center. Concierge. On harbor. Totally nonsmoking.

D 🏃🏼 🏊 🏋 ✈ 🔲 🏃

★ ★ ★ **SHERATON BOSTON HOTEL.** *39 Dalton St (02199). Phone 617/236-2000; toll-free 800/325-3535; fax*

617/236-1702. www.sheraton.com. Ideally located in the historic Back Bay and adjacent to the Hynes Convention Center, this hotel offers guests attentive service along with an elegant atmosphere. 1,215 rooms, 29 story. S, D $179-$479; each additional $20; suites from $450-$1,000; under 18 free; weekend rates. Pets accepted, some restrictions. Check-out noon, check-in 3 pm. TV; cable (premium). In-room modem link. Room service 24 hours. Restaurant, bar; entertainment. In-house fitness room. Indoor pool; outdoor pool; whirlpool. Business center. Luxury level.

D 🏃🏼 🏊 🏋 ✈ 🔲 🏃

★ ★ ★ ★ **XV BEACON.** *15 Beacon St (02108). Phone 617/670-1500; fax 617/670-2525. www.xvbeacon.com.* Dazzling and daring, XV Beacon is the hipster's answer to the luxury hotel. This turn-of-the-century Beaux Arts building in Beacon Hill belies the sleek décor found within. This highly stylized, seductive hotel flaunts a refreshing change of pace in traditional Boston. Decidedly contemporary, XV Beacon employs whimsical touches, like the plaster busts found at reception, to wink at the city's past. Original artwork, commissioned specifically for the hotel by well-known artists, decorates the walls of both public and private spaces. The guest rooms and suites are furnished in an eclectic style in a palette of rich chocolate browns, blacks, and creams. Rooms feature canopy beds with luxurious Italian linens and gas fireplaces covered in cool stainless steel. Completed in crisp white with simple fixtures, the bathrooms are a modernist's dream. The nouvelle cuisine at The Fed is delicious and fresh, thanks to the chef's rooftop garden and in-kitchen fish tanks. *Secret Inspector's Notes:* XV Beacon is a luxury lover's dream. The rooms are stocked with everything from private-label lip balms and Kiehl's shampoos to decadent minibars full of Stags Leap, Dominus, and Krug wines. The rooftop sundeck is a hidden spot to enjoy the sunshine or sunset with room service gladly providing cool drinks or snacks. 60 rooms, 10 story. Pets accepted, some restrictions. Check-out noon, check-in 3 pm. TV; cable (premium), VCR available, CD available. Room service 24 hours. Restaurant, bar. Babysitting services available. In-house fitness room; health club privileges. Whirlpool. Valet parking. Concierge. **$$$$**

D 🏃🏼 🏋 ✈ 🔲

All Suite

★ ★ ★ **THE ELIOT SUITE HOTEL.** *370 Commonwealth Ave (02215). Phone 617/267-1607; fax 617/536-9114. www.eliothotel.com.* This property is located in the prestigious Back Bay area of Boston and is convenient to the Hynes Convention Center and various shopping, entertainment, and cultural sites. All suites feature French doors to the bedrooms, Italian marble baths, and down comforters. The hotel, surrounded by lush greenery, is also home to the critically acclaimed

Clio restaurant serving contemporary French-American cuisine. 174 suites, 9 story. Pets accepted, some restrictions. Check-out noon, check-in 3 pm. TV; cable (premium), VCR available (movies). In-room modem link. Restaurant. Health club privileges. Valet parking. Business center. Concierge. **$$$$**

D 🐾 🏊 ⛷ 🏃

Brewster

B&B/Small Inn

★★ **POORE HOUSE INN.** *2311 Main St (02631). Phone 508/896-0004; toll-free 800/233-6662; fax 508/896-0005. www.capecodtravel.com/poore.* 5 rooms, 2 story. Pets accepted; fee. Children over 8 years only. Complimentary full breakfast. Check-out 11 am, check-in 2 pm. Built in 1837. Totally nonsmoking. **$$**

🐾 ⛷

Buzzards Bay

Motel/Motor Lodge

★ **BAY MOTOR INN.** *223 Main St (02532). Phone 508/759-3989; fax 508/759-3199. www.capecodtravel.com/baymotorinn.* 17 rooms, 1-2 story. Closed mid-Nov-Mar. Pets accepted, some restrictions; fee. Check-out 11 am. TV; cable (premium). Pool. **$**

🐾 🏊 ⛷

Cambridge

Motel/Motor Lodge

★★ **DOUBLETREE HARVARD SQUARE HOTEL.** *110 Mount Auburn St (02138). Phone 617/864-5200; toll-free 800/458-5886; fax 617/864-2409. www.doubletree.com.* 73 rooms, 4 story. Pets accepted, some restrictions; fee. Check-out noon, check-in 3 pm. TV; cable (premium). In-room modem link. Babysitting services available. **$$**

D 🐾 ⛷ SC

Hotel

★★★ **CHARLES HOTEL-HARVARD SQUARE.** *1 Bennett St (02138). Phone 617/864-1200; toll-free 800/882-1818; fax 617/864-5715. www.charleshotel.com.* This upscale hotel just off Harvard Square defines luxury lodging in Cambridge. For that reason, it attracts celebrities and other high-profile guests, as well as the wealthy parents of Harvard students. Its guest rooms mix Shaker-inspired design with a multitude of modern amenities: duvets, high-speed Internet access, three two-line phones, Bose Wave radios, color televisions in the bathrooms, and more. Dine in either of its two restaurants, and be sure to tune into the sweet sounds of jazz at the Regattabar, where swingin' national bands hit the stage. The hotel also has an onsite athletic center with indoor pool, a day spa, and indoor parking. 293 rooms, 10 story. Pets accepted, some restrictions; fee. Check-out noon, check-in 3 pm. TV; cable (premium), VCR available. In-room modem link. Room service 24 hours. Restaurant, bar. Babysitting services available. In-house fitness room; spa, massage, steam room. Indoor pool; whirlpool. Valet parking. Concierge. On Charles River. **$$**

D 🐾 🏊 🏋 ⛷ SC

Centerville

Motel/Motor Lodge

★ **CENTERVILLE CORNERS MOTOR LODGE.** *1338 Craigville Beach Rd (02632). Phone 508/775-7223; toll-free 800/242-1137; fax 508/775-4147. www.centervillecorners.com.* 48 rooms, 2 story. Closed Dec-Apr. Pets accepted, some restrictions; fee. Complimentary continental breakfast. Check-out 11 am. TV. Sauna. Indoor pool. Lawn games. **$**

🐾 🏊 ⛷

Fall River

Motel/Motor Lodge

★ **QUALITY INN.** *1878 Wilbur Ave (02725). Phone 508/678-4545; toll-free 800/228-5151; fax 508/678-9352. www.qualityinn.com.* 107 rooms, 2 story. Late May-Aug: S, D $69-$179; each additional $10; lower rates rest of year; under 18 free. Pets accepted, some restrictions. Complimentary continental breakfast. Check-out noon. TV; cable (premium), VCR available. In-room modem link. Indoor/outdoor pool.

D 🐾 🏊 ⛷

Gloucester

Motel/Motor Lodge

★ **THE MANOR INN.** *141 Essex Ave (01930). Phone 978/283-0614; fax 978/283-3154. www.themanorinnofgloucester.com.* 10 rooms. D $69-$79; lower rates Apr-late

June, early Sept-Oct. Closed rest of year. Pets accepted, some restrictions; fee. Complimentary continental breakfast. Check-out 11 am, check-in 2 pm. TV. Victorian manor house. Some rooms overlook the river.

Resort

★ ★ **OCEAN VIEW INN AND RESORT.** *171 Atlantic Rd (01930). Phone 978/283-6200; toll-free 800/315-7557; fax 978/283-1852. www.oceanviewinnandresort.com.* 62 rooms, 3 story. May-Oct: S, D $69-$190; lower rates rest of year. Pets accepted, some restrictions. Check-out 11 am, check-in 2 pm. TV; VCR available. In-room modem link. Restaurant. Two heated pools. Lawn games. Several buildings have accommodations, including a turn-of-the-century English manor house.

Great Barrington

B&B/Small Inn

★ ★ **RACE BROOK LODGE.** *864 S Undermountain Rd (01257). Phone 413/229-2916; toll-free 888/725-6343; fax 413/229-6629. www.rblodge.com.* 32 rooms, 3 story. No room phones. Pets accepted, some restrictions; fee. Complimentary full breakfast. Check-out 11 am, check-in 2-3 pm. TV; cable in common room. Bar. Downhill, cross-country ski 7 miles. Lawn games. Barn built in 1790s. Rustic décor. Totally nonsmoking. **$$**

Greenfield

Hotel

★ ★ ★ **BRANDT HOUSE.** *29 Highland Ave (01301). Phone 413/774-3329; toll-free 800/235-3329; fax 413/772-2908. www.brandthouse.com.* This turn-of-the-century Colonial-Revival mansion offers contemporary creature comforts. The owner is an interior decorator and has given each room its own personality. Antiques, fresh flowers, and feather beds allow guests to bask in comfort. 8 rooms, 3 story. June-Oct: suites $205; lower rates rest of year. Pets accepted, some restrictions; fee. Complimentary full breakfast. Check-out 11 am, check-in 2 pm. TV; VCR available. 18-hole golf. Tennis. Downhill skiing. Bike rentals. Hiking trail.

Harwich

B&B/Small Inn

★ ★ **CAPE COD CLADDAGH INN.** *77 Main St (02671). Phone 508/432-9628; toll-free 800/356-9628; fax 508/432-6039. www.capecodcladdaghinn.com.* 8 rooms, 3 story. No room phones. Closed Jan-Mar. Pets accepted. Complimentary breakfast. Check-out 10:30 am, check-in 2 pm. TV; cable (premium). Dining room. Pool. Parking. Former Baptist parsonage (circa 1900). **$**

Haverhill

Motel/Motor Lodge

★ **BEST WESTERN MERRIMACK VALLEY.** *401 Lowell Ave (01832). Phone 978/373-1511; toll-free 888/645-2025; fax 978/373-1517. www.bestwestern.com.* 127 rooms, 3 story. Apr-Oct: S, D $79-$159; under 18 free; higher rates special events. Pets accepted, some restrictions; fee. Complimentary continental breakfast. Check-out noon. TV; cable (premium). In-room modem link. Indoor pool; whirlpool. Airport transportation. Business center.

Hyannis

B&B/Small Inn

★ ★ **SIMMONS HOMESTEAD INN.** *288 Scudder Ave (02647). Phone 508/778-4999; toll-free 800/637-1649; fax 508/790-1342. www.simmonshomesteadinn.com.* 14 rooms, 2 story. No room phones. Pets accepted, some restrictions; fee. Complimentary full breakfast. Check-out 11 am, check-in 1 pm. TV in sitting room. Health club privileges. Lawn games. Bicycles. Concierge. Restored sea captain's home built in 1820; some canopied beds. Unique décor; all rooms have different animal themes. **$$**

Lenox

B&B/Small Inn

★ **WALKER HOUSE.** *64 Walker St (01240). Phone 413/637-1271; toll-free 800/235-3098; fax 413/637-2387. www.walkerhouse.com.* 8 rooms, 2 story. No room phones.

Late June-early Sept: S $90-$125; D $120-$190; each additional $5-$15; ski plans; lower rates rest of year. Pets accepted; fee. Children over 12 years only. Complimentary continental breakfast. Check-out noon, check-in 2 pm. TV in sitting room; VCR available. Restaurant opposite 11 am-10 pm. Downhill ski 6 miles, cross-country ski 1/2 mile. Built in 1804. Rooms named after composers. Totally nonsmoking.

Lowell

Hotel

★ ★ ★ **WESTFORD REGENCY INN AND CONFERENCE CENTER.** *219 Littleton Rd (01886). Phone 978/692-8200; toll-free 800/543-7801; fax 978/692-7403. www.westfordregency.com.* Take in the joys of New England at this inn and conference center with 20,000 square feet of meeting space. Every Thursday from June through August there's a classic lobster boil and clambake hosted outdoors under a 6,000-square-foot tent. 193 rooms, 4 story. S $114; D $140; each additional $8; suites $125-$235; under 18 free; weekend rates. Pets accepted, some restrictions; fee. Check-out noon. TV; cable (premium). In-room modem link. Restaurant, bar; entertainment. In-house fitness room; sauna. Indoor pool; whirlpool.

Lynn

B&B/Small Inn

★ ★ ★ **DIAMOND DISTRICT BREAKFAST INN.** *142 Ocean St (01902). Phone 781/599-4470; toll-free 800/666-3076; fax 781/599-5122. www.diamonddistrictinn.com.* Located just minutes away from Boston and only steps from the water, this 1911 Georgian-style inn offers a great location on a quiet block of town. Guest rooms are named for types of shoes or shoe parts. 11 rooms, 3 story. Pets accepted, some restrictions. Complimentary full breakfast. Check-out 11 am, check-in 3 pm. TV. In-room modem link. Health club privileges. Totally nonsmoking. **$$**

Marblehead

B&B/Small Inn

★ ★ **SEAGULL INN.** *106 Harbor Ave (01945). Phone 781/631-1893; fax 781/631-3535. www.seagullinn.com.* 6 rooms, 2 story. Pets accepted; fee. Complimentary

continental breakfast. Check-out 11 am, check-in 2 pm. TV; VCR available. Lawn games. Built in 1880; turn-of-the-century atmosphere. Totally nonsmoking. **$$**

Martha's Vineyard

B&B/Small Inn

★ ★ **POINT WAY INN.** *104 Main St (02539). Phone 508/627-8633; toll-free 888/711-6633; fax 508/627-3338. www.pointway.com.* 14 rooms, 1-3 story. Pets accepted, some restrictions; fee. Complimentary continental breakfast. Check-out 11 am, check-in 2 pm. TV. Totally nonsmoking. **$$**

Newburyport

B&B/Small Inns

★ ★ **MORRILL PLACE.** *209 High St (01950). Phone 978/462-2808; toll-free 888/594-4667; fax 978/462-9966.* 9 rooms, 4 share bath, 3 story. No A/C. Pets accepted, some restrictions. Complimentary continental breakfast. Check-out noon, check-in 4 pm. TV; VCR available. Built in 1806. Once owned by a law partner of Daniel Webster; Webster was a frequent visitor. **$**

★ ★ **WINDSOR HOUSE.** *38 Federal St (01950). Phone 978/462-3778; toll-free 888/873-5296; fax 978/465-3443. www.bbhost.com/windsorhouse.* 4 rooms, 3 story. Pets accepted, some restrictions. Complimentary full breakfast. Check-out 11 am, check-in 4 pm. TV in sitting room; VCR. Federal mansion (1786) built by a lieutenant of the Continental Army for his wedding. Totally nonsmoking. **$$**

Provincetown

B&B/Small Inn

★ ★ **WHITE WIND INN.** *174 Commercial St (02657). Phone 508/487-1526; toll-free 888/49WIND; fax 508/487-4792. www.whitewindinn.com.* 12 rooms, 3 story. 8 rooms with shower only. No elevator. No room phones. Pets accepted, some restrictions; fee. Complimentary continental breakfast. Check-out 11 am, check-in 2 pm. TV; VCR available (movies). Concierge. Built in 1845; former shipbuilder's home. Opposite harbor. Totally nonsmoking. **$**

Rockport

Motel/Motor Lodge

★ ★ **SANDY BAY MOTOR INN.** *173 Main St (01966). Phone 978/546-7155; toll-free 800/437-7155; fax 978/546-9131. www.sandybaymotorinn.com.* This inn is conveniently located just a short walk from downtown's quaint shops and galleries and is close to many beaches, theaters, and churches. 80 rooms, 23 kitchen units, 2 story. Late June-Labor Day: S, D $98-$142; each additional $10; family rates; lower rates rest of year. Pets accepted, some restrictions; fee. Check-out 11 am. TV; cable (premium), VCR available. In-room modem link. Restaurant. Sauna. Indoor pool; whirlpool. Outdoor tennis. Free transportation.

▢ ▧ ▧ ▧ ▧

Salem

Hotel

★ ★ **HAWTHORNE HOTEL.** *18 Washington Sq W (01970). Phone 978/744-4080; toll-free 800/729-7829; fax 978/745-9842. www.hawthornehotel.com.* 89 rooms, 6 story. July-Oct: S $125-$154; D $125-$172; each additional $12; suites $285; under 18 free; lower rates rest of year. Pets accepted, some restrictions; fee. Check-out 11 am. TV; cable (premium). In-room modem link. Laundry services. Restaurant. Health club privileges. In-house fitness room.

▧ ▧ ▧ SC

B&B/Small Inn

★ ★ ★ **SALEM INN.** *7 Summer St; Rte 114 (01970). Phone 978/741-0680; toll-free 800/446-2995; fax 978/744-8924. www.saleminnma.com.* With individually appointed rooms and suites, many of which feature whirlpools, kitchenettes, and fireplaces, this inn provides comfort and luxury without assaulting your wallet. Season packages are available. 33 rooms, 4 story. No elevator. S, D $139-$149; each additional $15; suites $169-$199. Pets accepted; fee. Complimentary continental breakfast. Check-out 11 am, check-in 3 pm. TV; cable (premium). In-room modem link.

▧ ▧

Sandwich

Motel/Motor Lodge

★ **EARL OF SANDWICH MOTEL.** *378 Rte 6A (02537). Phone 508/888-1415; toll-free 800/442-3275;*
fax 508/833-1039. www.earlofsandwich.com. 24 rooms. Late June-early Sept: S, D $65-$89; each additional $10; lower rates rest of year. Pets accepted, some restrictions. Complimentary continental breakfast. Check-out 11 am. TV. Tudor motif.

▢ ▧ ▧

South Yarmouth

B&B/Small Inn

★ ★ **COLONIAL HOUSE INN & RESTAURANT.** *277 Main St; Rte 6A (02675). Phone 508/362-4348; fax 508/362-8034.* 21 rooms, 3 story. Pets accepted; fee. Complimentary breakfast. Check-out noon, check-in 2 pm. TV; VCR available. In-room modem link. Dining room, bar. Massage. Indoor pool; whirlpool. Lawn games. Business center. Old mansion (1730s); many antiques, handmade afghans. **$**

▢ ▧ ▧ ▧ ▧ ▧ ▧ ▧

Springfield

Motel/Motor Lodge

★ ★ **HOLIDAY INN.** *711 Dwight St (01104). Phone 413/781-0900; toll-free 800/465-4329; fax 413/785-1410. www.holiday-inn.com.* 244 rooms, 12 story. S $85-$110; D $95-$120; suites $130-$210; under 19 free; weekend, family rates. Pets accepted; fee. Check-out noon. TV. Restaurant, bar. In-house fitness room. Game room. Indoor pool; whirlpool. Downhill, cross-country ski 10 miles.

▢ ▧ ▧ ▧ ▧ ▧ SC

Sudbury Center

B&B/Small Inn

★ ★ **THE ARABIAN HORSE INN.** *277 Old Sudbury Rd (01776). Phone 978/443-7400; toll-free 800/arabian; fax 978/443-0234. www.arabianhorseinn.com.* 5 rooms, 3 story. Pets accepted; fee. Complimentary full breakfast. Check-out 11 am, check-in 3 pm. TV; cable (premium). In-room modem link. Cross-country ski on site. Arabian horses, antique cars on site. Built in 1886. Totally non-smoking. **$$**

▧ ▧ ▧

Michigan

Alma

Motel/Motor Lodge

★ **PETTICOAT INN.** *2454 W Monroe Rd (48801). Phone 989/681-5728.* 11 rooms. Pets accepted, some restrictions. Check-out 11 am. TV; cable (premium). Country setting. **$**

🔲 ⬛ ⬛ **SC**

Alpena

Motels/Motor Lodges

★ **FLETCHER.** *1001 US 23 N (49707). Phone 989/354-4191; toll-free 800/334-5920; fax 989/354-4056.* 96 rooms, 2 story. Pets accepted. Check-out 11 am. TV. Restaurant, bar. Room service. Sauna. Indoor pool; whirlpool. Outdoor tennis. Nature trail. Free airport, bus depot transportation. Overlooks wooded acres. **$**

🔲 ⬛ ⬛ ⬛ ⬛ ⬛ ⬛

★ ★ **HOLIDAY INN.** *1000 US 23 N (49707). Phone 989/356-2151; toll-free 800/465-4329; fax 989/356-2151. www.holiday-inn.com.* 148 rooms, 2 story. Pets accepted, some restrictions. Check-out noon. TV. Laundry services. Restaurant, bar; entertainment. Room service. In-house fitness room; sauna. Game room. Indoor pool; whirlpool; poolside service. Cross-country ski 8 miles. Free airport, bus depot transportation. **$**

🔲 ⬛ ⬛ ⬛ ⬛ ⬛ ⬛ ⬛

Ann Arbor

Motels/Motor Lodges

★ **HAMPTON INN.** *2300 Green Rd (48105). Phone 734/996-4444; toll-free 800/426-7866; fax 734/996-0196. www.hamptoninn.com.* 130 rooms, 4 story. Pets accepted; fee. Complimentary continental breakfast. Check-out noon. TV; cable (premium). In-house fitness room. Indoor pool; whirlpool. Cross-country ski 3 miles. **$**

🔲 ⬛ ⬛ ⬛ ⬛ ⬛ **SC**

★ **RED ROOF INN.** *3621 Plymouth Rd (48105). Phone 734/996-5800; fax 734/996-5707. www.redroof.com.* 108

rooms, 2 story. Pets accepted. Check-out noon. TV; cable (premium). **$**

🔲 ⬛ ⬛

Extended Stay

★ ★ **RESIDENCE INN BY MARRIOTT.** *800 Victors Way (48108). Phone 734/996-5666; fax 734/996-1919. www.residenceinn.com.* 114 rooms, 2-3 story. Pets accepted; fee. Complimentary continental breakfast. Check-out noon. TV; cable (premium). Laundry services. Pool; whirlpool. **$$**

🔲 ⬛ ⬛ ⬛

Battle Creek

Motels/Motor Lodges

★ ★ **BATTLE CREEK INN.** *5050 Beckley Rd (49015). Phone 269/979-1100; toll-free 800/232-3405; fax 269/979-1899. www.battlecreekinn.com.* 211 rooms, 2 story. Pets accepted, some restrictions. Complimentary continental breakfast. Check-out noon. TV; cable (premium). Laundry services. Restaurant, bar. Room service. In-house fitness room. Health club privileges. Game room. Indoor heated pool; poolside service. **$**

🔲 ⬛ ⬛ ⬛ ⬛ ⬛ **SC**

★ **DAYS INN.** *4786 Beckley Rd (49017). Phone 269/979-3561; fax 269/979-1400. www.daysinn.com.* 88 rooms. Pets accepted; fee. Complimentary continental breakfast. Check-out noon, check-in 4 pm. TV; cable (premium). Health club privileges. Cross-country ski 4 miles. **$**

🔲 ⬛ ⬛ ⬛ ⬛ ⬛ ⬛

Bay City

Motel/Motor Lodge

★ ★ **HOLIDAY INN.** *501 Saginaw St (48708). Phone 989/892-3501; fax 989/892-9342. www.holiday-inn.com.* 100 rooms, 4 story. Pets accepted, some restrictions. Check-out noon. TV. Laundry services. Restaurant, bar. Room service. Sauna. Indoor pool; whirlpool. **$**

🔲 ⬛ ⬛ ⬛ ⬛

Cadillac

Motels/Motor Lodges

★ ★ ★ **MCGUIRE'S RESORT.** *7880 Mackinaw Trail (49601). Phone 231/775-9947; toll-free 800/632-7302; fax*

231/775-9621. *www.mcguiresresort.com.* This resort is the perfect spot for visitors to relax and enjoy their vacation, with walking and biking trails, two golf courses, a pool, tennis facilities, volleyball and basketball courts, and more. It is near shopping, a movie theater, and the lake. 122 rooms, 1-3 story. Pets accepted, some restrictions; fee. Check-out 11 am. TV. In-room modem link. Restaurant, bar; entertainment. Room service. Health club privileges. Sauna. Game room. Indoor pool; whirlpool. 27-hole golf, putting green, driving range. Greens fee $45-$62. Outdoor tennis. Downhill ski 15 miles, cross-country ski on site. Lawn games. Free airport transportation. Panoramic view of countryside. **$**

★ **SUN-N-SNOW MOTEL.** *301 S Lake Mitchell Dr (49601). Phone 231/775-9961. www.cadillacmichigan.com.* 29 rooms. Pets accepted, some restrictions; fee. Check-out 11 am. TV. Downhill ski 15 miles, cross-country ski 1/4 mile. Lawn games. Park opposite. **$**

Charlevoix

Motel/Motor Lodge

★ **LODGE.** *120 Michigan Ave (49720). Phone 231/547-6565; fax 231/547-0741.* 40 rooms, 2 story. Pets accepted, some restrictions; fee. Check-out 11 am. TV; cable (premium). Pool. Downhill, cross-country ski 1 mile. Overlooks harbor. **$**

Clare

Motel/Motor Lodge

★ **DOHERTY HOTEL.** *604 N McEwan St (48617). Phone 989/386-3441; toll-free 800/525-4115; fax 989/386-4231. www.dohertyhotel.com.* 92 rooms, 3 story. Pets accepted, some restrictions; fee. Complimentary full breakfast. Check-out noon. Restaurant, bar; entertainment Wed-Sat. Game room. Indoor pool; whirlpool; poolside service. Downhill ski 5 miles, cross-country ski 7 miles. Free airport transportation. **$**

Coldwater

Motel/Motor Lodge

★ ★ **RAMADA INN.** *1000 Orleans Blvd (49036). Phone 517/278-2017; toll-free 800/806-8226; fax 517/279-7214.*

www.ramada.com. 128 rooms, 2 story. Pets accepted; fee. Complimentary continental breakfast. Check-out 11 am. TV; cable (premium). Restaurant, bar; entertainment. Room service. Game room. Indoor pool; whirlpool. Cross-country ski 2 miles. **$**

Copper Harbor

Motel/Motor Lodge

★ **ASTOR HOUSE-MINNETONKA RESORT.** *560 Gratiot (49918). Phone 906/289-4449; toll-free 800/433-2770; fax 906/289-4326. www.exploringthenorth.com.* 33 rooms. No A/C. Closed late Oct-early May. Pets accepted, some restrictions; fee. Check-out 10:30 am. TV; cable (premium). Saunas. Astor House Museum on premises. **$**

Dearborn

Motel/Motor Lodge

★ **RED ROOF INN.** *24130 Michigan Ave (48124). Phone 313/278-9732; fax 313/278-9741. www.redroof.com.* 112 rooms, 2 story. Pets accepted, some restrictions. Check-out noon. TV; cable (premium). **$**

Detroit

Motel/Motor Lodge

★ ★ **PARKCREST INN.** *20000 Harper Ave (48225). Phone 313/884-8800; fax 313/884-7087.* 49 rooms, 2 story. Pets accepted; fee. Check-out 11 am. TV; cable (premium). Restaurant, bar. Room service. Pool. Cross-country ski 15 miles. **$**

Hotels

★ ★ ★ **MARRIOTT DETROIT METROPOLITAN AIRPORT TERMINAL.** *Detroit Metropolitan Airport (48242). Phone 734/941-9400. www.marriott.com.* 160 rooms, 5 story. Pets accepted; fee. Complimentary continental breakfast. Check-out noon. TV; cable (premium), VCR available. Business center. **$$**

★ ★ ★ **OMNI DETROIT RIVER PLACE.** *1000 River Place Dr (48207). Phone 313/259-9500; fax 313/259-3744. www.omnihotels.com.* This elegant hotel is located in downtown Detroit on the historic waterfront. Guest rooms boast views of the river and the Canadian border. The hotel has a championship croquet court, which is the only USCA sanctioned croquet court in Michigan. 108 rooms, 5 story. Pets accepted, some restrictions; fee. Check-out noon. TV; cable (premium), VCR available. In-room modem link. Restaurant, bar. In-house fitness room; massage, sauna. Indoor pool; whirlpool. Valet parking. **$**

D 🐾 ≈ 🏌 ⊠

Escanaba

Motel/Motor Lodge

★ **BAYVIEW.** *7110 US 2/41 (MI 35) (49837). Phone 906/786-2843; toll-free 800/547-1201; fax 906/786-6218. www.baydenoc.com/bayview.* 22 rooms, 1-2 story. Pets accepted, some restrictions; fee. Check-out 11 am. TV; cable (premium). Sauna. Indoor pool. **$**

D 🐾 ≈ 🏌 ⊠

Farmington

Motel/Motor Lodge

★ **RED ROOF INN.** *24300 Sinacola Ct NE (48335). Phone 248/478-8640; toll-free 800/843-7663; fax 248/478-4842. www.redroof.com.* 108 rooms. Pets accepted, some restrictions. Check-out noon. TV. **$**

D 🐾 ⊠

Frankfort

Motel/Motor Lodge

★ **BAY VALLEY INN.** *1561 Scenic Hwy (49635). Phone 231/352-7113; toll-free 800/352-7113; fax 231/352-7114.* 20 rooms. Pets accepted, some restrictions; fee. Complimentary continental breakfast. Check-out 11 am. TV; VCR available (free movies). Laundry services. Downhill, cross-country ski 18 miles. **$**

D 🐾 ≈ ⊠ SC

Resort

★★ **CHIMNEY CORNERS RESORT.** *1602 Crystal Dr (49635). Phone 231/352-7522; fax 616/352-7252. www.benzie.com.* 27 rooms, 1-2 story. No A/C. Closed Dec-Apr. Pets accepted, some restrictions; fee. Check-out 10 am, check-in 3 pm. TV in lobby. Laundry services. Dining room. Outdoor tennis. Sailboats. Private beach;

rowboats, hoists; paddleboats. 1,000-foot beach on Crystal Lake, 300 acres of wooded hills. **$**

🐾 ⚓ 🎿 ≈

Gaylord

Motels/Motor Lodges

★ **BEST VALUE INN.** *803 S Otsego Ave (49735). Phone 989/732-6451; toll-free 800/876-9252; fax 989/732-7634.* 44 rooms, 1-2 story. Pets accepted, some restrictions. Complimentary continental breakfast. Check-out 11 am. TV. In-house fitness room; sauna. Downhill, cross-country ski 3 miles. **$**

D 🐾 🎿 🏌 ⊠ SC

★★ **BEST WESTERN ALPINE LODGE.** *833 W Main St (49735). Phone 989/732-2431; toll-free 800/684-2233; fax 989/732-9640. www.bestwestern.com.* 137 rooms, 2 story. Pets accepted, some restrictions. Check-out 11 am. TV; VCR available (movies). Laundry services. Restaurant, bar. Room service. In-house fitness room; sauna. Game room. Indoor pool; whirlpool. Downhill, cross-country ski 4 miles. **$**

D 🐾 ⚓ 🎿 ≈ 🏌 ✈ ⊠

Grand Marais

Motel/Motor Lodge

★★ **WELKER'S LODGE.** *Canal St (49839). Phone 906/494-2361; fax 906/494-2371.* 41 rooms, 1-2 story. Some A/C. Some room phones. Pets accepted. Check-out 10 am. TV; cable (premium), VCR available. Restaurant, bar. Sauna. Indoor pool; whirlpool. Outdoor tennis. Lawn games. On Lake Superior; private beach. **$**

D 🐾 ⚓ 🎿 ≈ ⊠

Grand Rapids

Motels/Motor Lodges

★ **DAYS INN.** *310 NW Pearl St (49504). Phone 616/235-7611; toll-free 800/329-7466; fax 616/235-1995. www.daysinn.com.* 175 rooms, 8 story. Pets accepted, some restrictions; fee. Check-out 11 am. TV; cable (premium), VCR available. Restaurant, bar. Room service. In-house fitness room. Indoor pool; whirlpool. Downhill, cross-country ski 12 miles. **$**

D 🐾 ≈ 🏌 ⊠

★ **EXEL INN.** *4855 28th St SE (49512). Phone 616/957-3000; toll-free 800/367-3935; fax 616/957-0194. www.exelinns.com.* 110 rooms, 2 story. Pets accepted, some restrictions. Complimentary continental breakfast. Check-out noon. TV. Downhill ski 15 miles, cross-country ski 4 miles. **$**

★ **HAMPTON INN.** *4981 S 28th St (49512). Phone 616/956-9304; toll-free 800/426-7866; fax 616/956-6617. www.hamptoninn.com.* 120 rooms, 2 story. Pets accepted, some restrictions. Complimentary continental breakfast. Check-out noon. TV; cable (premium). In-house fitness room. Pool. Downhill ski 15 miles, cross-country ski 4 miles. **$**

★ **RED ROOF INN.** *5131 SE 28th St (49512). Phone 616/942-0800; toll-free 800/843-7663; fax 616/942-8341. www.redroof.com.* 107 rooms, 2 story. Pets accepted, some restrictions. Check-out noon. TV; cable (premium). Downhill ski 15 miles, cross-country ski 5 miles. **$**

Extended Stay

★★ **RESIDENCE INN BY MARRIOTT.** *2701 E Beltline Ave SE (49546). Phone 616/957-8111; fax 616/957-3699. www.residenceinn.com/grrgr.* 96 kitchen units, 2 story. Pets accepted; fee. Complimentary continental breakfast. Check-out noon. TV; cable (premium), VCR available. Laundry services. In-house fitness room. Health club privileges. Pool; whirlpool. Downhill ski 15 miles, cross-country ski 5 miles. Free airport transportation. **$**

Grayling

Motels/Motor Lodges

★★ **HOLIDAY INN.** *2650 I-75 Business Loop (49738). Phone 989/348-7611; toll-free 800/292-9095; fax 989/348-7984. www.holiday-inn.com.* 151 rooms, 2 story. Pets accepted, some restrictions. Check-out 11 am. TV; cable (premium), VCR available. Restaurant, bar; entertainment. Room service. In-house fitness room; sauna. Game room. Indoor pool; children's pool; whirlpool; poolside service. Downhill ski 5 miles, cross-country ski on site. Lawn games. Airport, bus depot transportation. On wooded property. **$**

★ **NORTH COUNTRY LODGE.** *615 I-75 Business Loop (49738). Phone 989/348-8471; toll-free 800/475-6300; fax 989/348-6114. www.grayling-mi.com/northcountrylodge.*

24 rooms. Pets accepted, some restrictions. Check-out 11 am. TV. Downhill, cross-country ski 3 miles. Free airport transportation. **$**

★ **SUPER 8.** *5828 Nelson A. Miles Pkwy (49738). Phone 989/348-8888; fax 989/348-2030. www.super8.com.* 61 rooms, 2 story. Pets accepted, some restrictions; fee. Complimentary continental breakfast. Check-out 11 am. TV. Laundry services. Downhill ski 1 mile, cross-country ski 6 miles. Lawn games. **$**

Houghton

Motels/Motor Lodges

★ **BEST WESTERN KING'S INN.** *215 Shelden Ave (49931). Phone 906/482-5000; toll-free 800/780-7234; fax 906/482-9795. www.bestwestern.com.* 68 rooms, 4 story. Pets accepted; fee. Complimentary continental breakfast. Check-out 11 am. TV; cable (premium), VCR available (movies). Sauna. Indoor pool; whirlpool. Downhill ski 2 miles, cross-country ski 3 miles. **$**

★ **SUPER 8.** *790 Michigan Ave (49908). Phone 906/353-6680; fax 906/353-7246. www.super8.com.* 40 rooms, 2 story. Pets accepted; fee. Complimentary continental breakfast. Check-out 11 am. TV. Cross-country ski 8 miles. **$**

Houghton Lake

Motel/Motor Lodge

★ **VAL HALLA MOTEL.** *9869 W Houghton Lake Dr (48629). Phone 989/422-5137.* 21 rooms. Pets accepted, some restrictions; fee. Check-out 11 am. TV. Pool. Downhill ski 17 miles, cross-country ski 2 miles. Lawn games. Free airport transportation. **$**

Iron Mountain

Motel/Motor Lodge

★ **BEST WESTERN EXECUTIVE INN.** *1518 S Stephenson Ave (US 2) (49801). Phone 906/774-2040; toll-free 800/528-1234; fax 906/774-0238. www.bestwestern.com.* 57 rooms, 2 story. Pets accepted; fee. Complimentary continental breakfast. Check-out 11 am. TV; cable (premium), VCR available. Indoor pool. Downhill, cross-country ski 3 miles. **$**

D 🐾 🏊 🏊 ⊠ SC

Ishpeming

Motel/Motor Lodge

★ ★ **BEST WESTERN COUNTRY INN.** *850 US 41 W (49849). Phone 906/485-6345; toll-free 800/780-7234; fax 906/485-6348. www.bestwestern.com.* 60 rooms, 2 story. Pets accepted, some restrictions. Complimentary continental breakfast. Check-out noon. TV; cable (premium). Health club privileges. Game room. Indoor pool; whirlpool. Downhill ski 15 miles, cross-country ski 2 miles. **$**

D 🐾 🏊 🏊 ⊠ SC

Jackson

Motels/Motor Lodges

★ **BAYMONT INN.** *2035 N Service Dr (49202). Phone 517/789-6000; toll-free 800/428-3438; fax 517/782-6836. www.baymontinns.com.* 67 rooms, 2 story. Pets accepted, some restrictions; fee. Complimentary continental breakfast. Check-out noon. TV; cable (premium). **$**

D 🐾 ⊠ SC

★ ★ **HOLIDAY INN.** *2000 Holiday Inn Dr (49202). Phone 517/783-2681; fax 517/783-5744. www.holiday-inn.com.* 184 rooms, 2 story. Pets accepted, some restrictions; fee. Check-out 11 am. TV; VCR available. Laundry services. Restaurant, bar. Room service. Sauna. Game room. Miniature golf. Pool; whirlpool. Cross-country ski 10 miles. **$**

D 🐾 🏊 🏊 ⊠ SC

Kalamazoo

Motels/Motor Lodges

★ **DAYS INN.** *3522 Sprinkle Rd (49001). Phone 269/381-7070; fax 269/381-4341. www.daysinn.com.* 146 rooms, 2 story. Pets accepted, some restrictions; fee. Check-out noon. TV; cable (premium), VCR available. Laundry services. Restaurant, bar. Room service. Sauna. Indoor pool; outdoor pool; whirlpool; poolside service. Downhill, cross-country ski 15 miles. Free airport transportation. Adjacent to stadium. **$**

D 🐾 🏊 🏊 🛫 ⊠

★ **QUALITY INN.** *3750 Easy St (49001). Phone 269/388-3551; toll-free 800/687-6667; fax 269/342-9132. www.qualityinn.com.* 116 rooms, 2 story. Pets accepted. Complimentary continental breakfast. Check-out noon. TV; cable (premium). Heated pool. Downhill, cross-country ski 15 miles. Free airport, train station transportation. **$**

D 🐾 🏊 🏊 🛫 ⊠ SC

★ **RED ROOF INN.** *5425 W Michigan Ave (49009). Phone 269/375-7400; fax 269/375-7533. www.redroof.com.* 108 rooms, 2 story. Pets accepted, some restrictions. Check-out noon. TV. Downhill ski 8 miles, cross-country ski 3 miles. **$**

D 🐾 🏊 🛠 ⊠

★ **SUPER 8.** *618 Maple Hill Dr (49009). Phone 269/345-0146; fax 269/345-0146. www.super8.com.* 62 rooms, 3 story. No elevator. Pets accepted; fee. Check-out 11 am. TV; cable (premium). Downhill ski 11 miles. **$**

D 🐾 🏊 ⊠ SC

Extended Stay

★ ★ **RESIDENCE INN BY MARRIOTT.** *1500 E Kilgore Rd (49001). Phone 269/349-0855; toll-free 800/331-3131; fax 269/373-5971. www.residenceinn.com.* 83 rooms, 2 story. Pets accepted; fee. Complimentary continental breakfast. Check-out noon. TV; VCR available (movies). In-room modem link. Laundry services. Health club privileges. Pool; whirlpool. Downhill, cross-country ski 20 miles. Free airport transportation. **$**

D 🐾 🏊 🏊 🛫 ⊠ SC

Lansing

Motels/Motor Lodges

★ ★ **BEST WESTERN MIDWAY.** *7111 W Saginaw Hwy (48917). Phone 517/627-8471; toll-free 877/772-6100; fax 517/627-8597. www.bestwestern.com.* 149 rooms, 2-3 story. Pets accepted, some restrictions. Check-out noon. TV; cable (premium). Restaurant, bar. Room service. In-house fitness room; sauna. Game room. Indoor pool; whirlpool. Free airport transportation. **$**

🐾 🏊 🛴

★ **RED ROOF INN.** *3615 Dunckel Rd (48910). Phone 517/332-2575; toll-free 800/843-7663; fax 517/332-1459. www.redroof.com.* 80 rooms, 2 story. Pets accepted. Check-out noon. TV. **$**

D 🐾 ⊠ SC

Mackinaw City

Motels/Motor Lodges

★ **GRAND MACKINAW INN AND SUITES.** *907 S Huron (49701). Phone 231/436-8831; toll-free 800/822-8314. www.grandmackinaw.com.* 40 rooms, 1-2 story. Closed Nov-Apr. Pet accepted, some restrictions; fee. Check-out 11 am. TV; cable (premium). Private sand beach; overlooks Lake Huron. Indoor pool; whirlpool. Lawn games. **$**

⬛ 🐾 ≋ ⛵ SC

★ **LIGHTHOUSE VIEW.** *699 N Huron St (49701). Phone 231/436-5304; fax 616/436-5304.* 25 rooms, 2 story. Closed Nov-Apr. Pets accepted, some restrictions. Check-out 11 am. TV. Beach opposite. Indoor pool; whirlpool. **$**

⬛ 🐾 ⛷ 🏋 ≋ ⛵

★ **MOTEL 6.** *206 N Nicolet St (49701). Phone 231/436-8961; toll-free 800/466-8356; fax 231/436-7317. www.motel6.com.* 53 rooms, 2 story. Pets accepted, some restrictions. Check-out 11 am. TV; cable (premium). Indoor pool; whirlpool. Cross-country ski on site. **$**

⬛ 🐾 ≋ ⛵ ⛷

★ **STARLITE BUDGET INN.** *116 Old US 31 (49701). Phone 231/436-5959; toll-free 800/288-8190; fax 616/436-5988. www.mackinawcity.com/lodging/starlite.* 33 rooms. Closed Nov-Apr. Pets accepted, some restrictions; fee. Check-out 10 am. TV; cable (premium). Pool. **$**

⬛ 🐾 ≋ ⛵

★ **SUPER 8.** *601 N Huron Ave (49701). Phone 231/436-5252; toll-free 800/800-8000; fax 231/436-7004. www.super8.com.* 50 rooms, 2 story. Pets accepted, some restrictions. Check-out 11 am. TV; VCR available. Laundry services. Sauna. Game room. Indoor pool; whirlpool. **$**

⬛ 🐾 ≋ ⛵ SC

Manistique

Motel/Motor Lodge

★ **HOLIDAY MOTEL.** *E US Hwy 2 (49854). Phone 906/341-2710.* 20 rooms. No A/C. Pets accepted, some restrictions; fee. Complimentary continental breakfast. Check-out 10 am. TV; cable (premium). Pool. Lawn games. **$**

🐾 ≋ ⛵ SC

Marquette

Motels/Motor Lodges

★ ★ **HOLIDAY INN.** *1951 US 41 W (49855). Phone 906/225-1351; toll-free 800/465-4329; fax 906/228-4329. www.holiday-inn.com.* 203 rooms, 5 story. Pets accepted. Check-out noon. TV; cable (premium). Restaurant, bar. Room service. Health club privileges. Sauna. Indoor pool; whirlpool. Downhill ski 7 miles, cross-country ski 3 miles. Nature trails. Free airport transportation. **$**

⬛ 🐾 ⛷ ≋ ✈ ⛵

★ ★ **RAMADA INN.** *412 W Washington St (49855). Phone 906/228-6000; toll-free 800/272-6232; fax 906/228-2963. www.ramada.com.* 113 rooms, 2-7 story. Pets accepted, some restrictions. Check-out noon. TV; cable (premium). Laundry services. Restaurant, bar. Room service. Health club privileges. Sauna. Indoor pool; whirlpool. Downhill ski 3 miles, cross-country ski 1/2 mile. Airport transportation. **$**

⬛ 🐾 🏋 ⛷ ≋ 🎿 ✈ ⛵

Midland

Motels/Motor Lodges

★ ★ **BEST WESTERN VALLEY PLAZA RESORT.** *5221 Bay City Rd (48642). Phone 989/496-2700; toll-free 800/825-2700; fax 989/496-9233. www.valleyplazaresort.com.* 162 rooms, 2 story. Pets accepted, some restrictions. Complimentary continental breakfast. Check-out noon. TV. In-room modem link. Restaurant, bar. Room service. In-house fitness room. Game room. Indoor pool; children's pool. Lawn games. Free airport transportation. Movie theater. **$**

⬛ 🐾 🏋 ⛷ 🎿 ✈ ⛵

★ ★ **HOLIDAY INN.** *1500 W Wackerly St (48640). Phone 989/631-4220; toll-free 800/622-4220; fax 989/631-3776. www.holiday-inn.com.* 235 rooms, 2 story. Pets accepted, some restrictions. Check-out 11 am. TV; cable (premium). In-room modem link. Restaurant, bar; entertainment. Room service. In-house fitness room; sauna. Game room. Indoor pool; whirlpool; poolside service. Cross-country ski 2 miles. Free airport transportation. Business center. **$**

⬛ 🐾 ⛷ ≋ ⛵ 🎿 ✈ ⛵ 🚶

Mount Pleasant

Motel/Motor Lodge

★ ★ **HOLIDAY INN.** *5665 E Pickard St (48858). Phone 989/772-2905; toll-free 800/299-8891; fax 989/772-4952. www.holiday-inn.com.* 184 rooms, 2-3 story. Pets accepted, some restrictions. Check-out 11 am. TV; cable (premium). In-room modem link. Restaurant, bar; entertainment. Room service. In-house fitness room; sauna. Indoor pool; outdoor pool; whirlpool. 36-hole golf, greens fee $35-$65. Lighted tennis. Lawn games. Free airport transportation. **$**

⬜🐾👫🏊🏊🚶⛷🏊SC

Munising

Motels/Motor Lodges

★ **ALGER FALLS MOTEL.** *M28 E (49862). Phone 906/387-3536; fax 906/387-5228.* 17 rooms. Pets accepted, some restrictions. Check-out 11 am. TV. Cross-country ski 3 miles. Wooded area with trails. **$**

🐾⛷🏊

★ ★ **BEST WESTERN.** *MI 28 E (49895). Phone 906/387-4864; toll-free 800/528-1234; fax 906/387-2038. www.bestwestern.com.* 80 rooms, 2 story. Pets accepted, some restrictions. Check-out 11 am. TV. Restaurant, bar. Sauna. Indoor pool; whirlpool. **$**

⬜🐾🏊🏊SC

★ **COMFORT INN.** *MI 28 E (49862). Phone 906/387-5292; fax 906/387-3753. www.comfortinn.com.* 61 rooms, 2 story. Pets accepted, some restrictions. Complimentary continental breakfast. Check-out 11 am. TV; cable (premium), VCR available. Laundry services. In-house fitness room. Game room. Indoor pool; whirlpool. Cross-country ski 6 miles. **$**

⬜🐾⛷🏊🚶

★ **DAYS INN.** *MI 28 E (49862). Phone 906/387-2493; toll-free 800/329-7466; fax 906/387-5214. www.daysinn.com.* 66 rooms. Pets accepted, some restrictions. Check-out 11 am. TV; cable (premium), VCR (movies). Sauna. Indoor pool; whirlpool. Cross-country ski 1 mile. **$**

⬜🐾🏊🏊✈

★ **SUNSET RESORT MOTEL.** *1315 Bay St (49862). Phone 906/387-4574. www.exploringthenorth.com.* 16 rooms. No A/C. Closed 3rd week in Oct-Apr. Pets accepted, some restrictions; fee. Check-out 11 am. TV. Lawn games. **$**

🐾

Muskegon

Motel/Motor Lodge

★ **SUPER 8.** *3380 Hoyt St (49444). Phone 231/733-0088; fax 616/733-0088. www.super8.com.* 62 rooms, 2 story. Pets accepted; fee. Check-out 11 am. TV; cable (premium), VCR available. **$**

⬜🐾⛷🚶🏊🏊

Newberry

Motels/Motor Lodges

★ **GATEWAY MOTEL.** *MI 123 S (49868). Phone 906/293-5651; toll-free 800/791-9485.* 11 rooms, 1 story. No room phones. Pets accepted, some restrictions. Check-out 10 am. TV; cable (premium). Cross-country ski 4 miles. **$**

🐾⛷✈🏊

★ **MANOR MOTEL.** *MI 123 Newberry Ave (49868). Phone 906/293-5000.* 12 rooms. Pets accepted, some restrictions. Check-out 10 am. TV; cable (premium). Game room. Lawn games. **$**

🐾🐾⛷🏊

★ **ZELLAR'S VILLAGE INN.** *MI 123 S (Newberry Ave) (49868). Phone 906/293-5114; fax 906/293-5116.* 20 rooms. Pets accepted, some restrictions; fee. Check-out 11 am. TV; cable (premium). In-room modem link. Restaurant, bar. Room service. Game room. **$**

⬜🐾🐾⛷🏊

Ontonagon

Motel/Motor Lodge

★ ★ **AMERICINN.** *120 Lincoln (49953). Phone 906/885-5311; fax 906/885-5847. www.americinns.com.* 71 rooms, 3 story. Pets accepted, some restrictions; fee. Complimentary continental breakfast. Check-out 11 am. TV; cable (premium), VCR available. Restaurant, bar. Sauna. Game room. Indoor pool; whirlpool. Downhill, cross-country ski 3 miles. Airport transportation. **$**

⬜🐾🐾🏊🏊🏊

Paw Paw

Motel/Motor Lodge

★ **MROCZER INN.** *139 Ampey Rd (49079). Phone 269/ 657-2578.* 43 rooms, 2 story. Pets accepted; fee. Check-out 11 am. TV. Downhill ski 20 miles. **$**

⊡ 🐾 🏊 🕾

Plymouth

Motel/Motor Lodge

★ **RED ROOF INN.** *39700 Ann Arbor Rd (48170). Phone 734/459-3300; toll-free 800/843-7663; fax 734/459- 3072. www.redroof.com.* 109 rooms, 2 story. Pets accepted, some restrictions. Check-out noon. TV; cable (premium). In-room modem link. **$**

⊡ 🐾 🕾

Port Huron

Motel/Motor Lodge

★ **KNIGHTS INN.** *2160 Water St (48060). Phone 810/982-1022; toll-free 800/843-5644; fax 810/982-0927. www.knightsinn.com.* 104 rooms. Pets accepted; fee. Check-out noon. TV; cable (premium), VCR available. Pool. **$**

⊡ 🐾 🏊 🕾 SC

Saginaw

Motels/Motor Lodges

★ ★ **FOUR POINTS BY SHERATON.** *4960 Towne Centre Rd (48604). Phone 989/790-5050; toll-free 800/428- 1470; fax 989/790-1466. www.fourpoints.com.* 156 rooms, 6 story. Pets accepted, some restrictions; fee. Check-out noon. TV; cable (premium), VCR available. Restaurant, bar; entertainment. Room service. In-house fitness room; sauna. Health club privileges. Game room. Indoor pool; outdoor pool; whirlpool. Free airport transportation. Country French décor. **$**

⊡ 🐾 🏊 🕅 🕾 SC

★ **SUPER 8.** *4848 Towne Center Rd (48603). Phone 989/ 791-3003; fax 989/791-3003. www.super8.com.* 62 rooms, 3 story. Pets accepted; fee. Check-out 11 am. TV; cable (premium). Health club privileges. **$**

⊡ 🐾 🕾

Saint Ignace

Motels/Motor Lodges

★ **BAY VIEW BEACHFRONT MOTEL.** *1133 N State St (49781). Phone 906/643-9444.* 19 rooms. Closed late Oct-mid-May. Pets accepted, some restrictions; fee. Check-out 10 am. TV. Free airport transportation. On Lake Huron; private beach. **$**

⊡ 🐾 ⛵ 🏊 🕾

★ **BUDGET HOST INN.** *700 N State St (49781). Phone 906/643-9666; toll-free 800/872-7057; fax 906/643- 9126. www.stignacebudgethost.com.* 56 rooms, 2 story. Pets accepted, some restrictions. Check-out 11 am. TV; cable (premium). In-room modem link. Laundry services. Indoor pool; whirlpool. Downhill, cross-country ski 5 miles. Overlooks Moran Bay. Ferry 1 block. **$**

⊡ 🐾 🏊 🛫 🕾

★ ★ **QUALITY INN.** *913 Boulevard Dr (49781). Phone 906/643-9700; toll-free 800/906-4656; fax 906/643-6762. www.qualityinn.com.* 57 rooms, 2 story. Pets accepted, some restrictions; fee. Complimentary continental breakfast. Check-out noon. TV; VCR available. Laundry services. Game room. Indoor pool; whirlpool. Cross-country ski 7 miles. **$**

⊡ 🐾 🏊 🕾 SC

Saint Joseph

Motels/Motor Lodges

★ ★ **BEST WESTERN TWIN CITY INN & SUITES.** *1598 Mall Dr (49022). Phone 269/925-1880; toll-free 800/228-5150; fax 269/925-1880. www.comfortinn.com.* 52 rooms, 2 story. Pets accepted; fee. Complimentary continental breakfast. Check-out 11 am. TV; cable (premium). Health club privileges. Game room. Indoor pool; whirlpool. **$**

⊡ 🐾 🏊 🕾 SC

★ **ECONO LODGE.** *2723 Niles Ave (49085). Phone 269/982-3333; fax 269/983-7630. www.econolodge.com.* 36 rooms, 2 story. Pets accepted, some restrictions; fee. Complimentary continental breakfast. Check-out noon. TV; cable (premium). Pool. Cross-country ski 5 miles. **$**

⊡ 🐾 ⛵ 🏊 🕅 🕾

★ **SUPER 8.** *1950 E Napier Ave (49022). Phone 269/926-1371; toll-free 800/800-8000; fax 269/926-1371. www.super8.com.* 62 rooms, 3 story. Pets accepted, some restrictions; fee. Check-out 11 am. TV; cable (premium). **$**

⊡ 🐾 🕾

Sault Sainte Marie

Motels/Motor Lodges

★ **BUDGET HOST INN.** *1200 Ashmun St (49783).* Phone 906/635-5213; toll-free 800/955-5213; fax 906/635-9672. www.crestviewinn.com. 44 rooms. Pets accepted, some restrictions. Complimentary continental breakfast. Check-out 11 am. TV; cable (premium). In-room modem link. Health club privileges. Locks 1 mile. **$**

★ **SEAWAY MOTEL.** *1800 Ashmun St (49783).* Phone 906/632-8201; toll-free 800/782-0466; fax 906/632-8210. 18 rooms. Closed mid-Oct-May. Pets accepted, some restrictions. Check-out 10 am. TV. Downhill ski 18 miles, cross-country ski 1/4 mile. Free airport transportation. **$**

★ **SUPER 8.** *3826 I-75 Business Spur (49783).* Phone 906/632-8882; toll-free 800/800-8000; fax 906/632-3766. www.super8.com. 61 rooms, 2 story. Pets accepted, some restrictions. Complimentary continental breakfast. Check-out 11 am. TV; cable (premium). Laundry services. **$**

Southfield

Motel/Motor Lodge

★★ **HOLIDAY INN.** *26555 Telegraph Rd (48034).* Phone 248/353-7700; toll-free 800/465-4329; fax 248/353-8377. www.holiday-inn.com. 417 rooms, 2 story. Pets acccpted, some restrictions; fee. Check-out noon. TV; cable (premium). Restaurant, bar. Room service. In-house fitness room. Game room. Indoor pool; whirlpool. Downhill, cross-country ski 20 miles. Many rooms in circular tower. **$**

Tawas City

Motel/Motor Lodge

★ **TAWAS MOTEL - RESORT.** *1124 US 23 (48763).* Phone 989/362-3822; toll-free 888/263-3260; fax 989/362-3822. www.tawasmotel.com. 21 rooms. Pets accepted. Check-out 11 am. TV; cable (premium). Sauna. Game room. Pool; whirlpool. Cross-country ski 15 miles. Lawn games. **$**

Traverse City

Motels/Motor Lodges

★★ **HOLIDAY INN.** *615 E Front St (49686).* Phone 231/947-3700; toll-free 800/888-8020; fax 231/947-0361. www.holiday-inn.com. 179 rooms, 4 story. Pets accepted, some restrictions; fee. Check-out 11 am. TV; cable (premium). Restaurant. Room service. In-house fitness room; sauna. Game room. Indoor pool; whirlpool. Downhill ski 5 miles, cross-country ski 8 miles. Lawn games. Free airport transportation. **$$**

★ **MAIN STREET INN.** *618 E Front St (49686).* Phone 231/929-0410; toll-free 800/255-7180; fax 231/929-0489. www.mainstreetinnusa.com. 93 rooms. Pets accepted, some restrictions. Check-out 11 am. TV; cable (premium), VCR available. Laundry services. Pool. Downhill ski 5 miles, cross-country ski 8 miles. **$**

★ **TRAVERSE BAY INN.** *2300 US 31 N (49686).* Phone 231/938-2646; toll-free 800/968-2646; fax 231/938-5845. www.traversebayinn.com. 24 rooms, 2 story. Pets accepted, some restrictions; fee. Check-out 11 am. TV; cable (premium), VCR available (movies). Laundry services. Game room. Beach opposite. Pool; whirlpool. Downhill, cross-country ski 1 mile. **$**

Troy

Motels/Motor Lodges

★ **DRURY INN.** *575 W Big Beaver Rd (48084).* Phone 248/528-3330; toll-free 800/325-8300; fax 248/528-3330. www.druryinn.com. 153 rooms, 4 story. Pets accepted. Complimentary continental breakfast. Check-out noon. TV; cable (premium), VCR available. In-room modem link. Health club privileges. Pool. Cross-country ski 4 miles. **$**

★★ **HOLIDAY INN.** *2537 Rochester Ct (48083).* Phone 248/689-7500; toll-free 800/465-4329; fax 248/689-9015. www.holiday-inn.com. 150 rooms, 4 story. Pets accepted, some restrictions; fee. Check-out noon. TV. In-room modem link. Laundry services. Restaurant, bar. Room service. In-house fitness room; sauna. Pool. Cross-country ski 5 miles. **$**

★ **RED ROOF INN.** *2350 Rochester Ct (48083). Phone 248/689-4391; toll-free 800/REDROOF; fax 248/689-4397. www.redroof.com.* 109 rooms, 2 story. Pets accepted. Check-out noon. TV; cable (premium). In-room modem link. Cross-country ski 10 miles. **$**

🐾 ⛷ ⌗ SC

Hotel

★★★ **HILTON NORTHFIELD.** *5500 Crooks Rd (48098). Phone 248/879-2100; fax 248/879-6054. www.hilton.com.* 191 rooms, 3 story. Pets accepted, some restrictions. Check-out noon. TV; cable (premium). In-room modem link. Restaurant, bar; entertainment. Room service. In-house fitness room; sauna. Health club privileges. Game room. Indoor pool. Cross-country ski 3 miles. Business center. **$$**

D 🐾 ⛷ ⌗ 🏃 ⌗ SC 🏃

Extended Stay

★★ **RESIDENCE INN BY MARRIOTT.** *2600 Livernois Rd (48083). Phone 248/689-6856; fax 248/689-3788. www.residenceinn.com.* 152 rooms, 2 story. Pets accepted; fee. Complimentary continental breakfast. Check-out noon. TV; cable (premium), VCR available. In-room modem link. Laundry services. Health club privileges. Pool; whirlpool. Downhill, cross-country ski 20 miles. **$**

D 🐾 ⛷ ⌗ ⌗

Wakefield

Resort

★★ **INDIANHEAD MOUNTAIN RESORT.** *500 Indianhead Mountain Rd (49968). Phone 906/229-5181; toll-free 800/346-3426; fax 906/229-5920. www.indianheadmtn.com.* 62 rooms, 2-3 story. Closed mid-Apr-June, Oct-mid-Nov. Pets accepted, some restrictions; fee. Complimentary continental breakfast. Check-out 11 am, check-in 4 pm. TV; VCR available (movies). Dining room, bar. Supervised children's activities (Nov-mid-Apr). In-house fitness room; sauna. Game room. Indoor pool; whirlpool. Golf on premises, greens fee $6-$10. Outdoor tennis. Downhill ski on site. Hiking, nature trails. **$**

D 🐾 ⛷ 🏃 ⌗ ⌗ 🏃 ⌗ SC

Warren

Motels/Motor Lodges

★★ **BEST WESTERN GEORGIAN INN.** *31327 Gratiot Ave (48066). Phone 586/294-0400; toll-free 800/446-1866; fax 586/294-1020.* 111 rooms, 2 story. Pets accepted, some restrictions; fee. Check-out noon. TV. In-room modem link. Laundry services. Restaurant, bar. Room service. In-house fitness room. Game room. Pool; poolside service. **$**

🐾 ⌗ 🏃 ⌗ ⌗

★ **RED ROOF INN.** *26300 Dequindre Rd (48091). Phone 586/573-4300; fax 586/573-6157. www.redroof.com.* 136 rooms, 2 story. Pets accepted, some restrictions. Check-out noon. TV; cable (premium). In-room modem link. **$**

D 🐾 ⌗

All Suite

★ **HOMEWOOD SUITES.** *30180 N Civic Center Blvd (48093). Phone 586/558-7870; toll-free 800/225-5466; fax 586/558-8072. www.homewoodsuites.com.* 76 rooms, 3 story. Pets accepted, some restrictions; fee. Complimentary continental breakfast. Check-out noon. TV; cable (premium), VCR available. In-room modem link. In-house fitness room. Health club privileges. Pool; whirlpool. Downhill, cross-country ski 20 miles. Business center. **$**

D 🐾 ⛷ ⌗ ⌗ 🏃 ⌗ ⌗

Extended Stay

★★ **RESIDENCE INN BY MARRIOTT.** *30120 Civic Center Blvd (48093). Phone 586/558-8050; fax 586/558-8214. www.marriott.com.* 133 rooms, 3 story. Pets accepted; fee. Complimentary continental breakfast. Check-out noon. TV; cable (premium), VCR available. In-room modem link. Laundry services. In-house fitness room. Health club privileges. Pool; whirlpool. **$**

D 🐾 ⌗ 🏃 ⌗ SC

Minnesota

Albert Lea

Motels/Motor Lodges

★ **BUDGET HOST INN.** *2301 E Main St (56007). Phone 507/373-8291; toll-free 800/218-2989; fax 507/373-4043. www.budgethost.com.* 124 rooms, 3 story. Pets accepted; fee. Check-out 11 am. TV. Laundry services. Restaurant, bar; entertainment weekends. In-house fitness room; sauna. Game room. Indoor pool; children's pool; whirlpool. Cross-country ski 1 mile. **$**

D 🐾 ⛵ 🏊 🏋 🏂 SC

★ **SUPER 8.** *2019 E Main St (56007). Phone 507/377-0591. www.super8.com.* 60 rooms, 3 story. No elevator. Pets accepted, some restrictions; fee. Check-out 11 am. TV; VCR available. Cross-country ski 1 mile. Snowmobile trail adjacent. **$**

🐾 ⛷ ✈

Alexandria

Motel/Motor Lodge

★ ★ **HOLIDAY INN.** *5637 MN 29 S (56308). Phone 320/763-6577; toll-free 800/465-4329; fax 320/762-2092. www.holiday-inn.com.* 149 rooms, 2 story. Pets accepted, some restrictions. Check-out noon. TV; cable (premium), VCR (movies). In-room modem link. Laundry services. Restaurant, bar; entertainment. Room service. In-house fitness room; sauna. Indoor pool; children's pool; whirlpool. **$**

D 🐾 🏊 🏋 🏂

Austin

Motel/Motor Lodge

★ ★ **HOLIDAY INN.** *1701 4th St NW (55912). Phone 507/433-1000; toll-free 800/985-8850; fax 507/433-8749. www.holiday-inn.com.* 121 rooms, 2 story. Pets accepted, some restrictions. Check-out 11 am. TV; cable (premium). In-room modem link. Laundry services. Restaurant, bar; entertainment. Room service. In-house fitness room; sauna. Game room. Indoor pool; children's pool; whirlpool; poolside service. Airport, train station transportation. **$**

D 🐾 🏊 🏋 🏂 SC

Bemidji

Motel/Motor Lodge

★ ★ **NORTHERN INN.** *3600 Moberg Dr NW (56601). Phone 218/751-9500; toll-free 800/667-8485; fax 218/751-8122.* The only full-service hotel in Bemidji. Try Gangelhoff's for dinner. Every Saturday, the hotel has stand-up comedy at The InnProv. 123 rooms, 2 story. Pets accepted, some restrictions; fee. Check-out noon. TV; VCR available (movies). In-room modem link. Restaurant, bar. Room service. In-house fitness room; sauna. Game room. Indoor pool; whirlpool; poolside service. Downhill ski 10 miles, cross-country ski 4 miles. Free airport transportation. **$**

D 🐾 ⛵ 🏊 🏋 ✈ 🏂

Bloomington

Motel/Motor Lodge

★ ★ **RAMADA INN AIRPORT & THUNDERBIRD CONFERENCE CENTER.** *2201 E 78th St (55425). Phone 952/854-3411; toll-free 800/328-1931; fax 952/854-1183. www.thunderbirdhotel.com.* 263 rooms, 2 story. Pets accepted, some restrictions; fee. Check-out 11 am, check-in 3 pm. TV. Restaurant, bar; entertainment. Room service. In-house fitness room; sauna. Game room. Indoor pool; outdoor pool; children's pool; whirlpool. Downhill ski 10 miles, cross-country ski 1 mile. Free airport transportation. Business center. **$**

D 🐾 ⛵ 🏊 🏋 ✈ 🏂 SC 🏋

Hotels

★ **CLARION HOTEL.** *8151 Bridge Rd (55437). Phone 952/830-1300; toll-free 800/328-7947; fax 952/830-1535. www.thebloomingtonhotel.com.* 252 rooms, 18 story. Pets accepted, some restrictions; fee. Check-out 11 am, check-in 3 pm. TV. In-room modem link. Restaurant, bar. Sauna. Game room. Indoor pool; whirlpool. Downhill ski 5 miles, cross-country ski 1 mile. Free airport transportation. **$**

D 🐾 ⛵ 🏊 ✈ 🏂 SC

★ ★ **RADISSON HOTEL SOUTH & PLAZA TOWER.** *7800 Normandale Blvd (55439). Phone 952/835-7800; toll-free 800/333-3333; fax 952/893-8419. www.radisson.com/minneapolismn_south.* 565 rooms, 22 story. Pets accepted, some restrictions; fee. Check-out noon, check-in 3 pm. TV; VCR available. In-room modem link. Restaurant, bar. In-house fitness room; sauna. Indoor pool; whirlpool. Downhill, cross-country ski 2 miles. Airport transportation. **$$**

D 🐾 ⚡ ⛵ 🏊 🏋 🏂 SC

★ ★ ★ **SOFITEL.** *5601 W 78th St (55439). Phone 952/ 835-1900; fax 952/835-2696. www.sofitel.com.* 282 rooms, 6 story. Pets accepted, some restrictions. Check-out noon, check-in 3 pm. TV; cable (premium), VCR available. In-room modem link. Restaurant, bar. In-house fitness room; massage. Indoor pool. Downhill, cross-country ski 1 mile. Valet parking. Airport transportation. Business center. Concierge. **$$**

D ⌂ ⛵ ⛱ ✕ ✈ ⤢ ⛷

Brainerd

Motels/Motor Lodges

★ **COUNTRY INN & SUITES BY CARLSON BAXTER.** *1220 Dellwood Dr N (56401). Phone 218/828- 2161; fax 218/825-8419. www.countryinns.com.* 68 rooms, 2 story. Pets accepted, some restrictions. Complimentary continental breakfast. Check-out noon. TV; cable (premium), VCR available (movies). In-room modem link. Sauna. Indoor pool; whirlpool. Cross-country ski 1 1/2 miles. **$**

D ⌂ ⛵ ⛱ ⛷

★ **DAYS INN.** *1630 Fairview Rd (56425). Phone 218/ 829-0391; fax 218/828-0749. www.daysinn.com.* 60 rooms, 2 story. Pets accepted, some restrictions. Complimentary continental breakfast. Check-out 11 am. TV; cable (premium). Downhill ski 15 miles, cross-country ski 1 mile. **$**

D ⌂ ⛵ ⛱ SC

★ **DAYS INN.** *45 N Smiley Rd (56468). Phone 218/ 963-3500; toll-free 800/329-7466; fax 218/963-4936. www.daysinn.com.* 43 rooms, 2 story. Pets accepted; fee. Complimentary continental breakfast. Check-out 11 am. TV; VCR available (movies). Laundry services. Indoor pool; whirlpool. Downhill ski 15 miles, cross-country ski 3 blocks. **$**

D ⌂ ⛵ ⛱ SC

★ ★ **RAMADA INN.** *2115 S 6th St (56401). Phone 218/829-1441; fax 218/829-1444. www.ramada.com.* 150 rooms, 2 story. Pets accepted; fee. Check-out noon. TV. In-room modem link. Restaurant, bar. Room service. Sauna. Indoor pool; whirlpool; poolside service. Outdoor tennis. Downhill ski 7 miles, cross-country ski 3 miles. Free airport transportation. **$**

D ⌂ ⛵ ⤢ ⛱ ⛷

Cloquet

Motel/Motor Lodge

★ **AMERICINN.** *111 Big Lake Rd (55720). Phone 218/879-1231; toll-free 800/634-3444; fax 218/879-2237.*

www.americinn.com. 51 rooms, 2 story. Pets accepted, some restrictions; fee. Complimentary continental breakfast. Check-out 11 am. TV; cable (premium). Sauna. Indoor pool; whirlpool. **$**

D ⌂ ⛱ ⛷

Cook

Motel/Motor Lodge

★ **NORTH COUNTRY INN.** *4483 US 53 (55771). Phone 218/757-3778; fax 218/757-3116. www.northcountryinn.com.* 12 rooms. Pets accepted, some restrictions; fee. Check-out 11 am. TV; cable (premium), VCR available. **$**

D ⌂ ⛷

Duluth

Motels/Motor Lodges

★ **ALLYNDALE MOTEL.** *510 N 66th Ave W (55807). Phone 218/628-1061; toll-free 800/341-8000.* 21 rooms. Pets accepted, some restrictions; fee. Check-out 11 am. TV; cable. Downhill, cross-country ski 1 1/2 miles. **$**

⌂ ⛱ ⛷

★ **BEST WESTERN EDGEWATER.** *2400 London Rd (55812). Phone 218/728-3601; toll-free 800/777-7925; fax 218/728-3727. www.bestwestern.com.* 282 rooms, 5 story. Pets accepted, some restrictions; fee. Complimentary continental breakfast. Check-out noon. TV; cable (premium). In-house fitness room; sauna. Game room. Indoor pool; whirlpool. Downhill ski 7 miles, cross-country ski 1 mile. Miniature golf. Lawn games. Business center. **$**

D ⌂ ⛵ ⛱ ✕ ⛷

★ **DAYS INN.** *909 Cottonwood Ave (55811). Phone 218/ 727-3110; fax 218/727-3110. www.daysinn.com.* 86 rooms, 2-3 story. No elevator. Pets accepted. Complimentary continental breakfast. Check-out noon. TV; cable (premium), VCR available. **$**

D ⌂ ⛷

Hotel

★ ★ **RADISSON HOTEL.** *505 W Superior St (55802). Phone 218/727-8981; fax 218/727-0162. www.radisson.com.* Located downtown and connected to the indoor skyway system. 268 rooms, 16 story. Pets accepted, some restrictions; fee. Check-out noon. TV; VCR available. Restaurant. Bar. Sauna. Indoor pool; whirlpool; poolside service. Downhill, cross-country ski 10 miles. **$**

D ⌂ ⛵ ⛱ ⛷

Elk River

Motel/Motor Lodge

★ **AMERICINN.** *17432 US Hwy 10 (55330). Phone 763/ 441-8554; toll-free 800/634-3444. www.americinn.com.* 40 rooms, 2 story. Pets accepted; fee. Complimentary continental breakfast. Check-out 11 am, check-in 3 pm. TV; VCR (movies). Sauna. Indoor pool; whirlpool. Cross-country ski 3 blocks. Mississippi River 1 block. **$**

D 🐾 🏊 ⛖ 🖭

Ely

Motel/Motor Lodge

★ **WESTGATE MOTEL.** *110 N 2nd Ave W (55731). Phone 218/365-4513; toll-free 800/806-4979; fax 218/365-5364.* 17 rooms, 2 story. Pets accepted, some restrictions; fee. Complimentary continental breakfast. Check-out 10:30 am. TV. Downhill ski 20 miles, cross-country ski 1 mile. Free airport transportation. **$**

🐾 🏊 ⛖

Eveleth

Motel/Motor Lodge

★ ★ **DAYS INN.** *US 53 (55734). Phone 218/744-2703; fax 218/744-5865.* This inn offers guests a kid-friendly environment with an Olympic-sized pool, mini golf course, volleyball court, and on-site restaurant. 145 rooms, 2 story. Pets accepted, some restrictions; fee. Check-out noon. TV; cable (premium). Restaurant, bar. Room service. Sauna. Indoor pool. **$**

D 🐾 🏊 ⛖

Fairmont

Motel/Motor Lodge

★ **SUPER 8.** *1200 Torgerson Dr (56031). Phone 507/238-9444; toll-free 800/800-8000; fax 507/238-9371. www.super8.com.* 47 rooms, 2 story. Pets accepted; fee. Check-out noon. TV. Free airport transportation. Continental breakfast. **$**

D 🐾 ⛖ 🆂🅲

Faribault

Motel/Motor Lodge

★ **SELECT INN.** *4040 Hwy 60 W (55021). Phone 507/334-2051; toll-free 800/641-1000; fax 507/334-2051. www.selectinn.com.* 67 rooms, 2 story. Pets accepted; fee. Complimentary continental breakfast. Check-out 11 am. TV; cable (premium). Game room. Indoor pool. **$**

D 🐾 🏊 ⛖ 🆂🅲

Fergus Falls

Motel/Motor Lodge

★ **DAYS INN.** *610 Western Ave (56537). Phone 218/ 739-3311; toll-free 800/329-7466; fax 218/736-6576. www.daysinn.com.* 57 rooms, 2 story. Pets accepted, some restrictions; fee. Complimentary continental breakfast. Check-out 11 am. TV. Indoor pool; whirlpool. Downhill, cross-country ski 2 miles. **$**

D 🐾 🏊 ⛖ 🖭 🆂🅲

Grand Marais

Motels/Motor Lodges

★ **ASPEN LODGE.** *E US Hwy 61 (55604). Phone 218/387-2500; fax 218/387-2647.* 52 rooms. Pets accepted, some restrictions. Complimentary continental breakfast. Check-out 11 am. TV; cable (premium). In-room modem link. Laundry services. Sauna. Indoor pool; whirlpool. Downhill ski 18 miles, cross-country ski 1 mile. Snowmobiling. **$**

D 🐾 🏊 ⛖ 🖭

★ **BEST WESTERN SUPERIOR INN AND SUITES.** *Hwy 61 E (55604). Phone 218/387-2240; fax 218/387-2244. www.bestwestern.com.* 66 rooms, 2-3 story. Pets accepted, some restrictions. Complimentary continental breakfast. Check-out 11 am. TV; cable (premium), VCR available (movies). Fireplaces. Private beach on lake. Whirlpool. Downhill ski 18 miles, cross-country ski 1/2 mile. Snowmobiling. Views of Lake Superior. **$**

D 🐾 🏊 🖭 🆂🅲

★ ★ **EAST BAY HOTEL AND DINING ROOM.** *Wisconsin St (55604). Phone 218/387-2800; toll-free 800/ 414-2807; fax 218/387-2801. www.eastbayhotel.com.* 36 rooms, 2-3 story. No A/C. Pets accepted; fee. Check-out 11 am. TV. Fireplace. Restaurant, bar; entertainment. Room service. Massage. Whirlpool. Downhill ski 18 miles, cross-country ski 5 miles. **$**

★ **SUPER 8.** *1711 W US 61 (55604). Phone 218/ 387-2448; toll-free 800/247-6020; fax 218/387-9859. www.super8.com.* 35 rooms. Pets accepted, some restrictions. Complimentary continental breakfast. Check-out 11 am. TV; cable (premium). In-room modem link. Laundry services. Sauna. Whirlpool. Downhill ski 18 miles, cross-country ski 2 miles. Snowmobiling. **$**

Grand Rapids

Motels/Motor Lodges

★ **COUNTRY INN BY CARLSON.** *2601 S US 169 (55744). Phone 218/327-4960; fax 218/327-4964.* 59 rooms, 2 story. Pets accepted, some restrictions. Complimentary continental breakfast. Check-out noon. TV; cable (premium). Indoor pool; whirlpool. Downhill ski 10 miles, cross-country ski 2 miles. **$**

★ ★ **SAWMILL INN.** *2301 S Pokegama Ave (55744). Phone 218/326-8501; toll-free 800/235-6455; fax 218/ 326-1039. www.sawmillinn.com.* 124 rooms, 2 story. Pets accepted, some restrictions. Check-out noon. TV. Restaurant, bar. Room service. Sauna. Game room. Indoor pool; whirlpool; poolside service. Downhill, cross-country ski 18 miles. Free airport transportation. **$**

Hibbing

Motel/Motor Lodge

★ **SUPER 8.** *1411 E 40th St (55746). Phone 218/263-8982. www.super8.com.* 49 rooms, 2 story. Pets accepted, some restrictions. Check-out 11 am. TV; cable (premium), VCR available. Cross-country ski 2 miles. **$**

Hinckley

Motels/Motor Lodges

★ **DAYS INN.** *104 Grindstone Ct (55037). Phone 320/384-7751; toll-free 800/559-8951; fax 320/384-6403.*

www.daysinn.com. 69 rooms, 2 story. Pets accepted; fee. Complimentary continental breakfast. Check-out 11 am. TV; VCR available. Sauna. Indoor pool; whirlpool. Cross-country ski 10 miles. **$**

★ **SUPER 8.** *2811 Hwy 23 (55735). Phone 320/245-5284; fax 320/245-2233. www.super8.com.* 31 rooms, 2 story. Pets accepted, some restrictions; fee. Complimentary continental breakfast. Check-out 11 am. TV; cable (premium). Game room. Whirlpool. Cross-country ski opposite. **$**

International Falls

Motels/Motor Lodges

★ **DAYS INN.** *2331 Hwy 53 S (56649). Phone 218/283-9441; toll-free 800/329-7466. www.daysinn.com.* 60 rooms, 2 story. Pets accepted, some restrictions. Complimentary continental breakfast. Check-out noon. TV; cable (premium). In-house fitness room; sauna. Whirlpool. **$**

★ ★ **HOLIDAY INN.** *1500 Hwy 71 (56649). Phone 218/283-8000; toll-free 800/331-4443; fax 218/283-3774. www.holidayinnifalls.com.* 127 rooms, 2 story. Pets accepted, some restrictions. Check-out noon. TV; cable (premium). In-room modem link. Restaurant, bar. Room service. Sauna. Indoor pool; children's pool; whirlpool. Free airport transportation. View of Rainy River. **$**

Lakeville

Motel/Motor Lodge

★ **MOTEL 6.** *11274 210th St (55044). Phone 952/469-1900; toll-free 800/466-8356; fax 952/469-5359. www.motel6.com.* 85 rooms, 2 story. Pets accepted, some restrictions. Check-out noon. Downhill ski 5 miles, cross-country ski 2 miles. **$**

Litchfield

Motel/Motor Lodge

★ **SCOTWOOD.** *1017 E Hwy 12 (55355). Phone 320/693-2496; toll-free 800/225-5489; fax 320/693-2496.*

35 rooms, 2 story. Pets accepted, some restrictions. Complimentary continental breakfast. Check-out 11 am. TV; cable (premium). **$**

[D] [icons]

Lutsen

Motels/Motor Lodges

★ ★ ★ **BLUEFIN BAY ON LAKE SUPERIOR.** *US 61 (55615). Phone 218/663-7296; toll-free 800/258-3346; fax 218/663-8025. www.bluefinbay.com.* On Lake Superior in a wilderness area, visitors can relax in front of their fireplace or in their private Jacuzzi. 56 kitchen units, 2 story. No A/C. Pets accepted, some restrictions; fee. Check-out noon. TV; VCR available (movies). Restaurant, bar. Supervised children's activities. In-house fitness room; massage, sauna. Game room. Indoor pool; outdoor pool; whirlpool. Downhill ski 9 miles, cross-country ski opposite. Lawn games. **$**

[D] [icons]

★ **MOUNTAIN INN.** *County Rd 5 (55612). Phone 218/663-7244; toll-free 800/686-4669; fax 218/663-7248. www.mtn-inn.com.* 30 rooms, 2 story. Pets accepted, some restrictions; fee. Complimentary continental breakfast. Check-out noon. TV; cable (premium). Sauna. Downhill ski 1 block, cross-country ski on site. **$**

[D] [icons] SC

Luverne

Motel/Motor Lodge

★ **SUPER 8.** *I-90 and US 75 (56156). Phone 507/283-9541. www.super8.com.* 36 rooms, 2 story. Pets accepted, some restrictions; fee. Check-out 11 am. TV; cable (premium). **$**

[D] [icons]

Mankato

Motel/Motor Lodge

★ **DAYS INN.** *1285 Range St (56001). Phone 507/387-3332. www.daysinn.com.* 50 rooms, 2 story. Pets accepted, some restrictions; fee. Complimentary continental breakfast. Check-out 11 am. TV. In-room modem link. Indoor pool; whirlpool. Downhill, cross-country ski 5 miles. **$**

[D] [icons]

Marshall

Motels/Motor Lodges

★ ★ **BEST WESTERN MARSHALL INN.** *1500 E College Dr (56258). Phone 507/532-3221; fax 507/532-4089. www.bestwestern.com.* 100 rooms, 2 story. Pets accepted; fee. Check-out noon. TV. In-room modem link. Restaurant, bar. Room service. Sauna. Indoor pool; whirlpool; poolside service. Cross-country ski 1 mile. Free airport transportation. **$**

[D] [icons]

★ **SUPER 8.** *1106 E Main St (56258). Phone 507/537-1461. www.super8.com.* 50 rooms, 2 story. Pets accepted, some restrictions; fee. Check-out 11 am. TV; cable (premium). Cross-country ski 1 mile. **$**

[D] [icons]

★ ★ **TRAVELER'S LODGE.** *1425 E College Dr (56258). Phone 507/532-5721; toll-free 800/532-5721; fax 507/532-4911.* 90 rooms, 1-2 story. Pets accepted, some restrictions. Complimentary continental breakfast. Check-out noon. TV; cable (premium), VCR available (movies, fee). Cross-country ski 1 mile. Free airport transportation. **$**

[icons]

Minneapolis

Motels/Motor Lodges

★ **AMERICINN.** *21800 Industrial Blvd (55374). Phone 763/428-4346; toll-free 800/634-3444; fax 763/428-2117. www.americinn.com.* 61 rooms, 2 story. Pets accepted, some restrictions. Complimentary continental breakfast. Check-out 11 am, check-in 3 pm. TV; cable (premium), VCR available. Indoor pool; whirlpool. **$**

[D] [icons]

★ **BEST WESTERN KELLY INN.** *5201 NE Central Ave (55441). Phone 763/571-9440; toll-free 800/780-7234; fax 763/571-1720. www.bestwestern.com.* 95 rooms, 2 story. Pets accepted, some restrictions. Complimentary continental breakfast. Check-out 11 am, check-in 3 pm. TV; cable (premium). Room service. Sauna. Game room. Indoor pool; whirlpool. **$**

[D] [icons]

Hotels

★ ★ **HILTON MINNEAPOLIS NORTH.** *2200 Freeway Blvd (55430). Phone 763/566-8000. www.hilton.com.* 176

rooms, 10 story. Pets accepted, some restrictions; fee. Check-out noon, check-in 3 pm. TV; cable (premium), VCR available. Restaurant, bar. In-house fitness room. Pool. Business center. **$$**

★ ★ **HOLIDAY INN MINNEAPOLIS METRO-DOME.** *1500 Washington Ave S (55454). Phone 612/ 333-4646; toll-free 800/448-3663; fax 612/333-7910. www.metrodome.com.* 265 rooms, 14 story. Pets accepted; fee. Check-out noon, check-in 3 pm. TV; cable (premium). In-room modem link. Restaurant, bar. In-house fitness room. Indoor pool; whirlpool. Airport transportation. **$**

★ ★ ★ **THE MARQUETTE.** *710 Marquette Ave (55402). Phone 612/333-4545; toll-free 800/328-4782; fax 612/288-2188. www.marquettehotel.com.* Located in the downtown area, this hotel is connected to shops, restaurants, and entertainment by the city's skywalk system. 277 rooms, 19 story. Pets accepted, some restrictions; fee. Check-out noon, check-in 3 pm. TV; cable (premium), VCR available. In-room modem link. Restaurant, bar. In-house fitness room. Cross-country ski 1 mile. Business center. Luxury level. **$$$**

★ ★ ★ **MARRIOTT MINNEAPOLIS CITY CENTER.** *30 S 7th St (55402). Phone 612/349-4000; toll-free 800/228-9290; fax 612/332-7165. www.marriott.com.* Linked by the enclosed skywalk to many of the city's offices and shopping complexes in the downtown area, this hotel is very convenient. Golf courses and tennis facilities are nearby. 583 rooms, 31 story. Pets accepted; fee. Check-out noon, check-in 3 pm. TV; cable (premium), VCR available (movies). In-room modem link. Restaurant, bar. In-house fitness room. Health club privileges. Massage, sauna. Cross-country ski 1 mile. Valet parking. Business center. Luxury level. **$$**

★ ★ ★ **MARRIOTT MINNEAPOLIS SOUTH-WEST.** *5801 Opus Pkwy (55343). Phone 952/935-5500; fax 952/935-0753. www.marriott.com.* 321 rooms, 17 story. Pets accepted, some restrictions. Complimentary continental breakfast. Check-out noon, check-in 4 pm. TV; cable (premium), VCR available. Restaurant, bar. In-house fitness room. Indoor pool; whirlpool. Business center. **$$**

★ ★ ★ **MILLENNIUM HOTEL.** *1313 Nicollet Mall (55403). Phone 612/332-6000; fax 612/359-2160. www.millennium-hotels.com.* Located on downtown's Nicollett Mall and near theaters, museums, and other attractions. 322 rooms, 14 story. Pets accepted, some

restrictions; fee. Check-out noon, check-in 3 pm. TV; cable (premium). In-room modem link. Restaurant, bar. In-house fitness room; sauna. Health club privileges. Indoor pool. Cross-country ski 1 mile. Airport transportation available. **$$**

★ ★ **RADISSON HOTEL AND CONFERENCE CENTER.** *3131 Campus Dr (55441). Phone 763/559-6600; fax 763/559-1053. www.radisson.com.* Set in picturesque marshlands, this hotel is near many attractions, including French Regional Park, the Ridgedale Shopping Mall, and more. 243 rooms, 6 story. Pets accepted, some restrictions. Check-out noon, check-in 3 pm. TV; cable (premium), VCR available. In-room modem link. Restaurant, bar. In-house fitness room; sauna. Indoor pool; whirlpool; poolside service. Lighted tennis courts. Downhill ski 20 miles, cross-country ski 2 miles. Racquetball. On wooded site. **$**

Morris

Motel/Motor Lodge

★ ★ **BEST WESTERN PRAIRIE INN.** *200 Hwy 28 E (56267). Phone 320/589-3030; toll-free 800/565-3035. www.bestwestern.com.* 78 rooms, 2 story. Pets accepted, some restrictions. Complimentary continental breakfast. Check-out 11 am. TV; cable (premium). Restaurant, bar. Sauna. Game room. Indoor pool; children's pool; whirlpool; poolside service. **$**

Pipestone

Motel/Motor Lodge

★ **ARROW MOTEL.** *600 8th Ave NE (56164). Phone 507/825-3331; fax 507/825-5638.* 17 rooms. Pets accepted, some restrictions; fee. Complimentary continental breakfast. Check-out 11 am. TV; cable (premium). Pool. Shaded lawn. **$**

Red Wing

Motels/Motor Lodges

★ **BEST WESTERN QUIET HOUSE & SUITES.** *752 Withers Harbor Dr (55066).; fax 612/388-1150. www.quiethouse.com.* 51 rooms, 2 story. Pets accepted, some restrictions; fee. Check-out 11 am. TV. In-room modem link. In-house fitness room. Indoor pool; outdoor pool; whirlpool. **$**

[icons]

★ **DAYS INN.** *955 E 7th St (55066). Phone 651/388-3568; toll-free 800/329-7466; fax 651/385-1901. www.daysinn.com.* 48 rooms. Pets accepted; fee. Complimentary continental breakfast. Check-out 11 am. TV. Indoor pool; whirlpool. Downhill ski 7 miles, cross-country ski 1 mile. Municipal park, marinas opposite. **$**

[icons]

Rochester

Motels/Motor Lodges

★ **BEST WESTERN FIFTH AVENUE MOTEL.** *20 NW 5th Ave (55901). Phone 507/289-3987. www.bestwestern.com.* 63 rooms, 3 story. Pets accepted, some restrictions. Check-out noon. TV; cable (premium). Indoor pool. Cross-country ski 1 mile. **$**

[icons]

★ **COMFORT INN.** *1625 S Broadway (55904). Phone 507/281-2211; toll-free 800/305-8470; fax 507/288-8979. www.comfortinn.com.* 162 rooms, 5 story. Pets accepted, some restrictions; fee. Complimentary continental breakfast. Check-out noon. TV; cable (premium). In-room modem link. Restaurant, bar. Room service. Sauna. Indoor pool; whirlpool. **$**

[icons]

★ **DAYS INN.** *111 28th SE St (55904). Phone 507/286-1001; toll-free 800/329-7466. www.daysinn.com.* 128 rooms. Pets accepted, some restrictions. Complimentary continental breakfast. Check-out noon. TV; cable (premium). Cross-country ski 2 miles. Free airport transportation. **$**

[icons]

★★ **EXECUTIVE SUITES AND INN.** *9 3rd Ave NW (55901). Phone 507/289-8646; toll-free 800/533-1655; fax 507/282-4478. www.kahler.com.* 266 rooms, 9 story. Pets accepted, some restrictions. Complimentary continental breakfast. Check-out 2 pm. TV; cable (premium). In-room modem link. Laundry services. Restaurant, bar. In-house fitness room; sauna. Indoor pool; whirlpool. Cross-country ski 1 mile. **$**

[icons]

★★ **HOLIDAY INN.** *1630 S Broadway (55904). Phone 507/288-1844. www.holiday-inn.com.* 195 rooms, 2 story. Pets accepted. Check-out 2 pm, Sat noon. TV. Laundry services. Restaurant, bar. Room service. Indoor pool. Free airport, bus depot transportation. **$**

[icons]

★★ **QUALITY INN.** *1620 1st Ave SE (55904). Phone 507/282-8091; toll-free 800/228-5151. www.qualityinn.com.* 41 rooms, 2 story. Pets accepted. Complimentary continental breakfast. Check-out noon. TV; cable (premium). In-room modem link. Airport transportation. **$**

[icons]

★ **SUPER 8.** *1230 S Broadway (55904). Phone 507/288-8288. www.super8.com.* 88 rooms. Pets accepted; fee. Check-out noon. TV. In-room modem link. Cross-country ski adjacent. **$**

[icons]

★ **TRAVELODGE.** *435 16th Ave NW (55901). Phone 507/288-9090; fax 507/292-9442. www.travelodge.com.* 120 rooms, 3 story. Pets accepted, some restrictions. Check-out noon. TV; cable (premium). Laundry services. Restaurant. Indoor pool. **$**

[icons]

★ **TRAVELODGE.** *1837 S Broadway (55904). Phone 507/288-2031; toll-free 800/890-3871. www.travelodge.com.* 27 rooms. Pets accepted; fee. Check-out noon. TV; cable. Cross-country ski 1 mile. **$**

[icons]

Hotels

★★★ **KAHLER HOTEL.** *20 2nd Ave SW (55902). Phone 507/282-2581; toll-free 800/533-1655; fax 507/285-2775. www.kahler.com.* Located across from the Mayo Clinic in the downtown area. 700 rooms, 11 story. Pets accepted, some restrictions; fee. Check-out 2 pm. TV. In-room modem link. Restaurant, bar; entertainment. In-house fitness room; sauna. Health club privileges. Game room. Indoor pool; whirlpool; poolside service. Cross-country ski 2 miles. Airport transportation. Original section English Tudor; vaulted ceilings, paneling. Walkway to Mayo Clinic. **$**

[icons]

★★★ **MARRIOTT ROCHESTER MAYO CLINIC.** *101 1st Ave SW (55902). Phone 507/280-6000; fax 507/280-8531. www.kahler.com.* Near the Galleria Mall, Miracle Mile Shopping Complex, tennis facilities, and many golf courses. 194 rooms, 9 story. Pets accepted, some restrictions. Check-out 2 pm. TV. In-room modem link. Restaurant, bar; entertainment. In-house fitness room; sauna. Game room. Indoor pool; whirlpool. Concierge. Luxury level. Mayo Clinic medical complex adjacent. **$$**

[icons]

Saint Cloud

Motels/Motor Lodges

★★ **BEST WESTERN AMERICANNA INN AND CONFERENCE CENTER.** *520 S US 10 (56304). Phone 320/252-8700; toll-free 800/950-8701. www.bestwestern.com.* 63 rooms, 2 story. Pets accepted; fee. Check-out 11 am. TV; cable (premium). In-room modem link. Restaurant, bar; entertainment. Room service. Sauna. Game room. Indoor pool; whirlpool. **$**

★ **DAYS INN.** *420 Hwy 10 SE (56304). Phone 320/253-0500; toll-free 800/329-7466. www.daysinn.com.* 78 rooms, 2 story. Pets accepted; fee. Complimentary continental breakfast. Check-out 11 am. TV; cable (premium). Indoor pool; whirlpool. Downhill ski 10 miles, cross-country ski 1 mile. **$**

★★ **QUALITY INN.** *70 S 37th Ave (56301). Phone 320/253-4444; fax 320/259-7809. www.qualityinn.com.* 89 rooms, 2 story. Pets accepted; fee. Check-out noon. TV; cable (premium). Sauna. Whirlpool. **$**

★ **SUPER 8.** *50 Park Ave S (56302). Phone 320/253-5530; toll-free 800/843-1991; fax 320/253-5292. www.super8.com.* 68 rooms, 2 story. Pets accepted; fee. Complimentary continental breakfast. Check-out 11 am. TV; cable (premium). Downhill ski 8 miles, cross-country ski 1 mile. **$**

St. Paul

Motels/Motor Lodges

★★ **BEST WESTERN MAPLEWOOD INN.** *1780 E County Rd D (55109). Phone 651/770-2811; toll-free 800/780-7234. www.bestwesternmaplewood.com.* 118 rooms, 2 story. Pets accepted, some restrictions; fee. Check-out noon. TV; cable (premium). In-room modem link. Restaurant, bar; entertainment. Room service. Sauna. Game room. Indoor pool; whirlpool. **$**

★ **EXEL INN.** *1739 Old Hudson Rd (55106). Phone 651/771-5566; fax 651/771-1262. www.exelinns.com.* 100 rooms, 3 story. Pets accepted, some restrictions. Complimentary continental breakfast. Check-out noon, check-in 3 pm. TV; cable (premium). In-room modem link. Laundry services. Game room. Downhill ski 15 miles, cross-country ski 2 miles. **$**

★★ **HOLIDAY INN EXPRESS.** *1010 W Bandana Blvd (55108). Phone 651/647-1637; toll-free 800/465-4329; fax 651/647-0244. www.holiday-inn.com.* 109 rooms, 2 story. Pets accepted, some restrictions; fee. Complimentary continental breakfast. Check-out noon, check-in 3 pm. TV; cable (premium). In-room modem link. In-house fitness room; sauna. Indoor pool; children's pool; whirlpool. Downhill ski 15 miles, cross-country ski 1 mile. Motel built within the exterior structure of an old railroad repair building; an old track runs through the lobby. **$**

Stillwater

Motel/Motor Lodge

★ **BEST WESTERN STILLWATER INN.** *1750 W Frontage Rd (55082). Phone 651/430-1300; toll-free 800/647-4039; fax 651/430-0596. www.bestwestern.com/stillwaterinn.* 59 rooms, 2 story. Pets accepted; fee. Complimentary continental breakfast. Check-out 11 am, check-in 3 pm. TV; cable (premium). In-room modem link. Indoor pool; whirlpool. Downhill ski 20 miles, cross-country ski 2 miles. **$**

Thief River Falls

Motel/Motor Lodge

★ **C'MON INN.** *1586 Hwy 59 S (56701). Phone 218/681-3000; toll-free 800/950-8111; fax 218/681-3060.* 44 rooms, 2 story. Pets accepted, some restrictions. Complimentary continental breakfast. Check-out noon. TV; cable (premium). In-room modem link. Game room. Indoor pool; whirlpool. **$**

Two Harbors

Resort

★★★ **SUPERIOR SHORES RESORT.** *1521 Superior Shores Dr (55616). Phone 218/834-5671; toll-free 800/242-1988; fax 218/834-5677. www.superiorshores.com.* 104 rooms, 3 story. Pets accepted, some restrictions; fee. Check-out 11 am, check-in by arrangement. TV; VCR (movies). Restaurant, bar. Sauna. Game room. Indoor pool; two outdoor pools, whirlpool. Cross-country ski opposite. Hiking trails. Snowmobiles. **$**

[icons]

Virginia

Motel/Motor Lodge

★ **SKI VIEW.** *903 17th St N (55792). Phone 218/741-8918; toll-free 800/255-7106; fax 218/749-3279.* 59 rooms, 2 story. Pets accepted, some restrictions; fee. Complimentary continental breakfast. Check-out 11 am. TV; cable (premium). Sauna. Downhill, cross-country ski 20 miles. Snowmobile trails adjacent. **$**

[icons]

Willmar

Motels/Motor Lodges

★ **DAYS INN.** *225 28th St SE (56201). Phone 320/231-1275; toll-free 877/241-5235; fax 320/231-1275. www.daysinn.com.* 59 rooms, 2 story. Pets accepted. Complimentary continental breakfast. Check-out 11 am. TV; cable (premium). In-house fitness room; sauna. **$**

[icons]

★ ★ **HOLIDAY INN.** *2100 E Hwy 12 (56201). Phone 320/235-6060; toll-free 877/405-4466; fax 320/235-4231. www.holiday-inn.com.* 98 rooms, 2 story. Pets accepted, some restrictions. Check-out noon. TV; cable (premium). In-room modem link. Restaurant, bar. Room service. Indoor pool; children's pool; whirlpool; poolside service. **$**

[icons]

★ **SUPER 8.** *2655 S 1st St (56201). Phone 320/235-7260; toll-free 800/800-8000; fax 320/235-5580. www.super8.com.* 60 rooms, 3 story. No elevator. Pets accepted, some restrictions. Check-out 11 am. TV; cable (premium). **$**

[icons]

Winona

Motel/Motor Lodge

★ ★ **BEST WESTERN RIVERPORT INN & SUITES.** *900 Bruski Dr (55987). Phone 507/452-0606; toll-free 800/595-0606; fax 507/452-6489. www.bestwestern.com.* 106 rooms, 3 story. Pets accepted, some restrictions; fee. Complimentary continental breakfast. Check-out 11 am. TV; cable (premium), VCR available. Restaurant, bar. Room service. Game room. Indoor pool; whirlpool. Downhill ski 8 miles, cross-country ski 1 mile. **$**

[icons]

Mississippi

Biloxi

Motels/Motor Lodges

★ **BREAKERS INN.** *2506 Beach Blvd (39531). Phone 228/388-6320; toll-free 800/624-5031; fax 228/388-7185.* 28 suites, 1-2 story. May-Sept: S, D $121-$171; higher rates: Memorial Day weekend, July 4, Labor Day; lower rates rest of year. Pets accepted; fee. Check-out 11 am. TV. In-room modem link. Laundry services. Pool; children's pool. Tennis. Lawn games. Opposite the Gulf.

★ ★ **HOLIDAY INN.** *2400 Beach Blvd (39531). Phone 228/388-3551; toll-free 800/441-0882; fax 228/385-2032. www.holiday-inn.com.* 268 rooms, 4 story. S $59-$64; D $93-$98; each additional $10; golf plan; higher rates holidays (3-day minimum). Pets accepted; fee. TV. In-room modem link. Restaurant, bar; entertainment. Room service. Game room. Pool; poolside service. Free airport transportation.

Grenada

Motel/Motor Lodge

★ ★ **BEST WESTERN GRENADA.** *1750 Sunset Dr (38901). Phone 662/226-7816; toll-free 800/880-8866; fax 662/226-5623. www.bestwestern.com.* 61 rooms, 2 story. S $42-$49; D $54-$66. Pets accepted, some restrictions; fee. Complimentary full breakfast. Check-out noon. TV. In-room modem link. Restaurant. Room service. Pool. Lawn games.

Hattiesburg

Motel/Motor Lodge

★ **COMFORT INN.** *6595 Hwy 49 N (39401). Phone 601/268-2170; fax 601/268-1820. www.choicehotels.com.* 119 rooms, 2 story. S, D $50-$64; each additional $6; suites $90-$100; under 18 free. Pets accepted; fee. Complimentary full breakfast. Check-out noon. TV; cable (premium). Restaurant, bar; entertainment. Room service. Pool.

Jackson

Motels/Motor Lodges

★ **BEST VALUE INN.** *5035 I-55 N (39206). Phone 601/982-1011. www.bestvalueinn.com.* 133 rooms, 2 story. S $46-$50; D $48-$54; each additional $5; suites $70-$100; under 17 free. Pets accepted, some restrictions; fee. Check-out noon. TV; cable (premium). In-room modem link. Laundry services. Restaurant, bar. Room service. Pool.

★ **LA QUINTA INN.** *150 Angle St (39204). Phone 601/373-6110; fax 601/373-6115. www.laquinta.com.* 101 rooms, 2-3 story. S $51; D $57; suites $69-$81; each additional $6; under 18 free. Pets accepted; fee. Check-out noon. TV. In-room modem link. Pool. Airport transportation.

★ **LA QUINTA INN.** *616 Briarwood Dr (39211). Phone 601/957-1741; fax 601/956-5764. www.laquinta.com.* 101 rooms, 2-3 story. S $51; D $57; suites $69-$81; each additional $6; under 18 free. Pets accepted. Check-out noon. TV. In-room modem link. Pool. Airport transportation.

Hotel

★ ★ ★ **EDISON WALTHALL HOTEL.** *225 E Capitol St (39201). Phone 601/948-6161; toll-free 800/932-6161; fax 601/948-0088. www.edisonwalthallhotel.com.* 208 rooms, 8 story. S $69-$75; D $79-$85; each additional $8; suites $90-$185; under 18 free. Pets accepted; fee. Check-out noon. TV. In-room modem link. Restaurant, bar. In-house fitness room. Pool; whirlpool. Free airport transportation.

Meridian

Motel/Motor Lodge

★ **QUALITY INN.** *1401 Roebuck Dr (39301). Phone 601/693-4521; toll-free 800/465-4329. www.qualityinn.com.* 172 rooms, 1-2 story. S, D $49-$54; under 12 free. Pets accepted. Check-out noon. TV; cable (premium). In-room modem link. Laundry services. Pool.

Natchez

Motel/Motor Lodge

★ ★ **RAMADA INN.** *130 John R. Junkin Dr (39120). Phone 601/446-6311; toll-free 800/256-6311; fax 601/446-6321. www.ramada.com.* 162 rooms, 1-3 story. No elevator. S $48-$60; D $48-$70; each additional $5; suites $140; under 18 free. Pets accepted. Check-out 1 pm. TV; cable (premium), VCR available. In-room modem link. Restaurant, bar; entertainment. Room service. Pool; children's pool; poolside service. Airport transportation. On a hilltop overlooking the Mississippi River.

Hotel

★ ★ **NATCHEZ EOLA HOTEL.** *110 N Pearl St (39120). Phone 601/445-6000; fax 601/446-5310. www.radisson.com.* This historic hotel is located in the heart of downtown. 125 rooms, 7 story. S, D $75-$195; suites $120-$225. Pets accepted; fee. Check-out 11 am. TV. Restaurant, bar.

Oxford

Motel/Motor Lodge

★ ★ **DOWNTOWN INN.** *400 N Lamar Blvd (38655). Phone 662/234-3031; toll-free 800/606-1497; fax 662/234-2834. www.downtowninnoxford.com.* 123 rooms, 2 story. S, D $63-$85; under 19 free. Pets accepted; fee. Check-out 1 pm. TV; cable (premium), VCR available. In-room modem link. Restaurant, bar. Room service. Pool. Free airport transportation.

Pascagoula

Motel/Motor Lodge

★ ★ ★ **LA FONT INN.** *2703 Denny Ave (39567). Phone 228/762-7111; fax 228/934-4324. www.lafont.com.* A festive atmosphere; located conveniently near the Mississippi Gulf golf courses. 192 rooms, 2 story. S $61-$78; D $66-$78; each additional $5; suites $121-$148; under 14 free. Pets accepted, some restrictions; fee. Check-out 1 pm. TV; cable (premium). In-room modem link. Restaurant, bar. Room service. In-house fitness room; sauna, steam room.

Pool; children's pool; whirlpool; poolside service. Lighted tennis. Lawn games.

Starkville

Motel/Motor Lodge

★ **RAMADA INN.** *403 Hwy 12 (39759). Phone 662/323-6161; fax 662/323-8073. www.ramada.com.* 173 rooms, 2 story. S, D $55; each additional $6; under 18 free; higher rates football weekends. Pets accepted. Check-out noon. TV; cable (premium). Restaurant, bar. Room service. Pool.

Tupelo

Motel/Motor Lodge

★ **HOLIDAY INN EXPRESS.** *923 N Gloster St (38801). Phone 662/842-8811; toll-free 800/800-6891; fax 662/844-6884. www.holiday-inn.com.* 124 rooms, 2 story. Feb-Aug: S $50; D $54; each additional $7; under 12 free; lower rates rest of year. Pets accepted, some restrictions; fee. Complimentary continental breakfast. TV; cable (premium). Pool.

Vicksburg

Motels/Motor Lodges

★ ★ **BATTLEFIELD INN.** *4137 I-20 N Frontage Rd (39183). Phone 601/638-5811; toll-free 800/359-9363; fax 601/638-9249. www.battlefieldinn.org.* 117 rooms, 2 story. S $35-$57; D $45-$67; each additional $5; under 16 free. Pets accepted, some restrictions; fee. Complimentary breakfast buffet. Check-out 12:30 pm. TV; cable (premium). In-room modem link. Restaurant, bar; entertainment. Room service. Pool.

★ ★ **HOLIDAY INN.** *3330 Clay St (39180). Phone 601/636-4551; toll-free 800/847-0372; fax 601/634-1105. www.holiday-inn.com.* 173 rooms, 2 story. S, D $65-$72; each additional $7; under 18 free. Pets accepted; fee. Check-out noon. TV; cable (premium). In-room modem link. Restaurant, bar. Room service. Sauna. Game room. Indoor pool.

B&B/Small Inn

★ ★ ★ **DUFF GREEN MANSION.** *1114 First East St (39181). Phone 601/638-6662; toll-free 800/992-0037; fax 601/661-0079. www.duffgreenmansion.com.* This Paladian mansion (1856), used as both a Confederate and Union hospital during Civil War, was shelled during the siege of Vicksburg. Each of the bedrooms has a fireplace and porch; luxuriously furnished in period antiques and reproductions. A complimentary bar is offered during happy hour. 7 rooms, 3 story. Pets accepted. Complimentary full breakfast. Check-out 11 am, check-in 3 pm. TV; VCR available. Pool; whirlpool. Business center. **$**

Missouri

Bethany

Motel/Motor Lodge

★ ★ **FAMILY BUDGET INN.** *4014 Miller St (64424). Phone 660/425-7915; toll-free 877/283-4388; fax 660/425-3697.* 78 rooms. Pets accepted; fee. Check-out 11 am. TV. **$**

D ⬚ ⬚ ⬚ ⬚

Branson/Table Rock Lake Area

Motels/Motor Lodges

★ **DAYS INN.** *3524 Keeter St (65616). Phone 417/334-5544; toll-free 800/325-2525; fax 417/334-2935. www.daysinn.com.* 425 rooms, 4 story. Pets accepted; fee. Complimentary continental breakfast. Check-out 11 am. TV. Restaurant. Pool, children's pool, whirlpool. **$**

D ⬚ ⬚ ⬚

★ ★ **SETTLE INN RESORT.** *3050 Green Mountain Dr (65616). Phone 417/335-4700; toll-free 800/677-6906; fax 417/335-3906. www.bransonsettleinn.com.* 300 rooms, 3-4 story. Pets accepted; fee. Complimentary continental breakfast. Check-out 11 am. TV; cable (premium). Restaurant, bar; entertainment. Room service. In-house fitness room, sauna. Game room. Two indoor pools, whirlpool. Business services available. Concierge. **$**

D ⬚ ⬚ ⬚ ⬚

Cameron

Motel/Motor Lodge

★ **ECONO LODGE.** *220 E Grand Ave (64429). Phone 816/632-6571. www.econolodge.com.* 36 rooms, 1-2 story. Pets accepted; fee. Complimentary continental breakfast. Check-out 11 am. TV. Outdoor pool. **$**

⬚ ⬚ ⬚

Cape Girardeau

Motels/Motor Lodges

★ ★ **DRURY LODGE.** *104 S Vantage Dr (63701). Phone 573/334-7151; toll-free 800/378-7946. www.druryinn.com.* 139 rooms, 2 story. Pets accepted. Complimentary breakfast buffet. Check-out noon. TV; cable (premium), VCR available. Restaurant, bar. Room service. In-house fitness room. Health club privileges. Game room. Outdoor pool, children's pool. **$**

D ⬚ ⬚ ⬚ ⬚

★ ★ **DRURY SUITES.** *3303 Campster Dr (63701). Phone 573/339-9500; toll-free 800/378-7946. www.druryinn.com.* 87 rooms, 5 story. Pets accepted, some restrictions. Complimentary continental breakfast. Check-out noon. TV; cable (premium). Bar. Room service. Indoor pool, whirlpool. **$**

D ⬚ ⬚ ⬚ SC

★ ★ **HOLIDAY INN.** *3257 William St (63701). Phone 573/334-4491; toll-free 800/645-3379; fax 573/334-7459. www.holiday-inn.com.* 186 rooms, 2 story. Pets accepted, some restrictions; fee. Check-out 11 am. TV; cable (premium). In-room modem link. Restaurant, bar. Room service. In-house fitness room. Indoor pool, outdoor pool, children's pool. Airport transportation. **$**

D ⬚ ⬚ ⬚ ⬚ SC

★ **PEAR TREE INN.** *3248 William St, I-55 and Rte K (63703). Phone 573/334-3000; toll-free 800/378-7946. www.peartreeinn.com.* 78 rooms, 3 story. No elevator. Pets accepted, some restrictions. Complimentary continental breakfast. Check-out noon. TV; cable (premium). Outdoor pool, children's pool. **$**

D ⬚ ⬚ ⬚ SC

Chillicothe

Motels/Motor Lodges

★ **BEST WESTERN INN & SUITES.** *1020 S Washington St (64601). Phone 660/646-0572; toll-free 800/990-9150; fax 660/646-1274. www.bestwestern.com.* 60 rooms, 1-2 story. Pets accepted; fee. Complimentary continental breakfast. Check-out noon. TV. In-room modem link. Outdoor pool. **$**

D ⬚ ⬚ ⬚ ⬚

★ ★ **GRAND RIVER INN.** *Hwy 36 & 65 (64601). Phone 660/646-6590. www.grandriverinn.com.* 60 rooms, 2 story. Pets accepted. Complimentary continental breakfast. Check-out noon. TV; cable (premium), VCR available (movies). In-room modem link. Restaurant, bar. Room service. Sauna. Outdoor pool, whirlpool. **$**

Clayton

Hotel

★ ★ ★ **DANIELE HOTEL.** *216 N Meramac (63105). Phone 314/721-0101; toll-free 800/325-8302; fax 314/721-0609.* Guests will enjoy the complimentary limousine service that takes visitors to and from the airport and the local area. 82 rooms, 4 story. Pets accepted, some restrictions. Check-out noon. TV; cable (premium), VCR available. In-room modem link. Restaurant, bar. Outdoor pool. Airport transportation. **$**

★ ★ ★ ★ **THE RITZ-CARLTON, ST. LOUIS.** *100 Carondelet Plaza (63105). Phone 314/863-6300; toll-free 800/241-3333; fax 314/863-3525. www.ritzcarlton.com.* The Ritz-Carlton is the jewel in the crown of Clayton, an exclusive residential and shopping area just outside St. Louis. This sophisticated hotel shares the best of the city with its privileged guests. The guest rooms are spacious and plush, and all have private balconies with sweeping views of the city skyline. A comprehensive fitness center includes lap and hydrotherapy pools. The restaurants and lounges, characterized by their convivial spirit, fine dining, and seamless service, are popular with locals and hotel guests alike. Cigar aficionados head straight for the Cigar Lounge for its clubby setting and wide selection of premium cigars, while oenophiles delight in the Wine Room's delicious dishes expertly paired with special vintages. 301 rooms, 18 story. Pets accepted; fee. Check-out noon, check-in 3 pm. TV; cable (premium), VCR available. In-room modem link. Restaurants, bars; entertainment. Room service. Babysitting services available. In-house fitness room, massage, sauna, steam room. Indoor pool, whirlpool, poolside service. Business center. Concierge. **$$**

Columbia

Motels/Motor Lodges

★ ★ **HOLIDAY INN.** *2200 I-70 Dr SW (65203). Phone 573/445-8531; toll-free 800/465-4329; fax 573/445-7607. www.holiday-inn.com.* 311 rooms, 6 story. Pets accepted. Check-out 11 am. TV; VCR available. In-room modem link. Restaurant 24 hours. Bar. Room service. In-house fitness room, sauna. Indoor pool, outdoor pool, whirlpool, poolside service. Concierge. Luxury level. Adjacent to the Exposition Center. **$**

★ ★ **QUALITY INN.** *1612 N Providence Rd (65202). Phone 573/449-2491; fax 573/874-6720. www.qualityinncolumbiamo.com.* 142 rooms, 2 story. Pets accepted, some restrictions; fee. Check-out noon. TV. Restaurant, bar. Room service. In-house fitness room, sauna. Indoor pool, whirlpool. **$**

★ **TRAVELODGE.** *900 Vandiver Dr (65202). Phone 573/449-1065; toll-free 800/456-1065; fax 573/442-6266. www.travelodge.com.* 162 rooms, 2 story. Pets accepted; fee. Complimentary continental breakfast. Check-out 11 am. TV. Outdoor pool. **$**

Hannibal

Motel/Motor Lodge

★ ★ ★ **HANNIBAL INN AND CONFERENCE CENTER.** *4141 Market St (63401). Phone 573/221-6610; toll-free 800/325-0777; fax 573/221-3840.* This inn offers a variety of rooms and suites to accommodate its guests. It also offers a continental breakfast, an indoor pool, game room, tennis courts, and a restaurant and lounge. There is plenty to do in the surrounding area as well. 241 rooms, 2 story. Pets accepted. Complimentary continental breakfast. Check-out 11 am. TV; cable (premium). In-room modem link. Restaurant, bar. Room service. Sauna. Indoor pool, whirlpool, poolside service. Tennis. **$**

Independence

Motels/Motor Lodges

★ **COMFORT INN EAST.** *4200 S Noland Rd (64055). Phone 816/373-8856; toll-free 800/228-5150; fax 816/373-3312. www.comfortinn.com.* 171 rooms, 2 story. Pets accepted; fee. Complimentary continental breakfast. Check-out noon. TV; cable (premium). In-room modem link. Sauna. Indoor pool, outdoor pool, whirlpool. **$**

⓪ 🐾 ⌦ ⌧ SC

★ **RED ROOF INN.** *13712 E 42nd Terrace (64055). Phone 816/373-2800; toll-free 800/843-7663; fax 816/373-0067. www.redroof.com.* 108 rooms, 2 story. Pets accepted, some restrictions. Check-out noon. TV. **$**

⓪ 🐾 ⌦

Jefferson City

Motel/Motor Lodge

★★ **RAMADA INN.** *1510 Jefferson St (65109). Phone 573/635-7171; toll-free 800/392-0202; fax 573/635-8006. www.ramadajeffcity.com.* 232 rooms, 2 story. Pets accepted; fee. Check-out 11 am. TV; cable (premium). Restaurant, bar; entertainment. Room service. In-house fitness room. Game room. Outdoor pool. Business center. Airport transportation. **$**

⓪ 🐾 ⌦ ⌧ ⌧ SC 🏃

Joplin

Motels/Motor Lodges

★ **DRURY INN.** *3601 S Range Line Rd (64804). Phone 417/781-8000; toll-free 800/378-7946. www.druryinn.com.* 109 rooms, 4 story. Pets accepted, some restrictions. Complimentary continental breakfast. Check-out noon. TV; cable (premium), VCR available. In-room modem link. In-house fitness room. Health club privileges. Indoor pool, whirlpool. **$**

⓪ 🐾 ⌦ ⌧ ⌧

★★ **HOLIDAY INN.** *3615 S Range Line Rd (64804). Phone 417/782-1000; toll-free 800/465-4329; fax 417/623-4093. www.holiday-inn.com.* 262 rooms, 2-5 story. Pets accepted, some restrictions. Check-out noon. TV; cable (premium), VCR available. In-room modem link. Restaurant, bar; entertainment. Room service. In-house

fitness room, sauna, steam room. Game room. Indoor pool, outdoor pool, whirlpool. **$**

⓪ 🐾 ⌦ ⌧ ⌧ ⌧

★ **RAMADA INN.** *3320 Range Line Rd (64804). Phone 417/781-0500; fax 417/781-9388. www.ramada.com.* 171 rooms, 2-3 story. Pets accepted, some restrictions; fee. Check-out noon. TV; cable (premium). In-room modem link. Restaurant, bar. Room service. Sauna. Indoor pool, outdoor pool, whirlpool. Lighted tennis. Airport transportation. **$**

⓪ 🐾 ⌧ ⌦ ⌧ ⌧ SC

Kansas City

Motels/Motor Lodges

★ **BAYMONT INN.** *2214 Taney St (64116). Phone 816/221-1200; toll-free 800/301-0200; fax 816/471-6207. www.baymontinn.com.* 94 rooms, 3 story. Pets accepted, some restrictions. Complimentary continental breakfast. Check-out noon. TV; cable (premium). In-room modem link. **$**

⓪ 🐾 ⌦ SC

★ **SUPER 8.** *6900 NW 83rd Terrace (64152). Phone 816/587-0808; toll-free 800/800-8000. www.super8.com.* 50 rooms, 3 story. Pets accepted; fee. Check-out 11 am. TV; cable (premium). In-room modem link. **$**

⓪ 🐾 ⌦

Hotels

★★ **DOUBLETREE HOTEL.** *1301 Wyandotte St (63801). Phone 816/474-6664; toll-free 800/843-6664; fax 816/474-0424. www.doubletree.com.* This hotel, located in the downtown business district, near the Kansas City Convention Center, has guest rooms with European charm. 388 rooms, 28 story. Pets accepted, some restrictions; fee. Check-out noon. TV; cable (premium), VCR available. In-room modem link. Restaurant, bar. In-house fitness room. Health club privileges. Indoor/Outdoor pool, poolside service. Valet parking. Business center. Concierge. Luxury level. **$$**

⓪ 🐾 ⌦ ⌧ ⌧ SC 🏃

★★★ **THE WESTIN CROWN CENTER.** *One Pershing Rd (64108). Phone 816/474-4400; toll-free 800/228-3000; fax 816/391-4438. www.westin.com.* Located in the downtown area within Hallmark's Crown Center where visitors will find shops, restaurants, and theaters. The hotel is also near the Liberty Memorial and the Bartle Convention Center and offers many amenities and facilities. 729 rooms, 13 story. Pets accepted; fee. Check-out noon. TV; VCR available. In-room modem link. Restaurant, bar; entertainment. Supervised children's activities, ages 6-12. In-house fitness room, sauna, steam room. Outdoor pool, whirlpool, poolside service. Lighted tennis. Lawn games. Business center. Airport transportation. Luxury level. **$**

[D] [icons] SC [icon]

Kirksville

Motels/Motor Lodges

★ **BUDGET HOST INN.** *1304 S Baltimore (63501). Phone 660/665-3722; toll-free 800/283-4678; fax 660/665-8277. www.budgethost.com.* 30 rooms, 1-2 story. Pets accepted; fee. Check-out noon. TV; cable (premium). In-room modem link. In-room steam baths. **$**

[icons] SC

★ **SHAMROCK INN.** *2501 S Business 63 (63501). Phone 660/665-8352; fax 660/665-0072.* 45 rooms. Pets accepted, some restrictions; fee. Check-out 11 am. TV; cable (premium), VCR available (movies). Outdoor pool. **$**

[icons] SC

Lake Ozark

Motel/Motor Lodge

★ ★ **HOLIDAY INN SUNSPREE.** *120 Holiday Ln (65049). Phone 573/365-2334; toll-free 800/532-3575; fax 573/365-6887. www.holiday-inn.com.* 207 rooms, 3 story. Pets accepted, some restrictions; fee. Complimentary continental breakfast. Check-out 11 am. TV; cable (premium). In-room modem link. Restaurant, bar. Room service. In-house fitness room, sauna. Game room. Indoor pool, two outdoor pools, whirlpool. Lawn games. **$**

[D] [icons] SC

Lebanon

Motel/Motor Lodge

★ ★ **BEST WESTERN WYOTA INN.** *I-44 at exit 130 (65536). Phone 417/532-6171; toll-free 800/780-7234; fax 417/532-6174. www.bestwestern.com.* 52 rooms, 1-2 story. Pets accepted, some restrictions; fee. Complimentary continental breakfast. Check-out 11 am. TV; cable (premium). Restaurant. Outdoor pool. **$**

[icons]

Lexington

Motel/Motor Lodge

★ **LEXINGTON INN.** *1078 N Outer Rd W (64067). Phone 660/259-4641; toll-free 800/289-4641; fax 660/259-6604.* 60 rooms, 2 story. Pets accepted, some restrictions; fee. Check-out 11 am. TV. Laundry services. Restaurant, bar; entertainment. Outdoor pool. **$**

[D] [icons]

Macon

Motel/Motor Lodge

★ ★ **BEST WESTERN INN.** *28933 Sunset Dr (63552). Phone 660/385-2125; toll-free 800/901-2125; fax 660/385-4900. www.bestwestern.com.* 46 rooms, 2 story. Pets accepted, some restrictions; fee. Complimentary continental breakfast. Check-out 11 am. In-room modem link. Outdoor pool. **$**

[icons] SC

Mount Vernon

Motel/Motor Lodge

★ **BUDGET HOST INN.** *1015 E Mount Vernon Blvd (65712). Phone 417/466-2125; toll-free 800/283-4678; fax 417/466-4440. www.budgethost.com.* 21 rooms. Pets accepted; fee. Check-out 11 am. TV; cable (premium), VCR available. Outdoor pool. **$**

[icons]

Nevada

Motels/Motor Lodges

★ **SUPER 8.** *2301 E Austin St (64772). Phone 417/667-8888; toll-free 800/800-8000; fax 417/667-8883. www.super8.com.* 59 rooms, 2 story. Pets accepted, some restrictions. Complimentary continental breakfast. Check-out 11 am. TV; cable (premium), VCR available. Indoor pool, whirlpool. **$**

[D] [icons] SC

★ **WELCOME INN.** *2345 Marvel Dr (64772). Phone 417/667-6777; fax 417/667-6135.* 46 rooms, 2 story. Pets accepted. Complimentary continental breakfast. Check-out 11 am. TV; cable (premium). Laundry services. Indoor pool, whirlpool. **$**

D ◈ ☲ ⇗ SC

Poplar Bluff

Motels/Motor Lodges

★ **DRURY INN.** *Business 60 and US 67 N (63901). Phone 573/686-2451; toll-free 800/325-8300. www.druryinn.com.* 78 rooms, 3 story. Pets accepted, some restrictions. Complimentary breakfast. Check-out noon. TV. In-room modem link. Indoor/Outdoor pool, whirlpool. **$**

D ◈ ☲ ⇗ SC

★★ **THREE RIVERS INN.** *2115 N Westwood Blvd (63901). Phone 573/785-7711; fax 573/785-5215.* 143 rooms, 1-2 story. Pets accepted, some restrictions; fee. Check-out noon. TV; cable (premium). Restaurant, bar; entertainment. Room service. Pool. **$**

D ◈ ☲ ⇗ ⇗

Rolla

Motels/Motor Lodges

★ **BEST WESTERN COACHLIGHT.** *1403 Martin Springs Dr (65401). Phone 573/341-2511; toll-free 800/780-7234; fax 573/308-3055. www.bestwestern.com.* 88 rooms, 2 story. Pets accepted, some restrictions. Complimentary continental breakfast. Check-out noon. TV; cable (premium). In-room modem link. Laundry services. **$**

D ◈ ⇗

★ **DRURY INN.** *2006 N Bishop Ave (65401). Phone 573/364-4000; toll-free 800/436-3310; fax 573/364-4000. www.druryinn.com.* 86 rooms, 2 story. Pets accepted, some restrictions. Complimentary continental breakfast. Check-out noon. TV. Outdoor pool. **$**

D ◈ ☲ ⇗ SC

Saint Charles

Motel/Motor Lodge

★★ **HOLIDAY INN SELECT.** *4341 Veteran's Memorial Pkwy (63376). Phone 636/928-1500; toll-free 800/767-3837. www.holiday-inn.com.* 195 rooms, 6 story.

Pets accepted; fee. Check-out noon. TV. Restaurant, bar; entertainment weekends. Room service. In-house fitness room, sauna. Game room. Indoor pool, outdoor pool, whirlpool, poolside service. Business center. Airport transportation. Luxury level. **$**

D ◈ ☲ ⇗ ✈ ⇗ ⇗

Saint Joseph

Motels/Motor Lodges

★ **DRURY INN.** *4213 Frederick Blvd (64506). Phone 816/364-4700; toll-free 800/378-7946. www.druryinn.com.* 133 rooms, 4 story. Pets accepted. Complimentary continental breakfast. Check-out noon. TV; cable (premium). In-room modem link. In-house fitness room. Indoor pool, whirlpool. **$**

D ◈ ☲ ⇗ ⇗

★★ **HOLIDAY INN.** *102 S 3rd St (64501). Phone 816/279-8000; toll-free 800/824-7402; fax 816/279-1484. www.holiday-inn.com.* 170 rooms, 6 story. Pets accepted. Check-out noon. TV. Restaurant, bar. Room service. In-house fitness room, sauna. Health club privileges. Game room. Indoor pool, whirlpool. Opposite river. **$**

D ◈ ☲ ⇗ ⇗

Sedalia

Motel/Motor Lodge

★★ **BEST WESTERN STATE FAIR MOTOR INN.** *3120 S Limit Ave (US 65 S and 32nd) (65301). Phone 660/826-6100; toll-free 800/780-7234; fax 660/827-3850. www.bestwestern.com.* 117 rooms, 2 story. Pets accepted. Check-out 11 am. TV; cable (premium). Restaurant, bar. Room service. In-house fitness room, sauna. Game room. Indoor pool, children's pool, whirlpool, poolside service. Airport transportation. **$**

D ◈ ☲ ⇗ ⇗ ⇗

Sikeston

Motels/Motor Lodges

★★ **BEST WESTERN COACH HOUSE INN.** *220 S Interstate Dr (63801). Phone 573/471-9700; toll-free 887/471-9700; fax 573/471-4285. www.bestwestern.com.* 63 rooms, 2 story. Pets accepted, some restrictions; fee. Check-out noon. TV. In-room modem link. Laundry services. Restaurant, bar; entertainment. Game room. Outdoor pool, poolside service. **$**

D 🐾 ≈ ⇘ SC

★ **DRURY INN.** *2602 E Malone Ave (63801). Phone 573/471-4100; toll-free 800/325-8300. www.druryinn.com.* 80 rooms, 4 story. Pets accepted, some restrictions. Complimentary continental breakfast. Check-out noon. TV; cable (premium), VCR available (movies). Indoor pool, outdoor pool, whirlpool. **$**

D 🐾 ≈ ⇘ SC

★ ★ **PEAR TREE INN.** *2602 Rear E Malone (63801). Phone 573/471-8660; toll-free 800/378-7946; fax 573/471-8660.* 67 rooms, 3 story. No elevator. Pets accepted, some restrictions. Complimentary continental breakfast. TV; cable (premium). In-room modem link. Outdoor pool. **$**

D 🐾 ≈ ⇘

Springfield

Motels/Motor Lodges

★ **BEST WESTERN ROUTE 66 RAIL HAVEN.** *203 S Glenstone Ave (65802). Phone 417/866-1963; toll-free 800/780-7234. www.bestwestern.com.* 93 rooms. Pets accepted, some restrictions. Complimentary continental breakfast. Check-out noon. TV; cable (premium), VCR available (movies). In-room modem link. Outdoor pool, whirlpool. **$**

🐾 ≈ ⇘ SC

★ ★ **CLARION HOTEL.** *3333 S Glenstone Ave (65803). Phone 417/883-6550; toll-free 800/756-7318; fax 417/883-5720. www.clarionhotel.com.* 199 rooms, 2 story. Pets accepted; fee. Check-out noon. TV; cable (premium). In-room modem link. Restaurant, bar. Room service. Outdoor pool. Airport transportation. **$**

D 🐾 ≈ ✈ ⇘ SC

★ **HAWTHORN SUITES.** *1550 E Raynell Pl (65804). Phone 417/520-7300; toll-free 877/570-7300; fax 417/520-7900. www.hawthorn.com.* 80 rooms, 2 story. Pets accepted; fee. Complimentary continental breakfast. Check-out noon. TV; cable (premium). Outdoor pool, whirlpool. **$**

D 🐾 ≈ ⇘

★ **LAMPLIGHTER INN & SUITES.** *2820 N Glenstone Ave (65803). Phone 417/869-3900; toll-free 800/707-0326; fax 417/865-5378. www.lamplighternorth.com.* 130 rooms, 3 story. Pets accepted, some restrictions. Complimentary continental breakfast. Check-out noon. TV; cable

(premium). In-room modem link. Restaurant, bar. In-house fitness room. Health club privileges. Outdoor pool. Business center. Airport transportation. **$**

D 🐾 ≈ ✕ ⇘ SC 🚶

Hotel

★ ★ **HOLIDAY INN UNIVERSITY PLAZA.** *333 John Q Hammons Pkwy (65806). Phone 417/864-7333; toll-free 800/465-4329; fax 417/831-5893. www.holiday-inn.com.* 271 rooms. Pets accepted, some restrictions; fee. Check-out noon. TV; cable (premium), VCR available. In-room modem link. Restaurant, bar; entertainment. In-house fitness room, sauna. Game room. Indoor pool, outdoor pool, whirlpool, poolside service. Lighted tennis. **$**

D 🐾 ⛷ ≈ ✕ ⇘ SC

St. Louis

Motels/Motor Lodges

★ **DRURY INN & SUITES.** *711 N Broadway (21001). Phone 314/231-8100; toll-free 800/325-8300. www.druryinn.com.* 178 rooms. Pets accepted, some restrictions. Complimentary continental breakfast. Check-out noon. TV; cable (premium). In-room modem link. Indoor pool, whirlpool, poolside service. **$**

D 🐾 ≈ ⇘ SC

★ ★ **DRURY INN UNION STATION.** *201 S 20th St (63103). Phone 314/231-3900; toll-free 800/378-7946. www.druryinn.com.* 176 rooms, 7 story. Pets accepted, some restrictions. Complimentary continental breakfast. Check-out noon. TV; cable (premium), VCR available. In-room modem link. Laundry services. Restaurant, bar. In-house fitness room. Indoor pool, whirlpool. Restored 1907 railroad hotel. **$**

D 🐾 ≈ ✕ ⇘

★ **HAMPTON INN.** *2211 Market St (63103). Phone 314/241-3200; toll-free 800/426-7866; fax 314/241-9351. www.hamptoninn.com.* 239 rooms, 11 story. Pets accepted, some restrictions. Complimentary continental breakfast. Check-out noon. TV; cable (premium). In-room modem link. Laundry services. Bar. In-house fitness room. Health club privileges. Indoor pool, whirlpool. **$**

D 🐾 ≈ ✕ ⇘ SC

★ ★ **HOLIDAY INN.** *5915 Wilson Ave (63110). Phone 314/645-0700; toll-free 800/465-4329. www.holiday-inn.com.* 120 rooms, 7 story. Pets accepted; fee. Check-out noon. TV; VCR available. In-room modem link. Restaurant, bar. Room service. Outdoor pool. Business center. **$**

[D] [icons]

★ **STAYBRIDGE SUITES.** *1855 Craigshire Rd (63121). Phone 314/878-1555; toll-free 800/238-8000; fax 314/878-9203. www.staybridge.com.* This all-suite property offers a choice between one- and two-room suites. Each room features a kitchen and a living area with a TV and VCR along with a pull-out sofa bed. A buffet breakfast is included. 106 rooms, 2 story. Pets accepted; fee. Check-out noon. TV; cable (premium), VCR (movies). In-room modem link. Laundry services. In-house fitness room. Health club privileges. Outdoor pool, whirlpool. Airport transportation. **$**

[D] [icons] [SC]

Hotels

★ ★ ★ **MILLENNIUM HOTEL.** *200 S 4th St (63102). Phone 314/241-9500; toll-free 800/325-7353; fax 314/241-9601. www1.millenniumhotels.com.* This large hotel is located in downtown St. Louis across from the Gateway Arch and near the Mississippi Riverfront and other attractions. It offers state-of-the-art facilities and great service. 780 rooms, 28 story. Pets accepted, some restrictions; fee. Check-out noon. TV; cable (premium), VCR available. In-room modem link. Restaurant, bar. In-house fitness room. Health club privileges. Game room. Indoor pool, outdoor pool, children's pool, poolside service. Business center. Luxury level. **$$**

[D] [icons]

★ ★ ★ **SHERATON CLAYTON PLAZA.** *7730 Bonhomme Ave (63105). Phone 314/863-0400; toll-free 800/325-3535; fax 314/863-8513. www.sheraton.com.* 257 rooms, 15 story. Pets accepted. Check-out noon. TV; cable (premium), VCR available. Restaurant. In-house fitness room. Indoor pool. Business center. **$$**

[D] [icons] [SC]

★ ★ **WYNDHAM MAYFAIR HOTEL.** *806 St. Charles St (63101). Phone 314/421-2500; toll-free 877/999-3223; fax 314/421-6254. www.wyndham.com.* 132 rooms, 18 story. Pets accepted, some restrictions; fee. Check-out noon. TV; cable (premium). In-room modem link. Restaurant, bar. In-house fitness room. Business center. Concierge. Luxury level. **$**

[D] [icons] [SC]

St. Louis Lambert Airport Area

Motels/Motor Lodges

★ **DRURY INN.** *10490 Natural Bridge Rd (63134). Phone 314/423-7700; toll-free 800/378-7946. www.druryinn.com.* 172 rooms, 6 story. Pets accepted, some restrictions. Complimentary continental breakfast. Check-out noon. TV; cable (premium), VCR available. In-room modem link. Indoor pool, whirlpool. Airport transportation. **$**

[D] [icons]

★ **HAMPTON INN.** *10800 Pear Tree Ln, Saint Ann (63074). Phone 314/427-3400; toll-free 800/426-7866; fax 314/423-7765. www.hamptoninn.com.* 155 rooms, 4 story. Pets accepted. Complimentary continental breakfast. Check-out noon. TV; cable (premium). In-room modem link. Outdoor pool. Airport transportation. **$**

[D] [icons]

★ ★ **RAMADA INN.** *3551 Pennridge (63044). Phone 314/291-5100; toll-free 800/298-2054; fax 314/291-3546. www.ramada.com.* 245 rooms, 4 story. Pets accepted; fee. Check-out noon. TV; cable (premium), VCR available. In-room modem link. Restaurant, bar. Room service. In-house fitness room, sauna. Game room. Indoor pool, whirlpool. Business center. Airport transportation. Luxury level. **$**

[D] [icons]

Sullivan

Motel/Motor Lodge

★ **SUPER 8.** *601 N Service Rd W (63080). Phone 573/468-8076; toll-free 800/800-8000. www.super8.com.* 60 rooms, 3 story. No elevator. Pets accepted; fee. Check-out 11 am. TV. Laundry services. **$**

[D] [icons]

Theodosia

Motel/Motor Lodge

★ **THEODOSIA MARINA RESORT.** *Lake Rd 160-25 (65761). Phone 417/273-4444; fax 417/273-4263. www.tmrbullshoals.net.* 20 rooms. Pets accepted, some restrictions; fee. Check-out 11 am. TV. Restaurant. Outdoor pool. Lighted tennis. **$**

[icons]

Waynesville

Motels/Motor Lodges

★ **BEST WESTERN MONTIS INN.** *14086 Hwy Z (65584). Phone 573/336-4299; toll-free 800/780-7234; fax 573/336-2872. www.bestwestern.com.* 45 rooms, 2 story. Pets accepted, some restrictions. Complimentary continental breakfast. Check-out noon. TV; VCR available (movies). Outdoor pool. **$**

[icons] D [icons] SC

★ **RAMADA INN.** *I-44 exit 16A (65583). Phone 573/336-3121; toll-free 800/272-6232; fax 573/336-4752. www.ramada.com.* 82 rooms, 2 story. Pets accepted; fee. Check-out noon. TV; cable (premium), VCR available. In-room modem link. Restaurant, bar; entertainment. In-house fitness room, sauna. Game room. Indoor pool, outdoor pool, whirlpool. Business center. Near Fort Leonard Wood. **$**

[icons] D [icons] SC [icons]

Wentzville

Motel/Motor Lodge

★ ★ **HOLIDAY INN.** *900 Corporate Pkwy (63385). Phone 636/327-7001; toll-free 800/465-4329; fax 636/327-7019. www.holiday-inn.com.* 138 rooms, 4 story. Pets accepted, some restrictions; fee. Check-out 1 pm. TV; cable (premium). In-room modem link. Restaurant, bar. Room service. Outdoor pool, poolside service. **$**

[icons] D [icons]

West Plains

Motel/Motor Lodge

★ **RAMADA INN.** *1301 Preacher Roe Blvd (65775). Phone 417/256-8191; toll-free 800/272-6232; fax 417/256-8069. www.ramada.com.* 80 rooms, 2 story. Pets accepted; fee. Check-out noon. TV; cable (premium), VCR available. Restaurant, bar. Room service. Outdoor pool. **$**

[icons] D [icons] SC

Montana

Bigfork

Motels/Motor Lodges

★ **SUPER 8.** *Hwy 83, Mile Marker 46.5 (59826). Phone 406/754-2688; toll-free 800/800-8000; fax 406/754-2688. www.super8.com.* 22 rooms, 2 story. No A/C. Pets accepted. Check-out 11 am. TV. **$**

⊡ ⬤ ⬤ ⬤ ⬤

★ **TIMBERS MOTEL.** *8540 Hwy 35 S (59911). Phone 406/837-6200; toll-free 800/821-4546; fax 406/837-6203. www.timbersmotel.com.* 40 rooms, 1-2 story. Pets accepted, some restrictions; fee. Complimentary continental breakfast. Check-out 11 am, check-in 3 pm. TV; cable (premium). Sauna. Outdoor pool, whirlpool. Cross-country ski 7 miles. **$**

⊡ ⬤ ⬤ ⬤ ⬤ ⬤ ⬤

B&B/Small Inn

★ ★ **O'DUACHAIN COUNTRY INN.** *675 Ferndale Dr (59911). Phone 406/837-6851; toll-free 800/837-7460; fax 406/837-0778. www.montanainn.com.* 5 rooms, 3 story. No A/C. No room phones. Pets accepted, some restrictions; fee. Complimentary full breakfast. Check-out 11 am, check-in 2 pm. Massage, sauna. Whirlpool. Authentic log home. Totally nonsmoking. **$**

⊡ ⬤ ⬤ ⬤ ⬤

Big Sky

Motels/Motor Lodges

★ **BEST WESTERN BUCK'S T-4 LODGE.** *Hwy 191, 46625 Gallatin Rd (59716). Phone 406/995-4111; toll-free 800/822-4484; fax 406/995-2191. www.buckst4.com.* 74 rooms, 2 story. Pets accepted; fee. Complimentary continental breakfast. Check-out 11 am, check-in 4 pm. TV; VCR available. Laundry services. Restaurant. Game room. Whirlpool. **$**

⊡ ⬤ ⬤

★ **COMFORT INN.** *47214 Gallatin Rd (59716). Phone 406/995-2333; fax 406/995-2277. www.comfortinnbigsky.com.* 62 rooms, 3 story. No elevator. Pets accepted, some restrictions; fee. Complimentary continental breakfast. Check-out 11 am. TV; cable (premium), VCR available.

Laundry services. In-house fitness room. Indoor pool, whirlpool. Downhill ski 10 miles, cross-country ski 2 miles. **$**

⊡ ⬤ ⬤ ⬤ ⬤ ⬤ ⬤ SC

★ ★ **RAINBOW RANCH.** *42950 Gallatin Rd (59716). Phone 406/995-4132; toll-free 800/937-4132; fax 406/995-2861. www.rainbowranch.com.* 16 rooms. No A/C. Pets accepted; fee. Complimentary continental breakfast. Check-out 11 am, check-in 3 pm. TV; VCR (movies). Restaurant. Whirlpool. On river. **$$**

⊡ ⬤ ⬤ ⬤ ⬤ ⬤ SC

Big Timber

Motel/Motor Lodge

★ **SUPER 8.** *I-90 and Hwy 10 W (59011). Phone 406/932-8888; toll-free 800/800-8000; fax 406/932-4103. www.super8.com.* 41 rooms, 2 story. Pets accepted, some restrictions; fee. Complimentary continental breakfast. Check-out 11 am, check-in 2 pm. TV. In-room modem link. **$**

⊡ ⬤ ⬤ SC

Billings

Motels/Motor Lodges

★ **BEST WESTERN.** *5610 S Frontage Rd (59101). Phone 406/248-9800; toll-free 800/780-7234; fax 406/248-2500. www.bestwestern.com.* 80 rooms, 3 story. Pets accepted, some restrictions. Complimentary continental breakfast. Check-out noon, check-in 2 pm. TV; cable (premium). In-room modem link. In-house fitness room, sauna. Indoor pool, whirlpool. **$**

⊡ ⬤ ⬤ ⬤ ⬤ ⬤

★ ★ **BEST WESTERN PONDEROSA INN.** *2511 1st Ave N (59101). Phone 406/259-5511; toll-free 800/628-9081; fax 406/245-8004. www.bestwesternponderosainn.com.* 131 rooms, 2 story. Pets accepted, some restrictions. Check-out 11 am, check-in 1 pm. TV; cable (premium). In-room modem link. Restaurant open 24 hours. Bar. Room service. Sauna. Outdoor pool. Airport transportation. **$**

⬤ ⬤ ⬤ SC

★ **BILLINGS INN.** *880 N 29th St (59101). Phone 406/252-6800; toll-free 800/231-7782; fax 406/231-7782. www.billingsinn.com.* 60 rooms, 4 story. Pets accepted, some restrictions; fee. Complimentary continental breakfast. Check-out 11 am, check-in 2 pm. TV; cable (premium). **$**

⬤ ⬤

★ **COMFORT INN.** *2030 Overland Ave (59102). Phone 406/652-5200; toll-free 800/228-5150; fax 406/652-5200.*

www.comfortinn.com. 60 rooms, 2 story. Pets accepted; fee. Complimentary continental breakfast. Check-out 11 am, check-in 2 pm. TV; cable (premium). In-room modem link. Game room. Indoor pool, whirlpool. **$**

D 🐾 🏊 ⛷ SC

★ **DAYS INN.** 843 Parkway Ln (59101). Phone 406/252-4007; toll-free 800/329-7466; fax 406/896-1147. www.daysinn.com. 62 rooms, 2 story. Pets accepted, some restrictions; fee. Complimentary continental breakfast. Check-out noon, check-in 3 pm. TV; VCR available (movies). In-room modem link. Laundry services. Whirlpool. **$**

D 🐾 🛥 🏋 ⛷

★ **HILLTOP INN.** 1116 N 28th St (59101). Phone 406/245-5000; toll-free 800/878-9282; fax 406/245-7851. www.hilltopinn-billings.com. 57 rooms, 3 story. Pets accepted, some restrictions; fee. Complimentary continental breakfast. Check-out 11 am, check-in 2 pm. TV; cable (premium). In-room modem link. **$**

🐾 ✈ ⛷

★ **HOWARD JOHNSON.** 1001 S 27th St (59101). Phone 406/248-4656; toll-free 800/654-2000; fax 406/248-7268. www.hojo.com. 170 rooms, 3 story. Pets accepted, some restrictions. Complimentary continental breakfast. Check-out noon, check-in 3 pm. TV. In-room modem link. Laundry services. In-house fitness room. Airport transportation. **$**

D 🐾 🛥 🏋 🍽 ⛷

★ ★ **QUALITY INN.** 2036 Overland Ave (59102). Phone 406/652-1320; toll-free 800/228-5151; fax 406/652-1320. www.qualityinn.com. 119 rooms, 2 story. Pets accepted, some restrictions; fee. Complimentary full breakfast. Check-out noon, check-in 3 pm. TV; cable (premium), VCR available (movies). In-room modem link. Sauna. Indoor pool, whirlpool. Airport transportation. **$**

D 🐾 🏊 ✈ ⛷ SC

★ **RAMADA LIMITED.** 1345 Mullowney Ln (59101). Phone 406/252-2584; fax 406/252-2584. www.ramada.com. 114 rooms, 2 story. Pets accepted, some restrictions; fee. Complimentary continental breakfast. Check-out noon, check-in 2 pm. TV; cable (premium). In-room modem link. In-house fitness room. Indoor pool. **$**

D 🐾 🏊 🍽 ⛷

★ **SUPER 8.** 5400 Southgate Dr (59102). Phone 406/248-8842; toll-free 800/800-8000; fax 406/248-8842. www.super8.com. 113 rooms, 3 story. Pets accepted, some restrictions; fee. Complimentary continental breakfast. Check-out 11 am, check-in 2 pm. TV; cable (premium), VCR available (movies). In-room modem link. **$**

D 🐾 ⛷ SC

Hotels

★ ★ **THE HISTORIC NORTHERN HOTEL.** 19 N 28th St (59101). Phone 406/245-5121; toll-free 800/542-5121; fax 406/259-9862. In the heart of downtown, just steps away from local shopping and the arts, this hotel provides a warm, friendly place to stay. Start your day off with the complimentary breakfast, and relax during the day while you work out in the state-of-the-art fitness facility. 160 rooms, 10 story. Pets accepted, some restrictions. Check-out noon, check-in 3 pm. TV; cable (premium). Restaurant, bar. In-house fitness room. Airport transportation. **$**

D 🐾 🍽 ⛷ SC

★ ★ **HOLIDAY INN THE GRAND MONTANA.** 5500 Midland Rd (59101). Phone 406/248-7701; toll-free 877/554-7263; fax 406/248-8954. www.holiday-inn.com/billings-west. 317 rooms, 7 story. Pets accepted, some restrictions; fee. Check-out noon, check-in 3 pm. TV; cable (premium). In-room modem link. Restaurant, bar; entertainment. Room service. Sauna. Game room. Indoor pool, whirlpool. Business center. Concierge. Airport transportation. **$**

D 🐾 🏊 🏋 ✈ ⛷ 🚶

★ ★ ★ **SHERATON BILLINGS HOTEL.** 27 N 27th St (59101). Phone 406/252-7400; toll-free 800/588-7666; fax 406/252-2401. www.sheraton.com. Offering a great view of both the city and the mountains, the 20th floor lounge is a great place to relax during your stay. Pleasant modern rooms are loaded with features for the business traveler. 282 rooms, 23 story. Pets accepted, some restrictions. Check-out noon, check-in 3 pm. TV; cable (premium). Internet access. In-room modem link. Restaurant, bar. Room service. In-house fitness room, sauna. Game room. Indoor pool, children's pool, whirlpool. Business center. Airport transportation. **$**

D 🐾 🏊 🏋 ✈ ⛷ SC 🚶

Bozeman

Motels/Motor Lodges

★ **BOZEMAN'S WESTERN HERITAGE INN.** 1200 E Main St (59715). Phone 406/586-8534; toll-free 800/877-1094; fax 406/587-8729. www.avicom.net/westernheritage. 37 rooms, 3 story. Pets accepted; fee. Complimentary continental breakfast. Check-out 11 am, check-in 2 pm. TV; cable (premium). In-room modem link. In-house fitness room, sauna. **$**

🐾 🏋 ⛷ SC

★ **COMFORT INN.** 1370 N 7th Ave (59715). Phone 406/587-2322; toll-free 800/587-3833; fax 406/587-2423. www.comfortinnbozeman.com. 121 rooms, 3 story. Pets accepted, some restrictions. Complimentary continental breakfast. Check-out 11 am, check-in 2 pm. TV; cable (premium). In-room modem link. In-house fitness room, sauna. Indoor pool, whirlpool. Business center. **$**

★ **DAYS INN.** *1321 N 7th Ave (59715). Phone 406/ 587-5251; toll-free 800/329-7466; fax 406/587-5351. www.the.daysinn.com/bozeman06765.* 79 rooms, 2 story. Pets accepted; fee. Complimentary full breakfast. Check-out 11 am, check-in 3 pm. TV; cable (premium), VCR available (movies). In-room modem link. In-house fitness room, sauna. Whirlpool. **$**

★★ **HOLIDAY INN.** *5 Baxter Ln (59715). Phone 406/587-4561; toll-free 800/366-5101; fax 406/587-4413. www.holiday-inn.com.* 179 rooms, 2 story. Pets accepted. Check-out noon, check-in 4 pm. TV; cable (premium). In-room modem link. Restaurant, bar. Room service. In-house fitness room, massage. Indoor pool, whirlpool. Lawn games. Airport transportation. **$**

★ **HOLIDAY INN EXPRESS.** *6261 Jackrabbit Ln (59714). Phone 406/388-0800; toll-free 800/542-6791; fax 406/388-0804. www.hiexpress.com.* 67 rooms, 3 story. Pets accepted. Complimentary continental breakfast. Check-out 11 am, check-in 3 pm. TV; cable (premium). In-room modem link. In-house fitness room. Airport transportation. **$**

★ **RAMADA LIMITED.** *2020 Wheat Dr (59715). Phone 406/585-2626; fax 406/585-2727. www.ramada.com.* 50 rooms, 2 story. Shower only. Pets accepted. Complimentary continental breakfast. Check-out noon, check-in 2 pm. TV; cable (premium). In-room modem link. Laundry services. Indoor pool, whirlpool. **$**

★ **ROYAL 7.** *310 N 7th Ave (59715). Phone 406/587-3103; toll-free 800/587-3103. www.avicom.net/Royal.* 47 rooms, 1 story. Pets accepted, some restrictions. Complimentary continental breakfast. Check-out 11 am, check-in 2 pm. TV; cable (premium). In-room modem link. Whirlpool. **$**

★ **TLC INN.** *805 Wheat Dr (59715). Phone 406/587-2100; toll-free 877/466-7852; fax 406/587-4941. www.tlc-inn.com.* 42 rooms, 3 story. No elevator. Pets accepted, some restrictions; fee. Complimentary continental breakfast. Check-out 11 am, check-in 3 pm. TV. In-room modem link. Sauna. Whirlpool. **$**

B&B/Small Inn

★★ **GALLATIN GATEWAY INN.** *76405 Gallatin Rd (Hwy 191) (59718). Phone 406/763-4672; toll-free 800/676-3522; fax 406/763-4777. www.gallatingatewayinn .com.* This historic, restored railroad hotel (1927) is located in the heart of Yellowstone Country and is close to all the outdoor activities offered there. Guest rooms are individually decorated in a Western theme, with many antiques. 33 rooms, 2 story. Pets accepted; fee. Complimentary continental breakfast. Check-out 11 am, check-in 3 pm. TV; cable (premium). Restaurant, bar. Outdoor pool, whirlpool. Lighted tennis. Lawn games. Mountain bike rentals. Concierge. Airport transportation. On river. **$$**

Butte

Motels/Motor Lodges

★ **COMFORT INN.** *2777 Harrison Ave (59701). Phone 406/494-8850; toll-free 877/424-6423; fax 406/494-2801. www.comfortinn.com.* 145 rooms, 3 story. No elevator. Pets accepted; fee. Complimentary continental breakfast. Check-out 11 am, check-in 2 pm. TV; cable (premium), VCR available (movies). In-room modem link. In-house fitness room, sauna. Indoor pool, whirlpool. Airport transportation. **$**

★ **DAYS INN.** *2700 Harrison Ave (59701). Phone 406/494-7000; toll-free 800/329-7466; fax 406/494-7000. www.daysinn.com.* 74 rooms, 3 story. Pets accepted, some restrictions. Complimentary continental breakfast. Check-out 11 am, check-in 3 pm. TV; VCR available. In-room modem link. In-house fitness room, sauna. Indoor pool, whirlpool. **$**

★ **RAMADA INN COPPER KING.** *4655 Harrison Ave (59701). Phone 406/494-6666; toll-free 800/332-8600; fax 406/494-3274. www.ramada.com.* 146 rooms, 2 story. Pets accepted, some restrictions; fee. Check-out noon, check-in 3 pm. TV. In-room modem link. Restaurant, bar; entertainment Fri-Sat. Room service. In-house fitness room, sauna. Indoor pool. Indoor tennis. Airport transportation. **$**

★ **SUPER 8.** *2929 Harrison Ave (59701). Phone 406/ 494-6000; toll-free 800/800-8000. www.super8.com.* 106 rooms, 3 story. No elevator. Pets accepted, some restrictions; fee. Complimentary continental breakfast. Check-out 11 am, check-in 3 pm. TV; VCR available (movies). In-room modem link. **$**

D 🐾 🏊 SC

Columbia Falls

Resort

★ ★ ★ **MEADOW LAKE.** *100 Saint Andrews Dr (59912). Phone 406/892-8700; toll-free 800/321-4653; fax 406/892-8731. www.meadowlake.com.* This resort provides year-round fun for the entire family. Enjoy golf, tennis, volleyball in the summer, or ice skating and other indoor recreation in the recreation center for kids. Large, comfortable rooms, each with private veranda area, are available. 24 rooms, 1-3 story. Pets accepted, some restrictions; fee. Check-out 10 am, check-in 4 pm. TV; cable (premium), VCR (movies). In-room modem link. Some wood-burning fireplaces. Laundry services. Restaurant. Room service. Supervised children's activities, ages 4-12. In-house fitness room, massage, sauna. Indoor pool, outdoor pool, children's pool, whirlpool. Golf. Outdoor tennis. Cross-country ski on site. Business center. Concierge. Airport transportation. **$**

D 🐾 ⛷ 🏊 🏌 ⛷ 🎿 🏊 ✈ 🏊 🚶

Deer Lodge

Motel/Motor Lodge

★ **SUPER 8.** *1150 N Main (59722). Phone 406/846-2370; toll-free 800/800-8000; fax 406/846-2373. www.super8.com.* 54 rooms, 2 story. Pets accepted, some restrictions; fee. Check-out 11 am. TV. **$**

D 🐾

Dillon

Motels/Motor Lodges

★ ★ **BEST WESTERN PARADISE INN.** *650 N Montana St (59725). Phone 406/683-4214; toll-free 800/780-7234; fax 406/683-4216. www.bestwestern.com.* 65 rooms, 2 story. Pets accepted. Check-out 11 am. TV; cable. Restaurant, bar. Indoor pool, whirlpool. **$**

🐾 🏊 🏊 SC

★ **COMFORT INN.** *450 N Interchange (59725). Phone 406/683-6831; toll-free 877/424-6423; fax 406/683-2021. www.comfortinn.com.* 48 rooms, 2 story. Pets accepted, some restrictions; fee. Check-out 11 am. TV; cable (premium). Laundry services. Bar. Indoor pool. **$**

D 🐾 🏊 🏊 SC

★ **SUPER 8.** *550 N Montana St (59725). Phone 406/683-4288; toll-free 800/800-8000; fax 406/683-4288. www.super8.com.* 48 rooms, 3 story. No elevator. Pets accepted, some restrictions; fee. Check-out 11 am. TV; cable (premium). **$**

🐾 🏊 SC

Ennis

Motel/Motor Lodge

★ **FAN MOUNTAIN INN.** *204 N Main St (59729). Phone 406/682-5200; toll-free 877/682-5200; fax 406/682-5266.* 27 rooms, 2 story. Pets accepted, some restrictions; fee. Check-out 11 am, check-in noon. TV. **$**

D 🐾 ⛷ 🏊 🏊

Gardiner

Motels/Motor Lodges

★ **ABSAROKA LODGE.** *Hwy 89 and Yellowstone River Bridge (59030). Phone 406/848-7414; toll-free 800/755-7414; fax 406/848-7560. www.yellowstonemotel.com.* 41 rooms, 2 story. Pets accepted; fee. Check-out 11 am, check-in 2 pm. TV. In-house fitness room. **$**

D 🐾 ⛷ 🏊 🚶 🏊

★ **BEST WESTERN MAMMOTH HOT SPRINGS.** *Hwy 89 W (59030). Phone 406/848-7311; toll-free 800/828-9080; fax 406/848-7120. www.bestwestern.com/mammothhotsprings.* 85 rooms, 2 story. Pets accepted, some restrictions; fee. Check-out 11 am, check-in 4 pm. TV. In-room modem link. Restaurant. Sauna, steam room. Indoor pool, whirlpool. On the Yellowstone River. **$**

D 🐾 ⛷ 🏊 🏊 🏊

★ **SUPER 8.** *Hwy 89 S (59030). Phone 406/848-7401; toll-free 800/800-8000; fax 406/848-9410. www.super8.com.* 66 rooms, 3 story. Pets accepted, some restrictions; fee. Complimentary continental breakfast. Check-out 10 am. TV; cable (premium). Indoor pool. Opposite river. **$**

D 🐾 ⛷ 🏊 🏊 🏊

Great Falls

Motels/Motor Lodges

★ ★ **BEST WESTERN HERITAGE INN.** *1700 Fox Farm Rd (59404). Phone 406/761-1900; toll-free 800/548-8256; fax 406/761-0136. www.bestwestern.com/heritageinngreatfalls.* 236 rooms, 2 story. Pets accepted, some restrictions. Check-out noon, check-in

2 pm. TV. In-room modem link. Restaurant, bar. Room service. Children's activity center. In-house fitness room, sauna. Indoor pool, whirlpool. Airport transportation. **$**

[D] [icons]

★ **COMFORT INN.** *1120 9th St S (59405). Phone 406/454-2727; toll-free 877/424-6423. www.comfortinn.com.* 64 rooms, 3 story. Pets accepted; fee. Complimentary continental breakfast. Check-out 11 am. TV; cable (premium). In-room modem link. Indoor pool, whirlpool. **$**

[D] [icons]

★ **DAYS INN.** *101 14th Ave NW (59404). Phone 406/727-6565; toll-free 800/329-7466; fax 406/727-6308. www.daysinn.com.* 61 rooms, 2 story. Pets accepted, some restrictions; fee. Complimentary continental breakfast. Check-out 11 am, check-in 2 pm. TV. In-room modem link. Laundry services. **$**

[D] [icons]

★ **HERITAGE INN EXPRESS.** *2 Treasure State Dr (59404). Phone 406/453-1602; toll-free 800/362-4842.* 60 rooms, 2 story. Pets accepted, some restrictions. Complimentary continental breakfast. Check-out noon, check-in 2 pm. TV; cable (premium). In-room modem link. Restaurant. Airport transportation. **$**

[D] [icons]

★ **TOWNHOUSE INNS.** *1411 S 10th Ave (59405). Phone 406/761-4600; toll-free 800/442-4667; fax 406/761-7603. www.townpump.com.* 109 rooms, 2 story. Pets accepted; fee. Check-out 11 am, check-in 3 pm. TV; cable (premium). In-room modem link. Laundry services. Restaurant, bar. Room service. Sauna. Game room. Indoor pool, whirlpool. Airport transportation. **$**

[D] [icons]

Hotel

★ ★ **HOLIDAY INN.** *400 10th Ave S (59405). Phone 406/727-7200; toll-free 800/626-8009; fax 406/268-0472. www.holiday-inn.com/greatfallsmt.* 168 rooms, 7 story. Pets accepted, some restrictions; fee. Check-out noon, check-in 3 pm. TV. In-room modem link. Laundry services. Restaurant, bar. Room service. In-house fitness room, sauna. Health club privileges. Indoor pool, whirlpool. Business center. Airport transportation. **$**

[D] [icons]

Hamilton

Motels/Motor Lodges

★ **BEST WESTERN HAMILTON INN.** *409 S 1st St (59840). Phone 406/363-2142; toll-free 800/426-4586. www.bestwestern.com.* 36 rooms, 1-2 story. Pets accepted, some restrictions; fee. Complimentary continental breakfast. Check-out 11 am, check-in 2 pm. TV; cable (premium). In-room modem link. Whirlpool. **$**

[D] [icons]

★ **COMFORT INN.** *1113 N 1st St (59840). Phone 406/363-6600; toll-free 877/424-6423; fax 406/363-5644. www.comfortinn.com.* 64 rooms, 2 story. Pets accepted, some restrictions; fee. Complimentary continental breakfast. Check-out 11 am, check-in 2 pm. TV; cable (premium), VCR available (movies). In-room modem link. Room service. Sauna. Whirlpool. **$**

[D] [icons]

Guest Ranch

★ ★ ★ **TRIPLE CREEK RANCH.** *5551 W Fork Rd (59829). Phone 406/821-4600; toll-free 800/654-2943; fax 406/821-4666. www.triplecreekranch.com.* With the mountains of Montana as a backdrop, this ranch allows guests to experience the wilderness in its natural setting. Log cabins, trout-filled lakes, horseback riding, and hiking trails keep guests coming back for the fresh mountain air and relaxing atmosphere. 20 cabins. Pets accepted, some restrictions. Children over 16 years only. Complimentary full breakfast. Check-out noon, check-in 3 pm. TV; cable (premium), VCR (movies). In-room modem link. Fireplaces. Restaurant, bar; entertainment Wed, Sat-Sun. Room service. In-house fitness room, massage. Indoor pool, outdoor pool, poolside service. Outdoor tennis. Cross-country ski on site. Lawn games. Horse stables. Snowmobiles. Business center. Concierge. Airport transportation. **$$$$**

[icons]

Havre

Motel/Motor Lodge

★ **TOWNHOUSE INNS.** *601 W 1st St (59501). Phone 406/265-6711; toll-free 800/442-4667; fax 406/265-6213. www.townpump.com.* 102 rooms, 2 story. Pets accepted; fee. Complimentary continental breakfast. Check-out noon, check-in 2 pm. TV; cable (premium). Laundry services. Bar. Sauna. Indoor pool, whirlpool. Business center. **$**

[D] [icons]

Helena

Motels/Motor Lodges

★ **COMFORT INN.** *750 Fee St (59601). Phone 406/443-1000; toll-free 800/228-5150; fax 406/443-1000.*

www.comfortinn.com. 56 rooms, 2 story. Pets accepted; fee. Complimentary continental breakfast. Check-out 11 am, check-in 2 pm. TV; cable (premium). In-room modem link. Indoor pool, whirlpool. **$**

D 🐾 ≈ ⊠ SC

★ **SHILO INN.** *2020 Prospect Ave (59601). Phone 406/442-0320; toll-free 800/222-2244; fax 406/449-4426. www.shiloinns.com.* 48 rooms, 3 story. No elevator. Pets accepted. Complimentary continental breakfast. Check-out noon. TV; cable (premium), VCR (movies, fee). Internet access, in-room modem link. Laundry services. Sauna, steam room. Indoor pool. Airport transportation. **$**

🐾 ⚓ ⚕ ✈ ≈ ✈ ⊠

★ **SUPER 8.** *2200 11th Ave (59601). Phone 406/443-2450; toll-free 800/800-8000. www.super8.com.* 102 rooms, 3 story. No elevator. Pets accepted; fee. Complimentary continental breakfast. Check-out 11 am. TV; cable (premium). In-room modem link. Laundry services. **$**

🐾 ⊠ SC

Hotel

★ ★ **RED LION COLONIAL HOTEL.** *2301 Colonial Dr (59601). Phone 406/443-2100; toll-free 800/733-5466; fax 406/442-0301. www.redlion.com.* 153 rooms, 2 story. Pets accepted, some restrictions; fee. Complimentary continental breakfast. Check-out 1 pm, check-in 3 pm. TV; cable (premium). In-room modem link. Laundry services. Restaurant, bar. Room service. Indoor pool, outdoor pool, whirlpool, poolside service. Airport transportation. **$**

D 🐾 ≈ ⊠ SC

Kalispell

Motels/Motor Lodges

★ **DAYS INN.** *1550 Hwy 93 N (59901). Phone 406/756-3222; toll-free 800/329-7466; fax 406/756-3277. www.daysinn.com.* 53 rooms, 2 story. Pets accepted; fee. Complimentary continental breakfast. Check-out 11 am, check-in 1 pm. TV; cable (premium). In-room modem link. **$**

D 🐾 ⊠ SC

★ ★ **WESTCOAST OUTLAW HOTEL.** *1701 Hwy 93 S (59901). Phone 406/755-6100; toll-free 800/325-4000; fax 406/756-8994. www.westcoasthotels.com/outlaw.* 220 rooms, 3 story. Pets accepted; fee. Check-out 11 am, check-in 4 pm. TV; cable (premium). In-room modem link. Restaurant, bar. Room service. In-house fitness room, massage, sauna. Game room. Two indoor pools, whirlpool. Outdoor tennis. Airport transportation. Casino. **$**

D 🐾 ⚕ ≈ ✈ ⊠ SC

Lewistown

Motel/Motor Lodge

★ **SUPER 8.** *102 Wendell Ave (59457). Phone 406/538-2581; toll-free 800/800-8000; fax 406/538-2702. www.super8.com.* 44 rooms, 2 story. Pets accepted; fee. Check-out 11 am, check-in 1 pm. TV; cable (premium). In-room modem link. **$**

D 🐾 ⊠

Livingston

Motels/Motor Lodges

★ ★ **BEST WESTERN YELLOWSTONE INN.** *1515 W Park St (59047). Phone 406/222-6110; toll-free 800/770-1874; fax 406/222-3357. www.bestwestern.com.* 98 rooms, 3 story. Pets accepted; fee. Check-out noon, check-in 3 pm. TV; cable (premium). In-room modem link. Restaurant, bar. Room service. Indoor pool. Airport transportation. **$**

D 🐾 ≈ ✈ ⊠ SC

★ ★ **CHICO HOT SPRINGS RESORT.** *1 Chico Rd (59065). Phone 406/333-4933; toll-free 800/468-9232; fax 406/333-4694. www.chicohotsprings.com.* 102 rooms, 7 story. No A/C. Some room phones. Pets accepted, some restrictions; fee. Check-out 11 am, check-in 3 pm. Restaurant, dining room, bar; entertainment Fri-Sat. Supervised children's activities (summer only). In-house fitness room, spa, massage. Two outdoor pools. Cross-country ski 3 miles. Lawn games. Bicycle rentals. Fishing/hunting guides. Hiking. **$**

D 🐾 ⚕ ✈ ≈ ✈ ⊠

★ ★ **PARADISE INN.** *Park Rd and Rogers Ln (59047). Phone 406/222-6320; toll-free 800/437-6291; fax 406/222-2204.* 43 rooms, 1 story. Pets accepted, some restrictions; fee. Complimentary continental breakfast. Check-out 11 am, check-in 1 pm. TV; cable (premium). Restaurant, bar. Room service. Indoor pool. **$**

D 🐾 ⚕ ✈ ≈ ⊠

Miles City

Hotel

★ **BEST WESTERN WAR BONNET INN.** *1015 S Haynes Ave (59301). Phone 406/232-4560; toll-free 800/780-7234; fax 406/232-0363. www.bestwestern.com.* 54 rooms, 2 story. Pets accepted; fee. Complimentary continental breakfast. Check-out noon. TV; cable (premium). Indoor pool, whirlpool. **$**

🐾 ≈ ⊠ SC

Missoula

Motels/Motor Lodges

★ **BEST INN.** *4953 N Reserve St (59808). Phone 406/542-7550; toll-free 800/272-9500; fax 406/721-5931. www.bestinn.com.* 67 rooms, 3 story. Pets accepted; fee. Complimentary continental breakfast. Check-out 11 am, check-in 2 pm. TV; cable (premium). In-room modem link. Laundry services. Whirlpool. Airport transportation. **$**

D 🐾 ✕ ⊠ SC

★ **BEST INN.** *3803 Brooks St (59804). Phone 406/251-2665; toll-free 800/272-9500; fax 406/251-5733. www.bestinn.com.* 81 rooms, 3 story. Pets accepted; fee. Complimentary continental breakfast. Check-out 11 am, check-in 2 pm. TV; cable (premium). Whirlpool. Airport transportation. **$**

D 🐾 ✕ ⊠ SC

★ **BEST WESTERN GRANT CREEK INN.** *5280 Grant Creek Rd (59808). Phone 406/543-0700; toll-free 888/543-0700; fax 406/543-0777. www.bestwestern.com/grantcreekinn.* 126 rooms, 4 story. Pets accepted. Complimentary continental breakfast. Check-out noon, check-in 3 pm. TV; cable (premium), VCR available (movies). In-room modem link. Room service 24 hours. In-house fitness room, sauna, steam room. Indoor pool, whirlpool. Downhill, cross-country ski 5 miles. Airport transportation. **$**

D 🐾 ➤ ≈ 🏃 ✕ ⊠ SC

★ **HAMPTON INN.** *4805 N Reserve St (59802). Phone 406/549-1800; toll-free 800/426-7866; fax 406/549-1737. www.hamptoninn.com.* 60 rooms, 4 story. Pets accepted; fee. Complimentary continental breakfast. Check-out noon, check-in 3 pm. TV; cable (premium). In-room modem link. Laundry services. In-house fitness room. Indoor pool, whirlpool. Business center. Airport transportation. **$**

D 🐾 ≈ 🏃 ✕ ⊠ SC 🏃

★★ **HOLIDAY INN.** *200 S Pattee St (59802). Phone 406/721-8550; toll-free 800/379-0408; fax 406/728-3472. www.holiday-inn.com.* 297 rooms, 4 story. Pets accepted, some restrictions. Check-out noon, check-in 4 pm. TV; cable (premium). Internet access, in-room modem link. Restaurant, bar; entertainment Fri-Sat. Room service. In-house fitness room, sauna. Indoor pool, whirlpool. Downhill ski 12 miles, cross-country ski 5 miles. Airport transportation. **$**

D 🐾 ➤ ≈ 🏃 ✕ ⊠ SC

★ **RAMADA LIMITED.** *801 N Orange St (59806). Phone 406/721-3610; toll-free 800/328-0801; fax 406/721-8875. www.ramada.com.* 81 rooms, 3 story. Pets accepted, some restrictions; fee. Complimentary continental breakfast. Check-out 11 am, check-in 3 pm. TV; cable (premium), VCR available (movies). In-room modem link. In-house fitness room. Airport transportation. **$**

D 🐾 🏃 ✕ ⊠

★ **RED LION.** *700 W Broadway (59802). Phone 406/728-3300; toll-free 800/733-5466; fax 406/728-4441. www.redlion.com.* 76 rooms, 2 story. Pets accepted; fee. Complimentary continental breakfast. Check-out noon, check-in 3 pm. TV; cable (premium). In-room modem link. In-house fitness room. Outdoor pool, whirlpool. Airport transportation. **$**

D 🐾 ≈ 🏃 ✕ ⊠ SC

★ **SLEEP INN.** *3425 Dore Ln (59801). Phone 406/543-5883; toll-free 800/228-5050; fax 406/543-5883. www.sleepinn.com.* 59 rooms, 3 story. Pets accepted; fee. Complimentary continental breakfast. Check-out 11 am, check-in 3 pm. TV; cable (premium). In-room modem link. Indoor pool, whirlpool. **$**

D 🐾 ≈ ⊠ SC

★ **SUPER 8.** *3901 Brooks St (59801). Phone 406/251-2255; toll-free 888/900-9010; fax 406/251-2989. www.super8mt.com.* 103 rooms, 2-3 story. No elevator. Pets accepted, some restrictions; fee. Check-out 11 am, check-in 2 pm. TV; cable (premium). **$**

D 🐾 🐾

Hotel

★★ **DOUBLETREE HOTEL.** *100 Madison (59802). Phone 406/728-3100; toll-free 800/222-8733; fax 406/728-2530. www.doubletree.com.* 172 rooms, 2-3 story. Pets accepted, some restrictions; fee. Check-out noon, check-in 3 pm. TV; VCR available. In-room modem link. Restaurant. Room service. In-house fitness room. Indoor pool, whirlpool. Business center. Airport transportation. **$**

D 🐾 ≈ 🏃 ✕ 🏃

Polson

Resort

★★ **BEST WESTERN KWATAQNUK RESORT.** *303 Hwy 93 E (59860). Phone 406/883-3636; toll-free 800/882-6363; fax 406/883-5392. www.kwataqnuk.com.* 112 rooms, 3 story. Pets accepted; fee. Check-out 11 am, check-in 3 pm. TV; cable (premium), VCR available. In-room modem link. Restaurant. Room service. Game room. Indoor pool, outdoor pool, whirlpool. On Flathead Lake; swimming, boat cruises (fee). **$**

D 🐾 🐾 ≈ ⊠ SC

Red Lodge

Motels/Motor Lodges

★ **BEST WESTERN LUPINE INN.** *702 S Hauser Ave (59068). Phone 406/446-1321; toll-free 888/567-1321; fax 406/446-1465. www.bestwesternlupine.com.* 47 rooms, 2 story. Pets accepted, some restrictions. Complimentary continental breakfast. Check-out noon, check-in 3 pm. TV; cable (premium). In-room modem link. In-house fitness room, sauna. Game room. Indoor pool, whirlpool. Downhill, cross-country ski 6 miles. **$**

🄳 ⬚ ⬚ ⬚ ⬚ ⬚

★ **COMFORT INN.** *612 N Broadway (59068). Phone 406/446-4469; toll-free 800/228-5150; fax 406/446-4669. www.comfortinn.com.* 53 rooms, 2 story. Pets accepted, some restrictions. Complimentary continental breakfast. Check-out 11 am, check-in 2 pm. TV; cable; VCR available. In-room modem link. In-house fitness room. Indoor pool, whirlpool. Downhill, cross-country ski 6 miles. **$**

🄳 ⬚ ⬚ ⬚ ⬚ ⬚ ⬚ ⬚

★ **SUPER 8.** *1223 S Broadway Ave (59068). Phone 406/446-2288; toll-free 800/813-8335; fax 406/446-3162. www.super8.com.* 50 rooms, 2 story. Pets accepted, some restrictions; fee. Complimentary continental breakfast. Check-out 11 am, check-in 2 pm. TV; cable (premium). Game room. Indoor pool, whirlpool. Downhill, cross-country ski 5 miles. **$**

🄳 ⬚ ⬚ ⬚ ⬚ ⬚ ⬚

Three Forks

Motel/Motor Lodge

★ **FORT THREE FORKS.** *10776 Hwy 287 (59752). Phone 406/285-3233; toll-free 800/477-5690; fax 406/285-4362. www.fortthreeforks.com.* 24 rooms, 2 story. Pets accepted, some restrictions; fee. Complimentary continental breakfast. Check-out 11 am. TV; cable (premium). In-room modem link. Outdoor pool, whirlpool. **$**

🄳 ⬚ ⬚ ⬚ ⬚ ⬚

West Yellowstone

Motels/Motor Lodges

★ **DAYS INN.** *301 Madison Ave (59758). Phone 406/646-7656; toll-free 800/548-9551; fax 406/646-7965. www.daysinn.com.* 116 rooms, 2 and 3 story. Pets accepted, some restrictions; fee. Check-out 11 am, check-in 3 pm. TV; cable (premium). Restaurant. Indoor pool, whirlpool. **$**

🄳 ⬚ ⬚ ⬚ ⬚ ⬚

★ **GRAY WOLF INN & SUITES.** *250 S Canyon St (59758). Phone 406/646-0000; toll-free 800/852-8602; fax 406/646-4232. www.graywolf-inn.com.* 103 rooms, 3 story. Pets accepted, some restrictions; fee. Complimentary continental breakfast. Check-out 11 am, check-in 4 pm. TV; cable (premium). Sauna. Indoor pool, whirlpool. Cross-country ski 3 blocks. **$**

⬚ ⬚ ⬚ ⬚ ⬚

★ **KELLY INN.** *104 S Canyon St (59758). Phone 406/646-4544; toll-free 800/259-4672; fax 406/646-9838. www.wyellowstone.com/kellyinn.* 78 rooms, 3 story. Pets accepted, some restrictions. Complimentary continental breakfast. Check-out 11 am, check-in 4 pm. TV. Sauna. Indoor pool, whirlpool. Cross-country ski 3 blocks. **$**

🄳 ⬚ ⬚ ⬚ ⬚ ⬚ ⬚

Whitefish

Motels/Motor Lodges

★ **BEST WESTERN ROCKY MOUNTAIN LODGE.** *6510 Hwy 93 S (59937). Phone 406/862-2569; toll-free 800/862-2569; fax 406/862-1154. www.rockymtnlodge.com.* 79 rooms, 3 story. Pets accepted, some restrictions; fee. Complimentary continental breakfast. Check-out 11 am, check-in 3 pm. TV. In-room modem link. In-house fitness room. Outdoor pool, whirlpool. Downhill ski 8 miles, cross-country ski 1 mile. **$**

🄳 ⬚ ⬚ ⬚ ⬚ ⬚ ⬚ ⬚ ⬚ SC

★ **PINE LODGE.** *920 Spokane Ave (59937). Phone 406/862-7600; toll-free 800/305-7463; fax 406/862-7616. www.thepinelodge.com.* 76 rooms, 4 story. Pets accepted; fee. Check-out 11 am, check-in 4 pm. TV; cable (premium). In-room modem link. In-house fitness room. Game room. Indoor pool, whirlpool. **$**

🄳 ⬚ ⬚ ⬚ ⬚ ⬚ SC

★ **SUPER 8.** *800 Spokane Ave (59937). Phone 406/862-8255; toll-free 800/800-8000. www.super8.com.* 41 rooms, 3 story. No elevator. Pets accepted; fee. Check-out 11 am, check-in 1 pm. TV; cable (premium). Whirlpool. **$**

⬚ ⬚ ⬚ SC

Nebraska

Auburn

Motels/Motor Lodges

★ **AUBURN INN.** *517 J St (68305). Phone 402/274-3143; toll-free 800/272-3143; fax 402/274-4404.* 36 rooms. Pets accepted, some restrictions; fee. Check-out 11 am. TV; cable (premium). **$**

★ **PALMER HOUSE.** *1918 J St (68305). Phone 402/274-3193; toll-free 800/272-3143; fax 402/274-4165.* 22 rooms. Pets accepted, some restrictions; fee. Check-out 11 am. TV; cable (premium). **$**

Beatrice

Motels/Motor Lodges

★ ★ **BEATRICE INN.** *3500 N 6th St (68501). Phone 402/223-4074.* 63 rooms, 2 story. Pets accepted, some restrictions. Check-out 11 am. TV; cable (premium). Laundry services. Restaurant, bar. Heated pool. **$**

★ **HOLIDAY VILLA MOTEL.** *1820 N 6th St (68310). Phone 402/223-4036; fax 402/228-3875.* 46 rooms, 1-2 story. Pets accepted, some restrictions. Check-out 11 am. TV. **$**

★ **VICTORIAN INN 4 LESS.** *1903 N 6th St (68310). Phone 402/228-5955; fax 402/228-2020.* 44 rooms, 2 story. Pets accepted, some restrictions. Complimentary continental breakfast. Check-out 11 am. TV; cable (premium), VCR available. **$**

Blair

Motel/Motor Lodge

★ **ECONO LODGE.** *1355 US 30 S (68008). Phone 402/426-2340; fax 402/426-8703.* 32 rooms, 2 story. Pets accepted; fee. Check-out 11 am. TV; cable (premium). **$**

Broken Bow

Motel/Motor Lodge

★ **THE BIG 12 MOTEL.** *853 E SE St (68822). Phone 308/872-2412; fax 308/872-6376.* 28 rooms. Pets accepted, some restrictions; fee. Check-out 10 am. TV; cable (premium). **$**

Chadron

Motel/Motor Lodge

★ ★ **BEST WESTERN WEST HILLS INN.** *1100 W 10th St (69337). Phone 308/432-3305; toll-free 877/432-3305; fax 308/432-5990. www.bestwestern.com.* 66 rooms, 2 story. Pets accepted, some restrictions. Complimentary continental breakfast. Check-out 11 am. TV; cable (premium). In-house fitness room. Game room. Indoor pool; whirlpool. **$**

Cozad

Motel/Motor Lodge

★ **CIRCLE S BEST VALUE INN.** *440 S Meridian St (69130). Phone 308/784-2290; toll-free 800/237-5852; fax 308/784-3917.* 49 rooms, 2 story. Pets accepted, some restrictions; fee. Check-out 11 am. TV; cable (premium). Heated pool. Restaurant. **$**

Fremont

Motels/Motor Lodges

★ **COMFORT INN.** *1649 E 23rd St (68025). Phone 402/721-1109; fax 402/721-1109. www.comfortinn.com.* 48 rooms, 2 story. Pets accepted; fee. Complimentary continental breakfast. Check-out 11 am. TV; cable (premium). Indoor pool; whirlpool. **$**

★ ★ **HOLIDAY LODGE.** *1220 E 23rd St (68025). Phone 402/727-1110; toll-free 800/743-7666; fax 402/727-4579.* 100 rooms, 2 story. Pets accepted, some restrictions; fee. Check-out noon. TV; cable (premium). Restaurant, bar. In-house fitness room. Indoor pool; whirlpool. **$**

Grand Island

Motels/Motor Lodges

★ ★ **HOWARD JOHNSON.** *3333 Ramada Rd (68801). Phone 308/384-5150; toll-free 800/780-7234; fax 308/384-6551. www.hojo.com.* 181 rooms, 2 story. Pets accepted; fee. Complimentary continental breakfast. Check-out noon. TV; cable (premium). Restaurant, bar. Room service. Game room. Heated pool; whirlpool. **$**

D ☜ ⇌ ⊠

★ **SUPER 8.** *2603 S Locust St (68801). Phone 308/384-4380; fax 308/384-5015. www.super8.com.* 80 rooms, 2 story. Pets accepted, some restrictions. Complimentary continental breakfast. Check-out 11 am. TV. Indoor pool; whirlpool. **$**

D ☜ ⇌ ⊠ SC

Hastings

Motels/Motor Lodges

★ ★ **HOLIDAY INN.** *2205 Osborne Dr E (68901). Phone 402/463-6721; toll-free 888/905-1200; fax 402/463-6874. www.holiday-inn.com.* 100 rooms, 2 story. Pets accepted. Check-out 11 am. TV; cable (premium). In-room modem link. Restaurant, bar. Room service. Sauna. Indoor pool; whirlpool. **$**

D ☜ ⇌ ⊠

★ **SUPER 8.** *2200 N Kansas Ave (68901). Phone 402/463-8888; fax 402/463-8899. www.super8.com.* 50 rooms, 2 story. Pets accepted, some restrictions. Check-out 11 am. TV; cable (premium). **$**

D ☜ ⊠ SC

Kearney

Motels/Motor Lodges

★ ★ **BEST WESTERN INN OF KEARNEY.** *1010 3rd Ave (68845). Phone 308/237-5185; toll-free 800/359-1894; fax 308/234-1002. www.bestwestern.com.* 62 rooms, 2 story. Pets accepted; fee. Complimentary full breakfast. Check-out noon. TV; cable (premium), VCR available (movies). Restaurant. Room service. In-house fitness room; sauna. Pool; children's pool; whirlpool. **$**

☜ ⇌ 🏋 ⊠

★ ★ **FIRST INN GOLD FORT KEARNEY.** *S 2nd Ave and I-80 (68848). Phone 308/234-2541; toll-free 800/652-7245; fax 308/237-4512.* 104 rooms, 3 story. Pets accepted.

Check-out noon. TV; cable (premium). Restaurant, bar. Heated pool. **$**

D ☜ ⇌ ⊠

★ **RAMADA INN.** *301 2nd Ave (68847). Phone 308/237-3141; fax 308/234-4675. www.ramada.com.* 210 rooms, 2 story. Pets accepted, some restrictions; fee. Complimentary continental breakfast. Check-out 11 am. TV; cable (premium). Restaurant, bar; entertainment. Room service. Sauna. Indoor pool; children's pool; whirlpool; poolside service. **$**

D ☜ ⇌ ⊠

Lexington

Motel/Motor Lodge

★ ★ **FIRST INTERSTATE INN.** *2503 Plum Creek Pkwy (68850). Phone 308/324-5601; toll-free 800/IN2-INNS; fax 308/324-4284. www.firstinns.com.* 52 rooms, 2 story. Pets accepted; fee. Complimentary continental breakfast. Check-out noon. TV; cable (premium). Heated pool. Laundry services. **$**

☜ ⇌ ⊠

Lincoln

Motels/Motor Lodges

★ ★ **BEST WESTERN VILLAGER COURTYARD & GARDENS.** *5200 O St (68510). Phone 402/464-9111; fax 402/467-0505. www.bestwestern.com.* 186 rooms, 2 story. Pets accepted. Complimentary continental breakfast. Check-out noon. TV; cable (premium), VCR available. Restaurant, bar. Room service. In-house fitness room. Pool; whirlpool. **$**

D ☜ ⇌ 🏋 ⊠ SC

★ **COMFORT INN.** *2940 NW 12th St (68521). Phone 402/475-2200; toll-free 800/228-5150; fax 402/475-2200. www.comfortinn.com.* 67 rooms, 2 story. Pets accepted; fee. Complimentary continental breakfast. Check-out 11 am. TV; cable (premium). Game room. **$**

D ☜ ⊠ SC

All Suite

★ ★ **WOODFIN SUITES.** *200 S 68th Pl (68510). Phone 402/483-4900; toll-free 888/433-6183; fax 402/483-4464. www.woodfinsuitehotels.com.* 120 kitchen suites, 2 story. Pets accepted; fee. Complimentary full breakfast. Check-out noon. TV; cable (premium), VCR available. Health club privileges, in-house fitness room. Heated pool; whirlpool. Lighted tennis. **$**

D ☜ 🏋 ⇌ 🏋

McCook

Motels/Motor Lodges

★ ★ **BEST WESTERN CHIEF MOTEL.** *612 West B St (69001). Phone 308/345-3700; fax 308/345-7182. www.bestwestern.com.* 111 rooms, 2 story. Pets accepted, some restrictions. Complimentary continental breakfast. Check-out 11 am. TV; cable (premium). Laundry services. Restaurant. In-house fitness room. Indoor pool; whirlpool; poolside service. **$**

⬛ 🐾 ⊠ 🏃 🏊

★ **SUPER 8.** *1103 E B St (69001). Phone 308/345-1141; toll-free 800/800-8000; fax 308/345-1144. www.super8.com.* 40 rooms. Pets accepted, some restrictions. Check-out 11 am. TV; cable (premium). **$**

⬛ 🐾 ⊠ SC

North Platte

Motels/Motor Lodges

★ **1ST INTERSTATE INN.** *US 83 and I-80 (69101). Phone 308/532-6980; toll-free 800/IN2-INNS; fax 308/532-6981. www.firstinns.com.* 29 rooms. Pets accepted, some restrictions; fee. Check-out 11 am. TV; cable (premium). **$**

⬛ 🐾 ⊠

★ **BEST WESTERN CHALET LODGE.** *920 N Jeffers St (69101). Phone 308/532-2313; fax 308/532-8823. www.bestwestern.com.* 38 rooms, 2 story. Pets accepted; fee. Complimentary continental breakfast. Check-out 11 am. TV; cable (premium). Pool. **$**

⬛ 🐾 ⊠

★ **BLUE SPRUCE MOTEL.** *821 S Dewey St (69101). Phone 308/534-2600; toll-free 800/434-2602.* 14 rooms. Pets accepted, some restrictions. Check-out 11 am. TV; cable (premium). **$**

🐾 ⊠ SC

★ ★ **COUNTRY INN.** *321 S Dewey St (69101). Phone 308/532-8130; toll-free 800/532-8130; fax 308/534-0588.* 40 rooms, 2 story. Pets accepted, some restrictions; fee. TV; cable (premium). Pool; whirlpool. **$**

🐾 ⊠

★ ★ **STOCKMAN INN.** *1402 S Jeffers St (69101). Phone 308/534-3630; toll-free 800/624-4643; fax 308/534-0110.* 140 rooms, 2 story. Pets accepted, some restrictions; fee. Complimentary continental breakfast. Check-out

noon. TV; cable (premium). Restaurant, bar. Room service. Heated pool. **$**

⬛ 🐾 ⊠ ⊠

O'Neill

Motels/Motor Lodges

★ **BEST VALUE INN.** *414 E Hwy 20 (68763). Phone 402/336-3800; toll-free 800/315-2378; fax 402/336-1419. www.bestvalueinn.com.* 21 rooms. Pets accepted, some restrictions. Check-out 11 am. TV; cable (premium). **$**

🐾 ⊠ SC

★ **GOLDEN HOTEL.** *406 E Douglas St (68763). Phone 402/336-4436; toll-free 800/658-3148; fax 402/336-3549. www.historicgoldenhotel.com.* 27 rooms, 3 story. Pets accepted. Complimentary continental breakfast. Check-out 11 am. TV; cable (premium), VCR (movies). Restored hotel built in 1913. **$**

⬛ 🐾

Ogallala

Motels/Motor Lodges

★ ★ **BEST WESTERN STAGECOACH INN.** *201 Stagecoach Trail (69153). Phone 308/284-3656; toll-free 800/662-2993; fax 308/284-6734. www.bestwestern.com.* 100 rooms, 2 story. Pets accepted; fee. Complimentary continental breakfast. Check-out noon. TV; VCR (movies). Restaurant, bar. Indoor pool; outdoor pool; children's pool; whirlpool. Free airport transportation. **$**

⬛ 🐾 ⊠ ⊠ SC

★ **RAMADA INN.** *201 Chuckwagon Rd (69153). Phone 308/284-3623; fax 308/284-4949. www.ramada.com.* 152 rooms, 2 story. Pets accepted; fee. Check-out noon. TV; cable (premium). Restaurant, bar. Room service. In-house fitness room. Game room. Pool; children's pool; poolside service. Free airport transportation. **$**

⬛ 🐾 ⊠ 🏃 ⊠

Omaha

Motels/Motor Lodges

★ **BAYMONT INN.** *10760 M St (68127). Phone 402/592-5200; fax 402/592-1416. www.baymontinns.com.* 96 rooms, 2 story. Pets accepted, some restrictions. Complimentary continental breakfast. Check-out noon. TV; cable (premium). **$**

🐾

★ **BEST INN.** *9305 S 145th St (68138). Phone 402/895-2555; fax 402/895-1565. www.bestinn.com.* 56 rooms, 3 story. No elevator. Pets accepted, some restrictions; fee. Complimentary continental breakfast. Check-out noon. TV; cable (premium). Bar. Whirlpool. **$**

D ● ≈ ≋

★ **HAMPTON INN.** *10728 L St (68127). Phone 402/593-2380; toll-free 800/426-7866; fax 402/593-0859. www.hamptoninn.com.* 133 rooms, 4 story. Pets accepted. Complimentary continental breakfast. TV; VCR available (movies). In-room modem link. Pool. **$**

D ● ≈ ≋ SC

★ **LA QUINTA INN.** *3330 N 104th Ave (68134). Phone 402/493-1900; fax 402/496-0750. www.laquinta.com.* 130 rooms, 2 story. Pets accepted. Check-out noon. TV; cable (premium). In-room modem link. Heated pool. **$**

D ● ≈ ≋

★★ **RED LION.** *7007 Grover St (68106). Phone 402/397-7030; toll-free 800/RED-LION; fax 402/397-8449. www.redlionhotelomaha.com.* 215 rooms, 9 story. Pets accepted. Check-out noon. TV; cable (premium). In-room modem link. Restaurant, bar. Sauna. Indoor pool; whirlpool. Free airport transportation. **$**

D ● ≈ ≋

Hotels

★★ **CLARION HOTEL.** *3650 S 72nd St (68124). Phone 402/397-3700; toll-free 800/CLARION; fax 402/397-8362. www.clarioninn.com.* 212 rooms, 5 story. Pets accepted, some restrictions. Check-out noon. TV; cable (premium). In-room modem link. Laundry services. Restaurant, bar. Room service. Sauna. Game room. Indoor pool; whirlpool. Airport transportation. **$**

D ● ≈ ≋ SC

★★ **CLARION HOTEL.** *4888 S 118th St (68137). Phone 402/895-1000; toll-free 888/625-5144; fax 402/896-9247. www.clarioninn.com.* 168 rooms, 6 story. Pets accepted; fee. Check-out noon. TV; cable (premium). Restaurant, bar. Room service. Sauna. Game room. Indoor pool; children's pool; whirlpool. Free airport transportation. **$**

D ● ≈ ✈ ≋

South Sioux City

Motels/Motor Lodges

★★★ **MARINA INN CONFERENCE CENTER.** *4th and B sts (68776). Phone 402/494-4000; toll-free 800/798-7980; fax 402/494-2550.* This hotel is located on the river near a city park, the downtown center, and other attractions. 182 rooms, 5 story. Pets accepted, some restrictions; fee. Check-out 11 am. TV; VCR available. Restaurant, bar. Room service. Indoor pool; whirlpool. Free airport transportation. **$**

D ● ≈ ✈ ≋

★ **REGENCY.** *400 Dakota Ave (68776). Phone 402/494-3046; fax 402/494-8299.* 61 rooms, 2 story. Pets accepted; fee. Complimentary continental breakfast. Check-out 11 am. TV; cable (premium). Airport transportation. **$**

D ● ≋ SC

Valentine

Motels/Motor Lodges

★ **MOTEL RAINE.** *W US 20 (69201). Phone 402/376-2030; toll-free 800/999-3066.* 34 rooms. Pets accepted, some restrictions. Check-out 11 am. TV. Free airport transportation. **$**

●

★ **TRADE WINDS LODGE.** *US 20 and US 83 (69201). Phone 402/376-1600; fax 402/376-3651.* 32 rooms. Pets accepted, some restrictions; fee. Check-out 11 am. TV. Heated pool. Free airport transportation. **$**

● ≈ ✈ ≋

Nevada

Battle Mountain

Motels/Motor Lodges

★ **BEST INN.** *650 W Front St (89820). Phone 775/635-5200; fax 775/635-5699. www.bestinn.com.* 72 rooms, 2 story. Pets accepted; fee. Check-out 11 am. TV; cable (premium). Western theme. **$**

D 🐾 ☒

★ **COMFORT INN.** *521 E Front St (89820). Phone 775/635-5880; toll-free 800/228-5150; fax 775/635-5788. www.comfortinn.com.* 72 rooms, 3 story. Pets accepted; fee. Complimentary continental breakfast. Check-out 11 am. TV; cable (premium). Laundry services. Heated pool; whirlpool. **$**

🐾 ☒ ☒ SC

Elko

Motels/Motor Lodges

★ ★ **RED LION.** *2065 E Idaho St (89801). Phone 775/738-2111; fax 775/753-9859.* 223 rooms, 3 story. Pets accepted, some restrictions; fee. Check-out noon. TV; cable (premium). Restaurant open 24 hours. Bar; entertainment. Game room. Pool. Free airport transportation. Casino. **$**

D 🐾 ☒ ☒

★ **SHILO INN.** *2401 Mountain City Hwy (89801). Phone 775/738-5522; toll-free 800/222-2244; fax 775/738-6247. www.shiloinns.com.* 70 rooms, 2 story. Pets accepted, some restrictions; fee. Complimentary continental breakfast. Check-out noon. TV; cable (premium), VCR available. In-room modem link. Laundry services. In-house fitness room; sauna. Indoor pool; whirlpool. **$**

D 🐾 ☒ ☒ ☒ ☒ SC

Hotel

★ ★ **HIGH DESERT INN.** *3015 E Idaho St (89801). Phone 775/738-8425; toll-free 888/394-8303; fax 775/753-7906.* 170 rooms, 4 story. Pets accepted, some restrictions; fee. Check-out noon. TV. Laundry services. Restaurant, bar. Room service. In-house fitness room. Indoor pool; whirlpool. Free airport transportation. **$**

D 🐾 ☒ ☒ ☒ ☒ SC

Fallon

Motels/Motor Lodges

★ **BONANZA INN AND CASINO.** *855 W Williams Ave (89406). Phone 775/423-6031; fax 775/423-6282.* 75 rooms, 2 story. Pets accepted, some restrictions; fee. Check-out 11 am. TV; cable (premium). Restaurant open 24 hours. Bar. Casino. RV park. **$**

D 🐾 ☒ SC

★ **WESTERN MOTEL.** *125 S Carson St (89407). Phone 775/423-5118; fax 775/423-4973.* 22 rooms, 2 story. Pets accepted; fee. Complimentary continental breakfast. Check-out 11 am. TV. Pool. **$**

🐾 ☒ ☒ SC

Hawthorne

Motels/Motor Lodges

★ **EL CAPITAN RESORT CASINO.** *540 F St (89415). Phone 775/945-3321; toll-free 800/922-2311; fax 775/945-2193.* 103 rooms, 1-2 story. Pets accepted; fee. Check-out 1 pm. TV. Restaurant open 24 hours. Bar. Game room. Pool. Casino. **$**

D 🐾 ☒ ☒ ☒ ☒

★ **SAND & SAGE LODGE.** *1301 E Fifth (89415). Phone 775/945-3352; fax 775/945-3353.* 37 rooms, 2 story. Pets accepted, some restrictions. Check-out 11 am. TV; cable (premium). Pool. **$**

🐾 ☒ ☒

Las Vegas

Motel/Motor Lodge

★ **LA QUINTA INN.** *3970 Paradise Rd (89109). Phone 702/796-9000; toll-free 800/531-5900; fax 702/796-3537. www.laquinta.com.* 251 kitchen units, 3 story. Pets accepted, some restrictions. Complimentary continental breakfast. Check-out noon, check-in 3 pm. TV; cable (premium). In-room modem link. Laundry services. Pool. Free airport transportation. **$**

D 🐾 ☒ ☒ SC

Extended Stay

★ ★ **RESIDENCE INN BY MARRIOTT.** *370 Hughes Center Dr (89109). Phone 702/650-0040; fax 702/650-5510. www.residenceinn.com.* Guests will enjoy the spacious guest rooms and the convenient location near the

Las Vegas Strip. 256 rooms, 11 story. Pets accepted, some restrictions; fee. Complimentary continental breakfast. Check-out noon, check-in 4 pm. TV; cable (premium). In-room modem link. In-house fitness room. Outdoor pool; whirlpool. **$**

🐾 ≋ 🚶 ⛷

Hotel

★ ★ **FLAMINGO LAS VEGAS.** *3555 Las Vegas Blvd S (89109). Phone 702/733-3111; toll-free 800/308-8899; fax 702/733-3528. www.flamingolasvegas.com.* This large, self-contained casino resort predates the recent explosion of megahotels on the Strip while bridging the old and new Vegas charm. Amenities include a water sports area and the Radio City Music Hall Review, featuring the Rockettes. 3,655 rooms, 28 story. Pets accepted, some restrictions. Check-out noon, check-in 3 pm. TV; cable (premium). In-room modem link. Restaurant, bar. In-house fitness room; spa, sauna, steam room. Outdoor pool. Outdoor tennis. Valet parking. Business center. Casino. **$**

D 🐾 ⛷ ≋ 🚶 ⛷ SC ⛷

★ ★ ★ ★ **FOUR SEASONS HOTEL LAS VEGAS.** *3960 Las Vegas Blvd S (89119). Phone 702/632-5000; toll-free 877/632-5000; fax 702/632-5195. www.fourseasons.com.* The Four Seasons Hotel is a palatial refuge in glittering Las Vegas. Located on the southern tip of the famous strip, the Four Seasons remains close to the attractions of this dynamic city while providing a welcome respite from the hustle and bustle. This non-gaming hotel occupies the 35th through 39th floors of the Mandalay Bay Resort tower, yet it is distinctively Four Seasons with its sumptuous décor and inimitable service. Guests surrender to plush furnishings in stylish rooms, and floor-to-ceiling windows showcase exhilarating views of the strip's neon lights or the stark beauty of the Nevada desert. Steak lovers rejoice at Charlie Palmer Steak, while the sun-filled Verandah offers a casual dining alternative. The glorious pool is a lush oasis with its swaying palm trees and attentive poolside service. Lucky visitors retreat to the sublime spa, where JAMU Asian techniques soothe the weary. 424 rooms, 5 story. Pets accepted, some restrictions. Check-out noon, check-in 3 pm. TV; cable (premium). Room service 24 hours. Restaurant, bar. Outdoor pool; children's pool. Concierge. **$$**

D 🐾 ≋ SC

Laughlin

Hotel

★ ★ **DON LAUGHLIN'S RIVERSIDE HOTEL.** *1650 Casino Dr (89029). Phone 702/298-2535; fax 702/298-2695. www.riversideresort.com.* 1,404 rooms, 28 story.

Pets accepted, some restrictions; fee. Check-out 11 am, check-in 3 pm. TV. In-room modem link. Restaurant open 24 hours. Bar; entertainment. Outdoor pool. Boat dockage on Colorado River; RV spaces. Free airport transportation. Business center. Casino. Movie theaters. Bus depot on premises. **$**

D 🐾 ⛵ 🚤 ≋ ⛷ 🚶

Reno

Motels/Motor Lodges

★ **LA QUINTA INN.** *4001 Market St (89502). Phone 775/348-6100; fax 775/348-8794. www.laquinta.com.* 130 rooms, 2 story. Pets accepted, some restrictions. Complimentary continental breakfast. Check-out noon. TV. Pool. Free airport transportation. **$**

D 🐾 ≋ 🛫 ⛷

★ **RODEWAY INN.** *2050 Market St (89502). Phone 775/786-2500; toll-free 800/648-3800; fax 775/786-3884. www.choicehotels.com.* 211 rooms, 4 story. Pets accepted; fee. Complimentary continental breakfast. Check-out noon. TV. Laundry services. Sauna. Pool; whirlpool. Airport, casino transportation. **$$**

D 🐾 ≋ ⛷

★ **VAGABOND INN.** *3131 S Virginia St (89502). Phone 775/825-7134; fax 775/825-3096. www.vagabondinns.com.* 129 rooms, 2 story. Pets accepted; fee. Complimentary continental breakfast. Check-out 11 am. TV; cable (premium). Health club privileges. Pool. Airport, train station, bus depot transportation. **$**

🐾 ≋ 🚶 ⛷ ⛷

Hotels

★ ★ ★ **ATLANTIS CASINO RESORT.** *3800 S Virginia St (89502). Phone 775/825-4700; fax 775/826-7860. www.atlantiscasino.com.* Experience the mystery of a sunken city at this glass-enclosed casino. Full health spa facilities, 9-foot-ceiling guest rooms, several restaurants, and the Entertainment Fun Center with over 100 casino games add to the gaming experience. 973 rooms, 27 story. Pets accepted, some restrictions; fee. Check-out 11 am. TV. Restaurant, bar; entertainment. Spa. Pool; whirlpool. Free valet parking. Free airport transportation. Casino. **$**

D 🐾 ≋ ⛷ ⛷

★ ★ ★ **HARRAH'S HOTEL RENO.** *219 N Center St (89504). Phone 775/786-3232; toll-free 800/427-7247; fax 775/788-3274. www.harrahs.com.* 952 rooms, 26 story. Pets accepted, some restrictions. Check-out noon. TV. In-room modem link. Restaurant open 24 hours. Bar; entertainment. Massage, sauna, steam room. Game room.

Pool; whirlpool. Covered parking; valet. Free airport transportation. Business center. Casino. **$**

Stateline

Hotel

★ ★ ★ **HARRAH'S LAKE TAHOE.** *Hwy 50 (89449). Phone 775/588-6611; toll-free 800/648-3773; fax 775/586-6607. www.harrahstahoe.com.* This hotel offers 18,000 square feet of function space and plenty of recreation options for leisure visitors. Shop at the Galleria, swim in the glass-domed pool, tan on the sun deck, or do the obvious at the casino. 532 rooms, 18 story. Pets accepted, some restrictions; fee. Check-out noon. TV; VCR available. Room service 24 hours. Restaurant, bar; entertainment. In-house fitness room; massage, sauna, steam room. Game room. Indoor pool; whirlpool; poolside service. Free covered valet parking. Concierge. Casino. Butler service in suites. **$**

Tonopah

Motels/Motor Lodges

★ ★ **BEST WESTERN HI-DESERT INN.** *320 Main St (89049). Phone 775/482-3511; toll-free 877/286-2208; fax 775/482-3300. www.bestwestern.com.* 62 rooms, 2 story. Pets accepted, some restrictions. Complimentary continental breakfast. Check-out 11 am. TV; cable (premium). Pool; whirlpool. **$**

★ **JIM BUTLER MOTEL.** *100 S Main St (89049). Phone 775/482-3577; toll-free 800/635-9455; fax 775/482-5240.* 24 rooms, 2 story. Pets accepted, some restrictions. Check-out 11 am. TV; cable (premium). **$**

★ **SILVER QUEEN MOTEL.** *255 Erie Main (89049). Phone 775/482-6291; toll-free 800/210-9218; fax 775/482-3190.* 85 rooms, 1-2 story. No elevator. Pets accepted. Check-out 11 am. TV; cable (premium), VCR available. Bar. Pool. **$**

Winnemucca

Motels/Motor Lodges

★ **BEST INN.** *125 E Winnemucca Blvd (89445). Phone toll-free 800/443-7777; fax 775/623-4722. www.bestinn.com.* 80 rooms, 3 story. No elevator. Pets accepted. Check-out noon. TV; cable (premium), VCR available. Sauna, steam room. Pool. **$**

★ **BEST WESTERN GOLD COUNTRY INN.** *921 W Winnemucca Blvd (89445). Phone 775/623-6999; toll-free 800/346-5306; fax 775/623-9190. www.bestwestern.com.* 71 rooms, 2 story. Pets accepted; fee. Check-out noon. TV; cable (premium). In-room modem link. Pool. Airport transportation. **$**

★ **DAYS INN.** *511 W Winnemucca Blvd (89445). Phone 775/623-3661; toll-free 800/548-0531; fax 775/623-4234. www.daysinn.com.* 50 rooms, 2 story. Pets accepted, some restrictions; fee. Check-out noon. TV; cable (premium). Pool. **$**

★ ★ **RED LION.** *741 W Winnemucca Blvd (89445). Phone 775/623-2565; toll-free 800/633-6435; fax 775/623-2527.* 105 rooms, 2 story. Pets accepted. Check-out noon. TV; cable (premium), VCR available. Restaurant open 24 hours. Bar. Game room. Pool. Airport transportation. Casino. **$**

Hotel

★ **WINNERS HOTEL & CASINO.** *185 W Winnemucca Blvd (89445). Phone 775/623-2511; toll-free 800/648-4770; fax 775/623-3976. www.winnerscasino.com.* 37 rooms, 2 story. Pets accepted; fee. Check-out 11 am. TV; cable (premium). Laundry services. **$**

New Hampshire

Colebrook

Motel/Motor Lodge

★ **NORTHERN COMFORT MOTEL.** *RR 1 (03576). Phone 603/237-4440. www.northerncomfortmotel.com.* 19 rooms. S, D $56-$68; each additional $8-$10. Pets accepted; fee. Complimentary continental breakfast June-Sept. Check-out 11 am. TV. In-house fitness room. Heated pool; whirlpool. Downhill, cross-country ski 12 miles.

Concord

Motel/Motor Lodge

★ **COMFORT INN.** *71 Hall St (03301). Phone 603/226-4100; fax 603/228-2106. www.comfortinn.com.* 100 rooms, 3 story. S $92-$165; D $99-$165; each additional $10; suites $199-$209; under 18 free. Pets accepted, some restrictions; fee. Complimentary continental breakfast. Check-out noon. TV. In-room modem link. Sauna. Game room. Indoor pool; whirlpool.

Dover

Motel/Motor Lodge

★ **DAYS INN.** *481 Central Ave (03820). Phone 603/742-0400; toll-free 800/329-7466; fax 603/742-7790. www.dover-durham-daysinn.com.* 50 rooms, 2 story, 13 kitchen suites. June-Oct: S, D $72-$99; each additional $5-$8; kitchen suites $85-$160; under 12 free; lower rates rest of year. Pets accepted. Check-out 11 am. Complimentary continental breakfast. TV. Pool; whirlpool.

Franconia

Motel/Motor Lodge

★ **GALE RIVER.** *1 Main St (03580). Phone toll-free 800/255-7989; fax 603/823-5280. www.galerivermotel.com.* 10 rooms. A/C in motel. Winter/spring $65-$75; summer $75-$85, foliage $85-$95; each additional $10; cottages $110-$120 (3-day minimum off season); cottages $725/week (summer); package plans, weekly rates (cottages); higher rates: weekends, fall foliage; lower rates rest of year. Pets accepted, some restrictions; fee. TV. Check-out 11 am. Heated pool; whirlpool. Downhill ski 4 miles. Lawn games.

B&B/Small Inns

★ **THE HORSE & HOUND INN.** *205 Wells Rd (03580). Phone 603/823-5501; toll-free 800/450-5501; fax 603/823-5501.* 8 rooms, 2 story. No A/C. S $75; D $90; under 6 free; ski plans; holidays (2-day minimum). Closed Apr. Pets accepted, some restrictions; fee. Complimentary full breakfast. Check-out 11 am, check-in 3-6 pm. TV; VCR in common room. Restaurant. Downhill ski 2 miles, cross-country ski on site. Secluded country inn near Cannon Mountain.

★ ★ **LOVETTS INN.** *1474 Profile Rd, Rte 18 (03580). Phone 603/823-7761; toll-free 800/356-3802; fax 603/823-8802. www.lovettsinn.com.* 6 rooms, 2 story. Some A/C. S $100-$150; D $140-$190; MAP available; package plans. Closed Apr. Pets accepted, some restrictions; fee. Check-out 11 am, check-in 2 pm. TV. Fireplaces in cottages. Restaurant, bar. Game room. Pool. Downhill ski 3 miles, cross-country ski on site. Lawn games.

Gorham

Motels/Motor Lodges

★ **GORHAM MOTOR INN.** *324 Main St (03581). Phone 603/466-3381; toll-free 800/445-0913; fax 603/752-2604. www.gorhammotorinn.com.* 39 rooms. S $58-$72; D $68-$84; each additional $6; higher rates fall foliage. Pets accepted, some restrictions; fee. Check-out 11 am. TV; cable (premium). Pool. Downhill, cross-country ski 8 miles.

★ ★ **ROYALTY INN.** *130 Main St (03581). Phone 603/466-3312; toll-free 800/437-3529; fax 603/466-5802. www.royaltyinn.com.* 90 rooms, 1-2 story. July-Labor Day, mid-Sept-Oct: S $66-$79; D $72-$86; each additional $6; kitchen units $82; lower rates rest of year. Pets accepted, some restrictions; fee. Check-out 11 am. TV; VCR available. Restaurant, bar. Health club privileges. In-house fitness room. Game room. Two pools, one indoor. Downhill ski 9 miles, cross-country ski 7 miles.

B&B/Small Inn

★ ★ ★ **PHILBROOK FARM INN.** *881 North Rd (03581). Phone 603/466-3831. www.philbrookfarminn .com.* The fifth generation of Philbrooks now runs this historic inn, set on 900 acres of forested property bordered by the Androscoggin River. Built in 1861, the building has been modernized without sacrificing any of the original charm. 18 rooms, 3 story. No A/C. No elevator, no room phones. Closed Oct 31-Dec 25; also Apr. Pets accepted. Check-out 10 am, check-in after noon. Full breakfast. Dining room. Pool. Downhill ski 15 miles, cross-country ski on site. Lawn games. **$**

Hampton Beach

Hotel

★ ★ **HAMPTON FALLS INN.** *11 Lafayette Rd (03844). Phone 603/926-9545; toll-free 800/356-1729; fax 603/926-4155. www.hamptonfallsinn.com.* 47 rooms, 3 story. Mid-June-mid-Oct: S, D $59-$169; each additional $10; suites $129; under 12 free; weekly, weekend, holiday rates (2-day minimum weekends, holidays); lower rates rest of year. Pets accepted, some restrictions; fee. Check-out 11 am. TV; VCR available. Restaurant. Health club privileges. Game room. Indoor pool; whirlpool.

Hanover

Motel/Motor Lodge

★ ★ ★ **HANOVER INN.** *Main St and Wheelock St (03755). Phone 603/643-4300; toll-free 800/443-7024; fax 603/646-3744. www.hanoverinn.com.* This inn is located just minutes from Dartmouth College. The guest rooms are decorated with a colonial motif, and guests have access to athletic facilities at the school. 92 rooms, 5 story. D $257-$307. Pets accepted, some restrictions; fee. Check-out noon. TV; VCR available. Restaurant, bar. Health club privileges, in-house fitness room; sauna. Covered parking $5; free valet parking. Free airport transportation. Georgian-style brick structure owned by the college; used as a guest house since 1780.

Resort

★ **LOCH LYME LODGE.** *70 Orford Rd, Rte l0 (03768). Phone 603/795-2141; toll-free 800/423-2141; fax 603/* 795-2141. www.lochlymelodge.com. 12 kitchen units. No A/C. No room phones. S, D $52-$97; cottages $575-$850; under 4 free; MAP available. Cottages closed Sept-May. Pets accepted, some restrictions. Check-out 10 am, check-in 2 pm. Downhill ski 4 miles, cross-country ski 10 miles. Lawn games.

B&B/Small Inn

★ ★ ★ **DOWD'S COUNTRY INN.** *On the Common (03768). Phone 603/795-4712; toll-free 800/482-4712; fax 603/795-4220. www.dowdscountryinn.com.* This charming New England inn is located just 10 miles north of Dartmouth College. Close to the Lyme Commons, this property is surrounded by trees and provides a wonderful place to relax. 23 rooms, 2 story. Pets accepted, some restrictions; fee. Complimentary full breakfast. Check-out 11 am, check-in 3 pm. TV in common room. In-room modem link. Downhill ski 2 miles. Built in 1780. Totally nonsmoking. **$$**

Jackson

B&B/Small Inn

★ ★ **DANA PLACE INN.** *Pinkham Notch, Rte 16 (03846). Phone 603/383-6822; toll-free 800/537-9276; fax 603/383-6022. www.danaplace.com.* 30 rooms, 2 story, 5 suites. Dec-Feb, July-Oct: D $225; suites $250; each additional $50; children $20; under 17 free; lower rates rest of year. Pets accepted. Complimentary full breakfast. TV; cable (premium). Restaurant, bar. Indoor pool; children's pool; whirlpool. Golf. Outdoor tennis. Downhill skiing. Hiking trail. Business center.

Keene

Motel/Motor Lodge

★ ★ **BEST WESTERN SOVEREIGN HOTEL.** *401 Winchester St (03431). Phone 603/357-3038; toll-free 800/528-1234; fax 603/357-4776. www.bwkeene.com.* 131 rooms, 2 story. S $69-$150; D $79-$175; each additional $10; studio rooms $90; under 18 free. Pets accepted; fee. Complimentary full breakfast. Check-out noon. TV. In-room modem link. Restaurant, bar; entertainment. Game room. Indoor pool.

Littleton

Motel/Motor Lodge

★ ★ **EASTGATE MOTOR INN.** *335 Cottage St (03561). Phone 603/444-3971; toll-free 866/640-3561. www.eastgatemotorinn.com.* 55 rooms. S $44-$74; D $50-$80; each additional $7; under 6 free. Pets accepted, some restrictions. Complimentary continental breakfast. Check-out 11 am. TV; cable (premium). Restaurant, bar. Heated pool; children's pool. Downhill ski 7 miles, cross-country ski 6 miles. Lawn games.

Manchester

Motels/Motor Lodges

★ **COMFORT INN.** *298 Queen City Ave (03102). Phone 603/668-2600. www.comfortinn.com.* 100 rooms, 5 story. D $75-$350; each additional $5; suites $135-$250; under 18 free; higher rates some weekends. Pets accepted, some restrictions. Complimentary continental breakfast. Check-out 11 am. TV; cable (premium). In-room modem link. Laundry services. In-house fitness room; sauna. Indoor pool. Free airport transportation.

★ **ECONO LODGE.** *75 W Hancock St (03102). Phone 603/624-0111; toll-free 800/553-2666; fax 603/623 0268. www.econolodge.com.* 120 rooms, 5 story. D $60-$70; each additional $5; under 18 free; weekly, monthly rates. Pets accepted; fee. Complimentary continental breakfast. Check-out 11 am. TV. Laundry services.

Meredith

Motel/Motor Lodge

★ **MEADOWS LAKESIDE LODGING.** *Rte 25 (03226). Phone 603/253-4347; fax 603/253-6171.* 35 rooms, 4 story. Some room phones. June-Sept: S, D $89-$155; each additional $20; kitchen units $120; under 4 free; weekly rates; lower rates May, Oct. Closed rest of year. Pets accepted, some restrictions. Check-out 11 am. TV; VCR available (movies).

Nashua

Motels/Motor Lodges

★ ★ **HOLIDAY INN.** *9 Northeastern Blvd (03062). Phone 603/888-1551; toll-free 888/801-5661; fax 603/888-7193. www.holiday-inn.com.* 208 rooms, 24 suites, 3-4 story. May-Nov: S, D $79-$119; each additional $4; suites $99-$129; under 19 free; package plans; lower rates rest of year. Pets accepted; fee. Check-out noon. TV; cable (premium), VCR available. Laundry services. Restaurant, bar; entertainment. Room service. In-house fitness room. Pool.

★ **RED ROOF INN.** *77 Spit Brook Rd (03060). Phone 603/888-1893; fax 603/888-5889. www.redroof.com.* 115 rooms, 3 story. D $49-$79; under 19 free. Pets accepted. Check-out noon. TV; cable (premium).

Hotel

★ ★ ★ **MARRIOTT NASHUA.** *2200 Southwood Dr (03063). Phone 603/880-9100; toll-free 800/362-0962; fax 603/886-9489. www.marriott.com.* Fully renovated in 1997, this medium-sized hotel is close to the high-tech industrial corridor Czechoslovakian chandeliers and Oriental objets d'art accent the lobby. 241 rooms, 4 story. Mar-mid-Sept: S, D $79-$139; weekend rates; higher rates mid-Sept-Nov; lower rates rest of year. Pets accepted, some restrictions. Check-out 1 pm. TV; cable (premium). In-room modem link. Restaurant, bar; entertainment. In-house fitness room. Indoor pool; whirlpool. Lawn games. Airport transportation. Business center. Concierge. Luxury level.

Extended Stay

★ ★ **RESIDENCE INN BY MARRIOTT.** *246 Daniel Webster Hwy (03054). Phone 603/424-8100; fax 603/424-3128. www.residenceinn.com.* 129 rooms, 2 story. D $119-$179. Pets accepted, some restrictions; fee. Complimentary continental breakfast. Check-out noon. TV; cable (premium). In-room modem link. Health club privileges. Pool; whirlpool. Sport court.

North Conway

Motel/Motor Lodge

★ **SWISS CHALETS VILLAGE INN.** *Rte 16A (03845). Phone 603/356-2232; toll-free 800/831-2727; fax 603/356-7331. www.swisschaletsvillage.com.* 42 rooms, 1-3 story. No elevator. S $69-$139; D $79-$169; each additional $10; suites $109-$179; under 13 free; ski plans; higher rates fall foliage. Pets accepted; fee. Complimentary continental breakfast. Check-out 11 am. TV. Some fireplaces. Game room. Downhill ski 4 miles, cross-country ski on site. Rooms in Swiss chalet-style buildings; on 12 acres.

Plymouth

Motel/Motor Lodge

★ **BEST INN.** *304 Main St (03264). Phone 603/536-2330; toll-free 800/237-8466; fax 603/536-2686. www.bestinn.com.* 38 rooms, 2 story. S $58-$79; D $68-$89; each additional $10; suite $90; family rates; ski, golf, bicycle plans. Pets accepted. Complimentary continental breakfast. Check-out 11 am. TV; VCR available. In-room modem link. Laundry services. Pool. Downhill, cross-country ski 15 miles.

Sunapee

B&B/Small Inn

★ ★ **DEXTERS INN & TENNIS CLUB.** *258 Stagecoach Rd (03782). Phone 603/763-5571; toll-free 800/232-5571. www.dextersnh.com.* 2 story. No room phones. Pets accepted, some restrictions; fee. Complimentary full breakfast. Check-out 11 am, check-in 3 pm. TV in lobby. Pool. Outdoor tennis. Lawn games. On a 20-acre estate.

Wolfeboro

Motel/Motor Lodge

★ **LAKE MOTEL.** *280 S Main St (03894). Phone 603/569-1100; toll-free 888/569-1110; fax 603/569-1258. www.thelakemotel.com.* 29 rooms, 5 kitchen units. July-Labor Day: S, D $88-$104; each additional $6; kitchen units for 2, $630/week; each additional $8; lower rates mid-May-June and after Labor Day-mid-Oct. Closed rest of year. Pets accepted, some restrictions. Check-out 11 am. TV. Tennis. Lawn games.

New Jersey

Bernardsville

Hotel

★ ★ ★ **SOMERSET HILLS HOTEL.** *200 Liberty Corner Rd (07059). Phone 908/647-6700; fax 908/647-8053. www.shh.com.* This hotel combines the service of a country inn with the facilities, entertainment, and accommodations expected from a large hotel. 111 rooms, 4 story. S $170; D $180; each additional $10; suites $250-$310; kitchens. Pets accepted, some restrictions; fee. Check-out noon. TV; cable (premium). In-room modem link. Restaurant, bar. In-house fitness room. Pool; poolside service. Business center. Concierge. Nestled in the Watchung Mountains near the crossroads of historical Liberty Corner.

Cape May

Resort

★ ★ **MARQUIS DE LAFAYETTE HOTEL.** *501 Beach Ave (08204). Phone 609/884 3500; fax 609/884-0669. www.marquiscapemay.com.* 43 kitchen units, 6 story. July-Labor Day: S $99-$249; $129-$279; each additional $18; kitchen units $259-$339; under 8 free; weekend rates; lower rates rest of year. Pets accepted; fee. Complimentary full breakfast. Check-out 1 pm. TV. Restaurant, bar; entertainment. Pool; poolside service.

Cherry Hill

Motel/Motor Lodge

★ ★ **HOLIDAY INN.** *Rte 70 and Sayer Ave (08034). Phone 856/663-5300; toll-free 800/465-4329; fax 856/662-2913. www.holiday-inn.com.* 186 rooms, 6 story. S, D $99-$109; each additional $8; under 19 free; weekend rates. Pets accepted, some restrictions. Check-out noon. TV; cable (premium), VCR available. In-room modem link. Restaurant, bar. In-house fitness room; sauna. Indoor pool; outdoor pool; children's pool. Business center.

Eatontown

Motel/Motor Lodge

★ **RED ROOF INN.** *11 Centre Plaza (07724). Phone 732/389-4646; toll-free 800/843-7663; fax 732/389-4509. www.redroof.com.* 119 rooms, 3 story. May-Labor Day: S, D $85-$89; each additional $7; under 18 free; lower rates rest of year. Pets accepted, some restrictions. Check-out noon. TV; cable (premium).

Flemington

Motel/Motor Lodge

★ ★ **RAMADA INN.** *250 Rte 202, at NJ 31 (08822). Phone 908/782-7472; fax 908/782-1975. www.ramada.com.* 104 rooms, 24 kitchen units, 2 story. S $95, D $103; each additional $10; suites $125; kitchen units $114. Pets accepted, some restrictions; fee. Check-out noon. TV; cable (premium). In-room modem link. Restaurant, bar. Pool.

Fort Lee

Hotel

★ ★ ★ **RADISSON HOTEL ENGLEWOOD.** *401 S Van Brunt St (07631). Phone 201/871-2020; fax 201/871-6904. www.radisson.com.* This hotel offers quality service and access to an abundance of shopping in New York City. 192 rooms, 9 story. Late Nov-mid-Dec: S, D $145-$165; suites $185-$275; weekend rates; lower rates rest of year. Pets accepted, some restrictions; fee. Check-out noon. TV; cable (premium), VCR available. Restaurant, bar. In-house fitness room. Indoor pool. Business center. Concierge. Luxury level.

Freehold

Hotel

★ ★ **FREEHOLD GARDENS HOTEL.** *50 Gibson Place (07728). Phone 732/780-3870; fax 732/780-8725. www.freeholdgardens.com.* 114 rooms, 5 story. S, D $69-$90; each additional $10; under 13 free; higher rates late May-early Sept. Pets accepted, some restrictions.

Complimentary continental breakfast. Check-out noon. TV. Restaurant; entertainment Fri, Sat. Health club privileges. Pool.

Matawan

Motel/Motor Lodge

★ **WELLESLEY INN.** *3215 NJ 35 (07730). Phone 732/888-2800; toll-free 800/444-8888; fax 732/888-2902. www.wellesleyinnandsuites.com.* 89 rooms, 3 story. S $63-$129; D $65-$129; each additional $5; under 18 free. Pets accepted, some restrictions; fee. Complimentary continental breakfast. Check-out 11 am. TV; cable (premium). Health club privileges.

Parsippany

Hotel

★ ★ **HILTON PARSIPPANY.** *1 Hilton Ct (07054). Phone 973/267-7373; toll-free 800/774-1500; fax 973/984-2896. www.hilton.com.* In a prime location, this hotel is only 25 minutes from the Newark International Airport, 3 miles from New Jersey, and 27 miles from New York. 516 rooms, 6 story. D $229-$239; each additional $20; family, weekend rates. Pets accepted, some restrictions; fee. Check-out noon, check-in 3 pm. TV; cable (premium), VCR available. In-room modem link. Restaurant, bar; entertainment. Room service. In-house fitness room. Indoor/outdoor pool; whirlpool. Outdoor tennis. Airport transportation. Business center.

Plainfield

Motel/Motor Lodge

★ ★ **HOLIDAY INN.** *4701 Stelton Rd (07080). Phone 908/753-5500; toll-free 877/214-6161; fax 908/753-5500. www.holiday-inn.com.* 173 rooms, 4 story. S, D $149; under 12 free; weekend rates. Pets accepted. Check-out 1 pm. TV; cable (premium). In-room modem link. Restaurant, bar. Room service. In-house fitness room; sauna. Indoor pool; whirlpool.

Princeton

Hotel

★ ★ **NASSAU INN.** *10 Palmer Sq (08542). Phone 609/921-7500; toll-free 800/862-7728; fax 609/921-9385. www.nassauinn.com.* Visitors to Princeton University are lucky to have this inn in such a convenient downtown location. Red armchairs, oriental rugs, and beamed ceilings create a rustic country charm, and the nightly, fresh-baked chocolate chip cookies are a welcome treat. 216 rooms, 5 story. S $139-$189; D $159-$209; each additional $20; suites $325-$780; under 13 free. Pets accepted; fee. Check-out noon. TV; cable (premium). In-room modem link. Colonial atmosphere, beamed ceilings, fireplaces in public rooms. Restaurant, bar; entertainment Fri, Sat. In-house fitness room. Business center.

B&B/Small Inn

★ ★ **PEACOCK INN.** *20 Bayard Ln (08540). Phone 609/924-1707; fax 609/924-0788. www.peacockinn.com.* 17 rooms, 3 story. Pets accepted. Complimentary breakfast buffet. Check-out 11 am, check-in 2 pm. TV; cable (premium). Dining room. Historic late Georgian colonial house, built in 1775 and relocated from Nassau St to its present site. Two blocks from the Princeton University campus. **$$**

Ramsey

Hotels

★ ★ ★ **SHERATON CROSSROADS HOTEL.** *One International Blvd, Rte 17 N (07495). Phone 201/529-1660; fax 201/529-4709. www.sheraton.com.* Choose a room with a garden or a fountain view. 251 rooms, 22 story. D $229; each additional $10; under 18 free; weekend rates. Pets accepted, some restrictions. Check-out noon, check-in 3 pm. TV; cable (premium). Restaurant, bar; entertainment. In-house fitness room; sauna. Indoor pool. Outdoor tennis. Business center. Concierge. Luxury level.

★ ★ **WELLESLEY INN.** *946 NJ 17N (07446). Phone 201/934-9250; toll-free 800/444-8888; fax 201/934-9719. www.wellesleyinnandsuites.com.* 89 rooms, 3 story. D $89-$109; each additional $5; under 18 free; weekend, monthly rates. Pets accepted, some restrictions. Complimentary continental breakfast. Check-out 11 am, check-in 2 pm. TV; cable (premium). Health club privileges.

Rutherford

Hotel

★ ★ ★ **SHERATON MEADOWLANDS HOTEL AND CONFERENCE CENTER.** *2 Meadowlands Plaza (07073). Phone 201/896-0500; fax 201/896-9696. www.sheraton.com.* This hotel is only minutes from Manhattan and is perfect for business or leisure travelers. With its conference facilities and ballroom, it is suited for large groups. A restaurant, sports pub, and lounge are available along with recreational facilities. 443 rooms, 21 story. D $99-$265; each additional $20; under 18 free; weekend rates. Pets accepted; fee. Check-out noon, check-in 3 pm. TV; cable (premium), VCR available. In-room modem link. Restaurant, bar. In-house fitness room; sauna. Indoor pool; whirlpool; poolside service. Business center. Concierge.

D 🐾 ≈ 🏃 🚶

Toms River

Motel/Motor Lodge

★ ★ **HOWARD JOHNSON.** *955 Hooper Ave (08753). Phone 732/244-1000; fax 732/505-3194. www.tomsriverhojos.com.* 96 rooms, 2 story. S $60-$199; D $70-$229; each additional $10; under 18 free; higher rates some holidays. Pets accepted, some restrictions; fee. Check-out noon. TV; VCR available (movies). In-room modem link. Restaurant, bar. Indoor/outdoor pool.

D 🐾 ≈ 🚫 SC

Trenton

Motel/Motor Lodge

★ ★ **HOWARD JOHNSON.** *Rte 1 S (08648). Phone 609/896-1100; toll-free 800/654-2000; fax 609/895-1325. www.hojo.com.* 104 rooms, 2 story. S $62.50-$88; D $68.50-$110; each additional $10; under 18 free; higher rates special events. Pets accepted; fee. Complimentary continental breakfast. Check-out noon. TV; cable (premium). In-room modem link. Restaurant open 24 hours. Pool.

D 🐾 ≈ 🚫 SC

Wayne

Motel/Motor Lodge

★ **WELLESLEY INN.** *1850 NJ 23 and Ratzer Rd (07470). Phone 973/696-8050; toll-free 800/444-8888; fax 973/696-8050. www.wellesleyonline.com.* 146 rooms, 2 story. D $94-$104; each additional $10; under 16 free. Pets accepted, some restrictions. Complimentary continental breakfast. Check-out noon, check-in 2 pm. TV; cable (premium). In-room modem link. Laundry services. Pool.

D 🐾 ≈ 🚫 SC

New Mexico

Alamogordo

Motels/Motor Lodges

★ **BEST WESTERN DESERT AIRE HOTEL.** *1021 S White Sands Blvd (88310). Phone 505/437-2110; fax 505/437-1898. www.bestwestern.com.* 100 rooms, 2 story. Pets accepted; fee. Complimentary continental breakfast. Check-out noon. TV. Sauna. Game room. Pool; whirlpool. **$**

D 🐾 🏊 ⊠

★ **SATELLITE INN.** *2224 N White Sands Blvd (88310). Phone 505/437-8454; toll-free 800/221-7690. www.satelliteinn.com.* 40 rooms, 1-2 story. Pets accepted. Check-out noon. TV; cable (premium), VCR available (movies). Pool. **$**

🐾 🏊 ⊠

Albuquerque

Motels/Motor Lodges

★★ **BEST WESTERN RIO RANCHO INN AND CONFERENCE CENTER.** *1465 Rio Rancho Blvd (87124). Phone 505/892-1700; toll-free 800/658-9558; fax 505/892-4628. www.innatriorancho.com.* 121 rooms. Pets accepted; fee. Check-out 11 am. TV; cable (premium). In-room modem link. Restaurant, bar; entertainment. Room service. In-house fitness room. Pool; whirlpool; poolside service. Downhill, cross-country ski 20 miles. Lawn games. Free airport transportation. **$**

🐾 ➤ 🏊 🎿 ✈ ⊠

★ **COMFORT INN.** *13031 Central Ave NE (87123). Phone 505/294-1800; toll-free 800/748-3278; fax 505/293-1088. www.comfortinn.com.* 122 rooms, 2 story. Pets accepted; fee. Complimentary full breakfast. Check-out noon. TV; cable (premium). Restaurant. Pool; whirlpools. Downhill ski 9 miles. **$**

D 🐾 ➤ 🏊 ⊠ SC

★ **DAYS INN.** *6031 Iliff Rd NW (87123). Phone 505/836-3297; toll-free 800/329-7466; fax 505/836-1214. www.daysinn.com.* 80 rooms, 2 story. Pets accepted; fee. Complimentary continental breakfast. Check-out 11 am. TV; cable (premium). Laundry services. Sauna. Indoor pool; whirlpool. Downhill, cross-country ski 10 miles. **$**

D 🐾 ➤ 🏊 ⊠ SC

★ **HAMPTON INN.** *5101 Ellison NE (87109). Phone 505/344-1555; toll-free 800/426-7866; fax 505/345-2216. www.hamptoninn.com.* 125 rooms, 3 story. Pets accepted. Complimentary continental breakfast. Check-out noon. TV; cable (premium). Coin laundry. Pool. **$**

D 🐾 🏊 ⊠ SC

★★★ **HOLIDAY INN.** *2020 Menaul NE (87107). Phone 505/884-2511; fax 505/884-5720. www.holiday-inn.com.* Parents can play virtual golf at the Sandia Springs golf course lounge, which features two full-swing golf simulators, while the kids play in the indoor pool and hot tub. 360 rooms, 4-5 story. Pets accepted; fee. Check-out noon. TV; cable (premium). Restaurant, bar. Room service. In-house fitness room; sauna. Pool; whirlpool; poolside service. Downhill ski 15 miles. Free airport transportation. **$**

D 🐾 ➤ 🏊 🎿 ✈ ⊠

★ **HOLIDAY INN EXPRESS.** *10330 Hotel Ave NE (87123). Phone 505/275-8900; fax 505/275-6000. www.holiday-inn.com.* 104 rooms, 2 story. Pets accepted; fee. Complimentary continental breakfast. Check-out noon. TV; cable (premium), VCR available. In-room modem link. Restaurant. Room service. In-house fitness room; sauna. Indoor pool; whirlpool. Downhill, cross-country ski 15 miles. **$**

D 🐾 ➤ 🏊 🎿 ⊠

★ **LA QUINTA INN.** *2116 Yale Blvd SE (87106). Phone 505/243-5500; toll-free 800/531-5900; fax 505/247-8288. www.laquinta.com.* 105 rooms, 3 story. Pets accepted, some restrictions. Check-out noon. TV; cable (premium). Laundry services. Pool. Downhill ski 20 miles. Free airport transportation. **$**

D 🐾 ➤ 🏊 ✈ ⊠ SC

★★ **PLAZA INN.** *900 Medical Arts NE (87102). Phone 505/243-5693; toll-free 800/237-1307; fax 505/843-6229. www.plazainnabq.com.* 120 rooms, 5 story. Pets accepted; fee. Check-out noon. TV. Laundry services. Restaurant, bar. In-house fitness room. Health club privileges. Indoor pool; whirlpools. Downhill ski 14 miles. Free airport, train station, bus depot transportation. **$**

D 🐾 ➤ 🏊 🎿 ⊠

★★ **RAMADA INN.** *25 Hotel Cir NE (87123). Phone 505/271-1000; toll-free 888/298-2054; fax 505/291-9028. www.ramada.com.* 205 rooms, 2 story. Pets accepted, some restrictions; fee. Check-out noon. TV; cable (premium). Laundry services. Restaurant, bar. Room service. Pool. Downhill ski 10 miles. Free airport transportation. **$**

D 🐾 🏊 ➤ ✈ ⊠ SC

★ **TRAVELODGE.** *13139 Central Ave NE (87123). Phone 505/292-4878; fax 505/299-1822. www.travelodge.com.* 41 rooms, 2 story. Pets accepted, some restrictions; fee. Complimentary continental breakfast. Check-out 11 am. TV; cable (premium). Downhill, cross-country ski 8 miles. **$**

⬛🐾📶🖥

Hotel

★★★ **RADISSON INN ALBUQUERQUE AIRPORT.** *1901 University Blvd SE (87106). Phone 505/247-0512; fax 505/247-1063. www.radisson.com.* Located near the University of New Mexico, this recently redecorated hotel features a heated outdoor pool that is open year-round and a hot tub in the large Southwestern-style courtyard. 148 rooms, 2-3 story. Pets accepted; fee. Check-out noon. TV; cable (premium). In-room modem link. Restaurant, bar. Room service. Pool; whirlpool; poolside service. Downhill ski 20 miles. Free airport transportation. **$**

🐾📶🏊✈🖥

All Suite

★★ **AMBERLEY SUITES HOTEL.** *7620 Pan American Fwy NE (87109). Phone 505/823-1300; toll-free 800/333-9806; fax 505/823-2896. www.amberleysuite.com.* 170 rooms, 3 story. Pets accepted, some restrictions; fee. Complimentary full breakfast. Check-out noon. TV; cable (premium). In-room modem link. Restaurant, bar. In-house fitness room; sauna. Game room. Pool; whirlpool. Downhill ski 5 miles. Free airport transportation. Business center. Courtyard; fountain. **$**

⬛🐾📶🏊🏃✈🖥 SC 🚶

B&B/Small Inns

★★★ **BRITTANIA W.E. MAUGER ESTATE B&B.** *701 Roma Ave NW (87102). Phone 505/242-8755; toll-free 800/719-9189; fax 505/842-8835. www.maugerbb.com.* "Mi Casa es Su Casa!" is the mantra of this warm bed-and-breakfast. The 8 suites in this restored Queen Anne house (1987) offer fresh flowers, antique furniture, private baths, data ports with ISDN Internet connections, and air conditioning. Centrally located near the business district and Old Town. 10 rooms, shower only, 3 story. Pets accepted, some restrictions; fee. Complimentary full breakfast. Check-out 11 am, check-in 4-6 pm. TV; cable (premium), VCR available. In-room modem link. Downhill, cross-country ski 12 miles. Sun porch. **$**

🐾📶🖥

★★★ **CASA DEL GRANJERO B&B.** *414C De Baca Ln NW (87114). Phone 505/897-4144; toll-free*

800/701-4144; fax 505/897-9788. www.innewmexico.com. This 1880 bed-and-breakfast fits its Spanish name, which translates as "farmer's house." Guests will enjoy the Old West décor, huge sculpted adobe fireplace, and Indian artifacts. Suites feature hand-painted murals, kiva fireplaces, and two-headed showers. 7 rooms. No room phones. Pets accepted, some restrictions; fee. Children of any age welcome. Complimentary full breakfast. Check-out 11 am, check-in 11 am-2 pm. TV in common room; VCR (movies). Sauna. Whirlpool. Downhill, cross-country ski 10 miles. Lawn games. Business center. Concierge service. Hacienda built in 1880; carved Mexican furniture. Totally nonsmoking. **$**

⬛🐾📶🖥🚶

★★★ **LA HACIENDA GRANDE.** *21 Baros Ln (87004). Phone 505/867-1887; toll-free 800/353-1887; fax 505/771-1436. www.lahaciendagrande.com.* Cathedral ceilings, beautiful views, and an open-air center courtyard grace this bed-and-breakfast. 6 rooms. Pets accepted. Complimentary full breakfast. Check-out 11 am, check-in 4-6 pm. TV; cable (premium), VCR available (movies). Downhill, cross-country ski 15 miles. Concierge. Spanish hacienda built in the 1750s. Totally nonsmoking. **$**

🐾📶🖥

Carlsbad

Motels/Motor Lodges

★★ **BEST WESTERN STEVENS INN.** *1829 S Canal St (88220). Phone 505/887-2851; toll-free 800/780-7234; fax 505/887-6338. www.bestwestern.com.* 202 rooms, 1-2 story. Pets accepted, some restrictions; fee. Check-out noon. TV; cable (premium), VCR (movies fee). Restaurant, bar; entertainment except Sun. Room service. Pool. Complimentary breakfast buffet. **$**

⬛🐾🏊🖥

★ **CONTINENTAL INN.** *3820 National Park Hwy (88220). Phone 505/887-0341; toll-free 877/887-0341; fax 505/885-1186.* 58 rooms, 2 story. Pets accepted. Check-out 11 am. TV; cable (premium). In-room modem link. Pool. **$**

🐾🏊🖥

★★★ **HOLIDAY INN.** *601 S Canal St (88220). Phone 505/885-8500; fax 505/887-5999. www.holiday-inn.com.* 100 rooms, 2 story. Pets accepted; fee. Check-out 11 am. TV; cable (premium), VCR available (movies). In-room modem link. Laundry services. Restaurant. Room service. In-house fitness room; sauna. Pool; whirlpool; poolside service. **$**

🐾🏊🏃🖥

Chama

Motel/Motor Lodge

★ **ELK HORN LODGE.** *HC 75 Box 45 (87520). Phone 505/756-2105; toll-free 800/532-8874; fax 505/756-2638. www.elkhornlodge.net.* 23 rooms, 1-2 story, 11 cabins. Pets accepted, some restrictions; fee. Check-out 11 am. TV. Restaurant. Cross-country ski 5 miles. Porches on cottages. On Chama River. **$**

Cloudcroft

Resort

★★★ **LODGE AT CLOUDCROFT.** *1 Corona Pl (88317). Phone 505/682-2566; toll-free 800/395-6343; fax 505/682-2715. www.thelodge-nm.com.* 60 rooms, 3 story. No elevator. Pets accepted, some restrictions; fee. Check-out noon, check-in after 4 pm. TV; cable (premium), VCR available. Restaurant, bar; entertainment. Massage, sauna. Pool; whirlpool. 9-hole golf, putting green, pro shop. Downhill ski 2 miles, cross-country ski on site. Historic building (1899). **$**

Deming

Motels/Motor Lodges

★ **DAYS INN.** *1601 E Pine St (88030). Phone 505/546-8813; fax 505/546-7095. www.daysinn.com.* 57 rooms, 2 story. Pets accepted, some restrictions; fee. Complimentary continental breakfast. Check-out 11 am. TV; cable (premium). Pool. **$**

★ **GRAND MOTOR INN.** *1721 E Spruce St (88031). Phone 505/546-2632; fax 505/546-4446.* 62 rooms, 2 story. Pets accepted. Check-out noon. TV; cable (premium). Restaurant, bar. Room service. Pool; children's pool; poolside service. Free airport, train station, bus depot transportation. **$**

★★ **HOLIDAY INN.** *I-10 E exit 85 (88031). Phone 505/546-2661; toll-free 888/546-2661; fax 505/546-6308. www.holiday-inn.com.* 120 rooms, 2 story. Pets accepted. Check-out 11 am. TV; cable (premium). Coin laundry. Restaurant. Pool. Free airport, train station, bus depot transportation. **$**

Farmington

Motels/Motor Lodges

★★ **BEST WESTERN INN & SUITES.** *700 Scott Ave (87401). Phone 505/327-5221; toll-free 800/780-7234; fax 505/327-1565. www.bestwestern.com.* 194 rooms, 3 story. Pets accepted, some restrictions; fee. Check-out noon. TV; cable (premium), VCR available (movies). Restaurant, bar. Room service. In-house fitness room; sauna. Indoor pool; whirlpool; poolside service. Free airport transportation. **$**

★ **COMFORT INN.** *555 Scott Ave (87401). Phone 505/325-2626; fax 505/325-7675. www.comfortinn.com.* 60 rooms, 2 story. Pets accepted; fee. Complimentary continental breakfast. Check-out 11 am. TV; cable (premium). In-room modem link. Pool. **$**

★★ **HOLIDAY INN.** *600 E Broadway (87499). Phone 505/327-9811; toll-free 888/327-9812; fax 505/325-2288. www.holiday-inn.com.* 149 rooms, 2 story. Pets accepted; fee. Check-out noon. TV; cable (premium). Restaurant, bar. Room service. In-house fitness room; sauna. Pool; whirlpool. Free airport transportation. **$**

★ **LA QUINTA INN.** *675 Scott Ave (87401). Phone 505/327-4706; fax 505/325-6583. www.laquinta.com.* 106 rooms, 2 story. Pets accepted, some restrictions. Complimentary continental breakfast. Check-out noon. TV; cable (premium). Pool. **$**

Gallup

Motels/Motor Lodges

★★ **BEST WESTERN INN & SUITES.** *3009 W 66, I-40 (87301). Phone 505/722-2221; toll-free 800/780-7234; fax 505/722-7442. www.bestwestern.com.* 126 rooms, 2 story. Pets accepted, some restrictions; fee. Check-out noon. TV; cable (premium). Laundry services. Restaurant, bar. Room service. Sauna. Game room. Indoor pool; whirlpool. **$**

★ **DAYS INN.** *1603 W US 66 (87301). Phone 505/863-3891. www.daysinn.com.* 78 rooms, 2 story. Pets accepted, some restrictions; fee. Complimentary continental breakfast. Check-out 11 am. TV; cable (premium). Laundry services. Pool. **$**

★ ★ **EL RANCHO.** *1000 E US 66 (87301). Phone 505/ 863-9311; toll-free 800/543-6351; fax 505/722-5917.* 75 rooms. Pets accepted. Check-out noon. TV. Restaurant, bar. **$**

D 🐾 ≈

Grants

Motel/Motor Lodge

★ ★ **BEST WESTERN INN & SUITES.** *1501 E Santa Fe Ave (87020). Phone 505/287-7901; toll-free 800/780-7234; fax 505/285-5751. www.bestwestern.com.* 126 rooms, 2 story. Pets accepted, some restrictions; fee. Check-out noon. TV; cable (premium). Laundry services. Restaurant, bar. Room service. Sauna. Game room. Indoor pool; whirlpool. **$**

D 🐾 ≈ SC

Hobbs

Motels/Motor Lodges

★ ★ **HOWARD JOHNSON.** *501 N Marland Blvd (88240). Phone 505/397-3251; fax 505/393-3065. www.hojo.com.* 75 rooms, 2 story. Pets accepted; fee. Check-out 11 am. TV. In-room modem link. Laundry services. Restaurant, bar; entertainment. Room service. Pool. **$**

D 🐾 ≈

★ **TRAVELODGE.** *1301 E Broadway (88240). Phone 505/393-4101; toll-free 888/963-9663; fax 505/393-4101. www.travelodge.com.* 72 rooms. Pets accepted; fee. Complimentary full breakfast. Check-out noon. TV; cable (premium). In-room modem link. Pool. **$**

D 🐾 ≈

Las Cruces

Motels/Motor Lodges

★ ★ **BEST WESTERN MESILLA VALLEY INN.** *901 Avenida De Mesilla (88005). Phone 505/524-8603; toll-free 800/528-1234; fax 505/526-8437. www.bestwestern.com.* 167 rooms, 2 story. Pets accepted, some restrictions; fee. Check-out 11 am. TV. Laundry services. Restaurant, bar; entertainment. Room service. Pool; whirlpool. **$**

D 🐾 ≈

★ **DAYS INN.** *2600 S Valley Dr (88005). Phone 505/ 526-4441; toll-free 800/329-7466; fax 505/526-1980. www.daysinn.com.* 130 rooms, 2 story. Pets accepted; fee.

Check-out noon. TV; cable (premium). Laundry services. Restaurant, bar. Sauna. Indoor pool; poolside service. **$**

D 🐾 ≈ SC

★ **HAMPTON INN.** *755 Avenida De Mesilla (88005). Phone 505/526-8311; toll-free 888/846-6741; fax 505/527- 2015. www.hamptoninn.com.* 117 rooms, 2 story. Pets accepted. Complimentary continental breakfast. Check-out noon. TV; cable (premium). In-room modem link. Pool. **$**

D 🐾 ≈ SC

★ ★ **HOLIDAY INN.** *201 E University Ave (88005). Phone 505/526-4411; toll-free 800/465-4329; fax 505/524-0530. www.holiday-inn.com.* 114 rooms, 2 story. Pets accepted; fee. Check-out noon. TV; cable (premium). Restaurant, bar. Room service. In-house fitness room. Game room. Indoor pool; children's pool. Free airport transportation. Enclosed courtyard re-creates Mexican plaza. **$**

D 🐾 ≈ 🏋 ≈ SC

Hotel

★ ★ ★ **HILTON LAS CRUCES.** *705 S Telshor Blvd (88011). Phone 505/522-4300; toll-free 800/445-8667; fax 505/521-4707. www.hilton.com.* This hotel is minutes from New Mexico State University, Las Cruces International Airport, NASA, White Sands Missile Range, and Historic Old Mesilla. Activities such as golfing, bowling, horseback riding, and fishing are just minutes away. 203 rooms, 7 story. Pets accepted; fee. Check-out 1 pm. TV; VCR available (movies). In-room modem link. Restaurant, bar; entertainment. Room service. In-house fitness room. Health club privileges. Pool, whirlpool; poolside service. Free airport transportation. Overlooks valley. **$**

D 🐾 ≈ 🏋 ≈ SC

Resort

★ ★ **MESON DE MESILLA RESORT HOTEL.** *1803 Avenida Demesilla (88046). Phone 505/525- 9212; toll-free 800/732-6025; fax 505/527-4196. www. mesondemesilla.com.* 15 rooms, 2 story. Pets accepted; fee. Complimentary full breakfast. Check-out 11 am, check-in 1 pm. TV; cable (premium). Restaurant, bar. Pool. Scenic views. Totally nonsmoking. **$**

🐾 ≈

B&B/Small Inn

★ ★ **LUNDEEN INN OF THE ARTS.** *618 S Alameda Blvd (88005). Phone 505/526-3326; toll-free 888/526-3326; fax 505/647-1334. www.innofthearts.com.* 21 rooms, 2 story. Pets accepted, some restrictions; fee. Complimentary full breakfast. Check-out 11 am, check-in 4 pm. TV in sitting room; cable (premium), VCR available. Lawn games.

Built in 1890; antique furnishings. Art gallery; each room is named for an artist. **$**

Las Vegas

Motel/Motor Lodge

★ **BUDGET INN.** *1216 N Grand Ave (87701). Phone 505/425-9357.* 45 rooms, 2 story. Pets accepted, some restrictions; fee. Check-out 11 am. TV; cable (premium). **$**

Hotel

★ ★ **PLAZA HOTEL.** *230 Plaza (87701). Phone 505/425-3591; toll-free 800/328-1882; fax 505/425-9659. www.plazahotel-nm.com.* 37 rooms, 3 story. Pets accepted; fee. Check-out 11 am. TV; cable (premium). Restaurant, bar. Cross-country ski 5 miles. Historic hotel built in 1882 in the Victorian Italianate-bracketed style; interior renovated; period furnishings, antiques. **$**

Resort

★ ★ **INN ON THE SANTA FE TRAIL.** *1133 Grand Ave (87701). Phone 505/425-6791; toll-free 888/448-8438; fax 505/425-0417. www.innonthesantafetrail.com.* 42 rooms. Pets accepted; fee. Complimentary continental breakfast. Check-out 11 am. TV; cable (premium). In-room modem link. Pool; whirlpool. Lawn games. **$**

Los Alamos

Motel/Motor Lodge

★ ★ **BEST WESTERN HILLTOP HOUSE HOTEL.** *400 Trinity Dr at Central (87544). Phone 505/662-2441; toll-free 800/462-0936; fax 505/662-5913. www.vla.com/hilltophouse.* 98 rooms, 3 story. Pets accepted, some restrictions. Complimentary breakfast. Check-out 11 am. TV; cable (premium). In-room modem link. Laundry services. Restaurant. Room service. In-house fitness room; massage, sauna. Indoor pool; whirlpool. Downhill, cross-country ski 10 miles. Airport transportation. **$**

Portales

Motel/Motor Lodge

★ **ECONOMY INN.** *1613 W 2nd St (88130). Phone 505/356-6668; toll-free 800/901-9466.* 40 rooms. Pets accepted, some restrictions; fee. Complimentary continental breakfast. Check-out noon. TV; cable (premium), VCR available. In-room modem link. Pool. Airport transportation. Adjacent to Eastern New Mexico University. **$**

Raton

Motel/Motor Lodge

★ **BUDGET HOST INN.** *136 Canyon Dr (87740). Phone 505/445-3655; toll-free 800/283-4678; fax 505/445-3461. www.budgethost.com.* 27 rooms. Pets accepted, some restrictions; fee. Check-out 11 am. TV; cable (premium). Continental breakfast. **$**

Red River

Motel/Motor Lodge

★ **TERRACE TOWERS LODGE.** *712 W Main St (87558). Phone 505/754-2962; toll-free 800/695-6343; fax 505/754-2990. www.redriver.com/terracetowers.* 26 rooms, 2 story. Pets accepted. Check-out 10 am. TV; cable (premium), VCR available. Whirlpool. Downhill, cross-country ski 1/2 mile. View of valley and mountains. **$**

Roswell

Motels/Motor Lodges

★ ★ **BEST WESTERN SALLY PORT INN & SUITES.** *2000 N Main St (88201). Phone 505/622-6430; fax 505/623-7631. www.bestwestern.com.* 124 rooms, 2 story. Pets accepted, some restrictions; fee. Complimentary full breakfast. Check-out noon. TV; cable (premium). Laundry services. Restaurant, bar. Room service. In-house fitness room. Indoor pool; whirlpool. Outdoor tennis. Free airport transportation. **$**

★ **FRONTIER MOTEL.** *3010 N Main St (88201). Phone 505/622-1400; toll-free 800/678-1401; fax 505/622-1405. www.frontiermotelroswell.com.* 38 rooms. Pets accepted, some restrictions. Complimentary continental breakfast. Check-out 11 am. TV; cable (premium). Pool. **$**

⊡ ◪ ⊠

★ **RAMADA INN.** *2803 W 2nd St (88201). Phone 505/623-9440; fax 505/622-9708. www.ramada.com.* 61 rooms, 2 story. Pets accepted, some restrictions. Check-out noon. TV. Pool. **$**

⊡ ◪ ⊠ ⊠

Ruidoso

Motel/Motor Lodge

★ ★ **SWISS CHALET INN.** *1451 Mechem Dr (88355). Phone 505/258-3333; toll-free 800/477-9477; fax 505/258-5325. www.ruidoso.net/swisschalet.* 81 rooms, 2 story. Pets accepted, some restrictions; fee. Check-out noon. TV; cable (premium), VCR available (movies). Restaurant, bar. Room service. Sauna. Indoor pool; whirlpool. On a hilltop. **$**

◪ ⊠ ⊠ SC

Resort

★ **HIGH COUNTRY LODGE.** *Hwy 48 (88312). Phone 505/336-4321; toll-free 800/845-7265; fax 505/336-8205. www.ruidoso.net.* 32 rooms. No A/C. Pets accepted; fee. Check-out 11 am. TV; cable (premium). Fireplaces. In-house fitness room; sauna. Game room. Indoor pool; whirlpool. Outdoor tennis. Lawn games. **$**

◪ ⊁ ⊠ ⊼ ⊠

Santa Fe

Motels/Motor Lodges

★ **BEST WESTERN INN OF SANTA FE.** *3650 Cerrillos Rd (87505). Phone 505/438-3822; fax 505/438-3795. www.bestwestern.com.* 97 rooms, 3 story. Pets accepted, some restrictions. Complimentary continental breakfast. Check-out 11 am. TV; cable (premium). Laundry services. Indoor pool; whirlpool. Downhill, cross-country ski 20 miles. **$**

⊡ ◪ ⊠ ⊠ ⊼ ⊠

★ **LA QUINTA INN.** *4298 Cerrillos Road (87505). Phone 505/471-1142; fax 505/438-7219. www.laquinta.com.* 130 rooms, 3 story. Pets accepted; fee. Complimentary continental breakfast. Check-out noon. TV; cable (premium).

Laundry services. Pool. Downhill, cross-country ski 14 miles. **$**

⊡ ◪ ⊠ ⊠ ⊠

★ **PARK INN.** *2907 Cerrillos Rd (87505). Phone 505/471-3000; fax 505/424-7561.* 101 rooms, 2 story. Pets accepted; fee. TV; cable (premium). Restaurant, bar. Game room. Pool. Downhill, cross-country ski 20 miles. **$**

⊡ ◪ ⊠ ⊠ ⊠

★ ★ **QUALITY INN.** *3011 Cerrillos Rd (87505). Phone 505/471-1211; fax 505/438-9535. www.qualityinn.com.* 99 rooms, 2 story. Pets accepted, some restrictions; fee. Check-out noon. TV; cable (premium). Restaurant. Room service. Pool. Downhill, cross-country ski 17 miles. Airport transportation. **$**

⊡ ◪ ⊠ ⊠ ✈ ⊠

Hotels

★ ★ ★ **ELDORADO HOTEL.** *309 W San Francisco (87501). Phone 505/988-4455; toll-free 800/286-6755; fax 505/995-4555. www.eldoradohotel.com.* The Eldorado Hotel's imposing pueblo-revival style building is one of Santa Fe's largest and most important landmarks. Its lobby and interiors are lavishly decorated with more than a quarter million dollars of original southwest art. The Lobby Lounge serves drinks and is a great spot for snacking, people watching, and enjoying live entertainment. Sunday brunch is served in the cozy Eldorado Court, voted "Best Brunch" by the residents of Santa Fe. 219 rooms, 5 story. Pets accepted; fee. Garage parking, fee. Check-out noon. TV; cable (premium), VCR available (movies). In-room modem link. Restaurant, bar; entertainment. In-house fitness room; massage, sauna. Rooftop pool; whirlpool; poolside service. Downhill ski 16 miles, cross-country ski 7 miles. Business center. Concierge. **$$$**

⊡ ◪ ⊠ ⊠ ⊼ ⊠ SC ⊼

★ ★ ★ ★ **INN OF THE ANASAZI.** *113 Washington Ave (87501). Phone 505/988-3030; toll-free 800/688-8100; fax 505/988-3277. www.innoftheanasazi.com.* Native American, Hispanic, and cowboy cultures collide at the Inn of the Anasazi, where a masterful blend of New Mexican legacies results in a stunning and unusual lodging. The true spirit of Santa Fe is captured here, where enormous handcrafted doors open to a world of authentic artwork, carvings, and textiles synonymous with the Southwest. The lobby sets a sense of place for arriving guests with its rough-hewn tables, leather furnishings, unique objects, and huge cactus plants in terracotta pots. Located just off the historic Plaza, the inn was designed to resemble the traditional dwellings of the Anasazi. The region's integrity is maintained in the guest rooms, where fireplaces and four-poster beds stand beneath ceilings of vigas and latillas, and guests discover toiletries made locally with native cedar extract. Artfully prepared, the meals of the Anasazi's restaurant earn praise for honoring the area's culinary heritage. 59 rooms, 3 story. Pets accepted; fee. Valet parking. Check-out noon. TV; cable (premium), VCR available. Restaurant. In-house fitness room. Massage. Health club privileges. Downhill ski 13 miles, cross-country ski 7 miles. Concierge. **$$**

★★★ **INN ON THE ALAMEDA.** *303 E Alameda (87501). Phone 505/984-2121; toll-free 800/984-2121; fax 505/986-8325. www.inn-alameda.com.* Sitting unassumingly behind adobe walls near the start of Canyon Road, this inn offers all the comforts of a luxury hotel with the quiet elegance of a smaller bed-and-breakfast. Guest rooms feature Egyptian cotton sheets, fireplaces, robes, hairdryers, cable television, and data ports. 69 rooms, 2-3 story. Pets accepted, some restrictions; fee. Complimentary continental breakfast. Check-out noon. TV; cable (premium). In-room modem link. Kiva fireplaces. Bar. In-house fitness room. Massage. Health club privileges. Whirlpool. Downhill, cross-country ski 15 miles. Concierge. **$$**

B&B/Small Inns

★★★ **ALEXANDER'S INN.** *529 E Palace Ave (87501). Phone 505/986-1431; toll-free 888/321-5123; fax 505/982-8572. www.alexanders-inn.com.* With a location only a short walk to shopping, restaurants, and galleries, this inn keeps a quiet and peaceful atmosphere. Built in 1903, the rooms are full of elegance with hardwood floors, stained-glass windows or lace curtains, and more. 16 rooms, 2 story. Pets accepted; fee. Complimentary continental breakfast. Check-out 11 am, check-in by arrangement. TV; VCR available. Whirlpool. Downhill ski 17 miles, cross-country ski 10 miles. Concierge. Five rooms in a renovated house built in 1903. Totally nonsmoking. **$**

★★ **EL PARADERO EN SANTA FE.** *220 W Manhattan Ave (87501). Phone 505/988-1177; fax 505/ 988-3577. www.elparadero.com.* 12 rooms. Pets accepted. Children over 3 years only. Complimentary full breakfast. Check-out 11 am, check-in 2-8 pm. TV in sitting room. Downhill ski 18 miles, cross-country ski 9 miles. Renovated Spanish adobe house (circa 1820) with details from 1880 and 1912 remodelings. **$**

Santa Rosa

Motels/Motor Lodges

★ **BEST WESTERN ADOBE INN.** *1501 Will Rogers Dr (88435). Phone 505/472-3446; fax 505/472-5759. www.bestwestern.com.* 58 rooms, 2 story. Pets accepted, some restrictions. Complimentary continental breakfast. Check-out 11 am. TV. In-room modem link. Pool. Airport transportation. **$**

★ **LA QUINTA INN.** *1701 Will Rogers Dr (88435). Phone 505/472-4800; fax 505/472-4809. www.laquinta.com.* 60 air-cooled rooms, 2 story. Pets accepted. Complimentary continental breakfast. TV; VCR available (movies). In-room modem link. Indoor pool; whirlpool. **$**

Silver City

Motels/Motor Lodges

★ **COPPER MANOR MOTEL.** *710 Silver Heights Blvd (88062). Phone 505/538-5392; toll-free 800/853-2916; fax 505/538-5830.* 68 rooms, 2 story. Pets accepted. Complimentary continental breakfast. Check-out 11 am. TV. Restaurant. Indoor pool. **$**

★★ **HOLIDAY MOTOR HOTEL.** *3420 Hwy 180 E (88061). Phone 505/538-3711; toll-free 800/828-8291. www.holidayhotel.com.* 79 rooms, 2 story. Pets accepted; fee. Check-out noon. TV; cable (premium). Laundry services. Restaurant. Room service. Pool. Free airport transportation. **$**

Socorro

Motels/Motor Lodges

★ **DAYS INN.** *507 N California Ave (87801). Phone 505/ 835-0230; fax 505/835-1993. www.daysinn.com.* 41 rooms, 2 story. Pets accepted; fee. Check-out 11 am. TV; cable (premium). Restaurant. Room service. Pool. **$**

★ **THE WESTERN.** *404 First St (87825). Phone 505/ 854-2417; fax 505/854-3217. www.thewesternmotel.com.* 6 rooms. No A/C. Pets accepted, some restrictions; fee. Check-out 11 am. TV; cable (premium). **$**

Taos

Motels/Motor Lodges

★ ★ **EL PUEBLO LODGE.** *412 Paseo Del Pueblo N (87571). Phone 505/758-8700; toll-free 800/433-9612; fax 505/758-7321.* 60 rooms, 1-2 story. Pets accepted; fee. Complimentary continental breakfast. Check-out 11:30 am. TV; cable (premium). Pool; whirlpool. Downhill ski 17 miles, cross-country ski 5 miles. **$**

★ ★ ★ **HOLIDAY INN.** *1005 Paseo Del Pueblo Sur (87571). Phone 505/758-4444; toll-free 800/759-2736; fax 505/758-0055. www.holiday-inn.com.* The six buildings of this Pueblo Indian adobe-style property are connected by walkways leading through courtyards and landscaped grounds. Guest rooms feature in-room ski storage and hand-carved furnishings. 124 rooms, 2 story. Pets accepted; fee. Check-out 11 am. TV; VCR available. Fireplace in suites. Restaurant, bar. Room service. Indoor pool; whirlpool; poolside service. Outdoor tennis. Downhill ski 20 miles, cross-country ski 5 miles. **$**

★ ★ **QUALITY INN.** *1043 Paseo Del Pueblo Sur (87571). Phone 505/758-2200; toll-free 800/845-0648; fax 505/758-9009. www.qualityinn.com.* 99 rooms, 2 story. Pets accepted, some restrictions; fee. Check-out 11 am. TV; cable (premium), VCR available. In-room modem link. Restaurant, bar. Room service. Pool; poolside service. Downhill ski 20 miles, cross-country ski 5 miles. **$**

Hotel

★ ★ ★ **SAGEBRUSH INN.** *1508 S Santa Fe Rd (87571). Phone 505/758-2254; toll-free 800/428-3626; fax 505/758-5077. www.sagebrushinn.com.* Built in 1929, this adobe inn houses a large collection of paintings, Indian rugs, and other regional art. The most recent addition, an 18,000-square-foot conference center, features hand-hewn vigas and fireplaces. Guest rooms feature handmade furniture. 100 rooms, 2 story. Pets accepted, some restrictions. Complimentary full breakfast. Check-out 11 am. TV; cable (premium). Restaurant, bar; entertainment. Pool; whirlpools. Cross-country ski 10 miles. Business center. **$**

B&B/Small Inns

★ ★ ★ **ADOBE AND STARS INN.** *584 NM 150 (87571). Phone 505/776-2776; toll-free 800/211-7076; fax 505/776-2872. www.taosadobe.com.* Located near the historic Taos Plaza and the Taos Ski Valley, this Southwestern inn offers panoramic views of the Sangre de Christo Mountains. Guest rooms feature kiva fireplaces, private baths with terra-cotta tile, and ceiling fans. 8 rooms. No A/C. Pets accepted, some restrictions; fee. Complimentary full breakfast. Check-out 11 am, check-in 4 pm. TV in common room; VCR (movies). Downhill, cross-country ski 8 miles. Concierge service. Totally nonsmoking. **$**

★ ★ **AUSTING HAUS B&B.** *1282 NM 150 (87525). Phone 505/776-2649; toll-free 800/748-2932; fax 505/776-8751. www.taoswebb.com/hotel/austinghaus.* 45 rooms, 2 story. No A/C. Closed mid-Apr-mid-May. Pets accepted, some restrictions. Complimentary continental breakfast. Check-out 10 am, check-in 2 pm. TV. Laundry services. Dining room. Whirlpool. Downhill ski 2 miles. Constructed of oak-pegged heavy timbers with beams exposed inside and out; built by hand entirely without nails or metal plates. **$**

★ ★ ★ **LA DONA LUZ INN, AN HISTORIC BED AND BREAKFAST.** *114 Kit Carson Rd (87571). Phone 505/758-4874; toll-free 800/758-9187; fax 505/758-4541. www.ladonaluz.com.* This 200-year-old pueblo-style adobe will delight visitors with its fascinating history and large collection of fine art. The unique guest rooms all have private baths and many feature fireplaces, mountain views, and art. Continental breakfast is served on the patio during the warm months. 15 rooms, 3 story. No room phones. Pets accepted, some restrictions; fee. Complimentary continental breakfast. Check-out 11 am, check-in 3 pm. TV; VCR (free movies). Downhill ski 18 miles, cross-country ski 5 miles. **$**

Truth or Consequences

Motels/Motor Lodges

★ **ACE LODGE AND MOTEL.** *1302 N Date St (87901). Phone 505/894-2151.* 38 rooms. Pets accepted; fee. Check-out 11 am. TV. Restaurant, bar. Pool. Free airport transportation. **$**

★ ★ **QUALITY INN.** *401 Hwy 195 (87935). Phone 505/744-5431; fax 505/744-5044. www.qualityinn.com.* 48 rooms, 2 story. Pets accepted; fee. Check-out 11 am. TV; cable (premium). Restaurant, bar. Room service. Pool. Outdoor tennis. **$**

Tucumcari

Motels/Motor Lodges

★ **COMFORT INN.** *2800 E Tucumcari Blvd (88401). Phone 505/461-4094; fax 505/461-4099. www.comfortinn.com.* 59 rooms, 2 story. Pets accepted; fee. Complimentary continental breakfast. Check-out noon. TV. Pool. **$**

D 🐾 🛏 🕂 🏊 🏃 🖘

★ **COUNTRY INN.** *1302 W Tucumcari Blvd (88401). Phone 505/461-3140; fax 505/461-3143.* 57 rooms, 2 story. Pets accepted, some restrictions; fee. Complimentary continental breakfast. Check-out noon. TV; cable (premium). Pool. **$**

🐾 🏊 🖘

★ **ECONO LODGE.** *3400 Rte 66 E (88401). Phone 505/461-4194; fax 505/461-4911. www.econolodge.com.* 41 rooms, 2 story. Pets accepted; fee. Check-out 11 am. TV. **$**

D 🐾 🖘

★ ★ **HOLIDAY INN.** *3716 E Tucumcari Blvd (88401). Phone 505/461-3780; toll-free 800/335-3780; fax 505/461-3931. www.holiday-inn.com.* 100 rooms, 2 story. Pets accepted, some restrictions; fee. Check-out noon. TV. In-room modem link. Restaurant, bar. Room service. In-house fitness room. Pool; whirlpool. **$**

🐾 🏊 🧍

New York

Albany

Motels/Motor Lodges

★ ★ **BEST WESTERN ALBANY AIRPORT INN.** *200 Wolf Rd (12205). Phone 518/458-1000; toll-free 800/458-1016; fax 518/458-2807. www.bestwestern.com.* 153 rooms, 2 story. S, D $65-$109; each additional $10; under 18 free; weekly, weekend, holiday rates. Pets accepted, some restrictions. Check-out noon. TV; cable (premium), VCR available. In-room modem link. Restaurant, bar. Health club privileges. Indoor pool. Free airport transportation.

⊡ 🔄 🐾 ⚕ 🏊 ✈ 🚫

★ ★ **BEST WESTERN SOVEREIGN HOTEL-ALBANY.** *1228 Western Ave (12203). Phone 518/489-2981; toll-free 888/963-7666; fax 518/489-8967. www.bestwestern.com.* 195 rooms, 5 story. S $95-$105; D $105-$115; each additional $10; suites $150-$195; under 18 free; weekend plan; higher rates special events. Pets accepted, some restrictions; fee. Full breakfast. Check-out noon. TV; cable (premium). In-room modem link. Restaurant, bar. Room service. In-house fitness room; sauna. Indoor pool.

⊡ 🔄 🐾 🏊 ⚕ 🔄 ✈ 🚫 SC

★ ★ **HOWARD JOHNSON.** *416 Southern Blvd (12209). Phone 518/462-6555; toll-free 800/562-7253; fax 518/462-2547. www.hojo.com.* 135 rooms, 1-2 story. S $65; D $75; each additional $8; suites $95; under 18 free. Pets accepted; fee. Check-out noon. TV; cable (premium). Laundry services. Restaurant open 24 hours. Bar. In-house fitness room. Pool.

⊡ 🔄 🐾 🏊 ⚕

★ **MICROTEL.** *7 Rensselaer Ave (12110). Phone 518/782-9161; toll-free 800/782-9121; fax 518/782-9162. www.microtelinn.com.* 100 rooms, 2 story. S $50-$89; D $53-$89; under 14 free. Pets accepted, some restrictions. Check-out noon. TV; cable (premium). In-room modem link.

🔄 🐾 ✈ 🚫

★ **RAMADA INN.** *1630 Central Ave (12205). Phone 518/456-0222; toll-free 800/354-0223; fax 518/452-1376. www.ramadaatalbany.com.* 105 rooms, 2 story. July-Aug: S $62-$80; D $72-$85; under 18 free; lower rates rest of year. Pets accepted, some restrictions; fee. Complimentary continental breakfast. Check-out noon. TV; cable (premium), VCR available. In-house fitness room.

⊡ 🔄 🐾 ⚕ 🚫 SC

Hotel

★ ★ ★ **CENTURY HOUSE HOTEL.** *997 New London Rd (12110). Phone 518/785-0931; toll-free 888/674-6873; fax 518/785-3274. www.thecenturyhouse.com.* This full-service bed-and-breakfast offers its guests a pool, restaurant, nature trails, a tennis court, complimentary breakfast, and much more. The rooms are elegantly decorated in colonial style with cherry wood furnishing. 68 rooms, 2 story. S $95-$129; D $105-$129; each additional $12; suites $125-$225; under 12 free; higher rates: Saratoga racing season, special events. Pets accepted, some restrictions; fee. Complimentary breakfast. Check-out noon. TV. In-room modem link. Restaurant, bar. Room service. In-house fitness room. Nature walk/trail. Pool. Tennis.

⊡ 🔄 🐾 🏊 ⚕ 🔄 🚫

B&B/Small Inn

★ ★ **MANSION HILL INN.** *115 Philip St at Park Ave (12202). Phone 518/465-2038; toll-free 888/299-0455; fax 518/434-2313. www.mansionhill.com.* 8 rooms, 2 story. D $145-$175; under 17 free; weekend rates. Pets accepted. Complimentary breakfast. Check-out 11:30 am, check-in 4 pm. TV; cable (premium), VCR available. Restaurant. Room service. Health club privileges. Concierge.

🔄 🔄 🚫

Alexandria Bay

Motel/Motor Lodge

★ **LEDGES RESORT MOTEL ALEXANDRIA BAY.** *71 Anthony St (13607). Phone 315/482-9334; fax 315/482-9334. www.thousandislands.com/ledges.* 27 rooms. Late June-Labor Day: D $88-$108; each additional $8; lower rates early May-late June and after Labor Day-mid-Oct. Closed rest of year. Pets accepted, some restrictions. Check-out 11 am. TV. Pool. Private dock.

🔄 🐾 🏊 SC

Resorts

★ **NORTH STAR RESORT.** *116 Church St (13607). Phone 315/482-9332; toll-free 877/417-7827; fax 315/482-5825. www.northstarresort.com.* 70 rooms. S $29-$89; D $39-$109; each additional $10. Pets accepted, some restrictions; fee. Check-out 11 am. TV. Restaurant. Pool. Boat launch, docks.

⊡ 🔄 🐾 ⚕ 🏊 🚫

★ ★ **RIVEREDGE RESORT HOTEL.** *17 Holland St (13607). Phone 315/482-9917; toll-free 800/365-6987; fax 315/482-5010. www.riveredge.com.* Found on the St. Lawrence River, this resort hotel features 129 rooms, most with a river view, casual and fine dining, an indoor and outdoor pool, a dock with power, water and cable hook-ups and so much more. 129 rooms, 4 story. June-Labor Day: S, D $174-$218; each additional $20; suites $178-$238; under 12 free; AP, MAP available; ski, golf plans; lower rates rest of year. Pets accepted, some restrictions; fee. Check-out 11 am, check-in 3 pm. TV. Laundry services. Bar; entertainment. Room service. In-house fitness room; massage, sauna. Indoor pool; outdoor pool; whirlpool; poolside service. Cross-country ski 5 miles. Lawn games, boats, fishing, hiking, sleighing/sleigh rides, snowmobiles, waterskiing. Concierge. Luxury level. On river.

Amsterdam

Motel/Motor Lodge

★★ **BEST WESTERN AMSTERDAM.** *10 Market St (12010). Phone 518/843-5760; fax 518/842-0940. www.bestwestern.com.* 125 rooms, 5 story. S $55-$72; D $58-$89; each additional $6; under 18 free; weekly rates; higher rates Aug. Pets accepted, some restrictions; fee. Check-out noon. TV; VCR available (movies). In-room modem link. Restaurant, bar. Indoor pool.

Auburn

Motel/Motor Lodge

★ **DAYS INN.** *37 William St (13021). Phone 315/252-7567; toll-free 800/329-7466. www.daysinn.com.* 51 rooms, 2 story. May-Sept: S $52; D $62; each additional $5; under 12 free; higher rates graduation; lower rates rest of year. Pets accepted; fee. Complimentary continental breakfast. Check-out 11 am. TV. In-room modem link. Laundry services. Health club privileges.

Batavia

Motels/Motor Lodges

★★ **BEST WESTERN BATAVIA INN.** *8204 Park Rd (14020). Phone 585/343-1000; toll-free 800/228-2842; fax 585/343-8608. www.bestwestern.com.* 75 rooms, 2 story. Mid-June-mid-Sept: S $74-$84; D $79-$99; each additional $6; under 18 free; lower rates rest of year. Pets accepted. Check-out noon. TV; cable (premium), VCR available. In-room modem link. Restaurant, bar; entertainment Fri, Sat. Pool; poolside service. Lawn games.

★ **DAYS INN.** *200 Oak St (14020). Phone 585/343-1440; fax 585/343-5322. www.daysinn.com.* 120 rooms, 2 story. May-Sept: S $62-$82; D $69-$99; each additional $7; under 18 free; lower rates rest of year. Pets accepted, some restrictions; fee. Complimentary continental breakfast. Check-out noon. TV; cable (premium). Health club privileges. Pool.

Bath

Motel/Motor Lodge

★ **DAYS INN.** *330 W Morris (14810). Phone 607/776-7644; fax 607/776-7650. www.daysinn.com.* 104 rooms, 5 story. Pets accepted. Complimentary continental breakfast. Check-out 11 am, check-in 2 pm. TV; cable (premium), VCR available. Indoor pool. **$**

Binghamton

Motels/Motor Lodges

★ **COMFORT INN.** *1156 Front St (13905). Phone 607/722-5353; fax 607/722-1823. www.choicehotels.com.* 67 rooms, 2 story. S $55-$70; D $60-$75; each additional $10; kitchen suites $60-$105; under 18 free; higher rates special events. Pets accepted, some restrictions. Complimentary continental breakfast. Check-out noon. TV; cable (premium). In-room modem link. Laundry services.

★★ **HOLIDAY INN.** *2-8 Hawley St (13901). Phone 607/722-1212; toll-free 800/465-4329; fax 607/722-6063. www.holiday-inn.com.* 241 rooms, 8 story. S, D $93-$99; each additional $10; suites $130; under 19 free; weekend plans. Pets accepted; fee. Check-out noon. TV; cable (premium). In-room modem link. Laundry services. Restaurant, bar; entertainment. Room service. Health club privileges. Indoor pool. Airport transportation.

★ **HOWARD JOHNSON.** *690 Front St (13905). Phone 607/724-1341; toll-free 800/446-4656; fax 607/773-8287. www.hojo.com.* 107 rooms, 2 story. S $40-$60; D $46-$70; each additional $5; higher rates special events. Pets accepted, some restrictions; fee. Complimentary continental breakfast. Check-out noon. TV; VCR available. Health club privileges.

Hotel

★ ★ ★ **GRAND ROYALE HOTEL.** *80 State St (13901). Phone 607/722-0000; fax 607/722-7912. www.villager.com.* 61 rooms, 6 story. S $75-$95; D $85-$95; each additional $7; suites $150; under 18 free. Pets accepted. Complimentary breakfast. Check-out noon. TV; cable (premium). In-room modem link. Bar. Health club privileges. Cross-country ski 5 miles. Valet parking. Renovated city hall (1897).

🄳 🐾 🏊 🏂 🛏 SC

Boonville

Motel/Motor Lodge

★ **HEADWATERS MOTOR LODGE.** *13524 RR 12 (13309). Phone 315/942-4493; toll-free 877/787-4606; fax 315/942-4626. www.headwatersmotorlodge.com.* 37 rooms, 4 kitchen units, 1-2 story. S $45; D $55; each additional $8; under 12 free. Pets accepted, some restrictions. Complimentary continental breakfast. Check-out 11 am. TV; cable (premium). In-room modem link. Health club privileges. Game room. Downhill, cross-country ski 9 miles.

🄳 🐾 🏊 🛏 SC

Buffalo

Motels/Motor Lodges

★ **MICROTEL.** *1 Hospitality Centre Way (14150). Phone 716/693-8100; toll-free 800/227-6346; fax 716/693-8750. www.microtelinn.com.* 100 rooms, 2 story. Mid-June-early Sept: S $45.95-$60.95; D $50.95-$65.95; under 18 free; lower rates rest of year. Pets accepted; fee. Complimentary continental breakfast. Check-out noon. TV.

🄳 🐾 🛏

★ **RED ROOF INN.** *42 Flint Rd (14226). Phone 716/689-7474; fax 716/689-2051. www.redroof.com.* 108 rooms. June-Aug: S $69.99-$79.99; D $79.99-$89.99; under 18 free; higher rates special events; lower rates rest of year. Pets accepted, some restrictions. Check-out noon. TV; cable (premium).

🄳 🐾 🛏

Hotels

★ ★ ★ **BUFFALO/NIAGARA MARRIOTT.** *1340 Millersport Hwy (14221). Phone 716/689-6900; toll-free 800/228-9290; fax 716/689-0483. www.marriott.com.* In the heart of Amherst's business district, this hotel has ten meeting and banquet rooms, a restaurant, cocktail lounge, gift shop, indoor and outdoor pool, a full spa nearby, and tons of golf in the area. 356 rooms, 10 story. Pets accepted, some restrictions; fee. Check-out noon, check-in 3 pm. TV; cable (premium). In-room modem link. Restaurant, bar. Room service. In-house fitness room; sauna. Game room. Indoor pool; outdoor pool; whirlpool. Business center. Concierge. Luxury level. Free transportation.

🄳 🐾 🏊 🏂 ✈ 🛏 SC 🚶

★ **LORD AMHERST HOTEL.** *5000 Main St (14226). Phone 716/839-2200; toll-free 800/544-2200; fax 716/839-1538. www.lordamherst.com.* 101 rooms, 2 story. May-Sept: S $59-$75; D $69-$89; each additional $7; suites $95-$160; kitchen units $75-$150; under 18 free; lower rates rest of year. Pets accepted, some restrictions. Complimentary full breakfast. Check-out 1 pm. TV. In-room modem link. Laundry services. Restaurant, bar. In-house fitness room. Game room. Pool. Colonial décor.

🐾 🏊 🏂 🛏 SC

Canandaigua

Motel/Motor Lodge

★ **ECONO LODGE.** *170 Eastern Blvd (14424). Phone 585/394-9000; toll-free 800/797-1222; fax 585/396-2560. www.econolodge.com.* 65 rooms, 2 story. May-Oct: S $42-$80; D $49-$90; each additional $10; under 18 free; lower rates rest of year. Pets accepted, some restrictions. Check-out 11 am. TV; cable (premium), VCR available (movies). Downhill ski 12 miles.

🄳 🐾 🏊 🛏 SC

Cazenovia

Motel/Motor Lodge

★ ★ ★ **LINCKLAEN HOUSE.** *79 Albany St (13035). Phone 315/655-3461; fax 315/655-5443. www.cazenovia.com.* For 150 years, this property has been providing fine dining and lodging for such people as former President Grover Cleveland and John D. Rockefeller. Rooms are elegantly decorated, and the dining room serves painstakingly prepared American cuisine. 18 rooms, 3 story. S, D $99-$140; suites $120-$140. Pets accepted. Complimentary continental breakfast. Check-out 11 am, check-in 2 pm. TV. Built in 1835.

🄳 🐾 🧴 🔧 🛏

Chautauqua

B&B/Small Inn

★ ★ ★ **WILLIAM SEWARD INN.** *6645 S Portage Rd (14787). Phone 716/326-4151; fax 716/326-4163. www.williamsewardinn.com.* Southwest Chautauqua County is the perfect setting for this country inn. Various local destinations make it a year-round retreat: ski areas, Chautauqua Lake, and the well-known Chautauqua Institution for cultural and educational programs. 12 rooms, 2 story. No room phones. Jun-Oct: S, D $80-$185; each additional $15; weekends, holidays (2-day minimum). Pets accepted, some restrictions. Children over 12 years only. Complimentary full breakfast; afternoon refreshments. Check-out 11 am, check-in 2-8 pm. TV. In-room modem link. Restaurant. Downhill ski 20 miles, cross-country ski 7 miles. Restored Greek Revival mansion built in 1837; antiques. Totally nonsmoking.

Clayton

Motel/Motor Lodge

★ **WEST WINDS MOTEL & COTTAGES.** *38267 Rte 12E (13624). Phone 315/686-3352; toll-free 888/937-8963. www.thousandislands.com/westwinds.* 12 kitchen units. Late June-early Sept: S $38-$60; D $48-$67; each additional $6; kitchen cabins for 2, $520/week; kitchen cottages for 2, $760-$880/week; each additional $50; lower rates mid-May-late June, early Sept-mid-Oct. Closed rest of year. Pets accepted; fee. Check-out 10 am. TV; cable (premium). Game room. Pool. Boats; dockage.

Corning

Motel/Motor Lodge

★ **KNIGHTS INN.** *2707 Westinghouse Rd (14904). Phone 607/739-3807; toll-free 800/418-8977; fax 607/796-5293. www.knightsinn.com.* 40 rooms. Apr-Oct: S, D $32.95-$95.95; under 12 free; family rates; package plans; weekends 2-day minimum; higher rates special events; lower rates rest of year. Pets accepted; fee. Complimentary continental breakfast. TV; cable (premium), VCR available (movies). In-room modem link. Pool.

Hotel

★ ★ ★ **RADISSON HOTEL CORNING.** *125 Denison Pkwy E (14830). Phone 607/962-5000; toll-free 800/333-3333; fax 607/962-4166. www.radisson.com/corningny.* This hotel is located in downtown Corning. It is a short walk to local shops, galleries, and other attractions in the area. The location puts it only a short drive from Finger Lakes wineries, Watkins Glen International Racetrack, and more. 177 rooms, 3 story. S $107-$141; D $117-$151; each additional $10; suites $175-$255; under 18 free; weekend rates. Pets accepted, some restrictions. Check-out 1 pm. TV. Restaurant, bar; entertainment. Room service. Indoor pool.

Cortland

Motel/Motor Lodge

★ **COMFORT INN.** *2 1/2 Locust Ave (13045). Phone 607/753-7721; toll-free 800/221-2222; fax 607/753-7608. www.comfortinn.com.* 6 rooms, 2 story. May-Nov: S, D $79-$139; under 18 free; ski plans; higher rates special events; lower rates rest of year. Pets accepted; fee. Complimentary continental breakfast. Check-out 11 am. TV. In-room modem link. In-house fitness room. Game room.

Dunkirk

Motel/Motor Lodge

★ ★ **RAMADA INN.** *30 Lake Shore Dr E (14048). Phone 716/366-8350; toll-free 800/525-8350; fax 716/366-8890. www.ramada.com.* 132 rooms, 4 story. Pets accepted, some restrictions; fee. Check-out noon, check-in. TV. In-room modem link. Restaurant, bar. Room service. In-house fitness room; sauna. Indoor pool; outdoor pool; whirlpool; poolside service. Downhill, cross-country ski 15 miles. **$**

Hotels

★ **BEST WESTERN DUNKIRK & FREDONIA.** *3912 Vineyard Dr (14048). Phone 716/366-7100; toll-free 800/528-1234; fax 716/366-1606. www.bestwestern.com.* 61 rooms, 2 story. Pets accepted, some restrictions; fee. Complimentary continental breakfast. Check-out noon, check-in 2 pm. TV; cable (premium). In-house fitness room; health club privileges. Indoor pool; whirlpool. **$**

★ **DAYS INN.** *10455 Bennett Rd (14063).* Phone *716/673-1351; fax 716/672-6909. www.daysinn.com.* 135 rooms, 2 story. Pets accepted. Complimentary continental breakfast. Check-out 11 am, check-in 3 pm. TV; cable (premium), VCR available. Laundry services. Restaurant, bar. Indoor pool; whirlpool. Downhill, cross-country ski 20 miles. **$**

D 🐾 🏊 🏊 🏊 SC

East Hampton

B&B/Small Inn

★ ★ ★ **CENTENNIAL HOUSE.** *13 Woods Ln (11937).* Phone *631/324-9414; fax 631/324-0493. www.centhouse.com.* Situated at the eastern tip of Long Island, this bed-and-breakfast was built in 1876 and restored with English country décor in 1987. A charming guest cottage is a nice alternative to the main house, and hearty breakfasts accompany all rooms. 6 rooms, 2 story. Pets accepted, some restrictions. Children over 12 years only. Complimentary continental breakfast. Check-out 11 am, check-in 2 pm. TV. Outdoor pool. Totally nonsmoking. **$$$**

🐾 🛋 🏊 🏊 🏊

Elmira

Motels/Motor Lodges

★ ★ **BEST WESTERN MARSHALL MANOR.** *3527 Watkins Rd (14845).* Phone *607/739-3891; toll-free 800/528-1234. www.bestwestern.com.* 40 rooms. S $38-$69; D $42-$69; each additional $5; under 18 free; higher rates special events. Pets accepted; fee. Complimentary continental breakfast. Check-out 11 am. TV; VCR available. In-room modem link. Restaurant, bar. Pool.

🐾 🏊 🏊 SC

★ **COACHMAN MOTOR LODGE.** *908 Pennsylvania Ave (14904).* Phone *607/733-5526; fax 607/733-0961. www.coachmanmotorlodge.com.* 18 rooms, 2 story. Apr-Nov: S $40-$55; D $50-$65; under 18 free; each additional $5; weekly rates; lower rates rest of year. Pets accepted, some restrictions. Check-out noon. TV. Laundry services. Health club privileges.

D 🐾 🏊 SC

★ ★ **HOWARD JOHNSON.** *2671 Corning Rd (14845).* Phone *607/739-5636; toll-free 888/895-1403; fax 607/739-8630. www.hojo.com.* 76 rooms, 1-2 story. May-mid-Nov: S $48-$70; D $58-$80; each additional $8; studio rooms available; under 18 free; lower rates rest of year.

Pets accepted. Check-out noon. TV; cable (premium). In-room modem link. Restaurant. Pool.

D 🐾 🏊 🏊

Fishkill

Hotel

★ ★ **WELLESLEY INN.** *20 Schuyler Blvd (12524).* Phone *845/896-4995; fax 845/896-6631. www.wellesleyinnsandsuites.com.* 82 rooms, 4 story. Apr-Oct: S, D $89-$109; each additional $2; suites $95-$150; under 17 free; weekly rates; package plans; higher rates special events; lower rates rest of year. Pets accepted, some restrictions. Complimentary continental breakfast. Check-out 11 am. TV; cable (premium). In-room modem link. Bar. Health club privileges.

🐾 🏊 SC

Herkimer

Motels/Motor Lodges

★ ★ **BEST WESTERN LITTLE FALLS MOTOR INN.** *20 Albany St (13365).* Phone *315/823-4954; fax 315/823-4507. www.bestwestern.com.* 56 rooms, 2 story. May-Sept: S $57-$67; D $70-$80; each additional $6; under 12 free; lower rates rest of year. Pets accepted, some restrictions. Check-out noon. TV. Restaurant, bar. Game room.

D 🐾 🏊

★ **HERKIMER MOTEL.** *100 Marginal Rd (13350).* Phone *315/866-0490; toll-free 877/656-6835; fax 315/866-0416. www.herkimermotel.com.* 62 rooms, 2 story. S $59-$64; D $68-$88; each additional $7; kitchen units $83-$99; two-room suite $99-$125; under 13 free. Pets accepted, some restrictions. Check-out 11 am. TV; cable (premium). Laundry services. Restaurant open 24 hours. In-house fitness room. Pool.

D 🐾 🏊 🏋 🏊 SC

Hillsdale

Resort

★ ★ **SWISS HUTTE.** *Rt 23 (12529).* Phone *518/325-3333; fax 413/528-6201. www.swisshutte.com.* 15 rooms, 2 story. MAP: S, D $75-$110; lodge suites $95/person; EP available; weekly rates; lower rates Mar-Apr, Nov. Pets accepted. Check-out 11 am, check-in 2 pm. TV.

Restaurant. Bar. Pool. Tennis. Downhill, cross-country ski adjacent. Lawn games.

Hornell

Motel/Motor Lodge

★★ **ECONO LODGE.** 7462 Seneca Rd N (14843). Phone 607/324-0800; toll-free 800/4CHOICE; fax 607/324-0905. www.econolodge.com. 67 rooms, 2 story. Pets accepted; fee. Complimentary continental breakfast. Check-out 11 am, check-in 1 pm. TV; VCR available (movies). In-room modem link. Restaurant, bar. Downhill ski 10 miles. **$**

Howes Cave

Motel/Motor Lodge

★★ **BEST WESTERN INN OF COBLESKILL.** 12 Campus Dr Extension (12043). Phone 518/234-4321; fax 518/234-3869. www.bestwestern.com. 76 rooms, 2 story. S, D $69-$119; under 12 free. Pets accepted; fee. Check-out 11 am. TV; cable (premium), VCR available (movies, fee). Restaurant, bar. Room service. Game room. Indoor pool; children's pool.

Hudson

Hotel

★★★ **ST. CHARLES.** 16-18 Park Pl (12534). Phone 518/822-9900; fax 518/822-0835. www.stcharleshotel.com. Nearby shops, galleries, and picturesque mountains attract guests to this 120-year-old Hudson Valley property. All rooms have a clean, simple décor. 34 rooms, 6 suites, 3 story. S, D $79-$99; each additional $10; suites $99; under 18 free; ski plans. Pets accepted. Complimentary continental breakfast. Check-out noon. TV; VCR available. Restaurant, bar; entertainment. Health club privileges.

Hunter

Hotel

★ **HUNTER INN.** Rte 23A (12442). Phone 518/263-3777; fax 518/263-3981. www.hunterinn.com. 41 rooms, 2-3 story. No elevator. Mid-Nov-mid-Apr: S, D $100-

$150; each additional $10-$15; suites $115-$185; under 17 free; holidays (3-day minimum); weekend, package plans; higher rates holidays; lower rates rest of year. Pets accepted, some restrictions; fee. Complimentary continental breakfast. Check-out 11 am. TV. In-house fitness room. Whirlpool. Downhill, cross-country ski 1/2 mile.

Huntington

Hotel

★ **HUNTINGTON COUNTRY INN.** 270 W Jericho Tpke (11746). Phone 631/421-3900; toll-free 800/739-5777; fax 631/421-5287. www.huntingtoncountryinn.com. 64 rooms, 2 story. S $99-$109; D $109-$119; each additional $10; suite $150; under 16 free. Pets accepted. Complimentary continental breakfast. Check-out noon. TV; cable (premium). Health club privileges. Pool.

Ithaca

Hotels

★ **BEST WESTERN UNIVERSITY INN.** 1020 Ellis Hollow Rd (14850). Phone 607/272-6100; fax 607/272-1518. www.bestwestern.com. 101 rooms. Pets accepted, some restrictions; fee. Complimentary continental breakfast. Check-out noon, check-in 3 pm. TV; VCR available. In-house fitness room. Outdoor pool. Airport transportation. **$**

★★ **CLARION HOTEL.** One Sheraton Dr (14850). Phone 607/257-2000; toll-free 800/257-6992; fax 607/257-3998. www.clarion.com. 106 rooms, 3 story. Pets accepted, some restrictions; fee. Check-out noon, check-in 3 pm. TV. Restaurant. Room service. Sauna. Indoor pool. Free transportation. **$**

★★ **HOLIDAY INN.** 222 S Cayuga St (14850). Phone 607/272-1000; toll-free 800/465-4329; fax 607/277-1275. www.holidayinnithaca.com. 181 rooms, 10 story. Pets accepted, some restrictions; fee. Check-out noon, check-in 3 pm. TV; cable (premium). Restaurant, bar. Room service. In-house fitness room. Indoor pool. **$**

★★ **RAMADA INN.** 2310 N Triphammer Rd (14850). Phone 607/257-3100; toll-free 888/298-2054; fax 607/257-4425. www.ramada.com. 200 rooms, 2 story. Pets accepted, some restrictions; fee. Check-out noon, check-in 3 pm.

TV; VCR available. In-room modem link. Restaurant, bar. Room service. Sauna. Game room. Indoor pool; outdoor pool; whirlpool. **$**

[D] [icons] SC

B&B/Small Inn

★ ★ ★ **LA TOURELLE.** *1150 Danby Rd (14850). Phone 607/273-2734; toll-free 800/765-1492; fax 607/273-4821. www.latourelleinn.com.* If you enjoy walking on nature paths while listening to the sounds of cascading waterfalls, visit this European-style inn, located on 70 acres of rolling countryside adjacent to Buttermilk State Park. Guest can choose from a variety of accommodations, including romantic king rooms decorated in soft colors; the roomy, private Tennis Cottage; the Fireplace Room; or one of two Tower Honeymoon Rooms, located in a cylindrical-shaped building and featuring sunken circular beds and Jacuzzi tubs. The John Thomas Steakhouse offers hearty American cuisine. 35 rooms, 3 story. Pets accepted, some restrictions. Check-out noon, check-in 2 pm. TV; VCR available. In-room modem link. Fireplaces. Restaurant. Outdoor tennis, lighted courts. Cross-country skiing on site. Hiking. **$**

[D] [icons] SC

Jamestown

Motel/Motor Lodge

★ **COMFORT INN.** *2800 N Main St Extension (14701). Phone 716/664-5920; toll-free 800/453-7155; fax 716/664-3068. www.comfortinn.com.* 101 rooms, 2 story. June-mid-Sept: S $50-$139; D $64-$139; each additional $5; under 18 free; lower rates rest of year. Pets accepted; fee. Complimentary continental breakfast. Check-out noon. TV; cable (premium), VCR available. Bar. Health club privileges. Downhill ski 20 miles.

[D] [icons] SC

Johnstown

Motel/Motor Lodge

★ ★ **HOLIDAY INN.** *308 N Comrie Ave (12095). Phone 518/762-4686; toll-free 800/465-4329; fax 518/762-4034. www.holiday-inn.com.* 100 rooms, 3 story. No elevator. S $62-$72; D $68-$78; under 19 free; higher rates Aug. Pets accepted, some restrictions. Check-out 11 am. TV; cable (premium), VCR available (movies). In-room modem link. Laundry services. Restaurant, bar; entertainment. Room service. Pool. Downhill, cross-country ski 15 miles.

[D] [icons] SC

Kingston

Motel/Motor Lodge

★ **SUPER 8.** *487 Washington Ave (12401). Phone 845/338-3078; toll-free 800/800-8000. www.super8.com.* 84 rooms, 2 story. June-Oct: S $54.88; D $58.88-$63.88; each additional $6; under 12 free; lower rates rest of year. Pets accepted. Complimentary continental breakfast. Check-out 11 am. TV; VCR available (movies). Laundry services.

[D] [icons] SC

Lake George Village

Resort

★ ★ **FORT WILLIAM HENRY RESORT.** *48 Canada St (12845). Phone 518/668-3081; toll-free 800/234-6686; fax 518/668-4926. www.fortwilliamhenry.com.* 99 rooms, 2 story. Late June-Labor Day: S, D $140-$159; each additional $15; suite $200-$255; under 12 free; holiday weekends (2-day minimum); lower rates rest of year. Pets accepted, some restrictions; fee. Check-out 11 am. TV; VCR available (movies). Restaurant, bar. Sauna. Indoor pool; outdoor pool; whirlpool; poolside service. Downhill ski 20 miles, cross-country ski 8 miles. Bicycle rentals.

[D] [icons]

Lake Placid

Motels/Motor Lodges

★ **ART DEVLIN'S OLYMPIC MOTOR INN.** *348 Main St. (12946). Phone 518/523-3700; fax 518/523-3893. artdevlins.com.* 40 rooms, 2 story. Pets accepted, some restrictions. Complimentary continental breakfast. Check-out 11 am. TV. Pool; children's pool. Downhill ski 8 miles, cross-country ski 2 miles. Airport transportation. **$**

[icons]

★ ★ **BEST WESTERN GOLDEN ARROW HOTEL.** *150 Main St (12946). Phone 518/523-3353; toll-free 800/582-5540; fax 518/523-8063. www.golden-arrow.com.* 130 rooms, 4 story. Pets accepted, some restrictions; fee. Check-out 11 am. TV. In-room modem link. Restaurant, bar; entertainment. In-house fitness room; sauna. Indoor pool; children's pool; whirlpool. Downhill ski 9 miles, cross-country ski on site. Paddle boats, canoes, racquetball. Free airport transportation. **$**

[D] [icons]

★ ★ **RAMADA INN.** *8-12 Saranac Ave (12946). Phone 518/523-2587; fax 518/523-2328. www.ramada.com.* 90 rooms, 3 story. Pets accepted, some restrictions. Check-out noon. TV; VCR available. In-room modem link. Restaurant, bar. In-house fitness room. Game room. Indoor pool; whirlpool. Downhill ski 10 miles, cross-country ski 1 mile. **$**

Hotel

★ ★ ★ **LAKE PLACID LODGE.** *Whiteface Inn Rd (12946). Phone 518/523-2700; fax 518/523-1124. www.lakeplacidlodge.com.* Nestled on the wooded shores of Lake Placid with majestic views of Whiteface Mountain, Lake Placid Lodge may be the most restful spot around. The lodge is a celebration of the simple beauty of the Adirondacks. The rooms, suites, and log and timber cabins from the 1920s reflect the region's unique style with twig and birch bark furniture and one-of-a-kind decorative accents. Every piece of artwork and furniture is attributed to a local artist or craftsman, adding to the lodge's individual style. Stone fireplaces and deep-soaking tubs further enhance the rustic sophistication of the accommodations, and discriminating diners praise the restaurant's refined new American cuisine. The lakeside setting makes it ideal for water sports; during the winter months, ice skating, snowshoeing, and skiing are popular activities. The pristine setting is often experienced from the comfortable seat of a lakefront Adirondack chair. 17 cabins. No elevator. Pets accepted, some restrictions; fee. Complimentary full breakfast. Check-out noon. In-room modem link. Restaurant, bar. Game room. Downhill skiing 10 miles, cross-country skiing on site. Concierge. **$$$$**

Resorts

★ ★ ★ **HILTON LAKE PLACID RESORT.** *1 Mirror Lake Dr (12946). Phone 518/523-4411; toll-free 800/755-5598; fax 518/523-1120. www.lphilton.com.* 176 rooms, 5 story. Pets accepted; fee. Check-out noon. TV. Restaurant, bar; entertainment. Room service. In-house fitness room. Game room. Four pools, two indoor; poolside service. Downhill ski 8 miles, cross-country ski 1 mile. Boats. **$**

★ ★ **HOLIDAY INN.** *1 Olympic Dr (12946). Phone 518/523-2556; toll-free 800/874-1980; fax 518/523-9410. www.lakeplacidresort.com.* 199 rooms, 4 story. Pets accepted, some restrictions. Check-out 11 am. TV. In-room modem link. Restaurant, bar. Room service. In-house fitness room; sauna. Pool; whirlpool. Tennis. Downhill ski 9 miles, cross-country ski on site. **$**

★ **HOWARD JOHNSON.** *90 Saranac Ave (12946). Phone 518/523-9555; toll-free 800/858-4656; fax 518/523-4765. www.hojo.com.* 92 rooms, 2 story. Pets accepted, some restrictions. Check-out noon. TV; cable (premium). Restaurant, bar. Indoor pool; whirlpool. Outdoor tennis. Downhill ski 10 miles, cross-country ski on site. Lawn games. **$**

Malone

Motel/Motor Lodge

★ **ECONO LODGE.** *227 W Main St (12953). Phone 518/483-0500; toll-free 800/553-2666; fax 518/483-4356. www.maloneeconolodge.com.* 45 rooms, 1-2 story. S $42-$47; D $48-$52; each additional $5. Pets accepted, some restrictions. Complimentary continental breakfast. Check-out 11 am. TV. Pool.

Middletown

Motel/Motor Lodge

★ **SUPER 8.** *563 Rte 211 E (10940). Phone 845/692-5828. www.super8.com.* 82 rooms, 2 story. S $60-$80; D $68-$90; each additional $7; under 12 free; higher rates: special events, weekends. Pets accepted; fee. Complimentary continental breakfast. Check-out 11 am. TV. Downhill, cross-country ski 15 miles.

Mount Kisco

Motel/Motor Lodge

★ ★ **HOLIDAY INN.** *1 Holiday Inn Dr (10549). Phone 914/241-2600; toll-free 888/452-5771; fax 914/241-4742.* 122 rooms, 2 story. S, D $139-$159; under 12 free; weekend plans. Pets accepted, some restrictions; fee. Check-out 11 am. TV; cable (premium), VCR available. In-room modem link. Restaurant, bar; entertainment. Room service. Health club privileges. Pool. Business center.

New York City

Hotels

★ ★ **ALGONQUIN HOTEL.** *59 W 44th St (10036). Phone 212/840-6800; fax 212/944-1419. www.algonquinhotel.com.* 174 rooms, 12 story. Pets accepted, some restrictions. Check-out noon. Check-in 3 pm. TV; cable (premium). Restaurant, bar; entertainment. Babysitting services available. In-house fitness room. Parking. Business center. Visited by numerous literary and theatrical personalities. **$$**

★ ★ **THE BENJAMIN.** *125 E 50th St (10022). Phone 212/715-2500; fax 212/715-2525. www.thebenjamin.com.* Despite the fact that it's set in a classic 1927 building, this hotel has all the high-tech amenities a business traveler could want, including high-speed Internet access and Web TV. It offers comfortable accommodations in a sophisticated setting that features beige, silver, and brown tones throughout the property and in the marble and silver two-story lobby. A particularly nice amenity is the "pillow menu," which offers you a choice of ten different kinds of bed pillows and a guarantee of your money back if you do not wake well rested. The Benjamin's Woodstock Spa and Wellness Center offers many services and treatments with a holistic approach. 209 rooms. Pets accepted, some restrictions. Check-out noon, check-in 3 pm. TV; VCR available. Internet access. Restaurant, bar. Babysitting services available. In-house fitness room. Concierge. **$$**

★ ★ ★ ★ **THE CARLYLE.** *35 E 76th St (10021). Phone 212/744-1600; toll-free 800/227-5737; fax 212/717-4682. www.rosewoodhotels.com.* Discreetly tucked away on Manhattan's Upper East Side, The Carlyle has maintained the allure of being one of New York's best-kept secrets for more than 70 years. A favorite of many movie stars, presidents, and royals, The Carlyle feels like an exclusive private club with its white-glove service and impeccable taste. Its art collection is extraordinary, from Audubon prints and Piranesi architectural drawings to English country scenes by Kips. Art factors largely at The Carlyle, where all rooms are equipped with direct lines to Sotheby's. The rooms are completed in an Art Deco décor and are enhanced by striking antiques and bountiful bouquets. Populated by power brokers and socialites, The Carlyle Restaurant defines elegance. Bemelmans Bar proudly shows off its murals by Madeline creator Ludwig Bemelmans, while guests have been tapping their toes to the tunes of Bobby Short for more than 30 years in the Café Carlyle. 180 rooms, 35 story. Pets accepted, some restrictions. Check-out noon, check-in 3 pm. TV;

cable (premium), VCR available, CD available. In-room modem link. Room service 24 hours. Restaurant, bar; entertainment. In-house fitness room; massage, sauna, steam room. Valet parking. **$$$$**

★ ★ ★ **CHAMBERS.** *15 W 56th St (10013). Phone 212/974-5656; fax 212/974-5657. www.chambersahotel.com.* Located just steps from some of New York's finest retail shops, this trendy hotel has a modern, open-air feel to it. The public spaces—including the soaring lobby with a double-sided fireplace—and the loftlike guest rooms feature modern, funky works of art of all kinds. The spacious, high-tech rooms with hand-troweled cement walls offer amenities like slippers you can actually keep, umbrellas, robes, cordless phones, and flat-screen TVs. Just off the lobby, Town restaurant serves fine American cuisine accented with French and Asian influences. It is popular with locals, so reservations are suggested for dinner. 77 rooms, 30 story. Pets accepted. Check-out noon. Check-in 3 pm. TV; cable (premium), VCR available. In-room modem link. Restaurant, bar. In-house fitness room. Babysitting services available. Valet parking. Business center. Concierge. **$$$**

★ ★ ★ **DYLAN HOTEL.** *52 E 41st St (10017). Phone 212/338-0500. www.dylanhotel.com.* With a grand feeling throughout, the 1903 Beaux Arts-style building, with its ornate facade and spiraling marble staircase, used to be the home of the Chemists Club. The guest rooms are bright and airy, with 11-foot ceilings and elegant marble baths. The rooms' white and blue walls, deep amethyst and steel blue carpeting, and ebony-stained furniture give them a quiet, tailored look without being austere or cold. Situated on a quiet street, the hotel contains the Dylan restaurant, which serves basic fare like burgers and pastas, and a bar for relaxing with a drink. 107 rooms, 20 story. Pets accepted. Check-out noon, check-in 3 pm. TV; cable (premium), VCR available. In-room modem link. Restaurant, bar. Room service. In-house fitness room. Business center. Concierge. **$$$**

★ ★ ★ ★ **FOUR SEASONS HOTEL NEW YORK.** *57 E 57th St (10022). Phone 212/758-5700; fax 212/758-5711. www.fourseasons.com.* The bustling world of 57th Street's designer boutiques and office towers awaits outside the doors of the Four Seasons Hotel New York, yet this temple of modern elegance provides a serene escape from city life. Designed by legendary architect I. M. Pei, the Four Seasons pays homage to the city's beloved skyscrapers as the tallest hotel in New York. The rooms and suites are testaments to chic simplicity with neutral tones, English sycamore furnishings, and state-of-the-art technology, but it's the service that defines the Four Seasons experience. The staff makes guests feel completely at ease in the monumental building, with ready smiles and generous spirit. The views are terrific, too; floor-to-ceiling windows showcase the dazzling city skyline or the quietude of Central Park. Some rooms offer furnished terraces so that guests can further admire the sights. Fifty Seven Fifty Seven, the restaurant in the hotel, remains the place to see and be seen, while the bar and the Lobby Lounge provide perfect settings for lingering over drinks or casual fare. 368 rooms, 52 story. Pets accepted, some restrictions. Check-out noon, check-in 3 pm. TV; cable (premium), VCR. In-room modem link. Restaurant, bar. Room service. In-house fitness room; massage, sauna, steam room. Whirlpool. Garage, valet parking. Business center. Concierge. **$$$$**

⊡ 🐾 🏋 🈲 🚶

★ ★ ★ **THE HELMSLEY PARK LANE.** *36 Central Park S (10019). Phone 212/371-4000; toll-free 800/221-4982; fax 212/521-6666. www.helmsleyhotels.com.* Spectacular, unobstructed views of Central Park distinguish the upper-level rooms of this part-residential hotel. 637 rooms, 46 story. Pets accepted, some restrictions. Check-out noon, check-in 3 pm. TV; VCR available (movies). In-room modem link. Restaurant, bar. Room service. In-house fitness room. Business center. Concierge. **$$$**

⊡ 🐾 🏋 🈲 SC 🚶

★ ★ ★ **HILTON NEW YORK.** *1335 Avenue of the Americas (10019). Phone 212/586-7000; toll-free 212/261-5870; fax 212/315-1374. www.newyorktowers.hilton.com. com.* This large convention hotel has a bustling, urban charm. Several restaurants, shops, and services make it a convenient base from which to explore New York. 2,034 rooms, 44 story. Pets accepted. Check-out noon. TV; cable (premium), VCR available. In-room modem link. Restaurant, bar. Room service. In-house fitness room; massage, sauna, steam room. Parking. Business center. Concierge. **$$**

⊡ 🐾 🏋 🈲 🚶

★ ★ ★ **HOTEL PLAZA ATHENEE.** *37 E 64th St (10021). Phone 212/734-9100; toll-free 800/447-8800; fax 212/772-0958. www.plaza-athenee.com.* Hotel Plaza Athénée is the perfect place to enjoy a little bit of France while visiting New York. Located between Park and Madison avenues in one of the city's most exclusive neighborhoods, this elegant hotel is a perfect hideaway with a decidedly residential feel. Celebrating its place among the boutiques of Madison Avenue, the townhouses and apartment buildings of Park Avenue, and the greenery of Central Park, the Plaza Athénée indeed feels like a home away from home for its guests. A palette of blues, golds, and reds creates the French contemporary décor of the rooms and suites. Some suites have dining rooms, while

others have indoor terraces or outdoor balconies. The exotic flavor of the Bar Seine, with its vibrant colors and striking furnishings, transports guests to a faraway land, while Arabelle Restaurant combines gracious French style with delicious continental cuisine. 150 rooms, 17 story. Pets accepted, some restrictions. Check-out noon, check-in 3 pm. TV; cable (premium), VCR available. In-room modem link. Room service 24 hours. Restaurant, bar. In-house fitness room. Concierge. **$$$$**

⊡ 🐾 🏋 🈲

★ ★ ★ **LE PARKER MERIDIEN.** *118 W 57th St (10019). Phone 212/245-5000; fax 212/307-1776. www.parkermeridien.com.* 730 rooms, 42 story. Pets accepted. Check-out noon, check-in 3 pm. TV; VCR available. Internet access. Restaurant. Room service. In-house fitness room; massage, sauna, steam room. Indoor pool. Valet parking. Business center. Concierge. **$$$**

⊡ 🐾 🏊 🏋 🚶

★ ★ **THE MANSFIELD.** *12 W 44th St (10036). Phone 212/944-6050; toll-free 800/255-5167; fax 212/764-4477. www.mansfieldhotel.com.* 124 rooms, 13 story. Pets accepted, some restrictions. Check-out noon. Check-in 3 pm. TV; cable (premium), VCR available. Room service 24 hours. Restaurant, bar. Babysitting services available. In-house fitness room; health club privileges. Valet parking. Concierge. **$$**

⊡ 🐾 🛁 🈲 SC

★ ★ ★ **THE MARK NEW YORK.** *25 E 77th St (10021). Phone 212/744-4300; toll-free 800/THEMARK; fax 212/744-2749. www.mandarinoriental.com.* Take a break from the shopping of Madison Avenue and the museums of the Upper East Side and enter the haven of The Mark, New York, where style and comfort combine for an exceptional experience. Situated on a quiet tree-lined street, The Mark feels like an elegant private home. The hotel's eclectic décor perfectly blends the clean lines of Italian design with the lively spirit of English florals. Asian decorative objects and Piranesi prints complete the look in the hotel's rooms and suites. Sophisticated cuisine is highlighted at Mark's Restaurant, where the Master Sommelier also offers wine-tasting courses and themed dinners. Afternoon tea at The Mark is especially notable thanks to the Tea Master, who ensures that little bits of America and the Orient are brought to this British tradition. Mark's Bar, a jewel-toned boîte, is particularly popular with local denizens as well as hotel guests. 176 rooms, 16 story. Pets accepted, some restrictions; fee. Check-out noon, check-in 3 pm. TV; cable (premium), VCR available. In-room modem link. Room service 24 hours. Restaurant, bar. In-house fitness room; sauna, steam room. Valet parking. Concierge. **$$$**

⊡ 🐾 🏋 🈲

★ ★ **MAYFLOWER ON THE PARK.** *15 Central Park W (10023). Phone 212/265-0060; toll-free 800/223-4164; fax 212/265-0227. www.mayflowerhotelny.com.* 365 rooms, 18 story. Pets accepted, some restrictions. Check-out noon, check-in 3 pm. TV; cable (premium). In-room modem link. Restaurant, bar. Room service. In-house fitness room. Valet parking. Concierge. **$$$**

★ ★ ★ ★ **MERCER HOTEL.** *147 Mercer St (10012). Phone 212/966-6060; toll-free 888/918-6060; fax 212/965-3838. www.mercerhotel.com.* Catering to a fashion-forward clientele in New York's SoHo, Mercer Hotel is a boutique hotel in the midst of one of the city's most exciting neighborhoods. This former artists' community stays true to its roots in its many cutting-edge boutiques and galleries. The loft-style Mercer Hotel epitomizes bohemian chic with its exposed brick, steel beams, and hardwood floors. Christian Liaigre, darling of the minimalist décor movement, has designed a sophisticated look for the hotel with simple furnishings and serene neutral colors. The uncluttered look extends to the bathrooms, with clean white tiles and luxurious two-person bathtubs or spacious showers with assorted spray fixtures. The lobby also serves as a lending library stocked with favorite books and videos, and the nearby trend-setting Crunch Gym is accessible to all guests. Mercer Kitchen and Bar reign as hotspots on the local scene, for both their sensational food under the direction of Jean-Georges Vongerichten and their fabulous people-watching. 75 rooms, 6 story. Pets accepted. Check-out 3 pm, check-in 11 am. In-room modem link. Fireplaces. Room service 24 hours. Restaurant. Babysitting services available. Valet parking. Concierge. **$$$$**

★ ★ ★ **METROPOLITAN HOTEL.** *569 Lexington Ave (10022). Phone 212/752-7000; toll-free 800/836-6471; fax 212/758-6311. www.metropolitanhotelnyc.com.* Recently renovated, this East Side business traveler's hotel (formerly the Loews New York) has a casual elegance in its soft tones and king-bed rooms. The Lexington Avenue Grill serves contemporary American cuisine, and the popular Lexy Lounge features a signature cocktail called the Sexy Lexy that is a hit with locals. The business center offers everything from secretarial services to fax capabilities to workstation rentals. The premium business-class program includes a separate check-in and check-out area; private lounge with wine and cheese, continental breakfast, and snacks; and special in-room amenities like fax machines. 667 rooms, 20 story. Pets accepted. Check-out noon. Check-in 3 pm. TV; cable (premium). In-room modem link. Restaurant, bar. Room service. In-house fitness room; sauna. Airport transportation. Business center. Concierge. Luxury level. **$$**

★ ★ ★ **MILLENNIUM HOTEL NEW YORK BROADWAY.** *145 W 44th St (10036). Phone 212/768-4400; toll-free 800/622-5569; fax 212/768-0847. www.millenniumbroadway.com.* Colorful murals that evoke the 1930s adorn the lobby of this fine midtown hotel. There are several grades of guest rooms, all of which are tastefully appointed, from "classic" to "premier" providing accomodations to meet the needs of most travelers. 750 rooms, 52 story. Pets accepted, some restrictions. Check-out noon. Check-in 4 pm. TV; cable (premium), VCR available. In-room modem link. Restaurant, bar. Room service. Babysitting services available. In-house fitness room. Valet parking. Business center. Concierge. Postmodern skyscraper with Moderne setbacks, Deco detailing; incorporates landmark Beaux Arts Hudson Theatre (1903), which has been restored. **$$**

★ ★ ★ **THE MUSE.** *130 W 46th St (10036). Phone 212/485-2400; fax 212/485-2900. www.themusehotel.com.* A designers' dream, this hotel has restored its unique, triple-arched, limestone and brick facade to give it a dramatic feel. Adding to the drama is a 15-foot vaulted ceiling with a commissioned mural depicting the nine muses in the lobby. Original artwork celebrating the theater and the performing arts hangs in each room, decorated in a warm color scheme of rust, burgundy, pear green, and muted blue-green and cherry wood furniture. Custom linens and duvet-covered feather beds add to guests' comfort. Guest baths feature green marble with stone vanities. Other distinguishing features include in-room spa services, balconies, and DVD players. 200 rooms, 19 story. Pets accepted. Check-out noon. Check-in 3 pm. TV; cable (premium), VCR available. In-room modem link. Restaurant, bar. Babysitting services available. In-house fitness room. Business center. Concierge. **$$$**

★ ★ ★ ★ **THE NEW YORK PALACE.** *455 Madison Ave (10022). Phone 212/888-7000; toll-free 800/697-2522; fax 212/303-6000. www.newyorkpalace.com.* Return to the Gilded Age at The New York Palace. Marrying the historic 1882 Villard Houses with a 55-story contemporary tower, The Palace brings the best of both worlds together under one roof. Directly across from St. Patrick's Cathedral, The Palace is convenient for sightseeing or conducting business. First impressions are memorable, and the grand entrance through the gated courtyard of twinkling lights is no exception. The glorious public rooms are masterfully restored and recall their former incarnations as part of the private residences of America's wealthiest citizens at the turn of the century. Set against the backdrop of New York City, The Palace's rooms and suites are a blend of contemporary flair and period décor. The Villard Bar & Lounge captures the imagination of its patrons with its Victorian design. Home to Le Cirque 2000, one of the world's most famous restaurants, The New York Palace is in its own class. 896 rooms, 55 story. Pets accepted, some restrictions. Check-out 3 pm, check-in noon. TV; VCR available. In-room modem link. Room service 24 hours. Restaurant, bar. In-house fitness room; health club privileges, spa, massage, steam room. Parking. Business center. Concierge. **$$$$**

D 🖐 🏃 🏊 🚶 .

★ ★ ★ **OMNI BERKSHIRE PLACE.** *21 E 52nd St at Madison Ave (10022). Phone 212/753-5800; toll-free 800/843-6664; fax 212/754-5018. www.omnihotels.com.* A soaring atrium—with a wood-burning fireplace—is the focal point of the lobby of this understated hotel. The rooms are designed with an Asian aesthetic, and business travelers will find all they need for a hassle-free stay. 396 rooms, 21 story. Pets accepted, some restrictions; fee. Check-out noon, check-in 3 pm. TV; cable (premium), VCR available. In-room modem link. Room service 24 hours. Restaurant, bar. Babysitting services available. In-house fitness room. Valet parking. Business center. Concierge. **$$$**

D 🖐 🏃 🏊 🚶

★ ★ ★ ★ **THE PIERRE NEW YORK, A FOUR SEASONS HOTEL.** *2 E 61st St (10021). Phone 212/838-8000; toll-free 800/743-7734; fax 212/940-8109. www.fourseasons.com.* Regal and esteemed, The Pierre New York is the definition of a grand old hotel. Relishing its location across from Central Park on Fifth Avenue, The Pierre has been a city landmark since 1930. Owned by Charles Pierre and John Paul Getty, among others, The Pierre is now managed by Four Seasons, which carefully maintains the integrity of this historic building while imparting its signature service levels with mixed success. Guests linger for hours in the impressive lobby, soaking up the ambience of old-world Europe. The rooms and suites are traditional with floral prints and antique reproductions. The Rotunda, where breakfast, light lunch, and afternoon tea are served, is a magical place where the cares of the world disappear under a ceiling of trompe l'oeil murals. Influenced by Renaissance paintings, the murals depict pastoral scenes of mythological figures intertwined with icons of the 1960s, including Jacqueline Kennedy Onassis. *Secret Inspector's Notes:* Don't be disappointed by the small rooms, aging bathrooms, and occasionally brusque service. This is still a hotel in the ultimate location for accessing all the wonders of Manhattan in the surrounding blocks. 201 rooms, 41 story. Pets accepted, some restrictions. Check-out noon, check-in 3 pm. TV; cable (premium), VCR available. In-room modem link. Room service 24 hours. Restaurant, bar; entertainment. Babysitting services available. In-house fitness room; health club privileges, massage. 24-hour valet parking. Business center. Concierge. **$$$$**

D 🖐 🏃 🏊 🚶

★ ★ ★ **THE PLAZA.** *5th Ave at Central Park S (10019). Phone 212/759-3000; toll-free 800/527-4727; fax 212/759-3167.* Considered by many to be the grande dame of New York City lodgings, this massive, opulent hotel filled with lush furniture, pricey stores, and chandeliers has played host to dignitaries, celebrities, and just about every rich and famous person who has lived throughout its history. It's located near Central Park on Fifth Ave. The rooms are elegant, too, with crystal chandeliers, formal furnishings, and 14-foot ceilings. The Oak Room is a classic steakhouse with an equally formal feel, and the Palm Court is legendary for its high tea and overflowing Sunday brunch. Bring an extra credit card to dine at either venue. 805 rooms, 18 story. Pets accepted, some restrictions; fee. Check-out noon. TV; cable (premium), VCR available. In-room modem link. Restaurant, bar. Room service. In-house fitness room. Business center. Concierge. **$$$**

D 🖐 🏃 🏊 🚶

★ ★ ★ ★ **THE REGENCY HOTEL.** *540 Park Ave (10021). Phone 212/759-4100; toll-free 800/233-2356; fax 212/826-5674. www.loewshotels.com.* Home of the original power breakfast, where deals are sealed and fortunes are made, The Regency consistently ranks as one of New York's top hotels. Combining the appearance of a library and a private club, The Regency provides attentive service that extends above and beyond the ordinary to create a memorable stay. International design influences create a warm atmosphere throughout the well-appointed rooms, while the fitness and business centers cater to guests with specific goals in mind. Creature comforts abound in the luxurious rooms and suites, from the Frette linens to the "Did You Forget" closet stocked with items often left at home. Pets are even welcomed in grand style with room service designed exclusively for man's best friend, as well as dog-walking services and listings of pet-friendly establishments. Unwind at Feinstein's, where Grammy-nominated Michael Feinstein entertains nightly, or savor a delectable meal at 540 Park or The Library. 351 rooms, 20 story. Pets accepted. Check-out noon, check-in 3 pm. TV; cable (premium), VCR available, CD available. In-room modem link. Room service 24 hours. Restaurant, bar. In-house fitness room; massage, sauna. Valet parking. Business center. Concierge. **$$$**

D 🖐 🏃 🏊 🚶

★ ★ ★ ★ **THE REGENT WALL STREET.** *55 Wall St (10005). Phone 212/845-8600; fax 212/845-8601. www.regenthotels.com.* The Regent Wall Street is the premier address in the heart of one of the world's most influential financial capitals. Just a short walk from the New York Stock Exchange, The Regent welcomes tired guests after a long day of trading or touring nearby SoHo, Chinatown, and South Street Seaport. The Regent's landmark Greek Revival building dates from 1842 and in former incarnations served as the Merchants Exchange and the Customs House, where writer Herman Melville toiled for many years. Rooms and suites are a beautiful blend of Italian contemporary décor with a masculine feel, and the fabulous bathrooms offer deep-soaking bathtubs. Fitness-minded guests will appreciate the terrific Health Club & Spa, with state-of-the-art equipment and relaxing treatments. Casual American dining is available at 55 Wall or 55 Wall Terrace, where the many ethnic neighborhoods of New York influence the inventive menu. *Secret Inspector's Notes:* The Regent's lounge plays host to many of New York's financial players seeking a place to unwind and enjoy a cigar, martini, or exceptional glass of wine at the conclusion of a fast-paced day. 144 rooms, 15 story. Pets accepted, some restrictions. Check-out noon. TV; cable (premium), VCR available. In-room modem link. Restaurant, bar. In-house fitness room; sauna. Business center. Concierge. **$$$**

D �’ 🛉 ⊠ 🏃

★ ★ ★ ★ **THE RITZ-CARLTON NEW YORK, BATTERY PARK.** *2 West St (10004). Phone 212/344-0800; fax 212/344-3801. www.ritzcarlton.com.* Watch the world from The Ritz-Carlton New York, Battery Park. While only a five-minute walk from Wall Street and the Financial District, The Ritz-Carlton feels light years away with its staggering views of the Hudson River, the Statue of Liberty, and Ellis Island from its location on the southern tip of Manhattan. This 38-story glass and brick tower is a departure from the traditional Ritz-Carlton European style, from the contemporary glass artwork bestowed upon the public and private spaces to the modern furnishings in rooms and suites. The service is distinctly Ritz-Carlton, however, with exceptional concierge service and Bath Butlers who create special concoctions for bath time. The view is omnipresent throughout the hotel, whether you're gazing through a telescope in a harbor view room, enjoying a cocktail while viewing Lady Liberty at Rise, the 14th-floor bar, or savoring a delicious meal at 2 West. 298 rooms, 39 story. Pets accepted, some restrictions; fee. Check-out noon, check-in 3 pm. TV; VCR available, CD player. In-room modem link. Room service 24 hours. Restaurant, bar. Babysitting services available. In-house fitness room; spa, massage, sauna. Parking. Business center. Concierge. Luxury level. **$$$$**

D �’ 🛉 ⊠ 🏃

★ ★ ★ ★ ★ **THE RITZ-CARLTON NEW YORK CENTRAL PARK.** *50 Central Park S (10019). Phone 212/308-9100; fax 212/207-8831. www.ritzcarlton.com.* Rising above Central Park and flanked by prestigious Fifth Avenue and fashionable Central Park West, the Ritz-Carlton has one of the most coveted locations in town. This genteel hotel is exquisite down to every last detail, from the priceless antiques and artwork to the bountiful floral displays. The light-filled rooms and suites are a pastel-hued paradise, with sumptuous fabrics and plush fur-

nishings. No detail is overlooked; rooms facing the park include telescopes for closer viewing. The distinguished ambience and white-glove service make this a top choice of well-heeled travelers. Atelier garners praise from top critics for its modern French cuisine. Dedicated to excellence in all areas, the hotel even includes an outpost of the renowned European La Prairie Spa. 277 rooms, 15 story. Pets accepted. Complimentary continental breakfast. Check-out noon. Check-in 3 pm. TV; cable (premium), DVD available. In-room modem link. Room service 24 hours. Restaurant, bar. In-house fitness room; spa, massage, steam room. Business center. Concierge. Luxury level. **$$$$**

D �’ 🛉 ⊠ 🏃

★ ★ ★ **SOFITEL.** *45 W 44th St (10036). Phone 212/354-8844; fax 212/354-2450. www.accor-hotels.com.* 398 rooms, 30 story. Pets accepted. Check-out 1 pm, check-in 12 pm. TV; cable (premium), VCR available. In-room modem link. Room service 24 hours. Restaurant, bar. Babysitting services available. In-house fitness room; massage. Concierge. **$$$**

D �’ 🛉

★ ★ ★ **SOHO GRAND HOTEL.** *310 W Broadway (10013). Phone 212/965-3000; fax 212/965-3200. www.sohogrand.com.* Calculated cool is the best way to describe this trendy downtown hotel. The second-floor lobby doubles as a popular lounge. The guest rooms are simple in design, with tones of black and white and clean, uncluttered baths. All rooms have stereos, and some have rocking chairs. The lobby provides a comfortable gathering place, with high ceilings, couches, and exotic plants. Each floor also features a pantry with complimentary coffee, tea, and espresso. The Grand Bar & Lounge serves a mix of dishes, from macaroni and cheese to lobster tea sandwiches to chickpea-fried rock shrimp. The lounge also features music and DJs—a good place to hang out after a day of sightseeing. 364 rooms, 17 story. Pets accepted, some restrictions. Check-out noon. TV; cable (premium), VCR available. In-room modem link. Restaurant, bar. Room service. In-house fitness room; massage. Garage parking. Concierge. **$$$**

D �’ 🛉 ⊠

★ ★ ★ ★ **THE STANHOPE, A PARK HYATT HOTEL.** *995 5th Ave at 81st St (10028). Phone 212/774-1234; toll-free 800/233-1234; fax 212/517-0088. www.hyatt.com.* Since 1926, The Stanhope Park Hyatt New York has endured as one of New York's favorite hotels. Directly across from the prestigious Metropolitan Museum of Art on Fifth Avenue, The Stanhope is situated in the middle of famed Museum Mile, with the Guggenheim, Whitney, and Cooper-Hewitt museums enticing visitors just blocks away. The Stanhope's gracious European style is evident in its public spaces, where antiques and gold-leafing details catch the eye. The rooms and suites are richly decorated with pastel walls, antique reproduction furnishings, and Chinoiserie accents. The dark wood paneling of the Bar makes it an intimate spot for gatherings, while Melrose entertains in grand style with contemporary American cuisine. In perhaps one of the most enviable dining spots in New York, Melrose opens its outdoor terrace for dining with a view of the Met in warmer months. 185 rooms, 17 story. Pets accepted, some restrictions; fee. Check-out noon. TV; cable (premium), VCR available. Restaurant, bar. Room service. In-house fitness room; massage, sauna. Valet parking. Business center. Concierge. **$$$**

D ⬛ 🏃 ⬛ SC 🏃

★ ★ ★ **THE SURREY HOTEL.** *20 E 76th St (10021). Phone 212/288-3700; toll-free 800/637-8483; fax 212/628-1549. www.mesuite.com.* Like staying at the home of a rich great-aunt, this hotel has the understated grandeur of a faded residence. You'll see old-world charm upon entering the lobby, with its 18th-century English décor, wood-paneled elevators, and leather sofas. The studio, one-bedroom, and two-bedroom suites have a similar look, with molded ceilings, beveled-glass mirrors, and antique accents. Some have kitchenettes, and others have full kitchens. Suites also offer Web TV, Nintendo, VCRs, and bathrobes—all the comforts of home. The hotel's best feature is its restaurant—world-renowned chef Daniel Boulud's Café Boulud serves up gourmet French cuisine (at prices to match). 131 rooms, 16 story. Pets accepted, some restrictions. Check-out noon, check-in 3 pm. TV; cable (premium), VCR available. In-room modem link. Restaurant, bar. Room service. In-house fitness room. Concierge. **$$**

D ⬛ 🏃 ⬛

★ ★ ★ **SWISSOTEL NEW YORK, THE DRAKE.** *440 Park Ave and 56th St (10022). Phone 212/421-0900; toll-free 800/637-9477; fax 212/371-4190. www.swissotel.com.* 495 rooms, 21 story. Pets accepted; fee. Check-out noon. TV; VCR available. In-room modem link. Room service 24 hours. Restaurant, bar. In-house fitness room; spa, massage, sauna, steam room. Garage, valet parking available. Business center. Concierge. **$$$**

D ⬛ 🏃 ⬛ 🏃

★ ★ ★ ★ **TRUMP INTERNATIONAL HOTEL & TOWER.** *1 Central Park W (10023). Phone 212/299-1000; toll-free 888/448-7867; fax 212/299-1150. www.trumpintl.com.* Occupying an enviable site across from Central Park on Manhattan's Upper West Side, the 52-story Trump International Hotel & Tower makes guests feel like they are on top of the world. The lobby's warm brass tones and polished marble welcome visitors to the world of Trump, where attention to detail results in perfection and everyone feels like a tycoon. The rooms

and suites are elegantly decorated with a contemporary European flavor, while the floor-to-ceiling windows focus attention on the mesmerizing views of Central Park framed by the impressive skyline. The Personal Attaché service ensures that all guests are properly coddled, while the extensive fitness center caters to exercise enthusiasts. All suites and most rooms are complete with kitchens, and in-room chefs are available to craft memorable dining experiences. Room service is world-class and created by one of New York's top chefs, Jean-Georges Vongerichten, whose Five-Star restaurant, Jean-Georges, is located here. *Secret Inspector's Notes:* Dinner at Jean-Georges is the one component of this hotel not to be missed. It is one of the finest dining experiences you'll find. 168 rooms, 52 story. Pets accepted, some restrictions; fee. Check-out noon, check-in 4 pm. Valet parking. TV; cable (premium), VCR available. In-room modem link. Restaurant, bar. Room service. Babysitting services available. In-house fitness room; sauna, steam room, massage, spa. Indoor pool. Business center. Concierge. **$$$$**

D ⬛ 🏊 🏃 ⬛ 🏃

★ ★ ★ **W NEW YORK.** *541 Lexington Ave (10022). Phone 212/755-1200; toll-free 888/625-5144; fax 212/319-8344. www.whotels.com.* The chic lobby has the air of an urban ski lodge, with a sunken lobby bar that has tree trunk end tables and colorful rugs. The guest rooms have an organic feel with natural cotton linens and neutral tones. 713 rooms, 18 story. Pets accepted, some restrictions; fee. Check-out noon, check-in 3 pm. TV; cable (premium), VCR available. In-room modem link. Restaurant, bar. Room service. In-house fitness room; spa, massage, sauna, steam room. Valet parking. Concierge. **$$$**

D ⬛ 🏃 ⬛

★ ★ ★ **W NEW YORK - UNION SQUARE.** *201 Park Ave S (10016). Phone 212/253-9119. www.whotels.com.* 270 rooms, 25 story. Pets accepted. Check-out noon. Check-in 3 pm. TV; cable (premium). In-room modem link. Restaurant, bar. In-house fitness room. Business center. Concierge. Game tables. **$$$$**

⬛ 🏃 🏃

Niagara Falls

Motel/Motor Lodge

★ **PORTAGE HOUSE.** *280 Portage Rd (14092). Phone 716/754-8295.* 21 rooms, 2 story. No room phone. May-Nov: S $57-$80.25; D $61-$80.25; each additional $7; under 12 free; lower rates rest of year. Pets accepted, some restrictions. Check-out 11 am. TV.

⬛ 🐾 ⬛

Hotels

★ **BEST WESTERN SUMMIT INN.** *9500 Niagara Falls Blvd (14304). Phone 716/297-5050; toll-free 800/404-8217; fax 716/297-0802. www.bestwestern.com.* 88 rooms, 2 story. Pets accepted, some restrictions; fee. Complimentary continental breakfast. Check-out 11 am, check-in 3 pm. TV; VCR available (movies). Restaurant, bar. Sauna. Game room. Indoor pool. **$**

★ **HOWARD JOHNSON.** *454 Main St (14301). Phone 716/285-5261; toll-free 800/282-5261; fax 716/285-8536. www.the.hojo.com/niagarafalls00139.* 80 rooms, 5 story. Pets accepted; fee. Complimentary continental breakfast. Check-out noon, check-in 4 pm. TV. Sauna. Game room. Indoor pool. Near falls. **$**

North Creek

Motel/Motor Lodge

★★ **BLACK MOUNTAIN SKI LODGE & MOTEL.** *2999 NY 8 (12853). Phone 518/251-2800; toll-free 888/846-4858; fax 518/251-5326. blackmountainskilodge.com.* 25 rooms. Pets accepted, some restrictions; fee. Check-out 11 am. TV. Restaurant. Pool. Downhill, cross-country ski 5 miles. **$**

Norwich

Motel/Motor Lodge

★★ **HOWARD JOHNSON.** *75 N Broad St (13815). Phone 607/334-2200; fax 607/336-5619. www.hojo.com.* 86 rooms, 3 story. S $79-$149; D $89-$159; each additional $10; suites $75-$125; some weekend rates; higher rates special events. Pets accepted, some restrictions; fee. Check-out 11 am. TV; cable (premium). Restaurant, bar. Health club privileges. Indoor pool.

Ogdensburg

Resort

★★ **STONEFENCE LODGING INC.** *7191 State Hwy 37 (13669). Phone 315/393-1545; toll-free 800/253-1545; fax 315/393-1749. www.stonefenceresort.com.* 31 rooms. May-Sep: S $69-$89; D $79-$119; each additional $5; suites $79-$145; weekly rates; lower rates rest of year.

Pets accepted, some restrictions; fee. Check-out 11 am. TV. Restaurant. Sauna. Pool; whirlpool. Outdoor tennis. On river; dockage, boat rentals, beach.

Old Forge

Motel/Motor Lodge

★ **BEST WESTERN SUNSET INN.** *NY 28 (13420). Phone 315/369-6836; toll-free 800/780-7234; fax 315/369-2607. www.bestwestern.com.* 52 rooms, 2 story. Pets accepted, some restrictions. Complimentary continental breakfast. Check-out 11 am. TV; cable (premium). Laundry services. Sauna. Indoor pool; whirlpool. Tennis. Downhill ski 3 miles, cross-country ski opposite. **$**

Oneonta

Motels/Motor Lodges

★★ **HOLIDAY INN.** *Rte 23 Southside (13820). Phone 607/433-2250; toll-free 800/465-4329; fax 607/432-7028. www.holiday-inn.com.* 120 rooms, 2 story. S, D $77-$199; under 19 free; higher rates special events. Pets accepted, some restrictions. Check-out 11 am. TV; cable (premium). In-room modem link. Laundry services. Restaurant, bar; entertainment Wed, Fri, Sat. Game room. Pool; children's pool.

★ **SUPER 8.** *4973 NY 23 (13820). Phone 607/432-9505. www.super8.com.* 60 rooms, 2 story. July-Aug: S $53-$103; D $63-$107; each additional $5; under 12 free; higher rates weekends, special events; lower rates rest of year. Pets accepted, some restrictions. Complimentary continental breakfast. Check-out 11 am. TV; VCR available (movies). Laundry services.

Oswego

Motel/Motor Lodge

★ **DAYS INN.** *101 NY 104 (13126). Phone 315/343-3136; fax 315/343-6187. www.daysinn.com.* 44 rooms, 2 story. S $49-$70; D $59-$100; each additional $5; suites $89; under 13 free; weekly rates; higher rates special events. Pets accepted, some restrictions. Complimentary continental breakfast. Check-out 11 am. TV.

Owego

Motel/Motor Lodge

★ **SUNRISE MOTEL.** *3778 Waverly Rd (13827). Phone 607/687-5666; toll-free 800/806-9074; fax 607/687-5667.* 20 rooms. S $43; D $47; each additional $4. Pets accepted, some restrictions; fee. Check-out 11 am. TV.
🅳 🐾 🕯 🔀 SC

Palmyra

Motel/Motor Lodge

★ ★ **QUALITY INN.** *125 N Main St (14513). Phone 315/331-9500; fax 315/331-5264. www.qualityinn.com.* 107 rooms, 2 story. S $68-$88; D $78-$108; each additional $10; under 18 free; monthly rates; ski plans. Pets accepted, some restrictions; fee. Check-out 11 am. TV; cable (premium). Restaurant, bar. Sauna. Pool. Downhill ski 8 miles, cross-country ski 9 miles. On barge canal.
🅳 🐾 🕯 🎿 🏊 🔀

Peekskill

Hotel

★ ★ **PEEKSKILL INN.** *634 Main St (10566). Phone 914/739-1500; toll-free 800/526-9466; fax 914/739-7067. www.peekskillinn.* 53 rooms, 2 story. S $89-$102; D $95-$110; suite $125-$159; higher rates West Point graduation. Pets accepted; fee. Complimentary continental breakfast; full breakfast on weekends. Check-out 11 am. TV; cable (premium). Restaurant, bar. Room service. Pool.
🐾 🏊 🔀

Penn Yan

Resort

★ ★ **VIKING RESORT.** *680 E Lake Rd (14527). Phone 315/536-7061; fax 315/536-0737. www.vikingresort.com.* 31 rooms, 2 story. S $48; D $65; each additional $15; kitchen units $75-$160; family, weekly rates. Closed mid-Oct-mid-May. Pets accepted; fee. Check-out 11 am. TV. Pool; whirlpool. Lawn games. Rental boats.
🐾 🏊 🔀

Plattsburgh

Motel/Motor Lodge

★ ★ **BEST WESTERN THE INN AT SMITHFIELD.** *446 Cornelia St (12901). Phone 518/561-7750; toll-free 800/780-7234; fax 518/561-9431. www.bestwestern.com.* 120 rooms, 2 story. Pets accepted. Check-out noon. TV; cable (premium), VCR available. In-room modem link. Laundry services. Restaurant, bar. In-house fitness room. Indoor pool; poolside service. $
🅳 🐾 🏊 🏋 🔀 SC

Poughkeepsie

Motel/Motor Lodge

★ **ECONO LODGE.** *2625 South Rd (12601). Phone 845/452-6600; toll-free 800/553-2666; fax 845/454-2210. www.econolodge.com.* 111 rooms, 1-2 story. S, D $99-$110; each additional $5; under 16 free; weekly rates. Pets accepted, some restrictions. Complimentary continental breakfast. Check-out 11 am. TV. In-room modem link. Laundry services.
🐾 🔀 SC

B&B/Small Inn

★ ★ ★ **OLD DROVERS INN.** *Old Rte 22 (12522). Phone 845/832-9311; fax 845/832-6356. www.olddroversinn.com.* This historic inn was built in 1750 and may be the oldest continuously operated inn in the US. Each room is delicately decorated with fine antiques. 4 rooms. No room phones. Closed Tues, Wed. Pets accepted, some restrictions; fee. Complimentary full breakfast. Check-out 11 am, check-in 3 pm. TV; VCR available. Restaurant. $$$
🐾 🔀

Rochester

Motels/Motor Lodges

★ **COMFORT INN.** *1501 Ridge Rd W (14615). Phone 585/621-5700; toll-free 800/892-9348; fax 585/621-8446. www.comfortinn.com.* 83 rooms, 5 story. Pets accepted, some restrictions; fee. Complimentary continental breakfast. Check-out noon, check-in 3 pm. TV; cable (premium). In-room modem link. $
🅳 🐾

★ **ECONO LODGE.** *940 Jefferson Rd (14623). Phone 585/427-2700; toll-free 800/228-5150; fax 716/427-8504. www.econolodgerochester.com.* 101 rooms, 3 story. Pets accepted. Complimentary continental breakfast. Check-out 11 am, check-in 3 pm. TV; cable (premium). Laundry services. Free transportation. **$**

D 🐾 ✈ 🖼

★ ★ **HOLIDAY INN.** *911 Brooks Ave (14624). Phone 585/328-6000; toll-free 800/465-4329; fax 585/328-1012. www.holiday-inn.com.* 280 rooms, 3 suites, 2 story. Pets accepted, some restrictions. Check-out noon, check-in 3 pm. TV; cable (premium). In-room modem link. Restaurant, bar; entertainment. Room service. In-house fitness room; sauna. Indoor pool; whirlpool. Business center. Concierge. Free transportation. **$**

D 🐾 ⛱ 🏃 ✈ 🖼 SC 🏃

★ **RED ROOF INN.** *4820 W Henriette Rd (14467). Phone 585/359-1100; fax 585/359-1121. www.redroof.com.* 108 rooms, 2 story. S $37-$60; D $44-$70; each additional $7; under 18 free. Pets accepted, some restrictions. Check-out noon. TV; cable (premium).

D 🐾 🖼

★ **WELLESLEY INN.** *1635 W Ridge Rd (14615). Phone 585/621-2060; toll-free 800/444-8888; fax 585/621-7102. www.wellesleyinnandsuites.com.* 97 rooms, 4 story. Pets accepted, some restrictions. Complimentary continental breakfast. Check-out noon, check-in 3 pm. TV; cable (premium). **$**

D 🐾 🖼

Hotels

★ ★ ★ **CROWNE PLAZA.** *70 State St (14614). Phone 585/546-3450; fax 585/546-8714. www.rochester crowne.com.* 362 rooms, 7 story. Pets accepted, some restrictions. Check-out noon, check-in 3 pm. TV; cable (premium). In-room modem link. Restaurant, bar. Room service. In-house fitness room. Game room. Outdoor pool. Downhill ski 20 miles. Airport transportation. Business center. Concierge. Luxury level. On river. **$**

D 🐾 ⛱ ⛱ 🏃 ✈ 🖼 🏃

★ **HAMPTON INN.** *500 Center Place Dr (14615). Phone 585/663-6070; fax 585/663-9158. www.hamptoninn.com.* 118 rooms, 4 story. Pets accepted, some restrictions. Complimentary continental breakfast. Check-out noon, check-in 3 pm. TV; cable (premium). In-room modem link. In-house fitness room. **$**

D 🐾 🏃 🖼

★ ★ **RAMADA INN.** *800 Jefferson Rd (14623). Phone 585/475-9190; toll-free 800/888-8102; fax 585/424-2138.* *www.ramada.com.* 143 rooms, 3 story. Pets accepted. Complimentary breakfast buffet. Check-out noon, check-in 3 pm. TV; cable (premium), VCR available. In-room modem link. Restaurant, bar. In-house fitness room; health club privileges. Indoor pool. Free transportation. **$**

D 🐾 ⛱ 🏃 🖼

★ **WELLESLEY INN.** *797 E Henrietta Rd (14623). Phone 585/427-0130; fax 585/427-0903. www.wellesleyinn andsuites.com.* 96 rooms, 4 story. Pets accepted, some restrictions; fee. Complimentary continental breakfast. Check-out noon, check-in 2 pm. TV; cable (premium). In-room modem link. **$**

D 🐾 🖼 SC

Rome

Motel/Motor Lodge

★ ★ **INN AT THE BEECHES.** *7900 Turin Rd (Rte 26 N) (13440). Phone 315/336-1775; toll-free 800/765-7251; fax 315/339-2636. www.thebeeches.com.* 75 rooms, 1-2 story. S $56-$63; D $62-$69; each additional $5; kitchen units $85-$99; under 12 free; weekly rates; weekend rates. Pets accepted, some restrictions; fee. Check-out 11 am. TV. Restaurant. Pool. Downhill, cross-country ski 8 miles. Lawn games. Business center. 52 acres with pond.

D 🐾 ⛱ 🖼 SC 🏃

Roscoe

Motel/Motor Lodge

★ **ROSCOE MOTEL.** *2045 NY 17 (12776). Phone 607/498-5220; fax 607/498-4643.* 18 rooms. S $45; D $60; each additional $10; kitchen units $60; Apr-Oct weekends (2-day minimum). Pets accepted, some restrictions; fee. Complimentary continental breakfast. Check-out 11 am. TV. Pool. On Beaverkill River.

🐾 ⛱ 🖼 🖼

B&B/Small Inn

★ ★ ★ **THE GUEST HOUSE.** *408 Debruce Rd (12758). Phone 845/439-4000; fax 845/439-3344. www.theguesthouse.com.* Come visit this 40-acre estate on the Willowemoc River for the nearby outdoor activities. 7 rooms, 1-2 story. Pets accepted; fee. Complimentary full breakfast. Check-out noon, check-in 11 am. TV; cable (premium). In-house fitness room; massage. Indoor pool; whirlpool. Outdoor tennis. Downhill ski nearby; cross-country ski on site. Airport transportation. On river. **$$**

D 🐾 ⛱ 🏃 ⛱ 🖼 🖼 🏃 ✈

Sackets Harbor

Hotel

★ ★ **ONTARIO PLACE HOTEL.** *103 Gen Smith Dr (13685). Phone 315/646-8000; toll-free 800/564-1812. www.ontarioplacehotel.com.* 38 rooms, 3 story. Mid-May–mid-Oct: D $29-$59; each additional $10; suites $125-$150; under 14 free; weekly rates; lower rates rest of year. Pets accepted; fee. Check-out 11 am. TV; VCR available. In-room modem link. Bicycles available.

Saranac Lake

B&B/Small Inn

★ ★ ★ ★ ★ **THE POINT.** *HC1, Box 65 NY 30 (12983). Phone 518/891-5674; toll-free 800/255-3530; fax 518/891-1152. www.thepointresort.com.* Well-heeled travelers seeking a gentleman's version of "roughing it" head straight for The Point. This former great camp of William Avery Rockefeller revives the spirit of the early 19th century in the Adirondacks, when the wealthy came to rusticate in this sylvan paradise. No signs direct visitors to this intimate and discreet country house hotel, and a decidedly residential ambience is maintained. The resort enjoys a splendid location on a 10-acre peninsula on Upper Saranac Lake. Adirondack twig furnishings, regional decorative objects, and antiques finish the rustic yet sophisticated décor in the accommodations. From snowshoeing and cross-country skiing to water sports and trail hikes, a variety of outdoor activities beckon. Thoughtful touches include morning bread baskets delivered to guests' doors; everyone feels cosseted here. Gourmet dining figures largely in the experience, and with a nod to the patrician past, guests don black-tie attire twice weekly. 11 rooms, 1 story. No room phones. Pets accepted. Adults only. Restaurant, bar. **$$$$**

Saratoga Springs

Motels/Motor Lodges

★ ★ **GRAND UNION MOTEL.** *120 S Broadway (12866). Phone 518/584-9000; fax 518/584-9001. www.grandunionmotel.com.* 64 rooms. S $149-$189; D $149-$199; each additional $10; higher rates special events. Pets accepted, some restrictions; fee. Check-out 11 am. TV. Sauna. Pool; mineral bath spa; only private mineral bath spa in NY. Lawn games. Victorian-style lobby.

★ ★ **HOLIDAY INN.** *232 Broadway (Rte 9) (12866). Phone 518/584-4550; fax 518/584-4417. www.holiday-inn.com.* 168 rooms, 4 story. S, D $89-$229; each additional $10; suites $199-$459; under 19 free; weekly, ski rates. Pets accepted. Check-out 11 am. TV. In-room modem link. Restaurant, bar. Room service. Health club privileges, in-house fitness room. Pool; poolside service. Downhill ski 20 miles, cross-country ski 1 mile.

★ ★ **PLAYMORE FARMS INN.** *3291 S Broadway; NY 9 (12866). Phone 518/584-2350; toll-free 800/813-9559; fax 518/584-2480. www.playmorefarms.com.* 36 rooms. S $45-$75; D $50-$85; each additional $10; suites $75-$120; family, weekly rates (racing season). Pets accepted, some restrictions; fee. Check-out 11 am. TV; cable (premium). Pool. Cross-country ski 2 miles. State park nearby.

Schenectady

Motel/Motor Lodge

★ ★ ★ **HOLIDAY INN.** *100 Nott Terrace (12308). Phone 518/393-4141; fax 518/393-4174. www.holiday-inn.com.* 184 rooms, 4 story. S $69-$100; D $75-$125; suites $250; under 18 free; higher rates: college events, racing season. Pets accepted, some restrictions. Complimentary breakfast. Check-out noon. TV; cable (premium). In-room modem link. Laundry services. Restaurant, bar. Room service. In-house fitness room; sauna. Indoor pool; whirlpool. Downhill, cross-country ski 20 miles. Free airport transportation.

Skaneateles

Motel/Motor Lodge

★ **THE BIRD'S NEST.** *1601 E Genesee St and Rte 20 (13152). Phone 315/685-5641; toll-free 888/447-7417. www.thebirdsnest.net.* 30 rooms. Pets accepted, some restrictions; fee. Check-out noon, check-in 3 pm. TV. Babysitting services available. Outdoor pool; whirlpool. Lawn games. Duck pond. **$**

Southampton

Motel/Motor Lodge

★ ★ **SOUTHAMPTON INN.** *91 Hill St (11968). Phone 631/283-6500; toll-free 800/732-6500; fax 631/283-6559.* 90 rooms, 2 story. Pets accepted, some restrictions; fee. Check-out 11 am, check-in 4 pm. TV; cable (premium). In-room modem link. Restaurant, bar; entertainment, dancing Fri, Sat. Children's activity center. Outdoor pool; poolside service. Outdoor tennis. Lawn games. Concierge. **$$**

⬛⬛⬛ SC

B&B/Small Inn

★ ★ **THE VILLAGE LATCH INN.** *101 Hill St (11968). Phone 631/283-2160; fax 631/283-3236.* 67 rooms, 2 story. Pets accepted; fee. Complimentary breakfast. Check-out 11 am, check-in 4 pm. TV; cable (premium), VCR available. Pool. Outdoor tennis. **$$**

⬛⬛⬛⬛

Spring Valley

Hotel

★ ★ **WELLESLEY INN.** *17 N Airmont Rd (10901). Phone 845/368-1900; fax 845/368-1927.* 95 rooms, 4 story. Apr-Oct: S, D $82-$102; each additional $10; suites $110-$160; under 18 free; higher rates West Point graduation, Dec 31; lower rates rest of year. Pets accepted. Complimentary continental breakfast. Check-out 11 am. TV; cable (premium).

⬛⬛⬛⬛

Syracuse

Motels/Motor Lodges

★ **ECONO LODGE.** *401 N 7th St (13088). Phone 315/451-6000; toll-free 800/424-4777; fax 315/451-0193. www.econolodge.com.* 83 rooms, 4 story. May-Sep: S $42-$59; D $49-$79; each additional $4; suites $49-$59; under 18 free; higher rates special events; lower rates rest of year. Pets accepted, some restrictions; fee. Complimentary continental breakfast. Check-out 11 am. TV.

⬛⬛⬛ SC

★ ★ **HOLIDAY INN.** *441 Electronics Pkwy (13088). Phone 315/457-1122; fax 315/451-0675. www.holiday-inn.com.* 280 rooms, 6 story. S $99; D $109; each additional $10; under 18 free; weekend rates. Pets accepted. Check-out 1 pm. TV. In-room modem link. Restaurant, bar; entertainment. Room service. In-house fitness room. Game room. Indoor pool; whirlpool.

⬛⬛⬛⬛⬛⬛

★ **JOHN MILTON INN.** *6578 Thompson Rd (13206). Phone 315/463-8555; fax 315/432-9240.* 55 rooms, 2 story. Pets accepted, some restrictions; fee. Complimentary continental breakfast. Check-out 11:30 am. Check-in 3 pm. TV; cable (premium). **$**

⬛⬛

★ **KNIGHTS INN.** *430 Electronics Pkwy (13088). Phone 315/453-6330; toll-free 800/843-5644; fax 315/457-9240. www.knightsinn.com.* 8 kitchen units. S $39-$44; D $44.95-$51; each additional $5; under 18 free; weekly rates. Pets accepted, some restrictions; fee. Complimentary continental breakfast. Check-out 11 am. TV; cable (premium), VCR (movies). Downhill ski 20 miles, cross-country ski 1 mile.

⬛⬛⬛⬛

★ **RED ROOF INN.** *6614 N Thompson Rd (13206). Phone 315/437-3309; toll-free 800/843-7663; fax 315/437-7865. www.redroof.com.* 115 rooms, 3 story. S $31.99-$64.99; D $35.99-$71.99; under 18 free. Pets accepted, some restrictions. Check-out noon. TV; cable (premium).

⬛⬛⬛ SC

Hotels

★ **COMFORT INN.** *7010 Interstate Island Rd (13209). Phone 315/453-0045; toll-free 800/638-3247; fax 315/453-3689. www.choicehotels.com.* 109 rooms, 4 story. Pets accepted; fee. Complimentary breakfast. Check-out 11 am, check-in 3 pm. TV; VCR available. Restaurant. In-house fitness room. **$**

⬛⬛⬛⬛

★ ★ ★ **SHERATON UNIVERSITY HOTEL AND CONFERENCE CENTER.** *801 University Ave (13210). Phone 315/475-3000; toll-free 800/395-2105; fax 315/475-2266.* Bordering Syracuse University and hospitals, this is a perfect choice for campus visits or area business. Within easy walking distance to downtown civic centers, restaurants, entertainment arenas, and other attractions, the hotel provides convenience and friendly, helpful service. 235 rooms, 9 story. Pets accepted, some restrictions; fee. Check-out noon, check-in 3 pm. TV. In-room modem link. Restaurant, bar; entertainment. Room service. In-house fitness room; sauna. Game room. Indoor pool; whirlpool. Business center. Luxury level. **$$**

⬛⬛⬛⬛⬛⬛

Ticonderoga

Motel/Motor Lodge

★ **CIRCLE COURT.** *440 Montcalm St W (12883). Phone 518/585-7660.* 14 rooms. June-mid-Oct: S $51-$55; D $56-$59; each additional $5; weekly rates off-season; lower rates rest of year. Pets accepted, some restrictions. Check-out 11 am. TV.

[icons]

Tupper Lake

Motel/Motor Lodge

★ **SUNSET PARK.** *71 Demars Blvd (12986). Phone 518/359-3995; fax 518/359-9577.* 11 rooms. No A/C. Mid-June-Oct: S $42-$48; D $44-$54; each additional $4; kitchen units $56-$62; lower rates rest of year. Pets accepted, some restrictions. Check-out 11 am. TV. Downhill ski 3 miles. Lawn games. Private sand beach, dock for small boats.

[icons]

Utica

Motels/Motor Lodges

★★ **BEST WESTERN GATEWAY ADIRONDACK INN.** *175 N Genesee St (13502). Phone 315/732-4121; fax 315/797-8265. www.bestwestern.com.* 89 rooms, 1-2 story. S $79-$129; D $79-$149; each additional $10; under 12 free; higher rates special events. Pets accepted. Complimentary continental breakfast. Check-out 11 am. TV. In-house fitness room. Game room.

[icons]

★★ **HOLIDAY INN.** *1777 Burrstone Rd (13413). Phone 315/797-2131; toll-free 800/465-4329; fax 315/797-5817. www.holiday-inn.com.* 100 rooms, 2 story. S, D $97-$129; under 18 free; higher rates some weekends. Pets accepted. Check-out noon. TV. In-room modem link. Restaurant, bar; entertainment Fri, Sat. Room service. In-house fitness room. Game room. Pool; whirlpool.

[icons]

★ **RED ROOF INN.** *20 Weaver St (13502). Phone 315/724-7128; fax 315/724-7158. www.redroof.com.* 112 rooms, 2 story. S $39.99-$59.99; D $47.99-$78.99; each additional $7-$9; under 18 free. Pets accepted, some restrictions. Check-out noon. TV; cable (premium).

[icons]

Hotel

★★★ **RADISSON HOTEL-UTICA CENTRE.** *200 Genesee St (13502). Phone 315/797-8010; toll-free 800/333-3333; fax 315/797-1490. www.radisson.com.* 158 rooms, 6 story. S, D $99-$124; suites $175; under 18 free; weekend rates. Pets accepted, some restrictions; fee. Check-out noon. TV. In-room modem link. Restaurant, bar; entertainment Fri-Sat. In-house fitness room. Game room. Downhill ski 10 miles, cross-country ski 5 miles. Garage parking.

[icons] SC

Victor

Hotel

★★ **SUNRISE HILL INN.** *6108 Loomis Rd (14425). Phone 585/924-2131; toll-free 800/333-0536; fax 585/924-1876.* 89 rooms, 2 story. Mid-June-mid-Sept: S $35-$60; $43-$68; each additional $8; suites $85; under 18 free; lower rates rest of year. Pets accepted. Check-out 11 am. TV; VCR available (movies). In-room modem link. Bar. Health club privileges. Pool. Countryside view. Near race track.

[icons]

Waterloo

Motel/Motor Lodge

★★ **HOLIDAY INN.** *2468 Mound Rd (13165). Phone 315/539-5011; toll-free 800/465-4329; fax 315/539-8355. www.holiday-inn.com.* 148 rooms, 2 story. June-mid-Oct: S, D $79-$150; higher rates special events; under 19 free; package plans; lower rates rest of year. Pets accepted, some restrictions. Check-out noon. TV; cable (premium), VCR available. In-room modem link. Restaurant, bar; entertainment Fri, Sat. In-house fitness room; sauna. Pool; whirlpool. Outdoor tennis.

[icons]

Watertown

Motels/Motor Lodges

★ **ECONO LODGE.** *1030 Arsenal St (13601). Phone 315/782-5500; toll-free 800/553-2666; fax 315/782-7608. www.econolodge.com.* 60 rooms, 2 story. May-Sep: S $59.95-$64.95; D $69.95-$74.95; each additional $5; under 18 free; lower rates rest of year. Pets accepted, some restrictions; fee. Complimentary continental breakfast in lobby. Check-out 11 am. TV; cable (premium). Indoor pool.

[icons]

★ ★ **THE INN.** *1190 Arsenal St (13601). Phone 315/788-6800; toll-free 800/799-5224; fax 315/788-5366.* 96 rooms, 2 story. May-Oct: S $48-$56; D $60-$70; each additional $6; under 18 free; lower rates rest of year. Pets accepted, some restrictions; fee. Check-out noon. TV; cable (premium). Laundry services. Health club privileges. Game room. Pool.

D 🐕 ⚓ 🛠 🏊 🆓

★ **NEW PARROT MOTEL.** *19325 Outer Washington St (13601). Phone 315/788-5080; toll-free 800/479-9889; fax 315/788-5080.* 26 rooms. June-Oct: S $34-$36; D $45-$55; each additional $5; family rates off-season; lower rates rest of year. Pets accepted; fee. Check-out 11 am. TV. Indoor pool.

🐕 🏊

Wilmington

Motel/Motor Lodge

★ **LEDGE ROCK AT WHITEFACE.** *Rte 86 (12997). Phone 518/946-2302; toll-free 800/336-4754; fax 518/946-7594.* 18 rooms, 2 story. Pets accepted; fee. Check-out 11 am. TV. Game room. Children's pool. Pond with paddleboats. **$**

D 🐕 ⚓ 🛠 🏊 🆓

Hotel

★ ★ **HUNGRY TROUT MOTOR INN.** *Rte 86 (12997). Phone 518/946-2217; toll-free 800/766-9137; fax 518/946-7418.* 20 rooms. Closed Apr, Nov. Pets accepted, some restrictions; fee. Check-out 11 am. TV. Bar. Pool; children's pool. Downhill ski 1/2 mile, cross-country ski 12 miles. On Ausable River. **$**

D 🐕 ⚓ 🏊 🆓

B&B/Small Inn

★ ★ **WHITEFACE CHALET.** *Springfield Rd (12997). Phone 518/946-2207; toll-free 800/932-0859. www.whitefacechalet.com.* 16 rooms. Pets accepted, some restrictions; fee. Check-out 11 am, check-in 1 pm. TV. Dining room, bar. Pool. Tennis. Lawn games. Airport transportation. **$**

🐕 🛠 🏊 SC

North Carolina

Albemarle

Motel/Motor Lodge

★ **COMFORT INN.** *735 Hwy 24/27 Bypass (28001). Phone 704/983-6990; fax 704/983-5597. www.comfortinn.com.* 86 rooms, 2 story. Pets accepted, some restrictions; fee. Complimentary continental breakfast. Check-out noon, check-in 2 pm. TV; cable (premium). Laundry services. Health club privileges. Pool. Parking. **$**

D 🐾 🛌 🏊

Asheboro

Motel/Motor Lodge

★ **DAYS INN.** *901 Albemarle Rd (27205). Phone 336/629-2101; toll-free 800/329-7466; fax 336/626-7944. www.daysinn.com.* 132 rooms, 2 story. Pets accepted, some restrictions; fee. Complimentary continental breakfast. Check-out 11 am, check-in 4 pm. TV; cable (premium). Laundry services. Health club privileges. Game room. Outdoor pool. Parking. **$**

D 🐾 🛌 🏋 🏊 SC

Asheville

Motels/Motor Lodges

★ **DAYS INN.** *1445 Tunnel Rd (28805). Phone 828/298-4000. www.daysinn.com.* 84 rooms, 3 story. Pets accepted, some restrictions; fee. Complimentary continental breakfast. Check-out noon, check-in 3 pm. TV; cable (premium), VCR available (movies, fee). Outdoor pool. **$**

🐾 🛌 🏊

★ **RED ROOF INN.** *16 Crowell Rd (28806). Phone 828/667-9803; fax 828/667-9810. www.redroof.com.* 109 rooms, 3 story. Pets accepted, some restrictions. Check-out noon, check-in 1 pm. TV; cable (premium). **$**

D 🐾 🛌 🏊

Resort

★ ★ **HOLIDAY INN.** *1 Holiday Inn Dr (28806). Phone 828/254-3211; toll-free 800/733-3211; fax 828/285-2688.*

www.sunspree.com. 272 rooms, 5 story. Pets accepted, some restrictions; fee. Check-out 11 am, check-in 3 pm. TV; cable (premium). Restaurant, bar. Room service. Children's activity center. In-house fitness center. Health club privileges. Outdoor pool. 18-hole golf, pro, putting green; greens fee $31. Outdoor tennis. **$$**

D 🐾 🏋 🏌 🏊 🏊 🏋 🏊 SC

All Suites

★ **COMFORT INN.** *890 Brevard Rd (28806). Phone 828/665-4000; toll-free 800/622-4005; fax 828/665-9082. www.ashevillenccomfort.com.* 125 rooms, 5 story. Pets accepted; fee. Complimentary continental breakfast. Check-out noon, check-in 3 pm. TV; cable (premium). In-room modem link. In-house fitness room. Pool; whirlpool. Free airport transportation. **$**

D 🐾 🛌 🏋 ✈ 🏊

Banner Elk

Motel/Motor Lodge

★ ★ **HOLIDAY INN.** *Hwy 184 (28604). Phone 828/898-4571; toll-free 877/877-4553; fax 828/898-8437. www.holidayinnbannerelk.com.* 101 rooms, 2 story. Pets accepted. Check-out 11 am, check-in 3 pm. TV; cable (premium). In-room modem link. Restaurant, bar. Room service. In-house fitness room. Game room. Outdoor pool. Downhill, cross-country ski 1 mile. **$**

D 🐾 🎿 🛌 🏋 🏊 SC

Brevard

Motel/Motor Lodge

★ **SUNSET MOTEL.** *415 S Broad St (28712). Phone 828/884-9106; fax 828/883-4919.* 18 rooms. Pets accepted, some restrictions. Check-out 11 am. TV. **$**

🐾 🏊

Burlington

Motels/Motor Lodges

★ **DAYS INN.** *978 Plantation Dr (27215). Phone 336/227-3681; fax 336/570-0900. www.comfortinn.com.* 111 rooms, 2 story. Pets accepted; fee. Complimentary continental breakfast. Check-out noon. TV; cable (premium). Laundry services. Pool; children's pool. **$**

D 🐾 🛌 🏊 SC

★ **RED ROOF INN.** *2133 W Hanford Rd (27215). Phone 336/227-1270; toll-free 800/329-7466; fax 336/227-1702. www.redroof.com.* 126 rooms, 2 story. Pets accepted, some restrictions. Complimentary continental breakfast. Check-out 11, check-in 2 pm. TV; cable (premium). Laundry services. Restaurant. Outdoor pool. Parking. **$**

D 🐾 🏊 🚭 SC

Cashiers

Resort

★★★ **HIGH HAMPTON INN AND COUNTRY CLUB.** *NC 107 S (28717). Phone 828/743-2411; toll-free 800/334-2551; fax 828/743-5991. www.highhamptoninn.com.* Nestled in the Blue Ridge Mountains, this 1,400-acre property boasts a private lake and a quiet, wooded landscape. Guests of the inn, private cottages, or colony homes stay busy with the inn's scenic golf course, six clay tennis courts, and hiking trails. 86 rooms, 3 story. No A/C. Closed late Nov-Apr. Pets accepted, some restrictions; fee. Check-out 1 pm, check-in 3 pm. TV room. Laundry services. Dining room. Supervised children's activities (June-Labor Day), ages 3-12. In-house fitness room. 18-hole golf, two putting greens, driving range; greens fee $29. Tennis. Lawn games. Entertainment. Bicycle rentals. Boats; dockage. Airport transportation. Archery. Trail guides. Kennels. Outdoor, indoor games. **$$**

D 🐾 🏌 ⛳ 🎿 🚶

Cedar Island

Motel/Motor Lodge

★ **DRIFTWOOD MOTEL & RESTAURANT.** *NC 12 (28520). Phone 252/225-4861; fax 252/225-1113.* 37 rooms. Pets accepted. Check-out noon. TV; cable (premium). Restaurant. On ocean. **$**

D 🐾 🚭

Chapel Hill

Hotels

★★★ **DOUBLETREE HOTEL.** *211 Pittsboro St (27516). Phone 919/933-2001; toll-free 800/222-8733; fax 919/918-2795. www.carolinainn.com.* 184 rooms, 3 story. Pets accepted, some restrictions; fee. Check-out noon, check-in 3 pm. TV; cable (premium). In-room modem link. Laundry services. Restaurant, bar. Health club privileges. Valet parking. Concierge. **$$**

D 🐾 🚭

★★★ **SIENA HOTEL–A SUMMIT HOTEL.** *1505 E Franklin St (27514). Phone 919/929-4000; toll-free 800/223-7379; fax 919/968-8527. www.sienahotel.com.* This hotel offers guests the spirit and flavor of Italy with a location in the heart of North Carolina. Visitors get the Italian feel from the hotel's elegant aromas, warm ambience, friendly service, and fine cuisine. 80 rooms, 4 story. Pets accepted, some restrictions; fee. Complimentary continental breakfast. Check-out noon, check-in 4 pm. TV; cable (premium), VCR available. In-room modem link. Restaurant, bar; entertainment. Health club privileges. Airport transportation. Concierge. **$$**

D 🐾 ✈ 🚭 SC

Charlotte

Motel/Motor Lodge

★ **RED ROOF INN.** *131 Red Roof Dr (28217). Phone 704/529-1020; fax 704/529-1054. www.redroof.com.* 115 rooms, 3 story. Pets accepted. Check-out 11 am. TV; cable (premium). Health club privileges. Parking. **$**

D 🐾 🚭

Hotels

★★★ **OMNI CHARLOTTE HOTEL.** *132 E Trade St (28202). Phone 704/377-0400; fax 704/347-4835. www.omnihotels.com.* The hotel is located near a science center, a performance and cultural center, and an amusement park. 365 rooms, 15 story. Pets accepted, some restrictions; fee. Check-out noon, check-in 3 pm. TV; cable (premium), VCR available. Restaurant, bar. Health club privileges. Sauna. Outdoor pool. Valet parking. Business center. Concierge. Luxury level. **$**

D 🐾 🏊 🚭 🚶

★★★ **SHERATON CHARLOTTE AIRPORT HOTEL.** *3315 I-85 and Billy Graham Pkwy (28208). Phone 704/392-1200; fax 704/393-2035. www.sheraton.com.* Old-fashioned Southern hospitality and newly renovated rooms will place guests in the heart of Charlotte. 225 rooms, 8 story. Pets accepted, some restrictions. Check-out noon, check-in 3 pm. TV; cable (premium). Laundry services. Restaurant, bar; entertainment. Room service. In-house fitness room; sauna. Health club privileges. Game room. Indoor, outdoor pool; whirlpool; poolside service. Parking. **$**

D 🐾 🏊 ✈ 🚭

All Suite

★★ **SUMMERFIELD SUITES CHARLOTTE.** *4920 S Tryon St (28217). Phone 704/525-2600; fax 704/521-9932. www.summerfieldsuites.com.* Centrally located just 10 minutes from uptown Charlotte, this hotel is perfect for family vacations. 135 rooms, 5 story. Pets accepted, some restrictions; fee. Complimentary full breakfast. Check-out noon, check-in 3 pm. TV; cable (premium), VCR (movies). In-room modem link. In-house fitness room. Health club privileges. Game room. Pool; whirlpool. Parking. Free airport transportation. **$**

Cornelius

Hotels

★ **BEST WESTERN LAKE NORMAN.** *19608 Liverpool Pkwy (28031). Phone 704/896-0660; toll-free 888/207-0666; fax 704/896-8633. www.bestwesternlakenorman.com.* 80 rooms, 4 story. Pets accepted, some restrictions; fee. Complimentary continental breakfast. Check-out 11 am, check-in 3 pm. TV; cable (premium), VCR available (movies, fee). In-house fitness room. Outdoor pool; whirlpool. **$**

★★ **HOLIDAY INN.** *19901 Holiday Ln (28031). Phone 704/892-9120; toll-free 800/HOLIDAY; fax 704/892-3854. www.holiday-inn.com.* 119 rooms, 2 story. Pets accepted; fee. Check-out 11 am, check-in 3 pm. TV; cable (premium). Laundry services. Restaurant, bar. Room service. In-house fitness room. Outdoor pool. **$**

Dunn

Motels/Motor Lodges

★ **ECONO LODGE.** *1125 E Broad St (28334). Phone 910/892-1293; fax 910/891-1038. www.econolodge.com.* 105 rooms, 2 story. Pets accepted, some restrictions; fee. Complimentary continental breakfast. Check-out 11 am, check-in 11 am. TV; cable (premium). Laundry services. Pool. **$**

★ **RAMADA INN.** *I-95 and US 421 (28334). Phone 910/892-8101; fax 910/892-2836. www.ramada.com.* 100 rooms, 2 story. Pets accepted, some restrictions; fee. Complimentary continental breakfast. Check-out noon.

Check-in 1 pm. TV; cable (premium). In-room modem link. Restaurant. Pool; whirlpool. **$**

Durham

Motels/Motor Lodges

★ **BEST WESTERN SKYLAND INN.** *5400 US 70 (27705). Phone 919/383-2508; fax 919/383-7316. www.bestwestern.com.* 31 rooms, 1 story. Pets accepted; fee. Complimentary continental breakfast. Check-out noon. TV; cable (premium). Outdoor pool. Parking.

★ **RED ROOF INN.** *1915 N Pointe Dr (27705). Phone 919/471-9882; fax 919/477-0512. www.redroof.com.* 117 rooms, 3 story. Pets accepted; some restrictions. Check-out noon, check-in 2 pm. TV; cable (premium). Internet access. Parking. **$**

★★ **WYNDHAM GARDEN HOTEL.** *4620 S Miami Blvd (27703). Phone 919/941-6066; fax 919/941-6363. www.wyndham.com.* 176 rooms, 7 story. Pets accepted, some restrictions. Check-out noon, check-in 3 pm. TV; cable (premium). In-room modem link. Laundry services. Restaurant, bar. In-house fitness room. Health club privileges. Pool; whirlpool. Parking. Airport transportation. **$**

All Suite

★★ **HAWTHORN SUITES.** *300 Meredith Dr (27713). Phone 919/361-1234; toll-free 800/527-1133; fax 919/361-1213. www.hawthorn.com.* 100 rooms, 2-3 story. Pets accepted, some restrictions; fee. Complimentary full breakfast. Check-out noon, check-in 3 pm. TV; cable (premium). Laundry services. Health club privileges. Outdoor pool. Parking. Free airport transportation. **$**

Fayetteville

Motels/Motor Lodges

★ **COMFORT INN.** *1957 Cedar Creek Rd (28301). Phone 910/323-8333; toll-free 800/621-6596; fax 910/323-3946. www.comfortinn.com.* 120 rooms, 2 story. Pets accepted. Complimentary breakfast buffet. Check-out noon, check-in 3 pm. TV; cable (premium). In-house fitness room. Outdoor pool. Parking. **$**

★ ★ **HOLIDAY INN.** *1707 Owen Dr (28304). Phone 910/323-0111; fax 910/484-9444. www.holiday-inn.com.* 289 rooms, 3-6 story. Pets accepted; fee. Complimentary continental breakfast. Check-out 11 am. Check-in 3 pm. TV; cable (premium). In-room modem link. Laundry services. Restaurant, bar. In-house fitness room. Outdoor pool. Free parking. Free airport transportation. **$**

⊡ ☞ ⇌ 大 ✈ ⇘

★ ★ **HOLIDAY INN.** *1944 Cedar Creek Rd (28301). Phone 910/323-1600; toll-free 800/465-4329; fax 910/323-0691. www.holiday-inn.com.* 206 rooms, 2 story. Pets accepted; fee. Check-out noon, check-in 3 pm. TV; cable (premium). In-room modem link. Laundry services. Restaurant, bar. Room service. In-house fitness room. Indoor pool; whirlpool. Parking. Free airport transportation. **$**

⊡ ☞ ⇌ 大 ✈ ⇘ SC

Franklin

Motel/Motor Lodge

★ **DAYS INN.** *1320 E Main St (28734). Phone 828/524-6491; fax 704/369-9636. www.daysinn.com.* 41 rooms. Pets accepted; fee. Complimentary continental breakfast. TV; cable (premium). Pool. Scenic view of mountains. **$**

⊡ ☞ ⇌ ⇘

Goldsboro

Motels/Motor Lodges

★ ★ **BEST WESTERN GOLDSBORO INN.** *801 US 70 Bypass E (27534). Phone 919/735-7911; fax 919/735-5030. www.bestwestern.com.* 116 rooms, 2 story. Pets accepted, some restrictions; fee. Complimentary continental breakfast. Check-out noon. TV; cable (premium). In-room modem link. Laundry services. Restaurant, bar. Room service. In-house fitness room. Pool. **$**

⊡ ☞ ⇌ 大 ⇘

★ **DAYS INN.** *2000 Wayne Memorial Dr (27534). Phone 919/734-9471; fax 919/736-2623. www.daysinn.com.* 121 rooms, 2 story. Pets accepted, some restrictions; fee. Check-out 11 am. TV. Restaurant. In-house fitness room. Health club privileges. Pool. **$**

⊡ ☞ ⇌ 大 ⇘

★ ★ **QUALITY INN.** *708 US 70 (27534). Phone 919/735-7901; fax 919/734-2946. www.qualityinn.com.* 108 rooms, 2 story. Pets accepted; fee. Check-out noon. TV; cable (premium). In-room modem link. Restaurant, bar.

Room service. In-house fitness room. Health club privileges. Pool. **$**

⊡ ☞ ⇌ 大 ⇘ SC

Greensboro

Motels/Motor Lodges

★ **AMERISUITES.** *1619 Stanley Rd (27407). Phone 336/852-1443; toll-free 800/833-1516; fax 336/854-9339. www.amerisuites.com.* 126 rooms, 6 story. Pets accepted, some restrictions. Complimentary continental breakfast. Check-out 11 am, check-in 3 pm. TV; cable (premium), VCR available, DVD available. In-room modem link. Health club privileges. Outdoor pool. Parking. Free airport transportation. **$**

☞ ⇌ 大 ✈

★ ★ **RAMADA INN.** *7067 Albert Pick Rd (27409). Phone 336/668-3900; toll-free 800/272-6232; fax 336/664-1042. www.ramada.com.* 167 rooms, 2 story. Pets accepted, some restrictions. Complimentary continental breakfast. Check-out noon, check-in 2 pm. TV; cable (premium). Restaurant, bar. Room service. In-house fitness room. Indoor, outdoor pools; whirlpool; poolside service. Parking. Free airport transportation. **$**

⊡ ☞ ⇌ 大 ⇘

★ **TRAVELODGE.** *2112 W Meadowview (27403). Phone 336/292-2020; toll-free 800/578-7878; fax 336/852-3476. www.travelodge.com.* 108 rooms, 2 story. Pets accepted; fee. Check-out noon, check-in 3 pm. TV; cable (premium). Laundry services. Restaurant. Outdoor pool. Parking. Airport transportation. **$**

☞ ⇌

Hendersonville

Motel/Motor Lodge

★ **COMFORT INN.** *206 Mitchell Dr (28792). Phone 828/693-8800; toll-free 800/882-3843; fax 828/693-8800. www.comfortinn.com.* 85 rooms, 2 story. Pets accepted; fee. Complimentary continental breakfast. Check-out 11 am. TV; VCR available. In-room modem link. Pool. **$**

⊡ ☞ ⇌ ⇘

Hickory

Motel/Motor Lodge

★ **RED ROOF INN.** *1184 Lenoir Rhyne Blvd (28602). Phone 828/323-1500; fax 828/323-1509. www.redroof.com.*

108 rooms, 2 story. Pets accepted. Check-out noon, check-in 2 pm. TV. In-room modem link. **$**

D 🐾

Highlands

Motel/Motor Lodge

★★ **MOUNTAIN HIGH LODGE.** *200 Main St (28741). Phone 828/526-2790; fax 828/526-2750. www. mountainhighinn.com.* 55 rooms, 1-2 story. Pets accepted, some restrictions; fee. Complimentary continental breakfast. Check-out noon. TV; cable (premium). Downhill ski 7 miles. **$**

D 🐾 ⇆

High Point

Motel/Motor Lodge

★★ **RADISSON HOTEL HIGH POINT.** *135 S Main St (27260). Phone 336/889-8888; fax 336/889-8870. www.radisson.com.* 262 rooms, 8 story. Pets accepted; fee. Check-out noon, check-in 3 pm. TV; cable (premium). In-room modem link. Restaurant, bar. In-house fitness room. Indoor pool; whirlpool. Parking. Free airport transportation. **$**

D 🐾 ⇆ 🏋 ✈ ⇟

Kill Devil Hills

Motel/Motor Lodge

★ **TRAVELODGE.** *804 N Virginia Dare Trail (27948). Phone 252/441-0411; fax 252/441-7811. www. travelodge.com.* 96 rooms, 4 story. Pets accepted, some restrictions; fee. Complimentary continental breakfast. Check-out 11 am. TV; cable (premium). Pool. **$**

D 🐾 ⇆ ⇟ SC

Resort

★ **RAMADA INN.** *1701 S Virginia Dare Trail (27948). Phone 252/441-2151; toll-free 800/635-1824; fax 252/441-1830. www.ramada.com.* 172 rooms, 5 story. Pets accepted, some restrictions; fee. Check-out 11 am. TV; VCR available (free movies). In-room modem link. Restaurant, bar; entertainment. Room service. Indoor pool; whirlpool. Lawn games. **$**

D 🐾 ⇆ ⇟

Laurinburg

Motel/Motor Lodge

★ **PINE ACRES LODGE.** *11860 McCall Rd (28352). Phone 910/276-1531; toll-free 800/348-8242; fax 910/ 277-1481.* 72 rooms. Pets accepted, some restrictions. Complimentary continental breakfast. TV. Laundry services. Restaurant. Parking. Outdoor pool. **$**

D 🐾 ⇆

Lumberton

Motel/Motor Lodge

★★ **QUALITY INN.** *3608 Kahn Dr (28358). Phone 910/ 738-8261; fax 910/671-9075.* 147 rooms, 2 story. D $59.95-79.95; each additional $6; under 17 free. Pets accepted; fee. Complimentary continental breakfast. Check-out noon, check-in 3 pm. TV. Laundry services. Restaurant, bar. Health club privileges. Outdoor pool. Parking.

D 🐾 ⇆ ⇟

Nags Head

Motel/Motor Lodge

★★ **QUALITY INN.** *7123 S Virginia Dare Trail (27959). Phone 252/441-7191; toll-free 800/228-5151; fax 919/441-1961. www.qualityinn.com.* 111 rooms, 1-3 story. Pets accepted, some restrictions. Check-out 11 am. TV; cable (premium), VCR available (movies). Pool; children's pool. Some rooms across street. **$**

D 🐾 ⛱ ⇆ ⇟

New Bern

Hotel

★★★ **SHERATON NEW BERN HOTEL AND MARINA.** *100 Middle St (28560). Phone 252/ 638-3585; toll-free 800/326-3745; fax 252/638-8112. www.sheraton.com.* With a downtown, waterfront location, this hotel offers all the amenities a visitor could want, with an outdoor pool and historic paddlewheel rides; golf, tennis and beaches are nearby. 171 rooms, 5 story. Pets accepted, some restrictions. Check-out noon. TV; cable (premium). In-room modem link. Restaurant, bar; entertainment Fri, Sat. In-house fitness room. Health club privileges. Pool. On river; marina facilities. Free airport transportation. Business center. $

Ocracoke

Resort

★ ★ **ANCHORAGE INN.** *Hwy 12 (27960). Phone 252/928-1101; fax 252/928-6322. www.theanchorageinn.com.* 35 rooms, 4 story. Pets accepted; fee. Complimentary continental breakfast. Check-out 11 am. TV; cable (premium). Pool. Marina. $

Raleigh

Motels/Motor Lodges

★ **RED ROOF INN.** *3520 Maitland Dr (27610). Phone 919/231-0200; toll-free 800/843-7663; fax 919/231-0228. www.redroof.com.* 115 rooms, 3 story. Pets accepted. Check-out noon. TV; cable (premium). $

★ **RED ROOF INN.** *3201 Wake Forest Rd (27609). Phone 919/878-9310; toll-free 800/843-7663; fax 919/790-1451. www.redroof.com.* 147 rooms, 2 story. Pets accepted. Complimentary continental breakfast. Check-out noon, check-in 3 pm. TV; cable (premium). Outdoor pool. $

Hotel

★ ★ **THE CRABTREE SUMMIT HOTEL.** *3908 Arrow Dr (27612). Phone 919/782-6868; fax 919/881-9340. www.crabtreesummithotel.com.* 90 rooms, 4 story. Pets accepted, some restrictions; fee. Complimentary full breakfast. Check-out noon, check-in 3 pm. TV; cable (premium). In-room modem link. Fireplaces. Restaurant. In-house fitness room. Outdoor pool. Free airport transportation. $

Salisbury

Motel/Motor Lodge

★ **HAMPTON INN.** *1001 Klumack Rd (28144). Phone 704/637-8000; toll-free 800/426-7866; fax 704/639-9995. www.hamptoninn.com.* 121 rooms, 4 story. Pets accepted.

Complimentary continental breakfast. Check-out noon. TV; cable (premium). Health club privileges. Pool. $

Sanford

Motel/Motor Lodge

★ **PALOMINO MOTEL.** *US 1 South (27331). Phone 919/776-7531; toll-free 800/641-6060; fax 919/776-9670.* 108 rooms, 1 story. Pets accepted, some restrictions; fee. Check-out noon, check-in 1 pm. TV; cable (premium). Restaurant, bar. In-house fitness room; sauna. Outdoor pool. Parking. $

Southern Pines

Motel/Motor Lodge

★ ★ **HOLIDAY INN.** *US 1 at Morganton Rd exit (28387). Phone 910/692-8585; toll-free 800/262-5737; fax 910/692-5213. www.holiday-inn.com.* 172 rooms, 2 story. Pets accepted; fee. Check-out noon, check-in 3 pm. TV; cable (premium). In-room modem link. Restaurant, bar. Room service. In-house fitness room. Health club privileges. Game room. Outdoor pool. Outdoor tennis. $

Williamston

Motel/Motor Lodge

★ ★ **HOLIDAY INN.** *101 East Blvd (27892). Phone 252/792-3184; toll-free 800/792-3101; fax 252/792-9003. www.holiday-inn.com.* 100 rooms, 2 story. Pets accepted. Check-out noon. TV; cable (premium). In-room modem link. Restaurant, bar. Room service. Pool. $

Wilmington

Motel/Motor Lodge

★ ★ **DAYS INN.** *5040 Market St (28405). Phone 910/799-6300; toll-free 800/DAYS INN; fax 910/791-7414. www.daysinn.com.* 122 rooms, 2 story. Pets accepted; fee. Check-out 11 am, check-in 2 pm. TV; cable (premium). Restaurant. Outdoor pool. $

Hotels

★ **COMFORT INN.** *151 S College Rd (28403). Phone 910/791-4841; fax 910/790-9100. www.choicehotels.com.* 146 rooms, 6 story. Pets accepted; fee. Complimentary continental breakfast. Check-out noon, check-in 3 pm. TV; cable (premium). Outdoor pool. **$**

D ⬛ ⬛

★ ★ ★ **HILTON WILMINGTON RIVERSIDE.** *301 N Water St (28401). Phone 910/763-5900; fax 910/763-0038. www.wilmingtonhilton.com.* Located a short walk from shops, restaurants, and cultural attractions as well as the city's riverwalk and cobblestone streets. 274 rooms, 9 story. Pets accepted, some restrictions; fee. Check-out noon. TV; cable (premium). In-room modem link. Restaurant, bar. In-house fitness room. Pool; whirlpool. Boat dock. Free airport transportation. Luxury level. **$$$**

D ⬛ ⬛ ⬛ ⬛

Winston-Salem

B&B/Small Inn

★ ★ **AUGUSTUS T ZEVELY.** *803 S Main St (27101). Phone 336/748-9299; toll-free 800/928-9299; fax 336/721-2211. www.winston-salem-inn.com.* 12 rooms, 3 story. Pets accepted, some restrictions; fee. Children over 12 years only. Complimentary continental breakfast; complimentary full breakfast on weekends. Check-out 11:30 am, check-in 3-9 pm. TV; cable (premium). Health club privileges. Built in 1844; restored to its mid-19th-century appearance. Moravian ambience. **$**

D ⬛ ⬛

North Dakota

Bismarck

Motels/Motor Lodges

★ **BEST WESTERN DOUBLEWOOD INN.** *1400 E Interchange Ave (58501). Phone 701/258-7000; toll-free 800/554-7077; fax 701/258-2001. www.bestwestern.com.* 143 rooms, 2 story. Pets accepted, some restrictions; fee. Complimentary full breakfast. Check-out noon, check-in 3 pm. TV; VCR available. In-room modem link. Laundry services. Restaurant, bar. Room service. Sauna. Indoor pool; whirlpool. Parking. Free airport transportation. Business center. **$**

D ⟍ 🐾 🛏 🚶 ⊠

★ **COMFORT INN.** *1030 Interstate Ave (58501). Phone 701/223-1911; toll-free 800/424-6423; fax 701/323-6977. www.comfortinn.com.* 148 rooms, 3 story. No elevator. Pets accepted, some restrictions. Complimentary continental breakfast. Check-out noon, check-in 2 pm. TV; cable (premium). In-room modem link. Game room. Indoor pool; whirlpool. Parking. Free airport transportation. **$**

D ⟍ 🛏 ⊠

★ **COMFORT INN.** *929 Gateway Ave (58501). Phone 701/223-4009; fax 701/223-9119. www.comfortinn.com.* 60 rooms, 2 story. Pets accepted, some restrictions. Complimentary continental breakfast. Check-out noon, check-in 2 pm. TV; cable (premium). In-room modem link. Guest laundry. In-house fitness room. Game room. Indoor pool; waterslide; whirlpool. Parking. Free airport transportation. **$**

D ⟍ 🛏 🚶 ✈ ⊠

★ **DAYS INN.** *1300 E Capitol Ave (58501). Phone 701/223-9151; fax 701/223-9423. www.daysinn.com.* 101 rooms, 2 story. Pets accepted, some restrictions; fee. Complimentary full breakfast. Check-out noon, check-in 3 pm. TV; cable (premium). In-room modem link. In-house fitness room; sauna. Indoor pool; whirlpool. Parking. **$**

D ⟍ 🛏 🚶 ⊠

★ **EXPRESSWAY INN.** *200 E Bismarck Expy (58504). Phone 701/222-2900; toll-free 800/456-6388; fax 701/222-2901. www.expresswayinns.com.* 160 rooms, 5 story. Pets accepted, some restrictions; fee. Complimentary continental breakfast. Check-out 11:30 am, check-in 2 pm. TV; cable (premium), VCR available. In-room modem link. Game room. Outdoor pool; whirlpool. Parking. Free airport transportation. **$**

D ⟍ 🛏 ✈ ⊠ SC

★★ **KELLY INN - BISMARCK.** *1800 N 12th St (58501). Phone 701/223-8001; toll-free 800/635-3559; fax 701/221-2685. www.kellyinns.com.* 101 rooms, 2 story. Pets accepted, some restrictions. Check-out noon, check-in 2 pm. TV; cable (premium). In-room modem link. Restaurant, bar. Room service. In-house fitness room; sauna. Game room. Indoor pool; whirlpool. Parking. Free airport transportation. **$**

D ⟍ 🛏 🚶 ⊠

★ **RAMADA INN.** *3808 E Divide Ave (58501). Phone 701/221-3030; fax 701/221-3030. www.ramada.com.* 66 rooms, 3 story. Pets accepted, some restrictions; fee. Complimentary continental breakfast. Check-out 11 am, check-in 3 pm. TV; cable (premium), VCR available. In-room modem link. In-house fitness room. Game room. Indoor pool; whirlpool. Parking. Free airport transportation. **$**

D ⟍ 🛏 ✈ 🚶 ✈ ⊠ 🚶

Hotels

★★ **BEST WESTERN RAMKOTA HOTEL.** *800 S 3rd St (58504). Phone 701/258-7700; toll-free 800/528-1234; fax 701/224-8212. www.bestwestern.com.* 288 rooms, 3 story. Pets accepted, some restrictions; fee. Check-out noon, check-in 3 pm. TV. In-room modem link. Restaurant, bar. Room service. In-house fitness room; sauna. Game room. Indoor pool; children's pool; whirlpool. Parking. Free airport transportation. Business center. Casino. **$**

D ⟍ 🛏 🚶 ⊠ 🚶

★★ **RADISSON HOTEL BISMARCK.** *605 E Broadway Ave (58501). Phone 701/255-6000; toll-free 800/465-4329; fax 701/223-0400. www.radisson.com.* 181 rooms, 9 story. Pets accepted, some restrictions. Check-out noon, check-in 2 pm. TV; VCR available. In-room modem link. Restaurant, bar. Room service. In-house fitness room; sauna. Game room. Indoor pool; whirlpool; poolside service. Parking. Free airport transportation. **$**

D ⟍ 🛏 🚶 ⊠ SC

Carrington

Motel/Motor Lodge

★ **SUPER 8.** *101 4th Ave S (58421). Phone 701/652-3982; fax 701/652-3984. www.super8.com.* 40 rooms, 2 story. Pets accepted, some restrictions; fee. Complimentary continental breakfast. Check-out 11 am. TV. In-room modem link. **$**

◻ ▦ ◺

Devils Lake

Motels/Motor Lodges

★ **COMFORT INN.** *215 Hwy 2E (58301). Phone 701/662-6760; fax 701/662-8440. www.comfortinn.com.* 87 rooms, 2 story. Pets accepted; fee. Complimentary continental breakfast. Check-out 11 am. TV; cable (premium). Game room. Indoor pool; whirlpool. **$**

◻ ▦ ≈ ◺ SC

★ **DAYS INN.** *Rte 5 (58301). Phone 701/662-5381; toll-free 800/622-1191; fax 701/662-3578. www.daysinn.com.* 45 rooms, 2 story. Pets accepted, some restrictions; fee. Complimentary continental breakfast. Check-out 11 am. TV. **$**

◻ ▦ ◺

Dickinson

Motels/Motor Lodges

★★ **AMERICINN.** *229 15th St W (58601). Phone 701/225-1400; toll-free 800/634-3444; fax 701/225-5230. www.americinn.com.* 46 rooms, 2 story. Pets accepted, some restrictions. Complimentary continental breakfast. Check-out noon, check-in 3 pm. TV; cable (premium). In-room modem link. Game room. Indoor pool; whirlpool. Parking. Free airport transportation. **$**

◻ ▦ ≈ ✈ ◺

★ **COMFORT INN.** *493 Elk Dr, Exit 61 (58601). Phone 701/264-7300; toll-free 800/424-6423; fax 701/264-7300. www.comfortinn.com.* 118 rooms, 2 story. Pets accepted. Complimentary continental breakfast. Check-out 11 am, check-in 4 pm. TV; cable (premium). In-room modem link. Indoor pool; whirlpool. Parking. Free airport transportation. **$**

◻ ▦ ≈ ◺

Fargo

Motels/Motor Lodges

★ **AMERICINN.** *1423 35th St SW (58103). Phone 701/234-9946; toll-free 800/634-3444; fax 701/234-9946. www.americinn.com.* 43 rooms, 2 story. Pets accepted, some restrictions; fee. Complimentary continental breakfast. Check-out 11 am. TV; cable (premium), VCR

available (movies). In-room modem link. Laundry services. Sauna. Indoor pool; whirlpool. **$**

◻ ▦ ≈ ◺ SC

★★ **BEST WESTERN KELLY INN.** *3800 Main Ave (58103). Phone 701/282-2143; fax 701/281-0243. www.bestwestern.com.* 133 rooms, 2 story. Pets accepted, some restrictions. Check-out 11 am. TV; cable (premium), VCR available. Restaurant, bar. Sauna. Indoor, outdoor pool; whirlpool. Free airport, train station, bus depot transportation. **$**

◻ ▦ ≈ ✈ ◺

★ **COMFORT INN.** *1407 35th St S (58103). Phone 701/280-9666; toll-free 800/228-5150; fax 701/280-9666. www.comfortinn.com.* 66 rooms, 2 story. Pets accepted, some restrictions. Complimentary continental breakfast. Check-out 11 am. TV. Game room. Indoor pool; whirlpool. **$**

◻ ▦ ≈ ◺ SC

★ **COMFORT INN.** *3825 9th Ave SW (58103). Phone 701/282-9596; toll-free 800/228-5150; fax 701/282-9596. www.comfortinn.com.* 56 rooms, 2 story. Pets accepted, some restrictions; fee. Complimentary continental breakfast. Check-out 11 am. TV. In-room modem link. Game room. Indoor pool; whirlpool. **$**

◻ ▦ ≈ ◺ SC

★ **COMFORT INN.** *1415 35th St S (58103). Phone 701/237-5911; toll-free 800/517-4000; fax 701/237-5911. www.comfortinn.com.* 66 rooms, 2 story. Pets accepted, some restrictions. Complimentary continental breakfast. Check-out 11 am. TV. In-room modem link. Game room. Indoor pool; whirlpool. **$**

◻ ▦ ≈ ◺ SC

★ **ECONO LODGE.** *1401 35th St (58103). Phone 701/232-3412; fax 701/232-3412. www.econolodge.com.* 44 rooms, 2 story. Pets accepted, some restrictions; fee. Complimentary continental breakfast. Check-out 11 am. TV. In-room modem link. **$**

◻ ▦ ◺

★★ **HOLIDAY INN.** *3803 13th Ave S (58103). Phone 701/282-2700; fax 701/281-1240. www.holiday-inn.com.* 309 rooms, 2-7 story. Pets accepted, some restrictions. Check-out noon. TV; cable (premium). In-room modem link. Restaurant, bar; entertainment. Room service. In-house fitness room. Indoor pool; children's pool; whirlpool; poolside service. Free airport transportation. Concierge. Casino. **$**

◻ ▦ ≈ 🛄 🛄 ◺

★ **HOLIDAY INN EXPRESS.** *1040 40th St S (58103). Phone 701/282-2000; fax 701/282-4721. www.holiday-inn.com.* 77 rooms, 4 story. Pets accepted, some restrictions; fee. Complimentary continental breakfast. Check-out noon. TV. Game room. Indoor pool; whirlpool. **$**

D ⬚ ≈ ⬚ ⬚ ⬚

★ **KELLY INN - FARGO.** *4207 13th Ave SW (58103). Phone 701/277-8821; fax 701/277-0208.* 59 rooms, 2 story. Pets accepted. Complimentary continental breakfast. Check-out 11 am. TV; cable (premium). Sauna. Game room. Indoor pool; whirlpool. **$**

D ⬚ ≈ ⬚

★ **SLEEP INN.** *1921 44th St SW (58103). Phone 701/281-8240; toll-free 800/905-7533; fax 701/281-2041. www.sleepinn.com.* 61 rooms, 2 story. Pets accepted, some restrictions. Complimentary continental breakfast. Check-out 11 am. TV; cable (premium). In-house fitness room. **$**

D ⬚ ⬚ ⬚ ⬚

★ **SUPER 8.** *3518 Interstate Blvd (58103). Phone 701/232-9202; fax 701/232-4543. www.super8.com.* 109 rooms, 2 story. Pets accepted, some restrictions; fee. Complimentary continental breakfast. Check-out 11 am. TV; cable (premium). Indoor pool; whirlpool. **$**

D ⬚ ≈ ⬚

Hotel

★★ **RADISSON HOTEL FARGO.** *201 5th St N (58102). Phone 701/232-7363; toll-free 800/333-3333; fax 701/298-9134. www.radisson.com.* 151 rooms, 18 story. Pets accepted, some restrictions; fee. Check-out noon. TV. In-room modem link. Restaurant, bar. In-house fitness room; sauna. Game room. Free airport transportation. **$**

D ⬚ ⬚ ⬚ ⬚ SC

Grand Forks

Motel/Motor Lodge

★ **COMFORT INN.** *3251 30th Ave S (58201). Phone 701/775-7503; toll-free 800/228-5150; fax 701/775-7503. www.comfortinn.com.* 67 rooms, 2 story. Pets accepted, some restrictions. Complimentary continental breakfast. Check-out 11 am. TV. Game room. Indoor pool; whirlpool. **$**

D ⬚ ≈ ⬚ SC

Jamestown

Motels/Motor Lodges

★ **COMFORT INN.** *811 SW 20th St (58401). Phone 701/252-7125; fax 701/252-7125. www.comfortinn.com.* 52

rooms, 2 story. Pets accepted. Complimentary continental breakfast. Check-out 11 am. TV. Game room. Indoor pool; whirlpool. **$**

D ⬚ ≈ ⬚

★★ **DAKOTA INN.** *US 281 S (58402). Phone 701/252-3611; toll-free 800/726-7924; fax 701/252-5711.* 120 rooms, 2 story. Pets accepted; fee. Check-out 11 am. TV. Restaurant, bar; entertainment Fri, Sat. Room service. Game room. Indoor pool; whirlpool. Lawn games. **$**

D ⬚ ≈ ⬚ ⬚

★★ **GLADSTONE SELECT HOTEL.** *111 2nd St NE (58401). Phone 701/252-0700; toll-free 800/641-1000; fax 701/252-0700. www.selectinn.com.* 117 rooms, 2 story. Pets accepted, some restrictions. Check-out 11 am. TV. Restaurant, bar. Room service. Indoor pool; whirlpool. Free airport, bus depot transportation. Casino. **$**

D ⬚ ≈ ⬚ ⬚ SC

Mandan

Motel/Motor Lodge

★★ **BEST WESTERN SEVEN SEAS INN & CONFERENCE CENTER.** *2611 Old Red Trail (58554). Phone 701/663-7401; toll-free 800/597-7327; fax 701/663-0025. www.bestwestern.com.* 163 rooms, 3 story. Pets accepted, some restrictions. Check-out noon, check-in 3 pm. TV; cable (premium). In-room modem link. Restaurant, bar; entertainment. Indoor pool; whirlpool. Parking. Free airport transportation. **$**

D ⬚ ≈ ⬚

Medora

Motel/Motor Lodge

★★ **AMERICINN.** *75 E River Rd S (58645). Phone 701/623-4800; fax 701/623-4890. www.americinn.com.* 56 rooms, 2 story. Pets accepted, some restrictions; fee. Complimentary continental breakfast. Check-out 11 am. TV; cable (premium). In-room modem link. Game room. Indoor pool; whirlpool. Parking. **$**

D ⬚ ≈ ⬚

Minot

Motels/Motor Lodges

★ **BEST WESTERN KELLY INN.** *1510 26th Ave SW (58701). Phone 701/852-4300; toll-free 800/780-7234; fax 701/838-1234. www.bestwestern.com/kellyinnminot.*

100 rooms, 2 story. Pets accepted, some restrictions. Complimentary continental breakfast. Check-out 11 am, check-in 3 pm. TV; cable (premium), VCR (movies). In-room modem link. Bar. Game room. Indoor pool; whirlpool. Parking. **$**

⊡ 🔖 🛏 📵

★ **COMFORT INN.** *1515 22nd Ave SW (58701). Phone 701/852-2201; fax 701/852-2201. www.comfortinn.com.* 140 rooms, 3 story. Pets accepted, some restrictions. Complimentary continental breakfast. Check-out 11 am. TV; cable (premium). In-room modem link. Game room. Indoor pool; whirlpool. Parking. **$**

⊡ 🔖 🛏 📵

★ **DAYS INN.** *2100 4th St SW (58701). Phone 701/852-3646; toll-free 888/327-6466; fax 701/852-0501. www.daysinn.com.* 82 rooms, 2 story. Pets accepted. Complimentary continental breakfast. Check-out noon. TV. Sauna. Indoor pool; whirlpool. Parking. **$**

⊡ 🔖 🛏 📵

★ ★ **HOLIDAY INN.** *2200 Burdick Expy E (58701). Phone 701/852-2504; toll-free 800/468-9968; fax 701/852-2630. www.holiday-inn.com.* 182 rooms, 7 story. Pets accepted, some restrictions. Check-out noon, check-in 3 pm. TV; cable (premium). In-room modem link. Laundry services. Restaurant, bar. Room service. In-house fitness room; sauna. Game room. Indoor pool; whirlpool; poolside service. Parking. Airport transportation. **$**

⊡ 🔖 🛏 🏋 ✈ SC

Ohio

Akron

Motels/Motor Lodges

★ **HOLIDAY INN EXPRESS.** *2940 Chenoweth Rd (44312). Phone 330/644-7126; toll-free 800/465-4329; fax 330/644-1776. www.holiday-inn.com.* 129 rooms, 2 story. Pets accepted; fee. Check-out noon. TV. Restaurant, bar; entertainment. Room service. Pool; poolside service. Airport transportation. **$**

D 🐾 ⊠ ✈ 🏊 SC

★ **RED ROOF INN.** *99 Rothrock Rd (44321). Phone 330/666-0566; toll-free 800/733-7663; fax 330/666-6874. www.redroof.com.* 108 rooms, 2 story. Pets accepted, some restrictions. Check-out noon. TV; cable (premium). **$**

D 🐾 🏊

Alliance

Motel/Motor Lodge

★ **COMFORT INN.** *2500 W State St (44601). Phone 330/821-5555; toll-free 800/948-5555; fax 330/821-4919. www.comfortinn.com.* 113 rooms, 5 story. Pets accepted; fee. Complimentary continental breakfast. Check-out noon. TV; cable (premium), VCR available. Laundry services. In-house fitness room. Indoor pool; whirlpool. **$**

D 🐾 🏊 ⚓ ✈ 🏊

Ashtabula

Motels/Motor Lodges

★ **CEDARS MOTEL.** *2015 W Prospect Rd (44004). Phone 440/992-5406.* 15 rooms. Pets accepted; fee. Check-out 11 am. TV; cable (premium). Health club privileges. **$**

D 🐾 🏊

★ **COMFORT INN.** *1860 Austinburg Rd (44010). Phone 440/275-2711; toll-free 800/228-5150; fax 440/275-7314. www.comfortinn.com.* 119 rooms, 2 story. Pets accepted, some restrictions; fee. Check-out noon. TV; cable (premium), VCR available. In-room modem link.

Laundry services. Restaurant, bar. Room service. Heated pool. **$**

D 🐾 ⚓ 🏊

Athens

Motels/Motor Lodges

★ **DAYS INN.** *330 Columbus Rd (45701). Phone 740/592-4000; toll-free 800/329-7466; fax 740/593-7687. www.daysinn.com.* 60 rooms, 2 story. Pets accepted; fee. Complimentary continental breakfast. Check-out noon. TV; cable (premium). **$**

D 🐾 🏊

★ ★ ★ **OHIO UNIVERSITY INN AND CONFERENCE CENTER.** *331 Richland Ave (45701). Phone 740/593-6661; fax 740/592-5139. www.ouinn.com.* In the foothills of the Appalachian Mountains, this beautiful hotel prides itself on customer service and comfort. With newly renovated rooms and a conference center with a range of services, guests will enjoy hospitality and efficiency here. 139 rooms, 2-3 story. Pets accepted, some restrictions; fee. Check-out noon. TV. In-room modem link. Restaurant, bar. Room service. Health club privileges. Pool. **$**

D 🐾 ⚓ 🏊 🏊 SC

Beachwood

Motel/Motor Lodge

★ **SUPER 8.** *3795 Orange Pl (44122). Phone 216/831-7200; fax 216/831-0616. www.super8.com.* 128 rooms, 2 story. Pets accepted; fee. Complimentary continental breakfast. Check-out 11 am. TV. Airport transportation. **$**

D 🐾 🏊

Hotel

★ ★ ★ **HILTON CLEVELAND EAST/ BEACHWOOD.** *3663 Park East Dr (44122). Phone 216/464-5950; fax 216/464-6539. www.hilton.com.* 403 rooms, 4-7 story. Pets accepted, some restrictions; fee. Check-out noon. TV; cable (premium), VCR available. Laundry services. Restaurant, bar. Room service. In-house fitness room; sauna. Health club privileges. Game room. Indoor pool; outdoor pool; whirlpool; poolside service. Downhill ski 15 miles, cross-country ski 10 miles. Business center. Concierge. Luxury level. **$**

D 🐾 ⛷ 🏊 ⚓ 🏊 🏊

Bellefontaine

Motel/Motor Lodge

★ **COMFORT INN.** *260 Northview Dr (43311). Phone 937/599-5555; toll-free 800/589-3666; fax 937/599-2300. www.comfortinn.com.* 73 rooms, 2 story. Pets accepted; fee. Complimentary continental breakfast. Check-out noon. TV; cable (premium), VCR available. In-room modem link. Laundry services. Bar; entertainment. In-house fitness room. Pool. Downhill ski 8 miles. **$**

⊡ 🐾 ⌇ ⋔ ⇌ ⋈

Bowling Green

Motel/Motor Lodge

★ **DAYS INN.** *1550 E Wooster St (43402). Phone 419/352-5211; fax 419/354-8030. www.daysinn.com.* 100 rooms, 2 story. Pets accepted; fee. Complimentary continental breakfast. Check-out 11 am. TV; cable (premium). **$**

⊡ 🐾 ⋔ ⋈

Cambridge

Motels/Motor Lodges

★ **BEST WESTERN CAMBRIDGE.** *1945 Southgate Pkwy (43725). Phone 740/439-3581; toll-free 800/528-1234; fax 740/439-1824. www.bestwestern.com.* 95 rooms, 2 story. Pets accepted. Check-out 11 am. TV; VCR available. In-room modem link. Bar. Pool. **$**

⊡ 🐾 ⇌ ⋈

★★ **HOLIDAY INN.** *2248 Southgate Pkwy (43725). Phone 740/432-7313; toll-free 800/465-4329; fax 740/432-2337. www.holiday-inn.com.* 108 rooms, 2 story. Pets accepted. Check-out noon. TV. In-room modem link. Laundry services. Restaurant, bar. Room service. Health club privileges. Pool. **$**

⊡ 🐾 ⇌ ⋈ SC

Canton

Motels/Motor Lodges

★★ **FOUR POINTS BY SHERATON.** *4375 Metro Circle NW (44720). Phone 330/494-6494; toll-free 877/867-7666; fax 330/494-7129. www.fourpoints.com.* 152 rooms, 6 story. Pets accepted, some restrictions; fee. Check-out

noon. TV; cable (premium). Restaurant, bar. Room service. In-house fitness room; sauna. Game room. Indoor pool; outdoor pool; poolside service. Free airport transportation. Business center. **$**

⊡ 🐾 ⇌ ⋔ ✈ ⋈ SC ⋔

★★ **HOLIDAY INN.** *4520 Everhard Rd NW (44718). Phone 330/494-2770; toll-free 800/465-4329; fax 330/494-6473. www.holiday-inn.com.* 194 rooms, 2-3 story. Pets accepted, some restrictions. Check-out noon. TV. In-room modem link. Restaurant, bar; entertainment. Room service. In-house fitness room. Health club privileges. Pool; poolside service. Free airport transportation. **$**

⊡ 🐾 ⇌ ⋔ ⋈ SC

★ **RED ROOF INN.** *5353 Inn Circle Ct NW (44720). Phone 330/499-1970; toll-free 800/733-7663; fax 330/499-1975. www.redroof.com.* 108 rooms, 2 story. Pets accepted, some restrictions. Check-out noon. TV. **$**

⊡ 🐾 ⋈

Chillicothe

Motels/Motor Lodges

★ **COMFORT INN.** *20 N Plaza Blvd (45601). Phone 740/775-3500; toll-free 800/542-7919; fax 740/775-3588. www.comfortinn.com.* 106 rooms, 2 story. Pets accepted. Complimentary continental breakfast. Check-out noon. TV. Bar; entertainment Fri, Sat. Health club privileges. Pool. **$**

⊡ 🐾 ⇌ ⋈

★ **DAYS INN.** *1250 N Bridge St (45601). Phone 740/775-7000; toll-free 800/329-7466; fax 740/773-1622. www.daysinn.com.* 42 rooms, 2 story. Pets accepted. Complimentary full breakfast. Check-out noon. TV; cable (premium). Laundry services. Restaurant, bar; entertainment. Room service. Pool; poolside service. **$**

⊡ 🐾 ⇌ ⋈ SC

Cincinnati

Motels/Motor Lodges

★ **AMERISUITES.** *11435 Reed Hartman Hwy (45241). Phone 513/489-3666; toll-free 800/833-1516; fax 513/489-4187. www.amerisuites.com.* 127 rooms, 6 story. Pets accepted, some restrictions. Complimentary continental breakfast. Check-out noon. TV; cable (premium), VCR available. In-room modem link. In-house fitness room. Pool. Business center. **$**

⊡ 🐾 ⇌ ⋔ ⋈ SC ⋔

★ **BAYMONT INN.** *11029 Dowlin Dr (45241). Phone 513/771-0300; fax 513/771-6411. www.woodfieldsuites.com.* 103 rooms, 8 story. Pets accepted, some restrictions; fee. Complimentary continental breakfast. Check-out noon. TV; cable (premium), VCR available. In-room modem link. Laundry services. In-house fitness room. Indoor pool; whirlpool. **$**

D 🐾 🏊 🧍 🈁

★ ★ **BEST WESTERN SPRINGDALE HOTEL & CONFERENCE CENTER.** *11911 Sheraton Ln (45246). Phone 513/671-6600; fax 513/671-0507. www.bestwestern.com.* 267 rooms, 10 story. Pets accepted; fee. Check-out noon. TV; cable (premium). In-room modem link. Laundry services. Restaurant, bar. In-house fitness room. Game room. Indoor pool; whirlpool. **$**

D 🐾 🏊 🧍 🈁

★ ★ **HOLIDAY INN.** *800 W 8th St (45203). Phone 513/241-8660; fax 513/241-9057. www.holiday-inn.com.* 243 rooms, 12 story. Pets accepted; fee. Check-out noon. TV; cable (premium). In-room modem link. Laundry services. Restaurant, bar. In-house fitness room. Pool. **$**

D 🐾 🏊 🧍 🈁

★ ★ **IMPERIAL HOUSE HOTEL.** *5510 Rybolt Rd (45248). Phone 513/574-6000; toll-free 800/543-3018; fax 513/574-6566. www.imperialhousehotel.com.* 197 rooms, 2-5 story. Pets accepted, some restrictions; fee. Check-out noon. TV; cable (premium). In-room modem link. Laundry services. Restaurant, bar; entertainment. Pool. **$**

D 🐾 🏊 🈁 SC

All Suite

★ ★ **GARFIELD SUITES HOTEL.** *2 Garfield Pl (45202). Phone 513/421-3355; toll-free 800/367-2155; fax 513/421-3729. www.garfieldsuiteshotel.com.* 152 rooms, 16 story. Pets accepted; fee. Check-out noon. TV; cable (premium), VCR available. In-room modem link. Laundry services. Restaurant, bar. Room service. In-house fitness room. Valet parking. **$$**

D 🐾 🧍 🈁

Extended Stay

★ ★ **RESIDENCE INN BY MARRIOTT.** *11689 Chester Rd (45246). Phone 513/771-2525; fax 513/771-3444. www.residenceinn.com.* 144 rooms, 1-2 story. Pets accepted; fee. Complimentary breakfast. Check-out noon. TV; cable (premium). Laundry services. Pool; whirlpool. **$**

D 🐾 🏊 🈁

Cleveland

Motels/Motor Lodges

★ ★ **CLARION HOTEL.** *17000 Bagley Rd (44130). Phone 440/243-5200; fax 440/243-5244. www.choicehotels.com.* 223 rooms, 2 story. Pets accepted, some restrictions; fee. Check-out 11 am. TV; cable (premium). In-room modem link. Laundry services. Restaurant, bar; entertainment Fri, Sat. Room service. Sauna. Indoor pool; outdoor pool; children's pool. Free airport transportation. **$**

🐾 🏊

★ **COMFORT INN.** *17550 Rosbough Dr (44130). Phone 440/234-3131; fax 440/234-6111. www.comfortinn.com.* 136 rooms, 3 story. Pets accepted, some restrictions; fee. Complimentary continental breakfast. Check-out noon. TV; cable (premium). Pool. Free airport transportation. Business center. **$**

D 🐾 🏊 🈁 🧍

Hotels

★ ★ ★ **MARRIOTT CLEVELAND AIRPORT.** *4277 W 150th St (44135). Phone 216/252-5333; fax 216/251-9404. www.marriott.com.* Located only 2 miles from the Cleveland Hopkins Airport and 10 miles from downtown, this hotel is near tennis courts, golf courses, and attractions. 371 rooms, 4-9 story. Pets accepted; fee. Check-out noon. TV; cable (premium), VCR available. In-room modem link. Laundry services. Restaurant, bar. In-house fitness room; sauna. Indoor pool; whirlpool; poolside service. Free airport transportation. **$$**

D 🐾 🏊 🧍 ✈

★ ★ ★ ★ **THE RITZ-CARLTON CLEVELAND.** *1515 W Third St (44113). Phone 216/623-1300; toll-free 800/241-3333; fax 216/623-0515. www.ritzcarlton.com.* The Ritz-Carlton is Cleveland's premier destination. This hotel enjoys a coveted downtown location with views of Lake Erie and the Cuyahoga River, and all of the city's attractions and businesses are within walking distance. Visitors are hosted in grand style here, where thoughtful service grants every wish. The guest rooms, with commanding city and water views, are luxury defined to the last detail. The marble bathrooms are sumptuous, and guests are graciously provided with every imaginable service. All-day dining at the Century Restaurant & Bar is always a delight, its clean, modern design providing a soothing alternative to urban life. Seafood is a specialty here, and the sushi bar is an ever-popular choice. By day, the Lobby Lounge is ideal for traditional afternoon tea, while in the evening, its live entertainment attracts hotel guests and local residents alike. 208 rooms, 7 story. Pets accepted, some restrictions; fee. Check-out noon. TV; VCR available. In-room modem link. Room service 24 hours. Restaurant. Afternoon tea. Bar. In-house fitness room, massage, sauna. Health club privileges. Indoor pool; whirlpool; poolside service. Business center. Concierge. Luxury level. **$$**

[icons]

Extended Stay

★ ★ **RESIDENCE INN BY MARRIOTT.** *17525 Rosbough Dr (44130). Phone 440/234-6688; toll-free 800/331-3131; fax 440/234-3459. www.marriott.com.* 158 rooms, 2 story. Pets accepted; fee. Complimentary continental breakfast. Check-out noon. TV; cable (premium), VCR available. Laundry services. In-house fitness room. Pool; whirlpool. Downhill ski 15 miles, cross-country ski 5 miles. Lawn games. Airport transportation. **$**

[icons]

Columbus

Motels/Motor Lodges

★ **AMERISUITES.** *7490 Vantage Dr (43235). Phone 614/846-4355; fax 614/846-4493. www.amerisuites.com.* 126 rooms, 6 story. Pets accepted, some restrictions. Complimentary continental breakfast. Check-out noon. TV; cable (premium), VCR available. Laundry services. In-house fitness room. Pool. Free airport transportation. Business center. **$**

[icons]

★ ★ **BEST WESTERN COLUMBUS NORTH.** *888 E Dublin Granville Rd (43229). Phone 614/888-8230; fax 614/888-8223. www.bestwestern.com.* 180 rooms, 2 story. Pets accepted; fee. Check-out noon. TV; cable (premium). Laundry services. Restaurant, bar. Room service. In-house fitness room. Indoor pool; outdoor pool. **$**

[icons]

★ ★ **HOLIDAY INN.** *175 E Town St (43215). Phone 614/221-3281; toll-free 800/367-7870; fax 614/221-5266. www.holiday-inn.com.* 240 rooms, 12 story. Pets accepted, some restrictions; fee. Check-out noon. TV; cable (premium). Restaurant, bar. Pool. Free airport transportation. **$**

[icons]

★ ★ **HOLIDAY INN.** *175 Hutchinson Ave (43235). Phone 614/885-3334; fax 614/846-4353. www.holiday-inn*

.com. 306 rooms, 6 story. Pets accepted, some restrictions. Check-out noon. TV; cable (premium), VCR available. In-room modem link. Laundry services. Restaurant, bar. Room service. In-house fitness room. Indoor pool. Business center. **$**

[icons]

★ **MOTEL 6.** *7480 N High St (43235). Phone 614/431-2525; fax 614/431-0272. www.motel6.com.* 105 rooms, 3 story. Pets accepted. Check-out noon. TV; cable (premium). In-room modem link. Laundry services. **$**

[icons]

★ ★ **UNIVERSITY PLAZA HOTEL AND CONFERENCE CENTER.** *3110 Olentangy River Rd (43202). Phone 614/267-7461; toll-free 877/677-5292; fax 614/267-3978. www.universityplazaosu.com.* 243 rooms, 5 story. Pets accepted, some restrictions; fee. Check-out noon. TV; cable (premium), VCR available. Restaurant. Health club privileges. Pool; poolside service. Free airport transportation. **$**

[icons]

Hotels

★ ★ ★ **COLUMBUS MARRIOTT NORTH.** *6500 Doubletree Ave (43229). Phone 614/885-1885; toll-free 800/228-9290; fax 614/885-7222. www.marriott.com.* This hotel is conveniently located to such area attractions as the Polaris Amphitheater, Columbus Zoo, and Center of Science and Industry. 300 rooms, 9 story. Pets accepted; fee. Check-out noon. TV; cable (premium). In-room modem link. Laundry services. Restaurant, bar. In-house fitness room; sauna. Indoor pool; outdoor pool; whirlpool; poolside service. Free airport transportation. Business center. **$**

[icons]

★ ★ **HOLIDAY INN.** *4560 Hilton Corp Dr (43232). Phone 614/868-1380; fax 614/863-3210. www.holiday-inn.com.* 278 rooms, 21 story. Pets accepted, some restrictions. Check-out noon. TV; cable (premium). In-room modem link. Restaurant, bar. In-house fitness room; sauna. Indoor pool; poolside service. Free airport transportation. Business center. **$**

[icons]

★ ★ ★ **MARRIOTT COLUMBUS NORTHWEST.** *5605 Paul G Blazer Memorial Pkwy (43017). Phone 614/791-1000; fax 614/336-4701. www.marriottnorthwest.com.* This hotel is located in one of Columbus' fastest growing entertainment and business districts. Guests enjoy the graciously elegant guest rooms, as well as friendly and attentive service. Nearby attractions include: Columbus Zoo, Murfield Village and Golf Club, and the Anheuser Busch Brewery. 303 rooms, 7 story. Pets accepted, some restrictions; fee. Check-out noon. TV; cable (premium). In-room modem link. Laundry services. Restaurant, bar. In-house fitness room. Indoor pool. Business center. Concierge. Luxury level. **$**

D 🐾 🏊 🏋 ⬆ ⬇ 🚶

★★ **WYNDHAM DUBLIN HOTEL.** *600 Metro Pl N (43017). Phone 614/764-2200; toll-free 800/996-3426; fax 614/764-1213. www.wyndhamdublin.com.* 217 rooms, 3 story. Pets accepted; fee. Check-out 1 pm. TV; cable (premium), VCR available. In-room modem link. Room service 24 hours. Restaurant, bar. In-house fitness room. Indoor pool. **$**

D 🐾 🏊 🏋 ⬇

All Suites

★★★ **DOUBLETREE GUEST SUITES.** *50 S Front St (43215). Phone 614/228-4600; fax 614/228-0297. www.doubletree.com.* Located in the heart of scenic downtown Columbus, this hotel boasts spacious guest rooms, some offering spectacular views of the Scioto River. 194 rooms, 10 story. Pets accepted, some restrictions; fee. Check-out noon. TV; cable (premium). In-room modem link. Restaurant, bar. Covered parking. Opposite river. **$$**

D 🐾 SC

★★★ **WOODFIN SUITES.** *4130 Tuller Rd (43017). Phone 614/766-7762; toll-free 888/433-9408; fax 614/761-1906. www.woodfinsuitehotels.com.* This cozy suite hotel, with one- and two-bedroom suites, has all the comforts of home. 88 rooms, 2 story. Pets accepted; fee. Complimentary breakfast buffet. Check-out noon. TV; cable (premium), VCR available. In-room modem link. Laundry services. Pool; whirlpool. Business center. **$$**

D 🐾 🏊 ⬆ ⬇ 🚶

Dayton

Motels/Motor Lodges

★ **DAYS INN.** *100 Parkview Dr (45309). Phone 937/833-4003; fax 937/833-4681. www.daysinn.com.* 62 rooms, 2 story. Pets accepted, some restrictions; fee. Complimentary continental breakfast. Check-out 11 am. TV. Pool. **$**

D 🐾 🏊 ⬇

★★ **HOLIDAY INN.** *2800 Presidential Dr (45324). Phone 937/426-7800; fax 937/426-1284. www.holiday-inn.com.* 204 rooms, 6 story. Pets accepted. Check-out noon. TV; cable (premium), VCR available. Restaurant, bar. Room service. In-house fitness room. Indoor pool. **$**

D 🐾 🏊 🏋 ⬆ ⬇

★ **HOWARD JOHNSON.** *7575 Poe Ave (45414). Phone 937/454-0550; toll-free 800/446-4656; fax 937/454-5566. www.hojo.com.* 121 rooms, 2 story. Pets accepted; fee. Complimentary continental breakfast. Check-out noon. TV; cable (premium), VCR available. Laundry services. Bar. Health club privileges. Pool. Free airport transportation. **$**

D 🐾 🏊 ⬇ SC

★ **RED ROOF INN.** *7370 Miller Ln (45414). Phone 937/898-1054; fax 937/898-1059. www.redroof.com.* 109 rooms, 2 story. Pets accepted. Check-out noon. TV; cable (premium). **$**

D 🐾 ⬇

Hotel

★★ **MARRIOTT DAYTON.** *1414 S Patterson Blvd (45409). Phone 937/223-1000; fax 937/223-7853. www.marriott.com.* 399 rooms, 6 story. Pets accepted, some restrictions; fee. Check-out noon. TV; cable (premium), VCR available. In-room modem link. Restaurant, bar; entertainment. In-house fitness room; sauna. Indoor pool; outdoor pool; whirlpool; poolside service. Business center. Luxury level. **$**

🐾 🏊 🏋 ⬇ SC 🚶

All Suite

★ **HOMEWOOD SUITES.** *2750 Presidential Dr (45324). Phone 937/429-0600; toll-free 800/225-5466; fax 937/429-6311. www.homewoodsuites.com.* 128 rooms, 3 story. Pets accepted, some restrictions; fee. Complimentary continental breakfast. Check-out noon. TV; cable (premium), VCR available. In-room modem link. Laundry services. In-house fitness room. Pool. Lawn games. Business center. **$**

D 🐾 🏊 🏋 ⬇ 🚶

Defiance

Motel/Motor Lodge

★ **QUALITY INN.** *2395 N Scott St (43545). Phone 419/592-5010; toll-free 800/592-6445; fax 419/592-6618. www.qualityinn.com.* 79 rooms, 2 story. Pets accepted, some restrictions; fee. Check-out noon. TV; cable (premium). Laundry services. Restaurant, bar. Room service. Pool. **$**

D 🐾 🏊 ⬇

Delaware

Motels/Motor Lodges

★ **DAYS INN.** *16510 Square Dr (43040). Phone 937/644-8821; toll-free 877/644-8821; fax 937/644-8821. www.daysinn.com.* 74 rooms, 2 story. Pets accepted; fee. Complimentary breakfast. Check-out noon. TV; cable (premium), VCR available. In-room modem link. Health club privileges. Business center. **$**

D ➟ ⌖ SC ✦

★ **TRAVELODGE.** *1001 US Hwy 23 N (43015). Phone 740/369-4421; fax 740/362-9090. www.travelodge.com.* 31 rooms, 1-2 story. Pets accepted; fee. Check-out noon. TV. Restaurant. **$**

➟ ⌖ SC

Elyria

Motel/Motor Lodge

★ **COMFORT INN.** *739 Leona St (44035). Phone 440/324-7676; fax 440/324-4046. www.comfortinn.com.* 66 rooms, 2 story. Pets accepted; fee. Complimentary continental breakfast. Check-out 11 am. TV; cable (premium). Laundry services. **$**

D ➟ ⌖ ✦ ⌖

Gallipolis

Motel/Motor Lodge

★ ★ **HOLIDAY INN.** *577 OH 7 N (45631). Phone 740/446-0090; fax 740/446-0090. www.holiday-inn.com.* 100 rooms, 2 story. Pets accepted, some restrictions. Check-out noon. TV. Laundry services. Restaurant, bar. Room service. Pool; children's pool. **$**

D ➟ ⌖ ✦ ⌖

Hamilton

Hotel

★ ★ **HAMILTONIAN HOTEL.** *1 Riverfront Plz (45011). Phone 513/896-6200; toll-free 800/522-5570; fax 513/896-9463.* 120 rooms, 6 story. Pets accepted; fee. Check-out noon. TV; cable (premium), VCR available. In-room modem link. Restaurant, bar. Pool. Luxury level. On river. **$**

D ➟ ⌖ ✦ ⌖ SC

Kent

Motels/Motor Lodges

★ ★ **HOLIDAY INN.** *4643 OH 43 (44240). Phone 330/678-0101; toll-free 800/240-1881; fax 330/677-5001. www.holiday-inn.com.* 152 rooms, 2 story. Pets accepted; fee. Check-out noon. TV; cable (premium). Laundry services. Restaurant, bar. Room service. In-house fitness room. Pool. **$**

D ➟ ⌖ ✦ ⌖

★ **INN OF KENT.** *303 E Main St (44240). Phone 330/673-3411; fax 330/673-9878. www.go.to/the-inn.com.* 56 rooms, 2 story. Pets accepted, some restrictions; fee. Check-out 11 am. TV. Laundry services. Indoor pool. **$**

D ➟ ⌖ ✦ ⌖

Lancaster

Motels/Motor Lodges

★ ★ **BEST WESTERN LANCASTER INN.** *1858 N Memorial Dr (43130). Phone 740/653-3040; toll-free 800/780-7234; fax 740/653-1172. www.bestwestern.com.* 168 rooms, 2 story. Pets accepted, some restrictions; fee. Check-out noon. TV. Laundry services. Restaurant, bar. Room service. Health club privileges. Pool. **$**

D ➟ ⌖ ⌖ SC

★ **KNIGHTS INN.** *1327 River Valley Blvd (43130). Phone 740/687-4823; toll-free 800/843-5644; fax 740/687-4823. www.knightsinn.com.* 60 rooms. Pets accepted. Check-out noon. TV; VCR available. **$**

D ➟ ⌖ SC

Lima

Motel/Motor Lodge

★ ★ **HOLIDAY INN.** *1920 Roschman Ave (45804). Phone 419/222-0004; toll-free 800/465-4329; fax 419/222-2176. www.holiday-inn.com.* 150 rooms, 4 story. Pets accepted. Check-out noon. TV. In-room modem link. Restaurant, bar; entertainment Fri, Sat. Room service. In-house fitness room; sauna. Game room. Indoor pool; whirlpool. **$**

D ➟ ⌖ ✦ ⌖ SC

Mansfield

Motels/Motor Lodges

★ **BEST VALUE INN.** *880 Laver Rd (44905). Phone 419/589-2200; fax 419/589-5624. www.bestvalueinn.com.* 99 rooms, 2 story. Pets accepted. Check-out noon. TV; cable (premium). Restaurant, bar. Room service. Pool. **$**

D ⬛ 🐾 ⬛ ⬛ ⬛

★ **COMFORT INN.** *500 N Trimble Rd (44906). Phone 419/529-1000; toll-free 800/918-9189; fax 419/529-2953. www.comfortinn.com.* 114 rooms, 2 story. Pets accepted; fee. Complimentary continental breakfast. Check-out noon. TV. In-room modem link. Laundry services. Bar. Room service. Health club privileges. Indoor pool. Downhill, cross-country ski 20 miles. **$**

D 🐾 ⬛ ⬛ ⬛

★ **KNIGHTS INN.** *555 N Trimble Rd (44906). Phone 419/529-2100; toll-free 800/843-5644; fax 419/529-6679. www.knightsinn.com.* 89 rooms. Pets accepted, some restrictions. Complimentary continental breakfast. Check-out noon. TV; cable (premium). Health club privileges. Pool. **$**

D 🐾 ⬛ ⬛ SC

★ **TRAVELODGE.** *90 W Hanley Rd (44903). Phone 419/756-7600; fax 419/756-7600. www.travelodge.com.* 93 rooms, 2 story. Pets accepted, some restrictions; fee. Check-out noon. TV. Restaurant open 24 hours. Pool. Downhill, cross-country ski 2 miles. **$**

D 🐾 ⬛ ⬛

Marietta

Motel/Motor Lodge

★ **KNIGHTS INN.** *506 Pike St (45750). Phone 740/373-7373; toll-free 800/526-5947; fax 740/374-9466. www.knightsinn.com.* 97 rooms. Pets accepted; fee. TV; cable (premium), VCR available. In-room modem link. Pool. **$**

D 🐾 ⬛ ⬛ SC

Hotel

★ ★ **LAFAYETTE.** *101 Front St (45750). Phone 740/373-5522; toll-free 800/331-9336; fax 740/373-4684. www.historiclafayette.com.* 78 rooms, 5 story. Pets accepted; fee. Check-out noon. TV. Restaurant, bar. Health club privileges. Free airport transportation. On Ohio River. **$**

D 🐾 ⬛

Marion

Motels/Motor Lodges

★ **COMFORT INN.** *256 James Way (43302). Phone 740/389-5552. www.comfortinn.com.* 56 rooms, 2 story. Pets accepted; fee. Complimentary continental breakfast. Check-out 11 am. TV; cable (premium). Indoor pool; whirlpool. **$**

🐾 ⬛ ⬛ SC

★ **TRAVELODGE.** *1952 Marion Mount Gilead Rd (43302). Phone 740/389-4671; toll-free 800/578-7878; fax 740/389-4671. www.travelodge.com.* 46 rooms, 2 story. Pets accepted; fee. Check-out noon. TV; cable (premium), VCR available. In-room modem link. Health club privileges. Pool. **$**

🐾 ⬛ ⬛ SC

Mason

Motels/Motor Lodges

★ **DAYS INN.** *9735 Mason-Montgomery Rd (45040). Phone 513/398-3297; toll-free 800/329-7466; fax 513/398-3297. www.daysinn.com.* 124 rooms, 2 story. Pets accepted; fee. Complimentary continental breakfast. Check-out 11 am. TV; cable (premium). Game room. Pool. **$**

D 🐾 ⬛ ⬛ SC

★ **RED ROOF INN.** *9847 Bardes Rd (45040). Phone 513/398-3633; fax 513/398-3633. www.redroof.com.* 124 rooms, 2 story. Pets accepted, some restrictions. Complimentary continental breakfast. Check-out 11 am. TV; cable (premium). Pool. **$**

D 🐾 ⬛ ⬛

Miamisburg

Motels/Motor Lodges

★ ★ **HOLIDAY INN.** *31 Prestige Plz Dr (45342). Phone 937/434-8030; toll-free 800/465-4329; fax 937/434-6452. www.holiday-inn.com.* 195 rooms, 3 story. Pets accepted, some restrictions; fee. Check-out 11 am. TV; cable (premium). In-room modem link. Laundry services. Restaurant, bar; entertainment. Room service. In-house fitness room; sauna. Game room. Indoor pool; outdoor pool; children's pool. **$**

D 🐾 ⬛ 🏃 ⬛ ⬛ SC

★ **RED ROOF INN.** *222 Byers Rd (45342). Phone 937/866-0705; fax 937/866-0700. www.redroof.com.* 107 rooms, 2 story. Pets accepted. Check-out noon. TV; cable (premium). In-room modem link. **$**

D 🐾 ⛓ SC

Extended Stay

★ ★ **RESIDENCE INN BY MARRIOTT.** *155 Prestige Pl (45342). Phone 937/434-7881; toll-free 800/331-3131; fax 937/434-9308. www.residenceinn.com.* 96 rooms, 2 story. Pets accepted; fee. Complimentary continental breakfast. Check-out noon. TV; cable (premium), VCR available. Fireplaces. Laundry services. Pool; whirlpool. **$**

D 🐾 ⛓ ⛓

Middletown

Motel/Motor Lodge

★ ★ **MANCHESTER INN & CONFERENCE CENTER.** *1027 Manchester Ave (45042). Phone 513/422-5481; toll-free 800/523-9126; fax 513/422-4615. www.manchesterinn.com.* 79 rooms, 5 story. Pets accepted; fee. Check-out noon. TV. In-room modem link. Restaurant, bar; entertainment Fri, Sat. Room service. **$**

D 🐾 ⛓ SC

Mount Vernon

Motel/Motor Lodge

★ ★ **HISTORIC CURTIS INN THE SQUARE.** *12 Public Sq (43050). Phone 740/397-4334; toll-free 800/934-6835; fax 740/397-4334.* 72 rooms, 2 story. Pets accepted, some restrictions; fee. Check-out noon. TV; VCR available. Laundry services. Restaurant, bar. Room service. **$**

🐾 ⛓

Painesville

B&B/Small Inn

★ ★ **RIDERS 1812.** *792 Mentor Ave (44077). Phone 440/942-2742. www.ridersinn.com.* 10 rooms, 2 story. Pets accepted, some restrictions. Complimentary full breakfast in room. Check-out, check-in times flexible. TV; VCR available. Restaurant. Room service. Health club privileges. Airport transportation. Concierge. Original stagecoach stop (1812); historic stop on the Underground Railroad, some original antiques. **$**

🐾 🔣

Piqua

Motel/Motor Lodge

★ **COMFORT INN.** *987 E Ash St and Miami Valley Centre (45356). Phone 937/778-8100; fax 937/778-9573. www.comfortinn.com.* 124 rooms, 5 story. Pets accepted; fee. Complimentary continental breakfast. Check-out noon. TV; cable (premium). In-house fitness room. Indoor pool; whirlpool. **$**

D 🐾 ⛓ 🏃 ⛓ SC

Portsmouth

Motels/Motor Lodges

★ ★ **DAYS INN.** *3762 US 23 (45662). Phone 740/354-2851; toll-free 800/465-4329; fax 614/353-2084.* 100 rooms, 2 story. Pets accepted; fee. Check-out noon. TV. In-room modem link. Restaurant, bar. Room service. Pool. **$**

D 🐾 ⛓ ⛓ SC

★ ★ **RAMADA INN.** *711 Second St (45662). Phone 740/354-7711; toll-free 888/298-2054; fax 740/353-1539. www.ramada.com.* 119 rooms, 5 story. Pets accepted. Complimentary continental breakfast. Check-out noon. TV; cable (premium). Restaurant. Room service. In-house fitness room. Health club privileges. Indoor pool; children's pool; whirlpool; poolside service. Dockage. **$**

D 🐾 ⛓ 🏃 ⛓ SC

Saint Clairsville

Motel/Motor Lodge

★ **KNIGHTS INN.** *51260 E National Rd (43950). Phone 740/695-5038; toll-free 800/843-5644; fax 740/695-3014. www.knightsinn.com.* 104 rooms. Pets accepted; fee. Check-out noon. TV; cable (premium), VCR available. In-room modem link. Pool. **$**

D 🐾 ⛓ 🔣 ⛓

Sandusky

Motel/Motor Lodge

★ ★ **CLARION HOTEL.** *1119 Sandusky Mall Blvd (44870). Phone 419/625-6280; fax 419/625-9080. www.clarionsandusky.com.* 143 rooms, 2 story. Pets accepted, some restrictions. Check-out 11 am. TV; cable (premium). In-room modem link. Restaurant, bar;

entertainment. Room service. In-house fitness room; sauna. Game room. Indoor pool; whirlpool; poolside service. **$**

Sidney

Motels/Motor Lodges

★ **COMFORT INN.** *1959 W Michigan Ave (45365). Phone 937/492-3001; toll-free 800/228-5150; fax 937/497-8150. www.comfortinn.com.* 71 rooms, 2 story. Pets accepted, some restrictions; fee. Complimentary continental breakfast. Check-out 11 am. TV; cable (premium). Pool; whirlpool. **$**

★★ **HOLIDAY INN.** *400 Folkerth Ave (45365). Phone 937/492-1131; toll-free 800/HOLIDAY; fax 937/498-4655. www.holiday-inn.com.* 134 rooms, 2 story. Pets accepted, some restrictions; fee. Check-out noon. TV; cable (premium), VCR available. In-room modem link. Laundry services. Restaurant, bar. Room service. In-house fitness room; sauna. Game room. Pool. **$**

Toledo

Motels/Motor Lodges

★ **CROWN INN.** *1727 W Alexis Rd (43613). Phone 419/473-1485; fax 419/473-0364.* 40 rooms. Pets accepted; fee. Complimentary continental breakfast. Check-out noon. TV; VCR available. Pool. **$**

★ **DAYS INN.** *150 Dussel Dr (43537). Phone 419/893-9960; toll-free 800/431-2574; fax 419/893-9559. www.daysinn.com.* 120 rooms, 2 story. Pets accepted, some restrictions; fee. Complimentary continental breakfast. Check-out noon. TV; cable (premium). Health club privileges. Game room. Pool. **$**

Wapakoneta

Motel/Motor Lodge

★★ **BEST WESTERN WAPAKONETA.** *1510 Saturn Dr (45895). Phone 419/738-8181; toll-free 877/738-8181; fax 419/738-6478. www.bestwestern.com/wapakoneta.* 94 rooms, 4 story. Pets accepted; fee. Complimentary

continental breakfast. Check-out noon. TV; cable (premium), VCR available. In-room modem link. Laundry services. Restaurant, bar. Room service. In-house fitness room. Pool. Neil Armstrong Museum adjacent. **$**

Warren

Motel/Motor Lodge

★★ **BEST WESTERN DOWNTOWN MOTOR INN.** *777 Mahoning Ave NW (44483). Phone 330/392-2515; fax 330/392-7099. www.bestwestern.com/downtownmotorinn.* 73 rooms, 2 story. Pets accepted, some restrictions. Complimentary continental breakfast. Check-out 11 am. TV; cable (premium). Restaurant, bar. Health club privileges. Pool. **$**

Hotel

★ **COMFORT INN.** *136 N Park Ave (44483). Phone 330/393-1200; fax 330/399-2875. www.comfortinn.com.* 55 rooms, 4 story. Pets accepted; fee. Check-out noon. TV. Restaurant, bar. Health club privileges. Airport transportation. Restored brick hotel (1887). **$**

Wauseon

Motel/Motor Lodge

★★ **BEST WESTERN DEL MAR.** *8319 OH 108 (43567). Phone 419/335-1565; toll-free 800/647-2260; fax 419/335-1828. www.bestwestern.com.* 48 rooms. Pets accepted; fee. Complimentary continental breakfast. Check-out 11 am. TV; cable (premium). Pool. **$**

Wilmington

Motel/Motor Lodge

★ **HOLIDAY INN EXPRESS.** *155 Holiday Dr (45177). Phone 937/382-5858; fax 937/382-0457. www.holiday-inn.com.* 61 rooms, 3 story. Pets accepted, some restrictions; fee. Complimentary continental breakfast. Check-out noon. TV; cable (premium). In-room modem link. In-house fitness room. Indoor pool; whirlpool. **$**

Wooster

Motel/Motor Lodge

★ **ECONO LODGE.** *2137 Lincoln Way E (44691). Phone 330/264-8883; toll-free 800/553-2666; fax 330/263-0792. www.econolodge.com.* 98 rooms, 2 story. Pets accepted; fee. Check-out 11 am. TV. Laundry services. Indoor pool; whirlpool. Airport transportation. Business center. **$**

D �¤ ≈ ≋ SC 🏃

B&B/Small Inn

★ ★ ★ **WOOSTER INN.** *801 E Wayne Ave (44691). Phone 330/263-2660; fax 330/263-2661.* This quaint country inn offers comfortable rooms and elegant dining experiences. Enjoy American-style fare served in the restaurant or a nightcap in the billiard parlor over a game of pool on the vintage table. 16 rooms, 2 story. Closed early Jan, Dec 25, 26. Pets accepted; fee. Check-out noon. TV. Restaurant. 9-hole golf, putting green, driving range. Greens fee $8-$9. Colonial décor. Owned and operated by College of Wooster; on campus. **$$**

D ➤ 🎱

Youngstown

Motels/Motor Lodges

★ ★ **BEST WESTERN MEANDER INN.** *870 N Canfield Niles Rd (44515). Phone 330/544-2378; toll-free 800/780-7234; fax 330/544-7926. www.bestwestern.com.* 57 rooms, 2 story. Pets accepted; fee. Complimentary continental breakfast. Check-out noon. TV. Laundry services. Restaurant, bar. Room service. Health club privileges. Pool. **$**

D ➤ ≈ ≋ SC

★ **MOTEL 6.** *5431 76 Dr (44515). Phone 330/793-9305; fax 330/793-2584. www.motel6.com.* 79 rooms. Pets accepted, some restrictions. Check-out 11 am. TV. Pool. **$**

D ➤ ≈ ≋

Zanesville

Motels/Motor Lodges

★ **COMFORT INN.** *500 Monroe St (43701). Phone 740/454-4144; fax 740/454-4144. www.comfortinn.com.* 81 rooms, 2 story. Pets accepted, some restrictions; fee. Complimentary continental breakfast. Check-out noon.

TV; VCR available. Laundry services. In-house fitness room; sauna. Indoor pool; whirlpool. **$**

D ➤ ≈ 🏃 ≋ SC

★ ★ **HOLIDAY INN.** *4645 East Pike (43701). Phone 740/453-0771; fax 740/453-0771. www.holiday-inn.com.* 130 rooms, 2 story. Pets accepted, some restrictions. Check-out noon. TV; cable (premium). In-room modem link. Laundry services. Restaurant, bar. Room service. In-house fitness room; sauna. Indoor pool; whirlpool; poolside service. **$**

D ➤ ≈ 🏃 ≋ SC

Oklahoma

Altus

Motels/Motor Lodges

★ **BEST WESTERN ALTUS.** *2804 N Main St (73521). Phone 580/482-9300; fax 580/482-2245. www.bestwestern.com.* 100 rooms, 2 story. Pets accepted, some restrictions; fee. Complimentary continental breakfast. Check-out noon. TV; cable (premium). In-room modem link. Laundry services. In-house fitness room; sauna. Game room. Indoor pool; outdoor pool. Business center. **$**

D 🐾 ≋ ✕ ≋ SC

★ **DAYS INN.** *3202 N Main St (73521). Phone 580/477-2300; toll-free 800/329-7466; fax 580/477-2379. www.daysinn.com.* 39 rooms, 2 story. Pets accepted; fee. Complimentary continental breakfast. Check-out 11 am. TV; cable (premium). **$**

🐾 ≋ SC

★ **RAMADA INN.** *2515 E Broadway St (73521). Phone 580/477-3000; toll-free 888/298-2054; fax 580/477-0078. www.ramada.com.* 12 rooms, 2 story. Pets accepted; fee. Check-out noon. TV; cable (premium). Restaurant, bar. Room service. Game room. Indoor pool. **$**

D 🐾 ≋ ≋ SC

Alva

Motel/Motor Lodge

★ **RANGER INN.** *420 E Oklahoma Blvd (73717). Phone 580/327-1981; fax 580/327-1981.* 41 rooms. Pets accepted, some restrictions. Check-out 11 am. TV; cable (premium). **$**

D 🐾 ≋

Ardmore

Motels/Motor Lodges

★ **DAYS INN.** *2614 W Broadway St (73401). Phone 580/226-1761; fax 580/223-3131.* 47 rooms, 2 story. Pets accepted; fee. Complimentary continental breakfast. Check-out 11 am. TV; cable (premium). **$**

D 🐾 ≋

★ **GUEST INN.** *2519 W Hwy 142 (73401). Phone 580/223-1234; toll-free 800/460-4064; fax 580/223-1234.* 126 rooms, 2 story. Pets accepted. Check-out 1 pm. TV; cable (premium), VCR available (movies). Laundry services. Pool. **$**

D 🐾 ≋ ≋ SC

★★ **HOLIDAY INN.** *2705 W Holiday Dr (73401). Phone 580/223-7130; toll-free 800/465-4329; fax 580/223-7130. www.holiday-inn.com.* 169 rooms, 2 story. Pets accepted, some restrictions; fee. Check-out 11 am. TV. In-room modem link. Tea maker. Restaurant open 24 hours. Live entertainment Mon, Tues, Thurs-Sat. Karaoke Wed. In-house fitness room. Pool; children's pool. Free airport transportation. **$**

D 🐾 ≋ ✈ ≋ SC

Resort

★ **LAKE MURRAY LODGE AND COUNTRY INN.** *3310 S Lake Murray Dr (73401). Phone 580/223-6600; fax 580/223-6154.* 131 rooms. Pets accepted. Check-out noon, check-in 3 pm. Some TV; VCR available (movies). Dining room, bar. Free supervised children's activities; ages 6-18. Pool. Miniature golf. Outdoor tennis. Lawn games. Paddleboats. Airport transportation. Movies. Chapel; services Sun. 2,500-foot lighted, paved airstrip. State operated. **$**

D 🐾 ⚡ ⛳ ≋ ≋ SC

Atoka

Motel/Motor Lodge

★★ **BEST WESTERN ATOKA INN.** *2101 S Mississippi Ave (74525). Phone 580/889-7381; fax 580/889-6695. www.bestwestern.com.* 54 rooms, 2 story. Pets accepted; fee. Check-out noon. TV. Restaurant open 24 hours. Pool. Free airport transportation. **$**

🐾 ≋ ≋ SC

Bartlesville

Motels/Motor Lodges

★★ **BEST WESTERN WESTON INN.** *222 SE Washington Blvd (74006). Phone 918/335-7755; fax 918/335-7763. www.bestwestern.com.* 109 rooms, 2 story. Pets accepted; fee. Complimentary continental breakfast. Check-out 11 am. TV; cable (premium). In-room modem link. Restaurant. Room service. Pool. **$**

D 🐾 ≋ ≋ SC

★ **TRAVELERS MOTEL.** *3105 E Frank Phillips Blvd (74006). Phone 918/333-1900; fax 918/333-6833.* 24 rooms. Pets accepted; fee. Check-out 11 am. TV; cable (premium). **$**

Chickasha

Motel/Motor Lodge

★ ★ **BEST WESTERN INN.** *2101 S 4th St (73023). Phone 405/224-4890; toll-free 877/489-0647; fax 405/224-3411. www.bestwestern.com.* 148 rooms, 2 story. Pets accepted, some restrictions; fee. Check-out noon. TV; cable (premium). In-room modem link. Restaurant, bar. Room service. Sauna. Pool; whirlpool. Free parking. **$**

Claremore

Motel/Motor Lodge

★ ★ **BEST WESTERN WILL ROGERS INN.** *940 S Lynn Riggs Blvd (74017). Phone 918/341-4410; toll-free 800/644-9455; fax 918/341-6045. www.bestwestern.com.* 52 rooms. Pets accepted. Check-out noon. TV; cable (premium). In-room modem link. Laundry services. Restaurant, bar. Pool. **$**

Duncan

Motel/Motor Lodge

★ ★ **HOLIDAY INN.** *1015 N Hwy 81 (73533). Phone 580/252-1500; fax 580/255-1851. www.holiday-inn.com.* 138 rooms, 2 story. Pets accepted, some restrictions. TV; cable (premium). In-room modem link. Restaurant, bar. Room service. Sauna. Indoor pool; children's pool. **$**

Durant

Motel/Motor Lodge

★ ★ **HOLIDAY INN.** *2121 W Main St (74701). Phone 580/924-5432; fax 580/924-9721. www.holiday-inn.com.* 81 rooms, 2 story. Pets accepted, some restrictions; fee. Check-out noon. TV; cable (premium). In-room modem link. Laundry services. Restaurant. Room service. Pool. **$**

Elk City

Motel/Motor Lodge

★ ★ **HOLIDAY INN.** *101 Meadow Ridge (73644). Phone 580/225-6637; fax 580/225-6637. www.holiday-inn.com.* 151 rooms, 2 story. Pets accepted, some restrictions. Complimentary breakfast. Check-out noon. TV; cable (premium), VCR available (movies). In-room modem link. Restaurant, bar. Room service. In-house fitness room; sauna. Game room. Indoor pool; whirlpool. Lawn games. **$**

El Reno

Motel/Motor Lodge

★ **BEST WESTERN HENSLEY'S.** *I-40 and Country Club Rd (73036). Phone 405/262-6490; toll-free 800/780-7234; fax 405/262-7642. www.bestwestern.com.* 60 rooms, 2 story. Pets accepted, fee. Complimentary breakfast. Check-out 11 am. TV; cable (premium). **$**

Enid

Motels/Motor Lodges

★ ★ **BEST WESTERN INN.** *2818 S Van Buren St (73703). Phone 580/242-7110; toll-free 800/378-6308; fax 580/242-6202. www.bestwestern.com.* 99 rooms, 2 story. Pets accepted; fee. Check-out noon. TV; cable (premium). In-room modem link. Restaurant, bar. In-house fitness room. Health club privileges. Game room. Indoor pool; whirlpool. **$**

★ **RAMADA INN.** *3005 W Garriott Rd (73703). Phone 580/234-0440; fax 580/233-1402. www.ramada.com.* 122 rooms, 2 story. Pets accepted, fee. Check-out noon. TV; cable (premium). Restaurant. Room service. In-house fitness room; sauna. Health club privileges. Game room. Pool; whirlpool. **$**

Guthrie

Motel/Motor Lodge

★ ★ **BEST WESTERN TERRITORIAL INN.** *2323 Territorial Trail (73044). Phone 405/282-8831; toll-free*

800/780-7234. www.bestwestern.com. 84 rooms, 2 story. Pets accepted. Check-out 11 am. TV; cable (premium). Restaurant, bar. Room service. Pool. **$**

D 🐾 ⛖ ⊠ SC

Guymon

Motels/Motor Lodges

★ ★ **AMBASSADOR INN.** *Hwy 64N at 21st St (73942). Phone 580/338-5555; toll-free 800/338-3301; fax 580/338-1784.* 70 rooms, 2 story. Pets accepted. Check-out 11 am. TV; cable (premium). Restaurant. **$**

D 🐾 ⊠

★ **ECONO LODGE.** *923 E Hwy 54 E (73942). Phone 580/338-5431; fax 580/338-0554. www.econolodge.com.* 40 rooms. Pets accepted; fee. Check-out 11 am. TV; cable (premium). **$**

D 🐾 ⊠

Henryetta

Motels/Motor Lodges

★ **HENRYETTA INN AND DOME.** *810 E Trudgeon St (74437). Phone 918/652-2581.* 85 rooms, 2 story. Pets accepted, some restrictions. Check-out noon. TV. Laundry services. Restaurant, bar. Room service. In-house fitness room; sauna. Indoor pool. **$**

D 🐾 ⛖ 🏋 ⊠ SC

★ **LE BARON MOTEL.** *1001 E Main St (74437). Phone 918/652-2531.* 24 rooms, 2 story. Pets accepted; fee. Check-out 11 am. TV; cable (premium). **$**

🐾 ⊠ SC

Lawton

Motels/Motor Lodges

★ **DAYS INN.** *3110 Cache Rd (73505). Phone 580/353-3104; toll-free 800/329-7466; fax 580/353-0992. www.daysinn.com.* 95 rooms, 2 story. Pets accepted; fee. Complimentary continental breakfast. Check-out noon. TV; cable (premium). In-room modem link. Laundry services. Indoor pool; outdoor pool; whirlpool. **$**

D 🐾 ⛖ ⊠ SC

★ **RAMADA INN.** *601 N 2nd St (73507). Phone 580/355-7155; toll-free 888/298-2054; fax 580/353-6162. www.ramada.com.* 98 rooms, 2 story. Pets accepted; fee.

Check-out noon. TV; cable (premium), VCR available (movies). Restaurant, bar. Room service. **$**

D 🐾 ⊠ SC

McAlester

Motels/Motor Lodges

★ ★ **BEST WESTERN INN OF MCALESTER.** *1215 George Nigh Expy (74502). Phone 918/426-0115; fax 918/426-3634. www.bestwestern.com.* 61 rooms, 2 story. Pets accepted. Complimentary continental breakfast. Check-out noon. TV; cable (premium). In-room modem link. Restaurant. Pool. **$**

🐾 ⛖ ⊠ SC

★ ★ **DAYS INN.** *1217 S George Nigh Expy (74502). Phone 918/426-5050; fax 918/426-5055. www.daysinn.com.* 100 rooms, 2 story. Pets accepted, some restrictions; fee. Check-out noon. TV; cable (premium). In-room modem link. Restaurant, bar. Room service. Indoor pool; whirlpool. Near Municipal Airport. **$**

D 🐾 ⛖ 🛫 ⊠

★ ★ **RAMADA INN.** *1500 S George Nigh Expy (74501). Phone 918/423-7766; fax 918/426-0068. www.ramada.com.* 161 rooms, 2 story. Pets accepted, some restrictions. Check-out noon. TV. Laundry services. Restaurant, bar. Room service. Sauna. Game room. Pool; whirlpool. Miniature golf. **$**

D 🐾 ⛖ ⊠ SC

Miami

Motel/Motor Lodge

★ ★ **BEST WESTERN INN OF MIAMI.** *2225 E Steve Owens Blvd (74354). Phone 918/542-6681; toll-free 877/884-5422; fax 918/542-3777. www.bestwestern.com.* 80 rooms. Pets accepted. Check-out noon. TV; cable (premium). Restaurant, bar. Room service. Pool. Airport transportation. **$**

🐾 ⛖ 🛫 ⊠ SC

Muskogee

Motels/Motor Lodges

★ ★ **RAMADA INN.** *800 S 32nd St (74401). Phone 918/682-4341; fax 918/682-7400. www.ramada.com.* 142 rooms, 2 story. Pets accepted; fee. Check-out noon. TV; cable (premium), VCR available. Restaurant, bar;

entertainment. In-house fitness room; sauna. Game room. Indoor pool; whirlpool. **$**

D 🐾 ⛱ 🕴 📠 SC

★ **TRAVELODGE.** *534 S 32nd St (74401). Phone 918/683-2951; toll-free 800/515-6375; fax 918/683-5848. www.travelodge.com.* 104 rooms, 2 story. Pets accepted, some restrictions; fee. Complimentary continental breakfast. Check-out 11 am. TV; cable (premium). In-room modem link. Bar. Pool; poolside service. **$**

D 🐾 ⛱ 📠 SC

Norman

Motels/Motor Lodges

★ ★ **GUEST INN.** *2543 W Main St (73069). Phone 405/360-1234; toll-free 800/460-4619.* 110 rooms, 2 story. Pets accepted. Complimentary continental breakfast. Check-out noon. TV; cable (premium). Laundry services. Restaurant open 24 hours. Pool. **$**

D 🐾 ⛱ 📠 SC

★ **TRAVELODGE.** *225 N Interstate Dr (73069). Phone 405/329-7194; fax 405/360-2618. www.travelodge.com.* 40 rooms, 2 story. Pets accepted, some restrictions; fee. Complimentary continental breakfast. Check-out 11 am. TV; cable (premium). In-room modem link. Laundry services. Pool; whirlpool. **$**

D 🐾 ⛱ 📠 SC

Oklahoma City

Motels/Motor Lodges

★ ★ **BEST WESTERN SADDLEBACK INN.** *4300 SW 3rd St (73108). Phone 405/947-7000; fax 405/948-7636. www.bestwestern.com.* 220 rooms, 2-3 story. Pets accepted, some restrictions; fee. Check-out noon. TV; cable (premium), VCR available. In-room modem link. Restaurant, bar. Room service. In-house fitness room; sauna. Pool; whirlpool; poolside service. Free airport transportation. Southwestern décor. **$**

D 🐾 ⛱ 🕴 ✈ 📠 SC

★ ★ **BILTMORE HOTEL OKLAHOMA.** *401 S Meridian Ave (73108). Phone 405/947-7681; fax 405/947-4253.* 509 rooms, 2 story. Pets accepted. Check-out noon. TV; cable (premium), VCR available. In-room modem link. Restaurant, bar; entertainment. Room service. In-house fitness room; sauna. Four pools; whirlpool; poolside service. Tennis. Free airport transportation. **$**

D 🐾 🏌 ⛱ 🕴 ✈ 📠

★ **DAYS INN.** *2801 NW 39th St (73112). Phone 405/946-0741; fax 405/942-0181. www.daysinn.com.* 117 rooms, 2 story. Pets accepted, some restrictions; fee. Complimentary continental breakfast. Check-out 11 am. TV; cable (premium). In-room modem link. Laundry services. Restaurant, bar. Room service. Pool. Free airport transportation. **$**

D 🐾 ⛱ ✈ 📠 SC

★ **DAYS INN.** *12013 N I-35 Service Rd (73131). Phone 405/478-2554; toll-free 800/329-7466; fax 405/478-5033. www.daysinn.com.* 47 rooms, 2 story. Pets accepted; fee. Complimentary breakfast. Check-out 11 am. TV; cable (premium). In-room modem link. Indoor pool. **$**

D 🐾 ⛱ 📠 SC

★ **HOWARD JOHNSON.** *400 S Meridian Ave (73108). Phone 405/943-9841; toll-free 800/458-8186; fax 405/942-1869. www.hojo.com.* 96 rooms, 2 story. Pets accepted, some restrictions; fee. Complimentary continental breakfast. Check-out noon. TV; cable (premium). In-house fitness room. Pool. Free airport transportation. **$**

D 🐾 ⛱ 🕴 ✈ 📠 SC

★ **LA QUINTA INN.** *800 S Meridian Ave (73108). Phone 405/942-0040; toll-free 800/531-5900; fax 405/942-0638. www.laquinta.com.* 168 rooms, 2 story. Pets accepted, some restrictions. Complimentary continental breakfast. Check-out noon. TV; cable (premium), VCR available. In-room modem link. Restaurant, bar. Room service. In-house fitness room. Pool; children's pool; poolside service. Free airport, bus depot transportation. **$**

D 🐾 ⛱ 🕴 📠 SC

★ **LA QUINTA INN.** *8315 S I-35 Service Rd (73149). Phone 405/631-8661; toll-free 800/531-5900; fax 405/631-1892. www.laquinta.com.* 121 rooms, 2 story. Pets accepted. Complimentary continental breakfast. Check-out noon. TV; cable (premium). In-room modem link. Health club privileges. Pool. **$**

D 🐾 ⛱ 📠 SC

★ ★ **QUALITY INN.** *12001 NE Expy (73131). Phone 405/478-0400; fax 405/478-2774. www.qualityinn.com.* 213 rooms, 2 story. Pets accepted, some restrictions; fee. Complimentary continental breakfast. Check-out noon. TV; cable (premium). Laundry services. Bar. Game room. Pool; whirlpool. **$**

D 🐾 🦮 ⛱ 🏄 📠

★ **RAMADA INN.** *1401 NE 63rd St (73111). Phone 405/478-5221; fax 405/478-5221. www.ramada.com.* 52 rooms, 2-3 story. No elevator. Pets accepted, some restrictions; fee. Complimentary continental breakfast. Check-out noon. TV; cable (premium). In-room modem link. Laundry services. Pool. **$**

D 🐾 ⛱ 📠

★ ★ **RAMADA INN.** *930 E 2nd St (73034). Phone 405/341-3577; toll-free 888/298-2054; fax 405/341-9279. www.ramada.com.* 145 rooms, 8 story. Pets accepted. Complimentary breakfast. Check-out 11 am. TV; cable (premium). In-room modem link. Restaurant, bar; entertainment Fri, Sat. Room service. In-house fitness room. Pool; whirlpool. Boats; water skiing; jet skiing. **$**

D ⬛ ⬛ ⬛ ⬛ SC

★ **SUPER 8.** *2821 NW 39th Expy (73112). Phone 405/946-9170; fax 405/942-0181. www.super8.com.* 71 rooms, 2 story. Pets accepted, some restrictions. Check-out 11 am. TV; cable (premium). In-room modem link. Laundry services. Room service. Pool. Free airport transportation. **$**

D ⬛ ⬛ ⬛ SC

Hotels

★ ★ **HOLIDAY INN.** *6200 N Robinson Ave (73118). Phone 405/843-5558; toll-free 800/682-0049; fax 405/840-3410. www.holiday-inn.com.* 200 rooms, 3 story. Pets accepted, some restrictions; fee. Check-out noon. TV; cable (premium). In-room modem link. Laundry services. Restaurant, bar. In-house fitness room. Health club privileges. Indoor pool; whirlpool; poolside service. **$**

D ⬛ ⬛ ⬛ ⬛

★ ★ ★ **MARRIOTT OKLAHOMA CITY.** *3233 NW Expy (73112). Phone 405/842-6633; fax 405/842-3152. www.marriott.com.* 354 rooms, 15 story. Pets accepted, some restrictions; fee. Check-out noon. TV; cable (premium), VCR available. In-room modem link. Restaurant, bar. Room service. In-house fitness room; sauna. Health club privileges. Indoor pool; outdoor pool; whirlpool. Business center. Concierge. Luxury level. **$**

D ⬛ ⬛ ⬛ ⬛ SC ⬛

★ ★ ★ **MARRIOTT WATERFORD.** *6300 Waterford Blvd (73118). Phone 405/848-4782; fax 405/848-7810. www.marriott.com.* Located in the city's premier suburb, this hotel is only 15 minutes from downtown and the airport. Guests can enjoy a drink in the waterfront lounge or take a swim in the outdoor pool. Volleyball and squash facilities are also available. 197 rooms, 9 story. Pets accepted, some restrictions; fee. Check-out noon. TV; cable (premium), VCR available. In-room modem link. Restaurant, bar; entertainment. Room service. In-house fitness room, massage, sauna. Pool; whirlpool; poolside service. Outdoor tennis. Business center. Concierge. Luxury level. **$**

D ⬛ ⬛ ⬛ ⬛ ⬛ ⬛ ⬛

All Suite

★ ★ **EMBASSY SUITES.** *1815 S Meridian Ave (73108). Phone 405/682-6000; toll-free 800/362-2779; fax 405/682-9835. www.embassysuites.com.* 236 rooms, 6 story. Pets accepted, some restrictions; fee. Complimentary

breakfast. Check-out noon. TV; cable (premium). In-room modem link. Laundry services. Restaurant, bar. Room service. In-house fitness room; sauna. Indoor pool; whirlpool. Airport transportation. Business center. **$**

D ⬛ ⬛ ⬛ ⬛ ⬛ ⬛

Okmulgee

Motel/Motor Lodge

★ ★ **BEST WESTERN OKMULGEE.** *3499 N Wood Dr (74447). Phone 918/756-9200; toll-free 800/552-9201; fax 918/752-0022. www.bestwestern.com.* 50 rooms, 2 story. Pets accepted; fee. Complimentary continental breakfast. Check-out 11 am. TV; cable (premium). In-room modem link. Restaurant, bar; entertainment. Pool. **$**

D ⬛ ⬛ ⬛

Pauls Valley

Motel/Motor Lodge

★ **DAYS INN.** *3203 W Grant Ave (73075). Phone 405/238-7548; toll-free 800/329-7466; fax 405/238-1262. www.daysinn.com.* 54 rooms, 2 story. Pets accepted, some restrictions. Complimentary continental breakfast. Check-out 11 am. TV. **$**

D ⬛ ⬛ ⬛ SC

Perry

Motel/Motor Lodge

★ ★ **BEST WESTERN CHEROKEE STRIP MOTEL.** *Hwy 64, 77 and I-35 (73077). Phone 580/336-2218; toll-free 800/780-7234; fax 580/336-9753. www.bestwestern.com.* 88 rooms. Pets accepted. Check-out noon. TV; cable (premium), VCR available. Restaurant, bar. Game room. Indoor pool. **$**

D ⬛ ⬛ ⬛ SC

Ponca City

Motel/Motor Lodge

★ **DAYS INN.** *1415 E Bradley Ave (74604). Phone 580/767-1406; fax 580/762-9589. www.daysinn.com.* 59 rooms, 3 story. No elevator. Pets accepted, some restrictions; fee. Complimentary continental breakfast. Check-out 11 am. TV; cable (premium). **$**

D ⬛ ⬛ ⬛

B&B/Small Inn

★ **ROSE STONE INN.** *120 S 3rd St (74601). Phone 580/765-5699; fax 580/762-0240.* 25 rooms, 3 suites, 2 story. Pets accepted, some restrictions; fee. Complimentary breakfast. Check-out 11 am, check-in 3 pm. TV; cable (premium), VCR available (movies). In-room modem link. Laundry services. Former home of one of the first savings & loans west of the Mississippi. Totally nonsmoking. **$**

D 🐾 ✈ 🏊 SC

Pryor

Motel/Motor Lodge

★ **PRYOR HOUSE MOTOR INN.** *123 S Mill St (74361). Phone 918/825-6677; fax 918/825-6678.* 35 rooms, 2 story. Pets accepted; fee. Complimentary continental breakfast. Check-out 11 am. TV; cable (premium). Restaurant open 24 hours. Pool. **$**

D 🐾 🏊 🏊

Sallisaw

Motels/Motor Lodges

★ **DAYS INN.** *1700 W Cherokee St (74955). Phone 918/775-4406; fax 918/775-4440. www.daysinn.com.* 33 rooms, 2 story. Pets accepted; fee. Complimentary continental breakfast. Check-out 11 am. TV; cable (premium). Room service. **$**

D 🐾 🐾 🏊

★ **GOLDEN SPUR MOTEL.** *Hwy 59 and I-40 (74955). Phone 918/775-4443.* 28 rooms, 2 story. Pets accepted; fee. Complimentary continental breakfast. Check-out 11 am. TV; cable (premium). Pool. **$**

🐾 🏊 🏊 SC

Shawnee

Motels/Motor Lodges

★ ★ **BEST WESTERN CINDERELLA MOTOR INN.** *623 Kickapoo Spur St (74801). Phone 405/273-7010; toll-free 800/480-5111. www.bestwestern.com.* 90 rooms, 2 story. Pets accepted, some restrictions; fee. Check-out noon. TV; cable (premium). Restaurant, bar. Room service. Health club privileges. Indoor pool; whirlpool; poolside service. **$**

D 🐾 🏊 🏊 SC

★ **RAMADA INN.** *4900 N Harrison Blvd (74801). Phone 405/275-4404; toll-free 800/298-2054; fax 405/275-4998. www.ramada.com.* 106 rooms, 2 story. Pets accepted; fee. TV; cable (premium). In-room modem link. Laundry services. Restaurant, bar; entertainment. Room service. Game room. Indoor pool; poolside service. **$**

D 🐾 🏊 🏊 SC

Stillwater

Motels/Motor Lodges

★ ★ **BEST WESTERN STILLWATER.** *600 E McElroy Rd (74075). Phone 405/377-7010; toll-free 800/353-6894; fax 405/743-1686. www.bestwestern.com.* 122 rooms, 4 story. Pets accepted. Check-out noon. TV; cable (premium). In-room modem link. Restaurant, bar. Room service. In-house fitness room; sauna. Game room. Indoor pool; whirlpool. Business center. **$**

D 🐾 🏊 🏋 🏊 SC 🚶

★ ★ **HOLIDAY INN.** *2515 W 6th Ave (74074). Phone 405/372-0800; fax 405/377-8212. www.holiday-inn.com.* 141 rooms, 2 story. Pets accepted. Check-out noon. TV; cable (premium). In-room modem link. Restaurant, bar. Room service. Sauna. Game room. Indoor pool; whirlpool. Business center. **$**

D 🐾 🏊 🏊 🚶

Tulsa

Motels/Motor Lodges

★ **BEST WESTERN GLENPOOL/TULSA.** *14831 S Casper, Hwy 75 S (74033). Phone 918/322-5201; toll-free 800/678-5201; fax 918/322-9604. www.bestwestern.com.* 64 rooms, 2 story. Pets accepted; fee. Complimentary continental breakfast. Check-out 11 am. TV; cable (premium). In-room modem link. **$**

D 🐾 🏊 SC

★ ★ **BEST WESTERN TRADE WINDS CENTRAL INN.** *3141 E Skelly Dr (74105). Phone 918/749-5561; fax 918/749-6312. www.bestwestern.com.* 164 rooms, 2 story. Pets accepted; fee. Complimentary continental breakfast. Check-out noon. TV; cable (premium), VCR available (movies). In-room modem link. Restaurant, bar; entertainment. Room service. In-house fitness room. Pool; whirlpool; poolside service. Free airport transportation. **$**

D 🐾 🏊 🏋 ✈ 🏊

★ **HAWTHORN SUITES.** *3509 S 79th E Ave (74145). Phone 918/663-3900; fax 918/664-0548. www.hawthorn.com.* 131 rooms, 3 story. Pets accepted, some restrictions; fee. Complimentary breakfast. TV; cable (premium). Fireplaces. Health club privileges. Pool; whirlpool. Sport court. Free airport transportation. **$**

[D] [✦] [≈] [✈] [≋] [SC]

★ ★ **HOLIDAY INN.** *1010 N Garnett Rd (74116). Phone 918/437-7660; fax 918/438-7538. www.holiday-inn.com.* 158 rooms, 2 story. Pets accepted, some restrictions; fee. Check-out noon. TV; cable (premium). In-room modem link. Restaurant, bar. Room service. In-house fitness room. Health club privileges. Game room. Indoor pool. Free airport transportation. **$**

[D] [✦] [≈] [✕] [✈] [✕] [≋]

★ **LA QUINTA INN.** *35 N Sheridan Rd (74115). Phone 918/836-3931; toll-free 800/531-5900; fax 918/836-5428. www.laquinta.com.* 101 rooms, 2 story. Pets accepted, some restrictions. Complimentary continental breakfast. Check-out noon. TV; cable (premium). In-room modem link. Pool. Free airport transportation. **$**

[D] [✦] [≈] [✈] [≋] [SC]

★ **TRAVELODGE.** *4717 S Yale Ave (74135). Phone 918/622-6776; fax 918/622-1809. www.travelodge.com.* 109 rooms, 3 story. Pets accepted; fee. Complimentary continental breakfast. Check-out 11 am. TV. In-room modem link. **$**

[D] [✦] [✚] [≋]

Hotels

★ ★ **DOUBLETREE HOTEL.** *6110 S Yale Ave (74136). Phone 918/495-1000; fax 918/495-1944. www.doubletree.com.* Near two major universities, great shopping, museums, and more. It is only 20 minutes from the Tulsa International Airport in a park-like setting with trees, a stream, and walking and jogging trails. 370 rooms, 10 story. Pets accepted; fee. Check-out noon. TV; cable (premium), VCR available. In-room modem link. Restaurant, bar. Children's activity center. In-house fitness room; sauna, steam room. Health club privileges. Indoor pool; whirlpool. Valet parking. Business center. Concierge. Luxury level. Common rooms decorated with Chippendale, Hepplewhite furniture. Free airport transportation. **$**

[D] [✦] [≈] [✕] [✈] [✕] [SC] [✚]

★ ★ **DOUBLETREE HOTEL.** *616 W 7th St (74127). Phone 918/587-8000; fax 918/587-3001. www.doubletree.com.* 417 rooms, 17 story. Pets accepted; fee. Check-out noon. TV; cable (premium), VCR available. In-room modem link. Restaurant, bar; entertainment. Room service. In-house fitness room. Indoor pool; whirlpool; poolside service. Valet parking. Business center. Free airport transportation. **$**

[D] [✦] [≈] [✕] [✈] [✕] [✚]

★ ★ ★ **SHERATON TULSA HOTEL.** *10918 E 41st St (74146). Phone 918/627-5000; toll-free 800/325-3535; fax 918/627-4003. www.sheraton.com.* This hotel is near the Tulsa International Airport, the Philbrook Museum, and the Big Splash Water Park. 325 rooms, 11 story. Pets accepted, some restrictions. Check-out 11 am. TV; cable (premium), VCR available (movies). In-room modem link. Restaurant, bar. Room service. In-house fitness room; sauna. Health club privileges. Indoor pool; outdoor pool; whirlpool; poolside service. Free airport transportation. Business center. Concierge. Luxury level. **$**

[D] [✦] [≈] [✕] [✈] [≋] [SC] [✚]

Weatherford

Motel/Motor Lodge

★ **BEST WESTERN MARK MOTOR HOTEL.** *525 E Main St (73096). Phone 580/772-3325; fax 580/772-8950. www.bestwestern.com.* 63 rooms, 1-2 story. Pets accepted, some restrictions. Complimentary breakfast. Check-out noon. TV; cable (premium), VCR available. In-room modem link. Pool. **$**

[D] [✦] [≈] [≋]

Woodward

Motels/Motor Lodges

★ ★ **NORTHWEST INN.** *US 270 S and 1st St (73802). Phone 580/256-7600; toll-free 800/727-7606; fax 580/254-2274.* 124 rooms, 2 story. Pets accepted; fee. Check-out noon. TV; cable (premium). Restaurant, bar; entertainment. Room service. Game room. Indoor pool. **$**

[D] [✦] [≈] [≋]

★ **SUPER 8.** *4120 Williams Ave (73801). Phone 580/254-2964. www.super8.com.* 60 rooms, 2 story. Pets accepted; fee. Complimentary continental breakfast. Check-out 11 am. TV; cable (premium). In-room modem link. Pool. **$**

[D] [✦] [≈] [≋] [SC]

Oregon

Albany

Motels/Motor Lodges

★ **BEST WESTERN PONY SOLDIER INN.** *315 Airport Rd SE (97321). Phone 541/928-6322; toll-free 800/634-7669; fax 541/928-8124. ponysoldierinns.com.* 72 rooms, 2 story. Pets accepted. Complimentary breakfast. Check-out noon. TV. In-room modem link. Laundry services. In-house fitness room. Pool; whirlpool. Airport transportation. **$**

★ **LA QUINTA INN.** *251 Airport Rd SE (97321). Phone 541/928-0921; fax 541/928-8055. www.laquinta.com.* 62 rooms, 2 story. Pets accepted, some restrictions. Complimentary continental breakfast. Check-out 1 pm. TV. Laundry services. In-house fitness room; sauna. Indoor pool; whirlpool. **$**

Ashland

Motels/Motor Lodges

★ **BEST WESTERN BARD'S INN.** *132 N Main St (97520). Phone 541/482-0049; toll-free 800/533-9627; fax 541/488-3259. www.bestwestern.com.* 91 rooms, 2-3 story. Pets accepted; fee. Complimentary continental breakfast. Check-out 11 am. TV; cable (premium). Pool; whirlpool. Downhill, cross-country ski 20 miles. Near Shakespeare Festival theater. **$**

★ **BEST WESTERN WINDSOR INN.** *2520 Ashland St (97520). Phone 541/488-2330;, toll-free 800/334-2330; fax 541/482-1068. www.bestwestern.com.* 92 rooms, 2 story. Pets accepted, some restrictions; fee. Complimentary continental breakfast. Check-out 11 am. TV. In-room modem link. Pool. Downhill, cross-country ski 15 miles. Airport transportation. **$**

★ **KNIGHTS INN.** *2359 Hwy 66 (97520). Phone 541/482-5111; toll-free 800/547-4566; fax 541/488-1589. www.brodeur-inns.com.* 40 rooms, 1-2 story. Pets accepted, some restrictions; fee. Check-out 11 am. TV. Restaurant, bar. Pool; whirlpool. Downhill ski 15 miles. **$**

★ **RODEWAY INN.** *1193 Siskiyou Blvd (97520). Phone 541/482-2641; toll-free 800/547-6414; fax 541/488-1656. www.rodewayinn.com.* 64 rooms, 1-3 story. Pets accepted; fee. Check-out 11 am. TV; cable (premium). Pool. Downhill, cross-country ski 18 miles. College opposite. **$**

★ ★ **WINDMILL INN AND SUITES OF ASHLAND.** *2525 Ashland St (97520). Phone 541/482-8310; toll-free 800/547-4747; fax 541/488-1783. www.windmillinns.com.* Located in downtown Ashland. Easily accessible from Interstate 5, this hotel features a hair salon, lending library, and bikes for guests to enjoy. 230 rooms, 3 story. Pets accepted. Complimentary continental breakfast. Check-out 11 am. TV. Laundry services. Restaurant, bar. Room service. In-house fitness room. Pool; whirlpool. Outdoor tennis. Downhill, cross-country ski 13 miles. Bicycles. Airport transportation. **$**

Astoria

Motels/Motor Lodges

★ **BEST WESTERN ASTORIA INN.** *555 Hamburg Ave (97103). Phone 503/325-2205; toll-free 800/621-0641. www.bestwestern.com.* 76 rooms, 4 story. Pets accepted; fee. Complimentary continental breakfast. Check-out 11 am. TV. In-room modem link. Laundry services. Sauna. Indoor pool; whirlpool. On river. Some A/C. **$**

★ **CREST MOTEL.** *5366 Leif Erickson Dr (97103). Phone 503/325-3141; toll-free 800/421-3141; fax 503/325-3141. www.crest-motel.com.* 40 rooms, 1-2 story. No A/C. Pets accepted. Complimentary continental breakfast. Check-out noon. TV; cable (premium). Laundry services. Whirlpool. On high bluff overlooking Columbia River. **$**

★ ★ **RED LION.** *400 Industry St (97103). Phone 503/325-7373; toll-free 800/733-5466; fax 503/325-5786. www.redlion.com.* 124 rooms, 2 story. No A/C. Pets accepted; fee. Check-out noon. TV. Laundry services. Restaurant, bar; entertainment. Free airport transportation. Overlooks harbor; on Columbia River. **$**

★★ **SHILO INN.** *1609 E Harbor Dr (97146). Phone 503/861-2181; toll-free 800/222-2244; fax 503/861-2980. www.shiloinns.com.* 63 rooms, 4 story. Pets accepted, some restrictions; fee. Check-out noon. TV; cable (premium), VCR available. Laundry services. Restaurant, bar. Room service. In-house fitness room; sauna. Indoor pool; whirlpool. Free airport transportation. **$**

Baker City

Motels/Motor Lodges

★★ **ELDORADO INN.** *695 Campbell St (97814). Phone 541/523-6494; toll-free 800/537-5756.* 56 rooms, 2 story. Pets accepted; fee. Check-out noon. TV; VCR available. Restaurant. Indoor pool. **$**

★ **QUALITY INN BAKER CITY.** *810 Campbell St (97814). Phone 541/523-2242. www.qualityinn.com.* 54 rooms, 2 story. Pets accepted, some restrictions; fee. Complimentary continental breakfast. Check-out noon. TV. **$**

Bandon

Motel/Motor Lodge

★ **SUNSET OCEANFRONT ACCOMMODATIONS.** *1865 Beach Loop Dr (97411). Phone 541/347-2453; toll-free 800/842-2407; fax 541/347-3636. www.sunsetmotel.com.* 70 rooms, 1-3 story. Pets accepted, some restrictions; fee. Check-out 11 am. TV. Laundry services. Restaurant. Indoor pool; whirlpool. Free airport transportation. Totally nonsmoking. **$**

Beaverton

Motels/Motor Lodges

★★★ **BEST WESTERN GREENWOOD INN & SUITES.** *10700 SW Allen Blvd (97005). Phone 503/643-7444; toll-free 800/289-1300; fax 503/626-4545. www.greenwoodinn.com.* 250 rooms, 2 story. Pets accepted; fee. Check-out 1 pm. TV; cable (premium). In-room modem link. Restaurant, bar; entertainment. Room service. Sauna. Pool; whirlpool. Business center. **$**

★ **RAMADA INN.** *13455 SW Canyon Rd (97005). Phone 503/643-9100; fax 503/643-0514. www.ramada.com.* 143 rooms, 3 story. Pets accepted, some restrictions; fee. Complimentary continental breakfast. Check-out noon. TV; cable (premium). In-house fitness room. Pool. **$**

Bend

Motels/Motor Lodges

★ **BEST WESTERN ENTRADA LODGE.** *19221 Century Dr (97702). Phone 541/382-4080. www.bestwestern.com/entradalodge.* 79 rooms. Pets accepted, some restrictions; fee. Complimentary continental breakfast. Check-out noon. TV. In-room modem link. Health club privileges. Pool; whirlpool. Downhill, cross-country ski 17 miles. Whitewater rafting. On 31 acres. **$**

★ **HAMPTON INN.** *15 NE Butler Market Rd (97701). Phone 541/388-4114; toll-free 800/426-7866; fax 541/389-3261. www.hamptoninn.com.* 99 rooms, 2 story. Pets accepted, some restrictions; fee. Complimentary continental breakfast. Check-out noon. TV; cable (premium). In-room modem link. Pool; whirlpool. **$**

★ **MOTEL 6.** *201 NE 3rd St (97701). Phone 541/382-8282; fax 541/388-6833. www.motel6.com.* 60 rooms, 2 story. Pets accepted. Complimentary continental breakfast. Check-out noon. TV; cable (premium). Pool. Downhill, cross-country ski 20 miles. **$**

★★ **RED LION.** *1415 NE 3rd St (97701). Phone 541/382-7011; fax 541/382-7934. www.redlion.com.* 75 rooms, 2 story. Pets accepted. Check-out noon. TV; cable (premium). In-room modem link. Restaurant. Room service. Sauna. Pool; whirlpool. **$**

★★ **RIVERHOUSE RESORT.** *3075 N Hwy 97 (97701). Phone 541/389-3111; toll-free 800/547-3928; fax 541/389-0870. www.riverhouse.com.* This resort is located on the Deschutes River and features such amenities as free movie channel, indoor/outdoor pool, and golfing and skiing packages. 220 rooms, 2 story. Pets accepted. Check-out noon. TV; cable (premium), VCR (movies). In-room modem link. Laundry services. Restaurant. Room service. Indoor, outdoor pool; poolside service. Golf, greens fee $28-$42. On the Deschutes River. **$**

★ ★ **SHILO INN.** *3105 NE O. B. Riley Rd (97701). Phone 541/389-9600; toll-free 800/222-2244; fax 541/382-4310. www.shiloinns.com.* 151 rooms, 2 story. Pets accepted, some restrictions; fee. Check-out noon. TV; cable (premium). Laundry services. Restaurant, bar. In-house fitness room; sauna. Indoor, outdoor pool; whirlpool. Downhill, cross-country ski 20 miles. Free airport transportation. On Deschutes River. **$**

D ➥ ⬧ ⚡ ⚲ ➤ 🅺 ⚓ ◹ **SC**

Biggs

Motel/Motor Lodge

★ **TRAVELODGE.** *91484 Biggs (97065). Phone 541/739-2501; toll-free 800/528-1234; fax 541/739-2091. www.travelodge.com.* 40 rooms, 1-2 story. Pets accepted; fee. Complimentary continental breakfast. Check-out noon. TV. Pool. **$**

➥ ⚲ ◹ **SC**

Burns

Motels/Motor Lodges

★ **DAYS INN.** *577 W Monroe St (97720). Phone 541/573-2047; fax 541/573-3828. www.daysinn.com.* 52 rooms, 2 story. Pets accepted; fee. Complimentary continental breakfast. Check-out 11 am. TV; cable (premium). Pool. **$**

D ➥ ⚲ ◹ **SC**

★ **SILVER SPUR MOTEL.** *789 N Broadway Ave (97720). Phone 541/573-2077; toll-free 800/400-2077; fax 541/573-3921.* 26 rooms, 2 story. Pets accepted; fee. Complimentary continental breakfast. Check-out 11:30 am. TV; cable (premium). Health club privileges. Free airport transportation. **$**

D ➥ 🅺 ✈

Cannon Beach

Motels/Motor Lodges

★ ★ **HALLMARK RESORT.** *1400 S Hemlock St (97110). Phone 503/436-1566; toll-free 800/345-5676; fax 503/436-0324. www.hallmarkinns.com.* Located in Cannon Beach, this property overlooks Haystack rock. 132 rooms, 5 cabins, 3 story. Pets accepted, some restrictions; fee. Check-out noon, check-in 4 pm. TV; cable (premium), VCR available (movies). Laundry services.

In-house fitness room. Health club privileges. Sauna. On beach. Indoor pool; children's pool; whirlpool. **$**

➥ ⚲ 🅺

★ ★ **SURFSAND RESORT.** *Oceanfront (97110). Phone 503/436-2274; toll-free 800/547-6100; fax 503/436-9116. www.surfsand.com.* 82 rooms, 2 story. No A/C. Pets accepted, some restrictions; fee. Check-out noon. TV; cable (premium), VCR (movies, fee). Fireplaces. Laundry services. Restaurant, bar. Health club privileges. On ocean, beach. Indoor pool; whirlpool. View of Haystack Rock. **$$**

D ➥ ⚲ ◹

★ ★ **TOLOVANA INN.** *3400 S Hemlock (97145). Phone 503/436-2211; toll-free 800/333-8890; fax 503/436-0134. www.tolovanainn.com.* 175 rooms, 3 story. No A/C. No elevator. Pets accepted, some restrictions; fee. Check-out noon. TV; VCR available (movies). Laundry services. Health club privileges. Game room. Indoor pool; whirlpool. Overlooks Haystack Rock. **$**

D ➥ ⬧ ⚲ 🅺 ◹

Coos Bay

Motel/Motor Lodge

★ ★ **RED LION.** *1313 N Bayshore Dr (97420). Phone 541/267-4141; fax 541/267-2884. www.redlion.com.* 143 rooms, 1-2 story. Pets accepted. Check-out noon. TV; cable (premium). In-room modem link. Laundry services. Restaurant, bar; entertainment. Room service. In-house fitness room. Pool. Free airport transportation. On Coos Bay. **$**

D ➥ ⬧ ⚲ 🅺 ✈ ◹ **SC**

Corvallis

Motels/Motor Lodges

★ **DAYS INN.** *1113 NW 9th St (97330). Phone 541/754-7474; toll-free 800/432-1233. www.daysinn.com.* 76 rooms, 3 story. Pets accepted, some restrictions; fee. Complimentary continental breakfast. Check-out noon. TV. Pool. **$**

D ➥ ⚲ ◹

★ **MOTEL ORLEANS.** *935 NW Garfield Ave (97330). Phone 541/758-9125; toll-free 800/626-1900; fax 541/758-0544.* 61 rooms, 3 story. No elevator. Pets accepted, some restrictions. Check-out 11 am. TV. Laundry services. Whirlpool. **$**

D ➥ ⬧ 🅺 ◹

Cottage Grove

Motel/Motor Lodge

★ ★ **VILLAGE GREEN RESORT.** *725 Row River Rd (97424). Phone 541/942-2491; toll-free 800/343-7666; fax 541/942-2386.* 96 rooms. Pets accepted. Check-out 11 am. TV; cable (premium). Laundry services. Restaurant, bar. Pool; whirlpool. Outdoor tennis. **$**

The Dalles

Motels/Motor Lodges

★ ★ **BEST WESTERN RIVER CITY INN.** *112 W 2nd St (97058). Phone 541/296-9107; toll-free 888/935-2378; fax 541/296-3002. www.bestwestern.com.* 65 rooms, 2-4 story. Pets accepted, some restrictions; fee. Check-out 11 am. TV; cable (premium). In-room modem link. Restaurant, bar. Room service. Health club privileges. Pool. **$**

★ **COMFORT INN.** *351 Lone Pine Dr (97058). Phone 541/298-2800; toll-free 800/955-9626; fax 541/298-8282. www.comfortinn.com.* 56 rooms, 2 story. Pets accepted, some restrictions; fee. Complimentary full breakfast. Check-out noon. TV; cable (premium). Laundry services. Bar. In-house fitness room. Indoor pool; whirlpool. Lawn games. Free airport transportation. **$**

★ **INN AT THE DALLES.** *3550 SE Frontage Rd (97058). Phone 541/296-1167; fax 541/296-3920.* 45 rooms. Pets accepted; fee. Check-out 11 am. TV. Indoor pool. Free airport transportation. View of the Columbia River, Mount Hood, and The Dalles Dam. **$**

★ ★ **QUALITY INN.** *2114 W 6th St (97058). Phone 541/298-5161; toll-free 800/848-9378; fax 541/298-6411. www.qualityinn-thedalles.com.* 85 rooms, 2 story. Pets accepted; fee. Check-out 11 am. TV. In-room modem link. Laundry services. Restaurant. Health club privileges. Pool; whirlpool. **$**

Eugene

Motels/Motor Lodges

★ **BEST WESTERN NEW OREGON MOTEL.** *1655 Franklin Blvd (97403). Phone 541/683-3669; toll-free 800/528-1234; fax 541/484-5556. www.bestwestern.com/neworegonmotel.* 129 rooms, 1-2 story. Pets accepted, some restrictions; fee. Check-out noon. TV; cable (premium). In-room modem link. Laundry services. In-house fitness room; sauna. Indoor pool; whirlpool. **$**

★ **DAYS INN.** *1859 Franklin Blvd (97403). Phone 541/342-6383; toll-free 800/444-6383. www.daysinn.com.* 60 rooms, 2-3 story. Pets accepted, some restrictions. Complimentary continental breakfast. Check-out 11 am. TV. Sauna. Whirlpool. **$**

★ **HOLIDAY INN EXPRESS.** *3480 Hutton St (97477). Phone 541/746-8471; toll-free 800/363-8471; fax 541/747-1541. www.hiexpress.com.* 58 rooms, 3 story. Pets accepted, some restrictions; fee. Complimentary continental breakfast. Check-out noon. TV; VCR available. In-room modem link. Laundry services. In-house fitness room. Indoor pool; whirlpool. **$**

★ ★ **RED LION.** *205 Coburg Rd (97401). Phone 541/342-5201; toll-free 800/733-5466; fax 541/485-2314. www.redlion.com.* 137 rooms, 2 story. Pets accepted. Check-out noon. TV; VCR available. In-room modem link. Restaurant, bar. Room service. In-house fitness room. Pool; whirlpool. Free airport, train station, bus depot transportation. **$**

★ ★ **SHILO INN.** *3350 Gateway St (97477). Phone 541/747-0332; toll-free 800/222-2244; fax 541/726-0587. www.shiloinn.com.* 143 rooms, 2 story. Pets accepted; fee. Complimentary continental breakfast. Check-out noon. TV; cable (premium), VCR available (movies). Laundry services. Restaurant, bar. Room service. Pool. Free airport transportation. **$**

★ ★ ★ **VALLEY RIVER INN.** *1000 Valley River Way (97401). Phone 541/687-0123; toll-free 800/543-8266; fax 541/683-5121. www.valleyriverinn.com.* This hotel is conveniently located in downtown and minutes from the airport, shopping, the University of Oregon, and the convention center. 257 rooms, 2-3 story. Pets accepted, some restrictions. Check-out 11 am. TV; cable (premium), VCR available. In-room modem link. Restaurant, bar; entertainment. Room service. In-house fitness room. Health club privileges. Sauna. Pool; children's pool; whirlpool; poolside service. Free airport, train station, bus depot transportation. Concierge. Logging memorabilia. Some rooms have views of Willamette River. **$$**

⧉ 🐾 ≋ 🏋 🛉 ✕ ⊠

Hotel

★★★ **HILTON EUGENE AND CONFERENCE CENTER.** *66 E 6th Ave (97401). Phone 541/342-2000; fax 541/342-6661. www.eugene.hilton.com.* Located in the heart of downtown, area attractions are just minutes away. 272 rooms, 12 story. Pets accepted; fee. Check-out noon. TV; cable (premium). Restaurant, bar; entertainment. Room service. In-house fitness room. Health club privileges. Indoor pool; whirlpool. Free airport, train station, bus depot transportation. Business center. Concierge. Luxury level. **$$**

⧉ 🐾 ≋ 🛉 🏋 ⊠ ✕

Florence

Motel/Motor Lodge

★ **MONEY SAVER MOTEL.** *170 Hwy 101 (97439). Phone 541/997-7131; toll-free 877/997-7131; fax 541/902-2303. www.moneysavermotel.com.* 40 rooms, 2 story. Pets accepted, some restrictions; fee. Check-out 11 am. TV. Old Town location. **$**

⧉ 🐾 ✕ ⊠ SC

Grants Pass

Motels/Motor Lodges

★★ **BEST WESTERN GRANTS PASS INN.** *111 NE Agness Ave (97526). Phone 541/476-1117; toll-free 800/553-7666; fax 541/479-4315. www.bestwestern.com.* 84 rooms, 2 story. Pets accepted, some restrictions; fee. Check-out 11 am. TV; cable (premium), VCR available. In-room modem link. Laundry services. Restaurant, bar. Health club privileges. Pool; whirlpool. Rogue River 1 mile. **$**

⧉ 🐾 ≋ ⊠

★ **BEST WESTERN INN AT THE ROGUE.** *8959 Rogue River Hwy (97527). Phone 541/582-2200; toll-free 800/238-0700; fax 541/582-1415. www.bestwestern.com.* 54 rooms, 2 story. Pets accepted,

some restrictions; fee. Complimentary continental breakfast. Check-out 11 am. TV; cable (premium), VCR available. Laundry services. Bar. Pool; whirlpool. **$**

⧉ 🐾 🏃 ≋ 🛉 ⊠ SC

★ **HOLIDAY INN EXPRESS.** *105 NE Agness Ave (97526). Phone 541/471-6144; toll-free 800/838-7666; fax 541/471-9248. www.rogueweb.com/holiday.* 80 rooms, 4 story. Pets accepted, some restrictions; fee. Complimentary continental breakfast. Check-out 11 am. TV; cable (premium). In-room modem link. Laundry services. Pool; whirlpool. Business center. **$**

⧉ 🐾 ≋ ⊠ 🏃

★ **REDWOOD MOTEL.** *815 NE 6th St (97526). Phone 541/476-0878; toll-free 888/535-8824; fax 541/476-1032. www.redwoodmotel.com.* 26 rooms. Pets accepted; fee. Complimentary continental breakfast. Check-out 11 am. TV; cable (premium). Laundry services. Pool; whirlpool. **$**

⧉ 🐾 ≋ ⊠ SC

★★★ **RIVERSIDE INN.** *971 SE 6th St (97526). Phone 541/476-6873; toll-free 800/334-4567; fax 541/474-9848. www.riverside-inn.com.* The largest hotel on the Rogue River, guests can enjoy river rafting, hiking, boating, and much more. 174 rooms, 3 story. Pets accepted, some restrictions; fee. Check-out 11 am. TV; VCR available (movies). Restaurant, bar. Health club privileges. Pool. Jet boat trips May-Sept. **$**

⧉ 🐾 🕊 ≋ 🏋 ⊠

★ **ROYAL VIEW MOTOR HOTEL.** *110 NE Morgan Ln (97526). Phone 541/479-5381; toll-free 800/547-7555. www.royalview.com.* 58 rooms, 2 story. Pets accepted, some restrictions. Check-out noon. TV; cable (premium), VCR available. Laundry services. Restaurant, bar; entertainment. Room service. Sauna; steam room. Pool; whirlpool; poolside service. **$**

🐾 ≋ ⊠ SC

★ **SHILO INN.** *1880 NW 6th St (97526). Phone 541/479-8391; fax 541/474-7344. www.shiloinn.com.* 70 rooms, 2 story. Pets accepted; fee. Check-out noon. TV; cable (premium). Sauna; steam room. Pool. **$**

⧉ 🐾 ≋ ⊠

Hermiston

Motel/Motor Lodge

★ **ECONOMY INN.** *835 N 1st St (97838). Phone 541/567-5516; toll-free 888/567-9521.* 39 rooms, 1-2 story. Pets accepted; fee. Check-out 11 am. TV; cable (premium). Pool. **$**

🐾 ≋ ⊠

Hood River

Motels/Motor Lodges

★ ★ **BEST WESTERN HOOD RIVER INN.** *1108 E Marina Way (97031). Phone 541/386-2200; toll-free 800/ 828-7873; fax 541/386-8905. www.hoodriverinn.com.* 149 rooms, 2-3 story. Pets accepted, some restrictions; fee. Check-out noon. TV; cable (premium). In-room modem link. Laundry services. Restaurant, bar; entertainment. Room service. Pool. Beach access; windsurfing. In Columbia River Gorge. **$**

[icons]

★ **VAGABOND LODGE HOOD RIVER.** *4070 Westcliff Dr (97031). Phone 541/386-2992; toll-free 877/ 386-2992; fax 541/386-3317. www.vagabondlodge.com.* 42 rooms. Pets accepted; fee. Check-out 11 am. TV. On 5 wooded acres; overlooks Columbia River Gorge. **$**

[icons]

Hotel

★ ★ ★ **COLUMBIA GORGE HOTEL.** *4000 Westcliff Dr (97031). Phone 541/386-5566; toll-free 800/345-1921; fax 541/387-5414. www.columbiagorgehotel.com.* Nestled in the Columbia Gorge National Scenic Area, trees and mountain peaks will adorn your scenery from this hotel. Featuring a waterfall and beautiful gardens guests can spend the day enjoying the beauty of the land. 40 rooms, 3 story. Pets accepted, some restrictions; fee. Complimentary full breakfast. Check-out noon. TV; VCR available. Dining room, bar. Health club privileges. Restored building (1920s) with formal gardens. Jazz Age atmosphere. **$$**

[icons]

B&B/Small Inn

★ ★ **INN OF THE WHITE SALMON.** *172 W Jewett Blvd (98672). Phone 509/493-2335; toll-free 800/972-5226. www.innofthewhitesalmon.com.* 16 rooms, 2 story. Pets accepted, some restrictions; fee. Complimentary full breakfast. Check-out noon, check-in 3 pm. TV. European-style inn built in 1937; antique décor, original art. **$**

[icons]

Jacksonville

B&B/Small Inn

★ **STAGE LODGE.** *830 N 5th St (97530). Phone 541/899-3953; toll-free 800/253-8254; fax 541/899-7556.* *www.stagelodge.com.* 27 rooms, 2 story. Pets accepted, some restrictions; fee. Complimentary continental breakfast. Check-out 11 am, check-in 2 pm. TV. **$**

[icons]

John Day

Motels/Motor Lodges

★ **DREAMERS LODGE MOTEL.** *144 N Canyon Blvd (97845). Phone 541/575-0526; toll-free 800/654-2849; fax 541/575-2733.* 25 rooms, 2 story. Pets accepted, some restrictions; fee. Check-out 11 am. TV; cable (premium). Cross-country ski 20 miles. Free airport transportation. **$**

[icons]

★ **JOHN DAY SUNSET INN.** *390 W Main St (97845). Phone 541/575-1462; toll-free 800/452-4899; fax 541/575-1471.* 43 rooms, 2 story. Pets accepted, some restrictions; fee. Check-out 11 am. TV; cable (premium). Restaurant, bar. Indoor pool; whirlpool. Free airport transportation. **$**

[icons]

Joseph

Motel/Motor Lodge

★ **INDIAN LODGE MOTEL.** *201 S Main (97846). Phone 541/432-2651; toll-free 888/286-5484; fax 541/432-4949.* 16 rooms. Pets accepted, some restrictions; fee. Check-out 11 am. TV; cable (premium). **$**

[icons]

Klamath Falls

Motels/Motor Lodges

★ **BEST WESTERN KLAMATH INN.** *4061 S 6th St (97603). Phone 541/882-1200; toll-free 877/ 882-1200; fax 541/882-2729. www.bestwestern.com/ klamathinn.* 52 rooms, 2 story. Pets accepted, some restrictions; fee. Complimentary continental breakfast. Check-out noon. TV; cable (premium), VCR available. Indoor pool. **$**

[icons]

★ **CIMARRON MOTOR INN–KLAMATH FALLS.** *3060 S 6th St (97603). Phone 541/882-4601; toll-free 800/742-2648; fax 541/882-6690.* 163 rooms, 2 story. Pets accepted; fee. Check-out noon. TV; cable (premium). Pool. **$**

[icons]

★ ★ **QUALITY INN.** *100 Main St (97601). Phone 541/882-4666; toll-free 800/732-2025; fax 541/883-8795. www.qualityinn.com.* 80 rooms, 2 story. Pets accepted. Complimentary continental breakfast. Check-out noon. TV; cable (premium). In-room modem link. Laundry services. Pool. **$**

D ⬛ ⬛ ⬛ SC

★ ★ **SHILO INN.** *2500 Almond St (97601). Phone 541/885-7980; toll-free 800/222-2244; fax 541/885-7959. www.shiloinn.com.* 4 story. Pets accepted, some restrictions; fee. Complimentary continental breakfast. Check-out noon. TV; cable (premium), VCR (movies). In-room modem link. Laundry services. Restaurant, bar. Room service. In-house fitness room; sauna. Health club privileges. Indoor pool; whirlpool. Free airport, train station transportation. Business center. **$**

D ⬛ ⬛ ⬛ ⬛ ⬛ SC ⬛

★ **SUPER 8.** *3805 Hwy 97 (97601). Phone 541/884-8880; fax 541/884-0235. www.super8.com.* 61 rooms, 3 story. No elevator. Pets accepted; fee. Check-out noon. TV. Laundry services. Whirlpool. **$**

D ⬛ ⬛ ⬛

La Grande

Motel/Motor Lodge

★ **HOWARD JOHNSON.** *2612 Island Ave (97850). Phone 541/963-7195; fax 541/963-4498. www.hojo.com.* 146 rooms, 2 story. Pets accepted; fee. Complimentary continental breakfast. Check-out noon. TV; cable (premium). Laundry services. Sauna. Pool; whirlpool. **$**

D ⬛ ⬛ ⬛ ⬛

Lakeview

Motels/Motor Lodges

★ **BEST WESTERN SKYLINE MOTOR LODGE.** *414 N G St (97630). Phone 541/947-2194; fax 541/947-3100. www.bestwestern.com.* 38 rooms, 2 story. Pets accepted, some restrictions; fee. Complimentary continental breakfast. Check-out 11 am. TV; cable (premium). In-room modem link. Laundry services. Indoor pool; whirlpool. Downhill, cross-country ski 10 miles. **$**

⬛ ⬛ ⬛ ⬛ ⬛

★ **LAKEVIEW LODGE MOTEL.** *301 N G St (97630). Phone 541/947-2181; fax 541/947-2572.* 40 rooms. Pets accepted, some restrictions. Check-out 11 am. TV; cable

(premium). In-house fitness room; sauna. Whirlpool. Downhill, cross-country ski 8 miles. **$**

D ⬛ ⬛ ⬛ ⬛ ⬛ SC

Lincoln City

Motels/Motor Lodges

★ **COHO INN.** *1635 NW Harbor Ave (97367). Phone 541/994-3684; toll-free 800/848-7006; fax 541/994-6244. www.thecohoinn.com.* 50 rooms, 3 story. No A/C. No elevator. Pets accepted, some restrictions; fee. Check-out 11 am. TV; cable (premium). Sauna. Whirlpool. **$**

⬛ ⬛

★ ★ **SHILO INN.** *1501 NW 40th Pl (97367). Phone 541/994-3655; fax 541/994-2199. www.shiloinn.com.* 247 rooms, 3-4 story. Pets accepted, some restrictions; fee. Check-out noon. TV; cable (premium), VCR available. Laundry services. Bar. Room service. In-house fitness room; sauna. Health club privileges. Indoor pool; whirlpool. Free airport, bus depot transportation. Business center. **$**

D ⬛ ⬛ ⬛ ⬛ ⬛ SC ⬛

Resort

★ ★ ★ **THE WESTIN SALISHAN LODGE AND GOLF RESORT.** *7760 Hwy 101 N (97388). Phone 541/764-2371; toll-free 800/452-2300; fax 541/764-3663. www.salishan.com.* 205 rooms, 2-3 story. Pets accepted; fee. Check-out noon. TV; cable (premium), VCR available. Dining room, bar; entertainment. Room service. In-house fitness room; massage; sauna. Game room. Indoor pool; whirlpool. Golf; greens fee $35-$50. Outdoor, indoor tennis, lighted courts. Self-guided nature trail. Art gallery. **$**

D ⬛ ⬛ ⬛ ⬛ ⬛ ⬛ ⬛ ⬛

Madras

Motel/Motor Lodge

★ ★ **SONNY'S MOTEL.** *1539 SW Hwy 97 (97741). Phone 541/475-7217; fax 541/475-6547. www.sonnysmotel.com.* 44 rooms, 2 story. Pets accepted; fee. Complimentary continental breakfast. Check-out 11 am. TV; cable (premium). Laundry services. Restaurant, bar. Pool; whirlpool. Lawn games. **$**

D ⬛ ⬛

Resort

★ ★ ★ **KAH-NEE-TA LODGE.** *100 Main St (97761). Phone 541/553-1112; toll-free 800/554-4786; fax 541/553-1071. www.kah-nee-taresort.com.* Overlooking the Warm Springs River, this resort gives guests a view of the sunrise from each room. For guests who enjoy testing their luck, this resort features a casino on-site. 139 rooms, 3-4 story. Pets accepted, some restrictions. Check-out 11:30 am, check-in 4:30 pm. TV; cable (premium). Dining room, bar; entertainment. In-house fitness room; massage; sauna. Game room. Pool; poolside service. Golf; greens fee $32. Outdoor tennis. Bicycles. Casino. Kayak float trips. Trails. Authentic Native American dances, Sun (May-Sept). RV and trailer spaces available. **$**

McMinnville

Guest Ranch

★ ★ **FLYING M RANCH.** *23029 NW Flying M Rd (97148). Phone 503/662-3222; fax 503/662-3202. www.flying-m-ranch.com.* 24 rooms, 7 cabins. Pets accepted. Check-out 11 am, check-in 4 pm. TV in lounge, some cabins. Dining room, bar; entertainment. Lawn games. Fishing. Hiking. Swimming pond. Overnight trail rides. **$**

Medford

Motels/Motor Lodges

★ **BEST INN.** *1015 S Riverside Ave (97501). Phone 541/773-8266; toll-free 800/237-8466; fax 541/734-5447. www.bestinn.com.* 112 rooms, 2 story. Pets accepted, some restrictions; fee. Complimentary continental breakfast. Check-out 11 am. TV; cable (premium). Bar. Pool. Downhill, cross-country ski 20 miles. **$**

★ ★ **BEST WESTERN HORIZON INN.** *1154 E Barnett Rd (97504). Phone 541/779-5085; toll-free 800/452-2255; fax 541/772-6878. www.bestwestern.com.* 123 rooms, 2 story. Pets accepted; fee. Check-out 11 am. TV; cable (premium), VCR available (movies). In-room modem link. Restaurant, bar. In-house fitness room; sauna. Pool; whirlpool. Downhill, cross-country ski 20 miles. Airport transportation. Business center. **$**

★ **BEST WESTERN PONY SOLDIER INN.** *2340 Crater Lake Hwy (94504). Phone 541/779-2011; toll-free 800/634-7669; fax 541/779-7304. www.bestwestern.com.* 74 rooms, 2 story. Pets accepted, some restrictions; fee. Complimentary continental breakfast. Check-out noon. TV; cable (premium), VCR available (movies). In-room modem link. Laundry services. Bar. Health club privileges. Pool; whirlpool. Downhill, cross-country ski 20 miles. **$**

★ **CEDAR LODGE MOTOR INN.** *518 N Riverside (97501). Phone 541/773-7361; toll-free 800/282-3419; fax 541/776-1033.* 79 rooms, 1-2 story. Pets accepted, some restrictions; fee. Complimentary continental breakfast. Check-out 11 am. TV. Pool. Downhill, cross-country ski 20 miles. **$**

★ **KNIGHTS INN.** *500 N Riverside Ave (97501). Phone 541/773-3676; toll-free 800/531-2655; fax 541/857-0493.* 83 rooms, 2 story. Pets accepted, some restrictions; fee. Check-out 11 am. TV. Pool. Downhill, cross-country ski 20 miles. **$**

★ ★ **RED LION.** *200 N Riverside Ave (97501). Phone 541/779-5811; fax 541/779-7961. www.redlionmedford.com.* 185 rooms, 2 story. Pets accepted; fee. Check-out noon. TV; cable (premium). In-room modem link. Laundry services. Restaurant, dining room, bar; entertainment. Room service. Health club privileges. Two pools. Downhill, cross-country ski 20 miles. Free airport transportation. **$**

★ ★ **RESTON HOTEL AND CONVENTION CENTER.** *2300 Crater Lake Hwy (97504). Phone 541/779-3141; toll-free 800/779-7829; fax 541/779-2623. www.restonhotel.com.* 164 rooms, 2 story. Pets accepted, some restrictions; fee. Complimentary continental breakfast. Check-out noon. TV. Restaurant, bar. Room service. Health club privileges. Indoor pool. Free airport transportation. **$**

★ **WINDMILL INN OF MEDFORD.** *1950 Biddle Rd (97504). Phone 541/779-0050; toll-free 800/547-4747. www.windmillinns.com.* 123 rooms, 2 story. Pets accepted. Complimentary continental breakfast. Check-out 11 am. TV; cable (premium). In-room modem link. Laundry services. In-house fitness room; sauna. Health club privileges. Pool; whirlpool. Bicycles. Free airport transportation. **$**

Mount Hood National Forest

Motel/Motor Lodge

★ **MOUNT HOOD INN.** *87450 E Government Camp Loop (97028). Phone 503/272-3205; toll-free 800/443-7777; fax 503/272-3307. www.mounthoodinn.com.* 56 rooms, 2 story. No A/C. Pets accepted, some restrictions; fee. Complimentary continental breakfast. Check-out noon. TV; cable (premium), VCR available. Laundry services. Whirlpool. Downhill ski 1/4 mile, cross-country ski adjacent. **$**

Newberg

Motel/Motor Lodge

★ **SHILO INN.** *501 Sitka Ave (97132). Phone 503/537-0303; toll-free 800/222-2244; fax 503/537-0442. www.shiloinns.com.* 60 rooms, 3 story. Pets accepted, some restrictions; fee. Complimentary continental breakfast. Check-out noon. TV; cable (premium), VCR available. Laundry services. In-house fitness room; sauna. Pool; whirlpool. **$**

Newport

Motel/Motor Lodge

★ ★ **SHILO INN.** *536 SW Elizabeth St (97365). Phone 541/265-7701; toll-free 800/222-2244; fax 541/265-5687. www.shiloinns.com.* 179 rooms, 4 story. Pets accepted, some restrictions; fee. Check-out noon. TV; cable (premium), VCR available. Laundry services. Restaurant, bar; entertainment. Room service. Indoor pool. **$**

North Bend

Motel/Motor Lodge

★ **BAY BRIDGE MOTEL.** *33 Coast Hwy (97459). Phone 541/756-3151; toll-free 800/557-3156; fax 541/756-0749.* 16 rooms. Pets accepted, some restrictions. Check-out 11 am. TV. On Pacific Bay. **$**

Ontario

Motels/Motor Lodges

★ **BEST WESTERN INN & SUITES.** *251 Goodfellow St (97914). Phone 541/889-2600; fax 541/889-2259. www.bestwestern.com.* 61 rooms, 2 story. Pets accepted, some restrictions; fee. Complimentary continental breakfast. Check-out 11 am. TV; cable (premium). Laundry services. In-house fitness room. Indoor pool; whirlpool. **$**

★ ★ **HOLIDAY INN.** *1249 Tapadera Ave (97914). Phone 541/889-8621; toll-free 800/525-5333; fax 541/889-8023. www.holiday-inn.com.* 98 rooms, 2 story. Pets accepted, some restrictions; fee. Check-out noon. TV. In-room modem link. Laundry services. Restaurant, bar. Room service. In-house fitness room. Health club privileges. Pool; whirlpool. Local airport, train station, bus depot transportation. **$**

★ **HOLIDAY MOTOR INN.** *615 E Idaho Ave (97914). Phone 541/889-9188; fax 541/889-4303.* 72 rooms, 2 story. Pets accepted. Check-out 11 am. TV; cable (premium). Restaurant. Pool. **$**

★ **MOTEL 6.** *275 NE 12th St (97914). Phone 541/889-6617; fax 541/889-8232. www.motel6.com.* 126 rooms, 2 story. Shower only. Pets accepted. Check-out noon. TV; cable (premium). In-room modem link. Laundry services. Pool. **$**

★ **YE OLDE COLONIAL MOTOR INN.** *1395 Tapadera Ave (97914). Phone 541/889-9615; toll-free 800/727-5014.* 84 rooms, 2 story. Pets accepted, some restrictions; fee. Check-out 11 am. TV. In-room modem link. Indoor pool; whirlpool. **$**

Oregon City

Motel/Motor Lodge

★ **RIVERSHORE HOTEL.** *1900 Clackamette Dr (97045). Phone 503/655-7141; toll-free 800/443-7777; fax 503/655-1927. www.rivershore.com.* 120 rooms, 4 story. Pets accepted, some restrictions; fee. Check-out noon. TV; cable (premium). Restaurant, bar. Room service. Pool; whirlpool. **$**

Pendleton

Motels/Motor Lodges

★ **ECONO LODGE.** *620 SW Tutilla Rd (97801). Phone 541/276-8654; fax 541/276-5808. www.econolodge.com.* 51 rooms, 1-3 story. Pets accepted, some restrictions; fee. Complimentary continental breakfast. Check-out 11 am. TV; cable (premium). Health club privileges. **$**

D 🐾 🏊 SC

★ **ECONOMY INN.** *201 SW Court Ave (97801). Phone 541/276-5252; fax 541/278-1213.* 51 rooms, 2 story. Closed during Pendleton Roundup. Pets accepted; fee. Complimentary continental breakfast. Check-out noon. TV; VCR available. Pool. **$**

🐾 🏊 🏊

★★ **RED LION.** *304 SE Nye Ave (97801). Phone 541/276-6111; fax 541/278-2413. www.redlion.com.* 168 rooms, 3 story. Pets accepted, some restrictions; fee. Check-out noon. TV. Restaurant, bar; entertainment. Room service. Health club privileges. Pool. Free airport transportation. **$**

D 🐾 🏊 🏊 SC

★ **TAPADERA MOTEL.** *105 SE Court Ave (97128). Phone 541/276-3231; toll-free 800/722-8277; fax 541/276-0754.* 47 rooms, 2 story. Pets accepted, some restrictions; fee. Check-out noon. TV; cable (premium). Restaurant, bar. Room service. Health club privileges. **$**

🐾 🕎 🏊 🏊

Portland

Motels/Motor Lodges

★ **DAYS INN.** *9930 N Whitaker Rd (97217). Phone 503/289-1800; toll-free 800/329-7466; fax 503/289-3778. www.daysinn.com.* 214 rooms, 4 story. Pets accepted; fee. Complimentary continental breakfast. Check-out noon. TV; cable (premium). In-room modem link. Laundry services. Free airport, train station, bus depot transportation. Park adjacent. **$**

D 🐾 🏊

★ **HAWTHORN SUITES.** *2323 NE 181st Ave (97230). Phone 503/492-4000; fax 503/492-3271. www.hawthorn.com.* 71 rooms, 3 story. Pets accepted, some restrictions; fee. Complimentary breakfast buffet. Check-out 1 pm. TV; cable (premium), VCR available (movies). In-room modem link. Laundry services. In-house fitness room; sauna. Indoor pool; whirlpool. **$**

D 🐾 🏊 🕎 🏊 SC

★★ **IMPERIAL HOTEL.** *400 SW Broadway at Stark (97205). Phone 503/228-7221; toll-free 800/452-2323; fax 503/223-4551. www.hotel-imperial.com.* 128 rooms, 9 story. Pets accepted. Check-out 2 pm. TV; cable (premium). In-room modem link. Restaurant, bar. Valet parking. **$**

D 🐾 🏊

★ **PHOENIX INN SUITES TROUTDALE.** *477 NW Phoenix Dr (97060). Phone 503/669-6500; toll-free 800/824-6824; fax 503/669-3500. www.phoenixinn.com.* 73 rooms, 3 story. Pets accepted; fee. Complimentary breakfast buffet. Check-out noon. TV; cable (premium). In-room modem link. Laundry services. Bar. In-house fitness room. Health club privileges. Indoor pool; whirlpool. Free airport transportation. **$**

D 🐾 🏊 🕎 🛫 🏊 SC

★ **SHILO INN.** *10830 SW Greenburg Rd (97223). Phone 503/620-4320; fax 503/620-8277. www.shiloinns.com.* 77 rooms, 4 story. Pets accepted; fee. Complimentary continental breakfast. Check-out noon. TV; cable (premium), VCR available (movies). Laundry services. In-house fitness room; sauna, steam room. Free airport transportation. **$**

D 🐾 🕎 🏊

★★ **SHILO INN.** *9900 SW Canyon Rd (97225). Phone 503/297-2551; toll-free 800/222-2244; fax 503/297-7708. www.shiloinns.com.* 142 rooms, 2-3 story. Pets accepted, some restrictions; fee. Complimentary breakfast buffet. Check-out noon. TV; cable (premium), VCR available. Restaurant, bar; entertainment. Room service. In-house fitness room. Pool; whirlpool. Free airport transportation. **$**

D 🐾 🏊 🕎 🏊 SC

★ **SUPER 8.** *25438 SW Parkway Ave (97070). Phone 503/682-2088; fax 503/682-0453. www.super8.com.* 72 rooms, 4 story. Pets accepted. Check-out noon. TV; cable (premium). Laundry services. **$**

D 🐾

★★ **SWEET BRIER INN & SUITES.** *7125 SW Nyberg Rd (97062). Phone 503/692-5800; toll-free 800/551-9167; fax 503/691-2894. www.sweetbrier.com.* 131 rooms. Pets accepted; fee. Complimentary continental breakfast. Check-out noon. TV; cable (premium). In-room modem link. Restaurant, bar; entertainment. Room service. In-house fitness room. Health club privileges. Pool. **$**

D 🐾 🏊 🕎 🏊

Hotels

★★★ **5TH AVENUE SUITES HOTEL.** *506 SW Washington St (97204). Phone 503/222-0001; toll-free 888/207-2201; fax 503/222-0004. www.5thavenuesuites.com.*

This historic hotel, built in 1912, was once the Lipman, Wolf & Co. department store. It has been renovated, and its guest rooms feature upholstered headboards, fluffy bedspreads, and Egyptian cotton robes to snuggle up in. The accommodations are decorated in soft colors, with subtle lighting and comfortable furniture adding to the cozy feel. The elegant lobby features soaring ceilings of molded plaster and wood, floor-to-ceiling windows, and a large corner fireplace surrounded by marble and topped with an antique mirror. Dine on Pacific Northwest cuisine at the Red Star Tavern & Roast House. 221 rooms, 10 story. Pets accepted, some restrictions. Check-out noon, check-in 2 pm. TV; cable (premium), VCR available. In-room modem link. Room service 24 hours. Restaurant, bar. Babysitting services available. In-house fitness room; spa. Health club privileges. Valet parking. Business center. Concierge. **$$**

★ ★ ★ **CROWNE PLAZA.** *14811 Kruse Oaks Blvd (97035). Phone 503/624-8400; toll-free 800/465-4329; fax 503/684-8324. www.crowneplaza.com.* 161 rooms, 6 story. Pets accepted; fee. Check-out noon. TV; cable (premium). In-room modem link. Laundry services. Restaurant, bar. Room service. In-house fitness room; sauna. Health club privileges. Indoor, outdoor pool; whirlpool. Valet parking, fee. Business center. Concierge. Luxury level. **$**

★ ★ **DOUBLETREE HOTEL.** *1401 N Hayden Island Dr (97217). Phone 503/283-2111; toll-free 800/222-8733; fax 503/283-4718. www.doubletree.com.* This hotel is located on the banks of the Columbia River, and just 15 minutes from the Portland International Airport. 352 rooms, 3 story. Pets accepted; fee. Check-out noon, check-in 3 pm. TV; cable (premium). In-room modem link. Laundry services. Restaurant, bar. Room service. In-house fitness room; spa. Golf on premise. Business center. On Columbia River. Free transportation. **$$**

★ ★ **DOUBLETREE HOTEL.** *909 N Hayden Island Dr (97217). Phone 503/283-4466; fax 503/283-4743. www.doubletree.com.* 320 rooms, 4 story. Pets accepted; fee. Check-out noon, check-in 3 pm. TV; cable (premium), VCR available. Laundry services. Restaurant, bar; entertainment. Room service. In-house fitness room. Outdoor pool; whirlpool. Outdoor tennis. Boats. Business center. Concierge. Free airport transportation. **$$**

★ ★ **FOUR POINTS BY SHERATON.** *50 SW Morrison; Front Ave (97204). Phone 503/221-0711; toll-free 888/627-8263; fax 503/484-1414. www.fourpointsportland .com.* 140 rooms, 5 story. Pets accepted, some restrictions. Complimentary continental breakfast. Check-out noon,

check-in 3 pm. TV; cable (premium). Restaurant, bar. Room service. Health club privileges. **$**

★ ★ ★ **THE HEATHMAN HOTEL.** *1001 SW Broadway (97205). Phone 503/241-4100; toll-free 800/551-0011; fax 503/790-7110. www.heathmanhotel.com.* Built in 1927, this grand "Arts Hotel of Portland" features a mix of artwork, from Art Deco mirrors in the Marble Bar to 18th-century French canvases in the historic Tea Court to silkscreens by Andy Warhol in the Heathman Restaurant. It's worth a tour for art lovers of any style and period. 150 rooms, 10 story. Pets accepted; fee. Check-out noon, check-in 3:30 pm. TV; cable (premium), VCR available. In-room modem link. Room service 24 hours. Restaurant, bar; entertainment. Babysitting services available. In-house fitness room. Health club privileges. Valet parking. Concierge. **$$**

★ ★ ★ **HOTEL VINTAGE PLAZA.** *422 SW Broadway (97205). Phone 503/228-1212; toll-free 800/263-2305; fax 503/228-3598. www.vintageplaza.com.* What started out as the Imperial Hotel in 1894 is now the elegant Hotel Vintage Plaza, listed on the National Register of Historic Places. The hotel celebrates local winemaking by offering tastings of Oregon vintages in the evenings in the warm and inviting lobby. Guest accommodations feature Tuscan wine country décor with Italian tapestries, ornately carved wooden mirrors, and bright colors and textures. Special rooms include the Garden Spa rooms, with their own outdoor patios and private spa tubs; and Starlight rooms, with slanted skylights and power shades. Pazzo Ristorante offers fine Italian cuisine and wines. 107 rooms, 10 story. Pets accepted. Check-out noon, check-in 3 pm. TV; cable (premium), VCR available. In-room modem link. Room service 24 hours. Restaurant. Babysitting services available. In-house fitness room. Valet parking. Business center. Concierge. **$**

★ **MALLORY HOTEL.** *729 SW 15th Ave (97205). Phone 503/223-6311; toll-free 800/228-8657; fax 503/223-0522. www.malloryhotel.com.* 136 rooms, 8 story. Pets accepted; fee. Check-out 1 pm. TV; cable (premium). In-room modem link. Restaurant, bar. **$**

★ **MARK SPENCER HOTEL.** *409 SW 11th Ave (97205). Phone 503/224-3293; toll-free 800/548-3934; fax 503/223-7848. www.markspencer.com.* 101 rooms, 6 story. Pets accepted; fee. Complimentary continental breakfast. Check-out noon. TV; VCR available (free movies). Laundry services. Health club privileges. **$**

★ ★ **MARRIOTT PORTLAND CITY CENTER.** *520 SW Broadway (97205). Phone 503/226-6300; fax 503/*

227-7515. *www.marriott.com.* 249 rooms, 20 story. Pets accepted; fee. Check-out noon, check-in 4 pm. TV; cable (premium), VCR available. Laundry services. Restaurant, bar. Room service. Babysitting services available. In-house fitness room. Whirlpool. Business center. Luxury level. **$**

[D] [icons]

★ ★ ★ **RIVER PLACE HOTEL.** *1510 SW Harbor Way (97201). Phone 503/228-3233; toll-free 800/227-1333; fax 503/295-6190. www.riverplacehotel.com.* Offering a full service restaurant and bar, valet parking, and room service, this hotel is located in a quiet neighborhood next to a park and near downtown and its attractions. 84 rooms, 4 story. Pets accepted; fee. Complimentary continental breakfast. Check-out 1 pm. TV; cable (premium), VCR available. In-room modem link. Room service 24 hours. Restaurant, bar; entertainment. Health club privileges. Spa; sauna. Whirlpool. Skyline, marina views. Valet parking, fee. Concierge. On river. **$$**

[D] [icons]

★ ★ ★ **SHERATON PORTLAND AIRPORT HOTEL.** *8235 NE Airport Way (97220). Phone 503/281-2500; fax 503/249-7602. www.sheratonpdx.com.* 218 rooms, 5 story. Pets accepted, some restrictions; fee. Check-out noon, check-in 3 pm. TV; cable (premium). Restaurant, bar. Room service. In-house fitness room; sauna. Indoor pool; whirlpool. Business center. Concierge. Free airport transportation. **$**

[D] [icons]

★ ★ ★ **THE BENSON.** *309 SW Broadway (97205). Phone 503/228-2000; fax 503/471-3924. www. bensonhotel.com.* Presidents and celebrities alike have stayed in this landmark downtown hotel, whose owners have spared no expense since it was built in 1912. Feast your eyes on the lobby's paneling and Russian pillars, Austrian crystal chandeliers, and Italian marble staircase. The guest rooms are equally elegant, offering pleasantries like complimentary coffee, tea, and apples. With the hotel's one-to-one ratio of employees to guests, expect top service from wine tastings to afternoon tea to the hotel's jazz club (the first ever to open in Portland). Don't miss the popular London Grill restaurant, which offers an extensive wine collection and live jazz. 287 suites, 14 story. Pets accepted; fee. Check-out 1 pm, check-in 3 pm. TV; VCR available, CD available. In-room modem link. Fireplaces. Restaurant, bar; entertainment. Room service 24 hours. In-house fitness room. Airport transportation. Business center. Concierge. **$$$**

[D] [icons]

★ ★ ★ **THE WESTIN PORTLAND.** *750 SW Alder St (97205). Phone 503/294-9000; fax 503/241-9565. www.westin.com.* Located in the center of downtown Portland, this hotel is within walking distance to such area attractions as the Portland Convention Center. This facility offers guests Internet access, coffee makers, in-room safes, and dual-line direct-dial telephones with fax and data ports. 205 rooms, 18 story. Pets accepted; fee. Check-out noon, check-in 3 pm. TV; cable (premium). Fireplaces. Room service 24-hours. Restaurant, bar. Babysitting services available. In-house fitness room. Downhill skiing. Valet parking. Business center. Concierge. **$$**

[D] [icons]

Extended Stays

★ ★ **RESIDENCE INN BY MARRIOTT.** *1710 NE Multnomah St (97232). Phone 503/288-1400; fax 503/288-0241. www.residenceinn.com.* 168 rooms, 3 story. Pets accepted; fee. Complimentary continental breakfast. Check-out noon. TV; cable (premium). In-room modem link. Laundry services. Pool; whirlpool. Outdoor tennis, lighted courts. Free airport, train station transportation. **$**

[D] [icons]

★ ★ **RESIDENCE INN BY MARRIOTT.** *15200 SW Banby Rd (97035). Phone 503/684-2603; fax 503/620-6712. www.residenceinn.com.* 112 rooms, 2 story. Pets accepted; fee. Complimentary continental breakfast. Check-out noon. TV; cable (premium), VCR available (free movies). Laundry services. Health club privileges. Pool; whirlpool. **$**

[D] [icons]

Redmond

Motels/Motor Lodges

★ **REDMOND INN.** *1545 Hwy 97 S (97756). Phone 541/548-1091; toll-free 800/833-3259; fax 541/548-0415.* 46 rooms, 3 story. No elevator. Pets accepted; fee. Complimentary continental breakfast. Check-out 11 am. TV. Pool. **$**

[D] [icons]

★ **VILLAGE SQUIRE MOTEL.** *629 SW 5th St (97756). Phone 541/548-2105; toll-free 800/548-2102; fax 541/548-5427. www.villagesquiremotel.com.* 24 rooms, 2 story. Pets accepted; fee. Check-out 11 am. TV; cable (premium), VCR available. **$**

[icon]

Reedsport

Motels/Motor Lodges

★ **ANCHOR BAY INN.** *1821 Hwy 101 (97467). Phone 541/271-2149; toll-free 800/767-1821; fax 541/271-1802.* 21 rooms, 2 story. Pets accepted, some restrictions;

fee. Complimentary continental breakfast. Check-out 10 am. TV; cable (premium), VCR available. Laundry services. Pool. **$**

★ **BEST WESTERN SALBASGEON INN OF REEDSPORT.** *1400 Hwy Ave (97467). Phone 541/271-4831; fax 541/271-4832. www.bestwestern.com.* 56 rooms, 2 story. Pets accepted, some restrictions; fee. Complimentary continental breakfast. Check-out 11 am. TV; cable (premium), VCR available. Laundry services. In-house fitness room. Indoor pool; whirlpool. Near Scholfield River. **$**

Rockaway

Motel/Motor Lodge

★ **SURFSIDE MOTEL.** *101 NW 11th Ave (97136). Phone 503/355-2312; toll-free 800/243-7786.* 79 rooms, 1-2 story. No A/C. Pets accepted, some restrictions; fee. Check-out noon. TV. Indoor pool. **$**

Roseburg

Motels/Motor Lodges

★★ **BEST INN & SUITES - ROSEBURG.** *427 NW Garden Valley Blvd (97470). Phone 541/673-5561; fax 541/957-0318.* 72 rooms, 1-2 story. Pets accepted, some restrictions; fee. Complimentary continental breakfast. Check-out 11 am. TV. Pool. **$**

★ **BEST WESTERN GARDEN VILLA MOTEL.** *760 NW Garden Valley Blvd (97470). Phone 541/672-1601; toll-free 800/547-3446; fax 541/672-1316. www.bestwestern.com.* 122 rooms, 2 story. Pets accepted, some restrictions. Complimentary continental breakfast. Check-out noon. TV; cable (premium), VCR available. Room service. In-house fitness room. **$**

★★ **WINDMILL INN OF ROSEBURG.** *1450 NW Mulholland Dr (97470). Phone 541/673-0901; toll-free 800/547-4747. www.windmillinns.com.* 128 rooms, 2 story. Pets accepted. Complimentary continental breakfast. Check-out 11 am. TV; cable (premium). In-room modem link. Laundry services. Restaurant, bar. In-house fitness room; sauna. Pool; whirlpool. Free airport, bus depot transportation. **$**

Salem

Motels/Motor Lodges

★ **BEST WESTERN NEW KINGS INN.** *1600 Motor Court NE (97301). Phone 503/581-1559; fax 503/364-4272. www.bestwestern.com.* 101 rooms, 2 story. Pets accepted, some restrictions; fee. Check-out noon. TV; cable (premium). In-house fitness room; sauna. Indoor pool; whirlpool. Outdoor tennis. **$**

★ **PHOENIX INN SUITES SOUTH SALEM.** *4370 Commercial St SE (97302). Phone 503/588-9220; toll-free 800/445-4498; fax 503/585-3616. www.phoenixinn.com.* 89 rooms, 4 story. Pets accepted, some restrictions; fee. Complimentary continental breakfast. Check-out noon. TV; cable (premium). Laundry services. In-house fitness room. Indoor pool; whirlpool. **$**

★★ **RED LION.** *3301 Market St (97301). Phone 503/370-7888; toll-free 800/248-6273; fax 503/370-6305. www.redlion.com.* 150 rooms, 4 story. Pets accepted; fee. Check-out 11 am. TV; cable (premium), VCR available. Restaurant, bar; entertainment. Room service. In-house fitness room; sauna. Indoor pool; whirlpool. **$**

★ **TIKI LODGE.** *3705 Market St NE (97305). Phone 503/581-4441.* 50 rooms, 2 story. Pets accepted. Check-out noon. TV; cable (premium). Sauna. Pool. **$**

Seaside

Motels/Motor Lodges

★★ **BEST WESTERN OCEAN VIEW RESORT.** *414 N Prom (97138). Phone 503/738-3334; toll-free 800/234-8439; fax 503/738-3264. www.oceanviewresort.com.* 104 rooms, 5 story. No A/C. Pets accepted, some restrictions; fee. Check-out 11 am. TV. In-room modem link. Restaurant, bar. Room service. Indoor pool; whirlpool. **$**

★★ **GEARHART BY THE SEA RESORT.** *1157 N Marion Ave (97138). Phone 503/738-8331; toll-free 800/547-0115; fax 503/738-0881. www.gearhartresort.com.* 80 rooms, 1-5 story. No A/C. Pets accepted, some restrictions; fee. Check-out 11 am. TV; VCR available. Restaurant, bar. Indoor pool. Golf; greens fee $27. **$**

Tillamook

Motel/Motor Lodge

★★**SHILO INN.** *2515 N Main St (97141). Phone 503/842-7971; toll-free 800/222-2244; fax 503/842-7960. www.shiloinns.com.* 101 rooms, 2 story. Pets accepted; fee. Check-out noon. TV; cable (premium), VCR available. Restaurant, bar. In-house fitness room. Indoor pool; whirlpool. **$**

D 🐾 🏊 🏋 🚫 ⛵

Yachats

Motels/Motor Lodges

★★**ADOBE RESORT MOTEL.** *1555 Hwy 101 N (97498). Phone 541/547-3141; toll-free 800/522-3623; fax 541/547-4234. www.adoberesort.com.* 93 rooms, 2-3 story. Pets accepted; fee. Check-out 11 am. TV; cable (premium), VCR available. Restaurant, bar. In-house fitness room; sauna. Whirlpool. **$**

D 🐾 🏋 🚫 SC

★**FIRESIDE MOTEL.** *1881 Hwy 101 N (97498). Phone 541/547-3636; toll-free 800/336-3573; fax 541/547-3152. www.overleaflodge.com/fireside.* 43 rooms, 2 story. Pets accepted; fee. Check-out 11 am. TV; VCR available. Health club privileges. **$**

D 🐾 🏋 🚫 SC

Pennsylvania

Allentown

Motels/Motor Lodges

★ **ALLENWOOD MOTEL.** *1058 Hausman Rd (18104). Phone 610/395-3707; fax 610/530-8166.* 21 rooms. Pets accepted, some restrictions; fee. Check-out 11 am. TV. **$**

[icons]

★ **SUPER 8.** *1715 Plaza Ln (18104). Phone 610/435-7880; toll-free 800/800-8000; fax 610/432-2555. www.super8.com.* 82 rooms, 4 story. Pets accepted; fee. Complimentary continental breakfast. Check-out 11 am. TV. **$**

[icons] D [icons] SC

Hotel

★★ **FOUR POINTS BY SHERATON.** *3400 Airport Rd (18109). Phone 610/266-1000; toll-free 888/610-2662; fax 610/266-1888.* 147 rooms, 3 story. Pets accepted; fee. Check-out noon. TV; cable (premium), VCR available. In-room modem link. Restaurant, bar; entertainment Tues-Sun. Room service. In-house fitness room; sauna. Indoor pool; whirlpool. **$**

[icons] D [icons] SC

Altoona

Motel/Motor Lodge

★ **RAMADA INN.** *1 Sheraton Dr (16601). Phone 814/946-1631; fax 814/946-0785. www.ramada.com.* 215 rooms, 2-3 story. Pets accepted, some restrictions; fee. Complimentary continental breakfast. Check-out noon. TV; cable (premium), VCR available. In-room modem link. Restaurant, bar. Room service. In-house fitness room. Indoor pool; children's pool; whirlpool. Downhill ski 20 miles. Airport transportation. Business center. **$**

[icons] D [icons] SC [icons]

Beaver Falls

Motel/Motor Lodge

★★ **HOLIDAY INN.** *7195 Eastwood Rd (15010). Phone 724/846-3700; toll-free 800/465-4329; fax 724/846-7008. www.holiday-inn.com.* 156 rooms, 3 story.

Pets accepted, some restrictions. Check-out noon. TV. In-room modem link. Restaurant, bar. Room service. Sauna. Game room. Indoor pool; whirlpool; poolside service. Miniature golf. **$**

[icons] D [icons] SC

Bedford

Motels/Motor Lodges

★★ **BEST WESTERN BEDFORD INN.** *4517 Business 220 (15522). Phone 814/623-9006; toll-free 800/752-8592; fax 814/623-7120. www.bestwestern.com.* 105 rooms, 2 story. Pets accepted, some restrictions; fee. Check-out noon. TV; cable (premium), VCR available (movies). Restaurant, bar. In-house fitness room; sauna. Game room. Pool; whirlpool. **$**

[icons] D [icons] SC

★ **ECONO LODGE.** *141 Hillcrest Dr (15522). Phone 814/623-5174; fax 814/623-5455. www.econolodge.com.* 32 rooms, 2 story. Pets accepted; fee. Check-out 11 am. TV; cable (premium). Bar. Game room. Downhill ski 15 miles. **$**

[icons] SC

★★ **QUALITY INN.** *4407 Business 220 (15522). Phone 814/623-5188; toll-free 800/228-5050; fax 814/623-0049. www.qualityinn.com.* 66 rooms. Pets accepted, some restrictions; fee. Complimentary continental breakfast. Check-out 11 am. TV; cable (premium). Restaurant, bar. Pool. Downhill ski 20 miles. **$**

[icons] D [icons] SC

Bethlehem

Motel/Motor Lodge

★ **COMFORT INN.** *3191 Highfield Dr (18020). Phone 610/865-6300; toll-free 800/732-2500; fax 610/865-5074. www.comfortinn.com.* 116 rooms, 2 1/2 story. Pets accepted; fee. Complimentary continental breakfast. Check-out noon. TV; VCR (movies, fee). Bar; entertainment Fri, Sat. **$**

[icons] D [icons] SC

Bloomsburg

Motel/Motor Lodge

★ **INN AT BUCKHORN.** *5 Buckhorn Rd (17815). Phone 570/784-5300; toll-free 888/754-6600; fax 570/387-0367. www.pavisnet.com/innatbuckhorn.* 120 rooms,

2 story. Pets accepted, some restrictions; fee. Check-out 11 am. TV. Bar. **$**

D 🐾 🏊

B&B/Small Inns

★ ★ ★ **INN AT TURKEY HILL.** *991 Central Rd (17815). Phone 570/387-1500; fax 570/784-3718. www.innatturkeyhill.com.* 18 rooms, 2 story. Pets accepted, some restrictions; fee. Complimentary continental breakfast. Check-out noon, check-in 2 pm. TV. In-room modem link. Dining room, bar. Room service. Airport, bus depot transportation. Old homestead (1839); guest rooms overlook landscaped courtyard; gazebo, lily pond. **$**

D 🐾 🏊 SC

★ ★ **MAGEE'S MAIN STREET INN.** *20 W Main St (17815). Phone 570/784-3200; toll-free 800/331-9815; fax 570/784-5517. www.magees.com.* 8 rooms, 3 story. Pets accepted, some restrictions. Complimentary continental breakfast. Check-out noon. TV. Dining room, bar. **$**

D 🐾 🦶 ⚡ 🏊

Breezewood

Motel/Motor Lodge

★ **RAMADA INN.** *US Rte 30 and I-70 (15533). Phone 814/735-4005; toll-free 814/535-4025; fax 814/735-3228. www.ramada.com.* 125 rooms, 2 story. Pets accepted, some restrictions; fee. Check-out noon. TV; cable (premium), VCR available (movies). In-room modem link. Restaurant, bar. Room service. In-house fitness room. Game room. Indoor pool. Business center. **$**

D 🐾 🏊 🏃 🏊 SC 🏃

Brookville

Motels/Motor Lodges

★ ★ **DAYS INN.** *US 322 and I-80, exit 13 (15825). Phone 814/849-8001; toll-free 800/329-7466; fax 814/849-9647. www.daysinn.com.* 118 rooms, 3 story. Pets accepted; fee. Check-out noon. TV. Laundry services. Restaurant, bar. Game room. Pool; children's pool; whirlpool; poolside service. Cross-country ski 17 miles. **$**

D 🐾 🏊 🏊 🏊 SC

★ **HOLIDAY INN EXPRESS.** *235 Allegheny Blvd (15825). Phone 814/849-8381; fax 814/849-8386. www.holiday-inn.com.* 68 rooms, 3 story. Pets accepted; fee. Complimentary continental breakfast. Check-out noon. TV; cable (premium). **$**

D 🐾 🦶 ⚡ 🏊

Butler

Motel/Motor Lodge

★ **DAYS INN.** *139 Pittsburgh Rd (16001). Phone 724/287-6761; toll-free 800/329-7466; fax 724/287-4307. www.daysinn.com.* 139 rooms, 2 story. Pets accepted; fee. Check-out 11 am. TV. Laundry services. Restaurant, bar; entertainment. Room service. In-house fitness room. Game room. Indoor pool; whirlpool. **$**

🐾 🏊 🏃 🏊 SC

Carlisle

Motels/Motor Lodges

★ ★ **CLARION HOTEL.** *1700 Harrisburg Pike (17013). Phone 717/243-1717; toll-free 800/692-7315; fax 717/243-6648. www.clarioncarlisle.com.* 270 rooms. Pets accepted; fee. Check-out 11 am. TV; cable (premium), VCR available (movies). In-room modem link. Restaurant, bar. Room service. Sauna. Indoor pool; whirlpool. Tennis. **$**

D 🐾 🦶 🏊 🏊 SC

★ ★ **HOLIDAY INN.** *1450 Harrisburg Pike (17013). Phone 717/245-2400; toll-free 800/465-4329; fax 717/245-9070.* 100 rooms, 2 story. Pets accepted; fee. Check-out noon. TV; cable (premium), VCR available. In-room modem link. Laundry services. Restaurant, bar. Room service. Health club privileges. Pool. **$**

D 🐾 🏊 🏊 SC

★ ★ **QUALITY INN.** *1255 Harrisburg Pike (17013). Phone 717/243-6000; fax 717/258-4123. www.qualityinn.com.* 96 rooms, 2 story. Pets accepted, some restrictions. Complimentary continental breakfast. Check-out noon. TV; cable (premium). Bar. Pool; children's pool.

D 🐾 🏊 🏊

Chambersburg

Motels/Motor Lodges

★ **DAYS INN.** *30 Falling Spring Rd (17201). Phone 717/263-1288; fax 717/263-6514. www.daysinn.com.* 107 rooms, 3 story. Pets accepted, some restrictions; fee. Complimentary continental breakfast. Check-out 11 am. TV; cable (premium). Downhill ski 15 miles. **$**

D 🐾 🏊 🏊

★ ★ **QUALITY INN.** *1095 Wayne Ave (17201). Phone 717/263-3400; toll-free 800/465-4329; fax 717/263-8386. www.qualityinn.com.* 139 rooms, 2 story. Pets accepted, some restrictions; fee. Check-out noon. TV; VCR available. Some in-room modem links. Restaurant, bar. Room service. Health club privileges. Pool; poolside service. **$**

D 🐾 ≈ ⊠ SC

★ ★ **TRAVELODGE.** *565 Lincoln Way E (17201). Phone 717/264-4187; fax 717/264-2446. www.travelodge.com.* 52 rooms, 3 story. Pets accepted; fee. Check-out noon. TV; cable (premium). Restaurant, bar. Room service. Health club privileges. **$**

D 🐾 ⊠

B&B/Small Inn

★ ★ **PENN NATIONAL INN AND GOLF CLUB.** *3809 Anthony Hwy (17237). Phone 717/352-2400; toll-free 800/231-0080; fax 717/352-3926. www.penngolf.com.* 48 rooms, 2 story. Pets accepted, some restrictions. Check-out 11 am. Check-in 2 pm. TV. Restaurant. Two 18-hole championship golf courses; greens fee $30-$70. Outdoor tennis. Georgian-style manor house built in 1847, additions built in 1989 and 2000. **$**

D 🐾 🏌 🏊 ≈ ⊠ SC

Clarion

Motels/Motor Lodges

★ ★ **DAYS INN.** *24 United Dr (16214). Phone 814/226-8682; fax 814/226-8372. www.daysinn.com.* 150 rooms, 2 story. Pets accepted; fee. Complimentary continental breakfast. Check-out noon. TV; cable (premium). Laundry services. Restaurant, bar; entertainment. Room service. Health club privileges. Pool. **$**

D 🐾 ≈ ⊠

★ ★ **HOLIDAY INN.** *45 Holiday Inn Dr (16214). Phone 814/226-8850; toll-free 800/596-1313; fax 814/226-9055. www.holiday-inn.com.* 122 rooms, 2 story. Pets accepted; fee. Check-out noon. TV; cable (premium), VCR available (movies). In-room modem link. Restaurant, bar. Room service. Sauna. Game room. Indoor pool. Airport transportation. **$**

D 🐾 ≈ ⊠

★ **SUPER 8.** *I-80 and Rte 68 (16214). Phone 814/226-4550; toll-free 800/800-8000; fax 814/227-2337. www.super8.com.* 99 rooms. Pets accepted. Complimentary continental breakfast. Check-out noon. TV; cable (premium), VCR available (movies). In-room modem link. Pool. **$**

D 🐾 ≈ ⊠ SC

Clearfield

Motel/Motor Lodge

★ **DAYS INN.** *PA 879 and I-80 (16830). Phone 814/765-5381; fax 814/765-7885. www.daysinn.com.* 119 rooms, 2 story. Pets accepted; fee. Complimentary continental breakfast. Check-out noon. TV; VCR available (movies). In-room modem link. In-house fitness room. Pool. **$**

D 🐾 ≈ 🏃 ⊠

Denver/Adamstown

Motel/Motor Lodge

★ ★ ★ **BLACK HORSE LODGE & SUITES.** *2180 N Reading Rd (17517). Phone 717/336-7563; toll-free 800/610-3805; fax 717/336-1110. www.blackhorselodge.com.* Located on 10 acres of land, this lodge is comprised of three buildings all found next to the outdoor pool. The property offers large suites with the living and bedroom areas separated by French doors, a king size bed and marble bathroom. 74 rooms, 2 story. Pets accepted. Complimentary full breakfast. Check-out noon. TV. Restaurant, bar. Pool. **$**

🐾 ≈ ⊠ SC

Du Bois

Motels/Motor Lodges

★ ★ **HOLIDAY INN.** *US 219 and I-80 (15801). Phone 814/371-5100; toll-free 800/959-3412; fax 814/375-0230. www.holiday-inn.com.* 160 rooms, 2 story. Pets accepted, some restrictions. Check-out noon. TV; cable (premium), VCR available. In-room modem link. Laundry services. Restaurant, bar. Room service. Health club privileges. Pool; children's pool; poolside service. Free airport transportation. **$**

D 🐾 ≈ ⊠ SC

★ ★ **RAMADA INN.** *I-80 and Rte 255 (15801). Phone 814/371-7070; toll-free 800/272-6232; fax 814/371-1055. www.ramada.com.* 96 rooms, 2-3 story. No elevator. Pets accepted; fee. Check-out noon. TV; cable (premium), VCR available. Restaurant, bar; entertainment. Room service. Health club privileges. Indoor pool; poolside service. Airport transportation. **$**

D 🐾 ≈ ⊠ SC

Edinboro

Motel/Motor Lodge

★ ★ **RAMADA.** *401 W Plum St (16412). Phone 814/734-5650; toll-free 888/449-0344; fax 814/734-7532. www.ramada.com.* 105 rooms, 2 story. Pets accepted; fee. Check-out noon. TV. Laundry services. Restaurant, bar; entertainment. Room service. Sauna. Indoor pool. Downhill ski 7 miles. **$**

⬚🐾⛷🏊⛱🔲SC

Erie

Motels/Motor Lodges

★ **MOTEL 6.** *7875 Peach St (16509). Phone 814/864-4811; toll-free 800/542-7674; fax 814/868-1277. www.motel6.com.* 83 rooms, 2 story. Pets accepted. Check-out noon. TV. Laundry services. In-house fitness room; sauna. Indoor pool; children's pool. Free airport transportation. **$**

⬚🐾🏊🏃⛱🔲SC

★ ★ **QUALITY INN & SUITES.** *8040 Perry Hwy (16509). Phone 814/864-4911; toll-free 800/550-8040; fax 814/864-3743. www.qualityinn.com.* 107 rooms, 2 story. Pets accepted, some restrictions; fee. Check-out 11 am. TV. In-room modem link. Restaurant, bar. Room service. Health club privileges. Pool. Free airport transportation. Business center. **$**

⬚🐾🏊✈⛱🔲SC🏃

★ **SUPER 8.** *8040 B Perry Hwy (16509). Phone 814/864-9200; fax 814/864-3743. www.super8.com.* 93 rooms, 4 story. Pets accepted; fee. Complimentary continental breakfast. Check-out 11 am. TV; cable (premium). In-room modem link. Laundry services. Game room. Airport transportation. **$**

⬚🐾⛱SC

Gettysburg

Motel/Motor Lodge

★ **BEST INN.** *301 Steinwehr Ave (17325). Phone 717/334-1188; toll-free 800/237-8466; fax 717/334-1188. www.bestinn.com.* 77 rooms, 2 story. Pets accepted. Check-out noon. TV; cable (premium), VCR available. Bar. Pool. Downhill ski 9 miles, cross-country ski adjacent. **$**

⬚🐾⛷🏊⛱SC

Harrisburg

Motels/Motor Lodges

★ **BAYMONT HARRISBURG-AIRPORT.** *200 N Mountain Rd (17112). Phone 717/540-9339; toll-free 800/428-3438; fax 717/540-9486. www.baymontinns.com.* 66 rooms, 3 story. Pets accepted. Complimentary continental breakfast. Check-out noon. TV; VCR available. In-room modem link. Business center. **$**

⬚🐾⛱SC🏃

★ ★ **BEST WESTERN HARRISBURG/ HERSHEY HOTEL & SUITES.** *300 N Mountain Rd (17112). Phone 717/652-7180; toll-free 800/528-1234; fax 717/541-8991. www.bestwestern.com.* 49 rooms, 2 story. Pets accepted, some restrictions; fee. Check-out 11 am. TV; cable (premium). In-room modem link. Restaurant, bar. **$**

🐾⛱SC

★ **COMFORT INN.** *4021 Union Deposit Rd (17109). Phone 717/561-8100; toll-free 800/253-1409; fax 717/561-1357. www.harrisburgpacomfortinn.com.* 115 rooms, 5 story. Pets accepted; fee. Complimentary continental breakfast. Check-out noon. TV; cable (premium). Laundry services. Health club privileges. Pool. Free airport, train station transportation. **$**

⬚🐾🏊⛱SC

★ ★ **HOLIDAY INN.** *148 Sheraton Dr (17070). Phone 717/774-2721; fax 717/774-2485. www.holilday-inn.com.* 196 rooms, 2 story. Pets accepted; fee. Check-out 11 am. TV; cable (premium). In-room modem link. Laundry services. Restaurant, bar; entertainment. Room service. Health club privileges. In-house fitness room. Game room. Indoor pool; whirlpool. Free airport, train station transportation. Business center. Luxury level. **$**

⬚🐾🏊🏃⛱SC🏃

★ ★ **HOLIDAY INN.** *5401 Carlisle Pike (17055). Phone 717/697-0321; toll-free 800/772-7829; fax 717/697-5917. www.holiday-inn.com.* 218 rooms, 2 story. Pets accepted; fee. Complimentary continental breakfast. Check-out noon. TV; cable (premium). Restaurant, bar; entertainment. Room service. In-house fitness room. Indoor, outdoor pool. Miniature golf. **$**

⬚🐾🏊🏃⛱SC

★ **RED ROOF INN.** *400 Corp Cir (17110). Phone 717/657-1445; toll-free 800/843-7663; fax 717/657-2775. www.redroof.com.* 110 rooms, 2 story. Pets accepted. Check-out noon. TV; cable (premium). In-room modem link. **$**

⬚🐾⛱SC

Hotels

★ ★ **RADISSON PENN HARRIS HOTEL & CONVENTION CENTER.** *1150 Camp Hill Byp (17011). Phone 717/763-7117; toll-free 800/333-3333; fax 717/763-7120. www.radisson.com.* This hotel offers a colonial setting, exceptional character and historic charm. It is located in a convenient central area near many of the area's attractions including the Gettysburg Battle Field. Rooms and suites are decorated in a colonial style. 250 rooms, 2-3 story. No elevator. Pets accepted, some restrictions; fee. Check-out 11 am. TV; cable (premium). In-room modem link. Restaurant, bar. Room service. In-house fitness room. Pool; poolside service. Free airport transportation. Business center. **$**

D 🐾 🏊 ⅍ ✕ ⤓ SC ⅍

★ ★ **WYNDHAM HARRISBURG - HERSHEY GARDEN HOTEL.** *765 Eisenhower Blvd (17111). Phone 717/558-9500; toll-free 800/528-1234; fax 717/558-8956. www.wyndham.com.* 167 rooms, 6 story. Pets accepted. Check-out noon. TV; cable (premium). In-room modem link. Restaurant, bar. Health club privileges. In-house fitness room. Pool. Downhill ski 20 miles. Free airport, train station, bus depot transportation. **$**

D 🐾 🏊 ⤓ ⅍ ⤓ SC

Hawley

B&B/Small Inn

★ **FALLS PORT INN & RESTAURANT.** *330 Main Ave (18428). Phone 570/226-2600; fax 570/226-6409.* 9 rooms, 3 story. No room phones. Pets accepted; fee. Complimentary continental breakfast. Check-out 11 am, check-in 1 pm. TV; VCR available. Restaurant. Room service. Downhill, cross-country ski 9 miles. Built in 1902 as an inn. **$**

🐾 🏊 ⤓

Hazleton

Motel/Motor Lodge

★ **RAMADA INN.** *Rte 309 N (18201). Phone 570/455-2061; fax 570/455-9387. www.ramada.com.* 107 rooms, 2 story. Pets accepted; fee. Check-out noon. TV. In-room modem link. Restaurant, bar. Room service. Pool. **$**

D 🐾 🏊 ⤓

Hershey

Motel/Motor Lodge

★ ★ **HOLIDAY INN.** *604 Station Rd (17028). Phone 717/469-0661; toll-free 800/465-4329; fax 717/469-7755. www.holiday-inn.com.* 195 rooms, 4 story. Pets accepted, some restrictions. Check-out noon. TV. In-room modem link. Laundry services. Restaurant, bar; entertainment. Room service. In-house fitness room; sauna. Indoor pool; outdoor pool; whirlpool. Lawn games. Airport, train station, bus depot transportation. Business center. **$**

D 🐾 🏊 ⅍ ✕ ⤓ SC ⅍

Huntingdon

Motel/Motor Lodge

★ ★ **HUNTINGDON MOTOR INN.** *US 22 (16652). Phone 814/643-1133; fax 814/643-1331.* 48 rooms, 2 story. Pets accepted; fee. Check-out 11 pm. TV. In-room modem link. Restaurant, bar. **$**

D 🐾 ⤓

Indiana

Motel/Motor Lodge

★ ★ **HOLIDAY INN.** *1395 Wayne Ave (15701). Phone 724/463-3561; toll-free 800/477-3561; fax 724/463-8006. www.holiday-inn.com.* 159 rooms, 2 story. Pets accepted. Check-out noon. TV; cable (premium). In-room modem link. Restaurant, bar; entertainment. Room service. Health club privileges. Sauna. Game room. Indoor pool; whirlpool; poolside service. **$**

D 🐾 🏊 ⤓ SC

Johnstown

Motels/Motor Lodges

★ **COMFORT INN.** *455 Theatre Dr (15904). Phone 814/266-3678; toll-free 800/228-5150; fax 814/266-9783. www.comfortinn.com.* 117 rooms, 5 story. Pets accepted, some restrictions; fee. Complimentary continental breakfast. Check-out noon. TV; VCR (movies). In-room modem link. Laundry services. Health club privileges. In-house fitness room. Indoor pool; whirlpool. Free airport transportation. Business center. **$**

D 🐾 🏊 ⅍ ⤓ SC ⅍

★ **SLEEP INN.** *453 Theatre Dr (15904). Phone 814/262-9292; fax 814/262-0486. www.sleepinn.com.* 62 rooms, 3 story. Shower only. Pets accepted; fee. Complimentary continental breakfast. Check-out noon. TV; cable (premium). In-room modem link. Airport transportation. **$**

D 🐾 🏊 SC

Hotel

★ ★ **HOLIDAY INN.** *250 Market St (15901). Phone 814/535-7777; toll-free 800/443-5663; fax 814/539-1393. www.holiday-inn.com.* 164 rooms, 6 story. Pets accepted, some restrictions. Check-out noon. TV; cable (premium). In-room modem link. Restaurant, bar. In-house fitness room; sauna. Health club privileges. Indoor pool; whirlpool; poolside service. Airport transportation. Business center. **$**

D 🐾 🏊 🏋 🏄 SC 🏃

Kennett Square

B&B/Small Inn

★ ★ ★ **BRANDYWINE RIVER HOTEL.** *US 1 and SR 100 (19317). Phone 610/388-1200; toll-free 800/274-9644; fax 610/388-1200.* 40 rooms, 2 story. Pets accepted, some restrictions; fee. Complimentary continental breakfast. Check-out 11 am, check-in 2 pm. TV. In-house fitness room. Airport, train station, bus depot transportation. Specialty shops on site. **$**

D 🐾 🏋 🏄 SC

King of Prussia

Motel/Motor Lodge

★ ★ **HOMEWOOD SUITES.** *12 E Swedesford Rd (19355). Phone 610/296-3500; fax 610/296-1941. www.homewoodsuites.com.* 123 suites, 4 story. Pets accepted; fee. Complimentary continental breakfast. Check-out noon. TV; cable (premium), VCR available. In-room modem link. Laundry services. Room service. In-house fitness room. Indoor pool; whirlpool. **$**

D 🐾 🏊 🏋 🏄 SC

Lancaster

Motel/Motor Lodge

★ ★ **BEST WESTERN EDEN RESORT INN & SUITES.** *222 Eden Rd (17601). Phone 717/569-6444; toll-free 800/528-1234; fax 717/569-4208. www.edenresort.com.*

276 rooms, 3 story. Pets accepted, some restrictions; fee. Check-out noon. TV; cable (premium). In-room modem link. Restaurant, bar; entertainment. Room service. In-house fitness room; sauna. Indoor, outdoor pool; whirlpool; poolside service. Outdoor tennis, lighted courts. Lawn games. Free airport transportation. Business center. **$**

D 🐾 🏋 🏊 🏄 🏋 SC 🏃

Hotel

★ ★ **BRUNSWICK HOTEL.** *N Queen St (17608). Phone 717/397-4801; toll-free 800/233-0182; fax 717/397-4991. www.hotelbrunswick.com.* 222 rooms, 7 story. Pets accepted, some restrictions; fee. Check-out noon. TV; VCR available (movies). Laundry services. Restaurant, bar; entertainment. In-house fitness room. Indoor pool. **$**

D 🐾 🏊 🏋 🏄

B&B/Small Inns

★ ★ **GENERAL SUTTER INN.** *14 E Main St (17543). Phone 717/626-2115; fax 717/626-0992. www.generalsutterinn.com.* Sixteen spacious rooms decorated in country and Victorian-style with local antiques are available to choose from at this inn. There are two restaurants on site, and a Victorian bar, as well as patio dining. 16 rooms, 3 story. Pets accepted; fee. Check-out noon, check-in 3 pm. TV. Fireplace in parlor. Dining room, bar. Built in 1764; antique country and Victorian furniture. **$**

🐾 🏄

★ ★ **HISTORIC STRASBURG INN.** *1 Historic Dr Rte 896 (17579). Phone 717/687-7691; toll-free 800/872-0201; fax 717/687-6098. www.historicstrasburginn.com.* Dating all the way back to 1793 and set on 58 acres, this elegant grand dame of an inn offers guests a truly memorable stay. Guests can relax amidst rooms handsomely appointed with 18th-century charm and 20th-century amenities. From the relaxing atmosphere which permeates this inn to the multitude of amenities guests are welcomed to enjoy. 101 rooms, 2 story. Pets accepted, some restrictions; fee. Complimentary full breakfast. Check-out noon. TV; VCR available (movies). Restaurant. Bar. In-house fitness room; sauna. Pool; whirlpool. Lawn games. **$**

D 🐾 🏊 🏋 🏄 SC

Lock Haven

B&B/Small Inn

★ ★ **VICTORIAN INN BED AND BREAKFAST.** *402 E Water St (17745). Phone 570/748-8688; toll-free 888/653-8688; fax 570/748-2444.* 12 rooms, 2 story. Pets accepted, some restrictions. Adults only. Complimentary full breakfast. Check-out 1 pm, check-in 2 pm. TV. Health club privileges. Built in 1859; garden atrium. **$**

◧ ◨

Mansfield

Motel/Motor Lodge

★ **COMFORT INN.** *300 Gateway Dr (16933).* *Phone 570/662-3000; toll-free 800/822-5470; fax 570/662-2551. www.comfortinn.com.* 100 rooms, 2 story. Pets accepted, some restrictions; fee. Complimentary continental breakfast. Check-out noon. TV. In-house fitness room. **$**

D ◧ ⌖ ◨ SC

Meadville

Motel/Motor Lodge

★ **DAYS INN.** *18360 Conneaut Lake Rd (16335).* *Phone 814/337-4264; toll-free 800/329-7466; fax 814/337-7304. www.daysinn.com.* 163 rooms, 2 story. Pets accepted, some restrictions; fee. Check-out 11 am. TV; cable (premium), VCR available (movies). Laundry services. Restaurant, bar. Indoor pool; whirlpool. **$**

◧ ◨ SC

Mercer

Motel/Motor Lodge

★★ **HOWARD JOHNSON.** *835 Perry Hwy (16137).* *Phone 724/748-3030; toll-free 800/542-7674; fax 724/748-3484. www.hojo.com.* 102 rooms, 2 story. Pets accepted. Check-out noon. TV; cable (premium), VCR available. In-room modem link. Restaurant, bar. Room service. In-house fitness room; sauna. Pool. Amish craft shop in lobby. **$**

D ◧ ◨ ⌖ ◨

Milford

Motel/Motor Lodge

★★ **BEST WESTERN INN AT HUNT'S LANDING.** *120 Rte 6 and 209 (18336).* *Phone 570/491-2400; toll-free 800/308-2378; fax 570/491-2422. www.bestwestern.com.* 108 rooms, 4 story. May-Oct. Pets accepted, some restrictions. Check-out 11 am. TV. In-room modem link. Laundry services. Restaurant, bar;

entertainment. Sauna. Game room. Indoor pool. Lawn games. **$**

D ◧ ⌖ ◨ ◨ SC

Mount Pocono

Motel/Motor Lodge

★★ **MEMORYTOWN.** *HC 1 Box 10 (18344).* *Phone 570/839-1680; fax 570/839-5846.* 30 rooms. Shower only. No A/C. No room phones. Pets accepted; fee. Complimentary continental breakfast; full breakfast weekends. Check-out 11 am, check-in 3 pm. TV. Restaurant. Game room. Downhill ski 10 miles, cross-country ski on site. Lawn games. Built in 1890; antiques. Country store, farmhouse on premises. **$**

◧ ⌖ ⌖ ◨ ◨

New Castle

Motel/Motor Lodge

★ **COMFORT INN.** *1740 New Butler Rd (16101).* *Phone 724/658-7700; fax 724/658-7727. www.comfortinn.com.* 79 rooms, 2 story. Pets accepted, some restrictions; fee. Complimentary continental breakfast. Check-out noon. TV. In-house fitness room; sauna. **$**

D ◧ ⌖ ◨

New Hope

B&B/Small Inns

★★★ **1870 WEDGWOOD INN OF NEW HOPE.** *111 W Bridge St (18938).* *Phone 215/862-3936; fax 215/862-3937. www.1870wedgwoodinn.com.* The wrap-around veranda invites you to relax at this historic inn in downtown New Hope. Unique touches include hand-painted and stenciled walls done by a local artist, and period antiques. 12 rooms, 2 story. Some room phones. Pets accepted, some restrictions; fee. Complimentary full breakfast. Check-out 11 am, check-in 3 pm. Health club privileges. Lawn games. Concierge service. Built 1870; antiques, large Wedgwood collection. Carriage rides. Totally nonsmoking. **$**

D ◧ ⌖ ◨ SC

★★★ **AARON BURR HOUSE.** *80 W Bridge St (18938).* *Phone 215/862-2343; fax 215/862-3937. www.new-hope-inn.com.* This year-round bed-and-breakfast is located in Bucks Country, just off the Delaware River. Activities include cross-country skiing, antiquing, and art shopping, both in New Hope and in its sister city, Lambertville, located across the river in New Jeresey. 5 rooms, 2 story. Pets accepted, some restrictions; fee. Complimentary full breakfast. Check-out 11 am, check-in 2 pm. TV in sitting room; VCR available. Health club privileges. Downhill ski 2 miles, cross-country ski adjacent. Lawn games. Concierge. Built in 1873. Swimming privileges. Totally nonsmoking. **$**

D 🔌🏊🛏🏊 SC

★ ★ ★ **GOLDEN PHEASANT INN.** *763 River Rd (18920). Phone 610/294-9595; fax 610/294-9882. www.goldenpheasant.com.* This is a cozy inn and restaurant providing French cuisine and a romantic setting. Located a little more than an hour from New York City and Philadelphia, this inn is a perfect place for a relaxing getaway. 6 rooms, 2 story. No room phones. Pets accepted, some restrictions; fee. Complimentary continental breakfast. Check-out noon, check-in 3 pm. TV. Restaurant. **$$**

🔌🐾🐾🏊

Oil City

Motel/Motor Lodge

★ ★ **HOLIDAY INN.** *1 Seneca St (16301). Phone 814/677-1221; fax 814/677-0492. www.holiday-inn.com.* 106 rooms, 5 story. Pets accepted; fee. Check-out noon. TV. In-room modem link. Restaurant, bar. Room service. Health club privileges. Pool. Cross-country ski 2 miles. **$**

D 🔌🐾🏊🏊

Philadelphia

Motel/Motor Lodge

★ ★ **BEST WESTERN CENTER CITY HOTEL.** *501 N 22nd St (19130). Phone 215/568-8300; fax 215/557-0259. www.bestwestern.com.* 183 rooms, 3 story. Pets accepted, some restrictions; fee. Check-out noon. TV; cable (premium). In-room modem link. Restaurant, bar. In-house fitness room. Pool. **$**

D 🔌🐾🏊🏊

Hotels

★ ★ ★ **FOUR SEASONS HOTEL PHILADELPHIA.** *1 Logan Sq (19103). Phone 215/963-1500; toll-free 800/332-3442; fax 215/963-9506. www.fourseasons.com/philadelphia.* Philadelphia's rich heritage comes alive at the Four Seasons Hotel. Located on historic Logan Square, the hotel puts the city's museums, shops, and businesses within easy reach. The eight-story Four Seasons is a Philadelphia institution in itself, from its

dramatic Swann Fountain to its highly rated Fountain Restaurant, considered one of the better dining establishments in town. The rooms and suites are a celebration of federalist décor, and some accommodations incorporate little luxuries like deep soaking tubs and high-speed Internet access. City views of the Academy of Natural Science, Logan Square, and the tree-lined Benjamin Franklin Parkway provide a sense of place for some guests, while other rooms offer tranquil views over the inner courtyard and gardens. The Four Seasons spa focuses on nourishing treatments, while the indoor pool resembles a tropical oasis with breezy palm trees and large skylights. 364 rooms, 8 story. Pets accepted, some restrictions. Check-out noon, check-in 3 pm. TV; cable (premium), VCR available. In-room modem link. Laundry services. Room service 24 hours. Restaurant, bar. Babysitting services available. In-house fitness room; spa; massage; sauna. Indoor pool; whirlpool; poolside service. Business center. Concierge. **$$$**

D 🔌🏊🏋🏊🏊

★ ★ ★ ★ **THE RITTENHOUSE HOTEL.** *210 W Rittenhouse Sq (19103). Phone 215/546-9000; toll-free 800/635-1042; fax 215/732-3364. www.rittenhousehotel.com.* The Rittenhouse Hotel is a jewel in the heart of Philadelphia. This intimate hotel occupies a particularly enviable address across from the leafy Rittenhouse Square and among the prestigious townhouses of this exclusive area. The accommodations are among the most spacious in the city and are decorated with a sophisticated flair. Guests at The Rittenhouse are treated to the highest levels of personalized service. Fitness and business centers cater to travelers visiting for work or pleasure, while the Adolf Biecker Spa and Salon pampers and primps its clients in a peaceful setting. From the mood-lifting décor of the gracious Cassatt Lounge and the striking contemporary style of Lacroix to the rowing memorabilia of the Boathouse Row Bar and the traditional steakhouse feel of Smith & Wollensky, the Rittenhouse Hotel also provides memorable dining experiences to match every taste. 98 rooms, 9 story. Pets accepted, some restrictions. Check-out 1 pm, check-in 3 pm. TV; cable (premium), VCR available. In-room modem link. Restaurant, bar; entertainment. Room service. Babysitting services available. In-house fitness room; sauna, steam room; spa, massage. Indoor pool. Business center. Garage; valet parking. Concierge. **$$**

D 🔌🏊🏋🏊🏊

★ ★ ★ ★ **THE RITZ-CARLTON, PHILADELPHIA.** *Ten Avenue of the Arts (19102). Phone 215/523-8000; toll-free 888/505-3914; fax 215/568-0942. www.ritzcarlton.com.* The Ritz-Carlton breathes new life into a magnificent historic building in the center of Philadelphia's downtown business district. This one-time home to Girard and Mellon Banks was designed in the 1900s by the architectural firm of McKim, Mead, and

White, and was inspired by Rome's Pantheon. Marrying historic significance with trademark Ritz-Carlton style, this Philadelphia showpiece boasts handsome and striking décor. Impressive marble columns dominate the lobby, where guests can pause for reflection over light meals in the Rotunda. The rooms and suites are the last word in luxury, while Club Level accommodations transport guests to heaven with a private lounge filled with five food and beverage selections daily. Dedicated to exceeding visitors' expectations, The Ritz-Carlton even offers a pillow menu, a bath butler, and other unique services. Dining options are plentiful, and the Sunday jazz brunch is a local favorite. 330 rooms, 31 story. Pets accepted, some restrictions; fee. Check-out noon, check-in 3 pm. TV; cable (premium). In-room modem link. Restaurant, bar. In-house fitness room. Business center. Concierge. **$$**

★ ★ ★ **SOFITEL.** *120 S 17th St (19103). Phone 215/569-8300; fax 215/569-1492. www.sofitel.com.* 306 rooms, 14 story. Pets accepted, some restrictions; fee. Check-out noon, check-in 3 pm. TV; cable (premium). In-room modem link. Restaurant, bar. In-house fitness room. Pool; whirlpool. Business center. Concierge. **$$**

B&B/Small Inn

★ ★ **TEN-ELEVEN CLINTON.** *1011 Clinton St (19107). Phone 215/923-8144; fax 215/923-5757.* 8 rooms, 3 story. Pets accepted, some restrictions. Complimentary continental breakfast. Check-out noon, check-in 3 pm. TV; VCR (movies). In-room modem link. Laundry services. Street parking. Concierge service. Built in 1836; enclosed courtyard. No elevators. Totally nonsmoking. **$**

Pittsburgh

Motels/Motor Lodges

★ **HAMPTON INN.** *555 Trumbull Dr (15205). Phone 412/922-0100; fax 412/921-7631. www.hamptoninn.com.* 132 rooms, 6 story. Pets accepted. Complimentary continental breakfast. Check-out noon. TV; cable (premium). In-room modem link. Health club privileges. Free airport transportation. **$**

★ **HAWTHORN SUITES.** *700 Mansfield Ave (15205). Phone 412/279-6300; toll-free 800/331-3131; fax 412/279-4993. www.hawthornsuitespittsburgh.com.* 151 suites, 2 story. Pets accepted; fee. Complimentary full breakfast. Check-out noon. TV; cable (premium). Fireplaces. Health

club privileges. Pool; whirlpool. Airport transportation. Chalet-style buildings. **$**

★ ★ **HOLIDAY INN.** *915 Brinton Rd (15221). Phone 412/247-2700; toll-free 800/465-4323; fax 412/371-9619. www.holiday-inn.com.* 177 rooms, 11 story. Pets accepted, some restrictions; fee. Check-out noon. TV; cable (premium). Laundry services. Restaurant, bar; entertainment Fri, Sat. Room service. Health club privileges. Indoor pool. **$**

★ ★ **HOLIDAY INN.** *401 Holiday Dr (15220). Phone 412/922-8100; toll-free 800/465-4329; fax 412/922-6511. www.holiday-inn.com.* 200 rooms, 4 story. Pets accepted. Check-out noon. TV; VCR available. In-room modem link. Restaurant, bar; entertainment. Room service. Health club privileges. In-house fitness room. Pool; poolside service. Free airport transportation. **$**

★ ★ **HOLIDAY INN.** *2750 Mosside Blvd (15146). Phone 412/372-1022; toll-free 800/465-4329; fax 412/373-4065. www.holiday-inn.com.* 188 rooms, 4 story. Pets accepted, some restrictions. Check-out noon. TV; cable (premium). In-room modem link. Laundry services. Restaurant, bar. Health club privileges. In-house fitness room. Pool. **$**

★ **RED ROOF INN.** *6404 Steubenville Pike (15205). Phone 412/787-7870; fax 412/787-8392. www.redroof.com.* 120 rooms, 2 story. Pets accepted. Check-out noon. TV; cable (premium). **$**

Hotels

★ ★ **RADISSON HOTEL PITTSBURGH GREEN TREE.** *101 Radisson Dr (15205). Phone 412/922-8400; toll-free 800/525-5902; fax 412/922-8981. www.radisson.com.* Conveniently located near downtown Pittsburgh, hotel guests can visit the Kennywood Amusement Park or the Pittsburgh Zoo. Sports enthusiasts can take in a Pittsburgh Steelers football game or a Pittsburgh Pirates baseball game. 467 rooms, 7 story. Pets accepted. Check-out noon. TV; cable (premium), VCR available. In-room modem link. Restaurant, bar; entertainment. Health club privileges. In-house fitness room; sauna. Three pools, one indoor, whirlpool; poolside service. Free airport transportation. Luxury level. **$**

★ ★ ★ **THE WESTIN CONVENTION CENTER PITTSBURGH.** *1000 Penn Ave (15222). Phone 412/281-3700; fax 412/227-4500. www.westin.com.* This 26 story hotel features rooms which are designed to be comfortable and work friendly. The rooms offer Internet access to guests as well as a telephone outlet for dataports. Amenities include a fitness center and pool. 616 rooms, 26 story. Pets accepted, some restrictions; fee. Check-out noon, check-in 3 pm. TV; cable (premium). In-room modem link. Room service 24 hours. Restaurant, bar. Babysitting services available. In-house fitness room; spa, sauna, steam room. Indoor pool; whirlpool. Business center. Concierge. **$**

[D] [⊠] [≈] [⅄] [≥] [SC] [⅄]

Pittsburgh International Airport Area

Motels/Motor Lodges

★ **AIRPORT PLAZA HOTEL MOON TOWNSHIP, PA.** *1500 Beers School Rd (15108). Phone 412/264-7900; fax 412/262-3229. www.plazaairport.com.* 193 rooms, 2 story. Pets accepted, some restrictions; fee. Complimentary deluxe continental breakfast. Check-out noon. TV; cable (premium). In-room modem link. In-house fitness room. Whirlpools. Free airport transportation. **$**

[⊠] [⅄] [≥] [SC]

★ **HAMPTON INN.** *1420 Beers School Rd (15108). Phone 412/264-0020; toll-free 800/426-7866; fax 412/264-3220. www.hamptoninn.com.* 129 rooms, 5 story. Pets accepted, some restrictions. Complimentary continental breakfast. Check-out noon. TV; cable (premium). Health club privileges. Free airport transportation. **$**

[D] [⊠] [≥] [SC]

★ **LA QUINTA INN.** *1433 Beers School Rd (15108). Phone 412/269-0400; toll-free 800/687-6667; fax 412/269-9258. www.laquinta.com.* 127 rooms, 3 story. Pets accepted. Complimentary continental breakfast. Check-out noon. TV. In-room modem link. Free airport transportation. **$**

[D] [⊠] [≥] [SC]

★ **RED ROOF INN.** *1454 Beers School Rd (15108). Phone 412/264-5678; fax 412/264-8034. www.redroof.com.* 119 rooms, 3 story. Pets accepted. Check-out noon. TV; cable (premium). Laundry services. Free airport transportation. **$**

[D] [⊠] [≥]

Pottstown

Motel/Motor Lodge

★ **COMFORT INN.** *Rte 100 and Shoemaker Rd (19464). Phone 610/326-5000; toll-free 800/879-2477; fax 610/970-7230. www.pottstownpacomfortinn.com.* 121 rooms, 4 story. Pets accepted, some restrictions; fee. Complimentary continental breakfast. Check-out noon. TV; cable (premium). In-room modem link. Laundry services. Room service. Health club privileges. Pool. **$**

[D] [⊠] [≈] [⅄] [≥] [SC]

Reading

Motels/Motor Lodges

★ ★ **BEST WESTERN DUTCH COLONY INN & SUITES.** *4635 Perkiomen Ave (19606). Phone 610/779-2345; toll-free 800/828-2830; fax 610/779-8348. www.bestwestern.com.* 71 rooms, 2 story. Pets accepted; fee. Check-out noon. TV. Restaurant, bar. Room service. Health club privileges. Pool. Lawn games. **$**

[D] [⊠] [≈] [≥]

★ **ECONO LODGE.** *635 Spring St (19610). Phone 610/378-5105; fax 610/373-3181. www.econolodge.com.* 84 rooms, 4 story. Pets accepted, some restrictions; fee. Complimentary continental breakfast. Check-out 11 am. TV; cable (premium). Laundry services. In-house fitness room. **$**

[D] [⊠] [⅄] [≥] [SC]

★ ★ **HOLIDAY INN.** *6170 Morgantown Rd (19543). Phone 610/286-3000; toll-free 800/339-0264; fax 610/286-1920. www.holiday-inn.com.* 191 rooms, 4 story. Pets accepted. Check-out noon. TV; cable (premium). In-room modem link. Restaurant, bar. Room service. In-house fitness room. Indoor pool; whirlpool. Business center. **$**

[D] [⊠] [≈] [⅄] [≥] [SC] [⅄]

Hotel

★ ★ **READING HOTEL.** *1741 W Papermill Rd (19610). Phone 610/376-3811; toll-free 800/325-3535; fax 610/375-7562.* Featuring 15,000 square feet of meeting space, the business traveler should find everything he or she needs to have a successful meeting. After a hard day at work enjoy the hotel's pools, sauna, or outdoor putting green. Basketball and tennis are also close by. 254 rooms, 5 story. Pets accepted; fee. Check-out noon. TV;

cable (premium), VCR available. In-room modem link. Restaurant, bar; entertainment. Room service. Health club privileges. In-house fitness room; massage, sauna. Indoor pool; whirlpool; poolside service. Free airport, bus depot transportation. **$**

D 🐾 ⛵ 🏃 🛏 SC

Scranton

Motels/Motor Lodges

★ **DAYS INN.** *1226 O'Neill Hwy (18512). Phone 570/348-6101; toll-free 888/246-3297; fax 570/348-5064. www.daysinn.com.* 90 rooms, 4 story. Pets accepted; fee. Complimentary continental breakfast. Check-out 11 am. TV; cable (premium), VCR available. **$**

D 🐾 🛏

★ ★ **HOLIDAY INN.** *200 Tigue St (18512). Phone 570/343-4771; fax 570/343-5171. www.holiday-inn.com.* 139 rooms, 2-3 story. Pets accepted, some restrictions; fee. Check-out noon. TV. In-room modem link. Restaurant, bar. Room service. Pool. **$**

D 🐾 ⛵ 🛏

Somerset

Motels/Motor Lodges

★ **BUDGET HOST INN.** *799 N Center Ave (15501). Phone 814/445-7988; toll-free 800/283-4678.* 28 rooms, 2 story. Pets accepted; fee. Check-out 11 am. TV; cable (premium). Downhill ski 10 miles, cross-country ski 13 miles. **$**

🐾 ⛵ 🛏 SC

★ **DOLLAR INN.** *1146 N Center Ave (15501). Phone 814/445-2977; toll-free 800/250-1505; fax 814/443-6205.* 16 rooms. Pets accepted; fee. Check-out 11 am. TV; cable (premium). **$**

🐾 🛏 SC

★ **KNIGHTS INN.** *585 Ramada Rd (15501). Phone 814/445-8933; fax 814/443-9745. www.knightsinn.com.* 112 rooms. Pets accepted. Check-out noon. TV; cable (premium), VCR available (movies). Laundry services. Pool. Downhill ski 15 miles. **$**

D 🐾 ⛵ 🛏 🏊

★ **RAMADA INN.** *215 Ramada Rd (15501). Phone 814/443-4646; fax 814/445-7539. www.ramada.com.* 152 rooms, 2 story. Pets accepted. Check-out noon. TV; cable (premium). Restaurant, bar; entertainment. Room service. Health club privileges. Sauna. Game room. Indoor

pool; whirlpool; poolside service. Downhill, cross-country ski 12 miles. **$**

D 🐾 ⛵ 🛏 🏊

B&B/Small Inn

★ ★ ★ **INN AT GEORGIAN PLACE.** *800 Georgian Place Dr (15501). Phone 814/443-1043; fax 814/443-6220. www.theinnatgeorgianplace.com.* Guests will delight in this 1918 Georgian-style mansion, charmingly restored to include modern amenities while retaining all the elegance and charm of that period. Some of the rooms are still appointed with the same elegant moldings and original silver and brass wall fixtures of a bygone era. 11 rooms, 3 story. Pets accepted, some restrictions. Children over 5 years only. Complimentary full breakfast. Check-out noon, check-in 3 pm. TV; cable (premium), VCR (movies). Restaurant. Room service. Downhill, cross-country ski 12 miles. Concierge service. Georgian mansion built in 1915; chandeliers, marble foyer. **$**

🐾 ⛵ 🛏

State College

Motels/Motor Lodges

★ ★ **DAYS INN.** *240 S Pugh St (16801). Phone 814/238-8454; toll-free 800/258-3297; fax 814/237-1607. www.daysinn.com.* 184 rooms, 6 story. S $59-$115; D $69-$115; each additional $10; suites $150; under 18 free; some weekend rates; higher rates special events. Pets accepted, some restrictions; fee. Complimentary continental breakfast. Check-out noon. TV. In-room modem link. Restaurant, bar; entertainment. Room service. In-house fitness room, sauna. Game room. Indoor pool. Free airport transportation. Business center.

🐾 🛏 🏃 🛏 SC 🏃

★ ★ **RAMADA INN.** *1450 S Atherton St (16801). Phone 814/238-3001; toll-free 800/465-4329; fax 814/237-1345. www.ramada.com.* 288 rooms, 2 story. Pets accepted; fee. Check-out noon. TV; cable (premium). In-room modem link. Restaurant, bar. Room service. Health club privileges. In-house fitness room. Game room. Two pools. **$**

D 🐾 🛏 🏃 🛏 SC

Stroudsburg

Motel/Motor Lodge

★ **BUDGET MOTEL.** *I-80 exit 51 (18301). Phone 570/424-5451; toll-free 800/233-8144; fax 570/424-0389. www.budmotel.com.* 115 rooms, 2-3 story. No elevator. Pets accepted, some restrictions; fee. Check-out 11 am.

TV; VCR available. In-room modem link. Restaurant, bar. Game room. $

D 🐾 🏊

Towanda

Motel/Motor Lodge

★★ **TOWANDA MOTEL & RESTAURANT.** *383 York Ave (18848). Phone 570/265-2178; fax 570/265-9060.* 48 rooms. Pets accepted; fee. Check-out noon. TV. Restaurant, bar. Pool. $

D 🐾 🏊 🏊

Uniontown

Motels/Motor Lodges

★★ **HOLIDAY INN.** *700 W Main St (15401). Phone 724/437-2816; toll-free 800/465-4329; fax 724/437-3505. www.holiday-inn.com.* 179 rooms, 2 story. Pets accepted, some restrictions. Check-out 11 am. TV; cable (premium), VCR available. In-room modem link. Restaurant, bar; entertainment. Room service. Sauna. Game room. Indoor pool; whirlpool; poolside service. Outdoor tennis, lighted courts. Lawn games. Miniature golf. $

D 🐾 🏌 🏊 🏊 SC

★★ **LODGE AT CHALK HILL.** *Rte 40E (15421). Phone 724/438-0168; toll-free 800/833-4283; fax 724/438-1685. www.thelodgeatchalkhill.com.* 60 suites. Pets accepted; fee. Complimentary continental breakfast. Check-out noon. TV; cable (premium), VCR available. $

D 🐾 🏌 🏊

Washington

Motels/Motor Lodges

★★ **HOLIDAY INN.** *340 Racetrack Rd (15301). Phone 724/222-6200; toll-free 800/465-4329; fax 724/228-1977. www.holiday-inn.com.* 138 rooms, 7 story. Pets accepted, some restrictions. Check-out noon. TV; cable (premium), VCR available. In-room modem link. Restaurant, bar; entertainment. Room service. In-house fitness room; sauna. Pool; whirlpool; poolside service. Airport transportation. Meadows Racetrack adjacent. $

D 🐾 🏊 🏋 🏊 SC

★ **MOTEL 6.** *1283 Motel 6 Dr (15301). Phone 724/223-8040; fax 724/228-6445. www.motel6.com.* 102 rooms. Pets accepted. Check-out noon. TV; cable (premium). Pool. $

D 🐾 🏊 🏊

★ **RED ROOF INN.** *1399 W Chestnut St (15301). Phone 724/228-5750; fax 724/228-5865. www.redroof.com.* 110 rooms, 2 story. Pets accepted, some restrictions. Check-out noon. TV; cable (premium). $

D 🐾 🏊

Wellsboro

Motel/Motor Lodge

★ **CANYON MOTEL.** *18 East Ave (16901). Phone 570/724-1681; toll-free 800/255-2718; fax 570/724-1681. www.canyonmotel.com.* 28 rooms. Pets accepted, some restrictions; fee. Complimentary continental breakfast. Check-out 11 am. TV. In-room modem link. Pool. Downhill, cross-country ski 17 miles. $

D 🐾 🏊 🏊 🏊 SC

West Chester

Motel/Motor Lodge

★ **ABBEY GREEN MOTOR LODGE.** *1036 Wilmington Pike (19382). Phone 610/692-3310; fax 610/431-0811. www.abbeygreen.com.* 6 rooms. Pets accepted, some restrictions; fee. Check-out 11 am. TV; cable (premium). $

D 🐾 🏊

West Middlesex

Motel/Motor Lodge

★★ **HOLIDAY INN.** *3200 S Hermitage Rd (16159). Phone 724/981-1530; toll-free 800/465-4329; fax 724/981-1518. www.holiday-inn.com.* 180 rooms, 3 story. Pets accepted, some restrictions. Check-out 11 am. TV; cable (premium). In-room modem link. Laundry services. Restaurant, bar; entertainment. Room service. Game room. Pool; poolside service. $

D 🐾 🏊 🏊 SC

Hotel

★★ **RADISSON HOTEL SHARON.** *I-80 and Rte 18 (16159). Phone 724/528-2501; toll-free 800/333-3333; fax 724/528-2306. www.radisson.com.* Upon arrival, guests are enveloped in a lobby filled with warmth and elegance, as well as an exquisite décor of authentic oriental furniture. 153 rooms, 3 story. S $80-$90; D $88-$98; each additional $8; suites $150-$200; under 12 free; weekend rates. Pets accepted, some restrictions. Check-out 11 am.

TV. Laundry services. Restaurant, bar; entertainment. Room service. In-house fitness room; sauna. Game room. Indoor pool; whirlpool; poolside service.

⊡ 🐾 ➳ 🛪 🏊 SC

White Haven

Motel/Motor Lodge

★ **RAMADA.** *Rte 940 (18624). Phone 570/443-8471; toll-free 800/251-2610; fax 570/443-0326. www.poconoramada.com.* 138 rooms, 4 story. Pets accepted, some restrictions; fee. Check-out noon. TV. Laundry services. Restaurant, bar. Room service. Sauna. Game room. Indoor pool; poolside service. Downhill, cross-country ski 4 miles. Lawn games. Airport transportation. **$**

⊡ 🐾 ➳ 🏊 🛏

Wilkes Barre

Motels/Motor Lodges

★ ★ **BEST WESTERN GENETTI HOTEL & CONVENTION CENTER.** *77 E Market St (18701). Phone 570/823-6152; toll-free 800/833-6152; fax 570/820-8502. www.bestwestern.com.* 72 rooms, 5 story. Apr-Dec: S $74-$79; D $79-$89; each additional $10; suites $89-$99; under 12 free; higher rates NASCAR races; lower rates rest of year. Pets accepted; fee. Check-out 11 am. TV; VCR available (movies). Restaurant, bar; entertainment. Room service. Pool; poolside service. Downhill, cross-country ski 12 miles.

🐾 ➳ 🏊 🛏

★ ★ **HOLIDAY INN.** *880 Kidder St (18702). Phone 570/824-8901; toll-free 888/466-9272; fax 570/824-9310.* 120 rooms, 2 story. S, D $69-$120; each additional $10; studio rooms $75; package plans. Pets accepted, some restrictions. Check-out noon. TV. In-room modem link. Restaurant, bar. Room service. Pool; children's pool; poolside service. Downhill ski 10 miles.

⊡ 🐾 ➳ 🏊 🛏 SC

Williamsport

Motels/Motor Lodges

★ **ECONO LODGE.** *2019 E 3rd St (17701). Phone 570/326-1501; fax 570/326-9776. www.econolodge.com.* 99 rooms, 2 story. S $45-$50; D $50-$55; each additional $5; higher rates Little League World Series. Pets accepted, some restrictions; fee. Check-out noon. TV; cable (premium). Restaurant, bar; entertainment.

⊡ 🐾 🛪 🛏

★ ★ **HOLIDAY INN.** *1840 E 3rd St (17701). Phone 570/326-1981; toll-free 800/369-4572; fax 570/323-9590. www.holiday-inn.com.* 170 rooms, 2 story. S, D $64-$79; each additional $10; under 18 free; higher rates Little League World Series. Pets accepted. Check-out 11 am. TV. In-room modem link. Restaurant, bar. Room service. Pool.

⊡ 🐾 ➳ 🛏

Hotels

★ ★ ★ **GENETTI HOTEL & SUITES.** *200 W 4th St (17701). Phone 570/326-6600; toll-free 800/321-1388; fax 570/326-5006. www.genetti.com.* Conveniently located in Center City, this property offers rooms and suites with European-style décor. 206 rooms, 10 story. S $29.95-$59, D $35.95-$65.95, each additional $6, suites $75.95-$139; under 10 free; higher rates Little League World Series. Pets accepted. Check-out 11 am. TV; cable (premium), VCR available. Laundry services. Restaurant, bar; entertainment Fri, Sat. In-house fitness room. Pool; poolside service. Downhill ski 20 miles. Free airport transportation.

⊡ 🐾 ➳ 🏊 🛪

★ ★ **RADISSON HOTEL WILLIAMSPORT.** *100 Pine St (17701). Phone 570/327-8231; toll-free 800/325-3535; fax 570/322-2957. www.radisson.com.* This hotel is conveniently located near the Williamsport Regional Airport. 148 rooms, 5 story. S, D $85-$95; suites $150; under 18 free. Pets accepted, some restrictions. Check-out noon. TV. Restaurant, bar; entertainment. Room service. Indoor pool. Downhill, cross-country ski 18 miles. Free airport transportation.

⊡ 🐾 ➳ 🏊 🛏 SC

York

Motel/Motor Lodge

★ ★ **HOLIDAY INN.** *2000 Loucks Rd (17404). Phone 717/846-9500; toll-free 800/465-4329; fax 717/764-5038. www.holiday-inn.com.* 181 rooms, 2 story. S, D $72-$98; under 18 free. Pets accepted. Check-out 11 am. TV; cable (premium). Restaurant, bar. Room service. In-house fitness room; sauna. Indoor pool; outdoor pool; whirlpool; poolside service. Miniature golf.

⊡ 🐾 ➳ 🛪 🛏 SC

Rhode Island

Providence

Kingston

B&B/Small Inn

★ ★ **LARCHWOOD INN.** *521 Main St (02879). Phone 401/783-5454; toll-free 800/275-5450; fax 401/783-1800. www.xpos.com/larchwoodinn.* 18 rooms, some A/C, 3 story. Pets accepted, some restrictions; fee. Check-out 11 am, check-in 1 pm. TV. Restaurant, bar. Built 1831. Some room phones. **$**

🐾 🏋 🎿 ⛶

Newport

Motels/Motor Lodges

★ ★ **HOWARD JOHNSON.** *351 W Main Rd (02842). Phone 401/849-2000; fax 401/849-6047. www.hojo.com.* 155 rooms, 2 story. Pets accepted, some restrictions; fee. Check-out 11 am. TV; cable (premium), VCR available. Restaurant, bar. Sauna. Pool; whirlpool. Outdoor tennis. **$**

🐾 🏊 🎿 ⛶

★ **RAMADA INN.** *936 W Main Rd (02842). Phone 401/846-7600; toll-free 800/836-8322; fax 401/849-6919. www.ramada.com.* 155 rooms, 2 story. Pets accepted; fee. Complimentary continental breakfast. Check-out noon. TV; cable (premium). In-room modem link. Laundry services. Bar. Indoor pool. **$**

Ⓓ 🐾 🏊 ⛶

Portsmouth

Motel/Motor Lodge

★ **FOUNDER'S BROOK MOTEL & SUITES.** *314 Boyd's Ln (02871). Phone 401/683-1244; toll-free 800/334-8765; fax 401/683-9129.* 24 kitchen kitchen units. Pets accepted, some restrictions; fee. Complimentary continental breakfast (weekends). Check-out 11 am. TV; VCR available. Laundry services. **$**

Ⓓ 🐾 ⛶

Hotel

★ ★ ★ **WESTIN HOTEL.** *1 W Exchange St (02903). Phone 401/598-8000; fax 401/598-8200. www.westin.com.* 363 rooms, 25 story. Pets accepted, some restrictions; fee. Check-out noon. TV; cable (premium), VCR available (movies). In-room modem link. Restaurant, bar. In-house fitness room; sauna. Indoor pool; whirlpool. Business center. Concierge. **$$**

Ⓓ 🐾 🏊 🏋 ⛶ 🚶

Warwick

Hotel

★ ★ ★ **CROWNE PLAZA.** *801 Greenwich Avenue (02886). Phone 401/732-6000; fax 401/732-4839. www.crowneplazari.com.* This hotel is just 8 miles from downtown and 3 miles from the airport. It is a suburban property with contemporary décor. 266 rooms, 6 story. Pets accepted, some restrictions. Check-out 11 am. TV. In-room modem link. Laundry services. Restaurant, bar. Room service. In-house fitness room; sauna. Indoor pool; whirlpool; poolside service. Business center. Free airport transportation. **$$**

Ⓓ 🐾 🏊 🏋 ⛶ ✈ SC 🚶

South Carolina

Aiken

Hotel

★★★ **THE WILLCOX.** *100 Colleton Ave (29801). Phone 803/648-1898; toll-free 877/648-2200; fax 803/648-6664. www.thewillcox.com.* Frederick Willcox welcomed the first guests to The Willcox in 1900. The same southern hospitality awaits travelers today. Aiken is home to some of the best thoroughbred horse trainers in the world and this inn, with all the amenities of a full-service hotel, serves as a perfect base to explore the area. 22 rooms, 3 story. Pets accepted, some restrictions; fee. Complimentary full breakfast. Check-out noon, check-in 3 pm. TV; cable (premium), VCR available. Restaurant; entertainment Fri, Sat. Room service. Babysitting services available. In-house fitness room; spa. Built 1898; antique furnishings. English country decor. **$$$**

D 🐾 🏋 🏊

Anderson

Motel/Motor Lodge

★★ **RAMADA INN.** *3025 N Main St (29621). Phone 864/226-6051; fax 864/964-9145. www.ramada.com.* 130 rooms, 2 story. Pets accepted, some restrictions; fee. Check-out noon. TV. Restaurant, bar. Room service. Pool. In-room modem link. **$**

D 🐾 🏊 ⊠

Camden

Motel/Motor Lodge

★★ **COLONY INN.** *2020 W Dekalb St (29020). Phone 803/432-5508; toll-free 800/356-9801; fax 803/432-0920.* 53 rooms, 2 story. Pets accepted, some restrictions. Check-out 11 am. TV. Restaurant. Pool. **$**

D 🐾 🏋 🏊

Charleston

B&B/Small Inn

★★★ **INDIGO INN.** *1 Maiden Ln (29401). Phone 843/577-5900; toll-free 800/845-7639; fax 843/577-0378. www.indigoinn.com.* Housed in an 1850 warehouse once used to store indigo for dying textiles, this colorful inn is located in the middle of the historic district, just one block from City Market. 40 rooms, 3 story. Pets accepted, some restrictions; fee. Complimentary continental breakfast. Check-out noon, check-in 3 pm. TV; cable (premium). In-room modem link. Parking. Built in 1850; courtyard. **$**

D 🐾 ⊠

Clemson

Motel/Motor Lodge

★★ **HOLIDAY INN.** *894 Tiger Blvd (29631). Phone 864/654-4450; toll-free 888/442-0422; fax 864/654-8451. www.holiday-inn.com.* 220 rooms, 2 story. Pets accepted. Check-out noon. TV; cable (premium). In-room modem link. Laundry services. Restaurant, bar. Pool. **$**

D 🐾 🏊 ⊠ SC

Clinton

Motel/Motor Lodge

★ **DAYS INN.** *12374 Hwy 56 N (29325). Phone 864/833-6600; toll-free 800/329-7466; fax 864/833-6600. www.daysinn.com.* 59 rooms, 2 story. Pets accepted; fee. Complimentary continental breakfast. Check-out 11 am. TV; cable (premium). In-house fitness room; sauna. Pool. **$**

D 🐾 🏊 🏋 ⊠ SC

Columbia

Motels/Motor Lodges

★ **AMERISUITES.** *7525 Two Notch Rd (29223). Phone 803/736-6666; fax 803/788-6011. www.amerisuites.com.* 112 rooms, 6 story. Pets accepted, some restrictions; fee. Complimentary continental breakfast. Check-out noon, check-in 3 pm. TV; cable (premium), VCR available. In-house fitness room. Outdoor pool. Business center. **$**

D 🐾 🏊 🏋 ⊠ 🏃

★ **BAYMONT INN.** *1538 Horseshoe Dr (29223). Phone 803/736-6400; toll-free 800/301-0200; fax 803/788-7875. www.baymontinn.com.* 98 rooms, 3 story. Pets accepted, some restrictions. Complimentary continental breakfast. Check-out noon, check-in 2 pm. TV; cable (premium). In-room modem link. Outdoor pool. **$**

D 🐾 🏊 🏂

★★ **HOLIDAY INN.** *7510 Two Notch Rd (29223). Phone 803/736-3000; toll-free 800/465-4329; fax 803/736-6399. www.holiday-inn.com.* 253 rooms, 2 story. Pets accepted, some restrictions; fee. Complimentary continental breakfast. Check-out noon, check-in 4 pm. TV; cable (premium). In-room modem link. Restaurant, bar. Room service. Children's activity center. In-house fitness room; sauna. Courtyard. Game room. Indoor, outdoor pool; whirlpool; poolside service. **$**

D 🐾 🏊 🏃 🏂 SC

★★ **RAMADA INN.** *8105 Two Notch Rd (29223). Phone 803/736-5600; fax 803/736-1241. www.ramada.com.* 186 rooms, 6 story. Pets accepted; fee. Check-out noon, check-in 3 pm. TV. In-room modem link. Restaurant, bar. Room service. In-house fitness room; sauna. Outdoor pool; whirlpool. **$**

D 🐾 🏊 🏃 🏂

★ **RED ROOF INN.** *7580 Two Notch Rd (29223). Phone 803/736-0850; toll-free 800/843-7663; fax 803/736-4270. www.redroof.com.* 108 rooms, 2 story. Pets accepted. Check-out noon, check-in 1 pm. TV; cable (premium). In-room modem link. **$**

D 🐾 🏂

Hotel

★★ **SHERATON COLUMBIA HOTEL AND CONFERENCE CENTER.** *2100 Bush River Rd (29210). Phone 803/731-0300; toll-free 800/325-3535; fax 803/731-2839. www.sheraton.com.* 237 rooms, 5 story. Pets accepted, some restrictions; fee. Check-out noon, check-in 3 pm. TV; cable (premium). In-room modem link. Restaurant, bar; entertainment. Babysitting services available. In-house fitness room; sauna. Indoor, outdoor pool; whirlpool. Free airport transportation. Business center. Luxury level. **$**

D 🐾 🏊 🏃 🏂 SC 🏃

Florence

Motels/Motor Lodges

★ **COMFORT INN.** *1916 W Lucas St (29501). Phone 843/665-4558; toll-free 800/882-3840. www.comfortinn.com.* 162 rooms, 2 story. Pets accepted, some restrictions; fee.

Complimentary continental breakfast. Check-out 11 am, check-in 2 pm. TV; cable (premium). In-house fitness room. Pool; whirlpool. **$**

D 🐾 🏊 🏃 🏂 SC

★ **DAYS INN.** *2111 W Lucas St (29501). Phone 843/665-4444; toll-free 800/489-4344. www.daysinn.com.* 108 rooms, 2 story. Pets accepted. Complimentary continental breakfast. Check-out 11 am, check-in 2 pm. TV; cable (premium). In-house fitness room; sauna. Pool; whirlpool. **$**

D 🐾 🏊 🏃 🏂 SC

★ **RAMADA INN.** *2038 W Lucas St (29501). Phone 843/669-4241; fax 843/665-8883. www.ramada.com.* 188 rooms, 2 story. Pets accepted. Check-out noon, check-in 3 pm. TV; cable (premium). Restaurant, bar; entertainment. Room service. In-house fitness room. Pool; whirlpool. Free airport transportation. **$**

D 🐾 🏊 🏃 🏂

★ **RED ROOF INN.** *2690 David H. McLeod Blvd (29501). Phone 843/678-9000; fax 843/667-1267. www.redroof.com.* 112 rooms, 2 story. Pets accepted, some restrictions. Check-out 11 am, check-in 3 pm. TV; cable (premium). **$**

D 🐾 🏂

Greenville

Motel/Motor Lodge

★ **LA QUINTA INN.** *31 Old Country Rd (29607). Phone 864/297-3500; fax 864/458-9818. www.laquinta.com.* 122 rooms, 2 story. Pets accepted. Complimentary continental breakfast. Check-out noon. TV; cable (premium). Pool. **$**

D 🐾 🏃 🏊 🏂

All Suites

★★ **GUESTHOUSE INTL.** *48 McPrice Ct (29615). Phone 864/297-0099; toll-free 800/214-8378; fax 864/288-8203. www.guesthouse.net.* 96 rooms, 2 story. Pets accepted, some restrictions; fee. Complimentary continental breakfast. Check-out noon. TV; cable (premium). Pool; whirlpool. **$**

D 🐾 🏊 🏂

Hardeeville

Motel/Motor Lodge

★ **HOWARD JOHNSON.** *I-95 and US 17 (29927). Phone 843/784-2271; toll-free 800/654-2000; fax 843/784-*

5334. www.hojo.com. 128 rooms, 2 story. Pets accepted; fee. Check-out noon. TV; cable (premium). Restaurant. Pool; children's pool. **$**

D 🐾 ≈ ⊠

Hilton Head Island

Motels/Motor Lodges

★ **HOLIDAY INN EXPRESS.** *40 Waterside Dr (29928). Phone 843/842-8888; toll-free 888/843-4136; fax 843/842-5948. www.holiday-inn.com.* 91 rooms, 3 story. Pets accepted; fee. Complimentary continental breakfast. Check-out 11 am, check-in 4 pm. TV; cable (premium). In-room modem link. Pool. **$**

D 🐾 ≈ ⊠ SC

★ **RED ROOF INN.** *5 Regency Pkwy (29928). Phone 843/686-6808; toll-free 800/733-7663; fax 843/842-3352. www.redroof.com.* 115 rooms, 2 story. Pets accepted. Check-out noon, check-in 3 pm. TV; cable (premium). Pool. **$**

D 🐾 ≈ ⊠

Kiawah Island

Resort

★ ★ ★ **KIAWAH ISLAND GOLF RESORT.** *12 Kiawah Beach Dr (29455). Phone 843/768-2121; toll-free 800/654-2924; fax 843/768-9339. www.kiawahresort.com.* This is the only resort located on the island. The island's beach was rated the "second most romantic beach in America" by *National Geographic Traveler.* Enjoy the resort's 10 miles of beaches or take a day trip to historic Charleston, located only 21 miles away. The resort also claims several opportunities to experience cuisine at its best. 610 rooms, 3 story. Pets accepted, some restrictions; fee. Check-out 11 am, check-in 4 pm. TV; cable (premium). Dining rooms. Bar; entertainment (in season). Room service. Supervised children's activities (Easter-Labor Day); ages 3-19. In-house fitness room. Game room. Snack bar. Seven pools; children's pool; poolside service. Golf on premise; greens fee $105-$185. Outdoor tennis, lighted courts. Lawn games. Bicycle rentals. Marina, boats. Canoe trips. Nature walks. Business center. Concierge. **$$**

🐾 🏌 🎾 ≈ 🏃 ⊠ SC 🚶

Myrtle Beach

Motels/Motor Lodges

★ **LA QUINTA INN.** *1561 21st Ave N (29577). Phone 843/916-8801; toll-free 800/687-6667; fax 843/916-8701.*

www.laquinta.com. 129 rooms, 4 story. Pets accepted, some restrictions. Complimentary continental breakfast. Check-out noon. TV; cable (premium). Laundry services. Room service. In-house fitness room. Pool; whirlpool. **$**

D 🐾 ≈ 🏃 ⊠ SC

★ **PALM CREST.** *701 S Ocean Blvd (29577). Phone 843/448-7141; toll-free 800/487-9233; fax 843/444-4799. www.palmcrestmotel.com.* 41 rooms, 3 story. No elevator. Pets accepted, some restrictions. Check-out 11 am. TV. Laundry services. Pool; children's pool. Free airport transportation. **$**

🐾 🎿 ≈ 🏃 ⊠

★ **ST. JOHN'S INN.** *6803 N Ocean Blvd (29572). Phone 843/449-5251; toll-free 800/845-0624; fax 843/449-3306. www.stjohnsinn.com.* 90 rooms, 3 story. Pets accepted, some restrictions; fee. Check-out 11 am. TV. Restaurant. Opposite beach. Pool; whirlpool. Lawn games. **$**

D 🐾 ≈ ⊠ SC

Rock Hill

Motel/Motor Lodge

★ ★ **HOLIDAY INN.** *2640 N Cherry Rd (29730). Phone 803/329-1122; toll-free 877/256-7399; fax 803/329-1072. www.holiday-inn.com.* 125 rooms, 2 story. Pets accepted, some restrictions; fee. Check-out noon. TV; cable (premium). In-room modem link. Restaurant, bar. Pool. Airport transportation. **$**

D 🐾 ≈ ⊠

Santee

Motel/Motor Lodge

★ **DAYS INN.** *9074 Old #6 Hwy (29142). Phone 803/854-2175; toll-free 800/329-7466; fax 803/854-2835. www.daysinn.com.* 119 rooms, 2 story. Pets accepted; fee. Complimentary full breakfast. Check-out noon. TV; cable (premium). Laundry services. Restaurant. Pool. **$**

🐾 ≈ ⊠ SC

Spartanburg

Motel/Motor Lodge

★ ★ **QUALITY INN.** *7136 Asheville Hwy (29303). Phone 864/503-0780; toll-free 800/228-5151; fax 864/503-0780. www.qualityinn.com.* 143 rooms, 6 story. Pets accepted; fee. Check-out noon. TV; cable (premium).

In-room modem link. Restaurant, bar. In-house fitness room. Pool; poolside service. **$**

D 🐾 🏊 🏃 ✈ 🖂

Sumter

Motel/Motor Lodge

★ **RAMADA INN.** *226 N Washington St (29150). Phone 803/775-2323; toll-free 800/457-6884; fax 803/773-9500. www.ramada.com.* 125 rooms, 2-3 story. Pets accepted, some restrictions; fee. Complimentary breakfast buffet. Check-out noon. TV; cable (premium). In-room modem link. Restaurant, bar. Room service. Pool. **$**

D 🐾 🏊 🖂

B&B/Small Inn

★ ★ ★ **MAGNOLIA HOUSE BED & BREAKFAST.** *230 Church St (29150). Phone 803/775-6694; toll-free 888/666-0296.* This hotel's architecture is reminiscent of the Old South including the four-column front porch, and the décor is antique French. Evening cocktails are served on the veranda overlooking the gardens. Pets are a part of the everyday atmosphere in the house. 4 rooms, 2 story. Pets accepted. Complimentary full breakfast. Check-out 11 am, check-in 3 pm. TV; VCR available (movies). Built in 1907; Greek Revival. Totally nonsmoking. **$**

🐾 ✈ 🖂

Walterboro

Motel/Motor Lodge

★ ★ **QUALITY INN.** *1286 Sniders Hwy (29488). Phone 843/538-5473; fax 843/538-5473. www.qualityinn.com.* 171 rooms, 2 story. Pets accepted, some restrictions; fee. Complimentary full breakfast. Check-out noon. TV; cable (premium). Restaurant. Room service. Pool; children's pool. **$**

D 🐾 🏊 🖂 SC

South Dakota

Aberdeen

Motels/Motor Lodges

★ ★ **BEST WESTERN RAMKOTA HOTEL.** *1400 NW 8th Ave (57401). Phone 605/229-4040; toll-free 800/528-1234; fax 605/229-0480. www.bestwestern.com.* 154 rooms, 2 story. Pets accepted, some restrictions. Check-out noon. TV. Restaurant, bar. Health club privileges. Sauna. Indoor pool; children's pool; whirlpool. Cross-country ski 2 miles. Free airport, train station, bus depot transportation. **$**

★ **RAMADA INN.** *2727 SE 6th Ave (57401). Phone 605/225-3600; toll-free 800/272-6232; fax 605/225-6704. www.ramada.com.* 153 rooms, 2 story. Pets accepted. Check-out 11 am. TV. Restaurant, bar. Room service. Indoor pool. Cross-country ski 1 mile. Free airport transportation. **$**

★ **WHITE HOUSE INN.** *500 SW 6th Ave (57402). Phone 605/225-5000; toll-free 800/225-6000; fax 605/225-6730.* 96 rooms, 3 story. Pets accepted; fee. Complimentary continental breakfast. Check-out 11 am. TV. Cross-country ski 1 1/2 miles. Airport transportation. **$**

Beresford

Motel/Motor Lodge

★ **CROSSROADS.** *1409 W Cedar St (57004). Phone 605/763-2020; fax 605/763-2504.* 32 rooms. Pets accepted, some restrictions; fee. Check-out 11 am. TV. **$**

Brookings

Motels/Motor Lodges

★ ★ **BROOKINGS INN.** *2500 E 6th St (57006). Phone 605/692-9471; toll-free 877/831-1562; fax 605/692-5807. www.brookingsinn.net.* 125 rooms, 2 story. Pets accepted, some restrictions. Complimentary continental breakfast. Check-out noon. TV. In-room modem link. Laundry services. Restaurant, bar; entertainment. Room service. In-house fitness room; sauna. Indoor pool; whirlpool. Cross-country ski 1 1/2 miles. Free airport transportation. Business center. **$**

★ ★ **QUALITY INN.** *2515 E 6th St (57006). Phone 605/692-9421; toll-free 800/228-5151; fax 605/692-9421. www.qualityinn.com.* 102 rooms, 2 story. Pets accepted; fee. Complimentary continental breakfast. Check-out 11 am. TV. In-room modem link. Restaurant, bar; entertainment. Room service. Health club privileges. Indoor pool; children's pool; whirlpool. Cross-country ski 1 mile. Free airport transportation. **$**

Chamberlain

Motel/Motor Lodge

★ **OASIS KELLY INN.** *1100 E Hwy 16 (57365). Phone 605/734-6061; toll-free 800/635-3559; fax 605/734-4161.* 69 rooms, 2 story. Pets accepted, some restrictions. Complimentary continental breakfast. Check-out 11 am. TV; cable (premium). Laundry services. Bar. Sauna. Pool; whirlpool. Miniature golf. Airport transportation. Pond. On river. **$**

Custer

Motels/Motor Lodges

★ ★ **BAVARIAN INN.** *Hwy 16 and 385 N (57730). Phone 605/673-2802; toll-free 800/657-4312; fax 605/673-4777. www.custer-sd.com/bavarian.* 65 rooms, 2 story. Pets accepted, some restrictions; fee. Check-out noon, check-in 2 pm. TV; cable (premium). Sauna. Game room. Two pools; whirlpool. Outdoor tennis, lighted courts. Lawn games. Parking. **$**

★ ★ **STATE GAME LODGE.** *Hwy 16A; Custer State Park (57730). Phone 605/255-4541; toll-free 800/658-3530; fax 605/255-4706. www.custerresorts.com.* 68 rooms, 2 and 3 story. No A/C in cabins, lodge, motel units. Some room phones. Closed Oct-Apr. Pets accepted, some restrictions; fee. Check-out 10 am, check-in 2 pm. TV. Restaurant, bar. Hiking trails. Parking. **$**

★ ★ **SYLVAN LAKE RESORT.** *HC 83, Box 74 (57730). Phone 605/574-2561; fax 605/574-4943. www.custerresorts.com.* 33 rooms, 3 story. No A/C. Closed

Oct-Apr. Pets accepted, some restrictions; fee. Check-out 10 am, check-in 2 pm. TV. Restaurant. Paddleboats. Hiking. Parking. **$**

D 🐾 🏊 ⊠

Hill City

Motel/Motor Lodge

★ ★ **BEST WESTERN GOLDEN SPIKE INN & SUITES.** *106 Main St (57745). Phone 605/574-2577; fax 605/574-4719. www.bestwesterngoldenspikeinn.com.* 80 rooms, 2 story. Closed Dec-Mar. Pets accepted, some restrictions; fee. Check-out 11 am, check-in 3 pm. TV. In-room modem link. Restaurant. In-house fitness room. Game room. Pool; whirlpool. Bicycle rentals. **$**

D 🐾 🏊 ✗ ⊠ SC

Huron

Motels/Motor Lodges

★ ★ **CROSSROADS HOTEL & CONVENTION CENTER.** *100 4th St SW (57350). Phone 605/352-3204; toll-free 800/876-5858. www.crossroadshotel.com.* This hotel is located near downtown in an area that gives a small town feeling with many shops and restaurants. 100 rooms, 3 story. Pets accepted, some restrictions; fee. Check-out 11 am. TV. In-room modem link. Restaurant, bar. Room service. Health club privileges. Sauna. Indoor pool; whirlpool; poolside service. Airport transportation. **$**

D 🐾 🏊 ⊠ SC

★ ★ **DAKOTA PLAINS INN.** *924 NE 4th St (57350). Phone 605/352-1400; toll-free 800/648-3735.* 77 rooms, 2 story. Pets accepted; fee. Check-out 11 am. TV. In-room modem link. Bar. Pool. Cross-country ski 1 1/2 miles. **$**

🐾 🏊 ⊠ ⊠

Keystone

Motel/Motor Lodge

★ **RUSHMORE EXPRESS.** *610 US 16A (57751). Phone 605/666-4483; fax 605/666-4883. www.rushmoreexpress.com.* 44 rooms, 2 story. Closed Nov-Apr. Pets accepted, some restrictions; fee. Complimentary continental breakfast. Check-out 11 am, check-in 3 pm. TV. Laundry services. In-house fitness room; sauna. Whirlpool. Parking. **$**

D 🐾 ✗ ⊠

Lead

Motel/Motor Lodge

★ ★ **GOLDEN HILLS INN.** *900 Miners Ave (57754). Phone 605/584-1800; toll-free 888/465-3080; fax 605/584-3933.* 96 rooms, 5 story. Pets accepted, some restrictions; fee. Check-out 11 am, check-in 3 pm. TV; cable (premium). Laundry services. Restaurant, bar. Downhill, cross-country ski 3 miles. Parking. **$**

D 🐾 🏊 ⊠

Madison

Motel/Motor Lodge

★ **SUPER 8.** *Junction of Hwys 34 and 81 (57042). Phone 605/256-6931; toll-free 800/800-8000. www.super8.com.* 34 rooms, 2 story. Pets accepted; fee. Check-out 11 am. TV. **$**

D 🐾 ⊠

Milbank

Motel/Motor Lodge

★ ★ **IMA MANOR MOTEL.** *E Hwy 12 (57252). Phone 605/432-4527; fax 605/432-4529.* 30 rooms, 1-2 story. Pets accepted. Check-out 11 am. TV. Restaurant. Sauna. Indoor pool; whirlpool. **$**

🐾 🏊 ⊠ SC

Mitchell

Motels/Motor Lodges

★ **COACHLIGHT.** *1000 W Havens St (57301). Phone 605/996-5686; fax 605/996-2798.* 20 rooms. Pets accepted, some restrictions. Check-out 11 am. TV. Cross-country ski 1 1/2 miles. Airport, bus depot transportation. **$**

D 🐾 🦮 🏊 ✗ ⊠

★ ★ **HOLIDAY INN.** *1525 W Havens St (57301). Phone 605/996-6501; toll-free 800/888-4702; fax 609/996-3228. www.holiday-inn.com.* 153 rooms, 2 story. Pets accepted; fee. Check-out noon. TV. In-room modem link. Laundry services. Restaurant, bar. Room service. Sauna. Indoor pool; children's pool; whirlpool; poolside service. Free airport, bus depot transportation. **$**

D 🐾 🏊 ✗ ⊠

★ **MOTEL 6.** *1309 S Ohlman St (57301). Phone 605/996-0530; fax 605/995-2019. www.motel6.com.* 122 rooms. Pets accepted, some restrictions. Check-out noon. TV. Pool. Cross-country ski 2 miles. **$**

⬚ 🐾 ➤ ⤢ ⊠

Pierre

Motels/Motor Lodges

★★ **BEST WESTERN RAMKOTA HOTEL.** *920 W Sioux Ave (57501). Phone 605/224-6877; fax 605/224-1042. www.ramkota.com.* 151 rooms, 2 story. Pets accepted. Check-out noon. TV. Laundry services. Restaurant, bar. Room service. In-house fitness room; sauna. Game room. Indoor pool; children's pool; whirlpool. Free airport, train station, bus depot transportation. At Missouri River. **$**

⬚ 🐾 ⚓ ⛄ 🏃 ⚓ ✈ ⊠

★ **CAPITOL INN & SUITES.** *815 E Wells Ave (57501). Phone 605/224-6387; toll-free 800/658-3055; fax 605/224-8083.* 83 rooms, 2 story. Pets accepted, some restrictions. Check-out 11 am. TV. Pool. **$**

⬚ 🐾 ➤ ⊠

★★ **KINGS INN HOTEL AND CONVENTION CENTER.** *220 S Pierre St (57501). Phone 605/224-5951; toll-free 800/232-1112; fax 605/224-5301.* 104 rooms, 2 story. Pets accepted, some restrictions; fee. Check-out 11 am. TV. Restaurant, bar. Room service. Sauna. Whirlpool. Cross-country ski 1 mile. **$**

🐾 ➤ ⊠

★ **SUPER 8.** *320 W Sioux Ave (57501). Phone 605/224-1617; fax 605/224-1617. www.super8.com.* 78 rooms, 3 story. Pets accepted, some restrictions; fee. Check-out 11 am. TV; cable (premium), VCR available. **$**

⬚ 🐾 ⚓ ⚓ ⊠

Platte

Motel/Motor Lodge

★ **KINGS INN OF PLATTE.** *221 E 7th St (57369). Phone 605/337-3385; toll-free 800/337-7756.* 34 rooms. Pets accepted, some restrictions; fee. Complimentary continental breakfast. Check-out 10 am. TV. **$**

🐾 ⊠

Rapid City

Motels/Motor Lodges

★ **FAIR VALUE INN.** *1607 N Lacrosse St (57701). Phone 605/342-8118; toll-free 800/954-8118.* 27 rooms, 2 story. Pets accepted, some restrictions. Check-out 11 am, check-in 1 pm. TV; cable (premium). Free parking. **$**

⬚ 🐾 ⊠ SC

★ **HOLIDAY INN EXPRESS.** *750 Cathedral Dr (57701). Phone 605/341-9300; fax 605/341-9333. www.holiday-inn.com.* 63 rooms, 3 story. Pets accepted, some restrictions. Complimentary continental breakfast. Check-out 11 am, check-in 3 pm. TV; cable (premium). In-room modem link. Laundry services. Indoor pool; whirlpool. Free parking. Airport transportation. **$**

⬚ 🐾 ➤ ✈ ⊠

★ **RAMADA INN.** *1721 N Lacrosse St (57701). Phone 605/342-1300; fax 605/342-0663. www.ramadamtrushmore.com.* 139 rooms, 4 story. Pets accepted; fee. Complimentary continental breakfast. Check-out noon, check-in 2 pm. TV; cable (premium). In-room modem link. Laundry services. Room service 24 hours. Restaurant open 24 hours. Bar. In-house fitness room; massage. Game room. Indoor pool; whirlpool. Free parking. **$**

⬚ 🐾 ➤ 🏃 ⊠ SC

★ **SUPER 8.** *2124 N Lacrosse St (57701). Phone 605/348-8070; fax 605/348-0833. www.super8.com.* 118 rooms, 3 story. No elevator. Pets accepted, some restrictions; fee. Complimentary continental breakfast. Check-out 11 am, check-in 3 pm. TV; cable (premium), VCR available (movies). In-room modem link. Game room. Free parking. **$**

⬚ 🐾 ⊠

Hotels

★★ **ALEX JOHNSON.** *523 Sixth St (57701). Phone 605/342-1210; toll-free 800/888-2539. www.alexjohnson.com.* 143 rooms, 10 story. Pets accepted, some restrictions; fee. Check-out 11 am, check-in 4 pm. TV; cable (premium). Laundry services. Restaurant, bar; entertainment Fri, Sat. Room service. Valet parking, free parking. Airport transportation. Concierge. **$**

⬚ 🐾 ⊠

★ ★ **HOLIDAY INN.** *505 N 5th St (57701). Phone 605/348-4000; fax 605/348-9777. www.holiday-inn.com.* 204 rooms, 8 story. Pets accepted; fee. Check-out 1 pm, check-in 3 pm. TV; cable (premium). In-room modem link. Laundry services. Restaurant, bar. Room service. In-house fitness room; sauna. Indoor pool; whirlpool; poolside service. Free parking. Free airport transportation. Business center. **$**

⬛🐾🏊🏃✈🈂🚶

Sioux Falls

Motels/Motor Lodges

★ **BAYMONT INN.** *3200 S Meadow Ave (57106). Phone 605/362-0835; fax 605/362-0836. www.baymontinns.com.* 82 rooms, 3 story. Pets accepted; fee. Check-out 11 am. TV; cable (premium). Indoor pool; whirlpool. Cross-country ski 2 miles. **$**

⬛🐾🏊🏊🈂

★ ★ **BEST WESTERN RAMKOTA HOTEL.** *2400 N Louise Ave (57107). Phone 605/336-0650; toll-free 800/528-1234; fax 605/336-1687. www.ramkota.com.* 226 rooms, 2 story. Pets accepted, some restrictions. Check-out 11 am. TV; cable (premium), VCR available. Restaurant, bar. Room service. Sauna. Game room. Two pools; whirlpool. Cross-country ski 2 miles. Free airport transportation. **$**

⬛🐾🏊🏊✈🈂

★ **BUDGET HOST INN.** *2620 E 10th St (57103). Phone 605/336-1550; fax 605/338-4752. www.budgethost.com.* 36 rooms. Pets accepted, some restricitons. Check-out 11 am. TV. **$**

🐾🈂

★ **COMFORT INN.** *3216 S Carolyn Ave (57106). Phone 605/361-2822; toll-free 800/638-7949; fax 605/361-2822. www.comfortinn.com.* 67 rooms, 2 story. Pets accepted; fee. Complimentary continental breakfast. Check-out 11 am. TV; cable (premium). Game room. Indoor pool; whirlpool. **$**

⬛🐾🏊🈂SC

★ **COMFORT INN.** *3208 Carolyn Ave (57106). Phone 605/362-9711; fax 605/362-9711. www.comfortinn.com.* 61 rooms, 3 story. Pets accepted; fee. Complimentary continental breakfast. Check-out 11 am. TV; cable (premium). Indoor pool; whirlpool. Cross-country ski 1 mile. **$**

⬛🐾🏊🏊🈂

★ **ECONO LODGE.** *1300 W Russell St (57104). Phone 605/331-5800; toll-free 800/55-ECONO; fax 605/331-4074. www.econolodge.com.* 105 rooms, 2 story. Pets accepted. Complimentary continental breakfast. Check-out 11 am. TV. Laundry services. In-house fitness room. Cross-country ski 1 1/2 miles. **$**

⬛🐾🏊🏃🈂

★ ★ **KELLY INN–SIOUX FALLS.** *3101 W Russell (57107). Phone 605/338-6242; fax 605/338-5453. www.kellyinns.com.* 43 rooms, 2 story. Pets accepted, some restrictions. Complimentary continental breakfast. Check-out 11 am. TV. Laundry services. Sauna. Whirlpool. Airport transportation. **$**

⬛🐾🏃✈🈂SC

★ **MOTEL 6.** *3009 W Russell St (57107). Phone 605/336-7800; fax 605/330-9273. www.motel6.com.* 87 rooms, 2 story. Pets accepted. Check-out noon. TV. Pool. **$**

⬛🐾🏊🈂

★ ★ **OAKS HOTEL.** *3300 W Russell St (57107). Phone 605/336-9000; toll-free 800/326-4656.* 200 rooms, 2 story. Pets accepted, some restrictions. Check-out noon. TV. Laundry services. Restaurant, bar; entertainment. Room service. Sauna. Game room. Indoor, outdoor pool; whirlpool. Cross-country ski 1 mile. Free airport, bus depot transportation. **$**

⬛🐾🏊🏊✈🈂

★ **RAMADA INN.** *1301 W Russell St (57104). Phone 605/336-1020; toll-free 888/298-2054; fax 605/336-3030. www.ramada.com.* 200 rooms, 2 story. Pets accepted, some restrictions; fee. Complimentary continental breakfast. Check-out noon. TV. In-room modem link. Restaurant, bar; entertainment. Room service. Game room. Indoor pool; whirlpool. Sauna. Free airport transportation. **$**

⬛🐾🏊🏊✈🈂

★ **SELECT INN.** *3500 Gateway Blvd (57106). Phone 605/361-1864; toll-free 800/641-1000; fax 605/361-9287. www.selectinn.com.* 100 rooms, 2 story. Pets accepted, some restrictions; fee. Complimentary continental breakfast. Check-out 11 am. TV; VCR available (movies). **$**

⬛🐾🈂SC

★ **SUPER 8.** *1508 W Russell St (57104). Phone 605/339-9330. www.super8.com.* 95 rooms, 3 story. No elevator. Pets accepted, some restrictions; fee. Complimentary continental breakfast. Check-out 11 am. TV; cable (premium). In-room modem link. Cross-country ski 1 mile. **$**

🐾🏊

Sisseton

Motel/Motor Lodge

★ **HOLIDAY MOTEL.** *E Hwy 10 and 127 (57262). Phone 605/698-7644; toll-free 888/460-9548; fax 605/742-0487.* 19 rooms. Pets accepted, some restrictions; fee. Check-out 11 am. TV. **$**

Ⓓ 🐾 ⊠

Spearfish

Motels/Motor Lodges

★ **BEST WESTERN BLACK HILLS LODGE.** *540 E Jackson (57783). Phone 605/642-7795; fax 605/642-7751.* 49 rooms, 2 story. Pets accepted; fee. Complimentary continental breakfast. Check-out 11 am. TV; cable (premium). Laundry services. Sauna. Whirlpool. **$**

Ⓓ 🐾 ⚓ 🕸 ⊠

★ **DAYS INN.** *240 Ryan Rd (57783). Phone 605/642-7101; toll-free 800/329-7466; fax 605/642-7120. www.daysinn.com.* 50 rooms, 2 story. Pets accepted; fee. Complimentary continental breakfast. Check-out 11 am, check-in 2 pm. TV; cable (premium). Free parking. **$**

Ⓓ 🐾 ⚓ ⊠

★ ★ **HOLIDAY INN.** *305 N 27th St (57783). Phone 605/642-4683; toll-free 800/999-3541; fax 605/642-0203. www.holidayinn-spearfish.com.* 145 rooms, 2 story. Pets accepted, some restrictions; fee. Check-out noon, check-in 4 pm. TV; cable (premium). In-room modem link. Laundry services. Restaurant, bar. Room service. In-house fitness room. Game room. Indoor pool; whirlpools. Downhill ski 15 miles. Free parking. **$**

Ⓓ 🐾 ☂ 🏊 🏋 ⊠ SC

★ **SPEARFISH CANYON RESORT.** *106 Roughlock Falls Rd (57754). Phone 605/584-3435; toll-free 877/975-6343; fax 605/584-3990. www.spfcanyon.com.* 55 rooms, 2 story. Pets accepted; fee. Check-out 11 am, check-in 3 pm. TV; cable (premium). In-room modem link. Laundry services. Restaurant, bar. Room service. Massage. Whirlpool. Downhill ski 6 miles, cross-country ski 8 miles. Bicycle rentals. Free parking. Concierge. **$**

Ⓓ 🐾 🐆 ⊠

Sturgis

Motel/Motor Lodge

★ **DAYS INN.** *HC 55, Box 3488 (57785). Phone 605/347-3027; fax 605/720-0313. www.daysinn.com.* 53 rooms, 2 story. Pets accepted, some restrictions; fee. Complimentary continental breakfast. Check-out 11 am, check-in 2 pm. TV. Laundry services. Whirlpool. Free parking. **$**

Ⓓ 🐾 ⊠

Vermillion

Motel/Motor Lodge

★ **COMFORT INN.** *701 W Cherry St (57069). Phone 605/624-8333; toll-free 800/228-5150; fax 605/624-8333. www.comfortinn.com.* 46 rooms, 2 story. Pets accepted; fee. Complimentary continental breakfast. Check-out 10 am. TV; cable (premium). In-house fitness room; sauna. Indoor pool; whirlpool. **$**

Ⓓ 🐾 🏊 🏋 ⊠ SC

Wall

Motels/Motor Lodges

★ **BEST WESTERN PLAINS MOTEL.** *712 Glenn St (57790). Phone 605/279-2145; fax 605/279-2977. www.bestwestern.com/plains.* 74 rooms, 2 story. Closed Dec-Feb. Pets accepted; fee. Check-out 11 am. TV; cable (premium). In-room modem link. Game room. Outdoor pool. Free parking. **$**

🐾 🏊 ⊠

★ **DAYS INN.** *210 Tenth Ave and Norris (57790). Phone 605/279-2000; fax 605/279-2004. www.daysinn.com.* 32 rooms, 2 story. Pets accepted, some restrictions; fee. Check-out 11 am, check-in noon. TV; cable (premium). Sauna. Whirlpool. Free parking. **$**

Ⓓ 🐾 ⊠ SC

Watertown

Motels/Motor Lodges

★ ★ **BEST WESTERN RAMKOTA HOTEL.** *1901 SW 9th Ave (57201). Phone 605/886-8011; toll-free 800/528-1234; fax 605/886-3667. www.ramoka.com.* 101 rooms, 2 story. Pets accepted, some restrictions. Check-out noon. TV. In-room modem link. Restaurant, bar. Room service. Sauna. Indoor pool; whirlpool. Free airport, bus depot transportation. **$**

🄳 ➔ ☖ ✈ 🕾

★ **TRAVELERS INN.** *920 SE 14th St (57201). Phone 605/882-2243; toll-free 800/568-7074; fax 605/882-0968.* 50 rooms, 2 story. Pets accepted. Complimentary continental breakfast. Check-out 11 am. TV. **$**

🄳 ➔ 🕾

★ **TRAVEL HOST.** *1714 SW 9th Ave (57201). Phone 605/886-6120; toll-free 800/658-5512; fax 605/886-5352.* 29 rooms, 2 story. Pets accepted, some restrictions. Complimentary continental breakfast. Check-out 11 am. TV. **$**

🄳 ➔ 🏃 ✈ 🕾

Winner

Motel/Motor Lodge

★ **BUFFALO TRAIL MOTEL.** *1030 W 2nd St (57580). Phone 605/842-2212; toll-free 800/485-0868; fax 605/842-3199. www.buffalotrailmotel.com.* 31 rooms. Pets accepted. Complimentary continental breakfast. Check-out 11 am. TV. Pool. Free airport transportation. **$**

🄳 ➔ ☖ 🕾

Yankton

Motels/Motor Lodges

★ **BEST WESTERN KELLY INN.** *1607 E SD 50 (57078). Phone 605/665-2906; fax 605/665-4318. www.bestwestern.com.* 123 rooms, 2 story. Pets accepted, some restrictions. Check-out 11 am. TV. In-house fitness room. Game room. Indoor pool; children's pool; whirlpool. **$**

🄳 ➔ ☖ 🏃 🕾

★ **BROADWAY INN MOTEL.** *1210 Broadway Ave (57078). Phone 605/665-7805; toll-free 800/336-3087; fax 605/668-9519.* 37 rooms. Pets accepted, some restrictions; fee. Check-out 11 am. TV; cable (premium), VCR available. Bar. Pool. Cross-country ski 1 mile. **$**

➔ 🏃 ☖

★ **RAMADA INN.** *2118 Broadway St (57078). Phone 605/665-8053; fax 605/665-8165. www.ramada.com.* 45 rooms, 2 story. Pets accepted; fee. Complimentary continental breakfast. Check-out 11 am. TV. In-room modem link. Whirlpool. **$**

🄳 ➔ 🕾

Tennessee

Caryville

Motels/Motor Lodges

★ **BUDGET HOST INN.** *115 Woods Ave (37714). Phone 423/562-9595; toll-free 800/283-4678; fax 423/566-0515. www.budgethost.com.* 22 rooms, 2 story. Pets accepted, some restrictions; fee. Check-out 10:30 am. TV; cable (premium). **$**

★ **SUPER 8.** *200 John McGhee Blvd (37714). Phone 423/562-8476; fax 423/562-8870. www.super8.com.* 98 rooms, 2 story. Pets accepted; fee. Complimentary continental breakfast. Check-out noon. TV; cable (premium). Pool; children's pool. **$**

Celina

Resort

★ **CEDAR HILL RESORT.** *2371 Cedar Hill Rd (38551). Phone 931/243-3201; toll-free 800/872-8393; fax 931/243-4892. www.cedarhillresort.com.* 47 rooms. Pets accepted; fee. Check-out 10 am, check-in 1 pm. TV. Dining room. Snack bar. Pool. Lawn games. Boats, motors, guides; waterskiing. **$**

Chattanooga

Motels/Motor Lodges

★ **BEST INN.** *7717 Lee Hwy (37421). Phone 423/894-5454; fax 423/499-9597. www.bestinn.com.* 64 rooms, 2 story. Pets accepted; fee. Complimentary continental breakfast. Check-out 11 am. TV; cable (premium). Pool. **$**

★ **DAYS INN.** *7725 Lee Hwy (37421). Phone 423/899-2288; toll-free 800/453-4511. www.daysinn.com.* 80 rooms, 2 story. Pets accepted, some restrictions; fee. Complimentary continental breakfast. Check-out 11 am. TV; cable (premium). Indoor pool; whirlpool. **$**

★ **ECONO LODGE.** *1417 St. Thomas St (37412). Phone 423/894-1417; toll-free 800/424-4777; fax 423/821-6840. www.econolodge.com.* 89 rooms, 2 story. Pets accepted, some restrictions; fee. Complimentary continental breakfast. Check-out 11 am. TV; cable (premium). Pool. **$**

★ ★ **KING'S LODGE MOTEL.** *2400 Westside Dr (37404). Phone 423/698-8944; toll-free 800/251-7702; fax 423/698-8949.* 138 rooms, 2 story. Pets accepted, some restrictions; fee. Check-out 11 am. TV; cable (premium). Restaurant, bar. Room service. Pool. **$**

★ **LA QUINTA INN.** *7015 Shallowford Rd (37421). Phone 423/855-0011; toll-free 800/687-6667; fax 423/499-5409. www.laquinta.com.* 132 rooms, 2 story. Pets accepted, some restrictions. Complimentary continental breakfast. Check-out noon. TV; cable (premium). Health club privileges. Pool. **$**

★ **RED ROOF INN.** *7014 Shallowford Rd (37421). Phone 423/899-0143; toll-free 800/843-7663; fax 423/899-8384. www.redroof.com.* 112 rooms, 2 story. Pets accepted. Check-out noon. TV; cable (premium). **$**

★ **SUPER 8.** *20 Birmingham Hwy (37419). Phone 423/821-8880; toll-free 800/800-8000. www.super8.com.* 74 rooms, 3 story. Pets accepted, some restrictions; fee. Check-out 11 am. TV; cable (premium). Laundry services. **$**

Clarksville

Motels/Motor Lodges

★ **DAYS INN.** *1100 Connector Rd (Hwy 76) (37043). Phone 931/358-3194; toll-free 800/329-7466; fax 931/358-9869. www.daysinn.com.* 84 rooms, 2 story. Pets accepted, some restrictions; fee. Complimentary continental breakfast. Check-out 11 am. TV; cable (premium). Pool. **$**

★ ★ **QUALITY INN.** *803 N 2nd St (37040). Phone 931/645-9084; toll-free 800/228-5151; fax 931/645-9084. www.qualityinn.com.* 130 rooms, 2 story. Pets accepted; fee. Complimentary continental breakfast. Check-out noon. TV; cable (premium). Laundry services. Bar. Sauna. Indoor pool; whirlpool. **$**

Cleveland

Motels/Motor Lodges

★ ★ **HOLIDAY INN.** *2400 Executive Park Dr NW (37312). Phone 423/472-1504; fax 423/479-5962. www. holiday-inn.com.* 146 rooms, 2 story. Pets accepted, some restrictions; fee. Check-out noon. TV; cable (premium). Restaurant. Room service. Health club privileges. Pool. **$**

★ ★ **QUALITY INN.** *2595 Georgetown Rd NW (37311). Phone 423/476-8511; toll-free 800/228-5151. www.qualityinn.com.* 97 rooms, 2-3 story. No elevator. Pets accepted; fee. Check-out noon. TV; cable (premium). Laundry services. Restaurant. Pool; children's pool. **$**

Columbia

Motel/Motor Lodge

★ **RAMADA INN.** *1208 Nashville Hwy (38401). Phone 931/388-2720; fax 931/388-2360. www.ramada.com.* 155 rooms, 2 story. Pets accepted; fee. Check-out noon. TV; cable (premium), VCR available. Restaurant, bar. Room service. Pool.

Cookeville

Motels/Motor Lodges

★ ★ **ALPINE LODGE & SUITES.** *2021 E Spring St (38506). Phone 931/526-3333; toll-free 800/213-2016; fax 931/528-9036. www.alpinelodge.org.* 64 rooms, 2 story. Pets accepted, some restrictions; fee. Complimentary continental breakfast. Check-out noon. TV; cable (premium), VCR available. In-room modem link. Laundry services. Restaurant. Pool; children's pool. **$**

★ **BEST WESTERN THUNDERBIRD MOTEL.** *900 S Jefferson Ave (38501). Phone 931/526-7115; toll-free 800/528-1234. www.bestwestern.com.* 76 rooms, 3 story. Pets accepted. Complimentary continental breakfast. Check-out noon. TV. In-house fitness room. Pool. **$**

★ **ECONO LODGE.** *1100 S Jefferson Ave (38506). Phone 931/528-1040; fax 931/528-5227. www.econolodge.com.* 71 air-cooled rooms, 2 story. Pets accepted; fee. Complimentary continental breakfast. Check-out 11 am. TV; cable (premium). Pool. **$**

★ ★ **HOLIDAY INN.** *970 S Jefferson Ave (38501). Phone 931/526-7125; fax 931/372-8508. www.holiday-inn.com.* This property is located 1 mile from downtown near the Cookeville Mall, and is within easy traveling distance of recreational areas. 200 rooms, 2-3 story. Pets accepted. Check-out noon. TV; cable (premium). In-room modem link. Restaurant, bar. Room service. In-house fitness room. Game room. Indoor, outdoor pool; whirlpool. Business center. **$**

Crossville

Motel/Motor Lodge

★ **DAYS INN.** *105 Executive Dr (38555). Phone 931/484-9691. www.daysinn.com.* 61 rooms, 2 story. Pets accepted; fee. Complimentary continental breakfast. Check-out 11 am. TV; cable (premium). Pool. On river. **$**

Franklin

Motel/Motor Lodge

★ **BEST WESTERN FRANKLIN INN.** *1308 Murfreesboro Rd (37064). Phone 615/790-0570; toll-free 800/251-3200; fax 615/790-0512. www.bestwesternfranklin.com.* 142 rooms, 2 story. Pets accepted, some restrictions. Complimentary continental breakfast. Check-out noon. TV; cable (premium). Pool. **$**

Gatlinburg

Motels/Motor Lodges

★ ★ **BEST WESTERN NEWPORT INN.** *1015 Cosby Hwy (37822). Phone 423/623-8713; toll-free 800/251-4022; fax 423/423-1804. www.bestwestern.com.* 111 rooms, 2 story. Pets accepted, some restrictions. Complimentary full breakfast. Check-out noon. TV; cable (premium). Restaurant. Pool; children's pool; whirlpool. **$**

★ **BON AIR LODGE.** *950 Parkway (37738). Phone 865/ 436-4857; toll-free 800/523-3919. www.smokymountain resort.com.* 74 rooms, 3 story. Pets accepted. Check-out 11 am. TV. Pool. Downhill ski 1 mile. **$**

D 🐾 ➤ ➳ ➳ SC

★ ★ **HOLIDAY INN.** *520 Historic Nature Trail (37738). Phone 865/436-9201; fax 865/436-7974. www.holiday- inn.com.* Just 2 blocks from downtown, this resort is adjacent to the Great Smoky Mountain National Park. Hop the convenient trolley for a short ride to Dollywood, music shows, theaters and shops. LeConte Creek winds through this mountain retreat. 402 rooms, 8 story. Pets accepted; fee. Check-out 11 am. TV; cable (premium). Laundry services. Restaurant, bar. Room service. Supervised children's activities (summer); ages 3-12. In- house fitness room. Indoor, outdoor pool; children's pool. Downhill ski 4 miles. **$**

D 🐾 🏋 ➤ ➤ ➳ ➳ SC

Greeneville

Motel/Motor Lodge

★ **DAYS INN.** *935 E Andrew Johnson Hwy (37743). Phone 423/639-2156. www.daysinn.com.* 60 rooms, 2 story. Pets accepted, some restrictions; fee. Complimentary continental breakfast. Check-out 11 am. TV; cable (premium). **$**

🐾 ➳ SC

Harrogate

Motel/Motor Lodge

★ ★ **RAMADA INN.** *TN 58 (37724). Phone 423/869- 3631; fax 423/869-5953. www.ramada.com.* 147 rooms, 4 story. Pets accepted; fee. Check-out noon. TV; cable (pre- mium), VCR available. Laundry services. Restaurant, bar. Room service. Pool. **$**

D 🐾 ➤ ➳

Hurricane Mills

Motels/Motor Lodges

★ ★ **BEST WESTERN OF HURRICANE MILLS.** *15542 TN 135 (37078). Phone 931/296-4251; fax 931/ 296-9104. www.bestwestern.com.* 89 rooms, 2 story. Pets accepted; fee. Check-out 11 am. TV; cable (premium), VCR available (movies). Restaurant. Pool; whirlpool. **$**

D 🐾 🏋 ➳ ➳

★ **DAYS INN.** *15415 TN 13 S (37078). Phone 931/ 296-7647; toll-free 800/329-7466; fax 931/296-5488. www.daysinn.com.* 78 rooms, 2 story. Pets accepted, some restrictions; fee. Check-out noon. TV; cable (premium). Restaurant. Pool. **$**

D 🐾 ➳ ➳ SC

Jackson

Motel/Motor Lodge

★ ★ **OLD HICKORY INN.** *1849 US 45 Bypass (38305). Phone 731/668-4222; toll-free 800/528-1234; fax 731/664- 8536. www.bestwestern.com.* 141 rooms, 2 story. Pets accepted, some restrictions; fee. Check-out noon. TV; cable (premium). Restaurant, bar; entertainment. Room service. Pool; children's pool. **$**

D 🐾 ➳ ➳ SC

Johnson City

Motels/Motor Lodges

★ **BEST WESTERN JOHNSON CITY HOTEL & CONFERENCE CENTER.** *2406 N Roan St (37601). Phone 423/282-2161; toll-free 877/504-1007; fax 423/282- 2488. www.hojo.com.* 197 rooms, 2-4 story. Pets accepted; fee. Check-out noon. TV; cable (premium). Laundry services. Restaurant, bar. Room service. Health club privi- leges. Pool. Free airport transportation. **$**

D 🐾 🏋 ➤ ➳ ✈ ➳

★ **DAYS INN.** *2312 Browns Mill Rd (37604). Phone 423/282-2211; toll-free 800/329-7466; fax 423/282-6111. www.daysinn.com.* 100 rooms, 2 story. Pets accepted, some restrictions; fee. Complimentary continental breakfast. Check-out 11 am. TV. Pool. **$**

🐾 🏋 ➳ ➳

Hotel

★ ★ ★ **GARDEN PLAZA–JOHNSON CITY.** *211 Mockingbird Ln (37604). Phone 423/929-2000; toll-free 800/342-7336; fax 423/929-1783. www.gardenplazahotel .com.* This hotel is adjacent to The Mall and convenient to the Rocky Mountain Museum and historic Jonesborough, Tennessee's first township. 186 rooms, 5 story. Pets accepted. Check-out noon. TV; VCR available (movies). Restaurant, bar. Room service. Indoor, outdoor pool; poolside service. Free airport transportation. Business center. Luxury level. **$**

D 🐾 ➳ ✈ ➳ 🏃

Kingsport

Motels/Motor Lodges

★ **COMFORT INN.** *100 Indian Center Ct (37660). Phone 423/378-4418; fax 423/246-5249. www.comfortinn.com.* 122 rooms, 2 story. Pets accepted, some restrictions; fee. Complimentary continental breakfast. Check-out noon. TV; cable (premium). Health club privileges. Sauna. Pool; whirlpool. **$**

[D] [pets] [pool] [no-smoking] [SC]

★ **ECONO LODGE.** *1704 E Stone Dr (37660). Phone 423/245-0286; toll-free 800/424-4777; fax 423/245-2985. www.econolodge.com.* 52. rooms, 2 story. Pets accepted, some restrictions; fee. Complimentary continental breakfast. Check-out 11 am. TV; cable (premium). **$**

[pets] [no-smoking] [SC]

Knoxville

Motels/Motor Lodges

★ **BAYMONT INN.** *11341 Campbell Lakes Dr (37922). Phone 865/671-1010; toll-free 800/301-0200; fax 865/675-5039. www.baymontinn.com.* 100 rooms, 3 story. Pets accepted, some restrictions. Complimentary continental breakfast. Check-out noon. TV; cable (premium), VCR available. In-house fitness room; sauna. Pool. **$**

[D] [pets] [pool] [fitness] [no-smoking] [SC]

★ ★ **BUDGET INNS OF AMERICA.** *323 Cedarbluff Rd (37923). Phone 865/693-7330; fax 865/693-7383.* 178 rooms, 2 story. Pets accepted; fee. Check-out noon. TV; cable (premium). Restaurant, bar; entertainment. Room service. Indoor pool. **$**

[D] [pets] [pool] [no-smoking] [SC]

★ **DAYS INN.** *200 Lovell Rd (37922). Phone 865/966-5801; fax 865/966-1755. www.daysinn.com.* 120 rooms, 2 story. Pets accepted, some restrictions; fee. Complimentary full breakfast. Check-out noon. TV; cable (premium). Pool. **$**

[D] [pets] [pool] [no-smoking]

★ ★ **HOLIDAY INN.** *1315 Kirby Rd (37909). Phone 865/584-3911; toll-free 800/854-8315; fax 865/588-0920. www.holiday-inn.com.* 240 rooms, 4 story. Pets accepted; fee. Check-out 11 am. TV; cable (premium). Restaurant, bar. Room service. Health club privileges. Pool; whirlpool. Free airport transportation. **$**

[D] [pets] [pool] [no-smoking]

★ **HOWARD JOHNSON.** *7621 Kingston Pike (37919). Phone 865/693-8111; fax 865/690-1031. www.hojo.com.* 162 rooms, 4 story. Pets accepted; fee. Check-out noon. TV; cable (premium). Restaurant, bar; entertainment. Room service. Pool. **$**

[D] [pets] [pool] [fitness] [pool] [no-smoking]

★ **LA QUINTA INN.** *258 Peters Rd N (37923). Phone 865/690-9777; toll-free 800/687-6667; fax 865/531-8304. www.laquinta.com.* 130 rooms, 3 story. Pets accepted. Complimentary continental breakfast. Check-out noon. TV. Laundry services. Health club privileges. Pool. **$**

[D] [pets] [pool] [no-smoking] [SC]

★ **SUPER 8.** *6200 Papermill Rd (37919). Phone 865/584-8511; fax 865/584. www.super8.com.* 139 rooms, 2-3 story. No elevator. Pets accepted. Complimentary continental breakfast. Check-out 11 am. TV; cable (premium). In-house fitness room. Pool; children's pool; whirlpool. **$**

[D] [pets] [pool] [fitness] [no-smoking] [SC]

Hotel

★ ★ **RADISSON SUMMIT HILL KNOXVILLE.** *401 Summit Hill Dr (37902). Phone 865/522-2600; toll-free 800/333-3333; fax 865/523-7200. www.radisson.com.* This hotel has a convenient location near many attractions including the historic shopping district and the Old City. 197 rooms, 12 story. Pets accepted, some restrictions; fee. Check-out noon. TV; VCR available. Restaurant, bar. In-house fitness room. Indoor pool. **$**

[D] [pets] [pool] [fitness] [no-smoking] [SC]

Lebanon

Motels/Motor Lodges

★ **BEST WESTERN EXECUTIVE INN.** *631 S Cumberland St (37087). Phone 615/444-0505; toll-free 800/528-1234; fax 615/449-8516. www.bestwestern.com.* 125 rooms, 2 story. Pets accepted, some restrictions. Check-out 11 am. TV; cable (premium). Sauna. Indoor, outdoor pool. **$**

[D] [pets] [pool] [no-smoking] [SC]

★ **DAYS INN.** *914 Murfreesboro Rd (37090). Phone 615/444-5635.* 52 rooms, 2 story. Pets accepted, some restrictions; fee. Complimentary continental breakfast. Check-out 11 am. TV; cable (premium). Laundry services. Pool. **$**

[D] [pets] [pool] [no-smoking]

★ **HAMPTON INN.** *704 S Cumberland St (37087). Phone 615/444-7400; fax 615/449-7969. www.hamptoninn.com.* 83 rooms, 2 story. Pets accepted, some restrictions.

Complimentary continental breakfast. Check-out 11 am. TV. Laundry services. In-house fitness room; sauna. Pool; whirlpool. $

Manchester

Motel/Motor Lodge

★ **SUPER 8.** 2430 Hillsboro Blvd (37355). Phone 931/728-9720; toll-free 800/800-8000. www.super8.com. 50 rooms, 2 story. Pets accepted; fee. Complimentary continental breakfast. Check-out 11 am. TV; cable (premium). Pool. $

Maryville

Motel/Motor Lodge

★ **PRINCESS MOTEL.** 2614 US Hwy 411 S (37801). Phone 865/982-2490; fax 865/984-1675. 33 rooms, 1-2 story. Pets accepted; fee. Check-out 11 am. TV; cable (premium). Pool. $

Memphis

Hotel

★ ★ ★ **THE PEABODY MEMPHIS.** 149 Union Ave (38103). Phone 901/529-4000; toll-free 800/732-2639; fax 901/529-3600. www.peabodymemphis.com. Located in downtown Memphis, this hotel is near many attractions, restaurants and businesses. It is also only two blocks from the river and offers a pool and full athletic club. 468 rooms, 13 story. Pets accepted, some restrictions; fee. Check-out 11 am, check-in 4 pm. TV; cable (premium), VCR available. In-room modem link. Room service 24 hours. Restaurant, bar. Babysitting services available. In-house fitness room; spa; massage; sauna; steam room. Health club privileges. Indoor pool; whirlpool. Business center. Concierge. $$

Monteagle

Motel/Motor Lodge

★ ★ **JIM OLIVER'S SMOKEHOUSE LODGE.** 850 Main St (37356). Phone 931/924-2268; toll-free 800/

489-2091; fax 931/924-3175. www.thesmokehouse.com. 85 rooms, 2 story. Pets accepted; fee. Check-out 11 am. TV; cable (premium). In-room modem link. Restaurant. Room service. Pool. Tennis. $

Morristown

Motels/Motor Lodges

★ **DAYS INN.** 2512 E Andrew Johnson Hwy (37814). Phone 423/587-2200; toll-free 800/329-7466; fax 423/587-9752. www.daysinn.com. 65 rooms, 2 story. Pets accepted, some restrictions. Complimentary continental breakfast. Check-out 11 am. TV; cable (premium). In-room modem link. $

★ ★ **HOLIDAY INN.** 5435 S Davy Crockett Pkwy (37815). Phone 423/587-2400; toll-free 800/465-4329; fax 423/581-7344. www.holiday-inn.com. 111 rooms, 3 story. No elevator. Pets accepted; fee. Check-out noon. TV. Restaurant. Room service. In-house fitness room. Game room. Two pools; children's pool. $

Murfreesboro

Motels/Motor Lodges

★ **HAMPTON INN.** 2230 Armory Dr (37129). Phone 615/896-1172; toll-free 800/426-7866; fax 615/895-4277. www.hamptoninn.com. 119 rooms, 2 story. Pets accepted, some restrictions. Complimentary continental breakfast. Check-out noon. TV; VCR available. Pool. $

★ ★ **HOLIDAY INN.** 2227 Old Park Pkwy (37129). Phone 615/896-2420; toll-free 800/465-4329; fax 615/896-8738. www.holiday-inn.com. 180 rooms, 4 story. Pets accepted, some restrictions. Check-out noon. TV; cable (premium). In-room modem link. Laundry services. Restaurant, bar. Room service. In-house fitness room. Game room. Indoor, outdoor pool; whirlpool. $

★ **HOWARD JOHNSON.** 2424 S Church St (37130). Phone 615/896-5522; toll-free 800/446-4656; fax 615/890-0024. www.hojo.com. 79 rooms, 2 story. Pets accepted, some restrictions; fee. Complimentary continental breakfast. Check-out 11 am. TV; cable (premium). Laundry services. Pool. $

★ **RAMADA INN.** *1855 S Church St (37130). Phone 615/896-5080; fax 615/898-0261. www.ramada.com.* 81 rooms, 2 story. Pets accepted; fee. Complimentary continental breakfast. Check-out noon. TV; cable (premium). Pool. **$**

D ◑ ⓚ ⚄ ≈ ⚐ ⊠

Hotel

★ ★ ★ **GARDEN PLAZA–MURFREESBORO.** *1850 Old Fort Pkwy (37129). Phone 615/895-5555; toll-free 800/342-7336; fax 615/895-3557.* Guests can enjoy the special attention to details, affordable rates, excellent dining, and quietly distinctive rooms. This hotel is conveniently located within minutes of business centers, hundreds of exciting Tennessee attractions, and the interstate system. 168 rooms, 5 story. Pets accepted; fee. Check-out noon. TV; cable (premium), VCR available. Restaurant, bar. Room service. Health club privileges. Indoor, outdoor pool; whirlpool; poolside service. **$**

D ◑ ≈ ⊠

Nashville

Motels/Motor Lodges

★ **AMERISUITES.** *220 Rudy's Cir (37214). Phone 615/872-0422; fax 615/872-9283. www.amerisuites.com.* 125 suites, 5 story. Pets accepted, some restrictions. Complimentary continental breakfast. Check-out 11 am, check-in 3 pm. TV; cable (premium), VCR available. In-house fitness room. Outdoor pool. Airport transportation. Business center. **$**

D ◑ ≈ ⓚ ✈ ⊠ ⚐

★ **BAYMONT INN.** *120 S Cartwright Ct (37072). Phone 615/851-1891; toll-free 800/301-0200; fax 615/851-4513. www.baymontinns.com.* 100 rooms, 3 story. Pets accepted, some restrictions. Complimentary continental breakfast. Check-out noon. TV; cable (premium). In-house fitness room. Pool. **$**

D ◑ ≈ ⓚ ⊠ SC

★ **BEST INN.** *5770 Old Hickory Blvd (37076). Phone 615/889-8940; fax 615/821-4444. www.bestinn.com.* 100 rooms, 3 story. Pets accepted, some restrictions; fee. Complimentary continental breakfast. Check-out noon. TV. Pool. **$**

D ◑ ≈ ⊠

★ **CLUBHOUSE INN.** *2435 Atrium Way (37214). Phone 615/883-0500; toll-free 800/258-2466; fax 615/889-4827. www.clubhouseinn.com.* 135 rooms, 3 story. Pets accepted, some restrictions. Complimentary breakfast. Check-out 11 pm, check-in 3 pm. TV; cable (premium), VCR available. Laundry services. Outdoor pool; whirlpool. Free airport transportation. **$**

D ◑ ≈ ✈ ⊠ SC

★ **DAYS INN.** *1009 TN 76 (37188). Phone 615/672-3746; fax 615/672-0929.* 100 rooms, 2 story. Pets accepted, some restrictions; fee. Complimentary continental breakfast. Check-out 11 am. TV; cable (premium). Pool. **$**

◑ ≈ ⊠

★ ★ **HOLIDAY INN.** *201 Crossings Pl (37013). Phone 615/731-2361; toll-free 800/465-4329; fax 615/731-6828. www.holiday-inn.com.* 138 rooms, 5 story. Pets accepted. Check-out noon. TV; cable (premium). In-room modem link. Restaurant, bar. Room service. Health club privileges. In-house fitness room. Pool. Free airport transportation.

D ◑ ≈ ⓚ ⊠ SC

★ ★ **HOLIDAY INN.** *2613 West End Ave (37203). Phone 615/327-4707; toll-free 800/465-4329; fax 615/327-8034. www.holiday-inn.com.* 300 rooms, 13 story. Pets accepted; fee. Check-out noon, check-in 3 pm. TV; cable (premium), VCR available. In-room modem link. Laundry services. Restaurant, bar; entertainment. In-house fitness room. Outdoor pool. Airport transportation. Business center. Concierge. Luxury level. **$**

D ◑ ≈ ⓚ ⊠ SC ⚐

★ **HOLIDAY INN EXPRESS.** *354 Hester Ln (37188). Phone 615/672-7200; fax 615/672-7100.* 54 rooms, 2 story. Pets accepted, some restrictions; fee. Complimentary continental breakfast. Check-out 11 am. TV; cable (premium). In-room modem link. Pool. **$**

D ◑ ≈ ⊠

Hotels

★ ★ ★ **THE HERMITAGE HOTEL.** *231 Sixth Ave N (37219). Phone 615/244-3121; toll-free 888/888-9414; fax 615/242-8715. www.thehermitagehotel.com.* 123 rooms, 10 story. Pets accepted. Check-out noon, check-in 3 pm. TV; cable (premium). Restaurant, bar. Babysitting services available. In-house fitness room; spa. **$$$**

D ◑ ⓚ

★ ★ ★ **LOEWS VANDERBILT HOTEL NASHVILLE.** *2100 West End Ave (37203). Phone 615/320-1700; toll-free 800/336-3335; fax 615/320-5019. www.loewshotels.com.* This well-kept, upscale property is conveniently located between Vanderbilt University and downtown. 340 rooms, 12 story. Pets accepted. Check-out noon, check-in 3 pm. TV; cable (premium), VCR available. In-room modem link. Restaurant, bar; entertainment. Room service. Children's activity center; babysitting services available. In-house fitness room; spa. Valet parking. Business center. Concierge. Luxury level. **$$**

D ◑ ⓚ ⊠ ⚐

★ ★ ★ **SHERATON MUSIC CITY.** *777 McGavok Pike (37214). Phone 615/885-2200; fax 615/231-1133. www.sheratonmusiccity.com.* Found on 23 landscaped acres, this hotel was built with Georgian architecture and is located 3 miles from the International Airport and 9 miles from downtown. 410 rooms, 4 story. Pets accepted. Check-out 11 am, check-in 3 pm. TV; cable (premium), VCR available. Restaurant, bar; entertainment. Babysitting services available. In-house fitness room; sauna. Indoor, outdoor pool; children's pool; whirlpool. Outdoor tennis, lighted courts. Airport transportation. Business center. Concierge. On 23 landscaped acres on top of hill. Semiformal décor. **$$**

🆔 🐾 🏊 🏃 🏋 🚶

★ ★ ★ **SHERATON NASHVILLE DOWNTOWN HOTEL.** *623 Union St (37219). Phone 615/259-2000; toll-free 800/447-9825; fax 615/742-6057. www.sheraton.com.* 476 rooms, 28 story. Pets accepted, some restrictions. Check-out noon, check-in 3 pm. TV; cable (premium), VCR available. Restaurant, bar. Room service. Babysitting services available. In-house fitness room. Indoor pool. Garage $10; valet parking $14. Airport transportation. Business center. Concierge. Luxury level. **$**

🆔 🐾 🏊 🏃 🏋 🚶

★ ★ ★ **WYNDHAM UNION STATION HOTEL.** *1001 Broadway (37203). Phone 615/726-1001; toll-free 800/9963426; fax 615/248-3554. www.wyndham.com.* This hotel is located only a few blocks from 2nd Avenue and Music Row. It was once a train station and now offers a unique place for visitors to stay with all the comforts and luxuries of a modern-day hotel. 124 rooms, 7 story. Pets accepted, some restrictions; fee. Check-out noon, check-in 3 pm. TV; cable (premium), VCR available. In-room modem link. Restaurant, bar. Valet parking. Business center. Concierge. In renovated historic train station (1897); stained-glass roof. **$$**

🐾 🏊 🚶

All Suites

★ **AMERISUITES.** *202 Summit View Dr (37027). Phone 615/661-9477; fax 615/661-9936. www.amerisuites.com.* 126 rooms, 6 story. Pets accepted. Complimentary continental breakfast. Check-out noon. TV; cable (premium), VCR available. In-house fitness room. Pool. Business center. **$**

🆔 🐾 🏊 🏋 🏃 🚶

★ ★ **EMBASSY SUITES.** *10 Century Blvd (37214). Phone 615/871-0033; fax 615/883-9245. www.embassy suitesnashville.com.* The suites in this hotel encircle a large atrium with waterfalls and exotic birds. Just two minutes from the airport and 10 minutes from the Grand Ole Opry, the hotel is convenient for all travelers. 296 suites, 9 story. Pets accepted, some restrictions; fee. Complimentary breakfast. Check-out noon, check-in 4 pm. TV; cable (premium), VCR available. Restaurant, bar. Room service. Children's activity center; babysitting services available. In-house fitness room; sauna. Game room. Indoor pool; whirlpool. Free airport transportation. Concierge. **$$**

🆔 🐾 🏊 🏃 ✈ 🚶

★ ★ ★ **HILTON SUITES BRENTWOOD.** *9000 Overlook Blvd (37027). Phone 615/370-0111; toll-free 800/445-8667; fax 615/370-0272. www.hilton.com.* Located just outside Nashville, this property is convenient to Opryland and a variety of attractions. 203 suites, 4 story. Pets accepted, some restrictions. Complimentary full breakfast. Check-out noon. TV; cable (premium), VCR available. Laundry services. Restaurant, bar. Room service. In-house fitness room. Indoor pool; whirlpool. Business center. **$**

🆔 🐾 🏊 🏃 🚶 SC 🏃

Oak Ridge

Motels/Motor Lodges

★ **COMFORT INN.** *433 S Rutgers Ave (37830). Phone 865/481-8200; toll-free 800/553-7830; fax 865/483-6142. www.oakridgetncomfortinn.com.* 122 rooms, 5 story. Pets accepted, some restrictions; fee. Complimentary continental breakfast. Check-out noon. TV. Health club privileges. Pool. **$**

🐾 🏊 🚶

★ **DAYS INN.** *206 S Illinois Ave (37830). Phone 865/483-5615; toll-free 800/329-7466. www.daysinn.com.* 80 rooms, 2 story. Pets accepted; fee. Complimentary continental breakfast. Check-out 11 am. TV. Pool. **$**

🆔 🐾 🏊 🚶 SC

Pigeon Forge

Motels/Motor Lodges

★ ★ **GRAND RESORT HOTEL AND CONVENTION CENTER.** *3171 N Parkway (37868). Phone 865/453-1000; toll-free 800/251-4444; fax 865/428-3944. www.grandresorthotel.com.* 425 rooms, 5 story. Pets accepted; fee. Complimentary continental breakfast. Check-out 11 am. TV. Restaurant. Room service. Pool; whirlpool. Downhill ski 7 miles. **$**

🆔 🐾 ⛷ 🏊 🚶 SC

★ ★ **HEARTLAND COUNTRY RESORT.** *2385 Parkway (37863). Phone 865/453-4106; toll-free 800/843-6686; fax 423/453-4106.* 160 rooms, 5 story. Pets accepted, some restrictions; fee. Check-out 11 am. TV. Game room. Indoor, outdoor pool; whirlpool. Continental breakfast. **$**

D 🐾 ☄ ☒ SC

Shelbyville

Motel/Motor Lodge

★ **SUPER 8.** *317 N Cannon Blvd (37160). Phone 931/684-6050; toll-free 800/622-0466; fax 931/684-2714. www.super8.com.* 72 rooms, 2 story. Pets accepted, some restrictions; fee. Check-out noon. TV; cable (premium). Restaurant. Pool. **$**

D 🐾 ✈ ☄ ☒

Sweetwater

Motel/Motor Lodge

★ **COMFORT INN.** *731 S Main St (37874). Phone 423/337-6646; toll-free 800/638-7949; fax 423/337-5409. www.comfortinn.com.* 60 rooms, 2 story. Pets accepted; fee. Complimentary continental breakfast. Check-out 11 am. TV. Pool; children's pool. **$**

D 🐾 ♣ ☄ ☒ SC

Townsend

Motel/Motor Lodge

★ **BEST WESTERN VALLEY VIEW LODGE.** *TN 321 (37882). Phone 865/448-2237; toll-free 800/292-4844; fax 865/448-9957. www.bestwestern.com.* 91 rooms, 2 story. Pets accepted, some restrictions; fee. Complimentary continental breakfast. Check-out 11 am. TV; cable (premium). Indoor, outdoor pool; whirlpool. Lawn games. **$**

D 🐾 ☄ ☒

Texas

Abilene

Motels/Motor Lodges

★ **BEST WESTERN MALL SOUTH.** *3950 Ridgemont Dr (79606). Phone 915/695-1262; toll-free 800/346-1574; fax 915/695-2593. www.bestwestern.com.* 61 rooms, 2 story. Pets accepted, some restrictions; fee. Complimentary continental breakfast. Check-out noon. TV; cable (premium). In-room modem link. Pool. Airport transportation. **$**

D 🐾 ⊠ 🖼

★ **LA QUINTA INN.** *3501 W Lake Rd (79601). Phone 915/676-1676; fax 915/672-8323. www.laquinta.com.* 106 rooms, 2 story. Pets accepted; some restrictions. Complimentary continental breakfast. Check-out noon. TV; cable (premium). Pool. **$**

D 🐾 ⊠ 🏃 🖼

★ ★ **QUALITY INN.** *505 Pine St (79601). Phone 915/676-0222; toll-free 800/588-0222; fax 915/673-6561. www.qualityinn.com.* 118 rooms, 2 story. Pets accepted; fee. Complimentary full breakfast. Check-out noon. TV; cable (premium). Restaurant, bar. Room service. Pool. Free airport transportation. **$**

D 🐾 ⊠ 🖼

★ **ROYAL INN.** *5695 S 1st St (79605). Phone 915/692-3022; toll-free 800/588-4386; fax 915/692-3137. www.royalinn-abilene.com.* 150 rooms. Pets accepted, some restrictions; fee. Check-out noon. TV; cable (premium). Restaurant, bar. Room service. Pool. **$**

D 🐾 ⊠ 🖼 SC

Hotel

★ ★ **CLARION HOTEL.** *5403 S 1st St (79605). Phone 915/695-2150; toll-free 800/252-7466; fax 915/698-6742. www.clarionhotel.com.* 178 rooms, 3 story. Pets accepted; fee. Check-out noon. TV; cable (premium). Laundry services. Restaurant, bar. Room service. Sauna. Indoor, outdoor pool; children's pool; whirlpool. Business center. **$**

D 🐾 ⊠ 🖼 SC 🏃

All Suite

★ ★ ★ **EMBASSY SUITES.** *4250 Ridgemont Dr (79606). Phone 915/698-1234; fax 915/698-2771. www.embassysuites.com.* This hotel is located directly across

the street from the Mall of Abilene, with shops, theaters, and other convenient services within walking distance. 176 rooms, 3 story. Pets accepted; fee. Complimentary full breakfast. Check-out noon. TV; cable (premium). Laundry services. Restaurant, bar; entertainment. Sauna, steam room. Game room. Indoor pool; whirlpool. Airport, train station, bus depot transportation. **$**

D 🐾 🏃 ⊠ 🖼

Alpine

Motel/Motor Lodge

★ **LIMPIA HOTEL.** *Main St (79734). Phone 915/426-3237; toll-free 800/662-5517; fax 915/426-3983. www.hotellimpia.com.* 36 rooms, 2 story. No room phones. Pets accepted, some restrictions. Check-out noon. TV; cable (premium). Built in 1912 of locally mined pink limestone. **$**

D 🐾 🖼 SC

Amarillo

Motels/Motor Lodges

★ **HAMPTON INN.** *1700 I-40 E (79103). Phone 806/372-1425; toll-free 800/426-7866; fax 806/379-8807. www.hamptoninn.com.* 116 rooms, 2 story. Pets accepted, some restrictions. Complimentary continental breakfast. Check-out noon. TV; cable (premium). Health club privileges. Pool. **$**

D 🐾 ⊠ 🖼 SC

★ ★ **HOLIDAY INN.** *1911 I-40 E (79102). Phone 806/372-8741; toll-free 800/465-4329; fax 806/372-2913. www.holiday-inn.com.* 248 rooms, 4 story. Pets accepted; fee. Check-out noon. TV; cable (premium). In-room modem link. Laundry services. Restaurant, bar. Room service. In-house fitness room. Game room. Indoor pool; children's pool. Free airport transportation. **$**

D 🐾 ⊠ 🏋 ✈ 🖼 SC

Arlington-Grand Prairie

Motel/Motor Lodge

★ **HAWTHORN SUITES.** *2401 Brookhollow Plaza Dr (76006). Phone 817/640-1188; fax 817/649-4720. www.hawthorn.com.* 130 rooms, 3 story. Pets accepted, some restrictions; fee. Complimentary full breakfast.

Check-out noon. TV; cable (premium), VCR available (movies). In-house fitness room. Pool; whirlpool. **$**

D ❧ ≈ 🎭 ⊠ SC

Austin

Motels/Motor Lodges

★ ★ **DRURY INN.** *6711 I-35 N (78752). Phone 512/467-9500; fax 512/323-6198. www.druryinn.com.* 224 rooms, 4 story. Pets accepted, some restrictions. Complimentary continental breakfast. Check-out noon. TV; cable (premium). In-room modem link. Laundry services. Pool. **$**

D ❧ ≈ ⊠

★ ★ **HOLIDAY INN.** *3401 S I-35 (78741). Phone 512/448-2444; toll-free 800/465-4329; fax 512/448-4999. www.holiday-inn.com.* 210 rooms, 5 story. Pets accepted; fee. Check-out noon, check-in 3 pm. TV; cable (premium). In-room modem link. Restaurant, bar. Room service. In-house fitness room. Outdoor pool; whirlpool; poolside service. Airport transportation. **$**

D ❧ ≈ 🎭 ✈ ⊠

★ ★ **HOLIDAY INN.** *20 N I-35 (78701). Phone 512/472-8211; fax 512/472-4636. www.holiday-inn.com.* 320 rooms, 14 story. Pets accepted; fee. Check-out noon. TV; cable (premium). In-room modem link. Laundry services. Restaurant, bar. Room service. Sauna. Pool; whirlpool. Free covered parking. Free airport transportation. Two towers. **$**

D ❧ ≈ 🎭 ⊠

★ **LA QUINTA INN.** *7100 I-35 N (78752). Phone 512/452-9401; fax 512/452-0856. www.laquinta.com.* 121 rooms, 2 story. Pets accepted, some restrictions. Complimentary continental breakfast. Check-out noon, check-in 1 pm. TV; cable (premium). In-room modem link. Outdoor pool. **$**

D ❧ ≈ ⊠

★ **LA QUINTA INN.** *2004 I-35 N (78681). Phone 512/255-6666; fax 512/388-3635. www.laquinta.com.* 116 rooms, 3 story. Pets accepted, some restrictions; fee. Complimentary continental breakfast. Check-out noon. TV; cable (premium). In-room modem link. In-house fitness room; sauna. Pool; whirlpool. **$**

D ❧ ≈ 🎭 ⊠ SC

★ **RED ROOF INN.** *8210 N Interregional Hwy 35 (78753). Phone 512/835-2200; fax 512/339-9043. www.redroof.com.* 143 rooms, 4 story. Pets accepted, some restrictions. Check-out noon. TV; cable (premium). In-room modem link. Pool. **$**

D ❧ ≈

Hotels

★ ★ ★ **THE DRISKILL.** *604 Brazos St (78701). Phone 512/474-5911; toll-free 800/252-9367; fax 512/474-2214. www.driskillhotel.com.* This historic hotel has been stunningly restored to the opulence of the past. A downtown location, it is within walking distance to the state capitol. 189 rooms, 4 story. Pets accepted, some restrictions; fee. Check-out noon. TV; cable (premium), VCR available. In-room modem link. Restaurant, bar. In-house fitness room. Business center. Concierge. **$$**

D ❧ 🎭 ⧗ ⊠ 🚶

★ ★ ★ ★ **FOUR SEASONS HOTEL AUSTIN.** *98 San Jacinto Blvd (78701). Phone 512/478-4500; fax 512/478-3117. www.fourseasons.com.* Texan hospitality and charm are particularly evident at the Four Seasons Hotel Austin. Close to downtown and the entertainment district, this hotel enjoys a parklike setting of rolling hills overlooking Town Lake. The traditional décor is enlivened with playful touches indicative of the region, including cow prints and wildflower arrangements. The guest rooms are luxurious without being pretentious, and the intuitive service is always on hand to exceed expectations. Guests absorb the tranquility here, whether lingering poolside or enjoying a gourmet picnic on the sprawling grounds. The peaceful setting is the focal point at this hotel; both the Café and the Lobby Lounge boast expansive views. Diners are introduced to renowned Hill Country cuisine, which blends elements from American, Asian, continental, and Southwestern cuisines to create palate-pleasing sensations. 291 rooms, 9 story. Pets accepted, some restrictions. Check-out noon. TV; cable (premium), VCR available. In-room modem link. Room service 24 hours. Restaurant. Bar. In-house fitness room; massage; sauna. Pool; whirlpool; poolside service. Valet parking. Business center. 24-hour concierge. **$$$**

D ❧ ≈ 🎭 ⊠ 🚶

★ ★ ★ **HILTON AUSTIN NORTH.** *6000 Middle Fiskville Rd (78752). Phone 512/451-5757; toll-free 800/347-0330; fax 512/467-7644. www.austinnorth.hilton.com.* 189 rooms, 10 story. Pets accepted, some restrictions; fee. Check-out noon, check-in 3 pm. TV; cable (premium). In-room modem link. Restaurant, bar. In-house fitness room. Pool. **$**

D ❧ ≈ 🎭 ⊠

★ ★ ★ **OMNI AUSTIN HOTEL.** *700 San Jacinto Blvd (78701). Phone 512/476-3700; toll-free 800/843-6664; fax 512/397-4888. www.omnihotels.com.* 427 rooms, 20 story. Pets accepted, some restrictions; fee. Check-out noon, check-in 3 pm. TV; cable (premium), VCR available. In-room modem link. Restaurant, bar. In-house fitness room; massage; sauna. Pool; whirlpool; poolside service. Valet parking. Business center. Luxury level. **$**

D ❧ ≈ 🎭 ⊠ SC 🚶

★ ★ **RED LION.** *6121 I-35 N (78752). Phone 512/ 323-5466; toll-free 800/733-5466; fax 512/453-1945. www.redlion.com.* 300 rooms, 7 story. Pets accepted; fee. Check-out noon, check-in 3 pm. TV; cable (premium). In-room modem link. Restaurant, bar. Room service. In-house fitness room; sauna. Outdoor pool; whirlpool; poolside service. **$**

D ◖ ⇌ ⚗ ⋈

★ ★ ★ **RENAISSANCE AUSTIN HOTEL.** *9721 Arboretum Blvd (78759). Phone 512/343-2626; toll-free 800/228-9290; fax 512/346-7953. www.renaissance hotels.com.* This hotel is part of the Aboretum complex, which holds over 50 clothing and specialty boutiques, 15 cinemas, and several restaurants. It is close to the high-tech companies in the area. 579 rooms, 8-10 story. Pets accepted, some restrictions. Check-out 1 pm, check-in 3 pm. TV; cable (premium). In-room modem link. Restaurant, bar. In-house fitness room; sauna. Indoor, outdoor pool; whirlpool; poolside service. Business center. Concierge. Luxury level. **$**

D ◖ ⇌ ⚗ ⋈ SC ⋈

All Suites

★ ★ ★ **DOUBLETREE HOTEL.** *303 W 15th St (78701). Phone 512/478-7000; fax 512/478-3562. www. doubletree.com.* Located just 2 blocks from the state capitol, this hotel has a contemporary design. 189 rooms, 15 story. Pets accepted, some restrictions; fee. Check-out noon, check-in 3 pm. TV; cable (premium), VCR available. In-room modem link. Laundry services. Restaurant, bar. In-house fitness room; sauna. Pool; whirlpool; poolside service. Valet parking. Business center. **$**

D ◖ ⇌ ⚗ ⋈ ⋈

★ ★ **HAWTHORN SUITES.** *4020 I-35 S (78704). Phone 512/440-7722; fax 512/440-4815. www.hawthorn .com.* 120 rooms, 2 story. Pets accepted; fee. Complimentary continental breakfast. Check-out noon, check-in 3 pm. TV; cable (premium). Laundry services. Outdoor pool; whirlpool. Outdoor tennis, lighted courts. **$**

D ◖ ⚗ ⇌ ⋈

Beaumont

Motels/Motor Lodges

★ **BEST WESTERN JEFFERSON INN.** *1610 I-10 S (77707). Phone 409/842-0037; fax 409/842-0057. www.bestwestern.com.* 120 rooms. Pets accepted. Complimentary continental breakfast. Check-out noon. TV; cable (premium). In-room modem link. Laundry services. Pool. **$**

◖ ⇌ ⋈

★ ★ **HOLIDAY INN.** *2095 N 11th St (77703). Phone 409/892-2222; toll-free 800/465-4329; fax 409/892-2231. www.holiday-inn.com.* 190 rooms, 6 story. Pets accepted; fee. Check-out noon. TV; cable (premium). In-room modem link. Laundry services. Restaurant, bar. Room service. Pool; poolside service. Free airport transportation. **$**

D ◖ ⇌ ✈ SC

★ ★ **HOLIDAY INN.** *3950 I-10 S (77705). Phone 409/842-5995; fax 409/842-0315. www.holiday-inn.com.* 253 rooms, 8 story. Pets accepted; fee. Check-out noon. TV; cable (premium), VCR available. In-room modem link. Restaurant, bar. In-house fitness room; sauna. Game room. Indoor pool; whirlpool; poolside service. Free airport transportation. Business center. **$**

D ◖ ⇌ ⚗ ⋈ ⋈

★ **LA QUINTA INN.** *220 I-10 N (77702). Phone 409/ 838-9991; fax 409/832-1266. www.laquinta.com.* 122 rooms, 2 story. Pets accepted. Complimentary continental breakfast. Check-out noon. TV. In-room modem link. Laundry services. Pool. **$**

D ◖ ⇌ ⋈ SC

Brazosport

Motels/Motor Lodges

★ **LA QUINTA INN.** *1126 W Hwy 332 (77531). Phone 979/265-7461; toll-free 800/687-6667; fax 979/265-3804.* 136 rooms, 2 story. Pets accepted, some restrictions. Complimentary continental breakfast. Check-out noon. TV; cable (premium). In-room modem link. Pool. **$**

D ◖ ⇌ ⋈ SC

★ ★ **RAMADA INN.** *925 Hwy 332 W (77566). Phone 979/297-1161; toll-free 800/544-2119; fax 979/297-1249. www.ramadainnlakejacksontx.com.* 144 rooms, 2 story. Pets accepted, some restrictions; fee. Check-out 1 pm. TV. In-room modem link. Restaurant, bar. Room service. Pool. **$**

D ◖ ⇌ ⋈

Brownsville

Motel/Motor Lodge

★ **RED ROOF INN.** *2377 N Expy 83 (78520). Phone 956/504-2300; fax 956/504-2303. www.redroof.com.* 124 rooms, 3 story. Pets accepted. Complimentary continental breakfast. Check-out 11 am. TV; cable (premium). Laundry services. Pool; whirlpool. **$**

D ◖ ⇌ ⋈

Brownwood

Motel/Motor Lodge

★ **DAYS INN.** *515 E Commerce St (76801). Phone 915/646-2551; fax 915/643-6064.* www.daysinn.com. 138 rooms, 2 story. Pets accepted; fee. Complimentary continental breakfast. Check-out noon. TV; cable (premium). In-room modem link. Laundry services. Sauna. Pool; whirlpool. **$**

D ⊁ ⩲ ⊠ SC

Bryan/College Station

Motels/Motor Lodges

★ ★ **HOLIDAY INN.** *1503 Texas Ave S (77840). Phone 979/693-1736.* www.holiday-inn.com. 125 rooms, 6 story. Pets accepted, some restrictions; fee. Check-out noon. TV; cable (premium). In-room modem link. Restaurant, bar. Room service. Pool; poolside service. Free airport transportation. **$**

D ⊁ ⩲ ✈ ⊠

★ **LA QUINTA INN.** *607 Texas Ave S (77840). Phone 979/696-7777; toll-free 800/531-5900; fax 979/696-0531.* www.laquinta.com. 176 rooms. Pets accepted. Complimentary continental breakfast. Check-out noon. TV; cable (premium). In-room modem link. Pool. Free airport transportation. Texas A & M University opposite. **$**

D ⊁ ⩲ ⊠

★ **MANOR HOUSE INN.** *2504 Texas Ave S (77840). Phone 979/764-9540; toll-free 800/231-4100; fax 979/693-2430.* www.manorhouseinn.com. 117 rooms, 2 story. Pets accepted; fee. Complimentary continental breakfast. Check-out noon. TV; cable (premium). In-room modem link. Pool. Free airport transportation. **$**

D ⊁ ⩲ ⊠ SC

Clarendon

Motel/Motor Lodge

★ **WESTERN SKIES MOTEL.** *800 W 2nd St (79226). Phone 806/874-3501; fax 806/874-5303.* 23 rooms. Pets accepted; fee. Check-out 11 am. TV. Pool. **$**

D ⊁ ⩲ ⊠

Corpus Christi

Motels/Motor Lodges

★ **DRURY INN.** *2021 N Padre Island Dr (78408). Phone 361/289-8200.* www.druryinn.com. 105 rooms, 4 story. Pets accepted; some restrictions. Complimentary continental breakfast. Check-out noon. TV; cable (premium), VCR available. In-room modem link. Laundry services. Pool. Free airport transportation. **$**

D ⊁ ⩲ ⊠ SC

★ ★ **HOLIDAY INN.** *1102 S Shoreline Blvd (78401). Phone 361/883-5731; toll-free 800/465-4329; fax 361/883-9079.* www.holiday-inn.com. 368 rooms, 2-7 story. Pets accepted, some restrictions; fee. Check-out noon. TV. In-room modem link. Restaurant, bar. Room service. In-house fitness room; sauna. Game room. Pool; whirlpool; poolside service. **$**

D ⊁ ⧗ ⩲ ⊀ ⊠ SC

★ **LA QUINTA INN.** *5155 I-37 N (78408). Phone 361/888-5721; toll-free 800/531-5900; fax 361/888-5401.* www.laquinta.com. 123 rooms, 2 story. Pets accepted. Complimentary continental breakfast. Check-out noon. TV; cable (premium). In-room modem link. Laundry services. Restaurant open 24 hours. Pool. **$**

D ⊁ ⩲ ⊠ SC

★ **RED ROOF INN.** *6301 I-37 (78409). Phone 361/289-6925; toll-free 800/843-7663; fax 361/289-2239.* www.redroof.com. 142 rooms, 3 story. Pets accepted, some restrictions; fee. Check-out 11 am. TV; cable (premium). In-room modem link. Pool; whirlpool. **$**

D ⊁ ⩲ ⊠ SC

Dalhart

Motel/Motor Lodge

★ **DAYS INN.** *701 Liberal St (79022). Phone 806/244-5246; fax 806/244-0805.* www.daysinn.com. 43 rooms, 2 story. Pets accepted, some restrictions. Complimentary continental breakfast. Check-out 11 am. TV; cable (premium). In-house fitness room. Indoor pool; whirlpool. **$**

D ⊁ ⩲ ⊀ ⊠

Dallas

Motels/Motor Lodges

★ ★ **BEST WESTERN DALLAS NORTH.** *13333 N Stemmons Fwy (75234). Phone 972/241-8521; toll-free 800/ 308-4593; fax 972/243-4103. www.bestwestern.com.* 185 rooms, 2 story. Pets accepted; fee. Check-out 11 am. TV; cable (premium). In-room modem link. Laundry services. Restaurant, bar. Room service. Sauna. Pool; whirlpool. Airport transportation. **$**

D 🐾 🏋 🏊 ✈ 🏊

★ ★ **BEST WESTERN PARK SUITES HOTEL.** *640 Park Blvd E (75074). Phone 972/578-2243; fax 972/ 578-0563. www.bestwestern.com.* 83 rooms, 3 story. Pets accepted, some restrictions; fee. Complimentary continental breakfast. Check-out noon. TV; cable (premium). In-room modem link. Laundry services. Bar. In-house fitness room. Pool; whirlpool. **$**

D 🐾 🏊 🏋 🏊

★ **LA QUINTA INN.** *8303 E. R. L. Thornton Fwy (75228). Phone 214/324-3731; toll-free 800/531-5900; fax 214/324-1652. www.laquinta.com.* 102 rooms, 2 story. Pets accepted. Complimentary continental breakfast. Check-out noon. TV; cable (premium). In-room modem link. Pool. **$**

D 🐾 🏊 🏊 SC

★ **LA QUINTA INN.** *13235 N Stemmons Fwy (75234). Phone 972/620-7333; toll-free 800/687-6667; fax 972/ 484-6533. www.laquinta.com.* 122 rooms, 2 story. Pets accepted. Complimentary continental breakfast. Check-out noon. TV; cable (premium). In-room modem link. Pool. Free airport transportation. **$**

D 🐾 🏊 🏊 SC

★ **SLEEP INN.** *4801 W Plano Pkwy (75093). Phone 972/867-1111; fax 972/612-6753. www.sleepinn.com.* 102 rooms, 2 story. Pets accepted, some restrictions; fee. Complimentary continental breakfast. Check-out noon. TV. In-room modem link. Pool. **$**

D 🐾 🏋 🏊 🏊

Hotels

★ ★ ★ **THE ADOLPHUS.** *1321 Commerce St (75202). Phone 214/742-8200; toll-free 800/221-9083; fax 214/651-3561. www.hoteladolphus.com.* Beer baron Adolphus Busch built this luxury property in 1912, and subsequent renovations have kept the downtown jewel sparkling, making it the grande dame of Dallas hotels. Through the years, queens, celebrities, and other notables have checked in and enjoyed its baroque splendor, not to mention its plush rooms and suites lavishly decorated with

Queen Anne and Chippendale furnishings. The elegant French Room rates as one of the city's best restaurants, with classic French cooking updated for contemporary tastes. The Bistro and Walt Garrison Rodeo Bar and Grill offer less formal dining. Wednesday through Sunday, the hotel serves high tea in the lobby living room. Its central location makes the Adolphus a good choice for business travelers, but its old-world charm sets just the right mood for a romantic getaway. 428 rooms, 21 story. Pets accepted; fee. Check-out 1 pm, check-in 3 pm. TV; cable (premium), VCR available. In-room modem link. Room service 24 hours. Restaurant, bar. Babysitting services available. In-house fitness room; massage. Health club privileges. Valet parking. Concierge. **$$**

D 🐾 🏋 🏊

★ ★ ★ **CROWNE PLAZA.** *7050 N Stemmons Fwy (75247). Phone 214/630-8500; fax 214/630-0037. www.dal-market-cp.crowneplaza.com.* The striking, modern façade of this hotel stands along an expressway-stretch of office buildings and attracts mostly corporate clients. The property is convenient to Market Center and the Dallas Convention Center. 357 rooms, 21 story. Pets accepted; fee. Check-out noon, check-in 3 pm. TV; cable (premium). In-room modem link. Laundry services. Restaurant, bar. In-house fitness room; sauna. Indoor pool; whirlpool. Business center. **$**

D 🐾 🏊 🏋 ✈ 🏊 SC 🏋

★ ★ ★ **CROWNE PLAZA.** *14315 Midway Rd (75001). Phone 972/980-8877; toll-free 800/222-7696; fax 972/788-2758. www.crowneplaza.com.* Located in the Addison business district outside of Dallas, this property caters to the business traveler. Complimentary shuttle service is provided to the nearby famous Galleria shopping mall. 429 rooms, 4 story. Pets accepted; fee. TV; cable (premium), VCR available. In-room modem link. Laundry services. Restaurant. Room service. In-house fitness room. Health club privileges. Pool; whirlpool. Airport transportation. Business center. **$$**

D 🐾 🏊 🏋 🏊 SC 🏋

★ ★ **HARVEY HOTEL–PLANO.** *1600 N Central Expy (75074). Phone 972/578-8555; toll-free 800/922-9222; fax 972/578-9720.* 279 rooms, 3 story. Pets accepted; fee. Check-out 1 pm. TV; VCR available. In-room modem link. Laundry services. Restaurant, bar. Room service. In-house fitness room. Game room. Pool; whirlpool; poolside service. **$**

D 🐾 🏊 🏋 🏊 SC

★ ★ ★ **HOTEL CRESCENT COURT.** *400 Crescent Ct (75201). Phone 214/871-3200; toll-free 800/654-6541; fax 214/871-3272. www.crescentcourt.com.* Located in the fashionable uptown area of Dallas, the recently renovated Hotel Crescent Court is the essence of chic European style. Designed by renowned architect Philip Johnson, the impressive exterior resembles a French chateau with a contemporary twist. Situated within a complex of luxury shops and trendy restaurants, this hotel has one of Dallas' finest addresses. Priceless antiques, artwork, and Louis XIV tapestries define the public spaces, while the guest rooms provide refined shelter. Spiral staircases add romance in the suites, and lovely French doors open out to the well-tended grounds. Little extras, like luxurious linens and warm and attentive service, make the guest experience exceptional. The fitness center and spa are committed to well-being, with state-of-the-art equipment, sensational treatments, and healthy cuisine. Patrons dine on superb New American dishes in the lovely setting of Beau Nash restaurant. This brasserie-style venue is one of the city's most popular restaurants. 220 rooms, 7 story. Pets accepted; fee. Check-out noon, check-in 4 pm. TV; cable (premium), VCR available. In-room modem link. Room service 24 hours. Restaurant, bar. Babysitting services available. In-house fitness room; spa; sauna; steam room. Outdoor pool; whirlpool; poolside service. Valet parking. Airport transportation. Business center. 24-hour concierge. **$$$$**

[D] [icons]

★ ★ ★ **HOTEL ZAZA.** 2332 Leonard St (75201). Phone 214/468-8399; toll-free 800/597-8399; fax 214/468-8397. www.hotelzaza.com. This luxury boutique hotel just recently came on the scene in the trendy Uptown district, where many young Dallas professionals live and hang out. Given the neighborhood, the developers gave the hotel a unique look to help attract the stylish crowd. The exterior says French chateau; the interior says hip, hip, hip. Although plenty of nightlife lies within blocks of its front door, you don't have to venture outside for your evening entertainment. Sip cocktails in the Dragonfly bar, a see-and-be-seen kind of place, and then dine at Dragonfly, where celebrated chef Stephan Pyles helped create a savory Mediterranean menu with Asian influences. Come bedtime, get comfy in your spacious guest room with an oversized television, or in one of the individually decorated suites with themes ranging from Bohemian to Out of Africa. 145 rooms, 4 story. Pets accepted, some restrictions. Check-out noon, check-in 3 pm. TV; cable (premium). Internet access. Restaurant, bar. Babysitting services available. In-house fitness room; spa. Outdoor pool; whirlpool. **$$**

[D] [icons]

★ ★ ★ ★ ★ **THE MANSION ON TURTLE CREEK.** 2821 Turtle Creek Blvd (75219). Phone 214/559-2100; toll-free 800/527-5432; fax 214/528-4187. www.mansiononturtlecreek.com. Situated on almost 5 acres in Dallas' exclusive residential neighborhood, The Mansion on Turtle Creek is only five minutes from the businesses of downtown. Once a private home, this 1920s Italian-Renaissance mansion retains the ambience of a distinguished residence. Together with a tower, the hotel welcomes guests to its refined accommodations, where French doors open to private balconies, suites have marble fireplaces, and original works of art adorn the walls. From the business and fitness centers to the salon and outdoor pool, guests are ensured a comfortable stay. The tradition of a gentlemen's club is alive at the bar, where hunting trophies decorate the hunter-green walls, while the Pool Terrace is perfect for light fare in the warm sunshine. No visit to Dallas is complete without reservations at the Restaurant, where culinary superstar Dean Fearing crafts sophisticated Southwestern cuisine in a magnificent setting. 143 rooms, 9 story. Pets accepted; fee. Check-out noon, check-in 3 pm. TV; cable (premium), VCR. In-room modem link. Room service 24 hours. Restaurant, bar; entertainment. Babysitting services available. In-house fitness room; sauna, steam room; spa; massage. Health club privileges. Outdoor pool; whirlpool; poolside service. Valet parking. Airport transportation. Business center. Concierge. **$$$**

[D] [icons]

★ ★ ★ **MARRIOTT SUITES DALLAS MARKET CENTER.** 2493 N Stemmons Fwy (75207). Phone 214/905-0050; fax 214/905-0060. www.marriott.com. 266 rooms, 12 story. Pets accepted; fee. Check-out noon, check-in 3 pm. TV; cable (premium), VCR available. In-room modem link. Laundry services. Restaurant, bar. Babysitting services available. In-house fitness room. Outdoor pool; whirlpool. Business center. Concierge. **$$**

[icons]

★ ★ ★ **THE MELROSE HOTEL DALLAS.** 3015 Oak Lawn Ave (75219). Phone 214/521-5151; toll-free 800/635-7673; fax 214/521-9306. www.melrosehotel.com. When just another chain hotel won't do, consider the inviting Melrose in the Oak Lawn/Turtle Creek area. Built in 1924, the hotel used to attract celebrities with its old-world charm, but guests now tend to be business travelers, people attending meetings, and couples on weekend getaways. No two of its 184 oversized rooms are alike, except for their stylish décor, European marble baths, and a few other amenities, all of which help ensure a comfortable stay. Locals crowd into the cozy Library Bar to sip cocktails (especially the martinis), chat with friends, and listen to relaxing piano music. Many then take a seat in the elegant Landmark Restaurant, where the eclectic menu features fresh, market-select items from around the country. 184 rooms, 8 story. Pets accepted, some restrictions; fee. Check-out noon, check-in 3 pm. TV; cable (premium), VCR available. In-room modem link. Room service 24 hours. Restaurant, bar; entertainment. Babysitting services available. In-house fitness room. Health club privileges. Valet parking. Free airport transportation. Concierge. Luxury level. Restored 1924 hotel. **$$**

[D] [icons]

★ ★ ★ **OMNI RICHARDSON HOTEL.** *701 E Campbell (75081). Phone 972/231-9600; fax 972/907-2578. www.omnihotels.com.* 342 rooms, 15 story. Pets accepted, some restrictions; fee. Check-out 11 am, check-in 3 pm. TV; cable (premium), VCR available. In-room modem link. Laundry services. Restaurant, bar. In-house fitness room. Outdoor pool; whirlpool. Business center. Concierge. Luxury level. **$$**

★ ★ ★ **RADISSON HOTEL CENTRAL DALLAS.** *6060 N Central Expy (75206). Phone 214/750-6060; fax 214/691-6581. www.radisson.com.* This hotel is centrally located a short distance from downtown. 296 rooms, 9 story. Pets accepted, some restrictions; fee. Check-out noon, check-in 3 pm. TV; cable (premium), VCR available. Restaurant, bar. Sauna. Indoor, outdoor pool; whirlpool; poolside service. Free airport transportation. Business center. **$**

★ ★ ★ **RENAISSANCE DALLAS HOTEL.** *2222 N Stemmons Fwy (75207). Phone 214/631-2222; toll-free 800/811-8893; fax 214/267-4989. www.renaissance hotels.com.* A sleek, 30-story, elliptical tower located in the Dallas Market Center, this hotel attracts corporate clients visiting the center's extensive wholesale collections or the nearby Texas Stadium and Dallas Convention Center. The pink granite façade houses 540 rooms and suites. 558 rooms, 30 story. Pets accepted; fee. Check-out noon, check-in 3 pm. TV; cable (premium), VCR available. In-room modem link. Restaurant, bar; entertainment. In-house fitness room. Health club privileges. Outdoor pool; whirlpool. Business center. Luxury level. **$$**

★ ★ ★ **SHERATON DALLAS BROOKHOLLOW HOTEL.** *1241 W Mockingbird Ln (75247). Phone 214/630-7000; toll-free 800/442-7547; fax 214/630-5232. www.sheraton.com.* Ideally located just 10 minutes from downtown Dallas, and 30 minutes from Six Flags and Hurricane Harbor, this hotel has something for everyone. 348 rooms, 13 story. Pets accepted, some restrictions; fee. Check-out noon, check-in 3 pm. TV; cable (premium). In-room modem link. Restaurant, bar. Room service. In-house fitness room. Health club privileges. Outdoor pool; poolside service. Free airport transportation. Luxury level. **$$**

★ ★ ★ **THE WESTIN GALLERIA DALLAS.** *13340 Dallas Pkwy (75240). Phone 972/934-9494; toll-free 800/228-3000; fax 972/851-2869. www.westin.com.* Located within the Galleria center, this hotel provides access to more than 200 shops, several restaurants, and entertainment. 432 rooms, 17 story. Pets accepted, some restrictions. Check-out noon, check-in 3 pm. TV; cable (premium), VCR available. In-room modem link. Restaurant, bar. Outdoor pool. Business center. Concierge. **$$$**

All Suites

★ **HAWTHORN SUITES.** *7900 Brookriver Dr (75247). Phone 214/688-1010; fax 214/638-5215. www.hawthorn.com.* 97 rooms, 2 story. Pets accepted; fee. Complimentary breakfast. Check-out noon, check-in 3 pm. TV; cable (premium). In-room modem link. Laundry services. Restaurant, bar. In-house fitness room. Health club privileges. Outdoor pool. Lawn games. **$**

★ ★ **RESIDENCE INN BY MARRIOTT.** *6950 N Stemmons Fwy (75247). Phone 214/631-2472; toll-free 800/331-3131; fax 214/634-9645. www.residenceinn.com.* 142 rooms, 3 story. Pets accepted; fee. Complimentary continental breakfast. Check-out noon, check-in 3 pm. TV; cable (premium). Laundry services. In-house fitness room. Health club privileges. Outdoor pool; whirlpool. Outdoor tennis. **$**

★ ★ ★ **SHERATON SUITES MARKET CENTER.** *2101 N Stemmons Fwy (75207). Phone 214/747-3000; toll-free 800/325-3535; fax 214/742-5713. www.sheraton.com.* French doors and marble baths grace each of this property's suites. The location is convenient to visitors of the nearby convention center or the Dallas Market Center, World Trade Center, and Apparel Mart, all of which are across the street. 251 rooms, 11 story. Pets accepted; fee. Check-out noon, check-in 3 pm. TV; cable (premium). In-room modem link. Restaurant, bar. Babysitting services available. In-house fitness room. Indoor, outdoor pool; whirlpool. **$**

B&B/Small Inn

★ ★ **HOTEL ST. GERMAIN.** *2516 Maple Ave (75201). Phone 214/871-2516; toll-free 800/683-2516; fax 214/871-0740. www.hotelstgermain.com.* Despite its location in the bustling Uptown district, this intimate boutique hotel offers its guests secluded getaways in grand style. All seven of its suites are richly decorated with turn-of-the-century antiques from France and New Orleans, and each has a working fireplace. Can you get any more romantic? Yes, come nightfall, with a candlelight dinner in a grand dining room that overlooks a New Orleans-style garden courtyard. The hotel serves the French cuisine on antique Limoges china. Before or after dinner, make a toast or two in the Parisian-style champagne bar in the parlor. 7 rooms, 3 story. Pets accepted, some restrictions; fee. Complimentary continental breakfast. Check-out noon, check-in 4 pm. TV; cable (premium), VCR available.

Room service 24 hours. Restaurant. Babysitting services available. Concierge. **$$$$**

D 🐾 ⊠

Dallas/Fort Worth Airport Area

Motels/Motor Lodges

★ **COUNTRY INN & SUITES BY CARLSON DFW AIRPORT-NORTH.** *4100 W John Carpenter Fwy (75063). Phone 972/929-4008; toll-free 800/456-4000; fax 972/929-4224. www.countryinns.com.* 72 rooms, 3 story. Pets accepted; fee. Complimentary continental breakfast. Check-out noon. TV; cable (premium). In-room modem link. Laundry services. In-house fitness room. Pool; children's pool; whirlpool. Free airport transportation. **$**

D 🐾 ⊠ 🏋 ✈ ⊠ SC

★ **DRURY INN.** *4210 W Airport Frwy (75062). Phone 972/986-1200. www.druryinn.com.* 129 rooms, 4 story. Pets accepted, some restrictions. Complimentary continental breakfast. Check-out noon. TV; cable (premium). In-room modem link. Pool. Free airport transportation. **$**

D 🐾 🐕 ⊠ ✈ ⊠

★ **HAMPTON INN.** *4340 W Airport Frwy (75062). Phone 972/986-3606; toll-free 800/426-7866; fax 972/986-6852. www.hamptoninn.com.* 81 rooms, 4 story. Pets accepted, some restrictions. Complimentary continental breakfast. Check-out noon. TV; cable (premium). Pool. Free airport transportation. **$**

D 🐾 ⊠ ✈ ⊠ SC

★★★ **HARVEY SUITES–D/FW AIRPORT.** *4550 W John Carpenter Frwy (75063). Phone 972/929-4499; fax 972/929-0774.* Built in 1984 and remodeled in 1995, this hotel offers guests a modern environment during their stay. The hotel is located near businesses and attractions. 164 rooms, 3 story. Pets accepted; fee. Complimentary continental breakfast. Check-out 1 pm. TV. In-room modem link. Laundry services. Restaurant, bar. Room service. In-house fitness room. Pool; whirlpool. Free airport transportation. **$$**

D 🐾 ⊠ 🏋 ✈ ⊠

★ **LA QUINTA INN.** *4105 W Airport Frwy (75062). Phone 972/252-6546; fax 972/570-4225. www.laquinta.com.* 169 rooms, 2 story. Pets accepted, some restrictions. Complimentary continental breakfast. Check-out noon. TV; cable (premium). In-room modem link. Pool. **$**

D 🐾 🐕 ⊠ ⊠

Resort

★★★★ **FOUR SEASONS RESORT AND CLUB DALLAS AT LAS COLINAS.** *4150 N MacArthur Blvd (75038). Phone 972/717-0700; toll-free 800/332-3442; fax 972/717-2550. www.fourseasons.com.* The Four Seasons Resort and Club Dallas at Las Colinas is only moments from downtown Dallas, yet it feels like it's a million miles away. Set on 400 rolling acres, the resort is a sports enthusiast's paradise. Home to the PGA's Byron Nelson Championship, the two golf courses accommodate players of all levels. Those guests looking to perfect their game appreciate the Byron Nelson Golf School and plentiful practice areas. The 12-court tennis facility attracts players with its climate-controlled indoor courts and sunny outdoor courts. Three outdoor pools, one indoor pool, and a children's pool keep swimmers satisfied, and the Sports Club's spa smoothes out the kinks with its variety of massages and treatments. Guests work up hearty appetites after active days, and the resort's six restaurants and bars serve up flavorful cuisine to meet the challenge. 357 rooms, 9 story. Pets accepted, some restrictions. Check-out noon, check-in 3 pm. TV; cable (premium), VCR available. In-room modem link. Room service 24 hours. Restaurant, bar. In-house fitness room; spa; massage; sauna; steam room. Outdoor pool; whirlpool; poolside service. Golf on premise; greens fee $150 (including cart). Indoor/outdoor tennis, lighted courts. Lawn games. Valet parking. Business center. Concierge. **$$$**

D 🐾 🏌 🎿 🏋 ⊠ 🏋 ⊠ 🏃

Del Rio

Motels/Motor Lodges

★ **BEST WESTERN INN OF DEL RIO.** *810 Ave F (78840). Phone 830/775-7511; toll-free 800/336-3537; fax 830/774-2194. www.bestwestern.com.* 62 rooms, 2 story. Pets accepted, some restrictions; fee. Complimentary full breakfast. Check-out noon. TV; cable (premium). Laundry services. Pool; whirlpool. **$**

D 🐾 ⊠ ⊠

★ **LA QUINTA INN.** *2005 Ave F (78840). Phone 830/775-7591; fax 830/774-0809. www.laquinta.com.* 101 rooms, 2 story. Pets accepted. Complimentary continental breakfast. Check-out noon. TV; cable (premium). In-room modem link. Laundry services. Pool. **$**

D 🐾 🐕 ⊠ ⊠

★★ **RAMADA INN.** *2101 Ave F (78840). Phone 830/775-1511; toll-free 800/272-6232; fax 830/775-1476. www.ramada.com.* 155 rooms. Pets accepted, some restrictions. Check-out noon. TV; cable (premium), VCR (movies). Laundry services. Restaurant, bar. Room service. In-house fitness room; sauna. Pool; whirlpool; poolside service. **$**

D 🐾 ⛖ 🏋 🔀 SC

Denton

Hotel

★ ★ ★ **RADISSON HOTEL DENTON AND EAGLE POINT GOLF CLUB.** *2211 I-35 E N (76205). Phone 940/565-8499; toll-free 800/333-3333; fax 940/ 384-2244. www.radisson.com.* 150 rooms, 8 story. Pets accepted, some restrictions; fee. TV; cable (premium), VCR available. Restaurant, bar. In-house fitness room. Health club privileges. Pool. Golf on premise. Business center. **$**

D 🐾 👬 ⛖ 🏋 🔀 SC 🚶

Dumas

Motels/Motor Lodges

★ **BEST WESTERN WINDSOR INN.** *1701 S Dumas Ave (79029). Phone 806/935-9644; fax 806/935-9730. www.bestwestern.com.* 57 rooms, 2 story. Pets accepted, some restrictions; fee. Check-out noon. TV; cable (premium). Laundry services. In-house fitness room; sauna. Indoor pool; whirlpool. **$**

D 🐾 ⛖ 🏋 🔀 SC

★ **COMFORT INN.** *1620 S Dumas Ave (79029). Phone 806/935-6988; toll-free 800/262-0038; fax 806/935-6924. www.comfortinn.com.* 50 rooms, 2 story. Pets accepted, some restrictions. Complimentary continental breakfast. Check-out noon. TV. In-house fitness room. Indoor pool; whirlpool. **$**

D 🐾 ⛖ 🏋 🔀

★ **ECONO LODGE.** *1719 S Dumas Ave (79029). Phone 806/935-9098; toll-free 800/344-2575; fax 806/935-7483. www.econolodge.com.* 40 rooms, 2 story. Pets accepted; fee. Complimentary continental breakfast. Check-out 11 am. TV; cable (premium). Laundry services. Pool; whirlpool. **$**

🐾 ⛖ 🔀

★ **SUPER 8.** *119 W 17th St (79029). Phone 806/ 935-6222; toll-free 800/800-8000; fax 806/935-6222. www.super8.com.* 30 rooms, 2 story. Pets accepted; fee. Complimentary continental breakfast. Check-out 11 am. TV. **$**

D 🐾 👬 🔀

Eagle Pass

Motels/Motor Lodges

★ **BEST WESTERN EAGLE PASS.** *1923 Loop 431 (78852). Phone 830/758-1234; toll-free 800/992-3245; fax 830/758-1235. www.bestwestern.com.* 40 rooms, 2 story. Pets accepted, some restrictions. Check-out noon. TV; cable (premium). In-room modem link. Pool. **$**

D 🐾 ⛖ 🔀

★ **LA QUINTA INN.** *2525 E Main St (78852). Phone 830/773-7000; fax 830/773-8852. www.laquinta.com.* 130 rooms, 2 story. Pets accepted, some restrictions. Complimentary continental breakfast. Check-out noon. TV; cable (premium). In-room modem link. Laundry services. Pool. **$**

D 🐾 🐾 ⛖ 🔀

El Paso

Motels/Motor Lodges

★ **COMFORT INN.** *900 N Yarbrough Dr (79915). Phone 915/594-9111; fax 915/590-4364. www.comfortinn.com.* 200 rooms, 3 story. Pets accepted. Complimentary continental breakfast. Check-out noon. TV; cable (premium). Laundry services. Pool; whirlpool. Airport transportation. **$**

D 🐾 ⛖ 🔀

★ ★ **HOLIDAY INN.** *900 Sunland Park Dr (79922). Phone 915/833-2900; toll-free 800/658-2744; fax 915/833-5588. www.holidayinnsunland.com.* 178 rooms, 2 story. Pets accepted; fee. Check-out noon. TV; cable (premium). Laundry services. Restaurant, bar. Room service. Pool; children's pool; whirlpool; poolside service. Airport transportation. On hill overlooking Sunland Park. **$**

D 🐾 🐾 ⛖ 🔀

★ **HOWARD JOHNSON.** *8887 Gateway West Blvd (79925). Phone 915/591-9471; fax 915/591-5602. www.hojoelpaso.com.* 140 rooms, 1-2 story. Pets accepted. Check-out 2 pm. TV; cable (premium). In-room modem link. Laundry services. In-house fitness room. Pool; children's pool. Free airport transportation. **$**

D 🐾 ⛖ 🏋 🔀

★ **LA QUINTA INN.** *6140 Gateway Blvd E (79905). Phone 915/778-9321; fax 915/779-1505. www.laquinta.com.* 121 rooms, 2 story. Pets accepted, some restrictions. Check-out noon. TV; cable (premium). In-room modem link. Pool. **$**

D 🐾 ⛖ 🔀

Hotels

★ ★ ★ **CAMINO REAL HOTEL EL PASO.** *101 S El Paso St (79901). Phone 915/534-3000; toll-free 800/769-4300; fax 915/534-3024. www.caminoreal.com.* Located downtown, next to the convention center and performing arts theatre, this hotel features a lobby bar covered by an original Tiffany glass dome. 359 rooms, 17 story. Pets accepted, some restrictions; fee. Check-out noon. TV. In-room modem link. Room service 24 hours. Restaurant, bar; entertainment. In-house fitness room; sauna. Pool. Business center. Luxury level. Renovated historic hotel (1912). **$**

⬛ 🐾 🏊 🧍 ✈ 🏊 🚶

★ ★ ★ **HILTON EL PASO AIRPORT.** *2027 Airway Blvd (79925). Phone 915/778-4241; fax 915/772-6871. www.hilton.com.* Located at the El Paso International Airport, this hotel has spacious courtyard rooms. 272 rooms, 4 story. Pets accepted; fee. Check-out noon. TV; cable (premium), VCR available. In-room modem link. Restaurant, bar. Room service. In-house fitness room. Pool. Free airport transportation. Business center. **$**

⬛ 🐾 🏊 🧍 ✈ 🏊 🚶

Fort Stockton

Motels/Motor Lodges

★ ★ **BEST WESTERN SWISS CLOCK INN.** *3201 W Dickinson (79735). Phone 915/336-8521; fax 915/336-6513. www.bestwestern.com.* 112 rooms, 2 story. Pets accepted, some restrictions. Check-out noon. TV; cable (premium). Laundry services. Restaurant. Room service. Pool. **$**

⬛ 🐾 🏊 🏊

★ **LA QUINTA INN.** *2601 W I-10 (79735). Phone 915/336-9781; fax 915/336-3634. www.laquinta.com.* 97 rooms, 2 story. Pets accepted. Check-out noon. TV; cable (premium), VCR available. Laundry services. Pool. **$**

⬛ 🐾 🏊 ✈ 🏊

Fort Worth

Motels/Motor Lodges

★ ★ **BEST WESTERN INNSUITES HOTEL AND SUITES FORT WORTH.** *2000 Beach St (76103). Phone 817/534-4801; toll-free 877/9-FORTWORTH; fax 817/534-3761. www.bestwestern.com.* 167 rooms, 2-3 story. Pets accepted; fee. Check-out noon, check-in 3 pm. TV; cable (premium). In-room modem link. Restaurant, bar. Room

service. In-house fitness room. Outdoor pool; whirlpool. Outdoor tennis, lighted courts. **$**

⬛ 🐾 🧍 🏊 🧍 🏊

★ **LA QUINTA INN.** *7888 W I-30 (76108). Phone 817/246-5511; toll-free 800/531-5900; fax 817/246-8870. www.laquinta.com.* 106 rooms, 3 story. Pets accepted, some restrictions. Complimentary continental breakfast. Check-out noon, check-in 1 pm. TV; cable (premium). In-room modem link. Outdoor pool. **$**

⬛ 🐾 🏊 🏊 SC

Hotels

★ ★ ★ **THE ASHTON.** *610 Main St (76102). Phone 817/332-0100; toll-free 866/327-4866. www.theashton hotel.com.* Small, intimate, and luxurious best describes this new boutique hotel, which occupies a historic downtown building built in 1915. All of its guest rooms have king-size beds that invite slumber with their Italian Frette linens, plush duvets, and down pillows. Some rooms have a claw-foot Jacuzzi tub nestled away in a corner, 12-foot ceilings, and good views of Main Street. Custom-designed mahogany furniture helps give the entire hotel a rich, inviting look. Sample the New American cuisine dished up in Café Ashton, or, if you're with a small group of up to 20, book the Wine Cellar for private dining. Work off the calories in the small fitness center. 39 rooms, 6 story. Pets accepted, some restrictions; fee. Check-out noon, check-in 3 pm. TV; cable (premium), VCR available. In-room modem link. Restaurant, bar. In-house fitness room. Concierge. **$$$**

🐾 🧍

★ ★ **GREEN OAKS HOTEL.** *6901 West Frwy (76116). Phone 817/738-7311; toll-free 800/772-2341; fax 817/377-1308. www.greenoakshotel.com.* This hotel is located in the suburban west side business district and just 8 miles from downtown Fort Worth. 260 rooms, 2-3 story. Pets accepted; fee. Complimentary full breakfast. Check-out noon, check-in 3 pm. TV; cable (premium), VCR available. In-room modem link. Restaurant, bar; entertainment. Room service. In-house fitness room; sauna. Two outdoor pools; poolside service. Lighted outdoor tennis courts. **$**

⬛ 🐾 🧍 🏊 🧍 🏊

★ ★ ★ **RENAISSANCE FORTH WORTH WORTHINGTON HOTEL.** *200 Main St (76102). Phone 817/870-1000; fax 817/338-9176. www.renaissancehotels .com.* This hotel, located in the historic Sundance Square, is just blocks from shops and museums, as well as restaurants and local points of interests. 531 rooms, 12 story. Pets accepted; fee. Check-out noon, check-in 3 pm. TV; cable (premium). In-room modem link. Room service 24 hours. Restaurant, bar. In-house fitness room; massage;

sauna. Indoor pool; whirlpool. Outdoor tennis. Valet parking. Business center. Concierge. Club level. **$**

★ ★ ★ **STOCKYARDS HOTEL.** *109 E Exchange Ave (76106). Phone 817/625-6427; toll-free 800/423-8471; fax 817/624-2571. www.stockyardshotel.com.* Check into this hotel and turn back time to the days of cattle drives and cattle rustlers. Located in Fort Worth's Stockyards, a national historic district, the hotel dates to the early 1900s, when it offered an elegant Old West theme to businessmen and ranchers in town for the booming livestock market. Completely restored in the 1980s, the property still has that Old West feel. The guest rooms have Western, Native American, Mountain Man, or Victorian décor. Instead of the typical lobby bar, there is Booger Red's Saloon, where saddles serve as barstools. The Western touch really heats up in H3 Ranch, a steakhouse with a hickory wood grill. 52 rooms, 3 story. Pets accepted, some restrictions; fee. Complimentary continental breakfast. Check-out noon, check-in 3 pm. TV. In-room modem link. Restaurant, bar. Valet parking. **$$**

Fredericksburg

Motels/Motor Lodges

★ **COMFORT INN.** *908 S Adams St (78624). Phone 830/997-9811; fax 830/997-2068. www.choicehotels.com.* 46 rooms, 2 story. Pets accepted, some restrictions; fee. Complimentary continental breakfast. Check-out noon, check-in 1 pm. TV; cable (premium). Outdoor pool. Outdoor tennis. **$**

★ ★ **SUNDAY HOUSE INN & SUITES.** *501 E Main St (78624). Phone 830/997-4484; toll-free 800/274-3762; fax 830/997-5607. www.sundayhouseinnandsuites.com.* 124 rooms, 2-3 story. Pets accepted, some restrictions; fee. Check-out noon, check-in 3 pm. TV. In-room modem link. Restaurant, bar. Outdoor pool. **$**

Gainesville

Motel/Motor Lodge

★ **BEST WESTERN SOUTHWINDS.** *2103 N I-35 (76240). Phone 940/665-7737; toll-free 800/731-1501; fax 940/668-2651. www.bestwestern.com.* 35 rooms. Pets accepted; fee. Complimentary continental breakfast. Check-out 11 am. TV; cable (premium). Pool. **$**

Galveston

Motel/Motor Lodge

★ **LA QUINTA INN.** *1402 Seawall Blvd (77550). Phone 409/763-1224; fax 409/765-8663. www. laquinta.com.* 117 rooms, 3 story. Pets accepted. Complimentary continental breakfast. Check-out noon. TV; cable (premium). In-room modem link. Pool. **$**

Georgetown

Motels/Motor Lodges

★ **COMFORT INN.** *1005 Leander Rd (78628). Phone 512/863-7504; toll-free 800/228-5150; fax 512/819-9016. www.comfortinn.com.* 55 rooms. Pets accepted, some restrictions; fee. Complimentary continental breakfast. Check-out noon. TV; VCR available (movies). Pool. **$**

★ **LA QUINTA INN.** *333 N I-35 (78628). Phone 512/869-2541; fax 512/863-7073. www.laquinta.com.* 98 rooms, 3 story. Pets accepted, some restrictions. Complimentary continental breakfast. Check-out noon. TV; cable (premium). In-room modem link. Laundry services. Restaurant. Room service. Pool. **$**

Glen Rose

Motel/Motor Lodge

★ ★ ★ **ROUGH CREEK LODGE.** *County Rd 2013. Phone 254/965-3700; toll-free 800/864-4705; fax 254/965-3170. www.roughcreek.com.* 39 rooms, 2 story. Pets accepted, some restrictions; fee. Check-out 11 am, check-in 3 pm. TV; cable (premium). Restaurant, bar. Children's activity center; babysitting services available. In-house fitness room; spa. Outdoor pool; whirlpool. Outdoor tennis. **$$$**

Graham

Motel/Motor Lodge

★ ★ **GATEWAY INN.** *1401 Hwy 16 S (76450). Phone 940/549-0222.* 77 rooms, 2 story. Pets accepted, some restrictions; fee. Check-out noon. TV; cable (premium).

Laundry services. Restaurant. Room service. Pool; whirlpool. Free airport transportation. **$**

D 🐾 🏊 🆖 SC

Granbury

Motels/Motor Lodges

★ **CLASSIC INN.** *1209 N Plaza Dr (76048). Phone 817/573-8874.* 42 rooms. Pets accepted, some restrictions. Complimentary continental breakfast. Check-out 11 am. TV; cable (premium). Pool. **$**

D 🐾 🏋 🏊 🆖

★ ★ **PLANTATION INN ON THE LAKE.** *1451 E Pearl St (76048). Phone 817/573-8846; toll-free 800/422-2403; fax 817/579-0917.* 53 rooms, 2 story. Pets accepted, some restrictions; fee. Complimentary continental breakfast. Check-out 11 am. TV; cable (premium). In-room modem link. Pool; children's pool. **$**

D 🐾 🏋 🏊 ✈ 🆖

Resort

★ **LODGE OF GRANBURY, ON LAKE GRANBURY.** *401 E Pearl St (76048). Phone 817/573-2606; fax 817/573-2077. www2.itexas.net/~lodgeofgby.* 58 rooms, 3 story. Pets accepted; fee. Check-out noon. TV; cable (premium). Pool; whirlpool. Outdoor tennis, lighted courts. **$**

D 🐾 🏋 🏌 🏊 🆖

Greenville

Motel/Motor Lodge

★ ★ **RAMADA INN.** *1215 E I-30 (75402). Phone 903/454-7000; fax 903/454-7001. www.ramada.com.* 138 rooms, 2 story. Pets accepted; fee. Complimentary full breakfast. Check-out noon. TV; cable (premium). In-room modem link. Laundry services. Restaurant. Room service. In-house fitness room; sauna. Health club privileges. Pool; whirlpool. **$**

D 🐾 🏊 🏌 🆖 SC

Harlingen

Motel/Motor Lodge

★ **LA QUINTA INN.** *1002 S Expy 83 (78552). Phone 956/428-6888; fax 956/425-5840. www.laquinta.com.* 130 rooms, 2 story. Pets accepted, some restrictions. Complimentary full breakfast. Check-out noon. TV; cable

(premium). In-room modem link. Laundry services. Pool. Free airport transportation. **$**

D 🐾 🏊 🆖 SC

Hereford

Motel/Motor Lodge

★ **BEST WESTERN RED CARPET INN.** *830 W 1st St (79045). Phone 806/364-0540; toll-free 877/512-6777; fax 806/364-0818. www.bestwestern.com.* 90 rooms, 2 story. Pets accepted, some restrictions. Check-out noon. TV. Pool. **$**

🐾 🏋 🏊 🆖

Hillsboro

Motel/Motor Lodge

★ **RAMADA INN.** *I-35 and US 22 (76645). Phone 254/582-3493; toll-free 877/200-3392; fax 254/582-2755. www.ramada.com.* 94 rooms, 2 story. Pets accepted. Check-out noon. TV; cable (premium). Pool. **$**

D 🐾 🏊 🆖

Houston

Motels/Motor Lodges

★ **DRURY INN.** *1615 W Loop S (77027). Phone 713/963-0700; toll-free 800/378-7946. www.druryinn.com.* 134 rooms, 5 story. Pets accepted. Complimentary continental breakfast. Check-out noon. TV; cable (premium). In-room modem link. Indoor, outdoor pool; whirlpool. **$**

D 🐾 🏊 🆖 SC

★ **HAMPTON INN.** *828 Mercury Dr (77013). Phone 713/673-4200; fax 713/674-6913. www.hamptoninn.com.* 90 rooms, 6 story. Pets accepted, some restrictions; fee. Complimentary continental breakfast. Check-out noon. TV; cable (premium). In-room modem link. Laundry services. Pool. **$**

D 🐾 🏊 🆖

★ ★ ★ **HOLIDAY INN.** *15222 John F Kennedy Blvd (77032). Phone 281/449-2311; fax 281/442-6833. www.holiday-inn.com.* This corporate-traveler hotel provides complimentary shuttles to George Bush Intercontinental Airport, located just 1 mile north. 413 rooms, 5 story. Pets accepted; fee. Check-out noon. TV; cable (premium), VCR available. In-room modem link. Laundry services. Restaurant, bar. Room service. In-house fitness room. Pool; children's pool; poolside service.

Outdoor tennis, lighted courts. Lawn games. Free airport transportation. **$**

⬡⬡⬡⬡⬡⬡⬡⬡ SC

★ **LA QUINTA INN.** *4015 SW Frwy (77027). Phone 713/623-4750; fax 713/963-0599. www.laquinta.com.* 131 rooms, 2-3 story. Pets accepted, some restrictions. Complimentary continental breakfast. Check-out noon. TV; cable (premium). Laundry services. Pool. **$**

D⬡⬡⬡

★ **LA QUINTA INN.** *11113 Katy Frwy (77079). Phone 713/932-0808; toll-free 800/687-6667; fax 713/973-2352. www.laquinta.com.* 176 rooms, 2 story. Pets accepted. Complimentary continental breakfast. Check-out noon. TV; cable (premium). In-room modem link. Laundry services. Pool. **$**

D⬡⬡⬡ SC

Hotels

★★★ **CROWNE PLAZA.** *12801 Northwest Frwy (77040). Phone 713/462-9977; toll-free 800/826-1606; fax 713/460-8725. www.crowneplaza.com/brookhollowtx.* This property is a short drive to Galleria shopping and Sam Houston Race Park. 291 rooms, 10 story. Pets accepted; fee. Check-out noon. TV; cable (premium). In-room modem link. Laundry services. Restaurant, bar. Room service. In-house fitness room. Health club privileges. Pool; poolside service. **$**

D⬡⬡⬡⬡ SC

★★★ **DOUBLETREE HOTEL.** *400 Dallas St (77002). Phone 713/759-0202; toll-free 800/772-7666; fax 713/759-1166. www.doubletree.com.* Located in Houston's business district, this hotel offers both business and leisure travelers a relaxing stay. Guests can enjoy spacious rooms offering a sensational skyline view and warm and friendly service. 350 rooms, 20 story. Pets accepted, some restrictions; fee. Check-out noon. TV; cable (premium). In-room modem link. Restaurant, bar; entertainment Mon-Fri. In-house fitness room. Health club privileges. Business center. Concierge. Elegant hanging tapestries. **$$**

D⬡⬡⬡ SC⬡

★★★ **DOUBLETREE HOTEL.** *5353 Westheimer Rd (77056). Phone 713/961-9000; fax 713/877-8835. www.doubletree.com.* This luxurious hotel is found in the Uptown/Galleria area. Its location puts it near premier shopping, restaurants and entertainment, as well as near many area attractions. 335 rooms, 26 story. Pets accepted; fee. Check-out noon, check-in 3 pm. TV; cable (premium). In-room modem link. Laundry services. Room service 24 hours. Restaurant, bar. In-house fitness room.

Health club privileges. Game room. Pool; whirlpool; poolside service. Garage, valet parking. **$$**

D⬡⬡⬡⬡⬡⬡

★★★★ **FOUR SEASONS HOTEL HOUSTON.** *1300 Lamar St (77010). Phone 713/650-1300; toll-free 800/332-3442; fax 713/652-6220. www.fourseasons.com.* The Four Seasons is a perfect complement to the urbane spirit of Houston. Close to the Convention Center and Enron Field Stadium, it is conveniently located near the downtown business and financial districts. Thoughtful car service makes doing business or visiting the sites carefree. Shoppers adore this hotel for its proximity to Park Shops, a three-level mall connected to the hotel via a climate-controlled skywalk. The guest rooms are a sophisticated blend of European furniture, Asian decorative objects, and Southwestern splash. The sparkling outdoor pool, fitness center, and spa give the hotel a resort-in-the-city ambience, perfect for guests after a long day. Guests sample tequila, taste wine, and savor tapas from around the world in the relaxing atmosphere of the Lobby Lounge. Quattro is a feast for the eyes and the senses with its vivacious décor and simply delicious Italian cuisine. 404 rooms, 30 story. Pets accepted, some restrictions. Check-out 1 pm, check-in 3 pm. TV; cable (premium), VCR available. In-room modem link. Room service 24 hours. Restaurant, bar; entertainment. Babysitting services available. In-house fitness room; spa; massage; sauna. Health club privileges. Outdoor pool; whirlpool; poolside service. Valet parking. Business center. Concierge. **$$$**

D⬡⬡⬡⬡⬡

★★★ **INTER-CONTINENTAL HOUSTON.** *2222 West Loop S (77459). Phone 713/627-7600; toll-free 866/342-0831; fax 713/961-5575. www.intercontinental.com.* 485 rooms, 23 story. Pets accepted, some restrictions; fee. Check-out noon, check-in 4 pm. TV; cable (premium). Internet access. Restaurant, bar. Room service. Babysitting services available. In-house fitness room; spa. Outdoor pool; whirlpool. Business center. **$$$**

D⬡⬡⬡⬡

★★★ **MARRIOTT HOUSTON HOBBY AIRPORT.** *9100 Gulf Frwy (77017). Phone 713/943-7979; toll-free 800/333-3333; fax 713/943-1621. www.marriott.com.* Within minutes from the Hobby Airport and just 7 miles from all of downtown Houston's attractions, this hotel offers travelers a relaxing and comfortable stay. Nearby attractions include the Nassau Space Center and Six Flags Astroworld. 288 rooms, 10 story. Pets accepted, some restrictions; fee. Check-out noon. TV; cable (premium). In-room modem link. Restaurant, bar. In-house fitness room; sauna. Indoor pool; whirlpool; poolside service. Free airport transportation. Concierge. Luxury level. **$**

D⬡⬡⬡⬡⬡

★★★ **OMNI HOUSTON HOTEL.** *4 Riverway (77056). Phone 713/871-8181; toll-free 800/843-6664; fax 713/871-0719. www.omnihotels.com.* Only 30 minutes from downtown, the Omni Houston Hotel occupies an enviable location in the Post Oak/Galleria section. Nestled on lush grounds overlooking a 3-acre lake, this hotel enables visitors to leave the world behind. The gracious lobby dazzles with its water garden of cascading waterfalls and brightly colored fish. Rich reds, golds, and persimmons are used in the public spaces, creating an exotic sophistication. Lush foliage dominates the lobby, and abundant floral displays add touches of beauty throughout the hotel. The guest rooms have a relaxed, contemporary style, while modern amenities allow visitors to keep in touch. A well-equipped fitness center, tennis and basketball courts, and the nearby jogging trails of Hershey Park provide athletic diversions. An American bistro and English-style pub offer pleasantly casual surroundings, while the refined French cuisine of La Reserve is an award-winning local sensation. 378 rooms, 11 story. Pets accepted, some restrictions; fee. Check-out noon, check-in 3 pm. TV; cable (premium), VCR available. In-room modem link. Room service 24 hours. Restaurant, bar; entertainment. Babysitting services available. In-house fitness room; spa; massage; sauna. Outdoor pool; whirlpool; poolside service. Outdoor tennis, lighted courts. Valet parking. Business center. Concierge. **$$**

★★★ **OMNI HOUSTON HOTEL WESTSIDE.** *13210 Katy Frwy I-10 (77079). Phone 281/558-8338; fax 281/558-4028. www.omnihotels.com.* This property offers 400 guest rooms and 25 meeting rooms. Guests will enjoy viewing the indoor lakes and scenery from glass elevators. Amenities include a pool, health club, tennis courts and more, while golf and other attraction are close by. 400 rooms, 5 story. Pets accepted, some restrictions; fee. Check-out noon. TV; cable (premium). In-room modem link. Restaurant, bar; entertainment. In-house fitness room. Health club privileges. Pool; whirlpool; poolside service. Outdoor tennis, lighted courts. Free garage parking. Business center. **$$**

★★★ **RENAISSANCE HOUSTON HOTEL.** *6 Greenway Plaza E (77046). Phone 713/629-1200; fax 713/629-4706. www.renaissancehotels.com.* This hotel is situated in the same complex as numerous corporate headquarters and adjacent to the Compaq Center Complex. 400 rooms, 20 story. Pets accepted, some restrictions. Check-out noon, check-in 1 pm. TV; cable (premium). In-room modem link. Room service 24 hours. Restaurant, bar. In-house fitness room; sauna. Health club privileges. Pool; poolside service. Valet parking. **$$**

★★★ **THE SAM HOUSTON HOTEL.** *1117 Prairie St (77002). Phone 832/200-8800; toll-free 877/348-8800; fax 832/200-8811. www.samhoustonhotel.com.* 100 rooms. Pets accepted; fee. Check-out noon, check-in 3 pm. Restaurant, bar. Babysitting services available. In-house fitness room. **$$**

★★★ **SHERATON HOUSTON BROOKHOLLOW HOTEL.** *3000 N Loop W (77092). Phone 713/688-0100; fax 713/688-9224. www.sheraton.com.* 382 rooms, 10 story. Pets accepted, some restrictions. Check-out 1 pm. TV; cable (premium). In-room modem link. Restaurant, bar. In-house fitness room; sauna. Pool; whirlpool; poolside service. Luxury level. **$$**

★★★★ **THE ST. REGIS, HOUSTON.** *1919 Briar Oaks Ln (77027). Phone 713/840-7600; fax 713/840-0616. www.stregis.com.* The St. Regis echoes the grace and elegance of its pedigreed neighbors in the River Oaks section of Houston. The world-class shopping of the Galleria is just a short distance, as are the businesses and attractions of downtown. This exceptional hotel combines sublime interiors and impeccable service under one roof. While staying here, guests are assured of a singular experience. The guest rooms are lovely homes away from home, with rich mahogany furnishings juxtaposed with subtle cream, white, and taupe color schemes. Large windows are swathed in luxurious fabrics, and appealing art adorns the walls. The climate-controlled outdoor pool offers a perfect place for reflection. Bathed in glorious sunshine, the Tea Lounge offers one of the most elegant ways to spend an afternoon, and the quality seafood and steaks at Remington Grill make for a memorable dining experience. 232 rooms, 12 story. Pets accepted, some restrictions. Check-out noon, check-in 3 pm. TV; cable (premium). Restaurant, bar; entertainment. Babysitting services available. In-house fitness room; spa; massage. Health club privileges. Outdoor pool; poolside service. Valet parking. Business center. Concierge. Luxury level. **$$$$**

Huntsville

Motels/Motor Lodges

★ **LA QUINTA INN.** *124 I-45 N (77320). Phone 936/295-6454; toll-free 800/687-6667; fax 936/295-9245. www.laquinta.com.* 120 rooms, 2 story. Pets accepted, some restrictions. Complimentary continental breakfast. Check-out noon. TV; cable (premium). Pool; children's pool. **$**

★ **UNIVERSITY HOTEL.** *1610 Ave H at 16th St (77341). Phone 936/291-2151; fax 936/294-1683.* 95 rooms, 4 story. Pets accepted. Check-out noon. TV. On Sam Houston State University campus. Totally nonsmoking. **$**

▫️🐾🏊

Jefferson

Motel/Motor Lodge

★ **INN AT JEFFERSON.** *400 S Walcott (75657). Phone 903/665-3983; fax 903/665-3536.* 65 rooms, 2 story. Pets accepted. Complimentary continental breakfast. Check-out noon. TV; cable (premium). Pool. **$**

▫️🐾🏊🏊

Kerrville

Motel/Motor Lodge

★★ **BEST WESTERN SUNDAY HOUSE INN.** *2124 Sidney Baker St (78028). Phone 830/896-1313; toll-free 800/677-9477; fax 830/896-1336. www.bestwestern.com.* 97 rooms, 2 story. Pets accepted, some restrictions; fee. Check-out noon. TV; cable (premium). Restaurant, bar. Pool. **$**

▫️🐾🏊🏊

Resort

★★ **Y.O. RANCH RESORT HOTEL.** *2033 Sidney Baker St (78028). Phone 830/257-4440; toll-free 877/967-3767; fax 830/896-8189. www.yoresort.com.* Visitors who are looking to experience the Old West will love this Texas hotel. Stepping into the lobby, which is filled with antiques and over forty game trophies, is like stepping back in time. Guest rooms are spacious with a western décor. 191 rooms, 2 story. Pets accepted, some restrictions. Check-out noon. TV; cable (premium). In-room modem link. Restaurant, bar. Room service. Pool; children's pool; whirlpool. Outdoor tennis. Lawn games. Airport transportation. Western décor; Mexican tile floors. **$**

▫️🐾🎾🏊🏊 SC

Killeen

Motel/Motor Lodge

★ **LA QUINTA INN.** *1112 S Fort Hood St (76541). Phone 254/526-8331; fax 254/526-0394. www.laquinta.com.* 105 rooms, 3 story. No elevator. Pets accepted. Complimentary continental breakfast. Check-out noon. TV; cable (premium). In-room modem link. Laundry services. Pool. Free airport transportation. **$**

▫️🐾🎾🏊🏊

Kingsville

Motels/Motor Lodges

★ **ECONO LODGE KINGSVILLE.** *221 S US Hwy 77 Bypass (78363). Phone 361/592-5251; toll-free 800/424-4777; fax 361/592-6197. www.econolodge.com.* 117 rooms, 2 story. Pets accepted, some restrictions. Complimentary continental breakfast. Check-out noon. TV; cable (premium). In-house fitness room. Pool; children's pool. **$**

▫️🐾🏊🏊🏊 SC

★★ **HOLIDAY INN.** *3430 S Hwy 77 Bypass (78363). Phone 361/595-5753; fax 361/595-4513. www.holiday-inn.com.* 75 rooms, 2 story. Pets accepted. Check-out noon. TV; cable (premium). Laundry services. Restaurant, bar. Room service. Pool; poolside service. **$**

▫️🐾🏊🏊

Laredo

Motel/Motor Lodge

★ **LA QUINTA INN.** *3610 Santa Ursula Ave (78041). Phone 956/722-0511; fax 956/723-6642. www.laquinta.com.* 152 rooms, 2 story. Pets accepted, some restrictions. Complimentary continental breakfast. Check-out noon, check-in 2 pm. TV; cable (premium). In-room modem link. Outdoor pool. **$**

▫️🐾🏊🏊

Hotel

★ **RED ROOF INN.** *1006 W Calton Rd (78041). Phone 956/712-0733; fax 956/712-4337. www.redroof.com.* 150 rooms, 4 story. Pets accepted, some restrictions. Check-out noon, check-in 3 pm. TV. Outdoor pool. **$**

▫️🐾🏊

Longview

Motel/Motor Lodge

★ **LA QUINTA INN.** *502 S Access Rd (75602). Phone 903/757-3663; toll-free 800/531-5900; fax 903/753-3780. www.laquinta.com.* 105 rooms, 2 story. Pets accepted, some restrictions. Complimentary continental breakfast. Check-out noon. TV; cable (premium). In-room modem link. Laundry services. Pool. **$**

D 🐾 🏊 🚫 SC

Lubbock

Motels/Motor Lodges

★ ★ **HOLIDAY INN.** *3201 S Loop 289 (79423). Phone 806/797-3241; fax 806/793-1203. www.holiday-inn.com.* 202 rooms, 2 story. Pets accepted, some restrictions. Check-out noon. TV; cable (premium). In-room modem link. Laundry services. Restaurant, bar. Room service. Indoor pool; children's pool. Free airport transportation. **$**

D 🐾 🏊 🚫

★ **LA QUINTA INN.** *601 Ave Q (79401). Phone 806/763-9441; toll-free 800/531-5900; fax 806/747-9325. www.laquinta.com.* 137 rooms, 2 story. Pets accepted, some restrictions. Complimentary continental breakfast. Check-out noon. TV. In-room modem link. Pool. **$**

🐾 🏊 🚫 SC

Lufkin

Motels/Motor Lodges

★ **DAYS INN.** *2130 S 1st St (75904). Phone 936/639-3301; toll-free 800/329-7466; fax 936/634-4266. www.daysinn.com.* 126 rooms, 2 story. Pets accepted; fee. Complimentary continental breakfast. Check-out noon. TV; cable (premium). Laundry services. Restaurant, bar. Room service. Pool; children's pool; whirlpool. **$**

D 🐾 🏊 🚫 SC

★ ★ **HOLIDAY INN.** *4306 S First St (75901). Phone 936/639-3333; toll-free 888/639-3382; fax 936/639-3382. www.holiday-inn.com.* 102 rooms, 2 story. Pets accepted, some restrictions; fee. Check-out noon. TV; cable (premium). In-room modem link. Laundry services. Restaurant, bar. Room service. Pool; poolside service. Free airport transportation. **$**

D 🐾 🏊 ✈ 🚫

★ **LA QUINTA INN.** *2111 S 1st St (75901). Phone 936/634-3351; fax 936/634-9475. www.laquinta.com.* 106 rooms, 2 story. Pets accepted, some restrictions. Complimentary continental breakfast. Check-out noon. TV. In-room modem link. Laundry services. Pool. **$**

D 🐾 🏊 🚫

Marshall

Motel/Motor Lodge

★ ★ **GUEST INN.** *100 W I-20 (75672). Phone 903/927-1718; fax 903/927-1747.* 46 rooms, 2 story. Pets accepted; fee. Complimentary continental breakfast. Check-out 11 am. TV; cable (premium). Pool. **$**

🐾 🕺 🏊 🚫

McAllen

Motels/Motor Lodges

★ **DRURY INN.** *612 W Expy 83 (78501). Phone 956/687-5100. www.druryinn.com.* 89 rooms. Pets accepted, some restrictions. Complimentary continental breakfast. Check-out noon. TV; cable (premium), VCR available. In-room modem link. Pool. **$**

D 🐾 🏊 ✈ 🚫

★ **HAMPTON INN.** *300 W Expy 83 (78501). Phone 956/682-4900; fax 956/682-6823. www.hamptoninn.com.* 91 rooms, 4 story. Pets accepted, some restrictions. Complimentary continental breakfast. Check-out noon. TV. In-room modem link. Pool. Near airport. **$**

D 🐾 🏊 ✈ 🚫

★ ★ **HOLIDAY INN.** *200 W Expy US 83 (78501). Phone 956/686-2471; fax 956/682-7609. www.holiday-inn.com.* 173 rooms, 2 story. Pets accepted, some restrictions; fee. Check-out noon. TV; cable (premium), VCR available. In-room modem link. Laundry services. Restaurant, bar. Room service. In-house fitness room; sauna. Game room. Indoor, outdoor pool; whirlpool. Free airport transportation. **$**

D 🐾 🏊 🕺 ✈ 🚫

★ **LA QUINTA INN.** *1100 S 10th St (78501). Phone 956/687-1101; toll-free 800/687-6667; fax 956/687-9265. www.laquinta.com.* 120 rooms, 3 story. Pets accepted. Complimentary continental breakfast. Check-out noon. TV; cable (premium). In-room modem link. Bar. Pool. Free airport, bus depot transportation. **$**

D 🐾 🏊 ✈ 🚫 SC

Midland

Motels/Motor Lodges

★ ★ **BEST INN.** *3100 W Wall St (79701). Phone 915/699-4144; fax 915/699-7639. www.bestinn.com.* 200 rooms, 3 story. Pets accepted, some restrictions; fee. Check-out noon. TV; cable (premium). Restaurant, bar. Room service. In-house fitness room. Indoor pool. Free airport transportation. **$**

🄳 🔊 ⇌ 🏃 ✈ 🔌 SC

★ **DAYS INN.** *1003 S Midkiff Ave (79701). Phone 915/697-3155; toll-free 800/329-7466; fax 915/699-2017. www.daysinn.com.* 182 rooms, 2 story. Pets accepted, some restrictions; fee. Complimentary continental breakfast. Check-out noon. TV; cable (premium). Laundry services. Pool; whirlpool. Airport transportation. **$**

🄳 🔊 ⇌ 🔌 SC

★ ★ **HOLIDAY INN.** *4300 W Wall St (79703). Phone 915/697-3181; fax 915/694-7754. www.holiday-inn.com.* 252 rooms, 2 story. Pets accepted, some restrictions; fee. Check-out noon. TV; cable (premium). Laundry services. Restaurant, bar. Room service. In-house fitness room; sauna. Indoor pool; whirlpool. Free airport transportation. Business center. **$**

🄳 🔊 ⇌ 🏃 ✈ 🔌 SC 🏃

★ ★ ★ **HOLIDAY INN.** *6201 E Business Loop 20 (79762). Phone 915/362-2311; toll-free 800/465-4329; fax 915/362-9810. www.holiday-inn.com.* 244 rooms, 3 story. Pets accepted, some restrictions. TV. In-room modem link. Laundry services. Restaurant, bar. Room service. In-house fitness room; sauna. Indoor, outdoor pool; whirlpool; poolside service. Free airport transportation. **$**

🄳 🔊 ⇌ 🏃 🔌

★ **LA QUINTA INN.** *4130 W Wall Ave (79703). Phone 915/697-9900; fax 915/689-0617. www.laquinta.com.* 146 rooms, 2 story. Pets accepted, some restrictions. Complimentary continental breakfast. Check-out noon. TV; cable (premium). Laundry services. Pool. **$**

🔊 ⇌ 🔌 SC

Mount Pleasant

Motel/Motor Lodge

★ **SUPER 8.** *401 W I-30 (75457). Phone 903/588-2882; fax 903/588-2844. www.super8.com.* 43 rooms, 2 story. Pets accepted, some restrictions; fee. Complimentary

continental breakfast. Check-out 11 am. TV; cable (premium). In-room modem link. Bar. **$**

🄳 🔊 🐾 🔌

Nacogdoches

Motel/Motor Lodge

★ **LA QUINTA INN.** *3215 South St (75961). Phone 936/560-5453; fax 936/560-4372. www.laquinta.com.* 106 rooms, 2 story. Pets accepted. Complimentary continental breakfast. Check-out noon. TV; cable (premium). In-room modem link. Laundry services. Pool. **$**

🄳 🔊 🐾 ⇌ 🔌

Hotel

★ **FREDONIA HOTEL & CONVENTION CENTER.** *200 N Fredonia St (75961). Phone 936/564-1234; toll-free 800/594-5323. www.fredoniahotel.com.* 113 rooms, 6 story. Pets accepted; fee. Check-out 1 pm. TV. Restaurant. Pool; poolside service. **$**

🄳 🔊 ⇌ ✈ 🔌

New Braunfels

Motel/Motor Lodge

★ **HOLIDAY INN.** *1051 I-35 E (78130). Phone 830/625-8017; toll-free 800/465-4329; fax 830/625-3130. www.holiday-inn.com.* 140 rooms, 2 story. Pets accepted; fee. Check-out noon. TV; cable (premium). In-room modem link. Laundry services. Restaurant, bar; entertainment. Room service. In-house fitness room. Pool; children's pool. **$**

🄳 🔊 ⇌ 🏃 🔌 SC

Odessa

Motels/Motor Lodges

★ ★ **BEST WESTERN GARDEN OASIS.** *110 W I-20 (79761). Phone 915/337-3006; toll-free 877/574-9231; fax 915/332-1956. www.bestwestern.com.* 118 rooms, 2 story. Pets accepted, some restrictions. Check-out noon. TV; cable (premium), VCR available. Laundry services. Restaurant. Room service. Sauna. Indoor pool; whirlpool; poolside service. Free airport transportation. **$**

🄳 🔊 ⇌ 🔌

★ **LA QUINTA INN.** *5001 E Business 20 (79761). Phone 915/333-2820; toll-free 800/531-5900; fax 915/333-4208. www.laquinta.com.* 122 rooms. Pets accepted, some restrictions. Check-out noon. TV; cable (premium). Pool. **$**

Orange

Motel/Motor Lodge

★ ★ **RAMADA INN.** *2610 I-H 10 (77632). Phone 409/883-0231; toll-free 800/272-6232; fax 409/883-8839. www.ramada.com.* 125 rooms, 2 story. Pets accepted, some restrictions. Check-out noon. TV; cable (premium). In-room modem link. Restaurant, bar; entertainment. Room service. Pool; children's pool. **$**

Palestine

Motel/Motor Lodge

★ ★ **BEST WESTERN PALESTINE INN.** *1601 W Palestine Ave (75801). Phone 903/723-4655; toll-free 800/523-0121; fax 903/723-2519. www.bestwestern.com.* 66 rooms, 2 story. Pets accepted. Check-out 1 pm. TV; cable (premium). In-room modem link. Restaurant. Pool. **$**

Plainview

Motel/Motor Lodge

★ **BEST WESTERN CONESTOGA.** *600 N I-27 (79072). Phone 806/293-9454; toll-free 800/780-7234. www.bestwestern.com.* 83 rooms, 2 story. Pets accepted; fee. Complimentary continental breakfast. Check-out noon. TV; cable (premium), VCR available. In-room modem link. Pool. **$**

Plano

Extended Stay

★ ★ **RESIDENCE INN BY MARRIOTT.** *5001 Whitestone Ln (75024). Phone 972/473-6761; fax 972/473-6628. www.residenceinn.com.* Guests will enjoy the spacious rooms featuring full kitchens and living rooms. 126 rooms, 3 story. Pets accepted; fee. Complimentary buffet breakfast. Check-out noon, check-in 3 pm. TV; cable (premium). In-room modem link. Laundry services. In-house fitness room. Outdoor pool. Outdoor tennis. **$**

Port Arthur

Motel/Motor Lodge

★ ★ **RAMADA INN.** *3801 Hwy 73 (77642). Phone 409/962-9858; fax 409/962-3685. www.ramada.com.* 125 rooms, 2 story. Pets accepted. Check-out noon. TV; cable (premium). Restaurant, bar. Room service. Pool; children's pool. Outdoor tennis, lighted courts. Free airport transportation. **$**

Port Lavaca

Motel/Motor Lodge

★ **DAYS INN.** *2100 N TX 35 Bypass (77979). Phone 361/552-4511; toll-free 800/329-7466. www.daysinn.com.* 99 rooms, 2 story. Pets accepted; fee. Complimentary continental breakfast. Check-out noon. TV. In-room modem link. Laundry services. Restaurant, bar. Pool. **$**

Rockport

Motel/Motor Lodge

★ **BEST WESTERN INN BY THE BAY.** *3902 US 35 N (78358). Phone 361/729-8351; toll-free 800/235-6076; fax 361/729-0950. www.bestwestern.com.* 72 rooms, 2 story. Pets accepted; fee. Complimentary breakfast. Check-out 11 am. TV; cable (premium). Laundry services. Pool. **$**

San Angelo

Motels/Motor Lodges

★ **EL PATIO MOTOR INN.** *1901 W Beauregard Ave (76901). Phone 915/655-5711; toll-free 800/677-7735; fax 915/653-2717.* 100 rooms, 2 story. Pets accepted, some restrictions. Check-out noon. TV; cable (premium), VCR available. Pool. **$**

★ ★ ★ **HOLIDAY INN.** *441 Rio Concho Dr (76903). Phone 915/658-2828; toll-free 800/465-4329; fax 915/658-8741. www.holiday-inn.com/sanangelotx.* This high rise features not only convention and meeting spaces, but also recreational facilities. 148 rooms, 6 story. Pets accepted; fee. Check-out noon. TV; cable (premium). Restaurant, bar. Indoor pool; whirlpool; poolside service. **$**

D 🐾 🛁 🏊 🛪 🕳

★ ★ **HOWARD JOHNSON.** *415 W Beauregard (76903). Phone 915/653-2995; toll-free 800/582-9668; fax 915/659-4393. www.hojo.com.* 75 rooms, 3 story. Pets accepted. Check-out noon. TV; cable (premium), VCR available. In-room modem link. Restaurant. Room service. Indoor pool. **$**

D 🐾 🛁 🕳

★ **INN OF THE CONCHOS.** *2021 N Bryant Blvd (76903). Phone 915/658-2811; toll-free 800/621-6091; fax 915/653-7560.* 125 rooms, 2 story. Pets accepted. Check-out noon. TV; cable (premium). Bar. Room service. Pool. **$**

D 🐾 🛁 🕳

★ **LA QUINTA INN.** *2307 Loop 306 (76904). Phone 915/949-0515; toll-free 800/687-6667; fax 915/944-1187. www.laquinta.com.* 170 rooms, 2 story. Pets accepted, some restrictions. Complimentary continental breakfast. Check-out noon. TV; cable (premium). In-room modem link. Laundry services. Pool. **$**

D 🐾 🛁 🕳 SC

San Antonio

Motels/Motor Lodges

★ ★ ★ **BAYMONT INN.** *100 W Durango (78204). Phone 210/212-5400; toll-free 877/211-0103; fax 210/212-5407. www.woodfieldsuitessa.com.* Very attractive guestrooms and public areas are complemented by a friendly, knowledgeable staff at this downtown hotel. 151 rooms, 6 story. Pets accepted, some restrictions; fee. Complimentary continental breakfast. Check-out noon, check-in 3 pm. TV; cable (premium). Laundry services. Bar. In-house fitness room. Pool; whirlpool. Parking lot. **$**

D 🐾 🛁 🏋 🕳 SC

★ **DRURY INN.** *95 NE Loop 410 (78216). Phone 210/308-8100; fax 210/341-6758. www.druryinn.com.* 286 rooms, 6 story. Pets accepted, some restrictions. Complimentary continental breakfast. Check-out noon. TV; cable (premium). In-room modem link. Pool; whirlpool. Free airport transportation. **$**

D 🐾 🛁 🕳

★ ★ **DRURY INN.** *143 NE Loop 410 (78216). Phone 210/366-9300. www.peartreeinn.com.* 125 rooms, 4 story. Pets accepted, some restrictions. Complimentary breakfast. Check-out noon. TV; cable (premium). In-room modem link. Laundry services. Pool. Free airport transportation. **$**

D 🐾 🛁 🕳

★ **HOLIDAY INN EXPRESS.** *91 NE Loop 410 (78216). Phone 210/308-6700. www.holiday-inn.com.* 154 rooms, 10 story. Pets accepted, some restrictions. Complimentary continental breakfast. Check-out noon. TV; cable (premium). In-room modem link. Laundry services. Pool. Free airport transportation. **$**

D 🐾 🛁 🕳

★ **RED ROOF INN.** *333 Wolf Rd (78216). Phone 210/340-4055; toll-free 800/843-7663; fax 210/340-4031. www.redroof.com.* 135 rooms, 3 story. Pets accepted. Check-out noon. TV; cable (premium). In-room modem link. Free airport transportation. **$**

D 🐾 🛪 🕳 SC

Hotels

★ ★ ★ **HILTON PALACIO DEL RIO.** *200 S Alamo St (78205). Phone 210/222-1400; toll-free 800/445-8667; fax 210/270-0761. www.palaciodelrio.hilton.com.* You can enjoy the views of the city either from your private balcony, or from the "Rincon Alegre", a casual lounge overlooking the adjacent River Walk. 493 rooms, 22 story. Pets accepted, some restrictions; fee. Check-out 11 am, check-in 3 pm. TV; cable (premium), VCR available. In-room modem link. Restaurant, bar; entertainment. In-house fitness room. Outdoor pool; whirlpool; poolside service. Parking. Business center. Concierge. Luxury level. **$**

D 🐾 🛁 🏋 🕳 SC 🚶 🏋

★ ★ **HOLIDAY INN.** *217 N Saint Mary's St (78205). Phone 210/224-2500; toll-free 800/445-8475; fax 210/527-9589. www.holiday-inn.com.* 313 rooms, 23 story. Pets accepted. Check-out noon, check-in 3 pm. TV. In-room modem link. Room service. Restaurant, bar. In-house fitness room. Outdoor pool; whirlpool; poolside service. Valet parking. **$$**

D 🐾 🛁 🏋 🕳 SC

★ ★ ★ **LA MANSION DEL RIO.** *112 College St (78205). Phone 210/518-1000; toll-free 800/292-7300; fax 210/226-0389. www.lamansion.com.* Overlooking the waterfront's Paseo del Rio, this graceful hacienda combines American comfort with Spanish-Colonial flair. 348 rooms, 7 story. Pets accepted, some restrictions. Check-out noon, check-in 3 pm. TV; VCR available. In-room modem link. Room service 24 hours. Restaurant, bar;

entertainment. In-house fitness room. Outdoor pool; poolside service. Valet parking. Airport transportation. Concierge. In building built in 1852. Overlooks San Antonio River, courtyard. **$$**

⊡ ⬛ ⬛ ⬛ ⬛

★ **LA QUINTA INN.** *900 Dolorosa St (78207). Phone 210/271-0001; toll-free 800/531-5900; fax 210/228-9816. www.laquinta.com.* 184 rooms, 2 story. Pets accepted, some restrictions. Complimentary continental breakfast. Check-out noon, check-in 3 pm. TV; cable (premium). In-room modem link. Outdoor pool. **$**

⊡ ⬛ ⬛ ⬛ SC

★★★ **MARRIOTT PLAZA SAN ANTONIO.** *555 S Alamo St (78205). Phone 210/229-1000; toll-free 800/727-3239; fax 210/229-1418. www.plazasa.com.* The fountains, courtyards and gardens of this hotel are a pleasant surprise in this downtown San Antonio location. The more adventuresome can explore the historic district by foot or complimentary bicycle. 258 rooms, 7 story. Pets accepted, some restrictions. Check-out noon, check-in 3 pm. TV; cable (premium), VCR available. In-room modem link. Room service 24 hours. Restaurant, bar. In-house fitness room; massage; sauna. Pool; whirlpool; poolside service. Outdoor tennis, lighted courts. Complimentary bicycles. Valet parking. Business center. Concierge. **$**

⊡ ⬛ ⬛ ⬛ ⬛ ⬛ SC ⬛

★★★ **MARRIOTT SAN ANTONIO RIVER-CENTER.** *101 Bowie St (78205). Phone 210/223-1000; toll-free 800/228-9290; fax 210/223-6239. www.marriott.com.* 1,087 rooms, 38 story. Pets accepted, some restrictions; fee. Check-out noon, check-in 3 pm. TV; cable (premium), VCR available. In-room modem link. Laundry services. Room service 24 hours. Restaurant, bar. In-house fitness room; massage; sauna. Indoor, outdoor pool; whirlpool; poolside service. Parking. Business center. Concierge. Luxury level. **$$**

⊡ ⬛ ⬛ ⬛ ⬛ ⬛

★★★ **MARRIOTT SAN ANTONIO RIVERWALK.** *711 E Riverwalk St (78205). Phone 210/224-4555; fax 210/224-2754. www.marriott.com.* Located on the famous River Walk, this hotel is directly in front of the convention center. 521 rooms, 28 story. Pets accepted, some restrictions; fee. Check-out noon, check-in 3 pm. TV; cable (premium), VCR available. In-room modem link. Laundry services. Room service 24 hours. Restaurant, bar; entertainment. In-house fitness room; massage; sauna. Indoor, outdoor pool; whirlpool. Valet parking. Business center. Luxury level. Many rooms overlook San Antonio River. **$$**

⊡ ⬛ ⬛ ⬛ ⬛ SC ⬛

★★★ **OMNI SAN ANTONIO HOTEL.** *9821 Colonnade Blvd (78230). Phone 210/691-8888; toll-free*

800/843-6664; fax 210/691-1128. www.omnihotels.com. Take in the views of the Texas hill country and the city skyline from this hotel. Some of the spacious rooms are especially equipped for guests' needs. 329 rooms, 20 story. Pets accepted, some restrictions; fee. Check-out noon, check-in 3 pm. TV. In-room modem link. Restaurant, bar; entertainment. In-house fitness room. Health club privileges. Game room. Indoor, outdoor pool; whirlpool; poolside service. Valet parking. Free airport transportation. Business center. Crystal chandelier, marble in lobby. **$**

⊡ ⬛ ⬛ ⬛ ⬛ SC ⬛

All Suite

★ **AMERISUITES.** *4325 Amerisuites Dr (78230). Phone 210/561-0099; toll-free 800/531-0013; fax 210/561-0513. www.amerisuites.com.* Located in the growing northwest side of the city, this property is convenient to Fiesta, Texas. This modern all-suites hotel offers attractive, well-appointed guestrooms and a host of amenities. 128 rooms, 6 story. Pets accepted, some restrictions. Complimentary continental breakfast. Check-out 11 am, check-in 4 pm. TV; VCR available. Laundry services. In-house fitness room. Outdoor pool. Free parking. Business center. **$**

⊡ ⬛ ⬛ ⬛ ⬛ SC ⬛

B&B/Small Inn

★★ **BRACKENRIDGE HOUSE.** *230 Madison (78204). Phone 210/271-3442; toll-free 800/221-1412; fax 210/226-3139. www.brackenridgehouse.com.* 10 rooms, 2 story. Pets accepted, some restrictions. Children over 12 years only. Complimentary full breakfast. Check-out 11 am, check-in 3-6 pm. TV; cable (premium). Parking. Individually decorated rooms. Totally nonsmoking. **$**

⬛ ⬛

San Marcos

Motel/Motor Lodge

★ **LA QUINTA INN.** *1619 I-35 N (78666). Phone 512/392-8800; fax 512/392-0324. www.laquinta.com.* 117 rooms, 2 story. Pets accepted, some restrictions. Complimentary continental breakfast. Check-out noon, check-in 3 pm. TV; cable (premium). In-room modem link. Outdoor pool; whirlpool. **$**

⊡ ⬛ ⬛ ⬛ SC

Hotel

★ **BEST WESTERN SAN MARCOS.** *917 I-35 N (78666). Phone 512/754-7557; toll-free 800/937-8376. www.stonebridgehotels.com.* 51 rooms, 2 story. Pets accepted, some restrictions; fee. Complimentary continental breakfast. Check-out noon, check-in 3 pm. TV; cable (premium). In-room modem link. Outdoor pool; whirlpool. **$**

D 🐾 ⛱ 🛂 SC

Shamrock

Motel/Motor Lodge

★ ★ **IRISH INN MOTEL.** *301 I-40 E (79079). Phone 806/256-2106; fax 806/256-2106.* 157 rooms, 2 story. Pets accepted, some restrictions; fee. Check-out 1 pm. TV; VCR available. In-room modem link. Laundry services. Restaurant open 24 hours. Indoor pool; whirlpool. **$**

D 🐾 ⛱ ✈ 🛂

Sherman

Hotel

★ ★ ★ **HOLIDAY INN.** *3605 S Hwy 75 (75090). Phone 903/868-0555; toll-free 800/325-3535; fax 903/892-9396.* 142 rooms, 2 story. Pets accepted; fee. Check-out noon. TV; cable (premium). In-room modem link. Laundry services. Restaurant. Room service. In-house fitness room. Pool; children's pool; whirlpool. **$**

D 🐾 ⛱ ✈ 🛂 SC

Snyder

Motel/Motor Lodge

★ **PURPLE SAGE MOTEL.** *1501 E Coliseum Dr (79549). Phone 915/573-5491; toll-free 800/545-5792; fax 915/573-9027.* 45 rooms. Pets accepted, some restrictions. Complimentary continental breakfast. Check-out noon. TV; cable (premium), VCR available. Pool. **$**

D 🐾 ⛱ ✈ 🛂

Sonora

Motel/Motor Lodge

★ **DAYS INN.** *1312 N Service Rd (76950). Phone 915/387-3516; fax 915/387-2854. www.daysinn.com.* 99 rooms, 2 story. Pets accepted, some restrictions; fee. Check-out noon. TV. Laundry services. Restaurant. Pool. **$**

D 🐾 ⛱ ✈

South Padre Island

Motel/Motor Lodge

★ **DAYS INN.** *3913 Padre Blvd (78597). Phone 956/761-7831; fax 956/761-2033. www.daysinn.com.* 57 rooms, 2 story. Pets accepted; fee. Check-out noon. TV; cable (premium). Laundry services. Pool; whirlpool. **$**

D 🐾 ⛵ ✈ ⛱ 🛂

Stephenville

Motels/Motor Lodges

★ ★ **HOLIDAY INN.** *2865 W Washington St (76401). Phone 254/968-5256; toll-free 800/465-4329; fax 254/968-4255. www.holiday-inn.com.* 100 rooms, 2 story. Pets accepted, some restrictions; fee. Check-out noon. TV; cable (premium). In-room modem link. Laundry services. Restaurant. Room service. Pool. **$**

D 🐾 ⛱ 🛂 SC

★ **TEXAN MOTOR INN.** *3030 W Washington (76401). Phone 254/968-5003; fax 254/968-5060.* 30 rooms. Pets accepted, some restrictions; fee. Complimentary continental breakfast. Check-out 11 am. TV; cable (premium). **$**

D 🐾 🛂

Sulphur Springs

Motel/Motor Lodge

★ ★ **HOLIDAY INN.** *1495 Industrial Dr E (75482). Phone 903/885-0562; toll-free 800/566-4431. www.holiday-inn.com/sulphursprngs.* 96 rooms, 2 story. Pets accepted; fee. Check-out noon. TV; cable (premium), VCR available. In-room modem link. Laundry services. Restaurant, bar. Room service. Pool. **$**

D 🐾 ⛱ ✈ 🛂

Sweetwater

Motels/Motor Lodges

★ ★ **HOLIDAY INN.** *500 NW Georgia St (79556). Phone 915/236-6887; toll-free 800/465-4329; fax 915/236-6887.* 107 rooms, 2 story. Pets accepted; fee. Check-out noon. TV; cable (premium). Laundry services. Restaurant open 24 hours. Room service. Pool. **$**

D 🐾 ⛵ ⛱ 🛂

★ **MOTEL 6.** *510 NW Georgia St (79556). Phone 915/235-4387; toll-free 800/466-8356; fax 915/235-8725. www.motel6.com.* 79 rooms, 2 story. Pets accepted, some restrictions. Check-out noon. TV; cable (premium). Laundry services. Restaurant. Pool. **$**

⬛⬛⬛ SC

Temple

Motel/Motor Lodge

★ **LA QUINTA INN.** *1604 W Barton Ave (76501). Phone 254/771-2980; fax 254/778-7565. www.laquinta.com.* 106 rooms, 3 story. Pets accepted, some restrictions. Check-out noon. TV; cable (premium). Pool. Continental breakfast. **$**

D ⬛⬛⬛⬛⬛

Hotel

★★ **THE INN AT SCOTT & WHITE.** *2625 S 31st St (76504). Phone 254/778-5511; toll-free 800/749-0318; fax 254/778-5485. www.theinnatscottandwhite.com.* 129 rooms, 1-2 story. Pets accepted, some restrictions. Check-out noon. TV. Restaurant. Room service. Pool. Near Scott & White Hospital. **$**

D ⬛⬛⬛ SC

Texarkana

Motels/Motor Lodges

★★ **BEST WESTERN KINGS ROW INN & SUITES.** *4200 State Line Ave (71854). Phone 870/774-3851; toll-free 800/643-5464; fax 870/772-8440. www.bestwestern.com.* 116 rooms, 2 story. Pets accepted, some restrictions; fee. Check-out noon. TV; cable (premium). Laundry services. Restaurant. Pool. Free airport transportation. **$**

D ⬛⬛⬛⬛

★ **LA QUINTA INN.** *5201 State Line Ave (75503). Phone 903/794-1900; fax 903/792-5506. www.laquinta.com.* 130 rooms, 2 story. Pets accepted. Complimentary continental breakfast. Check-out noon. TV; cable (premium). In-room modem link. Pool. Free airport transportation. **$**

D ⬛⬛⬛

Texas City

Motel/Motor Lodge

★ **LA QUINTA INN.** *1121 Hwy 146 N (77590). Phone 409/948-3101; toll-free 800/687-6667; fax 409/945-4412. www.laquinta.com.* 120 rooms, 2 story. Pets accepted, some restrictions. Complimentary continental breakfast. Check-out noon. TV; cable (premium). Laundry services. Pool. **$**

D ⬛⬛⬛⬛ SC

Uvalde

Motel/Motor Lodge

★★ **HOLIDAY INN.** *920 E Main St (78801). Phone 830/278-4511; toll-free 800/465-4329; fax 830/591-0413. www.holiday-inn.com.* 150 rooms, 2 story. Pets accepted. Check-out noon. TV; cable (premium). Laundry services. Restaurant, bar. Room service. Pool. **$**

D ⬛⬛⬛⬛ SC

Van Horn

Motels/Motor Lodges

★★ **BEST WESTERN INN OF VAN HORN.** *1705 W Broadway (79855). Phone 915/283-2410; toll-free 800/367-7589; fax 915/283-2143. www.bestwestern.com.* 60 rooms. Pets accepted; fee. Complimentary continental breakfast. Check-out noon. TV; cable (premium). Laundry services. Restaurant. Pool. **$**

D ⬛⬛⬛⬛⬛

★★ **RAMADA INN.** *200 Golf Course Dr (79855). Phone 915/283-2780; fax 915/283-2804. www.ramada.com.* 98 rooms, 2 story. Pets accepted, some restrictions; fee. Check-out 1 pm. TV; cable (premium), VCR available. In-room modem link. Laundry services. Bar; entertainment. Pool. **$**

D ⬛⬛⬛⬛ SC

Vernon

Motels/Motor Lodges

★ **DAYS INN.** *3110 W US Hwy 287 (76384). Phone 940/552-9982; toll-free 800/329-7466; fax 940/552-7851. www.daysinn.com.* 50 rooms, 2 story. Pets accepted, some restrictions; fee. Complimentary continental breakfast. Check-out 11 am. TV; cable (premium), VCR available (movies). Laundry services. Pool. **$**

⬛ ⬛ ⬛ SC

★ **GREEN TREE INN.** *3029 Morton St (76384). Phone 940/552-5421; toll-free 800/600-5421; fax 940/552-5421.* 30 rooms. Pets accepted, some restrictions. Complimentary continental breakfast. Check-out 11 am. TV; cable (premium). In-room modem link. Pool. **$**

D ⬛ ⬛ ⬛ ⬛

Waco

Motels/Motor Lodges

★ **BEST WESTERN OLD MAIN LODGE.** *I-35 at 4th St (76706). Phone 254/753-0316; toll-free 800/299-9226; fax 254/753-3811. www.bestwestern.com/oldmainlodge.* 84 rooms. Pets accepted, some restrictions; fee. Complimentary continental breakfast. Check-out 1 pm. TV; cable (premium). In-room modem link. Pool. Near Baylor University. **$**

⬛ ⬛ ⬛

★ **LA QUINTA INN.** *1110 S 9th St (76706). Phone 254/752-9741; toll-free 800/531-5900; fax 254/757-1600. www.laquinta.com.* 102 rooms, 2 story. Pets accepted. Complimentary continental breakfast. Check-out noon. TV; cable (premium). In-room modem link. Laundry services. Pool. Baylor University nearby. **$**

D ⬛ ⬛ ⬛ SC

Wichita Falls

Motels/Motor Lodges

★ **LA QUINTA INN.** *1128 Central Frwy N (76305). Phone 940/322-6971; fax 940/723-2573. www.laquinta.com.* 139 rooms, 2 story. Pets accepted, some restrictions. Complimentary continental breakfast. Check-out noon. TV; cable (premium). In-room modem link. Laundry services. Pool. Free airport transportation. **$**

D ⬛ ⬛ ⬛ ⬛

★ **RAMADA INN.** *3209 NW Frwy (76305). Phone 940/855-0085; fax 940/855-0040. www.ramada.com.* 83 rooms, 2 story. S $59; D $65; each additional $5; suites $69-$79; under 17 free; golf plans; higher rates special events. Pets accepted, some restrictions; fee. Complimentary continental breakfast. Check-out noon. TV; cable (premium). In-room modem link. Pool.

D ⬛ ⬛ ⬛

Utah

Beaver

Motels/Motor Lodges

★★ **BEST WESTERN BUTCH CASSIDY INN.** *161 S Main (84713). Phone 435/438-2438; fax 435/438-1053. www.bestwestern.com.* 35 rooms, 2 story. Pets accepted; fee. Check-out 11 am. TV; cable (premium). In-room modem link. Restaurant. Sauna. Pool; whirlpool. Downhill ski 18 miles. **$**

★ **DE LANO MOTEL.** *480 N Main St (84713). Phone 435/438-2418.* 11 rooms. Pets accepted, some restrictions; fee. Check-out 11 am. TV; cable (premium). Downhill ski 15 miles. Covered parking. **$**

★ **SLEEPY LAGOON MOTEL.** *882 S Main St (84713). Phone 435/438-5681; fax 435/438-9991.* 20 rooms. Pets accepted. Complimentary continental breakfast (summer). Check-out 11 am. TV. Pool. Small pond. **$**

Brigham City

Motel/Motor Lodge

★ **HOWARD JOHNSON.** *1167 S Main St (84302). Phone 435/723-8511; toll-free 800/446-4656; fax 435/723-0957. www.hojo.com.* 44 rooms, 2 story. Pets accepted, some restrictions. Complimentary continental breakfast. Check-out noon. TV; cable (premium). Indoor pool; whirlpool. **$**

Bryce Canyon

Motel/Motor Lodge

★★ **BEST WESTERN RUBY'S INN.** *UT 63 (84764). Phone 435/834-5341; fax 435/834-5265. www.rubysinn.com.* 368 rooms, 1-3 story. Pets accepted, some restrictions. Check-out 11 am, check-in 4 pm. TV; VCR (movies). Restaurant. Game room. Indoor pool; outdoor pool; whirlpool. Cross-country ski opposite. Rodeo in summer; general store. Lake on property. **$**

Capitol Reef National Park

Motel/Motor Lodge

★ **SUNGLOW MOTEL.** *63 E Main (84715). Phone 435/425-3821.* 12 rooms. Closed mid-Nov-Feb. Pets accepted; fee. Check-out 11 am, check-in noon. TV. Restaurant. **$**

Cedar City

Motel/Motor Lodge

★ **COMFORT INN.** *250 N 1100 W (84720). Phone 435/586-2082; toll-free 800/228-5750; fax 435/586-3193. www.comfortinn.com.* 93 rooms, 2 story. Pets accepted, some restrictions. Complimentary continental breakfast. Check-out 11 am. TV. Indoor pool; whirlpool. Free airport transportation. **$**

Fillmore

Resort

★ **BEST WESTERN PARADISE INN AND RESORT.** *905 N Main (84631). Phone 435/743-6895; fax 435/743-6892. www.bestwestern.com.* 80 rooms, 2 story. Pets accepted, some restrictions. Check-out 11 am. TV; cable (premium). Restaurant. Pool; whirlpool. **$**

Heber City

Motel/Motor Lodge

★ **DANISH VIKING LODGE.** *989 S Main St (84032). Phone 435/654-2202; toll-free 800/544-4066; fax 435/654-2770.* 34 rooms, 1-2 story. Pets accepted, some restrictions. Complimentary continental breakfast. Check-out 11 am. TV; cable (premium), VCR available. Health club privileges. Sauna. Pool; whirlpool. Downhill ski 12 miles, cross-country ski 7 miles. **$**

Kanab

Motels/Motor Lodges

★ **FOUR SEASONS INN.** *36 N 300 W (84741). Phone 435/644-2635; fax 435/644-5895.* 41 rooms, 2 story. Pets accepted. Check-out 11 am. TV. Restaurant. Pool; children's pool. **$**

⊡ ⊠ SC

★ **PARRY LODGE.** *89 E Center St (84741). Phone 435/644-2601; toll-free 800/748-4104; fax 435/644-2605. www.infowest.com/parry.* 89 rooms, 1-2 story. Closed Dec-mid-March. Pets accepted; fee. Check-out 11 am. TV. Laundry services. Restaurant. Autographed pictures of movie stars displayed in lobby. Heated pool. **$**

D ⊡ ⊠ ⊠

★ **SHILO INN.** *296 W 100 N (84741). Phone 435/ 644-2562; toll-free 800/222-2244; fax 435/644-5333. www.shiloinns.com.* 118 rooms, 3 story. Pets accepted; fee. Complimentary continental breakfast. Check-out noon. TV. Pool; whirlpool. Free airport transportation. **$**

D ⊡ ✈ ⊠ ✈ ⊠ SC

Lake Powell

Motel/Motor Lodge

★ **DEFIANCE HOUSE LODGE.** *Hwy 276 (84533). Phone 435/684-2233; toll-free 800/528-6154; fax 435/684-3114.* 48 rooms, 2 story. Pets accepted. Check-out 11 am, check-in 3 pm. TV. Dining room, bar. Airport transportation. Anasazi motif; décor, artifacts. **$**

D ⊡ ⊡

Logan

Motel/Motor Lodge

★ **DAYS INN.** *364 S Main (84321). Phone 435/753-5623. www.daysinn.com.* 64 rooms, 2 story. Pets accepted. Complimentary continental breakfast. Check-out 11 am. TV. Laundry services. Indoor pool. Cross-country ski 20 miles. **$**

D ⊡ ⊡ ⊡ ⊠ ⊠ ⊠

Moab

Motel/Motor Lodge

★ **BOWEN MOTEL.** *169 N Main St (84532). Phone 435/259-7132; toll-free 800/874-5439; fax 435/259-6641. www.bowenmotel.com.* 40 rooms, 2 story. Pets accepted, some restrictions; fee. Complimentary continental breakfast. Check-out 11 am, check-in 3 pm. TV; cable (premium). In-room modem link. Totally nonsmoking. **$**

⊡ ⊠

Guest Ranch

★★ **PACK CREEK RANCH.** *Pack Creek Ranch Rd (84532). Phone 435/259-5505. www.packcreekranch.com.* 10 rooms. No room phones. Pets accepted, some restrictions; fee. Check-out 11 am, check-in 3 pm. Dining room. Sauna. Pool; whirlpool. Cross-country skiing. Hiking. **$$**

D ⊡ ⊡ ⊡ ⊠ ⊠ ✈ ⊠ ⊠

Monticello

Motel/Motor Lodge

★ **BEST WESTERN WAYSIDE MOTOR INN.** *197 E Central Ave (84535). Phone 435/587-2261; toll-free 800/633-9700; fax 435/587-2920. www.bestwestern.com.* 38 rooms. Pets accepted; fee. Complimentary continental breakfast. Check-out 11 am, check-in 2 pm. TV; cable (premium). Restaurant. Cross-country ski 6 miles. **$**

⊡ ⊠ ⊠ SC

Nephi

Motel/Motor Lodge

★ **BEST WESTERN PARADISE INN OF NEPHI.** *1025 S Main (84648). Phone 435/623-0624. www.bestwestern.com.* 40 rooms, 2 story. Pets accepted; fee. Complimentary continental breakfast. Check-out noon. TV; cable (premium). Pool; whirlpool. **$**

⊡ ⊡ ⊠ ⊠

Ogden

Hotel

★ ★ **BEN LOMOND HISTORIC SUITE HOTEL.** *2510 Washington Blvd (84401). Phone 801/627-1900; toll-free 888/627-8897; fax 801/394-5342. www.benlomondhotel.com.* This beautiful historical building, built in 1890, welcomes guests with warm and friendly service, and offers a comfortable stay. Located in the historic district of Ogden, this hotel provides a charming atmosphere, perfect for relaxing. 122 suites, 11 story. Pets accepted, some restrictions. Complimentary breakfast. Check-out noon. TV; cable (premium). Restaurant, bar. In-house fitness room. Health club privileges. Downhill, cross-country ski 16 miles. Business center. **$**

⊡ 🐾 🏋 ⛷ 🏃 ✈ 🚶

Park City

Motel/Motor Lodge

★ **HOLIDAY INN EXPRESS.** *1501 W Ute Blvd (84098). Phone 435/658-1600. www.holiday-inn.com.* Conveniently located just off I-80 at the entrance to Park City, this hotel is well maintained and has a variety of accommodations. 76 rooms, 3 story. Pets accepted; fee. Check-out noon, check-in 3 pm. TV; cable (premium), VCR available. Laundry services. In-house fitness room; sauna. Indoor pool. **$**

⊡ 🐾 🏋 ⛷ 🏊 🏃 ✈ 🖼

Resort

★ ★ **RADISSON INN.** *2121 Park Ave (84060). Phone 435/649-5000; toll-free 800/333-3333; fax 435/649-2122. www.radisson.com.* 125 rooms. Pets accepted; fee. Complimentary full breakfast. Check-out noon. TV. Restaurant, bar. Steam room. Indoor pool; outdoor pool; whirlpool. Golf. Outdoor tennis. Downhill skiing. Bike rentals. Hiking trail. Concierge. **$**

⊡ 🐾 ⛷ 🎾 ⛷ 🏊 ✈ 🖼

Payson

Motel/Motor Lodge

★ **COMFORT INN.** *830 N Main St (84651). Phone 801/465-4861; fax 801/465-7686. www.comfortinn.com.* 62 rooms, 2 story. Pets accepted; fee. Complimentary continental breakfast. Check-out 11 am. TV; cable (premium). Laundry services. In-house fitness room; sauna. Indoor pool; whirlpool. **$**

⊡ 🐾 🏊 🏃 🖼

Provo

Motels/Motor Lodges

★ **COLONY INN NATIONAL 9.** *1380 S University Ave (84601). Phone 801/374-6800; fax 801/374-6803.* 80 rooms, 2 story. Pets accepted; fee. Complimentary continental breakfast. Check-out noon. TV; cable (premium). In-room modem link. Laundry services. Pool. Downhill ski 20 miles. **$**

🐾 🏊 🖼

★ **DAYS INN.** *1675 N 200 W (84604). Phone 801/375-8600; fax 801/374-6654. www.daysinn.com.* 49 rooms, 2 story. Pets accepted, some restrictions; fee. Complimentary continental breakfast. Check-out noon. TV. In-room modem link. Restaurant. Pool. Downhill, cross-country ski 15 miles. **$**

⊡ 🐾 ⛷ 🏊 🏃 🖼

Richfield

Motels/Motor Lodges

★ **DAYS INN.** *333 N Main (84701). Phone 435/896-6476; toll-free 888/275-8513; fax 435/996-6476. www.daysinn.com.* 51 rooms, 3 story. No elevator. Pets accepted; fee. Check-out 11 am. TV; cable (premium). In-room modem link. Restaurant. Sauna. Pool; whirlpool. **$**

🐾 🏋 🏊 🖼

★ **ROMANICO INN.** *1170 S Main St (84701). Phone 435/896-8471.* 29 rooms, 2 story. Pets accepted. Check-out noon. TV. Laundry services. **$**

⊡ 🐾 🏋 ⛷ 🏃 🖼

★ **TRAVELODGE.** *647 S Main St (84701). Phone 435/896-9271; toll-free 800/549-8208; fax 435/896-6864. www.travelodge.com.* 40 rooms, 2 story. Pets accepted, some restrictions; fee. Complimentary continental breakfast. Check-out noon. TV. Restaurant. Room service. Indoor pool; whirlpool. **$**

⊡ 🐾 🏊

Roosevelt

Motel/Motor Lodge

★ **FRONTIER MOTEL.** *75 S 200 E (98624). Phone 435/722-2201; fax 435/722-2212.* 54 rooms. Pets accepted, some restrictions. Check-out 11 am. TV; cable (premium). Restaurant. Pool. **$**

🐾 ⤬ ⊠ SC

Salt Lake City

Motels/Motor Lodges

★★ **BEST WESTERN SALT LAKE PLAZA HOTEL.** *122 W South Temple St (84101). Phone 801/521-0130; toll-free 800/366-3684; fax 801/322-5057. www.bestwestern.com.* 226 rooms, 13 story. Pets accepted; fee. Check-out noon. TV. In-room modem link. Laundry services. Restaurant. Room service. In-house fitness room. Pool; whirlpool. Airport transportation. Concierge. **$**

D 🐾 ⤬ ⊠ ✕ ✈ ⊠ SC

★ **COMFORT INN.** *200 N Admiral Byrd Rd (84116). Phone 801/537-7444; fax 801/532-4721. www.slccomfortinn.com.* 155 rooms, 4 story. Pets accepted; fee. Check-out 11 am. TV. Restaurant. Room service. In-house fitness room. Pool; whirlpool. Free airport transportation. **$**

🐾 ⤬ ✕ ⊠ SC

★ **DAYS INN.** *1900 W North Temple (84116). Phone 801/539-8538; toll-free 800/329-7466; fax 801/595-1041. www.daysinn.com.* 110 rooms, 2 story. Pets accepted, some restrictions. Complimentary continental breakfast. Check-out 11 am. TV; cable (premium). In-room modem link. Laundry services. In-house fitness room. Health club privileges. Indoor pool. Free airport, train station, bus depot transportation. **$**

D 🐾 ⤬ ✕ ✈ ⊠ SC

★ **HAMPTON INN.** *2393 S 800 W (84087). Phone 801/296-1211; toll-free 888/834-4470; fax 801/296-1222. www.hamptoninn.com.* 60 rooms, 3 story. Pets accepted. Complimentary continental breakfast. Check-out noon. TV; cable (premium). In-room modem link. Laundry services. Health club privileges. Indoor pool; whirlpool. Free airport transportation. **$**

D 🐾 ⤬ ⤬ ✕ ✈ ⊠ SC

★ **LA QUINTA INN.** *7231 S Catalpa Rd (84047). Phone 801/566-3291; fax 801/562-5943. www.laquinta.com.* 122 rooms, 2 story. Pets accepted. Check-out noon. TV; cable (premium). In-room modem link. Laundry services.

Health club privileges. Pool. Downhill ski 15 miles, cross-country ski 20 miles. Continental breakfast. **$**

D 🐾 ⤬ ⤬ ✕ ⊠

★ **QUALITY INN.** *4465 Century Dr S (84123). Phone 801/268-2533; fax 801/266-6206. www.qualityinn.com.* 131 rooms, 2 story. Pets accepted, some restrictions; fee. Complimentary continental breakfast. Check-out noon. TV; cable (premium). In-room modem link. Laundry services. Pool; whirlpool. **$**

D 🐾 ⤬ ✈ ⊠

★★ **RAMADA INN.** *230 W 600 S (84101). Phone 801/364-5200; toll-free 800/595-0505; fax 801/359-2542. www.ramadainnslc.com.* 160 rooms, 2 story. Pets accepted, some restrictions; fee. Check-out noon. TV. In-room modem link. Restaurant. Room service. In-house fitness room; sauna. Game room. Indoor pool; whirlpool. Free airport, train station, bus depot transportation. **$**

D 🐾 ⤬ ✕ ✈ ⊠ SC

★ **TRAVELODGE.** *524 SW Temple St (84101). Phone 801/531-7100; toll-free 800/578-7878; fax 801/359-3814. www.travelodge.com.* 60 rooms, 3 story. Pets accepted; fee. Check-out noon. TV; cable (premium). Pool; whirlpool. **$**

🐾 ⤬ ⊠ SC

Hotels

★★★ **HILTON SALT LAKE CITY AIRPORT.** *5151 Wiley Post Way (84116). Phone 801/539-1515; toll-free 800/999-3736; fax 801/539-1113. www.hilton.com.* This hotel is minutes from the airport with views of the Wasatch and Oquirrh Mountains. Amenities include an outdoor swimming pool and hot tub. Other activities are paddle boats, jogging path, fitness center and indoor pool. Grill 114 is a full-service restaurant with seating outside and great panoramas. 287 rooms, 5 story. Pets accepted; fee. Check-out 1 pm. TV; VCR available. Laundry services. Restaurant, bar. Pool; whirlpool. 9-hole golf; putting green. Free airport, train station transportation. Business center. Concierge. Luxury level. **$**

D 🐾 ⤬ ⤬ ✕ ✕ ✈ ⊠ ⤬

★★★ **HILTON SALT LAKE CITY CENTER.** *255 S West Temple (84101). Phone 801/328-2000; toll-free 800/445-8667; fax 801/238-4888. www.hilton.com.* Located in the heart of downtown, guests can enjoy all the comforts of home with spacious rooms and friendly service. 500 rooms, 18 story. Pets accepted, some restrictions; fee. Check-out noon. TV; VCR available. In-room modem link. Restaurant. In-house fitness room; sauna. Indoor pool; whirlpool; poolside service. Valet parking. Airport, train station, bus depot transportation available. Business center. Concierge. Luxury level. **$**

D 🐾 ⤬ ✕ ✈ ⊠ SC ⤬

★ ★ ★ **HOTEL MONACO SALT LAKE CITY.** *15 W 200 S (84101). Phone 801/595-0000; toll-free 877/294-9710; fax 801/532-8500. www.monaco-saltlakecity.com.* Located in the heart of the city, within a short walk of many major attractions, this former bank building offers visually striking décor in the public areas and handsomely-furnished guest rooms. 225 rooms, 15 story. Pets accepted, some restrictions. Check-out noon, check-in 3 pm. TV; CD available. Restaurant, bar. In-house fitness room. Golf. Outdoor tennis. Downhill skiing. Valet parking. **$**

All Suite

★ ★ **WOODFIN SUITES.** *765 E 400 S (84102). Phone 801/532-5511; toll-free 800/237-8811; fax 801/531-0416. www.woodfinsuitehotels.com.* 128 rooms, 2 story. Pets accepted; fee. Complimentary continental breakfast. Check-out noon. TV; cable (premium). In-room modem link. Fireplaces. Laundry services. Pool. Free airport, train station, bus depot transportation. Sports court. **$**

Extended Stay

★ ★ **RESIDENCE INN BY MARRIOTT.** *6425 S 3000 E (84121). Phone 801/453-0430; fax 801/453-0431. www.residenceinn.com.* Conveniently located at the base of the Wasatch Mountain range, this property offers complimentary shuttle service to local offices, ski rental facilities, ski bus stops, and restaurants. 144 rooms, 3 story. Pets accepted; fee. Complimentary buffet breakfast. Check-out noon, check-in 3 pm. TV; cable (premium). In-room modem link. Fireplaces. Laundry services. In-house fitness room. Outdoor pool. Outdoor tennis. **$**

St. George

Motel/Motor Lodge

★ ★ **SINGLETREE INN.** *260 E St. George Blvd (84770). Phone 435/673-6161; toll-free 800/528-8890; fax 435/673-7453.* 45 rooms, 2 story. Pets accepted, some restrictions; fee. Complimentary continental breakfast. Check-out 11 am. TV. Pool; whirlpool. **$**

Zion National Park

Motel/Motor Lodge

★ **DRIFTWOOD LODGE.** *1515 Zion Park Blvd (84767). Phone 435/772-3262; toll-free 888/801-8811; fax 435/772-3702. www.driftwoodlodge.net.* 42 rooms, 1-2 story. Pets accepted, some restrictions; fee. Complimentary continental breakfast. Check-out 11 am. TV. Pool; whirlpool. Shaded grounds; good views of park. **$**

Vermont

Barre

Motel/Motor Lodge

★ ★ ★ **HOLLOW INN AND HOTEL.** *278 S Main St (05641). Phone 802/479-9313; toll-free 800/998-9444; fax 802/476-5242. www.hollowinn.com.* Jim and Bunny Kelley are your hosts at this small country inn in scenic Vermont. Spacious rooms have contemporary décor. The inn is close to local attractions. 41 rooms, 2 story. Pets accepted; fee. Complimentary continental breakfast. Check-out 11 am. TV; cable (premium), VCR available. In-house fitness room; sauna. Pool; whirlpool. Cross-country ski 8 miles. **$**

Bennington

Motels/Motor Lodges

★ **FIFE 'N DRUM.** *693 US Rte 7 S (05201). Phone 802/442-4074; fax 802/442-8471.* 18 rooms, 1-2 story. Pets accepted, some restrictions; fee. Check-out 11 am. TV; cable (premium). Pool; whirlpool. Downhill ski 20 miles, cross-country ski 6 miles. Lawn games. **$**

★ ★ **VERMONTER MOTOR LODGE.** *2968 West Rd (05201). Phone 802/442-2529; fax 802/442-0879. www.the vermontermotorlodge.com.* Pets accepted, some restrictions; fee. Check-out 11 am. TV. Restaurant. Cross-country ski 20 miles. Lawn games. Swimming pond. **$**

Burlington

Motels/Motor Lodges

★ ★ **BEST WESTERN WINDJAMMER INN & CONFERENCE CENTER.** *1076 Williston Rd (05403). Phone 802/863-1125; toll-free 800/371-1125; fax 802/ 658-1296. www.bestwestern.com/windjammerinn.* 177 rooms, 2 story. Pets accepted, some restrictions; fee. Complimentary continental breakfast. Check-out 11 am. TV; cable (premium). Restaurant. In-house fitness room;

sauna. Pool; whirlpool. Nature trail. Free airport transportation. **$**

★ **DAYS INN.** *23 College Pkwy (05446). Phone 802/ 655-0900; toll-free 800/329-7466; fax 802/655-6851. www.daysinn.com.* 73 rooms, 4 story. Pets accepted, some restrictions; fee. Complimentary continental breakfast. Check-out 11 am. TV; cable (premium). Indoor pool. Cross-country ski 5 miles. **$**

★ ★ **HAMPTON INN.** *42 Lower Mountain View Dr (05446). Phone 802/655-6177; toll-free 800/426-7866; fax 802/655-4962. www.hampton-inn.com.* 188 rooms, 5 story. Pets accepted, some restrictions. Complimentary continental breakfast. Check-out 11 am. TV; cable (premium), VCR available. In-room modem link. Laundry services. Restaurant. In-house fitness room. Indoor pool; whirlpool. Downhill ski 20 miles, cross-country ski 5 miles. Free airport transportation. Business center. **$**

★ ★ **HOLIDAY INN.** *1068 Williston Rd (05403). Phone 802/863-6363; toll-free 800/799-6363; fax 802/863-3061. www.holiday-inn.com.* 174 rooms, 4 story. Pets accepted, some restrictions; fee. Check-out noon. TV. In-room modem link. Restaurant, bar; entertainment. Room service. In-house fitness room. Indoor pool; outdoor pool; whirlpool. Free airport transportation. **$**

Hotels

★ ★ **CLARION HOTEL.** *1117 Williston Rd (05403). Phone 802/658-0250; toll-free 800/272-6232; fax 802/660- 7516. www.clarionvermont.com.* 130 rooms, 2 story. Pets accepted, some restrictions; fee. Check-out noon. TV; VCR available (movies). In-room modem link. Restaurant, bar. Room service. In-house fitness room. Pool; children's pool. Downhill ski 20 miles, cross-country ski 6 miles. Free airport transportation. **$**

★ ★ ★ **SHERATON BURLINGTON HOTEL AND CONFERENCE CENTER.** *870 Williston Rd (05403). Phone 802/865-6600; toll-free 800/677-6576; fax 802/865- 6670. www.sheraton.com.* Surrounded by scenic trees and lush grass, this hotel offers guests attentive service amidst an elegant atmosphere. 309 rooms, 2-4 story. Pets accepted; fee. Check-out noon. TV; cable (premium), VCR available. In-room modem link. Restaurant, bar; entertainment. Room service. In-house fitness room. Game room. Indoor pool; whirlpool. Cross-country ski 6 miles. Free airport transportation. Business center. Luxury level. **$**

All Suite

★★ **WILSON INN.** *10 Kellogg Rd (05452). Phone 802/879-1515; toll-free 800/521-2334; fax 802/764-5149. www.wilsoninn.com.* 32 kitchen units, 3 story. No elevator. Pets accepted, some restrictions; fee. Complimentary breakfast buffet. Check-out 11 am. TV; cable (premium), VCR available. In-room modem link. Laundry services. Health club privileges. Game room. Pool. Downhill ski 15 miles, cross-country ski 8 miles. Lawn games. **$**

Extended Stay

★★ **RESIDENCE INN BY MARRIOTT.** *1 Hurricane Ln (05495). Phone 802/878-2001; fax 802/878-0025. www.residenceinn.com.* 96 suites, 2 story. Pets accepted; fee. Complimentary continental breakfast. Check-out noon. TV; cable (premium). In-room modem link. In-house fitness room. Indoor pool; whirlpool. Downhill, cross-country ski 15 miles. Free airport transportation. **$**

Dorset

B&B/Small Inn

★★ **BARROWS HOUSE INN.** *3156 VT 30 (05251). Phone 802/867-4455; toll-free 800/639-1620; fax 802/867-0132. www.barrowshouse.com.* 28 rooms, 3 kitchen units. No room phones. Pets accepted, some restrictions; fee. Check-out 11 am, check-in early afternoon. TV in some rooms; VCR available. Fireplaces. Restaurant, bar. Sauna. Game room. Poolside service. Tennis. Downhill ski 12 miles, cross-country ski 6 miles. Lawn games. Bicycles. Built in 1804. **$$**

Fairlee

B&B/Small Inn

★ **SILVER MAPLE LODGE & COTTAGES.** *520 US 5 S (05045). Phone 802/333-4326; toll-free 800/666-1946. www.silvermaplelodge.com.* 8 rooms. No A/C. No room phones. Pets accepted, some restrictions. Complimentary continental breakfast. Check-out 11 am, check-in 2 pm. TV in cottages. Lodge built as farmhouse in the 1790s. Wraparound porch. **$**

Killington

Motel/Motor Lodge

★ **VAL ROC MOTEL.** *8006 US 4 (05751). Phone 802/422-3881; toll-free 800/238-8762; fax 802/422-3236. www.valroc.com.* 24 rooms, 1-2 story, 2 kitchen units. Pets accepted, some restrictions; fee. Complimentary continental breakfast. Check-out 11 am. TV; cable (premium), VCR available. Game room. Heated pool; whirlpool. Tennis. Downhill ski 1/4 mile, cross-country ski 3 miles. Lawn games. **$**

B&B/Small Inn

★★★ **RED CLOVER INN.** *7 Woodward Rd (05701). Phone 802/775-2290; toll-free 800/752-0571; fax 802/773-0594. www.redcloverinn.com.* This 1840s country inn is situated on 13 acres and boasts wonderful views of the Green Mountains. The guest rooms are individually appointed with antiques and country woodwork. 14 rooms, 2 story. Pets accepted, some restrictions; fee. Children over 12 years only. Complimentary full breakfast. Check-out 11 am, check-in 2 pm. TV; VCR in parlor (movies). Dining room. Pool. Downhill, cross-country ski 6 miles. Built in 1840; former general's residence. Totally nonsmoking. **$$$**

Ludlow

B&B/Small Inn

★★ **COMBES FAMILY INN.** *953 E Lake Rd (05149). Phone 802/228-8799; toll-free 800/822-8799; fax 802/228-8704. www.combesfamilyinn.com.* 11 rooms, 2 story. No room phones. Pets accepted. Check-out 11 am, check-in 2 pm. Dining room. Room service. Game room. Downhill ski 4 miles, cross-country ski 3 miles. Lawn games. Restored farmhouse (1891) on 50 acres; near Lake Rescue. **$**

Lyndonville

B&B/Small Inn

★ **THE OLD CUTTER INN.** *143 Pinkham Rd (05832). Phone 802/626-5152; toll-free 800/295-1943. www.pbpub.com/cutter.htm.* 10 rooms, 2 story. Apr,

Nov. Pets accepted, some restrictions; fee. Check-out 11 am, check-in 1 pm. TV in lobby. Dining room. Pool. Downhill, cross-country ski 1/2 mile. Lawn games. In restored farmhouse (circa 1845) and renovated turn-of-the-century carriage house. **$**

Manchester & Manchester Center

B&B/Small Inn

★ ★ **SILAS GRIFFITH INN.** *178 S Main St (05739). Phone 802/293-5567; toll-free 800/545-1509; fax 802/293-5559. www.silasgriffith.com.* 17 rooms, 1-3 story. No room phones. Pets accepted, some restrictions; fee. Complimentary breakfast. Check-out 11 am, check-in 2 pm. TV. Game room. Pool. Downhill, cross-country skiing. Home of Vermont's first millionaire (1891). Totally nonsmoking. **$**

Marlboro

B&B/Small Inn

★ **WHETSTONE INN.** *550 South Rd (05344). Phone 802/254-2500; toll-free 877/254-2500. www.whetstoneinn.com.* 11 rooms, 3 share bath, 2 story, 3 kitchen units. No A/C. Pets accepted, some restrictions. Check-out 2 pm, check-in after 2 pm. Restaurant. Swimming pond. 18th-century country inn was originally a stagecoach stop; fireplaces in public rooms. **$**

Middlebury

Hotel

★ ★ **MIDDLEBURY INN.** *14 Court House Sq (05753). Phone 802/388-4961; toll-free 800/842-4666; fax 802/388-4563. www.middleburyinn.com.* 45 rooms, 2-3 story. Pets accepted, some restrictions. Complimentary continental breakfast. Check-out 11 am, check-in 3 pm. TV. Restaurant, bar. Downhill, cross-country ski 13 miles. Established in 1827. Porch dining in summer. **$$**

Montpelier

B&B/Small Inn

★ ★ ★ **THE INN ON THE COMMON.** *1162 N Craftsbury Rd (05827). Phone 802/586-9619; toll-free 800/521-2233; fax 802/586-2249. www.innonthecommon.com.* Nestled under a large maple tree, this inn, which consists of three restored Federal-style houses, offers colorful gardens and wooded hillsides. Individually-decorated guest rooms feature antiques, artwork, and sitting areas. 16 rooms, 2 story. No A/C. No room phones. Service charge 15%. Pets accepted, some restrictions; fee. Check-out 11 am, check-in 1 pm. TV; VCR available. Dining room, bar. Health club privileges. Pool. Tennis. Cross-country ski on site. Lawn games. Bicycle rentals. Restored Federal-period houses in scenic Vermont village; landscaped gardens. Afternoon refreshments. Extensive film collection. **$$**

Newfane

B&B/Small Inn

★ ★ ★ **FOUR COLUMNS INN.** *21 West St (05345). Phone 802/365-7713; toll-free 800/787-6633; fax 802/365-0022. www.fourcolumnsinn.com.* Built in 1833 and surrounded by 150 acres of scenic nature, this delightful inn exudes casual elegance and an ambiance of pure romance. Designed as a southern mansion, this inn offers the perfect weekend getaway where guests can enjoy the charmingly furnished guest rooms and dine on exquisite cuisine. 16 rooms. Pets accepted; fee. Complimentary full breakfast. Check-out 11 am, check-in 2 pm. TV in lounge; cable (premium). Bar. Pool. Stately 19th-century house; Colonial furnishings. On 150 wooded acres; walking paths. Totally nonsmoking. **$**

North Hero

Motel/Motor Lodge

★ ★ **SHORE ACRES INN.** *237 Shore Acres Dr (05474). Phone 802/372-8722. www.shoreacres.com.* 23 rooms. Pets accepted, some restrictions; fee. Check-out 10:30 am. TV. Restaurant, bar. Two tennis courts. Lawn games. **$**

Springfield

Motel/Motor Lodge

★ **HOLIDAY INN EXPRESS.** *818 Charlestown Rd (05156). Phone 802/885-4516; toll-free 800/465-4329; fax 802/885-4595. www.holiday-inn.com.* 88 rooms, 2 story. Pets accepted, some restrictions. Complimentary continental breakfast. Check-out noon. TV. In-room modem link. Restaurant, bar. In-house fitness room. Indoor pool. Downhill ski 20 miles, cross-country ski 14 miles. **$**

Stowe

Motel/Motor Lodge

★ ★ **INNSBRUCK INN AT STOWE.** *4361 Mountain Rd (05672). Phone 802/253-8582; toll-free 800/225-8582; fax 802/253-2260. www.innsbruckinn.com.* 25 rooms, 2 story. Pets accepted, some restrictions; fee. Check-out 11 am. TV; VCR available (movies). Restaurant, bar. In-house fitness room; sauna. Game room. Pool; whirlpool. Downhill ski 2 miles, cross-country ski adjacent. **$**

Resorts

★ ★ **COMMODORES INN.** *823 S Main St (05672). Phone 802/253-7131; toll-free 800/447-8693; fax 802/253-2360. www.commodoresinn.com.* 50 rooms, 2 story. Pets accepted; fee. Complimentary continental breakfast off-season. Check-out 11 am. TV; VCR available. In-room modem link. Restaurant. In-house fitness room; saunas. Game room. Indoor pool; children's pool; whirlpool. Downhill ski 9 miles, cross-country ski 6 miles. **$**

★ ★ ★ **GREEN MOUNTAIN INN.** *18 S Main St (05672). Phone 802/253-7301; toll-free 800/253-7302; fax 802/253-5096. www.greenmountaininn.com.* This inn is close to all the attractions of Stowe. 72 rooms, 1-3 story. Pets accepted, some restrictions; fee. Check-out 11 am, check-in 2 pm. TV; VCR available. Dining room, bar. Room service. In-house fitness room; massage; sauna. Pool; whirlpool. Downhill ski 6 miles, cross-country ski 5 miles. Historic inn (1833); paintings by Vermont artist. **$$**

★ ★ ★ **MOUNTAIN ROAD RESORT AT STOWE.** *1007 Mountain Rd (05672). Phone 802/253-4566; toll-free 800/367-6873; fax 802/253-7397.* There is plenty to do at this resort: tennis, biking and hiking, or relaxing by the pool with a glass of wine and enjoying the mountain views. Guests can find their ideal vacation in any season. 23 rooms. Pets accepted, some restrictions; fee. Check-out 11 am. TV; cable (premium), VCR available. Laundry services. In-house fitness room; sauna. Indoor pool; outdoor pool; whirlpool. Outdoor tennis. Downhill ski 4 miles, cross-country ski 2 1/2 miles. Lawn games. Bicycles. **$**

B&B/Small Inn

★ ★ ★ **YE OLDE ENGLAND INNE.** *433 Mountain Rd (05672). Phone 802/253-7558; toll-free 800/643-1553; fax 802/253-8944. www.englandinn.com.* This elegant English inn offers guests a truly delightful stay. From the charmingly-appointed rooms, furnished in the Laura Ashley style, to the Mr. Pickwick's Polo Pub where strangers are strangers no more, this warm and inviting inn is a welcome respite for those looking for the extraordinary. 30 rooms, 3-5 story. No elevator. Service charge 10%, cottages 5%. Pets accepted, some restrictions. Check-out 11 am, check-in 3 pm. TV; cable (premium), VCR available. Dining room; entertainment. Pool; whirlpool. Downhill ski 5 miles, cross-country ski 2 miles. Built in 1893. Totally nonsmoking. **$$**

Vergennes

Resort

★ ★ ★ **BASIN HARBOR CLUB.** *Basin Harbor Rd (05491). Phone 802/475-2311; toll-free 800/622-4000; fax 802/475-6545. www.basinharbor.com.* Located on Lake Champlain, this 700-acre property offers guest rooms in the lodge or cottages spread out over the acreage. Fresh local ingredients are used to prepare the breakfast or dinner meals served in the main dining room. The activities and amenities are too numerous to list but are all encompassing. 40 rooms. Pets accepted, some restrictions; fee. Check-out 11 am, check-in 4 pm. TV. Laundry services. Bar. Free supervised children's activities (July-Aug); ages 3-15. In-house fitness room. Massage. Pool; poolside service. 18-hole golf; putting green; driving range. Greens fee $42. Outdoor tennis. Lawn games. Bicycles. Beach; motorboats, sailboats, canoes, kayaks, cruise boat; windsurfing, waterskiing. Fitness, nature trails. Airport, train station, bus depot transportation. Concierge. Recreation directors. Family-owned since 1886; Colonial architecture. 3,200-foot airstrip available. **$$**

Waitsfield

B&B/Small Inn

★ **WHITE HORSE INN.** *999 German Flats Rd (05673). Phone 802/496-3260; toll-free 800/328-3260; fax 802/496-2476. www.whitehorseinnvermont.com.* 24 rooms, 2 story. No A/C. No room phones. Pets accepted, some restrictions; fee. Complimentary full breakfast. Check-out 11 am, check-in 3 pm. TV. Downhill ski 1/2 mile, cross-country ski 2 miles. Totally nonsmoking. **$**

Warren

Motel/Motor Lodge

★ **GOLDEN LION RIVERSIDE INN.** *731 VT 100 (05674). Phone 802/496-3084; toll-free 888/867-4491; fax 802/496-7438. www.madriver.com/lodging/goldlion.* 12 rooms. No A/C. Pets accepted; fee. Complimentary full breakfast. Check-out 11 am. TV. Downhill, cross-country ski 3 miles. **$**

White River Junction

Motels/Motor Lodges

★★ **BEST WESTERN AT THE JUNCTION.** *306 N Hartland Rd (05001). Phone 802/295-3015; toll-free 800/370-4656; fax 802/296-2581. www.bestwesternjunction.com.* 112 rooms, 2 story. Pets accepted; fee. Complimentary continental breakfast. Check-out 11 am. TV; cable (premium). Laundry services. Bar. In-house fitness room; sauna. Game room. Indoor pool; children's pool; whirlpool. Downhill ski 20 miles, cross-country ski 14 miles. **$**

★ **RAMADA INN.** *259 Holiday Dr (05001). Phone 802/295-3000; toll-free 800/648-6754; fax 802/295-3774. www.ramada.com.* 136 rooms, 2 story. S, D $85-$145; each additional $8; under 19 free; ski plan; weekend rates; higher rates fall foliage. Pets accepted, some restrictions;

fee. Check-out noon. TV; cable (premium). Restaurant, bar; entertainment. Room service. In-house fitness room; sauna. Game room. Indoor pool; whirlpool. Downhill ski 15 miles.

Wilmington

B&B/Small Inn

★ **THE INN AT QUAIL RUN.** *106 Smith Rd (05363). Phone 802/464-3362; toll-free 800/343-7227; fax 802/464-7784. www.theinnatquailrun.com.* 14 rooms, 2 story. No A/C. No room phones. Pets accepted, some restrictions; fee. Complimentary full breakfast. Check-out 11 am, check-in 3 pm. TV. Sauna. Pool. Downhill ski 4 1/2 miles, cross-country ski on site. Lawn games. On 12 acres in Green Mountains, view of Deerfield Valley. Totally nonsmoking. **$**

Woodstock

B&B/Small Inns

★★★ **KEDRON VALLEY INN.** *VT 106 (05071). Phone 802/457-1473; toll-free 800/836-1193; fax 802/457-4469. www.kedronvalleyinn.com.* Just 5 miles outside Woodstock, this small historic inn makes a good home while enjoying the local activities. Guests can partake in antique shopping or browsing in local shops. 37 rooms, 1-3 story. 10 rooms with A/C. No elevator, no room phones, closed Apr. Pets accepted. Check-out 11:30 am, check-in 3:30 pm. TV. Fireplaces. Restaurant, bar. Downhill skiing, cross-country skiing. Natural pond. **$$**

★★ **WINSLOW HOUSE.** *492 Woodstock Rd (05091). Phone 802/457-1820; fax 802/457-1820. www.thewinslowhousevt.com.* 5 rooms, 2 story. Pets accepted, some restrictions. Children over 8 years only. Complimentary full breakfast. Check-out 11 am, check-in 3 pm. TV; cable (premium). Downhill ski 8 miles, cross-country ski 3 miles. Farmhouse built in 1872; period furnishings. Totally nonsmoking. **$**

Virginia

Alexandria

Motel/Motor Lodge

★★ **HOLIDAY INN.** *480 King St (22314). Phone 703/549-6080; toll-free 800/465-4329; fax 703/684-6508. www.holiday-inn.com.* 227 rooms, 6 story. Pets accepted, some restrictions. Check-out noon. TV; cable (premium). In-room modem link. Laundry services. Restaurant, bar. In-house fitness room; sauna. Indoor pool. Free airport transportation. Business center. Concierge. **$$**

[icons]

Hotel

★★ **WASHINGTON SUITES ALEXANDRIA.** *100 S Reynolds St (22304). Phone 703/370-9600; fax 703/370-0467. www.washingtonsuiteshotel.com.* 225 rooms, 9 story. Pets accepted, some restrictions; fee. Complimentary continental breakfast. Check-out noon. TV; cable (premium). Laundry services. Restaurant, bar. In-house fitness room. Health club privileges. Pool. Business center. **$**

[icons]

Arlington County (Ronald Reagan Washington-National Airport Area)

Motels/Motor Lodges

★★ **BEST WESTERN KEY BRIDGE.** *1850 Fort Myer Dr (23692). Phone 703/522-0400; toll-free 800/528-1234; fax 703/524-5275. www.bestwestern.com.* 178 rooms, 11 story. Pets accepted; fee. Check-out noon. TV; cable (premium). Restaurant. In-house fitness room. Health club privileges. Pool. **$**

[icons]

★★ **BEST WESTERN KEY BRIDGE.** *1850 Fort Myer Dr (23692). Phone 703/522-0400; toll-free 800/528-1234; fax 703/524-5275. www.bestwestern.com.* 178 rooms, 11 story. Pets accepted; fee. Check-out noon. TV; cable (premium). Restaurant. In-house fitness room. Health club privileges. Pool. **$**

[icons]

★★ **QUALITY INN.** *1200 N Court House Rd (22201). Phone 703/524-4000; toll-free 800/221-2222; fax 703/522-6814. www.qualityhotelarlington.com.* 392 rooms, 1-10 story. Pets accepted, some restrictions; fee. Check-out noon. TV; cable (premium). In-room modem link. Laundry services. Restaurant, bar. In-house fitness room; sauna. Pool. Concierge. Luxury level. **$**

[icons]

Basye

Motel/Motor Lodge

★★ **BEST WESTERN SHENANDOAH VALLEY.** *250 Conickville Blvd (22842). Phone 540/477-2911; toll-free 800/528-1234; fax 540/477-2392. www.bestwestern.com.* 98 rooms, 2 story. Pets accepted, some restrictions; fee. Check-out 11 am. TV. Restaurant, bar. Game room. Pool; children's pool. Tennis. **$**

[icons]

B&B/Small Inn

★★★ **WIDOW KIP'S COUNTRY INN.** *355 Orchard Dr (22842). Phone 540/477-2400; toll-free 800/478-8714. www.widowkips.com.* This restored 1830 Victorian home is set on 7 acres of rural countryside with a view of the Shenandoah River and the valley. 5 rooms. No room phones. Pets accepted; fee. Complimentary full breakfast. Check-out 11 am, check-in 3 pm. TV; cable (premium). Pool. Bicycles. Federal-style saltbox house (1830); Victorian furnishings, handmade quilts. Totally nonsmoking. **$**

[icons]

Blacksburg

Motels/Motor Lodges

★ **COMFORT INN.** *3705 S Main St (24060). Phone 540/951-1500; toll-free 800/228-5150; fax 540/951-1530. www.comfortinn.com.* 80 rooms, 4 story. Pets accepted. Complimentary continental breakfast. Check-out 11 am. TV; cable (premium), VCR available. In-room modem link. In-house fitness room. Pool. **$$**

[icons]

★ **COMFORT INN.** *3705 S Main St (24068). Phone 540/382-0261; toll-free 800/329-7466; fax 540/382-0365. www.daysinn.com.* 122 rooms, 2 story. Pets accepted; fee. Complimentary continental breakfast. Check-out noon. TV; cable (premium). In-room modem link. Pool. **$**

D 🐾 ➰ ⛖ SC

★ ★ **RAMADA INN.** *3503 Holiday Ln (24060). Phone 540/951-1330; toll-free 800/684-9628; fax 540/951-4847. www.ramada.com.* 98 rooms, 2 story. Pets accepted, some restrictions; fee. Check-out noon. TV; cable (premium). Some in-room steam baths. Restaurant, bar. Room service. Pool; children's pool. Cross-country ski 20 miles. **$**

D 🐾 🎿 ➰ ⛖

Blue Ridge Parkway

Resort

★ ★ ★ **DOE RUN LODGE RESORT AND CONFERENCE CENTER.** *Blue Ridge Pkwy (24343). Phone 276/398-2212; toll-free 800/325-6189; fax 276/398-2833. www.doerunlodge.com.* Located along Blue Ridge Parkway, this true nature-lover's retreat with its fresh, clean mountain air will truly be delightful. Enjoy the beautiful scenery with deer and wildlife roaming in the forest with the scent of blossoms filling the air. 47 suites, 1-2 story. No elevator. Pets accepted, some restrictions; fee. Check-out noon. TV; VCR (movies, fee). Restaurant, bar; entertainment Fri, Sat. Sauna. Pool; poolside service. Lighted tennis. Lawn games. **$**

D 🐾 🏌 🎿 ➰ ⛖ SC

Bristol

Motels/Motor Lodges

★ **LA QUINTA INN.** *1014 Old Airport Rd (24201). Phone 276/669-9353; fax 276/669-6974. www.laquinta.com.* 123 rooms, 4 story. Pets accepted. Complimentary continental breakfast. Check-out noon. TV; cable (premium), VCR available. In-room modem link. Pool. **$**

D 🐾 ➰ ⛖

★ **RED CARPET INN.** *15589 Lee Hwy (24202). Phone 276/669-1151.* 60 rooms, 2 story. Pets accepted; fee. Check-out noon. TV; cable (premium). Pool. **$**

D 🐾 🏌 🎿 ➰ ⛖

★ **SUPER 8.** *2139 Lee Hwy (24201). Phone 276/466-8800. www.super8.com.* 62 rooms, 3 story. Pets accepted, some restrictions; fee. Check-out 11 am. TV. **$**

D 🐾 ⛖

Charlottesville

Motel/Motor Lodge

★ ★ **DAYS INN.** *1600 Emmet St N (22901). Phone 434/293-9111; toll-free 800/329-7466; fax 434/977-2780. www.daysinn.com.* 129 rooms, 3 story. Pets accepted; fee. Check-out noon, check-in 2 pm. TV; cable (premium). In-room modem link. Restaurant, bar. Room service. Health club privileges. In-house fitness room. Pool; children's pool. Free transportation. **$**

D 🐾 ➰ 🏌 ⛖ SC

Hotel

★ ★ ★ **OMNI CHARLOTTESVILLE HOTEL.** *235 W Main St (22902). Phone 434/971-5500; toll-free 800/843-6664; fax 434/979-4456. www.omnihotels.com.* Located on a downtown mall, this hotel is within walking distance of the government buildings. 211 rooms, 6 story. Pets accepted, some restrictions; fee. Check-out noon, check-in 3 pm. TV; cable (premium). Restaurant, bar. In-house fitness room; sauna. Indoor pool; outdoor pool; whirlpool. Free covered parking. **$**

D 🐾 ➰ 🏌 ⛖ SC

Chesapeake

Motel/Motor Lodge

★ **SUPER 8.** *3216 Churchland Blvd (23321). Phone 757/686-8888. www.super8.com.* 59 rooms, 3 story. Pets accepted, some restrictions. Complimentary continental breakfast. Check-out 11 am. TV; cable (premium). In-room modem link. **$**

D 🐾 ⛖ SC

Chincoteague

B&B/Small Inn

★ ★ **THE GARDEN AND THE SEA INN.** *4188 Nelson Rd (23415). Phone 757/824-0672; toll-free 800/824-0672. www.gardenandseainn.com.* This lovely Victorian inn offers romantically decorated rooms. The complimentary breakfast can be enjoyed in either the dining room overlooking the gardens or in the garden by the lily pond. 6 rooms. No room phones. Pets accepted. Complimentary continental breakfast. Check-out 11 am, check-in 3 pm. Restaurant. Concierge service. Built as Bloxom's Tavern (1802) and adjacent farmhouse. **$$**

D 🐾 ⛖

Covington

Motels/Motor Lodges

★★ **BEST WESTERN MOUNTAIN VIEW.** *820 E Madison St (24426). Phone 540/962-4951; toll-free 800/465-4329; fax 540/965-5714. www.bestwestern.com.* 79 rooms, 2 story. Pets accepted; fee. Check-out 11 am. TV; cable (premium). In-room modem link. Restaurant. Room service. Pool; children's pool. **$**

D 🐾 ⚊ 🔌 SC

★ **COMFORT INN.** *203 Interstate Dr (24426). Phone 540/962-2141; toll-free 800/228-5150; fax 540/965-0964.* 99 rooms, 2 story. Pets accepted; fee. Complimentary continental breakfast. Check-out 11 am, check-in 2 pm. TV; cable (premium), VCR available. Laundry services. Indoor pool; whirlpool. **$**

D 🐾 ⚊ 🔌 SC

B&B/Small Inn

★★★ **MILTON HALL BED AND BREAKFAST INN.** *207 Thorny Ln (24426). Phone 540/965-0196; fax 540/962-8232.* Built in 1874, this Gothic English manor is now an elegant bed-and-breakfast. The property and its formal English gardens sit on 44 acres of mostly-wooded land, adjoining the George Washington National Forest. At the forest, guests can enjoy hiking, horseback riding, fishing and hunting. 6 rooms, 2 story. Pets accepted, some restrictions. Complimentary full breakfast. Check-out noon, check-in 3 pm. TV in some rooms, sitting room; cable (premium). Lawn games. Some room phones. **$$**

🐾 SC

Culpeper

Motel/Motor Lodge

★ **COMFORT INN.** *890 Willis Ln (22701). Phone 540/825-4900; toll-free 800/228-5150; fax 540/825-4904. www.comfortinn.com.* 49 rooms, 2 story. Pets accepted; fee. Complimentary continental breakfast. Check-out 11 am. TV; cable (premium). In-room modem link. Pool. **$**

D 🐾 ⚊ 🔌 SC

Guest Ranch

★★ **GRAVES' MOUNTAIN LODGE.** *VA 670 (22743). Phone 540/923-4231; fax 540/923-4312. www.gravesmountain.com.* 40 rooms, 8 kitchen units. Closed rest of year. Pets accepted, some restrictions; fee. Check-out 11 am, check-in 3 pm. Some fireplaces; Laundry

services. Dining room. Pool; children's pool. Tennis. Lawn games. **$**

D 🐾 ⚒ ✦ 🏊 ⚊ 🔌

Danville

Motel/Motor Lodge

★ **STRATFORD INN.** *2500 Riverside Dr (24540). Phone 434/793-2500; fax 434/793-6960.* 151 rooms, 2 story. Pets accepted; fee. Complimentary full breakfast. Check-out noon. TV; cable (premium). In-room modem link. Laundry services. Restaurant, bar. Room service. Health club privileges. In-house fitness room. Pool; children's pool; whirlpool. **$**

D 🐾 ⚊ 🏋 ⚊ SC

Dulles International Airport Area

Motels/Motor Lodges

★★ **HOLIDAY INN.** *1000 Sully Rd (20166). Phone 703/471-7411; fax 703/709-0785. www.holiday-inn.com.* 296 rooms, 2 story. Pets accepted, some restrictions. Check-out noon. TV; cable (premium). In-room modem link. Laundry services. Restaurant, bar; entertainment. Room service. In-house fitness room; sauna. Game room. Indoor pool; whirlpool. Free airport transportation. Business center. **$$**

D 🐾 ⚒ ✦ 🏊 ⚊ 🏋 🔌 ✦

★ **HOLIDAY INN EXPRESS.** *485 Elden St (20170). Phone 703/478-9777; fax 703/471-4624. www.holiday-inn.com.* 115 rooms, 4 story. Pets accepted, some restrictions; fee. Complimentary continental breakfast. Check-out 11 am. TV; cable (premium). In-house fitness room. Free airport transportation. Business center. **$**

D 🐾 🏋 🔌 ✦

Resort

★★★ **MARRIOTT WESTFIELDS RESORT AND CONFERENCE CENTER.** *14750 Conference Center Dr (20151). Phone 703/818-0300; fax 703/818-3655. www.marriott.com.* Whether you are away on business or vacation, this hotel will accommodate all of your needs. The rooms are beautifully decorated and welcoming. 340 rooms, 4 story. Pets accepted, some restrictions; fee. Check-out 1 pm, check-in 3 pm. TV; cable (premium), VCR available. In-room modem link. Restaurant, bar; entertainment. Room service. Health club privileges. In-house fitness room; massage; sauna; steam room. Indoor pool; outdoor pool; whirlpool; poolside service. 18-hole golf; greens fee $85. Lighted tennis. Lawn games. Bicycles. Hiking. Valet parking. Free airport transportation. Business center. Concierge. **$$**

Extended Stay

★ ★ **RESIDENCE INN BY MARRIOTT.** *315 Elden St (20170). Phone 703/435-0044; fax 703/437-4007. www.residenceinn.com.* 168 kitchen units, 2 story. Pets accepted, some restrictions; fee. Complimentary continental breakfast. Check-out noon. TV; cable (premium), VCR available (movies). In-room modem link. Health club privileges. Pool; whirlpool. Lighted tennis. **$**

Emporia

Motels/Motor Lodges

★ **BEST WESTERN EMPORIA.** *1100 W Atlantic St (23847). Phone 434/634-3200; toll-free 800/528-1234; fax 434/634-5459. www.bestwestern.com.* 99 rooms, 2 story. Pets accepted; fee. Complimentary continental breakfast. Check-out 11 am. TV; cable (premium). In-room modem link. In-house fitness room. Pool. **$**

★ **COMFORT INN.** *1411 Skippers Rd (23847). Phone 434/348-3282; toll-free 800/228-5150. www.comfortinn .com.* 96 rooms, 2 story. Pets accepted. Complimentary continental breakfast. TV; cable (premium). In-room modem link. Pool. **$**

★ **DAYS INN.** *921 W Atlantic St (23847). Phone 434/634-9481; fax 434/348-0746. www.daysinn.com.* 122 rooms, 2 story. Pets accepted; fee. Complimentary full breakfast. Check-out noon. TV; cable (premium). Laundry services. Pool. **$**

★ **HAMPTON INN.** *1207 W Atlantic St (23847). Phone 434/634-9200; toll-free 800/426-7866; fax 434/348-0071. www.hamptoninn.com.* 115 rooms, 2 story. Pets accepted. Complimentary continental breakfast. Check-out 11 am. TV; cable (premium). Pool. **$**

Fairfax

Motel/Motor Lodge

★ ★ **HOLIDAY INN.** *11787 Lee-Jackson Memorial Hwy (22033). Phone 703/352-2525; fax 703/352-4471. www.holiday-inn.com.* 312 rooms, 6 story. Pets accepted; fee. Check-out noon. TV; cable (premium), VCR available. In-room modem link. Laundry services. Restaurant, bar; entertainment. In-house fitness room; sauna. Health club privileges. Game room. Indoor pool. Business center. Concierge. Luxury level. **$**

Falls Church

Extended Stay

★ ★ **RESIDENCE INN BY MARRIOTT.** *8125 Gatehouse Rd (22042). Phone 703/573-5200; fax 703/573-8100. www.residenceinn.com.* With a convenient location, this property has easy access to many area companies and is only 12 miles from Washington, D.C. 159 rooms, 4 story. Pets accepted; fee. Complimentary buffet breakfast. Check-out noon, check-in 3 pm. TV; cable (premium). In-room modem link. Laundry services. In-house fitness room. Outdoor pool. **$**

Fredericksburg

Motels/Motor Lodges

★ **BEST WESTERN CENTRAL PLAZA.** *3000 Plank Rd (22401). Phone 540/786-7404; toll-free 800/528-1234; fax 540/785-7415. www.bestwestern.com.* 76 rooms, 2-3 story. Pets accepted, some restrictions. Complimentary continental breakfast. Check-out noon. TV; cable (premium). Laundry services. Health club privileges. **$**

★ ★ **ECONO LODGE.** *2802 Plank Rd (22404). Phone 540/786-8361; toll-free 800/272-6232; fax 540/786-8811. www.econolodge.com.* 129 rooms, 2 story. Pets accepted, some restrictions; fee. Check-out 1 pm. TV. In-room modem link. Restaurant. Room service. Health club privileges. Pool. **$**

★ ★ **RAMADA INN.** *5324 Jefferson Davis Hwy (22408). Phone 540/898-1102; toll-free 800/465-4329; fax 540/898-2017. www.ramada.com.* 195 rooms, 2 story. Pets accepted, some restrictions. Check-out noon. TV; cable (premium). In-room modem link. Laundry services. Restaurant, bar; entertainment Wed-Sat. Room service. In-house fitness room. Game room. Indoor pool; whirlpool. **$**

⬜ 🐾 🏊 🏃 📶 SC

Hotel

★ ★ ★ **HOLIDAY INN.** *2801 Plank Rd (22404). Phone 540/786-8321; toll-free 800/544-5064; fax 540/786-3957. www.holiday-inn.com.* 195 rooms, 3 story. Pets accepted, some restrictions; fee. Check-out noon. TV; cable (premium). Restaurant, bar; entertainment. Room service. Health club privileges. In-house fitness room. Pool; children's pool; poolside service. Tennis. Lawn games. Airport transportation. **$**

⬜ 🐾 🏌 🏊 🏃 📶 SC

Harrisonburg

Motels/Motor Lodges

★ **COMFORT INN.** *1440 E Market St (22801). Phone 540/433-6066; fax 540/433-0793. www.comfortinn.com.* 60 rooms, 2 story. Pets accepted, some restrictions. Complimentary continental breakfast. Check-out noon. TV; cable (premium). Pool. **$**

⬜ 🐾 🏊 📶

★ **DAYS INN.** *1131 Forest Hill Rd (22801). Phone 540/433-9353; toll-free 800/329-7466; fax 540/433-5809. www.daysinn.com.* 89 rooms, 4 story. Pets accepted; fee. Complimentary continental breakfast. Check-out 11 am. TV; cable (premium). Health club privileges. Indoor pool; whirlpool. Downhill ski 12 miles. **$**

⬜ 🐾 🏊 📶 SC

★ ★ **FOUR POINTS BY SHERATON.** *1400 E Market St (22801). Phone 540/433-2521; toll-free 800/708-7037; fax 540/434-0253. www.fourpoints.com.* 140 rooms, 5 story. Pets accepted; fee. Check-out noon. TV; cable (premium). In-room modem link. Restaurant, bar; entertainment. Room service. Health club privileges. In-house fitness room; sauna. Indoor pool; children's pool; whirlpool; poolside service. **$**

⬜ 🐾 🏊 🏃 📶 SC

★ ★ **VILLAGE INN.** *4979 S Valley Pike (22801). Phone 540/434-7355; toll-free 800/736-7355. www.shenandoah.org/villageinn.* 36 rooms. Pets accepted; fee. Check-out noon. TV; cable (premium), VCR available (movies). Restaurant. Health club privileges. Pool. Lawn games. **$**

⬜ 🐾 🏊 📶

Hot Springs

B&B/Small Inn

★ ★ **VINE COTTAGE INN.** *US 220 (24445). Phone 540/839-2422; toll-free 800/410-9755. www.vinecottageinn.com.* 15 rooms, 3 story. No elevator. No room phones. Closed 2 weeks in Mar. Pets accepted; fee. Complimentary full breakfast. Check-out noon, check-in 3 pm. TV in common room; VCR available. Downhill ski 1 mile. Built in 1894; family-oriented Victorian inn. Totally nonsmoking. **$**

🐾 🌲 ⛷ 🏊 📶

Irvington

Resort

★ ★ ★ **TIDES INN.** *480 King Carter Dr (22480). Phone 804/438-5000; fax 804/438-5222. www.tidesinn.com.* 106 rooms. Pets accepted, some restrictions; fee. Check-out 1 pm, check-in 4 pm. TV; cable (premium), VCR available (free movies). Laundry services. Restaurant, bar noon-11 pm. Free supervised children's activities (late June-Labor Day); ages 5-12. In-house fitness room; sauna. Game room. Two pools, one saltwater, one heated; poolside service. 45-hole golf; pro, putting greens; driving range; greens fee $25-$40. Lighted tennis. Lawn games. Bicycles. Marina, cruises, boat rental. **$$**

⬜ 🐾 🌲 🏌 ⛷ 🏊 🏃 📶

Leesburg

Motels/Motor Lodges

★ **DAYS INN.** *721 E Market St (20176). Phone 703/777-6622; toll-free 800/329-7466; fax 703/777-4119. www.daysinn.com.* 81 rooms, 2 story. Pets accepted; fee. Complimentary continental breakfast. Check-out noon. TV; cable (premium). Laundry services. **$**

⬜ 🐾 📶 SC

★ ★ **HOLIDAY INN.** *1500 E Market St (20176). Phone 703/771-9200; toll-free 800/272-6232; fax 703/771-1575. www.holiday-inn.com.* 126 rooms, 2 story. Pets accepted, some restrictions. Check-out noon. TV; cable (premium). Laundry services. Restaurant, bar. In-house fitness room. Pool. Free airport transportation. Colonial mansion (1773). **$**

D 🐾 🛏 ✈ 🖥 SC

Lexington

Motels/Motor Lodges

★ ★ **BEST WESTERN INN AT HUNT RIDGE.** *Willow Springs Rd (24450). Phone 540/464-1500; toll-free 800/464-1501. www.bestwestern.com.* 100 rooms, 3 story. Pets accepted; fee. Check-out 11 am. TV; cable (premium). In-room modem link. Laundry services. Restaurant, bar. Room service. Health club privileges. Indoor pool; outdoor pool. **$**

D 🐾 🛏 🖥

★ **COMFORT INN.** *US 11 and I-64 (24450). Phone 540/463-7311; toll-free 800/628-1956; fax 540/463-4590. www.comfortinn.com.* 80 rooms, 4 story. Pets accepted, some restrictions; fee. Complimentary continental breakfast. Check-out 11 am. TV; cable (premium). Laundry services. Indoor pool. **$**

D 🐾 🛏 🖥 SC

★ **DAYS INN.** *325 W Midland Trail (24450). Phone 540/463-2143; fax 540/463-2143. www.daysinn.com.* 53 rooms, 10 kitchen units. Pets accepted; fee. Check-out 11 am. TV; cable (premium). View of mountains. **$**

D 🐾 🛏 🖥 🖥

★ **HOLIDAY INN EXPRESS.** *US 11 and I-64 (24450). Phone 540/463-7351; toll-free 800/465-4329; fax 540/463-7351. www.holiday-inn.com.* 72 rooms, 2 story. Pets accepted; fee. Complimentary continental breakfast. Check-out 11 am. TV; cable (premium). In-room modem link. View of mountains. **$**

D 🐾 🖥 SC

★ **HOWARD JOHNSON.** *2836 N Lee Hwy (24450). Phone 540/463-9181; toll-free 800/654-2000; fax 540/464-3448. www.hojo.com.* 100 rooms, 5 story. Pets accepted; fee. Check-out noon. TV; cable (premium). Laundry services. Restaurant. Pool. On hill; panoramic view of mountains. **$**

D 🐾 🛏 🖥 SC

★ **RAMADA INN.** *US 11 and I-64 (24450). Phone 540/463-7311; fax 540/464-3639. www.ramada.com.* 80 rooms, 4 story. Pets accepted, some restrictions; fee. Check-out noon. TV; cable (premium). Restaurant, bar. Room service. Indoor pool. **$**

D 🐾 🛏 🖥

B&B/Small Inn

★ ★ ★ **HUMMINGBIRD INN.** *30 Wood Ln (24439). Phone 540/997-9065; toll-free 800/397-3214; fax 540/997-0289. www.hummingbirdinn.com.* Located on the edge of Shenandoah Valley, near Goshen Pass, this historic bed-and-breakfast is made for relaxing. Sit on the wrap-around veranda, sleep late in one of the individually decorated rooms, or unwind with a day of trout fishing nearby. 5 rooms, 2 story. No room phones. Pets accepted, some restrictions; fee. Children over 12 years only. Complimentary full breakfast. Check-out 11 am, check-in 3 pm. TV in common room. Lawn games. Victorian Carpenter Gothic villa built in 1780. On river. Totally nonsmoking. **$**

🐾 🛶 🖥 SC

Luray

Motels/Motor Lodges

★ ★ **BEST WESTERN INTOWN OF LURAY.** *410 W Main St (22835). Phone 540/743-6511; fax 540/743-2917. www.bestwestern.com.* 40 rooms, 2 story. Pets accepted; fee. Check-out noon. TV; cable (premium). Restaurant. Room service. Pool. Lawn games. **$**

🐾 🛏 🖥 SC

★ ★ **MIMSLYN INN.** *401 W Main St (22835). Phone 540/743-5105; toll-free 800/296-5105; fax 540/743-2632. www.mimslyninn.com.* 49 rooms, 3 story. Pets accepted; fee. Check-out noon. TV. Restaurant. Health club privileges. Built in 1930 in the style of an antebellum mansion. **$**

🐾 🖥 SC

Lynchburg

Motels/Motor Lodges

★ **COMFORT INN.** *3125 Albert Lankford Dr (24501). Phone 434/847-9041; fax 434/847-8513. www.comfortinn.com.* 120 rooms, 5 story. Pets accepted, some restrictions; fee. Complimentary full breakfast. Check-out noon. TV; cable (premium), VCR available. Health club privileges. Pool. Free airport, train station transportation. **$**

D 🐾 🛏 🖥

★ ★ **HOLIDAY INN.** *601 Main St (24505). Phone 434/ 528-2500; fax 434/528-0062. www.holiday-inn.com.* 243 rooms, 8 story. Pets accepted; fee. Check-out noon. TV; cable (premium). In-room modem link. Restaurant, bar. In-house fitness room. Pool; poolside service. Free airport transportation. **$**

D 🐾 🏊 🏋 🚭

Manassas

Motels/Motor Lodges

★ ★ **BEST WESTERN BATTLEFIELD INN.** *10820 Balls Ford Rd (20109). Phone 703/361-8000; toll-free 800/528-1234; fax 703/361-8000. www.bestwestern.com.* 121 rooms, 2 story. Pets accepted, some restrictions; fee. Complimentary continental breakfast. Check-out 11 am. TV; cable (premium). In-room modem link. Laundry services. Restaurant, bar; entertainment Tues-Sat. Room service. Pool. **$**

D 🐾 🏊 🚭 SC

★ ★ **HOLIDAY INN.** *10800 Vandor Ln (20109). Phone 703/335-0000; fax 703/361-8440. www.holiday-inn.com.* 158 rooms, 5 story. Pets accepted, some restrictions; fee. Check-out noon. TV; cable (premium). In-room modem link. Laundry services. Restaurant, bar. Room service. In-house fitness room. Health club privileges. Pool. Near Manassas (Bull Run) Battlefield. **$**

D 🐾 🏊 🏋 🚭

★ **RED ROOF INN.** *10610 Automotive Dr (20109). Phone 703/335-9333; fax 703/335-9342. www.redroof.com.* 119 rooms, 3 story. Pets accepted. Check-out noon. TV; cable (premium). **$**

D 🐾 🚭

Martinsville

Motels/Motor Lodges

★ ★ **BEST WESTERN MARTINSVILLE INN.** *1755 Virginia Ave (24112). Phone 276/632-5611; toll-free 800/528-1234; fax 276/632-1168. www.bestwestern.com.* 97 rooms, 2 story. Pets accepted, some restrictions. Check-out noon. TV; cable (premium). In-room modem link. Laundry services. Restaurant, bar. Room service. In-house fitness room. Pool; children's pool. **$**

D 🐾 🏊 🏋 🚭 SC

★ ★ **DUTCH INN.** *2360 Virginia Ave (24078). Phone 276/647-3721; toll-free 800/800-3996; fax 276/647-4857. www.dutchinns.com.* 150 rooms, 2 story. Pets accepted,

some restrictions; fee. Check-out noon. TV; cable (premium). In-room modem link. Restaurant, bar. Room service. In-house fitness room; sauna. Pool; whirlpool; poolside service. **$**

D 🐾 🏊 🏋 🚭

Natural Bridge

Motel/Motor Lodge

★ ★ **WATTSTULL COURT.** *RR 1 Box 21 (24066). Phone 540/254-1551.* 26 rooms. Pets accepted, some restrictions; fee. Check-out 11 am. TV. Restaurant. Pool; children's pool. Panoramic view of Shenandoah Valley. **$**

🐾 🏊 🚭

New Market

Motel/Motor Lodge

★ **BUDGET INN.** *2192 Old Valley Pike (22844). Phone 540/740-3105; toll-free 800/296-6835; fax 540/740-3108. www.budgetinn.com.* 14 rooms. Pets accepted, some restrictions; fee. Check-out 11 am. TV; cable (premium). **$**

🐾 🚭 SC

Newport News

Motel/Motor Lodge

★ **COMFORT INN.** *12330 Jefferson Ave (23602). Phone 757/249-0200; toll-free 800/368-2477; fax 757/249-4736. www.comfortinn.com.* 124 rooms, 3 story. Pets accepted; fee. Complimentary continental breakfast. Check-out noon, check-in 2 pm. TV; cable (premium). In-room modem link. Laundry services. Health club privileges. Pool. Free airport transportation. **$**

D 🐾 🏊 🚭 SC

Norfolk

Motel/Motor Lodge

★ **ECONO LODGE.** *9601 4th View St (23503). Phone 757/480-9611; fax 757/480-1307. www.econolodge.com.* 71 rooms, 3 story. Pets accepted; fee. Complimentary continental breakfast. Check-out 11 am. TV; cable (premium), VCR available. Laundry services. In-house fitness room. Ocean; fishing pier. **$**

D 🐾 🏋 🚭

Hotel

★ ★ **CLARION HOTEL.** *345 Granby St (23510). Phone 757/622-6682; toll-free 888/402-6682; fax 757/623-5949.* 125 rooms, 8 story. Pets accepted, some restrictions; fee. Check-out noon, check-in 3 pm. TV; cable (premium). In-room modem link. Restaurant, bar. In-house fitness room. Health club privileges. **$**

⊡ 🐾 👤 🔁

Petersburg

Motels/Motor Lodges

★ ★ **BEST WESTERN STEVEN KENT.** *12205 S Crater Rd (23805). Phone 804/733-0600; fax 804/862-4549. www.bestwestern.com.* 138 rooms, 1-2 story. Pets accepted, some restrictions; fee. Check-out 11 am. TV; cable (premium). In-room modem link. Restaurant, bar. Pool; children's pool. Miniature golf. Lighted tennis. Lawn games. **$**

⊡ 🐾 ⛳ 🏊 🔁

★ **DAYS INN.** *12208 S Crater Rd (23805). Phone 804/733-4400; toll-free 877/512-4400; fax 804/861-9559. www.thedaysinn.com/petersburg.* 155 rooms, 2 story. Pets accepted, some restrictions; fee. Check-out 11 am. TV; cable (premium). In-room modem link. In-house fitness room. Pool; children's pool. **$**

⊡ 🐾 🏊 👤 🔁

Portsmouth

Hotel

★ ★ **HOLIDAY INN.** *8 Crawford Pkwy (23704). Phone 757/393-2573; toll-free 800/456-2811; fax 757/399-1248.* 222 rooms, 4 story. Pets accepted. Check-out 11 am, check-in 4 pm. TV; cable (premium). In-room modem link. Laundry services. Restaurant, bar. Room service. In-house fitness room. Pool. Dockage, marina adjacent. **$**

⊡ 🐾 🏊 👤 🔁

Radford

Motels/Motor Lodges

★ ★ **BEST WESTERN RADFORD INN.** *1501 Tyler Ave (24141). Phone 540/639-3000; toll-free 800/628-1955; fax 540/633-0251. www.bestwestern.com.* 72 rooms, 2 story. Pets accepted, some restrictions; fee. Check-out noon. TV; cable (premium). In-house fitness room; sauna. Indoor pool; children's pool; whirlpool. **$**

⊡ 🐾 🏊 👤 🔁 SC

★ **DOGWOOD LODGE.** *7073 Lee Hwy (24141). Phone 540/639-9338.* 15 rooms. Pets accepted; fee. Check-out 11 am. TV; cable (premium). **$**

🐾

★ **EXECUTIVE MOTEL.** *7498 Lee Hwy (24143). Phone 540/639-1664; toll-free 888/393-8483; fax 540/633-1737.* 27 rooms, 2 story. Pets accepted, some restrictions; fee. Check-out 11 am. TV; cable (premium), VCR. Health club privileges. **$**

⊡ 🐾 🐾 🔁

Richmond

Motels/Motor Lodges

★ **LA QUINTA INN.** *6910 Midlothian Tpke (23225). Phone 804/745-7100; toll-free 800/531-5900; fax 804/276-6660. www.laquinta.com.* 130 rooms, 3 story. Pets accepted. Complimentary continental breakfast. Check-out noon. TV; cable (premium). In-room modem link. Pool. **$**

⊡ 🐾 🏊 🔁 SC

★ **QUALITY INN.** *8008 W Broad St (23294). Phone 804/346-0000; fax 804/527-0284. www.qualityinn.com.* 191 rooms, 6 story. Pets accepted; fee. Complimentary continental breakfast. Check-out 11 am. TV; cable (premium). In-room modem link. In-house fitness room. Pool. **$**

⊡ 🐾 🏊 👤 🔁 SC

★ **RED ROOF INN.** *4350 Commerce Rd (23234). Phone 804/271-7240; fax 804/271-7245. www.redroof.com.* 108 rooms, 2 story. Pets accepted, some restrictions. Check-out noon. TV; cable (premium). **$**

⊡ 🐾 🔁

Hotel

★ ★ ★ ★ ★ **THE JEFFERSON HOTEL.** *101 W Franklin St (23220). Phone 804/788-8000; toll-free 800/424-8014; fax 804/225-0334. www.jeffersonhotel.com.* The Jefferson Hotel is an institution in the heart of Richmond. Imaginations run wild at this historic landmark, dating to 1895. It's easy to conjure a beautifully dressed debutante gliding down the hotel's sweeping staircase, or influential politicians having a heated debate under the impressive marble-style columns. The guest rooms are furnished in a traditional style defined by antique reproductions and fine art, while modern amenities and inimitable

Southern hospitality ensure the comfort of all guests. Pedigreed residents take afternoon tea here. TJ's provides a casual setting for fine dining with local dishes like oyster chowder and peanut soup. The hotel's star restaurant is Lemaire, with its sparkling ambience and refined menu. 264 rooms, 9 story. Pets accepted; fee. Check-out noon, check-in 3 pm. TV; cable (premium), VCR available. In-room modem link. Room service 24 hours. Restaurant, bar. Children's activity center, babysitting services available. In-house fitness room. Indoor pool. Valet parking. Business center. Concierge. **$$$**

D ⬛ ⬛ ⬛ SC ⬛

Extended Stay

★ ★ **RESIDENCE INN BY MARRIOTT.** *2121 Dickens Rd (23230). Phone 804/285-8200; fax 804/285-2530. www.residenceinn.com.* 80 rooms, 2 story. Pets accepted; fee. Complimentary continental breakfast. Check-out noon. TV; cable (premium), VCR available (movies). In-room modem link. Laundry services. Pool; whirlpool. Outdoor tennis. **$**

D ⬛ ⬛ ⬛ ⬛

Roanoke

Motels/Motor Lodges

★ ★ **CLARION HOTEL.** *2727 Ferndale Dr NW (24017). Phone 540/362-4500; toll-free 800/228-5050; fax 540/362-4506. www.clarionhotel.com.* 154 rooms, 5 story. Pets accepted, some restrictions; fee. Check-out noon. TV; cable (premium). In-room modem link. Restaurant, bar. Room service. In-house fitness room. Indoor pool; outdoor pool; whirlpool. Outdoor tennis, lighted courts. Free airport transportation. **$**

D ⬛ ⬛ ⬛ ⬛ ⬛ ⬛ SC

★ ★ **HOLIDAY INN.** *4468 Starkey Rd (24014). Phone 540/774-4400; toll-free 888/228-5040; fax 540/774-1195. www.holiday-inn.com.* 196 rooms, 5 story. Pets accepted; fee. Check-out noon. TV; cable (premium). In-room modem link. Restaurant, bar; entertainment. Room service. Health club privileges. Pool; poolside service. Free airport, bus depot transportation. Concierge. Luxury level. **$**

D ⬛ ⬛ ⬛

★ **RAMADA INN.** *1927 Franklin Rd SW (24014). Phone 540/343-0121; fax 540/342-2048. www.ramada.com.* 127 rooms, 4 story. Pets accepted; fee. Complimentary full breakfast. Check-out noon. TV. In-room modem link. Laundry services. Restaurant, bar. Health club privileges. Pool. Near river. **$**

D ⬛ ⬛ ⬛

★ **TRAVELODGE.** *2619 Lee Hwy S (24175). Phone 540/992-6700; toll-free 800/578-7878; fax 540/992-3991. www.travelodge.com.* 108 rooms. Pets accepted; fee. Complimentary continental breakfast. Check-out 11 am. TV; cable (premium). Pool. **$**

D ⬛ ⬛ ⬛ SC

Hotel

★ ★ **WYNDHAM ROANOKE AIRPORT HOTEL.** *2801 Hershberger Rd NW (24017). Phone 540/563-9300; fax 540/366-5846. www.wyndham.com.* 320 rooms, 8 story. Pets accepted, some restrictions; fee. Check-out noon. TV; cable (premium), VCR available. Restaurant, bar. In-house fitness room; sauna. Indoor pool; outdoor pool; whirlpool; poolside service. Lighted tennis. Free airport transportation. Concierge. Luxury level. **$**

D ⬛ ⬛ ⬛ ⬛ ⬛ ⬛ ⬛

Salem

Motel/Motor Lodge

★ ★ **QUALITY INN.** *179 Sheraton Dr (24153). Phone 540/562-1912; toll-free 800/459-4949; fax 540/562-0507. www.qualityinn.com.* 120 rooms, 2 story. Pets accepted, some restrictions; fee. Complimentary continental breakfast. Check-out 11 am. TV; cable (premium), VCR available. Laundry services. Restaurant, bar. In-house fitness room. Pool. Airport transportation. **$**

D ⬛ ⬛ ⬛ ⬛ ⬛

South Hill

Motel/Motor Lodge

★ **BEST WESTERN INN.** *I-85 and US 58 (23970). Phone 434/447-3123; toll-free 800/296-3123; fax 434/447-4237. www.bestwestern.com.* 151 rooms, 2 story. Pets accepted. Complimentary continental breakfast. Check-out 11 am. TV; cable (premium). Laundry services. Bar. Health club privileges. In-house fitness room. Game room. Pool; children's pool. Free airport transportation. **$**

D ⬛ ⬛ ⬛ ⬛ ⬛

Springfield

Motels/Motor Lodges

★ **COMFORT INN.** *6560 Loisdale Ct (22150). Phone 703/922-9000; toll-free 800/228-5150; fax 703/971-6944. www.comfortinn.com.* 112 rooms, 5 story. Pets accepted.

Complimentary continental breakfast. Check-out noon. TV; cable (premium). In-room modem link. Health club privileges. **$**

[D] [icons] [SC]

★ **HAMPTON INN.** *6550 Loisdale Ct (22150). Phone 703/924-9444; toll-free 800/426-7866; fax 703/924-0324. www.hamptoninn.com.* 153 rooms, 7 story. Pets accepted. Complimentary continental breakfast. Check-out noon. TV; cable (premium). Health club privileges. Pool. **$**

[D] [icons] [SC]

Staunton

Motels/Motor Lodges

★ **BUDGET HOST INN.** *3554 Lee Jackson Hwy (24401). Phone 540/337-1231; fax 540/337-0821.* 32 rooms, 2 story. Pets accepted, some restrictions; fee. Complimentary continental breakfast. Check-out 11 am. TV; cable (premium). Pool; children's pool. **$**

[icons] [SC]

★ **COMFORT INN.** *1302 Richmond Ave (24401). Phone 540/886-5000; fax 540/886-6643. www.comfortinn.com.* 98 rooms, 5 story. Pets accepted, some restrictions; fee. Complimentary continental breakfast. Check-out 11 am. TV; cable (premium). Pool. **$**

[D] [icons]

Tappahannock

Motel/Motor Lodge

★ **SUPER 8.** *US 17 and US 360 (22560). Phone 804/443-3888; fax 804/443-3888. www.super8.com.* 43 rooms, 2 story. Pets accepted, some restrictions; fee. Check-out 11 am. TV. **$**

[D] [icons]

Tysons Corner

Motel/Motor Lodge

★ **COMFORT INN.** *1587 Spring Hill Rd (22182). Phone 703/448-8020; toll-free 800/828-3297; fax 703/448-0343. www.comfortinntysons.com.* 250 rooms, 3 story. Pets accepted, some restrictions; fee. Complimentary continental breakfast. Check-out noon. TV; cable (premium). In-room modem link. Laundry services. Health club privileges. Pool. Free airport transportation. **$**

[D] [icons] [SC]

Virginia Beach

Motel/Motor Lodge

★ **DAYS INN.** *3107 Atlantic Ave (23451). Phone 757/428-7233; toll-free 800/292-3297; fax 757/491-1936. www.daysinn.com.* 8 story. Pets accepted; fee. Check-out 11 am. TV; cable (premium). In-room modem link. Restaurant, bar. Room service. Indoor pool; whirlpool. **$**

[D] [icons] [SC]

Warrenton

Motels/Motor Lodges

★ **COMFORT INN.** *7379 Comfort Inn Dr (20187). Phone 540/349-8900; fax 540/347-5759. www.comfortinn .com.* 97 rooms. Pets accepted, some restrictions; fee. Complimentary continental breakfast. Check-out 11 am. TV; cable (premium). In-room modem link. Laundry services. Health club privileges. In-house fitness room. Pool. **$**

[D] [icons]

★ **HAMPTON INN.** *501 Blackwell Rd (20186). Phone 540/349-4200; toll-free 800/426-7866; fax 540/349-0061. www.hamptoninn.com.* 101 rooms, 2 story. Pets accepted. Complimentary continental breakfast. Check-out noon. TV; cable (premium), VCR (movies). Laundry services. In-house fitness room. Pool. **$**

[D] [icons] [SC]

Waynesboro

Motels/Motor Lodges

★ **DAYS INN.** *2060 Rosser Ave (22980). Phone 540/943-1101; toll-free 800/943-1102; fax 540/949-7586. www.daysinn.com.* 98 rooms, 2 story. Pets accepted; fee. Check-out 11 am. TV; cable (premium). Game room. Pool. Lawn games. **$**

[D] [icons]

★ ★ **INN AT AFTON.** *US 250 and I-64 (22980). Phone 540/942-5201; toll-free 800/860-8559; fax 540/943-8746. www.comet.net/nelsoncty.* 118 rooms, 2-3 story. No elevator. Pets accepted. Check-out noon. TV. Restaurant, bar; entertainment Fri, Sat. Room service. Pool. Downhill ski 18 miles. **$**

[D] [icons] [SC]

★ ★ **QUALITY INN.** *640 W Broad St (22980). Phone 540/942-1171; fax 540/942-4785. www.qualityinn.com.* 75 rooms. Pets accepted, some restrictions. Check-out noon. TV; cable (premium). Health club privileges. Pool; children's pool. Downhill ski 20 miles. **$**

D 🐾 ⤢ ≈ SC

Williamsburg

Motel/Motor Lodge

★ **QUARTERPATH INN.** *620 York St (23185). Phone 757/220-0960; toll-free 800/446-9222; fax 757/220-1531. www.quarterpathinn.com.* 130 rooms, 2 story. Pets accepted. Check-out noon, check-in 2 pm. TV; cable (premium). Outdoor pool. **$**

D 🐾 ⤢ ≈ SC

Winchester

Motels/Motor Lodges

★ ★ **BEST WESTERN LEE-JACKSON MOTOR INN.** *711 Millwood Ave (22601). Phone 540/662-4154; toll-free 800/528-1234; fax 540/662-2618. www.bestwestern.com.* 140 rooms, 2 story. Pets accepted; fee. Check-out noon. TV; cable (premium). Laundry services. Restaurant, bar. Room service. Health club privileges. Pool. Free airport transportation. **$**

D 🐾 ⤢ ≈ SC

★ **TRAVELODGE.** *160 Front Royal Pike (22602). Phone 540/665-0685; toll-free 800/578-7878; fax 540/665-0689. www.travelodge.com.* 149 rooms, 3 story. Pets accepted; fee. Complimentary continental breakfast. Check-out 11 am. TV; cable (premium), VCR available (movies). In-room modem link. Laundry services. Health club privileges. Pool. **$**

D 🐾 ⤢ ≈ SC

Woodstock

Motel/Motor Lodge

★ **BUDGET HOST INN.** *1290 S Main St (22664). Phone 540/459-4086; fax 540/459-4043. www.budgethost.com.* 43 rooms, 1-2 story. Pets accepted, some restrictions. Check-out 11 am. TV. Laundry services. Restaurant. Pool. Downhill ski 20 miles. **$**

D 🐾 ⚓ ⚡ ⤢ ⤢ ≈

Wytheville

Motels/Motor Lodges

★ **BEST WESTERN WYTHEVILLE INN.** *355 Nye Rd (24382). Phone 276/228-7300; fax 276/228-4223. www.bestwestern.com.* 100 rooms, 2 story. Pets accepted, some restrictions; fee. Complimentary continental breakfast. Check-out noon. TV; cable (premium). Pool. **$**

D 🐾 ⤢ ≈ SC

★ ★ **HOLIDAY INN.** *1800 E Main St (24382). Phone 276/228-5483; toll-free 800/465-4329; fax 276/228-5417. www.holiday-inn.com.* 199 rooms, 1-4 story. Pets accepted, some restrictions; fee. Check-out 11 am. TV; cable (premium). Restaurant, bar. Room service. Pool; children's pool. **$**

D 🐾 ⤢ ≈ SC

★ **RAMADA INN.** *955 Peppers Ferry Rd (24382). Phone 276/228-6000; toll-free 800/272-6232; fax 276/228-6009. www.ramada.com.* 154 rooms, 2 story. Pets accepted. Check-out noon. TV; cable (premium). Laundry services. Restaurant, bar. Room service. Pool. **$**

D 🐾 ⤢ ≈ SC

★ **SHENANDOAH INN.** *140 Lithia Rd (24382). Phone 276/228-3188; fax 276/228-6458.* 100 rooms, 1-2 story. Pets accepted; fee. Check-out 11 am. TV. **$**

D 🐾 ≈ SC

Washington

Aberdeen

Motels/Motor Lodges

★ **OLYMPIC INN.** *616 W Heron St (98520). Phone 360/533-4200; toll-free 800/562-8618; fax 360/533-6223.* 55 rooms, 2 story. No A/C. Pets accepted; fee. Complimentary continental breakfast. Check-out noon. TV; cable (premium). Laundry services. **$**

D ⦾ ⊠

★ **RED LION.** *521 W Wishkah St (98520). Phone 360/532-5210; toll-free 800/RED-LION; fax 360/533-8483. www.redlion.com.* 67 rooms, 2 story. Pets accepted. Complimentary continental breakfast. Check-out noon. TV. **$**

D ⦾ ⚓ ⊠

Anacortes

Motels/Motor Lodges

★ **ANACORTES INN.** *3006 Commercial Ave (98221). Phone 360/293-3153; toll-free 800/327-7976; fax 360/293-0209. www.anacortesinn.com.* 44 rooms, 2 story. Pets accepted, some restrictions; fee. Check-out 11 am. TV; cable (premium). Pool. **$**

⦾ ⇌ ⊠ SC

★ **SHIP HARBOR INN.** *5316 Ferry Terminal Rd (98221). Phone 360/293-5177; toll-free 800/852-8568; fax 360/299-2412. www.shipharborinn.com.* 16 rooms, 1-2. story. No A/C. Pets accepted, some restrictions; fee. Complimentary continental breakfast. Check-out 11 am. TV. Laundry services. Bar. **$**

D ⦾ ✈ ⊠

Bellevue

Hotels

★ ★ ★ **BELLEVUE CLUB HOTEL.** *11200 SE 6th St (98004). Phone 425/454-4424; toll-free 800/579-1110; fax 425/688-3101. www.bellevueclub.com.* You instantly feel the hush of the Bellevue Club Hotel when you walk through the vine-covered entrance to this exquisite hotel. Visitors are welcomed to this temple of serenity and contemporary elegance set on 9 acres in the center of Bellevue. While the Bellevue Club feels very private and exclusive, hotel guests are warmly greeted with thoughtful touches and deluxe amenities. Each room has an inviting atmosphere, complete with luxurious bedding and baths crafted of marble, limestone, or granite. Stone fireplaces, oversized baths, or private balconies set each room apart from another. An Olympic-size pool, state-of-the-art equipment, racquet courts, and spa make the fitness facility a true sanctuary. Quick bites are provided at two other establishments for those on the go. 67 rooms, 4 story. Pets accepted, some restrictions; fee. Complimentary continental breakfast. Check-out 1 pm, check-in 3 pm. TV; cable (premium), VCR available. In-room modem link. Room service 24 hours. Restaurant, bar; entertainment. Children's activity center; supervised children's activities, ages 1-12. Outdoor pool; children's pool; whirlpool; poolside service. Outdoor tennis. Valet parking. Business center. Concierge. **$$$**

D ⦾ ⨂ ⇌ �⩎ ⊠ ⫞

★ ★ ★ **DOUBLETREE HOTEL.** *300 112th Ave (98004). Phone 425/455-1300; toll-free 800/222-TREE; fax 425/450-4119. www.doubletree.com.* This full-service hotel, located in downtown Bellevue, is only 10 minutes from Seattle and its many attractions. 353 rooms, 10 story. Pets accepted, some restrictions. Check-out noon, check-in 3 pm. TV; cable (premium). Restaurant, bar. Babysitting services available. In-house fitness room; spa. Outdoor pool; whirlpool. Business center. **$$**

D ⦾ ⇌ ⩎ ⊠ SC ⫞

★ ★ **RED LION.** *11211 Main St (98004). Phone 425/455-5240; toll-free 800/RED-LION; fax 425/455-0654. www.redlion.com.* 181 rooms, 2 story. Pets accepted, some restrictions; fee. Check-out noon, check-in 4 pm. TV; cable (premium). Restaurant, bar; entertainment. Room service. In-house fitness room. Outdoor pool; poolside service. **$**

D ⦾ ⇌ ⩎ ⊠

★ ★ ★ **THE WOODMARK HOTEL ON LAKE WASHINGTON.** *1200 Carillon Point (98033). Phone 425/822-3700; fax 425/822-3699. www.thewoodmark.com.* With the blinking lights of Seattle's skyline only 7 miles in the distance, the Woodmark Hotel gently rests on the shores of scenic Lake Washington. Convenient to Bellevue and Redmond, the Woodmark is an ideal stop for travelers to the pristine Pacific Northwest. Set within a complex of specialty shops, restaurants, and marina, the hotel is a true getaway enhanced by a marvelous destination spa. Characterized by the serenity and casual elegance of the region, the Woodmark instills a sense of belonging in its guests. From the friendly staff to the cozy furnishings, a relaxed, residential style pervades the hotel. The rooms are luxurious without being pretentious and feature lake, marina, or creek views. The region's fresh, delicious cuisine is the highlight at Waters Lakeside Bistro, and the Library Bar serves a wonderful afternoon tea, complete with a special menu and china service for children. 100 rooms, 4 story. Pets accepted; fee. Check-out noon, check-in 4 pm. TV; VCR available. In-room modem link. Room service 24 hours. Restaurant, bar. Babysitting services available. In-house fitness room; health club privileges, spa. Pool; poolside service. Marina; three lakeside parks. Valet parking. Concierge. **$$**

D ☟ ⇴ 🏃 ⊠

Bellingham

Motels/Motor Lodges

★ ★ **BEST WESTERN LAKEWAY INN.** *714 Lakeway Dr (98226). Phone 360/671-1011; toll-free 888/671-1011; fax 360/676-8519. www.bellingham-hotel.com.* 132 rooms, 4 story. Pets accepted, some restrictions; fee. Check-out noon. TV; cable (premium). Laundry services. Restaurant, bar; entertainment. Room service. In-house fitness room; sauna. Indoor pool; whirlpool. Free airport, bus depot transportation. Business center. **$**

D ☟ ⇴ 🏃 ✈ ⊠ SC 🏃

★ **DAYS INN.** *125 E Kellogg Rd (98226). Phone 360/671-6200; toll-free 800/831-0187; fax 360/671-9491. www.daysinn.com.* 70 rooms, 3 story. Pets accepted; fee. Complimentary continental breakfast. Check-out 11 am. TV; cable (premium). Laundry services. Health club privileges. Pool; whirlpool. **$**

D ☟ ⇴ ⊠

★ ★ **QUALITY INN.** *100 E Kellogg Rd (98226). Phone 360/647-8000; fax 360/647-8094. www.qualityinn.com.* 86 rooms, 3 story. Pets accepted, some restrictions; fee. Complimentary continental breakfast. Check-out noon. TV; cable (premium), VCR available. In-room modem link. Laundry services. In-house fitness room. Pool; whirlpool. Free airport, bus depot transportation. Business center. **$**

D ☟ ⇴ 🏃 ⊠ 🏃

★ **VAL-U INN.** *805 Lakeway Dr (98226). Phone 360/671-9600; toll-free 800/443-7777; fax 360/671-8323. www.bellinghamvaluinn.com.* 82 rooms, 3 story. Pets accepted, some restrictions; fee. Complimentary continental breakfast. Check-out noon. TV; cable (premium), VCR available. Laundry services. Whirlpool. Free airport, train station, ferry terminal transportation. **$**

☟ ✈ ⊠ SC

Blaine

Resort

★ ★ ★ **RESORT SEMIAHMOO.** *9565 Semiahmoo Pkwy (98230). Phone 360/318-2000; toll-free 800/770-7992; fax 360/318-2087. www.semiahmoo.com.* Found in the tall trees of Puget Sound, this beach-front resort offers tons of amenities. It is near hiking and biking trails, a marina, and other attractions. 261 rooms, 4 story. Pets accepted, some restrictions; fee. Check-out noon, check-in 3 pm. TV. In-room modem link. Laundry services. Dining room, bar; entertainment. Room service. In-house fitness room; spa; sauna; steam room. Game room. Indoor pool; outdoor pool; whirlpool; poolside service. Golf; greens fee $75. Outdoor, indoor tennis. Lawn games. Bicycle rentals. 300-slip marina; boat and water sports. Charter fishing, clam digging, oyster picking (seasonal). Concierge. Beachcombing. San Juan Island cruise yacht. On 1,100-acre wildlife preserve. **$**

D ☟ ⇔ 🏊 🏌 🎾 ⇴ 🏃 ⊠

Bremerton

Motel/Motor Lodge

★ **MIDWAY INN.** *2909 Wheaton Way (98310). Phone 360/479-2909; toll-free 800/231-0575; fax 360/479-1576. www.midway-inn.com.* 60 rooms, 3 story. Pets accepted, some restrictions; fee. Complimentary continental breakfast. Check-out 11 am. TV; cable (premium), VCR (free movies). Laundry services. **$**

D ☟ ⊠ SC

Centralia

Motel/Motor Lodge

★ **INN AT CENTRALIA.** *702 W Harrison Ave (98531). Phone 360/736-2875; toll-free 800/459-0035; fax 360/736-2651.* 89 rooms, 2 story. Pets accepted; fee. Complimentary continental breakfast. Check-out 11 am. TV. Pool. **$**

D ☟ ⇴ ⊠

Cheney

Motel/Motor Lodge

★ **WILLOW SPRINGS MOTEL.** *5 B St (99004). Phone 509/235-5138; fax 509/235-4528. www.nebsnow.com/*

manager. 44 rooms, 3 story. No elevator. Pets accepted, some restrictions; fee. Check-out 11 am. TV. Laundry services. **$**

D 🐾 🏊

Coulee Dam

Motel/Motor Lodge

★ **COULEE HOUSE MOTEL.** *110 Roosevelt Way (99116). Phone 509/633-1101; toll-free 800/715-7767; fax 509/633-1416. www.couleehouse.com.* 61 rooms, 2 story. Pets accepted, some restrictions; fee. Check-out 11 am. TV; cable (premium). Laundry services. Pool; whirlpool. View of dam. **$**

D 🐾 🏊

Coupeville

Motel/Motor Lodge

★ **HARBOUR INN.** *1606 Main St (98249). Phone 360/331-6900.* 20 rooms, 2 story. No A/C. Pets accepted, some restrictions; fee. Complimentary continental breakfast. Check-out 11 am. TV. **$**

D 🐾 🏊

Ellensburg

Motel/Motor Lodge

★★ **ELLENSBURG INN.** *1700 Canyon Rd (98926). Phone 509/925-9801; toll-free 800/321-8791; fax 509/925-2093.* 105 rooms, 2 story. Pets accepted; fee. Check-out noon. TV; cable (premium). Restaurant, bar. Room service. In-house fitness room. Indoor pool; children's pool; whirlpool. **$**

🐾 🏊 🏃 🏊 SC

Enumclaw

Motel/Motor Lodge

★★ **BEST WESTERN PARK CENTER HOTEL.** *1000 Griffin Ave (98022). Phone 360/825-4490; fax 360/825-3686. www.bestwestern.com.* 40 rooms, 2 story. Pets accepted; fee. Check-out 11 am. TV. In-room modem link. Restaurant, bar. Room service. In-house fitness room. **$**

D 🐾 🏃 🏋 🏊

Everett

Motel/Motor Lodge

★ **WELCOME MOTOR INN.** *1205 Broadway (98201). Phone 425/252-8828; toll-free 800/252-5512; fax 425/252-8880. www.welcomemotorinn.com.* 42 rooms, 2 story. Pets accepted, some restrictions; fee. Check-out 11 am. TV; cable (premium). **$**

D 🐾 🏊 SC

Forks

Resort

★★ **KALALOCH LODGE.** *157151 Hwy 101 (98331). Phone 360/962-2271; fax 306/962-3391. www.visitkalaloch.com.* 65 rooms, 2 story. No A/C. No room phones. Pets accepted, some restrictions; fee. Check-out 11 am, check-in 4 pm. Dining room. **$**

D 🐾 🏊

B&B/Small Inn

★ **MANITOU LODGE BED & BREAKFAST.** *813 Kilmer Rd (98331). Phone 360/374-6295; fax 360/374-7495. www.manitoulodge.com.* 7 rooms, 2 story. No A/C. No room phones. Pets accepted, some restrictions; fee. Complimentary full breakfast. Check-out 11 am, check-in 4-7 pm. Amidst 10 acres of rainforest. **$**

D 🐾 🏄 🏃 🏊

Goldendale

Motel/Motor Lodge

★ **PONDEROSA MOTEL.** *775 E Broadway St (98620). Phone 509/773-5842; fax 509/773-4049.* 28 rooms, 2 story. Pets accepted, some restrictions; fee. Check-out 11 am. TV. **$**

🐾 🏃 🏊

Kelso

Motel/Motor Lodge

★★ **RED LION.** *510 Kelso Dr (98626). Phone 360/636-4400; toll-free 800/733-5466; fax 360/425-3296. www.redlion.com.* 162 rooms, 2 story. Pets accepted; fee. Check-out noon. TV; cable (premium). Restaurant, bar;

entertainment. Room service. In-house fitness room. Pool; children's pool; whirlpool; poolside service. **$**

D 🐕 🏊 🎿 🖨 SC

Kennewick

Motels/Motor Lodges

★ **DAYS INN.** *2811 W 2nd Ave (99336). Phone 509/735-9511; toll-free 800/547-0106; fax 509/735-1944.* 104 rooms, 3 story. Pets accepted, some restrictions; fee. Complimentary continental breakfast. Check-out 11 am. TV. Pool. **$**

D 🐕 🏊 🖨 SC

★ ★ **RED LION.** *1101 N Columbia Center Blvd (99336). Phone 509/783-0611; toll-free 800/325-4000; fax 509/735-3087. www.redlion.com.* 162 rooms, 2 story. Pets accepted; fee. Check-out noon. TV; cable (premium). In-room modem link. Restaurant, bar; entertainment. Room service. Health club privileges. Pool; whirlpool. Airport, train station, bus depot transportation. **$**

D 🐕 🏊 🎿 ✈ 🖨

★ **TAPADERA INN.** *300-A N Ely St (99336). Phone 509/783-6191; toll-free 800/737-9804; fax 509/735-3854.* 61 rooms, 2 story. Pets accepted, some restrictions; fee. Check-out noon. TV; cable (premium). Laundry services. Pool. **$**

D 🐕 🏊 🖨

★ **TRAVELODGE.** *321 N Johnson St (99336). Phone 509/735-6385; fax 509/736-6631. www.travelodge.com.* 49 rooms, 3 story. No elevator. Pets accepted, some restrictions; fee. Complimentary continental breakfast. Check-out 11 am. TV; cable (premium). In-room modem link. Laundry services. Pool. **$**

D 🐕 🏊 🎿 🖨

Leavenworth

Motels/Motor Lodges

★ **DER RITTERHOFF MOTOR INN.** *190 US 2 (98826). Phone 509/548-5845; toll-free 800/255-5845; fax 509/548-4098. www.derritterhof.com.* 51 rooms, 2 story. Pets accepted, some restrictions; fee. Check-out 11 am. TV. Restaurant. Pool; whirlpool. Cross-country ski 1 mile. Lawn games. **$**

D 🐕 🎿 🏊 🖨

★ **RODEWAY INN.** *185 US 2 (98826). Phone 509/548-7992; toll-free 800/693-1225; fax 509/548-2193. www.leavenworthwa.com.* 78 rooms, 2 story. Pets accepted,

some restrictions; fee. Complimentary continental breakfast. Check-out 11 am. TV; cable (premium). In-room modem link. Indoor pool; whirlpool. Downhill, cross-country ski 1 mile. **$**

D 🐕 🎿 🏊 🖨

Long Beach

Motels/Motor Lodges

★ **THE BREAKERS MOTEL & CONDO.** *26th and Hwy 103 (98631). Phone 360/642-4414; toll-free 800/219-9833; fax 360/642-8772. www.breakerslongbeach.com.* 124 rooms, 3 story. No A/C. Pets accepted, some restrictions. Check-out 11 am. TV; VCR available. Pool; whirlpool. **$**

🐕 🎿 🏊 🖨

★ **CHAUTAUQUA LODGE.** *304 14th St NW (98631). Phone 360/642-4401; toll-free 800/869-8401; fax 360/642-2340. www.chautauqualodge.com.* 180 rooms, 3 story. No A/C. Pets accepted; fee. Check-out 11 am. TV. Laundry services. Bar. Sauna. Indoor pool; whirlpool. **$**

D 🐕 🏊 🖨

★ **EDGEWATER INN.** *409 10th St (98631). Phone 360/642-2311; toll-free 800/561-2456; fax 360/642-8018.* 84 rooms, 3 story. Pets accepted, some restrictions; fee. Check-out 11 am. TV; cable (premium). Restaurant, bar. **$**

D 🐕 🖨

★ **OUR PLACE AT THE BEACH.** *1309 South Blvd (98631). Phone 360/642-3793; toll-free 800/538-5107; fax 360/642-3896.* 25 rooms, 1-2 story. Pets accepted; fee. Check-out 11 am. TV; cable (premium). In-house fitness room; sauna. Whirlpool. **$**

🐕 🛥 🎿 🚶 🖨

★ **SHAMAN MOTEL.** *115 3rd St SW (98631). Phone 360/642-3714; toll-free 800/753-3750. www.shamanmotel.com.* 42 rooms, 2 story. No A/C. Pets accepted, some restrictions; fee. Check-out 11 am. TV; VCR available (movies). Pool. **$**

D 🐕 🏊 🖨

Marysville

Motel/Motor Lodge

★ **VILLAGE MOTOR INN.** *235 Beach Ave (98270). Phone 360/659-0005; toll-free 877/659-0005; fax 360/658-0866.* 45 rooms, 3 story. Pets accepted, some restrictions; fee. Complimentary continental breakfast. Check-out 11 am. TV; cable (premium). In-room modem link. **$**

D 🐕 🖨

Moclips

Motels/Motor Lodges

★ **HI-TIDE CONDOMINIUM RESORT.** *4890 Railroad Ave (98162). Phone 360/276-4142; toll-free 800/662-5477; fax 360/276-0156.* 25 rooms, 2 story. No A/C. Pets accepted, some restrictions; fee. Check-out 11 am. TV; VCR available. Lawn games. **$**

D 🐾 ⛖ SC

★★ **OCEAN CREST RESORT.** *4651 WA 109 (98562). Phone 360/276-4465; toll-free 800/684-8439; fax 360/276-4149. www.oceancrestresort.com.* 45 rooms, 1-3 story. No A/C. Pets accepted, some restrictions; fee. Check-out 11 am. TV; cable; VCR available (movies fee). Laundry services. Restaurant, bar. In-house fitness room; sauna. Indoor pool; whirlpool. **$**

🐾 ⛖ 🧍 ⛖

Moses Lake

Motels/Motor Lodges

★ **BEST VALUE INN.** *1214 S Pioneer Way (98837). Phone 509/765-9173; toll-free 888/315-BEST; fax 509/765-1137. www.bestvalueinn.com.* 20 rooms. Pets accepted, some restrictions. Check-out 11 am. TV; cable (premium), VCR available (movies). Pool. **$**

🐾 ⛖ ⛖

★★ **BEST WESTERN HALLMARK INN & CONFERENCE CENTER.** *3000 Marina Dr (98837). Phone 509/765-9211; toll-free 800/235-4255; fax 509/766-0493. www.hallmarkinns.com.* 161 rooms, 2-3. story. Pets accepted, some restrictions. Check-out noon. TV; cable (premium), VCR available. Laundry services. Restaurant, bar; entertainment. Room service. In-house fitness room; sauna. Pool; children's pool; whirlpool. Outdoor tennis. Kayak, bicycle rentals. Free airport transportation. **$**

D 🐾 ⛷ ⛖ 🧍 ✈ ⛖ SC

★ **INTERSTATE INN.** *2801 W Broadway (98837). Phone 509/765-1777; fax 509/766-9452.* 30 rooms, 2 story. Pets accepted, some restrictions; fee. Check-out 11 am. TV; cable (premium), VCR available. Sauna. Indoor pool; whirlpool. **$**

🐾 ⛖ ⛖

★ **MOTEL 6.** *2822 Wapato Dr (98837). Phone 509/766-0250; fax 509/766-7762. www.motel6.com.* 111 rooms, 2 story. Pets accepted. Check-out noon. TV; cable (premium). Pool. **$**

D 🐾 ⛖ ⛖

★★ **SHILO INN.** *1819 E Kittleson (98837). Phone 509/765-9317; fax 509/765-5058. www.shiloinn.com.* 100 rooms, 2 story. Pets accepted; fee. Check-out noon. TV; cable (premium). Laundry services. Restaurant. In-house fitness room; sauna. Indoor pool; whirlpool. Free airport, bus depot transportation. **$**

D 🐾 ⛖ 🧍 ✈ ⛖

Mount Vernon

Motels/Motor Lodges

★ **BEST WESTERN COLLEGE WAY INN.** *300 W College Way (98273). Phone 360/424-4287; toll-free 800/793-4024; fax 360/424-6036. www.bestwestern.com.* 66 rooms, 2 story. Pets accepted, fee. Complimentary continental breakfast. Check-out noon. TV; cable (premium). In-room modem link. Health club privileges. Pool; whirlpool. **$**

D 🐾 ⛖ ⛖

★ **BEST WESTERN COTTONTREE INN.** *2300 Market St (98273). Phone 360/428-5678; fax 360/428-1844. www.bestwestern.com.* 120 rooms, 3 story. Pets accepted, some restrictions; fee. Complimentary continental breakfast. Check-out noon. TV; cable (premium). In-room modem link. Laundry services. Bar. Health club privileges. Pool. **$**

D 🐾 ⛖ ⛖

Oak Harbor

Motel/Motor Lodge

★ **BEST WESTERN HARBOR PLAZA.** *33175 WA 20 (98277). Phone 360/679-4567; toll-free 800/927-5478; fax 360/675-2543. www.bestwestern.com.* 80 rooms, 3 story. Pets accepted, some restrictions; fee. Complimentary continental breakfast. Check-out noon. TV; cable (premium). In-room modem link. Bar. Pool; whirlpool. **$**

D 🐾 ⛖ ⛖ SC

Ocean Shores

Motel/Motor Lodge

★ **THE GREY GULL RESORT.** *647 Ocean Shores Blvd NW (98569). Phone 360/289-3381; toll-free 800/562-9712; fax 360/289-3673. www.thegreygull.com.* 36 rooms, 3 story. No A/C. Pets accepted, some restrictions; fee. Check-out noon, check-in 4 pm. TV. Laundry services. Sauna. Pool; whirlpool. **$**

D 🐾 ⛖ ⛖

Olympia

Motels/Motor Lodges

★ **BEST WESTERN TUMWATER INN.** *5188 Capitol Blvd (98501). Phone 360/956-1235. www.bestwestern.com.* 89 rooms, 2 story. Pets accepted; fee. Complimentary continental breakfast. Check-out 11 am. TV. In-room modem link. Laundry services. In-house fitness room; sauna. **$**

D 🐾 🏃 🎿 ⌝ SC

★ **RAMADA INN.** *621 S Capitol Way (98501). Phone 360/352-7700; toll-free 888/298-2054; fax 360/943-9349. www.ramada.com.* 123 rooms, 8 story. Pets accepted; fee. Check-out noon. TV; cable. In-room modem link. Laundry services. Restaurant, bar. In-house fitness room; sauna. Pool; whirlpool. **$$**

D 🐾 ⌂ 🎿 ⌝ ⌝ SC

★★ **RED LION.** *2300 Evergreen Park Dr (98502). Phone 360/943-4000; fax 360/357-6604. www.redlion.com.* This state capital property is near the beautiful Cascade Mountains and many recreational activities. 190 rooms, 3 story. Pets accepted, some restrictions; fee. Check-out noon. TV; cable (premium). In-room modem link. Laundry services. Restaurant, bar. Room service. In-house fitness room. Pool; whirlpool. Lawn games. **$**

🐾 ⌂ 🎿 ⌝

Omak

Motels/Motor Lodges

★ **CEDARS INN.** *1 Apple Way (98840). Phone 509/422-6431; fax 509/422-4214. www.cedarsinn.com.* 78 rooms, 3 story. No elevator. Pets accepted; fee. Check-out noon. TV; VCR available (movies, fee). Laundry services. Restaurant, bar. Pool. **$**

D 🐾 ⌂ ⌝ SC

★ **MOTEL NICHOLAS.** *527 E Grape Ave (98841). Phone 509/826-4611; toll-free 800/404-4611.* 21 rooms. Pets accepted; fee. Check-out 11 am. TV; cable (premium). City park opposite. **$**

🐾 ⌝

Othello

Motel/Motor Lodge

★ **BEST WESTERN LINCOLN INN.** *1020 E Cedar (99344). Phone 509/488-5671; toll-free 800/240-7865; fax* *509/488-5084. www.bestwestern.com.* 50 rooms, 2 story. Pets accepted; fee. Complimentary continental breakfast. Check-out 11 am. TV; cable (premium), VCR available. Restaurant. In-house fitness room; sauna. Pool. **$**

🐾 ⌂ 🎿 ⌝

Pasco

Hotel

★★ **RED LION.** *2525 N 20th Ave (99301). Phone 509/547-0701; fax 509/547-4278. www.redlion.com.* Located in the heart of Washington State wine country, this hotel offers plenty of shopping and many attractions. 279 rooms, 2-3 story. Pets accepted. Check-out noon. TV. In-room modem link. Restaurant, bar; entertainment. Room service. In-house fitness room. Pool; whirlpool; poolside service. Free airport, train station, bus depot transportation. Business center. **$**

D 🐾 ⌂ 🎿 ⌝ 🏃

Port Angeles

Motels/Motor Lodges

★ **QUALITY INN.** *101 E 2nd St (98362). Phone 360/457-9434; toll-free 800/858-3812; fax 360/457-5915. www.qualityinn.com.* 35 rooms, 1-3 story. No A/C. Pets accepted, some restrictions; fee. Complimentary continental breakfast. Check-out 11 am. TV; cable (premium). **$**

🐾 ⌝

★★ **RED LION.** *221 N Lincoln (98362). Phone 360/452-9215; fax 360/452-4734. www.redlion.com.* 186 rooms, 2 story. No A/C. Pets accepted, some restrictions; fee. Check-out noon. TV; cable. Restaurant. Health club privileges. Pool; whirlpool. Overlooks harbor. **$**

D 🐾 ⌂ 🎿

Port Townsend

Motel/Motor Lodge

★★ **INN AT PORT HADLOCK.** *310 Alcohol Loop Rd (98339). Phone 360/385-7030; toll-free 800/785-7030; fax 360/385-6955. www.innatporthadlock.com.* 28 rooms, 3 story. Pets accepted, some restrictions; fee. Check-out 11 am. TV; cable (premium), VCR (movies fee). Restaurant, bar. Marina. Former alcohol plant built in 1910. **$**

D 🐾 🎿 ⌝

Hotel

★★ **PALACE.** *1004 Water St (98368). Phone 360/385-0773; toll-free 800/962-0741. www.olympus.net/palace.* 15 rooms, 2 story. No A/C. No room phones. Pets accepted; fee. Complimentary continental breakfast. Check-out noon. TV. Laundry services. Restaurant. **$**

All Suite

★★ **BISHOP VICTORIAN GUEST SUITES.** *714 Washington St (98368). Phone 360/385-6122; toll-free 800/824-4738. www.bishopvictorian.com.* 14 rooms, 3 story. No A/C. No elevator. Pets accepted, some restrictions; fee. Complimentary continental breakfast. Check-out 11 am, check-in 3 pm. TV; VCR available (movies). In-room modem link. Health club privileges. Built in 1890 as an office/warehouse; converted to English inn. Totally nonsmoking. **$**

B&B/Small Inn

★★ **THE SWAN HOTEL.** *216 Monroe St (98368). Phone 360/385-6122. www.rainshadowproperties.com.* 9 rooms, 3 story. Pets accepted, some restrictions; fee. Check-out 11 am, check-in 3 pm. TV; VCR available (movies). In-room modem link. **$**

Pullman

Motel/Motor Lodge

★★ **QUALITY INN.** *SE 1400 Bishop Blvd (99163). Phone 509/332-0500; fax 509/334-4271. www.qualityinn.com.* 66 rooms, 2 story. Pets accepted, some restrictions; fee. Check-out noon. TV; cable (premium), VCR available. In-room modem link. Health club privileges; sauna. Pool; whirlpool. Airport transportation. **$**

Quincy

Motel/Motor Lodge

★ **TRADITIONAL INNS.** *500 F St SW (98848). Phone 509/787-3525; fax 509/787-3528. www.traditionalinns.com.* 24 rooms, 2 story. Pets accepted, some restrictions; fee. Check-out 11 am. TV. Laundry services. **$**

Richland

Motels/Motor Lodges

★ **BALI HAI MOTEL.** *1201 George Washington Way (99352). Phone 509/943-3101; fax 509/943-6363.* 44 rooms, 2 story. Pets accepted, some restrictions; fee. Check-out noon. TV; cable (premium). Laundry services. Pool; whirlpool. **$**

★ **DAYS INN.** *615 Jadwin Ave (99352). Phone 509/943-4611; fax 509/946-2271. www.daysinn.com.* 98 rooms, 2 story. Pets accepted; fee. Complimentary continental breakfast. Check-out noon. TV; cable (premium). Pool. **$**

★★ **RED LION.** *802 George Washington Way (99352). Phone 509/946-7611; toll-free 800/733-5466; fax 509/943-8564. www.redlion.com.* 149 rooms, 2 story. Pets accepted; fee. Check-out noon. TV. Restaurant, bar. Room service. Pool; poolside service. Boat dock. Free airport, train station, bus depot transportation. **$**

★★ **ROYAL HOTEL AND CONFERENCE CENTER.** *1515 George Washington (99352). Phone 509/946-4121; toll-free 800/635-3980; fax 509/946-2222. www.bestwestern.com.* 195 rooms, 6 story. Pets accepted; fee. Complimentary full breakfast. Check-out noon. TV; cable (premium). Laundry services. Restaurant, bar; entertainment. Room service. Sauna. Pool; children's pool; whirlpool; poolside service. Lawn games. Free airport, train station, bus depot transportation. **$**

★★ **SHILO INN.** *50 Comstock St (99352). Phone 509/946-4661; fax 509/943-6741. www.shiloinns.com.* 150 rooms, 2 story. Pets accepted; fee. Complimentary breakfast buffet. Check-out noon. TV; cable (premium). In-room modem link. Laundry services. Restaurant, bar. In-house fitness room. Pool; children's pool; whirlpool. Airport, train station, bus depot transportation. On 12 acres. **$**

Ritzville

Motel/Motor Lodge

★ **LA QUINTA INN.** *1513 S Smittys Blvd (99169). Phone 509/659-1007; fax 509/659-1025. www.laquinta.com.* 54 rooms, 2 story. Pets accepted. Complimentary continental breakfast. Check-out 11 am. TV; cable (premium), VCR available. Laundry services. Pool; whirlpool. **$**

D 🐾 🏊 🚭

San Juan Islands

B&B/Small Inn

★ ★ **TUCKER HOUSE BED & BREAKFAST.** *260 B St (98250). Phone 360/378-2783; toll-free 800/965-0123; fax 360/378-8775. www.tuckerhouse.com.* 6 rooms, 2 story. No A/C. No room phones. Pets accepted; fee. Complimentary breakfast. Check-out 11 am, check-in 3 pm. TV; VCR available (movies). Victorian home built in 1898. Totally nonsmoking. **$**

D 🐾 ⛷ 🚭

Seattle

Motels/Motor Lodges

★ ★ **BEST WESTERN EXECUTIVE INN.** *200 Taylor Ave N (98109). Phone 206/448-9444; toll-free 800/351-9444; fax 206/441-7929. www.bwexec-inn.com.* 123 rooms, 5 story. Pets accepted, some restrictions; fee. Complimentary continental breakfast. Check-out noon, check-in 3 pm. TV. Restaurant, bar. Room service. In-house fitness room. Whirlpool. **$**

D 🐾 ⛷ 🚭

★ **LA QUINTA INN.** *2824 S 188th St (98188). Phone 206/241-5211; toll-free 866/725-1661; fax 206/246-5596. www.laquinta.com.* 143 rooms, 6 story. Pets accepted. Complimentary continental breakfast. Check-out noon. TV; cable (premium). In-house fitness room. Outdoor pool; whirlpool. Free airport transportation. **$**

🐾 🏊 ⛷ 🚭

Hotels

★ ★ ★ **ALEXIS HOTEL.** *1007 First Ave (98104). Phone 206/624-4844; toll-free 800/426-7033; fax 206/621-9009. www.alexishotel.com.* This is an historic hotel that has been offering fine accommodations in downtown Seattle since the turn of the century. The rooms are all finely decorated and furnished with European décor. 109 rooms, 6 story. Pets accepted, some restrictions. Check-out noon. TV; cable (premium), VCR available. In-room modem link. Room service 24 hours. Restaurant, bar. Massage; steam room. Valet parking. Concierge. **$$$**

D 🐾 ⛷ 🚭

★ ★ **CROWNE PLAZA.** *1113 Sixth Ave (98101). Phone 206/464-1980; toll-free 800/2CROWNE; fax 206/340-1617.* www.crowneplaza.com. 415 rooms, 34 story. Pets accepted; fee. Check-out noon, check-in 4 pm. TV; cable (premium), VCR available. Restaurant, bar. In-house fitness room. Concierge. Luxury level. **$$**

D 🐾 ⛷ 🚭

★ ★ ★ **ELLIOTT GRAND HYATT SEATTLE.** *721 Pine St (98101). Phone 206/774-1234; fax 206/774-6311. www.hyatt.com.* 425 rooms, 30 story. Pets accepted, some restrictions; fee. Check-out noon, check-in 3 pm. TV; cable (premium), VCR available. Restaurant, bar. Room service. In-house fitness room; spa. Whirlpool. Business center. **$$$**

D 🐾 ⛷ ⛷

THE FAIRMONT OLYMPIC HOTEL. *(Unrated due to new management.) 411 University St (98101). Phone 206/621-1700; toll-free 877/441-1414; fax 206/682-9633. www.fairmont.com.* 450 rooms, 13 story. Pets accepted, some restrictions; fee. Check-out noon, check-in 3 pm. TV; cable (premium), VCR available (movies). In-room modem link. Room service 24 hours. Babysitting services available. In-house fitness room; spa; massage; sauna. Indoor pool; whirlpool; poolside service. Valet parking. Airport transportation. Business center. Concierge. **$$$**

D 🐾 🏊 ⛷ 🚭 ⛷

★ ★ ★ **HOTEL MONACO.** *1101 4th Ave (98101). Phone 206/621-1770; toll-free 800/945-2240; fax 206/621-7779. www.monaco-seattle.com.* A hip hotel decorated with imagination, guests will enjoy the intimate feel here. For lonely pet owners, the hotel will even provide a temporary pet goldfish in each guest suite upon request. 189 rooms, 11 story. Pets accepted. Check-out noon. TV; cable (premium), VCR available. Room service 24 hours. Restaurant, bar. In-house fitness room. Health club privileges. Valet parking. Business center. Concierge. **$$$**

D 🐾 ⛷ 🚭 ⛷

★ ★ ★ **HOTEL VINTAGE PARK.** *1100 Fifth Ave (98101). Phone 206/624-8000; toll-free 800/624-4433; fax 206/623-0568. www.vintagepark.com.* This hotel offers well-appointed and finely furnished guest rooms, each named after a local winery or vineyard. Visitors can enjoy the comfortable lobby while they sit by the fireplace and taste local wines and microbeers. 127 rooms, 11 story. Pets accepted, some restrictions. Check-out noon, check-in 3 pm. TV; VCR available. Room service 24 hours. Restaurant. Health club privileges. Valet parking. Concierge. **$$$**

D 🐾 ⛷ 🚭

★ ★ ★ **SORRENTO HOTEL.** *900 Madison St (98104). Phone 206/622-6400; toll-free 800/426-1265; fax 206/343-6155. www.hotelsorrento.com.* This small hotel offers the services and amenities expected from a larger hotel. It is located near the city water park and other attractions. 76 rooms, 7 story. Pets accepted; fee. Check-out noon, check-in 4 pm. TV; VCR available. Stereos and CD players. Restaurant, bar. Babysitting services available. In-house fitness room; massage. Airport transportation available. Concierge. Turndown service nightly. **$$**

⬜🖐🏃⛵

★ ★ **UNIVERSITY INN.** *4140 Roosevelt Way NE (98105). Phone 206/632-5055; toll-free 800/733-3855; fax 206/547-4937. www.universityinnseattle.com.* 102 rooms, 4 story. Pets accepted, some restrictions; fee. Complimentary continental breakfast. Check-out noon, check-in 3 pm. TV; cable (premium). Laundry services. Restaurant. Outdoor pool. **$**

⬜🖐≈⛵

★ ★ ★ **THE WESTIN SEATTLE.** *1900 Fifth Ave (98101). Phone 206/728-1000; fax 206/728-2259. www.westin.com.* 919 rooms, 40 story. Pets accepted, some restrictions; fee. Check-out noon. Check-in. TV; VCR available. Room service 24 hours. Restaurant, bar; entertainment. In-house fitness room. Pool; whirlpool. Business center. Concierge. Tower rooms with panoramic view. **$**

⬜🖐≈🏃🏃

★ ★ ★ **W SEATTLE HOTEL.** *1112 4th Ave (98101). Phone 206/264-6000; toll-free 877/WHOTELS; fax 206/264-6100. www.whotels.com.* Since this hotel is designed for style-conscious, tech-savvy business travelers, rooms offer CD players, high-speed Ethernet access, and cordless phones at a well-equipped work station. Dream up desires to test the "whatever you want, whenever you want it" service motto. The lobby, adjacent bar, and dining room are new contenders in the 'now' scene of Seattle. 426 rooms, 26 story. Pets accepted, some restrictions; fee. Check-out noon, check-in 3 pm. TV; cable (premium), VCR available, CD available. High-speed Internet access. Room service 24 hour. Restaurant, bar. Babysitting services available. In-house fitness room. Valet parking. Business center. Concierge. **$$$$**

⬜🖐🏃🏃

Seattle-Tacoma International Airport Area

Motels/Motor Lodges

★ ★ **HOLIDAY INN.** *17338 International Blvd (98188). Phone 206/248-1000; toll-free 800/HOLIDAY; fax 206/242-7089. www.holiday-inn.com.* 259 rooms, 12 story. Pets accepted, some restrictions; fee. Check-out noon,

check-in 3 pm. TV; cable (premium). In-room modem link. Revolving rooftop dining room. Room service. In-house fitness room. Indoor pool; whirlpool. Free airport transportation. **$**

⬜🖐≈🏃✈⛵

★ **RED ROOF INN.** *16838 International Blvd (98188). Phone 206/248-0901; toll-free 800/REDROOF; fax 206/242-3170. www.redroof.com.* 152 rooms, 3 story. Pets accepted, some restrictions. Complimentary continental breakfast. Check-out noon, check-in 3 pm. TV; cable (premium). In-room modem link. Laundry services. In-house fitness room. Free airport transportation. **$**

⬜🖐🏃⛵

Hotels

★ ★ ★ **DOUBLETREE HOTEL.** *18740 International Blvd (98188). Phone 206/246-8600; toll-free 800/222-8733; fax 206/431-8687. www.doubletree.com.* 850 rooms, 14 story. Pets accepted; fee. Check-out noon, check-in 3 pm. TV. In-room modem link. Restaurant, bar; entertainment. Room service. In-house fitness room. Outdoor pool; whirlpool; poolside service. Business center. Concierge. Free airport transportation. **$**

⬜🖐≈🏃🏃⛵🏃

★ ★ ★ **HILTON SEATTLE AIRPORT.** *17620 Pacific Hwy S (98188). Phone 206/244-4800; fax 206/248-4499. www.seattleairport.hilton.com.* This hotel and conference center is conveniently located at the airport. 402 rooms, 4 story. Pets accepted; fee. Check-out noon, check-in 3 pm. TV; cable (premium), VCR available. In-room modem link. Restaurant, bar. Room service. In-house fitness room. Pool; whirlpool; poolside service. Free airport transportation. Business center. Concierge. **$**

⬜🖐≈🏃🏃✈⛵🏃

★ ★ ★ **MARRIOTT SEA-TAC AIRPORT.** *3201 S 176th St (98188). Phone 206/241-2000; toll-free 800/228-9290; fax 206/248-0789. www.marriott.com.* 464 rooms. Pets accepted. Check-out 1 pm, check-in 3 pm. TV; cable (premium). In-room modem link. Restaurant, bar. Room service. In-house fitness room; massage; sauna. Game room. Pool; whirlpool; poolside service. Free airport transportation. Business center. Luxury level. **$**

⬜🖐≈🏃🏃⛵SC 🏃

★ ★ **RED LION.** *18220 International Blvd (98188). Phone 206/246-5535; toll-free 800/426-0670; fax 206/246-9733. www.redlion.com.* 146 rooms, 5 story. Pets accepted, some restrictions. Check-out noon, check-in 3 pm. TV; cable (premium). Restaurant. Room service. In-house fitness room; sauna. Outdoor pool; whirlpool; poolside service. Free valet parking. Free airport transportation. **$**

⬜🖐≈🏃⛵SC

Sequim

Motels/Motor Lodges

★ **ECONO LODGE.** *801 E Washington St (98382). Phone 360/683-7113. www.econolodge.com.* 43 rooms, 2 story. Pets accepted; fee. Complimentary continental breakfast. Check-out 11 am. TV; VCR available. Laundry services. Lawn games. **$**

D 🐾 ✈ 🖼

★ **SEQUIM BAY LODGE.** *268522 US 101 (59730). Phone 360/683-0691; toll-free 800/622-0691; fax 360/683-3748.* 54 rooms, 3 story. No elevator. Pets accepted, some restrictions; fee. Complimentary continental breakfast. Check-out 11 am. TV. Pool. Lawn games. **$**

🐾 🖼 🖼

B&B/Small Inn

★ ★ **GROVELAND COTTAGE BED & BREAKFAST.** *4861 Sequim Dungeness Way (98382). Phone 360/683-3565; toll-free 800/879-8859; fax 360/683-5181. www.northolympic.com/groveland.* 4 rooms, 2 story. No A/C. Pets accepted, some restrictions; fee. Children over 12 years only. Complimentary full breakfast. Check-out noon, check-in 3 pm. TV; VCR (free movies). Totally nonsmoking. **$**

🐾 🏃 🖼 🖼

Soap Lake

Motel/Motor Lodge

★ ★ **NOTARAS LODGE.** *13 Canna St (98851). Phone 509/246-0462; fax 509/246-1054. www.notaraslodge.com.* 21 rooms, 2 story. Pets accepted; fee. Check-out 11 am. TV. Restaurant. **$**

D 🐾 🖼 🖼

Spokane

Motels/Motor Lodges

★ **COMFORT INN.** *905 N Sullivan Rd (99037). Phone 509/924-3838; fax 509/921-6976. www.comfortinn.com.* 76 rooms, 2 story. Pets accepted, some restrictions; fee. Complimentary continental breakfast. Check-out 11 am. TV. Pool; whirlpool. **$**

D 🐾 🖼 🖼

★ **DAYS INN.** *4212 W Sunset Blvd (99224). Phone 509/747-2021; toll-free 888/318-2611; fax 509/747-5950.* www.daysinn.com. 130 rooms, 2 story. Pets accepted, some restrictions; fee. Check-out noon. Check-in. TV. In-room modem link. Restaurant. Outdoor pool. Free airport, train station, bus depot transportation. **$**

D 🐾 🖼 🖼

★ ★ **DOUBLETREE HOTEL.** *1100 N Sullivan Rd (99037). Phone 509/924-9000; fax 509/922-4965. www.doubletreevalley.com.* This hotel is located near the Spokane International Airport and other attractions. 236 rooms, 2-3 story. Pets accepted, some restrictions; fee. Check-out noon. Restaurant, bar; entertainment. Room service. In-house fitness room. Pool; whirlpool; poolside service. Free airport transportation. **$**

D 🐾 🖼 🏃 🏃 ✈ 🖼 SC

★ **MOTEL 6.** *1919 N Hutchinson Rd (99212). Phone 509/926-5399; fax 509/928-5974. www.motel6.com.* 92 rooms, 2 story. Pets accepted, some restrictions; fee. Check-out 11, check-in 4 pm. TV; cable (premium). **$**

D 🐾 🏃 🖼

★ ★ **QUALITY INN.** *8923 E Mission Ave (99212). Phone 509/928-5218; toll-free 800/777-7355; fax 509/928-5211. www.spokanequalityinn.com.* 128 rooms, 3-4 story. Pets accepted, some restrictions; fee. Complimentary breakfast. Check-out 11 am. Check-in 3 pm. TV; VCR available. In-house fitness room; sauna. Indoor pool; whirlpool. Business center. **$**

D 🐾 🖼 🏃 🏃 🖼 🏃

★ **SUPER 8.** *N 2020 Argonne Rd (99212). Phone 509/928-4888; toll-free 800/800-8000; fax 509/928-4888. www.super8.com.* 181 rooms, 3 story. Pets accepted; fee. Complimentary continental breakfast. Check-out 11 am. Check-in 3 pm. TV; cable (premium). In-house fitness room. Indoor pool; whirlpool. **$**

🐾 🖼 🏃 🖼

★ **TRADE WINDS NORTH MOTEL.** *3033 N Division St (99207). Phone 509/326-5500; toll-free 800/621-8593; fax 509/328-1357.* 63 rooms, 3 story. No elevator. Pets accepted, some restrictions; fee. Complimentary continental breakfast. Check-out noon. TV; cable (premium). Indoor pool. **$**

🐾 🖼 🖼 SC

Hotels

★ ★ ★ **THE DAVENPORT HOTEL.** *10 S Post St (99201). Phone 509/455-8888; toll-free 800/899-1482; fax 509/624-4455. www.thedavenporthotel.com.* Step back in time to this grand downtown hotel that opened in 1914 and has recently undergone a massive renovation. As soon as you enter the soaring lobby, you can see the attention to design and detail that has been put into this property. The rooms feature hand-carved mahogany furniture, imported Irish linens, and travertine marble bathrooms with spacious showers. Some suites and deluxe rooms have fireplaces, wet bars, and jetted tubs for extra comfort and luxury. The upscale Palm Court restaurant serves Euro-Asian cuisine. The hotel also offers a cigar bar, espresso bar, and candy shop. 284 rooms, 14 story. Pets accepted; fee. Check-out noon. Check-in 3 pm. TV; cable (premium). In-room modem link. Restaurant, bar. Room service 24 hours. Babysitting services available. In-house fitness room; spa; sauna. Indoor pool; whirlpool. Valet parking. Business center. Concierge. **$$**

★★ **RAMADA INN.** *Spokane International Airport (99219). Phone 509/838-5211; toll-free 888/298-2054; fax 509/838-1074. www.ramada.com.* 165 rooms, 2 story. Pets accepted; fee. Check-out noon. Check-in 3 pm. TV. Restaurant, bar; entertainment. Room service. In-house fitness room. Outdoor pool; whirlpool. Free airport transportation. **$**

★★ **RED LION.** *N 700 Division St (99202). Phone 509/326-5577; toll-free 800/REDLION; fax 509/326-1120. www.redlion.com.* 245 rooms, 2 story. Pets accepted. Complimentary continental breakfast. Check-out noon. Check-in 3 pm. TV. Restaurant, bar; entertainment. Room service. In-house fitness room. Outdoor pool; whirlpool. Outdoor tennis. Airport, train station, bus depot transportation. On river. **$**

★★ **RED LION.** *515 W Sprague Ave (99201). Phone 509/838-2711; fax 509/747-6970. www.redlion.com.* 342 rooms, 3-12 story. Pets accepted; fee. Check-out noon. TV; VCR available. In-room modem link. Restaurant, bar; entertainment. In-house fitness room. Pool; poolside service. Free airport transportation. **$**

Tacoma

Motels/Motor Lodges

★ **BEST INN.** *3100 Pacific Hwy E (98424). Phone 253/922-9520; toll-free 877/982-3781; fax 253/922-2002. www.bestinnhotel.com.* 115 rooms, 2 story. Pets accepted, some restrictions; fee. Check-out 11 am. TV; cable (premium). In-room modem link. Laundry services. Health club privileges. **$**

★★ **BEST WESTERN TACOMA INN.** *8726 S Hosmer St (98444). Phone 253/535-2880; fax 253/537-8379. www.bwtacomainn.com.* 149 rooms, 2 story. Pets accepted; fee. Check-out noon. TV; cable (premium). In-room modem link. Restaurant, bar; entertainment. Room service. In-house fitness room. Pool; poolside service. **$**

★ **DAYS INN.** *6802 Tacoma Mall Blvd (98409). Phone 253/475-5900; toll-free 800/329-7466; fax 253/475-3540. www.daysinn.com.* 123 rooms, 2 story. Pets accepted, some restrictions; fee. Check-out 11 am. Check-in 3 pm. TV; cable (premium). In-room modem link. Restaurant. Health club privileges. Pool. Business center. **$**

★ **LA QUINTA INN.** *1425 E 27th St (98421). Phone 253/383-0146; fax 253/627-3280. www.laquinta.com.* 157 rooms, 7 story. Pets accepted. Complimentary continental breakfast. Check-out noon. TV; cable (premium). In-room modem link. Restaurant, bar. Room service. In-house fitness room. Pool; whirlpool. Business center. View of both Mount Rainier and Commencement Bay. **$**

★ **ROYAL COACHMAN INN.** *5805 Pacific Hwy E (98424). Phone 253/922-2500; toll-free 800/422-3051; fax 253/922-6443. www.royalcoachmaninn.com.* 94 rooms, 2 story. Pets accepted; fee. Check-out noon. TV; cable (premium), VCR available. **$**

★ **SHILO INN.** *7414 S Hosmer (98408). Phone 253/475-4020; fax 253/475-1236. www.shiloinns.com.* 132 rooms, 4 story. Pets accepted; fee. Complimentary continental breakfast. Check-out noon. TV; cable (premium). In-room modem link. Sauna; steam room. Indoor pool; whirlpool. **$**

Hotel

★★★ **SHERATON TACOMA HOTEL.** *1320 Broadway Plz (98402). Phone 253/572-3200; toll-free 800/845-9466; fax 253/591-4105. www.sheratontacoma.com.* This hotel is located in downtown Tacoma, near the Tacoma Dome and Sea-Tac International Airport. 319 rooms, 26 story. Pets accepted, some restrictions; fee. Check-out noon. TV; cable (premium), VCR available. In-room modem link. Restaurant, bar; entertainment. Health club privileges; sauna. Business center. Concierge. Luxury level. **$$**

Vancouver

Motels/Motor Lodges

★ **COMFORT INN.** *13207 NE 20th (98686). Phone 360/574-6000; toll-free 888/522-6122; fax 360/573-3746.*

www.comfortinn.com. 58 rooms, 2 story. Pets accepted; fee. Complimentary continental breakfast. Check-out 11 am, check-in 2 pm. TV; cable (premium). In-room modem link. In-house fitness room. Indoor pool; whirlpool. **$**

★ **DAYS INN.** *221 NE Chkalov Dr (98684). Phone 360/256-7044; toll-free 800/426-5110; fax 360/256-1231. www.daysinn.com.* 115 rooms, 2 story. Pets accepted; fee. Complimentary continental breakfast. Check-out noon, check-in 3 pm. TV; cable (premium). Indoor pool; whirlpool. Free transportation. **$**

★ **SHILO INN.** *13206 NE Hwy 99 (98686). Phone 360/573-0511; fax 360/573-0396. www.shiloinns.com.* 66 rooms, 2 story. Pets accepted; fee. Complimentary continental breakfast. Check-out noon, check-in 3 pm. TV; cable (premium). Health club privileges, sauna, steam room. Indoor pool; whirlpool. **$**

Walla Walla

Motels/Motor Lodges

★ **HOWARD JOHNSON.** *325 E Main (99362). Phone 509/529-4360; fax 509/529-7463. www.hojo.com.* 85 rooms, 2 story. Pets accepted. Complimentary continental breakfast. Check-out noon. TV; cable (premium). In-room modem link. Laundry services. In-house fitness room; sauna. Pool; whirlpool. **$**

★ **TRAVELODGE.** *421 E Main St (99362). Phone 509/529-4940; toll-free 800/578-7878; fax 509/529-4943. www.travelodge.com.* 39 rooms, 2 story. Pets accepted, some restrictions; fee. Check-out noon. TV; cable (premium). Pool; whirlpool. **$**

Wenatchee

Motels/Motor Lodges

★ **HOLIDAY LODGE.** *610 N Wenatchee (98801). Phone 509/663-8167; toll-free 800/722-0852.* 59 rooms, 2 story. Pets accepted; fee. Complimentary continental breakfast. Check-out noon. TV; cable (premium), VCR available. Laundry services. In-house fitness room; sauna. Pool; whirlpool. **$**

★★ **RED LION.** *1225 N Wenatchee Ave (98801). Phone 509/663-0711; toll-free 800/733-5466; fax 509/662-8175. www.redlion.com.* 149 rooms, 3 story. Pets accepted. Check-out noon. TV. In-room modem link. Restaurant, bar; entertainment. Room service. In-house fitness room. Pool; whirlpool; poolside service. **$**

★ **WENATCHEE ORCHARD INN.** *1401 N Miller St (98801). Phone 509/662-3443; toll-free 800/368-4571; fax 509/665-0715.* 103 rooms, 3 story. Pets accepted, some restrictions; fee. Check-out 11 am. TV; cable (premium). Restaurant. Pool; whirlpool. Downhill ski 12 miles, cross-country ski 10 miles. **$**

Hotel

★★ **COAST WENATCHEE CENTER HOTEL.** *201 N Wenatchee Ave (98801). Phone 509/662-1234; fax 509/662-0782. www.coasthotels.com.* 147 rooms, 9 story. Pets accepted, some restrictions; fee. Check-out noon. TV. Laundry services. Restaurant, bar; entertainment. In-house fitness room. Indoor pool; outdoor pool; whirlpool; poolside service. Downhill ski 12 miles. Free airport, train station, bus depot transportation. **$**

Winthrop

Motel/Motor Lodge

★ **BEST WESTERN CASCADE INN.** *960 Hwy 20 (98862). Phone 509/996-2217; toll-free 800/444-1972; fax 509/996-3923. www.bestwestern.com.* 30 rooms, 2 story. Pets accepted, some restrictions; fee. Check-out 11 am. TV. In-room modem link. Pool; whirlpool. Downhill ski 15 miles, cross-country ski on site. **$**

Woodinville

Hotel

★★★ **WILLOWS LODGE.** *14580 NE 145th St (98072). Phone 425/424-3900; toll-free 877/424-3930; fax 425/424-2585. www.willowslodge.com.* 86 rooms, 2 story. Pets accepted, some restrictions. Complimentary continental breakfast. Check-out noon, check-in 4 pm. TV; cable (premium), VCR available. Restaurant, bar. Babysitting services available. In-house fitness room; spa. Whirlpool. Concierge. **$$$**

Yakima

Motels/Motor Lodges

★ ★ **DOUBLETREE HOTEL.** *1507 N First St (98901). Phone 509/248-7850; fax 509/575-1694. www.doubletree.com.* This hotel is located near the city center, wineries, the Yakima Mall, Sundome, and Mount Rainier National Park. 208 rooms, 2 story. Pets accepted; fee. Check-out noon. TV. Restaurant, bar; entertainment. Room service. In-house fitness room. Two pools; whirlpool; poolside service. **$**

D 🐾 🏊 🏋 ✈ 🚫 SC

★ ★ **QUALITY INN.** *12 E Valley Mall Blvd (98903). Phone 509/248-6924; toll-free 800/228-5151; fax 509/575-8470. www.qualityinn.com.* 86 rooms, 2 story. Pets accepted, some restrictions; fee. Complimentary continental breakfast. Check-out 11 am. TV. Pool. **$**

D 🐾 🏊 🚫

★ ★ **RED LION.** *607 E Yakima Ave (98901). Phone 509/248-5900; fax 509/575-8975. www.redlion.com.* 153 rooms, 2 story. Pets accepted; fee. Check-out noon. TV; cable (premium). In-room modem link. Restaurant, bar; entertainment. Room service. Health club privileges. Two pools; poolside service. Airport, bus depot transportation. Business center. **$**

D 🐾 🏊 🚫 🏋

★ ★ **RED LION.** *9 N 9th St (98901). Phone 509/452-6511; fax 509/457-4931. www.redlion.com.* 171 rooms, 2-3 story. Pets accepted, some restrictions; fee. Check-out noon. TV; cable (premium), VCR available. In-room modem link. Restaurant, bar. Room service. Pool; poolside service. Free airport transportation. **$**

D 🐾 🏊 🚫

West Virginia

Beckley

Motel/Motor Lodge

★ **COMFORT INN.** *1909 Harper Rd (25801). Phone 304/255-2161; toll-free 800/888-2598; fax 304/255-2161. www.comfortinn.com.* 130 rooms, 3 story. Pets accepted. Complimentary continental breakfast. Check-out noon, check-in 2 pm. TV; cable (premium). In-room modem link. In-house fitness room. Downhill ski 15 miles. **$**

D ⬧ ⬧ ⬧ ⬧ SC

Bluefield

Motels/Motor Lodges

★ **ECONO LODGE.** *3400 Cumberland Rd (24701). Phone 304/327-8171; fax 304/324-4259. www.econolodge.com.* 47 rooms, 2 story. Pets accepted, some restrictions; fee. Complimentary continental breakfast. Check-out 11 am. Check-in 3 pm. TV; cable (premium). In-room modem link. **$**

D ⬧ ⬧ SC

★ ★ **HOLIDAY INN.** *3350 Big Laurel Hwy (24701). Phone 304/325-6170; toll-free 800/465-4329; fax 304/323-2451. www.holiday-inn.com.* 122 rooms, 2 story. Pets accepted, some restrictions. Check-out noon, check-in 2 pm. TV; cable (premium), VCR available. In-room modem link. Restaurant. Room service. In-house fitness room; sauna. Pool. **$**

D ⬧ ⬧ ⬧ ⬧ SC

★ **RAMADA INN.** *3175 E Cumberland Rd (24701). Phone 304/325-5421; toll-free 888/613-9080; fax 304/325-6045. www.ramada.com.* 98 rooms, 2 story. Pets accepted, some restrictions; fee. Check-out noon, check-in 2 pm. TV; cable (premium), VCR available. In-room modem link. Room service 24 hours. Restaurant, bar; entertainment. In-house fitness room; sauna. Game room. Indoor pool; children's pool; whirlpool. **$**

D ⬧ ⬧ ⬧ ⬧

Buckhannon

Motel/Motor Lodge

★ **BICENTENNIAL MOTEL.** *90 E Main St (26201). Phone 304/472-5000; fax 304/472-9159.* 45 rooms, 2 story. Pets accepted, some restrictions. Check-out 11 am, check-in 2 pm. TV; cable (premium). In-room modem link. Bar. Room service. Outdoor pool. **$**

D ⬧ ⬧ ⬧ SC

Charleston

Motels/Motor Lodges

★ **DAYS INN.** *6400 SE MacCorkle Ave (25304). Phone 304/925-1010; toll-free 800/304-3809; fax 304/925-1364. www.daysinn.com.* 147 rooms, 2-3 story. Pets accepted, some restrictions. Complimentary continental breakfast. Check-out 11 am, check-in 3 pm. TV; cable (premium). In-room modem link. In-house fitness room. Pool. **$**

D ⬧ ⬧ ⬧ ⬧

★ **HOLIDAY INN EXPRESS.** *100 Civic Center Dr (25301). Phone 304/345-0600; fax 304/343-1322. www.charleston-holidayinn.com.* 196 rooms, 6 story. Pets accepted, some restrictions; fee. Complimentary continental breakfast. Check-out noon, check-in 2 pm. TV; VCR available. In-room modem link. Laundry services. In-house fitness room. Free airport transportation. **$**

D ⬧ ⬧ ⬧ SC

★ **RED ROOF INN.** *6305 MacCorkle Ave SE (25304). Phone 304/925-6953; toll-free 800/843-7663; fax 304/925-8111. www.redroof.com.* 108 rooms, 2 story. Pets accepted. Check-out noon, check-in 2 pm. TV; cable (premium). Restaurant. **$**

D ⬧ ⬧ SC

Charles Town

Motel/Motor Lodge

★ **TURF MOTEL.** *608 E Washington St (25414). Phone 304/725-2081; toll-free 800/422-8873; fax 304/728-7605.* 47 rooms, 2 story. Pets accepted, some restrictions; fee. Check-out 11:30 am, check-in 2 pm. TV; cable (premium). In-room modem link. Restaurant, bar. Room service. Pool. **$**

D ⬧ ⬧ ⬧ SC

Clarksburg

Motels/Motor Lodges

★ ★ **HOLIDAY INN.** *100 Lodgeville Rd (26330). Phone 304/842-5411; fax 304/842-7258. www.holiday-inn.com.* 159 rooms, 2 story. Pets accepted. Check-out noon. TV; cable (premium). In-room modem link. Restaurant. Room service. Pool. Airport transportation. **$**

D ➔ ⚓ ➳ ⊠

★ **SLEEP INN.** *115 Tolley Dr (26330). Phone 304/842-1919; fax 304/842-9524. www.sleepinn.com.* 73 rooms, 2 story. Pets accepted. Complimentary continental breakfast. Check-out 11 am. TV; cable (premium), VCR available. **$**

D ➔ ⊠

Elkins

Motels/Motor Lodges

★ **ECONO LODGE.** *40 Cherry St; Rte 1 Box 15 (26241). Phone 304/636-5311; toll-free 800/446-6900; fax 304/636-5311. www.econolodge.com.* 72 rooms, 1-2 story. Pets accepted; fee. Complimentary continental breakfast. Check-out 11 am. TV; cable (premium). In-room modem link. Laundry services. Indoor pool. **$**

D ➔ ➳ ⊠ SC

★ ★ **ELKINS MOTOR LODGE.** *Harrison Ave (26241). Phone 304/636-1400; fax 304/636-6318.* 55 rooms, 1-2 story. S, D $41-$50; each additional $3; suites $75. Pets accepted; fee. Check-out noon. TV; cable (premium). In-room modem link. Restaurant. Room service. Free airport transportation.

D ➔ ⊠

★ **SUPER 8.** *350 Beverly Pike; Rte 219 S (26241). Phone 304/636-6500; fax 304/636-6500. www.super8.com.* 44 rooms, 2 story. Pets accepted. Complimentary continental breakfast. Check-out 11 am. TV; cable (premium). In-room modem link. **$**

D ➔ ⊠ SC

Fairmont

Motels/Motor Lodges

★ ★ **HOLIDAY INN.** *930 E Grafton (26554). Phone 304/366-5500; toll-free 800/465-4329; fax 304/363-3975. www.holiday-inn.com.* 106 rooms, 2 story. Pets accepted, some restrictions. Check-out noon. TV; cable (premium).

In-room modem link. Restaurant, bar. Room service. Pool. **$**

D ➔ ⚓ ➳ ⊠ SC

★ **RED ROOF INN.** *50 Middletown Rd (26554). Phone 304/366-6800; toll-free 800/733-7663; fax 304/366-6812. www.redroof.com.* 108 rooms, 2 story. Pets accepted, some restrictions. Check-out noon. TV. **$**

D ➔ ⊠ SC

Grafton

Motel/Motor Lodge

★ **CRISLIP MOTOR LODGE.** *300 Moritz Ave (26354). Phone 304/265-2100; fax 304/265-2017.* 40 rooms, 2 story. Pets accepted. Check-out 11 am. TV; cable (premium). In-room modem link. Pool. **$**

D ➔ ⚓ ➳ ⊠

Huntington

Motel/Motor Lodge

★ **RED ROOF INN.** *5190 US Rte 60E (25705). Phone 304/733-3737; toll-free 800/733-7663; fax 304/733-3786. www.redroof.com.* 108 rooms, 2 story. Pets accepted, some restrictions. Check-out noon. TV. In-room modem link. **$**

D ➔ ⊠ SC

Lewisburg

Motels/Motor Lodges

★ ★ **BRIER INN.** *540 N Jefferson St (24901). Phone 304/645-7722; fax 304/645-7865. www.brierinn.com.* 164 rooms, 2 story. Pets accepted, some restrictions; fee. Check-out 11 am, check-in 2 pm. TV; VCR available (movies). In-room modem link. Restaurant, bar; entertainment Fri. Room service. In-house fitness room. Pool. **$**

D ➔ ➳ 🏋 🏃 ✈ ⊠

★ **DAYS INN.** *635 N Jefferson St (24901). Phone 304/645-2345; toll-free 800/325-2525; fax 304/645-5501. www.daysinn.com.* 26 rooms. Pets accepted, some restrictions; fee. Check-out 11 am, check-in 1 pm. TV; cable (premium). Health club privileges. Airport transportation. **$**

➔ ⊠ SC

★ **ECONO LODGE.** *204 N Jefferson St (24901). Phone 304/645-3055; toll-free 800/283-4678; fax 304/645-3033.* 68 rooms, 1-3 story. Pets accepted; fee. Check-out 11 am, check-in 2 pm. TV. Restaurant. Room service. Pool; whirlpool. Airport transportation. **$**

D 🐾 ⛱ ⊠ SC

Martinsburg

Motels/Motor Lodges

★ ★ **HOLIDAY INN.** *301 Foxcroft Ave (25401). Phone 304/267-5500; toll-free 800/465-4329; fax 304/264-9157. www.holiday-inn.com.* 120 rooms, 5 story. Pets accepted, some restrictions. Check-out noon. TV; cable (premium). In-room modem link. Laundry services. Restaurant, bar. Room service. In-house fitness room; sauna. Indoor pool; outdoor pool; whirlpool; poolside service. Lighted tennis. Lawn games. **$**

D 🐾 🎿 ⛱ 🏃 ✈ ⊠ SC

★ **KNIGHTS INN.** *1997 Edwin Miller Blvd (25401). Phone 304/267-2211; toll-free 800/843-5644; fax 304/267-9606. www.knightsinn.com.* 59 rooms, 1-2 story. Pets accepted; fee. Check-out 11 am. TV; cable (premium), VCR available. In-room modem link. **$**

D 🐾 ⊠ SC

★ **SUPER 8.** *2048 Edwin Miller Blvd (25401). Phone 304/263-0801; toll-free 800/800-8000; fax 304/263-0801. www.super8.com.* 43 rooms, 3 story. Pets accepted, some restrictions. Check-out 11 am. TV; cable (premium). In-room modem link. **$**

D 🐾 ⊠ SC

Morgantown

Motels/Motor Lodges

★ **COMFORT INN.** *225 Comfort Inn Dr (26508). Phone 304/296-9364; toll-free 800/228-5150; fax 304/296-0469. www.comfortinn.com.* 80 rooms, 2 story. Pets accepted, some restrictions; fee. Complimentary continental breakfast. Check-out noon. TV; cable (premium), VCR available. In-room modem link. In-house fitness room. Pool; whirlpool. **$**

D 🐾 ⛱ 🏃 ⊠ SC

★ **ECONO LODGE.** *3506 Monongahela Blvd (26505). Phone 304/599-8181; fax 304/599-8181. www.econolodge.com.* 71 rooms, 2 story. Pets accepted, some restrictions. Complimentary continental breakfast. Check-out 11 am. TV; cable (premium). In-room modem link. **$**

D 🐾 ⊠

★ ★ **HOLIDAY INN.** *1400 Saratoga Ave (26505). Phone 304/599-1680; toll-free 800/465-4329; fax 304/598-0989. www.holiday-inn.com.* 147 rooms, 2-4 story. Pets

accepted; fee. Check-out noon. TV; cable (premium). In-room modem link. Restaurant, bar. Pool. **$**

D 🐾 ⛱ ⊠ SC

★ **RAMADA INN.** *US Rte 119 N, I-68 and I-79 (26506). Phone 304/296-3431; toll-free 800/834-9766; fax 304/296-8841. www.ramada.com.* 151 rooms, 4 story. Pets accepted. Complimentary continental breakfast. Check-out noon. TV; cable (premium). In-room modem link. Restaurant, bar; entertainment Wed, Fri, Sat. In-house fitness room. Pool. Free airport transportation. **$**

D 🐾 ⛱ 🏃 ⊠ SC

Nitro

Motel/Motor Lodge

★ **SUPER 8.** *419 Hurricane Creek Rd (25526). Phone 304/562-3346; toll-free 1-800/726-7016; fax 304/562-7408. www.super8.com.* 146 rooms, 2 story. Pets accepted; fee. Complimentary continental breakfast. Check-out noon. TV; cable (premium). In-room modem link. Laundry services. Game room. Pool. **$**

D 🐾 ⛱ ⊠ SC

Parkersburg

Motel/Motor Lodge

★ **RED ROOF INN.** *3714 E 7th St (26104). Phone 304/485-1741; toll-free 800/733-7663; fax 304/485-1746. www.redroof.com.* 106 rooms, 2 story. Pets accepted. Check-out noon. TV; cable (premium). In-room modem link. In-house fitness room. **$**

D 🐾 🏃 ⊠ SC

Philippi

Motel/Motor Lodge

★ **SUPER 8.** *US 250 S Rte 4 Box 155 (26416). Phone 304/457-5888; fax 304/457-5888. www.super8.com.* 39 rooms, 2 story. Pets accepted. Check-out 11 am. TV; cable (premium). In-room modem link. **$**

D 🐾 ⊠

Princeton

Motel/Motor Lodge

★ **DAYS INN.** *347 Meadowfield Ln (24740). Phone 304/425-8100; fax 304/487-1734. www.daysinn.com.* 122

rooms, 2 story. Pets accepted, some restrictions; fee. Complimentary continental breakfast. Check-out 11 am. TV; cable (premium). In-room modem link. Indoor pool; whirlpool. Downhill ski 15 miles. **$**

Summersville

Motels/Motor Lodges

★ ★ **BEST WESTERN SUMMERSVILLE LAKE MOTOR LODGE.** *1203 S Broad St (26651). Phone 304/872-6900; toll-free 800/214-9551; fax 304/872-6908. www.bestwestern.com.* 57 rooms, 3 story. Pets accepted; fee. Complimentary continental breakfast. Check-out 11 am. TV; cable (premium), VCR available. In-room modem link. Restaurant, bar. **$**

★ **COMFORT INN.** *903 Industrial Dr N (26651). Phone 304/872-6500; toll-free 800/872-1752; fax 304/872-3090. www.comfortinn.com.* 99 rooms, 2 story. Pets accepted, some restrictions; fee. Complimentary continental breakfast. Check-out 11 am. TV; cable (premium), VCR available (movies). In-room modem link. In-house fitness room; sauna. Pool; children's pool. **$**

★ **SLEEP INN.** *701 Professional Park Dr (26651). Phone 304/872-4500; toll-free 800/872-1751; fax 304/872-0288. www.sleepinn.com.* 97 rooms, 2 story. Pets accepted, some restrictions; fee. Complimentary continental breakfast. Check-out 11 am. TV; cable (premium), VCR available (movies). In-room modem link. Laundry services. Pool. Lawn games. **$**

Weston

Motel/Motor Lodge

★ ★ **COMFORT INN.** *Rte 33 E and I-79 (26452). Phone 304/269-7000; toll-free 800/228-5150; fax 304/269-7011. www.comfortinn.com.* 62 rooms, 2 story. Pets accepted, some restrictions; fee. Complimentary continental breakfast. Check-out noon, check-in 3 pm. TV; cable (premium). In-room modem link. Pool. **$**

Wheeling

Motels/Motor Lodges

★ ★ **BEST WESTERN WHEELING INN.** *949 Main St (26003). Phone 304/233-8500; toll-free 800/780-7234; fax 304/233-8500. www.bestwestern.com.* 82 rooms, 4 story. Pets accepted; fee. Complimentary continental breakfast. Check-out 11 am. TV; cable (premium). In-room modem link. Restaurant, bar. In-house fitness room; sauna. **$**

★ **DAYS INN.** *I-70 and Dallas Pike Exit 11 (26059). Phone 304/547-0610; fax 304/547-9029. www.daysinn.com.* 106 rooms, 2 story. Pets accepted, some restrictions. Complimentary continental breakfast. Check-out noon. TV; cable (premium), VCR available. In-room modem link. Bar. Pool. **$**

Resort

★ ★ ★ **OGLEBAY CONFERENCE CENTER.** *Oglebay Park (26003). Phone 304/243-4000; toll-free 800/624-6988; fax 304/243-4070. www.oglebay-resort.com.* This 1,650-acre resort features beautiful gardens and fine accommodations. 261 rooms, 2 story. Pets accepted, some restrictions. Check-out 11 am, check-in 3 pm. TV; cable (premium), VCR available (movies). In-room modem link. Fireplaces. Laundry services. Dining room. Snack bar. Supervised children's activities (June-Aug); ages 6-14. In-house fitness room; massage. Game room. Two pools, one indoor, wading pool; whirlpool; poolside service. Three 18-hole golf courses; pro; driving range; par-3; greens fee $26-$50. Miniature golf. Lighted tennis courts. Downhill ski 1/2 mile. Lawn games. Paddleboats. Fishing. Valet parking available. Airport transportation. Business center. Stables. Mansion museum, garden center. Children's zoo. Lounge noon-midnight. Rustic setting in Oglebay Park. **$**

White Sulphur Springs

Motel/Motor Lodge

★ **OLD WHITE MOTEL.** *865 E Main St (24986). Phone 304/536-2441; toll-free 800/867-2441; fax 304/536-1836. www.oldwhitemotel.com.* 26 rooms. Pets accepted, some restrictions. Check-out 11 am, check-in 11 am. TV; cable (premium). Pool. **$**

Wisconsin

Algoma

Motel/Motor Lodge

★ **RIVER HILLS MOTEL.** *820 N Water St (54201). Phone 920/487-3451; toll-free 800/236-3451; fax 920/487-2031.* 30 rooms. Pets accepted; fee. Check-out 11 am. TV; cable (premium). Boat dock, public ramps nearby. **$**

D 🐾 ⚓

Appleton

Motels/Motor Lodges

★ ★ **BEST WESTERN MIDWAY HOTEL.** *3033 W College Ave (54914). Phone 920/731-4141; toll-free 800/528-1234; fax 920/731-6343. www.bestwestern.com.* 105 rooms, 2 story. Pets accepted; fee. Complimentary full breakfast. Check-out 11 am. TV. In-room modem link. Restaurant, bar. Room service. In-house fitness room; sauna. Health club privileges. Indoor pool; whirlpool. Free airport transportation. **$**

D 🐾 ➤ 🏃 ✈ 🖹 SC

★ ★ **DAYS INN.** *200 N Perkins St (54914). Phone 920/735-2733; fax 920/735-5588. www.daysinn.com.* 91 rooms, 2 story. Pets accepted. Complimentary breakfast buffet. Check-out noon. TV; cable (premium), VCR available. Laundry services. Bar. In-house fitness room. Indoor pool; whirlpool. Free airport, bus depot transportation. **$**

D 🐾 ➤ 🏃 ✈ 🖹

★ **EXEL INN APPLETON.** *210 N Westhill Blvd (54914). Phone 920/733-5551; toll-free 800/367-3935; fax 920/733-7199. www.exelinns.com.* 104 rooms, 2 story. Pets accepted, some restrictions. Complimentary continental breakfast. Check-out noon. TV; cable (premium). In-room modem link. In-house fitness room. Health club privileges. **$**

D 🐾 🏃 🖹 SC

★ **ROADSTAR INN.** *3623 W College Ave (54914). Phone 920/731-5271; toll-free 800/445-4667; fax 920/731-0227.* 102 rooms, 2 story. Pets accepted, some restrictions; fee. Complimentary continental breakfast. Check-out noon. TV; cable (premium). Laundry services. **$**

D 🐾 🏃 🖹

Ashland

Motel/Motor Lodge

★ **SUPER 8.** *1610 W Lake Shore Dr (54806). Phone 715/682-9377; fax 715/682-9377. www.super8.com.* 70 rooms, 2 story. Pets accepted; fee. Check-out 11 am. TV; cable (premium), VCR available. In-room modem link. Laundry services. Indoor pool; whirlpool. Cross-country ski 10 miles. **$**

D 🐾 ⚓ 🏃 ➤ 🏊 🚶 🖹

Baraboo

Motel/Motor Lodge

★ **SPINNING WHEEL MOTEL.** *809 8th St (53913).* 25 rooms. Pets accepted, some restrictions; fee. TV; cable (premium). Downhill ski 10 miles, cross-country ski 5 miles. **$**

D 🐾 ➤ 🖹 SC

Bayfield

Motels/Motor Lodges

★ **SUPER 8.** *Harbor View Dr (54891). Phone 715/373-5671; fax 715/373-5674. www.super8.com.* 35 rooms, 2 story. Pets accepted. Complimentary continental breakfast. Check-out 11 am. TV. Sauna. Game room. Whirlpool. Downhill, cross-country skiing 8 miles. **$**

🐾 ⚓ ➤ 🚶 🖹

★ **WINDFIELD INN.** *225 E Lynde Ave (54814). Phone 715/779-3252; fax 715/779-5180.* 31 rooms, 1-2 story. Pets accepted, some restrictions; fee. Check-out 11 am. TV. Downhill, cross-country ski 8 miles. **$**

🐾 ➤ ✈

Beaver Dam

Motel/Motor Lodge

★ **GRAND VIEW.** *1510 N Center St (53916). Phone 920/885-9208; fax 920/887-8706.* 22 rooms. Pets accepted. Check-out 11 am. TV; cable (premium). **$**

🐾

Beloit

Motel/Motor Lodge

★ **COMFORT INN.** *2786 Milwaukee Rd (53511). Phone 608/362-2666; fax 608/362-2666. www.comfortinn.com.* 56 rooms, 2 story. Pets accepted, some restrictions; fee. Complimentary continental breakfast. Check-out 11 am. TV; cable (premium), VCR available (movies). Game room. Indoor pool; whirlpool. **$**

D 🐾 ≋ ⊠

Black River Falls

Motels/Motor Lodges

★★ **BEST WESTERN ARROWHEAD LODGE & SUITES.** *600 Oasis Rd (54615). Phone 715/284-9471; toll-free 800/284-9471; fax 715/284-9664. www.bestwestern.com.* 144 rooms, 3 story. Pets accepted, some restrictions. Complimentary full breakfast. Check-out noon. TV. In-room modem link. Restaurant, bar; entertainment. Sauna. Indoor pool; whirlpool. Nature/fitness trail. Snowmobile trails. **$**

D 🐾 🏂 ≋ ⊠

★ **DAYS INN.** *919 Hwy 54 E (54615). Phone 715/284-4333; toll-free 800/356-8018; fax 715/284-9068. www.daysinn.com.* 86 rooms, 2 story. Pets accepted, some restrictions; fee. Complimentary continental breakfast. Check-out noon. TV; VCR available. In-room modem link. Laundry services. Health club privileges. Sauna. Game room. Indoor pool; whirlpool. Downhill ski 15 miles, cross-country ski 1 mile. **$**

D 🐾 ≋ ≋ ⊠ SC

Cedarburg

Motels/Motor Lodges

★ **BEST WESTERN QUIET HOUSE & SUITES.** *10330 N Port Washington Rd (53092). Phone 262/241-3677; fax 414/241-3707. www.bestwestern.com.* 54 rooms, 2 story. Pets accepted, some restrictions; fee. Complimentary continental breakfast. Check-out 11 am. TV; cable (premium). In-room modem link. In-house fitness room. Indoor pool; outdoor pool; whirlpool. **$**

D 🐾 ≋ 🏋 ⊠

★ **BREEZE INN TO THE CHALET.** *10401 N Port Washington Rd (53092). Phone 262/241-4510; toll-free 800/343-4510; fax 414/241-5542.* 41 rooms, 2 story. Pets

accepted, some restrictions; fee. Check-out 11 am. TV; cable (premium). Restaurant, bar. **$**

D 🐾 ⊠

Chippewa Falls

Motels/Motor Lodges

★★ **AMERICINN.** *11 W South Ave (54729). Phone 715/723-5711; toll-free 800/634-3444; fax 715/723-5254. www.americinn.com.* 62 rooms, 2 story. Pets accepted; fee. Check-out 11 am. TV; cable (premium). In-room modem link. Indoor pool; whirlpool. **$**

D 🐾 ≋ ⊠

★ **IMA INDIANHEAD.** *501 Summit Ave (54729). Phone 715/723-9171; fax 715/723-6142.* 27 rooms. Pets accepted, some restrictions; fee. Check-out 11 am. TV; cable (premium), VCR available. On bluff overlooking city. **$**

D 🐾 ⊠

★★ **PARK INN.** *1009 W Park Ave (54729). Phone 715/723-2281; toll-free 800/446-9320; fax 715/723-2281. www.parkinn.com.* 67 rooms. Pets accepted, some restrictions; fee. Check-out noon. TV. Restaurant, bar. Room service. Indoor pool; whirlpool. **$**

D 🐾 ≋ ⊠ SC

Eagle River

Motels/Motor Lodges

★ **DAYS INN.** *844 WI 45 N, 844 Railroad St N (54521). Phone 715/479-5151; toll-free 800/356-8018; fax 715/479-8259. www.daysinn.com.* 93 rooms, 2 story. Pets accepted, some restrictions; fee. Complimentary continental breakfast. Check-out 11 am. TV. Laundry services. Sauna. Game room. Indoor pool; whirlpool. Cross-country skiing 1/2 mile. **$**

🐾 ≋ ≋ ✈

★ **WHITE EAGLE.** *4948 WI 70 W (54521). Phone 715/479-4426; toll-free 800/782-6488; fax 715/479-3570. www.whiteeaglemotel.com.* 22 rooms. No A/C. Pets accepted, some restrictions; fee. Check-out 10:30 am. TV; cable (premium). Sauna. Pool; whirlpool. Cross-country skiing 3 miles. Paddleboat, pontoon boat. Snowmobile trails. On Eagle River; private piers. **$**

🐾 🏂 ≋ ≋ 🏂 ⊠

Resort

★ **GYPSY VILLA RESORT.** *950 Circle Dr (54521). Phone 715/479-8644; toll-free 800/232-9714; fax 715/479-*

8780. www.gypsyvilla.com. 21 kitchen units. Some A/C. Pets accepted, some restrictions; fee. Check-out noon, check-in 3 pm. TV; VCR available. Laundry services. Free supervised children's activities (June-Aug). In-house fitness room; sauna. Game room. Children's pool; whirlpool. Outdoor tennis. Lawn games. Bicycles. Boats, waterskiing. Garage parking, fee. Fish/hunt guides. Phone available. Most cottages on Cranberry Island. **$**

⊠ ⚓ ⛄ ⛱ ⛷ ⟓ SC

Eau Claire

Motels/Motor Lodges

★ **COMFORT INN.** *3117 Craig Rd (54701). Phone 715/833-9798; fax 715/833-9798. www.comfortinn.com.* 56 rooms, 2 story. Pets accepted, some restrictions; fee. Complimentary continental breakfast. Check-out 11 am. TV; cable (premium). In-room modem link. Indoor pool. Cross-country skiing 2 miles. **$**

D ⚓ ⛷ ⛱ ⟓

★ **EXEL INN.** *2305 Craig Rd (54701). Phone 715/834-3193; toll-free 800/367-3935; fax 715/839-9905.* 100 rooms, 2 story. Pets accepted, some restrictions. Complimentary continental breakfast. Check-out noon. TV; cable (premium). In-house fitness room. **$**

D ⚓ ⟓ ⛱ SC

★ **HEARTLAND INN EAU CLAIRE.** *4075 Commonwealth Ave (54701). Phone 715/839-7100; toll-free 800/334-3277; fax 715/839-7050. www.heartlandinn.com.* 88 rooms, 2 story. Pets accepted; fee. Complimentary continental breakfast. Check-out noon. TV; cable (premium), VCR available. In-room modem link. Sauna. Indoor pool; whirlpool. Cross-country skiing 5 miles. **$**

D ⚓ ⛷ ⛱ SC

★ **MAPLE MANOR MOTEL.** *2507 S Hastings Way (54701). Phone 715/834-2618; toll-free 800/624-3763; fax 715/834-1148. www.themaplemanor.com.* 36 rooms. Pets accepted, some restrictions. Complimentary full breakfast. Check-out 11:30 am. TV; cable (premium). Restaurant, bar. **$**

⚓ ⛱ SC

★★ **QUALITY INN.** *809 W Clairmont Ave (54701). Phone 715/834-6611; toll-free 800/638-7949; fax 715/834-6611. www.qualityinn.com.* 120 rooms, 2 story. Pets accepted; fee. Complimentary full breakfast. Check-out noon. TV; cable (premium), VCR available. In-room modem link. Restaurant, bar; entertainment. Room service. Sauna. Indoor pool; outdoor pool; whirlpool. **$**

D ⚓ ⛱ ⛱ SC

Egg Harbor

Motel/Motor Lodge

★★ **ALPINE INN.** *7715 Alpine Rd (54209). Phone 920/868-3000.* 52 rooms, 3 story. No elevator. No room phones. Closed Nov-Memorial Day. Pets accepted, some restrictions; fee. Check-out 10 am. TV. Restaurant, bar. Supervised children's activities (July-Aug), ages 3-8. Game room. Pool. 27-hole golf; putting green. Outdoor tennis. **$**

D ⚓ ⛄ ⛱ ⟓ ⛷ ⛱

Ellison Bay

B&B/Small Inn

★★ **HARBOR HOUSE INN.** *12666 WI 42 (54210). Phone 920/854-5196; fax 920/854-9917. www.door-county-inn.com.* 15 rooms, 2 story. 9 rooms with shower only. No room phones. Closed Nov-Apr. Pets accepted, some restrictions; fee. Complimentary continental breakfast. Check-out 10 am, check-in 3 pm. TV. Sauna. Whirlpool. Victorian-style house built in 1904; many antiques. Totally nonsmoking. **$**

⚓ ⛄ ⛱

Fish Creek

Motel/Motor Lodge

★ **JULIE'S PARK CAFE AND MOTEL.** *4020 WI 42 (54212). Phone 920/868-2999; fax 920/868-9837. www.juliesmotel.com.* 12 rooms. Pets accepted, some restrictions; fee. Check-out 10 am. TV; cable (premium). Restaurant. Cross-country skiing adjacent. Totally nonsmoking. **$**

⚓ ⛱ ⟓

Fond du Lac

Motels/Motor Lodges

★ **DAYS INN.** *107 N Pioneer Rd (54935). Phone 920/923-6790; toll-free 800/329-7466; fax 920/923-6790. www.daysinn.com.* 59 rooms, 2 story. Pets accepted, some restrictions; fee. Complimentary continental breakfast. Check-out 11 am. TV; cable (premium). In-room modem link. **$**

D ⚓ ⛱ SC

★ ★ **HOLIDAY INN.** *625 W Rolling Meadows Dr (54937). Phone 920/923-1440; fax 920/923-1366. www.holiday-inn.com.* 141 rooms, 2 story. Pets accepted, some restrictions. Check-out 11 am. TV; cable (premium), VCR available. In-room modem link. Laundry services. Restaurant, bar. Room service. In-house fitness room; sauna. Indoor pool; whirlpool. Free airport transportation. **$**

D🐾🏊🏃🛏SC

★ **NORTHWAY MOTEL.** *301 S Pioneer Rd (54935). Phone 920/921-7975; toll-free 800/850-7339; fax 920/921-7983. www.visitwisconsin.com/fondulac.* 19 rooms. Pets accepted; fee. Complimentary continental breakfast. Check-out 11 am. TV. Cross-country skiing 10 miles. **$**

D🐾🏊🛏SC

Fort Atkinson

Motel/Motor Lodge

★ **SUPER 8.** *225 S Water St E (53538). Phone 920/563-8444; toll-free 800/800-8000; fax 920/563-8444. www.super8.com.* 40 rooms, 3 story. Pets accepted; fee. Complimentary continental breakfast. Check-out 11 am. TV. Bar; entertainment. Downhill, cross-country ski 5 miles. Overlooks Rock River. **$**

D🐾🐾🏊🛏SC

Green Bay

Motels/Motor Lodges

★ **BAYMONT INN.** *2840 S Oneida St (54304). Phone 920/494-7887; toll-free 877/229-6668; fax 920/494-3370. www.baymontinn.com.* 80 rooms, 2 story. Pets accepted, some restrictions. Complimentary continental breakfast. Check-out noon. TV; cable (premium), VCR available (movies). Health club privileges. Cross-country skiing 10 miles. Business center. **$**

D🐾🏊🛏🏃

★ **DAYS INN.** *406 N Washington St (54301). Phone 920/435-1478; fax 920/435-3120. www.daysinn.com.* 98 rooms, 5 story. Pets accepted; fee. Check-out noon. TV. In-room modem link. Restaurant, bar. Room service. Health club privileges. Indoor pool. Overlooks Fox River. **$**

D🐾🏊🛏🏃

★ **EXEL INN.** *2870 Ramada Way (54304). Phone 920/499-3599; fax 920/498-4055. www.exelinns.com.* 105 rooms, 2 story. Pets accepted, some restrictions. Complimentary continental breakfast. Check-out noon. TV. In-room modem link. Health club privileges. **$**

D🐾🛏

★ ★ **HOLIDAY INN.** *200 Main St (54301). Phone 920/437-5900; toll-free 800/457-2929; fax 920/437-1192. www.holiday-inn.com.* 149 rooms, 7 story. Pets accepted, some restrictions. Check-out noon. TV; cable (premium). Restaurant, bar; entertainment. Room service. Health club privileges. Sauna. Indoor pool; whirlpool. On Fox River; marina. Luxury level. **$**

D🐾🏊🛏

★ **ROAD STAR INN.** *1941 True Ln (54304). Phone 920/497-2666; toll-free 800/445-4667; fax 920/497-4754.* 63 rooms, 2 story. Pets accepted, some restrictions; fee. Complimentary continental breakfast. Check-out 11 am. TV. **$**

D🐾🛏

★ **SKY LITE.** *2120 S Ashland Ave (54304). Phone 920/494-5641; fax 920/494-4032.* 23 rooms. Pets accepted; fee. Check-out 11 am. TV; cable (premium). Laundry services. **$**

D🐾🛏

★ **SUPER 8.** *2868 S Oneida St (54304). Phone 920/494-2042; fax 920/494-6959. www.super8.com.* 84 rooms, 2 story. Pets accepted; fee. Complimentary continental breakfast. Check-out 11 am. TV; VCR available. Laundry services. Health club privileges. Sauna. Whirlpool. **$**

D🐾🐾🏃🛏

Hayward

Motels/Motor Lodges

★ **AMERICINN.** *15601 US 63 N (54843). Phone 715/634-2700; toll-free 800/634-3444; fax 715/634-3958. www.americinn.com.* 42 rooms, 2 story. Pets accepted, some restrictions; fee. Complimentary continental breakfast. Check-out 11 am. TV; cable (premium), VCR available. Sauna. Game room. Indoor pool; whirlpool. Downhill ski 20 miles, cross-country ski adjacent. **$**

D🐾🏊🛏

★ **NORTHWOODS MOTEL.** *9854 WI 27 N (54843). Phone 715/634-8088; toll-free 800/232-9202; fax 715/634-0714.* 9 rooms. Pets accepted, some restrictions; fee. Check-out 10 am. TV. Downhill ski 19 miles, cross-country ski 3 miles. **$**

D🐾🐾🏃🛏SC

★ **SUPER 8.** *10444 N WI 27 (54843). Phone 715/634-2646; fax 715/634-6482. www.super8.com.* 46 rooms, 1-2 story. Pets accepted. Check-out 11 am. TV; cable (premium). Game room. Indoor pool; whirlpool. Cross-country ski 2 miles. **$**

D🐾🏊🛏

Hudson

Motel/Motor Lodge

★ **COMFORT INN.** *811 Dominion Dr (54016). Phone 715/386-6355; toll-free 800/725-8987; fax 715/386-9778. www.comfortinn.com.* 60 rooms, 2 story. Pets accepted, some restrictions; fee. Complimentary continental breakfast. Check-out 11 am. TV; cable (premium), VCR available. Laundry services. Indoor pool; whirlpool. **$**

⊡ ⬧ ⬧ ⬧ ⬧

Janesville

Motel/Motor Lodge

★★ **BEST WESTERN JANESVILLE.** *3900 Milton Ave (53545). Phone 608/756-4511; fax 608/756-0025. www.bestwestern.com.* 106 rooms, 3 story. Pets accepted, some restrictions; fee. Check-out noon. TV. Restaurant, bar. Room service. In-house fitness room. Game room. Indoor pool; whirlpool. Airport transportation. **$**

⊡ ⬧ ⬧ ⬧ SC

Kenosha

Motel/Motor Lodge

★ **BAYMONT INN.** *7540 118th Ave (53158). Phone 262/857-7911; fax 414/857-2370. www.baymontinn.com.* 95 rooms, 2 story. Pets accepted, some restrictions. Complimentary continental breakfast. Check-out noon. TV; cable (premium). In-room modem link. Downhill ski 15 miles. **$**

⊡ ⬧ ⬧ ⬧ ⬧ SC

Lac du Flambeau

Resort

★★ **DILLMAN'S BAY PROPERTIES.** *3285 Sandlake Lodge Ln (54538). Phone 715/588-3143; fax 715/588-3110. www.dillmans.com.* 34 rooms. No A/C. Closed mid-Oct-mid-May. Pets accepted; fee. Check-out 10 am, check-in noon. TV in lobby, some rooms. Outdoor tennis. Lawn games. Bicycles. Fishing clean and store area. Hiking trails. Dining by reservations. Sand beaches; waterskiing; windsurfing; scuba diving; boats, motors, kayaks, sailboats, canoes, pontoon boats; private launch, covered boathouse. On 250 acres. Practice fairway. Nature study, photography, painting workshops. **$**

⊡ ⬧ ⬧ ⬧ ⬧ ⬧ ⬧ ⬧ SC

La Crosse

Hotel

★★ **RADISSON HOTEL LA CROSSE.** *200 Harborview Plz (54601). Phone 608/784-6680; fax 608/784-6694. www.radisson.com.* Providing a lovely view of the river, the spacious accommodations at this hotel are designed to make guests feel at home. 169 rooms, 8 story. Pets accepted. Check-out noon. TV. Restaurant, bar; entertainment. In-house fitness room. Indoor pool. Downhill, cross-country ski 8 miles. Free airport transportation. Overlooks Mississippi River. **$**

⊡ ⬧ ⬧ ⬧ ⬧ ⬧ SC

Ladysmith

Motel/Motor Lodge

★★ **BEST WESTERN EL RANCHO.** *8500 W Flambeau Ave (54848). Phone 715/532-6666; fax 715/532-7551. www.bestwestern.com.* 27 rooms. Pets accepted; fee. Check-out 11 am. TV; cable (premium). Restaurant, bar. Downhill ski 15 miles, cross-country ski on site. **$**

⊡ ⬧ ⬧ ⬧

Land O Lakes

Motel/Motor Lodge

★ **PINEAIRE RESORT MOTEL.** *2091 WI 45 (95449). Phone 906/544-2313.* 9 rooms. 7 rooms with shower only. No A/C. No room phones. Pets accepted; fee. Check-out 10 am. TV. Cross-country ski on site. Snowmobiling. **$**

⬧ ⬧ ⬧

Resort

★★ **SUNRISE LODGE.** *5894 W Shore Rd (54540). Phone 715/547-3684; toll-free 800/221-9689; fax 715/547-6110. www.sunriselodge.com.* 22 kitchen units. No A/C. Pets accepted. Dining room. Miniature golf. Outdoor tennis. Cross-country ski on site. Lawn games. Bicycles. Private beach; boats, motors, canoes. Nature trail. Airport, bus depot transportation. Fitness trail. Fish/hunt guides; clean and store area. Spacious grounds. On Lac Vieux Desert. **$$**

⊡ ⬧ ⬧ ⬧ ⬧

Madison

Motels/Motor Lodges

★ **BEST WESTERN WEST TOWNE SUITES.** *650 Grand Canyon Dr (53719). Phone 608/833-4200; toll-free 800/847-7919; fax 608/833-5614. www.bestwestern.com.* 101 rooms, 2 story. Pets accepted, some restrictions. Complimentary full breakfast. Check-out noon. TV. In-room modem link. Laundry services. In-house fitness room. Health club privileges. **$**

⬚ 🐾 🏃 ⤓ SC

★ ★ ★ **EDGEWATER HOTEL.** *666 Wisconsin Ave (53703). Phone 608/256-9071; toll-free 800/922-5512; fax 608/256-0910. www.theedgewater.com.* Lake view rooms loaded with the latest in modern features await guests at this getaway on Lake Mendota. 116 rooms, 8 story. Pets accepted. Check-out noon. TV; cable (premium). Restaurant, bar. Room service. Health club privileges. Massage. Free garage parking. Free airport transportation. **$**

⬚ 🐾 ⚓ ✈ ⤓

★ **EXEL INN.** *4202 E Towne Blvd (53704). Phone 608/241-3861; toll-free 800/356-8013; fax 608/241-9752. www.exelinns.com.* 101 rooms, 2 story. Pets accepted, some restrictions. Complimentary continental breakfast. Check-out noon. TV; cable (premium). In-room modem link. Laundry services. In-house fitness room. Health club privileges. Game room. Cross-country ski 3 miles. **$**

⬚ 🐾 ⚓ 🏃 ⤓ SC

★ **SELECT INN.** *4845 Hayes Rd (53704). Phone 608/249-1815; toll-free 800/641-1000; fax 608/249-1815. www.selectinn.com.* 96 rooms, 3 story. Pets accepted; fee. Complimentary continental breakfast. Check-out 11 am. TV. Whirlpool. **$**

⬚ 🐾 ⤓ SC

Hotel

★ ★ ★ **MARRIOTT MADISON WEST.** *1313 John Q. Hammons Dr (53582). Phone 608/831-2000. www.marriott.com.* 295 rooms, 10 story. Pets accepted, some restrictions. Check-out noon. TV; cable (premium), VCR available. Restaurant. Indoor pool. Business center. **$**

🐾 ⤓ 🏃

Extended Stay

★ ★ **RESIDENCE INN BY MARRIOTT.** *501 D'Onofrio Dr (53719). Phone 608/833-8333; fax 608/833-2693. www.residenceinn.com.* 80 rooms, 2 story. Pets accepted, some restrictions; fee. Complimentary continental breakfast. Check-out noon. TV. Laundry services.

In-house fitness room. Health club privileges. Pool; whirlpool. **$**

⬚ 🐾 ⚓ 🏃 ⤓

Manitowish Waters

Motel/Motor Lodge

★ **GREAT NORTHERN.** *US 51 S (54547). Phone 715/476-2440; fax 715/476-2205.* 80 rooms, 2 story. No A/C. Pets accepted, some restrictions; fee. Complimentary continental breakfast. Check-out 11 am. TV; cable (premium). Restaurant, bar. Sauna. Game room. Indoor pool; whirlpool. Cross-country ski 1 mile. On lake; swimming beach, boats. **$**

⬚ 🐾 ⚓ ⛷ 🎿 ⚓ ⤓

Marinette

Motel/Motor Lodge

★ **SUPER 8.** *1508 Marinette Ave (54143). Phone 715/735-7887; fax 715/735-7455. www.super8.com.* 68 rooms, 2 story. Pets accepted, some restrictions; fee. Complimentary continental breakfast. Check-out 11 am. TV; cable (premium). Sauna. Whirlpool. Cross-country ski 5 miles. **$**

⬚ 🐾 ⤓ ⤓ SC

Mauston

Motel/Motor Lodge

★ **K AND K MOTEL.** *219 US 12/16 (54618). Phone 608/427-3100; fax 608/427-3824. rkelsingamwt.net.* 14 rooms. Pets accepted, some restrictions; fee. Check-out 10 am. TV; VCR available. Laundry services. **$**

⬚ 🐾 ⚓ ⤓ SC

Guest Ranch

★ ★ **WOODSIDE RANCH TRADING POST.** *W 4015 WI 82 (53948). Phone 608/847-4275; toll-free 800/646-4275. www.woodsideranch.com.* 37 rooms, 2 story. No room phones. Pets accepted; fee. Check-out 10 am, check-in 1:30 pm. TV in lobby. Fireplace in cottages. Laundry services. Dining room, bar; entertainment Tues, Sat. Free supervised children's activities. Sauna. Game room. Pool; children's pool; poolside service. Outdoor tennis. Downhill, cross-country ski on site. Boats. Hiking. Sleighing, sledding. Swimming. On 1,400 acres. **$**

⬚ 🐾 ⚓ 🎿 ⛷ 🏃 ⚓ ⤓

Menomonee Falls

Motel/Motor Lodge

★ **SUPER 8.** *N96 W17490 County Line Rd (53022). Phone 262/255-0880; toll-free 800/800-8000; fax 262/255-7741. www.super8.com.* 81 rooms, 2 story. Pets accepted, some restrictions. Complimentary continental breakfast. Check-out 11 am. TV; cable (premium). Laundry services. **$**

D 🐾 🏊 SC

Menomonie

Motel/Motor Lodge

★ **BEST WESTERN INN OF MENOMONIE.** *1815 N Broadway (54751). Phone 715/235-9651; toll-free 800/622-0504; fax 715/235-6568. www.bestwestern.com.* 135 rooms. Pets accepted; fee. Check-out 11 am. TV; cable (premium). Bar. Cross-country ski 2 miles. **$**

D 🐾 🏊 ⛷ SC

Milwaukee

Motels/Motor Lodges

★ **BAYMONT INN.** *5442 N Lovers Ln (53225). Phone 414/535-1300; toll-free 800/428-3438; fax 414/535-1724. www.baymontinns.com.* 140 rooms, 3 story. Pets accepted, some restrictions. Complimentary continental breakfast. Check-out noon. TV; cable (premium), VCR available. In-room modem link. **$**

D 🐾 🏊

★ **EXEL INN.** *5485 N Port Washington Rd (53217). Phone 414/961-7272; toll-free 800/367-3935; fax 414/961-1721. www.exelinn.com.* 125 rooms, 3 story. Pets accepted, some restrictions. Complimentary continental breakfast. Check-out noon. TV; cable (premium). In-room modem link. Laundry services. Game room. **$**

D 🐾 🏊 SC

★ **EXEL INN.** *1201 W College Ave (53154). Phone 414/764-1776; fax 414/762-8009. www.exelinn.com.* 110 rooms, 2 story. Pets accepted, some restrictions. Complimentary continental breakfast. Check-out noon. TV; cable (premium). In-room modem link. Laundry services. Free airport transportation. **$**

D 🐾 ⚡ ✈ ✈ 🏊

★ **RED ROOF INN.** *6360 S 13th St (53154). Phone 414/764-3500; toll-free 800/843-7663; fax 414/764-5138.* www.redroof.com. 108 rooms, 2 story. Pets accepted. Check-out noon. TV; cable (premium). **$**

D 🐾 🏊

Hotels

★ ★ **HOTEL WISCONSIN.** *720 N Old World 3rd St (53203). Phone 414/271-4900; fax 414/271-9998.* 234 rooms, 11 story. Pets accepted, some restrictions. Check-out 11 am. TV; cable (premium), VCR available. Laundry services. Restaurant. Health club privileges. Game room. Concierge. **$**

🐾 🏊

★ ★ ★ **SHERATON MILWAUKEE BROOKFIELD HOTEL.** *375 S Moorland Rd (53005). Phone 262/786-1100.* 389 rooms, 12 story. Pets accepted, some restrictions. Check-out noon. TV; cable (premium), VCR available. Laundry services. Restaurant. In-house fitness room. Indoor pool; outdoor pool; whirlpool. Free parking. Business center. **$$**

🐾 🏊 🏋 🏃

Minocqua

Motels/Motor Lodges

★ **AQUA AIRE MOTEL.** *806 WI 51N (54548). Phone 715/356-3433; fax 715/358-9701. www.north-wis.com/aquaaire.* 10 rooms. Shower only. Pets accepted, some restrictions; fee. Check-out 11 am. TV; cable (premium). Cross-country ski 7 miles. **$**

🐾 🎣 ⚡ 🏊 🏃 ✈ 🏊

★ ★ **LAKEVIEW MOTOR LODGE.** *311 E Park Ave (54548). Phone 715/356-5208; toll-free 800/852-1021; fax 715/356-1412. www.lakeviewmotorlodgeminocqua.com.* 41 rooms, 2 story. Pets accepted, some restrictions; fee. Complimentary continental breakfast. Check-out 11 am. TV; cable (premium). Sauna. Whirlpool. Cross-country ski 10 miles. Snowmobiling. On Lake Minocqua; dock. **$**

🐾 🏊 🏊

Mount Horeb

Motel/Motor Lodge

★ ★ **KARAKAHL COUNTRY INN.** *1405 US 18 Business and 151 E (53572). Phone 608/437-5545; fax 608/437-5908. www.karakahl.com.* 76 rooms, 1-2 story. Pets accepted, some restrictions; fee. Complimentary continental breakfast. Check-out noon. TV. Restaurant, bar. Sauna. Indoor pool. Cross-country ski 2 blocks. **$**

D 🐾 🏊 🏊 ⛷ 🏊

New Glarus

Motel/Motor Lodge

★ **SWISS-AIRE MOTEL.** *1200 WI 69 (53574). Phone 608/527-2138; toll-free 800/798-4391; fax 608/527-5818.* 26 rooms. Pets accepted, some restrictions; fee. Complimentary continental breakfast. Check-out 11 am. TV. Pool. **$**

Oconomowoc

B&B/Small Inn

★★ **INN AT PINE TERRACE.** *351 E Lisbon Rd (53066). Phone 920/893-0552; toll-free 800/421-4667; fax 262/567-7532. www.innatpineterrace.com.* 13 rooms, 3 story. Pets accepted; fee. Complimentary continental breakfast. Check-out 10:30 am, check-in 3 pm. TV; cable (premium). Pool. Restored mansion (1879); antique furnishings. **$$**

Oshkosh

Motels/Motor Lodges

★ **BAYMONT INN.** *1950 Omro Rd (54901). Phone 920/233-4190; fax 920/233-8197. www.baymontinn.com.* 100 rooms, 2 story. Pets accepted, some restrictions. Complimentary continental breakfast. Check-out noon. TV. In-room modem link. Cross-country ski 2 miles. **$**

★ **HOLIDAY INN EXPRESS.** *2251 Westowne Ave (54904). Phone 920/303-1300; toll-free 888/522-9472; fax 920/303-9330. www.hiexpress.com.* 68 rooms, 3 story. Pets accepted. Complimentary continental breakfast. Check-out 11 am. TV. In-room modem link. Laundry services. In-house fitness room. Indoor pool; whirlpool. Downhill, cross-country ski 2 miles. Free airport transportation. **$**

★ **HOWARD JOHNSON.** *1919 Omro Rd (54902). Phone 920/233-1200; fax 920/233-1135. www.hojo.com.* 100 rooms, 2 story. Pets accepted, some restrictions. Check-out noon. TV. Bar. Indoor pool; whirlpool. **$**

★★ **RAMADA INN.** *500 S Koeller St (54902). Phone 920/235-3700; fax 920/233-1909. www.ramada.com.* 129 rooms, 2 story. Pets accepted, some restrictions; fee.

Check-out noon. TV; cable (premium). Laundry services. Restaurant. Room service. In-house fitness room; sauna. Indoor pool; whirlpool; poolside service. Free airport transportation. Business center. **$**

Platteville

Motels/Motor Lodges

★★ **BEST WESTERN GOVERNOR DODGE MOTOR INN.** *300 W US 151 (53818). Phone 608/348-2301; toll-free 800/528-1234; fax 608/348-8579. www.bestwestern.com.* 74 rooms, 2 story. Pets accepted, some restrictions. Check-out noon. TV. Restaurant. In-house fitness room; sauna. Game room. Indoor pool; whirlpool. State university 5 blocks away. **$**

★ **SUPER 8.** *100 WI 80/81 S (53818). Phone 608/348-8800; fax 608/348-7233. www.super8.com.* 73 rooms, 2 story. Pets accepted; fee. Complimentary continental breakfast. Check-out 11 am. TV; cable (premium). Laundry services. Sauna. Whirlpool. Overlooks stream. **$**

Port Washington

Motel/Motor Lodge

★★ **BEST WESTERN HARBORSIDE.** *135 E Grand Ave (53074). Phone 262/284-9461; fax 414/284-3169. www.bestwestern.com.* 96 rooms, 5 story. Pets accepted, some restrictions; fee. Check-out 11 am. Restaurant, bar. In-house fitness room; sauna. Game room. Indoor pool; whirlpool. **$**

Prairie du Chien

Motels/Motor Lodges

★ **BEST WESTERN QUIET HOUSE & SUITES.** *Hwys 18 and 35 S (53821). Phone 608/326-4777; fax 608/326-4787. www.bestwestern.com.* 42 rooms, 2 story. Pets accepted, some restrictions; fee. Check-out 11 am. TV; cable (premium). In-room modem link. In-house fitness room. Indoor pool; whirlpool. **$**

★ **BRISBOIS MOTOR INN.** *533 N Marquette Rd (53821). Phone 608/326-8404; toll-free 800/356-5850; fax 608/326-8404. www.brisboismotorinn.com.* 46 rooms. Pets accepted, some restrictions; fee. Check-out 11 am. TV; cable (premium). Pool. Cross-country ski 2 miles. Free airport transportation. **$**

★ **PRAIRIE MOTEL.** *1616 S Marquette Rd (53821). Phone 608/326-6461; toll-free 800/526-3776.* 32 rooms. Pets accepted, some restrictions; fee. Check-out 11 am. TV; cable (premium). Pool. Cross-country ski 2 miles. Lawn games. Miniature golf. **$**

Racine

Motels/Motor Lodges

★ **DAYS INN.** *3700 Northwestern Ave (53405). Phone 262/637-9311; toll-free 888/242-6494; fax 414/637-4575. www.daysinn.com.* 112 rooms, 2 story. Pets accepted, some restrictions; fee. Check-out noon. TV; cable (premium). In-room modem link. Laundry services. Restaurant, bar. Room service. Game room. Pool. Cross-country ski 3 miles. Lawn games. On Root River. **$**

★ **KNIGHTS INN.** *1149 Oakes Rd (53406). Phone 262/886-6667; toll-free 800/843-5644; fax 414/886-6667. www.knightsinn.com.* 107 rooms, 1 story. Pets accepted; fee. Complimentary continental breakfast. Check-out noon. TV; cable (premium), VCR available (movies). **$**

Rhinelander

Motels/Motor Lodges

★ **AMERICINN.** *648 W Kemp St (54501). Phone 715/369-9600; toll-free 800/634-3444; fax 715/369-9613. www.americinn.com.* 52 rooms, 2 story. Pets accepted, some restrictions. Complimentary continental breakfast. Check-out 11 am. TV; cable (premium), VCR available. Laundry services. Sauna. Indoor pool; whirlpool. Cross-country ski 1 mile. **$**

★ ★ **BEST WESTERN CLARIDGE MOTOR INN.** *70 N Stevens St (54501). Phone 715/362-7100; toll-free 800/427-1377; fax 715/362-3883. www.bestwestern.com.* 81 rooms, 2-4 story. Pets accepted, some restrictions; fee. Check-out 11 am. TV. Laundry services. Restaurant, bar. Room service. In-house fitness room. Indoor pool; whirlpool. Cross-country ski 5 miles. Free airport transportation. **$**

Resort

★ **HOLIDAY ACRES RESORT.** *4060 S Shore Dr (54501). Phone 715/369-1500; toll-free 800/261-1500; fax 715/369-3665.* 56 rooms, 2 story. Pets accepted, some restrictions; fee. Check-out 11 am. TV; VCR available (movies). Dining room, bar. Room service. Sauna. Indoor pool. Outdoor tennis. Downhill ski 20 miles, cross-country ski on site. Lawn games. Bicycles. Snowmobile trails. Sand beach; boats, motors, rafts, canoes, sailboat, windsurfing. Airport transportation. **$**

Rice Lake

Motel/Motor Lodge

★ **CURRIER'S LAKEVIEW MOTEL.** *2010 E Sawyer St (54868). Phone 715/234-7474; toll-free 800/433-5253; fax 715/736-1501. www.currierslakeview.com.* 19 rooms, 2 story. Pets accepted. Check-out 11 am. TV; cable (premium). Continental breakfast. Private beach. Downhill, cross-country ski 18 miles. Boats, motors, dockage; paddle boats, canoes, pontoons. Snowmobile trails. Free airport transportation. **$**

Saint Croix Falls

Motel/Motor Lodge

★ ★ **DALLES HOUSE MOTEL.** *WI 35 S (54024). Phone 715/483-3206; fax 715/483-3207.* 50 rooms, 2 story. Pets accepted, some restrictions. Check-out 11 am. TV; cable (premium). In-room modem link. Laundry services. Restaurant. Sauna. Indoor pool; whirlpool. Downhill ski 3 miles; cross-country ski 1/4 mile. Interstate State Park adjacent. **$**

Sheboygan

Motels/Motor Lodges

★ **BAYMONT INN.** *2932 Kohler Memorial Dr (53081). Phone 920/457-2321; toll-free 800/301-0200; fax 920/457-0827. www.baymontinn.com.* 98 rooms, 2 story. Pets accepted, some restrictions. Complimentary continental breakfast. Check-out noon. TV; cable (premium). **$**

★ **BEST VALUE INN.** *3900 Motel Rd (53081). Phone 920/458-8338; fax 920/459-7470. www.bestvalueinn.com.* 32 rooms. Pets accepted, some restrictions; fee. Check-out 11 am. TV; cable (premium). Cross-country ski 2 miles. $

Sister Bay

Motels/Motor Lodges

★ **EDGE OF TOWN MOTEL.** *11092 WI 42 (54234). Phone 920/854-2012.* 10 rooms. No room phones. Pets accepted, some restrictions; fee. Check-out 11 am. TV; cable (premium). $

★ **SCANDIA COTTAGES.** *11062 Beach Rd (54234). Phone 920/854-2447. www.scandiacottages.com.* 6 rooms. No room phones. Pets accepted; fee. Check-out 10 am. TV. Cross-country ski 4 miles. Bay nearby. Totally non-smoking. $

Sparta

Motels/Motor Lodges

★ **BUDGET HOST INN.** *704 W Wisconsin St (54656). Phone 608/269-6991; toll-free 800/658-9484.* 22 rooms, 2 story. Pets accepted, some restrictions. Check-out 11 am. TV; cable (premium). Pool; whirlpool. $

★ **COUNTRY INN & SUITES BY CARLSON SPARTA.** *737 Avon Rd (54656). Phone 608/269-3110; fax 608/269-6726.* 61 rooms, 2 story. Pets accepted; fee. Complimentary continental breakfast. Check-out noon. TV; cable (premium), VCR available (movies). Laundry services. Bar. Indoor pool; whirlpool. Downhill ski 7 miles, cross-country ski 1 mile. $

Spooner

Motels/Motor Lodges

★ **COUNTRY HOUSE.** *717 S River St (54801). Phone 715/635-8721.* 22 rooms. Pets accepted, some restrictions; fee. Check-out 11 am. TV; VCR available. $

★ **GREEN ACRES MOTEL.** *N 4809 US 63 S (54801). Phone 715/635-2177.* 21 rooms. Pets accepted, some

restrictions; fee. Check-out 10 am. TV; cable (premium). Cross-country ski 2 miles. Lawn games. $

Stevens Point

Motels/Motor Lodges

★ **BAYMONT INN.** *4917 Main St (54481). Phone 715/344-1900; fax 715/344-1254. www.baymontinn.com.* 80 rooms, 3 story. Pets accepted, some restrictions. Complimentary continental breakfast. Check-out noon. TV; cable (premium). In-room modem link. Laundry services. Cross-country ski 1 mile. $

★ ★ **HOLIDAY INN.** *800 Victor's Way (54481). Phone 715/341-1340; toll-free 800/922-7880; fax 715/341-9446. www.holiday-inn.com.* 295 rooms, 2-6 story. Pets accepted, some restrictions; fee. Check-out 11 am. TV; VCR (movies). In-room modem link. Restaurant, bar; entertainment. Room service. In-house fitness room; sauna. Indoor pool; whirlpool; poolside service. Downhill ski 20 miles; cross-country ski 1 mile. Free airport transportation. $

★ **POINT MOTEL.** *209 Division St (54481). Phone 715/344-8312; fax 715/344-8312.* 44 rooms, 2 story. Pets accepted, some restrictions; fee. Complimentary continental breakfast. Check-out 11 am. TV; VCR available. $

Sturgeon Bay

Motel/Motor Lodge

★ **HOLIDAY MOTEL.** *29 N 2nd Ave (54235). Phone 920/743-5571; fax 920/743-5395.* 18 rooms, 2 story. Pets accepted, some restrictions; fee. Complimentary continental breakfast. Check-out 11 am. TV; VCR available (free movies). Cross-country ski 4 miles. $

Superior

Motels/Motor Lodges

★ **BEST WESTERN BAY WALK INN.** *1405 Susquehanna Ave (54880). Phone 715/392-7600; fax 715/392-7680. www.bestwestern.com.* 50 rooms, 2 story. Pets accepted, some restrictions. Complimentary continental breakfast. Check-out 11 am. TV; cable (premium), VCR available (movies). Laundry services. Sauna. Game room.

Indoor pool; whirlpool. Downhill ski 7 miles; cross-country ski 1 mile. **$**

D 🦮 🏊 🏊 🚭

★ **BEST WESTERN BRIDGEVIEW MOTOR INN.**
415 Hammond Ave (54880). Phone 715/392-8174; toll-free 800/777-5572; fax 715/392-8487. www.bestwestern.com.
96 rooms, 2 story. Pets accepted, some restrictions. Complimentary continental breakfast. Check-out noon. TV; cable (premium). Laundry services. Bar. Sauna. Indoor pool; whirlpool. Downhill, cross-country ski 8 miles. **$**

D 🦮 🏊 🏊 🚭 SC

Tomah

Motels/Motor Lodges

★ **COMFORT INN.** *305 Wittig Rd (54660). Phone 608/372-6600; toll-free 800/288-5150; fax 608/372-6600. www.comfortinn.com.* 52 rooms, 2 story. Pets accepted, some restrictions. Complimentary continental breakfast. Check-out 11 am. TV; cable (premium). Indoor pool; whirlpool. Downhill ski 15 miles; cross-country ski 1/2 mile. **$**

D 🦮 🏊 🏊 🚭 SC

★ **LARK INN.** *229 N Superior Ave (54660). Phone 608/372-5981; toll-free 800/447-5275; fax 608/372-3009. www.larkinn.com.* 25 rooms, 1-2 story. Pets accepted; fee. Check-out 11 am. TV; cable (premium), VCR available. Laundry services. Restaurant. Room service. Downhill ski 10 miles; cross-country ski 1 mile. **$**

D 🦮 🛗 🏊 🏃 🚭

★ **REST WELL MOTEL.** *25491 US 12 (54660). Phone 608/372-2471.* 12 rooms. 10 rooms with shower only. No room phones. Pets accepted, some restrictions; fee. Check-out 10 am. TV. Downhill ski 10 miles; cross-country ski 1 mile. **$**

🦮 🏊 ✈ 🚭

★ **SUPER 8.** *1008 E McCoy Blvd (54660). Phone 608/372-3901; fax 608/372-5792. www.super8.com.* 64 rooms, 2 story. Pets accepted; fee. Complimentary continental breakfast. Check-out 11 am. TV. Laundry services. Downhill ski 12 miles; cross-country ski 1 mile. **$**

D 🦮 🛗 🏃 🏊 🚭

Washington Island

Motel/Motor Lodge

★ **VIKING VILLAGE MOTEL.** *Main Rd (54246). Phone 920/847-2551; toll-free 800/522-5469; fax 920/847-2752. www.holidayinn.net.* 12 kitchen units. No A/C.

Pets accepted, some restrictions. Check-out 10 am. TV. Restaurant. Health club privileges. **$**

D 🦮 ⛷

Waukesha

Motel/Motor Lodge

★ **SELECT INN.** *2510 Plaza Ct (53186). Phone 262/786-6015; toll-free 800/641-1000; fax 262/786-5784. www.selectinn.com.* 101 rooms, 2-3 story. No elevator. Pets accepted, some restrictions; fee. Complimentary continental breakfast. Check-out 11 am. TV. Cross-country ski 5 miles. **$**

D 🦮 🏊 🚭 SC

Waupaca

Motel/Motor Lodge

★ ★ **BAYMONT INN.** *110 Grand Seasons Dr (54981). Phone 715/258-9212; toll-free 877/880-1054; fax 715/258-4294. www.baymontinns.com.* 90 rooms, 3 story. Pets accepted. Complimentary continental breakfast. Check-out 11 am. TV; cable (premium). Restaurant, bar. In-house fitness room; sauna; massage. Game room. Indoor pool; whirlpool. Downhill ski 10 miles; cross-country ski 2 miles. **$**

D 🦮 🏊 🏊 🏃 🚭 SC

Waupun

Motel/Motor Lodge

★ **INN TOWN.** *27 S State St (53963). Phone 920/324-4211; toll-free 800/433-6231; fax 920/324-6921.* 16 rooms. Pets accepted, some restrictions; fee. Check-out 10 am. TV; cable (premium). **$**

🦮 ✈

Wausau

Motels/Motor Lodges

★ **BAYMONT INN.** *1910 Stewart Ave (54401). Phone 715/842-0421; fax 715/845-5096. www.baymontinns.com.* 96 rooms, 2 story. Pets accepted, some restrictions. Check-out noon. TV. In-room modem link. Indoor pool. Downhill, cross-country ski 2 miles. **$**

🦮 🏊 🏊 🚭

★★ **BEST WESTERN MIDWAY HOTEL.** *2901 Martin Ave (54401). Phone 715/842-1616; toll-free 800/528-1234; fax 715/845-3726. www.bestwestern.com.* 98 rooms, 2 story. Pets accepted, some restrictions; fee. Check-out noon. TV. In-room modem link. Restaurant, bar; entertainment. Room service. In-house fitness room; sauna. Indoor pool; whirlpool. Downhill ski 1 mile; cross-country ski 3 miles. Lawn games. Free airport transportation. **$**

D

★ **EXEL INN.** *116 S 17th Ave (54401). Phone 715/842-0641; toll-free 800/367-3935; fax 715/848-1356. www.exelinns.com.* 122 rooms, 2 story. Pets accepted, some restrictions. Complimentary continental breakfast. Check-out noon. TV. Laundry services. Game room. Downhill, cross-country ski 3 miles. View of Rib Mountain. **$**

D SC

★ **RIB MOUNTAIN INN.** *2900 Rib Mountain Way (54401). Phone 715/848-2802; toll-free 877/960-8900; fax 715/848-1908.* 16 rooms, 2 story. Pets accepted; fee. Complimentary continental breakfast. Check-out 11 am. TV; cable (premium), VCR (movies). Fireplaces. Sauna. Downhill ski 1/4 mile; cross-country ski 7 miles. Lawn games. On Rib Mountain. Adjacent to state park. **$**

D

★ **SUPER 8.** *2006 Stewart Ave (54401). Phone 715/848-2888; fax 715/842-9578. www.super8.com.* 88 rooms, 2 story. Pets accepted, some restrictions; fee. Complimentary continental breakfast. Check-out noon. TV. Indoor pool; whirlpool. **$**

D

Wauwatosa

Motel/Motor Lodge

★ **EXEL INN.** *115 N Mayfair Rd (53226). Phone 414/257-0140; toll-free 800/367-3935; fax 414/475-7875. www.exelinns.com.* 123 rooms, 2 story. Pets accepted, some restrictions. Complimentary continental breakfast. Check-out noon. TV; cable (premium). **$**

D SC

Wisconsin Dells

Motels/Motor Lodges

★ **INTERNATIONAL MOTEL.** *1311 E Broadway (53965). Phone 608/254-2431.* 45 rooms. Closed mid-Oct-Apr. Pets accepted, some restrictions. Check-out 11 am. TV; cable (premium). Game room. Pool; children's pool. **$**

D

★ **SUPER 8.** *800 Cty Hwy H (53965). Phone 608/254-6464; fax 608/254-2692. www.super8.com.* 124 rooms, 3 story. Pets accepted, some restrictions. Complimentary continental breakfast. Check-out 11 am. TV. Sauna. Indoor pool; whirlpool. Downhill ski 5 miles; cross-country ski 3 miles. **$**

D

Wisconsin Rapids

Motels/Motor Lodges

★ **BEST WESTERN RAPIDS MOTOR INN.** *911 Huntington Ave (54494). Phone 715/423-3211; toll-free 800/528-1234; fax 715/423-2875. www.bestwestern.com.* 43 rooms, 2 story. Pets accepted. Check-out 11 am. TV; cable (premium). In-room modem link. Cross-country ski 2 miles. **$**

D SC

★ **ECONO LODGE.** *3300 8th St S (54494). Phone 715/423-7000; toll-free 800/755-1488. www.econolodge.com.* 55 rooms, 2 story. Pets accepted, some restrictions; fee. Check-out 11 am. TV. In-room modem link. Restaurant, bar. **$**

D

★★★ **HOTEL MEAD.** *451 E Grand Ave (54494). Phone 715/423-1500; toll-free 800/843-6323; fax 715/422-7064. www.hotelmead.com.* Centrally located and considered by many as the hospitality center of central Wisconsin, this hotel caters to business travelers, leisure travelers and adventure travelers. 157 rooms, 5 story. Pets accepted, some restrictions; fee. Check-out noon. TV; cable (premium). In-room modem link. Restaurant, bar. Room service. In-house fitness room. Indoor pool; whirlpool; poolside service. Cross-country ski 2 miles. **$**

D

★ **MAPLES MOTELS.** *4750 8th St S (54494). Phone 715/423-2590; fax 715/423-2592.* 27 rooms, 16 kitchen units. Pets accepted, some restrictions. Check-out 11 am. TV; VCR available. In-room modem link. Game room. Pool. Cross-country ski 2 miles. **$**

Wyoming

Afton

Motel/Motor Lodge

★ **CORRAL MOTEL.** *161 Washington (83110). Phone 307/886-5424; fax 307/886-5464.* 15 rooms. No A/C. Closed Nov-mid-Apr. Pet accepted, some restrictions. Check-out 10 am. TV; cable (premium). Totally non-smoking. **$**

Alpine

Motels/Motor Lodges

★★ **BEST WESTERN FLYING SADDLE LODGE.** *118878 Jct Hwy 89 and 26 (83128). Phone 307/654-7561; toll-free 866/666-2937; fax 307/654-7563. www.flyingsaddle.com.* 20 rooms, 6 cabins. Pets accepted; fee. Complimentary continental breakfast. Check-out 11 am, check-in 2 pm. TV; cable (premium), VCR available (free movies). In-room modem link. Restaurant, bar. In-house fitness room. Pool; whirlpools. Outdoor tennis. On Snake River. **$**

★ **ROYAL RESORT.** *Jct US 26 and 89 (83128). Phone 307/654-7545; toll-free 800/343-6755; fax 307/654-7546. www.royal-resort.com.* 45 rooms, 3 story. Pets accepted, some restrictions; fee. Complimentary continental breakfast. Check-out 11 am, check-in 4 pm. TV; VCR available (movies). Restaurant, bar. Whirlpool. Cross-country ski on site. Free parking. **$**

Buffalo

Motels/Motor Lodges

★ **COMFORT INN.** *65 US 16 E (82834). Phone 307/684-9564. www.comfortinn.com.* 41 rooms, 2 story. Pets accepted, some restrictions; fee. Complimentary continental breakfast. Check-out 11 am, check-in 2 pm. TV; cable (premium). In-room modem link. Whirlpool. Free parking. **$**

★★ **THE RANCH AT UCROSS.** *2673 US Hwy 14 E (82835). Phone 307/737-2281; toll-free 800/447-0194; fax 307/737-2211. www.blairhotels.com.* 31 rooms, 2 story. Closed Oct-mid-May. Pets accepted, some restrictions; fee. Complimentary full breakfast. Check-out 11 am, check-in 3 pm. Restaurant, bar. Outdoor pool. Outdoor tennis. Free parking. Airport transportation. On creek. **$$**

Casper

Motels/Motor Lodges

★ **COMFORT INN.** *480 Lathrop Rd (82636). Phone 307/235-3038. www.comfortinn.com.* 56 rooms, 2 story. Pets accepted, some restrictions. Complimentary continental breakfast. Check-out 11 am, check-in 2 pm. TV; cable (premium). In-room modem link. Indoor pool; whirlpool. Free parking. **$**

★★ **HOLIDAY INN.** *300 West F St (82601). Phone 307/235-2531; toll-free 877/576-8636; fax 307/473-3100. www.holiday-inn.com.* 200 rooms, 2 story. Pets accepted; fee. Check-out noon. TV; cable (premium). In-room modem link. Restaurant, bar. Room service. In-house fitness room. Game room. Indoor pool; whirlpool. Downhill, cross-country ski 7 miles. Free parking. Airport transportation. On river. **$**

Hotel

★★ **RADISSON HOTEL.** *800 N Poplar St (82601). Phone 307/266-6000; fax 307/473-1010. www.radisson.com/casper.* 236 rooms, 6 story. Pets accepted; fee. Check-out noon, check-in 3 pm. TV; cable (premium). Restaurant, bar. Game room. Indoor pool; whirlpool. Downhill, cross-country ski 7 miles. Parking. Free airport transportation. **$**

B&B/Small Inn

★★ **HOTEL HIGGINS.** *416 W Birch St (82637). Phone 307/436-9212; toll-free 800/458-0144; fax 307/436-9213. www.hotelhiggins.com.* 10 rooms, 2 story. Pets accepted, some restrictions. Complimentary continental breakfast. Check-out noon, check-in noon. TV; cable (premium). Restaurant, bar. Room service. Free parking. Airport transportation. **$**

Cheyenne

Motels/Motor Lodges

★ ★ ★ **BEST WESTERN HITCHING POST INN RESORT & CONFERENCE CENTER.** *1700 W Lincolnway (82001). Phone 307/638-3301; toll-free 800/ 221-0125; fax 307/778-7194. www.hitchingpostinn.com.* 179 rooms, 2 story. Pets accepted, some restrictions. Check-out noon, check-in 3 pm. TV; cable (premium). Restaurant, bar; entertainment. Room service. In-house fitness room; massage; sauna; steam room. Game room. Indoor pool; outdoor pool; whirlpool. Free airport transportation. Business center. **$**

⊡ ⌷ ⌷ ⌷ ✈ ⌷ SC ⌷

★ **COMFORT INN.** *2245 Etchepare Dr (82007). Phone 307/638-7202; toll-free 800/228-5150; fax 307/635-8560. www.comfortinn.com.* 77 rooms, 2 story. Pets accepted; fee. Complimentary continental breakfast. Check-out noon. TV; cable (premium). Heated pool. **$**

⊡ ⌷ ⌷ ⌷ SC

★ **DAYS INN.** *2360 W LincolnWay (82001). Phone 307/ 778-8877; fax 307/778-8697. www.daysinn.com.* 72 rooms, 2 story. Pets accepted; fee. Complimentary continental breakfast. Check-out noon. TV; cable (premium). In-house fitness room; sauna. **$**

⊡ ⌷ ⌷ SC

★ **LA QUINTA INN.** *2410 W Lincolnway (82009). Phone 307/632-7117; toll-free 800/531-5900; fax 307/638-7807. www.laquinta.com.* 108 rooms, 3 story. Pets accepted. Complimentary continental breakfast. Check-out noon, check-in 3 pm. TV; cable (premium). Outdoor pool. **$**

⊡ ⌷ ⌷ ⌷ SC

★ **SUPER 8.** *1900 W Lincolnway (82001). Phone 307/635-8741. www.super8.com.* 61 rooms, 3 story. No elevator. Pets accepted, some restrictions; fee. Check-out 11 am, check-in noon. TV; cable (premium). **$**

⊡ ⌷ ⌷ ⌷

Cody

Motel/Motor Lodge

★ ★ **ELEPHANT HEAD LODGE.** *1170 Yellowstone Hwy (82450). Phone 307/587-3980; fax 307/527-6850. www.elephantheadlodge.com.* 14 cabins. No A/C. Closed mid-Oct-mid-May. Pets accepted. Check-out noon, check-in noon. Dining room, bar. Hiking, nature trails. Free parking. On river in Shoshone National Forest. Trail rides available. Totally nonsmoking. **$**

⌷ ⌷ ⌷ ⌷

Guest Ranch

★ ★ ★ **DOUBLE DIAMOND X RANCH.** *3453 Southfork Rd (82414). Phone 307/527-6276; toll-free 800/ 833-7262; fax 307/587-2708. www.ddxranch.com.* This resort provides an unforgettable dude ranch vacation. It features comfortable accommodations, excellent food, lots of entertainment, and a relaxed environment situated among the scenic mountains of Wyoming. 13 cabins. Closed mid-Oct-mid-Apr. Pets accepted, some restrictions. Check-out 11 am. Laundry services. Entertainment. Supervised children's activities (June-Sept). Indoor pool; whirlpool. Fishing/hunting trips. Fly fishing instruction. Hiking. Free parking. Free airport transportation. Square dancing. On the south fork of the Shoshone River. Cookouts. **$$$**

⊡ ⌷ ⌷ ⌷ ⌷

Douglas

Motel/Motor Lodge

★ ★ **BEST WESTERN DOUGLAS INN AND CONFERENCE CENTER.** *1450 Riverbend Dr (82633). Phone 307/358-9790; fax 307/358-6251. www.bwdouglas .com.* 117 rooms, 2 story. Pets accepted. Complimentary continental breakfast. Check-out 11 am, check-in 3 pm. TV; cable (premium), VCR. DVD available, fee. In-room modem link. Restaurant, bar. Room service. In-house fitness room; sauna. Game room. Indoor pool; whirlpool; poolside service. Hiking trail. Free parking. **$**

⊡ ⌷ ⌷ ⌷ ⌷ ⌷ SC

Dubois

Motel/Motor Lodge

★ **SUPER 8.** *1414 Warm Springs Dr (82513). Phone 307/455-3694; fax 307/455-3640. www.super8.com.* 35 rooms, 2 story. Pets accepted; fee. Check-out 11 am. TV. Whirlpool. Free parking. **$**

⊡ ⌷ ⌷

Evanston

Motel/Motor Lodge

★ **PRAIRIE INN MOTEL.** *264 Bear River Dr (82920). Phone 307/789-2920.* 31 rooms, 1 story. Pets accepted, some restrictions; fee. Complimentary continental breakfast. Check-out 11 am, check-in 2 pm. TV; cable (premium). In-room modem link. **$**

⬛⬛⬛

Gillette

Motel/Motor Lodge

★★ **BEST WESTERN TOWER WEST LODGE.** *109 N US 14 and 16 (82716). Phone 307/686-2210; toll-free 800/762-7375; fax 307/682-5105. www.bestwestern.com.* 189 rooms, 2 story. Pets accepted; fee. Check-out noon, check-in 2 pm. TV; cable (premium). Internet access, in-room modem link. Laundry services. Restaurant, bar; entertainment. Room service. In-house fitness room; sauna. Game room. Indoor pool; whirlpool. Free parking. Airport transportation. Business center. **$**

⬛⬛⬛⬛⬛⬛

Hotel

★★ **CLARION HOTEL.** *2009 S Douglas Hwy (82718). Phone 307/686-3000; toll-free 800/686-3368; fax 307/686-4018. www.westernplaza.com.* 159 rooms, 3 story. Pets accepted, some restrictions. Check-out 11 am, check-in 2 pm. TV; cable (premium). In-room modem link. Laundry services. Restaurant, bar; entertainment. Room service. In-house fitness room; steam room. Game room. Indoor pool; whirlpool. Free airport transportation. Business center. **$**

⬛⬛⬛⬛⬛⬛⬛

Grand Teton National Park

Motels/Motor Lodges

★★ **HATCHET RESORT.** *Hwy 287 (83013). Phone 307/543-2413; fax 307/543-2034. www.hatchetresort.com.* 22 cabins. No A/C. Closed Labor Day-Memorial Day. Pets accepted. Check-out 10 am. Restaurant. Totally nonsmoking. **$**

⬛⬛⬛

★★ **SIGNAL MOUNTAIN LODGE.** *Inner Park Rd (83013). Phone 307/543-2831; toll-free 800/672-6012; fax 307/543-2569. www.signalmtnlodge.com.* 79 cabins, 1-2 story. No A/C. Closed mid-Oct-mid-May. Pets accepted; fee. Check-out 11 am. Restaurant, bar. Marina; boat rentals; guided fishing trips. Scenic float trips on the Snake River. **$**

⬛⬛⬛

Jackson

Motels/Motor Lodges

★★★ **ALPENHOF LODGE.** *3255 W Village Dr (83025). Phone 307/733-3242; toll-free 800/732-3244; fax 307/739-1516. www.alpenhoflodge.com.* This Bavarian-style lodge is located at the base of Jackson Hole's ski hill. 43 rooms, 3 story. No A/C. Closed mid-Oct-Nov and Apr-mid-May. Pets accepted; fee. Complimentary continental breakfast. Check-out 11 am, check-in 3 pm. TV; cable (premium). In-room modem link. Fireplace in lounge. Room service. Restaurant, bar. Outdoor pool; whirlpool. Downhill, cross-country ski in and out of lodge. Valet parking. Free parking. **$$**

⬛⬛⬛⬛⬛⬛

★ **ANTLER INN.** *43 W Pearl St (83001). Phone 307/733-2535; toll-free 800/4-TETONS; fax 307/733-4158. www.townsquareinns.com.* 106 rooms, 2 story. Pets accepted, some restrictions. Check-out 11 am, check-in 2 pm. TV; cable (premium). In-room modem link. Laundry services. In-house fitness room, sauna. Whirlpool. Downhill, cross-country ski 12 miles. Free parking. **$**

⬛⬛⬛⬛⬛⬛

★ **FLAT CREEK INN.** *1935 N US Hwys 26/89 (83002). Phone 307/733-5276; toll-free 800/438-9338; fax 307/733-0374. www.flatcreekmotel.com.* 75 rooms, 2 story. Pets accepted, some restrictions; fee. Complimentary continental breakfast. Check-out 11 am, check-in 3 pm. TV. In-room modem link. Laundry services. Sauna. Whirlpool. Free parking. **$**

⬛⬛⬛

★★ **QUALITY INN.** *330 W Pearl St (83001). Phone 307/733-7550; toll-free 800/451-2980; fax 307/733-2002. www.townsquareinns.com.* 142 rooms, 2 and 3 story. Pets accepted, some restrictions. Complimentary continental breakfast. Check-out 11 am, check-in 3 pm. TV; cable (premium). In-room modem link. In-house fitness room, sauna. Whirlpool. Downhill, cross-country ski 12 miles. Free parking. **$**

⬛⬛⬛⬛⬛⬛⬛

★ ★ ★ **SNOW KING RESORT HOTEL.** *400 E Snow King Ave (83001). Phone 307/733-5200; toll-free 800/522-5464; fax 307/733-4086. www.snowking.com.* This western lodge is located in Jackson Hole, a few blocks from downtown and near Grand Teton National Park. 204 rooms, 7 story. Pets accepted, some restrictions; fee. Check-out noon, check-in 4 pm. TV. Restaurant, bar. Room service. In-house fitness room; massage; sauna. Game room. Outdoor pool; whirlpools, poolside service. Downhill ski adjacent; cross-country ski 5 miles. Free airport transportation. Concierge. Alpine slide. Located at the foot of Snow King Mountain. **$$**

D ▭ ⬚ ⬚ ⬚ ⬚ 🕇 ✈ ⬚ SC

Lander

Motel/Motor Lodge

★ **PRONGHORN LODGE.** *150 E Main St (82520). Phone 307/332-3940; toll-free 800/283-4678; fax 307/332-2651. www.pronghornlodge.com.* 60 rooms, 2 story. Pets accepted, some restrictions; fee. Complimentary continental breakfast. Check-out 11 am, check-in 4 pm. TV. In-room modem link. Laundry services. Restaurant. Room service. In-house fitness room. Whirlpool. Parking. Airport transportation. On river. **$**

D ▭ 🕇 ⬚

Laramie

Motels/Motor Lodges

★ **BEST VALUE INN.** *523 S Adams St (82070). Phone 307/721-8860; toll-free 866/721-8395; fax 307/721-6290.* 33 rooms, 2 story. Pets accepted, some restrictions. Check-out 11 am, check-in 2 pm. TV; cable. Parking. **$**

D ▭ ⬚ SC

★ ★ **HOLIDAY INN.** *2313 Soldier Springs Rd (82070). Phone 307/742-6611; fax 307/745-8371. www.holiday-inn.com.* 100 rooms, 2 story. Pets accepted, some restrictions; fee. Check-out noon, check-in 3 pm. TV; cable (premium). In-room modem link. Laundry services. Restaurant, bar. Room service. In-house fitness room. Indoor pool; whirlpool. Airport transportation. **$**

D ▭ ⬚ 🕇 ⬚ SC

Lovell

Motel/Motor Lodge

★ **SUPER 8.** *595 E Main (82431). Phone 307/548-2725; toll-free 800/800-8000. www.super8.com.* 34 rooms, 2 story. Pets accepted; fee. Complimentary continental breakfast. Check-out 11 am, check-in 3 pm. TV. Free parking. **$**

D ▭ ⬚ SC

Pinedale

Motel/Motor Lodge

★ **BEST WESTERN PINEDALE INN.** *850 W Pine St (82941). Phone 307/367-6869; toll-free 800/937-8376; fax 307/367-6897. www.bestwestern.com.* 59 rooms, 2 story. Pets accepted, some restrictions. Complimentary continental breakfast. Check-out 11 am, check-in 3 pm. TV. In-room modem link. Indoor pool; whirlpool. Free parking. **$**

D ▭ ⬚ ⬚ SC

Rawlins

Motels/Motor Lodges

★ **DAYS INN.** *2222 E Cedar St (82301). Phone 307/324-6615; toll-free 888/324-6615. www.daysinn.com.* 118 rooms, 2 story. Pets accepted; fee. Complimentary continental breakfast. Check-out noon, check-in 2 pm. TV; cable (premium). Laundry services. Restaurant, bar. Pool. Free parking. **$**

D ▭ ⬚ ⬚ SC

★ **SLEEP INN.** *1400 Higley Blvd (82301). Phone 307/328-1732; fax 307/328-0412. www.sleepinn.com.* 81 rooms, 2 story. Many rooms with shower only. Pets accepted; fee. Complimentary continental breakfast. Check-out 11 am, check-in 3 pm. TV; cable (premium), VCR available (movies, fee). In-room modem link. In-house fitness room, sauna. Game room. Free parking. **$**

D ▭ 🕇

Riverton

Motels/Motor Lodges

★ ★ **HOLIDAY INN.** *900 E Sunset Dr (82501). Phone 307/856-8100; fax 307/856-0266. www.holiday-inn.com.* 176 rooms, 2 story. Pets accepted, some restrictions; fee. Check-out noon, check-in 2 pm. TV. In-room modem link. Laundry services. Restaurant, bar. In-house fitness room. Indoor pool; poolside service. Free parking. Free airport transportation. **$**

⊡ 🐾 🛋 🏋 🏊 🏃

★ ★ **SUNDOWNER STATION.** *1616 N Federal Blvd (82501). Phone 307/856-6503; toll-free 800/874-1116.* 61 rooms, 2 story. Pets accepted. Check-out 11 am, check-in 11 am. TV. Laundry services. Restaurant, bar. Sauna. Free parking. Free airport transportation. **$**

🐾 🏊 SC

Rock Springs

Motels/Motor Lodges

★ **COMFORT INN.** *1670 Sunset Dr (82901). Phone 307/382-9490; fax 307/382-7333. www.comfortinn.com.* 103 rooms. Pets accepted; fee. Complimentary continental breakfast. Check-out 11 am, check-in 3 pm. TV; cable (premium). In-room modem link. Laundry services. In-house fitness room. Pool; whirlpool. Free parking. Airport transportation. **$**

⊡ 🐾 🏊 🏃 🏊 🏊

★ ★ **HOLIDAY INN.** *1675 Sunset Dr (82901). Phone 307/382-9200; fax 307/362-1064. www.holiday-inn.com.* 114 rooms, 4 story. Pets accepted; fee. Check-out noon, check-in 2 pm. TV. In-room modem link. Laundry services. Restaurant, bar. Room service. In-house fitness room. Game room. Indoor pool; whirlpool. Free parking. Airport transportation. **$**

⊡ 🐾 🛋 🏊 🏃 🏊 🏊

★ **RAMADA INN.** *2717 Dewar Dr (82901). Phone 307/362-1770; toll-free 800/272-6232; fax 307/362-2830. www.ramada.com.* 129 rooms, 2 story. Pets accepted, some restrictions; fee. Complimentary continental breakfast. Check-out noon, check-in noon. TV; cable (premium). In-room modem link. In-house fitness room. Outdoor pool. Free parking. **$**

⊡ 🐾 🏊 🏃

Sheridan

Motel/Motor Lodge

★ ★ **HOLIDAY INN.** *1809 Sugarland Dr (82801). Phone 307/672-8931; toll-free 877/672-4011; fax 307/672-6388. www.holiday-inn.com.* 219 rooms, 5 story. Pets accepted, some restrictions; fee. Check-out noon, check-in 3 pm. TV. In-room modem link. Laundry services. Restaurant, bar. Room service. In-house fitness room; sauna. Game room. Indoor pool; whirlpool; poolside service. Free parking. Airport transportation. Concierge. **$**

⊡ 🐾 🛋 🏋 🏊 🏃 🏊 SC

Thermopolis

Motel/Motor Lodge

★ **SUPER 8.** *Ln 5, Hwy 20 S (82443). Phone 307/864-5515. www.super8.com.* 52 rooms, 2 story. Pets accepted, some restrictions; fee. Check-out 11 am. TV; cable (premium). Indoor pool; whirlpool. **$**

⊡ 🐾 🛋 🏊 🏊

Wheatland

Motel/Motor Lodge

★ **BEST WESTERN TORCHLITE MOTOR INN.** *1809 N 16th St (82201). Phone 307/322-4070; fax 307/322-4072. www.bestwestern.com.* 50 rooms, 2 story. Pets accepted; fee. Check-out 11 am, check-in 2 pm. TV; cable (premium). In-room modem link. Outdoor pool. Free parking. **$**

⊡ 🐾 🛋 🏊 🏊

Alberta

Banff

Motels/Motor Lodges

★ **AKAI MOTEL.** *1717 Mountain Ave (T1W 2W1). Phone 403/678-4664; toll-free 877/900-2524; fax 403/678-4775.* 42 kitchen units. D $80-$100; each additional $5; under 12 free; family rates; package plans. Pets accepted, some restrictions; fee. Check-out 11 am, check-in 2 pm. TV; cable. Downhill ski 15 miles, cross-country ski 3 miles.

★ **BEST WESTERN SIDING 29 LODGE.** *453 Marten St (T0L 0C0). Phone 403/762-5575; fax 403/762-8866. www.bestwesternbanff.com.* 57 rooms, 3 story. No A/C. July-Aug: S, D $95-$200; suites $219-$304; lower rates rest of year. Pets accepted, some restrictions. Complimentary continental breakfast. Check-out 11 am, check-in 3 pm. TV. Indoor pool; whirlpool. Downhill ski 5 miles, cross-country ski 2 miles. Heated underground parking.

★ ★ **CASTLE MOUNTAIN CHALETS.** *Jct Hwy 1-A, 93 S (T1L 1B5). Phone 403/762-3868; toll-free 800/ 661-1315; fax 403/762-8629. www.castlemountain.com.* 33 rooms. No A/C. No room phones. June-Sept: S, D $185-$250; each additional $10; under 17 free; package plans; lower rates rest of year. Pets accepted; fee. Check-out 10:30 am, check-in 3 pm. TV; VCR available. In-house fitness room. Downhill ski 20 miles, cross-country ski on site.

★ ★ **NORQUAY'S TIMBERLINE INN.** *1 Norquay Rd (T1L 1A2). Phone 403/762-2281; toll-free 877/762-2281; fax 403/762-8331. www.banfftimberline.com.* 52 rooms, 3 story. No A/C. June-early Oct: S, D $155-$165; each additional $15; suites $250-$300; kitchen chalet $285; under 16 free; MAP available; lower rates rest of year; 2-day minimum (late Dec-early Jan). Pets accepted, some restrictions; fee. Check-out 11 am, check-in 4 pm. TV. Dining room. Outdoor whirlpool. Downhill, cross-country ski 1/2 mile.

★ **RED CARPET INN.** *425 Banff Ave (T0L 0C0). Phone 403/762-4184; toll-free 800/563-4609; fax 403/762-4894. www.motels.ab.ca/m/redcrpet.html.* 52 rooms, 3 story. D

$125-$190. Pets accepted, some restrictions. Check-out 11 am, check-in 4 pm. TV; VCR available. Whirlpool. Free garage parking.

Hotels

★ ★ **MOUNT ROYAL HOTEL.** *138 Banff Ave (T1L 1A7). Phone 403/762-3331; toll-free 800/267-3035; fax 403/762-8938. www.mountroyalhotel.com.* 134 rooms, 3-4 story. June-early Oct: S, D $270-$295; each additional $15; suites $385-$475; under 16 free; ski plans; lower rates rest of year. Pets accepted, some restrictions; fee. Check-out 11 am, check-in 4 pm. TV. Restaurant, bar. Health club privileges, exercise equipment; sauna. Downhill, cross-country ski 5 miles. Airport transportation.

★ ★ **RADISSON HOTEL AND CONFERENCE CENTER CANMORE.** *511 Bow Valley Trail (T1W 1N7). Phone 403/678-3625; fax 403/678-3765. www.radisson.com.* This hotel nestled in the Canadian Rockies offers spectacular mountain views as well as access to outdoor activities in both summer and winter. 224 rooms, 3 story. Late June-early Sept: S, D $139-$186; each additional $10; suites $159-$229; under 16 free; lower rates rest of year. Pets accepted, some restrictions; fee. Check-out 11 am, check-in 4 pm. TV. Restaurant, bar. Room service. In-house fitness room, steam room. Indoor pool; whirlpool. Downhill ski 14 miles, cross-country ski 2 miles.

Resorts

★ ★ **BANFF ROCKY MOUNTAIN RESORT.** *1029 Banff Ave (T1L 1A2). Phone 403/762-5531; toll-free 800/ 661-9563; fax 403/762-5166. www.rockymountainresort .com.* 172 rooms, 2 story. Mid-June-mid-Sept: S, D $213-$315; condos $220-$290; each additional $15; under 18 free; package plans; higher rates Christmas holiday; lower rates rest of year. Pets accepted; fee. Check-out 11 am. TV. Fireplaces. Restaurant, bar. Room service. Supervised children's activities. In-house fitness room; massage; sauna. Indoor pool; whirlpool. Outdoor tennis. Downhill, cross-country ski 2 miles. Squash.

★ ★ ★ **THE FAIRMONT BANFF SPRINGS.** *405 Spray Ave (T1L 1J4). Phone 403/762-2211; toll-free 800/ 441-1414; fax 403/762-8469. www.fairmont.com.* Located in Banff National Park, this hotel, with its breathtaking scenery and accommodating staff, is a true getaway. 770 rooms, 9 story. No A/C. June-Aug: S, D $325-$685; each additional $21; suites $527-$837; under 18 free; package plans; lower rates rest of year. Pets accepted, some restrictions; fee. Check-out noon. TV. Restaurant, bar. In-house fitness room; massage; sauna. Two pools, one indoor, two whirlpools. 27-hole golf, greens fee $75-$150. Outdoor tennis. Downhill ski 2 miles. Horseback riding. Business center. Concierge.

Calgary

Motels/Motor Lodges

★ ★ **BEST WESTERN HOSPITALITY INN.** *135 Southland Dr SE (T2J 5X5). Phone 403/278-5050; toll-free 800/780-7234. www.bestwestern.com/ca/hospitalityinn.* 260 rooms, 8 story. S, D $99-$169; each additional $5; suites $175-$325; under 17 free; weekend rates Oct-May. Pets accepted, some restrictions. Check-out noon, check-in 4 pm. TV; cable (premium). Restaurant, bar. Room service. Indoor pool; whirlpool.

★ ★ **BLACKFOOT INN.** *5940 Blackfoot Trail SE (T2H 2B5). Phone 403/252-2253; toll-free 800/661-1151; fax 403/252-3574. www.blackfootinn.com.* 200 rooms, 7 story. S, D $189-$225; each additional $10; suite $199-$235; under 16 free; monthly rates. Pets accepted, some restrictions. Check-out noon, check-in 3 pm. TV; VCR (movies). Restaurant, bar; entertainment. Room service. In-house fitness room; sauna. Pool; whirlpool; poolside service. Business center.

★ **DAYS INN.** *1818 16th Ave NW (Trans-Can Hwy 1) (T2M 0L8). Phone 403/289-1961; toll-free 800/661-9564; fax 403/289-3901. www.daysinn.com.* 130 rooms, 4 story. Mid-June-Sept: S, D $79-$109; suites $130-$170; each additional $10; under 16 free; higher rates special events; lower rates rest of year. Pets accepted, some restrictions; fee. Check-out 11 am, check-in 3 pm. TV; cable (premium), VCR available. Restaurant, bar. Room service. Pool; poolside service. Airport transportation.

★ ★ **HOLIDAY INN.** *1250 McKinnon Dr NE (T2E 7T7). Phone 403/230-1999; toll-free 877/519-7113; fax 403/277-2623. www.holiday-inn.com/calgary-apt.* 170 rooms, 5 story. D $129-$179; each additional $10; under 18 free. Pets accepted; fee. Check-out noon. TV. In-room modem link. Laundry services. Restaurant, bar. Room service. In-house fitness room; sauna. Indoor pool. Free airport transportation. Business center.

★ ★ **HOLIDAY INN.** *4206 Macleod Trail S (T2G 2R7). Phone 403/287-2700; toll-free 800/661-1889; fax 403/243-4721. www.calgaryholidayinn.com.* 152 rooms, 4 story. May-Sept: S, D $99-$169; each additional $5; under 18 free; weekend, weekly rates; lower rates rest of year. Pets accepted, some restrictions; fee. Check-out noon. TV; cable (premium). In-room modem link. Restaurant, bar. Room service. Health club privileges, exercise equipment. Pool; whirlpool.

★ **HOLIDAY INN EXPRESS.** *2227 Banff Trail NW (T2M 4L2). Phone 403/289-6600; fax 403/289-6767. www.holiday-inn.com.* 63 rooms, 3 story. D $110-$175; each additional $10; under 18 free. Pets accepted. Complimentary continental breakfast. Check-out noon, check-in 4 pm. TV. In-room modem link. Laundry services. Sauna. Pool; whirlpool.

★ ★ **QUALITY INN.** *3828 Macleod Trail (T2G 2R2). Phone 403/243-5531; toll-free 800/361-3422; fax 403/243-6962. www.qualityinn.com.* 134 rooms, 4 story. S, D $99-$159; suites $119-$129; each additional $10; under 18 free. Pets accepted, some restrictions; fee. Check-out noon. TV; cable (premium). Restaurant, bar. Room service. In-house fitness room. Heated indoor pool; whirlpool. Luxury level.

★ ★ **QUALITY INN.** *2359 Banff Trail NW (1A) (T2M 4L2). Phone 403/289-1973; toll-free 800/661-4667; fax 403/282-1241. www.qualityinnmotelvillage.com.* 105 rooms, 2 story. July-Sept: S, D $99-$129; suites $149-$189; under 18 free; higher rates: Calgary Stampede, first two weeks in July; lower rates rest of year. Pets accepted, some restrictions; fee. Complimentary continental breakfast. Check-out 11 am. TV; cable (premium), VCR (movies). Restaurant, bar. Room service. In-house fitness room; sauna, steam room. Indoor pool; whirlpool. Casino.

Hotels

★ ★ **THE CARRIAGE HOUSE INN.** *9030 Macleod Trail S (T2H 0M4). Phone 403/253-1101; toll-free 800/661-9566; fax 403/259-2414. www.carriagehouse.net.* 157 rooms, 10 story. S, D $105-$140; each additional $10; suites $205-$245; under 18 free. Pets accepted, some restrictions; fee. Check-out noon. TV; cable (premium). In-room modem link. Restaurant, bar. Health club privileges; sauna. Heated pool; whirlpool; poolside service. Bakery.

★ ★ ★ **THE COAST PLAZA HOTEL.** *1316 33rd St NE (T2A 6B6). Phone 403/248-8888; toll-free 800/661-1464; fax 403/248-0749. www.calgaryplaza.com.* 248 rooms, 12 story. Pets accepted; fee. Check-out noon, check-in 3 pm. TV; VCR available. Restaurant, bar. Room service 24 hours. In-house fitness room; sauna. Indoor pool; whirlpool. Free airport transportation. Concierge. $

CALGARY/ALBERTA **429**

www.mobiltravelguide.com

★★ **DELTA BOW VALLEY.** *209 4th Ave SE (T2G 0C6). Phone 403/266-1980; toll-free 800/268-1133. www.deltabowvalley.com.* 398 rooms, 21 story. S, D $199-$229; each additional $15; suites $249-$265; under 18 free; weekend, family rates. Pets accepted, some restrictions. Check-out 11 am. TV; cable (premium). Room service 24 hours. Restaurant, bar. Supervised children's activities (weekends), ages 3-16. In-house fitness room; sauna. Indoor pool; whirlpool; poolside service. Concierge. Canadian artwork on display. Overlooks river.

D 🐾 ⌘ 🏃 ⌀

★★ **DELTA CALGARY AIRPORT.** *2001 Airport Rd NE (T2E 6Z8). Phone 403/291-2600; toll-free 800/268-1133; fax 403/250-8722. www.deltahotels.com.* 296 rooms, 8 story. S, D $159-$160; each additional $20; suites $260-$280; under 18 free. Pets accepted, some restrictions. Check-out noon. TV. Room service 24 hours. Restaurant, bar. In-house fitness room; sauna. Indoor pool; whirlpool. Business center. Concierge.

D 🐾 ⌘ 🏃 ✈ ⌀ 🏃

★★★ **DELTA LODGE AT KANANASKIS.** *209 4th Ave SE (T0L 2H0). Phone 403/591-7711; toll-free 888/244-8666; fax 888/315-1515. www.deltalodgeatkananskis.ca.* This resort is a mountain paradise located among 1,500 square miles of rugged mountains. It offers year-round recreational fun. 321 rooms, 3 story. S, D $150-$589; each additional $20. Pets accepted; fee. Check-out noon. TV. Restaurant, bar; entertainment. Room service. In-house fitness room; sauna, steam room. Game room. Indoor pool; whirlpool. 36-hole golf course, greens fee. Outdoor tennis. Downhill ski 1 mile, cross-country ski on site. Valet parking. Business center. Concierge.

D 🐾 ⛷ 🏃 ⌀ 🎿 ⛷ ⌘ 🏃 ⌀ 🏃

★★★ **THE FAIRMONT PALLISER.** *133 9th Ave SW (T2P 2M3). Phone 403/262-1234; fax 403/260-1260. www.fairmont.com.* Opened in 1914, this hotel is a historic landmark for the city of Calgary. It is connected by a skywalk to the Telus Convention Center and the Calgary Tower and is near many other area attractions, shopping, and restaurants. 405 rooms, 11 story. Pets accepted, some restrictions; fee. Check-out noon, check-in 3 pm. TV; cable (premium), VCR available. In-room modem link. Room service 24 hours. Restaurant, bar. In-house fitness room, spa, massage, steam room. Indoor pool; whirlpool. Valet, self-parking. Airport transportation. Business center. Concierge. **$$**

D 🐾 ⛷ 🏊 ⌘ 🏃 ⌀

★★★ **MARRIOTT.** *110 9th Ave SE (T2G 5A6). Phone 403/266-7331; toll-free 800/896-6878. www.marriott.com/marriott/yycdt.* This hotel is located in downtown, near the Calgary Tower, the Glenbow Museum, and the Calgary Zoo. 384 rooms, 22 story. S, D $89-$245; each additional $20; suites $245-$350; under 18 free; family, weekend rates; higher rates special events. Pets accepted, some restrictions. Check-out noon. TV; cable (premium). Restaurant, bar. Room service. In-house fitness room; sauna. Pool; whirlpool; poolside service. Business center. Concierge. Luxury level.

D 🐾 ⌘ 🏃 ✈ ⌀ SC 🏃

★★ **RADISSON HOTEL CALGARY AIRPORT.** *2120 16th Ave NE (T2E 1L4). Phone 403/291-4666; toll-free 800/333-3333; fax 403/291-6498. www.radisson.com.* This hotel is central to many attractions in the downtown Calgary area. Great shopping is located only 5 minutes away. 185 rooms, 10 story. S, D $109-$129; each additional $10; suites $225-315; under 12 free. Pets accepted, some restrictions; fee. Check-out 11 am. TV; cable (premium). Restaurant, bar; entertainment. In-house fitness room. Indoor pool; whirlpool. Free airport transportation. Business center.

D 🐾 ⌘ 🏃 ✈ ⌀ SC 🏃

★★★ **WESTIN.** *320 4th Ave SW (T2P 2S6). Phone 403/508-5182; toll-free 800/937-8461; fax 403/508-5240. www.westin.com.* This hotel is located in downtown Calgary, across from a park and near shopping, restaurants, and nightclubs. 525 rooms, 19 story. S, D $115-$349; each additional $20; suites $285-$700; under 18 free; weekend rates. Pets accepted, some restrictions. Check-out 1 pm. TV; cable (premium), VCR available. In-room modem link. Room service 24 hours. Restaurant, bar. In-house fitness room; sauna. Indoor pool; whirlpool; poolside service. Indoor valet parking. Concierge.

D 🐾 ⌘ 🏃 ⌀ SC

Edmonton

Motels/Motor Lodges

★★ **BEST WESTERN CEDAR PARK INN.** *5116 Calgary Trail N (T6H 2H4). Phone 780/434-7411; toll-free 800/528-1234; fax 780/437-4836. www.bestwestern.com.* 190 rooms, 5 story. S, D $99-$109; each additional $7; suites $149-$160; under 18 free; family rates. Pets accepted, some restrictions; fee. Check-out noon. TV. In-room modem link. Restaurant, bar. Room service. In-house fitness room; sauna. Indoor pool. Free airport transportation.

D 🐾 ⌘ 🏃 ✈ ⌀ SC

★★ **CHATEAU LOUIS HOTEL & CONFERENCE CENTER.** *11727 Kingsway (T5G 3A1). Phone 780/452-7770; toll-free 800/661-9843; fax 780/454-3436. www.chateaulouis.com.* 142 rooms, 3 story. S $90; D $110; each additional $10; suites $281-$290; weekend rates; under 12 free. Pets accepted, some restrictions; fee. Check-out noon. TV. Room service 24 hours. Restaurant, bar; entertainment.

D ✈ ❄

★★ **DAYS INN.** *1101 4th St (T5J 2T2). Phone 780/955-7744; toll-free 800/661-6966; fax 780/955-7743. www.daysinnedmontonairport.com.* 156 rooms, 2 story. S, D $98-$108; each additional $10; suites $119-$199; under 18 free; weekend rates. Pets accepted, some restrictions; fee. Check-out noon. TV. In-room modem link. Restaurant, bar. Room service. In-house fitness room. Indoor pool; whirlpool. Free airport transportation.

D ✈ ❄

★★ **HOLIDAY INN.** *4235 Gateway Blvd N (T6J 5H2). Phone 780/438-1222; toll-free 800/565-1222; fax 780/438-1222. www.holidayinn.ca/edmonton.* 125 rooms, 5 story. S, D $180-$200; suite $270-$280. Pets accepted, some restrictions; fee. Check-out 11 am. TV. Restaurant, bar. Room service. In-house fitness room; sauna, steam room. Free airport transportation.

D ✈ SC

Hotels

★★★ **COAST TERRACE INN.** *4440 Gateway Blvd (T6H 5C2). Phone 780/437-6010; toll-free 888/837-7223; fax 780/431-5801. www.coasthotels.com.* 235 rooms, 4 story. S, D $150; suites $139-$169; under 18 free; weekend rates; package plans. Pets accepted, some restrictions. Check-out noon. TV. Room service 24 hours. Restaurant, bar; entertainment. In-house fitness room; sauna; steam room. Heated indoor pool; whirlpool. Racquetball court. Underground parking. Luxury level.

D ❄

★★★ **CROWNE PLAZA.** *10111 Bellamy Hill (T5J 1N7). Phone 780/428-6611; toll-free 800/661-8801; fax 780/425-6564. www.chateaulacombe.com.* Located in downtown Edmonton, this hotel overlooks the river valley. It is near many attractions, including the well-known West Edmonton Mall, Telus Field, an art gallery, and golf courses. 307 rooms, 24 story. S, D $99-$160; each additional $15; suites $129-$210; under 18 free; weekend rates. Pets accepted, some restrictions. Check-out 1 pm. TV. Restaurant, bar. In-house fitness room. Valet parking. Luxury level.

D ❄ SC

★★★ **DELTA CENTRE SUITES.** *10222 102nd St (T5J 4C5). Phone 780/429-3900; toll-free 800/268-1133; fax 780/426-0562. www.deltahotels.com.* 169 rooms, 7 story. S, D $99-$299; each additional $15; suites $129-$329; under 18 free; weekend rates. Pets accepted, some restrictions. Check-out noon. TV; VCR available. In-room modem link. Laundry services. Restaurant, bar. Room service. In-house fitness room, steam room. Valet parking, fee. Business center. Concierge. Miniature golf.

D ❄

★★★ **THE FAIRMONT HOTEL MACDONALD.** *10065 100th St (T5J 0N6). Phone 780/424-5181; toll-free 800/441-1414; fax 780/429-6481. www.fairmont.com.* Originally built in 1915 during the era of grand hotels in Canada, the MacDonald has been fully restored to its original old-world elegance. High on the banks of the North Saskatchewan River and only minutes from the Shaw Convention Center and the city's main cultural attractions, this French chateau-style hotel has a first-class, fully equipped health club, squash courts, swimming pool and whirlpools, and a fully equipped 24-hour business center. 198 rooms, 8 story. S, D $129-$269; each additional $20; suites $359-$659; under 18 free; weekend rates. Pets accepted, some restrictions; fee. Check-out 1 pm. TV; cable (premium). In-room modem link. Room service 24 hours. Restaurant, bar. In-house fitness room; massage; sauna, steam room. Game room. Indoor pool; children's pool; whirlpool; poolside service. Valet parking. 24-hour business center. Concierge.

D ❄

★★★ **SHERATON GRANDE EDMONTON HOTEL.** *10235 101st St (T5J 3E9). Phone 780/428-7111; toll-free 800/263-9030; fax 780/441-3098. www.sheratonedmonton.com.* This hotel is located near the Edmonton International Airport, the Space and Science Center, and many other area attractions. 313 rooms, 26 story. S, D $155; each additional $20; suites $209-$249. Pets accepted, some restrictions; fee. Check-out noon. TV; cable (premium), VCR available. Room service 24 hours. Restaurant, bar; entertainment. Heated pool. Cross-country ski 2 miles. Valet parking. Business center. Concierge. Connected by walkway to Edmonton Centre.

❄

★ **TOWER ON THE PARK HOTEL.** *9715 110th St (T5K 2M1). Phone 780/488-1626; toll-free 800/720-2179; fax 780/488-0659. toweronthepark.com.* 98 kitchen units, 14 story. 1-bedroom $100; 2-bedroom $120-$150; weekly, monthly rates. Pets accepted, some restrictions. Complimentary continental breakfast. Check-out noon. TV. Laundry services. Italian marble, mirrored lobby.

D ❄

Fort Macleod

Motel/Motor Lodge

★ **SUNSET MOTEL.** *104 Hwy 3W (T0L 0Z0). Phone 403/553-4448; toll-free 888/553-2784; fax 403/553-2784.* 22 rooms. D $54-$60; each additional $5. Pets accepted, some restrictions. Check-out 11 am, check-in 3 pm. TV. In-room modem link.

Jasper National Park

Motels/Motor Lodges

★★ **LOBSTICK LODGE.** *94 Geikie St (T0E 1E0). Phone 780/852-4431; toll-free 888/852-7737; fax 780/852-4142. www.mtn-park-lodges.com.* 139 rooms, 3 story. No A/C. June-Sept: S, D $187-$210; each additional $10; suites, kitchen. units $200-$225; under 15 free; MAP available; ski plans; lower rates rest of year. Pets accepted, some restrictions. Check-out 11 am, check-in 4 pm. TV; cable (premium). Restaurant, bar. Sauna, steam room. Pool; whirlpool. Downhill, cross-country ski 15 miles.

★★ **MARMOT LODGE.** *86 Connaught Dr (T0E 1E0). Phone 780/852-4471; toll-free 888/852-7737; fax 403/852-3280. www.mtn-park-lodges.com.* 106 rooms, 2 story. June-Sept: S, D $189-$233; each additional $10; suites $410-$420; under 16 free; ski plan; lower rates rest of year. Pets accepted, some restrictions. Check-out 11 am. TV. Restaurant, bar. Sauna. Pool; whirlpool. Downhill, cross-country ski 15 miles.

Resort

★★★ **THE FAIRMONT JASPER PARK LODGE.** *Old Lodge Rd (T0E 1E0). Phone 780/852-3301; fax 780/852-5107. www.fairmont.com.* This resort gives guests the option of a lake view or a mountain view. Guests can enjoy many outdoor adventures, including boating and rafting. 390 rooms. No A/C. Late May-mid-Oct: S, D $250-$750; each additional $25; under 18 free; MAP available; lower rates rest of year. Pets accepted, some restrictions; fee. Check-out noon, check-in 4 pm. TV. Fireplaces. Dining room, bar; entertainment. Room service. Supervised children's activities; ages 2 and up. In-house fitness room; massage; sauna, steam room. Game room. Pool; whirlpool. Outdoor tennis. Downhill, cross-country ski 11 miles. Lawn games, bicycles, boats, canoes, fishing. Airport transportation. Swimming. Whitewater rafting.

Lake Louise

Resort

★★★ **THE FAIRMONT CHATEAU LAKE LOUISE.** *111 Lake Louise Dr (T0L 1E0). Phone 403/522-3511; toll-free 800/441-1414; fax 403/522-3834. www.fairmont.com.* This hotel offers cozy accommodations with a Swiss alpine feel and a great mountain view. 487 rooms, 8 story. Mid-May-mid-Oct: S, D $569-$739; each additional $20; suites $1,089-$1,259; under 18 free; lower rates rest of year. Pets accepted, some restrictions; fee. Check-out noon. TV. Dining room, bar; entertainment. In-house fitness room, steam room. Indoor pool; whirlpool. Downhill, cross-country ski on site. Ice skating. Sleighing/sleigh rides. Airport transportation.

Lethbridge

Hotel

★★★ **LETHBRIDGE LODGE.** *320 Scenic Dr (T1J 4B4). Phone 403/328-1123; toll-free 800/661-1232; fax 403/328-0002. www.lethbridgelodge.com.* This hotel is located in downtown Lethbridge. It is built around a tropical courtyard. Guests can choose a room that has a courtyard or a city view. 154 rooms, 4 story. S $109-$129; D $124-$159; each additional $10; suites $149-$179; under 18 free. Pets accepted, some restrictions; fee. Check-out noon. TV. Restaurant, bar.

Medicine Hat

Motels/Motor Lodges

★★ **BEST WESTERN INN.** *722 Redcliff Dr (T1A 5A3). Phone 403/527-3700; toll-free 888/527-6633; fax 403/526-8689. www.bestwestern.com.* 122 rooms, 2 story. D $85-$229. Pets accepted, some restrictions. Complimentary continental breakfast. Check-out 11 am, check-in 3 pm. TV; cable (premium). Laundry services. Bar. In-house fitness room; sauna. Game room. Indoor pool; whirlpool.

★ ★ ★ **MEDICINE HAT LODGE.** *1051 Ross Glen Dr SE (T1B 3T8). Phone 403/529-2222; toll-free 800/661-8095; fax 403/529-1538. www.medhatlodge.com.* This lodge features one of the largest indoor waterparks in Canada, as well as a steam room, in-house fitness room, swimming pool, and wading pool. Conveniently located to most area attractions, guests can enjoy golfing, skiing, and hiking. 221 rooms, 4 story. S $89-$109; D $119-$154 suites $154-$169; under 18 free. Pets accepted, some restrictions. Check-out noon. TV; VCR available. In-room modem link. Restaurant, bar. Room service. Sauna. Pool; whirlpool.

D 🐕 🏊 🎿 ⛷ 🔲 SC

★ **SUPER 8.** *1280 Trans-Canada Way SE (T1B 1J5). Phone 403/528-8888; toll-free 800/800-8000; fax 403/526-4445. www.super8.com.* 70 rooms, 2-3 story. D $75-$88; each additional $4; under 12 free; weekly rates. Pets accepted, some restrictions; fee. Complimentary continental breakfast. Check-out 11 am, check-in 4 pm. TV. Indoor pool; whirlpool.

D 🐕 🏊 🔲

Red Deer

Motels/Motor Lodges

★ **HOLIDAY INN EXPRESS.** *2803 50th Ave (T4R 1H1). Phone 403/343-2112; toll-free 800/223-1993; fax 403/340-8540. www.holiday-inn.com.* 92 rooms, 2 story. S, D $109-$118; each additional $6; suites $140; under 18 free. Pets accepted, some restrictions; fee. Check-out 11 am. Check-in 3 pm. TV; cable (premium). In-room modem link. In-house fitness room; sauna. Pool; whirlpool. Downhill ski 10 miles, cross-country ski 3 miles. Courtyard.

D 🐕 🏊 🎿 🏃 ⛷ 🔲 SC

★ **NORTH HILL INN.** *7150 50th Ave (T4N 6A5). Phone 403/343-8800; toll-free 800/662-7152; fax 403/342-2334. www.northhillsinnreddear.com.* 116 rooms, 4 story. S $72; D $89-$105; under 18 free; weekend rates. Pets accepted, some restrictions. Check-out noon, check-in 2 pm. TV; cable (premium). Restaurant, bar. Room service. In-house fitness room; sauna. Pool; whirlpool. Downhill ski 10 miles, cross-country ski 3 miles. Business center.

D 🐕 🏊 🎿 ⛷ 🔲 🏃

★ **TRAVELODGE.** *2807 50th Ave (T4R 1H6). Phone 403/346-2011; toll-free 800/578-7878; fax 403/346-1075. www.travelodge.com.* 136 rooms, 10 kitchen units, 3 story. S $79; D $95; suites $120. Pets accepted, some restrictions. Check-out 11 am. Check-in 3 pm. TV. In-room modem link. Restaurant. Room service. In-house fitness room. Indoor pool; whirlpool. Downhill ski 10 miles, cross-country ski 3 miles.

D 🐕 🏊 🎿 🔲

Hotel

★ ★ **HOLIDAY INN.** *6500 67th St (T3P 1A2). Phone 403/342-6567; toll-free 800/661-4961; fax 403/343-3600. www.holidayinnreddear.com.* 97 rooms, 4 story. S, D $99-$129 suites $199-$249; under 18 free. Pets accepted, some restrictions; fee. Check-out 11 am. Check-in 3 pm. TV; cable (premium). Restaurant, bar. In-house fitness room, massage; sauna. Downhill ski 10 miles, cross-country ski 2 miles. Business center.

D 🐕 🏊 🎿 🔲 SC 🏃

British Columbia

Kamloops

Motels/Motor Lodges

★ **ACCENT INN KAMLOOPS.** *1325 Columbia St W (V2C 6P4). Phone 250/374-8877; fax 250/372-0507.* 83 rooms, 25 kitchen units, 3 story. S,D $109-$119; each additional $10; suites $120; kitchen units $99-$130; under 16 free; ski plans. Pets accepted, some restrictions; fee. Check-out 11 am. TV. In-room modem link. Restaurant open 24 hours. In-house fitness room; sauna. Heated pool; whirlpool. Cross-country ski 15 miles.

[D] [symbols]

★ ★ **THE COAST CANADIAN INN.** *339 St. Paul St (V2E 1J7). Phone 250/372-5201; fax 250/372-9363.* 94 rooms, 5 story. May-Sept: S $120; D $130; each additional $10; under 18 free; ski plans; lower rates rest of year. Pets accepted; fee. Check-out noon. TV; cable (premium), VCR available. In-room modem link. Restaurant, bar; entertainment. Room service. In-house fitness room. Health club privileges. Business center.

[D] [symbols] [SC]

★ **DAYS INN.** *1285 W Trans Canada Hwy (V2E 2J7). Phone 250/374-5911; toll-free 800/561-5002; fax 250/374-6922. www.daysinn.com.* 60 rooms. June-Sept: S $99; D $109; each additional $10; suites $125-$250; kitchen units. $150-$250; under 12 free; lower rates rest of year. Pets accepted; fee. Check-out noon. TV; cable (premium), VCR available. Restaurant 7 am-9 pm. Heated pool; whirlpool.

[D] [symbols]

★ ★ **HOSPITALITY INN.** *500 W Columbia St (V2C 1K6). Phone 250/374-4164; toll-free 800/663-5733; fax 250/374-6971.* 77 rooms, 2 story. June-Sept: S $92.50; D $96.50; each additional $6; kitchen units $6 additional; under 12 free; lower rates rest of year. Pets accepted; fee. Check-out 11 am. TV; cable (premium). Restaurant. Sauna. Pool; whirlpool.

[symbols]

★ **RAMADA INN.** *555 W Columbia St (V2C 1K7). Phone 250/374-0358; toll-free 800/663-2832; fax 250/374-0691. www.ramada.com.* 90 rooms, 12 kitchen units, 3 story. May-Sept: S $109; D $119; each additional $10;

suites $100-$175; kitchen units $10 additional; under 18 free; lower rates rest of year. Pets accepted, some restrictions; fee. Check-out 11 am. TV; cable (premium), VCR available. Restaurant, bar; entertainment. Room service. Health club privileges; sauna. Pool; whirlpool.

[D] [symbols]

Kelowna

Motels/Motor Lodges

★ **ACCENT INNS KELOWNA.** *1140 Harvey Ave (V1Y 6E7). Phone 250/862-8888; toll-free 800/663-0298; fax 250/862-8884.* 101 rooms, 12 suites, 26 kitchen units, 3 story. Mid-May-Sept: S $79-$119; D $89-$129; each additional $10; suites $120; kitchen units $109; under 16 free; lower rates rest of year. Pets accepted, some restrictions; fee. Check-out 11 am. TV. Restaurant. In-house fitness room; sauna. Heated pool; whirlpool.

[D] [symbols] [SC]

★ ★ **RAMADA LODGE HOTEL.** *2170 Harvey Ave (V1Y 6G8). Phone 250/860-9711; toll-free 800/665-2518; fax 250/860-3173. www.rpbhotels.com.* 135 rooms, 39 suites, 3 story. Mid-May-mid-Sept: S,D $99-$119; each additional $10; suites $110-$199; under 19 free; golf plans; lower rates rest of year. Pets accepted; fee. Check-out noon. TV; cable (premium). Restaurant open 24 hours. Bar. Room service. In-house fitness room. Indoor pool; whirlpool. 18-hole golf 4 miles.

[D] [symbols] [SC]

★ **SANDMAN HOTEL.** *2130 Harvey Ave (V1Y 6J8). Phone 250/860-6409; toll-free 888/526-1988; fax 250/860-7377. www.sandman.ca.* 120 rooms, 3 story. S $77-$87; D $85-$89; each additional $5; kitchen units $10 additional; under 12 free. Pets accepted, some restrictions; fee. Check-out noon. TV. Restaurant open 24 hours. Bar. Sauna. Pool; whirlpool.

[symbols] [SC]

Hotel

★ ★ ★ **COAST CAPRI HOTEL.** *1171 Harvey Ave (Hwy 97) (V1Y 6E8). Phone 250/860-6060; toll-free 800/663-1144; fax 250/762-3430. www.coasthotels.com.* Surrounded by mountains and orchards, this hotel is located near golf courses, water sports, and Lake Okanagan. 185 rooms, 4-7 story. May-Sept: S $125-$135; D $135-$145; each additional $10; suites $205; under 18 free; ski, golf plans; lower rates rest of year. Pets accepted; fee. Check-out noon. TV; VCR available. In-room modem link. Room service 24 hours. Restaurant, bar. Health club privileges. Heated pool; whirlpool; poolside service. Business center.

D ⬤🏊➰SC🏃

Nanaimo

Motel/Motor Lodge

★ **DAYS INN.** 809 Island Hwy S (V9R 5K1). Phone 250/754-8171; fax 250/754-8557. www.daysinn.com. 79 rooms, 16 kitchen units, 2 story. June-Sept: S $95; D $115; each additional $10; suites $145; kitchen units $85-$115; under 12 free; lower rates rest of year. Pets accepted; fee. Check-out 11 am. TV; cable (premium), VCR available. Restaurant. Room service. Indoor pool; whirlpool. Overlooking Nanaimo's inner harbor.

D ⬤🐕➰🏃➰

Hotel

★ ★ **COAST BASTION INN.** 11 Bastion St (V9R 2Z9). Phone 250/753-6601; fax 250/753-4155. www.coasthotels.com. 179 rooms, 14 story. Mid-May-mid-Sept: S $140-$165, D $150-$175; each additional $10; suites $198-$208; under 18 free; package plans; lower rates rest of year. Pets accepted; fee. Check-out 11 am. TV; cable (premium). Restaurant, bar. In-house fitness room; sauna.

D ⬤🐕➰🏃➰

Resorts

★ ★ ★ **FAIRWINDS SCHOONER COVE RESORT & MARINA.** 3521 Dolphin Dr (V9P 9J7). Phone 250/468-7691; toll-free 800/663-7060; fax 250/468-5744. www.fairwinds.bc.ca. Whether you enjoy golfing, boating, fishing, kayaking, or tennis, this resort can accommodate your vacation adventures. Located on the east coast of Vancouver Island, the Strait of Georgia provides a beautiful view while dining, golfing, or just relaxing. May-Oct: S, D $154; each additional $10; under 12 free; lower rates rest of year. Pets accepted, some restrictions; fee. Check-out noon. TV; VCR available(movies). Dining room 7 am-9 pm. Room service. Pool; whirlpool. Outdoor tennis. 405-slip marina, boat (rentals). Extensive landscaping; outstanding views.

D ⬤🐕➰🏃➰SC

★ ★ ★ **KINGFISHER OCEANSIDE RESORT AND SPA.** 4330 S Island Hwy (V9N 8R9). Phone 250/338-1323; toll-free 800/663-7929; fax 250/338-0058. www.kingfisherresortspa.com. 27 rooms, 2 story. S, D $100-$150. Pets accepted, some restrictions; fee. Check-out 11 am, check-in 3 pm. TV; cable (premium), VCR available, CD available. Restaurant, bar. In-house fitness

room; sauna, steam room. Pool; whirlpool. Golf, 18 holes. Outdoor tennis. Downhill skiing. Hiking trail. Business center. Concierge.

D ⬤🐕➰🏃➰

Penticton

Motels/Motor Lodges

★ **BEL-AIR MOTEL.** 2670 Skaha Lake Rd (V2A 6G1). Phone 250/492-6111; toll-free 800/766-5770; fax 250/492-8035. www.belairmotel.bc.ca. 42 rooms, 16 kitchen units, 2 story. Mid-June-mid-Sept: S $69-$79; D $69-$89; each additional $5; kitchen units $84-$98; lower rates rest of year. Pets accepted, some restrictions. Check-out 11 am. TV; cable (premium). Sauna. Heated pool; whirlpool.

🐕➰🏃➰

★ **RAMADA INN.** 1050 Eckhardt Ave W (V2A 2C3). Phone 250/492-8926; toll-free 800/665-4966; fax 250/492-2778. www.ramada.com. 50 rooms. Mid-May-mid-Sept: S, D $95; each additional $10; under 12 free; lower rates rest of year. Pets accepted; fee. Check-out 11 am. TV; cable (premium). Laundry services. Bar. Pool. Lawn games.

🐕➰➰

★ **SPANISH VILLA.** 890 Lakeshore Dr W (V2A 1C1). Phone 250/492-2922; toll-free 800/552-9199. 60 rooms, 45 kitchen units, 1-2 story. Mid-June-Sept: S $58-$108; D $68-$118; each additional $20; suites, kitchen units $80-$150; under 12 free; lower rates rest of year. Pets accepted, some restrictions; fee. Check-out 11 am. TV. In-room modem link. Indoor pool. Free airport transportation.

D ⬤🐕➰➰SC

Hotel

★ ★ ★ **PENTICTON LAKESIDE RESORT AND CONFERENCE CENTER.** 21 Lakeshore Dr W (V2A 7M5). Phone 250/493-8221; toll-free 800/663-9400; fax 250/493-0607. www.rpbhotels.com. This resort and conference center is located on the southern shore of the pristine Lake Okanagan. 204 rooms, 6 story. July-Aug: S, D $175-$195; each additional $15; under 16 free; golf plans; lower rates rest of year. Pets accepted, some restrictions; fee. TV; cable (premium). In-room modem link. Restaurant, bar; entertainment. Supervised children's activities (late May-Labor Day); ages 3-14. In-house fitness room; sauna. Indoor pool; whirlpool. Golf on premises. Downhill, cross-country ski 20 miles. Swimming in Lake Okanagan. Boat rides.

D ⬤🐕➰🏃➰

Revelstoke

Motel/Motor Lodge

★ **CANYON MOTOR INN.** *1911 Fraser Dr (V0E 2S0). Phone 250/837-5221; toll-free 877/837-5221; fax 250/837-3160.* 40 rooms, 12 kitchen units, 1-2 story. May-Oct: S $44-$76; D $50-$100; each additional $7; kitchen units $7 additional; lower rates rest of year. Pets accepted. Check-out 11 am. TV. Restaurant. Room service. Sauna. Downhill, cross-country ski 5 miles.

D ⊷ ⚓ ⚡ ✈ 🏃 ✈ ⊠

Vancouver

Motel/Motor Lodge

★ ★ **ACCENT INNS RICHMOND.** *10551 St. Edward Dr (V6X 3L8). Phone 604/273-3311; toll-free 800/663-0298; fax 604/273-9522. www.accentinns.com.* 206 rooms, 3 story. Mid-May-Sept: S $89-$124; D $99-$134; each additional $10; suites $120-$130; kitchen units. $10 additional; under 16 free; lower rates rest of year. Pets accepted; fee. Check-out 11 am. TV; VCR available (movies free). Restaurant. In-house fitness room. Free transportation.

D ⊷ 🏃 ✈ ⊠ SC

Hotels

★ ★ **BEST WESTERN SANDS BY THE SEA.** *1755 Davie St (Z6G 1W5). Phone 604/682-1831; toll-free 800/663-9400; fax 604/682-3546. www.rpbhotels.com.* 121 rooms, 5 story. Pets accepted; fee. Complimentary continental breakfast. Check-out noon, check-in 4 pm. TV. In-room modem link. Restaurant, bar. Room service. In-house fitness room; sauna. Beach. **$$**

D ⊷ 🏃 ✈ ⊠ SC

★ ★ ★ **CLUB INTRAWEST.** *1088 Burrard St (V6Z 2R9). Phone 604/331-1000; toll-free 800/663-9255; fax 604/893-7122. www.sheratonvancover.com.* 733 rooms, 25 story. Pets accepted; fee. Check-out noon, check-in 3 pm. TV; cable (premium), VCR available. Restaurant, bar. Babysitting services available. In-house fitness room, spa. Indoor pool; whirlpool. Business center. **$$$**

⊷ ⊠ 🏃 🏃

★ ★ ★ **THE FAIRMONT HOTEL VANCOUVER.** *900 W Georgia St (V6C 2W6). Phone 604/684-3131; toll-free 800/441-1414; fax 604/662-1929. www.fairmont.com.* The Fairmont Hotel echoes the vibrancy of its home city. This gracious hotel offers guests the perfect blend of history and cosmopolitan panache. Grand, yet inviting, it has been a preeminent destination since 1939, when it opened to celebrate the royal visit of King George VI and Queen Elizabeth. The guest rooms employ rich jewel tones and sumptuous fabrics to create a wonderful English castle ambience. The décor gives a nod to the past, but the dining and entertainment venues are cutting edge and are hotspots on the local scene. Business and fitness centers keep guests focused on goals, while world-renowned boutiques, including Louis Vuitton and St. John, tempt shoppers. 550 rooms, 14 story. Late April-early Oct: S $180-$340; D $205-$365; each additional $25; suites $305-$1,830; family, weekend rates; lower rates rest of year. Pets accepted; fee. Check-out noon. TV; cable (premium), VCR available. In-room modem link. Restaurant 6 am-10 pm, bar 11-1 am; entertainment. Room service 24 hours. In-house fitness room; sauna. Indoor pool; children's pool; whirlpool. Business center. Concierge. Luxury level.

D ⊷ ⚓ ⚡ ⊠ 🏃 🏃 ⊠ 🏃

★ ★ ★ **THE FAIRMONT VANCOUVER AIRPORT.** *3111 Grant McConachie Way (V7B 1X9). Phone 604/207-5200; toll-free 800/676-8922; fax 604/248-3219. www.fairmont.com.* Not the stereotypical airport hotel, this elegant property has technology-friendly and very comfortable guest rooms for busy international travelers. Rooms include complimentary high-speed Internet access and portable phones. Floor-to-ceiling soundproof windows offer great views of the mountains and Georgia Straits. This elegant full-service hotel offers a fully-equipped in-house fitness room, spa, dining room and lounge, and full concierge service. 392 rooms, 2 suites, 14 story. May-Oct: S, D $189-$299; each additional $20; suites $600; under 17 free; lower rates rest of year. Pets accepted, some restrictions; fee. Check-out noon, check-in 3 pm. TV; cable (premium), VCR available, CD available. Restaurant 6:30 am-11 pm, bar. Room service 24 hours. Sauna. Indoor pool; whirlpool. Bike rentals. Valet parking. Business center.

D ⊷ ⊠ 🏃 🏃 ⊠ ⊠

★ ★ ★ **THE FAIRMONT WATERFRONT.** *900 Canada Way (V6C 3L5). Phone 604/691-1991; fax 604/691-1838. www.fairmont.com.* Guests can enjoy mountain and harbor views from this hotel, which is located in downtown Vancouver near the cruise ship terminal. 489 rooms, 23 story. May-Oct: S, D $280-$395; each additional $25; suites $465-$1,700; under 18 free; lower rates rest of year. Pets accepted, some restrictions; fee. Check-out noon. TV; VCR available. In-room modem link. Restaurant 6:30 am-midnight. Bar; entertainment except Sun. Room service 24 hours. In-house fitness room. Heated pool; whirlpool; poolside service. Business center. Concierge. Luxury level.

D ⊷ ⊠ 🏃 🏃 ⊠ 🏃

★★★★ **FOUR SEASONS HOTEL VANCOUVER.** *791 W Georgia St (V6C 2T4). Phone 604/689-9333; toll-free 800/819-5053; fax 604/689-3466. www.fourseasons.com.* Impeccable service and an ideal location make the Four Seasons Hotel a natural choice in Vancouver. The city's vibrant arts and entertainment area is just a short walk from this hotel, situated above the shops of the Pacific Centre. The guest rooms are comfortably elegant. Moods are instantly brightened in the accommodations, where plaid and floral fabrics add a cheery feel and unencumbered views of the city, mountains, and harbor delight visitors. Fitness and business centers assist travelers with their needs, and the indoor-outdoor pool is an urban oasis with its flower-filled outdoor terrace. The signature restaurant, Chartwell, looked to Winston Churchill's favorite country home for its design influences, and the walnut-paneled walls, clubby furnishings, and parquet floors capture that spirit perfectly. Blooming plants and large windows impart a greenhouse atmosphere at the Garden Terrace, where patrons enjoy informal dining. *Secret Inspector's Notes:* The concierge service at the Four Seasons is impeccable; the staff is capable of suggesting such a variety of options for your pleasure that you may find it difficult to decide what to do. Although the bar makes for an excellent spot to enjoy an evening cocktail or beer, avoid Chartwell, as the staff is often disorganized and unprofessional, unusual and disappointing in a luxury hotel at which every other detail is close to perfect. 385 rooms, 28 story. D $315-$465; each additional $30; under 18 free. Pets accepted. Check-out noon. TV; cable (premium), VCR available (movies). In-room modem link. Room service 24 hours. Restaurant, bar. In-house fitness room; sauna. Pool; whirlpool. Downhill ski 10 miles. Business center. Concierge. Shuffleboard.

★★ **GOLDEN TULIP GEORGIAN COURT HOTEL.** *773 Beatty St (V6B 2M4). Phone 604/682-5555; toll-free 800/663-1155; fax 604/682-8830. www.georgiancourt.com.* 180 rooms, 12 story. Pets accepted; fee. Check-out 1 pm, check-in 3 pm. TV; cable (premium). In-room modem link. Restaurant, bar. Babysitting services available. In-house fitness room; sauna. Whirlpool. Parking. Concierge. Italian marble in bathrooms. **$$**

★★ **HOLIDAY INN.** *711 W Broadway (V5Z 3Y2). Phone 604/879-0511; toll-free 800/465-4329; fax 604/872-7520. holidayinnvancouver.com.* 196 rooms, 16 story. May-Oct: S $169-$189; D $179-$209; each additional $20; suites $275-$325; under 18 free; weekend rates; lower rates rest of year. Pets accepted. Check-out noon. TV. In-room modem link. Restaurant 7 am-10 pm, bar 11-1 am. In-house fitness room; sauna. Indoor pool.

★★★★ **METROPOLITAN HOTEL VANCOUVER.** *645 Howe St (V6C 2Y9). Phone 604/687-1122; toll-free 800/667-2300; fax 604/602-7846. www.metropolitan.com.* Wired for the new millennium, the Metropolitan Hotel Vancouver is the hotel of choice for executives, VIPs, and technology aficionados. This contemporary hotel makes it easy to stay in touch, with dual-line telephones, modem and fax jacks, and broadband Internet connections in all accommodations, and even in public spaces. Contemporary artwork adorns the walls of the guest rooms. Light woods and neutral colors result in a soothing ambience in the private spaces, and luxurious bed linens ensure a good night's sleep. Guests enjoy views of this beautiful city from the privacy of their rooms, and many of the suites feature balconies. A fitness center, indoor pool, and squash court are available, and the hotel's convenient location makes it popular with joggers and walkers who want to experience the city by foot. Diva at the Met earns bravos from diners who feast on sensational regional specialties. 197 rooms, 18 story. D $265-$310; each additional $20; under 18 free; weekend rates. Pets accepted. Covered parking. Check-out 1 pm. TV; cable (premium), VCR available. In-room modem link. Room service 24 hours. Restaurant, bar. Steam room. Indoor pool; whirlpool; poolside service. Business center. Concierge. Artwork, antiques; elaborate floral arrangements. Elegant Asian touches.

★★★ **PACIFIC PALISADES HOTEL.** *1277 Robson St (V6E 1C4). Phone 604/688-0461; toll-free 800/663-1815; fax 604/688-4374. www.pacificpalisades.com.* 233 suites, 20-23 story. Pets accepted; fee. Check-out noon, check-in 3 pm. TV; VCR available. In-room modem link. Room service 24 hours. Restaurant, bar; entertainment. In-house fitness room, spa; sauna. Indoor pool; whirlpool. Parking. Business center. Concierge. **$**

★★★ **PAN PACIFIC VANCOUVER.** *300-999 Canada Pl (V6C 3B5). Phone 604/662-8111; toll-free 800/937-1515; fax 604/685-8690. www.panpacific.com.* Awe-inspiring views take center stage at Vancouver's Pan Pacific Hotel, located on the waterfront. This contemporary hotel enjoys a serene setting on the harbor, yet is only minutes from the alluring shopping of Robson Street. The guest rooms are a testament to subtle luxury, with clean lines and neutral tones. Large windows look out over unobstructed, picture-perfect views of the mountains and sea, and many accommodations include private balconies for further enjoyment. Whether taking advantage of the fitness center or relaxing in the privacy of their accommodations, guests reap the rewards of the hotel's commitment to the latest technology. Diners traverse the world in the four distinctive restaurants, where sushi, Italian, and other international dishes tantalize taste buds. 504 rooms, 23 story. Pets accepted, some restrictions. Check-out noon, check-in 3 pm. TV; VCR available. Steam room. Room service 24 hours. Restaurant, bar. Babysitting services available. In-house fitness room, spa, massage, steam room; sauna. Outdoor pool; whirlpool. Sailing 6:30 am-11 pm. Business center. Concierge. **$$$**

D 🐾 🏊 🏃 🚭 🏃

★ ★ **QUALITY INN.** *1335 Howe St (V6Z 1R7). Phone 604/682-0229; toll-free 800/663-8474; fax 604/662-7566. www.qualityhotelvancouver.com.* 157 rooms, 7 story. Pets accepted; fee. Check-out 11 am, check-in 3 pm. TV. Restaurant, bar. Room service. Babysitting services available. Outdoor pool. **$**

D 🐾 🏊 🚭 SC

★ ★ ★ **RENAISSANCE VANCOUVER HARBOURSIDE HOTEL.** *1133 W Hastings (V6E 3T3). Phone 604/689-9211; toll-free 800/HOTELS-1; fax 604/689-4358. www.renaissancevancouver.com.* This hotel is located on the waterfront overlooking Vancouver Harbor, Burrard Inlet, and the North Shore Mountains and is easy walking distance to the Robson Street and the Pacific Centre shopping area. 438 rooms, 19 story. Pets accepted; fee. Check-out noon, check-in 3 pm. TV; cable (premium). In-room modem link. Restaurant, bar; entertainment. Babysitting services available. In-house fitness room; sauna. Indoor pool; whirlpool. **$$**

D 🐾 🐕 🏊 🚭 🏃 🚭

★ ★ ★ **THE WESTIN GRAND, VANCOUVER.** *433 Robson St (V6B 6L9). Phone 604/602-1999; toll-free 888/680-9393; fax 604-647-2502. www.westingrandvancouver.com.* All of Vancouver is within reach of the Westin Grand. This high-rise tower is perfectly located for business travelers conducting meetings or leisure visitors absorbing the local culture. Sleek and stylish, this all-suite property introduces visitors to the hip side of this western Canadian city. The accommodations define city chic with modern, polished-wood furnishings and floor-to-ceiling windows with skyline vistas. Guests never leave behind the comforts of home here, where all suites feature well-stocked kitchenettes. The hotel caters to the sophisticated, and many services, including the fitness center, are offered 24 hours daily. Diners feast on Pacific Rim dishes at the Aria Restaurant & Lounge and dance the night away at the fashionable Club Voda. 207 rooms, 31 story. Pets accepted; fee. Check-out noon, check-in 3 pm. TV; CD available. Restaurant, bar. Room service 24 hours. Babysitting services available. In-house fitness room;

sauna, steam room. Outdoor pool; whirlpool. Downhill skiing. Bicycles, hiking. Business center. Concierge. **$$**

D 🐾 🐕 🏃 🏊 🚭 🏃 🚭 🏃

Resort

★ ★ **RAMADA PLAZA.** *10251 St. Edward's Dr (V6X 2M9). Phone 604/278-9611; toll-free 800/268-1133; fax 604/276-1121.* 438 rooms, 15 and 21 story. Apr-Oct: S, D $200-$300; each additional $15; suites $299-$1,000; under 18 free; lower rates rest of year. Pets accepted, some restrictions; fee. Check-out noon. TV. In-room modem link. Room service 24 hours. Restaurant, bar. Supervised children's activities, ages 5-12. In-house fitness room; massage; sauna. Three pools, one indoor, whirlpool; poolside service. Outdoor tennis, lighted courts, indoor tennis. Business center. Squash courts.

D 🐾 🏊 🏃 🎾 🖑 🚭 🏃 🎾 ✈ 🚭 🏃

B&B/Small Inn

★ ★ ★ **RIVER RUN COTTAGES.** *4551 River Rd W (V4K 1R9). Phone 604/946-7778; fax 604/940-1970. www.riverruncottages.com.* Located on the Fraser River Delta, this bed-and-breakfast allows guests to experience a tranquil and relaxing getaway. Kayaks, canoes and rowboats are available for guests to venture out to watch eagles, seals, otters, and beavers in their natural environment. Guests can pack a picnic and enjoy a romantic getaway on No Name Island. 4 rooms, 1 story. Pets accepted; fee. Complimentary full breakfast. Check-out noon, check-in 4 pm. Bicycles available. On river. Totally nonsmoking. **$**

🐾 🚭

Victoria

Motel/Motor Lodge

★ **ACCENT INN.** *3233 Maple St (V8X 4Y9). Phone 250/475-7500; toll-free 800/663-0298; fax 250/475-7599. www.accentinns.com.* 118 rooms, 3 story. Pets accepted, some restrictions; fee. Check-out 11 am, check-in 2 pm. TV. In-room modem link. Restaurant. Health club privileges. **$**

D 🐾 🚭 SC

Hotels

★ ★ **BEST WESTERN CARLTON PLAZA HOTEL.** *642 Johnson St (V8W 1M6). Phone 250/388-5513; toll-free 800/663-7241; fax 250/388-5343. www.bestwesterncarlton.com.* 103 rooms, 47 kitchen units, 6 story. Pets accepted; fee. Check-out 11 am, check-in 3 pm. TV; cable (premium). In-room modem link. Restaurant. In-house fitness room. Health club privileges. Valet parking. **$**

D 🐾 🖑 🏃

★ ★ **CHATEAU VICTORIA HOTEL AND SUITES.**
740 Burdett Ave (V8W 1B2). Phone 250/382-4221; toll-free 800/663-5891; fax 250/380-1950. www.chateauvictoria.com. 177 rooms, 49 kitchen units, 19 story. Pets accepted, some restrictions; fee. Check-out 11 am, check-in 3 pm. TV; cable (premium), VCR available (movies). In-room modem link. Restaurant, bar. In-house fitness room. Indoor pool; whirlpool. Free parking. **$**

D ⊁ ⊱ ⋉ ⊠

★ ★ ★ **COAST HARBOURSIDE HOTEL & MARINA.** *146 Kingston St (V9B 5X3). Phone 250/ 360-1211; toll-free 800/663-1144; fax 250/360-1418. www.coasthotels.com.* Located just blocks from downtown, this hotel offers a beautiful harbor view. 140 rooms, 10 story. Pets accepted; fee. Check-out 11 am, check-in 4 pm. TV; VCR available. In-room modem link. Restaurant, bar. Room service. Babysitting services available. In-house fitness room; sauna. Indoor pool; outdoor pool; whirlpool. Concierge. **$**

D ⊁ ⊱ ⋉ ⊁ ✈ ⊠

★ ★ **EXECUTIVE HOUSE HOTEL.** *777 Douglas St (V8W 2B5). Phone 250/388-5111; toll-free 800/663-7001; fax 250/385-1323. executivehouse.com.* 181 rooms, 17 story. Pets accepted, some restrictions; fee. Check-out noon, check-in 3 pm. TV. Restaurant, bar; entertainment. In-house fitness room, massage; sauna, steam room. Whirlpool. **$**

⊁ ⋉

★ ★ ★ **THE FAIRMONT EMPRESS.** *721 Government St (V8W 1W5). Phone 250/384-8111; toll-free 800/441-1414; fax 250/381-5959. www.fairmont.com.* This restored heritage hotel is described as "the Grande Dame of the Pacific Northwest" and overlooks Victoria's busy inner harbor. It is near many attractions, including the Convention Center, Parliament Buildings, the Royal British Columbia Museum, and many shops and restaurants. 477 rooms, 7 story. No A/C. Pets accepted, some restrictions; fee. Check-out 11 am, check-in 4 pm. TV; cable (premium), VCR available. In-room modem link. Restaurant, bar; entertainment except Sun. In-house fitness room; spa; sauna. Indoor pool; children's pool; whirlpool. Opened in 1908. **$$**

D ⊁ ⊱ ⋉ ⊠

★ ★ **HARBOUR TOWERS HOTEL & SUITES.** *345 Quebec St (V8V 1W4). Phone 250/385-2405; toll-free 800/ 663-5896; fax 250/480-6593. www.harbourtowers.com.* 195 rooms, 72 kitchen units, 12 story. No A/C. Pets accepted, some restrictions; fee. Complimentary continental breakfast. Check-out 11 am. TV; cable (premium). In-room modem link. Laundry services. Restaurant, bar. Room service. Children's activity center, babysitting services available. In-house fitness room, spa; sauna. Indoor pool; whirlpool. Airport transportation. Business center. Luxury level. Totally nonsmoking. **$**

D ⊁ ⊱ ⋉ ⊁ ⊱ ⋉

★ ★ ★ **HOTEL GRAND PACIFIC.** *463 Belleville St (V8V 1X3). Phone 250/386-2421; toll-free 800/663-7550; fax 250/380-4489. www.hotelgrandpacific.com.* 304 rooms, 10 story. Pets accepted, some restrictions; fee. Check-out noon, check-in 3 pm. TV; VCR available. Restaurant, bar. Babysitting services available. In-house fitness room, spa. Indoor pool; whirlpool. Massage; sauna. Free parking. In-room modem link. **$$**

D ⊁ ⊱ ⋉ ⊠ **SC**

★ ★ ★ **LAUREL POINT INN.** *680 Montreal St (V8V 1Z8). Phone 250/386-8721; toll-free 800/663-7667; fax 250/386-9547. www.laurelpoint.com.* 200 rooms, 3 story. Pets accepted, some restrictions; fee. Check-out 11:30 am, check-in 3 pm. TV; VCR available. In-room modem link. Restaurant, bar. Babysitting services available. Indoor pool; whirlpool. Tudor-Style hotel (1927); some four-poster beds, many antiques. **$$$**

D ⊁ ⊱ ⊥ ⋉ ⊁ ⊱ ⊠

★ ★ ★ **MAGNOLIA HOTEL AND SPA.** *623 Courtney St (V8W 1B8). Phone 250/381-0999; toll-free 877/624-6654; fax 250/381-0988. www.magnoliahotel.com.* This boutique hotel is located downtown just 1 block from the Inner Harbour and within walking distance of shops and the conference center. 63 rooms, 7 story. Pets accepted, some restrictions; fee. Complimentary continental breakfast. Check-out noon, check-in 3 pm. TV; cable (premium), VCR available. Restaurant, bar. Babysitting services available. In-house fitness room, spa. Valet parking. **$$**

D ⊁ ⊱ ⊥ ⋉ ⊠

Resort

★ ★ ★ **DELTA VICTORIA OCEAN POINTE RESORT AND SPA.** *45 Songhees Rd (V9A 6T3). Phone 250/360-2999; toll-free 888/244-8666; fax 250/360-1041. www.oprhotel.com.* Situated on Victoria's Inner Harbour, this hotel offers guests a wide array of activities to enjoy. Take a ferry ride to downtown Victoria for shopping adventures or book an excursion to view the area's whales, sea lions, and porpoises. 242 rooms, 7 suites, 8 story. Pets accepted, some restrictions. Check-out noon, check-in 3 pm. TV; VCR available. In-room modem link. Restaurant, bar. Room service 24 hours. Children's activity center, babysitting services available. In-house fitness room, spa; sauna. Outdoor pool. Outdoor tennis, lighted courts. Business center. Concierge. On harbor. **$$**

D ⊁ ⊱ ⊥ ⊁ ⋉ ⊱ ⋉ ⊠ ⋉

B&B/Small Inns

★ ★ ★ **ENGLISH INN & RESORT.** *429 Lampson St (V9A 5Y9). Phone 250/388-4353; toll-free 866/388-4353; fax 250/382-8311. www.englishinnresort.com.* 40 rooms, 6 kitchen units, 3 story. Pets accepted, some restrictions; fee. Complimentary continental breakfast. Check-out 11 am, check-in 3 pm. TV. Restaurant, bar. Children's activity center, babysitting services available. Replica of Shakespeare's 16th-century birthplace on grounds. **$$**

★ ★ ★ **SOOKE HARBOUR HOUSE.** *1528 Whiffen Spit Rd (V0S 1N0). Phone 250/642-3421; toll-free 800/ 889-9688; fax 250/642-6988. www.sookeharbourhouse .com.* Located on Vancouver Island by the sea, this bed-and-breakfast features beautifully designed guest rooms with fireplaces and spectacular ocean views. Guests can enjoy such area activities as hiking, whale watching and cross-country skiing. Ideal for a romantic getaway. 28 rooms, 4 story. No A/C. Closed 3 weeks in Jan. Pets accepted; fee. Complimentary continental breakfast. Check-out noon, check-in 3 pm. TV; cable (premium), VCR available (movies). Restaurant. Room service. Babysitting services available. Massage. Totally nonsmoking. **$$$**

★ **SPINNAKERS GUESTHOUSE.** *308 Catherines St (V9A 3S8). Phone 250/386-2739; fax 250/384-3246. www.spinnakers.com.* 11 rooms. Pets accepted, some restrictions; fee. Complimentary breakfast. Check-out 11 am, check-in 3 pm. Restaurant, bar. No credit cards accepted. **$**

Whistler

Hotels

★ ★ **BEST WESTERN LISTEL WHISTLER HOTEL.** *4121 Village Green (V0N 1B4). Phone 604/ 932-1133; toll-free 800/663-5472; fax 604/932-8383. www.listelhotel.com.* 98 rooms, 3 story. Pets accepted; fee. Check-out 10 am, check-in 4 pm. TV. Restaurant, bar. Babysitting services available. Sauna. Outdoor pool; whirlpool. Downhill skiing, cross-country ski adjacent. Valet parking. **$$**

★ ★ **CRYSTAL LODGE.** *4154 Village Green (V0N 1B0). Phone 604/932-2221; toll-free 800/667-3363; fax 604/932-2635. www.crystal-lodge.com.* 137 rooms, 2-3

story. Pets accepted, some restrictions; fee. Check-out 11 am, check-in 4 pm. TV; cable; VCR available. Laundry services. Restaurant, bar; entertainment. In-house fitness room, steam room. Outdoor pool; whirlpool; poolside service. Downhill, cross-country ski adjacent. Garage parking. Airport transportation. Concierge. **$**

Resorts

★ ★ ★ **DELTA WHISTLER RESORT.** *4050 Whistler Way (V0N 1B4). Phone 604/932-1982; toll-free 888/244-8666; fax 888/315-1515. www.deltahotels.com.* 288 rooms, 99 kitchen units, 8 story. Pets accepted, some restrictions; fee. Check-out 11 am, check-in 4 pm. TV; cable (premium). Restaurant, bar. Babysitting services available. In-house fitness room, spa, steam room. Outdoor pool; whirlpool; poolside service. Indoor tennis. Downhill, cross-country ski adjacent. Concierge.

★ ★ ★ **THE FAIRMONT CHATEAU WHISTLER.** *4599 Chateau Blvd (V0N 1B4). Phone 604/938-8000; toll-free 800/606-8244; fax 604/938-2291. www.fairmont.com.* 550 rooms, 10-12 story. Pets accepted, some restrictions; fee. Check-out noon, check-in 4 pm. TV. Room service 24 hours. Restaurant, bar; entertainment. Supervised children's activities (June-Sept). Babysitting services available. In-house fitness room, spa; sauna. Indoor pool; outdoor pool; children's pool; whirlpool. Golf on premises, greens fee. Outdoor tennis, lighted courts. Downhill, cross-country ski adjacent. Valet parking. Concierge. **$$**

All Suite

★ **SUMMIT LODGE.** *4359 Main St (V0N 1B4). Phone 604/932-2778; toll-free 888/913-8811; fax 604/932-2716. www.summitlodge.com.* 81 rooms, 4 story. Pets accepted, some restrictions; fee. Complimentary continental breakfast. Check-out 11 am, check-in 4 pm. TV; cable (premium), VCR available. Restaurant. Babysitting services available. In-house fitness room; sauna. Outdoor pool; whirlpool. Downhill skiing. Business center. Concierge. Free airport transportation. **$$**

Manitoba

Brandon

Motels/Motor Lodges

★ **COMFORT INN.** *925 Middleton Ave (R7C 1A8). Phone 204/727-6232; fax 204/727-2246. www.choicehotels.ca.* 81 rooms, 2 story. Apr-Oct: S $79-$85; D $89-$95; each additional $4; under 18 free; weekend rates; lower rates rest of year. Pets accepted, some restrictions. Check-out 11 am. TV. In-room modem link.

D ⛷ ☃ SC

★ ★ **ROYAL OAK INN & SUITES.** *3130 Victoria Ave (R7B 0N2). Phone 204/728-5775; toll-free 800/852-2709; fax 204/726-2709. www.royaloakinn.com.* 96 rooms, 2 story. S $89.99; D, suites $109.99-$114.99; package plans. Pets accepted, some restrictions; fee. Check-out noon. TV; VCR available. Laundry services. Restaurant, bar. In-house fitness room. Indoor pool; children's pool; whirlpool; poolside service.

D ⛷ ☃ ☂ ☃

★ ★ ★ **VICTORIA INN.** *3550 Victoria Ave (R7B 2R4). Phone 204/725-1532; fax 204/727-8282. www.victoriainn.ca.* 131 rooms, 2 story. S, D $89.99; suites $99.99; studio rooms $75-$125; under 18 free; package plans. Pets accepted; fee. Check-out noon. TV. In-room modem link. Restaurant, bar. Room service. In-house fitness room; sauna. Indoor pool; whirlpool; poolside service.

D ⛷ ☃ ☂ ☃ SC

Winnipeg

Motels/Motor Lodges

★ ★ **BEST WESTERN VICTORIA INN.** *1808 Wellington Ave (R3H 0G3). Phone 204/786-4801; toll-free 800/928-4067; fax 204/786-1329. www.bestwestern.com.* 288 rooms, 5 story. S $79; D $84; suites $175; under 16 free. Pets accepted, some restrictions; fee. Check-out noon. TV. In-room modem link. Restaurant, bar. Room service. Indoor pool; whirlpool; poolside service. Free airport transportation.

⛷ ☃ ☂ ☃ SC

★ **COMFORT INN.** *1770 Sargent Ave (R3H 0C8). Phone 204/783-5627; fax 204/783-5661. www.hotelchoice.com.* 81 rooms, 2 story. Mid-June-mid-Sept: S, D $85-$95; each

additional $10; under 18 free; weekend rates; lower rates rest of year. Pets accepted, some restrictions. Check-out 11 am. TV. In-room modem link.

D ⛷ ☃ ☃

★ ★ **COUNTRY INN & SUITES BY CARLSON.** *730 King Edward St (R3H 1B4). Phone 204/783-6900; fax 204/775-7197. www.countryinns.com.* 77 suites, 3 story. S $65-$95; D $75-$105; each additional $10; under 18 free; weekend rates. Pets accepted. Complimentary continental breakfast. Check-out noon. TV; cable (premium), VCR (free movies). Laundry services.

D ⛷ ☃ ☃

★ ★ **HOLIDAY INN.** *1330 Pembina Hwy (R3T 2B4). Phone 204/452-4747; toll-free 800/423-1337; fax 204/284-2751. www.hi-winnipeg.mb.ca.* 170 rooms, 11 story. S $159; D $179; each additional $10; suites $250; under 19 free; weekend rates. Pets accepted. Check-out noon. TV; VCR available. In-room modem link. Restaurant, bar. Room service. In-house fitness room. Indoor pool; children's pool; whirlpool; poolside service. Free airport transportation.

D ⛷ ☃ ☂ ☃

Hotels

★ ★ **RADISSON HOTEL DOWNTOWN.** *288 Portage Ave (R3C 0B8). Phone 204/956-0410; fax 204/947-1129. www.radisson.com.* 272 rooms, 29 story. S, D $129-$199; each additional $15; suites $229; under 18 free; weekend rates. Pets accepted. Check-out 1 pm. TV; cable (premium), VCR available. In-room modem link. Room service 24 hours. Restaurant, bar. In-house fitness room; sauna. Indoor pool; poolside service. Business center. Concierge.

D ⛷ ☃ ☂ ☃ ☂

★ ★ ★ **SHERATON WINNIPEG HOTEL.** *161 Donald St. (R3C 1M3). Phone 204/942-5300; toll-free 800/463-6400; fax 204/943-7975. www.sheraton.com.* This hotel is conveniently located three blocks from the convention center. 271 rooms, 21 story. S $130-$145; D $140-$155; under 18 free; weekend rates. Pets accepted, some restrictions; fee. Check-out noon. TV; cable (premium). In-room modem link. Room service 24 hours. Restaurant, bar. Health club privileges. Sauna. Indoor pool; whirlpool. Underground, valet parking. Concierge.

D ⛷ ☃ ☃

New Brunswick

Fredericton

Motels/Motor Lodges

★ ★ **RAMADA INN.** *480 Riverside Dr (E3B 5E3). Phone 506/460-5500; toll-free 800/596-4656; fax 506/472-0170. www.ramada.com.* 116 rooms, 2 story. S $65-$76; D $74-$79; each additional $8; suites $136; under 18 free. Pets accepted, some restrictions. Check-out noon. TV; cable (premium), VCR available. In-room modem link. Restaurant, bar. Room service. In-house fitness room; sauna. Pool; whirlpool; poolside service. Indoor tennis. Downhill ski 10 miles, cross-country ski 5 miles. Lawn games. Airport transportation.

$\boxed{D}$ ⬛ ⬛ ⬛ ⬛ ⬛ ⬛ ⬛

★ ★ **WANDLYN INN.** *958 Prospect St (E3B 4Y9). Phone 506/462-4444; toll-free 506/561-0000; fax 506/452-7658. www.wandlyn.com.* 100 rooms, 3 story. S, D $70-$99; studio rooms $75-$100; each additional $10; suites $125-$199; under 18 free. Pets accepted, some restrictions; fee. Check-out 11 am. TV; cable (premium), VCR available. Laundry services. Restaurant, bar. Sauna. Indoor pool; outdoor pool; whirlpool; poolside service.

⬛ ⬛

Hotel

★ ★ ★ **LORD BEAVERBROOK HOTEL.** *659 Queen St (E3B 5A6). Phone 506/455-3371; fax 506/455-1441. www.lordbeaverbrookhotel.com.* Located on the banks of the majestic Saint John River, this convenient downtown hotel is one of the finest the city has to offer. 168 rooms, 7 story. S $139; D $149; each additional $10; suites $90-$150; under 19 free; package plans. Pets accepted, some restrictions. Check-out noon. TV; VCR available. In-room modem link. Restaurant, bar; entertainment. Supervised children's activities. Sauna. Game room. Pool; children's pool; whirlpool; poolside service. Bicycle, boat, canoe rentals. Airport transportation. Concierge. Docking facilities.

$\boxed{D}$ ⬛ ⬛ ⬛ ⬛

Moncton

Motels/Motor Lodges

★ ★ **COLONIAL INN.** *42 Highfield St (E1C 8T6). Phone 506/382-3395; toll-free 800/561-4667; fax 506/858-*

8991. www.colonial-inn.com. 61 rooms, 1-2 story. S $62 D $68; each additional $5; studio rooms $75; under 16 free. Pets accepted, some restrictions. Check-out noon-2 pm. TV. Restaurant open 24 hours. Bar. Room service. Sauna. Pool; whirlpool.

⬛ ⬛ ⬛ **SC**

★ **ECONO LODGE.** *1905 W Main St (E1E 1H9). Phone 506/382-2587; fax 506/858-5998. www.econolodge.com.* 67 rooms, 2 story. S $59; D $79; each additional $5; studio rooms $79; kitchen units $89; each additional $5; under 12 free; weekly rates. Pets accepted, some restrictions. Check-out 11 am. TV. Restaurant, bar. Pool.

$\boxed{D}$ ⬛ ⬛ ⬛ ⬛ ⬛

★ **RODD PARK HOUSE INN.** *434 Main St (E1C 1B9). Phone 506/382-1664; fax 506/855-9494. www.rodd-hotels.ca.* 97 rooms, 4 story. S $79; D $99; each additional $10; under 19 free. Pets accepted, some restrictions. Check-out noon. TV; cable (premium). Restaurant, bar. Pool.

⬛ ⬛

Hotel

★ ★ ★ **DELTA BEAUSEJOUR.** *750 Main St (E1C 1E6). Phone 506/854-4344; fax 506/858-0957. www.deltahotels.com.* 310 rooms, 9 story. S, D $109-$151; each additional $15; suites $240-$950; under 18 free; weekend rates. Pets accepted, some restrictions; fee. Check-out noon. TV; cable (premium). In-room modem link. Room service 24 hours. Restaurant, bar. In-house fitness room. Pool; poolside service. Concierge.

$\boxed{D}$ ⬛ ⬛ ⬛ ⬛ ⬛

St. Andrews

Motels/Motor Lodges

★ **SEASIDE BEACH RESORT.** *339 Water St (E5B 2R2). Phone 506/529-3846; toll-free 800/506-8677; fax 506/529-4479. www.seaside.nb.ca.* 24 rooms, 1-2 story. No A/C. No room phones. June-Labor Day: S, D $65-$75; each additional $5; weekly rates; lower rates May, early Sept-Oct. Closed rest of year. Pets accepted, some restrictions; fee. Check-out 11 am. TV. Laundry services. Overlooks bay.

$\boxed{D}$ ⬛ ⬛ ⬛ ⬛

★ **ST. STEPHEN INN.** *99 King St (E3L 2C6). Phone 506/466-1814; toll-free 800/565-3088; fax 506/466-6148.* 52 rooms, 2 story. July-Dec: S $65; D $80; each additional $8; under 17 free; lower rates rest of year. Pets accepted; fee. TV; VCR available. Restaurant.

⬛

★ **TRAVELODGE.** *310 Mowat Dr (E5B 2P3). Phone 506/529-3245; toll-free 877/534-5271.* 39 rooms. May-Oct: S $45-$55; D $55-$75; each additional $7; kitchen units $5 additional; under 6 free. Closed rest of year. Pets accepted, some restrictions; fee. Check-out 11 am. TV.

Hotel

★ ★ ★ **KINGSBRAE ARMS.** *219 King St (E5B 1Y1). Phone 506/529-1897; fax 506/529-1197. www.kingsbrae.com.* Fresh sea air and heady fragrances from the garden leave an indelible mark on guests of Kingsbrae Arms. Nestled in the historic resort of St. Andrew's in the Atlantic Maritime Provinces of eastern Canada, this winsome country house hotel speaks to travelers celebrating special occasions. Cherished memories are created in this intimate hotel, where eight rooms set the mood for romance with canopy beds, fireplaces, and balconies with enchanting views of the formal garden and the crashing sea beyond. Guests greet the morning with hearty country breakfasts before setting out for sea kayaking or whale-watching adventures or simply strolling through the adjacent 27-acre public Kingsbrae Garden. Whether gathering for cocktails and hors d'oeuvres in the library or under the shade of an umbrella, or savoring each bite of a four-course dinner enhanced by fresh herbs and vegetables from the garden, gourmet dining is the centerpiece here. 8 rooms, 3 story. Mid-Mar-mid-Oct: S, D $225; suites $250-$350; package plans; weekends 2-day minimum; lower rates rest of year. Pets accepted, some restrictions. Children over 9 years only. Complimentary full breakfast; afternoon refreshments. Check-out noon, check-in 3 pm. TV; VCR available (movies). In-room modem link. Fireplaces. Room service 24 hours. Bar. Health club privileges. Pool. Lawn games. Airport transportation. Business center. Concierge. Totally nonsmoking.

Resort

★ ★ ★ **THE ALGONQUIN.** *184 Adolphus St (E5B 1T7). Phone 506/529-8823; fax 506/529-7162.* This seaside resort overlooks Passamaquoddy Bay and offers guests an array of recreation, including an in-house fitness room, tennis, racquetball, squash; saunas, heated outdoor pool, whirlpool, and golf. Several rooms have fully equipped kitchens. 250 rooms, 4 story. Mid-May-mid-Oct: S, D $119-$219; each additional $20; suites $189-$369; under 18 free. Pets accepted, some restrictions; fee. Check-out noon, check-in 4 pm. TV; VCR available. Fireplaces. Laundry services. Restaurant, bar; entertainment. Room service. Supervised children's activities (mid-Jun-Aug); ages 12 and under. In-house fitness room; sauna; whirlpool. 18-hole golf, pro, putting green, greens fee $25-$39. Tennis. Aerobics. Lawn games. Bicycle rentals. Free parking. Concierge. On hill; view of water from most rooms.

St. John

Motels/Motor Lodges

★ ★ **COLONIAL INN.** *175 City Rd (E2L 3T5). Phone 506/652-3000; toll-free 800/561-4667; fax 506/658-1664.* 94 rooms, 2 story. S $65; D $71; each additional $6; suites $85; under 18 free. Pets accepted, some restrictions. Check-out noon-2 pm. TV. Restaurant open 24 hours. Bar. Room service. Sauna. Pool; whirlpool.

★ ★ **HOTEL COURTENAY BAY.** *350 Haymarket Sq (E2L 3P1). Phone 506/657-3610; toll-free 800/563-2489; fax 506/633-1773.* 125 rooms, 5 story. S $59-$69; D $69-$79; each additional $8; under 18 free. Pets accepted, some restrictions. Check-out 1 pm. TV; cable (premium). Laundry services. Restaurant, bar. Room service. Pool.

Hotels

★ ★ **DELTA BRUNSWICK.** *39 King St (E2L 4W3). Phone 506/648-1981; toll-free 800/268-1133; fax 506/658-0914. www.deltahotels.com.* 255 rooms, 5 story. May-mid-Oct: S, D $125-$135; each additional $10; suites $135-$500; studio rooms $135-$145; under 18 free; lower rates rest of year. Pets accepted, some restrictions. Check-out 1 pm. TV. Room service 24 hours. Restaurant, bar. Free supervised children's activities (weekends), over age 2. In-house fitness room; sauna, steam room. Game room. Indoor pool; whirlpool. Covered parking; valet. Covered walkway to downtown offices, Market Square.

★ ★ ★ **HILTON ST. JOHN.** *1 Market Sq (E2L 4Z6). Phone 506/693-8484; toll-free 800/561-8282; fax 506/657-6610. www.hilton.com.* Located on the historic waterfront and connected to the convention center and historic market, this hotel is within walking distance of Saint John's major venues. 197 rooms, 12 story. May-Sept: S, D $109-$149; each additional $15; suites $305-$439; lower rates rest of year. Pets accepted, some restrictions; fee. Check-out noon. TV. Restaurant, bar; entertainment. Health club privileges. In-house fitness room; sauna. Game room. Indoor pool; whirlpool. Cross-country ski 2 miles. Business center. Concierge. Underground access to Market Square shopping mall. Harbor view.

Nova Scotia

Antigonish

Motels/Motor Lodges

★ ★ **BEST WESTERN CLAYMORE INN.** *Church St (B2G 2M5). Phone 902/863-1050; toll-free 800/565-1234; fax 902/863-1238. www.bestwestern.com.* 76 rooms, 3 story. July-mid-Oct: S $77-$85; D $99-$119; each additional $10; under 18 free; lower rates rest of year. Pets accepted, some restrictions. Check-out noon. TV. Restaurant, bar. In-house fitness room; sauna. Indoor pool; whirlpool. Downhill, cross-country ski 7 miles.

★ ★ **MARITIME INN ANTIGONISH.** *158 Main St (B2G 2B7). Phone 902/863-4001; toll-free 888/662-7484; fax 902/863-2672. www.maritimeinns.com.* 34 rooms, 2 story. Mid-June-mid-Oct: S, D $103-$145; each additional $10; suites $124-$145; under 12 free; lower rates rest of year. Pets accepted, some restrictions. Check-out 11 am. TV. Restaurant, bar.

Hotel

★ ★ **HEATHER HOTEL AND CONVENTION CENTRE.** *Foord St (B0K 1S0). Phone 902/752-8401; toll-free 800/565-4500; fax 902/755-4580. www.heatherhotel.com.* 77 rooms, 2 story. S $64-$89; D $69-$99; each additional $10; under 12 free. Pets accepted; fee. Check-out noon. TV. Restaurant, bar. Room service. Cross-country ski 5 miles.

Dartmouth

Motel/Motor Lodge

★ ★ **RAMADA INN.** *240 Brownlow Ave (B3B 1X6). Phone 902/468-8888; fax 902/468-8765. www.ramada.com.* 178 rooms, 5 story, 31 suites. May-Oct: S $150-$180; D $160-$190; each additional $10; suites $129; under 15 free; package plans; lower rates rest of year. Pets accepted, some restrictions; fee. TV. Restaurant, bar. In-house fitness room; sauna. Indoor pool; children's pool; whirlpool. Cross-country ski 1 mile. Business center.

Hotel

★ ★ **HOLIDAY INN.** *101 Wyse Rd (B3A 1L9). Phone 902/463-1100; toll-free 800/465-4329; fax 902/464-1227. www.holiday-inn.com.* 196 rooms, 7 story. May-Oct: S, D $129-$139; each additional $10; suites $195-$395; under 19 free; weekend rates; lower rates rest of year. Pets accepted, some restrictions; fee. Check-out noon. TV. In-room modem link. Restaurant, bar. Health club privileges. Pool. Cross-country ski 15 miles. Airport transportation.

Digby

Motels/Motor Lodges

★ ★ **ADMIRAL DIGBY INN.** *441 Shore Rd (B0V 1A0). Phone 902/245-2531; toll-free 800/465-6262; fax 902/245-2533. www.digbyns.com.* 46 rooms. Mid-June-mid-Sept: S, D $99-$110; each additional $10; kitchen cottages $135; under 12 free; lower rates Apr-mid-June and mid-Sept-Oct. Closed Nov-Mar. Pets accepted, some restrictions. Check-out 11 am. TV. Laundry services. Restaurant, bar. Pool. Overlooks Annapolis Basin.

★ ★ **COASTAL INN KINGFISHER.** *111 Warwick St (B0V 1A0). Phone 902/245-4747; toll-free 800/401-1155; fax 902/245-4866.* 36 rooms. S $84; D $89; each additional $8; under 10 free; some lower rates. Pets accepted, some restrictions. Check-out 11 am. TV. Laundry services. Restaurant.

Resort

★ ★ **MOUNTAIN GAP INN.** *217 Hwy 1 (B0V 1A0). Phone 902/245-5841; toll-free 800/565-5020; fax 902/245-2277. www.mountaingap.ns.ca.* 96 rooms. No A/C. Mid-May-mid-Oct: S, D $90; each additional $10; kitchen units, kitchen cottages $159-$199; under 18 free; weekly rates. Closed rest of year. Pets accepted, some restrictions. Check-out 11 am, check-in 2 pm. TV; VCR available (movies). Dining room, bar. Game room. Pool. Tennis. Private beach. Lawn games. Bicycle rentals. Rustic setting on 45 acres.

Grand Pre

Motels/Motor Lodges

★ **GREENSBORO INN.** *9016 Commercial St (B4N 3E2). Phone 902/681-3201; fax 902/681-3399.*

www.greensboroinn.com. 26 rooms, 1 kitchen unit. Mid-May-Oct: S $70; D $70-$90, kitchen unit $110; under 18 free; each additional $6; lower rates rest of year. Pets accepted, some restrictions; fee. Check-out 11 am. TV. Indoor pool. Downhill, cross-country ski 20 miles.

★ ★ ★ **WANDLYN INN.** *7270 Hwy 1 (B4R 1B9). Phone 902/678-8311; fax 902/679-1253. www.wandlyn.com.* 70 units, 3 story. Mid-June-Oct: S $85-$110; D $95-$120; each additional $10; suites $110-$125; under 18 free; lower rates rest of year. Pets accepted, some restrictions; fee. Check-out 11 am, check-in 3 pm. TV; VCR available. Restaurant, bar. Indoor pool.

Resort

★ ★ **OLD ORCHARD INN.** *Hwy 101, exit 11 (B0P 1X0). Phone 902/542-5751; toll-free 800/561-8090; fax 902/542-2276. www.oldorchardinn.com.* 105 rooms, 3 story. May-Oct: S, D $115-$125; each additional $8; suites $150; cabins $59-$64 (with kitchen $15 additional); family rates; ski plans. Pets accepted, some restrictions; fee. Check-out 11 am, check-in 3 pm. TV. Dining room, bar. Supervised children's activities (winter); ages 5-12. Sauna. Indoor pool. Lighted tennis. Downhill ski 20 miles, cross-country ski on site. Lawn games. Sleigh rides.

Halifax

Motels/Motor Lodges

★ **GRAND VIEW.** *Black Point (B0J 1B0). Phone 902/857-9776; toll-free 881/591-5122. www.grandviewmotelandcottages.com.* 13 rooms, 10 kitchen units. No A/C. No room phones. Mid-June-early Sept: S, D $55-$85; each additional $10; cottages $95-$110; under 5 free; weekly rates; lower rates rest of year. Pets accepted, some restrictions; fee. Check-out 10:30 am. TV.

★ ★ **HOLIDAY INN.** *1980 Robie St (B3H 3G5). Phone 902/423-1161; toll-free 800/465-4329; fax 902/423-9069. www.holiday-inn.com.* 232 rooms, 14 story. S, D $125-$149.95; each additional $10; suites $195-$225; under 19 free; weekend rates. Pets accepted. Check-out 1 pm. TV. In-room modem link. Restaurant, bar. Room service. Health club privileges. In-house fitness room; sauna. Indoor pool; children's pool; whirlpool; poolside service. Indoor parking. Business center.

★ **SEASONS MOTOR INN.** *4 Melrose Ave (B3N 2E2). Phone 902/443-9341; toll-free 800/792-2498; fax 902/443-9344.* 37 rooms, 4 story. June-Oct: S $70; D $80; each additional $5; under 12 free; lower rates rest of year. Pets accepted, some restrictions. Complimentary continental breakfast. Check-out 11 am. TV.

Hotels

★ ★ ★ **AIRPORT HOTEL.** *60 Bell Blvd (B2T 1K3). Phone 902/873-3000; toll-free 800/667-3333; fax 902/873-3001.* 151 rooms, 3 story. No elevator. May-Nov: S $124; D, kitchen units $134; each additional $10; suites $160; under 18 free; lower rates rest of year. Pets accepted, some restrictions. Check-out noon. TV. In-room modem link. Restaurant, bar. Room service. In-house fitness room; sauna. Indoor pool; outdoor pool; whirlpool. Free airport transportation.

★ ★ ★ **CASINO NOVA SCOTIA HOTEL.** *1919 Upper Water St (B3J 3J5). Phone 902/421-1700; fax 902/422-5805. www.casinonovascotia.com.* This hotel is the home of the only Halifax casino and is located right downtown. 352 rooms, 6 story. S, D $94-$335; each additional $20; suites $335-$1,100; under 18 free. Pets accepted. Check-out noon. TV. In-room modem link. Restaurant, bar; entertainment. In-house fitness room; sauna. Indoor pool; whirlpool. Parking. Business center. Concierge.

★ ★ ★ **CITADEL HALIFAX HOTEL.** *1960 Brunswick St (B3J 2G7). Phone 902/422-1391; fax 902/429-6672. www.citadelhalifax.com.* This downtown hotel is located at the base of the historic Fort Citadel. 264 rooms, 7 and 11 story. S, D $139-$189; each additional $15; suites $250-$305; weekend rates; under 18 free. Pets accepted, some restrictions. Check-out 1 pm. TV. In-room modem link. Restaurant, bar. In-house fitness room; sauna. Indoor pool; whirlpool; poolside service. Business center.

★ ★ ★ **DELTA BARRINGTON.** *1875 Barrington St (B3J 3L6). Phone 902/429-7410; fax 902/420-6524. www.deltahotels.com.* 202 rooms, 4 story. S, D $189-$249; each additional $15; suites $289-$475; under 18 free; weekend rates; some lower rates. Pets accepted. Check-out 1 pm. TV. In-room modem link. Restaurant, bar. Room service. In-house fitness room; sauna. Indoor pool; whirlpool.

★ ★ ★ **DELTA HALIFAX.** *1990 Barrington St (B3J 1P2). Phone 902/425-6700; fax 902/425-6214. www.deltahotels.com.* 300 rooms, 8 story. S, D $109-$389; each additional $20; suites $195-$400; under 18 free. Pets accepted, some restrictions. Check-out noon. TV. Restaurant, bar. In-house fitness room; sauna. Heated pool; whirlpool. Valet parking. Business center. On Halifax Harbour.

⬛🈳🏊🏃🚶

★ ★ **HOWARD JOHNSON.** *20 St. Margaret's Bay Rd (B3N 1J4). Phone 902/477-5611; fax 902/479-2150. www.hojo.com.* 135 rooms, 9 story. S, D $79-$139; each additional $10; suites $109-$199; kitchen units $57-$99; under 19 free; lower rates rest of year. Pets accepted. Complimentary continental breakfast. Check-out noon. TV; VCR available. In-room modem link. Restaurant, bar. Sauna. Indoor pool.

🈳🏊

★ ★ **LORD NELSON HOTEL.** *1515 S Park St (B3J 2L2). Phone 902/423-6331; fax 902/423-7148. www.lordnelsonhotel.com.* 243 rooms, 9 story. S, D $79-$109; each additional $15; suites $199-$220; under 18 free. Pets accepted; fee. Check-out 1 pm. TV.

⬛🈳⚓🈳🏊

★ ★ ★ **PRINCE GEORGE HOTEL.** *1725 Market St (B3J 3N9). Phone 902/425-1986; toll-free 800/565-7567; fax 902/429-6048. www.princegeorgehotel.com.* This downtown hotel is a favorite for business and leisure travelers alike. Guest rooms have mahogany furnishings and are laid out to accommodate the needs of the business traveler. A covered walkway connects the hotel to the World Trade & Convention Centre, the Halifax Metro Centre, and the Halifax Casino. 203 rooms, 6 story. S, D $149-$270; suites $250-$550; under 18 free. Pets accepted. Check-out 1 pm. TV; cable (premium), VCR available. Restaurant. Room service. In-house fitness room. Indoor pool; poolside service. Business center. Concierge.

⬛🈳⚓🈳🏊🏃🈳🚶

Resort

★ ★ ★ **OAK ISLAND RESORT AND SPA.** *51 Vaughan Rd (B0J 3M0). Phone 902/627-2600; toll-free 800/565-5075; fax 902/627-2020. www.oakislandinn.com.* This hotel overlooks Mahone Bay and its many islands, including the famous Oak Island, rumored to be the hiding place of Captain Kidd's buried treasure. In addition to the many activities offered at the hotel, it is close to many others, such as Peggy's Cove, theaters, museums, golf, ocean kayaking, and whale watching. 120 rooms, 3 story. No elevator. June-Sept: S, D $79-$89; each additional $15; suites $54-$209; under 16 free; weekend rates; lower rates

rest of year. Pets accepted, some restrictions; fee. Check-out noon, check-in 3 pm. TV; cable (premium), VCR available. Dining room, bar. Room service. Sauna. Indoor pool; whirlpool; poolside service. Tennis. Cross-country ski 1 mile. Lawn games. Fishing guides, charter boats. Hiking. Business center.

⬛🈳🏊🈳🏊🈳🏃

B&B/Small Inn

★ **FRESH START.** *2720 Gottingen St (B3K 3C7). Phone 902/453-6616; toll-free 888/453-6616; fax 902/453-6617. www.bbcanada.com/2262.html.* 8 rooms, 2-3 story. No A/C. Room phones available. Pets accepted, some restrictions. Complimentary full breakfast. Check-out 1 pm, check-in 4 pm. TV in sitting room; VCR available. Victorian house (1880). Maritime Command Museum opposite. Totally nonsmoking. **$**

🈳🈳

Peggy's Cove

Motel/Motor Lodge

★ ★ **WINDJAMMER.** *4070 Hwy 3 (B0J 1J0). Phone 902/275-3567.* 18 rooms. Mid-June-mid-Sept: S, D $50-$65; each additional $6; under 12 free; lower rates rest of year. Pets accepted. Check-out 11 am. TV; VCR available.

⬛🈳⚓🈳🏊

Truro

Motel/Motor Lodge

★ **PALLISER MOTEL.** *103/104 Tidal Bore Rd (B2N 5B3). Phone 902/893-8951.* 42 rooms. No A/C. No room phones. Early May-late-Oct: S $45; D $53; each additional $7. Closed rest of year. Pets accepted. Complimentary continental breakfast. Check-out 11 am. TV. Restaurant, bar.

⬛🈳

Yarmouth

Motels/Motor Lodges

★ **BEST WESTERN MERMAID.** *545 Main St (B5A 1J6). Phone 902/742-7821; toll-free 800/528-1234; fax 902/742-2966. www.bestwestern.com.* 45 rooms, 2 story. No A/C. June-Oct: S, D $110-$170; each additional $8; kitchen units $110-$135; under 18 free; lower rates rest of year.

Pets accepted. Check-out 11 am. TV. Laundry services. Pool. Business center.

★ **LAKELAWN MOTEL.** *641 Main St (B5A 1K2). Phone 902/742-3588; toll-free 877/664-0664.* 31 rooms, 2 story. No room phones. July-Sept: S, D $64-$79; each additional $5; under 12 free; lower rates May-June, Oct. Closed rest of year. Pets accepted, some restrictions. Check-out 11 am. TV. Free airport transportation. Full breakfast available.

★ ★ **RODD COLONY HARBOUR INN.** *6 Forest St (B5A 3K8). Phone 902/742-9194; toll-free 800/565-7633; fax 902/742-6291. www.rodd-hotels.ca.* 65 rooms, 4 story. May-Sept: S $85; D $95; under 16 free; suites $101; lower rates rest of year. Pets accepted. TV; VCR available (movies). Restaurant, bar. Room service. Health club privileges. Airport transportation.

Hotel

★ ★ ★ **RODD GRAND YARMOUTH.** *417 Main St (B5A 4B2). Phone 902/742-2446; toll-free 800/565-7633; fax 902/742-4645. www.rodd-hotels.ca.* This hotel is located in the downtown core of Yarmouth. Many of the guest rooms have views of the waterfront. 138 rooms, 7 story. June-Oct: S, D $95-$105; each additional $10; suites $120-$130; under 16 free; lower rates rest of year. Pets accepted. Check-out 11 am. TV. In-room modem link. Restaurant, bar. In-house fitness room. Indoor pool. Free airport transportation. Business center.

Ontario

Brantford

Motel/Motor Lodge

★ ★ **DAYS INN.** *460 Fairview Dr (N3R 7A9). Phone 519/759-2700; fax 519/759-2089. www.daysinn.com.* 75 rooms, 2 story. Apr-Oct: S $91.95-$101.95; D $98.95-$101.95; each additional $7; under 12 free; weekly, weekend rates; lower rates rest of year. Pets accepted. Check-out 11 am. TV; cable (premium). In-room modem link. Restaurant. Health club privileges.

D 🐾 ⇟ SC

Brockville

Motel/Motor Lodge

★ ★ **BEST WESTERN WHITE HOUSE MOTEL.** *1843 Hwy 2 E (K6V 5T1). Phone 613/345-1622; fax 613/345-4284. www.bestwestern.com.* 56 rooms. S $67; D $72-$77; each additional $5. Pets accepted, some restrictions; fee. Complimentary continental breakfast. Check-out 11 am. TV. In-room modem link. Restaurant. Pool.

D 🐾 ≈ ⇟ SC

Cornwall

Motel/Motor Lodge

★ ★ **BEST WESTERN PARKWAY INN & CONFERENCE CENTRE.** *1515 Vincent Massey Dr (Hwy 2) (K6H 5R6). Phone 613/932-0451; fax 613/938-5479.* 91 rooms, 2 story. S $86; D $110-$145; each additional $6; suites $200; under 18 free. Pets accepted, some restrictions. Check-out noon. TV; cable (premium). In-room modem link. Restaurant, bar. In-house fitness room; sauna. Pool; whirlpool. Cross-country ski 2 miles.

🐾 ≈ ⇟ 🏋 ⇟ SC

Hamilton

Motels/Motor Lodges

★ ★ **HOWARD JOHNSON.** *112 King St E (L8N 1A8). Phone 905/546-8111; fax 905/546-8144. www.hojo.com.* 206 rooms, 11 story. S $99; D $109; each additional $10; suites from $139; under 18 free; weekend rates. Pets accepted, some restrictions; fee. Check-out noon. TV; cable (premium), VCR available. Room service 24 hours. Restaurant open 24 hours. Bar. In-house fitness room; sauna. 124-foot (38-meter) pool slide. Indoor pool; whirlpool.

D 🐾 ≈ 🏋 ⇟ SC

★ **RAMADA INN.** *150 King St E (L8N 1B2). Phone 905/528-3451; fax 905/522-2281. www.ramada.com.* 215 rooms, 12 story. S, D $69-$110; each additional $10; suites $187.50-$325; under 19 free. Pets accepted, some restrictions; fee. Check-out 11 am. TV; VCR available. Restaurant, bar. Health club privileges. In-house fitness room; sauna. Pool; children's pool; whirlpool.

D 🐾 ≈ 🏋 ⇟ SC

★ **TRAVELODGE.** *2020 Lakeshore Rd (L7S 1Y2). Phone 905/681-0762; fax 905/634-4398. www.travelodge.com.* 122 rooms, 7 story. S $95; D $105; each additional $10; suites $159; under 18 free. Pets accepted, some restrictions; fee. TV. Bar; entertainment. Sauna. Indoor pool; whirlpool.

D 🐾 🛍 ≈ ⇟ SC

Hotel

★ ★ ★ **SHERATON HAMILTON HOTEL.** *116 King St W (L8P 4V3). Phone 905/529-5515; fax 905/529-8266. www.sheraton.com.* Eight miles from the Hamilton airport, this hotel is located downtown. Nearby is the famous Royal Botanical Gardens. 299 rooms, 18 story. S, D $185-$200; each additional $15; suites from $225; under 17 free; weekend rates. Pets accepted. Check-out noon. TV; cable (premium). In-room modem link. Restaurant, bar; entertainment. Room service. Health club privileges. In-house fitness room; sauna. Indoor pool; whirlpool. Downhill, cross-country ski 4 miles. Parking, fee. Business center. Direct access to Convention Centre and Hamilton Place Concert Hall.

D 🐾 ≈ 🏋 ⇟ SC 🏃

Kenora

Motels/Motor Lodges

★ **COMFORT INN.** *1230 Hwy 17E (P9N 1L9). Phone 807/468-8845; toll-free 800/228-5150; fax 807/468-1588. www.comfortinn.com.* 77 rooms, 2 story. Mid-June-mid-Sept: S $70-$90; D $75-$100; each additional $4; under 18 free; lower rates rest of year. Pets accepted, some restrictions. Check-out 11 am. TV.

D 🐾 🏊 ☒ SC

★ ★ **TRAVELODGE.** *800 Sunset Strip (P9N 1L9). Phone 807/468-3155; fax 807/468-4780. www.travelodge.com.* 42 rooms, 5 kitchen units, 1-2 story. Mid-June-mid-Sept: S $75-$80; D $75-$104; lower rates rest of year. Pets accepted, some restrictions. Check-out noon. TV; cable (premium). Restaurant, bar. Room service. Health club privileges. In-house fitness room; sauna. Indoor pool; outdoor pool; whirlpool. Downhill, cross-country ski 6 miles.

D 🐾 🏊 🏖 🏋 ☒ SC

Kingston

Motels/Motor Lodges

★ **FIRST CANADA INN.** *1 First Canada Ct (K7K 6W2). Phone 613/541-1111; fax 613/549-5735.* 74 rooms, 2 story. June-Sept: S, D $61.95-$99.95; each additional $5; suites $85.95-$165.95; under 12 free; lower rates rest of year. Pets accepted, some restrictions. Complimentary continental breakfast. TV; VCR available (movies).

D 🐾 ☒ SC

★ ★ **HOWARD JOHNSON.** *237 Ontario St (K7L 2Z4). Phone 613/549-6300; fax 613/549-1508. www.hojo.com.* 94 rooms, 6 story. May-late Sept: S, D $99-$160; each additional $10; suites $225-$250; under 18 free; higher rates special events; lower rates rest of year. Pets accepted; fee. Check-out 11 am. TV. Restaurant. Room service. Health club privileges. In-house fitness room. Pool; whirlpool; poolside service. Cross-country ski 3 miles. Underground free parking. On waterfront.

🐾 🏊 🏖 🏋 ☒ SC

★ **KNIGHTS INN.** *2327 Princess St (Hwy 2) and Sybenham Rd (K7M 3G1). Phone 613/531-8929. www.knightsinn.com.* 32 rooms. May-Labour Day: S $48; D $58-$78; each additional $7; kitchen units $7 additional; lower rates rest of year. Pets accepted; fee. Check-out 11 am. TV. Pool.

D 🐾 🏊 ☒ SC

★ **SEVEN OAKES.** *2331 Princess St (Hwy 2) (K7M 3G1). Phone 613/546-3655; fax 613/546-0293.* 40 rooms. June-Sept: S $64; D $68-$74; each additional $5; package plans; lower rates rest of year. Pets accepted, some restrictions. Check-out 11 am. Laundry services. Bar. Sauna. Pool; whirlpool. Lighted tennis.

🐾 🏋 🏊 ☒ SC

Kitchener-Waterloo

Motels/Motor Lodges

★ **COMFORT INN.** *220 Holiday Inn Dr (N3C 1Z4). Phone 519/658-1100; fax 519/658-6979. www.comfortinn.com.* 84 rooms, 2 story. S $59-$80; D $67-$95; each additional $4; under 18 free. Pets accepted, some restrictions. Check-out 11 am. TV; cable (premium). Downhill, cross-country ski 4 miles.

🐾 ☒ ☒ SC

★ ★ **FOUR POINTS BY SHERATON.** *105 E King St (N2G 2K8). Phone 519/744-4141; fax 519/578-6889. www.sheraton.com.* This hotel is located in the business district. The famous Kitchener Farmers' Market is connected to the hotel. 201 rooms, 9 story. S, D $119-$139; each additional $10; suites $130-$269; studio rooms $79; under 18 free; weekend package. Pets accepted, some restrictions; fee. Check-out noon. TV; cable. In-room modem link. Restaurant, bar. In-house fitness room; sauna. Game room. Pool; whirlpool; poolside service. Miniature golf. Downhill, cross-country ski 4 miles. Free covered parking. Business center.

D 🐾 🏊 🏖 🏋 ☒ SC 🚶

★ ★ **HOLIDAY INN.** *30 Fairway Rd S (N2A 2N2). Phone 519/893-1211; fax 519/894-8518. www.holiday-inn.com.* 182 rooms, 2-6 story. S $125.95-$145.95; D $136.95-$156.95; each additional $10; suites $205.95-$305.95; under 19 free. Pets accepted, some restrictions; fee. Check-out noon. TV; cable (premium). In-room modem link. Restaurant, bar. Supervised children's activities (July-Aug). In-house fitness room. Indoor pool; outdoor pool; poolside service. Downhill, cross-country ski 2 miles.

D 🐾 🏊 🏖 🏋 ☒ SC

★ ★ **HOWARD JOHNSON.** *1333 Weber St E (N2A 1C2). Phone 519/893-1234; fax 519/893-2100. www.hojo.com.* 102 rooms, 2-4 story. S $89-$109; D $99-$129; each additional $10; under 18 free; higher rates Oktoberfest. Pets accepted, some restrictions; fee. Check-out 11:30 am. TV. Restaurant, bar; entertainment Thurs-Sat. Room service. Sauna. Pool; whirlpool; poolside service. Business center.

D 🐾 🏊 ☒ SC 🚶

★ ★ ★ **WATERLOO INN.** *475 King St N (N2J 2Z5). Phone 519/884-0220; toll-free 800/361-4708; fax 519/884-0321. www.waterlooinn.com.* This inn is close to the famous St. Jacob's Farmers Market, the Elora Gorge, and the Stratford Festival. 155 rooms, 4 story. S $93; D $103; each additional $12; suites from $125; under 16 free. Pets accepted; fee. TV. In-room modem link. Room service 24 hours. Restaurant, bar. In-house fitness room; sauna. Game room. Indoor pool; whirlpool; poolside service. Downhill ski 10 miles, cross-country ski 1/2 mile. Landscaped courtyard.

[D] [icons] SC

Hotel

★ ★ ★ **LANGDON HALL COUNTRY HOUSE.** *RR 33 (N3H 5R8). Phone 519/740-2100; fax 519/740-8161. www.langdonhall.ca.* This inn has been restored and decorated with period furniture and feather beds. 43 rooms, 3 story. 2-day minimum: S, D $229-$269; suites $369; under 10 free. Pets accepted, some restrictions. Complimentary continental breakfast. Check-out noon. TV; cable (premium), VCR available. In-room modem link. Room service 24 hours. Restaurant, bar. In-house fitness room, massage; sauna, steam room. Pool; whirlpool; poolside service. Outdoor tennis. Downhill ski 4 miles, cross-country ski on site. Lawn games. Hiking trail. Antebellum-style building in a rural setting.

[D] [icons]

London

Motel/Motor Lodge

★ ★ **BEST WESTERN LAMPLIGHTER INN & CONFERENCE CENTRE.** *591 Wellington Rd (N6C 4R3). Phone 519/681-7151; toll-free 888/232-6747; fax 519/681-3271. www.bestwestern.com.* 126 rooms, 2 story. S $79; D $109; each additional $8; suites $119-$209; under 12 free. Pets accepted, some restrictions; fee. Check-out 11 am. TV. Restaurant, bar. Pool.

[D] [icons] SC

Hotels

★ ★ **DELTA LONDON ARMOURIES HOTEL.** *325 Dundas St (N6B 1T9). Phone 519/679-6111; fax 519/679-3957. www.deltahotels.com.* 250 rooms, 20 story. S $189; D $199; each additional $10; suites $250-$450; under 18 free; weekend rates. Pets accepted, some restrictions. Check-out noon. TV; cable (premium), VCR available (movies). Restaurant, bar. Supervised children's activities

(July and Aug, daily; rest of year, Fri-Sun); ages 5-12. Health club privileges. In-house fitness room; sauna. Indoor pool; children's pool; whirlpool. Valet parking. Business center. Concierge. Luxury level.

[D] [icons] SC

★ ★ ★ **HILTON LONDON ONTARIO.** *300 King St (N6R 1S2). Phone 519/439-1661; toll-free 800/210-9336; fax 519/439-9672. www.hilton.com.* 331 rooms, 22 story. S, D $135-$155; suites $300; under 18 free; weekend rates. Pets accepted, some restrictions; fee. Check-out 1 pm. TV; VCR available. In-room modem link. Restaurant, bar; entertainment. Health club privileges. In-house fitness room; sauna. Pool; children's pool; whirlpool. Concierge. Luxury level.

[D] [icons] SC

Mississauga

Motels/Motor Lodges

★ **COMFORT INN.** *2420 Surveyor Rd (L5N 4E6). Phone 905/858-8600; fax 905/858-8574. www.comfortinn.com.* 117 rooms, 2 story. June-Sept: S $69-$74; D $74-$84; each additional $5; under 18 free; package plans; lower rates rest of year. Pets accepted; fee. Complimentary continental breakfast. Check-out 1 pm. TV; cable (premium). Laundry services. Game room. Downhill, cross-country ski 15 miles.

[icons] SC

★ ★ **DELTA TORONTO AIRPORT WEST.** *5444 Dixie Rd (L4W 2L2). Phone 905/624-1144; toll-free 800/737-3211; fax 905/624-9477. www.fourpoints.com/torontoairport.* 296 rooms, 10 story. S, D $99-$209; each additional $15; suites $225-$395; under 18 free; package plans. Pets accepted. Check-out 1 pm. TV; cable (premium), VCR available. In-room modem link. Restaurant, bar. Supervised children's activities; ages 2-12. In-house fitness room; sauna. Game room. Pool. Garage parking. Free airport transportation. Business center.

[D] [icons] SC

★ ★ **HOLIDAY INN.** *100 Britannia Rd (L4Z 2G1). Phone 905/890-5700; fax 905/568-0868. www.holiday-inn.com.* 132 rooms, 6 story. S, D $145; each additional $8; under 20 free. Pets accepted, some restrictions; fee. Check-out noon. TV; cable (premium), VCR available. In-room modem link. Restaurant, bar. Room service. In-house fitness room; sauna. Whirlpool. Free airport transportation.

[D] [icons] SC

★ ★ **NOVOTEL.** *3670 Hurontartio St (L5B 1P3). Phone 905/896-1000; fax 905/896-2521.* 325 rooms, 14 story. S, D $169-$189; each additional $15; suite $250; under 16 free; weekend rates. Pets accepted, some restrictions; fee. Check-out 1 pm. TV; cable (premium). In-room modem link. Restaurant, bar. In-house fitness room. Health club privileges. Indoor pool. Covered parking. Free airport transportation.

D ⬛🐾🏊🏋️🚫 SC

★ ★ **QUALITY INN.** *5599 Ambler Dr (L4W 3Z1). Phone 905/624-9500; toll-free 866/247-6204; fax 905/624-1382. www.qualityinn.com.* 222 rooms, 6 story. S $85; D $95; under 18 free; suites $115. Pets accepted, some restrictions. Complimentary breakfast. Check-out noon. TV. Laundry services. Restaurant, bar. Indoor pool; whirlpool. Free airport transportation.

D 🐾🏊🚫 SC

Hotels

★ ★ **DELTA MEADOWVALE RESORT & CONFERENCE CENTRE.** *6750 Mississauga Rd (L5N 2L3). Phone 905/821-1981; fax 905/542-4036. www.deltahotels.com.* 374 rooms, 15 story. S, D $190-$205; each additional $15; suites $150-$300; under 18 free. Pets accepted, some restrictions. Check-out 1 pm. TV; cable (premium), VCR available. Room service 24 hours. Restaurant, bar. Supervised children's activities; ages 2-14. In-house fitness room. Indoor pool; outdoor pool; whirlpool; poolside service. Indoor tennis. Airport transportation.

D 🐾🎿🏊🏋️🚫 SC

★ ★ ★ **HILTON TORONTO AIRPORT.** *5875 Airport Rd (L4V 1N1). Phone 905/677-9900; fax 905/677-5073. www.hilton.com.* 413 rooms, 11 story. S, D $165-$185; each additional $20; suites $185-$225; family rates; weekend packages. Pets accepted, some restrictions. Check-out noon. TV. Restaurant, bar; entertainment. In-house fitness room; sauna. Pool; poolside service. Garage parking. Free airport transportation. Business center.

D 🐾🏊🏋️✈️🚫 SC 🧗

Niagara Falls

Motel/Motor Lodge

★ **PILGRIM MOTOR INN.** *4955 Clifton Hill (L2G 3N5). Phone 905/374-7777; toll-free 800/471-4913; fax 905/354-8086.* 40 rooms, 3 story. Pets accepted, some restrictions. Check-out noon, check-in 1 pm. TV.

🐾🚫 SC

Ottawa

Hotels

★ ★ **DELTA OTTAWA HOTEL & SUITES.** *361 Queen St (K1R 7F9). Phone 613/238-6000; fax 613/238-2290. www.deltahotels.com.* 328 rooms, 18 story. May-June, Sept-Oct: S, D $155-$175; each additional $15; suites $180-$200; under 18 free; weekend rates; special summer rates; lower rates rest of year. Pets accepted; fee. Check-out noon. TV. In-room modem link. Restaurant, bar. Room service. In-house fitness room; sauna. Indoor pool; whirlpool. Downhill, cross-country ski 12 miles. Business center. Luxury level.

D 🐾🏊🏋️🚫 SC 🧗

★ ★ **LORD ELGIN HOTEL.** *100 Elgin St (K1P 5K8). Phone 613/235-3333; toll-free 800/267-4298; fax 613/235-3223. www.lordelginhotel.ca.* 311 rooms, 11 story. S $115-$160; D $120-$170; each additional $5; suites $180-$200; under 18 free; weekend rates. Pets accepted, some restrictions. Check-out 1 pm. TV. In-room modem link. Restaurant, bar. In-house fitness room. Downhill, cross-country ski 12 miles. Originally opened in 1941; completely renovated.

D 🐾🏊🏋️🚫 SC

★ ★ ★ **MARRIOTT OTTAWA.** *100 Kent St (K1P 5R7). Phone 613/238-1122; fax 613/783-4229. www.marriott.com.* This hotel is located only a block from a pedestrian street mall. 478 rooms, 26 story. S, D $125-$155; each additional $10; suites $300-$400; under 19 free; weekend rates. Pets accepted, some restrictions. Check-out 1 pm. TV; cable (premium). In-room modem link. Restaurant, dining room, bar. In-house fitness room; sauna. Indoor pool; whirlpool. Downhill ski 15 miles. Luxury level.

D 🐾🏊🏋️🚫 SC

★ ★ ★ **TAWA HOTEL.** *150 Albert St (K1P 5G2). Phone 613/238-1500; toll-free 800/489-8333; fax 613/235-2723. www.sheraton.com.* This hotel is located within walking distance of the Canadian Parliament Buildings. 236 rooms, 18 story. S $200; D $215; each additional $20; suites $280-$450; family rates; package plans. Pets accepted, some restrictions. Check-out noon. TV. In-room modem link. Restaurant. In-house fitness room; sauna. Indoor pool; poolside service. Downhill, cross-country ski 12 miles. Business center. Luxury level.

D 🐾🎿🏊🏋️🚫 SC 🧗

★ ★ ★ **THE WESTIN OTTAWA.** *11 Colonel By Dr (K1N 9H4). Phone 613/560-7000; fax 613/234-5396. www.westin.com.* Located only blocks from the historic

Byward Market, this hotel is connected to the Rideau Center Shopping Complex and the Ottawa Congress Center. 484 rooms, 24 story. Mid-Apr-June, mid-Sept-mid-Nov: S, D $190-$211; each additional $20; suites $265-$700; under 18 free; weekend rates; lower rates rest of year. Pets accepted. Check-out 1 pm. TV. Room service 24 hours. Restaurant, bar. In-house fitness room; massage; sauna. Indoor pool; whirlpool. Downhill, cross-country ski 12 miles. Valet parking. Business center. Concierge. Opposite Rideau Canal; near Parliament Hill.

[D] [icons]

Resort

★ ★ ★ **FAIRMONT LE CHATEAU MONTEBELLO.** *392 rue Notre Dame (J0V 1L0). Phone 819/423-6341; toll-free 800/441-1414; fax 819/423-5283. www.fairmont.com.* This stunning red cedar log chateau is a perfect choice for business or leisure travel. The property has terrific meeting facilities and a wide breadth of recreational facilities, including a fitness center, pools, and squash courts. The location offers year-round outdoor activities such as horseback riding, skiing, and more. 210 rooms, 3 story. Mid-May-mid-Oct, MAP: S $186.50; D $238; each additional $71.50; under 4 free; lower rates rest of year. Pets accepted, some restrictions; fee. Check-out noon, check-in 3 pm. TV. In-room modem link. Restaurant, bar; entertainment Fri, Sat. Room service. Supervised children's activities (mid-June-early Sept), ages 3-12. In-house fitness room; massage; sauna, steam room. Game room. Indoor pool; outdoor pool; whirlpool. 18-hole golf, pro, putting green, greens fee (including cart) $62. Outdoor tennis, indoor tennis. Cross-country ski on site (rentals). Lawn games. Bicycles. Marina. Fishing, hunting guides. Sleighing. Curling. Squash courts. Business center. On 65,000 acres.

[icons]

Sarnia

Motels/Motor Lodges

★ ★ ★ **DRAWBRIDGE INN.** *283 N Christina St (N7T 5V4). Phone 519/337-7571; toll-free 800/663-0376; fax 519/332-8181.* Located downtown on the waterfront. 97 rooms, 3 story. S, D $82; each additional $9; suites $115-$135; under 12 free; weekend rates. Pets accepted. Check-out noon. TV. In-room modem link. Restaurant, bar. Room service. Health club privileges. Sauna. Indoor pool. Business center.

[icons]

★ **HARBOURFRONT INN.** *505 Harbour Rd (N7T 5R8). Phone 519/337-5434; toll-free 800/787-5010; fax 519/332-5882.* 102 rooms, 2 story. Pets accepted. Complimentary continental breakfast. Check-out 11 am. TV. On river. **$**

[D] [icons]

★ ★ **HOLIDAY INN.** *1498 Venetian Blvd (N7T 7W6). Phone 519/336-4130; fax 519/332-3326. www.holiday-inn.com.* 151 rooms, 2 story. S, D $69-$89; suites $180-$240; under 19 free; weekend rates. Pets accepted, some restrictions; fee. Check-out 1 pm. TV; cable (premium). Restaurant, bar. Room service. In-house fitness room; sauna. Indoor pool; outdoor pool; whirlpool. Lawn games.

[D] [icons]

Sault Ste. Marie

Motels/Motor Lodges

★ ★ ★ **ALGOMAS WATER TOWER INN.** *360 Great Northern Rd (P6A 5N3). Phone 705/949-8111; toll-free 800/461-0800; fax 705/949-1912. www.watertowerinn.com.* Take a stroll through the waterfall garden and enjoy the beautiful outdoors! 180 rooms, 5 story. S, D $79-$99; each additional $7; suites $130-$290; under 18 free; ski plans. Pets accepted. Check-out noon. TV; cable (premium), VCR available. Restaurant, bar. Room service. In-house fitness room. Pool; whirlpool. Cross-country ski 5 miles. Airport transportation.

[D] [icons]

★ ★ **BEST WESTERN GREAT NORTHERN.** *229 Great Northern Rd; Hwy 17N (P6B 4Z2). Phone 705/942-2500; fax 705/942-2570. www.bestwestern.com.* 211 rooms, 2-7 story. S $86-$109; D $96-$122; each additional $10; suites $150-$275; under 18 free; package plans. Pets accepted, some restrictions. Check-out noon. TV; VCR available. Restaurant, bar. Room service. In-house fitness room. Indoor pool; outdoor pool; whirlpool. Downhill ski 20 miles, cross-country ski 3 miles. Miniature golf. Game rooms.

[D] [icons]

★ ★ **HOLIDAY INN.** *208 St. Mary's River Dr (P6A 5V4). Phone 705/949-0611; fax 705/945-6972. www.holiday-inn.com.* 195 rooms, 9 story. June-mid-Oct: S, D $92-$139; each additional $10; suites $175-$275; under 12 free; lower rates rest of year. Pets accepted. Check-out 4 pm. TV; cable (premium). In-room modem link. Restaurant, bar. Room service. In-house fitness room; sauna. Game room. Indoor pool; whirlpool. Airport transportation.

[D] [icons]

St. Catharines

Motels/Motor Lodges

★ ★ **HOLIDAY INN.** *2 N Service Rd (L2N 4G9). Phone 905/934-8000; toll-free 800/465-4329; fax 905/934-9117. www.holiday-inn.com.* 140 rooms, 2 story. July-Sept: S $105-$135; D $115-$145; each additional $10; under 18 free; lower rates rest of year. Pets accepted, some restrictions; fee. Check-out noon. TV; cable (premium), VCR available (movies). In-room modem link. Restaurant, bar. Room service. In-house fitness room; sauna. Indoor pool; outdoor pool.

D ⊠ ⊠ ⊠ ⊠ SC

★ ★ **HOWARD JOHNSON.** *89 Meadowvale Dr (L2N 3Z8). Phone 905/934-5400; fax 905/646-8700. www.hojo.com.* 96 rooms, 5 story. S $69-$149; D $79-$159; each additional $10; under 18 free. Pets accepted, some restrictions. Check-out noon. TV. In-room modem link. Laundry services. Restaurant open 24 hours. Bar. In-house fitness room; sauna. Indoor pool. Cross-country ski 10 miles.

D ⊠ ⊠ ⊠ ⊠ ⊠ SC

All Suite

★ ★ **FOUR POINTS BY SHERATON.** *3530 Schmon Pkwy (L2V 4Y6). Phone 905/984-8484; toll-free 877/848-3782; fax 905/984-6691. www.fourpointsuites.com.* 129 kitchen units, 4 story. Pets accepted, some restrictions; fee. Check-out 11 am, check-in 3 pm. TV; VCR available. In-room modem link. Laundry services. Restaurant, bar. Room service. Babysitting services available. In-house fitness room; sauna. Indoor pool; whirlpool. Lawn games. Business center. **$**

D ⊠ ⊠ ⊠ ⊠ SC ⊠

Stratford

B&B/Small Inn

★ ★ ★ **QUEEN'S INN.** *161 Ontario St (N5A 3H3). Phone 519/271-1400; fax 519/271-7373. www.queensinn stratford.ca.* This lovely inn was built in 1850. 32 rooms, 3 story. Pets accepted. Check-out 11 am, check-in 3 pm. TV; VCR available. Restaurant. Room service. In-house fitness room. Downhill, cross country skiing. Concierge, Built in 1850. **$$$$**

D ⊠ ⊠ ⊠ ⊠ SC

Thunder Bay

Motels/Motor Lodges

★ **BEST WESTERN CROSSROADS MOTOR INN.** *655 W Arthur St (P7E 5R6). Phone 807/577-4241; fax 807/475-7059. www.bestwestern.com.* 60 rooms, 2 story. May-Oct: S $73; D $78; under 12 free; lower rates rest of year. Pets accepted, some restrictions; fee. Check-out 11 am. TV. In-room modem link. Free airport transportation.

⊠ ⊠ ⊠ SC

★ **COMFORT INN.** *660 W Arthur St (P7E 5R8). Phone 807/475-3155; fax 807/475-3816. www.comfortinn.com.* 80 rooms, 2 story. S $70-$85; D $75-$93; each additional $8; under 19 free. Pets accepted, some restrictions. Check-out 11 am. TV. In-room modem link.

D ⊠ ⊠ ⊠ SC

★ ★ ★ **GOLDEN TULIP VALHALLA INN THUNDER BAY.** *1 Valhalla Inn Rd (P7E 6J1). Phone 807/577-1121; fax 807/475-4723. www.valhallainn.com.* 267 rooms, 5 story. S $175-$190; D $185-$200; each additional $10; suites $295 $305; under 18 free; ski, weekend rates. Pets accepted, some restrictions; fee. Check-out 1 pm. TV. In-room modem link. Restaurant, bar. Room service. In-house fitness room; sauna. Game room. Indoor pool; whirlpool. Downhill ski 3 miles, cross-country ski 4 miles. Bicycle rentals. Free airport transportation. Luxury level.

D ⊠ ⊠ ⊠ ⊠ ⊠ ⊠ SC

★ ★ **PRINCE ARTHUR.** *17 N Cumberland (P7A 4K8). Phone 807/345-5411; fax 807/345-8565. www.princearthur.on.ca.* 121 rooms, 6 story. S $59-$77; D $67-$85; each additional $8; suites $115-$145; under 16 free. Pets accepted, some restrictions. Check-out noon. TV. In-room modem link. Restaurant, bar. Room service. Health club privileges. Sauna. Indoor pool; children's pool; whirlpool. Downhill ski 10 miles. Free airport transportation. Overlooks harbor.

D ⊠ ⊠ ⊠ ⊠ ⊠ SC

★ ★ **RAMADA INN.** *1010 Dawson Rd (P7B 5J4). Phone 807/767-1681; fax 807/767-1439.* 106 rooms, 4 story. S $80; D $86; each additional $8; under 12 free. Pets accepted. Complimentary continental breakfast. Check-out 11 am. TV. In-room modem link. Restaurant, bar. Room service. Sauna. Indoor pool; whirlpool; poolside service. Downhill ski 20 miles. Free airport transportation.

D ⊠ ⊠ ⊠ ⊠ SC

★ **TRAVELODGE.** *450 Memorial Ave (P7B 3Y7). Phone 807/345-2343; fax 807/345-3246. www.travelodge.com.* 93 rooms, 3 story. S $75; D $85; each additional $10; under 20 free. Pets accepted, some restrictions. Complimentary continental breakfast. Check-out 1 pm. TV. In-room modem link. Sauna. Indoor pool. Downhill ski 15 miles.

🐾 ✕ 🏊 ⛷ SC

★★★ **VICTORIA INN.** *555 W Arthur St (P7E 5R5). Phone 807/577-8481; toll-free 800/387-3331; fax 807/475-8961. www.tbaytel.net/vicinn.* Claiming to have the largest indoor recreation area in northern Ontario, this is a terrific place to take the family for a getaway. The indoor water slide is three stories high! 182 rooms, 3 story. S $76.95-$155; D $86.95-$155; each additional $10; suites $179-$229; under 16 free. Pets accepted, some restrictions; fee. Check-out noon. TV. In-room modem link. Laundry services. Restaurant, bar. Room service. Health club privileges. In-house fitness room; sauna. Indoor pool; children's pool; whirlpool; poolside service. Downhill ski 8 miles, cross-country ski 5 miles. Free airport transportation.

D 🐾 🏊 🏃 ✕ ⛷ SC

Toronto

Motels/Motor Lodges

★ **HOWARD JOHNSON.** *89 Avenue Rd (M5R 2G3). Phone 416/964-1220; toll-free 800/446-4656; fax 416/964-8692. www.hojo.com.* 71 rooms, 8 story. S $124; D $134; each additional $10; under 19 free; weekend rates off-season. Pets accepted. Complimentary continental breakfast. Check-out noon, check-in 4 pm. TV; cable (premium), VCR available. Health club privileges. Parking $6.50/day.

🐾 ⛷ SC

★★ **QUALITY INN.** *2180 Islington Ave (N9P 3P1). Phone 416/240-9090; fax 416/240-9944. www.qualityinn.com.* 198 rooms, 12 story. S, D $89-$139; each additional $10; under 18 free; package plans; higher rates special events. Pets accepted. Check-out 11 am. TV; cable (premium). In-room modem link. Restaurant, bar.

D 🐾 ✕ ⛷ SC

★★ **QUALITY INN.** *111 Lombard St (M5C 2T9). Phone 416/367-5555; fax 416/367-3470. www.qualityinn.com.* 196 rooms, 16 story. S $139; D $149; each additional $10; under 18 free. Pets accepted, some restrictions. Check-out 11 am. TV. Health club privileges. In-house fitness room.

D 🐾 🏃 ⛷ SC

★★ **QUALITY INN & SUITES.** *262 Carlingview Dr (M9W 5G1). Phone 416/674-8442; toll-free 800/228-5151; fax 416/674-3088. www.qualityinn.com.* 254 suites, 12 story. S, D $120-$145; each additional $5; under 18 free; weekend, holiday rates. Pets accepted. Check-out 11 am. TV; cable (premium). Restaurant, bar. Health club privileges. In-house fitness room. Downhill, cross-country ski 15 miles.

D 🐾 🏊 🏃 ⛷ SC

★★ **TRAVELODGE.** *925 Dixon Rd (M9W 1J8). Phone 416/674-2222; toll-free 888/483-6887; fax 416/674-5757. www.travelodge.com.* 283 rooms, 17 story. S $120; D $140; each additional $10; suites $140-$275; under 18 free; weekend rates. Pets accepted, some restrictions. Complimentary continental breakfast. Check-out 1 pm. TV; cable (premium). In-room modem link. Restaurant, bar. Health club privileges. Sauna. Indoor pool; whirlpool. Airport transportation.

D 🐾 🏊 ✕ ⛷ SC

Hotels

★★★ **DELTA CHELSEA.** *33 Gerrard St W (M5G 1Z4). Phone 416/595-1975; toll-free 800/268-1133; fax 416/585-4375. www.deltahotels.com.* 1,590 rooms, 26 story. Pets accepted, some restrictions. Check-out 11 am, check-in 3 pm. TV; VCR available. Room service 24 hours. Restaurant, bar; entertainment. Supervised children's activities, ages 2-13. Children's activity center, babysitting services available. In-house fitness room, health club privileges; sauna. Game room. Indoor pool; whirlpool. Valet parking. Business center. **$$**

D 🐾 🏊 🏃 ⛷ SC 🏃

★★ **DELTA TORONTO AIRPORT.** *801 Dixon Rd (N9W 1J5). Phone 416/675-6100; fax 416/675-4022. www.deltahotels.com.* 251 rooms, 8 story. S, D $115-$165; each additional $15; suites $170-$220; under 18 free; package plans. Pets accepted, some restrictions. Check-out 1 pm. TV; cable (premium). Restaurant, bar. Room service 24 hours. Supervised children's activities (June-Aug). Health club privileges. In-house fitness room; sauna. Indoor pool. Business center.

D 🐾 🏊 🏃 ⛷ SC 🏃

★★ **DELTA TORONTO EAST.** *2035 Kennedy Rd (M1T 3G2). Phone 416/299-1500; fax 416/299-8959. www.deltahotels.ca.* 368 rooms, 14 story. S, D $219; each additional $15; suites $365-$620; under 18 free; weekend rates. Pets accepted; fee. Check-out noon. TV. In-room modem link. Room service 24 hours. Restaurant, bar. Free supervised children's activities (weekends, school holidays); ages 3-15. In-house fitness room; sauna. Game room. Indoor pool; children's pool; whirlpool. Covered valet parking. Concierge. Luxury level.

D 🐾 🏊 🏃 ⛷ SC

★ ★ ★**THE FAIRMONT ROYAL YORK.** *100 Front St W (M5J 1E3). Phone 416/368-2511; fax 416/368-2884. www.fairmont.com.* In 1929, the largest hotel in the British Commonwealth opened on the site of the old Queen's Hotel, which had been an integral part of Toronto's boomtown. It was also rumored to have been the site of Sir John Macdonald's meeting with American Civil War sympathizers who plotted retaliation. The Royal York became known as a city within a city, its 1.5 acres of public rooms including a 12-bed hospital, a 12,000-book library, a concert hall with a 50-ton pipe organ, its own bank, and ten ornate passenger elevators. A $100 million project from 1988-1993 restored the guest rooms and public spaces to their original elegance and added a health club. Still, many of the hotel's original features are still intact, such as the marvelous hand-painted ceilings, travertine pillars, ornate furnishings, and wall hangings. Even if you aren't a guest of the hotel, take a walk through it and think about the illustrious guests who have walked before you. And don't forget to sneak a peak at ornate elevator #9, the designated lift for Her Majesty Queen Elizabeth II. 1,365 rooms, 22 story. S, D $189-$289; each additional $20; suites $295-$1,750; under 18 free; package plans. Pets accepted, some restrictions; fee. Check-out noon. TV. Room service 24 hours. Restaurant, bar; entertainment. In-house fitness room; massage; sauna. Health club privileges. Pool; children's pool; whirlpool. Business center. Concierge. Luxury level.

★ ★ ★ ★ **FOUR SEASONS HOTEL TORONTO.** *21 Avenue Rd (M5R 2G1). Phone 416/964-0411; toll-free 800/819-5053; fax 416/964-2301. www.fourseasons.com.* The standard-setting Four Seasons Hotel has a stylish home in Toronto. The 32-story headquarters is located in the Yorkville District, a fashionable and dynamic neighborhood filled with specialty shops and galleries. The guest rooms are sublimely comfortable and feature fine furnishings and impressive artwork. Guests stay on track with fitness regimes, enjoying both a fitness center and an indoor-outdoor pool. The spa offers a variety of massages, all of which are also available in the privacy of a guest room. Toronto's dining scene is well represented at the Four Seasons, with four sensational restaurants. The eclectic décor and the striking glass art make the Studio Café a favorite place for casual dining, while the contemporary, sleek style of Avenue attracts the chic. No visit is complete without dining at Truffles, where a mouthwatering menu transports diners to the French countryside. 380 rooms, 32 story. Pets accepted, some restrictions. Complimentary continental breakfast. Check-out noon, check-in 3 pm. TV; cable (premium), VCR available (movies). In-room modem link. Room service 24 hours. Restaurant, bar; entertainment. Babysitting services available. In-house fitness room; sauna. Massage.

Indoor/outdoor pool; whirlpool. Valet parking. Business center. Concierge. **$$$**

★ ★ ★ **INTERNATIONAL PLAZA HOTEL.** *655 Dixon Rd (M9W 1J4). Phone 416/244-1711; fax 416/244-8031. www.internationalplaza.com.* 415 rooms, 12 story. S, D $170; each additional $10; suites $350-$500; under 18 free; weekend rates. Pets accepted. Check-out noon. TV; cable (premium). Room service 24 hours. Restaurant, bar. Supervised children's activities, ages 3-12. In-house fitness room; sauna. Game room. Indoor pool; children's pool; poolside service. Valet parking. Business center. Concierge. Massages.

★ ★ ★ ★ **METROPOLITAN HOTEL TORONTO.** *108 Chestnut St (M5G 1R3). Phone 416/977-5000; fax 416/599-3317. www.metropolitan.com.* All of Toronto is within easy reach from the Metropolitan Hotel, making it an obvious choice for discerning travelers. Not far from the Financial District, the hotel also enjoys close proximity to world-renowned shopping, art galleries, and museums. The has the services of a large property and the intimacy of a private residence. Blonde woods, earth tones, and simple furnishings deliver a calming sense to guests in the guest rooms. The accommodations are a dream, featuring the latest technology, from faxes, laser printers, modems, and multi-line telephones to stereo equipment. Fully staffed fitness and business centers are also on hand to assist all guests with their goals. Hemispheres scours the globe for culinary inspiration, and the beige and black dining room of Lai Wah Heen is a serene setting for its luscious Cantonese cuisine. Considered an excellent example of authentic dim sum, this restaurant is a local sensation. 425 rooms, 26 story. S, D $240-$380; each additional $30; suites $490-$1,800; weekend rates. Pets accepted, some restrictions. Check-out noon. TV; cable (premium), VCR available (free movies). In-room modem link. Restaurant, bar. In-house fitness room; sauna. Indoor pool; whirlpool. Business center. Concierge. Eaton Centre 2 blocks.

★ ★ **NOVOTEL TORONTO CENTRE.** *45 The Esplanade (M5E 1W2). Phone 416/367-8900; fax 416/360-8285. www.novotel.com.* This property has a great location near the CN Tower, the Eaton Centre, and other attractions. Also nearby are many restaurants and stores. The hotel itself offers a plethora of amenities. 262 rooms, 9 story. S, D $205; each additional $20; suites $215; under 16 free; weekend rates. Pets accepted, some restrictions; fee. Check-out 1 pm. TV; cable (premium). Restaurant, bar. In-house fitness room; sauna. Indoor pool; whirlpool.

★★★ **SHERATON GATEWAY HOTEL.** *Toronto International Airport, Terminal 3 (L5P 1C4). Phone 905/ 672-7000; fax 905/672-7100. www.sheraton.com.* This hotel is conveniently located at the Toronto airport. 474 rooms, 8 story. S, D $190-$240; each additional $15; suites $420-$800; under 18 free; weekly, weekend rates. Pets accepted, some restrictions. Check-out noon. TV; cable (premium), VCR available. Room service 24 hours. Restaurant, bar. In-house fitness room, massage; sauna. Indoor pool; whirlpool. Garage, valet parking. Free airport transportation. Business center. Concierge. Modern facility connected by climate-controlled walkway to Terminal 3.

★★★ **THE SUTTON PLACE HOTEL.** *955 Bay St (M5S 2A2). Phone 416/924-9221; fax 416/324-5617. www.suttonplace.com.* A landmark for more than 30 years, this hotel has a central location adjacent to Queen's Park and minutes from fashionable Yorkville. Guests can still catch flashes of luxury within the historic décor, including crystal chandeliers and an overall European elegance. 292 rooms, 33 story. Pets accepted; fee. Check-out noon, check-in 3 pm. TV; cable (premium), VCR available. Internet access. Room service 24 hours. Restaurant, bar; entertainment. Babysitting services available. In-house fitness room. Health club privileges; spa; massage; sauna. Indoor pool; poolside service. Valet parking. Business center. Concierge. **$$**

Motel/Motor Lodge

★★ **QUALITY INN.** *280 Bloor St W (M5S 1V8). Phone 416/968-0010; toll-free 800/424-6423; fax 416/968-7765. www.choicehotels.ca.* 209 rooms, 14 story. Pets accepted. Check-out 11 am, check-in 1 pm. TV. Restaurant, bar. Health club privileges. **$**

Windsor

Motels/Motor Lodges

★ **COMFORT INN.** *1100 Richmond St (N7M 5J5). Phone 519/352-5500; fax 519/352-2520. www.comfortinn.com.* 81 rooms, 2 story. May-Sept: S $57-$95; D $65-$105; each additional $4; under 19 free; weekend rates; lower rates rest of year. Pets accepted, some restrictions. Check-out 11 am. TV.

★ **MARQUIS PLAZA.** *2530 Ouellette Ave (N8X 1L7). Phone 519/966-1860; fax 519/966-6619. www. royalmarquis.com.* 97 rooms, 2 story. S $48-$150; D $60; each additional $5; suites $90-$150. Pets accepted, some restrictions; fee. Check-out noon. TV; cable (premium), VCR available.

★★★ **ROYAL MARQUIS.** *590 Grand Marais E (N8X 3H4). Phone 519/966-1900; toll-free 800/265-5032; fax 519/966-4689. www.royalmarquis.com.* 99 rooms, 5 story. S $70; D $80; each additional $5; suites $90-$175; under 12 free; weekend rates; higher rates prom. Pets accepted; fee. Check-out noon. TV; cable (premium), VCR available. Restaurant, bar; entertainment. Room service. Supervised children's activities; ages 5-10. In-house fitness room; sauna. Indoor pool; whirlpool. Cross-country ski 5 miles. Concierge. Luxurious furnishings, atmosphere.

Hotel

★ **RADISSON RIVERFRONT HOTEL WINDSOR.** *333 Riverside Dr W (N9A 5K4). Phone 519/977-9777; toll-free 800/267-9777; fax 519/977-1411. www.radisson.com.* Located on the waterfront, this hotel offers a spectacular view of the Detroit skyline. 207 rooms, 19 story. S, D $95; under 12 free. Pets accepted, some restrictions. Complimentary full breakfast. Check-out noon. TV; cable (premium). In-room modem link. In-house fitness room; sauna. Indoor pool; whirlpool.

Prince Edward Island

Charlottetown

Motels/Motor Lodges

★ ★ **BEST WESTERN CHARLOTTETOWN.** *238 Grafton St (C1A 1L5). Phone 902/892-2461; toll-free 800/528-1234; fax 902/566-2979. www.bestwestern.com.* 143 rooms, 2-3 story. June-mid-Oct: S $139-$149; D $149-$159; each additional $10; studio rooms $149-$159; suites $169-$209; kitchen units $149-$159; under 18 free; lower rates rest of year. Pets accepted, some restrictions. Check-out noon. TV. Restaurant. In-house fitness room; sauna. Indoor pool; whirlpool.

D 🦅 ≈ 🏃 ⊠ SC

★ ★ **ISLANDER MOTOR LODGE.** *146-148 Pownal St (C1A 7N4). Phone 902/892-1217; toll-free 800/268-6261; fax 902/566-1623. www.islandermotorlodge.com.* 49 rooms, 2 story. Mid-May-mid-Oct: S, D $86-$96; each additional $8; suites, kitchen units $96-$120; under 12 free; lower rates rest of year. Pets accepted, some restrictions. Check-out 11 am. TV. Restaurant.

D 🦅

★ ★ **QUALITY INN.** *150 Euston St (C1A 1W5). Phone 902/894-8572; fax 902/368-3556. www.qualityinn.com.* 48 rooms, 5 story. Late June-mid-Oct: S $116; D $127; each additional $9; studio rooms $137-$142; suites $152-$174; under 16 free; lower rates rest of year. Pets accepted. Check-out noon. TV. Restaurant, bar. Room service. Health club privileges.

🦅 ⊠

★ ★ ★ **RODD CONFEDERATION INN & SUITES.** *Trans-Canada Hwy (C1A 7K7). Phone 902/892-2481; fax 902/368-3247. www.rodd-hotels.ca.* 62 rooms, 2 story. Mid-June-Sept: S, D $85-$94; suites $99-$115; under 16 free; lower rates rest of year. Pets accepted. Check-out 11 am. TV. Restaurant, bar. Health club privileges. Pool.

🦅 ≈ ⊠ SC

★ **SUNNY KING.** *Hwy 1. Phone 902/566-2209; fax 902/566-4209.* 37 rooms, 1-2 story. No A/C. Late June-early Sept: S $54-$64; D $60-$70; each additional $8; suites, kitchen units $68-$92; under 16 free; lower rates rest of year. Pets accepted, some restrictions. Check-out 11 am.

TV. Laundry services. Free supervised children's activities (May-mid-Nov). Pool.

D 🦅 ≈ ⊠ SC

Hotels

★ ★ **THE CHARLOTTETOWN.** *75 Kent St (C1A 7K4). Phone 902/894-7371; toll-free 800/565-7633; fax 902/368-2178. www.rodd-hotels.ca.* 115 rooms, 5 story. June-mid-Oct: S, D $135-$215; each additional $10; under 16 free; lower rates rest of year. Pets accepted, some restrictions. Check-out 11 am. TV. Restaurant, bar. In-house fitness room; sauna. Indoor pool; whirlpool.

D 🦅 ≈ 🏃 ⊠ SC

★ ★ ★ **DELTA PRINCE EDWARD.** *18 Queen St (C1A 8B9). Phone 902/566-2222; toll-free 800/441-1414; fax 902/566-1745. www.deltahotels.com.* 211 rooms, 10 story. May-mid-Oct: S $139-$229; D $159-$249; each additional $20; suites $299-$799; lower rates rest of year. Pets accepted; fee. Check-out noon. TV. Restaurant, bar; entertainment. In-house fitness room; massage; sauna. Indoor pool; children's pool; whirlpool. Business center. On the waterfront in Olde Charlottetown.

D 🦅 ≈ 🏃 ⊠ SC 🏃

Québec

Drummondville

Motel/Motor Lodge

★ ★ **HOTEL UNIVERSEL.** *915 Hains St (J2C 3A1). Phone 819/478-4971; toll-free 800/668-3521; fax 819/477-6604. www.hoteluniversal.qc.ca.* 115 rooms, 4 story. S $75.95; D $85.95; each additional $10; suites $120-$150; under 15 free. Pets accepted, some restrictions. Check-out noon. TV. Restaurant, bar; entertainment Wed-Sat. Room service. Indoor pool; poolside service.

⊡ 🐾 ☎ ⊠

Montréal

Motel/Motor Lodge

★ ★ **QUALITY INN.** *7700 Cote de Liesse (H4T 1E7). Phone 514/731-7821; toll-free 800/361-2643; fax 514/731-7267. www.qualityinn.com.* 159 rooms, 4 story. S, D $145-$170; kitchen suites $185-$395; each additional $10; weekend rates. Pets accepted. Check-out noon. TV; cable (premium). Restaurant, bar. Room service. Health club privileges. In-house fitness room, massage; sauna. Outdoor heated pool; two whirlpools. Parking. Free airport transportation. Concierge.

⊡ 🐾 ☎ ⊀ ☎ ⊠ ✈ ⊠

Hotels

★ ★ ★ **DELTA MONTRÉAL.** *475 President Kennedy Ave (H3A 1J7). Phone 514/286-1986; toll-free 800/268-1133; fax 514/284-4342. www.deltahotels.com.* 456 rooms, 23 story. Pets accepted; fee. Check-out noon, check-in 3 pm. TV; cable (premium). In-room modem link. Restaurant, bar. Room service. Supervised children's activities, ages 4-12. Babysitting services available. In-house fitness room, spa, massage; sauna. Indoor pool; whirlpool. Business center. Concierge. Located in the heart of downtown Montréal, near Cultural Arts Center, Place des Arts. **$$**

⊡ 🐾 ☎ ⊀ ⊠ ⊠

★ ★ **FOUR POINTS BY SHERATON.** *475 Sherbrooke St W (H3A 2L9). Phone 514/842-3961; toll-free 800/842-3961; fax 514/844-0945. www.fourpoints.com.* 195 rooms, 20 story. Pets accepted, some restrictions. Check-

out noon, check-in 3 pm. TV; VCR available. In-room modem link. Restaurant, bar. Room service. Babysitting services available. In-house fitness room; sauna. Valet parking. Business center. Concierge. **$**

⊡ 🐾 ⊀ ⊠ SC ⊠

★ ★ ★ **HILTON MONTRÉAL BONAVENTURE.** *1 Place Bonaventure (H5A 1E4). Phone 514/878-2332; fax 514/878-3881. www.hiltonmontreal.com.* Penthouse life is glorious inside this hotel perched on top of the Place Bonaventure Exhibition Hall. There are acres of rooftop gardens to explore and a year-round outdoor pool. The central city location is perfect for sightseeing in Old Montréal, gambling at the casino, or shopping the underground boutiques. 370 rooms, 2 story. S, D $155-$425; under 18 free. Pets accepted, some restrictions. Check-out noon. TV. Restaurant, bar. In-house fitness room. Pool. Business center. Concierge.

⊡ 🐾 ☎ ⊀ ⊠ ⊠

★ ★ ★ **HOTEL INTER-CONTINENTAL MONTRÉAL.** *360 rue Ste. Antoine W (H2Y 3X4). Phone 514/987-9900; toll-free 800/361-3600; fax 514/847-8550. www.interconti.com.* Located in downtown Montréal, a short walk from the popular Old Town, which has cobblestone roads, art galleries, shops, and restaurants. 357 rooms, 17 story. May-mid-Oct: S, D $189-$245; each additional $25; suites $360-$2,200; under 17 free; family, weekend rates; lower rates rest of year. Pets accepted, some restrictions. Check-out 1 pm, check-in 3 pm. TV; cable (premium), VCR available. In-room modem link. Room service 24 hours. Restaurant, bar; entertainment. In-house fitness room; massage. Indoor heated pool. Valet parking. Business center. Concierge. Connected to shop and boutiques, metro system. Near Old Montréal. Next to Convention Center.

🐾 ☎ ⊀ ⊠ ⊠ ⊠

★ ★ ★ **HOTEL LE GERMAIN.** *2050 Mansfield (H3A 1Y9). Phone 514/849-2050; toll-free 877/333-2050; fax 514/849-1437. www.hotelboutique.com.* This distinctive boutique hotel offers hospitality, comfort, and relaxation in a very elegant setting, while providing state-of-the-art work equipment. The convenient downtown location makes it close to shopping, museums, concert halls, and movie theaters. Guest rooms feature original photos by Louis Ducharme, natural lighting, down duvets, and dual-line phones. 99 rooms, 13 story. July-Aug: S, D $210-$315; lower rates rest of year. Pets accepted; fee. Complimentary full breakfast. Check-out noon, check-in 3 pm. TV; cable (premium), VCR available, CD available. Bar. Tennis. Downhill skiing. Bike rentals. Valet parking.

⊡ 🐾 ☎ ⊀ ✈ ⊠

★ **HOTEL LE SAINTE-ANDRE.** *1285 rue Ste.-Andre (H2L 3T1). Phone 514/849-7070; toll-free 800/265-7071; fax 514/849-8167. www.hotelsaintandre.ca.* 62 rooms, 4 story. Pets accepted. Complimentary continental breakfast. Check-out noon. Check-in 1 pm. TV. Located near the main metro system Barrie-Uqam, walking distance to Old Montréal, Chinatown, and shopping district. Small, contemporary hotel. **$**

★ ★ ★ **HOTEL LE ST. JAMES.** *355 Saint Jacques St (H2Y 1N9). Phone 514/841-3111; toll-free 800/223-6800; fax 866/841-3311. www.hotellestjames.com.* 61 rooms. Closed for Grand Prix in June. Pets accepted, some restrictions. Check-out noon, check-in 3 pm. Restaurant, bar. Babysitting services available. In-house fitness room, spa. **$$$$**

★ ★ ★ **HOTEL OMNI MONT-ROYAL.** *1050 Sherbrooke St W (H3A 2R6). Phone 514/284-1110; toll-free 800/842-6664; fax 514/284-1162. www.omnihotels.com.* 300 rooms, 31 story. May-Oct: S, D $149-$585; each additional $30; suites $250-$1,975; under 18 free; weekend rates; lower rates rest of year. Pets accepted, some restrictions; fee. Check-out 1 pm, check-in 3 pm. TV; cable (premium), VCR available. In-room modem link. Room service 24 hours. Restaurant, bar. In-house fitness room, massage; sauna, steam room. Outdoor pool; whirlpool; poolside service. Valet parking. Business center. Concierge. Located at the foot of Mount Royal; near attractions and shopping.

★ ★ ★ ★ **LOEWS HOTEL VOGUE.** *1425 rue de la Montagne (H3G 1Z3). Phone 514/285-5555; toll-free 800/465-6654; fax 514/849-8903. www.loewshotels.com.* The fresh spirit and chic modernity of the Loews Hotel Vogue breathes new life into old-world Montreal. Located in the business district of this "Paris of Canada," this hip hotel's vivid colors, plush amenities, and superb service make it a favorite of the jet set. The accommodations provide sleek shelter with silk upholstered furnishings, while creature comforts like oversized bathrooms appeal to the sybarite in every guest. Visitors are well cared for here, with a gracious concierge who attends to all needs and efficient business and fitness centers. From bistros to brasseries, Montreal is known for its food, and this hotel is no exception. Chez Georges delights both the eye and the palate with its atmospheric setting and inventive French fusion cuisine, while patrons enjoy watching the world go by at L'Opéra Bar, the place to see and be seen in this charming city. 142 rooms, 9 story. Pets accepted, some restrictions. Check-out 1 pm, check-in 3 pm. TV; VCR available. In-room modem link. Restaurant, bar. Room service. Babysitting services available. In-house fitness room. Health club privileges; massage. Valet parking. **$$**

★ ★ ★ **NOVOTEL.** *1180 rue de la Montagne (H3G 1Z1). Phone 514/861-6000; fax 514/861-6470. www.novotel.com.* Walk to everything from this hotel, one block north of the Molson Centre, a venue for both sporting events and concerts. 227 rooms, 9 story. May-Oct: S, D $129-$400; each additional $15; suites $500-$1,500; family, weekend and holiday rates; higher rates during Grand Prix; lower rates rest of year. Pets accepted; fee. Check-out 1 pm. TV; cable (premium). In-room modem link. Restaurant, bar. In-house fitness room.

★ ★ ★ **RENAISSANCE MONTRÉAL HOTEL.** *3625 Ave du Parc (H2X 3P8). Phone 514/288-6666; toll-free 800/200-5909; fax 514/288-2469. www.renaissance hotels.com.* Located in downtown Montréal, this hotel is the perfect place to stay for those visitors looking to explore the city. Shopping, restaurants, and attractions are all nearby. 457 rooms, 16 story. May-Oct: S, D $109-$260; each additional $15; suites $250-$1,500; under 18 free; weekend rates; lower rates rest of year. Pets accepted, some restrictions. Check-out noon. TV; VCR available. Restaurant, bar. Health club privileges. In-house fitness room. Business center. Luxury level.

All Suite

★ ★ **CHATEAU ROYAL HOTEL SUITES.** *1420 Crescent St (H3G 2B7). Phone 514/848-0999; toll-free 800/363-0335; fax 514/848-1891. www.chateauroyal.com.* 113 rooms, 21 story. Pets accepted, some restrictions; fee. Check-out noon, check-in 3 pm. TV; cable (premium). Restaurant. Room service. Valet parking. **$**

Québec City

Motels/Motor Lodges

★ ★ **MOTEL SPRING.** *8520 Blvd Ste. Anne (G0A 1N0). Phone 418/824-4953; toll-free 888/824-4953; fax 418/824-4117.* 25 rooms. No room phones. July-early Sept: S, D $45; weekly rates; higher rates major holidays; lower rates mid-May-June, early Sept-late Oct. Closed rest of year. Pets accepted, some restrictions. Check-out noon. TV. Restaurant. On river. Family-owned.

★ **ONCLE SAM.** *7025 W Hamel Blvd (G2G 1V6). Phone 418/872-1488; toll-free 800/414-1488; fax 418/871-5519.* 44 rooms, 1-2 story. Mid-June-mid-Sept: S, D $59-$79; each additional $10; under 14 free; lower rates rest of year. Pets accepted, some restrictions. Check-out noon.

TV; VCR available. Laundry services. Pool. Cross-country ski 5 miles.

D 🐕 ⛷ 🏊 ⛵ SC

Hotels

★ ★ ★ **HILTON QUÉBEC.** *1100 Blvd Rene Levesque E (G1K 7M9). Phone 418/647-2411; fax 418/647-3737. www.hilton.com.* This property is connected to the Québec government buildings by the Place Québec, a modern underground shopping center with many stores, restaurants, and entertainment. 571 rooms, 23 story. Mid-May-mid-Oct: S $138-$187; D $160-$209; each additional $22; suites $355-$835; weekend rates. Pets accepted. Check-out noon. TV. Restaurant, bar. In-house fitness room; massage; sauna. Pool; poolside service. Downhill ski 11 miles, cross-country ski nearby. Parking. Business center. Luxury level.

D 🐕 ⛷ 🏊 🏃 🎿 SC 🏃

★ ★ ★ **LOEWS LE CONCORDE.** *1225 Cours du General De Montcalm (G1R 4W6). Phone 418/647-2222; toll-free 800/463-5256; fax 418/647-4710. www.loewshotels.com.* See a vision of Paris out your window from this hotel on Québec City's "Champs-Elysees." Just 15 minutes from the airport, the tower has views of the St. Lawrence River, the city lights, and the historic Plains of Abraham. A visit is not complete without a peek, and hopefully a meal, at L'Astral, the revolving rooftop restaurant. 404 rooms, 26 story. May-Oct: S, D $135-$290; each additional $25; suites $180-$750; weekend, ski plans; lower rates rest of year. Pets accepted, some restrictions. Check-out 1 pm. TV. In-room modem link. Fireplaces. Restaurant, bar. In-house fitness room; sauna. Health club privileges. Pool; whirlpool; poolside service. Downhill ski 11 miles, cross-country ski on site. Garage, valet parking. Business center. Concierge. Luxury level.

D 🐕 ⛷ 🏊 🏃 🎿 SC 🏃

Trois-Rivières

Hotel

★ ★ **DELTA.** *1620 Notre Dame St (G9A 6E5). Phone 819/376-1991; fax 819/372-5975. www.deltahotels.com.* 159 rooms, 12 story. S, D $72-$150; each additional $15; suites $150-$300; under 18 free; higher rates Formula Grand Prix (Aug). Pets accepted, some restrictions; fee. Check-out noon. TV. In-room modem link. Restaurant, bar. In-house fitness room, massage; sauna. Indoor pool; whirlpool. Downhill ski 15 miles, cross-country ski 5 miles. Free garage parking.

D 🐕 ⛷ 🏊 🏃 🎿 SC

Saskatchewan

Regina

Hotels

★ **COUNTRY INN & SUITES BY CARLSON.** *3321 Eastgate Bay (S4Z1A4). Phone 306/789-9117; fax 306/789-3010. www.countryinns.com.* 76 rooms. Pets accepted, some restrictions. Complimentary continental breakfast. Check-out noon, check-in 3 pm. TV. Babysitting services available. In-house fitness room. **$**

★★★ **DELTA REGINA.** *1919 Saskatchewan Dr (S4P 4H2). Phone 306/525-5255; toll-free 800/209-3555; fax 306/781-7188. www.deltahotels.com.* 274 rooms. Pets accepted, some restrictions; fee. Check-out noon, check-in 3 pm. Restaurant, bar. Children's activity center, babysitting services available. In-house fitness room. Indoor pool; children's pool; whirlpool. **$$**

★★★ **RADISSON PLAZA HOTEL.** *2125 Victoria Ave (S4P0S3). Phone 306/522-7691; toll-free 800/667-5828; fax 306/757-5521. www.hotelsask.com.* 224 rooms. Pets accepted, some restrictions; fee. Check-out noon, check-in 3 pm. TV; cable (premium). Restaurant, bar. In-house fitness room. Whirlpool. **$$**

★★★ **REGINA INN HOTEL AND CONFERENCE CENTRE.** *1975 Broad St (S4P 1Y2). Phone 306/525-6767; toll-free 800/667-8162; fax 306/352-1858. www.reginainn.com.* 235 rooms. Pets accepted, some restrictions. Check-out noon, check-in 4 pm. Restaurant, bar. In-house fitness room. **$**

Saskatoon

Hotels

★ **COUNTRY INN & SUITES BY CARLSON.** *617 Cynthia St (S7L6B7). Phone 306/934-3900; fax 306/652-3100.* 77 rooms. Pets accepted, some restrictions; fee. Check-out noon, check-in 3 pm. TV. **$**

★★ **RADISSON HOTEL.** *405 20th St E (S7K 6X6). Phone 306/665-3322; toll-free 800/333-3333; fax 306/665-5531. www.radisson.com.* 291 rooms. Pets accepted, some restrictions; fee. Check-out noon, check-in 3 pm. TV; cable (premium). Restaurant, bar. Babysitting services available. In-house fitness room. Indoor pool; whirlpool. **$**

Swift Current

Motel/Motor Lodge

★ **SUPER 8.** *405 N Service Rd (S9H 3X6). Phone 306/778-6088; fax 306/778-0803. www.super8.com.* 63 rooms. Pets accepted, some restrictions; fee. Check-out 11 am, check-in 3 pm. TV. In-house fitness room. Indoor pool; whirlpool. **$**

Yorkton

Motel/Motor Lodge

★ **COMFORT INN.** *22 Dracup Ave (S3N 3W1). Phone 306/783-0333; toll-free 800/228-5150; fax 306/783-1239.* 80 rooms. Pets accepted, some restrictions; fee. Complimentary continental breakfast. Check-out 11 am, check-in 3 pm. TV. In-house fitness room. Indoor pool; whirlpool. **$**

Appendix A: First Aid for Your Pet

It's important to know what is normal for your pet so that you can spot any abnormal signs or behaviors that could indicate a health problem. You should know your animal's normal vital signs, including temperature, heart rate, respiration rate, and how often she eats, drinks, urinates, and defecates. When you take your pet in for her pre-trip check-up (see page A-21), your veterinarian can help you compile this list.

First-Aid Kit

Always have a first-aid kit for your pet, whether you're at home or on the road. You can save space in your suitcase by combining your first-aid kit with your pet's—many of the items will be the same, anyway.

A first-aid kit should contain:
- antibiotic ointment
- antiseptic cleansing wipes
- Benadryl liquid
- blunt tweezers
- cotton balls
- cotton swabs
- disposable razors
- extra collar and leash
- gauze pads
- hydrogen peroxide
- Kaopectate
- nail clippers
- Pepto-Bismol
- rectal thermometer
- rolls of gauze
- rolls of surgical tape
- saline eye wash
- scissors
- soft cloth muzzle

When Is It an Emergency?

The stress of travel can take its toll on both you and your pet. Loss of appetite, diarrhea, or constipation may be the result. Sometimes these problems clear up on their own, as your pet settles down. Sometimes they require medical attention. If you are unsure, *always be cautious and take your pet to a veterinarian.* However, in general, you can treat the following conditions yourself

and wait 24 hours to see if they clear up. If they don't, take your pet to a veterinarian without further delay.
- Loss of appetite
- Bleeding that can quickly be stopped
- Small amounts of blood in the urine or stool
- Constipation
- Mild coughing
- Diarrhea
- Mild fever
- Runny nose or eyes
- Squinting
- Vomiting
- Weight-bearing lameness

The following conditions are true emergencies that require a trip to the nearest 24-hour emergency veterinary clinic:
- Abnormal body posture
- Burns
- Difficulty breathing
- Excessive slobbering
- High fever
- Inability to urinate
- Ingesting poison
- Jaundice
- Inability to stand
- Inability to put weight on a limb
- Seizures
- Snake bites
- Uncontrolled bleeding
- Vomiting blood

If your pet has been hit by a car, has been attacked by a larger animal, or has suffered a serious blow or fall, take her to a veterinarian immediately, even if she seems to be okay. Again, if you are unsure, *always be cautious and take your pet to a veterinarian.*

Finding a Veterinarian

Finding a veterinarian when you're on the road is not always easy. Start by asking at the place you're staying. Pet-friendly lodgings are often run by pet lovers, and they may be able to recommend their own veterinarian.

If you have access to the Internet (many lodgings have Internet access that they generally do not make available to their guests, but in an emergency they will often make an exception), try www.vetlocator.petplace.com. You click on the home page, enter your zip code (or in Canada, your postal code), and list the distance you're willing to travel, and you will find vets in your area. Another Web site that lists veterinarians is www.vetquest.com.

If you are involved with a particular breed of dog or cat, find out the names of some breeders who live in the areas to which you will be traveling before you go. If you need a vet, call one of them and ask for a recommendation.

If you need an emergency clinic, try the Yellow Pages. Hotels have them, as do gas stations and convenience markets. Often, veterinarians have a recorded message in their office after hours that refers callers to the nearest emergency clinic. You can also call directory information, the nearest animal shelter, or the local police department. All are likely to know about the nearest 24-hour animal hospital.

A friend of mine had an emergency with her dog at midnight in a big-city hotel. She called the front desk, which recommended a clinic about a 30-minute drive away. She asked them to get her a taxi while she hustled downstairs with her dog. When she got in the taxi, the driver told her about an emergency veterinary clinic that was much closer and took her there. Taxi drivers who work the night shift often know what's open after hours and exactly where it is.

Treating Minor Problems

The scrapes and bumps of everyday life can be treated on the road, often with common over-the-counter medications that you can get at any drugstore. Look for infant formulas in liquid form and dose according to body weight. If you're not absolutely certain of the dosage, call your veterinarian, who should be able to advise you over the phone.

Constipation. Constipation is most often due to a lack of exercise and not enough water. Try to make sure that your pet gets enough exercise on the road. Pets can take unflavored Milk of Magnesia once a day at a dose of 1/2 teaspoon per 5 pounds of body weight. One to three teaspoons of Metamucil powder can also be mixed into canned food or liquids (if your pet will drink it) once a day. One tablespoon of plain canned pumpkin (not pumpkin pie filling) two to three times a day also works as a laxative.

Call a veterinarian if constipation persists for more than a day, especially if you see blood in the stool. Also, if your pet is straining to urinate, especially if you have a male cat, the problem may be a urinary blockage. This is a life-threatening emergency, and you must take your cat to a veterinary clinic at once.

Coughing. Robitussin Pediatric Cough Formula is safe to give every six hours, but make sure that there is no other cold medication in the formula you buy. You must never give a cat aspirin, acetaminophen (Tylenol), ibuprofen (Advil), or any other anti-inflammatory medication made for humans. Cats lack the enzymes needed to metabolize these drugs, and they can be life-threatening.

Cuts and scrapes. Clean cuts and scrapes with hydrogen peroxide, shave or clip the hair away from the area, and apply an over-the-counter antibacterial ointment (such as Neosporin, Betadine, or triple antibiotic ointment) twice a day to prevent infection. If bleeding persists, apply direct pressure with a clean cloth and take your pet to a veterinarian. Seek veterinary care if the scrape is on the eye or if there is any discharge. Any wound inflicted by another animal should be seen by a veterinarian.

Diarrhea. One loose stool is usually not enough to cause major concern. Stress, overeating, or a change in diet often causes loose stools. However, if there is any blood in the stool or if diarrhea persists for more than 24 hours, call a veterinarian immediately. Cats, in particular, dehydrate very quickly, so make sure that your cat is drinking plenty of water. When you pull up the skin on the scruff of her neck, it should immediately fall smoothly back into place. Pedialyte can help a pet with diarrhea regain her electrolyte balance. But a dehydrated pet also needs to see a veterinarian.

Dogs and cats can take Kaopectate or Pepto-Bismol. A safe dosage is 1 teaspoon (5 ml) of these medications per 5 pounds of body weight, twice a day for two or three days. Imodium can be used safely for a short period as well. The dose is 1/8 teaspoon per 10 pounds of body weight, three times a day, for no more than two days.

Eye irritations. If your pet has a little dust in her eyes, you can use a saline solution made for people with contact lenses, or artificial tears, to clean the eyes and nose. Clean any discharge around the eyes and nose with warm water on a cotton ball. If your pet is pawing at her eye or squinting nonstop, she needs to see a veterinarian.

Hairballs. If your cat is spitting up hairballs and you do not have any type of hairball remedy, try putting half a teaspoon of white petroleum jelly on her nose. Cats hate this and will lick it off right away. Do not give your cat petroleum jelly (or any hairball remedy or treat that contains mineral oil or petroleum jelly) right before a meal. Both of these substances leach out the fat-soluble vitamins A, D, E, and K from the intestines and will unbalance your cat's diet.

Insect bites and stings. If an insect has bitten your pet, you will likely hear her yelp and see her begin to lick the affected area frantically. Have someone hold and in some cases muzzle her and gently scrape the stinger out, if there is one. Cool water, ice, or rubbing alcohol is usually all you need to apply to the area. Calamine lotion or Cortaid can be used to relieve the itching. Benadryl can help prevent the localized allergic reaction that sometimes occurs with bee stings. You can give half a 25 mg tablet or 12.5 mg of the liquid. Be sure the medication you use contains only diphenhydramine, because many antihistamine preparations also contain acetaminophen (Tylenol), which can be fatal to cats. Chlortrimeton, the brand name for chlorpheniramine, can also be given to pets. It comes as a 4 mg tablet, and your pet can take half a tablet twice a day. This antihistamine can be used for a mild allergic reaction or for itchy skin. If you know your pet is allergic to certain insect bites, consult a veterinarian. If you notice severe swelling at the site or your pet goes into shock, take her to an emergency clinic.

Oil on the coat. If your pet gets oil or grease from a car on her coat, or any kind of oily substance, wash it off right away. A safe way to remove grease or oil from a pet's coat is to bathe the animal in Dawn dishwashing liquid. Using any type of detergent is normally not recommended, especially on a cat, but Dawn does not contain phosphates.

Skin irritations. Hydrocortisone cream or ointment can be applied to a minor, itchy rash. It is useful for itching and inflammation if there is no infection, but if bacteria or fungus are present, it can make the infection worse. Desitin can also help soothe irritated skin.

Ticks. Ticks can carry diseases that can be dangerous to both dogs and humans. Examine your pet carefully at the end of every day, even if your only experience in the great outdoors has been at roadside rest stops. If you find a tick on your pet—they usually attach near the neck and ears—drip a little rubbing alcohol on the tick and use tweezers to grab it as near to the head (that is, as close to your pet's skin) as possible and slowly pull it out. After extracting the tick, soak the area with hydrogen peroxide to clean it and dab it with an antibiotic ointment. If the area becomes red or inflamed, consult a veterinarian.

Never dispose of a tick by crushing it between your fingers, because you will expose yourself to any disease it is carrying. Flushing it down the toilet will not kill the tick, either. It is best to put a tick in a glass jar or plastic container with a drop of alcohol and put the lid on tightly, and then dispose of it safely.

Travel sickness. Some pets vomit when they travel in a car. You can give a dog or cat half of a 25 mg tablet of Dramamine 30 minutes before travel to calm the stomach. This drug is an antihistamine, so your pet may become sleepy. Removing food and water for a few hours before travel also decreases the likelihood of vomiting during a car ride.

Travel or motion sickness is a common cause of excessive drooling. Some drugs, especially tranquilizers, can also cause drooling. Foreign objects (for example, sticks) in the mouth can cause drooling as well. If drooling persists, contact your veterinarian.

Vomiting. Regurgitation—marked by repeated gulping sounds and production of semi-digested food—is normal for pets under stress. Sometimes they simply eat too fast. Make sure your pet has a safe, quiet place to eat and is not hurried through her meals.

Vomiting is much more violent and usually produces a yellow, viscous solution. If your pet is vomiting but is still able to hold down water and small bits of food, you can try treating her with Pepcid A/C. A safe dosage is 1/4 to 1/2 of a 10 mg tablet once a day. For dehydration, see Diarrhea (page 447).

If your pet vomits more than once in a day, vomits several days in a row, or the vomiting is accompanied by any other symptoms, consult a vet immediately, especially if there is any blood in the vomit.

Treating Emergencies

Animal bites. If your pet is bitten by another animal, take her to a veterinarian even if she seems to be okay. On the way, check for wounds. If she is bleeding, try to stop the bleeding by applying direct pressure to the wound.

Bleeding. If your pet has been injured and is bleeding, try to slow or stop the bleeding before you take her to an emergency animal hospital. For an oozing wound, use a gauze pad or a clean cloth to put pressure on the wound. Bandage tightly (but not so tight that you cut off circulation) and take your pet to the hospital. If the wound is spurting, a blood vessel has been broken. A small animal can bleed to death very quickly, so do what you can to slow the loss of blood. Try covering the wound with one hand while wrapping a finger and thumb around the limb to constrict blood flow. Release the finger and thumb every 15 seconds—do not close off blood flow for more than one minute at a time. If two people are available, one should drive while the other tends to the injured animal. If only one person is available, use a length of gauze or a shoelace or string to make a tourniquet between the wound and the heart. Tie the gauze or string around the wound then insert a pencil or small stick and twist it until the bleeding slows. Untwist the tourniquet every few minutes to allow circulation back into the limb. A tourniquet can do more harm than good to a limb, so use it only if you are alone and you're sure a large vessel has been cut.

Broken bones. A broken bone is very painful, so muzzle your pet before you do anything else. Even the most loving and loyal pet may bite out of pain or panic in this situation. Immobilize the limb by using something rigid as a splint. A stick, a rolled-up magazine or newspaper, a ruler—anything that's a little longer than the broken limb is fine. Secure it with some rolled-up gauze (don't try to straighten the limb; just immobilize it) and take your pet to the hospital.

Burns. Heat, electric shock, and chemicals can cause burns. A superficial burn is indicated by redness of the skin and in some cases mild swelling. A veterinarian should look at most burns, because shock can set in quickly. If your pet has come in contact with any kind of chemical irritant, wash the area for five minutes with large amounts of cool water, bandage loosely, and get your pet to the hospital. For other kinds of burns, apply cool compresses and get your pet to the hospital.

If your pet has received an electric shock, check first to make sure that she is not still in contact with the source of electricity. If she is, *do not touch her.* Throw the switch, pull the plug, or move the animal by using a piece of wood first. Then check for breathing and a heartbeat and administer CPR, if needed (see page 451). Treat any burns on the skin and get your pet to the hospital right away.

For mild burns, apply cold water or an ice pack to cool the skin and ease the pain. Neosporin (a topical antibiotic) can be applied, and you may want to wrap the area in light gauze to protect it until the vet can take a look.

Car accident. If your pet has been in a car accident, gently move her to a safe place, changing her position as little as possible (see "Carrying an injured animal" on page 451). Secure your pet in a crate or carrier while you wait for help, or sit with her to make sure that she doesn't move. It's a disaster when an injured and disoriented animal jumps up and runs loose at an accident site. Injuries from a car accident may not be immediately apparent, but your pet should see a veterinarian no matter how she appears.

Choking. Cats are difficult to restrain when they are panicked, but you may be able to perform the Heimlich maneuver on your dog. Hold your dog sitting up in your lap, with her back against your chest. Reach around her waist from behind, make a fist with one hand, and grasp it with the other hand. Place the fist in the dog's upper mid-abdomen close to the breastbone, where the rib cage forms a V. Forcefully thrust up and in with your fist four times in quick succession. This usually dislodges the object. If it doesn't come flying out of your pet's mouth, pull out the tongue and use your fingers to sweep the mouth. If the object is still not dislodged, use the heel of your hand to give your pet a sharp thump on the back between the shoulder blades. Once the object is dislodged, check for breathing and administer artificial respiration (see page 451), if necessary.

You can try this method with a cat (using less force than you would with a dog), but it may not be possible. You can also try holding the cat upside down by placing your hands around the lower abdomen and gently swinging the cat back and forth for 30 seconds. If the cat faints, you can open her mouth, look for the object, hold her neck behind where it is, and then use your finger to hook it and extract it. Check for breathing and administer artificial respiration (see page 451), if necessary.

Choking is always an emergency. Even if you manage to dislodge the object, your pet needs to be seen right away by a veterinarian.

Dehydration. Dehydration can be caused by lack of fluid intake, fever, prolonged vomiting, or diarrhea. Symptoms are a dry mouth and a lack of skin elasticity. When you pick up the fold of skin on your pet's back, it should spring back. If it doesn't, your pet might be dehydrated. Sunken eyes are also an indication of dehydration. If your pet is noticeably dehydrated, consult a vet immediately. For mild cases, see Diarrhea (page 447).

Frostbite. The areas most exposed to cold with the least amount of fur protection are most susceptible to frostbite. These include the ears, toes, tail, and scrotum. The skin will turn pale and white, and, as circulation returns, it will become red and swollen. Warm frostbitten areas by immersing or bathing in warm (not hot) water for 20 minutes, until the tissue begins to turn red. If you cannot get warm water, try to place the affected area next to your body, in a cupped hand, under your arm or another area where your body temperature is warmer. Do not rub or massage the affected parts. Apply a soft, dry bandage and take your pet to the hospital.

Heatstroke. On a warm day, the temperature in a parked car can reach 120 degrees F in a matter of minutes—even with the car windows partially open. Your pet can quickly suffer brain damage or die from heatstroke or suffocation when trapped in high temperatures. Signs of heatstroke include heavy panting, glazed eyes, a rapid pulse, unsteadiness, a staggering gait, vomiting, a deep red or purple tongue, foaming at the mouth, and unconsciousness. The color of your pet's gums is also an indication of her health. Normally, gums are a light pink, and if you press them, the white spot caused by the pressure fades back to pink within a couple of seconds. If the animal is suffering from heatstroke, the gums will be dark pink, and it will take a bit longer for the white spot to refill with color.

If your pet becomes overheated, you must lower her body temperature immediately. Move her into the shade and apply cool (not cold) water all over her body to gradually lower her temperature. Let your pet drink small amounts of cool water or lick ice cubes; apply cool water packs to the armpits, chest, and abdomen; and get her to a veterinarian immediately.

Hypothermia. Prolonged exposure to cold can result in a dangerous drop in body temperature. Violent shivering followed by listlessness and lethargy are signs of hypothermia. Hypothermia is especially serious if your pet is wet. Vigorously rub her dry and keep her warm by wrapping her in a blanket and snuggling her close to you. If you can, apply warm water packs to the armpits, chest, and abdomen. Call a veterinarian, who will advise you about bringing your pet in for emergency care.

Poisons. If you suspect that your pet has been poisoned, contact a veterinarian or the poison control hotline immediately (phone 888/ANU-HELP or 900/443-0000; see Appendix B). The most obvious symptoms of poisoning are profuse salivation, vomiting, staggering, and convulsions. Common poisons include car antifreeze, rat poison, and insecticides. Antifreeze, especially, is a quick killer, so be sure to get your pet to an emergency hospital immediately. If possible, bring the poison with you to help the veterinarian treat your pet appropriately.

Shock. An animal in shock does not have sufficient blood flow to meet the body's basic needs. Shock can quickly become life-threatening. Symptoms of shock are a racing pulse, fast breathing, a lower-than-normal temperature, shivering, listlessness, weakness, cold feet and legs, a weak pulse, and, in some cases, a loss of consciousness.

In cases of shock, lay the animal on her side and be sure the breathing passages are not obstructed. Evaluate the pet's vital signs and administer artificial respiration or CPR if needed. Pull out the tongue to keep the airway clear and keep the head lower than the body. Do not give your pet anything to drink, do not muzzle her, and do not force her to lie in any particular position. Calm her as best you can, wrap her in a warm blanket, and get her to a veterinarian immediately.

Snake bites. Symptoms of snakebites are swelling, vomiting, difficulty breathing, weakness, and convulsion. If you suspect that a snake has bitten your pet, get to a veterinarian immediately. On the way, keep the animal as quiet as you can. If the bite is on the leg, apply a constricting bandage (but not a tourniquet) between the bite and the animal's heart. Do not wash the wound, do not apply ice, and do not make cuts over the wound or attempt to suck out the venom. Do not attempt to capture the snake, either, but do your best to get a good look so you can describe it to the vet.

Emergency Procedures

Restraint. Even the most docile, loving animal may lash out or bite in an emergency or when she is in pain. If at all possible, muzzle your pet before you begin any emergency treatment. You should have a muzzle in your first-aid kit, but you can also make one from a leash, a leg of pantyhose, a bandanna, a length of gauze, or anything similar. Wrap it quickly around the animal's muzzle, then bring the ends under the chin, pull them back behind the animal's neck, and tie them off. Make sure that your pet can still breathe freely.

A cat or small dog can be restrained in a pillowcase or cloth sack. Hold the animal by the scruff of the neck and drop her in the pillowcase. If she is panicking too much, throw a towel loosely over her head first.

Cats, especially, can be very effective with their back claws. If you are carrying an injured cat, hold her at your hip with her back feet projecting behind you, where they can't do any harm. However, it's best to transport her in a carrier if you can.

Carrying an injured animal. As you transport any animal, make sure that you do not aggravate any injuries. Find something you can slip under the animal—a towel, a cutting board, a piece of plywood, an old door, some rigid cardboard, or a blanket—and carry the animal with as little jostling as possible. Do your best to keep your pet quiet in the car on the way to the hospital.

Artificial respiration. Check to see if your pet is breathing. (Do not attempt artificial respiration if she is!) If she is not breathing, place your pet on her side, open her mouth, and pull the tongue to one side. Make sure the airway is clear by sweeping it with your finger. Then close the mouth and pull the lips over the teeth. For a cat or small dog, place your hand completely around the animal's muzzle. For a large dog, gently hold the muzzle closed. Now take a deep breath and gently exhale into the animal's nose. Watch to see that the chest rises. Repeat every five seconds. Continue until the animal can breathe on her own, or until help arrives.

CPR. CPR is the combination of artificial respiration and cardiac massage. If your pet is not breathing but has a heartbeat, do not do CPR. Do cardiac massage only if your pet has no heartbeat. To check a dog or cat's pulse, feel the femoral artery, which is located in the inside of the thigh, where the leg joins the body. If there is no pulse, for cats and small dogs, place three fingers over the heart (at about the fifth rib) and press gently with medium pressure, and then release. The ribs should compress about 1 inch. Repeat five times. Do 12 breaths, then five chest compressions, and repeat until your pet starts to breathe on her own or until help arrives. For larger dogs, with the dog on her side, place both hands over the dog's heart and push down in short bursts. Do ten breaths, then five chest compressions, and repeat until the dog breathes on her own or until help arrives.

Appendix B: Resources for You and Your Pet

Government Organizations

US Department of Agriculture-APHIS. *Animal Care Staff, 6505 Belcrest Rd, Hyattsville, MD 20782. Phone 301/436-7833 or toll-free 800/545-USDA. www.usda.gov.* Direct inquiries regarding airline reimbursements, pets lost in transport, or mistreatment of animals by airline personnel here. The USDA also maintains a database of rules for transporting animals into and out of each state, which can be found at www.aphis.usda.gov/vs/sregs.

US Department of Transportation. *Office of Consumer Affairs/I-25, 400 Seventh St SW, Washington, DC 20590. Phone 202/366-2220. airconsumer.ost.dot.gov/publications/animals.htm.* The Department of Transportation offers tips for safe airline travel with your pet and a place to complain if things go wrong.

Travel Industry Organizations

Air Transport Association of America. *1301 Pennsylvania Ave NW, Suite 1100, Washington, DC 20004-1707. Phone 202/626-4000. www.airlines.org/public/publications/display1.asp?nid=926.* The Air Transport Association of America is a trade association for US airlines. It offers detailed advice and information about airline travel with your pet.

International Air Transport Association. *703 Waterford Ave, Suite 600, Miami, FL 33126. Phone 305/264-7772. www.iata.org/cargooperations/liveanimals/pets.htm.* The International Air Transport Association is an international airline trade group. Its members subscribe to a lengthy code of conduct, which includes detailed guidelines for the humane transport of animals.

Health Organizations

American Animal Hospital Association (AAHA). *12575 W Bayaud Ave, Lakewood, CO 80228. Phone 303/986-2800 or toll-free 800/252-2242. www.healthypet.com.* This association includes more than 16,000 veterinary care providers. You can call for veterinary referrals; the group's Web site is full of tips on pet health and safety.

American Veterinary Medical Association. *1931 N Meacham Rd, Suite 100, Schaumburg, IL 60173. Phone 847/925-8070. www.avma.org.* This association can provide veterinarian referrals from a list that includes more than 50,000 vets in the United States.

ASPCA Animal Poison Control Center. *1717 Thilo Rd, Suite 36, Urbana, IL 61802. Phone 888/426-4435 (888/ANU-HELP) or 900/443-0000. www.napcc.aspca.org.* The ASPCA Animal Poison Control Center has specially trained veterinary toxicologists on duty around the clock. The center provides 24-hour service for emergency calls. Note that a $45 consultation fee will be charged to your credit card if you call the 888 number, and a $45 charge will appear on your phone bill if you call the 900 number. The fee includes as many follow-up calls as necessary, including calls to your veterinarian. Be prepared to give relevant information regarding your pet and, if possible, the suspected poison.

Canadian Veterinary Medical Association. *339 Booth St, Ottawa, ON, Canada K1R 7K1. Phone 613/236-1162. www.cvna-acmv.org.* The Canadian Veterinary Medical Association is a good source for veterinary referrals if you are traveling in Canada.

Poisonous Plant Guides

Cornell University. *www.ansci.cornell.edu/plants/index.html.*

Purdue University. *vet.purdue.edu/depts/addl/toxic/cover1.htm.*

University of Illinois at Urbana-Champaign. *gateway.library.uiuc.edu/vex/vetdocs/toxic.htm.*

Pet Sitting and Boarding

American Boarding Kennel Association. *1702 E Pikes Peak Ave, Colorado Springs, CO 80909. Phone 719/667-0116. www.abka.com.* Referrals for boarding kennels are available from this association.

National Association of Professional Pet Sitters. *17000 Commerce Pkwy, Suite C, Mount Laurel, NJ 08054. Phone toll-free 800/296-PETS. www.petsitters.org.* The NAPPS provides referrals for certified pet sitters by zip code.

Pet Sitters International. *201 E King St, King, NC 27021-9161. Phone 336/983-9222. www.petsit.com.* The world's largest organization for professional pet sitters will refer you to member pet sitters in your area.

Catalog and Internet Shopping, Pet Supplies

Cherrybrook. *Rte 57, PO Box 15, Broadway, NJ 08808. Phone 908/689-7979 or toll-free 800/524-0820. www.cherrybrook.com.*

Doctors Foster & Smith. *2253 Air Park Rd, PO Box 100, Rhinelander, WI 54501. Phone toll-free 800/381-7179. www.drsfostersmith.com.*

JB Wholesale Pet Supplies. *5 Raritan Rd, Oakland, NJ 07436. Phone toll-free 800/526-0388. www.jbpet.com.*

Pet Identification (Tattoos and Microchips)

AKC Companion Animal Recovery. *Phone toll-free 800/252-7894. www.akccar.org.* This service, run by the American Kennel Club, registers pets with tattoos and microchips. You and any other contacts you designate will be called if your pet is found.

Help 4 Pets. *Phone toll-free 800/HELP-4-PETS (435-7473). www.help4pets.com.* Help 4 Pets services include a national veterinarian referral system and a 24-hour pet-recovery system.

National Dog Registry (NDR). *Box 116, Woodstock, NY 12498. Phone 914/679-BELL or 914/277-4485; toll-free 800/NDR-DOGS (548-2423). www.natldogregistry.com.* The NDR was established in 1966 and currently has more than 4 million registered pets. NDR members' dogs are registered with a tattooed number or an implanted microchip. You and any other contacts you designate will be called if your pet is found.

Pet Finders. *661 High St, Athol, NY 12810. Phone 518/623-2164; toll-free 800/666-5678.* Pet Finders keeps a medical history of your pet as well as your travel itinerary on file. Your pet will wear a tag with Pet Finders' 800 number. If someone finds your lost pet, he can call the number and Pet Finders can tell him how to find you and whether the animal needs any special medical care. Also, if you lose your pet while traveling, Pet Finders will fax a description of your pet to every shelter, veterinarian, and boarding kennel in the area.

PetTrac. *Phone toll-free 800/336-2843. www.avidid.com.* PetTrac registers animals who have the AVID microchip. If a pet is found, the company will contact you or the veterinarian who implanted the microchip.

Tattoo-A-Pet International. *6571 SW 20th Ct, Fort Lauderdale, FL 33317. Phone toll-free 800/TATTOOS. www.tattoo-a-pet.com.* Tattoo-A-Pet has been in business for more than 30 years and has more than 2 million registered pets. You and any other contacts you designate will be called if your pet is found.

Online Dog Park Directories

Dog Park. *www.dogpark.com.* Finds dog parks all over the US and Canada.

The Dog Park. *www.thedogpark.com.* Lists dog parks throughout the United States.

Dog Fun Directory. *www.ilovethisplace.com/dogfun/.* The original dog park directory. Lists parks all over the US and in some Canadian provinces.

Urban Hound. *www.urbanhound.com.* Lists dog parks in New York City and provides a community for dog owners.

Canine Camps

Camp Dances With Dogs (Lebanon, NJ). *234 Gabryszewski Rd, St. Johnsville, NY 13452. www.flyingdogpress.com/camp.html.*

Camp Dogwood (Ingleside, IL). *3540 N Southport Ave, PMB 178, Chicago, IL 60657-1436. Phone 312/458-9549. www.campdogwood.com.*

Camp Gone to the Dogs (Stowe or Marlboro, VT). *PO Box 600, Putney, VT 05346. Phone 802/387-5673. www.camp-gone-tothe-dogs.com.*

Camp Jackpot. *1144 Reynolds Rd, Cross Junction, VA 22625. Phone 540/888-4124. www.campjackpot.com.*

Camp Ruffin' It (Lytton, BC). *Gordon Park, PO Box 37002, Vancouver, British Columbia, Canada V5P 4W7. Phone 604/439-8450. www.webcrosser.com/campruffinit/main.htm.*

Camp Winnaribbun (Lake Tahoe, NV). *PO Box 50300, Reno, NV 89513. Phone 775/348-8412. www.campw.com.*

Competitive Edge Sports Camp. *Cornwall-on-the-Hudson, NY. Phone 508/529-3568. www.dogsofcourse.com.*

Dog Days of Wisconsin Summer Camp. *235 S Greenfield Ave, Waukesha, WI 53186. Phone 800/CAMP-4-DOGS. www.dogcamp.com.*

The Dog's Camp (Weaverville, NC). *121 Webb Dr, Marshall, NC 28753. Phone 828/649-3691. www.thedogscamp.com.*

Dog Scouts of America. *5068 Nestel Rd, St. Helen, MI 48656. Phone 989/389-2000. www.dogscouts.com.*

Dogskills Adventure (Oxford, OH). *4937 Thornhill Ln, Dublin, OH 43017. www.dogskillsadventure.com.*

Hand-in-Paw Productions. *PO Box 413, Garrisonville, VA 22463. Phone 540/659-6868. E-mail highintrial@aol.com.*

Iron Dogs. *PO Box 17643, Encino, CA 91416. Phone 310/491-9973, ext 777-1000. www.iron-dogs.com/index.html.*

Legacy Canine Behavior and Training. *PO Box 3909, Sequim, WA 98382. Phone 360/683-1522. www.legacycanine.com.*

Pine Meadows Farm Agility Camp. *6125 Woodman Rd SW, South Boardman, MI 49680. Phone toll-free 877/276-6215. www.pinemeadowsfarm.com/dogcamp.htm.*

Ready for Prime Time Dog Performance Camp (Friendsville, PA). *PO Box 413, Garrisonville, VA 22463. Phone 540/659-6868. www.members.aol.com/highintrial/rfpt.html.*

Splash Camp. *PO Box 842, Monroe, CT 06468. Phone 203/521-0934. www.splashcamp.com.*

Wiz Kid Dog Camp (PA). *4 Brookside Pl, Westport, CT 06880. Phone 203/226-9556. E-mail wizkid@netaxis.com.*

Notes

Notes

Notes

Notes

Notes

Notes

Notes

Notes

Notes

Notes

Notes

Notes

Notes

Notes